University of Massachusetts, Amherst

COMPREHENSIVE EDITION

PROGRAMMING AND PROBLEM SOLVING WITH C++

SIXTH EDITION

JONES & BARTLETT
LEARNING

World Headquarters
Jones & Bartlett Learning
5 Wall Street
Burlington, MA 01803
978-443-5000
info@jblearning.com
www.jblearning.com

Jones & Bartlett Learning books and products are available through most bookstores and online booksellers. To contact Jones & Bartlett Learning directly, call 800-832-0034, fax 978-443-8000, or visit our website, www.jblearning.com.

> Substantial discounts on bulk quantities of Jones & Bartlett Learning publications are available to corporations, professional associations, and other qualified organizations. For details and specific discount information, contact the special sales department at Jones & Bartlett Learning via the above contact information or send an email to specialsales@jblearning.com.

Copyright © 2014 by Jones & Bartlett Learning, LLC, an Ascend Learning Company

All rights reserved. No part of the material protected by this copyright may be reproduced or utilized in any form, electronic or mechanical, including photocopying, recording, or by any information storage and retrieval system, without written permission from the copyright owner.

Programming and Problem Solving with C++, Comprehensive Sixth Edition is an independent publication and has not been authorized, sponsored, or otherwise approved by the owners of the trademarks or service marks referenced in this product.

Some images in this book feature models. These models do not necessarily endorse, represent, or participate in the activities represented in the images.

The screenshots in this product are for educational and instructive purposes only. All trademarks displayed are the trademarks of the parties noted therein. Such use of trademarks is not an endorsement by said parties of Jones & Bartlett Learning, its products, or its services, nor should such use be deemed an endorsement by Jones & Bartlett Learning of said third party's products or services.

Production Credits
Chief Executive Officer: Ty Field
President: James Homer
SVP, Editor-in-Chief: Michael Johnson
SVP, Chief Marketing Officer: Alison M. Pendergast
Executive Publisher: Kevin Sullivan
Senior Developmental Editor: Amy Bloom
Director of Production: Amy Rose
Production Assistant: Eileen Worthley
Marketing Manager: Lindsay White
Associate Marketing Manager: Cassandra Peterson
V.P., Manufacturing and Inventory Control: Therese Connell
Composition: Northeast Compositors, Inc.
Cover and Title Page Design: Scott Moden
Cover and Title Page Image: © Toncsi/ShutterStock, Inc.
Matters of Style box: © iStockphoto/Thinkstock
Theoretical Foundations box: © iStockphoto/Thinkstock
Background Information box: © SergeyIT/Shutterstock, Inc.
Software Engineering Tip box: © iStockphoto/Thinkstock
Illustration of George Boole: © Photos.com/Thinkstock
Printing and Binding: Edwards Brothers Malloy
Cover Printing: Edwards Brothers Malloy

To order this product, use ISBN: 978-1-284-02876-8

Library of Congress Cataloging-in-Publication Data
Dale, Nell B.
  Programming and problem solving with C++ : comprehensive sixth edition / Nell Dale and Chip Weems. -- Comprehensive sixth edition.
     pages cm.
  Includes index.
  ISBN-13: 978-1-4496-9426-5 (pbk.)
  ISBN-10: 1-4496-9426-8 (pbk.)
  1. C++ (Computer program language) I. Weems, Chip. II. Title.
  QA76.73.C153D34 2014
  005.13'3--dc23
                              2012043491

6048

Printed in the United States of America
17 16 15 14 13   10 9 8 7 6 5 4 3 2 1

Contents

Preface   xix

1 Overview of Programming and Problem Solving   1

1.1   Overview of Programming   2
  What Is Programming?   2
  How Do We Write a Program?   3
  What Is an Algorithm?   4
  What Is a Programming Language?   5

1.2   How Does a Computer Run a Program?   9
  What Kinds of Instructions Can Be Written in a Programming Language?   13
  What Is Software Maintenance?   13

  Software Maintenance Case Study: An Introduction to Software Maintenance   16

1.3   What's Inside the Computer?   20

1.4   Ethics and Responsibilities in the Computing Profession   24
  Software Piracy   24
  Privacy of Data   25
  Use of Computer Resources   25
  Software Engineering   26

1.5   Problem-Solving Techniques   27
  Ask Questions   27
  Look for Things That Are Familiar   28
  Solve by Analogy   28
  Means-Ends Analysis   28
  Divide and Conquer   29
  The Building-Block Approach   29
  Merging Solutions   30

Mental Blocks: The Fear of Starting   30
Algorithmic Problem Solving   31
Problem-Solving Case Study: Leap Year Algorithm   33
Summary   36
Quick Check Answers   37
Exam Preparation Exercises   38
Programming Warm-Up Exercises   40
Case Study Follow-Up   41
Line Number   42

2 C++ Syntax and Semantics, and the Program Development Process   43

2.1 The Elements of C++ Programs   44
    C++ Program Structure   44
    Syntax and Semantics   46
    Syntax Templates   47
    Naming Program Elements: Identifiers   49
    Data and Data Types   50
    Naming Elements: Declarations   53
    Taking Action: Executable Statements   57
    Beyond Minimalism: Adding Comments to a Program   62

2.2 Program Construction   64
    Blocks (Compound Statements)   66
    The C++ Preprocessor   68
    Software Maintenance Case Study: Adding Titles to Names   70

2.3 More About Output   74
    Creating Blank Lines   74
    Inserting Blanks Within a Line   75
    Special Characters   75

2.4 Program Entry, Correction, and Execution   76
    Entering a Program   76
    Compiling and Running a Program   77
    Problem-Solving Case Study: Printing a Chessboard   78
    Testing and Debugging   82
    Summary   83
    Quick Check Answers   83
    Exam Preparation Exercises   84
    Programming Warm-Up Exercises   86
    Programming Problems   88
    Case Study Follow-Up   89

3 Numeric Types, Expressions, and Output   91

- 3.1 Overview of C++ Data Types   92
- 3.2 Numeric Data Types   92
    - Integral Types   92
    - Floating-Point Types   94
- 3.3 Declarations for Numeric Types   95
    - Named Constant Declarations   95
    - Variable Declarations   96
- 3.4 Simple Arithmetic Expressions   97
    - Arithmetic Operators   97
    - Increment and Decrement Operators   99
- 3.5 Compound Arithmetic Expressions   100
    - Precedence Rules   101
    - Type Coercion and Type Casting   101
    - **Software Maintenance Case Study:** Precedence Error   104
- 3.6 Function Calls and Library Functions   107
    - Value-Returning Functions   107
    - Library Functions   108
    - Void Functions   110
- 3.7 Formatting Output   110
    - Integers and Strings   111
    - Floating-Point Numbers   113
- 3.8 Additional `string` Operations   119
    - The `length` and `size` Functions   119
    - The `find` Function   120
    - The `substr` Function   122
    - Accessing Characters Within a String: The `at` Function   123
    - Converting to Lowercase and Uppercase   123
- **Problem-Solving Case Study:** Mortgage Payment Calculator   126
- Testing and Debugging   129
- Summary   129
- Quick Check Answers   130
- Exam Preparation Exercises   130
- Programming Warm-Up Exercises   132
- Programming Problems   133
- Case Study Follow-Up   135

4 Program Input and the Software Design Process   137

- 4.1 Getting Data into Programs   138
    - Input Streams and the Extraction Operator (>>)   139

The Reading Marker and the Newline Character   142
Reading Character Data with the `get` Function   143
Skipping Characters with the `ignore` Function   146
Reading String Data   147
4.2 Interactive Input/Output   149
4.3 Noninteractive Input/Output   152
4.4 File Input and Output   152
Files   152
Using Files   153
Software Maintenance Case Study: Adding File Input/Output to a Program   156
Run-Time Input of File Names   160
4.5 Input Failure   162
4.6 Software Design Methodologies   163
4.7 Functional Decomposition   164
Modules   165
Implementing the Design   166
A Perspective on Design   170
Problem-Solving Case Study: Displaying a Name in Multiple Formats   171
Testing and Debugging   175
Summary   177
Quick Check Answers   178
Exam Preparation Exercises   178
Programming Warm-Up Exercises   180
Programming Problems   182
Case Study Follow-Up   184

5 Conditions, Logical Expressions, and Selection Control Structures   185

5.1 Flow of Control   186
Selection   186
5.2 Conditions and Logical Expressions   187
The `bool` Data Type   188
Logical Expressions   188
5.3 The If Statement   192
The If-Then-Else Form   193
Blocks (Compound Statements)   195
The If-Then Form   198
A Common Mistake   199
Software Maintenance Case Study: Incorrect Output   200
5.4 Nested If Statements   203
The Dangling `else`   206

5.5 Logical Operators   207
    Precedence of Operators   213
    Relational Operators with Floating-Point Types   214
5.6 Testing the State of an I/O Stream   215
    Problem-Solving Case Study: BMI Calculator   217
    Testing and Debugging   223
        Testing in the Problem-Solving Phase: The Algorithm Walk-Through   223
        Testing in the Implementation Phase   225
        The Test Plan   229
        Tests Performed Automatically During Compilation and Execution   230
    Summary   233
    Quick Check Answers   233
    Exam Preparation Exercises   233
    Programming Warm-Up Exercises   235
    Programming Problems   237
    Case Study Follow-Up   241

6 Looping   243

6.1 The While Statement   244
6.2 Phases of Loop Execution   246
6.3 Loops Using the While Statement   246
    Count-Controlled Loops   247
    Event-Controlled Loops   249
    Looping Subtasks   255
    Software Maintenance Case Study: Make a Program General   259
6.4 How to Design Loops   263
    Designing the Flow of Control   263
    Designing the Process Within the Loop   265
    The Loop Exit   266
6.5 Nested Logic   267
    Designing Nested Loops   271
    Problem-Solving Case Study: Recording Studio Design   278
    Testing and Debugging   290
        Loop-Testing Strategy   290
        Test Plans Involving Loops   290
    Summary   293
    Quick Check Answers   293
    Exam Preparation Exercises   294
    Programming Warm-Up Exercises   297
    Programming Problems   298
    Case Study Follow-Up   302

7 Additional Control Structures 303

- 7.1 The Switch Statement 304
- 7.2 The Do-While Statement 310
- 7.3 The For Statement 314
   Software Maintenance Case Study: Changing a Loop Implementation 318
- 7.4 The Break and Continue Statements 321
- 7.5 Guidelines for Choosing a Looping Statement 322
- 7.6 Additional C++ Operators 323
   Assignment Operators and Assignment Expressions 324
   Increment and Decrement Operators 325
   Bitwise Operators 326
   The Cast Operation 326
   The `sizeof` Operator 327
   The ?: Operator 328
   Operator Precedence 328
   Type Coercion in Arithmetic and Relational Expressions 330
   Problem-Solving Case Study: The Rich Uncle 332
   Testing and Debugging 336
   Summary 337
   Quick Check Answers 337
   Exam Preparation Exercises 338
   Programming Warm-Up Exercises 340
   Programming Problems 341
   Case Study Follow-Up 344

8 Functions 345

- 8.1 Functional Decomposition with Void Functions 346
   When to Use Functions 346
   Why Do Modules Need an Interface Design? 347
   Designing Interfaces 347
   Writing Modules as Void Functions 349
- 8.2 An Overview of User-Defined Functions 353
   Flow of Control in Function Calls 353
   Function Parameters 354
- 8.3 Syntax and Semantics of Void Functions 356
   Function Call (Invocation) 356
   Function Declarations and Definitions 357
   Local Variables 359
   The Return Statement 360

8.4 Parameters   361
   Value Parameters   362
   Reference Parameters   363
   Software Maintenance Case Study: Refactoring a Program   365
   Using Expressions with Parameters   371
   A Last Word of Caution About Argument and Parameter Lists   372
   Writing Assertions as Function Documentation   374
   Problem-Solving Case Study: Lawn Care Company Billing   377
   Testing and Debugging   387
   The `assert` Library Function   387
   Summary   390
   Quick Check Answers   390
   Exam Preparation Exercises   391
   Programming Warm-Up Exercises   392
   Programming Problems   394
   Case Study Follow-Up   400

9 Scope, Lifetime, and More on Functions   401

9.1 Scope of Identifiers   402
   Scope Rules   404
   Variable Declarations and Definitions   407
   Namespaces   407
9.2 Lifetime of a Variable   410
   Initializations in Declarations   411
   Software Maintenance Case Study: Debug a Simple Program   412
9.3 Interface Design   416
   Side Effects   417
   Global Constants   419
9.4 Value-Returning Functions   422
   Complete Example   425
   Boolean Functions   429
   Interface Design and Side Effects   431
   When to Use Value-Returning Functions   432
9.5 Type Coercion in Assignments, Argument Passing, and Return of a Function Value   433
   Problem-Solving Case Study: Health Profile   436
   Testing and Debugging   445
   Stubs and Drivers   446
   Summary   451
   Quick Check Answers   452

Exam Preparation Exercises   452
Programming Warm-Up Exercises   455
Programming Problems   456
Case Study Follow-Up   460

10 User-Defined Data Types   461

10.1 Built-In Simple Types   462
  Numeric Types   463
  Characters   464
10.2 User-Defined Simple Types   466
  The Typedef Statement   466
  Enumeration Types   467
  Named and Anonymous Data Types   476
10.3 Simple Versus Structured Data Types   476
10.4 Records (Structs)   478
  Accessing Individual Components   480
  Aggregate Operations on Structs   481
  More About Struct Declarations   483
  Binding Like Items   484
  Software Maintenance Case Study: Changing a Loop Implementation   484
10.5 Hierarchical Records   486
10.6 Unions   488
10.7 Pointers   490
  Pointer Variables   490
  Pointers Expressions   493
10.8 Reference Types   495
  Problem-Solving Case Study: Stylistical Analysis of Text   496
  Testing and Debugging   504
    Coping with Input Errors   504
    Debugging with Pointers   505
  Summary   507
  Quick Check Answers   508
  Exam Preparation Exercises   508
  Programming Warm-Up Exercises   510
  Programming Problems   510
  Case Study Follow-Up   513

11 Arrays   515

11.1 One-Dimensional Arrays   516
  Declaring Arrays   518

　　　　Accessing Individual Components of an Array　519
　　　　Out-of-Bounds Array Indexes　521
　　　　Initializing Arrays in Declarations　523
　　　　(Lack of) Aggregate Array Operations　523
　　　　Examples of Declaring and Accessing Arrays　524
　　　　Passing Arrays as Arguments　530
　　　　Commenting Arrays　533
　　　Software Maintenance Case Study: Modularizing a Program　534
　　　　Using Typedef with Arrays　537
　　　　Pointer Expressions and Arrays　537
　　　　C-Style Strings　538
　　　　Strings as Arrays　538
　　　　C String Operations　540
　　　　Converting C Strings to C++ Strings　540
　　　　Which String Representation to Use　541
11.2　Arrays of Records　541
　　　　Arrays of Records　541
11.3　Special Kinds of Array Processing　545
　　　　Subarray Processing　545
　　　　Indexes with Semantic Content　548
11.4　Two-Dimensional Arrays　548
11.5　Passing Two-Dimensional Arrays as Arguments　552
11.6　Processing Two-Dimensional Arrays　554
　　　　Sum the Rows　555
　　　　Sum the Columns Revised　556
　　　　Sum the Columns　557
　　　　Initialize the Array　558
　　　　Print the Array　559
11.7　Another Way of Defining Two-Dimensional Arrays　562
11.8　Multidimensional Arrays　563
　　　Problem-Solving Case Study: Calculating Exam Statistics　566
　　　Problem-Solving Case Study: Favorite Rock Group　574
　　　Testing and Debugging　581
　　　　One-Dimensional Arrays　581
　　　　Complex Structures　582
　　　　Multidimensional Arrays　583
　　　Summary　585
　　　Quick Check Answers　586
　　　Exam Preparation Exercises　586
　　　Programming Warm-Up Exercises　589

Programming Problems   591
Case Study Follow-Up   594

12 Classes and Abstraction   595

12.1 Abstract Data Types   596
12.2 C++ Classes   599
    Implementing the Member Functions   604
    Classes, Objects, and Members   607
    Built-in Operations on Objects   608
    Class Scope   609
12.3 Information Hiding   610
    User-Written Header Files   611
    Specification and Implementation Files   612
    Compiling and Linking a Multifile Program   618
12.4 What Is an Object?   619
12.5 Class Design Principles   623
    Encapsulation   623
    Abstraction   625
    Designing for Modifiability and Reuse   626
    Mutability   627
Software Maintenance Case Study: Comparing Two TimeOfDay Objects   629
12.6 The Name ADT   634
    Specification of the ADT   635
    Implementation File   637
12.7 Composition   639
    Design of an Entry Class   640
12.8 UML Diagrams   644
    Diagramming a Class   644
    Diagramming Composition of Classes   645
Problem-Solving Case Study: Create an Array of Name Objects   645
Testing and Debugging   652
Summary   656
Quick Check Answers   657
Exam Preparation Exercises   657
Programming Warm-Up Exercises   658
Programming Problems   659
Case Study Follow-Up   662

13 Array-Based Lists   663

13.1 What Is a List?   664
13.2 The List as an Abstract Data Type   664
       Refining Responsibilities   666
       Data Representation   668
       Example Program   670
13.3 Implementation of List ADT   673
       Basic Operations   673
       Insertion and Deletion   674
       Sequential Search   675
       Iterators   676
       Software Maintenance Case Study: Enhancing Class List with a Sort   677
13.4 Sorted Lists   681
       Basic Operations   682
       Insertion   683
       Sequential Search   685
       Binary Search   686
       Deletion   690
13.5 Sorted List of Classes   695
       IsThere   696
       Insert and Delete   697
13.6 More on UML Diagrams   699
       Problem-Solving Case Study: Calculating Exam Statistics Revisited   700
       Testing and Debugging   711
       Summary   712
       Quick Check Answers   712
       Exam Preparation Exercises   712
       Programming Warm-Up Exercises   713
       Programming Problems   714
       Case Study Follow-Up   715

14 Dynamic Data and Linked Lists   717

14.1 Dynamic Data   718
       Allocating Dynamic Data   718
       Deleting Dynamic Data   720
       Constants and Dynamic Data   724
14.2 Sequential Versus Linked Structures   725
14.3 Creating a Dynamic Linked List: A Walk-Through Example   727
14.4 Dynamic Implementation of ADT List   734
       Creating an Empty Linked List   735

Inserting into a Linked List 736
Traversals of a Linked List 737
Deleting from a Linked List 738
Resetting the List 740
Getting the Next Item 741
Testing for the Full Linked List 741
Searching the List 741
14.5 Destructors and Copy Constructors 746
Destructor 746
Shallow Versus Deep Copying 746
Copy-Constructor 748
14.6 Sorted Linked List 750
Insert(20) 753
Insert(60) (pick up with loop) 753
Insert(100) 755
Deleting from a Linked List 755
Delete(30) 756
Delete(50) 757
Problem-Solving Case Study: Creating a Sorted List of Entry Objects 757
Testing and Debugging 760
Summary 762
Quick Check Answers 763
Exam Preparation Exercises 763
Programming Warm-Up Exercises 766
Programming Problems 768
Case Study Follow-Up 770

15 Inheritance, Polymorphism, and Object-Oriented Design 771

15.1 Object-Oriented Programming 772
15.2 Inheritance 774
An Analogy 774
Inheritance and the Object-Oriented Design Process 775
Deriving One Class from Another Class 777
Specification of the `ExpandedEntry` Class 778
Implementation of the `ExpandedEntry` Class 779
Constructor Execution Order 784
Software Maintenance Case Study: Extending `TimeOfDay` with Support for a Time Zone 785
15.3 Dynamic Binding and Virtual Functions 791
The Slicing Problem 792

Virtual Functions   793
15.4 Object-Oriented Design   795
    Brainstorming   796
    Filtering   797
    Scenario Exploration   797
    Responsibility Algorithms   799
    A Final Word   799
15.5 Implementing a Design   801
    Problem-Solving Case Study: Creating an Appointment Calendar   802
    Testing and Debugging   819
    Summary   821
    Quick Check Answers   821
    Exam Preparation Exercises   822
    Programming Warm-Up Exercises   824
    Programming Problems   826
    Case Study Follow-Up   828

16 Templates, Operator Overloading, and Exceptions   829

16.1 Template Classes   830
    Defining a Class Template   831
    Instantiating a Class Template   832
    Another Way of Implementing Incoming Parameters: `const` References   834
    Organization of Program Code   835
    A Word of Caution   841
16.2 Generic Functions   842
    Function Overloading   842
    Defining a Function Template Outside a Class   843
    Instantiating a Function Template   843
16.3 Operator Overloading   845
    Using `*this`   847
16.4 Exceptions   848
    The `throw` Statement   849
    The `try-catch` Statement   851
    Nonlocal Exception Handlers   854
    Rethrowing an Exception   856
    Standard Exceptions   857
    Software Maintenance Case Study: Adding Exceptions to the Date Class   859
    Problem-Solving Case Study: Starship Weight and Balance   865
    Testing and Debugging   877
    Summary   878

Quick Check Answers 879
Exam Preparation Exercises 880
Programming Warm-Up Exercises 881
Programming Problems 883
Case Study Follow-Up 884

17 Introduction to Data Structures Using the Standard Template Library 885

17.1 Abstract Data Structures versus Implementations 886
17.2 Additional Linear Structures 888
  Stacks 889
  Queues 891
  Priority Queues 891
17.3 Bidirectional Linear Structures 893
  Bidirectional Lists 893
  Deques 894
17.4 An Introduction to the STL 895
  Iterators 896
  The `vector` Template 898
  The `list` Template 904
  The `stack` Template 906
  The `queue` Template 908
  The `priority_queue` Template 909
  The `deque` Template 911
  Software Maintenance Case Study: Appointment Calendar Using STL List 913
17.5 Nonlinear Structures 924
  Binary Trees 924
  Hash Tables 928
17.6 Associative Containers 929
  The `set` Template 930
  The `map` Template 933
  Problem-Solving Case Study: Creating a Deck of Cards 935
  Testing and Debugging 948
  Summary 949
  Quick Check Answers 950
  Exam Preparation Exercises 950
  Programming Warm-Up Exercises 952
  Programming Problems 954
  Case Study Follow-Up 957

18 Recursion 959

18.1 What Is Recursion? 960
18.2 Recursive Algorithms with Simple Variables 963
18.3 Towers of Hanoi 965
18.4 Recursive Algorithms with Structured Variables 969
Software Maintenance Case Study: Substituting Binary Search for Linear Search 972
18.5 Recursion Using Pointer Variables 977
Printing a Dynamic Linked List in Reverse Order 977
Copying a Dynamic Linked List 979
18.6 Recursion or Iteration? 983
Problem-Solving Case Study: Quicksort 984
Testing and Debugging 992
Summary 992
Quick Check Answers 993
Exam Preparation Exercises 993
Programming Warm-Up Exercises 995
Programming Problems 998
Case Study Follow-Up 999

Appendices 1001

Appendix A: Reserved Words 1001
Appendix B: Operator Precedence 1002
Appendix C: A Selection of Standard Library Routines 1003
Appendix D: Using This Book with a Prestandard Version of C++ 1011
Appendix E: Character Sets 1015
Appendix F: Program Style, Formatting, and Documentation 1016
Appendix G: More on Floating-Point Numbers 1022
Appendix H: Using C Strings 1031
Appendix I: C++ `char` Constants 1038

Index 1041

Preface

Introduction to the Comprehensive *Sixth Edition*

The first five editions of *Programming and Problem Solving with C++* have consistently been among the best-selling computer science textbooks in the United States. These editions, as well as the Java, Ada, and Pascal versions, have been accepted widely as model textbooks for ACM/IEEE-recommended curricula for the CS1/C101 course, and for the Advanced Placement exam in computer science.

Throughout the successive editions of this book, one thing has not changed: our commitment to the student. As always, our efforts are directed toward making the sometimes difficult concepts of computer science more accessible to all students. This edition of *Programming and Problem Solving with C++* continues to reflect our philosophy that a textbook should be like a guide, blazing a trail and leading its readers through territory that can initially seem difficult to navigate.

Changes to the *Sixth Edition*

Programming and Problem Solving with C++, Comprehensive Sixth Edition continues to offer expanded coverage with the goal of making the book suitable for use across two terms, thereby providing greater value for students.

In this edition we have replaced the use of function-notation casting with the more modern `static_cast<type>` throughout the text. The Quick Check exercises now appear at the end of each section with their answers following the chapter summary. We have moved coverage of pointers so that Chapter 10 now introduces pointers and reference types, while Chapter 11 adds coverage of using pointers with arrays plus dynamic allocation and deallocation of memory. Also added in Chapter 11 is a new section on C strings and using them in combination with the C++ `string` class. We have not yet adopted features of the C++11 standard because many users are still working with C++03.

Pedagogical Approach

Our approach, as always, is to provide a gradual layering of concepts, rather than piling on details and related alternatives that can be overwhelming. For example, many texts begin by introducing numeric types. Instead, we start with `char` and `string` types in Chapter 2 so that students can focus on the mechanics of constructing a C++ program that performs basic output and quickly get a working demonstration running. Once they are comfortable with the basics, in Chapter 3 we add numeric types. By separating the conceptual hurdles of statement and program syntax from the complexities of types that involve numeric precision, signedness, casting and precedence, we make it possible for more students to succeed early in the course.

Based on the research of Elliot Soloway with novice programmers, we continue to initially cover selection using only the If statement, and loops using only the While statement. However, because many instructors like to cover all selection control structures together and all looping control structures together, the chapter on additional control structures is directly after the chapters on selection and looping.

Similarly, students find it easier to comprehend the `struct` type, with its named fields that can mix types, than the array type with indexes that often involve arithmetic expressions for access. Thus, Chapter 10 introduces `struct` and `union` types, whereas arrays are deferred to Chapter 11. We also present simple uses of pointers and reference types in Chapter 10 and defer usage of pointers with arrays and dynamic allocation until Chapter 11 so that students can become comfortable with indirect access prior to working with values on the heap.

Recognizing that many students learn programming from mimicking existing solutions, we include numerous short example programs in every chapter. These programs illustrate chapter concepts in a more complete context than code segments and appear immediately after the introduction of new concepts. We have also organized chapters so that the discussion moves more quickly from a concept to its practical application early in the chapter, before moving on to related concepts. Chapters thus offer a series of concrete examples that serve as intermediate waypoints on the path to the major case studies.

C++ and Object-Oriented Programming

Some educators reject C and C++ as too permissive and too conducive to writing cryptic, unreadable programs. Our experience does not support this view, *provided that the use of language features is modeled appropriately*. The fact that the C family permits a terse, compact programming style cannot be labeled simply as "good" or "bad." Almost *any* programming language can be used to write in a style that is too terse and clever to be easily understood. Although the C family may, indeed, be used in this manner more often than other languages, we have found that with careful instruction in software engineering and use of a programming style that is straightforward, disciplined, and free of intricate language features, students can learn to use C++ to produce clear, readable code.

It must be emphasized that although we use C++ as a vehicle for teaching computer science concepts, the book is not a language manual: it does not attempt to cover the whole of the C++ language. Instead, the language constructs are introduced in parallel with the appropriate theory as a way to demonstrate its practical application.

There are diverse opinions about when to introduce the topic of object-oriented programming (OOP). Some educators advocate an immersion in OOP from the very beginning, whereas others (for whom this book is intended) favor a more heterogeneous approach, in which both functional decomposition and object-oriented design are presented as design tools. The chapter organization of *Programming and Problem Solving with C++, Comprehensive Sixth Edition* reflects a transitional approach to OOP. Classes and object-oriented terminology are presented in Chapter 12, but inheritance, polymorphism, and object-oriented design are deferred until Chapter 15. The intervening chapters offer ample time and experience for students to become comfortable with the practice of using classes.

Synopsis

Chapter 1 is designed to create a comfortable rapport between students and the subject. The basics of hardware and software are presented, issues in computer ethics are raised, C++ syntax is first encountered in a Software Maintenance Case Study, and problem-solving techniques are introduced and reinforced in a Problem-Solving Case Study.

Instead of overwhelming the student right away with the various numeric types available in C++, Chapter 2 concentrates on only two types: `char` and `string`. (For the latter type, we use the ISO/ANSI string class provided by the standard library.) With fewer data types to keep track of, students can focus on overall program structure and get an earlier start on creating and running a simple program. Chapter 3 follows with a discussion of the C++ numeric types and then moves on to cover arithmetic expressions, function calls, and output. Unlike many books that detail *all* of the C++ data types and *all* of the C++ operators at once, these two chapters focus on only the `int`, `float`, `char`, and `string` types, as well as the basic arithmetic operators. The discussion of other data types is postponed until Chapter 10.

Input and programming methodology are the major topics of Chapter 4. The distinction between object-oriented design (OOD) and functional decomposition is explained, and the functional decomposition methodology is then presented in more depth. Students thus gain the perspective early that there are two—not just one—design methodologies in widespread use and that each serves a specific purpose. Chapter 4 also covers file I/O. The early introduction of files permits the assignment of programming problems that require the use of sample data files.

Chapter 5 begins with the concept of flow of control and branching before moving into relational and Boolean operations. Selection, using the If-Then and If-Then-Else structures, demonstrates the distinction between physical ordering of statements and logical ordering. We also develop the concept of nested control structures. Chapter 5 concludes with a lengthy "Testing and Debugging" section that expands on the modular design discussion by introducing preconditions and postconditions. The algorithm walk-through and code walk-through are introduced as means of preventing errors, and the execution trace is used to find errors that may have made their way into the code. We also cover data validation and testing strategies extensively in this section.

Chapter 6 is devoted to loop control strategies and looping operations using the syntax of the While statement. Rather than introduce multiple syntactical structures, our approach is to teach the concepts of looping using only the While statement. Chapter 7 then covers the remaining "ice cream and cake" control structures in C++ (Switch, Do-While, and For), along with the Break and Continue statements. Like their dessert counterparts, these structures are nice to have, but not essential. The section on additional C++ operators has been moved into this chapter, as these operators are also useful but not indispensable.

By Chapter 8, students are already comfortable with breaking problems into modules and using library functions, and they are receptive to the idea of writing their own functions. Chapter 8 focuses on passing arguments by value and covers flow of control in function calls, arguments and parameters, local variables, and interface design. Coverage of interface design includes preconditions and postconditions in the interface documentation, control abstraction, encapsulation, and physical versus conceptual hiding of an implementation. Chapter 9 expands on this discussion to include value-returning functions, reference parameters, scope and lifetime, stubs and drivers, and more on interface design, including side effects.

Chapter 10 begins the transition between the control structure orientation of the first part of the book and the data structure orientation of the second part. We revisit the built-in simple data types in terms of the set of values represented by each type and the allowable operations on those values. Enumeration types, structs, and unions are covered. In addition, Chapter 10 includes a discussion of simple versus structured data types. In this edition we have added pointers and reference types.

In Chapter 11, the array is introduced as a homogeneous data structure whose components are accessed by position rather than by name. One-dimensional arrays are examined in depth, including arrays of structs. Material on C strings, two-dimensional arrays, three-dimensional arrays, and multidimensional arrays rounds out the discussion of the array type. The chapter concludes with using pointers with arrays and the dynamic allocation of data.

Chapter 12 formalizes the concept of an abstract data type as an introduction to the discussion of the class construct. Object-oriented terminology is presented, emphasizing the distinction between a class and an object. Good class design principles are stressed. The use of specification files and implementation files is presented as a form of information hiding. Although mutability is discussed and illustrated in a brief example, all of the classes developed in this chapter are intentionally immutable: students have enough new software design concepts to digest at this point without adding this aspect to the mix.

Mutable classes are demonstrated repeatedly in the next chapter, however. Chapter 13 integrates the material from Chapters 11 and 12 by defining the list as an ADT, which is then implemented by a class containing an array. Because we have already introduced classes and arrays, we can clearly distinguish between arrays and lists from the very beginning of this discussion. The array is a built-in, fixed-size data structure. The list is a user-defined, variable-size structure, represented in this chapter as a length variable and an array of items bound together in a class object. In Chapter 13, we design C++ classes for unsorted and sorted list ADTs, and we code the list algorithms as class member functions. Chapter 14 examines dynamic allocation and deallocation of data. Pointers are then used to provide a dynamic linked implementation of the unsorted and sorted list ADTs from Chapter 13.

Chapter 15 extends the concepts of data abstraction and C++ classes to an exploration of object-oriented software development. The notion of inheritance is introduced, and students learn to distinguish between inheritance and composition. This chapter also introduces C++ virtual functions, which support polymorphism in the form of run-time binding of operations. Object-oriented design, introduced briefly in Chapter 4 and further developed in Chapter 12, is revisited in greater depth here as well. We present an outline of how to move from the problem statement through the design phase of a software solution. We then follow this outline in the case study, implement the design, and discuss testing strategies.

Chapter 16 introduces C++ templates, operator overloading, and exception handling. Chapter 17 discusses classic data structures and introduces their STL equivalents. Several of the STL container classes are used to reimplement programs from previous chapters.

Chapter 18 concludes the text by introducing the concept of recursion. This chapter is broken into three parts: recursion with simple variables, recursion with arrays, and recursion with pointers. Its organization allows an instructor to cover all of recursion as a separate topic or piece-by-piece in conjunction with the presentation of value-returning functions, arrays, and pointers, according to his or her preference.

Additional Features

Special Sections

Five kinds of features are set off from the main text:

- Theoretical Foundations sections present material related to the fundamental theory behind various branches of computer science.
- Software Engineering Tips discuss methods of making programs more reliable, robust, or efficient.
- Matters of Style address stylistic issues in the coding of programs.
- Background Information sections explore side issues that enhance the student's general knowledge of computer science.
- May We Introduce sections contain biographies of computing pioneers such as Blaise Pascal, Charles Babbage, Ada Lovelace, and Grace Murray Hopper.

Goals

Each chapter begins with a list of goals for the student, broken into two categories: knowledge goals and skill goals. Both types of goals are reinforced and tested in the end-of-chapter exercises.

Demonstration Programs

Much shorter and simpler than the case study examples, demonstration programs provide a bridge between syntactic concepts and their application in a problem-solving context. Each chapter now includes multiple complete demonstration programs, interspersed with coverage of new programming and language topics. All of these programs are available at go.jblearning.com/PPS6e so that students can easily experiment with them and reuse the code in their own projects.

Software Maintenance Case Studies

The majority of modern software engineering work involves maintaining legacy code. Given this fact, it is essential that students learn the skills associated with reading, understanding, extending, and fixing existing programs. Such skills are rarely taught in an introductory course, where the focus tends to be on writing new programs from problem specifications. It turns out that these same maintenance skills are actually an important aspect of successfully writing new programs: Once a modest amount of code has been written, the process of getting it to work correctly is, at its essence, synonymous with maintenance. These case studies are intended to build the skills of reading, dissecting, modifying, and testing existing code.

Problem-Solving Case Studies

Problem solving is best demonstrated through case studies. In each of the Problem-Solving Case Studies, we present a problem and use problem-solving techniques to develop a manual solution. Next, we expand the solution to an algorithm, using functional decomposition, object-oriented design, or both; then we code the algorithm in C++. We show sample test data and output, and then follow up with a discussion of what is involved in thoroughly testing the program.

Testing and Debugging

Testing and Debugging sections follow the case studies in each chapter and consider in depth the implications of the chapter material with regard to the thorough testing of programs. These sections conclude with a list of testing and debugging hints.

Quick Checks
At the end of each section are questions that test the student's recall of major points associated with the chapter goals. On reading each question, the student immediately should know the answer, which he or she can then verify by glancing at the answers at the end of the chapter. The page number where the concept is discussed appears at the end of each question, allowing the student to readily review the material in the event of an incorrect response.

Exam Preparation Exercises
The Exam Preparation Exercises are intended to help the student prepare for tests. The questions usually have objective answers and are designed to be answered with only a few minutes of work.

Programming Warm-Up Exercises
The Programming Warm-Up Exercises provide the student with experience in writing C++ code fragments. The student can practice the syntactic constructs in each chapter without the burden of writing a complete program.

Programming Problems
Programming Problems, which are drawn from a wide range of disciplines, require the student to design solutions and write complete programs. Some of the problems are carried through multiple chapters, with subsequent chapters' Programming Problems asking the student to reimplement the solution using new constructs or techniques as a way of illustrating that one problem can be solved by many different approaches.

Case Study Follow-Up
The Case Study Follow-Up exercises give the student an opportunity to strengthen his or her software maintenance skills by answering questions that require reading the case study code or making changes to it.

Supplements

Instructor's Resources
The online resources are powerful teaching aids available to adopters on request from the publisher. They include a complete set of exercise answers, a Test Bank, PowerPoint lecture outlines, and the complete programs from the text. To request access, contact your account representative or visit go.jblearning.com/PPS6e.

Programs
The source code for all of the complete programs that appear within the textbook is available as a free download for instructors and students from the publisher's website (go.jblearning.com/PPS6e). This code includes all of the case study programs, plus the demonstration programs that appear interspersed within the various chapters. The program files can be viewed or edited using any standard text editor, but a C++ compiler must be used to compile and run the programs.

A Laboratory Course in C++, Sixth Edition
The digital lab manual that accompanies this book follows the organization of this edition of the text. It is designed to allow the instructor maximum flexibility in making assignments and may be used in both open and closed laboratory settings. Each chapter contains three types of activities: Prelab, Inlab, and Postlab. Each chapter is broken into lessons that

thoroughly demonstrate the concepts covered in the corresponding chapter. The programs, program shells (partial programs), and data files that accompany the lab manual can be found on the website for this book.

Acknowledgments

We would like to thank the many individuals who have helped us in the preparation of this *Sixth Edition*. In particular, we are indebted to the members of the faculties of the Computer Science Departments at the University of Texas at Austin and the University of Massachusetts at Amherst.

We extend special thanks to Jeff Brumfield for developing the syntax template metalanguage and allowing us to use it in the text. Special thanks also to Tim Richards for his help with developing the *Sixth Edition* and its ancillary materials.

For their many helpful suggestions, we thank the lecturers, teaching assistants, consultants, and student proctors who run the courses for which this book was written, as well as the students themselves.

We are grateful to the following people who took the time to offer their comments on potential changes for this and previous editions: Ziya Arnavut, SUNY Fredonia; Trudee Bremer, Illinois Central College; Mira Carlson, Northeastern Illinois University; Kevin Daimi, University of Detroit, Mercy; Bruce Elenbogen, University of Michigan, Dearborn; Letha Etzkorn, University of Alabama–Huntsville; Ilga Higbee, Black Hawk College; Sue Kavli, Dallas Baptist University; Sandria Kerr, Winston-Salem State University; Alicia Kime, Fairmont State College; Shahadat Kowuser, University of Texas, Pan America; Bruce Maxim, University of Michigan, Dearborn; William McQuain, Virginia Tech; Xiannong Meng, Bucknell University, PA; William Minervini, Broward University; Janet Remen, Washtenaw Community College; Viviana Sandor, Oakland University; Mehdi Setareh, Virginia Tech; Katherine Snyder, University of Detroit, Mercy; Tom Steiner, University of Michigan, Dearborn; John Weaver, West Chester University; Charles Welty, University of Southern Maine; Cheer-Sun Yang, West Chester University.

We also thank the many people at Jones & Bartlett Learning who contributed so much to this book, especially Tim Anderson, Senior Acquisitions Editor; Amy Bloom, Senior Developmental Editor; and Amy Rose, Director of Production.

Anyone who has ever written a book—or is related to someone who has—can appreciate the amount of time involved in such a project. To our families—all of the Dale clan and the extended Dale family (too numerous to name), and to Lisa, Charlie, and Abby—thanks for your tremendous support and indulgence.

N. D.
C. W.

To quote Mephistopheles, one of the chief devils and tempter of Faust,

...My friend, I shall be pedagogic,
And say you ought to start with Logic...
...Days will be spent to let you know
That what you once did at one blow,
Like eating and drinking so easy and free,
Can only be done with One, Two, Three.
Yet the web of thought has no such creases
And is more like a weaver's masterpieces;
One step, a thousand threads arise,
Hither and thither shoots each shuttle,
The threads flow on, unseen and subtle,
Each blow effects a thousand ties.
The philosopher comes with analysis
And proves it had to be like this;
The first was so, the second so,
And hence the third and fourth was so,
And were not the first and second here,
Then the third and fourth could never appear.
That is what all the students believe,
But they have never learned to weave.

J. W. von Goethe, *Faust*, Walter Kaufman trans., New York, 1963, 199.

As you study this book, do not let the logic of algorithms bind your imagination, but rather make it your tool for weaving masterpieces of thought.

Overview of Programming and Problem Solving

KNOWLEDGE GOALS

- To understand what a computer program is.
- To understand what an algorithm is.
- To learn what a high-level programming language is.
- To understand the compilation and execution processes.
- To learn the history of the C++ language.
- To learn what the major components of a computer are and how they work together.
- To learn about some of the basic ethical issues confronting computing professionals.

SKILL GOALS

To be able to:
- List the basic stages involved in writing a computer program.
- Describe what a compiler is and what it does.
- Distinguish between hardware and software.
- Choose an appropriate problem-solving method for developing an algorithmic solution to a problem.

1.1 Overview of Programming

com•put•er \kəm–pyōō′tər\ n. often attrib (1646): one that computes; *specif* : a programmable electronic device that can store, retrieve, and process data.[1]

What a brief definition for something that has, in just a few decades, changed the way of life in industrialized societies! Computers touch all areas of our lives: paying bills, driving cars, using the telephone, shopping. In fact, it would be easier to list those areas of our lives that are *not* affected by computers.

It is sad that a device that does so much good is so often maligned and feared. How many times have you heard someone say, "I'm sorry, our computer fouled things up" or "I just don't understand computers; they're too complicated for me"? The very fact that you are reading this book, however, means that you are ready to set aside prejudice and learn about computers. But be forewarned: This book is not just about computers in the abstract. This is a text to teach you how to program computers.

What Is Programming?

Much of human behavior and thought is characterized by logical sequences. Since infancy, you have been learning how to act, how to do things. You have also learned to expect certain behavior from other people.

A lot of what you do every day, you do automatically. Fortunately, it is not necessary for you to consciously think of every step involved in a process as simple as turning a page by hand:

1. Lift hand.
2. Move hand to right side of book.
3. Grasp top-right corner of page.
4. Move hand from right to left until page is positioned so that you can read what is on the other side.
5. Let go of page.

> **Programming** Planning or scheduling the performance of a task or an event.
>
> **Computer** A programmable device that can store, retrieve, and process data.
>
> **Computer program** A sequence of instructions to be performed by a computer.
>
> **Computer programming** The process of planning a sequence of steps for a computer to follow.

Think how many neurons must fire and how many muscles must respond, all in a certain order or sequence, to move your arm and hand. Yet you do it unconsciously.

Much of what you do unconsciously you once had to learn. Watch how a baby concentrates on putting one foot before the other while learning to walk. Then watch a group of three-year-olds playing tag.

On a broader scale, mathematics never could have been developed without logical sequences of steps for solving problems and proving theorems. Mass production never would have worked without operations taking place in a certain order. Our whole civilization is based on the order of things and actions.

We create order, both consciously and unconsciously, through a process we call programming. This book is concerned with the programming of one of our tools, the computer.

Just as a concert program lists the order in which the players perform pieces, so a computer program lists the sequence of steps the computer performs. From now on, when we use the words *programming* and *program*, we mean computer programming and *computer program*.

---

1. By permission. From *Merriam-Webster's Collegiate Dictionary*, tenth edition. © 1994 by Merriam-Webster Inc.

The computer allows us to do tasks more efficiently, quickly, and accurately than we could by hand—if we could do them by hand at all. To use this powerful tool, we must specify what we want done and the order in which we want it done. We do this through programming.

How Do We Write a Program?

A computer is not intelligent. It cannot analyze a problem and come up with a solution. Instead, a human (the *programmer*) must analyze the problem, develop a sequence of instructions for solving the problem, and then communicate it to the computer. What's the advantage of using a computer if it can't solve problems? Once we have written the solution as a sequence of instructions for the computer, the computer can repeat the solution very quickly and consistently, again and again. The computer frees people from repetitive and boring tasks.

To write a sequence of instructions for a computer to follow, we must go through a two-phase process: *problem solving* and *implementation* (see **FIGURE 1.1**).

Problem-Solving Phase

1. *Analysis and specification.* Understand (define) the problem and what the solution must do.
2. *General solution (algorithm).* Develop a logical sequence of steps that solves the problem.
3. *Verify.* Follow the steps exactly to see if the solution really does solve the problem.

FIGURE 1.1 Programming Process

Implementation Phase

1. *Concrete solution (program).* Translate the algorithm into a programming language.
2. *Test.* Have the computer follow the instructions, then manually check the results. If you find errors, analyze the program and the algorithm to determine the source of the errors, and then make corrections.

Once a program has been written, it enters a third phase: *maintenance*.

Maintenance Phase

1. *Use.* Use the program.
2. *Maintain.* Modify the program to meet changing requirements or to correct any errors that show up in using it.

This series of stages is known as the *waterfall model* of software development. Other development models exist that are used in different situations. For example, the *spiral model* involves developing an initial specification of the problem, programming a portion of the solution, having the client evaluate the result, and then revising the specification and repeating the process until the client is satisfied. The spiral model is appropriate when a problem is not well defined initially or when aspects of the problem are changing during the development. Solutions to scientific or engineering research problems are often developed using the spiral model. We use the waterfall model throughout this book because it is well suited for solving the kinds of clearly defined problems that you'll encounter in an introductory programming course.

What Is an Algorithm?

The programmer begins the programming process by analyzing the problem and developing a general solution called an algorithm. Understanding and analyzing a problem take up much more time than Figure 1.1 implies. These steps are the heart of the programming process.

Algorithm A step-by-step procedure for solving a problem in a finite amount of time.

If our definitions of a computer program and an algorithm look similar, it is because all programs are algorithms. A program is simply an algorithm that has been written for a computer.

An algorithm is a verbal or written description of a logical sequence of actions. We use algorithms every day. Recipes, instructions, and directions are all examples of algorithms that are not programs.

When you start your car, you follow a step-by-step procedure. The algorithm might look something like this:

1. Insert the key.
2. Depress the brake pedal.
3. Make sure the transmission is in Park (or Neutral).
4. Turn the key to the start position.
5. If the engine starts within six seconds, release the key to the ignition position.
6. If the engine doesn't start in six seconds, release the key and gas pedal, wait ten seconds, and repeat Steps 3 through 6, but not more than five times.
7. If the car doesn't start, call the garage.

Without the phrase "but not more than five times" in Step 6, you could be trying to start the car forever. Why? Because if something is wrong with the car, repeating Steps 3 through 6 over and over again will not start it. This kind of never-ending situation is called an *infinite loop*. If we leave the phrase "but not more than five times" out of Step 6, the procedure does not fit our definition of an algorithm. An algorithm must terminate in a finite amount of time for all possible conditions.

Suppose a programmer needs an algorithm to determine an employee's weekly wages. The algorithm reflects what would be done by hand:

1. Look up the employee's pay rate.
2. Determine the number of hours worked during the week.
3. If the number of hours worked is less than or equal to 40, multiply the number of hours by the pay rate to calculate regular wages.
4. If the number of hours worked is greater than 40, multiply 40 by the pay rate to calculate regular wages, and then multiply the difference between the number of hours worked and 40 by 1.5 times the pay rate to calculate overtime wages.
5. Add the regular wages to the overtime wages (if any) to determine total wages for the week.

The steps the computer follows are often the same steps you would use to do the calculations by hand.

After developing a general solution, the programmer tests the algorithm, walking through each step mentally or manually. If the algorithm doesn't work, the programmer repeats the problem-solving process, analyzing the problem again and coming up with another algorithm. Often the second algorithm is just a variation of the first. When the programmer is satisfied with the algorithm, he or she translates it into a programming language. We use the C++ programming language in this book.

> **Programming language** A set of rules, symbols, and special words used to construct a computer program.

What Is a Programming Language?

A programming language is a simplified form of English (with math symbols) that adheres to a strict set of grammatical rules. English is far too complicated a language for today's computers to follow. Programming languages, because they limit vocabulary and grammar, are much simpler.

Although a programming language is simple in form, it is not always easy to use. Try giving someone directions to the nearest airport using a vocabulary of no more than 45 words, and you'll begin to see the problem. Programming forces you to write very simple, exact instructions.

Translating an algorithm into a programming language is called *coding* the algorithm. The product of that translation—the program—is tested by running (*executing*) it on the computer. If the program fails to produce the desired results, the programmer must *debug* it—that is, determine what is wrong and then modify the program, or even the algorithm, to fix it. The combination of coding and testing an algorithm is called *implementation*.

There is no single way to implement an algorithm. For example, an algorithm can be translated into more than one programming language, and each translation produces a different implementation. Even when two people translate the same algorithm into the same programming language, they are likely to come up with different implementations (see **FIGURE 1.2**). Why? Because every programming language allows the programmer some flexibility in how an algorithm is translated. Given this flexibility, people adopt their own styles in writing programs, just as they do in writing short stories or essays. Once you have some programming experience, you will develop a style of your own. Throughout this book, we offer tips on good programming style.

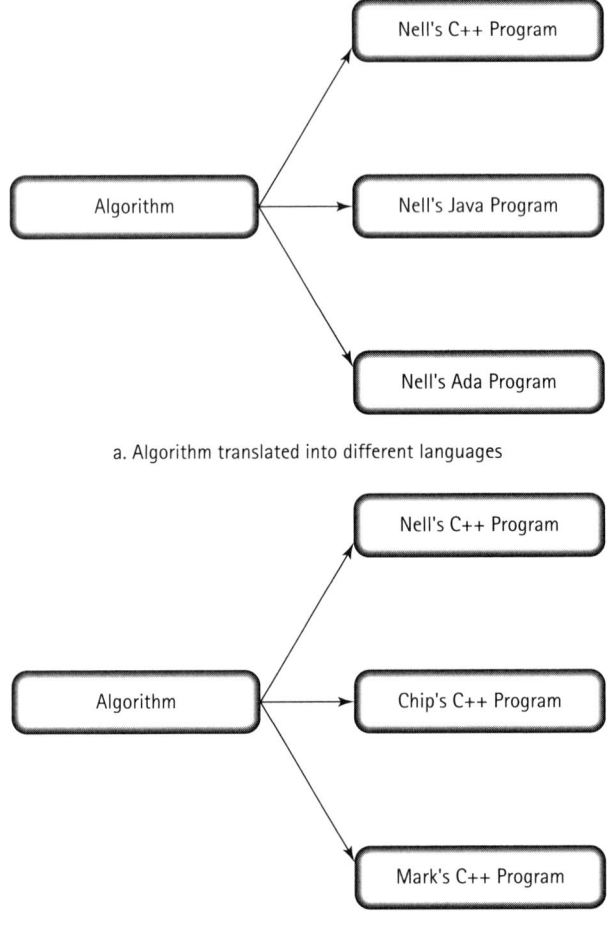

a. Algorithm translated into different languages

b. Algorithm translated by different people

FIGURE 1.2 Differences in Implementations

Some people try to speed up the programming process by going directly from the problem definition to coding the program (see **FIGURE 1.3**). A shortcut here is very tempting and at first seems to save a lot of time. However, for many reasons that will become obvious to you as you read this book, this kind of shortcut actually takes *more* time and effort. Developing a general solution before you write a program helps you manage the problem, keep your thoughts straight, and avoid mistakes. If you don't take the time at the beginning to think out and polish your algorithm, you'll spend a lot of extra time debugging and revising your program. So think first and code later! The sooner you start coding, the longer it takes to write a program that works.

Once a program has been put into use, it may become necessary to modify it. Modification may involve fixing an error that is discovered during the use of the program or changing the program in response to changes in the user's requirements. Each time the program is modified, the problem-solving and implementation phases must be repeated for those aspects of the program that change. This phase of the programming process, which is known as maintenance, actually accounts for the majority of the effort expended on most programs.

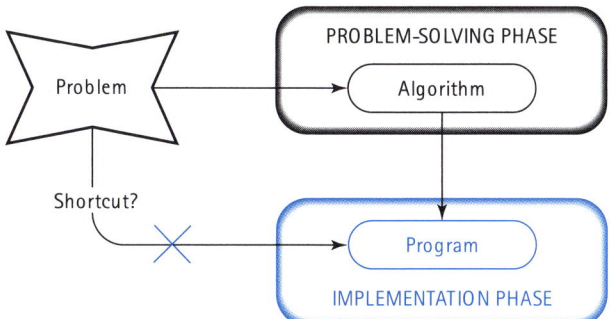

FIGURE 1.3 Programming Shortcut?

For example, a program that is implemented in a few months may need to be maintained over a period of many years. Thus it is a cost-effective investment of time to develop the initial problem solution and program implementation carefully. Together, the problem-solving, implementation, and maintenance phases constitute the program's *life cycle*.

In addition to solving the problem, implementing the algorithm, and maintaining the program, documentation is an important part of the programming process. Documentation includes written explanations of the problem being solved and the organization of the solution, comments embedded within the program itself, and user manuals that describe how to use the program. Most programs are worked on by many different people over a long period of time. Each of those people must be able to read and understand your code.

> **Documentation** The written text and comments that make a program easier for others to understand, use, and modify.
> **Information** Any knowledge that can be communicated.
> **Data** Information in a form a computer can use.

After you write a program, you must give the computer the information or data necessary to solve the problem. Information is any knowledge that can be communicated, including abstract ideas and concepts such as "the earth is round." Data is information in a form the computer can use—for example, the numbers and letters making up the formulas that relate the earth's radius to its volume and surface area. Data can represent many kinds of information, such as sounds, images, video, rocket telemetry, automobile engine functions, weather, global climate, interactions of atomic particles, drug effects on viruses, and so forth. Part of the programming process involves deciding how to represent the information in a problem as data.

THEORETICAL FOUNDATIONS
Binary Representation of Data

In a computer, data are represented electronically by pulses of electricity. Electric circuits, in their simplest form, are either on or off. A circuit that is on represents the number 1; a circuit that is off represents the number 0. Any kind of data can be represented by combinations of enough 1s and 0s. We simply have to choose

> **THEORETICAL FOUNDATIONS** Binary Representation of Data, continued

which combination represents each piece of data we are using. For example, we could arbitrarily choose the pattern 1101000110 to represent the name "C++."

Data represented by 1s and 0s are in binary form. The binary, or base-2, number system uses only 1s and 0s to represent numbers. (The decimal, or base-10, number system uses the digits 0 through 9.) The word bit (short for <u>bi</u>nary dig<u>it</u>) refers to a single 1 or 0. Thus the pattern 1101000110 has ten bits. A binary number with three bits can represent 2^3, or eight, different patterns. The eight patterns are shown here, together with some examples of base-2 arithmetic:

Binary	Decimal Equivalent	Examples of Binary Addition	Decimal Equivalent
000	0	001 + 001 = 010	1 + 1 = 2
001	1	011 + 010 = 101	3 + 2 = 5
010	2	111 + 001 = 1000	7 + 1 = 8
011	3		
100	4	*Examples of Binary Subtraction*	
101	5	011 − 011 = 000	3 − 3 = 0
110	6	110 − 010 = 100	6 − 2 = 4
111	7	101 − 011 = 010	5 − 3 = 2

A ten-digit binary number can represent 2^{10} (1024) distinct patterns. Thus you can use your fingers to count in binary from 0 to 1023! A byte is a group of eight bits; it can represent 2^8 (256) patterns. Inside the computer, each character (such as the letter A, the letter g, the digit 7, a question mark, or a blank) is usually represented by either one or two bytes.[2] For example, in one scheme 01001101 represents M and 01101101 represents m (look closely—the third bit from the left is the only difference). Groups of 16, 32, and 64 bits are generally referred to as words (the terms "short word" and "long word" sometimes are used to refer to 16-bit and 64-bit groups, respectively).

The process of assigning bit patterns to pieces of data is called coding—the same name we give to the process of translating an algorithm into a programming language. The names are the same because the first computers recognized only one language, which was binary in form. Thus, in the early days of computers, programming meant translating both data and algorithms into patterns of 1s and 0s. The resulting programs looked like messages in a secret code that were being passed from the programmer to the computer. It was very difficult for one programmer to understand a program written by another programmer. In fact, after leaving a program alone for a while, many programmers could not even understand their own programs!

The patterns of bits that represent data vary from one family of computers to another. Even on the same computer, different programming languages may use different binary representations for the same data. A single programming language may even use the same pattern of bits to represent different things in different contexts. (People do this, too: The four

---

2. Most programming languages use the American Standard Code for Information Interchange (ASCII) to represent the English alphabet and other symbols. Each ASCII character is stored in a single byte. The Java language uses a newer standard called Unicode, which includes the alphabets of many other languages. A single Unicode character takes up two bytes in the computer's memory. With a little extra work on the part of the programmer, C++ can also process Unicode.

THEORETICAL FOUNDATIONS Binary Representation of Data, continued

letters that form the word *tack* have different meanings depending on whether you are talking about upholstery, sailing, sewing, paint, or horseback riding.) The point is that patterns of bits by themselves are meaningless. Rather, it is the way in which the patterns are used that gives them their meaning. That's why we combine data with operations to form meaningful objects.

Fortunately, we no longer have to work with binary coding schemes. Today, the process of coding is usually just a matter of writing down the data in letters, numbers, and symbols. The computer automatically converts these letters, numbers, and symbols into binary form. Still, as you work with computers, you will continually run into numbers that are related to powers of 2—numbers such as 256, 32,768, and 65,536. They are reminders that the binary number system is lurking somewhere in the background.

QUICK CHECK

1.1.1 What do we call a sequence of instructions that is executed by a computer? (p. 2)
1.1.2 Is a computer capable of analyzing a problem to come up with a solution? (p. 3)
1.1.3 How does an algorithm differ from a computer program? (p. 4)
1.1.4 Describe the three important phases of the *waterfall model* we must go through to write a sequence of instructions for a computer. (p. 3–4)
1.1.5 How does a programming language differ from a human language? (p. 5)

Answers to Quick Check questions are given at the end of each chapter.

1.2 How Does a Computer Run a Program?

In the computer, all data, whatever its form, is stored and used in binary codes—that is, as strings of 1s and 0s. Instructions and data are stored together in the computer's memory using these binary codes. If you were to look at the binary codes representing instructions and data in memory, you could not tell the difference between them; they are distinguished only by the manner in which the computer uses them. This scheme makes it possible for the computer to process its own instructions as a form of data.

When computers were first developed, the only programming language available was the primitive instruction set built into each machine, the machine language, or *machine code*.

Even though most computers perform the same kinds of operations, their designers choose different sets of binary codes for each instruction. Thus the machine code for one computer is not the same as the machine code for another computer.

When programmers used machine language for programming, they had to enter the binary codes for the various instructions, a tedious process that was prone to error. Moreover, their programs were difficult to read and modify. In time, assembly languages were developed to make the programmer's job easier.

Machine language The language, made up of binary-coded instructions, that is used directly by the computer.

Assembly language A low-level programming language in which a mnemonic is used to represent each of the machine language instructions for a particular computer.

Instructions in an assembly language are in an easy-to-remember form called a *mnemonic* (pronounced nee-MAHN-ik). Typical instructions for addition and subtraction might look like this:

Although assembly language is easier for humans to work with, the computer cannot directly execute the instructions. One of the fundamental discoveries in computer science is that, because a computer can process its own instructions as a form of data, it is possible to write a program to translate the assembly language instructions into machine code.

Such a program is called an assembler. The name comes from the fact that much of what an assembler does is to look up the pieces of an instruction in a table to find the corresponding binary code (such as ADD = 1001, R1 = 001, R3 = 011, R5 = 101), and then assemble these binary coded pieces of the instruction into a complete machine language instruction (1001 001 011 101). The assembler also puts the instructions together in the specified sequence to create a complete program.

Assembler A program that translates an assembly language program into machine code.

Assembly language is a step in the right direction, but it still forces programmers to think in terms of individual machine instructions. Eventually, computer scientists developed high-level programming languages. These languages are easier to use than assembly languages or machine code because they are closer to English and other natural languages (see **FIGURE 1.4**).

FIGURE 1.4 Levels of Abstraction

A program called a compiler translates programs written in certain high-level languages (C++, Java, Visual Basic, and Ada, for example) into machine language. If you write a program in a high-level language, you can run it on any computer that has the appropriate compiler. This is possible because most high-level languages are *standardized*, which means that an official description of the language exists.

A program in a high-level language is called a source program. To the compiler, a source program is just input data. It translates the source program into a machine language program called an object program (see **FIGURE 1.5**). If there are errors in the program, the compiler instead generates one or more error messages indicating the nature and location of the errors.

> **Compiler** A program that translates a high-level language into machine code.
> **Source program** A program written in a high-level programming language.
> **Object program** The machine language version of a source program.

One benefit of using standardized high-level languages is that they allow you to write *portable* (or *machine-independent*) code. As Figure 1.5 emphasizes, a single C++ program can be used on different machines, whereas a program written in assembly language or machine language is not portable from one computer to another. Because each computer has its own machine language, a machine language program written for computer A will not run on computer B.

It is important to understand that compilation and execution are two distinct processes. During compilation, the computer runs the compiler program. During execution, the object program is loaded into the computer's memory unit, replacing the compiler program. The computer then runs the object program, doing whatever the program instructs it to do (see **FIGURE 1.6**).

FIGURE 1.5 High-Level Programming Languages Allow Programs to Be Compiled on Different Systems

FIGURE 1.6 Compilation and Execution

BACKGROUND INFORMATION
Compilation Versus Interpretation

Some programming languages—LISP, Prolog, and many versions of BASIC, for example—are translated by an *interpreter* rather than by a compiler. An interpreter translates *and executes* each instruction in the source program, one instruction at a time. In contrast, a compiler translates the entire source program into machine language, after which execution of the object program takes place. The difference between compilation and interpretation is like the difference between translating a book of poetry into another language (say, translating Goethe's *Faust* from German to English) and having a human interpreter provide a live interpretation of a dramatic reading of some poems.

The Java language uses both a compiler and an interpreter. First, a Java program is compiled not into a particular computer's machine language, but rather into an intermediate code called bytecode. Next, a program called the Java Virtual Machine (JVM) takes the bytecode program and interprets it (that is, translates a bytecode instruction into machine language and executes it, translates the next instruction and executes it, and so on). Thus, a Java program compiled into bytecode is portable to many different computers, as long as each computer has its own specific JVM that can translate bytecode into the computer's machine language.

What Kinds of Instructions Can Be Written in a Programming Language?

The instructions in a programming language reflect the operations a computer can perform:

- A computer can transfer data from one place to another.
- A computer can input data from an input device (a keyboard or mouse, for example) and output data to an output device (a screen, for example).
- A computer can store data into and retrieve data from its memory and secondary storage (parts of a computer that we discuss in the next section).
- A computer can compare two data values for equality or inequality.
- A computer can perform arithmetic operations (addition and subtraction, for example) very quickly.

Programming languages require that we use certain *control structures* to express algorithms as programs. There are four basic ways of structuring statements (instructions) in most programming languages: sequentially, conditionally, repetitively, and with subprograms (see **FIGURE 1.7**). A *sequence* is a series of statements that are executed one after another. *Selection*, the conditional control structure, executes different statements depending on certain conditions. The *repetitive* control structure, called a *loop*, repeats statements while certain conditions are met. The *subprogram* allows us to structure a program by breaking it into smaller units. Each of these ways of structuring statements controls the order in which the computer executes the statements, which is why they are called control structures.

Imagine you're driving a car. Going down a straight stretch of road is like following a sequence of instructions. When you come to a fork in the road, you must decide which way to go and then take one or the other branch of the fork. This is what the computer does when it encounters a selection control structure (also called a *branch*) in a program. Sometimes you have to go around the block several times to find a place to park. The computer does the same sort of thing when it encounters a loop in a program.

A subprogram is a process that consists of multiple steps. Every day, for example, you follow a procedure to get from home to work. It makes sense, then, for someone to give you directions to a meeting by saying, "Go to the office, then go four blocks west" without specifying all the steps you have to take to get to the office. Subprograms allow us to write parts of our programs separately and then assemble them into final form. They can greatly simplify the task of writing large programs.

What Is Software Maintenance?

In the life cycle of a program, the maintenance phase accounts for the majority of a typical program's existence. As we said earlier, programs are initially written in a fairly short time span, and then are used for many years after. The original designers develop the program to meet a set of specifications, and they cannot possibly foresee all the ways that the program will be used in the future. Decisions that were made in the initial implementation may prove to be inadequate to support some future use, and a new team of programmers may then be called in to modify the program. After going through many modifications, the code may become so complicated that it is difficult to identify the purpose of some of the original instructions.

For example, at the turn of the millennium, the software industry faced a major maintenance effort known collectively as the "Y2K Problem." For much of the preceding 50

14 CHAPTER 1 Overview of Programming and Problem Solving

SEQUENCE

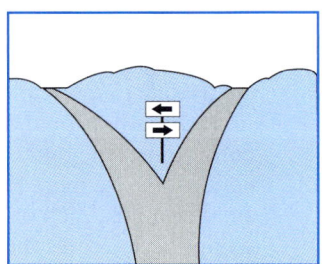

SELECTION (also called *branch* or *decision*)
IF condition THEN statement1 ELSE statement2

LOOP (also called *repetition* or *iteration*)
WHILE condition DO statement1

SUBPROGRAM (also called *procedure*, *function*, *method*, or *subroutine*)

FIGURE 1.7 Basic Control Structures of Programming Languages

years, programmers had been encoding dates with a two-digit integer representing the year, as shown here:

Year Code	Actual Year
00	1900
01	1901
.	.
.	.
.	.
64	1964
.	.
.	.
.	.
99	1999

There was no way for these programs to make the transition to the new millennium and be able to distinguish a year such as 2005 from 1905. There were dire predictions for the failure of much of our modern infrastructure, such as the shutdown of the electric power grid, telecommunication networks, and banking systems.

In the end, the software industry spent billions of dollars finding all of the places where programs used a two-digit year and changing the code to use four digits. Some of this code dated back to the 1960s, and the original programmers were not available to help with the conversion. A new generation of programmers had to read and understand the programs well enough to make the necessary changes.

While the rest of the world was celebrating New Year's Eve in 1999, many of these programmers were sitting at their computers, watching nervously as the date ticked over to 2000, just in case they had missed something. A few problems were encountered, but the vast majority of computers made the transition without skipping a beat.

In retrospect, it is easy to find fault with the decisions of the original programmers to use a two-digit date. But at the time, computers had very small memories (in the 1960s, a large computer had only 65,000 bytes of main memory), and saving even a byte or two in representing a date could make the difference between a working program and one that wouldn't fit in memory. None of those programmers expected their code to be used for 40 years. It is impossible to know which programming decisions are being made today that will turn out to be problematic in the future.

Successive attempts to extend the capabilities of a program will often produce errors because programmers fail to comprehend the ways that earlier changes to the program will interact with new changes. In some cases, testing fails to reveal those errors before the modified program is released, and it is the user who discovers the error. Then, fixing the bugs becomes a new maintenance task and the corrections are usually done hastily because users are clamoring for their software to work. The result is code that is even harder to understand. In time, the software grows so complex that attempts to fix errors frequently produce new errors. In some cases the only solution is to start over, rewriting much of the software anew with a clean design.

SOFTWARE MAINTENANCE CASE STUDY: An Introduction to Software Maintenance

The preceding discussion is intended to illustrate the importance of developing skills not just in writing new code, but also in working with existing code. These Software Maintenance Case Study sections walk you through the process of typical maintenance tasks. Unlike the Problem-Solving Case Study sections, where we begin with a problem, solve it, and then code a program, here we begin with a program and see how to understand what it does before making some change.

Let's start with something extremely simple, just to get a sense of what we'll be doing in future Software Maintenance Case Study sections. We keep this example so simple that you don't even have to know anything about C++ to follow what's happening. But in following our steps through this process, you'll get a sense of what's involved in working with programs.

MAINTENANCE TASK: Enter the "Hello World" application program, changing it to output "Hello Universe" instead.

EXISTING CODE

```
//***********************************
// This program prints Hello World!.
//***********************************
#include <iostream>
using namespace std;
int main ()
{
  cout << "Hello World!";
  return 0;
}
```

DISCUSSION: The classic first application that is written by many beginners is generically known as "Hello World." Its sole purpose is to print out a greeting from the computer to the programmer, and then quit. There are many variations of the message, but the traditional one is "Hello World!" Here, we are being asked to change the existing message to "Hello Universe!"

Looking at this code, you can immediately see the message, enclosed in quotes. Your first temptation would be to just change the word "World" to "Universe". (Even without knowing any C++, you're already programming!) In a simple case like this, that strategy may be adequate; with a larger application, however, such an approach could result in the creation of more problems. With any maintenance effort, we must first observe and record the current behavior of the application. If it isn't working initially, you may think that your changes are the source of a preexisting problem and spend many hours in a futile attempt to fix the problem by correcting your changes.

Thus the first step in this maintenance task is to enter the application exactly as it is written and run it to ensure that it works. Unless you've written programs before, it is hard to appreciate how precisely you must type C++ code. Every letter, every capitalization, every punctuation mark is significant. There are exceptions, which we'll see later, but for now, it is good practice to enter this application exactly as it appears here. For example, can you spot the error in the following version of the code that fails to run? All you have to do is compare it, letter by letter, with the preceding version, to find the difference.[3]

---

3. In the fifth line, the word "cout" has been capitalized instead of being typed entirely in lowercase.

SOFTWARE MAINTENANCE CASE STUDY: An Introduction to Software Maintenance

```
//***********************************
// This program prints Hello World!.
//***********************************
#include <iostream>
using namespace std;
int main ()
{
  Cout << "Hello World!";
  return 0;
}
```

Once we are sure that the program works as claimed, we can change it with the knowledge that any new problems are associated with our modifications.

Entering an application involves typing it into the computer with an editor, which is just a program that lets us record our typing in a file. A word processor is an example of an editor. Most programming systems use a specialized code editor that has features to help us enter programs. For example, a code editor will indent the lines of an application automatically in a pattern similar to what is shown in the preceding example, and it may color-code certain elements of the program to help us locate them more easily.

Depending on the programming system that you are using, you may need to begin by creating a new "project," which is the system's way of organizing the information it keeps about your application. Typically, creating a new project involves selecting the "New Project" item from the File menu of the programming system, and then entering a name for the project in a dialog box that appears.

In another programming system, you may need to create a new file directory manually and tell the editor to store your code file there. There are too many different C++ programming systems for us to show them all here. You should consult the manual or help screens for your particular system to learn the specifics.

Once you type the application into the editor window, you need to save it (with another menu selection) and then run it. Here's what happens when we try to run the erroneous version of Hello World. A red mark appears in the margin next to the line with the offending name, and the error message, "error: 'Cout' was not declared within this scope" appears on another screen.

SOFTWARE MAINTENANCE CASE STUDY: An Introduction to Software Maintenance

Every programmer gets these kinds of error messages at some time. Very few of us are perfect typists! Rather than being afraid of seeing such messages, we just come to expect them, and are pleasantly surprised on the rare occasions when we discover that we've entered a long stretch of code without typos. Usually, we enter some code, look it over carefully for mistakes, and run it to see if the computer finds any more. We then use the error messages to help us find remaining typos and fix them. Here's what happens when the application is at last correct:

```
Hello World!
```

Now we know that the program works as advertised, and we can start changing it. Of the seven lines in this application, the first three and the sixth are general instructions that appear in almost all programs. The braces are a form of punctuation in a C++ application. It is the fifth line that is specific to this problem.

```
//***********************************
// This program prints Hello World!
//***********************************
#include <iostream>
using namespace std;
int main ()
{
  cout << "Hello World!";
  return 0;
}
```

Now, let's try making our change, substituting "Universe" for "World"—in two places. We must also change the documentation. Here's the revised application, with "Universe" substituted for "World".

SOFTWARE MAINTENANCE CASE STUDY: An Introduction to Software Maintenance

```
//*************************************
// This program prints Hello Universe!
//*************************************
#include <iostream>
using namespace std;
int main ()
{
  cout << "Hello Universe!";
  return 0;
}
```

```
Hello Universe!
```

   Is that it? Could it really be as simple as changing one word? Well, actually no. We edited our existing Hello World code file, and when we saved it, we overwrote the existing application, so we no longer have the original code. It's always a good idea to keep the working version of a program separate from a new version. That way, we have a working baseline to compare against the new version. And if things really go wrong with our modifications, we have a place to go back to, and start over.

   To correct this situation, we really should have created a new project, perhaps called HelloUniverse, and copied the code from our existing project into the new one. Then we can edit the fifth line, and save the change without affecting the original.

Software Maintenance Tips

1. Check that the existing code works as claimed.
2. Make changes to a *copy* of the existing code.
3. A maintenance task isn't necessarily complete once the desired functionality has been achieved. Change related aspects of the program to leave clean, consistent code for the next programmer who has to do maintenance.
4. Keeping backup copies of code is also useful in developing new programs. Before making any significant change in a program that you're developing, save a copy of the current version so that you can go back to it if necessary.

QUICK CHECK

1.2.1 What is the input and output of a compiler? (p. 11)
1.2.2 Which of the following tools translates a C++ program into machine language: editor, operating system, compiler, or assembler? (pp. 10–11)
1.2.3 What are the four basic ways of structuring statements in most programming languages? (p. 13)
1.2.4 What happens when a program encounters a *selection* statement during execution? (p. 13)
1.2.5 What happens when a program encounters a *loop* statement during execution? (p. 13)
1.2.6 What are subprograms used for? (p. 13)

FIGURE 1.8 Basic Components of a Computer

1.3 What's Inside the Computer?

You can learn a programming language, including how to write programs and how to run (execute) these programs, without knowing much about computers. But if you know something about the parts of a computer, you can better understand the effect of each instruction in a programming language.

Most computers have six basic components: the memory unit, the arithmetic/logic unit, the control unit, input devices, output devices, and auxiliary storage devices. **FIGURE 1.8** is a stylized diagram of the basic components of a computer.

The memory unit is an ordered sequence of storage cells, each capable of holding a piece of data. Each memory cell has a distinct address to which we refer so as to store data into it or retrieve data from it. These storage cells are called *memory cells*, or *memory locations*.[4] The memory unit holds data (input data or the product of computation) and instructions (programs), as shown in **FIGURE 1.9**.

The part of the computer that follows instructions is called the central processing unit (CPU). The CPU usually has two components. The arithmetic/logic unit (ALU) performs arithmetic operations (addition, subtraction, multiplication, and division) and logical operations (comparing two values). The control unit controls the actions of the other components so that program instructions are executed in the correct order.

For us to use computers, there must be some way of getting data into and out of them. Input/output (I/O) devices accept data to be processed (input) and present data values that have been processed (output). A keyboard is a common input

> **Memory unit** Internal data storage in a computer.
> **Central processing unit (CPU)** The part of the computer that executes the instructions (program) stored in memory; made up of the arithmetic/logic unit and the control unit.
> **Arithmetic /logic unit (ALU)** The component of the central processing unit that performs arithmetic and logical operations.
> **Control unit** The component of the central processing unit that controls the actions of the other components so that instructions (the program) are executed in the correct sequence.
> **Input /output (I/O) devices** The parts of the computer that accept data to be processed (input) and present the results of that processing (output).

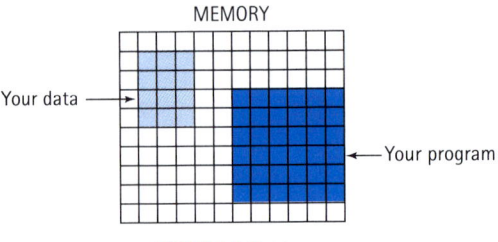

FIGURE 1.9 Memory

---
4. The memory unit is also referred to as RAM, an acronym for random-access memory (so called because we can access any location at random).

device. Another is a *mouse*, a pointing device. Trackpads and touch screens are also used as pointing devices. A liquid crystal display (LCD) screen is a common output device, as are printers. Some devices, such as a connection to a computer network, are used for both input and output.

For the most part, computers simply move and combine data in memory. The many types of computers differ primarily in the size of their memories, the speed with which data can be recalled, the efficiency with which data can be moved or combined, and limitations on I/O devices.

When a program is executing, the computer proceeds through a series of steps, the *fetch–execute cycle*:

1. The control unit retrieves (*fetches*) the next coded instruction from memory.
2. The instruction is translated into control signals.
3. The control signals tell the appropriate unit (arithmetic/logic unit, memory, I/O device) to perform (*execute*) the instruction.
4. The sequence repeats from Step 1.

Computers can have a wide variety of peripheral devices attached to them. An auxiliary storage device, or *secondary storage device*, holds coded data for the computer until we actually want to use the data. Instead of inputting data every time, we can input it once and have the computer store it onto an auxiliary storage device. Whenever we need to use this data, we can tell the computer to transfer the data from the auxiliary storage device to its memory. An auxiliary storage device therefore serves as both an input device and an output device. Typical auxiliary storage devices are disk drives and flash memory. A *disk drive* uses a thin disk made out of magnetic material. A read/write head containing an electromagnet travels across the spinning disk, retrieving or recording data in the form of magnetized spots on the surface of the disk. A *flash memory* is a silicon chip containing specialized electronic switches that can be locked into either the on or off state, representing a binary 1 or 0, respectively. Unlike normal computer memory, flash memory retains its contents when the power is turned off. Flash is typically used to transfer data between computers, and to *back up* (make a copy of) the data on a disk in case the disk is ever damaged.

> **Peripheral device** An input, output, or auxiliary storage device attached to a computer.
> **Auxiliary storage device** A device that stores data in encoded form outside the computer's main memory.
> **Hardware** The physical components of a computer.
> **Software** Computer programs; the set of all programs available on a computer.

Other examples of peripheral devices include the following:

- Scanners, which "read" visual images on paper and convert them into binary data
- CD-ROM (compact disc–read-only memory) disks, which can be read (but not written)
- CD-R (compact disc–recordable), which can be written to once only but can be read many times
- DVD-ROM (digital versatile disc–read-only memory), which has greater storage capacity than CDs, and is often used to store video
- Modems (modulator/demodulators), which convert back and forth between binary data and signals that can be sent over conventional telephone lines
- Audio sound cards and speakers
- Microphones and electronic musical instruments
- Game controllers
- Digital cameras

Together, all of these physical components are known as hardware. The programs that allow the hardware to operate are called software. Hardware usually is fixed in design; software

> **User/computer interface** A connecting link that translates between the computer's internal representation of data and representations that humans are able to work with.
>
> **Interactive system** A system that allows direct communication between user and computer.
>
> **Operating system** A set of programs that manages all of the computer's resources

is easily changed. In fact, the ease with which software can be manipulated is what makes the computer such a versatile, powerful tool.

In addition to the programs that we write or purchase, some programs in the computer are designed to simplify the user/computer interface, making it easier for humans to use the machine. The interface between user and computer is a set of I/O devices—for example, a keyboard, mouse, and screen—that allow the user to communicate with the computer. We work with the keyboard, mouse, and screen on our side of the interface boundary; wires attached to these devices carry the electronic pulses that the computer works with on its side of the interface boundary. At the boundary itself is a mechanism that translates information for the two sides.

When we communicate directly with the computer, we are using an interactive system. Interactive systems allow direct entry of programs and data and provide immediate feedback to the user. In contrast, *batch systems* require that all data be entered before a program is run and provide feedback only after a program has been executed. In this text we focus on interactive systems, although in Chapter 4 we discuss file-oriented programs, which share certain similarities with batch systems.

The set of programs that simplify the user/computer interface and improve the efficiency of processing is collectively called *system software*. It includes the compiler as well as the operating system and the editor (see **FIGURE 1.10**). The operating system manages all of the computer's resources. It can input programs, call the compiler, execute object programs, and

FIGURE 1.10 User/Computer Interface

carry out any other system commands. The editor is an interactive program used to create and modify source programs or data.

> **Editor** An interactive program used to create and modify source programs or data.

Although solitary (*standalone*) computers are often used in private homes and small businesses, it is very common for many computers to be connected together, forming a *network*. A *local area network* (*LAN*) is one in which the computers are connected by wires or a wireless router and must be reasonably close together, as in a single office building. In a *wide area network* (*WAN*) or *long-haul network*, the computers can be far apart geographically and communicate through phone lines, fiberoptic cable, and other media. The most well-known long-haul network is the Internet, which was originally devised as a means for universities, businesses, and government agencies to exchange research information. The Internet exploded in popularity with the establishment of the World Wide Web, a system of linked Internet computers that support specially formatted documents (*web pages*) that contain text, graphics, audio, and video.

BACKGROUND INFORMATION
What Makes One Computer Faster Than Another?

The faster a computer is, the more quickly it responds to our commands and the more work it can do in less time. But which factors affect the speed of a computer? The answer is quite complex, but let's consider some of the essential issues.

In computer advertising you often see numbers such as 3.2 GHz, and the ads clearly want you to believe that this is an important contributor to speed. But what does it really mean? The abbreviation GHz is short for gigahertz, which means billions of cycles per second. What's cycling at this speed is the pulse of the computer—an electrical signal called the clock, which generates a continuous sequence of precisely regulated on/off pulses that are used to coordinate all of the actions of the other circuitry within the computer. It's called a clock because it bears a similarity to the steady ticking of a mechanical clock. But if you want a better sense of what it does, think of it like the rhythmic swinging of an orchestra conductor's baton, which keeps all of the instruments playing in time with each other. The clock ensures that all the components of the computer are doing their jobs in unison. It's clear that the faster the clock, the faster the components work. But that's just one factor that affects speed.

> **Clock** An electrical circuit that sends out a train of pulses to coordinate the actions of the computer's hardware components. The speed of the clock is measured in Hertz (cycles per second).

Although we have described the fetch–execute cycle as if the computer always fetches just one instruction at a time and executes that instruction to completion before fetching the next one, modern computers are not so simple. They often fetch and execute multiple instructions at once (for example, most can simultaneously do integer and real arithmetic, while retrieving values from memory). In addition, they start fetching the next instruction from memory while executing prior instructions. The number of instructions that the computer can execute simultaneously also has a significant effect on speed.

Different computers also work with data in chunks of different sizes. The computer in a microwave oven may work with 8 bits at a time, whereas a smartphone computer typically handles 32 bits at once. Higher-performance machines work with data in units of 64 bits. The more data the computer can process at once, the faster it will be, assuming that the application has need of working with larger quantities of data. The computer in the microwave is plenty fast enough to do its job—your popcorn would not pop any faster if it had a 64-bit processor!

> **BACKGROUND INFORMATION** — **What Makes One Computer Faster Than Another? continued**
>
> It is not uncommon to see, for example, a 1.8 GHz, 64-bit computer that can process many instructions at once, which is significantly faster than a 3.6 GHz, 32-bit computer that handles fewer instructions in parallel. The only way to accurately judge the speed of a computer is to run an application on it, and measure the time it takes to execute.
>
> Other major hardware factors that affect speed are the amount of memory (RAM) and speed of the hard disk. When a computer has more memory, it can hold more programs and data in its memory. With less memory, it must keep more of the programs and data on the hard disk drive, shuffling them between disk and memory as it needs them. The hard disk takes as much as a million times longer to access than RAM, so you can see that a computer with too little RAM can be slowed down tremendously. Disks themselves vary significantly in the speed with which they access data.
>
> Software also affects speed. As we will see in later chapters, problems can be solved more or less efficiently. A program that is based on an inefficient solution can be vastly slower than one that is more efficient. Different compilers do a better job of translating high-level instructions into efficient machine code, which also affects speed. Operating systems also vary in their efficiency. The raw speed of the hardware is masked by the overall efficiency of the software. As a programmer, then, you can have a strong influence on how fast the computer seems to be.

QUICK CHECK

1.3.1 What are the six basic components most computers have? (p. 20)
1.3.2 What two important types of data are held by the memory unit? (p. 20)
1.3.3 What do we call the combination of the control unit and the arithmetic/logic unit? (p. 20)
1.3.4 What is the general term that we use to refer to the physical components of the computer? (p. 21)
1.3.5 What are the steps taken by the computer's fetch–execute cycle? (p. 21)

1.4 Ethics and Responsibilities in the Computing Profession

Every profession operates with a set of ethics that help to define the responsibilities of its practitioners. For example, medical professionals have an ethical responsibility to keep information about their patients confidential. Engineers must protect the public and environment from harm that may result from their work. Writers are ethically bound not to plagiarize, and so on.

The computer can affect people and the environment in dramatic ways. As a consequence, it challenges society with new ethical issues. Some existing ethical practices apply to the computer, whereas other situations require new rules. In some cases, it will be up to you to decide what is ethical.

Software Piracy

Software piracy The unauthorized copying of software for either personal use or use by others.

Computer software is easy to copy. But just like books, software is usually copyrighted—it is illegal to copy software without the permission of its creator. Such copying is called software piracy.

Copyright laws exist to protect the creators of software (and books and art) so that they can make a profit. A major software package can cost millions of dollars to develop, which is reflected in its purchase price. If people make unauthorized copies of the software, then the company loses sales.

Software pirates sometimes rationalize their theft with the excuse that they're just making one copy for their own use. It's not as if they're selling a bunch of bootleg copies, after all. Nevertheless, they have failed to compensate the company for the benefit they received. If thousands of people do the same thing, the losses can add up to millions of dollars, which leads to higher prices for everyone.

Computing professionals have an ethical obligation to not engage in software piracy and to try to stop it from occurring. You should never copy software without permission. If someone asks to copy some software that you have, you should refuse to supply it. If someone says that he or she just wants to "borrow" the software to "try it out," tell the person that he or she is welcome to try it out on your machine but not to make a copy.

This rule isn't restricted to duplicating copyrighted software; it includes plagiarism of all or part of code that belongs to anyone else. If someone gives you permission to copy some of his or her code, then, just like any responsible writer, you should acknowledge that person with a citation in the comments.

Privacy of Data

The computer enables the compilation of databases containing useful information about people, companies, and so on. These databases allow employers to issue payroll checks, banks to cash a customer's check at any branch, the government to collect taxes, and mass merchandisers to send out junk mail. Even though we may not care for every use of databases, they generally have positive benefits. However, they can also be used in negative ways.

For example, a car thief who gains access to a state's motor vehicle database could print out a "shopping list" of car models together with their owners' addresses. An industrial spy might steal customer data from a company database and sell it to a competitor. Although these are obviously illegal acts, computer professionals face other situations that are not as clearly unethical.

Suppose your job includes managing the company payroll database, which includes the names and salaries of the firm's employees. You might be tempted to poke around in the data and see how your salary compares to others—but this act is an unethical invasion of your associates' right to privacy. Any information about a person that is not clearly public should be considered confidential. An example of public information is a phone number listed in a telephone directory. Private information includes any data that has been provided with an understanding that it will be used only for a specific purpose (such as the data on a credit card application).

A computing professional has a responsibility to avoid taking advantage of special access that he or she may have to confidential data. The professional also has a responsibility to guard that data from unauthorized access. Guarding data can involve such simple things as shredding old printouts, keeping backup copies in a locked cabinet, using passwords that are difficult to guess, and implementing more complex measures such as file encryption.

Use of Computer Resources

A computer is an unusual resource because there is no significant physical difference between a computer that is working and one that is sitting idle. By contrast, a car is in motion when it is working. Thus to use a car without permission requires taking it physically—stealing it. However, someone can make unauthorized use of a computer without physically taking it, by using its time and resources.

For some people, theft of computer resources is a game. The thief doesn't really want the resources, but likes the challenge of breaking through a computer's security system. Such people may think that their actions are acceptable if they don't do any harm. Whenever real work is displaced by such activities, however, harm is done. If nothing else, the thief is trespassing. By analogy, consider that even though no physical harm may be done by someone who breaks into your bedroom and takes a nap while you are away, that is certainly disturbing to you because it poses a threat of harm.

Other thieves have malicious intentions and destroy data. Sometimes they leave behind programs that act as time bombs, causing harm later. Another destructive kind of program is a virus—a program that replicates itself, with the goal of spreading to other computers, usually via email or shared files. Some viruses may be benign, merely using up some resources. Others can be destructive. Incidents have occurred in which viruses have cost millions of dollars in data losses. In contrast to a virus, which is spread by contact between users, a worm exploits gaps in a computer's security, hijacking it to search the Internet for other computers with the same gaps. When a computer is taken over and used for some other purpose, such as sending spam email, it is called a zombie.

Harmful programs such as these are collectively known as malware. Now that spam accounts for the majority of worldwide email traffic, some viruses have attempted to extort money from their victims, and zombies have been used to shut down parts of the Internet, the effects of malware on the computing industry are significant.

Computing professionals should never use computer resources without permission. We also have a responsibility to help guard computers to which we have access by watching for signs of unusual use, writing applications without introducing security loopholes, installing security updates as soon as they are released, checking files for viruses, and so on.

> **Virus** Malicious code that replicates and spreads to other computers through email messages and file sharing, without authorization, and possibly with the intent of doing harm.
>
> **Worm** Malicious code that replicates and spreads to other computers through security gaps in the computer's operating system, without authorization, and possibly with the intent of doing harm.
>
> **Zombie** A computer that has been taken over for unauthorized use, such as sending spam email.
>
> **Malware** Software written with malicious purposes in mind.

Software Engineering

Humans have come to depend greatly on computers in many aspects of their lives. That reliance is fostered by the perception that computers function reliably; that is, they work correctly most of the time. However, the reliability of a computer depends on the care that is taken in writing its software.

Errors in a program can have serious consequences, as the following examples of real incidents involving software errors illustrate:

- An error in the control software of the F-18 jet fighter caused it to flip upside down the first time it flew across the equator.
- A rocket launch went out of control and had to be blown up because a comma was typed in place of a period in its control software.
- A radiation therapy machine killed several patients because a software error caused the machine to operate at full power when the operator typed certain commands too quickly.

Even when software is used in less critical situations, errors can have significant effects. Examples of such errors include the following:

- An error in your word processor causes your term paper to be lost just hours before it is due.
- An error in a statistical program causes a scientist to draw a wrong conclusion and publish a paper that must later be retracted.
- An error in a tax preparation program produces an incorrect return, leading to a fine for the taxpayer.

Programmers have a responsibility to develop software that is free from errors. The process that is used to develop correct software is known as software engineering.

Software engineering has many aspects. The software life cycle described at the beginning of this chapter outlines the stages in the development of software. Different techniques are used at each of these stages. We address many of these techniques in this text. In Chapter 4, we introduce methodologies for developing correct algorithms. We discuss strategies for testing and validating programs in every chapter. We use a modern programming language that enables us to write readable, well-organized programs, and so on. Some aspects of software engineering, such as the development of a formal, mathematical specification for a program, are beyond the scope of this text.

> **Software engineering** The application of traditional engineering methodologies and techniques to the development of software.

QUICK CHECK

1.4.1 How can you help to keep confidential data private? (p. 25)

1.5 Problem-Solving Techniques

You solve problems every day, often unaware of the process you are going through. In a learning environment, you usually are given most of the information you need: a clear statement of the problem, the necessary input, and the required output. In real life, the process is not always so simple. You often have to define the problem yourself and then decide what information you have to work with and what the results should be.

After you understand and analyze a problem, you must come up with a solution—an algorithm. Earlier we defined an algorithm as a step-by-step procedure for solving a problem in a finite amount of time. Although you work with algorithms all the time, most of your experience with them is in the context of *following* them. You follow a recipe, play a game, assemble a toy, take medicine. In the problem-solving phase of computer programming, you will be *designing* algorithms, not following them. This means you must be conscious of the strategies you use to solve problems so as to apply them effectively to programming problems.

Ask Questions

If you are given a task orally, you ask questions—When? Why? Where?—until you understand exactly what you have to do. If your instructions are written, you might put question marks in the margin, underline a word or a sentence, or in some other way indicate that the task is not clear. Your questions may be answered by a later paragraph, or you might have to discuss them with the person who gave you the task.

These are some of the questions you might ask in the context of programming:

- What do I have to work with—that is, what is my data?
- What do the data items look like?
- How much data is there?
- How will I know when I have processed all the data?
- What should my output look like?
- How many times will the process be repeated?
- What special error conditions might come up?

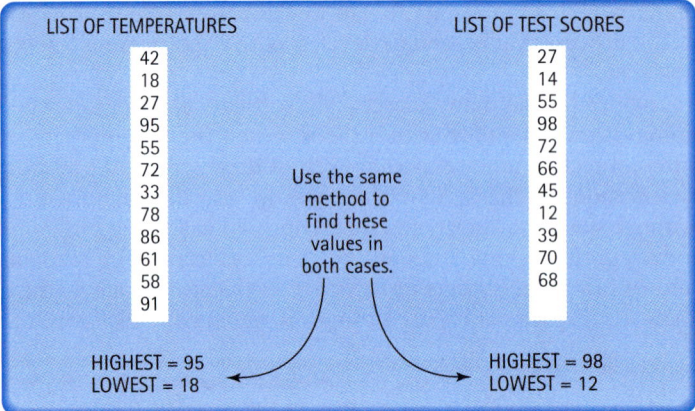

FIGURE 1.11 Look for Things That Are Familiar

Look for Things That Are Familiar

Never reinvent the wheel. If a solution exists, use it. If you've solved the same or a similar problem before, just repeat your solution. People are good at recognizing similar situations. We don't have to learn how to go to the store to buy milk, then to buy eggs, and then to buy candy. We know that going to the store is always the same; only what we buy is different.

In programming, certain problems occur again and again in different guises. A good programmer immediately recognizes a subtask he or she has solved before and plugs in the solution. For example, finding the daily high and low temperatures is really the same problem as finding the highest and lowest grades on a test: You want the largest and smallest values in a set of numbers (see **FIGURE 1.11**).

Solve by Analogy

Often a problem may remind you of a similar problem you have seen before. You may find solving the problem at hand easier if you remember how you solved the other problem. In other words, draw an analogy between the two problems. For example, a solution to a perspective-projection problem from an art class might help you figure out how to compute the distance to a landmark when you are on a cross-country hike. As you work your way through the new problem, you may come across things that are different than they were in the old problem, but usually these are just details that you can deal with one at a time.

Analogy is really just a broader application of the strategy of looking for things that are familiar. When you are trying to find an algorithm for solving a problem, don't limit yourself to computer-oriented solutions. Step back and try to get a larger view of the problem. Don't worry if your analogy doesn't match perfectly—the only reason for using an analogy is that it gives you a place to start (see **FIGURE 1.12**). The best programmers are people who have broad experience solving all kinds of problems.

Means-Ends Analysis

Often the beginning state and the ending state are given; the problem is to define a set of actions that can be used to get from one to the other. Suppose you want to go from Boston, Massachusetts to Austin, Texas. You know the beginning state (you are in Boston) and the ending state (you want to be in Austin). The problem is how to get from one to the other. In this example, you have lots of choices. You can fly, walk, hitchhike, ride a bike, or what-

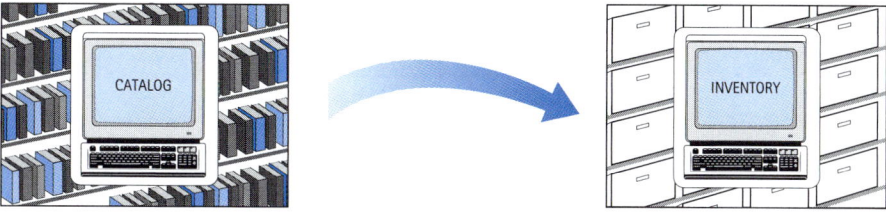

A library catalog system can give insight into how to organize a parts inventory.

FIGURE 1.12 Analogy

Start: Boston Goal: Austin	Means: *Fly*, walk, hitchhike, bike, drive, sail, bus
Start: Boston Goal: Austin	Revised Means: Fly to Chicago and then Austin; *fly to Newark and then Austin;* fly to Atlanta and then Austin
Start: Boston Intermediate Goal: Newark Goal: Austin	Means to Intermediate Goal: *Commuter flight*, walk, hitchhike, bike, drive, sail, bus
Solution: Take commuter flight to Newark and then catch cheap flight to Austin	

FIGURE 1.13 Means-Ends Analysis

ever. The method you choose depends on your circumstances. If you're in a hurry, you'll probably decide to fly.

Once you've narrowed down the set of actions, you have to work out the details. It may help to establish intermediate goals that are easier to meet than the overall goal. Suppose there is a really cheap, direct flight to Austin out of Newark, New Jersey. You might decide to divide the trip into legs: Boston to Newark, and then Newark to Austin. Your intermediate goal is to get from Boston to Newark. Now you just have to examine the means of meeting that intermediate goal (see **FIGURE 1.13**).

The overall strategy of means-ends analysis is to define the ends and then to analyze your means of getting between them. This process translates easily to computer programming. You begin by writing down what the input is and what the output should be. Then you consider the actions a computer can perform and choose a sequence of actions that can transform the data into the results.

Divide and Conquer

We often break up large problems into smaller units that are easier to handle. Cleaning the whole house may seem overwhelming; cleaning the rooms one at a time seems much more manageable. The same principle applies to programming: We can break up a large problem into smaller pieces that we can solve individually (see **FIGURE 1.14**). In fact, the functional decomposition and object-oriented methodologies, which we describe in Chapter 4, are based on the principle of divide and conquer.

The Building-Block Approach

Another way of attacking a large problem is to see if any solutions for smaller pieces of the problem exist. It may be possible to put some of these solutions together end to end to solve most of the big problem. This strategy is just a combination of the look-for-familiar-things

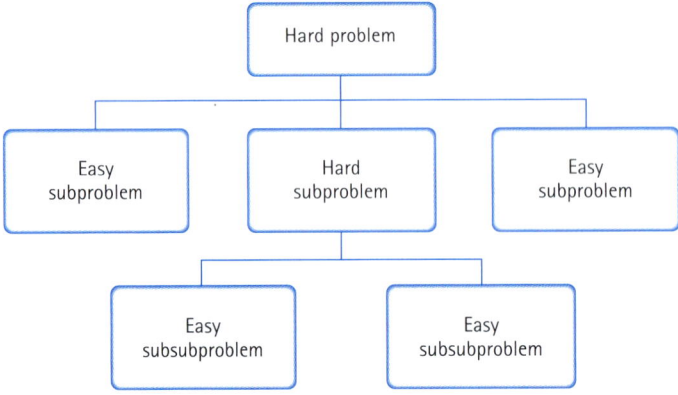

FIGURE 1.14 Divide and Conquer

and divide-and-conquer approaches. You look at the big problem and see that it can be divided into smaller problems for which solutions already exist. Solving the big problem is just a matter of putting the existing solutions together, like mortaring together blocks to form a wall (see **FIGURE 1.15**).

Merging Solutions

Another way to combine existing solutions is to merge them on a step-by-step basis. For example, to compute the average of a list of values, we must both sum and count the values. If we already have separate solutions for summing values and for counting values, we can combine them. But if we first do the summing and then do the counting, we have to read the list twice. We can save steps if we merge these two solutions: Read a value, add it to the running total, and add 1 to our count before going on to the next value. Whenever the solutions to subproblems duplicate steps, think about merging them instead of joining them end to end. (See **FIGURE 1.16**.)

Mental Blocks: The Fear of Starting

Writers are all too familiar with the experience of staring at a blank page, not knowing where to begin. Programmers have the same difficulty when they first tackle a big problem. They look at the problem and it seems overwhelming.

FIGURE 1.15 Building-Block Approach

FIGURE 1.16 Merging Solutions

Remember that you always have a way to begin solving any problem: Write it down on paper in your own words so that you understand it. Once you paraphrase the problem, you can focus on each of the subparts individually instead of trying to tackle the entire problem at once. This process gives you a clearer picture of the overall problem. It helps you see pieces of the problem that look familiar or that are analogous to other problems you have solved, and it pinpoints areas where something is unclear and you need more information.

As you write down a problem, you tend to group things together into small, understandable chunks, which may be natural places to split the problem up—to divide and conquer. Your description of the problem may collect all of the information about data and results into one place for easy reference. Then you can see the beginning and ending states necessary for means-ends analysis.

Most mental blocks are caused by a failure to really understand the problem. Rewriting the problem in your own words is a good way to focus on the subparts of the problem, one at a time, and to understand what is required for a solution.

Algorithmic Problem Solving

Coming up with a step-by-step procedure for solving a particular problem is not always a cut-and-dried process. In fact, it is usually a trial-and-error process requiring several attempts and refinements. We test each attempt to see if it really solves the problem. If it does, great. If it doesn't, we try again. Solving any nontrivial problem typically requires a combination of the techniques we've described.

Remember that the computer can only do certain things (see page 13). Your primary concern, then, is how to make the computer transform, manipulate, calculate, or process the input data to produce the desired output. If you keep in mind the allowable instructions in your programming language, you won't design an algorithm that is difficult or impossible to code.

In the Problem-Solving Case Study that follows, we develop a program to determine whether a year is a leap year. This case study typifies the thought processes involved in writing an algorithm and coding it as a program, and it shows you what a complete C++ program looks like.

BACKGROUND INFORMATION
The Origins of C++

In the late 1960s and early 1970s, Dennis Ritchie created the C programming language at AT&T Bell Labs. At the time, a group of people within Bell Labs were designing the UNIX operating system. Initially, UNIX was written in assembly language, as was the custom for almost all system software in those days. To escape the difficulties of programming in assembly language, Ritchie invented C as a system programming language. C combines the low-level features of an assembly language with the ease of use and portability of a high-level language. UNIX was reprogrammed so that approximately 90% was written in C and the remainder in assembly language.

People often wonder where the cryptic name "C" came from. In the 1960s, a programming language named BCPL (Basic Combined Programming Language) had a small but loyal following, primarily in Europe. From BCPL, another language arose with its name abbreviated to B. For his language, Dennis Ritchie adopted features from the B language and decided that the successor to B naturally should be named C. So the progression was from BCPL to B to C.

In 1985, Bjarne Stroustrup, also of Bell Labs, invented the C++ programming language. To the C language he added features for data abstraction and object-oriented programming (topics we discuss later in this book). Instead of naming the language D, the Bell Labs group, following a humorous vein, named it C++. As we see later, ++ signifies the increment operation in the C and C++ languages. Given a variable *x*, the expression x++ means to increment (add one to) the current value of *x*. Therefore, the name C++ suggests an enhanced ("incremented") version of the C language.

In the years since Dr. Stroustrup invented C++, the language began to evolve in slightly different ways in different C++ compilers. Although the fundamental features of C++ were nearly the same in all companies' compilers, one company might add a new language feature, whereas another would not. As a result, C++ programs were not always portable from one compiler to the next. The programming community agreed that the language needed to be standardized, so a joint committee of the International Standards Organization (ISO) and the American National Standards Institute (ANSI) began the long process of creating a C++ language standard. After several years of discussion and debate, the ISO/ANSI language standard for C++ was officially approved in mid-1998. Most of the current C++ compilers support the ISO/ANSI standard (hereafter called *standard C++*).

Although C originally was intended as a system programming language, both C and C++ are widely used today in business, industry, and personal computing. C++ is powerful and versatile, embodying a wide range of programming concepts. In this book you will learn a substantial portion of the language, but C++ incorporates sophisticated features that go well beyond the scope of an introductory programming course.

QUICK CHECK

1.5.1 Who invented the C++ programming language? (p. 32)
1.5.2 When would you use the building-block approach to solve a problem? (pp. 29–30)
1.5.3 What does it mean to use divide and conquer to solve a problem? (p. 29)
1.5.4 What is the overall strategy of means-ends analysis? (p. 29)
1.5.5 Which problem-solving technique should be used as an alternative to the building-block approach when we want to save steps? (p. 30)

Problem-Solving Case Study

Leap Year Algorithm

PROBLEM: You need to write a set of instructions that can be used to determine whether a year is a leap year. The instructions must be very clear because they will be used by a class of fourth graders who have just learned about multiplication and division. They plan to use the instructions as part of an assignment to determine whether any of their relatives were born in a leap year. To check that the algorithm works correctly, you will code it as a C++ program and test it.

DISCUSSION: The rule for determining whether a year is a leap year is that a year must be evenly divisible by 4, but not a multiple of 100. When the year is a multiple of 400, it is a leap year anyway. We need to write this set of rules as a series of steps (an algorithm) that can be followed easily by the fourth graders.

First, we break this into major steps using the divide-and-conquer approach. There are three obvious steps in almost any problem of this type:

1. Get the data.
2. Compute the results.
3. Output the results.

What does it mean to "get the data"? By *get*, we mean *read* or *input* the data. We need one piece of data: a four-digit year. So that the user will know when to enter the value, we must have the computer output a message that indicates when it is ready to accept the value (this is called a *prompting message,* or a *prompt*). Therefore, to have the computer get the data, we have it do these two steps:

Get Data

Prompt the user to enter a four-digit year
Read the year

Next, we check whether the year that was read can be a leap year (is divisible by 4), and then we test whether it is one of the exceptional cases. Our high-level algorithm is as follows:

Is Leap Year

IF the year is not divisible by 4
    then the year is not a leap year
ELSE check for exceptions

Clearly, we need to expand these steps with more detailed instructions, because neither the fourth graders nor the computer knows what "divisible" means. We use means-ends analysis to solve the problem of how to determine when something is divisible by 4. Our fourth graders know how to do simple division that results in a quotient and a remainder. We can tell them to divide the year by 4, and if the remainder is zero, then it is divisible by 4. Thus the first line is expanded into the following:

Is Leap Year revised

Divide the year by 4
IF the remainder is not 0
    then the year is not a leap year
ELSE check for exceptions

Problem-Solving Case Study

Checking for exceptions when the year is divisible by 4 can be further divided into two parts: checking whether the year is also divisible by 100 and whether it is further divisible by 400. Given how we did the first step, this is easy:

Checking for exceptions

```
Divide the year by 100
IF the remainder is 0
    then the year is not a leap year
Divide the year by 400
IF the remainder is 0
    then the year is a leap year
```

These steps are confusing by themselves. When the year is divisible by 400, it is also divisible by 100, so we have one test that says it is a leap year and one that says it is not. What we need to do is to treat the steps as building blocks and combine them. One of the operations that we can use in such situations is to check when a condition does *not* exist. For example, if the year is divisible by 4 but not by 100, then it must be a leap year. If it is divisible by 100 but not by 400, then it is definitely not a leap year. Thus the third step (check for exceptions when the year is divisible by 4) expands to the following three tests:

Checking for exceptions revised

```
IF the year is not divisible by 100
    then it is a leap year
IF the year is divisible by 100 but not by 400
    then it is not a leap year
IF the year is divisible by 400
    then it is a leap year
```

We can simplify the second test because the check for being divisible by 100 is just the opposite of the first test—if the subalgorithm determines that year is not a leap year in the first test, it can return to the main algorithm, conveying this fact. The second test will then be performed only if the year is actually divisible by 100. Similarly, the last test is really just the "otherwise" case of the second test. If the second test did not return, then we know that the year has to be divisible by 400. Once we translate these simplified tests into steps that the fourth graders know how to perform, we can write the subalgorithm that returns true if the year is a leap year and false otherwise. Let's call this subalgorithm `IsLeapYear`, and put the year it is to test in parentheses beside the name.

IsLeapYear(year)

```
Divide the year by 4
IF the remainder isn't 0
    RETURN with false        (We know the year is not a leap year)

Divide the year by 100       (To get to this step, the year must be divisible by 4)
```

Problem-Solving Case Study

```
IF the remainder isn't 0
    RETURN true            (We know the year is a leap year)

Divide the year by 400     (To get to this step, the year must be divisible by 100)
IF the remainder isn't 0
    RETURN false           (We know the year is not a divisible-by-400 leap year)
                           (To get to this point, the year is divisible by 400)
RETURN true                (The year is a divisible-by-400 leap year)
```

The only piece left is to write the results. If **IsLeapYear** returns true, then we write that the year is a leap year; otherwise, we write that it is not a leap year. Now we can write the complete algorithm for this problem.

Main Algorithm

```
Prompt the user to enter a four-digit year
Read the year
IF IsLeapYear(year)
    Write year is a leap year
ELSE
    Write year is not a leap year
```

Not only is this algorithm clear, concise, and easy to follow, but once you have finished the next few chapters, you will see that it is easy to translate into a C++ program. We present the program here so that you can compare it to the algorithm. You do not need to know how to read C++ programs to begin to see the similarities. Note that the symbol **%** is what C++ uses to calculate the remainder, and whatever appears between **//** and the end of the line is a comment that is ignored by the compiler.

```cpp
//************************************************************
// LeapYear program
// This program inputs a year and prints whether the year
// is a leap year
//************************************************************

#include <iostream>            // Access output stream

using namespace std;

bool IsLeapYear( int year );   // Prototype for subalgorithm

int main()
{
  int year;                    // Year to be tested
  cout << "Enter a year AD, for example, 1997."
       << endl;                // Prompt for input
```

Problem-Solving Case Study

```
  cin >> year;                    // Read year

  if (IsLeapYear(year))           // Test for leap year
    cout << year << " is a leap year." << endl;
  else
    cout << year << " is not a leap year." << endl;

  return 0;                       // Indicate successful completion
}

//************************************************************

bool IsLeapYear( int year )

// IsLeapYear returns true if year is a leap year and
// false otherwise.

{
  if (year % 4 != 0)       // Is year not divisible by 4?
    return false;          // If so, can't be a leap year
                           // Must be divisible by 4 at this point
  if (year % 100 != 0)     // Is year not a multiple of 100?
    return true;           // If so, is a leap year
                           // Must be divisible by 100 at this point
  if (year % 400 != 0)     // Is year not a multiple of 400?
    return false;          // If so, is not a leap year
                           // Must be divisible by 400 at this point
  return true;             // Is a leap year
}
```

Here is the input and the output of a test run:

```
Enter a year AD, for example, 1997.
2008
2008 is a leap year.
```

Summary

We think nothing of turning on the television and sitting down to watch it. The television is a communication tool we use to enhance our lives. Computers are becoming as common as televisions, just a normal part of our lives. And like televisions, computers are based on complex principles but are designed for easy use.

Computers are dumb; they must be told what to do. A true computer error is extremely rare (usually due to a component malfunction or an electrical fault). Because we tell the computer what to do, most errors in computer-generated output are really human errors.

Computer programming is the process of planning a sequence of steps for a computer to follow. It involves a problem-solving phase and an implementation phase. After analyzing a problem, we develop and test a general solution (algorithm). This general solution becomes a concrete solution—our program—when we write it in a high-level programming language. The sequence of instructions that makes up our program is then compiled into machine code, the language the computer uses. After correcting any errors ("bugs") that show up during testing, our program is ready to use.

Once we begin to use the program, it enters the maintenance phase. Maintenance involves correcting any errors discovered while the program is being used and changing the program to reflect changes in the user's requirements.

Data and instructions are represented as binary numbers (numbers consisting of just 1s and 0s) in electronic computers. The process of converting data and instructions into a form usable by the computer is called coding.

A programming language reflects the range of operations a computer can perform. The basic control structures in a programming language—sequence, selection, loop, and subprogram—are based on these fundamental operations. In this text, you will learn to write programs in the high-level programming language called C++.

Computers are composed of six basic parts: the memory unit, the arithmetic/logic unit, the control unit, input and output devices, and auxiliary storage devices. The arithmetic/logic unit and control unit together are called the central processing unit. The physical parts of the computer are called hardware. The programs that are executed by the computer are called software.

System software is a set of programs designed to simplify the user/computer interface. It includes the compiler, the operating system, and the editor.

Computing professionals are guided by a set of ethics, as are members of other professions. Copying software only with permission, including attribution to other programmers when we make use of their code, guarding the privacy of confidential data, using computer resources only with permission, and carefully engineering our programs so that they work correctly are among the responsibilities that we have.

Problem solving is an integral part of the programming process. Although you may have little experience programming computers, you have lots of experience solving problems. The key is to stop and think about which strategies you use to solve problems, and then to use those strategies to devise workable algorithms. Among those strategies are asking questions, looking for things that are familiar, solving by analogy, applying means-ends analysis, dividing the problem into subproblems, using existing solutions to small problems to solve a larger problem, merging solutions, and paraphrasing the problem to overcome a mental block.

The computer is used widely today in science, engineering, business, government, medicine, consumer goods, and the arts. Learning to program in C++ can help you use this powerful tool effectively.

Quick Check Answers

The Quick Checks are intended to help you decide if you've met the goals set forth at the beginning of each chapter. If you understand the material in the chapter, the answer to each question should be fairly obvious. After reading a question, check your response against the answers listed at the end of the chapter. If you don't know an answer or don't understand the answer that's provided, turn to the page(s) listed at the end of the question to review the material.

1.1.1 A computer program. 1.1.2 No, a computer is not intelligent. A human must analyze the problem and create a sequence of instructions for solving the problem. A computer can repeat that sequence of instructions over and over again. 1.1.3 An algorithm can be written in any language, to be carried out by a person or a processor of any kind. A program is written in a programming language, for execution by a computer. 1.1.4 The Problem-Solving phase focuses on understanding the problem and developing a general solution, the Implementation phase translates the algorithm into a computer program, and the Maintenance phase emphasizes the use and maintenance of a computer program. 1.1.5 A programming language has a very small vocabulary of words and symbols, and a very precise set of rules that specify the form and meaning of valid language constructs. 1.2.1 The compiler inputs a source program written in a high-level language, and outputs an equivalent program in machine language. Some compilers also output a listing, which is a copy of the source program with error messages inserted. 1.2.2 Compiler. 1.2.3 sequentially, conditionally, repetitively, and subprograms. 1.2.4 It will execute different statements depending on certain conditions. 1.2.5 The program repeats statements while a certain condition is met. 1.2.6 They allow us to write parts of a program separately. 1.3.1 the memory unit, the arithmetic/logic unit, the control unit, input devices, output devices, and auxiliary storage devices. 1.3.2 The memory unit holds data that is input to the program or the result of computation and the program instructions. 1.3.3 The central processing unit. 1.3.4 Hardware. 1.3.5 (1) fetch an instruction, (2) the instruction is translated into control signals, (3) the control signals tell the computer how to execute the instruction, and (4) repeat this sequence starting at (1). 1.4.1 Use passwords that are difficult to guess, and change them periodically. Encrypt stored data. Ensure that data storage media are kept in a secure area. 1.5.1 Bjarne Stroustrup at Bell Laboratories. 1.5.2 When you see that a problem can be divided into pieces that may correspond to subproblems for which solutions are already known. 1.5.3 We can break up a large problem into smaller pieces that we can solve individually to make it easier to handle. 1.5.4 The overall strategy of means-ends analysis is to define the ends and then to analyze your means of getting between them. 1.5.5 Merging solutions.

Exam Preparation Exercises

1. Match the following terms to their definitions, given below:
    a. Programming
    b. Computer
    c. Algorithm
    d. Computer program
    e. Programming language
    f. Documentation
    g. Information
    h. Data
        i. A programmable device that can store, retrieve, and process data.
        ii. Information in a form a computer can use.
        iii. A sequence of instructions to be performed by a computer.
        iv. A set of rules, symbols, and special words used to construct a computer program.
        v. Planning or scheduling the performance of a task or event.
        vi. Any knowledge that can be communicated.
        vii. The written text and comments that make a program easier for others to understand, use, and modify.
        viii. A step-by-step procedure for solving a problem in a finite amount of time.
2. List the three steps in the problem-solving phase of the software life cycle.
3. List the steps in the implementation phase of the software life cycle.
4. If testing uncovers an error, to which step in the software life cycle does the programmer return?

5. Explain why the following series of steps isn't an algorithm, and then rewrite the steps to make a valid algorithm:

   Wake up.
   Go to school.
   Come home.
   Go to sleep.
   Repeat from first step.

6. Match the following terms with their definitions, given here:
   a. Machine language
   b. Assembly language
   c. Assembler
   d. Compiler
   e. Source program
   f. Object program
      i. A program that translates a high-level language into machine code.
      ii. A low-level programming language in which a mnemonic is used to represent each of the instructions for a particular computer.
      iii. The machine language version of a source program.
      iv. A program that translates an assembly language program into machine code.
      v. The language, made up of binary coded instructions, that is used directly by the computer.
      vi. A program written in a high-level programming language.

7. What is the advantage of writing a program in a standardized programming language?
8. What does the control unit do?
9. The editor is a peripheral device. True or false?
10. Memory (RAM) is a peripheral device. True or false?
11. Is it a case of software piracy if you and a friend buy a piece of software together and install it on both of your computers? The license for the software says that it can be registered to just one user.
12. Match the following problem-solving strategies to the descriptions below:
    a. Ask questions.
    b. Look for things that are familiar.
    c. Solve by analogy.
    d. Means-ends analysis.
    e. Divide and conquer.
    f. Building-block approach.
    g. Merging solutions.
       i. Break up the problem into more manageable pieces.
       ii. Gather more information to help you discover a solution.
       iii. Identify aspects of the problem that are similar to a problem in a different domain.
       iv. Combine the steps in two or more different algorithms.
       v. Identify aspects of the problem that you've solved before.
       vi. Join existing problem solutions together.
       vii. Look at the input, output, and available operations and find a sequence of operations that transform the input into the output.

CHAPTER 1 Overview of Programming and Problem Solving

■ **Programming Warm-Up Exercises**

1. In the following algorithm for making black-and-white photographs, identify the steps that are branches (selection), loops, or references to subalgorithms defined elsewhere.
   a. Mix developer according to instructions on package.
   b. Pour developer into tray.
   c. Mix stop bath according to instructions on package.
   d. Pour stop bath into tray.
   e. Mix fixer according to instructions on package.
   f. Pour fixer into tray.
   g. Turn off white lights and turn on safelight.
   h. Place negative in enlarger and turn on.
   i. Adjust size of image and focus, and then turn off enlarger.
   j. Remove one piece of printing paper from paper safe and place in enlarging easel.
   k. Turn enlarger on for 30 seconds and then off.
   l. Place paper in developer for 1 minute, stop bath for 30 seconds, and fixer for 1 minute.
   m. Turn on white lights and inspect the first print, and then turn off white lights.
   n1. If first print is too light:
       Remove one piece of paper from paper safe, place on easel, and expose for 60 seconds to create a too-dark print. Then place in developer for 1 minute, stop bath for 30 seconds, and fixer for 1 minute.
   n2. If first print is too dark:
       Remove one piece of paper from paper safe, place on easel, and expose for 15 seconds to create a too-light print. Then place in developer for 1 minute, stop bath for 30 seconds, and fixer for 1 minute.
   n3. If first print is about right:
       Remove one piece of paper from paper safe, place on easel, and expose for 60 seconds to create a too-dark print. Then place in developer for 1 minute, stop bath for 30 seconds, and fixer for 1 minute. Remove one piece of paper from paper safe, place on easel, and expose for 15 seconds to create a too-light print. Then place in developer for 1 minute, stop bath for 30 seconds, and fixer for 1 minute.
   o. Analyze too-light and too-dark prints to estimate base exposure time, and then identify highlights and shadows that require less or more exposure and estimate the necessary time for each area.
   p. Remove one piece of paper from paper safe, place on easel, and expose for base exposure time, covering shadow areas for estimated time, and then cover entire print except for highlight areas, which are further exposed as estimated. Then place print in developer for 1 minute, stop bath for 30 seconds, and fixer for 1 minute.
   q. Analyze print from Step p and adjust estimates of times as appropriate.
   r. Repeat Steps p and q until a print is obtained with the desired exposure.
   s. Document exposure times that result in desired print.
   t. Remove one piece of paper from paper safe, place on easel, and expose according to documentation from Step s. Then place in developer for 1 minute, stop bath for 30 seconds, and fixer for 4 minutes. Place print in print washer.
   u. Repeat step t to create as many prints as needed.
   v. Wash all prints for 1 hour.
   w. Place prints in print dryer.

2. Write an algorithm for brushing teeth. The instructions must be very simple and exact because the person who will follow them has never done this activity before, and takes every word literally.
3. Identify the steps in your solution to Exercise 2 that are branches, loops, and references to subalgorithms defined elsewhere.
4. Change the algorithm in Exercise 1 so that 10 properly exposed prints are created each time it is executed.

Case Study Follow-Up

1. Use the algorithm in the leap year case study to decide whether the following years are leap years.
    a. 1900
    b. 2000
    c. 1996
    d. 1998
2. Given the algorithm from the leap year case study with the lines numbered as follows:

    1. Divide the year by 4
    2. IF the remainder isn't 0
    3.   RETURN false   (We know the year is not a leap year)
    4. Divide the year by 100 (To get to this step, year must be divisible by 4)
    5. IF the remainder isn't 0
    6.   RETURN true   (We know the year is a leap year)
    7. Divide the year by 400
    8. IF the remainder isn't 0
    9.   RETURN false   (We know the year is not a divisible-by-400 leap year)
    10. RETURN true   (The year is a divisible-by-400 leap year)

    Indicate which line of the algorithm tells you whether the date is a leap year in each of the following cases.
    a. 1900   Line =
    b. 1945   Line =
    c. 1600   Line =
    d. 1492   Line =
    e. 1776   Line =
3. How would you extend the leap year algorithm to tell you when a year is a millennium year (a multiple of 1000)?
4. Use the leap year algorithm to determine whether you were born in a leap year.
5. Extend the leap year algorithm so that it tells you when the next leap year will be, if the input year is not a leap year.
6. Compare the algorithm for determining the leap year with the C++ program that is shown in the Problem-Solving Case Study. Using the numbering scheme for the algorithm from Question 2, decide which line (or lines) of the algorithm corresponds to which line (or lines) of the program shown here.

■ **Line Number**

	`{`
_____	`if (year % 4 != 0)`
_____	`    return false;`
_____	`if (year % 100 !=  0)`
_____	`    return true;`
_____	`if (year % 400 != 0)`
_____	`    return false;`
_____	`return true;`
	`}`

2 C++ Syntax and Semantics, and the Program Development Process

KNOWLEDGE GOALS

- To understand how a C++ program is composed of one or more subprograms (functions).
- To know what a metalanguage is, and how it is used.
- To understand the concept of a data type.
- To learn the steps involved in entering and running a program.

SKILL GOALS

To be able to:
- Read syntax templates so as to understand the formal rules governing C++ programs.
- Create and recognize legal C++ identifiers.
- Declare named constants and variables of type **char** and **string**.
- Distinguish reserved words in C++ from user-defined identifiers.
- Assign values to variables.
- Construct simple string expressions made up of constants, variables, and the concatenation operator.
- Construct a statement that writes to an output stream.
- Determine what is printed by a given output statement.
- Use comments to clarify your programs.
- Construct simple C++ programs.

2.1 The Elements of C++ Programs

Programmers develop solutions to problems using a programming language. In this chapter, we start looking at the rules and symbols that make up the C++ programming language. We also review the steps required to create a program and make it work on a computer.

C++ Program Structure

In Chapter 1, we talked about the four basic structures for expressing actions in a programming language: sequence, selection, loop, and subprogram. We said that subprograms allow us to write parts of our program separately and then assemble them into final form. In C++, all subprograms are referred to as *functions*, and a C++ program is a collection of one or more functions.

Function A subprogram in C++.

Each function performs some particular task, and collectively they all cooperate to solve the entire problem.

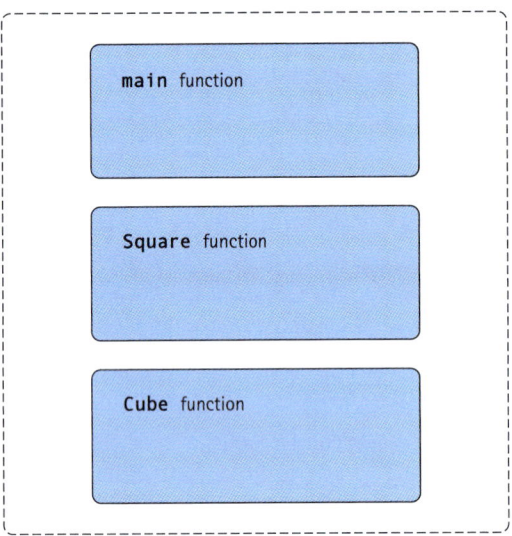

Every C++ program must have a function named `main`. Execution of the program always begins with the `main` function. You can think of `main` as the master and the other functions as the servants. When `main` wants the function `Square` to perform a task, `main` *calls* (or *invokes*) `Square`. When the `Square` function completes execution of its statements, it obediently returns control to the master, `main`, so the master can continue executing.

Let's look at an example of a C++ program with three functions: `main`, `Square`, and `Cube`. Don't be too concerned with the details in the program—just observe its overall look and structure.

```
//************************************************************
// This program demonstrates the use of three functions.
//************************************************************

#include <iostream>

using namespace std;
```

```
int Square( int );
int Cube( int );

int main()
{
  cout << "The square of 27 is " << Square(27) << endl;
  cout << "and the cube of 27 is " << Cube(27) << endl;
  return 0;
}

int Square( int n )
{
  return n * n;
}

int Cube( int n )
{
  return n * n * n;
}
```

In each of the three functions, the left brace ({) and the right brace (}) mark the beginning and the end of the statements to be executed. Statements appearing between the braces are known as the *body* of the function.

Execution of a program always begins with the first statement of the **main** function. In our program, the first statement is

```
cout << "The square of 27 is " << Square(27) << endl;
```

This output statement causes information to be printed on the computer's display screen. You will learn how to construct output statements later in the chapter. Briefly, this statement prints two items. The first is the message

```
The square of 27 is
```

The second item to be printed is the value obtained by calling (invoking) the **Square** function, with the value 27 as the number to be squared. As the servant, the **Square** function performs its task of squaring the number and sending the computed result (729) back to its *caller*, the **main** function. Now **main** can continue executing by printing the value 729 and proceeding to its next statement.

In a similar fashion, the second statement in **main** prints the message

```
and the cube of 27 is
```

and then invokes the **Cube** function and prints the result, 19683. The complete output produced by executing this program is, therefore,

```
The square of 27 is 729
and the cube of 27 is 19683
```

Both **Square** and **Cube** are examples of value-returning functions. A value-returning function returns a single value to its caller. The word **int** at the beginning of the first line of the **Square** function

```
int Square( int n )
```

states that the function returns an integer value.

Now look at the `main` function again. You'll see that the first line of the function is

```
int main()
```

The word `int` indicates that `main` is a value-returning function that should return an integer value. And it does: After printing the square and cube of 27, `main` executes the statement

```
return 0;
```

to return the value 0 to its caller. But who calls the `main` function? The answer: the computer's operating system.

When you work with C++ programs, the operating system is considered to be the caller of the `main` function. The operating system expects `main` to return a value when `main` finishes executing. By convention, a return value of 0 means everything went okay. A return value of anything else (typically 1, 2, . . .) means something went wrong. Later in this book we look at situations in which you might want to return a value other than 0 from `main`. For the time being, we always conclude the execution of `main` by returning the value 0.

We have looked only briefly at the overall picture of what a C++ program looks like—a collection of one or more functions, including `main`. We have also mentioned what is special about the `main` function—it is a required function, execution begins there, and it returns a value to the operating system. Now it's time to begin looking at the details of the C++ language.

Syntax and Semantics

A programming language is a set of rules, symbols, and special words used to construct a program. In particular, there are rules for both syntax (grammar) and semantics (meaning).

Syntax The formal rules governing how valid instructions are written in a programming language.

Semantics The set of rules that determines the meaning of instructions written in a programming language.

Metalanguage A language that is used to write the syntax rules for another language.

Syntax is a formal set of rules that defines exactly which combinations of letters, numbers, and symbols can be used in a programming language. There is no room for ambiguity in the syntax of a programming language because the computer can't think; it doesn't "know what we mean." To avoid ambiguity, syntax rules themselves must be written in a very simple, precise, formal language called a metalanguage.

Learning to read a metalanguage is like learning to read the notations used in the rules of a sport. Once you understand the notations, you can read the rule book. It's true that many people learn a sport simply by watching others play, but what they learn is usually just enough to allow them to take part in casual games. You could learn C++ by following the examples in this book, but a serious programmer, like a serious athlete, must take the time to read and understand the rules.

Syntax rules are the blueprints we use to build instructions in a program. They allow us to take the elements of a programming language—the basic building blocks of the language—and assemble them into *constructs*, which are syntactically correct structures. If our program violates any of the rules of the language—by misspelling a crucial word or leaving out an important comma, for instance—the program is said to have *syntax errors* and cannot compile correctly until we fix them.

> ## THEORETICAL FOUNDATIONS
> ### Metalanguages
>
>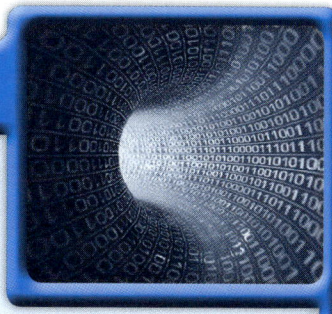
>
> Metalanguage is the word language with the prefix *meta*, which means "beyond" or "more comprehensive." In other words, a metalanguage is a language that goes beyond a normal language by allowing us to speak precisely about that language. It is a language for talking about languages.
>
> One of the first computer-oriented metalanguages was the *Backus–Naur Form (*BNF), which is named for John Backus and Peter Naur, who developed it in 1960. BNF is an extremely simple language. When we say simple, however, we mean that the metalanguage itself has very few symbols and rules. Unfortunately, that simplicity forces each syntax definition to be written using many symbols, so that it becomes long and difficult to read. In this book, we use another metalanguage, called a syntax template. Syntax templates show at a glance the form of a C++ construct.
>
> One final note: Metalanguages show only how to write instructions that the compiler can translate. They do not define what those instructions do (their semantics). Formal languages for defining the semantics of a programming language exist, but they are beyond the scope of this text. Throughout this book, we will describe the semantics of C++ in English.

Syntax Templates

In this book, we write the syntax rules for C++ using a metalanguage called a *syntax template*. A syntax template is a generic example of the C++ construct being defined. Graphic conventions show which portions are optional and which portions can be repeated. A boldface word or symbol is a literal word or symbol in the C++ language. A nonboldface word can be replaced by another template. A curly brace is used to indicate a list of items, from which one item can be chosen.

Let's look at an example. This template defines an identifier in C++:

Identifier

The shading indicates a part of the definition that is optional. The three dots (. . .) mean that the preceding symbol or shaded block can be repeated. Thus an identifier in C++ must begin with a letter or underscore and is optionally followed by one or more letters, underscores, or digits.

Remember that a word not in boldface type can be replaced with another template. Here are the templates for Letter and Digit:

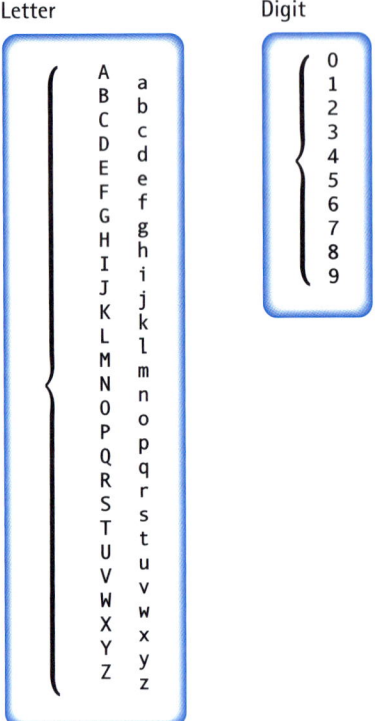

In these templates, the braces again indicate lists of items from which any one item can be chosen. So a letter can be any one of the uppercase or lowercase letters, and a digit can be any of the numeric characters 0 through 9.

Now let's look at the syntax template for the C++ **main** function:

MainFunction

```
int main()
{
    Statement
       ⋮
}
```

The **main** function begins with the word **int**, followed by the word **main** and then left and right parentheses. This first line of the function is the *heading*. After the heading, the left brace signals the start of the statements in the function (its body). The shading and the three dots indicate that the function body consists of zero or more statements. (In this diagram we have placed the three dots vertically to suggest that statements usually are arranged vertically, one above the next.) Finally, the right brace indicates the end of the function.

In principle, the syntax template allows the function body to have no statements at all. In practice, the body should include a **return** statement because the word **int** in the function heading states that `main` returns an integer value. Thus the shortest C++ program possible is

```
int main()
{
   return 0;
}
```

As you might guess, this program does absolutely nothing useful when executed!

As we introduce C++ language constructs throughout the book, we use syntax templates to display the proper syntax. When you finish this chapter, you should know enough about the syntax and semantics of statements in C++ to write simple programs. But before we can talk about writing statements, we must look at how names are written in C++ and at some of the elements of a program.

Naming Program Elements: Identifiers

As we noted in our discussion of metalanguages, identifiers are used in C++ to name things—things such as subprograms and places in the computer's memory. Identifiers are made up of letters (A–Z, a–z), digits (0–9), and the underscore character (_), but must begin with a letter or underscore.

> **Identifier** A name associated with a function or data object and used to refer to that function or data object.

Remember that an identifier *must* start with a letter or underscore:

Identifier

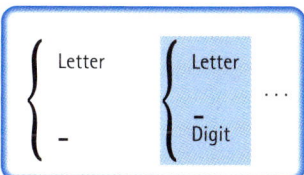

(Identifiers beginning with an underscore have special meanings in some C++ systems, so it is best to begin an identifier with a letter.) Here are some examples of valid identifiers:

`sum_of_squares   J9   box_22A   GetData   Bin3D4   count`

And here are some examples of invalid identifiers and the reasons why they are invalid:

Invalid Identifier	Explanation
`40Hours`	Identifiers cannot begin with a digit.
`Get Data`	Blanks are not allowed in identifiers.
`box-22`	The hyphen (-) is a math symbol (minus) in C++.
`cost_in_$`	Special symbols such as `$` are not allowed.
`int`	The word `int` is predefined in the C++ language.

The last identifier in the table, `int`, is an example of a reserved word. Reserved words are words that have specific uses in C++; you cannot use them as programmer-defined identifiers. Appendix A lists all of the reserved words in C++.

> **Reserved word** A word that has special meaning in C++; it cannot be used as a programmer-defined identifier.

The `LeapYear` program in Chapter 1 uses the programmer-defined identifiers in the following list. (Most of the other identifiers in the program are C++ reserved words.) Notice that we chose the names to convey how the identifiers are used.

Identifier	How It Is Used
`year`	Year to be tested
`IsLeapYear`	Whether year is a leap year

MATTERS OF STYLE Using Meaningful, Readable Identifiers

The names we use to refer to things in our programs are totally meaningless to the computer. The computer behaves in the same way whether we call the value 3.14159265 `pi` or `cake`, as long as we always call it the same thing. However, it is much easier for someone to figure out how a program works if the names we choose for elements actually tell something about them. Whenever you have to make up a name for something in a program, try to pick one that is meaningful to a person reading the program.

C++ is a *case-sensitive* language, which means that it considers uppercase letters to be different from lowercase letters. The identifiers

`PRINTTOPPORTION   printtopportion   pRiNtToPpOrTiOn   PrintTopPortion`

are four distinct names and are not interchangeable in any way. As you can see, the last of these forms is the easiest to read. In this book, we use combinations of uppercase letters, lowercase letters, and underscores in identifiers. We explain our conventions for choosing between uppercase and lowercase as we proceed through this chapter.

Now that we've seen how to write identifiers, let's look at some of the things that C++ allows us to name.

Data and Data Types

A computer program operates on data (stored internally in memory, stored externally on disk, or input from a device such as a keyboard, scanner, network, or electrical sensor) and produces output. In C++, each piece of data must be of a specific data type. The data type determines how the data is represented in the computer and the kinds of processing the computer can perform on it.

Data type A specific set of data values, along with a set of operations on those values.

Some types of data are used so frequently that C++ defines them for us. Examples of these *standard* (or *built-in*) *types* include `int` (for working with integer numbers), `float` (for working with real numbers having decimal points), and `char` (for working with character data).

Additionally, C++ allows programmers to define their own data types—known as *programmer-defined* (or *user-defined*) *types*. Beginning in Chapter 10, we show you how to define your own data types.

In this chapter, we focus on two data types—one for representing data consisting of a single character, the other for representing strings of characters. In Chapter 3, we examine the numeric types (such as `int` and `float`) in detail.

BACKGROUND INFORMATION
Data Storage

Where does a program get the data it needs to operate? Data is stored in the computer's memory. Recall that memory is divided into a large number of separate locations or cells, each of which can hold a piece of data. Each memory location has a unique address to which we refer when we store or retrieve the data there. We can visualize memory as a set of post office boxes, with the box numbers as the addresses used to designate particular locations.

Of course, the actual address of each location in memory is a binary number in a machine language code. In C++, we use identifiers to name memory locations; the compiler then translates them into binary for us. This is one of the advantages of a high-level programming language: It frees us from having to keep track of the numeric addresses of the memory locations in which our data and instructions are stored.

The `char` Data Type

The built-in type `char` describes data consisting of one alphanumeric character—a letter, a digit, or a special symbol:

```
'A'    'a'    '8'    '2'    '+'    '-'    '$'    '?'    '*'    ' '
```

Each machine uses a particular *character set*, the set of alphanumeric characters it can represent. (See Appendix E for some sample character sets.) Notice that each character is enclosed in single quotes (apostrophes). The C++ compiler needs the quotes to differentiate, say, between the character data `'8'` and the integer value 8 because the two are stored differently inside the machine. Notice also that the blank, `' '`, is a valid character.[1]

You wouldn't want to add the character `'A'` to the character `'B'` or subtract the character `'3'` from the character `'8'`, but you might want to compare character values. Each character set has a *collating sequence*, a predefined ordering of all the characters. Although this sequence varies from one character set to another, `'A'` always compares less than `'B'`, `'B'` less than `'C'`, and so forth. Also, `'1'` compares less than `'2'`, `'2'` less than `'3'`, and so on. None of the identifiers in the `LeapYear` program is of type `char`.

The `string` Data Type

Whereas a value of type `char` is limited to a single character, a *string* is a sequence of characters, such as a word, name, or sentence, enclosed in double quotes. For example, the following are strings in C++:

```
"Problem Solving"    "C++"    "Programming and "    " "    "."
```

A string must be typed entirely on one line. For example, the string

```
"This string is invalid because it
is typed on more than one line."
```

is not valid because it is split across two lines. In this situation, the C++ compiler issues an error message at the first line. The message may say something like **UNTERMINATED STRING**, depending on the particular compiler.

The quotes are not considered to be part of the string but are simply there to distinguish the string from other parts of a C++ program. For example, `"amount"` (in double quotes) is the character string made up of the letters *a*, *m*, *o*, *u*, *n*, and *t* in that order. By contrast, `amount` (without the quotes) is an identifier, perhaps the name of a place in memory. The symbols `"12345"` represent a string made up of the characters *1, 2, 3, 4,* and *5* in that order. If we write `12345` without the quotes, it is an integer quantity that can be used in calculations.

A string containing no characters is called the *null string* (or *empty string*). We write the null string using two double quotes with nothing (not even spaces) between them:

```
""
```

The null string is not equivalent to a string of spaces; it is a special string that contains no characters.

To work with string data, this book uses a data type named `string`. This data type is not part of the C++ language (that is, it is not a built-in type). Rather, `string` is a programmer-defined type that is supplied by the C++ *standard library*, a large collection of prewritten functions and data types that any C++ programmer can use. Operations on `string` data include comparing the values of strings, searching a string for a particular character, and joining one string to another. We look at some of these operations later in this chapter and cover additional string operations in subsequent chapters. None of the identifiers in the `LeapYear` program is of type `string`, although string values are used directly in several places in the program.

---

[1]. As noted in Chapter 1, most programming languages use the ASCII character code. C++ provides the data type `wchar_t` (for "wide character") to accommodate larger character sets such as Unicode. In C++, the notation `L'something'` denotes a value of type `wchar_t`, where the *something* depends on the particular wide character set being used. We do not examine wide characters any further in this book.

Naming Elements: Declarations

Identifiers can be used to name both constants and variables. In other words, an identifier can be the name of a memory location whose contents are not allowed to change or it can be the name of a memory location whose contents can change.

How do we tell the computer what an identifier represents? By using a declaration, a statement that associates a name (an identifier) with a description of an element in a C++ program (just as a dictionary definition associates a name with a description of the thing being named). In a declaration, we name an identifier and indicate what it represents. For example, the `LeapYear` program uses the declaration

> **Declaration** A statement that associates an identifier with a data object, a function, or a data type so that the programmer can refer to that item by name.

```
int year;
```

to announce that `year` is the name of a variable whose contents are of type `int`. When we declare a variable, the compiler picks a location in memory to be associated with the identifier. We don't have to know the actual address of the memory location because the computer automatically keeps track of it for us.

Suppose that when we mailed a letter, we only had to put a person's name on it and the post office would look up the address. Of course, everybody in the world would need a different name; otherwise, the post office wouldn't be able to figure out whose address was whose. The same is true in C++. Each identifier can represent just one thing (except under special circumstances, which we talk about in Chapters 7 and 8). Every identifier you use in a program must be different from all others.

Constants and variables are collectively called *data objects*. Both data objects and the actual instructions in a program are stored in various memory locations. You have seen that a group of instructions—a function—can be given a name. A name also can be associated with a programmer-defined data type.

In C++, you must declare every identifier before it is used. This practice allows the compiler to verify that the use of the identifier is consistent with what it was declared to be. If you declare an identifier to be a constant and later try to change its value, for example, the compiler detects this inconsistency and issues an error message.

There is a different form of declaration statement for each kind of data object, function, or data type in C++. The forms of declarations for variables and constants are introduced here; others are covered in later chapters.

Variables

A program operates on data, which is stored in memory. While a program is executing, different values may be stored in the same memory location at different times. This kind of memory location is called a variable, and its content is the *variable value*. The symbolic name that we associate with a memory location is the *variable name* or *variable identifier* (see **FIGURE 2.1**). In practice, we often refer to the variable name more briefly as the *variable*.

> **Variable** A location in memory, referenced by an identifier, that contains a data value that can be changed.

Declaring a variable means specifying both the variable's name and its data type. The declaration tells the compiler to associate a name with a memory location whose contents are of a specific type (for example, `char` or `string`). The following statement declares `myChar` to be a variable of type `char`:

```
char myChar;
```

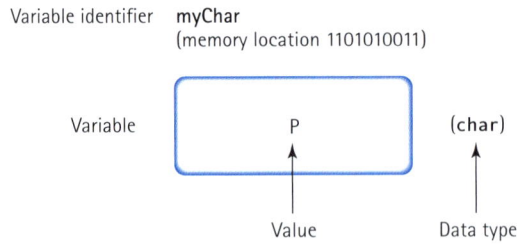

FIGURE 2.1 Variable

In C++, a variable can contain a data value only of the type specified in its declaration. Because of the preceding declaration, the variable `myChar` can contain *only* a `char` value. If the C++ compiler comes across an instruction that tries to store a `float` value into `myChar`, it generates extra instructions to convert the `float` value to the proper type. In Chapter 3, we examine how such type conversions take place.

Here's the syntax template for a variable declaration:

VariableDeclaration

```
DataType Identifier , Identifier ... ;
```

where `DataType` is the name of a data type such as `char` or `string`. Notice that a variable declaration always ends with a semicolon.

From the syntax template, you can see that it is possible to declare several variables in one statement:

```
char letter, middleInitial, ch;
```

Here, all three variables are declared to be `char` variables. Our preference, though, is to declare each variable with a separate statement:

```
char letter;
char middleInitial;
char ch;
```

This form makes it easier, when modifying a program, to add new variables to the list or delete ones you no longer want.

Declaring each variable with a separate statement also allows you to attach comments to the right of each declaration, as shown here:

```
float payRate;      // Employee's pay rate
float hours;        // Hours worked
float wages;        // Wages earned
int empNum;         // Employee ID number
```

These declarations tell the compiler to reserve memory space for three `float` variables—`payRate`, `hours`, and `wages`—and one `int` variable, `empNum`. The comments explain to someone reading the program what each variable represents.

Now that we've seen how to declare variables in C++, let's look at how to declare constants.

Constants

All single characters (enclosed in single quotes) and strings (enclosed in double quotes) are constants.

```
'A'    '@'    "Howdy boys"    "Please enter an employee number:"
```

In C++, as in mathematics, a constant is something whose value never changes. When we use the actual value of a constant in a program, we are using a literal value (or *literal*).

An alternative to the literal constant is the named constant (or symbolic constant), which is introduced in a declaration statement. A named constant is just another way of representing a literal value. Instead of using the literal value in an instruction, we give it a name in a declaration statement, then use that name in the instruction. For example, we can write an instruction that prints the title of this book using the literal string `"Programming and Problem Solving with C++"`. Alternatively, we can declare a named constant called `BOOK_TITLE` that equals the same string and then use the constant name in the instruction. That is, we can use either

> **Literal value** Any constant value written in a program.
>
> **Named constant (symbolic constant)** A location in memory, referenced by an identifier, that contains a data value that cannot be changed.

```
"Programming and Problem Solving with C++"
```

or

```
BOOK_TITLE
```

in the instruction.

Using a literal value may seem easier than declaring a named constant and then referring to it. But, in fact, named constants make a program easier to read because they make the meaning clearer. Named constants also make it easier to change a program at a later time.

Here is the syntax template for a constant declaration:

ConstantDeclaration

```
const DataType Identifier = LiteralValue;
```

Notice that the reserved word `const` begins the declaration, and an equal sign (=) appears between the identifier and the literal value.

The following are examples of constant declarations:

```
const string STARS = "********";
const char   BLANK = ' ';
const string BOOK_TITLE = "Programming and Problem Solving with C++";
const string MESSAGE = "Error condition";
```

As we have done above, many C++ programmers capitalize the entire identifier of a named constant and separate the English words with an underscore. The idea is to let the reader quickly distinguish between variable names and constant names when they appear in the middle of a program.

It's a good idea to add comments to constant declarations as well as variable declarations. We describe in comments what each constant represents:

```
const float MAX_HOURS = 40.0; // Maximum normal work hours
const float OVERTIME = 1.5;   // Overtime pay rate factor
```

Here is a program that contains just declarations:

```cpp
//****************************************************
// This program contains only declarations.
//****************************************************
#include <iostream>
#include <string>
using namespace std;

int main()
{
    const string NAME = "Susy Sunshine";
    const char INITIAL = 'S';
    const float TAX_RATE = 12.5;
    float hourlyWage;
    int numberOfDependents;
    string jobDescription;
    // Rest of program
}
```

MATTERS OF STYLE   Capitalization of Identifiers

Programmers often use capitalization as a quick visual clue to what an identifier represents. Different programmers adopt different conventions for using uppercase letters and lowercase letters. Some people use only lowercase letters, separating the English words in an identifier with the underscore character:

```
pay_rate    emp_num    pay_file
```

The conventions we use in this book are as follows:

- For identifiers representing variables, we begin with a lowercase letter and capitalize each successive English word.

    ```
    lengthInYards    middleInitial    hours
    ```

- Names of programmer-written functions and programmer-defined data types (which we examine later in the book) are capitalized in the same manner as variable names, except that they begin with capital letters.

    ```
    CalcPay(payRate, hours, wages)    Cube(27)    MyDataType
    ```

MATTERS OF STYLE   Capitalization of Identifiers, continued

Capitalizing the first letter allows a person reading the program to tell at a glance that an identifier represents a function name or data type rather than a variable. However, we cannot use this capitalization convention everywhere. C++ expects every program to have a function named `main`—all in lowercase letters—so we cannot name it `Main`. Nor can we use `Char` for the built-in data type `char`. C++ reserved words use all lowercase letters, as do most of the identifiers declared in the standard library (such as `string`).

- For identifiers representing named constants, we capitalize every letter and use underscores to separate the English words.

```
BOOK_TITLE    OVERTIME    MAX_LENGTH
```

This convention, which is widely used by C++ programmers, is an immediate signal that `BOOK_TITLE` is a named constant and not a variable, a function, or a data type.

These conventions are only that—conventions. In other words, C++ does not *require* this particular style of capitalizing identifiers. You may wish to capitalize identifiers in a different fashion. But whatever system you use, it is essential that you use a consistent style throughout your program. A person reading your program will be confused or misled if you use a random style of capitalization.

Taking Action: Executable Statements

Up to this point, we've looked at ways of declaring data objects in a program. Now we turn our attention to ways of acting, or performing operations, on data.

Assignment

The value of a variable can be set or changed through an assignment statement. For example,

```
lastName = "Lincoln";
```

assigns the string value `"Lincoln"` to the variable `lastName`; that is, it stores the sequence of characters `"Lincoln"` into the memory associated with the variable named `lastName`.

Here's the syntax template for an assignment statement:

AssignmentStatement

> Variable = Expression;

> **Assignment statement** A statement that stores the value of an expression into a variable.
>
> **Expression** An arrangement of identifiers, literals, and operators that can be evaluated to compute a value of a given type.

The semantics (meaning) of the assignment operator (=) is "store"; the value of the expression is *stored* into the variable. Any previous value in the variable is destroyed and replaced by the value of the expression.

Evaluate To compute a new value by performing a specified set of operations on given values.

Only one variable can be on the left-hand side of an assignment statement. An assignment statement is *not* like a math equation (x + y = z + 4); the expression (what is on the right-hand side of the assignment operator) is evaluated, and the resulting value is stored into the single variable on the left of the assignment operator. A variable keeps its assigned value until another statement stores a new value into it.

Given the declarations

```
string firstName;
string middleName;
string lastName;
string title;
char middleInitial;
char letter;
```

the following assignment statements are valid:

```
firstName = "Abraham";
middleName = firstName;
middleName = "";
lastName = "Lincoln";
title = "President";
middleInitial = ' ';
letter = middleInitial;
```

However, these assignments are not valid:

Invalid Assignment Statement	Reason
`middleInitial = "A.";`	`middleInitial` is of type `char`; `"A."` is of type `string`.
`letter = firstName;`	`letter` is of type `char`; `firstName` is of type `string`.
`firstName = Thomas;`	`Thomas` is an undeclared identifier.
`"Edison" = lastName;`	Only a variable can appear to the left of `=`.
`lastName = ;`	The expression to the right of `=` is missing.

String Expressions

Although we can't perform arithmetic on strings, the **string** data type provides a special string operation, called *concatenation*, that uses the + operator. The result of concatenating (joining) two strings is a new string containing the characters from both strings. For example, given the statements

```
string bookTitle;
string phrase1;
string phrase2;

phrase1 = "Programming and ";
phrase2 = "Problem Solving";
```

we could write

```
bookTitle = phrase1 + phrase2;
```

This statement retrieves the value of `phrase1` from memory and concatenates the value of `phrase2` to form a new, temporary string containing the characters

`"Programming and Problem Solving"`

This temporary string (which is of type `string`) is then assigned to (stored into) `bookTitle`.

The order of the strings in the expression determines how they appear in the resulting string. If we write

`bookTitle = phrase2 + phrase1;`

then `bookTitle` contains

`"Problem SolvingProgramming and "`

Concatenation works with named `string` constants, literal strings, and `char` data, as well as with `string` variables. The only restriction is that at least one of the operands of the + operator *must* be a `string` variable or named constant (so you cannot use expressions like `"Hi" + "there"` or `'A' + 'B'`). For example, if we have declared the following constants

```
const string WORD1 = "Programming";
const string WORD3 = "Solving";
const string WORD5 = "C++";
```

then we could write the following assignment statement to store the title of this book into the variable `bookTitle`:

`bookTitle = 'P' + WORD1 + " and Problem " + WORD3 + " with " + WORD5;`

As a result, `bookTitle` contains the string

`"Programming and Problem Solving with C++"`

The preceding example demonstrates how we can combine identifiers, `char` data, and literal strings in a concatenation expression. Of course, if we simply want to assign the complete string to `bookTitle`, we can do so directly:

`bookTitle = "Programming and Problem Solving with C++";`

Occasionally we may encounter a situation in which we want to add some characters to an existing string value. Suppose that `bookTitle` already contains `"Programming and Problem Solving"` and now we wish to complete the title. We could use a statement of the form

`bookTitle = bookTitle + " with C++";`

Such a statement retrieves the value of `bookTitle` from memory, concatenates the string `"with C++"` to form a new string, and then stores the new string back into `bookTitle`. The new string replaces the old value of `bookTitle` (which is destroyed).

Keep in mind that concatenation works only with values of type `string`. Even though an arithmetic plus sign is used for the operation, we cannot concatenate values of numeric data types, such as `int` and `float`, with strings.

Here is a program that shows how declarations and assignment statements could be arranged with respect to one another.

```
//*******************************************
// This program shows the placement
// of declarations and assignment operations
//*******************************************
#include <string>
using namespace std;
int main ()
{
  const string firstPart = "Programming and Problem ";
  const string secondPart = "Solving with C++";
  string bookTitle;
  string newEdition;
  bookTitle = firstPart + secondPart;
  newEdition = bookTitle + ", 6th Edition";
}
```

Output

Have you ever asked someone, "Do you know what time it is?" only to have the person smile smugly, say, "Yes, I do," and walk away? This situation is like the one that currently exists between you and the computer. You now know enough C++ syntax to tell the computer to assign values to variables and to concatenate strings, but the computer won't give you the results until you tell it to write them out.

In C++, we write out the values of variables and expressions by using a special variable named **cout** (pronounced "see-out") along with the *insertion operator* (<<):

```
cout << "Hello";
```

This statement displays the characters **Hello** on the *standard output device*, usually the display screen.

The variable **cout** is predefined in C++ systems to denote an *output stream*. You can think of an output stream variable as a doorway through which we send a sequence of characters to an output device.

The insertion operator << (often pronounced as "put to") takes two operands. Its left-hand operand is a stream expression (in the simplest case, just a stream variable such as **cout**). Its right-hand operand is an expression, as in the following two examples:

```
cout << "The title is ";
cout << bookTitle + ", 6th Edition";
```

The insertion operator converts its right-hand operand to a sequence of characters and sends them to the output device through the stream variable.[2] Notice how the << operator points in the direction the data is going—*from* the expression written on the right *to* the output stream on the left.

You can use the << operator several times in a single output statement. Each occurrence appends the next data item to the output stream. For example, we can write the preceding two output statements as

```
cout << "The title is " << bookTitle + ", 6th Edition";
```

If **bookTitle** contains "American History", both versions produce the same output:

```
The title is American History, 6th Edition
```

---

2. In C++ terminology, it is said that the stream expression is "appended to" the output stream.

The output statement has the following form:

OutputStatement

```
cout << Expression << Expression ···;
```

The following output statements yield the output shown. These examples assume that the `char` variable `ch` contains the value `'2'`, the `string` variable `firstName` contains `"Marie"`, and the `string` variable `lastName` contains `"Curie"`.

Statement	What Is Printed (□ means blank)
`cout << ch;`	2
`cout << "ch = " << ch;`	ch□=□2
`cout << firstName + " " + lastName;`	Marie□Curie
`cout << firstName << lastName;`	MarieCurie
`cout << firstName << ' ' << lastName;`	Marie□Curie
`cout << "ERROR MESSAGE";`	ERROR□MESSAGE
`cout << "Error=" << ch;`	Error=2

An output statement prints literal strings exactly as they appear. To let the computer know that you want to print a literal string—and not a named constant or variable—you must remember to use double quotes to enclose the string. If you don't put quotes around a string, you'll probably get an error message (such as **UNDECLARED IDENTIFIER**) from the C++ compiler. If you want to print a string that includes a double quote, you must type a backslash (\) character and a double quote, with no space between them, in the string. For example, to print the characters

```
Al "Butch" Jones
```

the output statement would look like this:

```
cout << "Al \"Butch\" Jones";
```

To conclude this introductory look at C++ output, we should mention how to terminate an output line. Normally, successive output statements cause the output to continue along the same line of the display screen. For example, the sequence

```
cout << "Hi";
cout << "there";
```

writes the following to the screen, all on the same line:

```
Hithere
```

To print the two words on separate lines, we can write this:

```
cout << "Hi" << endl;
cout << "there" << endl;
```

The output from these statements is

```
Hi
there
```

The identifier **endl** (meaning "end line") is a special C++ feature called a *manipulator*. We discuss manipulators in detail in Chapter 3. For now, the important thing to note is that **endl** lets you finish an output line and go on to the next line whenever you wish.

Here is a program that contains declarations, assignment statements, and output statements.

```cpp
//*********************************************
// Example program containing declarations,
// string assignment statements, and output
// statements
//*********************************************
#include <iostream>      // For cout, endl
#include <string>
using namespace std;
int main ()
{
  const string BORDER = "***********************************";
  const string NAME = "Susy Sunshine";
  const string MESSAGE = "Good Morning";
  string outMessage;
  cout << BORDER << endl;
  outMessage = MESSAGE + " to " + "Miss " +  NAME;
  cout << outMessage << '!' << endl;
  cout << BORDER << endl;
  return 0;
}
```

```
***********************************
Good Morning to Miss Susy Sunshine!
***********************************
```

Beyond Minimalism: Adding Comments to a Program

All you need to create a working program is the correct combination of declarations and executable statements. The compiler ignores comments, but they are of enormous help to anyone who must read the program. Comments can appear anywhere in a program except in the middle of an identifier, a reserved word, or a literal constant.

C++ comments come in two forms. The first is any sequence of characters enclosed by the /* */ pair. The compiler ignores anything within the pair. Here's an example:

```cpp
string idNumber;   /* Identification number of the aircraft */
```

The second, and more common, form begins with two slashes (`//`) and extends to the end of that line of the program:

```
string idNumber;   // Identification number of the aircraft
```

The compiler ignores anything after the two slashes.

Writing fully commented programs is good programming style. A comment should appear at the beginning of a program to explain what the program does:

```
// This program computes the weight and balance of a Beechcraft
// Starship-1 airplane, given the amount of fuel, number of
// passengers, and weight of luggage in fore and aft storage.
// It assumes that there are two pilots and a standard complement
// of equipment, and that passengers weigh 170 pounds each.
```

Another good place for comments is in constant and variable declarations, where the comments explain how each identifier is used. In addition, comments should introduce each major step in a long program and should explain anything that is unusual or difficult to read (for example, a lengthy formula).

It is important to make your comments concise and to arrange them in the program so that they are easy to see and it is clear what they refer to. If comments are too long or crowd the statements in the program, they make the program more difficult to read—just the opposite of what you intended!

QUICK CHECK

2.1.1 What is the name of the one function that every C++ program must have? (p. 44)

2.1.2 What is the purpose of a metalanguage? (p. 47)

2.1.3 What is a data type? (p. 50)

2.1.4 Use the following syntax template to decide if the string "C++ 6th edition" is a valid "Sentence." (pp. 47–48)

Sentence

$$\left\{ \begin{array}{l} \text{Letter} \\ \text{Digit} \\ \text{Space} \\ + \end{array} \right\} \ldots \left\{ \begin{array}{l} . \\ ! \\ ? \end{array} \right\}$$

2.1.5 Which of the following are valid C++ identifiers? (pp. 49–50)

```
Hello    Bob    6th-edition    C++    maximum    all_4_one
```

2.1.6 The only difference between a variable declaration and a constant declaration is that the reserved word `const` precedes the declaration. True or false? (pp. 55–56)

2.1.7 The reserved words listed in Appendix A cannot be used as identifiers. True or false? (p. 49)

2.1.8 Write a statement to assign the letter "A" to the `char` variable `initial`. (pp. 57–60)

> **QUICK CHECK**
>
> 2.1.9 What value is stored in the variable **name** by the following statement? (pp. 57–60)
>
> ```
> name = "Alexander" + " Q. " + "Smith";
> ```
>
> 2.1.10 Write a statement that sends the value in variable **name** to the stream **cout**. (pp. 60–62)
>
> 2.1.11 What is printed by the following statement, given the value assigned to **name** in Exercise 2.1.10? (pp. 60–62)
>
> ```
> cout << name << " Jr." << endl;
> ```
>
> 2.1.12 What are the two ways to write comments in C++? (pp. 62–63)

2.2 Program Construction

We have looked at basic elements of C++ programs: identifiers, declarations, variables, constants, expressions, statements, and comments. Now let's see how to collect these elements into a program. As you saw earlier, C++ programs are made up of functions, one of which must be named **main**. A program also can have declarations that lie outside of any function. The syntax template for a program looks like this:

A function definition consists of the function heading and its body, which is delimited by left and right braces:

FunctionDefinition

```
Heading
{
    Statement
        ⋮
}
```

Here's an example of a program with just one function, the **main** function:

```cpp
//*****************************************************************
// PrintName program
// This program prints a name in two different formats
//*****************************************************************
#include <iostream>              // For cout, endl
#include <string>

using namespace std;

const string FIRST = "Herman";   // Person's first name
const string LAST = "Smith";     // Person's last name
const char   MIDDLE = 'G';       // Person's middle initial

int main()
{
  string firstLast;  // Name in first-last format
  string lastFirst;  // Name in last-first format

  firstLast = FIRST + " " + LAST;
  cout << "Name in first-last format is " << firstLast << endl;

  lastFirst = LAST + ", " + FIRST + ", ";
  cout << "Name in last-first-initial format is ";
  cout << lastFirst << MIDDLE << '.' << endl;

  return 0;
}
```

The program begins with a comment that explains what the program does. Immediately after the comment, the following lines appear:

```
#include <iostream>
#include <string>

using namespace std;
```

The `#include` lines instruct the C++ system to insert into our program the contents of the files named `iostream` and `string`. The first file contains information that C++ needs to output values to a stream such as `cout`. The second file contains information about the programmer-defined data type `string`. We discuss the purpose of these `#include` lines and the `using` statement a little later in the chapter.

Next comes a declaration section in which we define the constants FIRST, LAST, and MIDDLE.[3] Comments explain how each identifier is used. The rest of the program is the function definition for our `main` function. The first line is the function heading: the reserved word `int`, the name of the function, and then opening and closing parentheses. (The parentheses inform the compiler that `main` is the name of a function, and not a variable or named constant.) The body of the function includes the declarations of two variables, `firstLast` and `lastFirst`, followed by a list of executable statements. The compiler translates these

---

3. As with our earlier demonstration programs, we could have declared these constants within `main`. Here we place them before `main` as an example of what are called *global declarations*. We return to this topic in a later chapter.

executable statements into machine language instructions. During the execution phase of the program, these instructions will be executed.

Our `main` function finishes by returning 0 as the function value:

```
return 0;
```

Recall that `main` returns an integer value to the operating system when it completes execution. This integer value is called the *exit status*. On most computer systems, you return an exit status of 0 to indicate successful completion of the program; otherwise, you return a nonzero value. Here is the output from the program.

```
Name in first-last format is Herman Smith
Name in last-first-initial format is Smith, Herman, G.
```

Notice how we use spacing in the `PrintName` program to make it easy for someone to read. We use blank lines to separate statements into related groups, and we indent the entire body of the `main` function. The compiler doesn't require us to format the program this way; we do so only to make it more readable. We will have more to say about formatting a program in Chapter 3.

Blocks (Compound Statements)

The body of a function is an example of a *block* (or *compound statement*). This is the syntax template for a block:

Block

A block is just a sequence of zero or more statements enclosed (delimited) by a `{ }` pair. Now we can redefine a function definition as a heading followed by a block:

FunctionDefinition

```
Heading
Block
```

In later chapters, when we learn how to write functions other than `main`, we will define the syntax of the heading in detail. In the case of the `main` function, the heading is simply

```
int main()
```

Here is the syntax template for a statement, limited to the C++ statements discussed in this chapter:

Statement

{
NullStatement
Declaration
AssignmentStatement
OutputStatement
Block
}

A statement can be empty (the *null statement*). The null statement is just a semicolon (;) and looks like this:

;

It does absolutely nothing at execution time; execution just proceeds to the next statement. The null statement is not used often.

As the syntax template shows, a statement can also be a declaration, an executable statement, or even a block. The last term means that you can use an entire block wherever a single statement is allowed. In later chapters in which we introduce the syntax for branching and looping structures, this fact is very important.

We use blocks often, especially as parts of other statements. Leaving out a { } pair can dramatically change the meaning as well as the execution of a program. This is why we always indent the statements inside a block—the indentation makes a block easy to spot in a long, complicated program.

Notice in the syntax templates for the block and the statement that there is no mention of semicolons—yet the `PrintName` program contains many semicolons. If you look back at the templates for constant declaration, variable declaration, assignment statement, and output statement, you can see that a semicolon is required at the end of each kind of statement. However, the syntax template for the block shows no semicolon after the right brace. The rule for using semicolons in C++, then, is quite simple: Terminate each statement *except* a compound statement (block) with a semicolon.

One more thing about blocks and statements: According to the syntax template for a statement, a declaration is officially considered to be a statement. A declaration, therefore, can appear wherever an executable statement can. In a block, we can mix declarations and executable statements if we wish:

```
{
  char ch;
  ch = 'A';
  cout << ch;
  string str;
  str = "Hello";
  cout << str;
}
```

We prefer, however, to group the declarations together before the start of the executable statements:

```
{
  char    ch;
  string  str;

  ch = 'A';
  cout << ch;
  str = "Hello";
  cout << str;
}
```

The C++ Preprocessor

Imagine that you are the C++ compiler. You are presented with the following program. You are to check it for syntax errors and, if there are no syntax errors, you are to translate it into machine language code.

```
//**************************************
// This program prints Happy Birthday
//**************************************

int main()
{
  cout << "Happy Birthday" << endl;
  return 0;
}
```

You, the compiler, recognize the identifier `int` as a C++ reserved word and the identifier `main` as the name of a required function. But what about the identifiers `cout` and `endl`? The programmer has not declared them as variables or named constants, and they are not reserved words. You have no choice but to issue an error message and give up.

To fix this program, the first thing we must do is insert a line near the top that says

```
#include <iostream>           // For cout, endl
```

just as we did in the **PrintName** program (as well as in the sample program at the beginning of this chapter and the **LeapYear** program of Chapter 1). This line says to insert the contents of a file named `iostream` into the program. This file contains declarations of `cout`, `endl`, and other items needed to perform stream input and output. The `#include` line is not handled by the C++ compiler, but rather by a program known as the *preprocessor*.

The preprocessor concept is fundamental to C++. The preprocessor is a program that acts as a filter during the compilation phase. Your source program passes through the preprocessor on its way to the compiler (see **FIGURE 2.2**).

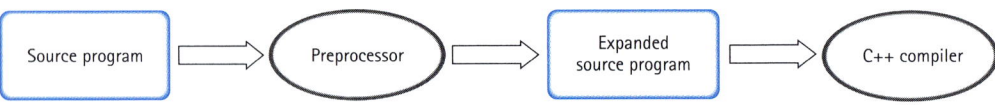

FIGURE 2.2 C++ Preprocessor

A line beginning with a pound sign (#) is not considered to be a C++ language statement (and thus is not terminated by a semicolon). Instead, it is called a *preprocessor directive*. The preprocessor expands an `#include` directive by physically inserting the contents of the named file into your source program. A file whose name appears in an `#include` directive is called a *header file*. Header files contain constant, variable, data type, and function declarations needed by a program.

In the directives

```cpp
#include <iostream>        // For cout, endl
#include <string>
```

the angle brackets < > are required. They tell the preprocessor to look for the files in the standard *include directory*—which contains all the header files that are related to the C++ standard library. The file `iostream` contains declarations of input/output facilities, and the file `string` contains declarations for the `string` data type. In Chapter 3, we make use of header files other than `iostream` and `string`.[4]

Using the std Namespace

In our `HappyBirthday` program, even if we add the preprocessor directive `#include <iostream>`, the program will not compile. The compiler *still* doesn't recognize the identifiers `cout` and `endl`. The problem is that the header file `iostream` (and, in fact, every standard header file) declares all of its identifiers to be in a *namespace* block called `std`:

```cpp
namespace std
{          // Start of namespace block
    :      // Declarations of variables, data types, and so forth
}          // End of namespace block
```

Don't worry about writing namespace block declarations for now; the important point is that an identifier declared within a namespace block can be accessed directly only by statements within that same block. To access an identifier that is "hidden" inside a namespace, the programmer has several options. We describe the simplest one here. Chapter 8 describes namespaces in more detail.

If we insert a statement called a *using directive*

```cpp
using namespace std;
```

near the top of the program before the `main` function, then we make *all* the identifiers in the `std` namespace accessible to our program.

```cpp
//*************************************
// This program prints Happy Birthday.
//*************************************
#include <iostream>     // For cout, endl
using namespace std;

int main()
{
  cout << "Happy Birthday" << endl;
  return 0;
}
```

---

4. In the C language and in prestandard C++, the standard header files end in the suffix `.h` (for example, `iostream.h`), where the `h` suggests "header file." In ISO/ANSI C++, the standard header files no longer use the `.h` suffix.

This option is the one we used in the **PrintName** program and in sample programs earlier in the chapter. In many of the following chapters, we continue to use this method. However, in Chapter 8 we discuss why the approach is not advisable in large programs.

SOFTWARE MAINTENANCE CASE STUDY: Adding Titles to Names

In Chapter 1, we saw the essential steps of any software maintenance process:

1. Check the operation of the existing code.
2. Understand sufficiently how the code works to do the maintenance task.
3. Create a working copy of the code.
4. Make the modifications.
5. Test the new code.
6. Clean up any inconsistencies and update any related documentation.

For the **HelloWorld** program in Chapter 1, the code was so trivial that we could understand its operation and make the changes without any knowledge of C++ syntax. In the following scenario, the code is not so simple. We'll need to study it more consciously to discover how it works and what needs to be changed.

MAINTENANCE TASK: Add the title "Mr." to each of the name formats in the **PrintName** application.

EXISTING CODE

```cpp
//***************************************************************
// PrintName program
// This program prints a name in two different formats
//***************************************************************
#include <iostream>            // For cout, endl
#include <string>
using namespace std;

const string FIRST = "Herman";  // Person's first name
const string LAST = "Smith";    // Person's last name
const char   MIDDLE = 'G';      // Person's middle initial

int main()
{
  string firstLast;   // Name in first-last format
  string lastFirst;   // Name in last-first format

  firstLast = FIRST + " " + LAST;
  cout << "Name in first-last format is " << firstLast << endl;

  lastFirst = LAST + ", " + FIRST + ", ";
  cout << "Name in last-first-initial format is ";
  cout << lastFirst << MIDDLE << '.' << endl;
  return 0;
}
```

SOFTWARE MAINTENANCE CASE STUDY: Adding Titles to Names

CODE ANALYSIS: To understand any sizable piece of code, we look for recognizable chunks into which we can partition it. One of our goals is to set aside portions that are unlikely to be related to our maintenance task. In this case, we see that there are opening comments:

```
//*************************************************************
// PrintName program
// This program prints a name in two different formats
//*************************************************************
```

The next chunk is made up of the **include** and **using** statements. These also are unrelated to the maintenance task.

```
#include <iostream>           // For cout, endl
#include <string>
using namespace std;
```

Next comes the declaration of the three constants:

```
const string FIRST = "Herman";   // Person's first name
const string LAST = "Smith";     // Person's last name
const char   MIDDLE = 'G';       // Person's middle initial
```

Because the heading of **main** simply follows the standard formula, we can also set aside that line of code and its associated braces. Thus the portion of this application that we must focus on is the block within **main**. That block can be further partitioned into a section of declarations:

```
string firstLast;   // Name in first-last format
string lastFirst;   // Name in last-first format
```

There is also a section that generates and prints each of the two name formats:

```
firstLast = FIRST + " " + LAST;
cout << "Name in first-last format is " << firstLast << endl;

lastFirst = LAST + ", " + FIRST + ", ";
cout << "Name in last-first-initial format is ";
cout << lastFirst << MIDDLE << '.' << endl;
```

Thus the major steps in the application are declarations and output.

SOLUTION: Our task is to modify the application to incorporate a title in each of the formats. How are we to do this? We must begin with the problem-solving technique of asking questions.

How do we get the title? We need to declare a **string** constant TITLE that contains the string "Mr.".

```
const String TITLE = "Mr.";
```

How is the title to be incorporated into the formats? For the first format, it simply appears at the beginning of the name. For the second format, it appears after the last name. Now we must decide how to accomplish this within the application. There are two places where we could add the title to each format. One place is within the assignment statements that generate the format. For example:

```
firstLast = TITLE + " " + FIRST + " " + LAST;
```

SOFTWARE MAINTENANCE CASE STUDY: Adding Titles to Names

The other place is within the output statements that print the names:

```cpp
cout << "Name in first-last format is " << TITLE << " "
     << firstLast << endl;
```

With the second format, the change is not so simple, because the title must be inserted between the names. We could still change the output statement, but it would not make use of the contents of **lastFirst**, which would be wasteful.

In this short application, it doesn't really matter which approach we choose. But in a larger application, we would need to check whether the **firstLast** and **lastFirst** variables are used elsewhere. If they are, then we must understand how they are used. In this case, however, let's simply insert the title into the assignment statements.

REVISED CODE: Here is the revised application, with the inserted or modified code highlighted.

```cpp
//***************************************************************
// PrintName program
// This program prints a name in two different formats
//***************************************************************
#include <iostream>                    // For cout, endl
#include <string>

using namespace std;

const string FIRST = "Herman";         // Person's first name
const string LAST = "Smith";           // Person's last name
const char   MIDDLE = 'G';             // Person's middle initial
const string TITLE = "Mr.";
int main()
{
    string firstLast;                  // Name in first-last format
    string lastFirst;                  // Name in last-first format

    firstLast = TITLE + " " + FIRST + " " + LAST;
    cout << "Name in first-last format is " << firstLast << endl;

    lastFirst = LAST + ", " + TITLE + " " + FIRST + ", ";
    cout << "Name in last-first-initial format is ";
    cout << lastFirst << MIDDLE << '.' << endl;
    return 0;
}
```

As you can see, the actual changes are quite small. By analyzing the original code and breaking it into meaningful sections, we could isolate the steps that required modification. It was then obvious how and where to make each of the changes. Here is the output:

SOFTWARE MAINTENANCE CASE STUDY: Adding Titles to Names

Software Maintenance Tips

1. Break a long block of code into smaller chunks that have distinct purposes.
2. Identify portions of the code that you are sure you can ignore.
3. Focus on those code sections that are clearly related to the maintenance task.
4. Make sure that you understand which changes are required. Ask questions about anything that is unclear. Formally, this information would be written as a specification document.
5. Consider the major steps that you've identified in the existing code. Then establish how you would solve the maintenance task within that overall approach. For example, in a simple application whose steps are input, process, and output, think about how the task relates to each of these steps. It doesn't help to develop a solution for a maintenance task that takes a completely different approach from the existing code. You must work within the given context.
6. Look for how your changes affect other parts of the application. If you're changing the content of an existing variable, check whether it is used elsewhere and how it is used.
7. Document your changes. In our example, we highlighted the updated code. Some companies have standards for how code changes are recorded. For example, each line may have a comment that identifies the programmer and the date of the change. There are also code management tools that automatically record this information.

QUICK CHECK

2.2.1 What is an exit status? (p. 66)
2.2.2 What value is given to the exit status on most computing systems when a program completes successfully? (p. 66)
2.2.3 What is a block (compound statement)? (p. 66)
2.2.4 What is an example of a block in this section? (p. 66)
2.2.5 What are the five statements discussed in this section? (p. 67)
2.2.6 What character is used to terminate a statement? (p. 67)
2.2.7 Which statement does not need to be terminated? (p. 67)
2.2.8 Which compilation phase expands `#include<iostream>`? (p. 68)
2.2.9 What is the `#include` called? (p. 69)
2.2.10 Every standard header file declares all of its identifiers to be in a "hidden" place called `std`. What is the general term used for `std`? (p. 69)
2.2.11 Fill in the blanks in the following statements, which appear at the beginning of a program. (pp. 70–72)

```
#include <_____>
#include <_____>

using namespace _____;
```

2.3 More About Output

We can control both the horizontal and vertical spacing of our output to make it more appealing (and understandable). Let's look first at vertical spacing.

Creating Blank Lines

We control vertical spacing by using the **endl** manipulator in an output statement. You have seen that a sequence of output statements continues to write characters across the current line until an **endl** terminates the line. Here are some examples:

Statements	Output Produced[5]

`cout << "Hi there, ";`
`cout << "Lois Lane. " << endl;`
`cout << "Have you seen ";`
`cout << "Clark Kent?" << endl;`
	Hi there, Lois Lane.
	
	Have you seen Clark Kent?

`cout << "Hi there, " << endl;`
`cout << "Lois Lane. " << endl;`
`cout << "Have you seen " << endl;`
`cout << "Clark Kent?" << endl;`
	Hi there,
	Lois Lane.
	Have you seen
	Clark Kent?

`cout << "Hi there, " << endl;`
`cout << "Lois Lane. ";`
`cout << "Have you seen " << endl;`
`cout << "Clark Kent?" << endl;`
	Hi there,
	Lois Lane. Have you seen
	Clark Kent?

What do you think the following statements print out?

```
cout << "Hi there, " << endl;
cout << endl;
cout << "Lois Lane." << endl;
```

The first output statement causes the words *Hi there,* to be printed; the **endl** causes the screen cursor to go to the next line. The next statement prints nothing but goes on to the next line. The third statement prints the words *Lois Lane.* and terminates the line. The resulting output is the three lines

```
Hi there,

Lois Lane.
```

Whenever you use an **endl** immediately after another **endl**, a blank line is produced. As you might guess, three consecutive uses of **endl** produce two blank lines, four consecutive uses produce three blank lines, and so forth.

Note that we have a great deal of flexibility in how we write an output statement in a C++ program. We could combine the three preceding statements into two statements:

```
cout << "Hi there, " << endl << endl;
cout << "Lois Lane." << endl;
```

---

5. The output lines are shown next to the output statement that ends each of them. There are no blank lines in the actual output from these statements.

In fact, we could do it all in one statement. One possibility is this:

```
cout << "Hi there, " << endl << endl << "Lois Lane." << endl;
```

Here's another:

```
cout << "Hi there, " << endl << endl
        << "Lois Lane." << endl;
```

The last example shows that you can spread a single C++ statement onto more than one line of the program. The compiler treats the semicolon—not the physical end of a line—as the end of a statement.

Inserting Blanks Within a Line

To control the horizontal spacing of the output, one technique is to send extra blank characters to the output stream. (Remember that the blank character, which is generated by pressing the spacebar on a keyboard, is a perfectly valid character in C++.)

For example, to produce this output:

```
*   *   *   *   *   *   *   *   *

*  *  *  *  *  *  *  *  *  *

 *  *  *  *  *  *  *  *  *
```

you would use these statements:

```
cout << "  *   *   *   *   *   *   *   *    *" << endl << endl;
cout << "*  *  *  *  *  *  *  *  *    *" << endl << endl;
cout << "  *  *  *  *  *  *  *  *    *" << endl;
```

All of the blanks and asterisks are enclosed in double quotes, so they print literally as they are written in the program. The extra **endl** manipulators give you the blank lines between the rows of asterisks.

If you want blanks to be printed, you *must* enclose them in quotes. The statement

```
cout << '*' <<                              '*';
```

produces the following output:

```
**
```

Despite all of the blanks we included in the output statement, the asterisks print side by side because the blanks are not enclosed by quotes.

Special Characters

We have already mentioned that to include a double-quote mark within a string, it must be preceded by a backslash (\"). C++ defines some additional special characters using the backslash prefix. Here we discuss three that are particularly useful.

We use the **endl** manipulator in an output stream to go to the next line. You can also use the newline character **\n** to place a newline operation directly in a string. The following two output statements both produce the same output:

```
cout << "The answer is:\n42\n";
cout << "The answer is:" << endl << "42" << endl;
```

They each display:

```
The answer is:
42
```

The second statement is clearly more readable, of course. Starting with Chapter 8, we'll encounter cases where embedding **\n** in a string makes sense. For now, we recommend always using **endl**.

If you want to include a single quote mark as a **char** literal within an output stream, then it must also be preceded by a backslash: '\''. Note that there is no problem including single quote marks in strings or writing a double quote directly as a **char** literal. For example, to output a double quote followed by a single quote, we can write either:

```
cout << '"' << "'";        // Outputs "'
```

or

```
cout << "\"" << '\'';      // Also outputs "'
```

Given that the backslash has these special uses, it is natural to wonder how a backslash would be output. The answer is that we must write two backslashes in a row:

```
cout << "\\";              // Outputs \
```

QUICK CHECK

2.3.1 What is used to control vertical spacing in an output statement? (p. 74)
2.3.2 What is the special character for *newline*? (p. 76)

2.4 Program Entry, Correction, and Execution

In this section, we examine the program entry process in general. You should consult the manual for your specific computer to learn the details.

Entering a Program

The first step in entering a program is to get the computer's attention. With a personal computer, you just turn it on or wake it from sleep mode. If you're using a computer in an educational lab, you may need to *log on* by entering a user name and password.

Once the computer is ready to accept your commands, you tell it that you want to enter a program by having it run a development environment, which includes a code editor.

The code editor is a program that allows you to create and modify the code for a program, which is then stored on a file.

A file is a collection of data that has a name associated with it. You usually choose the name for the file when you create it with the editor. From that point on, you refer to the file by the name you've given it.

> **File** A named area in secondary storage that is used to hold a collection of data; the collection of data itself.

There are so many different types of editors, each with different features, that we can't begin to describe them all here. But we can describe some of their general characteristics.

A code editor is very much like a word processor. It allows you to type in a window and move around the file with your mouse and keyboard to make changes. In most development environments, the code editor also color-codes different parts of C++ syntax to make it easier to more distinctly see keywords, variables, comments, and so on. It will also help you to automatically indent lines of code. Some code editors check syntax as you type, flagging parts of your code that may not compile.

In many development environments, the compiler will automatically use the code editor to display the location where it detects an error in your code. Note, however, that a compiler sometimes detects an error in a place much different from where it actually occurred. For example, the compiler will point out the first place that an undeclared variable name is used, when the source of the error may be that you forgot a `using` statement.

Compiling and Running a Program

Once your program is stored in a file, you compile it by issuing a command to run the C++ compiler. The compiler translates the program, then stores the machine language version into a file. The compiler may display messages indicating errors in the program, either in a separate window or in the editor.

If the compiler finds errors in your program (syntax errors), you have to determine their cause, fix them in the editor, and then run the compiler again. Once your program compiles without errors, you can run (execute) it.

Some systems automatically run a program when it compiles successfully. On other systems, you have to issue a separate command to run the program. Still other systems require that you specify an extra step called *linking* between compiling and running a program. Whatever series of commands your system uses, the result is the same: Your program is loaded into memory and executed by the computer.

Even though a program runs, it may still have errors in its design. The computer does exactly what you tell it to do, even if that's not what you wanted it to do. If your program doesn't do what it should (a *logic error*), you have to return to the algorithm and fix it, and then go back to the editor and fix the program. Finally, you compile and run the program again. This *debugging* process is repeated until the program does what it is supposed to do (see **FIGURE 2.3**).

QUICK CHECK

2.4.1 What does a compiler translate a program into? (p. 77)

2.4.2 What do we call an error that occurs when the program is executing? (p. 77)

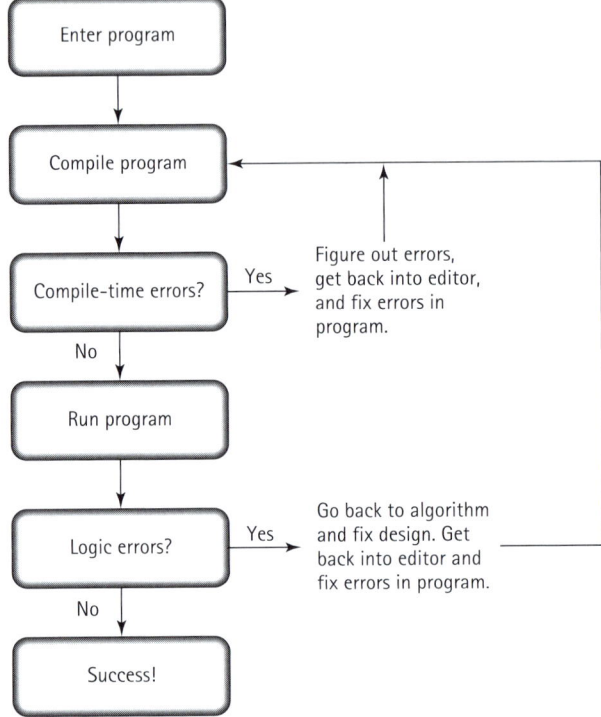

FIGURE 2.3 Debugging Process

Problem-Solving Case Study

Printing a Chessboard

PROBLEM: Your college is hosting a chess tournament, and the people running the tournament want to record the final positions of the pieces in each game on a sheet of paper with a chessboard preprinted on it. Your job is to write a program to preprint these pieces of paper. The chessboard is an eight-by-eight pattern of squares that alternate between black and white, with the upper-left square being white. You need to print out squares of light characters (spaces) and dark characters (such as *) in this pattern to form the chessboard.

DISCUSSION: You could simply type up a program consisting of a series of output statements with alternating patterns of blanks and asterisks. But the organizers of the tournament aren't sure exactly what they want the chessboard to look like, and you decide it would be safer to write the program in a manner that allows the design of the chessboard to be modified easily.

It is easy to make a changeable chessboard if the design is built up using string variables. You can begin by defining string constants for rows of characters that make up the black and white areas. Then you can

Problem-Solving Case Study

concatenate these constants to form variables containing the alternating patterns of black and white that are repeated to print a row of chessboard squares. For example, suppose your initial design for the chessboard looks like this:

```
        ********        ********        ********        ********
        ********        ********        ********        ********
        ********        ********        ********        ********
        ********        ********        ********        ********
        ********        ********        ********        ********
********        ********        ********        ********
********        ********        ********        ********
********        ********        ********        ********
********        ********        ********        ********
********        ********        ********        ********
        ********        ********        ********        ********
        ********        ********        ********        ********
        ********        ********        ********        ********
        ********        ********        ********        ********
        ********        ********        ********        ********
********        ********        ********        ********
********        ********        ********        ********
********        ********        ********        ********
********        ********        ********        ********
********        ********        ********        ********
        ********        ********        ********        ********
        ********        ********        ********        ********
        ********        ********        ********        ********
        ********        ********        ********        ********
        ********        ********        ********        ********
********        ********        ********        ********
********        ********        ********        ********
********        ********        ********        ********
********        ********        ********        ********
********        ********        ********        ********
        ********        ********        ********        ********
        ********        ********        ********        ********
        ********        ********        ********        ********
        ********        ********        ********        ********
        ********        ********        ********        ********
********        ********        ********        ********
********        ********        ********        ********
********        ********        ********        ********
********        ********        ********        ********
********        ********        ********        ********
```

You can begin by defining constants for **WHITE** and **BLACK** that contain eight blanks and eight asterisks respectively, and then concatenate these together into variables that follow the patterns

```
WHITE + BLACK + WHITE + BLACK + WHITE + BLACK + WHITE + BLACK
```

and

```
BLACK + WHITE + BLACK + WHITE + BLACK + WHITE + BLACK + WHITE
```

Problem-Solving Case Study

These variables can then be printed with `cout` statements the appropriate number of times to create the chessboard.

From this discussion we know that there are two constants and two variables, as summarized in the following tables:

CONSTANTS

Name	Value	Function
BLACK	"********"	Characters forming one line of a black square
WHITE	" "	Characters forming one line of a white square

VARIABLES

Name	Data Type	Description
whiteRow	string	A row beginning with a white square
blackRow	string	A row beginning with a black square

If we look carefully at the chessboard, the algorithm jumps out at us. We need to output five `whiteRow`s, five `blackRow`s, five `whiteRow`s, five `blackRow`s, five `whiteRow`s, five `blackRow`s, five `whiteRow`s, and five `blackRow`s. We can summarize this in our algorithm to output the five `whiteRow`s and five `blackRow`s four times.

```
Repeat four times
    Output five whiteRows
    Output five blackRows
```

```cpp
//************************************************************
// Chessboard program
// This program prints a chessboard pattern that is built up from
// basic strings of white and black characters.
//************************************************************
#include <iostream>                      // For cout, endl
#include <string>
using namespace std;

const string BLACK = "********";   // Define a line of a black square
const string WHITE = "        ";   // Define a line of a white square

int main ()
{
    string whiteRow;           // A row beginning with a white square
    string blackRow;           // A row beginning with a black square

    // Create a white-black row by concatenating the basic strings
    whiteRow = WHITE + BLACK + WHITE + BLACK +
               WHITE + BLACK + WHITE + BLACK;
    // Create a black-white row by concatenating the basic strings
    blackRow = BLACK + WHITE + BLACK + WHITE +
               BLACK + WHITE + BLACK + WHITE;
```

Problem-Solving Case Study

```cpp
    // Print five white-black rows
    cout << whiteRow << endl;
    cout << whiteRow << endl;
    cout << whiteRow << endl;
    cout << whiteRow << endl;
    cout << whiteRow << endl;
    // Print five black-white rows
    cout << blackRow << endl;
    cout << blackRow << endl;
    cout << blackRow << endl;
    cout << blackRow << endl;
    cout << blackRow << endl;
    // Print five white-black rows
    cout << whiteRow << endl;
    cout << whiteRow << endl;
    cout << whiteRow << endl;
    cout << whiteRow << endl;
    cout << whiteRow << endl;
    // Print five black-white rows
    cout << blackRow << endl;
    cout << blackRow << endl;
    cout << blackRow << endl;
    cout << blackRow << endl;
    cout << blackRow << endl;
    // Print five white-black rows
    cout << whiteRow << endl;
    cout << whiteRow << endl;
    cout << whiteRow << endl;
    cout << whiteRow << endl;
    cout << whiteRow << endl;
    // Print five black-white rows
    cout << blackRow << endl;
    cout << blackRow << endl;
    cout << blackRow << endl;
    cout << blackRow << endl;
    cout << blackRow << endl;
    // Print five white-black rows
    cout << whiteRow << endl;
    cout << whiteRow << endl;
    cout << whiteRow << endl;
    cout << whiteRow << endl;
    cout << whiteRow << endl;
    // Print five black-white rows
    cout << blackRow << endl;
    cout << blackRow << endl;
    cout << blackRow << endl;
    cout << blackRow << endl;
    cout << blackRow << endl;

    return 0;
}
```

Problem-Solving Case Study

There are eight blocks of five lines that look alike. In Chapter 6, we introduce a looping statement that allows us to shorten this program considerably.

After you show the printout from this program to the organizers of the tournament, they suggest that the board would look better with the "#" character instead of "*" filling the black squares. You cheerfully agree to make this change because you know that the only difference in the program is that the value of the constant `BLACK` becomes `"########"`.

Testing and Debugging

1. Every identifier that isn't a C++ reserved word must be declared. If you use a name that hasn't been declared—either by creating your own declaration statements or by including a header file—you get an error message.
2. If you try to declare an identifier that is the same as a reserved word in C++, you get an error message from the compiler. See Appendix A for a list of reserved words.
3. C++ is a case-sensitive language. Two identifiers that are capitalized differently are treated as two different identifiers. The word `main` and all C++ reserved words use only lowercase letters.
4. To use identifiers from the standard library, such as `cout` and `string`, you must put a `using` directive near the top of your program:

   ```
   using namespace std;
   ```

5. Check for mismatched quotes in `char` and string literals. Each `char` literal begins and ends with an apostrophe (a single quote). Each string literal begins and ends with a double quote.
6. Be sure to use only the apostrophe (') to enclose `char` literals. Most keyboards also have a reverse apostrophe (`), which is easily confused with the apostrophe. If you use the reverse apostrophe, the compiler will issue an error message.
7. To use a double quote within a literal string, use the two symbols \" in a row. If you use just a double quote, it ends the string, and the compiler then sees the remainder of the string as an error.
8. In an assignment statement, be sure that the identifier to the left of = is a variable and not a named constant.
9. In assigning a value to a `string` variable, the expression to the right of = must be a `string` expression, a string literal, or a `char`.

10. In a concatenation expression, at least one of the two operands of + must be of type `string`. For example, the operands cannot both be literal strings or `char` values.[6]

11. Make sure your statements end in semicolons (except blocks, which do not have a semicolon after the right brace).

■ Summary

The syntax (grammar) of the C++ language is defined by a metalanguage. In this text, we use a form of metalanguage called syntax templates. We describe the semantics (meaning) of C++ statements in English.

Identifiers are used in C++ to name things. Some identifiers, called reserved words, have predefined meanings in the language; others are created by the programmer. The identifiers you invent are restricted to those *not* reserved by the C++ language. Reserved words are listed in Appendix A.

Identifiers are associated with memory locations by declarations. A declaration may give a name to a location whose value does not change (a constant) or to one whose value can change (a variable). Every constant and variable has an associated data type. C++ provides many built-in data types; the most commonly used are `int`, `float`, and `char`. Additionally, C++ permits programmer-defined types, such as the `string` type from the standard library.

The assignment operator is used to change the value of a variable by assigning it the value of an expression. At execution time, the expression is evaluated and the result is stored into the variable. With the `string` type, the plus sign (+) is an operator that concatenates two strings. A string expression can concatenate any number of strings to form a new `string` value.

Program output is accomplished by means of the output stream variable `cout`, along with the insertion operator (<<). Each insertion operation sends output data to the standard output device. When an `endl` manipulator appears instead of a data item, the computer terminates the current output line and goes on to the next line.

Output should be clear, understandable, and neatly arranged. Messages in the output should describe the significance of values. Blank lines (produced by successive uses of the `endl` manipulator) and blank spaces within lines help to organize the output and improve its appearance.

A C++ program is a collection of one or more function definitions (and optionally some declarations outside of any function). One of the functions *must* be named `main`. Execution of a program always begins with the `main` function. Collectively, the functions all cooperate to produce the desired results.

■ Quick Check Answers

2.1.1 main **2.1.2** To provide a language for expressing the syntax rules of a programming language. **2.1.3** A specific set of values, together with a set of operations that can be applied to those values. **2.1.4** No. According to the template, a Sentence must end in a period, exclamation point, or question mark. **2.1.5** Hello, Bob, maximum, and all_4_one are the valid C++ identifiers. **2.1.6** False. The constant declaration also assigns a literal value to the identifier. **2.1.7** True. Identifiers must differ from reserved words. **2.1.8** initial = 'A'; **2.1.9** Alexander Q. Smith **2.1.10** cout << name; **2.1.11** The string Alexander Q. Smith Jr. is output and then successive output will appear on the next line. **2.1.12** Between the delimiters /* and */, or following // to the end of the line. **2.2.1** The

---

6. The invalid concatenation expression "Hi" + "there" results in a confusing syntax error message such as INVALID POINTER ADDITION. For now, just keep in mind that such a message may indicate a concatenation expression that doesn't include a variable.

exit status is an integer value that is returned from the main function to the operating system when it completes execution. **2.2.2** A 0 value indicates success. **2.2.3** A block is a sequence of zero or more statements enclosed by a { } pair. **2.2.4** The body of a function. **2.2.5** Null, Declaration, Assignment, Output, and Block. **2.2.6** A semicolon (;) **2.2.7** Block **2.2.8** Preprocessor phase. **2.2.9** A preprocessor directive. **2.2.10** A namespace.
2.2.11
```
#include <iostream>
#include <string>
using namespace std;
```
2.3.1 endl **2.3.2** '\n' **2.4.1** Machine language. **2.4.2** A logic error or runtime error.

Exam Preparation Exercises

1. Mark the following identifiers as either valid or invalid.

		Valid	Invalid
a.	theDog	___	___
b.	all-In-One	___	___
c.	const	___	___
d.	recycling	___	___
e.	DVD_ROM	___	___
f.	elizabeth_the_2nd	___	___
g.	2morrow	___	___
h.	page#	___	___

2. Match the following terms with the definitions given below.
   a. Function
   b. Syntax
   c. Semantics
   d. Metalanguage
   e. Identifier
   f. Data type
   g. Variable
   h. Named constant
   i. Literal
   j. Expression
     i. An identifier referring to a value that can be changed.
     ii. A specific set of values, along with operations that can be applied to those values.
     iii. A value that appears in a program.
     iv. The set of rules that determines the meaning of instructions written in a programming language.
     v. A language that is used to write the rules for another language.
     vi. A subprogram in C++.
     vii. A name that is used to refer to a function or data object.
     viii. An arrangement of identifiers, literals, and operators that can be evaluated.
     ix. The formal rules governing how valid instructions are written in a programming language.
     x. An identifier referring to a value that cannot be changed.
3. A reserved word is a named constant that is predefined in C++. True or false?

4. What is wrong with the following syntax template for a C++ identifier?

5. A **char** literal can be enclosed either in single or double quotes. True or false?
6. The null string represents a string containing no characters. True or false?
7. Concatenation works with a **char** value only when its other operand is a string value. True or false?
8. What is output by the following statement?

   ```
   cout << "Four score and" << endl << "seven years ago"
        << "our fathers" << endl
        << "brought forth on this" << endl
        << "continent a new nation..." << endl;
   ```

9. Given these assignments to string variables:

   ```
   string1 = "Bjarne Stroustrup";
   string2 = "C";
   string3 = "programming language";
   string4 = "++ because it is a successor to the ";
   string5 = " named his new ";
   ```

   What is the value of the following expression?

   ```
   string1 + string5 + string3 + " " + string2 + string4 +
         string2 + " " + string3 + "."
   ```

10. How do we insert a double quote into a string?
11. What danger is associated with the use of the /* and */ form of comment, and is avoided by use of the // comment form?
12. What are the limitations associated with the // form of comment?
13. What is the name of the << operator, and how might we pronounce it in reading a line of code that contains it?
14. Can we concatenate **endl** with a string in an expression? Explain.
15. What does the #include preprocessor directive do?
16. For the following output statement, the compiler reports this error message: UNDECLARED IDENTIFIER: cout.

    ```
    cout << "Hello everybody!" << endl;
    ```

    The program includes the statement

    ```
    using namespace std;
    ```

    What is the most likely source of this error?

17. What is the name of the C++ construct that begins with { and ends with }?
18. How do you write a string that is too long to fit on a single line?
19. Reorder the following lines to make a working program.

    ```
    {
    }
    #include <iostream>

    const string TITLE = "Dr.";
    cout << "Hello " + TITLE + " Stroustrup!";
    int main()
    #include <string>
    return 0;
    using namespace std;
    ```

■ Programming Warm-Up Exercises

1. Write an output statement that prints today's date and then goes to the next line.
2. Write a single output statement that outputs the following three lines:

    ```
    He said, "How is that possible?"
    She replied, "Using manipulators."
    "Of course!" he exclaimed.
    ```

3. Write declarations for the following:
    a. A named constant, called `ANSWER`, of type `string`, with the value `"True"`
    b. A `char` variable with the name `middleInitial`
    c. A `string` variable with the name `courseTitle`
    d. A named `char` constant, called `PERCENT`, with the value `'%'`
4. Change the three declarations in the `PrintName` program on page 65 so that it prints your name.
5. Given the following declarations:

    ```
    const string PART1 = "Pro";
    const string PART2 = "gramming and ";
    const string PART3 = "blem Solving with C++";
    ```

    Write an output statement that prints the title of this book, using only the `cout` stream, the stream insertion operator, and the above-named constants.
6. Write an expression that results in a string containing the title of this book, using only the concatenation operator and the declarations of Exercise 5.
7. Write C++ output statements to print the following exactly as shown (a portion of the text found in the preface of this book, relating the action of a weaver's loom to the complexity of human thought). You should write one output statement for each line of text.

    ```
    Yet the web of thought has no such creases
    And is more like a weaver's masterpieces;
    One step a thousand threads arise,
    Hither and thither shoots each shuttle,
    The threads flow on unseen and subtle,
    Each blow effects a thousand ties.
    ```

8. Fill in the missing lines in the following program, which outputs:

   ```
   Rev. H.G. Jones
   ```

   _____
   _____

   _____

   ```
   const string TITLE = "Rev. ";
   const char FIRST = 'H';
   const char MID 'G';
   ```

   _____

   _____
   ```
   {
   cout << TITLE << FIRST << DOT << MID << DOT << " Jones";
   ```
   _____

9. Enter and run the following program. Be sure to type it exactly as it appears here, but substitute your name and the date as indicated.

   ```
   //*************************************************************
   // Program entry and compilation exercise
   // Your name goes here
   // Today's date goes here
   //*************************************************************

   #include <iostream>
   #include <string>

   using namespace std;

   const string STARS35 = "***********************************";
   const char   STAR = '*';
   const string BLANKS33 = "                                 ";
   const string MSG = "Welcome to C++ Programming!";
   const string BLANKS3 = "   ";

   int main()
   {
      cout << STARS35 << endl << STAR << BLANKS33 << STAR << endl;
      cout << STAR << BLANKS3 << MSG << BLANKS3 << STAR << endl;
      cout << STAR << BLANKS33 << STAR << endl << STARS35 << endl;
   }
   ```

10. Find the 10 missing items in the following program.

    ```
    #include <iostream>

    const string A = "A";
    const string B = "B";
    const char C 'C';
    ```

```
int main
    string forward
    string backward;

    forward = A + " " + B + " " + C;
    cout "Forward order: " forward << endl;

    backward = C + " " + B + " ";
    cout << "Backward order: "
    cout << backward << A << endl;
}
```

Programming Problems

1. Write a program that prints out your course schedule for a single week. Here's an example of the output for one day:

   ```
   Monday   9:00 Computer Science 101
   Monday  11:00 Physics 201
   Monday   2:00 Dance 153
   ```

   Use named string constants wherever possible to avoid retyping any words or numbers. Be sure to include appropriate comments in your code, choose meaningful identifiers, and use indentation as we do with the programs in this chapter.

2. Write a program that prints out all six permutations of the ordering of the following three lines. Declare a named constant for each line and write an output statement for each permutation. Be sure to include appropriate comments in your code, choose meaningful identifiers, and use indentation as we do with the programs in this chapter.

   ```
   I saw the big brown bear.
   The big brown bear saw me.
   Oh! What a frightening experience!
   ```

3. Write a program that displays a checkerboard pattern made of stars and blanks, as shown below. A checkerboard is eight squares by eight squares. This will be easier if you first declare two named string constants representing the two different row patterns. Be sure to include appropriate comments in your code, choose meaningful identifiers, and use indentation as we do with the programs in this chapter.

   ```
       *   *   *   *
     *   *   *   *
       *   *   *   *
     *   *   *   *
       *   *   *   *
     *   *   *   *
       *   *   *   *
     *   *   *   *
   ```

4. Write a program that prints out business cards for yourself. A card should include your name, street address, phone number(s), and email address. You also can make up a company name and put that on the card if you wish. To save paper, the program should print eight cards per page, arranged in two columns of four cards. To reduce typing, you should declare a named string constant for each line of the card, and then write output statements to print the eight cards using those constants. Be sure to include

appropriate comments in your code, choose meaningful identifiers, and use indentation as we do with the programs in this chapter.

■ Case Study Follow-Up

1. What change would you have to make to the `Chessboard` program to cause the black squares to be printed with the `"%"` character instead of `"*"`?
2. How would you change the `Chessboard` program to print periods in the white squares instead of blanks?
3. How would you change the `Chessboard` program if you wanted to reverse the colors (that is, make black squares white, and vice versa) without changing the constant declarations or the values of `whiteRow` and `blackRow`?
4. Change the `Chessboard` program so that the squares are 10 characters wide by 8 rows high.
5. The organizers of the chess tournament find it difficult to write in the black squares of the printed chessboard. They want you to change the program so that the black squares have a blank space in their center that is four characters wide and two lines high. (*Hint:* You may have to define another string constant.)
6. How many characters are stored in each of the string variables in the `Chessboard` program?

Numeric Types, Expressions, and Output

KNOWLEDGE GOALS

- To understand implicit type coercion and explicit type conversion.
- To recognize and understand the purpose of function arguments.
- To learn and use additional operations associated with the `string` type.
- To learn how to format program statements in a clear and readable fashion.

SKILL GOALS

To be able to:
- Declare named constants and variables of type `int` and `float`.
- Construct simple arithmetic expressions.
- Evaluate simple arithmetic expressions.
- Construct and evaluate expressions that contain multiple arithmetic operations.
- Call (invoke) a value-returning function.
- Use C++ library functions in expressions.
- Call (invoke) a void function (one that does not return a function value).
- Use C++ manipulators to format output.

In Chapter 2, we examined enough C++ syntax to be able to construct simple programs using assignment and output. We focused on the `char` and `string` types and saw how to construct expressions using the concatenation operator. In this chapter, we continue to write programs that use assignment and output, but we concentrate on additional built-in data types: `int` and `float`. These numeric types are supported by numerous operators that allow us to construct complex arithmetic expressions. We show how to make expressions even more powerful by using *library functions*—prewritten functions that are part of every C++ system and are available for use by any program.

We also return to the subject of formatting output. In particular, we consider the special features that C++ provides for formatting numbers as they are output. We finish by looking at some additional operations on `string` data.

3.1 Overview of C++ Data Types

The C++ built-in data types are organized into simple types, structured types, and address types (see **FIGURE 3.1**). Do not feel overwhelmed by the quantity of data types shown in Figure 3.1. Our purpose is simply to give you an overall picture of what is available in C++. This chapter concentrates on the integral and floating types. Details of the other types come later in the book. First we look at the integral types (those used primarily to represent integers), and then we consider the floating types (used to represent real numbers containing decimal points).

3.2 Numeric Data Types

You already are familiar with the basic concepts of integer and real numbers in math. However, as used on a computer, the corresponding data types have certain limitations.

Integral Types

The data types `char`, `short`, `int`, and `long` are known as integral types (or integer types) because they refer to integer values—that is, whole numbers with no fractional part. (We postpone talking about the remaining integral type, `bool`, until Chapter 5.)

In C++, the simplest form of integer value is a sequence of one or more digits:

22   16   1   498   0   4600

Commas are not allowed.

In most cases, a minus sign preceding an integer value makes the integer negative:

-378   -912

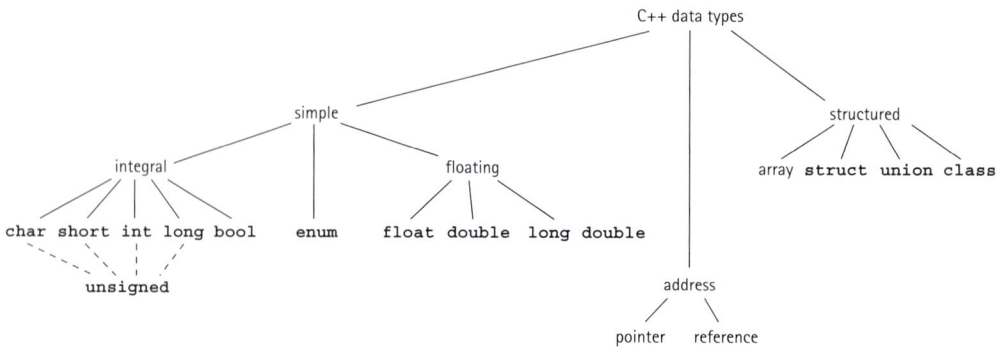

FIGURE 3.1 C++ Data Types

The exception is when you explicitly add the reserved word **unsigned** to the data type name:

```
unsigned int
```

An **unsigned** integer value is assumed to be only positive or zero. The unsigned types are used primarily in specialized situations. We rarely use **unsigned** in this book.

The data types **char**, **short**, **int**, and **long** are intended to represent different sizes of integers, from smaller (fewer bits) to larger (more bits). The sizes are machine dependent; that is, they may vary from machine to machine. The following table shows sample ranges:

Type	Size in Bytes*	Minimum Value*	Maximum Value*
char	1	-128	127
unsigned char	1	0	255
short	2	-32,768	32,767
unsigned short	2	0	65,535
int	4	-2,147,483,648	+2,147,483,647
unsigned int	4	0	+4,294,967,295
long	8	-9,223,372,036,854,775,808	+9,223,372,036,854,775,807
unsigned long	8	0	+18,446,744,073,709,551,615

*These values are for one particular machine. Your machine's values may be different.

On another machine, the size of an **int** might be the same as the size of a **long**. In general, the more bytes in the memory cell, the larger the integer value that can be stored there.

Although we used the **char** type in Chapter 2 to store character data such as **'A'**, C++ classifies **char** as an integral type because it also allows **char** to be used for storing integer values with a very limited range.

int is by far the most common data type for manipulating integer data. In the **LeapYear** program created in Chapter 1, the identifier, **year**, is of data type **int**. You nearly always use **int** for manipulating integer values, but sometimes you have to use **long** if your program requires values larger than the maximum **int** value. (On an embedded computer, such as the controller for a microwave oven, the range of **int** values might be from −32,768 through +32,767. More commonly, **int**s range from −2,147,483,648 through +2,147,483,647.) If your program tries to compute a value larger than your machine's maximum value, the result is *integer overflow*. Some machines display an error message when overflow occurs, but others don't. We talk more about overflow in later chapters.

One caution about integer values in C++: A literal constant beginning with a zero is taken to be an octal (base-8) number instead of a decimal (base-10) number. Thus, if you write

```
015
```

the C++ compiler takes this to mean the decimal number 13. If you aren't familiar with the octal number system, don't worry about why octal 15 is the same as decimal 13. The important thing to remember is that you should not start a decimal integer constant with a zero (unless you simply want the number 0, which is the same in both octal and decimal). In Chapter 10, we discuss the various integral types in more detail.

Floating-Point Types

Floating-point types (or floating types), the second major category of simple types in C++, are used to represent real numbers. Floating-point numbers have an integer part and a fractional part, with a decimal point in between. Either the integer part or the fractional part, but not both, may be missing. Here are some examples:

```
18.0    127.54    0.57    4.    193145.8523    .8
```

Starting `0.57` with a zero does not make it an octal number. It is only with integer values that a leading zero indicates an octal number.

Just as the integral types in C++ come in different sizes (`char`, `short`, `int`, and `long`), so do the floating-point types. In increasing order of size, the floating-point types are `float`, `double` (meaning double precision), and `long double`. Again, the exact sizes are machine dependent. Each larger size potentially gives us a wider range of values and more precision (the number of significant digits in the number), but at the expense of more memory space to hold the number.

Floating-point values also can have an exponent, as in scientific notation. (In scientific notation, a number is written as a value multiplied by 10 to some power.) Instead of writing 3.504×10^{12}, in C++ we write `3.504E12`. The `E` means exponent of base-10. The number preceding the letter `E` doesn't need to include a decimal point. Here are some examples of floating-point numbers in scientific notation:

```
1.74536E-12    3.652442E4    7E20
```

Most programs don't need the `double` and `long double` types. The `float` type usually provides sufficient precision and range of values for floating-point numbers. Most personal computers provide `float` values with a precision of six or seven significant digits and a maximum value of about `3.4E+38`. We use floating-point values to represent money and interest rate in the case study at the end of this chapter. The following table shows sample ranges for floating-point data types:

Type	Size in Bytes*	Minimum Positive Value*	Maximum Positive Value*
float	4	3.4E-38	3.4E+38
double	8	1.7E-308	1.7E+308
long double	10	3.4E-4932	1.1E+4932

*These values are for one particular machine. Your machine's values may be different.

There is one more thing you should know about floating-point numbers: Computers cannot always represent them exactly. You learned in Chapter 1 that the computer stores all data in binary (base-2) form. Many floating-point values can only be approximated in the binary number system. Don't be surprised if your program prints out the number `4.8` as `4.7999998`. In most cases, slight inaccuracies in the rightmost fractional digits are to be expected and are not the result of programmer error.

QUICK CHECK

3.2.1 What are the four integral types discussed in this section? (p. 92)

3.2.2 What does an integral type refer to? (p. 92)

3.2.3 What reserved word must be used for values that are only positive? (p. 93)

3.2.4 What is the smallest and largest integral types in terms of bytes studied in this section? (p. 93)

QUICK CHECK

3.2.5 What is the smallest and largest integral types in terms of values? (p. 93)
3.2.6 What is the result if your program tries to compute a value larger than your machine's maximum value? (p. 94)
3.2.7 What type is used to represent real numbers? (p. 94)
3.2.8 What are the floating-point types? (p. 94)
3.2.9 How do we write the real number 3.504×10^{12} as a C++ literal value? (p. 94)

3.3 Declarations for Numeric Types

Just as with the types `char` and `string`, we can declare named constants and variables of type `int` and `float`. Such declarations use the same syntax as before, except that the literals and the names of the data types are different.

Named Constant Declarations

In the case of named constant declarations, the literal values in the declarations are numeric instead of being characters in single or double quotes. Here are some example constant declarations that define values of type `int` and `float`. For comparison, declarations of `char` and `string` values are included.

```
const float   PI = 3.14159;
const float   E = 2.71828;
const int     MAX_SCORE = 100;
const int     MIN_SCORE = -100;
const char    LETTER = 'W';
const string  NAME = "Elizabeth";
```

Although character and string literals are put in quotes, literal integers and floating-point numbers are not, because there is no chance of confusing them with identifiers. Why? Because identifiers must start with a letter or underscore, and numbers must start with a digit or sign.

SOFTWARE ENGINEERING TIP   Using Named Constants Instead of Literals

It's a good idea to use named constants instead of literals. In addition to making your program more readable, named constants can make your program easier to modify. Suppose you wrote a program last year to compute taxes. In several places you used the literal 0.05, which was the sales tax rate at the time. Now the rate has gone up to 0.06. To change your program, you must locate every literal 0.05 and change it to 0.06. If 0.05 is used for some other reason—to compute deductions, for example—you also need to look at each place where it is used, figure out what it is used for, and then decide whether to change it.

The process is much simpler if you use a named constant. Instead of using a literal constant, suppose you had declared a named constant, **TAX_RATE**, with a value of 0.05. To change your program, you would simply change the declaration, setting **TAX_RATE** equal to 0.06. This one modification automatically changes all of the tax rate computations without affecting the other places

> **SOFTWARE ENGINEERING TIP** Using Named Constants Instead of Literals, continued
>
> where 0.05 is used.
>
> C++ allows us to declare constants with different names but the same value. If a value has different meanings in different parts of a program, it makes sense to declare and use a constant with an appropriate name for each meaning.
>
> Named constants are also reliable—they protect us from mistakes. If you mistype the name **PI** as **PO**, for example, the C++ compiler tells you that the name **PO** has not been declared. At the same time, even though we recognize that the number 3.14149 is a mistyped version of pi (3.14159), the number is perfectly acceptable to the compiler. As a consequence, it won't warn us that anything is wrong.

Variable Declarations

We declare numeric variables the same way in which we declare `char` and `string` variables, except that we use the names of numeric types. The following are valid variable declarations:

```
int     studentCount;     // Number of students
int     sumOfScores;      // Sum of their scores
float   average;          // Average of the scores
char    grade;            // Student's letter grade
string  stuName;          // Student's name
```

Given the declarations

```
int   num;
int   alpha;
float rate;
char  ch;
```

the following are appropriate assignment statements:

Variable   Expression
```
alpha  =  2856;
rate   =  0.36;
ch     =  'B';
num    =  alpha;
```

In each of these assignment statements, the data type of the expression matches the data type of the variable to which it is assigned. Later in the chapter we see what happens if the data types do not match.

QUICK CHECK

3.3.1 Write a named constant declaration for the mathematical value of $\pi = 3.14159$. (p. 95)

3.3.2 Given the variable declarations:

```
int numX = 17;
int numY;
```

What is the type of the expression: (p. 96)

```
numY = numX
```

> **QUICK CHECK**
>
> **3.3.3** How does the declaration of named constants and variables of type `int` and `float` differ from declarations of named constants and variables of type `string`? (pp. 95–96)

3.4 Simple Arithmetic Expressions

Now that we have looked at declaration and assignment, let's consider how to calculate with values of numeric types. Calculations are performed with expressions. Here, we look at simple expressions that involve at most one operator so that we may examine each operator in detail. Later, we move on to compound expressions that combine multiple operations.

Arithmetic Operators

Expressions are made up of constants, variables, and operators. The following are all valid expressions:

```
alpha + 2    rate - 6.0    4 - alpha    rate    alpha * num
```

The operators allowed in an expression depend on the data types of the constants and variables in the expression. The *arithmetic operators* are

- `+`   Unary plus
- `-`   Unary minus
- `+`   Addition
- `-`   Subtraction
- `*`   Multiplication
- `/`   { Floating-point division (floating-point result)
         Integer division (no fractional part)
- `%`   Modulus (remainder from integer division)

> **Unary operator** An operator that has just one operand.
>
> **Binary operator** An operator that has two operands.

The first two operators are unary operators—they take just one operand. The remaining five are binary operators, taking two operands. Unary plus and minus are used as follows:

```
-54    +259.65    -rate
```

Programmers rarely use the unary plus. Without any sign, a numeric constant is assumed to be positive anyway.

You may not be familiar with integer division and modulus (`%`). Let's look at these operations more closely. Note that `%` is used only with integers. When you divide one integer by another, you get an integer quotient and a remainder. Integer division gives only the integer quotient, and `%` gives only the remainder. (If either operand is negative, the sign of the remainder may vary from one C++ compiler to another.[1])

```
    3 ← 6 / 2         3 ← 7 / 2
  2)6               2)7
    6                 6
    ─                 ─
    0 ← 6 % 2         1 ← 7 % 2
```

---

1. This inconsistency between compilers can result in subtle bugs when a program is moved to a different computer system. We recommend avoiding the use of the remainder with negative integers. The `abs` function (described in Section 3.6) can be used to take the absolute value of an `int` before applying `%`. In Chapter 5, we see how to check for negative values and skip a computation that would otherwise use them.

In contrast, floating-point division yields a floating-point result. For example, the expression

```
7.0 / 2.0
```

yields the value 3.5.

Here are some expressions using arithmetic operators and their values:

Expression	Value
3 + 6	9
3.4 - 6.1	-2.7
2 * 3	6
8 / 2	4
8.0 / 2.0	4.0
8 / 8	1
8 / 9	0
8 / 7	1
8 % 8	0
8 % 9	8
8 % 7	1
0 % 7	0
5 % 2.3	error (Both operands must be integers)

Be careful with division and modulus. The expressions 7 / 0 and 7 % 0 both produce errors. With floating-point values, 7.0 / 0.0, produces a special infinity value that is displayed as "inf" when output. The computer cannot divide by zero.

Because variables are allowed in expressions, the following are valid assignments:

```
alpha = num + 6;
alpha = num / 2;
num = alpha * 2;
num = 6 % alpha;
alpha = alpha + 1;
num = num + alpha;
```

As we saw with assignment statements involving **string** expressions, the same variable can appear on both sides of the assignment operator. In the case of

```
num = num + alpha;
```

the value in **num** and the value in **alpha** are added together, and then the sum of the two values is stored back into **num**, replacing the previous value stored there. This example shows the difference between mathematical equality and assignment. The mathematical equality

num = num + alpha

is true only when *alpha* equals 0. The assignment statement

```
num = num + alpha;
```

is valid for *any* value of **alpha**.

Here's a simple program that uses arithmetic expressions.

```cpp
//*****************************************************************
// FreezeBoil program
// This program computes the midpoint between
// the freezing and boiling points of water
//*****************************************************************
#include <iostream>

using namespace std;

const float FREEZE_PT = 32.0;    // Freezing point of water
const float BOIL_PT = 212.0;     // Boiling point of water

int main()
{
  float avgTemp;                 // Holds the result of averaging
                                 //    FREEZE_PT and BOIL_PT

  cout << "Water freezes at " << FREEZE_PT << endl;
  cout << " and boils at " << BOIL_PT << " degrees." << endl;

  avgTemp = FREEZE_PT + BOIL_PT;
  avgTemp = avgTemp / 2.0;

  cout << "Halfway between is ";
  cout << avgTemp << " degrees." << endl;

  return 0;
}
```

The program begins with a comment that explains what the program does. Next comes a declaration section where we define the constants `FREEZE_PT` and `BOIL_PT`. The body of the `main` function includes a declaration of the variable `avgTemp` and then a sequence of executable statements. These statements print a message, add `FREEZE_PT` and `BOIL_PT`, divide the sum by 2, and finally print the result. Here is the output:

```
Water freezes at 32
 and boils at 212 degrees.
Halfway between is 122 degrees.
```

Increment and Decrement Operators

In addition to the arithmetic operators, C++ provides *increment* and *decrement* *operators*:

++   Increment
--   Decrement

These unary operators take a single variable name as an operand. For integer and floating-point operands, the effect is to add 1 to (or subtract 1 from) the operand. If **num** currently contains the value 8, the statement

```
num++;
```

causes **num** to contain 9. You can achieve the same effect by writing the following assignment statement:

```
num = num + 1;
```

C++ programmers typically prefer the increment operator, however. (Recall from Chapter 1 how the C++ language got its name: C++ is an enhanced ["incremented"] version of the C language.)

The ++ and -- operators can be either *prefix* operators:

```
++num;
```

or postfix operators:

```
num++;
```

Both of these statements behave in exactly the same way: They add 1 to whatever is in **num**. The choice between the two is a matter of personal preference.

C++ allows the use of ++ and -- in the middle of a larger expression:

```
alpha = num++ * 3;
```

In this case, the postfix form of ++ does *not* give the same result as the prefix form. In Chapter 7, we explain the ++ and -- operators in detail. In the meantime, you should use them only to increment or decrement a variable as a separate, standalone statement:

IncrementStatement

$$\begin{cases} \text{Variable ++ ;} \\ \text{++ Variable ;} \end{cases}$$

DecrementStatement

$$\begin{cases} \text{Variable -- ;} \\ \text{-- Variable ;} \end{cases}$$

QUICK CHECK

3.4.1 If **integer1** contains 37 and **integer2** contains 7, what is the result of the expression **37 % 7**? (pp. 97–98)

3.4.2 What does the expression 7 / 0 produce? (p. 98)

3.4.3 What value does the expression 7.0 / 0.0 produce? (p. 98)

3.4.4 What effect does the expression **num++** produce? (p. 100)

3.5 Compound Arithmetic Expressions

The expressions we have used so far have contained at most a single arithmetic operator. We have also been careful not to mix integer and floating-point values in the same expression. Now we look at more complicated expressions—ones that are composed of several operators and ones that contain mixed data types.

Precedence Rules

Arithmetic expressions can be made up of many constants, variables, operators, and parentheses. In what order are the operations performed? For example, in the assignment statement

`avgTemp = FREEZE_PT + BOIL_PT / 2.0;`

is `FREEZE_PT + BOIL_PT` calculated first or is `BOIL_PT / 2.0` calculated first?

The basic arithmetic operators (unary +, unary -, + for addition, - for subtraction, * for multiplication, / for division, and % for modulus) are ordered the same way mathematical operators are, according to *precedence rules*:

Precedence Level	Operators
Highest precedence level:	Unary + Unary -
Middle level:	* / %
Lowest level:	+ -

Because division has higher precedence than addition, the expression in the example given earlier is implicitly parenthesized as

`FREEZE_PT + (BOIL_PT / 2.0)`

That is, we first divide `BOIL_PT` by `2.0` and then add `FREEZE_PT` to the result.

You can change the order of evaluation by using parentheses. In the statement

`avgTemp = (FREEZE_PT + BOIL_PT) / 2.0;`

`FREEZE_PT` and `BOIL_PT` are added first, and then their sum is divided by `2.0`. We evaluate subexpressions in parentheses first and then follow the precedence of the operators.

When an arithmetic expression has several binary operators with the same precedence, their *grouping order* (or *associativity*) is from left to right. The expression

`int1 - int2 + int3`

means `(int1 - int2) + int3`, not `int1 - (int2 + int3)`. As another example, we would use the expression

`(float1 + float2) / float1 * 3.0`

to evaluate the expression in parentheses first, then divide the sum by `float1`, and finally multiply the result by `3.0`. Following are some more examples.

Expression	Value
10 / 2 * 3	15
10 % 3 - 4 / 2	-1
5.0 * 2.0 / 4.0 * 2.0	5.0
5.0 * 2.0 / (4.0 * 2.0)	1.25
5.0 + 2.0 / (4.0 * 2.0)	5.25

In C++, all unary operators (such as unary + and unary -) have right-to-left associativity. Although this fact may seem strange at first, it turns out to be the natural grouping order. For example, `- + x` means `- (+ x)` rather than the meaningless `(- +) x`.

Type Coercion and Type Casting

Integer values and floating-point values are stored differently inside a computer's memory. The pattern of bits that represents the constant `2` does not look at all like the pattern of bits that represents the constant `2.0`. What happens if we mix integer and floating-point values together in an assignment statement or an arithmetic expression? Let's look first at assignment statements.

Assignment Statements

If you make the declarations

```
int    someInt;
float  someFloat;
```

then `someInt` can hold *only* integer values, and `someFloat` can hold *only* floating-point values. The assignment statement

```
someFloat = 12;
```

may seem to store the integer value 12 into `someFloat`, but this is not true. The computer refuses to store anything other than a `float` value into `someFloat`. The compiler inserts extra machine language instructions that first convert 12 into 12.0 and then store 12.0 into `someFloat`. This implicit (automatic) conversion of a value from one data type to another is known as type coercion.

The statement

```
someInt = 4.8;
```

also causes type coercion. When a floating-point value is assigned to an `int` variable, the fractional part is truncated (cut off). As a result, `someInt` is assigned the value 4.

With both of the previously given assignment statements, the program would be less confusing for someone to read if we avoided mixing data types:

```
someFloat = 12.0;
someInt   = 4;
```

> **Type coercion** The implicit (automatic) conversion of a value from one data type to another.
>
> **Type casting** The explicit conversion of a value from one data type to another; also called type conversion.

More often, it is not just constants but entire expressions that are involved in type coercion. Both of the assignments

```
someFloat = 3 * someInt + 2;
someInt   = 5.2 / someFloat - anotherFloat;
```

lead to type coercion. Storing the result of an `int` expression into a `float` variable generally doesn't cause loss of information; a whole number such as 24 can be represented in floating-point form as 24.0. However, storing the result of a floating-point expression into an `int` variable can cause loss of information because the fractional part is truncated. It is easy to overlook the assignment of a floating-point expression to an `int` variable when we try to discover why our program is producing the wrong answers.

To make our programs as clear (and error free) as possible, we can use explicit type casting (or type conversion). A C++ *cast operation* consists of a data type name and then, within parentheses, the expression to be converted:[2]

```
someFloat = float(3 * someInt + 2);
someInt   = int(5.2 / someFloat - anotherFloat);
```

---

2. There are two other ways of writing a cast operation in C++, which have some advantages over this syntax. We will wait until Chapter 7 to introduce and explain them. Until then, this simpler notation will be adequate for your programming needs.

Both of the statements

```
someInt = someFloat + 8.2;
someInt = int(someFloat + 8.2);
```

produce identical results. The only difference is in clarity. With the cast operation, it is perfectly clear to the programmer and to others reading the program that the mixing of types is intentional, not an oversight. Countless errors have resulted from unintentional mixing of types.

There is a nice way to round off rather than truncate a floating-point value before storing it into an `int` variable. Here is the way to do it:

```
someInt = int(someFloat + 0.5);
```

With pencil and paper, see for yourself what gets stored into `someInt` when `someFloat` contains 4.7. Now try it again, assuming `someFloat` contains 4.2. (This technique of rounding by adding 0.5 assumes that `someFloat` is a positive number.)

Arithmetic Expressions

So far we have been talking about mixing data types across the assignment operator (=). It's also possible to mix data types within an expression:

```
someInt * someFloat
4.8 + someInt - 3
```

Such expressions are called mixed type (or mixed mode) expressions.

Whenever an integer value and a floating-point value are joined by an operator, implicit type coercion occurs:

> **Mixed type expression** An expression that contains operands of different data types; also called mixed mode expression.

1. The integer value is temporarily coerced to a floating-point value.
2. The operation is performed.
3. The result is a floating-point value.

Let's examine how the machine evaluates the expression `4.8 + someInt - 3`, where `someInt` contains the value 2. First, the operands of the + operator have mixed types, so the value of `someInt` is coerced to 2.0. (This conversion is only temporary; it does not affect the value that is stored in `someInt`.) The addition takes place, yielding a value of 6.8. Next, the subtraction (-) operator joins a floating-point value (6.8) and an integer value (3). The value 3 is coerced to 3.0, the subtraction takes place, and the result is the floating-point value 3.8.

Just as with assignment statements, you can use explicit type casts within expressions to lessen the risk of errors. Writing expressions such as

```
float(someInt) * someFloat
4.8 + float(someInt - 3)
```

makes it clear what your intentions are.

Explicit type casts are not only valuable for program clarity, but are also mandatory in some cases for correct programming. Given the declarations

```
int    sum;
int    count;
float  average;
```

suppose that `sum` and `count` currently contain 60 and 80, respectively. If `sum` represents the sum of a group of integer values and `count` represents the number of values, let's find the average value:

```
average = sum / count;      // Wrong
```

Unfortunately, this statement stores the value 0.0 into `average`. Here's why: The expression to the right of the assignment operator is not a mixed type expression. Both operands of the / operator are of type `int`, so integer division is performed. When 60 is divided by 80, it yields the integer value 0. Next, the machine implicitly coerces 0 to the value 0.0 before storing it into `average`.

Here is the way to find the average correctly, as well as clearly:

```
average = float(sum) / float(count);
```

This statement gives us floating-point division instead of integer division. As a result, the value 0.75 is stored into `average`.

As a final remark about type coercion and type conversion, you may have noticed that we have concentrated on the `int` and `float` types. It is also possible to stir `char` values, `short` values, and `double` values into the pot. The results can be confusing and unexpected. In Chapter 10, we return to this topic with a more detailed discussion. In the meantime, you should avoid mixing values of these types within an expression.

SOFTWARE MAINTENANCE CASE STUDY: Precedence Error

PROBLEM: Numerous programming errors result from writing expressions that fail to take the precedence rules into account. For example, take a look at the following program, which is supposed to compute the radius of a circle from its circumference.

```cpp
//*********************************************
// This program computes the radius of a circle
//*********************************************

#include <iostream>
using namespace std;

int main ()
{
  const double CIRCUMFERENCE = 10.0;
  double radius;
  radius = CIRCUMFERENCE / 2 * 3.14159265;
  cout << "The radius is " <<  radius;
  return 0;
}
```

The problem is that, given a circumference of 10, for which the radius is approximately 1.59, the program outputs 15.707963265. What's wrong? Because the circumference is stored as a constant, the only remaining potential source of error must be the expression that computes the radius.

SOFTWARE MAINTENANCE CASE STUDY: Precedence Error

We know that to get the radius from the circumference, we divide the circumference by 2 times pi, which is what the statement does. Or does it? Division and multiplication have the same precedence, so they are evaluated from left to right. The expression is really computing

```
radius = (circumference / 2) * 3.14159265;
```

In our test case, the application divides 10 by 2, giving 5, which is then multiplied by pi to get 15.707963265. What we really want is this:

```
radius = circumference / (2 * 3.14159265);
```

Whenever you face a debugging task, take the time first to narrow down your search for the bug by a process of elimination. Once you isolate the section of code that is the most likely source of the error, consider the common mistakes associated with those kinds of statements. Efficient debugging is not a hit-or-miss process. It takes careful thought and organization to zero in on a bug.

MAY WE INTRODUCE   Blaise Pascal

One of the great historical figures in the world of computing was the French mathematician and religious philosopher Blaise Pascal (1623–1662), the inventor of one of the earliest known mechanical calculators.

Pascal's father, Etienne, was a noble in the French court, a tax collector, and a mathematician. Pascal's mother died when Pascal was 3 years old. Five years later, the family moved to Paris and Etienne took over the education of the children. Pascal quickly showed a talent for mathematics. When he was only 17, he published a mathematical essay that earned the jealous envy of René Descartes, one of the founders of modern geometry. (Pascal's work actually had been completed before he was 16.) It was based on a theorem, which he called the hexagrammum mysticum, or mystic hexagram, that described the inscription of hexagons in conic sections (parabolas, hyperbolas, and ellipses). In addition to the theorem (now called Pascal's theorem), his essay included more than 400 corollaries.

When Pascal was about 20, he constructed a mechanical calculator that performed addition and subtraction of eight-digit numbers. The calculator required the user to dial in the numbers to be added or subtracted; the sum or difference then appeared in a set of windows. It is believed that his motivation for building this machine was to aid his father in collecting taxes. The earliest version of the machine did, indeed, split the numbers into six decimal digits and two fractional digits, as would be used for calculating sums of money. The machine was hailed by his contemporaries as a great advance in mathematics, and Pascal built several more in different forms. It achieved such popularity that many fake, nonfunctional copies were built by others and displayed as novelties. Several of Pascal's calculators are now exhibited in various museums.

Pascal's box, as it is called, was long believed to be the first mechanical calculator. However, in 1950, a letter from Wilhelm Shickard to Johannes Kepler, written in 1624, was discovered. This letter described an even more sophisticated calculator built by Shickard 20 years prior to Pascal's box. Unfortunately, the machine was destroyed in a fire and never rebuilt.

MAY WE INTRODUCE   Blaise Pascal, continued

During his twenties, Pascal solved several difficult problems related to the cycloid curve, indirectly contributing to the development of differential calculus. Working with Pierre de Fermat, he laid the foundation of the calculus of probabilities and combinatorial analysis. One of the results of this work came to be known as Pascal's triangle, which simplifies the calculation of the coefficients of the expansion of $(x + y)^n$, where n is a positive integer.

Pascal also published a treatise on air pressure and conducted experiments showing that barometric pressure decreases with altitude, which helped to confirm theories that had been proposed by Galileo and Torricelli. His work on fluid dynamics forms a significant part of the foundation of that field. Among the most famous of his contributions is Pascal's law, which states that pressure applied to a fluid in a closed vessel is transmitted uniformly throughout the fluid.

When Pascal was 23, his father became ill, and the family was visited by two disciples of Jansenism, a reform movement in the Catholic Church that had begun six years earlier. The family converted, and five years later one of his sisters entered a convent. Initially, Pascal was not so taken with the new movement, but by the time he was 31, his sister had persuaded him to abandon the world and devote himself to religion.

Pascal's religious works are considered no less brilliant than his mathematical and scientific writings. Some consider *Provincial Letters,* his series of 18 essays on various aspects of religion, to mark the beginning of modern French prose.

Pascal returned briefly to mathematics when he was 35. A year later his health, which had always been poor, took a turn for the worse. Unable to perform his usual work, he devoted himself to helping the less fortunate. Three years later, he died while staying with his sister, having given his own house to a poor family.

QUICK CHECK

3.5.1 What happens to the fractional portion of a floating-point number when it is converted to an integer type? (pp. 102–103)

3.5.2 What operators studied in this section have the highest precedence level? (p. 101)

3.5.3 What operators studied in this section have the lowest precedence level? (p. 101)

3.5.4 What must we use to force the evaluation of a subexpression outside of the regular precedence rules? (p. 101)

3.5.5 What must we use in order to mix integer and floating-point values in the same expression? (p. 101)

3.5.6 Assume we have a variable `x` declared as an `int` and a variable `y` declared as a `float` and the following expression: `x = y + 1.25`. What explicit type cast must be used to make this a valid expression? (p. 103)

3.5.7 How must the following expression be modified in order to correctly produce the correct percentage for a student's score and the total points available in an assignment. Assume that score and total have type int: (p. 104)

```
float percentage = (score / total) * 100.0;
```

3.5.8 What is the result of the following expression? (p. 101)

```
27 + 8 * 6 - 44 % 5
```

3.6 Function Calls and Library Functions

Value-Returning Functions

At the beginning of Chapter 2, we showed a program consisting of three functions: `main`, `Square`, and `Cube`. Here is a listing of a portion of the program:

```
int main()
{
  cout << "The square of 27 is " << Square(27) << endl;
  cout << "and the cube of 27 is " << Cube(27) << endl;
  return 0;
}

int Square( int n )
{
  return n * n;
}

int Cube( int n )
{
  return n * n * n;
}
```

At the time we introduced the program, we said that all three functions are value-returning functions. `Square` returns to its caller a value—the square of the number sent to it. `Cube` returns a value—the cube of the number sent to it. Likewise, `main` returns to the operating system a value—the program's exit status.

Let's focus for a moment on the `Cube` function. The `main` function contains the following statement:

```
cout << " and the cube of 27 is " << Cube(27) << endl;
```

In this statement, the master (`main`) causes the servant (`Cube`) to compute the cube of 27 and give the result back to `main`. The sequence of symbols

```
Cube(27)
```

is a *function call* or *function invocation*. The computer temporarily puts the `main` function on hold and starts the `Cube` function running. When `Cube` has finished doing its work, the computer goes back to `main` and picks up where it left off.

> **Function call (function invocation)** The mechanism that transfers control to a function.

In the preceding function call, the number 27 is known as an *argument* (or *actual parameter*). Arguments make it possible for the same function to work on many different values. For example, we can write statements like these:

```
cout << Cube(4);
cout << Cube(16);
```

Here's the syntax template for a function call:

FunctionCall

FunctionName (ArgumentList)

> **Argument list** A mechanism by which functions communicate with one another.

The argument list is a way for functions to communicate with one another. Some functions, such as `Square` and `Cube`, have a single argument in the argument list. Other functions, such as `main`, have no arguments. Finally, some other functions have two, three, or more arguments in the list, separated by commas.

Value-returning functions are used in expressions in much the same way that variables and constants are. The value computed by a function simply takes its place in the expression. For example, the statement

```
someInt = Cube(2) * 10;
```

stores the value 80 into `someInt`. First the `Cube` function is executed to compute the cube of 2, which is 8. The value 8—now available for use in the rest of the expression—is then multiplied by 10. Note that a function call has higher precedence than multiplication, which makes sense if you consider that the function result must be available before the multiplication takes place.

Here are several facts about value-returning functions:

- The function call is used within an expression; it does not appear as a separate statement.
- The function computes a value (*result*) that is then available for use in the expression.
- The function returns exactly one result—no more, no less.

The `Cube` function expects to be given (or *passed*) an argument of type `int`. What happens if the caller passes a `float` argument? The answer is that the compiler applies implicit type coercion. Thus the function call `Cube(6.9)` computes the cube of 6, not 6.9.

Although we have been using literal constants as arguments to `Cube`, the argument could just as easily be a variable or a named constant. In fact, the argument to this value-returning function can be any expression of the appropriate type. In the statement

```
alpha = Cube(int1 * int1 + int2 * int2);
```

the expression in the argument list is evaluated first, and only its result is passed to the function. For example, if `int1` contains 3 and `int2` contains 5, the preceding function call passes 34 as the argument to `Cube`.

An expression in a function's argument list can even include calls to functions. For example, we could use the `Square` function to rewrite the earlier assignment statement as follows:

```
alpha = Cube(Square(int1) + Square(int2));
```

Library Functions

Certain computations, such as taking square roots or finding the absolute value of a number, are very common in programs. It would be an enormous waste of time if every programmer had to start from scratch and create functions to perform these tasks. To help make the programmer's life easier, every C++ system includes a standard library—a large collection of prewritten functions, data types, and other items that any C++ programmer may use. The functions in the library are divided into separate files called header files. Here is a very small sample of some standard library functions:

3.6 Function Calls and Library Functions

Header File	Function	Argument Type	Result Type	Result (Value Returned)
`<cstdlib>`	`abs(i)`	`int`	`int`	Absolute value of **i**
`<cmath>`	`cos(x)`	`float`	`float`	Cosine of **x** (**x** is in radians)
`<cmath>`	`fabs(x)`	`float`	`float`	Absolute value of **x**
`<cstdlib>`	`labs(j)`	`long`	`long`	Absolute value of **j**
`<cmath>`	`pow(x, y)`	`float`	`float`	**x** raised to the power **y** (if **x** = 0.0, **y** must be positive; if **x** <= 0.0, **y** must be a whole number)
`<cmath>`	`sin(x)`	`float`	`float`	Sine of **x** (**x** is in radians)
`<cmath>`	`sqrt(x)`	`float`	`float`	Square root of **x** (**x** $\geq$ 0.0)

Technically, the entries in the table marked `float` should all say `double`. These library functions perform their work using double-precision floating-point values. Because of type coercion, however, the functions work just as you would like them to when you pass `float` values to them.

Using a library function is easy. First, you place an `#include` directive near the top of your program, specifying the appropriate header file. This directive ensures that the C++ preprocessor inserts declarations into your program that give the compiler some information about the function. Then, whenever you want to use the function, you just make a function call. Here's a sample program that calls functions, along with its output:

```cpp
//*********************************************
// This program demonstrates function calls.
//*********************************************

#include <iostream>
#include <cmath>        // For sqrt() and fabs()

using namespace std;
int main()
{
  float alpha;
  float beta;
  alpha = sqrt(7.3 + fabs(-100.0));
  cout << "alpha " << alpha << endl;
  beta = pow(alpha, 2);
  cout << "alpha squared " << beta << endl;
}
```

Output:

```
alpha 10.3586
alpha squared 107.3
```

Void Functions

Thus far, we have looked only at value-returning functions. In fact, C++ provides another kind of function. Look at the following definition for function `CalcPay`. Notice how it begins with the word `void` instead of a data type like `int` or `float`:

```
void CalcPay( . . . )
{
    :
}
```

> **Void function (procedure)** A function that does not return a function value to its caller and is invoked as a separate statement.
>
> **Value-returning function** A function that returns a single value to its caller and is invoked from within an expression.

`CalcPay` is an example of a function that doesn't return a value to its caller. Instead, it just performs some action and then quits. We refer to a function like this as a *non-value-returning function*, a *void-returning function*, or, most briefly, a *void function*. In some programming languages, a void function is known as a procedure.

Void functions are invoked differently from value-returning functions. With a value-returning function, the function call appears in an expression. With a void function, the function call is a separate, standalone statement. In the `LeapYear` program, `main` calls the `IsLeapYear` function using an expression like this:

```
if (IsLeapYear(year))
```

By comparison, a call to a void function has the flavor of a command or built-in instruction:

```
DoThis(x, y, z);
DoThat();
```

For the next few chapters, we won't be writing our own functions (except `main`). Instead, we'll be concentrating on how to use existing functions, including functions for performing stream input and output. Some of these functions are value-returning functions; others are void functions. Again, we emphasize the difference in how you invoke these two kinds of functions: A call to a value-returning function occurs in an expression, whereas a call to a void function occurs as a separate statement.

QUICK CHECK

3.6.1 Where do arguments appear, and what is their purpose? (pp. 107–108)
3.6.2 Write an expression that computes the square root of 17.5. (p. 109)
3.6.3 How does a call to a `void` function differ from a call to a value-returning function? (p. 110)
3.6.4 What does the computer do to `main` when a function is invoked? (p. 107)
3.6.5 What are in libraries and what are they used for? (p. 108)
3.6.6 How does a programmer use a library? (p. 109)

3.7 Formatting Output

To format a program's output means to control how it appears visually on the screen or on a printout. In Chapter 2, we considered two kinds of output formatting: creating extra blank lines by using the `endl` manipulator and inserting blanks within a line by putting extra blanks into literal strings. In this section, we examine how to format the output values themselves.

Integers and Strings

By default, consecutive integer and string values are output with no spaces between them. If the variables i, j, and k contain the values 15, 2, and 6, respectively, the statement

```
cout << "Results: " << i << j << k;
```

outputs the following stream of characters:

```
Results: 1526
```

Without spacing between the numbers, this output is difficult to interpret.

To separate the output values, you could print a single blank (as a **char** constant) between the numbers:

```
cout << "Results: " << i << ' ' << j << ' ' << k;
```

This statement produces the following output:

```
Results: 15 2 6
```

If you want even more spacing between items, you can use literal strings containing blanks, as we discussed in Chapter 2:

```
cout << "Results: " << i << "   " << j << "   " << k;
```

The resulting output is shown here:

```
Results: 15    2    6
```

Another way to control the horizontal spacing of the output is to use manipulators. For some time now, we have been using the **endl** manipulator to terminate an output line. In C++, a manipulator is a rather curious thing that behaves like a function but travels in the disguise of a data object. Like a function, a manipulator causes some action to occur. But like a data object, a manipulator can appear in the midst of a series of insertion operations:

```
cout << someInt << endl << someFloat;
```

Manipulators are used only in input and output statements.

Here's a revised syntax template for the output statement, showing that not only arithmetic and string expressions but also manipulators are allowed:

OutputStatement

```
cout << ExpressionOrManipulator << ExpressionOrManipulator ... ;
```

The C++ standard library supplies many manipulators, but for now we look at only five of them: **endl**, **setw**, **fixed**, **showpoint**, and **setprecision**. The **endl**, **fixed**, and **showpoint** manipulators come "for free" when we **#include** the header file **iostream** to perform I/O.

The other two manipulators, `setw` and `setprecision`, require that we also `#include` the header file `iomanip`:

```
#include <iostream>
#include <iomanip>
using namespace std;
    :
cout << setw(5) << someInt;
```

The manipulator `setw`—meaning "set width"—lets us control how many character positions the next data item should occupy when it is output (`setw` is typically used for formatting numbers and strings, rather than `char` data). The argument to `setw` is an integer expression called the *fieldwidth specification*; the group of character positions is called the *field*. The next data item to be output is printed *right-justified* (filled with blanks on the left to fill up the field).

Let's look at an example. Suppose two `int` variables have been assigned values as follows:

```
ans = 33;
num = 7132;
```

Then the following output statements produce the output shown to their right:

Statement   *Output (□ means blank)*

1. `cout << setw(4) << ans`
   `    << setw(5) << num`
   `    << setw(4) << "Hi";`   □□33□7132□□Hi
                                               ‾‾ ‾‾‾‾ ‾‾
                                                4   5   4

2. `cout << setw(2) << ans`
   `    << setw(4) << num`
   `    << setw(2) << "Hi";`   337132Hi
                                              ‾‾ ‾‾‾‾ ‾‾
                                              2   4   2

3. `cout << setw(6) << ans`
   `    << setw(3) << "Hi"`
   `    << setw(5) << num;`   □□□□33□Hi□7132
                                              ‾‾‾‾‾‾ ‾‾‾ ‾‾‾‾
                                                 6   3   5

4. `cout << setw(7) << "Hi"`
   `    << setw(4) << num;`   □□□□□Hi7132
                                              ‾‾‾‾‾‾‾ ‾‾‾‾
                                                 7   4

5. `cout << setw(1) << ans`
   `    << setw(5) << num;`   33□7132
                                              ↑ ‾‾‾‾‾
                                                 5
                                              Field automatically expands to fit
                                              the two-digit value

In Example 1, each value is specified to occupy enough positions so that there is at least one space separating them. In Example 2, the values all run together because the fieldwidth specified for each value is just large enough to hold the value. This output obviously is not very readable. It's better to make the fieldwidth larger than the minimum size required so that some space is left between values. Example 3 includes extra blanks for readability; Example 4 does not. In Example 5, the fieldwidth is not large enough for the value in `ans`, so it automatically expands to make room for all of the digits.

Setting the fieldwidth is a one-time action. This preference holds only for the very next item to be output. After this output, the fieldwidth resets to 0, meaning "extend the field to exactly as many positions as are needed." For example, in the statement

```
cout << "Hi" << setw(5) << ans << num;
```

the fieldwidth resets to 0 after `ans` is output. As a result, we get the output

```
Hi   337132
```

Here is a short program that illustrates these manipulators, followed by the output.

```
//***************************************************************
// This program demonstrates the use of manipulators.
//***************************************************************

#include <iostream>
#include <iomanip>

using namespace std;
int main ()
{
  const int num1 = 1066;
  const int num2 = 1492;
  cout << setw(3) << num1 << setw(5) << num2 << endl;
  cout << num1 << num2;
  cout << setw(4) << num1 << setw(6) << num2 << num1 << endl;
  return 0;
}
```

Output:

```
1066 1492
106614921066    14921066
```

Floating-Point Numbers

You can specify a fieldwidth for floating-point values just as for integer values. When doing so, you must remember to allow for the decimal point when you specify the number of character positions. For example, the value 4.85 requires four output positions, not three. If x contains the value 4.85, the statement

```
cout << setw(4) << x << endl
     << setw(6) << x << endl
     << setw(3) << x << endl;
```

produces the following output:

```
4.85
  4.85
4.85
```

In the third line, a fieldwidth of 3 isn't sufficient, so the field automatically expands to accommodate the number.

Several other issues arise when we are working with the output of floating-point numbers. First, large floating-point values are printed in scientific (E) notation. The value 123456789.5 may print on some systems as

```
1.23457e+08
```

You can use the manipulator named **fixed** to force all subsequent floating-point output to appear in decimal form rather than scientific notation:

```
cout << fixed << 3.8 * x;
```

Second, if the number is a whole number, C++ doesn't print a decimal point. Thus the value 95.0 is output as

```
95
```

To force decimal points to be displayed in subsequent floating-point output, even for whole numbers, you can use the manipulator **showpoint**:

```
cout << showpoint << floatVar;
```

Third, you often would like to control the number of *decimal places* (digits to the right of the decimal point) that are displayed. If your program is supposed to print the 5% sales tax on a certain amount, for example, the statement

```
cout << "Tax is $" << price * 0.05;
```

may produce the following output:

```
Tax is $17.7435
```

Obviously, you would prefer to display the result to two decimal places. To do so, use the **setprecision** manipulator as follows:

```
cout << fixed << setprecision(2) << "Tax is $" << price * 0.05;
```

Provided that `fixed` has already been specified, the argument to `setprecision` specifies the desired number of decimal places. Unlike `setw`, which applies only to the very next item printed, the value sent to `setprecision` remains in effect for all subsequent output (until you change it with another call to `setprecision`). Here are some examples in which `setprecision` is used in conjunction with `setw`, given that `x` is 310.0 and `y` is 4.827:

Statement   *Output (□ means blank)*

```
cout << fixed;
cout << setw(10)
     << setprecision(2) << x;          □□□□310.0
cout << setw(10)
     << setprecision(5) << x;          □310.00000
cout << setw(7)
     << setprecision(5) << x;          310.00000 (expands to nine positions)
cout << setw(6)
     << setprecision(2) << y;          □□4.83 (last displayed digit is rounded off)
cout << setw(6)
     << setprecision(1) << y;          □□□4.8 (last displayed digit is rounded off)
```

Again, the total number of print positions is expanded if the fieldwidth specified by `setw` is too narrow. However, the number of positions for fractional digits is controlled entirely by the argument to `setprecision`.

For a scientific application, it may be desirable to force output values to be in scientific notation, which is accomplished using the `scientific` manipulator. When the output stream is in `scientific` mode, `setprecision` determines the number of digits displayed after the decimal point. We should also note that if neither `fixed` nor `scientific` mode has been set, then `setprecision` determines the number of digits displayed preceding the exponent. Here are two examples:

Statement   *Output*

```
cout << setprecision(5) << 12345678.0;      1.2346e+07
cout << scientific
     << setprecision(5) << 12345678.0;      1.23457e+07
```

In the first case, scientific notation is output because the number is big enough to cause the output stream to automatically change to **e** notation. (If a smaller number is subsequently output, the stream switches back to normal formatting.) Because no manipulator for fixed or scientific formatting has previously been inserted into the stream, `setprecision` formats the number to have five digits preceding the **e**. In the second case, the `scientific` manipulator switches the stream into scientific mode. In this mode, `setprecision` formats the number with five digits between the decimal point and the **e**. Subsequent output will be in scientific notation until a `fixed` manipulator is used.

The following table summarizes the manipulators we have discussed in this section. Manipulators without arguments are available through the header file `iostream`. Those with arguments require the header file `iomanip`.

Header File	Manipulator	Argument Type	Effect
<iostream>	endl	None	Terminates the current output line
<iostream>	showpoint	None	Forces display of a decimal point in floating-point output
<iostream>	fixed	None	Activates fixed-point notation in floating-point output
<iostream>	scientific	None	Activates scientific notation in floating-point output
<iomanip>	setw(n)	int	Sets the fieldwidth to **n**
<iomanip>	setprecision(n)	int	Sets the floating-point precision to **n** digits

The following program and output demonstrates the use of these manipulators.

```cpp
//***********************************************************
// This program demonstrates floating-point manipulators.
//***********************************************************

#include <iostream>
#include <iomanip>

using namespace std;
int main ()
{
  double num = 1000;
  cout << setw(3) << 1776 << ' ' << 44 << endl;
  cout << setw(4) << showpoint << num << ' ' << 44.55 << endl;
  cout << setprecision(5) << 1776.12 << ' ' << num << endl;
  cout << num;
  return 0;
}
```

Output:

```
1776 44
1000.00 44.5500
1776.1 1000.0
1000.0
```

MATTERS OF STYLE   Program Formatting

As far as the compiler is concerned, C++ statements are *free format*: They can appear anywhere on a line, more than one can appear on a single line, and one statement can span several lines. The compiler needs blanks (or comments or new lines) only to separate important symbols, and it needs semicolons only to terminate statements. Of course, these restrictions are the bare minimum. In fact, it is extremely important that your programs be readable, both for your sake and for the sake of anyone else who has to examine them.

When you write an outline for an English paper, you follow certain rules of indentation to make it readable. These same kinds of rules can make your programs easier to read. It is much easier to spot a mistake in a neatly formatted program than in a messy one. Thus you should keep your program neatly formatted while you are working on it. If you've gotten lazy and let your program become messy while you were making a series of changes, take the time to straighten it up. Often the source of an error becomes obvious during the process of formatting the code.

Take a look at the following program for computing the cost per square foot of a house. Although it compiles and runs correctly, it does not conform to any formatting standards.

```cpp
// HouseCost program
// This program computes the cost per square foot of
// living space for a house, given the dimensions of


// the house, the number of stories, the size of the
// nonliving space, and the total cost less land
#include <iostream>
#include <iomanip>// For setw() and setprecision()
using namespace
std;
const float WIDTH = 30.0; // Width of the house
    const float LENGTH = 40.0; // Length of the house
const float STORIES = 2.5; // Number of full stories
const float NON_LIVING_SPACE - 825.0;// Garage, closets, etc.

const float PRICE = 150000.0; // Selling price less land
int main() { float grossFootage;// Total square footage
    float livingFootage;         // Living area
float costPerFoot;       // Cost/foot of living area
   cout << fixed << showpoint;   // Set up floating-pt.
//   output format

grossFootage = LENGTH * WIDTH * STORIES; livingFootage =
grossFootage - NON_LIVING_SPACE; costPerFoot = PRICE /
livingFootage; cout << "Cost per square foot is "
<< setw(6) << setprecision(2) << costPerFoot << endl;
return 0; }
```

MATTERS OF STYLE Program Formatting, continued

Now look at the same program with proper formatting:

```cpp
//*****************************************************************
// HouseCost program
// This program computes the cost per square foot of
// living space for a house, given the dimensions of
// the house, the number of stories, the size of the
// nonliving space, and the total cost less land
//*****************************************************************
#include <iostream>
#include <iomanip>     // For setw() and setprecision()

using namespace std;

const float WIDTH = 30.0;                // Width of the house
const float LENGTH = 40.0;               // Length of the house
const float STORIES = 2.5;               // Number of full stories
const float NON_LIVING_SPACE = 825.0;    // Garage, closets, etc.
const float PRICE = 150000.0;            // Selling price less land

int main()
{
  float grossFootage;        // Total square footage
  float livingFootage;       // Living area
  float costPerFoot;         // Cost/foot of living area

  cout << fixed << showpoint;   // Set up floating-pt. output format

  grossFootage = LENGTH * WIDTH * STORIES;
  livingFootage = grossFootage - NON_LIVING_SPACE;
  costPerFoot = PRICE / livingFootage;

  cout << "Cost per square foot is "
       << setw(6) << setprecision(2) << costPerFoot << endl;
  return 0;
}
```

Need we say more?
  Appendix F talks about programming style. Use it as a guide when you are writing programs.

> **QUICK CHECK**
>
> **3.7.1** Neatly formatting a program makes it easier to find errors. True or false? (pp. 117–118)
> **3.7.2** Which stream manipulator would you use to set the output precision for floating-point values? (pp. 114–115)
> **3.7.3** What library must be included to set the output precision for floating-point values? (p. 116)
> **3.7.4** What does the `setw` manipulator do for us? (p. 112)
> **3.7.5** What does the `showpoint` manipulator do? (p. 114)
> **3.7.6** What manipulator is used to output scientific notation? (p. 115)

3.8 Additional string Operations

Now that we have introduced numeric types and function calls, we can take advantage of additional features of the `string` data type. In this section, we introduce four functions that operate on strings: `length`, `size`, `find`, and `substr`.

The length and size Functions

The `length` function, when applied to a `string` variable, returns an unsigned integer value that equals the number of characters currently in the string. If `myName` is a `string` variable, a call to the `length` function looks like this:

`myName.length()`

You specify the name of a string variable (here, `myName`), then a dot (period), and then the function name and argument list. The length function requires no arguments to be passed to it, but you still must use parentheses to signify an empty argument list. Also, `length` is a value-returning function, so the function call must appear within an expression:

```
string firstName;
string fullName;
firstName = "Alexandra";
cout << firstName.length() << endl;      // Prints 9
fullName = firstName + " Jones";
cout << fullName.length() << endl;       // Prints 15
```

Perhaps you are wondering about the syntax in a function call like

`firstName.length()`

This expression uses a C++ notation called *dot notation*. There is a dot (period) between the variable name `firstName` and the function name `length`. Certain programmer-defined data types, such as `string`, have functions that are tightly associated with them, and dot notation is required in the function calls. Suppose you forget to use dot notation, writing the function call as

`length()`

You will get a compile-time error message, something like **UNDECLARED IDENTIFIER**. The compiler thinks you are trying to call an ordinary function named `length`, not the `length` function associated with the `string` type. In Chapter 4, we discuss the meaning behind dot notation.

Some people refer to the length of a string as its *size*. To accommodate both terms, the `string` type provides a function named `size`. Both `firstName.size()` and `firstName.length()` return the same value.

The **length** and **size** functions return an unsigned integer value of type **string::size_type**. Most C++ compilers, however, allow you to declare the results to be of type **int**.[3]

```
string firstName;
int len;

firstName = "Alexandra";
len = firstName.length();
```

Before leaving the **length** and **size** functions, we should remark on capitalization conventions for identifiers. In the guidelines given in Chapter 2, we said that in this book we begin the names of programmer-defined functions and data types with uppercase letters. We follow this convention when we write our own functions and data types in later chapters. However, we have no control over the capitalization of items supplied by the C++ standard library. Identifiers in the standard library generally use all lowercase letters.

The **find** Function

The **find** function searches a string to find the first occurrence of a particular substring and returns an unsigned integer value (of type **string::size_type**) giving the result of the search. The substring, passed as an argument to the function, can be a literal string or a **string** expression. If **str1** and **str2** are of type **string**, all of the following are valid function calls:

```
str1.find("the")     str1.find(str2)     str1.find(str2 + "abc")
```

In each of the three cases, **str1** is searched to see if the specified substring can be found within it. If so, the function returns the position in **str1** where the match begins. (Positions are numbered starting at 0, so the first character in a string is in position 0, the second is in position 1, and so on.) For a successful search, the match must be exact, including identical capitalization. If the substring could not be found, the function returns the special value **string::npos**, a named constant meaning "not a position within the string." (**string::npos** is the largest possible value of type **string::size_type**, a number like **4294967295** on many machines. This value is suitable for "not a valid position" because the **string** operations do not let any string become this long.)

Given the code segment

```
string phrase;
string::size_type position;

phrase = "The dog and the cat";
```

the statement

```
position = phrase.find("the");
```

assigns to **position** the value 12, whereas the statement

```
position = phrase.find("rat");
```

assigns to **position** the value **string::npos**, because there was no match.

The argument to the **find** function can also be a **char** value. In this case, **find** searches for the first occurrence of that character within the string and returns its position

---

3. In Chapter 10, we explain why it is better programming practice to use a type supplied by **string** itself. In all of the examples we see before raising that point, **int** is adequate.

(or `string::npos`, if the character was not found). For example, the following program

```
//*****************
// String demo
//*****************
#include <iostream>
#include <string>      // For string type
using namespace std;

int main()
{
  string theString;

  theString = "Abracadabra";
  cout << "Position: " << theString.find('a');
}
```

outputs

```
Position 3
```

which is the position of the first occurrence of a lowercase *a* in `theString`.

Below are some more examples of calls to the `find` function, assuming the following code segment has been executed:

```
string str1;
string str2;

str1 = "Programming and Problem Solving";
str2 = "gram";
```

Function Call	Value Returned by Function
`str1.find("and")`	12
`str1.find("Programming")`	0
`str2.find("and")`	`string::npos`
`str1.find("Pro")`	0
`str1.find("ro" + str2)`	1
`str1.find("Pr" + str2)`	`string::npos`
`str1.find(' ')`	11

In the fourth example, there are two copies of the substring `"Pro"` in `str1`, but `find` returns only the position of the first copy. Also notice that the copies can be either separate words or parts of words—`find` merely tries to match the sequence of characters given in the argument list. The final example demonstrates that the argument can be as simple as a single character, even a single blank.

The `substr` Function

The `substr` function returns a particular substring of a string. Assuming `myString` is of type `string`, here is a sample function call:

```
myString.substr(5, 20)
```

The first argument is an unsigned integer that specifies a position within the string, and the second is an unsigned integer that specifies the length of the desired substring. The function returns the piece of the string that starts with the specified position and continues for the number of characters given by the second argument. Note that `substr` doesn't change `myString`. Instead, it returns a new, temporary string value that is a copy of a portion of the string. Following are some examples, assuming the statement

```
myString = "Programming and Problem Solving";
```

has been executed.

Function Call	String Contained in Value Returned by Function
`myString.substr(0, 7)`	`"Program"`
`myString.substr(7, 8)`	`"ming and"`
`myString.substr(10, 0)`	`""`
`myString.substr(24, 40)`	`"Solving"`
`myString.substr(40, 24)`	None; program terminates with an execution error message

In the third example, specifying a length of 0 produces the null string as the result. The fourth example shows what happens if the second argument specifies more characters than are present after the starting position: `substr` returns the characters from the starting position to the end of the string. The last example illustrates that the first argument, the position, must not be beyond the end of the string.

Because `substr` returns a value of type `string`, you can use it with the concatenation operator (+) to copy pieces of strings and join them together to form new strings. The `find` and `length` functions can be useful in determining the location and end of a piece of a string to be passed to `substr` as arguments.

Here is a program that uses `find` and `substr` to break a string into parts.

```cpp
//***********************************************************
// SubstrOps program
// This program demonstrates find and substr operations
//***********************************************************
#include <iostream>
#include <string>       // For string type

using namespace std;

int main()
{
    string name = "Olivia Johnson Peterson";
    int index;
```

```
    index = name.find(' ');
    cout << "First Name: " << name.substr(0, index) << endl;
    name = name.substr(index+1, name.length()-1);
    index = name.find(' ');
    cout << "Middle Name: " << name.substr(0, index) << endl;
    name = name.substr(index+1, name.length()-1);
    cout << "Last Name: " << name;
    return 0;
}
```

Output:

The program uses **find** to locate the first blank and **substr** to extract the substring beginning with the first character and extending to just before the first blank. This substring is stored in **firstName**. The original string is redefined to contain the string following the first blank through to the end. The process is repeated to extract the middle name. The remaining string is stored in **lastName**. Perhaps this process seems trivial—after all, we could have just created the three separate strings. However, in Chapter 4, when we examine how to read a string from the keyboard, this general algorithm will prove useful in breaking an input string into different parts.

Accessing Characters Within a String: The `at` Function

Sometimes it would be very useful to access characters directly by their position. C++ allows us to do so easily. You can access an individual character in a string by using the **at** function. Here is an example call to this function:

`someCharVariable = someString.at(somePosition);`

Within a **string**, the first character is at position 0, the second is at position 1, and so forth. Therefore, the value of **somePosition** must be greater than or equal to 0 and less than or equal to the string length minus 1. For example, if **inputStr** is a **string** object and **letter** is a **char** variable, the statement

`letter = inputStr.at(2);`

accesses the character at position 2 of the string (the third character) and copies it into **letter**. Calling **at** with a value that lies outside the allowable range will generate an error message.

Converting to Lowercase and Uppercase

When working with character data, you may sometimes find that you need to convert a lowercase letter to uppercase, or vice versa. Fortunately, the programming technique required to do these conversions is easy—a simple call to a library function is all it takes. Through the header file `<cctype>`, the standard library provides two value-returning functions named `toupper` and `tolower`. Here are their descriptions:

Header File	Function	Function Type	Function Value
`<cctype>`	`toupper(ch)`	char*	Uppercase equivalent of **ch**, if **ch** is a lowercase letter; **ch**, otherwise
`<cctype>`	`tolower(ch)`	char	Lowercase equivalent of **ch**, if **ch** is an uppercase letter; **ch**, otherwise

*Technically, both the argument and the return value are of type `int`. Conceptually, the functions operate on character data.

The value returned by each function is just the original character if the condition is not met. For example, `tolower('M')` returns the character `'m'`, whereas `tolower('+')` returns `'+'`.

The following program uses `toupper` to ensure that the first letter of a string is uppercase. The first letter is accessed and changed to uppercase. Then the string is concatenated with the original string with the first character removed.

```cpp
//***********************************************************
// This program demonstrates the use of substr and toupper
//***********************************************************
#include <iostream>
#include <string>
#include <cctype>

using namespace std;
int main()
{
  string firstName = "mary";
  string lastName = "melrose";
  char ch;
  ch = toupper(lastName.at(0));
  lastName = ch + lastName.substr(1, lastName.length());
  ch = toupper(firstName.at(0));
  firstName = ch + firstName.substr(1, firstName.length());
  cout << firstName << " " << lastName << endl;
  return 0;
}
```

Output:

```
Mary Melrose
```

The following table summarizes the `string` and character operations we have looked at in this chapter.

3.8 Additional string Operations

Function Call (s is of type string)	Argument Type(s)	Result Type	Result (Value Returned)
s.length() s.size()	None	string::size_type	Number of characters in string.
s.find(arg)	string, literal string, or char	string::size_type	Starting position in s where arg was found; if not found, result is string::npos.
s.substr(pos,len)		string	Substring of at most len characters, starting at position pos of s. If len is too large, it means "to the end" of string s. If pos is too large, execution of the program is terminated.*
s.at(pos)		char	Returns char at pos position in s. If pos is too large, execution of the program is terminated.*
toupper(ch)	char	char	Returns uppercase of ch if lowercase; otherwise, ch is unchanged.
tolower(ch)	char	char	Returns lowercase of ch if uppercase; otherwise, ch is unchanged.

*Technically, if pos is too large, the program generates what is called an out-of-range exception. Unless we write additional program code to deal explicitly with this exception, the program simply terminates with a message such as ABNORMAL PROGRAM TERMINATION. Using more advanced capabilities in C++, it is possible to catch such errors before the program halts and take corrective action.

SOFTWARE ENGINEERING TIP Understanding Before Changing

When you are trying to get a program to run and you come across an error, it's tempting to start changing parts of the program in an attempt to make it work. Don't! You'll nearly always make things worse. It's essential that you understand what is causing the error and carefully think through the solution. The only thing you should try is running the program with different data to determine the pattern of the unexpected behavior.

There is no magic trick that can automatically fix a program. If the compiler tells you that a semicolon or a right brace is missing, you need to examine the program and determine precisely what the problem is. Perhaps you accidentally typed a colon instead of a semicolon. Or maybe there's an extra left brace.

If the source of a problem isn't immediately obvious, a good rule of thumb is to leave the computer and go somewhere else to quietly look over a printed copy of the program. Studies show that people who do all of their debugging away from the computer actually get their programs to work in less time and in the end produce better programs than those who continue to work on the machine—more proof that there is still no mechanical substitute for human thought.

Source: Basili, V. R., and Selby, R. W., "Comparing the Effectiveness of Software Testing Strategies," *IEEE Trans. on Software Engineering* SE-13, no. 12 (1987): 1278–1296.

QUICK CHECK

3.8.1 What is the value of the following expression, given that the string variable `quickCheck` contains the string `"My friend I shall be pedagogic"`? (p. 122)

```
quickCheck.substr(10, 20) + " " + quickCheck.substr(0, 9) + "."
```

3.8.2 What is the result of the following expression if `myString` contains `"Hello"`? (p. 123)

```
myString.at(2)
```

3.8.3 What is the result of the following expression if `myString` contains `"Hello"`? (p. 120)

```
myString.find("H");
```

3.8.4 What library function can be used to make a character lowercase? (p. 124)

Problem-Solving Case Study

Mortgage Payment Calculator

PROBLEM: Your parents are thinking about refinancing their mortgage and have asked you to help them with the calculations. Now that you're learning C++, you realize that you can save yourself a lot of calculator button-pressing by writing a program to do the calculations automatically.

DISCUSSION: In the case study in Chapter 1, we said that there are often three obvious steps in almost any problem of this type:

1. Get the data.
2. Compute the results.
3. Output the results.

The data we need in this case are the amount of money to borrow, the number of years for the loan, and the interest rate. From these three values, the monthly payment can be calculated. Although you could solve this problem for your parents using paper-and-pencil calculations, you might as well write a program to solve it. You can make the data values be constants now; later, when you learn how to input values, you can rewrite the program.

After a chat with your parents, you find that they still owe $50,000 on the house and have exactly 7 years worth of payments to go. The latest quote from their credit union is for an interest rate of 5.24% with no closing costs.

Define Constants

```
Set LOAN_AMOUNT = 50000.00
Set NUMBER_OF_YEARS = 7
Set INTEREST_RATE = 0.0524
```

Problem-Solving Case Study

You vaguely recall seeing the formula for determining payments, using compound interest, but you can't remember it. You decide to go to the Internet and look it up.

$$\frac{\text{Amount} * (1 + \text{Monthly Interest})^{\text{Number of Payments}} * \text{Monthly Interest}}{(1 + \text{Monthly Interest})^{\text{Number of Payments}} - 1}$$

Hmmm. This may actually be easier to do on the computer than on a calculator. Two values taken to the number of payments power looks daunting. Fortunately, the C++ `<cmath>` header file, which we looked at earlier, contains a number of mathematical functions including the power function. Before you actually enter the values in the formula, two intermediate values need to be calculated: monthly interest rate and number of payments.

Calculate Values

```
Set monthlyInterest to YEARLY_INTEREST divided by 12
Set numberOfPayments to NUMBER_OF_YEARS times 12
Set payment to (LOAN_AMOUNT * pow(1+monthlyInterest,
   numberOfPayments) * monthlyInterest) / (pow(1+monthlyInterest,
   numberOfPayments) — 1)
```

Now all that is left is to print out the answer in a clear, concise format. Let's use a precision of 2 for the floating-point values and a fixed format.

Output Results

```
Print "For a loan amount of " LOAN_AMOUNT " with an interest rate of
   " YEARLY_INTEREST " and a " NUMBER_OF_YEARS " year mortgage,"
Print "your monthly payments are $" payment "."
```

From the algorithm, we can create tables of constants and variables to help us write the declarations for the program.

CONSTANTS

Name	Value	Function
LOAN_AMOUNT	50000.00	Amount of the loan
YEARLY_INTEREST	0.0524	Yearly interest rato
NUMBER_OF_YEARS	7	Number of years

VARIABLES

Name	Data Type	Description
monthlyInterest	float	Monthly interest rate
numberOfPayments	int	Total number of payments
payment	int	Monthly payment

Problem-Solving Case Study

```cpp
//*****************************************************************
// Mortgage Payment Calculator program
// This program determines the monthly payments on a mortgage given
// the loan amount, the yearly interest, and the number of years.
//*****************************************************************

#include <iostream>                          // Access cout
#include <cmath>                             // Access power function
#include <iomanip>                           // Access manipulators
using namespace std;

const float LOAN_AMOUNT = 50000.00;          // Amount of the loan
const float YEARLY_INTEREST = 0.0524;        // Yearly interest rate
const int NUMBER_OF_YEARS = 7;               // Number of years

int main()
{
  // Local variables
  float monthlyInterest;                     // Monthly interest rate
  int numberOfPayments;                      // Total number of payments
  float payment;                             // Monthly payment

  // Calculate values
  monthlyInterest = YEARLY_INTEREST / 12;
  numberOfPayments = NUMBER_OF_YEARS * 12;
  payment = (LOAN_AMOUNT * pow(1 + monthlyInterest, numberOfPayments)
          * monthlyInterest)/
          (pow(1 + monthlyInterest, numberOfPayments) - 1 );

  // Output results
  cout << fixed << setprecision(2) << "For a loan amount of "
       << LOAN_AMOUNT  << " with an interest rate of "
       << YEARLY_INTEREST << " and a " << NUMBER_OF_YEARS
       << " year mortgage, " << endl;
  cout << " your monthly payments are $" << payment
       << "." << endl;
  return 0;
}
```

Output:

```
For a loan amount of 50000.00 with an interest rate of 0.05 and a 7 year mortgage,
 your monthly payments are $712.35.
```

Something looks strange about the output: The interest should be 0.0524, not 0.05. The decision to use a precision of 2 was correct for dollars and cents, but not for interest rates, which are rarely whole percentages. You are asked to make this correction in Case Study Follow-Up Exercise 1.

Testing and Debugging

1. An `int` constant other than 0 should not start with a zero. If it starts with a zero, it is an octal (base-8) number.
2. Watch out for integer division. The expression `47 / 100` yields 0, the integer quotient. This is one of the major sources of erroneous output in C++ programs.
3. When using the `/` and `%` operators, remember that division by zero is not allowed.
4. Double-check every expression against the precedence rules to be sure that the operations are performed in the desired order.
5. Avoid mixing integer and floating-point values in expressions. If you must mix them, consider using explicit type casts to reduce the chance of mistakes.
6. For each assignment statement, check that the expression result has the same data type as the variable to the left of the assignment operator (=). If not, consider using an explicit type cast for clarity and safety. Also, remember that storing a floating-point value into an `int` variable truncates the fractional part.
7. For every library function you use in your program, be sure to `#include` the appropriate header file.
8. Examine each call to a library function to confirm that you have the right number of arguments and that the data types of the arguments are correct.
9. With the `string` type, positions of characters within a string are numbered starting at 0, not 1.
10. If the cause of an error in a program is not obvious, leave the computer and study a printed listing. Change your program only after you understand the source of the error.

Summary

C++ provides several built-in numeric data types, of which the most commonly used are `int` and `float`. The integral types are based on the mathematical integers, but the computer limits the range of integer values that can be represented. The floating-point types are based on the mathematical notion of real numbers. As with integers, the computer limits the range of floating-point numbers that can be represented. Also, it limits the number of digits of precision in floating-point values. We can write literals of type `float` in several forms, including scientific (E) notation.

Much of the computation of a program is performed in arithmetic expressions. Expressions can contain more than one operator. The order in which the operations are performed is determined by precedence rules. In arithmetic expressions, multiplication, division, and modulus are performed first, followed by addition and subtraction. Multiple binary (two-operand) operations of the same precedence are grouped from left to right. You can use parentheses to override the precedence rules.

Expressions may include function calls. C++ supports two kinds of functions: value-returning functions and void functions. A value-returning function is called by writing its name and argument list as part of an expression. A void function is called by writing its name and argument list as a complete C++ statement.

The C++ standard library is an integral part of every C++ system. It contains many prewritten data types, functions, and other items that any programmer can use. These items are accessed by using `#include` directives to the C++ preprocessor, which then inserts the appropriate header files into the program.

In output statements, the `setw`, `showpoint`, `fixed`, and `setprecision` manipulators can be used to control the appearance of values in the output. These manipulators do not affect the values actually stored in memory—only their appearance when displayed on the output device.

Not only should the output produced by a program be easy to read, but the format of the program itself should also be clear and readable. C++ is a free-format language. Using a consistent style that incorporates indentation, blank lines, and spaces within lines will help you (and other programmers) understand and work with your programs.

The `string` type provides a collection of useful functions that can be applied to strings: `length` and `size` return the number of characters in a string, `find` looks for a substring within a larger string, and `substr` returns a specified substring of a string. The `char` type provides two functions, `toupper` and `tolower`, that allow the user to force a character to be uppercase or lowercase, respectively. Characters within a string can be accessed by using the `at` function.

■ Quick Check Answers

3.2.1 `char`, `short`, `int`, and `long` 3.2.2 integer values (whole numbers without a fractional part). 3.2.3 unsigned 3.2.4 smallest: `char` or `unsigned char`; largest: `long` or `unsigned long`. 3.2.5 smallest: `long`; largest: `unsigned long`. 3.2.6 The result is *integer overflow*. 3.2.7 The floating-point type. 3.2.8 `float`, `double`, `long double`. 3.2.9 `3.504E12` 3.3.1 `const float PI = 3.14159.` 3.3.2 `int` 3.3.3 The declarations are exactly the same, except that we use the reserved word `int` or `float` instead of `string`, and we assign a numerical value to the constant rather than a string value. 3.4.1 `37 % 7 = 2` 3.4.2 An error. 3.4.3 A special *infinity* value displayed as "inf". 3.4.4 It adds 1 to the value of the variable `num`. 3.5.1 The fractional part is truncated. 3.5.2 Unary + and -. 3.5.3 Binary + and -. 3.5.4 Parentheses ( ) 3.5.5 Type casting 3.5.6 `x = int(y + 1.25)`. 3.5.7 `float percentage = (float(score) / float(total)) * 100.0;` 3.5.8 `27 + ( 8 * 6) - (44 % 5) = 27 + 48 - 4 = 71` 3.6.1 They appear in the call to a function, between parentheses, and are used to pass data to or from a function. 3.6.2 `sqrt(17.5)` 3.6.3 A void function call appears as a separate statement rather than being part of an expression. 3.6.4 It puts main temporarily on hold. 3.6.5 Libraries contain commonly used functions so programmers do not need to start from scratch. 3.6.6 They use the #include directive to get access to the library. 3.7.1 True. 3.7.2 `setprecision` 3.7.3 `iomanip` 3.7.4 It lets us control how many character positions the next data item should occupy when it is output. 3.7.5 It forces a decimal point to be displayed in subsequent floating-point output. 3.7.6 `scientific` 3.8.1 "I shall be pedagogic My friend." 3.8.2 'l' 3.8.3 0 3.8.4 `tolower`.

■ Exam Preparation Exercises

1. The integer and floating-point types in C++ are considered (simple, address, structured) data types. (Circle one)
2. What are the four integral types in C++? List them in order of size, from smallest to largest.
3. What is the result if the computer tries to calculate a value that is larger than the maximum integer allowed for a given integral type?
4. In a floating-point value, what does it mean when the letter *E* appears as part of a number?
5. Label each of the following as an integer or floating-point declaration, and indicate whether it is a constant or a variable declaration.

	Integer / Floating Point	Constant / Variable
a. `const int tracksOnDisk = 17;`	_____	_____
b. `float timeOfTrack;`	_____	_____
c. `const float maxTimeOnDisk = 74.0;`	_____	_____
d. `short tracksLeft;`	_____	_____

e. `float timeLeft;`
   f. `long samplesInTrack;`
   g. `const double sampleRate = 262144.5;`
6. What are the two meanings of the / operator?
7. What is the result of each of the following expressions?
   a. `27 + 8 / 5 - 7`
   b. `27.0 + 8.0 / 5.0 - 7.0`
   c. `25 % 7 + 9.0`
   d. `17++`
   e. `int(15.0 + 12.0 * 2.2 - 3 * 7)`
   f. `23--`
   g. `18 / 1.0`
8. List the following operators in the order of highest precedence to lowest precedence. If a set of operators has the same precedence, write them enclosed in square brackets within the ordered list.

   `*   +   %   /   -   unary -   ()`

9. The increment and decrement operators can either precede or follow their operand. True or false?
10. Match the following terms to the definitions given below.
    a. Unary operator
    b. Binary operator
    c. Type coercion
    d. Type casting
    e. Mixed type expression
    f. Argument list
    g. Void function
       i. A computation involving both floating-point and integer values
       ii. An operator with two operands
       iii. A function that is called as a separate statement
       iv. Explicitly changing a value of one type into another
       v. The values that appear between the parentheses in a function call
       vi. An operator with just one operand
       vii. Implicitly changing a value of one type into another
11. The statement

    `count = count + 1;`

    is equivalent to which C++ operator?
12. How do you write a C++ cast operation?
13. Is `main` a value-returning function or a void function?
14. Show precisely what the following statement outputs:

    `cout << setw(6) << showpoint << setprecision(2) << 215.0;`

15. The prefix and postfix forms of the increment operator (++) always behave the same way. We can use them interchangeably anywhere in C++ code. True or false? Explain your answer.

16. Which data type do we use to declare a variable to hold the result of applying the length function to a string?
17. Given that the string variables `str1` and `str2` contain

    `"you ought to start with logic"`

    and

    `"ou"`

    respectively, what is the result of each of the following expressions?
    a. `str1.length()`
    b. `str1.find(str2)`
    c. `str1.substr(4, 25)`
    d. `str1.substr(4, 25).find(str2)`
    e. `str1.substr.(str1.find("logic"), 3)`
    f. `str1.substr(24, 5).find(str2.substr(0,1))`
    g. `str1.find("end")`
18. What does the manipulator `fixed` do?
19. What does the function `toupper` do?
20. What does the function `tolower` do?

■ Programming Warm-Up Exercises

1. Write an expression to convert a time stored in the `int` variables `hours`, `minutes`, and `seconds` into the number of seconds represented by the time. For example, if `hours` contains 2, `minutes` contains 20, and `seconds` contains 12, then the result of your expression should be 8412.
2. Given an `int` variable `days` that contains a number of days:
   a. Write an expression that gives the number of whole weeks corresponding to `days`. For example, if `days` contains 23, then the number of whole weeks is 3.
   b. Write an expression that gives the number of days remaining after taking the whole weeks out of the value in `days`. For example, if `days` contains 23, then the number of days remaining after 3 whole weeks is 2.
3. Given `int` variables called `dollars`, `quarters`, `dimes`, `nickels`, and `pennies`, write an expression that computes the total amount of the money represented in the variables. The result should be an integer value representing the number of pennies in the total.
4. Given the same variables as in Exercise 3, compute the total but store it in a floating-point variable so that the integral part is dollars and the fractional part is cents.
5. Write an assignment statement that adds 3 to the value in `int` variable `count`.
6. Write expressions that implement the following formulas.
   a. $3X + Y$
   b. $A^2 + 2B + C$
   c. $\left(\dfrac{A+B}{C-D}\right) \times \left(\dfrac{X}{Y}\right)$

d. $\left(\dfrac{A^2 + 2B + C}{D}\right) \Big/ XY$

e. $\sqrt{|A - B|}$

f. $X^{-\cos(Y)}$

7. Write a series of assignment statements that find the first three positions of the string "and" in a string variable sentence. The positions should be stored in int variables called first, second, and third. You may declare additional variables if necessary. The contents of sentence should remain unchanged.

8. Write an assignment statement to find the first blank in a string variable called name. Store the result plus one in the int variable startOfMiddle.

9. Write an output statement that prints the value in float variable money in eight spaces on the line, with a leading dollar sign ($), and two digits of decimal precision.

10. Write an output statement that prints the value in double variable distance in 15 spaces on a line with 5 digits of decimal precision.

11. If you include the header file climits in a program, the constants INT_MAX and INT_MIN are provided, which give the highest and lowest int values that can be represented. Write the include statement for this file as well as an output statement that displays the two values, identified with appropriate labels.

12. Write the statement that accesses the third character in string variable myString.

13. Write the statement that changes the char variable letter to lowercase.

14. Write the statement that changes the char variable letter to uppercase.

15. Complete the following C++ program. The program should compute and output the Celsius value corresponding to the given Fahrenheit value.

```
//************************************************
// Celsius program
// This program outputs the Celsius temperature
// corresponding to a given Fahrenheit temperature
//************************************************

#include <iostream>

using namespace std;

int main()
{
    const float FAHRENHEIT = 72.0;
```

Programming Problems

1. Write a C++ program that computes and outputs the volume of a cone, given the diameter of its base and its height. The formula for computing the cone's volume is:

   $1/3 \; \pi \times \text{Radius}^2 \times \text{Height}$

   Be sure to use proper formatting and appropriate comments in your code. The output should be labeled clearly.

2. Write a C++ program that computes the mean and standard deviation of a set of four integer values. The mean is the sum of the four values divided by 4, and the formula for the standard deviation is

$$s = \sqrt{\frac{\sum_{i=1}^{n}(x_i - \bar{x})^2}{n-1}}$$

Where $n = 4$, x_i refers to each of the four values, and $\bar{x}$ is the mean. Note that although the individual values are integers, the results are floating-point values. Be sure to use proper formatting and appropriate comments in your code. The output should be labeled clearly and formatted neatly.

3. The factorial of a number n (written $n!$) is the number times the factorial of itself minus one. This self-referential definition is easiest to understand through an example: The factorial of 2 is 2 * 1; the factorial of 3 is 3 * 2 * 1; the factorial of 4 is 4 * 3 * 2 * 1; and so on. Factorials grow very large, very quickly. An approximation to the factorial for larger values is given by Stirling's formula:

$$n! = e^{-n} n^n \sqrt{2\pi n}$$

The **exp** function in the `<cmath>` header file gives the value of *e* raised to given power (see Appendix C.5). We've already discussed all of the other functions that are needed to write this formula. Write a C++ program that computes the factorial of 15 both directly and with Stirling's formula, and outputs both results, together with their difference. You will need to use the **double** type for this computation. Be sure to use proper formatting and appropriate comments in your code. The output should be labeled clearly and formatted neatly.

4. Write a C++ program that computes a student's grade for an assignment as a percentage given the student's score and the total points. The final score should be rounded up to the nearest whole value using the **ceil** function in the `<cmath>` header file. You should also display the floating-point result up to 5 decimal places.

5. Given the following string:

"Program testing can be used to show the presence of bugs, but never to show their absence"

Write a C++ program that will construct a new string in uppercase from the string above such that the new string is:

"I CAN WRITE CODE THAT RUNS"

6. The number of permutations of a set of n items taken r at a time is given by the following formula:

$$\frac{n!}{r!(n-r)!}$$

where $n!$ is the factorial of n. (See Programming Problem 3 for a discussion of ways to compute the factorial.) If there are 18 people in your class and you want to divide the class into programming teams of 3 members, you can compute the number of different teams that can be arranged using this formula. Write a C++ program that determines the number of potential team arrangements. You will need to use the **double** type for this computation. Be sure to use proper formatting and appropriate comments in your code. The output should be labeled clearly and formatted neatly.

7. Write a C++ program that takes a string containing a full name and outputs each part of the name separately. The name should be in the form of first, middle, and last name, separated from each other by a single space. For example, if the name string contains

    ```
    "John Jacob Schmidt"
    ```

    then the program would output

    ```
    First name: John
    Middle name: Jacob
    Last name: Schmidt
    ```

8. Extend Programming Problem 7 to output the length of each name. This problem can be solved using a combination of the string operations presented in this chapter. Be sure to use proper formatting and appropriate comments in your code. The output should be labeled clearly and formatted neatly.

Case Study Follow-Up

1. Change the output statements so that the interest rate is printed with four decimal places, but the dollar amounts continue to have two decimal places.
2. The program assumes that the number of months left on the old mortgage is an even multiple of 12. Change the program so that the constant is the number of months left, not the number of years.
3. We usually speak of interest rates as percentages. Rewrite the program so that the interest rate is set as a percentage—that is, as 5.24 rather than 0.0524.
4. The calculation of `1 + monthlyInterest` is made twice. Rewrite the program so that it makes this calculation only once. In your judgment, which version of the program is better? Justify your answer.

Program Input and the Software Design Process

KNOWLEDGE GOALS

- To understand the value of appropriate prompting messages for interactive programs.
- To know when noninteractive input/output is appropriate and how it differs from interactive input/output.
- To understand the distinction between functional decomposition and object-oriented design.

SKILL GOALS

To be able to:

- Construct input statements to read values into a program.
- Determine the contents of variables assigned values by input statements.
- Write programs that use data files for input and output.
- Apply the functional decomposition methodology to solve a simple problem.
- Take a functional decomposition and code it in C++, using self-documenting code.

A program needs data on which to operate. Up to this point, we have been writing data values in the program itself, in literal and named constants. If this were the only way we could enter data, we would have to rewrite a program for each different set of values. In this chapter, we look at ways of entering data into a program while it is running.

Once we know how to input data, process it, and output results, we can begin to think about designing more complicated programs. We have talked about general problem-solving strategies and writing simple programs. For a simple problem, it's easy to choose a strategy, write the algorithm, and code the program. As problems become more complex, however, we have to use a more organized approach. In the second part of this chapter, we look at two general methodologies for developing software: object-oriented design and functional decomposition.

4.1 Getting Data into Programs

One of the major advantages offered by computers is that a program can be used with many different sets of data. To do so, we must keep the data separate from the program until the program is executed. Then instructions in the program copy values from the data set into variables in the program. After storing these values into the variables, the program can perform calculations with them (see **FIGURE 4.1**).

The process of placing values from an outside data set into variables in a program is called *input*. We say that the computer *reads* data into the variables. Data can come from an input device or from a file on an auxiliary storage device. We look at file input later in this chapter; here we consider the *standard input device*, the keyboard.

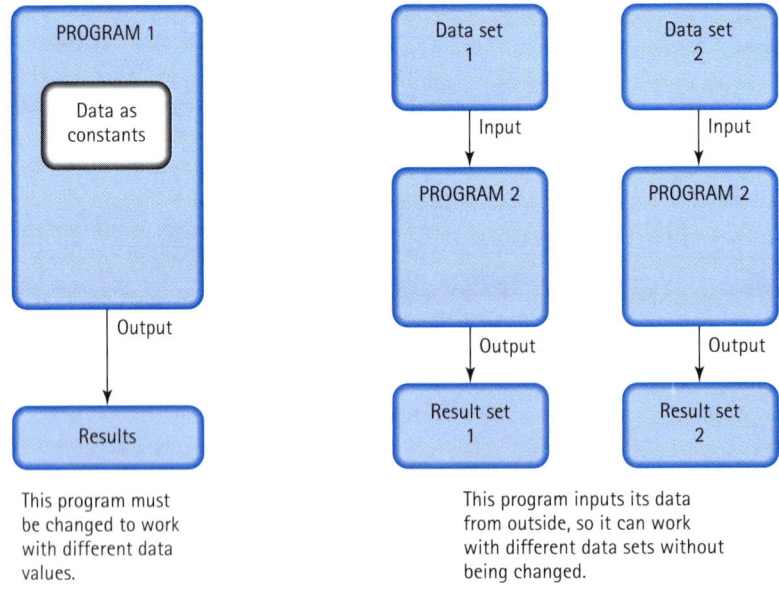

FIGURE 4.1 Separating the Data from the Program

Input Streams and the Extraction Operator (>>)

The concept of a stream is fundamental to input and output in C++. Similar to how we have described an output stream, you can think of an *input stream* as a doorway through which characters come into your program from an input device.

As we saw in Chapter 2, to use stream input/output (I/O), we write the preprocessor directive

```
#include <iostream>
```

The header file `iostream` contains, among other things, the definitions of two data types: `istream` and `ostream`. These data types represent input streams and output streams, respectively. The header file also contains declarations that look like this:

```
istream cin;
ostream cout;
```

The first declaration says that `cin` (pronounced "see-in") is a variable of type `istream`. The second says that our old friend `cout` is a variable of type `ostream`. The stream `cin` is associated with the standard input device (the keyboard).

As you have already seen, you can output values to `cout` by using the insertion operator (<<), which is sometimes pronounced "put to":

```
cout << 3 * price;
```

In a similar fashion, you can input data from `cin` by using the extraction operator (>>), sometimes pronounced "get from":

```
cin >> cost;
```

When the computer executes this statement, it inputs the next number you type on the keyboard (425, for example) and stores it into the variable `cost`.

The extraction operator >> takes two operands. Its left-hand operand is a stream expression (in the simplest case, just the variable `cin`). Its right-hand operand is a variable into which we store the input data. For now, let's assume the variable is of a simple type (`char`, `int`, `float`, and so forth). Later in the chapter we discuss the input of string data.

You can use the >> operator several times in a single input statement. Each occurrence extracts (inputs) the next data item from the input stream. For example, there is no difference between the statement

```
cin >> length >> width;
```

and the pair of statements

```
cin >> length;
cin >> width;
```

Using a sequence of extractions in one statement is very convenient for the programmer.

When you are new to C++, you may confuse the extraction operator (>>) with the insertion operator (<<). Here is an easy way to remember which is which: Always begin the statement with either **cin** or **cout**, and use the operator that points in the direction in which the data is going. The statement

```cpp
cout << someInt;
```

sends data *from* the variable **someInt** *to* the output stream. The statement

```cpp
cin >> someInt;
```

sends data *from* the input stream *to* the variable **someInt**. The following program demonstrates the use of **cin** and **cout**.

```cpp
//***********************************************************
// This program demonstrates cin and cout.
//***********************************************************

#include <iostream>
#include <string>
using namespace std;

int main ()
{
    int year;
    int month;
    int day;
    cout << "Enter the month, day, and year in integer form."
         << endl;
    cin >> month >> day >> year;

    cout << month << "/" << day << "/" << year;
    return 0;
}
```

Here is the output, with the data entered by the user highlighted:

```
Enter the month, day, and year in integer form.
12
7
1941
12/7/1941
```

Here's the syntax template for an input statement:

InputStatement

```
cin >> Variable >> Variable ... ;
```

Unlike the items specified in an output statement, which can be constants, variables, or complicated expressions, the items specified in an input statement can *only* be variable names. Why? Because an input statement indicates where input data values should be stored. Only variable names refer to memory locations where we can store values while a program is running.

When you enter input data at the keyboard, you must be sure that each data value is appropriate for the data type of the variable in the input statement.

Data Type of Variable in an >> Operation	Valid Input Data
char	A single printable character other than a blank
int	An int literal constant, optionally preceded by a sign
float	An int or float literal constant (possibly in scientific, or E, notation), optionally preceded by a plus or minus sign

When you input a number into a float variable, the input value doesn't need a decimal point. That's because the integer value is automatically coerced to a float value. Any other mismatches, such as trying to input a float value into an int variable or a char value into a float variable, can lead to unexpected and sometimes serious results. Later in this chapter we discuss what might happen.

When looking for the next input value in the stream, the >> operator skips any leading *whitespace characters*. Whitespace characters are blanks and certain nonprintable characters, such as the character that marks the end of a line. (We talk about this end-of-line character in the next section.) After skipping any whitespace characters, the >> operator proceeds to extract the desired data value from the input stream. If this data value is a char value, input stops as soon as a single character is input. If the data value is an int or float, input of the number stops at the first character that is inappropriate for the data type, such as a whitespace character. Here are some examples, where i, j, and k are int variables, ch is a char variable, and x is a float variable:

Statement	Data	Contents After Input
1. cin >> i;	32	i = 32
2. cin >> i >> j;	4 60	i = 4, j = 60
3. cin >> i >> ch >> x;	25 A 16.9	i = 25, ch = 'A', x = 16.9
4. cin >> i >> ch >> x;	25	
	A	
	16.9	i = 25, ch = 'A', x = 16.9
5. cin >> i >> ch >> x;	25A16.9	i = 25, ch = 'A', x = 16.9
6. cin >> i >> j >> x;	12 8	i = 12, j = 8 (Computer waits for a third number)
7. cin >> i >> x;	46 32.4 15	i = 46, x = 32.4 (15 is held for later input)

Examples 1 and 2 are straightforward examples of integer input. Example 3 shows that you do not use quotes around character data values when they are input (quotes around character constants are needed in a program, though, to distinguish them from identifiers). Example 4 demonstrates how the process of skipping whitespace characters includes going on to the next line of input if necessary. Example 5 shows that the first character encountered that is inappropriate for a numeric data type ends the number. Input for the variable i stops at the input character A, after which the A is stored into ch, and then input for x stops at the end of the input line. Example 6 shows that if you are at the keyboard and haven't entered enough values to satisfy the input statement, the computer waits (and waits and waits . . .) for more data. Example 7 shows that if you enter more values than there are variables in the input statement, the extra values remain waiting in the input stream until they can be read by the next input statement. If extra values are left over when the program ends, the computer disregards them.

The Reading Marker and the Newline Character

To help explain stream input in more detail, we introduce the concept of the *reading marker*. The reading marker works like a bookmark, but instead of marking a place in a book, it keeps track of the point in the input stream where the computer should continue reading. In other words, the reading marker indicates the next character waiting to be read. The extraction operator >> leaves the reading marker on the character following the last piece of data that was input.

Each input line has an invisible end-of-line character (the *newline character*) that tells the computer where one line ends and the next begins. To find the next input value, the >> operator crosses line boundaries (newline characters) if necessary.

Where does the newline character come from? What is it? The answer to the first question is easy. When you are working at a keyboard, you generate a newline character each time you press the Return or Enter key. Your program also generates a newline character when it uses the **endl** manipulator in an output statement. The **endl** manipulator outputs a newline, telling the screen cursor to go to the next line. The answer to the second question varies from computer system to computer system. The newline character is a nonprintable control character that the system recognizes as meaning the end of a line, whether it's an input line or an output line.

As we saw in Chapter 3, you can also refer directly to the newline character by using the symbols \n, consisting of a backslash and an **n** with no space between them.

Let's look at some examples of input using the reading marker and the newline character. In the following table, i is an **int** variable, ch is a **char** variable, and x is a **float** variable. The input statements produce the results shown. The part of the input stream printed in color is what has been extracted by input statements. The reading marker, denoted by the shaded block, indicates the next character waiting to be read. The \n denotes the newline character.

Statements	Contents After Input	Marker Position in the Input Stream
1.		25 A 16.9\n
cin >> i;	i = 25	25 A 16.9\n
cin >> ch;	ch = 'A'	25 A 16.9\n
cin >> x;	x = 16.9	25 A 16.9\n
2.		25\n
		A\n
		16.9\n
cin >> i;	i = 25	25\n
		A\n
		16.9\n
cin >> ch;	ch = 'A'	25\n
		A\n
		16.9\n
cin >> x;	x = 16.9	25\n
		A\n
		16.9\n
3.		25A16.9\n
cin >> i;	i = 25	25A16.9\n
cin >> ch;	ch = 'A'	25A16.9\n
cin >> x;	x = 16.9	25A16.9\n

Reading Character Data with the `get` Function

As we have discussed, the >> operator skips any leading whitespace characters (such as blanks and newline characters) while looking for the next data value in the input stream. Suppose that ch1 and ch2 are char variables and the program executes the following statement

`cin >> ch1 >> ch2;`

If the input stream consists of

`R 1`

then the extraction operator stores 'R' into ch1, skips the blank, and stores '1' into ch2. (Note that the char value '1' is not the same as the int value 1. The two are stored in completely different ways in a computer's memory. The extraction operator interprets the same data in different ways, depending on the data type of the variable that's being filled.)

What if we had wanted to input *three* characters from the input line, where one was a blank? With the extraction operator, it's not possible. Whitespace characters such as blanks are skipped over.

The `istream` data type provides a second way in which to read character data, in addition to the >> operator. You can use the **get** function, which inputs the very next character in the input stream without skipping any whitespace characters. The function call looks like this:

```
cin.get(someChar);
```

The **get** function is associated with the `istream` data type, and you must use dot notation to make a function call. (Recall that we used dot notation in Chapter 3 to invoke certain functions associated with the `string` type. Later in this chapter we explain the reason for dot notation.) To use the **get** function, you give the name of an `istream` variable (here, `cin`), then a dot (period), and then the function name and argument list. Notice that the call to **get** uses the syntax for calling a void function, not a value-returning function. The function call is a complete statement; it is not part of a larger expression.

The effect of this function call is to input the next character waiting in the stream—even if it is a whitespace character like a blank—and store it into the variable `someChar`. The argument to the **get** function *must* be a variable, not a constant or arbitrary expression; we must tell the function where we want it to store the input character.

The following program demonstrates the use of the **get** function to read three characters and store them in three different places.

```
//***********************************************************
// This program demonstrates the use of the get function.
//***********************************************************

#include <iostream>
using namespace std;
int main ()
{
    char ch1, ch2, ch3;
    cout << "Enter three characters including a space." << endl;
    cin.get(ch1);
    cin.get(ch2);
    cin.get(ch3);
    cout << "You entered: " << ch1 << ch2 << ch3 << endl;
    return 0;
}
```

Here is the output, with user input highlighted:

```
Enter three characters including a space.
* A
You entered: * A
```

Because the middle character is a blank, we could have used the following three lines to input the data.

```
cin >> ch1;
cin.get(ch2);
cin >> ch3;
```

However, the first version always works.

Here are some more examples of character input using both the >> operator and the **get** function. **ch1**, **ch2**, and **ch3** are all **char** variables. As before, \n denotes the newline character.

Statements	Contents After Input	Marker Position in the Input Stream
1.		A B\n
		CD\n
cin >> ch1;	ch1 = 'A'	A B\n
		CD\n
cin >> ch2;	ch2 = 'B'	A B\n
		CD\n
cin >> ch3;	ch3 = 'C'	A B\n
		CD\n
2.		A B\n
		CD\n
cin.get(ch1);	ch1 = 'A'	A B\n
		CD\n
cin.get(ch2);	ch2 = ' '	A B\n
		CD\n
cin.get(ch3);	ch3 = 'B'	A B\n
		CD\n
3.		A B\n
		CD\n
cin >> ch1;	ch1 = 'A'	A B\n
		CD\n
cin >> ch2;	ch2 = 'B'	A B\n
		CD\n
cin.get(ch3);	ch3 = '\n'	A B\n
		CD\n

THEORETICAL FOUNDATIONS
More About Functions and Arguments

When your **main** function tells the computer to go off and follow the instructions in another function, **SomeFunc**, the **main** function is calling **SomeFunc**. In the call to **SomeFunc**, the arguments in the argument list are *passed* to the function. When **SomeFunc** finishes, the computer *returns* to the **main** function.

With some functions you have seen, such as **sqrt** and **abs**, you can pass constants, variables, and arbitrary expressions to the function. The **get** function for reading character data, however, accepts only a variable as an argument. The **get** function stores a value into its argument when it returns, and only variables can have values stored into them while a program is running. Even though **get** is called as a void function—not a value-returning function—it *returns* or *passes back* a value through its argument list. The point to remember is that you can use arguments both to send data into a function and to get results back out.

Skipping Characters with the `ignore` Function

Most of us have a specialized tool lying in a kitchen drawer or in a toolbox. It gathers dust and cobwebs because we almost never use it. Of course, when we suddenly need it, we're glad we have it. The **ignore** function associated with the **istream** type is like this specialized tool. You rarely have occasion to use **ignore**; but when you need it, you're glad it's available.

The **ignore** function is used to skip (read and discard) characters in the input stream. It is a function with two arguments, called like this:

```
cin.ignore(200, '\n');
```

The first argument is an **int** expression; the second, a **char** value. This particular function call tells the computer to skip the next 200 input characters or to skip characters until a newline character is read, whichever comes first.

Here are some examples that use a **char** variable **ch** and three **int** variables, **i**, **j**, and **k**:

Statements	Contents After Input	Marker Position in the Input Stream
1.		957 34 1235\n
		128 96\n
cin >> i >> j;	i = 957, j = 34	957 34 1235\n
		128 96\n
cin.ignore(100, '\n');		957 34 1235\n
		128 96\n
cin >> k;	k = 128	957 34 1235\n
		128 96\n

Statements	Contents After Input	Marker Position in the Input Stream
2.		A 22, 16, 19\n
`cin >> ch;`	ch = 'A'	A 22, 16, 19\n
`cin.ignore(100, ',');`		A 22, 16, 19\n
`cin >> i;`	i = 16	A 22, 16, 19\n
3.		ABCDEF\n
`cin.ignore(2, '\n');`		ABCDEF\n
`cin >> ch;`	ch = 'C'	ABCDEF\n

Example 1 shows the most common use of the **ignore** function, which is to skip the rest of the data on the current input line. Example 2 demonstrates the use of a character other than \n as the second argument. We skip over all input characters until a comma has been found, and then read the next input number into **i**. In both Example 1 and Example 2, we are focusing on the second argument to the **ignore** function, and we arbitrarily choose any large number, such as 100, for the first argument. In Example 3, we change our focus and concentrate on the first argument. Our intention is to skip the next two input characters on the current line.

Reading String Data

To input a character string into a **string** variable, we have two options. First, we can use the extraction operator (>>). When reading input characters into a **string** variable, the >> operator skips any leading whitespace characters such as blanks and newlines. It then reads successive characters into the variable, stopping at the first *trailing* whitespace character (which is not consumed, but remains as the first character waiting in the input stream). For example, assume we have the following code:

```
string firstName;
string lastName;

cin >> firstName >> lastName;
```

If the input stream initially looks like this (where □ denotes a blank):

□□Mary□Smith□□□18

then our input statement stores the four characters **Mary** into **firstName**, stores the five characters **Smith** into **lastName**, and leaves the input stream as

□□□18

Although the >> operator is widely used for string input purposes, it has a potential drawback: It cannot be used to input a string that has blanks within it. (Remember that it stops reading as soon as it encounters a whitespace character.) This fact leads us to the second option for performing string input: the **getline** function. A call to this function looks like this:

`getline(cin, myString);`

This function call, which does not use dot notation, requires two arguments: an input stream variable (here, **cin**) and a **string** variable. The **getline** function does not skip leading whitespace characters and continues until it reaches the newline character \n. That is, **getline** reads and stores an entire input line, embedded blanks and all. Note that with **getline**, the newline character is consumed (but is not stored into the string variable). Given the code segment

```
string inputStr;

getline(cin, inputStr);
```

and the input line

☐☐Mary☐Smith☐☐☐18

the result of the call to **getline** is that all 17 characters on the input line (including blanks) are stored into **inputStr**, and the reading marker is positioned at the beginning of the next input line.

The following table summarizes the differences between the >> operator and the **getline** function when reading string data into **string** variables.

Statement	Skips Leading Whitespace?	Stops Reading When?
`cin >> inputStr;`	Yes	When a trailing whitespace character is encountered (which is not consumed)
`getline(cin, inputStr);`	No	When \n is encountered (which is consumed)

The following program demonstrates the use of **getline** and **cin**.

```
//*************************************************
// This program demonstrates the use of cin and
// and getline combined.
//*************************************************
#include <iostream>
#include <string>
using namespace std;

int main()
{
    int     partNumber;
    int     quantity;
    float   unitPrice;
    float   totalPrice;
    string  title;
    getline(cin, title);
    cin >> partNumber;
    cin >> quantity;
    cin >> unitPrice;
    totalPrice = quantity * unitPrice;
    cout << title << endl;
    cout << partNumber << " " << quantity << " "
         << unitPrice << " ";
    cout << totalPrice << endl;
    return 0;
}
```

Here is a sample run of the program. The data entered by the user are highlighted, and are followed by the output.

QUICK CHECK

4.1.1 Write an input statement that reads three integer values into variables **a**, **b**, and **c**. (pp. 139–142)

4.1.2 If an input line contains

Jones, Walker Thomas

what will be the values in the **string** variables **first**, **middle**, and **last** when the following statement is executed? (pp. 147–149)

cin >> first >> middle >> last;

4.1.3 What do we call the process of placing values from an outside data set into variables in a program? (p. 138)

4.1.4 Which operator do you use for program input, >> or <<? (p. 139)

4.1.5 Why can an input statement specify only variables as its operands? (p. 141)

4.1.6 What is a reading marker used for? (p. 142)

4.1.7 The << operator skips spaces when reading input from the console. What function can we use to read characters into a **char** variable **ch** and not skip spaces? (p. 144)

4.1.8 Write a C++ statement that invokes a function to skip 10 characters or skip characters until a space is encountered? (p. 146)

4.2 Interactive Input/Output

In Chapter 1, we defined an interactive program as one in which the user communicates directly with the computer. Many of the programs that we write are interactive. There is a certain "etiquette" involved in writing interactive programs that has to do with instructions for the user to follow.

To get data into an interactive program, we begin with *input prompts*—that is, printed messages explaining what the user should enter. Without these messages, the user has no idea which data values to type. In many cases, a program also should print out all of the data values typed in by the user so that the user can verify that they were entered correctly. Printing out the input values is called *echo printing*.

Here's a program showing the proper use of prompts:

```
//****************************************************************
// This program demonstrates the use of input prompts.
//****************************************************************
#include <iostream>
```

```cpp
#include <iomanip>                        // For setprecision()
#include <string>

using namespace std;

int main()
{
   int    partNumber;
   int    quantity;
   float  unitPrice;
   float  totalPrice;
   string title;

   cout << fixed << showpoint        // Set up floating-point
        << setprecision(2);          // output format

   cout << "Enter the title for this execution." << endl; // Prompt
   getline(cin, title);

   cout << "Enter the part number:" << endl;              // Prompt
   cin >> partNumber;
   cout << "Enter the quantity of this part ordered:"     // Prompt
        << endl;
   cin >> quantity;

   cout << "Enter the unit price for this part:"          // Prompt
        << endl;
   cin >> unitPrice;

   totalPrice = quantity * unitPrice;

   cout << title << endl;
   cout << "Part " << partNumber                          // Echo print
        << ", quantity " << quantity
        << ", at $ " << unitPrice << " each" << endl;
   cout << "totals $ " << totalPrice << endl;
   return 0;
}
```

Here is the output, with user input highlighted:

```
Enter the title for this execution.
Demonstrating interactive input/output
Enter the part number:
23
Enter the quantity of this part ordered:
6
Enter the unit price for this part:
33.4
Demonstrating interactive input/output
Part 23, quantity 6, at $ 33.40 each
totals $ 200.40
```

Go back and look at the program in the previous section. It is the same program with no prompts and no formatting. If you were the person entering the information, which program would you prefer to use? If your job required you to read the output, which version would you find more usable?

The amount of information you should put into your prompts depends on who will use the program. If you are writing a program for people who are not familiar with computers, your messages should be more detailed. For example, the prompt might read, "Type a four-digit part number, then press the key marked Enter." If the program will be used frequently by the same people, you might shorten the prompts: "Enter PN" and "Enter Qty." If the program is intended for very experienced users, you can prompt for several values at once and have them type all of the values on one input line:

```
Enter PN, Qty, Unit Price:
```

In programs that use large amounts of data, this method saves the user keystrokes and time. Of course, it also makes it easier for the user to enter values in the wrong order. In such situations, echo printing the data is especially important.

The decision about whether a program should echo print its input or not also depends on how experienced the users are and on which task the program is to perform. If the users are experienced and the prompts are clear, as in the first example, then echo printing is probably not required. If the users are novices or multiple values can be input at once, echo printing should be used. If the program takes a large quantity of data as input and the users are experienced, rather than echo print the data, the data may be stored in a separate file that can be checked after all of the data is input. We discuss how to store data into a file later in this chapter.

Prompts are not the only way in which programs interact with users. It can be helpful to have a program print out some general instructions at the beginning ("Press Enter after typing each data value. Enter a negative number when done."). When data are not entered in the correct form, a message that indicates the problem should be printed. For users who haven't worked much with computers, it's important that these messages be informative and "friendly." The message

is likely to upset an inexperienced user. Moreover, it doesn't offer any constructive information. A much better message would be

In Chapter 5, we introduce the statements that allow us to test for erroneous data.

QUICK CHECK

4.2.1 Why do we need to use prompts for interactive I/O? (pp. 147–148)
4.2.2 What is an *input* prompt? (p. 149)

4.3 Noninteractive Input/Output

Although we tend to use examples of interactive I/O in this text, many programs are written using noninteractive I/O. A common example of noninteractive I/O on large computer systems is batch processing (see Chapter 1). In batch processing, the user and the computer do not interact while the program is running. This method is most effective when a program will have large amounts of data as input or output. An example of batch processing is a program that takes as input a file containing semester grades for thousands of students and prints grade reports to be mailed out to those students.

When a program must read in many data values, the usual practice is to prepare the data ahead of time, storing them into a file. This allows the user to go back and make changes or corrections to the data as necessary before running the program. When a program is designed to print lots of data, the output can be sent directly to a high-speed printer or another disk file. After the program has been run, the user can examine the data at leisure. In the next section, we discuss input and output with disk files.

Programs designed for noninteractive I/O do not print prompting messages for input. It is a good idea, however, to echo print each data value that is read. Echo printing allows the person reading the output to verify that the input values were prepared correctly. Because noninteractive programs tend to print large amounts of data, their output often takes the form of a table—columns with descriptive headings.

Most C++ programs are written for interactive use. The flexibility of the language allows you to write noninteractive programs as well. The biggest difference is in the input/output requirements. Noninteractive programs are generally more rigid about the organization and format of the input and output data.

4.4 File Input and Output

In everything we've done so far, we've assumed that the input to our programs comes from the keyboard and that the output from our programs goes to the screen. We look now at input/output from and to files.

Files

Earlier we defined a file as a named area in secondary storage that holds a collection of information (for example, the program code we have typed into the editor). The information in a file usually is stored on an auxiliary storage device, such as a disk. Our programs can read data from a file in the same way they read data from the keyboard, and they can write output to a disk file in the same way they write output to the screen.

Why would we want a program to read data from a file instead of the keyboard? If a program will read a large quantity of data, it is easier to enter the data into a file with an editor than to enter it while the program is running. When we are working in the editor, we can easily go back and correct mistakes. Also, we do not have to enter the data all at once;

we can take a break and come back later. Finally, if we want to rerun the program, having the data stored in a file allows us to do so without retyping the data.

Why would we want the output from a program to be written to a file? The contents of a file can be displayed on a screen or printed. This gives us the option of looking at the output over and over again without having to rerun the program. Also, the output stored in a file can be read into another program as input.

Using Files

If we want a program to use file I/O, we have to do four things:

1. Request the preprocessor to include the header file `fstream`.
2. Use declaration statements to declare the file streams we will use.
3. Prepare each file for reading or writing by using a function named `open`.
4. Specify the name of the file stream in each input or output statement.

Including the Header File `fstream`

Suppose we want Chapter 3's Mortgage program (p. 126) to read data from a file and to write its output to a file. The first thing we must do is use the following preprocessor directive:

```
#include <fstream>
```

Through the header file `fstream`, the C++ standard library defines two data types, `ifstream` and `ofstream` (standing for *input file stream* and *output file stream*, respectively). Consistent with the general idea of streams in C++, the `ifstream` data type represents a stream of characters coming from an input file, whereas `ofstream` represents a stream of characters going to an output file.

All of the `istream` operations you have learned about—the extraction operator (>>), the `get` function, and the `ignore` function—are also valid for the `ifstream` type. Likewise, all of the `ostream` operations, such as the insertion operator (<<) and the `endl`, `setw`, and `setprecision` manipulators, apply to the `ofstream` type. To these basic operations, the `ifstream` and `ofstream` types add some more operations designed specifically for file I/O.

Declaring File Streams

In a program, you declare stream variables the same way that you declare any variable—you specify the data type and then the variable name:

```
int        someInt;
float      someFloat;
ifstream   inFile;
ofstream   outFile;
```

(You don't have to declare the stream variables `cin` and `cout`. The header file `iostream` already does so for you.)

For our Mortgage program, let's name the input and output file streams `inData` and `outData`. We declare them like this:

```
ifstream inData;    // Holds loan amount, interest, and length
ofstream outData;   // Holds input values and monthly payments
```

Note that the `ifstream` type is for input files only, and the `ofstream` type is for output files only. With these data types, you cannot read from and write to the same file.

Opening Files

The third thing we have to do is prepare each file for reading or writing, an act called *opening a file*. Opening a file causes the computer's operating system to perform certain actions that allow us to proceed with file I/O.

In our example, we want to read from the file stream **inData** and write to the file stream **outData**. We open the relevant files by using these statements:

```
inData.open("loan.in");
outData.open("loan.out");
```

Both of these statements are function calls (notice the telltale arguments—the mark of a function). In each function call, the argument is a literal string enclosed by quotes. The first statement is a call to a function named **open**, which is associated with the **ifstream** data type. The second statement is a call to another function (also named **open**) associated with the **ofstream** data type. As we have seen earlier, we use dot notation (as in **inData.open**) to call certain library functions that are tightly associated with data types.

Exactly what does an **open** function do? First, it associates a stream variable used in your program with a physical file on disk. Our first function call creates a connection between the stream variable **inData** and the actual disk file, named **loan.in**. (Names of file streams must be identifiers; they are variables in your program. But some computer systems do not use this syntax for file names on disk. For example, many systems allow or even require a dot within a file name.) Similarly, the second function call associates the stream variable **outData** with the disk file **loan.out**. Associating a program's name for a file (**outData**) with the actual name for the file (**loan.out**) is much the same as associating a program's name for the standard output device (**cout**) with the actual device (the screen).[1]

The next thing the **open** function does depends on whether the file is an input file or an output file. With an input file, the **open** function sets the file's reading marker to the first piece of data in the file. (Each input file has its own reading marker.)

With an output file, the **open** function checks whether the file already exists. If the file doesn't exist, **open** creates a new, empty file for you. If the file already exists, **open** erases the old contents of the file. Then the writing marker is set at the beginning of the empty file (see **FIGURE 4.2**). As output proceeds, each successive output operation advances the writing marker to add data to the end of the file.

Because the reason for opening files is to *prepare* the files for reading or writing, you must open the files before using any input or output statements that refer to the files. In a program, it's a good idea to open files right away to be sure that the files are prepared before the program attempts any file I/O.

---

1. C++ provides a second means to declare a file variable and associate a file name with it, all in one statement. You can instead write

```
ifstream inData("loan.in");
ofstream outData("loan.out");
```

These statements are examples of what C++ calls parameterized constructors. This term is related to the object-oriented aspect of C++, which we explore in Chapter 12. Until then, we continue to declare and open files in separate statements.

FIGURE 4.2 The Effect of Opening a File

```
int main()
{
    // Declarations
      ⋮
    // Open the files

    inData.open("loan.in");
    outData.open("loan.out");
      ⋮
}
```

In addition to the **open** function, a **close** function is associated with both the **ifstream** and **ofstream** types. This function has no arguments and may be used as follows:

```
ifstream inFile;

inFile.open("mydata.dat"); // Open the file
  ⋮                        // Read and process the file data
inFile.close();            // Close the file
  ⋮
```

Closing a file causes the operating system to perform certain wrap-up activities on it and to break the connection between the stream variable and the file.

Should you always call the **close** function when you're finished reading or writing a file? In some programming languages, it's extremely important that you remember to do so. In C++, however, a file is automatically closed when program control leaves the block (compound statement) in which the stream variable is declared. (Until we get to Chapter 8, this block is assumed to be the body of the **main** function.) When control leaves this block, a special function associated with each of **ifstream** and **ofstream** called a *destructor* is implicitly executed; this destructor function closes the file for you. Consequently, C++ programs rarely call the **close** function explicitly. Conversely, many programmers make it a regular habit to call the **close** function explicitly, and you may wish to do so yourself.

Specifying File Streams in Input/Output Statements

There is just one more thing we have to do to use files. As we said earlier, all `istream` operations also are valid for the `ifstream` type, and all `ostream` operations are valid for the `ofstream` type. So, to read from or write to a file, all we need to do in our input and output statements is substitute the appropriate file stream variable for `cin` or `cout`. In our Mortgage program, we would use a statement like

```
inData >> loanAmount >> yearlyInterest >> numberOfYears;
```

to instruct the computer to read data from the file `inData`. Similarly, all of the output statements that write to the file `outData` would specify `outData`, not `cout`, as the destination:

```
outData << fixed << setprecision(2) << "For a loan amount of "
        << loanAmount
        << " with an interest rate of " << setprecision(4)
        << yearlyInterest  << " and a "
        << numberOfYears << " year mortgage, " << endl;
outData << fixed << setprecision(2)
        << "your monthly payments are $" << payment
        << "." << endl;
```

What is nice about C++ stream I/O is that we have a uniform syntax for performing I/O operations, regardless of whether we're working with the keyboard and screen, with files, or with other I/O devices.

SOFTWARE MAINTENANCE CASE STUDY: Adding File Input/Output to a Program

We have used the **Mortgage** program as an example to demonstrate file input and output. In this maintenance case study, we rework the complete program to use files.

The first steps in any maintenance project involve examining the original program, understanding how the code works, and creating a copy of the original code with which to work. Here is a listing of the original program with comments interspersed as we examine the code.

```
#include <iostream>                  // Access cout
#include <cmath>                     // Access power function
#include <iomanip>                   // Access manipulators
using namespace std;
```

These first four lines remain the same for any program that uses screen input/output, math functions, and formatting manipulators. Now, however, we will use file input/output. Thus the first line must be changed to include `fstream` rather than `iostream`.

```
const float LOAN_AMOUNT = 50000.00;     // Amount of the loan
const float YEARLY_INTEREST = 0.0524;   // Yearly interest rate
const int NUMBER_OF_YEARS = 7;          // Number of years
```

SOFTWARE MAINTENANCE CASE STUDY: Adding File Input/Output to a Program

These constants must be removed, and variable declarations inserted for `loanAmount`, `yearlyInterest`, and `numberOfYears`. These declarations should be placed within the function `main` along with the other declarations.

```cpp
int main()
{
  // Local variables
  float monthlyInterest;        // Monthly interest rate
  int numberOfPayments;         // Total number of payments
  float payment;                // Monthly payment
```

These declarations should remain the same, followed by the declarations for the values that were previously constants.

```cpp
  // Calculate values
  monthlyInterest = YEARLY_INTEREST / 12;
  numberOfPayments = NUMBER_OF_YEARS * 12;
  payment = (LOAN_AMOUNT * pow(1 + monthlyInterest,
     numberOfPayments) * monthlyInterest)/
      (pow(1 + monthlyInterest, numberOfPayments) - 1 );
```

These assignment statements must have the names of the constants replaced with the corresponding variable names. But before we do that, we must enter the values for the variables from the files.

```cpp
  // Output results
  cout << fixed << setprecision(2) << "For a loan amount of "
       << LOAN_AMOUNT  << " with an interest rate of "
       << YEARLY_INTEREST << " and a " << NUMBER_OF_YEARS
       << " year mortgage, " << endl;
  cout << " your monthly payments are $" << payment
       << "." << endl;
```

The constants need to be replaced by the variable names in these output statements. While we are making the changes, let's change the output to be in tabular form rather than sentence form.

```cpp
  return 0;
}
```

> **SOFTWARE MAINTENANCE CASE STUDY:** Adding File Input/Output to a Program
>
> Let's list the tasks necessary to make the changes.
>
> - Remove constants and insert variable declarations.
> - Read in the values for the variables.
> - Change assignments to use variables instead of constants.
> - Change output statements from constants to appropriate variables.
> - Make the output in table form.
>
> Have we forgotten anything? Yes: We must declare the file variables, which in turn means we must include **fstream**, and open the files. Although it isn't required, we also close the files so that you can see an example of doing this.
>
> Here is a listing of the revised program with the changes highlighted.

```cpp
//*************************************************************
// Mortgage Payment Calculator program
// This program determines the monthly payments on a mortgage
// given the loan amount, the yearly interest rate, and the
// number of years.
//*************************************************************
#include <fstream>
#include <cmath>
#include <iomanip>

using namespace std;
int main()
{
   // Input variables
   float loanAmount;
   float yearlyInterest;
   int numberOfYears;
   ofstream outData;
   ifstream inData;

   // Local variables
   float monthlyInterest;
   int numberOfPayments;
   float payment;

   // Open files
   inData.open("loan.in");
   outData.open("loan.out");

   // Read values
   inData >> loanAmount >> yearlyInterest >> numberOfYears;

   // Calculate values
   monthlyInterest = yearlyInterest / 12;
```

SOFTWARE MAINTENANCE CASE STUDY: Adding File Input/Output to a Program

```
    numberOfPayments = numberOfYears * 12;
    payment = (loanAmount * pow(1 + monthlyInterest, numberOfPayments)
            * monthlyInterest)/
             (pow(1 + monthlyInterest, numberOfPayments) - 1 );

    // Output results
    outData << fixed << "Loan amount:      " << setprecision(2)
        << loanAmount << endl << "Interest rate:    "
        << setprecision(4) << yearlyInterest  << endl
        << "Number of years: " << numberOfYears << endl;
    outData << fixed
        << "Monthly payment: " <<  setprecision(2) << payment << endl;

    // Close files
    inData.close();
    outData.close();
    return 0;
}
```

Before running the program, you would use the editor to create and save a file **loan.in** to serve as input. The contents of **loan.in** and **loan.out** are shown here:

loan.in

```
50000.00 0.0524 7
```

loan.out

```
Loan amount:      50000.00
Interest rate:    0.0524
Number of years:  7
Monthly payment: 712.35
```

In writing the new **Mortgage** program, what happens if you mistakenly specify **cout** instead of **outData** in one of the output statements? Nothing disastrous—the output of that one statement merely goes to the screen instead of the output file. And what if, by mistake, you specify **cin** instead of **inData** in the input statement? The consequences are not as pleasant: When you run the program, the computer will appear to go dead (to *hang*). Here's the reason: Execution reaches the input statement and the computer waits for you to enter the data from the keyboard. Of course, you don't know that the computer is waiting, because no message on the screen prompts you for input, and you are assuming (wrongly) that the program is getting its input from a data file. So the computer waits, and you wait, and the computer waits, and you wait. Every programmer at one time or another has had the experience of thinking the computer has hung, when, in fact, it is working just fine, silently waiting for keyboard input.

Run-Time Input of File Names

Until now, our examples of opening a file for input have included code similar to the following:

```
ifstream inFile;

inFile.open("datafile.dat");
```

The **open** function associated with the **ifstream** data type requires an argument that specifies the name of the actual data file. By using a literal string, as in the preceding example, the file name is fixed at compile time. Therefore, the program works for only this particular file.

We often want to make a program more flexible by allowing the file name to be determined at *run time*. A common technique is to prompt the user for the name of the file, read the user's response into a variable, and pass the variable as an argument to the **open** function. In principle, the following code should accomplish what we want. Unfortunately, the compiler does not allow it.

```
ifstream inFile;
string   fileName;

cout << "Enter the input file name: ";
cin >> fileName;
inFile.open(fileName);                       // Compile-time error
```

The problem is that the **open** function does not expect an argument of type string. Instead, it expects a *C string*. A C string (so named because it originated in the C language, the forerunner of C++) is a limited form of string whose properties we discuss much later in this book. A literal string, such as **"datafile.dat"**, happens to be a C string and thus is acceptable as an argument to the **open** function.

To make this code work correctly, we need to convert a **string** variable to a C string. The **string** data type provides a value-returning function named **c_str** that is applied to a **string** variable as follows:

```
fileName.c_str()
```

This function returns the C string that is equivalent to the one contained in the **fileName** variable. (The original string contained in **fileName** is not changed by the function call.) The primary purpose of the **c_str** function is to allow programmers to call library functions that expect C strings, not **string** strings, as arguments.

The following program reads in a file name and prints the first line on the file. The file and output are shown following the program.

```
//**************************************************
// This program demonstrates inputting file names.
//**************************************************

#include <fstream>
#include <iostream>
#include <string>
```

```
using namespace std;
int main ()
{
  ifstream inFile;
  string fileName;
  string inputString;
  cout << "Enter the input file name: ";
  cin >> fileName;
  inFile.open(fileName.c_str());

  getline(inFile, inputString);
  cout << "First line of file: " << inputString << endl;
  return 0;
}
```

File `testData.in`:

```
Oh what a beautiful day!
Rest of the data
on the file
```

Output:

```
Enter the input file name: testData.in
First line of file: Oh what a beautiful day!
```

QUICK CHECK

4.4.1 What is a file? (p. 152)
4.4.2 Why might we want a program to read from a file instead of the keyboard? (p. 152)
4.4.3 Why might we want a program to write output to a file instead of the console? (p. 152)
4.4.4 What are the four things we must do to have a program use file I/O? (p. 153)
4.4.5 Which data type is used for a file input stream? (p. 153)
4.4.6 Which data type is used for a file output stream? (p. 153)
4.4.7 What is wrong with the following code. (p. 160)

```
string filename = "data.txt";
ifstream inFile;
inFile.open(filename);
```

4.4.8 What conditions would you look for in a problem to decide whether interactive or noninteractive input is appropriate? (p. 152)
4.4.9 After including the header file `fstream` and declaring a file stream, what is the next step in using a file I/O? (p. 153)

4.5 Input Failure

When a program inputs data from the keyboard or an input file, things can go wrong. Suppose that we're executing a program. It prompts us to enter an integer value, but we absentmindedly type some letters of the alphabet. The input operation fails because of the invalid data. In C++ terminology, the `cin` stream has entered the *fail state*. Once a stream has entered the fail state, any further I/O operations using that stream are considered to be null operations—that is, they have no effect at all. Unfortunately for us, *the computer does not halt the program or display any error message*. The computer just continues executing the program, silently ignoring each additional attempt to use that stream.

Invalid data is the most common reason for input failure. When your program takes an `int` value as input, it expects to find only digits in the input stream, possibly preceded by a plus or minus sign. If there is a decimal point somewhere within the digits, does the input operation fail? Not necessarily—it depends on where the reading marker is. Let's look at an example.

Assume that a program has `int` variables `i`, `j`, and `k`, whose contents are currently 10, 20, and 30, respectively. The program now executes the following two statements:

```
cin >> i >> j >> k;
cout << "i: " << i << "  j: " << j << "  k: " << k;
```

If we type these characters for the input data:

```
1234.56  7  89
```

then the program produces this output:

```
i: 1234   j: 20   k: 30
```

Let's see why.

Remember that when reading `int` or `float` data, the extraction operator >> stops reading at the first character that is inappropriate for the data type (whitespace or otherwise). In our example, the input operation for `i` succeeds. The computer extracts the first four characters from the input stream and stores the integer value 1234 into `i`. The reading marker is now on the decimal point:

```
1234.56  7  89
```

The next input operation (for `j`) fails; an `int` value cannot begin with a decimal point. The `cin` stream is now in the fail state, and the current value of `j` (20) remains unchanged. The third input operation (for `k`) is ignored, as are all the rest of the statements in our program that read from `cin`.

Another way to make a stream enter the fail state is to try to open an input file that doesn't exist. Suppose that you have a data file named `myfile.dat`. Your program includes the following statements:

```
ifstream inFile;
inFile.open("myfil.dat");
inFile >> i >> j >> k;
```

In the call to the **open** function, you misspelled the name of your file. At run time, the attempt to open the file fails, so the stream `inFile` enters the fail state. The next three input operations (for `i`, `j`, and `k`) are null operations. Without issuing any error message, the program proceeds to use the (unknown) contents of i, j, and k in calculations. The results of these calculations are certain to be puzzling.

The point of this discussion is not to make you nervous about I/O but rather to make you aware of its limitations. The "Testing and Debugging" section at the end of this chapter offers suggestions for avoiding input failure, and Chapters 5 and 6 introduce program statements that let you test the state of a stream.

4.6 Software Design Methodologies

Over the last two chapters and the first part of this one, we have introduced elements of the C++ language that let us input data, perform calculations, and output results. The programs we have written so far were short and straightforward because the problems to be solved were simple. We are now ready to write programs for more complicated problems—but first we need to step back and look at the overall process of programming.

As you learned in Chapter 1, the programming process consists of a problem-solving phase and an implementation phase. The problem-solving phase includes *analysis* (analyzing and understanding the problem to be solved) and *design* (designing a solution to the problem). Given a complex problem—one that results in a 10,000-line program, for example—it's simply not reasonable to skip the design process and go directly to writing C++ code. What we need is a systematic way of designing a solution to a problem, no matter how complicated the problem is.

In the remainder of this chapter, we describe two important methodologies for designing solutions to more complex problems: *functional decomposition* and *object-oriented design*. These methodologies will help you create solutions that can be easily implemented as C++ programs. The resulting programs are readable, understandable, and easy to debug and modify.

One software design methodology that is in widespread use is known as object-oriented design (OOD). C++ evolved from the C language primarily to facilitate the use of the OOD methodology. Here we present the essential concepts of OOD; we expand our treatment of the approach later in the book. OOD is often used in conjunction with the other methodology that we discuss more fully in this chapter, functional decomposition.

Object-oriented design (OOD) A technique for developing software in which the solution is expressed in terms of objects—self-contained entities composed of data and operations on that data.

Functional decomposition A technique for developing software in which the problem is divided into more easily handled subproblems, the solutions of which create a solution to the overall problem.

OOD focuses on entities (*objects*) consisting of data and operations on the data. In OOD, we solve a problem by identifying the components that make up a solution and identifying how those components interact with one another through operations on the data that they contain. The result is a design for a set of objects that can be assembled to form a solution to a problem. In contrast, functional decomposition views the solution to a problem as a task to be accomplished. It focuses on the sequence of operations that are required to complete the task. When the problem requires a sequence of steps that is long or complex, we divide it into subproblems that are easier to solve.

The choice of which methodology to use depends on the problem at hand. For example, a large problem might involve several sequential phases of processing, such as gathering data and verifying its correctness with noninteractive processing, analyzing the data interactively, and printing reports noninteractively at the conclusion of the analysis. This process has a natural functional decomposition. Each of the phases, however, may best be solved by a set of objects that represent the data and the operations that can be applied to it. Some of the individual operations may be sufficiently complex that they require further decomposition, either into a sequence of operations or into another set of objects.

If you look at a problem and see that it is natural to think about it in terms of a collection of component parts, then you should use OOD to solve it. For example, a banking problem may require a `checkingAccount` object with associated operations `OpenAccount`, `WriteCheck`, `MakeDeposit`, and `IsOverdrawn`. The `checkingAccount` object might consist of both data (the account number and current balance, for example) and these operations, all bound together into one unit.

By contrast, if you find that it is natural to think of the solution to the problem as a series of steps, you should use functional decomposition. For example, when computing some statistical measures on a large set of real numbers, it is natural to decompose the problem into a sequence of steps that read a value, perform calculations, and then repeat the sequence. The C++ language and the standard library supply all of the operations that we need, and we simply write a sequence of those operations to solve the problem.

To summarize, top-down design methods focus on the *process* of transforming the input into the output, resulting in a hierarchy of tasks. Object-oriented design focuses on the *data objects* that are to be transformed, resulting in a hierarchy of objects. In reality, these design methods are often combined, with functional decomposition used to describe the actions of the objects specified in an object-oriented design.

QUICK CHECK

4.6.1 What is the first step in the object-oriented design process? (p. 163)

4.7 Functional Decomposition

In functional decomposition (also called *structured design*, *top-down design*, *stepwise refinement*, and *modular programming*), we work from the abstract (a list of the major steps in our solution) to the particular (algorithmic steps that can be translated directly into C++ code). You can also think of this methodology as working from a high-level solution, leaving the details of the implementation unspecified, down to a fully detailed solution.

The easiest way to solve a problem is to give it to someone else and say, "Solve this problem." This is the most abstract level of a problem solution: a single-statement solution that encompasses the entire problem without specifying any of the details of implementation. It's at this point that we programmers are called in. Our job is to turn the abstract solution into a concrete solution, a program.

If the solution clearly involves a series of major steps, we break it down (decompose it) into pieces. In the process, we move to a lower level of abstraction—that is, some of the implementation details (but not too many) are now specified. Each of the major steps becomes an independent subproblem that we can work on separately. In a large project, one person (the *chief architect* or *team leader*) formulates the subproblems for other members of the team, saying to each one, "Solve this problem." In the case of a small project, we give the subproblems to ourselves. Then we choose one subproblem at a time to solve. We may break the subproblem into another series of steps that, in turn, become smaller subproblems. Or we may identify components that are naturally represented as objects. The process continues until each subproblem cannot be divided further or has an obvious solution.

Why do we work this way? Why not simply write out all of the details? Because it is much easier to focus on one problem at a time. For example, suppose you are working on a program and discover that you need a complex formula to calculate an appropriate fieldwidth for printing a value. Calculating fieldwidths is not the purpose of this part of the program. If you shift your focus to the calculation, you are likely to forget some detail of the overall process. So you write down an abstract step—"Calculate the fieldwidth"—and go on. Once you've written out the major steps, you can go back to working out the calculation.

By subdividing the problem, you create a hierarchical structure called a *tree structure*. Each level of the tree is a complete solution to the problem that is less abstract (more detailed) than the level above it. **FIGURE 4.3** shows a generic solution tree for a problem. Steps that are shaded have enough detail to be translated directly into C++ statements; these are concrete steps. Those that are not shaded are abstract steps; they reappear as subproblems in the next level down. Each box in the figure represents a module. Modules are the basic building blocks in a functional decomposition. The diagram in Figure 4.3 is also called a module structure chart.

Functional decomposition uses the divide-and-conquer approach to problem solving. In other words, it breaks up large problems into smaller units that are easier to handle. OOD does this, too, but in OOD the units are objects, whereas the units in functional decomposition are modules.

> **Concrete step** A step for which the implementation details are fully specified.
>
> **Abstract step** A step for which some implementation details remain unspecified.
>
> **Module** A self-contained collection of steps that solves a problem or subproblem; can contain both concrete and abstract steps.
>
> **Functional equivalence** A property of a module that performs exactly the same operation as the abstract step it defines. A pair of modules are also functionally equivalent to each other when they perform exactly the same operation.

Modules

A module begins life as an abstract step in the next-higher level of the solution tree. It is completed when it solves a given subproblem—that is, when it specifies a series of steps that does the same thing as the higher-level abstract step. At this stage, a module is functionally equivalent to the abstract step.

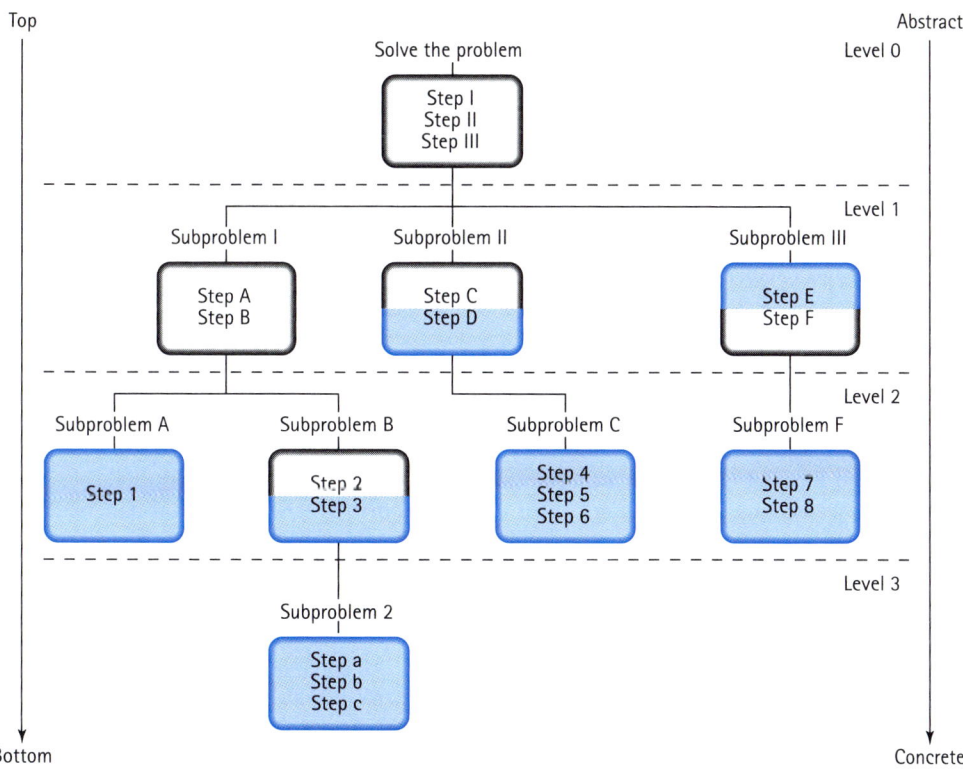

FIGURE 4.3 Hierarchical Solution Tree

> **Functional cohesion** A property of a module in which all concrete steps are directed toward solving just one problem, and any significant subproblems are written as abstract steps.

(Don't confuse our use of *function* here with C++ functions. Here we use the term to refer to the specific role that the module or step plays in an algorithmic solution.)

In a properly written module, the only steps that directly address the given subproblem are concrete steps; abstract steps are used for significant new subproblems. This is called functional cohesion.

The idea behind functional cohesion is that each module should do just one thing and do it well. Functional cohesion is not a well-defined property; there is no quantitative measure of cohesion. Rather, it is a product of the human need to organize things into neat chunks that are easy to understand and remember.

Knowing which details to make concrete and which to leave abstract is a matter of experience, circumstance, and personal style. For example, you might decide to include a fieldwidth calculation in a printing module if there isn't so much detail in the rest of the module that it becomes confusing. In contrast, if the calculation is performed several times, it makes sense to write it as a separate module and just refer to it each time you need it.

Writing Cohesive Modules

Here's one approach to writing modules that are cohesive:

1. Think about how you would solve the subproblem by hand.
2. Write down the major steps.
3. If a step is simple enough that you can see how to implement it directly in C++, it is at the concrete level; it doesn't need any further refinement.
4. If you have to think about implementing a step as a series of smaller steps or as several C++ statements, it is still at an abstract level.
5. If you are trying to write a series of steps and start to feel overwhelmed by details, you probably are bypassing one or more levels of abstraction. Stand back and look for pieces that you can write as more abstract steps.

We could call this the "procrastinator's technique." If a step is cumbersome or difficult, put it off to a lower level; don't think about it today, think about it tomorrow. Of course, tomorrow does come, but the whole process can be applied again to the subproblem. A trouble spot often seems much simpler when you can focus on it. And eventually the whole problem is broken up into manageable units.

As you work your way down the solution tree, you make a series of design decisions. If a decision proves awkward or wrong (and many times it does!), you can backtrack (go back up the tree to a higher-level module) and try something else. You don't have to scrap your whole design—only the small part you are working on. You may explore many intermediate steps and trial solutions before you reach a final design.

Pseudocode

You'll find it easier to implement a design if you write the steps in pseudocode. *Pseudocode* is a mixture of English statements and C++-like control structures that can be translated easily into C++. (We've been using pseudocode in the algorithms in the Problem-Solving Case Studies.) When a concrete step is written in pseudocode, it should be possible to rewrite it directly as a C++ statement in a program.

Implementing the Design

The product of functional decomposition is a hierarchical solution to a problem with multiple levels of abstraction. Figure 4.4 shows a functional decomposition for the revised Mortgage program. This kind of solution forms the basis for the implementation phase of programming.

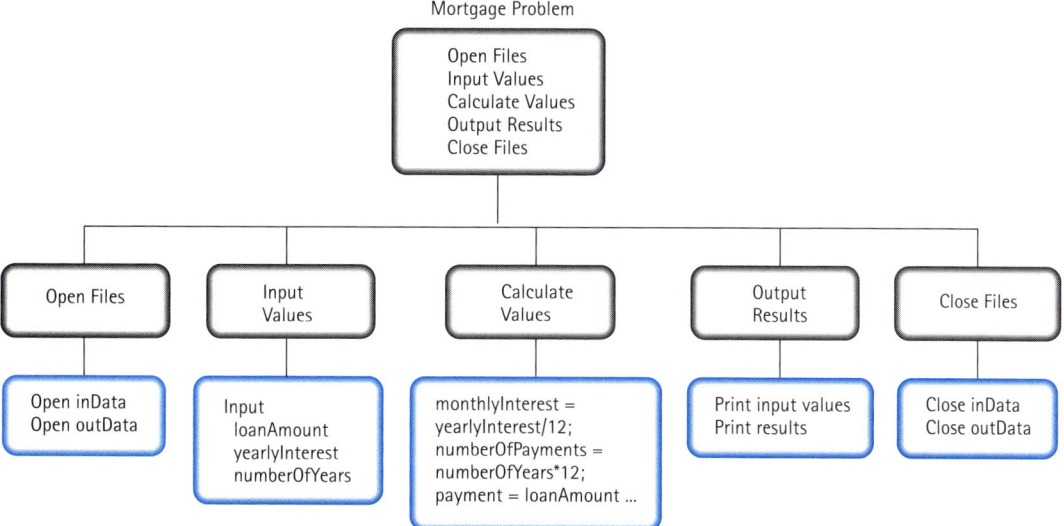

FIGURE 4.4 Solution Tree of Mortgage Program

How do we translate a functional decomposition into a C++ program? If you look closely at **FIGURE 4.4**, you can see that the concrete steps (which are shaded) can be assembled into a complete algorithm for solving the problem. The order in which they are assembled is determined by their position in the tree. We start at the top of the tree, at level 0, with the first step, "Open Files." Because it is abstract, we must go to the next level, level 1. There we find a series of concrete steps that correspond to this step; this series of steps becomes the first part of our algorithm. Because the conversion process is now concrete, we can go back to level 0 and go on to the next step, "Input Values." Because it is abstract, we go to level 1 and find a series of concrete steps that correspond to this step; this series of steps becomes the next part of our algorithm. Returning to level 0, we go on to the next step, "Calculate Values." Finally we return to level 0 for the last time and complete the last steps, "Output Results" and "Close Files."

```
Open inData
Open outData
Input loanAmount, yearlyInterest, numberOfYears
Set monthlyInterest to yearlyInterest divided by 12
Set numberOfPayments to numberOfYears times 12
Set payment to (loanAmount * pow(1 + monthlyInterest, numberOfPayments)
   * monthlyInterest) / (pow(1 + monthlyInterest, numberOfPayments) – 1)
Print "For a loan amount of " loanAmount "with an interest rate of "
   yearlyInterest " and a " numberOfYears " year mortgage, "
Print "your monthly payments are $" payment "."
Close inData
Close outData
```

From this algorithm we can construct a table of the variables required, and then write the declarations and executable statements of the program.

In practice, you write your design not as a tree diagram, but rather as a series of modules grouped by levels of abstraction.

Main — Level 0

Open Files
Input Values
Calculate Values
Output Results
Close Files

Open Files — Level 1

Open inData
Open outData

Input Values

Input loanAmount
Input yearlyInterest
Input numberOfyears

Calculate Values

Set monthlyInterest to yearlyInterest divided by 12
Set numberOfPayments to numberOfYears times 12
Set payment to (loanAmount * pow(1 + monthlyInterest, numberrOfPayments)
 * monthlyInterest) / (pow(1 + monthlyInterest, numberOfPayments) − 1)

Output

Print "Loan amount: " loanAmount
Print "Interest rate: " yearlyInterest
Print "Number of years: " numberOfYears
Print "Monthly payment: " payment

Close Files

Close inData
Close outData

If you look at the C++ program for **Mortgage**, you can see that it closely resembles this solution. The names of the modules are also paraphrased as comments in the code.

The type of implementation that we've introduced here is called a *flat* or *inline implementation*. We are flattening the two-dimensional, hierarchical structure of the solution by writing all of the steps as one long sequence. This kind of implementation is adequate when a solution is short and has only a few levels of abstraction. The programs it produces are clear and easy to understand, assuming appropriate comments and good style.

Longer programs, with more levels of abstraction, are difficult to work with as flat implementations. In Chapter 8, you'll see that it is preferable to implement a hierarchical solution by using a *hierarchical implementation*. There we implement many of the modules by writing them as separate C++ functions, and the abstract steps in the design are then replaced with calls to those functions.

One advantage of implementing modules as functions is that they can be called from different places in a program. For example, if a problem requires that the volume of a cylinder be computed in several places, we could write a single function to perform this calculation and simply call it in each place. This gives us a *semihierarchical implementation*. Such an implementation does not preserve a pure hierarchy because abstract steps at various levels of the solution tree share one implementation of a module (see **FIGURE 4.5**). A shared module actually falls outside the hierarchy because it doesn't really belong at any one level.

Another advantage of implementing modules as functions is that you can pick them up and use them in other programs. Over time, you will build a library of your own functions to complement those that are supplied by the C++ standard library.

We will postpone a detailed discussion of hierarchical implementations until Chapter 8. For now, our programs remain short enough for flat implementations to suffice. Chapters 5

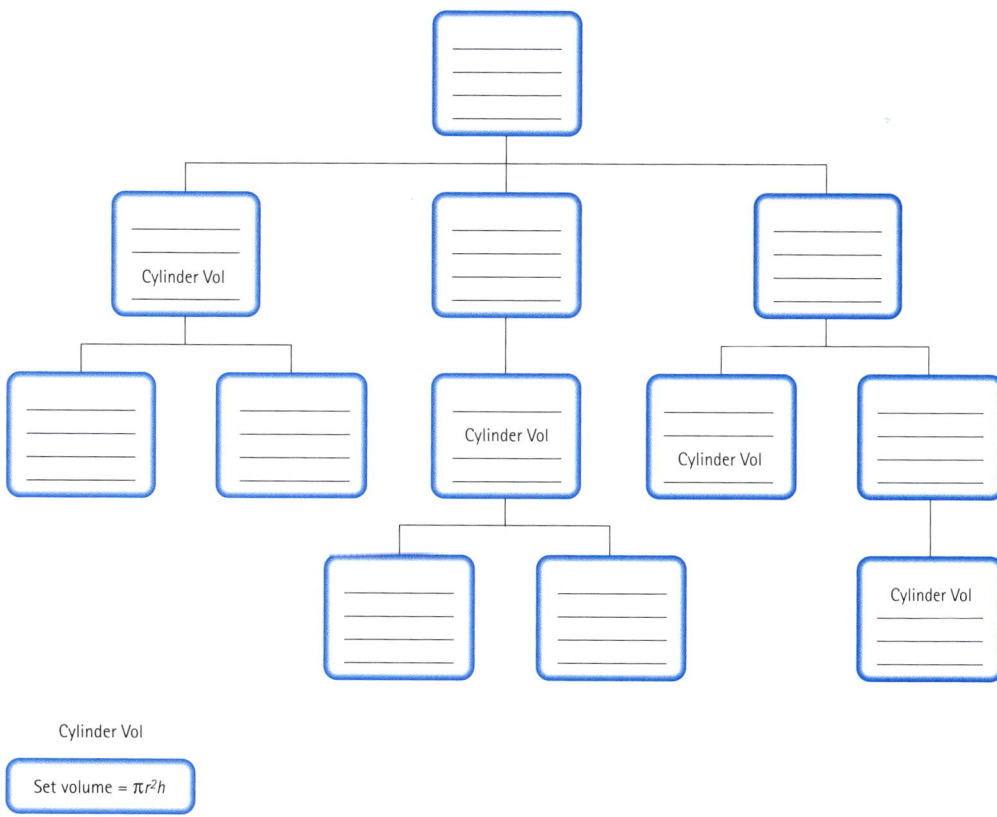

FIGURE 4.5 A Semihierarchical Module Structure Chart with a Shared Module

and 6 examine topics such as flow of control, preconditions and postconditions, interface design, and side effects that you'll need to develop hierarchical implementations.

From now on, we use the following outline for the functional decompositions in our case studies, and we recommend that you adopt a similar outline in solving your own programming problems:

Problem statement
Input description
Output description
Discussion
Assumptions (if any)
Main module
Remaining modules by levels
Module structure chart

In some of our case studies, this outline is reorganized a bit, so that the input and output descriptions follow the discussion. In later chapters, we also expand the outline with additional sections. Don't think of this outline as a rigid prescription—it is more like a "to-do list." We want to be sure to do everything on the list, but the individual circumstances of each problem guide the order in which we do them.

A Perspective on Design

We have looked at two design methodologies, object-oriented design and functional decomposition. Until we learn about additional C++ language features that support OOD, we will use functional decomposition in the next several chapters to come up with our problem solutions.

An important perspective to keep in mind is that functional decomposition and OOD are not separate, disjoint techniques. OOD decomposes a problem into objects. Objects not only contain data but also have associated operations. The operations on objects require algorithms. Sometimes the algorithms are complicated and must be decomposed into subalgorithms by using functional decomposition. Experienced programmers are familiar with both methodologies and know when to use one or the other, or a combination of the two.

Remember that the problem-solving phase of the programming process takes time. If you spend the bulk of your time analyzing and designing a solution, then coding and implementing the program should take relatively little time.

SOFTWARE ENGINEERING TIP   Documentation

As you create your functional decomposition or object-oriented design, you are developing documentation for your program. *Documentation* includes the written problem specifications, design, development history, and actual code of a program.

Good documentation helps other programmers read and understand a program and is invaluable when software is being debugged and modified (maintained). If you haven't looked at your program for six months and need

SOFTWARE ENGINEERING TIP Documentation, continued

to change it, you'll be happy that you documented it well. Of course, if someone else has to use and modify your program, documentation is indispensable.

Documentation is both external and internal to the program. External documentation includes the specifications, the development history, and the design documents. Internal documentation includes the program format and *self-documenting code*—meaningful identifiers and comments. You can use the pseudocode from the design process as comments in your programs.

> **Self-documenting code** Program code containing meaningful identifiers as well as judiciously used clarifying comments.

This kind of documentation may be sufficient for someone reading or maintaining your programs. However, if a program will be used by people who are not programmers, you must provide a user's manual as well.

Be sure to keep documentation up to date. Indicate any changes you make in a program in all of the pertinent documentation. Use self-documenting code to make your programs more readable.

QUICK CHECK

4.7.1 What characterizes a concrete step in a functional decomposition design? (pp. 164–166)
4.7.2 If you are given a functional decomposition design, how do you implement it? (pp. 166–167)
4.7.3 In functional decomposition we work from the _____ to the _____. (p. 164)
4.7.4 If a solution clearly involves a series of major steps, what must we do? (p. 164)
4.7.5 What is a module? (p. 165)
4.7.6 What is functional cohesion? (p. 166)
4.7.7 What is pseudocode? (p. 166)
4.7.8 Where do we start when translating a functional decomposition into a C++ program? (p. 167)

Now let's look at a case study that demonstrates functional decomposition.

Problem-Solving Case Study

Displaying a Name in Multiple Formats

PROBLEM: You are beginning to work on a problem that needs to output names in several formats along with the corresponding Social Security number. As a start, you decide to write a short C++ program that takes a Social Security number as input and a single name and displays them in the different formats so you can be certain that all of your string expressions are correct.

INPUT: The Social Security number and a name in three parts, on file `name.dat`, each separated by one or more whitespace characters.

Problem-Solving Case Study

OUTPUT: The name is to be written in four different formats on file `name.out`:

1. First name, middle name, last name, Social Security number
2. Last name, first name, middle name, Social Security number
3. Last name, first name, middle initial, Social Security number
4. First name, middle initial, last name

DISCUSSION: You could easily type the Social Security number and the name in the four formats as string literals in the code, but the purpose of this exercise is to develop and test the string expressions that you need for the larger problem. The problem statement doesn't say in which order the parts of the name are entered on the file, but it does say that they are separated by whitespace. You assume that they are in first name, middle name or initial, and last name order. Because the data are on a file, you don't need to prompt for the values. Once you have the Social Security number and the name, you just write them out in the various formats.

ASSUMPTION: The name is in first, middle, and last order on the file.

Main Module — Level 0

Open files
Get Social Security number
Get name
Write data in proper formats
Close files

Open Files — Level 1

Open inData
Open outData

The "Get Social Security number" step can be directly implemented by reading into the `string` variable. Thus it doesn't require expansion at Level 1 of our design.

Get Name

Get first name
Get middle name or initial
Get last name

Does reading the middle name present a problem if the file contains an initial rather than a middle name? Not really. You just assume that a middle name is entered and extract the initial from the middle name when you need it for the third and fourth formats. If the initial was entered for the middle name, then the second and third output forms will be the same.

What about punctuation in the output? If the last name comes first, it should be followed by a comma, and the middle initial should be followed by a period. Thus, if an initial is entered rather than a middle name, it must be followed by a period. This must be added to the assumptions.

Problem-Solving Case Study

ASSUMPTION: The name is in first, middle, and last order, and a period must follow the middle initial if it is entered instead of a middle name.

Write Data in Proper Formats

Write first name, blank, middle name, blank, last name, blank, Social Security number
Write last name, comma, blank first name, blank, middle name, blank, Social Security number
Write last name, comma, blank, first name, blank, middle initial, period, blank, Social Security number
Write first name, blank, middle initial, period, blank, last name

The only thing left to define is the middle initial. We can directly access the first character in the middle name.

Middle Initial   Level 2

Set initial to middleName.at(0)

Close Files

Close inData
Close outData

MODULE STRUCTURE CHART

Below is the program. The input data and the output follow the program.

```
//*************************************************************
// Format Names program
// This program reads in a Social Security number, a first name, a
// middle name or initial, and a last name from file inData.
// The name is written to file outData in three formats:
//   1. First name, middle name, last name, and Social Security
//      number.
//   2. Last name, first name, middle name, and Social
//      Security number
```

Problem-Solving Case Study

```cpp
//    3. Last name, first name, middle initial, and Social Security
//       number
//    4. First name, middle initial, last name
//*****************************************************************
#include <fstream>                  // Access ofstream
#include <string>                   // Access string

using namespace std;

int main()
{
  // Declare and open files
  ifstream inData;
  ofstream outData;
  inData.open("name.in");
  outData.open("name.out");

  // Declare variables
  string socialNum;                 // Social Security number
  string firstName;                 // First name
  string lastName;                  // Last name
  string middleName;                // Middle name
  char initial;                     // Middle initial

  // Read in data from file inData
  inData >> socialNum >> firstName >> middleName >> lastName;

  // Access middle initial and append a period
  initial = middleName.at(0);

  // Output information in required formats
  outData << firstName << ' ' << middleName << ' ' << lastName
          << ' ' << socialNum << endl;
  outData << lastName << ", " << firstName << ' ' << middleName
          << ' ' << socialNum  << endl;
  outData << lastName << ", " << firstName << ' ' << initial
          << ". " << socialNum  << endl;
  outData << firstName << ' ' << initial << ". " << lastName;

  // Close files
  inData.close();
  outData.close();
  return 0;
}
```

Input file:

```
333-55-3456 Clara Jones Jacobey
```

Problem-Solving Case Study

Testing and Debugging

An important part of implementing a program is testing it (checking the results). By now you should realize that there is nothing magical about the computer. It is infallible only if the person writing the instructions and entering the data is infallible. Don't trust the computer to give you the correct answers until you've verified enough of them by hand to convince yourself that the program is working.

From here on, these "Testing and Debugging" sections offer tips on how to test your programs and what to do if a program doesn't work the way you expect it to work. But don't wait until you've found a bug to read the "Testing and Debugging" sections—it's much easier to prevent bugs than to fix them.

When testing programs that receive data values from a file as input, it's possible for input operations to fail. And when input fails in C++, the computer doesn't issue a warning message or terminate the program. Instead, the program simply continues executing, ignoring any further input operations on that file. The two most common reasons for input failure are invalid data and the *end-of-file error*.

An end-of-file error occurs when the program has read all of the input data available in the file and needs more data to fill the variables in its input statements. It might be that the data file simply was not prepared properly. Perhaps it contains fewer data items than the program requires. Or perhaps the format of the input data is wrong. Leaving out whitespace between numeric values, for instance, is guaranteed to cause trouble.

As an example, suppose we want a data file to contain three integer values: 25, 16, and 42. Look what happens with this data:

2516 42

and this code:

```
inFile >> i >> j >> k;
```

The first two input operations use up the data in the file, leaving the third with no data to read. The stream `inFile` enters the fail state, so `k` isn't assigned a new value and the computer quietly continues executing at the next statement in the program.

If the data file is prepared correctly and an end-of-file error still occurs, the problem lies in the program logic. For some reason, the program is attempting too many input operations.

In this case, the error could be a simple oversight such as specifying too many variables in a particular input statement. It could be a misuse of the `ignore` function, causing values to be skipped inadvertently. Or it could be a serious flaw in the algorithm. You should check all of these possibilities.

The other major source of input failure—invalid data—has several possible causes. The most common is an error in the preparation or entry of the data. Numeric and character data mixed inappropriately in the input can cause the input stream to fail if it is supposed to read a numeric value but the reading marker is positioned at a character that isn't allowed in the number. Another cause is using the wrong variable name (which happens to be of the wrong data type) in an input statement. Declaring a variable to be of the wrong data type is a variation on the problem. Finally, leaving out a variable (or including an extra one) in an input statement can cause the reading marker to end up positioned on the wrong type of data.

Another oversight, which doesn't cause input failure but does cause programmer frustration, is to use `cin` or `cout` in an I/O statement when you meant to specify a file stream. If you mistakenly use `cin` instead of an input file stream, the program stops and waits for input from the keyboard. If you mistakenly use `cout` instead of an output file stream, you get unexpected output on the screen.

By giving you a framework that can help you organize and keep track of the details involved in designing and implementing a program, functional decomposition (and, later, object-oriented design) should help you avoid many of these errors in the first place.

In later chapters, you'll see that you can test modules separately. If you make sure that each module works by itself, your program should work when you put all the modules together. Testing modules separately is less work than trying to test an entire program. In a smaller section of code, it's less likely that multiple errors will combine to produce behavior that is difficult to analyze.

Testing and Debugging Hints

1. Input and output statements always begin with the name of a stream object, and the >> and << operators point in the direction in which the data is going. The statement

    ```
    cout << n;
    ```

    sends data to the output stream `cout`, and the statement

    ```
    cin >> n;
    ```

    sends data to the variable `n`.

2. When a program takes input from or sends output to a file, each I/O statement from or to the file should use the name of the file stream, not `cin` or `cout`.

3. The `open` function associated with an `ifstream` or `ofstream` object requires a C string as an argument. The argument cannot be a `string` object. At this point in the book, the argument can only be (a) a literal string or (b) the C string returned by the function call `myString.c_str()`, where `myString` is of type `string`.

4. When you open a data file for input, make sure that the argument to the `open` function supplies the correct name of the file.

5. When reading a character string into a `string` object, the >> operator stops at, *but does not consume*, the first trailing whitespace character.

6. Each input statement must specify the correct number of variables, and each of those variables must be of the correct data type.
7. If your input data is mixed (character and numeric values), be sure to deal with intervening blanks.
8. Echo print the input data to verify that each value is where it belongs and is in the proper format. (This is crucial, because an input failure in C++ doesn't produce an error message or terminate the program.)

Summary

Programs operate on data. If data and programs are kept separate, the data is available to use with other programs, and the same program can be run with different sets of input data.

The extraction operator (>>) inputs data from the keyboard or a file, storing the data into the variable specified as its right-hand operand. The extraction operator skips any leading whitespace characters and finds the next data value in the input stream. The `get` function does not skip leading whitespace characters; instead, it takes the very next character and stores it into the `char` variable specified in its argument list. Both the >> operator and the `get` function leave the reading marker positioned at the next character to be read. The next input operation begins reading at the point indicated by the marker.

The newline character (denoted by \n in a C++ program) marks the end of a data line. You create a newline character each time you press the Return or Enter key. Your program generates a newline each time you use the `endl` manipulator or explicitly output the \n character. Newline is a control character, so it is not a printable character. It controls the movement of the screen cursor.

Interactive programs prompt the user for each data entry and directly inform the user of results and errors. Designing interactive dialog through use of prompts is an exercise in the art of communication.

Noninteractive input/output allows data to be prepared before a program is run and allows the program to run again with the same data in the event that a problem crops up during processing.

Data files often are used for noninteractive processing and to permit the output from one program to be used as input to another program. To use these files, you must do four things: (1) include the header file `fstream`, (2) declare the file streams along with your other variable declarations, (3) prepare the files for reading or writing by calling the `open` function, and (4) specify the name of the file stream in each input or output statement that uses it.

Object-oriented design and functional decomposition are methodologies for tackling nontrivial programming problems. Object-oriented design produces a problem solution by focusing on objects and their associated operations. Functional decomposition begins with an abstract solution that then is divided into major steps. Each step becomes a subproblem that is analyzed and subdivided further. A concrete step is one that can be translated directly into C++; those steps that need more refining are called abstract steps. A module is a collection of concrete and abstract steps that solves a subproblem. Programs can be built out of modules using a flat implementation, a hierarchical implementation, or a semihierarchical implementation.

Careful attention to program design, program formatting, and documentation produces highly structured and readable programs.

Quick Check Answers

4.1.1 `cin >> a >> b >> c;` 4.1.2 `first = "Jones,"` `middle = "Walker"` `last = "Thomas"` 4.1.3 input. 4.1.4 `<<` 4.1.5 Because an input statement indicates where input data values should be stored. 4.1.6 To keep track of the point in the input stream where the computer should continue reading. 4.1.7 `cin.get(ch)` 4.1.8 `cin.ignore(10, ' ');` 4.2.1 To tell the user how and when to enter values as input. 4.2.2 A printed message explaining what the user should enter. 4.4.1 A named area in secondary storage that holds a collection of information. 4.4.2 If a program will read a large quantity of data, it is easier to enter the data into a file with an editor than to enter it while the program is running. 4.4.3 The contents of a file can be displayed on a screen, printed, or used as input to another program. 4.4.4 1. Include the `fstream` library, 2. Declare the file streams we will use, 3. Use the `open` function to open a file, 4. Use the file stream in each input or output statement. 4.4.5 `ifstream` 4.4.6 `ofstream` 4.4.7 we must use the `filename.c_str` function to return a C string because that is what the `inFile.open` function expects as its argument type. 4.4.8 The amount of data to be input, and whether the data can be prepared for entry before the program is run. 4.4.9 Preparing the file for reading or writing with the `open` function. 4.6.1 To identify the major objects in the problem. 4.7.1 It is a step that can be implemented directly in a programming language. 4.7.2 By identifying all of the concrete steps, starting from the top of the tree, and arranging them in the proper order. The sequence of steps is then converted step-by-step into code. 4.7.3 Abstract, particular. 4.7.4 We break the problem down into pieces. 4.7.5 A module is an abstract step in the next-higher level of the solution tree. 4.7.6 A property of a module in which all concrete steps are directed toward solving just one problem, and any significant subproblems are written as abstract. 4.7.7 A mixture of English statements and C++-like control structures that can be translated easily into C++. 4.7.8 We start with the concrete steps at the bottom of the decomposition tree.

Exam Preparation Exercises

1. The statement

   ```
   cin >> maximum >> minimum;
   ```

   is equivalent to the two statements:

   ```
   cin >> minimum;
   cin >> maximum;
   ```

   True or false?

2. What is wrong with each of the following statements?

   a. `cin << score;`
   b. `cout >> maximum;`
   c. `cin >> "Enter data";`
   d. `cin.ignore('Y', 35);`
   e. `getline(someString, cin);`

3. Suppose the input data are entered as follows:

   ```
   10  20
   30  40
   50  60
   70  80
   ```

   The input statements that read it are

   ```
   cin >> a >> b >> c;
   cin >> d >> e >> f;
   cin >> a >> b;
   ```

   What are the contents of the variables a, b, c, d, e, and f after the statements have executed?

4. Suppose the input data are entered as follows:

   ```
   10   20   30   40   50   60
   10   20   30   40   50   60
   10   20   30   40   50   60
   70   80
   ```

   The input statements that read it are

   ```
   cin >> a >> b >> c;
   cin.ignore(100, '\n');
   cin.get(ch1);
   cin >> d >> e >> f;
   cin.ignore(100, '\n');
   cin.ignore(100, '\n');
   cin >> a >> b;
   ```

   What are the contents of the variables a, b, c, d, e, and f after the statements have executed?

5. Given the input data

   ```
   January 25, 2005
   ```

   and the input statement

   ```
   cin >> string1 >> string2;
   ```

   a. What is contained in each of the string variables after the statement is executed?
   b. Where is the reading marker after the statement is executed?

6. Given the input data

   ```
   January 25, 2005
   ```

   and the input statement

   ```
   getline(cin, string1);
   ```

   a. What is contained in the string variable after the statement is executed?
   b. Where is the reading marker after the statement is executed?

7. Given the input data

   ```
   January 25, 2005
   ```

   and the input statement (where the type of each variable is given by its name)

   ```
   cin >> string1 >> int1 >> char1 >> string2;
   ```

   a. What is contained in each of the variables after the statement is executed?
   b. Where is the reading marker after the statement is executed?

8. If the reading marker is on the newline character at the end of a line, and you call the **get** function, what value does it return in its argument?

9. What do the two arguments to the **ignore** function specify?

10. You are writing a program whose input is a date in the form of mm/dd/yyyy.
    a. Write an output statement to prompt an inexperienced user to enter a date.
    b. Write an output statement to prompt an experienced user to input a date.
11. What are the four steps necessary to use a file for input or output?
12. What are the two file stream data types discussed in this chapter?
13. What is the purpose of the following statements?

    ```
    ifstream inFile;
    inFile.open("datafile.dat");
    ```

14. Correct the following code segment so that it opens the file whose name is entered via the input statement.

    ```
    ifstream inData;
    string name;

    cout << "Enter the name of the file: ");
    cin >> name;
    infile.open(name);
    ```

15. What happens when an input operation is performed on a file that is in the fail state?
16. When you try to open a file that doesn't exist, C++ outputs an error message and terminates execution of the program. True or false?
17. Just opening an input file stream cannot cause it to enter the fail state. True or false?
18. You're writing a program for a rental car company that keeps track of vehicles. What are the major objects in this problem?
19. Define the following terms:
    a. Concrete step
    b. Abstract step
    c. Module
    d. Functional equivalence
    e. Functional cohesion
20. Which C++ construct do we use to implement modules?
21. Which of the following are member functions of the `istream` class?
    a. `>>`
    b. `ignore`
    c. `get`
    d. `getline`
    e. `cin`
22. The `open` function is associated with both the `ifstream` and the `ofstream` data types. True or false?

▪ Programming Warm-Up Exercises

1. Write a C++ input statement that reads three integer values into the variables `int1`, `int2`, and `int3`, in that order.
2. Write a prompting output statement and then an input statement that reads a name into three string variables: `first`, `middle`, and `last`. The name is to be entered in the following format: first middle last.

3. Write a prompting output statement and then an input statement that reads a name into a single string variable, name. The name is to be entered on one line, in the following format: first middle last.

4. Write the statements necessary to prompt for and input three floating-point values, and then output their average. For this exercise, assume that the user has no prior experience with computers and needs very detailed instructions. To help avoid errors, the user should enter each value separately.

5. Write the statements necessary to prompt for and input three floating-point values, and then output their average. For this exercise, assume that the user has plenty of experience with computers and needs minimal instructions. The user should enter all three values on one line.

6. Write the declarations and input statements necessary to read each of the following sets of data values into variables of the appropriate types. You choose the names of the variables. In some cases, punctuation marks or special symbols must be skipped.

   a. 100 A 98.6
   b. February 23 March 19
   c. 19, 25, 103.876
   d. A a B b
   e. $56.45

7. Write a single input statement that reads the following lines of data into the variables streetNum, street1, street2, town, state, and zip.

   782 Maple Avenue
   Blithe, CO 56103

8. Write the statements necessary to prepare a file called temperatures.dat for reading as an ifstream called temps.

9. The file temperatures.dat contains a list of six temperatures, arranged one per line. Assuming that the file has already been prepared for reading, as described in Exercise 8, write the statements to read in the data from the file and print out the average temperature. You will also need to declare the necessary float variables to accomplish this task.

10. Fill in the blanks in the following program:

```
#include <iostream>
#include _____

using namespace std;

_____ inData;
_____ outData;
const float  PI = 3.14159265;
float  radius;
float  circumference;
float  area;

int main()
{
    _____("inData.dat");
    _____("outData.dat");
    _____ >> radius;
```

```
        circumference = radius * 2 * PI;
        area = radius * radius * PI;
        cout << "For the first circle, the circumference is "
             << circumference << " and the area is " << area << endl;
    ____ << radius << " " << circumference << " " << area
             << endl;
    _____ >> radius;
        circumference = radius * 2 * PI;
        area = radius * radius * PI;
        cout << "For the second circle, the circumference is "
             << circumference << " and the area is " << area << endl;
    _____ << radius << " " << circumference << " " << area
             << endl;
        return 0;
    }
```

11. Modify the program in Exercise 10 so that it allows the user to enter the name of the output file instead of having the program use `outData.dat`.
12. The file stream `inFile` contains two integer values. Write an input statement that will cause it to enter the fail state.
13. Write a code segment that prompts the user for a file name, reads the file name into a `string` called `filename`, and then opens the file stream `userFile` using the supplied name.
14. Use functional decomposition to write an algorithm for writing and mailing a business letter.

■ Programming Problems

1. Write a C++ program that computes a student's grade for an assignment as a percentage given the student's score and the total points. The final score should be rounded up to the nearest whole value using the `ceil` function in the `<cmath>` header file. You should also display the floating-point result up to 5 decimal places. The input to the program must come from a file containing a single line with the score and total separated by a space.

2. Write a program that reads a line from a file called `quote.txt` containing the text,

   `a b c d e f`

   And writes the uppercase version of that line in reverse to the output file named `upquote.txt`.

3. Write an interactive C++ program that inputs a name from the user in the following format:

   `last, first middle`

   The program should then output the name in the following format:

   `first middle last`

   The program will have to use string operations to remove the comma from the end of the last name. Be sure to use proper formatting and appropriate comments in your code. The input should have an appropriate prompt, and the output should be labeled clearly and formatted neatly.

4. Write an interactive C++ program whose input is a series of 12 temperatures from the user. It should write out on file `tempdata.dat` each temperature as well as the difference between the current temperature and the one preceding it. The difference is not output for the first temperature that is input. At the end of the program, the average temperature should be displayed for the user via `cout`. For example, given the input data

```
34.5 38.6 42.4 46.8 51.3 63.1 60.2 55.9 60.3 56.7 50.3 42.2
```

file `tempdata.dat` would contain

```
34.5
38.6   4.1
42.4   3.8
46.8   4.4
51.3   4.5
63.1   11.8
60.2   -2.9
55.9   -4.3
60.3   4.4
56.7   -3.6
50.3   -6.4
42.2   -8.1
```

Be sure to use proper formatting and appropriate comments in your code. The input should be collected through appropriate prompts, and the output should be labeled clearly and formatted neatly.

5. Write an interactive C++ program that computes and outputs the mean and standard deviation of a set of four integer values that are input by the user. (If you did Programming Problem 2 in Chapter 3, then you can reuse much of that code here.) The mean is the sum of the four values divided by 4, and the formula for the standard deviation is

$$s = \sqrt{\frac{\sum_{i=1}^{n}(x_i - \bar{x})^2}{n-1}}$$

where $n = 4$, x_i refers to each of the four values, and $\bar{x}$ is the mean. Although the individual values are integers, the results are floating-point values. Be sure to use proper formatting and appropriate comments in your code. Provide appropriate prompts to the user. The output should be labeled clearly and formatted neatly.

6. Write a C++ program that reads data from a file whose name is input by the user, and that outputs the first word following each of the first three commas in the file. For example, if the file contains the text of this problem, then the program would output

```
and
if
then
```

Assume that a comma appears within at least every 200 characters in the file. Be sure to use proper formatting and appropriate comments in your code. Provide appropriate prompts to the user. The output should be labeled clearly and formatted neatly.

7. Write a C++ program that allows the user to enter the percentage of the moon's face that appears illuminated, and that outputs the surface area of that portion of the moon. The formula for the surface area of a segment of a sphere is

$$S = 2R^2\theta$$

where R is the radius of the sphere (the moon's radius is 1738.3 km) and θ is the angle of the wedge in radians. There are 2π radians in a circle, so the hemisphere of the moon that we see accounts for at most π radians. Thus, if the user enters 100% (full moon), the angle of the wedge is π and the formula can be evaluated as follows:

$$S = 2 \times 1738.3^2 \times 3.14159 = 18985818.672 \text{ square kilometers}$$

If the user enters 50% (first or last quarter), then the angle of the wedge is $\pi \times 0.5$, and so on. Be sure to use proper formatting and appropriate comments in your code. Provide appropriate prompts to the user. The output should be labeled clearly and formatted neatly (limit the decimal precision to three places as in the example above).

■ Case Study Follow-Up

1. Replace Clara Jones Jacobey's information with your own name as input to the `Format Names` program.
2. Change this program so that the Social Security number is written on a line by itself with the various name formats indented five spaces on the next four lines.
3. Change the program so that the name of the input file name is read from the keyboard.
4. Change the program so that the names of both the input file and the output file are read from the keyboard.
5. Rewrite the `Mortgage` program, prompting for and reading the variables from the keyboard.

Conditions, Logical Expressions, and Selection Control Structures

KNOWLEDGE GOALS

- To understand how the Boolean operators work.
- To understand the flow of control in a branching statement.
- To understand the flow of control in a nested branching statement.
- To know what preconditions and postconditions are.

SKILL GOALS

To be able to:
- Construct a simple logical (Boolean) expression to evaluate a given condition.
- Construct a complex logical expression to evaluate a given condition.
- Construct an If-Then-Else statement to perform a specific task.
- Construct an If-Then statement to perform a specific task.
- Construct a set of nested If statements to perform a specific task.
- Trace the execution of a C++ program.
- Test and debug a C++ program.

CHAPTER 5 Conditions, Logical Expressions, and Selection Control Structures

So far, the statements in our programs have been executed in their physical order. The first statement is executed, then the second, and so on, until all of the statements have been executed. But what if we want the computer to execute the statements in some other order? Suppose we want to check the validity of input data and then perform a calculation *or* print an error message, but not both. To do so, we must be able to ask a question and then, based on the answer, choose one or another course of action.

The If statement allows us to execute statements in an order that is different from their physical order. We can ask a question with it and do one thing if the answer is yes (true) or another thing if the answer is no (false). In the first part of this chapter, we deal with asking questions; in the second part, we deal with the If statement itself.

5.1 Flow of Control

> **Flow of control** The order in which the computer executes statements in a program.
> **Control structure** A statement used to alter the normally sequential flow of control.

The order in which statements are executed in a program is called the **flow of control**. In a sense, the computer is under the control of one statement at a time. When a statement has been executed, control is turned over to the next statement (like a baton being passed in a relay race).

Flow of control is normally sequential (see **FIGURE 5.1**). That is, when one statement is finished executing, control passes to the next statement in the program. When we want the flow of control to be nonsequential, we use **control structures**, special statements that transfer control to a statement other than the one that physically comes next. Control structures are so important that we focus on them in the remainder of this chapter and in the next four chapters.

Selection

We use a selection (or branching) control structure when we want the computer to choose between alternative actions. Within the control structure, we make an assertion—a claim that is either true or false. We commonly refer to this assertion as the branching condition. If the assertion is true, the computer executes one statement. If it is false, it executes another (see **FIGURE 5.2**). The computer's ability to solve practical problems is a product of its ability to make decisions and execute different sequences of instructions.

The `LeapYear` program in Chapter 1 shows the selection process at work. The computer must decide whether a year is a leap year. It does so by testing the assertion that the year is

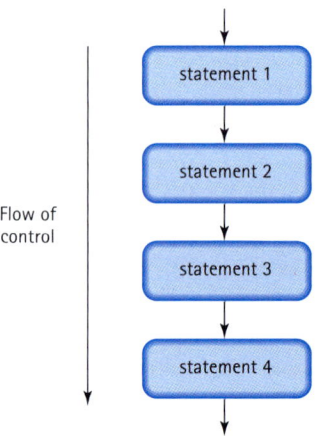

FIGURE 5.1 Flow of Control

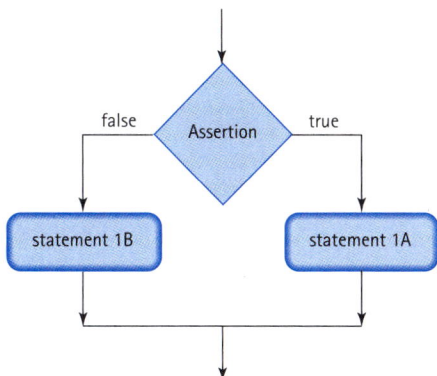

FIGURE 5.2 Selection (Branching) Control Structure

not divisible by 4. If the assertion is true, the computer follows the instructions to return false, indicating that the year is not a leap year. If the assertion is false, the computer goes on to check the exceptions to the general rule. In Chapter 1, we said that this construct is like a fork in a road.

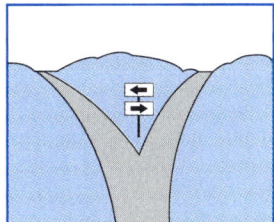

Before we examine selection control structures in C++, let's look closely at how we get the computer to make decisions.

QUICK CHECK

5.1.1 What does "flow of control" mean? (p. 186)
5.1.2 What is the "normal" flow of control for a program? (p. 186)
5.1.3 What control structure do we use when we want a computer to choose between alternative actions? (p. 186)
5.1.4 What does a branch allow the computer to do? (pp. 186–187)

5.2 Conditions and Logical Expressions

To ask a question in C++, we don't phrase it as a question; we state it as an assertion. If the assertion we make is true, the answer to the question is yes. If the statement is not true, the answer to the question is no. For example, if we want to ask, "Are we having spinach for dinner tonight?" we would say, "We are having spinach for dinner tonight." If the assertion is true, the answer to the question is yes. If not, the answer is no.

So, asking questions in C++ means making an assertion that is either true or false. The computer *evaluates* the assertion, checking it against some internal condition (the values stored in certain variables, for instance) to see whether it is true or false.

The `bool` Data Type

In C++, the `bool` data type is a built-in type consisting of just two values, the constants `true` and `false`. The reserved word `bool` is short for Boolean (pronounced "BOOL-e-un").[1] Boolean data is used for testing conditions in a program so that the computer can make decisions (with a selection control structure).

We declare variables of type `bool` in the same way we declare variables of other types—that is, by writing the name of the data type and then an identifier:

```
bool dataOK;     // True if the input data is valid
bool done;       // True if the process is done
bool taxable;    // True if the item has sales tax
```

Each variable of type `bool` can contain one of two values: `true` or `false`. It's important to understand right from the beginning that `true` and `false` are not variable names and they are not strings. They are special constants in C++ and, in fact, are reserved words.

Logical Expressions

In programming languages, assertions take the form of *logical expressions* (also called *Boolean expressions*). Just as an arithmetic expression is made up of numeric values and operations, so a logical expression is made up of logical values and operations. Every logical expression has one of two values: true or false.

Here are some examples of logical expressions:

- A Boolean variable or constant
- An expression followed by a relational operator followed by an expression
- A logical expression followed by a logical operator followed by a logical expression

Let's look at each of these in detail.

Boolean Variables and Constants

As we have seen, a Boolean variable is a variable declared to be of type `bool`, and it can contain either the value `true` or the value `false`. For example, if `dataOK` is a Boolean variable, then

```
dataOK = true;
```

is a valid assignment statement.

Relational Operators

Another way of assigning a value to a Boolean variable is to set it equal to the result of comparing two expressions with a *relational operator*. Relational operators test a relationship between two values.

Let's look at an example. In the following program fragment, `lessThan` is a Boolean variable and `i` and `j` are `int` variables:

```
cin >> i >> j;
lessThan = (i < j);   // Compare i and j with the "less than"
                      // relational operator, and assign the
                      // resulting Boolean value to lessThan
```

---

[1]. The word *Boolean* is a tribute to George Boole, a nineteenth-century English mathematician who described a system of logic using variables with just two values: true and false. (See the "May We Introduce" feature on page 212.)

By comparing two values, we assert that a relationship (such as "less than") exists between them. If the relationship does exist, the assertion is true; if not, it is false. We can test for the following relationships in C++:

Operator	Relationship Tested
==	Equal to
!=	Not equal to
>	Greater than
<	Less than
>=	Greater than or equal to
<=	Less than or equal to

An expression followed by a relational operator followed by an expression is called a *relational expression*. The result of a relational expression is of type `bool`. For example, if x is 5 and y is 10, the following expressions all have the value `true`:

```
x != y
y > x
x < y
y >= x
x <= y
```

If x is the character `'M'` and y is `'R'`, the values of the expressions are still `true` because the relational operator <, used with letters, means "comes before in the alphabet," or, more properly, "comes before in the collating sequence of the character set." For example, in the widely used ASCII character set, all of the uppercase letters are in alphabetical order, as are the lowercase letters, but all of the uppercase letters come before the lowercase letters. So

`'M' < 'R'`

and

`'m' < 'r'`

have the value `true`, but

`'m' < 'R'`

has the value `false`.

Of course, we have to be careful about data types when we compare things. The safest approach is to always compare `int`s with `int`s, `float`s with `float`s, `char`s with `char`s, and so on. If you mix data types in a comparison, implicit type coercion takes place, just as it does in arithmetic expressions. If an `int` value and a `float` value are compared, the computer temporarily coerces the `int` value to its `float` equivalent before making the comparison. As with arithmetic expressions, it's wise to use explicit type casting to make your intentions known:

`someFloat >= float(someInt)`

If you compare a `bool` value with a numeric value (probably by mistake), the value `false` is temporarily coerced to the number 0, and `true` is coerced to 1. Therefore, if `boolVar` is a `bool` variable, the expression

`boolVar < 5`

yields `true` because 0 and 1 are both less than 5.

Until you learn more about the **char** type in Chapter 10, be careful to compare **char** values only with other **char** values. For example, the comparisons

'0' < '9'

and

0 < 9

are appropriate, but

'0' < 9

generates an implicit type coercion and a result that probably isn't what you expect.

We can use relational operators not only to compare variables or constants, but also to compare the values of arithmetic expressions. In the following table, we compare the results of adding 3 to **x** and multiplying **y** by 10 for different values of **x** and **y**.

Value of x	Value of y	Expression	Result
12	2	x + 3 <= y * 10	true
20	2	x + 3 <= y * 10	false
7	1	x + 3 != y * 10	false
17	2	x + 3 == y * 10	true
100	5	x + 3 > y * 10	true

Caution: It's easy to confuse the assignment operator (=) and the == relational operator. These two operators have very different effects in a program. Some people pronounce the relational operator as "equals-equals" to remind themselves of the difference.

The following program shows the output from comparing five sets of integer values.

```
//***************************************
// This program compares integer values.
//***************************************
#include <iostream>
using namespace std;

int main ()
{
    cout << (2 == 2) << endl;
    cout << (3 == 2) << endl;
    cout << (-3 == 2) << endl;
    cout << (-3 == -3) << endl;
    cout << (-3 == -2) << endl;
    return 0;
}
```

Output from a test run:

```
1
0
0
1
0
```

What are those 1s and 0s? C++ stores **true** as the value 1 and **false** as the value 0. Later in the chapter, we will show you how to convert the numbers 1 and 0 to the words "true" and "false".

Comparing Strings

In C++, the **string** type is an example of a class—a programmer-defined type from which you declare variables that are called objects. Recall that C++ is an object-oriented language. Contained within each **string** object is a character string. The **string** class is designed such that you can compare these strings using the relational operators. Syntactically, the operands of a relational operator can either be two **string** objects, as in

```
myString < yourString
```

or a **string** object and a C string, as in

```
myString >= "Johnson"
```

However, both operands cannot be C strings.

Comparison of strings follows the collating sequence of the machine's character set (ASCII, for instance). When the computer tests a relationship between two strings, it begins with the first character of each string, compares those characters according to the collating sequence, and if they are the same repeats the comparison with the next character in each string. The character-by-character test proceeds until either a mismatch is found or the final characters have been compared and are equal. If all their characters are equal, then the two strings are equal. If a mismatch is found, then the string with the character that comes before the other is the "lesser" string.

For example, given the statements

```
string word1;
string word2;

word1 = "Tremendous";
word2 = "Small";
```

the relational expressions in the following table have the indicated values.

Expression	Value	Reason
`word1 == word2`	`false`	They are unequal in the first character.
`word1 > word2`	`true`	`'T'` comes after `'S'` in the collating sequence.
`word1 < "Tremble"`	`false`	Fifth characters don't match, and `'b'` comes before `'e'`.
`word2 == "Small"`	`true`	They are equal.
`"cat" < "dog"`	Unpredictable	The operands cannot both be C strings.[2]

In most cases, the ordering of strings corresponds to alphabetical ordering. But when strings have mixed-case letters, we can get nonalphabetical results. For example, in a phone book we expect to see Macauley before MacPherson, but the ASCII collating sequence places all uppercase letters before the lowercase letters, so the string `"MacPherson"` compares as less than `"Macauley"`. To compare strings for strict alphabetical ordering, all the characters must be in the same case. In a later chapter we show an algorithm for changing the case of a string.

If two strings with different lengths are compared and the comparison is equal up to the end of the shorter string, then the shorter string compares as less than the longer string. For example, if `word2` contains `"Small"`, the expression

`word2 < "Smaller"`

yields `true`, because the strings are equal up to their fifth character position (the end of the string on the left), and the string on the right is longer.

QUICK CHECK ✓

5.2.1 What are the two values that are the basis for Boolean logic? (p. 188)

5.2.2 Write a Boolean expression that is true when the value of the variable `temperature` is greater than 32. (pp. 188–190)

5.2.3 In C++, how many values does the bool data type consist of? (p. 188)

5.2.4 What is a logical expression made up of? (p. 188)

5.2.5 What are possible values for x and y such that the following boolean expression evaluates to false? (pp. 188–190)

`(x + 3) * 2 <= x * (y - 5)`

5.3 The If Statement

Now that we've seen how to write logical expressions, let's use them to alter the normal flow of control in a program. The If statement is the fundamental control structure that allows branches in the flow of control. With it, we can ask a question and choose a course of action: *If* a certain condition exists, *then* perform one action, *else* perform a different action.

At run time, the computer performs just one of the two actions, depending on the result of the condition being tested. Yet we must include the code for *both* actions in the program. Why? Because, depending on the circumstances, the computer can choose to execute *either* of them. The If statement gives us a way of including both actions in a program and gives the computer a way of deciding which action to take.

---

[2]. The expression is syntactically legal in C++ but results in a pointer comparison, not a string comparison. Pointers are not discussed until Chapter 10.

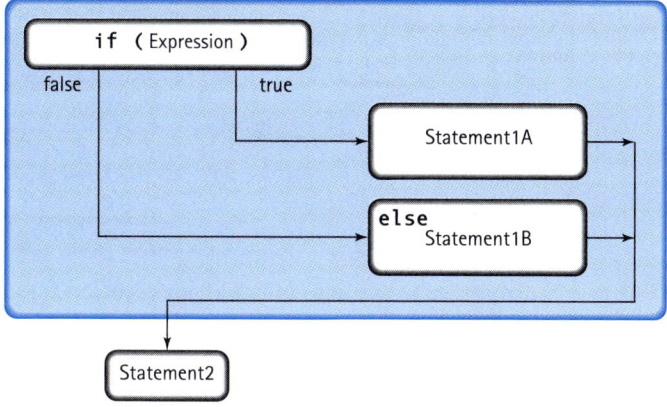

FIGURE 5.3 If-Then-Else Flow of Control

The If-Then-Else Form

In C++, the If statement comes in two forms: the *If-Then-Else* form and the *If-Then* form. Let's look first at the If-Then-Else. Here is its syntax template:

If Statement (the If-Then-Else form)

```
if ( Expression )
    Statement1A
else
    Statement1B
```

The expression in parentheses can be of any simple data type. Almost without exception, it will be a logical (Boolean) expression; if not, its value is implicitly coerced to type **bool**. At run time, the computer evaluates the expression. If the value is **true**, the computer executes Statement1A. If the value of the expression is **false**, it executes Statement1B. Statement1A often is called the *then-clause*; Statement1B, the *else-clause*. **FIGURE 5.3** illustrates the flow of control of the If-Then-Else. In the figure, Statement2 is the next statement in the program after the entire If statement.

Notice that a C++ If statement uses the reserved words **if** and **else** but does not include the word *then*. We use the term *If-Then-Else* because it corresponds to how we say things in English: "*If* something is true, *then* do this, *else* do that."

The following code fragment shows how to write an If statement in a program. Observe the indentation of the then-clause and the else-clause, which makes the statement easier to read. Also notice the placement of the statement following the If statement.

```
if (hours <= 40.0)
    pay = rate * hours;
else
    pay = rate * (40.0 + (hours - 40.0) * 1.5);
cout << pay;
```

In terms of instructions to the computer, this code fragment says, "If **hours** is less than or equal to 40.0, compute the regular pay and then go on to execute the output statement. But if **hours** is greater than 40, compute the regular pay and the overtime pay, and then go on to execute the output statement." **FIGURE 5.4** shows the flow of control of this If statement.

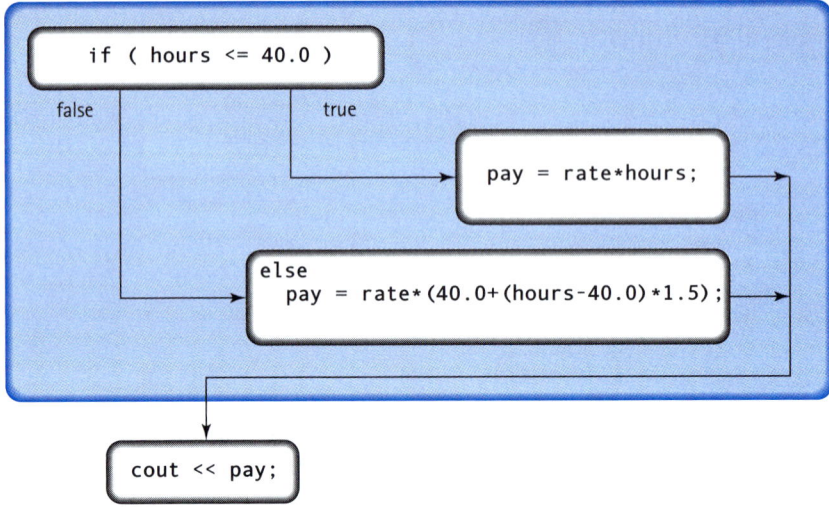

FIGURE 5.4 Flow of Control for Calculating Pay

If-Then-Else often is used to check the validity of input. For example, before we ask the computer to divide by a data value, we should make sure that the value is not zero. (Even computers can't divide something by zero. If you try, most computers halt the execution of your program.) If the divisor is zero, our program should print out an error message. Here's the code:

```
if (divisor != 0)
  result = dividend / divisor;
else
  cout << "Division by zero is not allowed." << endl;
```

As another example of an If-Then-Else, suppose we want to determine where in a string variable the first occurrence (if any) of the letter *A* is located and the first occurrence (if any) of the letter *B*. Recall from Chapter 3 that the `string` class has a member function named `find`, which returns the position where the item was found (or the named constant `string::npos` if the item wasn't found). The following program outputs the result of such a search, including one that succeeds and one that doesn't.

```
//*************************************************************
// This program demonstrates the string function find with
// with one successful and one unsuccessful application.
//*************************************************************
#include <iostream>
#include <string>
using namespace std;

int main ()
{
  string myString = "CAT";
  int pos;
```

```
  pos = myString.find('A');
  if (pos == string::npos)
    cout << "No 'A' was found" << endl;
  else
    cout << "An 'A' was found in position " << pos << endl;
  pos = myString.find('B');
  if (pos == string::npos)
    cout << "No 'B' was found" << endl;
  else
    cout << "A 'B' was found in position " << pos << endl;
  return 0;
}
```

Here is the result of running the program:

```
An 'A' was found in position 1
No 'B' was found
```

Before we look any further at If statements, take another look at the syntax template for the If-Then-Else. According to the template, there is no semicolon at the end of an If statement. In all of the program fragments we have seen so far—the worker's pay, division-by-zero, and string search examples—there seems to be a semicolon at the end of each If statement. Actually, these semicolons belong to the statements in the else-clauses in those examples; assignment statements end in semicolons, as do output statements. The If statement doesn't have its own semicolon at the end.

Blocks (Compound Statements)

In our division-by-zero example, suppose that when the divisor is equal to zero we want to do *two* things: print the error message *and* set the variable named `result` equal to a special value like 9999. We would need two statements in the same branch, but the syntax template seems to limit us to one.

What we really want to do is turn the else-clause into a *sequence* of statements. This is easy. Recall from Chapter 2 that the compiler treats the block (compound statement)

```
{
  :
}
```

like a single statement. If you put a { } pair around the sequence of statements you want in a branch of the If statement, the sequence of statements becomes a single block. For example:

```
if (divisor != 0)
  result = dividend / divisor;
```

```
else
{
  cout << "Division by zero is not allowed." << endl;
  result = 9999;
}
```

If the value of divisor is 0, the computer both prints the error message and sets the value of result to 9999 before continuing with whatever statement follows the If statement.

Blocks can be used in both branches of an If-Then-Else, as shown in the following program.

```
//*********************************************************
// Division program
// Dividend and divisor are prompted for and read.
// If divisor is 0, division is not performed;
// otherwise, division is performed and result is printed.
//*********************************************************
#include <iostream>
using namespace std;

int main()
{
  int dividend;
  int divisor;
  int result;
  cout << "Enter dividend and divisor" << endl;
  cin >> dividend >> divisor;

  if (divisor != 0)
  {
    result = dividend / divisor;
    cout << "Result is " << result << endl;
  }
  else
  {
    cout << "Division by zero is not allowed." << endl;
    result = 9999;
  }
  return 0;
}
```

Here is an example that succeeds:

```
Enter dividend and divisor
200 5
Result is 40
```

Here is one in which the division fails:

```
Enter dividend and divisor
200 0
Division by zero is not allowed.
```

When you use blocks in an If statement, you must remember this rule of C++ syntax: *Never use a semicolon after the right brace of a block.* Semicolons are used only to terminate simple statements such as assignment statements, input statements, and output statements. If you look at the previous examples, you won't see a semicolon after the right brace that signals the end of each block.

MATTERS OF STYLE Braces and Blocks

C++ programmers use different styles when it comes to locating the left brace of a block. The style we use in this book puts the left and right braces directly below the words `if` and `else`, with each brace appearing on its own line:

```
if (n >= 2)
{
  alpha = 5;
  beta = 8;
}
else
{
  alpha = 23;
  beta = 12;
}
```

Another popular style is to place the left braces at the end of the `if` line and the `else` line; the right braces still line up directly below the words `if` and `else`. This way of formatting the If statement originated with programmers using the C language, the predecessor of C++.

```
if (n >= 2) {
  alpha = 5;
  beta = 8;
}
else {
  alpha = 23;
  beta = 12;
}
```

It makes no difference to the C++ compiler which style you use (and there are other styles as well). It's a matter of personal preference. Whichever style you use, though, you should always use the same style throughout a program. Inconsistency can confuse the person reading your program and give the impression of carelessness.

The If-Then Form

Sometimes you run into a situation where you want to say, "*If* a certain condition exists, *then* perform some action; otherwise, don't do anything." In other words, you want the computer to skip a sequence of instructions if a certain condition isn't met. You could do this by leaving the **else** branch empty, using only the null statement:

```
if (a <= b)
  c = 20;
else
  ;
```

Better yet, you can simply leave off the **else** part. The resulting statement is the If-Then form of the If statement. This is its syntax template:

If Statement (the If-Then form)

> if   (Expression)
>   Statement

Here's an example of an If-Then. Notice the indentation and the placement of the statement that follows the If-Then.

```
if (age < 18)
  cout << "Not an eligible ";
cout << "voter." << endl;
```

This statement means that if **age** is less than 18, first print "Not an eligible " and then print "voter." If **age** is not less than 18, skip the first output statement and go directly to print "voter." **FIGURE 5.5** shows the flow of control for an If-Then statement.

Like the two branches in an If-Then-Else, the one branch in an If-Then can be a block. For example, suppose you are writing a program to compute income taxes. One of the lines

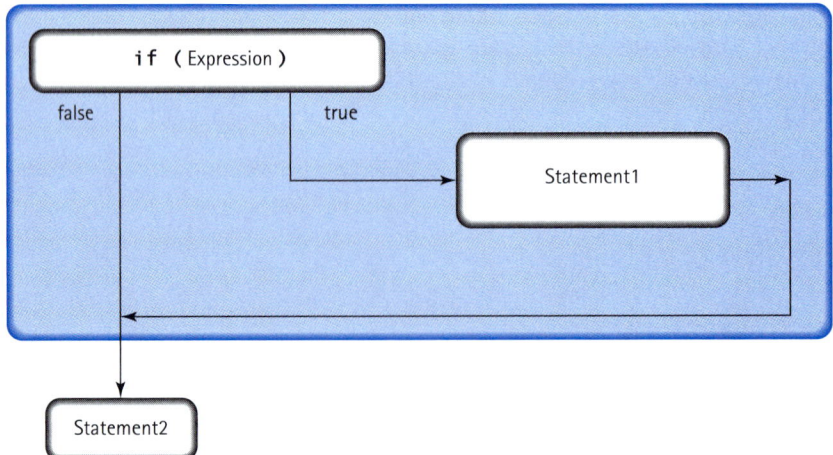

FIGURE 5.5 If-Then Flow of Control

on the tax form reads "Subtract line 23 from line 17 and enter result on line 24; if result is less than zero, enter zero and check box 24A." You can use an If-Then to do this in C++:

```
result = line17 - line23;
if (result < 0.0)
{
  cout << "Check box 24A" << endl;
  result = 0.0;
}
line24 = result;
```

This code does exactly what the tax form says it should: It computes the result of subtracting line 23 from line 17. Then it looks to see if `result` is less than 0. If it is, the fragment prints a message telling the user to check box 24A and then sets `result` to 0. Finally, the calculated result (or 0, if the result is less than 0) is stored into a variable named `line24`.

What happens if we leave out the left and right braces in the code fragment? Let's look at it:

```
result = line17 - line23;        // Incorrect version
if (result < 0.0)
  cout << "Check box 24A" << endl;
  result = 0.0;
line24 = result;
```

Despite the way we have indented the code, the compiler takes the then-clause to be a single statement—the output statement. If `result` is less than 0, the computer executes the output statement, then sets `result` to 0, and then stores `result` into `line24`. So far, so good. But if `result` is initially greater than or equal to 0? Then the computer skips the then-clause and proceeds to the statement following the If statement—the assignment statement that sets `result` to 0. The unhappy outcome is that `result` ends up as 0 no matter what its initial value was!

The moral here is not to rely on indentation alone; you can't fool the compiler. If you want a compound statement for a then- or else-clause, you must include the left and right braces.

A Common Mistake

Earlier we warned against confusing the = operator with the == operator. Here is an example of a mistake that every C++ programmer is guaranteed to make at least once in his or her career:

```
cin >> n;
if (n = 3)              // Wrong
  cout << "n equals 3";
else
  cout << "n doesn't equal 3";
```

This code segment *always* prints out

```
n equals 3
```

no matter what was input for `n`.

Here is the reason: We've used the wrong operator in the If test. The expression `n = 3` is not a logical expression; it's an *assignment expression*. (If an assignment is written as a separate statement ending with a semicolon, it's an assignment *statement*.) An assignment expression has a *value* (here, it's 3) and a *side effect* (storing 3 into n). In the If statement of our example, the computer finds the value of the tested expression to be 3. Because 3 is a nonzero value and thus is coerced to `true`, the then-clause is executed, no matter what the value of n is. Worse yet, the side effect of the assignment expression is to store 3 into n, destroying what was there.

Our intention is not to focus on assignment expressions; we discuss their use later in the book. What's important now is that you see the effect of using = when you meant to use ==. The program compiles correctly but runs incorrectly. When debugging a faulty program, always look at your If statements to see whether you've made this particular mistake.

SOFTWARE MAINTENANCE CASE STUDY: Incorrect Output

MAINTENANCE TASK: When you were helping your parents with their mortgage loan, you wrote a program to determine the monthly payments given the amount to be borrowed, the interest rate, and the number of years. You gave the same program to a friend to use when she was buying a car. She says that the program gives very strange results. You ask for an example of the erroneous output. She said it gave a ridiculously high rate for an amount of $3000, for 2 years at an interest rate of 6.8%.

VERIFYING THE BEHAVIOR: Whenever a user reports a bug, you should begin by making sure that you can generate the reported behavior yourself. This sets up the necessary conditions for isolating the problem and testing your modifications. You run the program using the data your friend supplied and the answers seem reasonable.

```
Loan amount:      3000.00
Interest rate:    0.0680
Number of years:  2
Monthly payment:  134.05
```

Because you can't get the program to exhibit the bug, you go back to your friend to ask more questions. (Remember, that's one of our problem-solving strategies, and they apply just as much to debugging as to writing new applications.) "What sort of ridiculously high rate did you get?" you ask her. Your friend says that she got 1700.03556473111262 as the payment amount. Clearly, $1700.03 per month for 2 years is not correct. What could have gone wrong?

Just as a mechanic may have to go for a drive with a car's owner to understand what's wrong, sometimes you have to sit and watch a user run your application. You ask your friend to show you what happened. Here's what she did:

```
Loan amount:      3000.00
Interest rate:    6.8000
Number of years:  2
Monthly payment:  1700.04
```

Aha! You wrote the code to read the interest rate as a decimal fraction, and she is entering it as a percentage! There's an easy solution to this problem. You can tell her to enter the interest rate as a decimal fraction, and you won't have to change the code at all. Such a "fix" is known as a *workaround*.

She can do this, but says, "It's annoying to have to do the math in my head. Why can't you fix the program so that it takes the percentage the way that people normally write it?" She has a good point. As a programmer, you wrote the code in a way that made it easier for you. But a good application should

SOFTWARE MAINTENANCE CASE STUDY: Incorrect Output

be designed to make it easier for the user, which is what we mean by *user friendly*. If other people will be using your application, you must think in those terms.

To make your friend happy, you have to change the program to first divide the input percentage by 100. But then you remember that you've also given the program to a friend who is a math major and who prefers to enter percentages as decimal fractions. The program could ask the user for his or her preference, but again, that's more work for the user. What to do? How to accommodate both kinds of users with the least hassle?

Obviously, there has to be a branch somewhere in the application that chooses between dividing the percentage by 100 and using it as entered. Interest rates on loans are generally no more than about 25% and no less than one-quarter of a percent. So we could simply say that any number greater than or equal to 0.25 is assumed to be a percentage, and any number less than that is a decimal fraction. Thus, the necessary If statement would be written as follows:

```
if (yearlyInterest >= 0.25)           // Assume percent entered
  yearlyInterest = yearlyInterest / 100.0;
```

Is that the only change? That's all that's required to make the program do the proper calculations. However, your friend indicated that it would be nice to have a version that used the keyboard for input and output rather than files. Let's make this version use keyboard input and output and include our assumptions in the input prompts.

MODIFIED CODE: You call up the file with your source code so that you can modify it. You also refamiliarize yourself with the compound interest formula:

$$\frac{Amount \times (1 + Monthly\ Interest)^{Number\ of\ Payments} \times Monthly\ Interest}{(1 + Monthly\ Interest)^{Number\ of\ Payments} - 1}$$

You then insert the revised input and output and the If statement. The changes are highlighted in the code below.

```
//****************************************************************
// Mortgage Payment Calculator program
// This program determines the monthly payments on a loan given
// the loan amount, the yearly interest rate, and the number of
// years.
//****************************************************************
#include <cmath>
#include <iomanip>
#include <iostream>
using namespace std;

int main()
{
  // Input variables
  float loanAmount;
  float yearlyInterest;
  int numberOfYears;
```

SOFTWARE MAINTENANCE CASE STUDY: Incorrect Output

```cpp
    // Local variables
    float monthlyInterest;
    int numberOfPayments;
    float payment;

    // Prompts
    cout << "Input loan amount, interest rate, and number of years."
        << endl;
    cout << "An interest rate of less than 0.25 is assumed to be "
        << endl;
    cout << "a decimal rather than a percent." << endl;

    // Read values
    cin >> loanAmount >> yearlyInterest >> numberOfYears;

    // Calculate values
    if (yearlyInterest >= 0.25)       // Assume percent entered
      yearlyInterest = yearlyInterest / 100.0;
    monthlyInterest = yearlyInterest / 12;
    numberOfPayments = numberOfYears * 12;
    payment = (loanAmount * pow(1 + monthlyInterest, numberOfPayments)
        * monthlyInterest)/
      (pow(1 + monthlyInterest, numberOfPayments) - 1 );

    // Output results
    cout << fixed << "Loan amount:        " << setprecision(2)
        << loanAmount << endl << "Interest rate:     "
        << setprecision(4) << yearlyInterest*100.0 << "%"  << endl
        << "Number of years: " << numberOfYears << endl;
    cout << fixed
        << "Monthly payment: " << setprecision(2) << payment << endl;
    return 0;
}
```

Here is the output from two test runs of the application, one with data entered as a percentage and one with data entered as a decimal:

```
Input loan amount, interest rate, and number of years.
An interest rate of less than 0.25 is assumed to be
a decimal rather than a percent.
3000 6.82
Loan amount:      3000.00
Interest rate:    6.80%
Number of years: 2
Monthly payment: 134.05
```

SOFTWARE MAINTENANCE CASE STUDY: Incorrect Output

```
Input loan amount, interest rate, and number of years.
An interest rate of less than 0.25 is assumed to be
a decimal rather than a percent.
3000 0.068 2
Loan amount:      3000.00
Interest rate:    6.80%
Number of years:  2
Monthly payment:  134.05
```

> **QUICK CHECK** ✓
>
> **5.3.1** Write an If-Then-Else statement that uses the test from Question 5.2.2 to output either `"Above freezing."` or `"Freezing or below."`. (pp. 193–195)
>
> **5.3.2** Why must we provide code for both actions of an If statement? (p. 192)
>
> **5.3.3** What data type must the expression in parentheses of an If statement evaluate to? (p. 193)

5.4 Nested If Statements

There are no restrictions on what the statements in an If can be. Therefore, an If within an If is okay. In fact, an If within an If within an If is legal. The only limitation here is that people cannot follow a structure that is too involved, and readability is one of the hallmarks of a good program.

When we place an If within an If, we are creating a *nested control structure*. Control structures nest much like mixing bowls do, with smaller ones tucked inside larger ones. Here's an example, written in pseudocode:

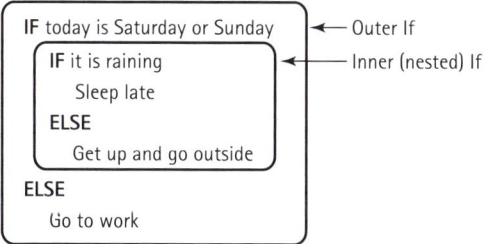

In general, any problem that involves a *multiway branch* (more than two alternative courses of action) can be coded using nested If statements. For example, to print out the name of a month given its number, we could use a sequence of If statements (unnested):

```
if (month == 1)
  cout << "January";
if (month == 2)
  cout << "February";
```

```
if (month == 3)
  cout << "March";
  ⋮
if (month == 12)
  cout << "December";
```

But the equivalent nested If structure,

```
if (month == 1)
  cout << "January";
else
  if (month == 2)        // Nested If
    cout << "February";
  else
    if (month == 3)      // Nested If
      cout << "March";
    else
      if (month == 4)    // Nested If
        .
        .
        .
```

is more efficient because it makes fewer comparisons. The first version—the sequence of independent If statements—always tests every condition (all 12 of them), even if the first one is satisfied. In contrast, the nested If solution skips all remaining comparisons after one alternative has been selected. As fast as modern computers are, many applications require so much computation that inefficient algorithms can waste hours of computer time. Always be on the lookout for ways to make your programs more efficient, as long as doing so doesn't make them difficult for other programmers to understand. It's usually better to sacrifice a little efficiency for the sake of readability.

In the last example, notice how the indentation of the then- and else-clauses causes the statements to move continually to the right. Alternatively, we can use a special indentation style with deeply nested If-Then-Else statements to indicate that the complex structure is just choosing one of a set of alternatives. This general multiway branch is known as an *If-Then-Else-If* control structure:

```
if (month == 1)
  cout << "January";
else if (month == 2)     // Nested If
  cout << "February";
else if (month == 3)     // Nested If
  cout << "March";
else if (month == 4)     // Nested If
  .
  .
  .
else
  cout << "December";
```

This style prevents the indentation from marching continuously to the right. More importantly, it visually conveys the idea that we are using a 12-way branch based on the variable month.

It's important to note one difference between the sequence of If statements and the nested If: More than one alternative can be taken by the sequence of Ifs, but the nested If can select only one option. To see why this is important, consider the analogy of filling out a questionnaire. Some questions are like a sequence of If statements, asking you to circle all the items in a list that apply to you (such as all your hobbies). Other questions ask you to circle only one item in a list (your age group, for example) and are thus like a nested If structure. Both kinds of questions occur in programming problems. Being able to recognize which type of question is being asked permits you to immediately select the appropriate control structure.

Another particularly helpful use of the nested If is when you want to select from a series of consecutive ranges of values. For example, suppose that we want to print out an appropriate activity for the outdoor temperature, given the following information:

Activity	Temperature
Swimming	temperature > 85
Tennis	70 < temperature <= 85
Golf	32 < temperature <= 70
Skiing	0 < temperature <= 32
Dancing	temperature <= 0

At first glance, you may be tempted to write a separate If statement for each range of temperatures. On closer examination, however, it is clear that these If conditions are interdependent. That is, if one of the statements is executed, none of the others should be executed. We are really selecting one alternative from a set of possibilities—just the sort of situation in which we can use a nested If structure as a multiway branch. The only difference between this problem and our earlier example of printing the month name from its number is that we must check ranges of numbers in the If expressions of the branches.

When the ranges are consecutive, we can take advantage of that fact to make our code more efficient. We arrange the branches in consecutive order by range. Then, if a particular branch has been reached, we know that the preceding ranges have been eliminated from consideration. Thus the If expressions must compare the temperature to only the lowest value of each range. To see how this works, look at the following **Activity** program.

```cpp
//*****************************************************************
// Activity program
// This program outputs an appropriate activity
// for a given temperature
//*****************************************************************
#include <iostream>
using namespace std;

int main()
{
  int temperature;   // The outside temperature

  // Read and echo temperature
  cout << "Enter the outside temperature:" << endl;
  cin >> temperature;
  cout << "The current temperature is " << temperature << endl;

  // Print activity
  cout << "The recommended activity is ";
  if (temperature > 85)
    cout << "swimming." << endl;
```

```
      else if (temperature > 70)
         cout << "tennis." << endl;
      else if (temperature > 32)
         cout << "golf." << endl;
      else if (temperature > 0)
         cout << "skiing." << endl;
      else
         cout << "dancing." << endl;
      return 0;
}
```

To understand how the If-Then-Else-If structure in this program works, consider the branch that tests for `temperature` greater than `70`. If it has been reached, we know that `temperature` must be less than or equal to `85` because that condition causes this particular `else` branch to be taken. Thus we need to test only whether `temperature` is above the bottom of this range (`> 70`). If that test fails, then we enter the next else-clause knowing that `temperature` must be less than or equal to `70`. Each successive branch checks the bottom of its range until we reach the final `else`, which takes care of all the remaining possibilities.

If the ranges aren't consecutive, however, we must test the data value against both the highest and lowest values of each range. We still use an If-Then-Else-If because that is the best structure for selecting a single branch from multiple possibilities, and we may arrange the ranges in consecutive order to make them easier for a human reader to follow. In such a case, there is no way to reduce the number of comparisons when there are gaps between the ranges.

The Dangling else

When If statements are nested, you may find yourself confused about the `if-else` pairings. That is, to which `if` does an `else` belong? For example, suppose that if a student's average is below 60, we want to print "Failing"; if the average is at least 60 but less than 70, we want to print "Passing but marginal"; and if it is 70 or greater, we don't want to print anything. We code this information with an If-Then-Else nested within an If-Then:

```
if (average < 70.0)
  if (average < 60.0)
    cout << "Failing";
  else
    cout << "Passing but marginal";
```

How do we know to which `if` the `else` belongs? Here is the rule that the C++ compiler follows: In the absence of braces, an `else` is always paired with the closest preceding `if` that doesn't already have an `else` paired with it. We indented the code to reflect this pairing.

Suppose we write the fragment like this:

```
if (average >= 60.0)      // Incorrect version
  if (average < 70.0)
    cout << "Passing but marginal";
else
  cout << "Failing";
```

Here we want the `else` branch attached to the outer If statement, not the inner If, so we indent the code as you see it. Of course, indentation does not affect the execution of the code. Even though the `else` aligns with the first `if`, the compiler pairs it with the second `if`. An `else` that follows a nested If-Then is called a *dangling* `else`. It doesn't logically belong with the nested If but is attached to it by the compiler.

To attach the `else` to the first `if`, not the second, you can turn the outer then-clause into a block:

```
if (average >= 60.0)       // Correct version
{
  if (average < 70.0)
  cout << "Passing but marginal";
}
else
  cout << "Failing";
```

The `{ }` pair indicates that the inner If statement is complete, so the `else` must belong to the outer `if`.

QUICK CHECK

5.4.1 What purpose does a nested branch serve? (pp. 203–205)

5.4.2 Write nested If statements to print messages indicating whether a temperature is below freezing, freezing, above freezing but not boiling, or boiling and above. (pp. 203–205)

5.4.3 What type of control structure do we have when an If statement is within another If statement? (p. 203)

5.4.4 What type of branching control structure is used when we have many (more than 2) alternative courses of action? (p. 204)

5.4.5 What problem does a C++ compiler solve using the rule: In the absence of braces, an `else` is always paired with the closest preceding `if` that doesn't already have an `else` paired with it. (p. 206)

5.5 Logical Operators

In mathematics, the *logical* (or *Boolean*) *operators* AND, OR, and NOT take logical expressions as operands. C++ uses special symbols for the logical operators: `&&` (for AND), `||` (for OR), and `!` (for NOT). By combining relational operators with logical operators, we can make more complex assertions. For example, in the last section we used two If statements to determine if an average was greater than 60.0 but less than 70.0. In C++, we would write the expression this way:

```
average >= 60.0  && average < 70.0
```

The AND operation (`&&`) requires both relationships to be true for the overall result to be true. If either or both of the relationships are false, the entire result is false.

The OR operation (`||`) takes two logical expressions and combines them. If *either* or *both* are true, the result is true. *Both* values must be false for the result to be false. For example, we can determine whether the midterm grade is an A *or* the final grade is an A. If either the midterm grade or the final grade equals A, the assertion is true. In C++, we write the expression like this:

```
midtermGrade == 'A' || finalGrade == 'A'
```

The `&&` and `||` operators always appear between two expressions; they are binary (two-operand) operators. The NOT operator (`!`) is a unary (one-operand) operator. It precedes a single logical expression and gives its opposite as the result. If `(grade == 'A')` is false, then `!(grade == 'A')` is true. NOT gives us a convenient way of reversing the meaning of an assertion. For example,

```
!(hours > 40)
```

is the equivalent of

```
hours <= 40
```

In some contexts, the first form is clearer; in others, the second makes more sense.

The following pairs of expressions are equivalent:

Expression	Equivalent Expression
!(a == b)	a != b
!(a == b || a == c)	a != b && a != c
!(a == b && c > d)	a != b || c <= d

Take a close look at these expressions to be sure you understand why they are equivalent. Try evaluating them with some values for **a**, **b**, **c**, and **d**. Notice the pattern: The expression on the left is just the one to its right with **!** added and the relational and logical operators reversed (for example, **==** instead of **!=** and **||** instead of **&&**). Remember this pattern. It allows you to rewrite expressions in the simplest form.[3]

Logical operators can be applied to the results of comparisons. They can also be applied directly to variables of type **bool**. For example, instead of writing

```
isElector = (age >= 18 && district == 23);
```

to assign a value to the Boolean variable **isElector**, we could use two intermediate Boolean variables, **isVoter** and **isConstituent**:

```
isVoter = (age >= 18);
isConstituent = (district == 23);
isElector = isVoter && isConstituent;
```

The following two tables summarize the results of applying **&&** and **||** to a pair of logical expressions (represented here by Boolean variables **x** and **y**).

Value of x	Value of y	Value of x && y
true	true	true
true	false	false
false	true	false
false	false	false

Value of x	Value of y	Value of x || y
true	true	true
true	false	true
false	true	true
false	false	false

The following table summarizes the results of applying the **!** operator to a logical expression (represented by Boolean variable **x**):

Value of x	Value of !x
true	false
false	true

---

3. In Boolean algebra, the pattern is formalized by a theorem called *DeMorgan's law*.

Technically, the C++ operators !, &&, and || are not required to have logical expressions as operands. Their operands can be of any simple data type, even floating-point types. If an operand is not of type **bool**, its value is temporarily coerced to type **bool** as follows: A 0 value is coerced to **false**, and any nonzero value is coerced to **true**. As an example, you sometimes encounter C++ code that looks like this:

```
float  height;
bool   badData;
    .
    .
    .
cin >> height;
badData = !height;
```

The assignment statement says to set **badData** to **true** if the coerced value of **height** is **false**. That is, the statement is really saying, "Set **badData** to **true** if **height** equals 0.0." Although this assignment statement works correctly in the C++ language, the following statement is more readable:

```
badData = (height == 0.0);
```

Throughout this text we apply the logical operators *only* to logical expressions, not to arithmetic expressions.

Caution: It's easy to confuse the logical operators **&&** and **||** with two other C++ operators, **&** and **|**. We don't discuss the **&** and **|** operators here, but we'll tell you that they are used for manipulating individual bits within a memory cell—a role quite different from that of the logical operators. If you accidentally use **&** instead of **&&**, or **|** instead of **||**, you won't get an error message from the compiler, but your program probably will compute wrong answers. Some programmers pronounce **&&** as "and-and" and **||** as "or-or" to avoid making mistakes.

The preceding assignment statement can also be implemented using an If statement. That is,

```
badData = (height == 0.0);
```

can be implemented as

```
if (height == 0.0)
  badData = true;
else
  badData = false;
```

As you can see, the first form is simpler to write and, with a little practice, is easier to read.

The following application sets the Boolean variables **walk**, **movie**, and **book** to **true** or **false** depending on what the temperature is and whether it is raining. An If statement is then used to print the results.

```
//*****************************************************************
// Activity program
// This program outputs an appropriate activity
// for a given temperature
//*****************************************************************
#include <iostream>
#include <string>
using namespace std;

int main()
{
  int temperature;      // The outside temperature
  bool raining;
  bool walk;
  bool movie;
  bool book;

  // Read and echo temperature
  cout << "Enter the outside temperature:" << endl;
  cin >> temperature;
  cout << "Enter 1 if it is raining and 0 if it is not.";
  cin >> raining;
  cout << "The current temperature is " << temperature;
  if (raining)
    cout << " and it is raining." << endl;
  else
    cout << " and it is not raining." << endl;

  // Print activity
  walk = temperature > 60 && !raining;
  movie = temperature > 60 && raining;
  book = temperature < 60;
  if (walk)
    cout << "Go for a walk." << endl;
  else
    if (movie)
      cout << "Go to a movie." << endl;
    else
      cout << "Read a good book" << endl;
  return 0;
}
```

Following are the results of running the program on four different sets of input:

```
Enter the outside temperature:
50
Enter 1 if it is raining and 0 if it is not.
0
The current temperature is 50 and it is not raining.
Read a good book
```

Short-Circuit Evaluation

Consider the logical expression

`i == 1 && j > 2`

Some programming languages use *full evaluation* of logical expressions. With full evaluation, the computer first evaluates both subexpressions (both `i == 1` and `j > 2`) before applying the `&&` operator to produce the final result.

In contrast, C++ uses short-circuit (or conditional) evaluation of logical expressions. Evaluation proceeds from left to right, and the computer stops evaluating subexpressions as soon as possible—that is, as soon as it knows the Boolean value of the entire expression. How can the computer know if a lengthy logical expression yields `true` or `false` if it doesn't examine all the subexpressions? Let's look first at the AND operation.

> **Short-circuit (conditional) evaluation** Evaluation of a logical expression in left-to-right order, with evaluation stopping as soon as the final truth value can be determined.

An AND operation yields the value `true` only if both of its operands are `true`. In the earlier expression, suppose that the value of `i` happens to be 95. The first subexpression yields `false`, so it isn't necessary even to look at the second subexpression. The computer stops evaluation and produces the final result of `false`.

With the OR operation, the left-to-right evaluation stops as soon as a subexpression yielding `true` is found. Remember that an OR produces a result of `true` if either one or both of its operands are `true`. Suppose we have this expression:

`c <= d || e == f`

If the first subexpression is `true`, evaluation stops and the entire result is `true`. The computer doesn't waste time with an unnecessary evaluation of the second subexpression.

MAY WE INTRODUCE George Boole

Boolean algebra is named for its inventor, English mathematician George Boole, who was born in 1815. His father, a tradesman, began teaching George mathematics at an early age. But Boole initially was more interested in classical literature, languages, and religion—interests he maintained throughout his life. By the time he was 20, he had taught himself French, German, and Italian. He was well versed in the writings of Aristotle, Spinoza, Cicero, and Dante, and wrote several philosophical papers himself.

At 16, to help support his family, Boole took a position as a teaching assistant in a private school. His work there and a second teaching job left him little time to study. A few years later, he opened a school and began to learn higher mathematics on his own. In spite of his lack of formal training, his first scholarly paper was published in the *Cambridge Mathematical Journal* when he was just 24. Boole went on to publish more than 50 papers and several major works before he died in 1864, at the peak of his career.

Boole's *The Mathematical Analysis of Logic* was published in 1847. It would eventually form the basis for the development of digital computers. In the book, Boole set forth the formal axioms of logic (much like the axioms of geometry) on which the field of symbolic logic is built.

Boole drew on the symbols and operations of algebra in creating his system of logic. He associated the value 1 with the universal set (the set representing everything in the universe) and the value 0 with the empty set, and restricted his system to these two quantities. He then defined operations that are analogous to subtraction, addition, and multiplication. Variables in the system have symbolic values. For example, if a Boolean variable P represents the set of all plants, then the expression $1 - P$ refers to the set of all things that are not plants. We can simplify the expression by using $-P$ to mean "*not* plants." ($0 - P$ is simply 0 because we can't remove elements from the empty set.) The subtraction operator in Boole's system corresponds to the ! (NOT) operator in C++. In a C++ program, we might set the value of the Boolean variable plant to true when the name of a plant is entered, whereas `!plant` is `true` when the name of anything else is input.

The expression $0 + P$ is the same as P. However, $0 + P + F$, where F is the set of all foods, is the set of all things that are either plants or foods. So the addition operator in Boole's algebra is the same as the C++ `||` (OR) operator.

The analogy can be carried to multiplication: $0 \times P$ is 0, and $1 \times P$ is P. But what is $P \times F$? It is the set of things that are both plants and foods. In Boole's system, the multiplication operator is the same as the `&&` (AND) operator.

In 1854, Boole published *An Investigation of the Laws of Thought, on Which Are Founded the Mathematical Theories of Logic and Probabilities.* In the book, he described theorems built on his axioms of logic and extended the algebra to show how probabilities could be computed in a logical system. Five years later, Boole published *Treatise on Differential Equations,* then *Treatise on the Calculus of Finite Differences.* The latter book is one of the cornerstones of numerical analysis, which deals with the accuracy of computations. (In Chapter 10, we examine the important role numerical analysis plays in computer programming.)

Boole received little recognition and few honors for his work. Given the importance of Boolean algebra in modern technology, it is hard to believe that his system of logic was not taken seriously until the early twentieth century. George Boole was truly one of the founders of computer science.

Precedence of Operators

In Chapter 3, we discussed the rules of precedence—the rules that govern the evaluation of complex arithmetic expressions. C++'s rules of precedence also govern relational and logical operators. Here's a list showing the order of precedence for the arithmetic, relational, and logical operators (with the assignment operator thrown in as well):

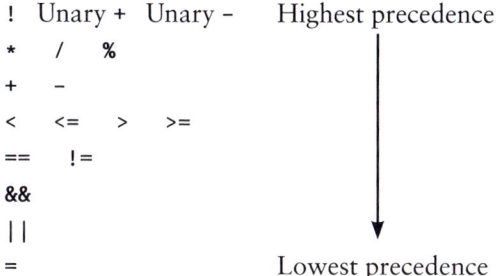

```
!   Unary +  Unary -       Highest precedence
*   /   %
+   -
<   <=  >   >=
==  !=
&&
||
=                          Lowest precedence
```

Operators on the same line in the list have the same precedence. If an expression contains several operators with the same precedence, most of the operators group (or *associate*) from left to right. For example, the expression

`a / b * c`

means `(a / b) * c`, not `a / (b * c)`. However, the unary operators (!, unary +, unary -) group from right to left. Although you'd never have occasion to use this expression,

`!!badData`

its meaning is `!(!badData)` rather than the meaningless `(!!)badData`. Appendix B, "Precedence of Operators," lists the order of precedence for all operators in C++. In skimming the appendix, you can see that a few of the operators associate from right to left (for the same reason we just described for the ! operator).

Parentheses are used to override the order of evaluation in an expression. If you're not sure whether parentheses are necessary, use them anyway. The compiler disregards unnecessary parentheses. So, if they clarify an expression, use them. Some programmers like to include extra parentheses when assigning a relational expression to a Boolean variable:

`dataInvalid = (inputVal == 0);`

The parentheses are not actually needed here; the assignment operator has the lowest precedence of all the operators we've just listed. So we could write the statement as

`dataInvalid = inputVal == 0;`

Some people find the parenthesized version more readable, however.

One final comment about parentheses: C++, like other programming languages, requires that parentheses always be used in pairs. Whenever you write a complicated expression, take a minute to go through and pair up all of the opening parentheses with their closing counterparts.

SOFTWARE ENGINEERING TIP   Changing English Statements into Logical Expressions

In most cases, you can write a logical expression directly from an English statement or mathematical term in an algorithm. But you have to watch out for some tricky situations. Remember our sample logical expression:

```
midtermGrade == 'A' || finalGrade == 'A'
```

In English, you would be tempted to write this expression: "Midterm grade or final grade equals A." In C++, you can't write the expression as you would in English. That is,

```
midtermGrade || finalGrade == 'A'
```

won't work because the `||` operator is connecting a `char` value (`midtermGrade`) and a logical expression (`finalGrade == 'A'`). The two operands of `||` should be logical expressions. (Note that this expression is wrong in terms of logic, but it isn't "wrong" to the C++ compiler. Recall that the `||` operator may legally connect two expressions of any data type, so this example won't generate a syntax error message. The program will run, but it won't work the way you intended.)

A variation of this mistake is to express the English assertion "*i* equals either 3 or 4" as follows:

```
i == 3 || 4
```

Again, the syntax is correct but the semantics are not. This expression always evaluates to `true`. The first subexpression, `i == 3`, may be `true` or `false`. But the second subexpression, `4`, is nonzero and, therefore, is coerced to the value `true`. Thus the `||` operator causes the entire expression to be `true`. We repeat: Use the `||` operator (and the `&&` operator) only to connect two logical expressions. Here's what we want:

```
i == 3 || i == 4
```

In math books, you might see a notation like this:

```
12 < y < 24
```

which means "*y* is between 12 and 24." This expression is legal in C++ but gives an unexpected result. First, the relation `12 < y` is evaluated, giving the result `true` or `false`. The computer then coerces this result to 1 or 0 to compare it with the number 24. Because both 1 and 0 are less than 24, the result is always `true`. To write this expression correctly in C++, you must use the `&&` operator as follows:

```
12 < y && y < 24
```

Relational Operators with Floating-Point Types

So far, we've talked about comparing `int`, `char`, and `string` values. Here we look at `float` values.

Do not compare floating-point numbers for equality. Because small errors in the rightmost decimal places are likely to arise when calculations are performed on floating-point numbers, two **float** values rarely are exactly equal. For example, consider the following code that uses two **float** variables named **oneThird** and **x**:

```
oneThird = 1.0 / 3.0;
x = oneThird + oneThird + oneThird;
```

We would expect **x** to contain the value 1.0, but it probably doesn't. The first assignment statement stores an *approximation* of 1/3 into **oneThird**, perhaps 0.333333. The second statement stores a value like 0.999999 into **x**. If we now ask the computer to compare **x** with 1.0, the comparison yields **false**.

Instead of testing floating-point numbers for equality, we test for *near* equality. To do so, we compute the difference between the two numbers and test whether the result is less than some maximum allowable difference. For example, we often use comparisons like this:

```
fabs(r - s) < 0.00001
```

where **fabs** is the floating-point absolute value function from the C++ standard library. The expression **fabs(r - s)** computes the absolute value of the difference between two float variables **r** and **s**. If the difference is less than 0.00001, the two numbers are close enough to call them equal.

QUICK CHECK

5.5.1 What are the C++ boolean operators that correspond to the logical operators AND, OR, and NOT? (p. 207)

5.5.2 Write an equivalent boolean expression for **(a != b && c < d)** that uses the operators **==** and **>=** and **!**. (p. 208)

5.5.3 Write a single assignment statement that corresponds to the following If statement (assuming that grade is type **float** and failed is type **bool**): (p. 209)

```
if (grade <= 50.0)
    failed = true;
else
    failed = false;
```

5.5.4 Which direction is a logical expression evaluated in in C++? (p. 211)

5.5.5 Write a boolean expression such that it demonstrates short-circuit evaluation. Highlight the part of the expression that *is not executed*. (p. 211)

5.6 Testing the State of an I/O Stream

In Chapter 4, we talked about the concept of input and output streams in C++. As part of that discussion, introduced the classes **istream**, **ostream**, **ifstream**, and **ofstream**. We said that any of the following can cause an input stream to enter the fail state:

- Invalid input data
- An attempt to read beyond the end of a file
- An attempt to open a nonexistent file for input

C++ provides a way to check whether a stream is in the fail state. In a logical expression, you simply use the name of the stream object (such as **cin**) as if it were a Boolean variable:

```
if (cin)
    .
    .
    .
```

```cpp
if (!inFile)
    .
    .
    .
```

Testing the state of a stream The act of using a C++ stream object in a logical expression as if it were a Boolean variable; the result is true if the last I/O operation on that stream succeeded, and false otherwise.

When you do this, you are said to be *testing the state of the stream*. The result of the test is either `true` (meaning the last I/O operation on that stream succeeded) or `false` (meaning the last I/O operation failed). Conceptually, you want to think of a stream object in a logical expression as being a Boolean variable with a value `true` (the stream state is okay) or `false` (the state isn't okay).

In an If statement, the way you phrase the logical expression depends on what you want the then-clause to do. The statement

```cpp
if (inFile)
    .
    .
    .
```

executes the then-clause if the last I/O operation on `inFile` succeeded. The statement

```cpp
if (!inFile)
    .
    .
    .
```

executes the then-clause if `inFile` is in the fail state. (Remember that once a stream is in the fail state, it remains so. Any further I/O operations on that stream are null operations.)

Here's an example that shows how to check whether an input file was opened successfully:

```cpp
//************************************************************
// StreamState program
// This program demonstrates testing the state of a stream
//************************************************************
#include <iostream>
#include <fstream>    // For file I/O

using namespace std;

int main()
{
    int height;
    int width;
    ifstream inFile;

    inFile.open("measures.dat");            // Attempt to open file
    if (!inFile)                            // Was it opened?
    {
        cout << "Can't open the input file.";   // No--print message
        return 1;                               // Terminate program
    }
    inFile >> height >> width;
    cout << "For a height of " << height << endl
         << "and a width of " << width << endl
         << "the area is " << height * width << endl;
    return 0;
}
```

In this program, we begin by attempting to open the file `measures.dat` for input. Immediately, we check whether the attempt succeeded. If it was successful, the value of the expression `!inFile` in the If statement is `false` and the then-clause is skipped. The program proceeds to read data from the file and then perform a computation. It concludes by executing the statement

```
return 0;
```

With this statement, the `main` function returns control to the operating system. Recall that the function value returned by `main` is known as the exit status. The value 0 signifies normal completion of the program. Any other value (typically 1, 2, 3, . . .) means that something went wrong.

Let's trace through the program again, assuming we weren't able to open the input file. Upon return from the `open` function, the stream `inFile` is in the fail state. In the If statement, the value of the expression `!inFile` is `true`. Thus the then-clause is executed. The program prints an error message to the user and then terminates, returning an exit status of 1 to inform the operating system of an abnormal termination of the program. (Our choice of the value 1 for the exit status is purely arbitrary. System programmers sometimes use several different values in a program to signal different reasons for program termination. But most people just use the value 1.)

Whenever you open a data file for input, be sure to test the stream state before proceeding. If you forget to do so, and the computer cannot open the file, your program quietly continues executing, and ignores any input operations on the file.

QUICK CHECK

5.6.1 Write an If statement that tests if the standard input stream is in the fail state. (pp. 215–217)
5.6.2 What terminology is used when you are trying to determine if a stream is in the fail state? (p. 216)
5.6.3 What happens if you **do not** test the state of a file input stream before using it? (p. 216)

Problem-Solving Case Study

BMI Calculator

PROBLEM: A great deal has been said about how overweight much of the American population is today. You can't pick up a magazine that doesn't have an article on the health problems caused by obesity. Rather than looking at a chart that shows the average weight for a particular height, a measure called the body mass index (BMI), which computes a ratio of your weight and height, has become a popular tool to determine an appropriate weight. The formula for nonmetric values is

$$BMI = weight \times 703 / height^2$$

BMI correlates with the amount of body fat, which can be used to determine whether a weight is unhealthy for a certain height.

Although the discussion of the BMI in the media is a fairly recent phenomenon, the formula was actually developed by Adolphe Quetelet, a nineteenth-century Belgian statistician. Do a search of the Internet for

Problem-Solving Case Study

"body mass index" and you will find more than a million hits. In these references, the formula remains the same but the interpretation of the result varies, depending upon age and gender. Here is the most commonly used generic interpretation:

BMI	Interpretation
< 20	Underweight
20–25	Normal
26–30	Overweight
> 30	Obese

Write a program that calculates the BMI given a weight and height and prints out an appropriate message.

INPUT: The problem statement says that the formula is for nonmetric values. In other words, the weight should be in pounds and the height should be in inches. Thus the input should be two float values: `weight` and `height`.

OUTPUT

- Prompts for the input values
- A message based on the BMI

DISCUSSION: To calculate the BMI, you read in the weight and height and plug them into the formula. If you square the height, you must include `<cmath>` to access the `pow` function. It is more efficient to just multiply height by itself.

$$BMI = weight \times 703 / (height \times height)$$

If you were calculating this index by hand, you would probably notice if the weight or height were negative and question it. If the semantics of your data imply that the values should be nonnegative, then your program should test to be sure that they are. The program should test each value and use a Boolean variable to report the results. Here is the main module for this algorithm.

Main Level 0

```
Test data
IF data are okay
    Calculate BMI
    Print message indicating status
ELSE
    Print "Invalid data; weight and height must be positive."
```

Which of these steps require expansion? Get data, Test data, and Print message indicating status all require multiple statements to solve their particular subproblem. By contrast, we can translate Print "Invalid data; . . ." directly into a C++ output statement. What about the step Calculate BMI? We can write it as a single C++ statement, but there's another level of detail that we must fill in—the actual formula to be used. Because the formula is at a lower level of detail than the rest of the main module, we choose to expand Calculate BMI as a Level 1 module.

Problem-Solving Case Study

Get Data — Level 1

Prompt for weight
Read weight
Prompt for height
Read height

Test Data

IF weight < 0 OR height < 0
   Set dataAreOk to false
ELSE
   Set dataAreOk to true

Calculate BMI

Set bodyMassIndex to weight * 703 / (height * height)
Print Message Indicating Status

Print Message Indicating Status

The problem doesn't say exactly what the message should be, other than reporting the status. Why not jazz up the output a little by printing an appropriate message along with the status.

Status	Message
Underweight	Have a milk shake.
Normal	Have a glass of milk.
Overweight	Have a glass of iced tea.
Obese	See your doctor.

Print "Your body mass index is ", bodyMassIndex, "."
Print "Interpretation and instructions."
IF bodyMassIndex <20
   Print "Underweight: Have a milk shake."
ELSE IF bodyMassIndex <= 25
   Print "Normal: Have a glass of milk."
ELSE IF bodyMassIndex <= 30
   Print "Overweight: Have a glass of iced tea."
ELSE
   Print "Obese: See your doctor."

Problem-Solving Case Study

MODULE STRUCTURE CHART

```
                        Main
          ┌──────────┬───────┴────┬──────────────┐
      Get Data   Test Data   Calculate BMI   Print Message
```

```cpp
//*****************************************************************
// BMI Program
// This program calculates the body mass index (BMI) given a weight
// in pounds and a height in inches and prints a health message
// based on the BMI. Input in English measures.
//*****************************************************************

#include <iostream>

using namespace std;

int main()
{
  const int BMI_CONSTANT = 703;   // Constant in nonmetric formula
  float weight;                    // Weight in pounds
  float height;                    // Height in inches
  float bodyMassIndex;             // Appropriate BMI
  bool dataAreOK;                  // True if data are nonnegative

  // Prompt for and input weight and height
  cout << "Enter your weight in pounds. " << endl;
  cin >> weight;
  cout << "Enter your height in inches. " << endl;
  cin >> height;

  // Test data
  if (weight < 0 || height < 0)
    dataAreOK = false;
  else
    dataAreOK = true;

  if ( dataAreOK)
  {
    // Calculate body mass index
    bodyMassIndex = weight * BMI_CONSTANT / (height * height);

    // Print message indicating status
    cout << "Your body mass index is " << bodyMassIndex
         << ". " << endl;
    cout << "Interpretation and instructions. " << endl;
```

Problem-Solving Case Study

```
    if (bodyMassIndex < 20)
      cout << "Underweight: Have a milk shake." << endl;
    else if (bodyMassIndex <= 25)
      cout << "Normal: Have a glass of milk." << endl;
    else if (bodyMassIndex <= 30)
      cout << "Overweight: Have a glass of iced tea." << endl;
    else
      cout << "Obese: See your doctor." << endl;
  }
  else
    cout << "Invalid data; weight and height must be positive."
         << endl;
  return 0;
}
```

Here are outputs of runs with various heights and weights and with both good and bad data.

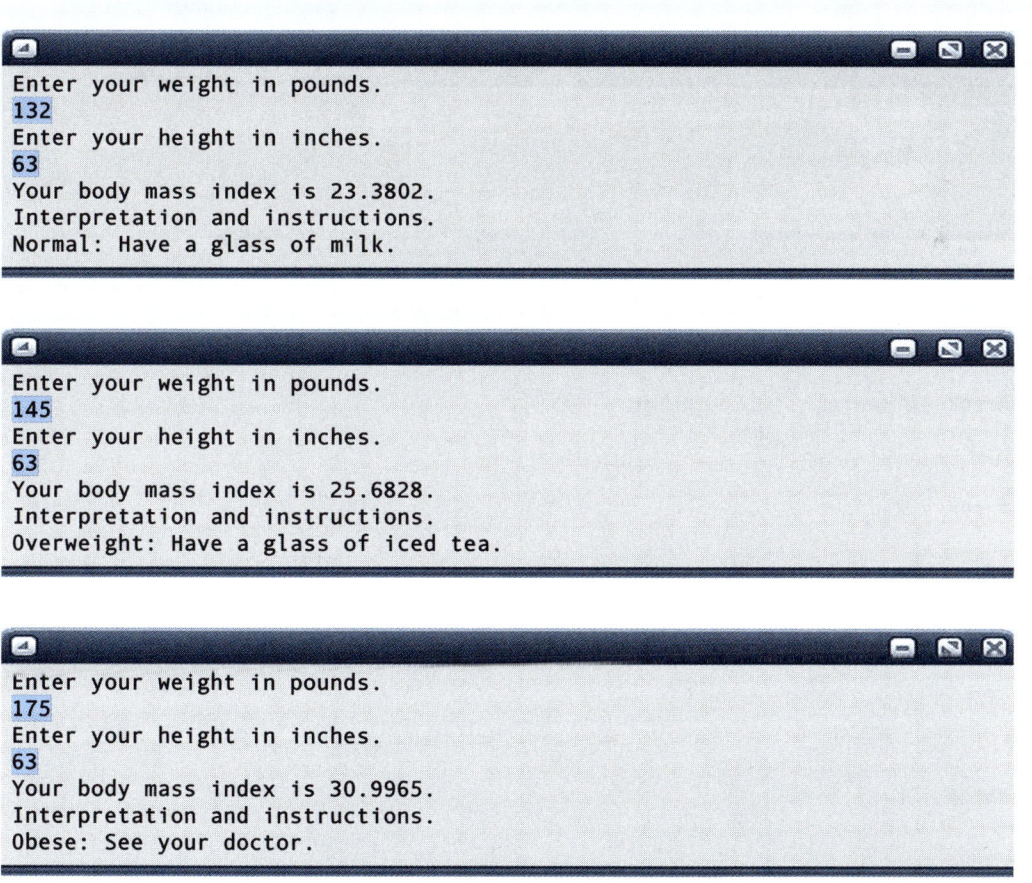

```
Enter your weight in pounds.
132
Enter your height in inches.
63
Your body mass index is 23.3802.
Interpretation and instructions.
Normal: Have a glass of milk.
```

```
Enter your weight in pounds.
145
Enter your height in inches.
63
Your body mass index is 25.6828.
Interpretation and instructions.
Overweight: Have a glass of iced tea.
```

```
Enter your weight in pounds.
175
Enter your height in inches.
63
Your body mass index is 30.9965.
Interpretation and instructions.
Obese: See your doctor.
```

Problem-Solving Case Study

```
Enter your weight in pounds.
175
Enter your height in inches.
68
Your body mass index is 26.6058.
Interpretation and instructions.
Overweight: Have a glass of iced tea.
```

```
Enter your weight in pounds.
-100
Enter your height in inches.
64
Invalid data; weight and height must be positive.
```

```
Enter your weight in pounds.
130
Enter your height in inches.
-65
Invalid data; weight and height must be positive.
```

In this program, we use a nested *If* structure that is easy to understand although somewhat inefficient. We assign a value to `dataAreOK` in one statement before testing it in the next. We could reduce the code by writing

`dataAreOK = !(weight < 0 || height < 0);`

Using DeMorgan's law, we also could write this statement as

`dataAreOK = (weight >= 0 && height >= 0);`

In fact, we could reduce the code even more by eliminating the variable `dataAreOK` and using

```
if (weight => 0 && height >= 0)
   .
   .
   .
```

in place of

```
if (dataAreOK)
   .
   .
   .
```

To convince yourself that these three variations work, try them by hand with some test data. If all of these statements do the same thing, how do you choose which one to use? If your goal is efficiency, the final variation—the compound condition in the main If statement—is the best choice. If you are trying to express as clearly as possible what your code is doing, the longer form shown in the program may be the best option. The other variations lie somewhere in between. (Some people would find the compound condition in the main If statement to be not only the most efficient, but also the clearest to understand.) There are no absolute rules to follow here, but the general guideline is to strive for clarity, even if you must sacrifice a little efficiency.

Testing and Debugging

In Chapter 1, we discussed the problem-solving and implementation phases of computer programming. Testing is an integral part of both phases. Here, we test both phases of the process used to develop the BMI program. Testing in the problem-solving phase is done after the solution is developed but before it is implemented. In the implementation phase, we do testing after the algorithm is translated into a program, and again after the program has compiled successfully. The compilation itself constitutes another stage of testing that is performed automatically.

Testing in the Problem-Solving Phase: The Algorithm Walk-Through

Determining Preconditions and Postconditions

To test during the problem-solving phase, we do a *walk-through* of the algorithm. For each module in the functional decomposition, we establish an assertion called a precondition and another called a postcondition. A precondition is an assertion that must be true before a module is executed for the module to execute correctly. A postcondition is an assertion that should be true after the module has executed, if it has done its job correctly. To test a module, we "walk through" the algorithmic steps to confirm that they produce the required postcondition, given the stated precondition.

> **Precondition** An assertion that must be true before a module begins executing.
> **Postcondition** An assertion that should be true after a module has executed.

Our algorithm has five modules: the `main` module, Get Data, Test Data, Calculate BMI, and Print Message Indicating Status. Usually there is no precondition for a `main` module. Our `main` module's postcondition is that it outputs the correct results, given the correct input. More specifically, the postcondition for the `main` module is as follows:

- The computer has input two real values into `weight` and `height`.
- If the input is invalid, an error message has been printed; otherwise, the body mass index has been calculated and an appropriate message has been printed based on the result.

Because Get Data is the first module executed in the algorithm and because it does not assume anything about the contents of the variables it is about to manipulate, it has no precondition. Its postcondition is that it has input two real values into `weight` and `height`.

The precondition for module Test Data is that `weight` and `height` have been assigned meaningful values. Its postcondition is that `dataAreOK` contains `true` if the values in `weight` and `height` are nonnegative; otherwise, `dataAreOK` contains `false`.

The precondition for module Calculate BMI is that `weight` and `height` contain meaningful values. Its postcondition is that the variable named `dataAreOK` contains the evaluation of the BMI formula (`weight * 703 / (height * height)`).

The precondition for module Print Message Indicating Status is that `dataAreOK` contains the result of evaluating the BMI formula. Its postcondition is that appropriate documentation and the value in `dataAreOK` have been printed, along with the messages: "Underweight: Have a milk shake." if the BMI value is less than 20; "Normal: Have a glass of milk." if the value is less than or equal to 26; "Overweight: Have a glass of iced tea." if the value is less than or equal to 30; and "Obese: See your doctor." if the value is greater than 30.

The module preconditions and postconditions are summarized in the following table. In the table, we use *AND* with its usual meaning in an assertion—the logical AND operation. Also, a phrase like "`someVariable` is assigned" is an abbreviated way of asserting that `someVariable` has already been assigned a meaningful value.

Module	Precondition	Postcondition
Main		Two float values have been input AND if the input is valid, the BMI formula is calculated and the value is printed with an appropriate message; otherwise, an error message has been printed.
Get Data		`weight` and `height` have been input.
Test Data	`weight` and `height` are assigned values.	`dataAreOK` contains `true` if `weight` and `height` are nonnegative; otherwise, `dataAreOK` contains `false`.
Calculate BMI	`weight` and `height` are assigned values.	`bodyMassIndex` contains the evaluation of the BMI formula.
Print Message	`bodyMassIndex` contains the evaluation of the BMI formula.	The value of `bodyMassIndex` has been printed, along with a message interpreting the value.

Performing the Algorithm Walk-Through

Now that we've established the preconditions and postconditions, we walk through the `main` module. At this point, we are concerned only with the steps in the `main` module, so for now we assume that each lower-level module executes correctly. At each step, we must determine the current conditions. If the step is a reference to another module, we must verify that the precondition of that module is met by the current conditions.

We begin with the first statement in the `main` module. Get Data does not have a precondition, and we assume that Get Data satisfies its postcondition that it correctly inputs two real values into `weight` and `height`.

The precondition for module Test Data is that `weight` and `height` are assigned values. This must be the case if Get Data's postcondition is true. Again, because we are concerned only with the step at Level 0, we assume that Test Data satisfies its postcondition that `dataAreOK` contains `true` or `false`, depending on the input values.

Next, the If statement checks to see if `dataAreOK` is `true`. If it is, the algorithm performs the then-clause. Assuming that Calculate BMI correctly evaluates the BMI formula and that Print Message Indicating Status prints the result and the appropriate message (remember, we're assuming that the lower-level modules are correct for now), then the If statement's then-clause is correct. If the value in `dataAreOK` is `false`, the algorithm performs the else-clause and prints an error message.

We now have verified that the `main` (Level 0) module is correct, assuming the Level 1 modules are correct. The next step is to examine each module at Level 1 and answer this question: If the Level 2 modules (if any) are assumed to be correct, does this Level 1 module do what it is supposed to do? We simply repeat the walk-through process for each module, starting with its particular precondition. In this example, there are no Level 2 modules, so the Level 1 modules must be complete.

Get Data correctly reads in two values—`weight` and `height`—thereby satisfying its postcondition. (The next refinement is to code this instruction in C++. Whether it is coded correctly is *not* an issue in this phase; we deal with the code when we perform testing in the implementation phase.)

Test Data checks whether both variables contain nonnegative values. The If condition correctly uses OR operators to combine the relational expressions so that if either of them is `true`, the then-clause is executed. It thus assigns `false` to `dataAreOK` if either of the numbers is negative; otherwise, it assigns `true`. The module, therefore, satisfies its postcondition.

Calculate BMI evaluates the BMI formula: `weight * 703 / (height * height)`. The required postcondition, therefore, is true. But what if the value of `height` is 0? Oh, dear! We checked that the inputs are nonnegative, but forgot that `height` is used as a divisor and thus cannot be 0. We'll need to fix this problem before we release this program for general use.

Print Message Indicating Status outputs the value in `bodyMassIndex` with appropriate documentation. It then compares the result to the standards and prints the appropriate interpretation. "Underweight: Have a milk shake." is printed if the value is less than 20; "Normal: Have a glass of milk." is printed if the value is less than or equal to 26; "Overweight: Have a glass of iced tea." is printed if the value is less than or equal to 30; and "Obese: See your doctor." is printed if the value is greater than 30. Thus the module satisfies its postcondition.

Once we've completed the algorithm walk-through, we have to correct any discrepancies and repeat the process. When we know that the modules do what they are supposed to do, we start translating the algorithm into our programming language.

A standard postcondition for any program is that the user has been notified of invalid data. You should *validate* every input value for which any restrictions apply. A data-validation If statement tests an input value and outputs an error message if the value is not acceptable. (We validated the data when we tested for negative scores in the BMI program.) The best place to validate data is immediately after it is input. To satisfy the data-validation postcondition, the algorithm should also test the input values to ensure that they aren't too large or too small.

Testing in the Implementation Phase

Now that we've talked about testing in the problem-solving phase, we turn to testing in the implementation phase. In this phase, you need to test at several points.

Code Walk-Through

After the code is written, you should go over it line by line to be sure that you've faithfully reproduced the algorithm—a process known as a *code walk-through*. In a team programming situation, you ask other team members to walk through the algorithm and code with you, to double-check the design and code.

Execution Trace

You also should take some actual values and hand-calculate what the output should be by doing an *execution trace* (or *hand trace*). When the program is executed, you can use these same values as input and check the results.

The computer is a very literal device—it does exactly what we *tell* it to do, which may or may not be what we *want* it to do. We try to make sure that a program does what we want by tracing the execution of the statements.

We use a nonsense program below to demonstrate the technique. We keep track of the values of the program variables on the right-hand side. Variables with undefined values are indicated with a dash. When a variable is assigned a value, that value is listed in the appropriate column.

	Value of		
Statement	a	b	c

`const int X = 5;`
`int main()`
`{`
  `int a, b, c;`
	—	—	—

`b = 1;`	—	1	—
`c = X + b;`	—	1	6
`a = X + 4;`	9	1	6
`a = c;`	6	1	6
`b = c;`	6	6	6
`a = a + b + c;`	18	6	6
`c = c % X;`	18	6	1
`c = c * a;`	18	6	18
`a = a % b;`	0	6	18
`cout << a << b << c;`	0	6	18
`return 0;` `}`	0	6	18

Now that you've seen how the technique works, let's apply it to the BMI program. We list only the executable statement portion here. The input values are 124 and 63.5.

The then-clause of the first If statement is not executed for these input data, so we do not fill in any of the variable columns to its right. The then-clause of the second If statement is executed; thus the else-clause is not. The else-clause of the third If statement is executed, which is another If statement. The then-clause is executed here, leaving the rest of the code unexecuted.

We always create columns for all of the variables, even if we know that some will stay empty. Why? Because it's possible that later we'll encounter an erroneous reference to an empty variable; having a column for the variable reminds us to check for just such an error.

Statement	weight	height	BMI	dataAreOK
`cout << "Enter your weight in pounds. " << endl;`	—	—	—	—
`cin >> weight;`	124	—	—	—
`cout << "Enter your height in inches. " << endl;`	124	—	—	—
`cin >> height;`	124	63.5	—	—

`if (weight < 0 || height < 0)`
  `dataAreOK = false;`
`else`
	124	63.5	—	—

`dataAreOK = true;`	124	63.5	—	true
`if (dataAreOK)` `{`	124	63.5	—	true
`bodyMassIndex = weight * BMI_CONSTANT /` `(height * height);`	124	63.5	21.087	true

Statement	weight	height	BMI	dataAreOK
`cout << "Your body mass index is "` `     << bodyMassIndex << ". " << endl;`	124	63.5	21.087	true
`cout << "Interpretation and instructions. "` `     << endl;`	124	63.5	21.087	true
`if (bodyMassIndex < 20)`	124	63.5	21.087	true
`  cout << "Underweight: Have a milk shake."` `       << endl;`				
`else if (bodyMassIndex <= 25)`	124	63.5	21.087	true
`  cout << "Normal: Have a glass of milk."` `       << endl;`	124	63.5	21.087	true

`else if (bodyMassIndex <= 30)`
`  cout`
`     << "Overweight: Have a glass of iced tea."`
`     << endl;`
`else`
`  cout << "Obese: See your doctor." << endl;`
`}`
`else`
`  cout << "Invalid data; weight "`
`       << "and height must be positive."`
`       << endl;`				

`return 0;`	124	63.5	21.087	true

When a program contains branches, it's a good idea to retrace its execution with different input data so that each branch is traced at least once. In the next section, we describe how to develop data sets that test all of a program's branches.

Testing Selection Control Structures

To test a program with branches, we need to execute each branch at least once and verify the results. For example, the BMI program contains five If-Then-Else statements (see **FIGURE 5.6**). We need a series of data sets to test the different branches. For example, the following sets of input values for `weight` and `height` cause all of the branches to be executed:

Data Set	Weight in Pounds	Height in Inches	Status
1	110.0	67.5	Underweight
2	120.0	63.0	Normal
3	145.0	62.0	Overweight
4	176.6	60.0	Obese
5	-100	65.0	Error message

FIGURE 5.7 shows the flow of control through the branching structure of the BMI program for each of these data sets. Every branch in the program is executed at least once through this series of test runs; eliminating any of the test data sets would leave at least one branch untested. This series of data sets provides what is called *minimum complete coverage* of the program's branching structure. Whenever you test a program with branches in it, you should design a series of tests that cover all of the branches. It may help to draw diagrams like those in Figure 5.7 so that you can see which branches are being executed.

Because an action in one branch of a program often affects processing in a later branch, it is critical to test as many *combinations of branches*, or paths, through a program as possible. By doing so, we can be sure that there are no interdependencies that could cause problems. Of course, some combinations of branches may be impossible to follow. For example, if the else-clause is executed in the first branch of the BMI program, the else-clause in the second

FIGURE 5.6 Branching Structure for BMI Program

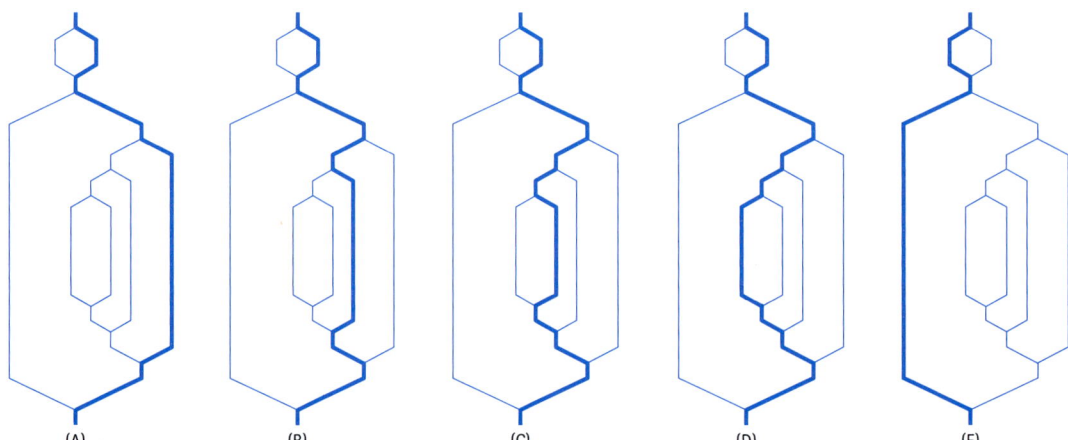

FIGURE 5.7 Flow of Control Through BMI Program for Each of Five Data Sets

branch cannot be executed. Shouldn't we try all possible paths? Yes, in theory we should. However, even in a small program the number of paths can be very large.

The approach to testing that we've used here is called *code coverage* because the test data are designed by looking at the code of the program. Code coverage also is called *white-box* (or *clear-box*) *testing* because we are allowed to see the program code while designing the tests. Another approach to testing, called *data coverage*, attempts to test as many allowable data values as possible without regard to the program code. Because we need not see the code in this form of testing, it also is called *black-box testing*—we would design the same set of tests even if the code were hidden in a black box.

Complete data coverage is as impractical as complete code coverage for many programs. For example, if a program has four `int` input values, there are approximately $(2 \times \text{INT\_MAX})^4$ possible inputs. (`INT_MAX` and `INT_MIN` are constants declared in the header file `<climits>`. They represent the largest and smallest possible `int` values, respectively, on your particular computer and C++ compiler.)

Often, testing entails a combination of these two strategies. Instead of trying every possible data value (data coverage), we examine the code (code coverage) and look for ranges of values for which processing is identical. Then we test the values at the boundaries and, sometimes, a value in the middle of each range. For example, a simple condition such as

```
alpha < 0
```

divides the integers into two ranges:

1. `INT_MIN` through `-1`
2. `0` through `INT_MAX`

Thus we should test the four values `INT_MIN`, `-1`, `0`, and `INT_MAX`. A compound condition such as

```
alpha >= 0 && alpha <= 100
```

divides the integers into three ranges:

1. `INT_MIN` through `-1`
2. `0` through `100`
3. `101` through `INT_MAX`

Thus we have six values to test. In addition, to verify that the relational operators are correct, we should test for values of `1` (`> 0`) and `99` (`< 100`).

Conditional branches are only one factor in developing a testing strategy. We consider more of these factors in later chapters.

The Test Plan

We've discussed strategies and techniques for testing programs, but how do you approach the testing of a specific program? You do it by designing and implementing a test plan—a document that specifies the test cases that should be tried, the reason for each test case, and the expected output. Implementing a test plan involves running the program using the data specified by the test cases in the plan and checking and recording the results.

> **Test plan** A document that specifies how a program is to be tested.
>
> **Test plan implementation** Using the test cases specified in a test plan to verify that a program outputs the predicted results.

The test plan should be developed together with the functional decomposition. As you create each module, write out its precondition and postcondition and note the test data required to verify them. Consider code coverage and data coverage to see if you've left out tests for any aspects of the program (if you've forgotten something, it probably indicates that a precondition or postcondition is incomplete).

The following table shows a partial test plan for the BMI program. It has six test cases. The first four cases test the different paths through the program for valid data. Two more test cases check that `weight` and `height` are validated appropriately by separately entering an invalid score for each.

We should test the program on the end cases—that is, where the BMI is exactly 20, 25, and 30. Because the BMI is calculated and not input, it is difficult to come up with the appropriate input values. The Case Study Follow-Up Exercises ask you to look at this problem, complete this test plan, and implement it.

Test Plan for BMI Program			
Reason for Test Case	Input Values	Expected Output	Observed Ouput
Underweight case	110, 67.5	Your body mass index is 16.9723. Interpretation and instructions. Underweight: Have a milk shake.	
Normal case	120, 63	Your body mass index is 21.2547. Interpretation and instructions. Normal: Have a glass of milk.	
Overweight case	145, 62	Your body mass index is 26.518. Interpretation and instructions. Overweight: Have a glass of iced tea.	
Obese case	176.6, 60	Your body mass index is 34.4861. Interpretation and instructions. Obese: See your doctor.	
Negative weight	−120, 63	Invalid data; weight and height must be positive.	
Negative height	120, −63	Invalid data; weight and height must be positive.	

Implementing a test plan does not guarantee that a program is completely correct. It means only that a careful, systematic test of the program has not demonstrated any bugs.

Tests Performed Automatically During Compilation and Execution

Once a program is coded and test data has been prepared, it is ready for compiling. The compiler has two responsibilities: to report any errors and (if there are no errors) to translate the program into object code.

Errors can be syntactic or semantic. The compiler finds syntactic errors. For example, the compiler warns you when reserved words are misspelled, identifiers are undeclared, semicolons are missing, and operand types are mismatched. But it won't find all of your typing errors. If you type > instead of <, for example, you won't get an error message; instead, you will get erroneous results when you test the program. It's up to you to design a test plan and carefully check the code to detect errors of this type.

FIGURE 5.8 Testing Process

Semantic errors (also called *logic errors*) are mistakes that give you the wrong answer. They are more difficult to locate than syntactic errors and usually surface when a program is executing. C++ detects only the most obvious semantic errors—those that result in an invalid operation (dividing by zero, for example). Although semantic errors sometimes are caused by typing errors, they are more often a product of a faulty algorithm design. The lack of checking whether `height` is 0—the potential problem that we found in the algorithm walk-through for the BMI problem—is a typical semantic error. By walking through the algorithm and the code, tracing the execution of the program, and developing a thorough test strategy, you should be able to avoid, or at least quickly locate, semantic errors in your programs.

FIGURE 5.8 illustrates the testing process we've been discussing. The figure shows where syntax and semantic errors occur and in which phase they can be corrected.

Testing and Debugging Hints

1. C++ has three pairs of operators that are similar in appearance but very different in effect: == and =, && and &, and || and |. Double-check all of your logical expressions to be sure you're using the "equals-equals," "and-and," and "or-or" operators.

2. If you use extra parentheses for clarity, be sure that the opening and closing parentheses match up. To verify that parentheses are properly paired, start with the innermost pair and draw a line connecting them. Do the same for the others, working your way out to the outermost pair. For example,

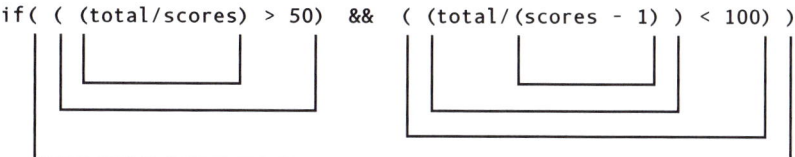

Here is a quick way to tell whether you have an equal number of opening and closing parentheses. The scheme uses a single number (the "magic number"), whose value

initially is 0. Scan the expression from left to right. At each opening parenthesis, add 1 to the magic number; at each closing parenthesis, subtract 1. At the final closing parenthesis, the magic number should be 0. For example,

```
if (((total/scores) > 50) && ((total/(scores - 1)) < 100))
 0   1 2 3              2    1   2 3            4       3 2      1 0
```

3. Don't use =< to mean "less than or equal to"; only the symbol <= works for this purpose. Likewise, => is invalid for "greater than or equal to"; you must use >= for this operation.

4. In an If statement, remember to use a { } pair if the then-clause or else-clause is a sequence of statements. Also, be sure not to put a semicolon after the right brace.

5. Echo print all input data. By doing so, you know that your input values are what they are supposed to be.

6. Test for bad data. If a data value must be positive, use an If statement to test the value. If the value is negative or 0, an error message should be printed; otherwise, processing should continue. For example, the following code segment tests whether three test scores are less than 0 or greater than 100:

```
dataOK = true;
if (test1 < 0 || test2 < 0 || test3 < 0)
{
  cout << "Invalid Data:  Score(s) less than zero." << endl;
  dataOK = false;
}
if (test1 > 100 || test2 > 100 || test3 > 100)
{
  cout << "Invalid Data:  Score(s) greater than 100." << endl;
  dataOK = false;
}
```

These If statements test the limits of reasonable scores, and the rest of the program continues only if the data values are reasonable.

7. When an If statement is inadvertently applied to an `int` value, it returns `true` if the value is nonzero and `false` otherwise. The compiler does not report this result as an error.

8. Take some sample values and try them by hand as we did for the BMI program. (There's more on this method in Chapter 6.)

9. If your program reads data from an input file, it should verify that the file was opened successfully. Immediately after the call to the `open` function, an If statement should test the state of the file stream.

10. If your program produces an answer that does not agree with a value you've calculated by hand, try these suggestions:
    a. Redo your arithmetic.
    b. Recheck your input data.
    c. Carefully go over the section of code that does the calculation. If you're in doubt about the order in which the operations are performed, insert clarifying parentheses.
    d. Check for integer overflow. The value of an `int` variable may have exceeded `INT_MAX` in the middle of a calculation. Some systems give an error message when this happens, but most do not.
    e. Check the conditions in branching statements to be sure that the correct branch is taken under all circumstances.

Summary

Using logical expressions is a way of asking questions while a program is running. The program evaluates each logical expression, producing the value `true` if the expression is true or the value `false` if the expression is not true.

The If statement allows you to take different paths through a program based on the value of a logical expression. The If-Then-Else statement is used to choose between two courses of action; the If-Then statement is used to choose whether to take a particular course of action. The branches of an If-Then or If-Then-Else can be any statement, simple or compound. They can even be other If statements.

The algorithm walk-through requires us to define a precondition and a postcondition for each module in an algorithm. Then we need to verify that those assertions are true at the beginning and end of each module. By testing our design in the problem-solving phase, we can eliminate errors that can be more difficult to detect in the implementation phase.

An execution trace is a way of finding program errors once we've entered the implementation phase. It's a good idea to trace a program before you run it, so that you have some sample results against which to check the program's output. A written test plan is an essential part of any program development effort.

Quick Check Answers

5.1.1 The order in which statements are executed in a program. **5.1.2** sequential **5.1.3** selection or branching control structure **5.1.4** It allows the computer to choose between alternative courses of action, depending on a test of certain conditions. **5.2.1** `true` and `false`.
5.2.2 `temperature > 32` **5.2.3** 2 **5.2.4** logical values and logical operations. **5.2.5** $x = 1, y = 5$
5.3.1
```
if (temperature > 32)
     cout << "Above freezing.";
else
     cout << "Freezing or below.";
```
5.3.2 Because the computer can choose to execute either of them depending on the circumstances. **5.3.3** It must evaluate to a `bool` data type. **5.4.1** It allows the computer to select among any number of alternative courses of action.
5.4.2
```
if (temperature < 32)
     cout << "Below freezing.";
else if (temperature = = 32)
     cout << "Freezing.";
else if (temperature < 212)
     cout << "Above freezing and below boiling.";
else
     cout << "Boiling and above.";
```
5.4.3 A nested control structure. **5.4.4** A multiway branch **5.4.5** The dangling `else` problem. **5.5.1** `&&, ||, !` **5.5.2** `!(a == b || c >= d)` **5.5.3** `failed = (grade <= 50.0);` **5.5.4** From left to right **5.5.5** `5 >= 2 && x != 7` **5.6.1** `if (cin) ...` **5.6.2** Testing the state of the stream **5.6.3** Your program will quietly continue to execute and ignore any input/output operations on the file.

Exam Preparation Exercises

1. Define the term "flow of control."
2. The values `true` and `false` are keywords in C++. True or false?
3. The "equals or greater" operator in C++ is written =>. True or false?
4. Why is it that `'A' < 'B'` and `'a' < 'b'` are both `true`, but `'a' < 'B'` is `false`?

5. If `int1` has the value 12, `int2` has the value 18, and `int3` has the value 21, what is the result of each of the following Boolean expressions?
   a. `int1 < int2 && int2 < int3`
   b. `int1 < int3 || int3 < int2`
   c. `int1 <= int2 - 6`
   d. `int2 <= int1 + 5 || int3 >= int2 + 5`
   e. `!(int1 < 30)`
   f. `!(int2 == int1 && int3 == int1)`
   g. `!(int1 > 25) && !(int2 < 17)`

6. If `string1` has the value `"miniscule"`, `string2` has the value `"minimum"`, and `string3` has the value `"miniature"`, what is the result of each of the following expressions?
   a. `string1 > string2`
   b. `string1 > string2 && string2 > string3`
   c. `string1.substr(0, 4) == string2.substr(0, 4)`
   d. `string1 > "maximum"`
   e. `string3.substr(0, 4) == "mini" || string1 == string2`
   f. `string3.length() > string1.length() && string1 > string3`
   g. `!((string1.substr(8, 1) == string3.substr(8, 1)) && string1.length() == 9)`

7. Why won't the following expression result in a division-by-zero error when `someInt` has the value `0`?

   `someInt != 0 && 5/someInt > 10`

8. The `bool` operators have lower precedence than the arithmetic operators, with the exception of the `!` operator, which has the same precedence as unary minus. True or false?

9. We enclose the logical expression in an If statement in parentheses only to make the code more readable. C++ doesn't require the parentheses. True or false?

10. What does the following If statement do when the value in `someInt` is 77?

    ```
    if (someInt <= 44) || (someInt - 37 < 40)
      cout << "The data is within range.";
    else
      cout << "The data doesn't make sense.";
    ```

11. What does the following If statement do when the value in `string1` is `"The"`?

    ```
    if (string1.length() == 3 && string1.substr(0, 1) = "T")
      cout << "The word may be \"The\"";
    else
    {
      string1 = "The";
      cout << "The word is now \"The\"";
    }
    ```

12. What does the following If statement do when the value in `float1` is `3.15`?

    ```
    if (fabs(float1 - 3.14) < 0.00000001)
    {
      cout << "The area of the circle of radius 6.0 "
           << "is approximately:" << endl;
      cout << 6.0 * 6.0 * float1;
    }
    ```

13. Why does the following If statement always output `"false"` regardless of the value in `someInt`?

    ```
    if (someInt = 0)
      cout << "true";
    else
      cout << "false";
    ```

14. What is output by the following code segment when `score` has the value `85`?

    ```
    if (score < 50)
      cout << "Failing";
    else if (score < 60)
      cout << "Below average";
    else if (score < 70)
      cout << "Average";
    else if (score < 80)
      cout << "Above average";
    else if (score < 90)
      cout << "Very good";
    else if (score < 100)
      cout << "Excellent";
    ```

15. What is output by the following code segment when `score` has the value `85`?

    ```
    if (score < 50)
      cout << "Failing";
    if (score < 60)
      cout << "Below average";
    if (score < 70)
      cout << "Average";
    if (score < 80)
      cout << "Above average";
    if (score < 90)
      cout << "Very good";
    if (score < 100)
      cout << "Excellent";
    ```

16. How do you fix a nested If statement that has a dangling `else`?
17. How would you write a Boolean expression in an If statement if you want the statement's then-clause to execute when file `inData` is in the fail state?
18. Is there any limit to how deeply we can nest If statements?

Programming Warm-Up Exercises

1. Write a Boolean expression that is true when the `bool` variable `moon` has the value `"blue"` or the value `"Blue"`.

2. Write a Boolean expression that is true when both `inFile1` and `inFile2` are in the fail state.
3. Write a branching statement that reads into a string variable called `someString`, from a file called `inFile`, if the file is not in the fail state.
4. Write a branching statement that tests whether one date comes before another. The dates are stored as integers representing the month, day, and year. The variables for the two dates are called `month1`, `day1`, `year1`, `month2`, `day2`, and `year2`. The statement should output an appropriate message depending on the outcome of the test. For example:

    `12/21/01 comes before 1/27/05`

    or

    `7/14/04 does not come before 7/14/04`

5. Change the branching statement that you wrote for Exercise 4 so that when the first date doesn't come before the second, it sets the first date equal to the second date in addition to printing the message.
6. Write a Boolean expression that is `true` when either of the `bool` variables `bool1` or `bool2` is `true`, but is `false` whenever both of them are `true` or neither of them is `true`.
7. Write a branching statement that tests whether `score` is in the range of 0 to 100, and outputs an error message if it is not within that range.
8. Change the branching statement that you wrote for Exercise 7 so that when `score` is in the proper range, it adds `score` to a running total variable called `scoreTotal` and increments a counter called `scoreCount`.
9. Write a code segment that reads an `int` value from each of two files, `infile1` and `infile2`. If neither file is in the fail state, the program writes the lesser value of the two to a file called `outfile`, and reads another value from the file that had the lesser value. If either of the files is in the fail state, then the value from the file that is not in the fail state is written to `outfile`. If both files are in the fail state, then an error message is output to `cout`. The `int` values can be input into variables `value1` and `value2`.
10. Change the following series of If-Then statements into a nested If-Else-If structure.

    ```
    if (score > 100)
      cout << "Duffer.";
    if (score <= 100 && score > 80)
      cout << "Weekend regular.";
    if (score <= 80 && score > 72)
      cout << "Competitive player.";
    if (score <= 72 && score > 68)
      cout << "Turn pro!";
    if (score <= 68)
      cout << "Time to go on tour!";
    ```

11. Write an If structure that outputs the least of three values, `count1`, `count2`, and `count3`. If more than one variable has the same lowest value, then output the value as many times as it is found in those variables.

12. The following program segment is not supposed to print anything, yet it outputs the first error message, `"Error in maximum: 100"`. What's wrong, and how would you correct it? Why doesn't the code output both error messages?

    ```
    maximum = 75;
    minimum = 25;
    if (maximum = 100)
      cout << "Error in maximum: " << maximum << endl;
    if (minimum = 0)
      cout << "Error in minimum: " << minimum << endl;
    ```

13. Write an If statement that takes the square root of the variable **area** only when its value is nonnegative. Otherwise, the statement should set **area** equal to its absolute value and then take the square root of the new value. The result should be assigned to the variable **root**.

14. Write a test plan for the following branching structure.

    ```
    cout << "The water is a ";
    if (temp >= 212)
      cout << "gas.";
    else if (temp > 32)
      cout << "liquid.";
    else
      cout << "solid.";
    ```

15. Write a test plan for the following branching structure. (Note that the test for a leap year given here does not include the special rules for century years.)

    ```
    if (month == 2 && day > 28)
      if (year%4 != 0)
        cout << "Date error. Not a leap year."
      else
        if (day > 29)
          cout << "Date error. Improper day for February."
    ```

Programming Problems

1. Write a C++ program that computes a student's grade for an assignment as a percentage given the student's score and the total points. The final score should be rounded up to the nearest whole value using the `ceil` function in the `<cmath>` header file. You should also display the floating-point result up to 5 decimal places. The input to the program must come from a file containing a single line with the score and total separated by a space. In addition, you should print to the console "Excellent" if the grade is greater than 90, "Well Done" if the grade is greater than 80, "Good" if the grade is greater than 70, "Need Improvement" if the grade is greater than or equal to 60, and "Fail" if the grade is less than 50.

2. ROT13 (rotate by 13 places) is a simple letter substitution cipher that is an instance of a Caesar cipher developed in ancient Rome and used by Julius Caesar who used it in

his private correspondence. ROT13 replaces a letter with the letter 13 letters after it in the alphabet. The following table demonstrates the translation in ROT13:

A ↔ N
B ↔ O
C ↔ P
D ↔ Q
E ↔ R
F ↔ S
G ↔ T
H ↔ U
I ↔ V
J ↔ W
K ↔ X
L ↔ Y
M ↔ Z

Thus, the translation of the word JULIUS using ROT13 would be WHYVHF. Write a C++ program that inputs a letter and outputs the corresponding letter using the ROT13 encoding scheme above. Your output should look like `G -> T`.

3. Use functional decomposition to write a C++ program that inputs a letter and outputs the corresponding International Civil Aviation Organization alphabet word (these are the words that pilots use when they need to spell something out over a noisy radio channel). The alphabet is as follows:

A	Alpha
B	Bravo
C	Charlie
D	Delta
E	Echo
F	Foxtrot
G	Golf
H	Hotel
I	India
J	Juliet
K	Kilo
L	Lima
M	Mike
N	November
O	Oscar
P	Papa
Q	Quebec
R	Romeo
S	Sierra

T	Tango
U	Uniform
V	Victor
W	Whiskey
X	X-ray
Y	Yankee
Z	Zulu

Be sure to use proper formatting and appropriate comments in your code. Provide appropriate prompts to the user. The output should be labeled clearly and formatted neatly.

4. Use functional decomposition to write a C++ program that asks the user to enter his or her weight and the name of a planet. The program then outputs how much the user would weigh on that planet. The following table gives the factor by which the weight must be multiplied for each planet. The program should output an error message if the user doesn't type a correct planet name. The prompt and the error message should make it clear to the user how a planet name must be entered. Be sure to use proper formatting and appropriate comments in your code. The output should be labeled clearly and formatted neatly.

Mercury	0.4155
Venus	0.8975
Earth	1.0
Moon	0.166
Mars	0.3507
Jupiter	2.5374
Saturn	1.0677
Uranus	0.8947
Neptune	1.1794
Pluto	0.0899

5. Use functional decomposition to write a C++ program that takes a number in the range of 1 to 12 as input, and outputs the corresponding month of the year, where 1 is January, and so on. The program should output an error message if the number entered is not in the required range. The prompt and the error message should make it clear to the user how a month number must be entered. Be sure to use proper formatting and appropriate comments in your code. The output should be labeled clearly and formatted neatly.

6. Use functional decomposition to write a C++ program that takes a number in the range of 0 to 6 and a second number in the range of 1 to 366 as input. The first number represents the day of the week on which the year begins, where 0 is Sunday, and so on. The second number indicates the day of the year. The program then outputs the name of the day of the week corresponding to the day of the year. The number of the day of the week can be computed as follows:

```
(start day + day of year - 1) % 7
```

The program should output an error message if the numbers entered are not in the required ranges. The prompt and the error message should make it clear to the user how the numbers must be entered. Be sure to use proper formatting and appropriate comments in your code. The output should be labeled clearly and formatted neatly.

7. Use functional decomposition to write a C++ program that takes a number in the range of 1 to 365 as input. The number represents the day of the year. The program then outputs the name of the month (assume the year is not a leap year). You can do this by comparing the day of the year to the number of days in the year that precede the start of each month. For example, 59 days precede March, which has 31 days. So, if the day of the year is in the range of 60 through 91, then your program would output `March`. The program should output an error message if the number entered is not in the required range. The prompt and the error message should make it clear to the user how the number must be entered. Be sure to use proper formatting and appropriate comments in your code. The output should be labeled clearly and formatted neatly.

8. Use functional decomposition to write a C++ program that takes as input three numbers representing the number of pins knocked down by a bowler in three throws. The rules of bowling are that if the first throw is a strike (all 10 pins knocked down), then the score is equal to those 10 points plus the number knocked down in the next two throws. Thus the maximum score (three strikes) is 30. If the first throw knocks down fewer than 10 pins, but the second throw knocks down the remainder of the 10 pins (a spare), then the score is those 10 points plus the number of pins knocked down on the third throw. If the first two throws fail to knock down all of the pins (a blow), then the score is just the total number of pins knocked down in the first two throws. Your program should output the computed score, and also should check for erroneous input. For example, a throw may be in the range of 0 through 10 points, and the total of the first two throws must be less than or equal to 10, except when the first throw is a strike. Be sure to use proper formatting and appropriate comments in your code. The output should be labeled clearly and formatted neatly, and the error messages should be informative.

9. Use functional decomposition to write a C++ program that computes a dance competition score. There are four judges who mark the dancers in the range of 0 to 10, and the overall score is the average of the three highest scores (the lowest score is excluded). Your program should output an error message, instead of the average, if any of the scores are not in the correct range. Be sure to use proper formatting and appropriate comments in your code. The output should be labeled clearly and formatted neatly, and the error message should indicate clearly which score was invalid.

10. Use functional decomposition to write a C++ program that determines the median of three input numbers. The median is the middle number when the three numbers are arranged in order by size. However, the user can input the values in any order, so your program must determine which value is between the other two. For example, if the user enters

    `41.52 27.18 96.03`

    then the program would output

    `The median of 41.52, 27.18, and 96.03 is 41.52.`

    Once you have the three-number case working, extend the program to handle five numbers. Be sure to use proper formatting and appropriate comments in your code. The output should be labeled clearly and formatted neatly.

Case Study Follow-Up

1. How might you go about choosing values for `weight` and `height` so that the BMI values of 20, 25, and 30 are tested?
2. Change the program so that the BMI is rounded. Choose appropriate cases to test the end conditions. Implement your test plan.
3. Change the program so that it takes metric values for the weight and height. Go on the Internet to find the correct formula.
4. Change the original program so that the height is entered in feet and inches. Prompt for and enter them separately.
5. A negative input value for `weight` or `height` was considered an error condition in the BMI program. Are there other values for `weight` or `height` that should be considered error conditions? Explain.

Looping

KNOWLEDGE GOALS

- To understand the flow of control in a loop.
- To understand the differences between count-controlled, event-controlled, and flag-controlled loops.
- To understand counting and summing operations within a loop.
- To know how to choose the correct type of loop for a given problem.

SKILL GOALS

To be able to:
- Construct syntactically correct While loops.
- Construct count-controlled, event-controlled, and flag-controlled loops using a While statement.
- Use the end-of-file condition to control the input of data.
- Construct counting and summing loops with a While statement.
- Construct nested While loops.
- Choose data sets that test a looping program comprehensively.

In Chapter 5, we said that the flow of control in a program can differ from the physical order of the statements. The *physical order* is the order in which the statements appear in a program; the order in which we want the statements to be executed is called the *logical order*.

The If statement is one way of making the logical order differ from the physical order. Looping control structures are another. A loop executes the same statement (simple or compound) over and over, as long as a condition or set of conditions is satisfied.

> **Loop** A control structure that causes a statement or group of statements to be executed repeatedly.

In this chapter, we discuss different kinds of loops and explore how they are constructed using the While statement. We also discuss *nested loops* (loops that contain other loops) and introduce a notation for comparing the amount of work done by different algorithms.

6.1 The While Statement

The While statement, like the If statement, tests a condition. Here is the syntax template for the While statement:

WhileStatement

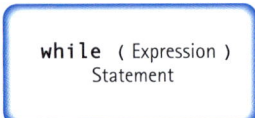

Here is an example of one:

```
while (inputVal != 25)
  cin >> inputVal;
```

The While statement is a looping control structure. The statement to be executed each time through the loop is called the *body* of the loop. In the preceding example, the body of the loop is the input statement that reads in a value for `inputVal`. This While statement says to execute the body repeatedly as long as the input value does not equal 25. The While statement is completed (hence, the loop stops) when `inputVal` equals 25. The effect of this loop, then, is to consume and ignore all the values in the input stream until the number 25 is read.

Just like the condition in an If statement, the condition in a While statement can be an expression of any simple data type. Nearly always, it is a logical (Boolean) expression; if not, its value is implicitly coerced to type **bool** (recall that a zero value is coerced to **false**, and any nonzero value is coerced to **true**). The While statement says, "If the value of the expression is **true**, execute the body and then go back and test the expression again. If the

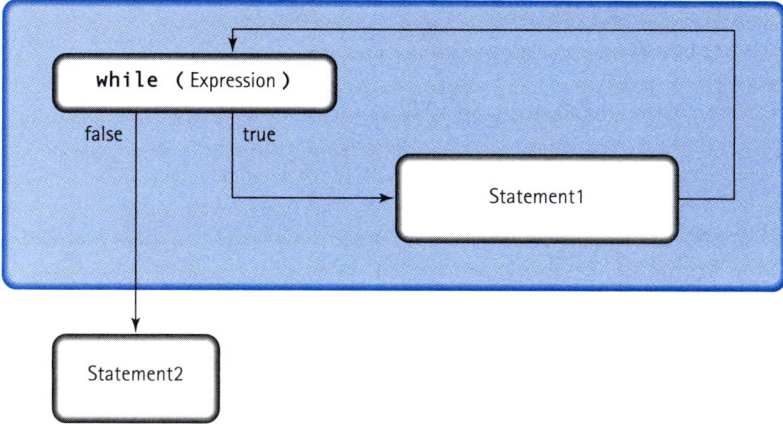

FIGURE 6.1 While Statement Flow of Control

expression's value is **false**, skip the body." The loop body is thus executed over and over as long as the expression is **true** when it is tested. When the expression is **false**, the program skips the body and execution continues at the statement immediately following the loop. Of course, if the expression is **false** initially, the body is never executed. **FIGURE 6.1** shows the flow of control of the While statement, where Statement1 is the body of the loop and Statement2 is the statement following the loop.

The body of a loop can be a compound statement (block), which allows us to execute any group of statements repeatedly. Most often we use While loops in the following form:

```
while (Expression)
{
    .
    .
    .
}
```

In this structure, if the expression is **true**, the entire sequence of statements in the block is executed, and then the expression is checked again. If it is still **true**, the statements are executed again. The cycle continues until the expression becomes **false**.

Although in some ways the If and While statements are alike, some fundamental differences distinguish them (see **FIGURE 6.2**). In the If structure, Statement1 is either skipped or executed exactly once. In the While structure, Statement1 can be skipped, executed once, or executed over and over. The If is used to *choose* a course of action; the While is used to *repeat* a course of action.

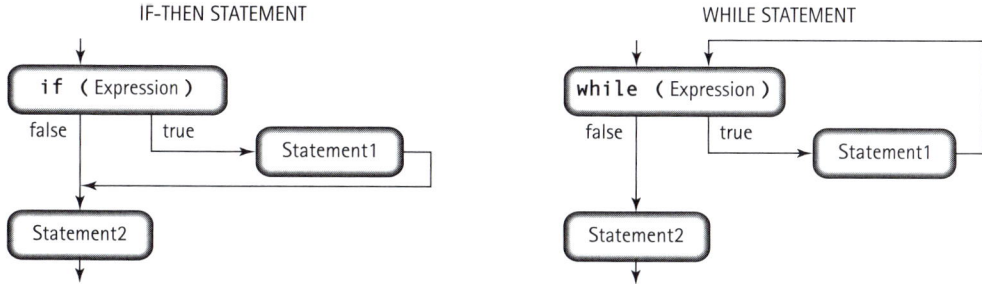

FIGURE 6.2 A Comparison of If and While

246 CHAPTER 6 Looping

QUICK CHECK

6.1.1 What is the name of the looping control structure studied in this section? (p. 244)
6.1.2 What is the data type of the condition expression used in a While statement? (p. 245)
6.1.3 What if the condition expression used in a While statement does not have type **bool**? (p. 245)
6.1.4 An If statement is used to *choose* a course of action where as the While statement is used to _____ a course of action. (p. 245)

6.2 Phases of Loop Execution

The body of a loop is executed in several phases:

Loop entry The point at which the flow of control reaches the first statement inside a loop.

Iteration An individual pass through, or repetition of, the body of a loop.

Loop test The point at which the While expression is evaluated and the decision is made either to begin a new iteration or to skip to the statement immediately following the loop.

Loop exit The point at which the repetition of the loop body ends and control passes to the first statement following the loop.

Termination condition The condition that causes a loop to be exited.

- The moment that the flow of control reaches the first statement inside the loop body is the loop entry.
- Each time the body of a loop is executed, a pass is made through the loop. This pass is called an iteration.
- Before each iteration, control is transferred to the loop test at the beginning of the loop.
- When the last iteration is complete and the flow of control has passed to the first statement following the loop, the program has exited the loop. The condition that causes a loop to be exited is the termination condition. In the case of a While loop, the termination condition is that the While expression becomes **false**.

Notice that the loop exit occurs at only one point: when the loop test is performed. Even though the termination condition may become satisfied midway through the execution of the loop, the current iteration is completed before the computer checks the While expression again.

The concept of looping is fundamental to programming. In this chapter, we spend some time looking at typical kinds of loops and ways of implementing them with the While statement. These looping situations come up again and again when you are analyzing problems and designing algorithms.

QUICK CHECK

6.2.1 What are the four phases of loop execution? (p. 246)

6.3 Loops Using the While Statement

Count-controlled loop A loop that executes a specified number of times.

Event-controlled loop A loop that terminates when something happens inside the loop body to signal that the loop should be exited.

In solving problems, you will come across two major types of loops: count-controlled loops, which repeat a specified number of times, and event-controlled loops, which repeat until something happens within the loop.

If you are making an angel food cake and the recipe reads, "Beat the mixture 300 strokes," you are executing a count-controlled loop. If you are making a pie crust and the recipe reads, "Cut with a pastry blender until the mixture resembles coarse meal," you are executing an event-controlled loop; you don't know ahead of time the exact number of loop iterations.

Count-Controlled Loops

A count-controlled loop uses a variable we call the *loop control variable* in the loop test. Before we enter a count-controlled loop, we have to *initialize* (set the initial value of) the loop control variable and then test it. Then, as part of each iteration of the loop, we must *increment* (increase by 1) the loop control variable. Here's an example in a program that repeatedly outputs "Hello!" on the screen:

```cpp
//***********************************************************
// This program demonstrates a count-controlled loop
//***********************************************************
#include <iostream>

using namespace std;

int main()
{
  int loopCount;                  // Loop control variable

  loopCount = 1;                  // Initialization
  while (loopCount <= 10)         // Test
  {
    cout << "Hello!" << endl;
    loopCount = loopCount + 1;    // Incrementation
  }
  return 0;
}
```

In the Hello program, `loopCount` is the loop control variable. It is set to 1 before loop entry. The While statement tests the expression

```
loopCount <= 10
```

and executes the loop body as long as the expression is **true**. Inside the loop body, the main action we want to be repeated is the output statement. The last statement in the loop body increments `loopCount` by adding 1 to it.

Notice the form of the statement in which we increment the loop control variable:

```
variable = variable + 1;
```

This statement adds 1 to the current value of the variable, and the result replaces the old value. Variables that are used this way are called *counters*. In the Hello program, `loopCount` is incremented with each iteration of the loop—we use it to count the iterations. The loop control variable of a count-controlled loop is always a counter.

Of course, we've encountered another way of incrementing a variable in C++. The incrementation operator (++) increments the variable that is its operand. The statement

```
loopCount++;
```

has precisely the same effect as the assignment statement

```
loopCount = loopCount + 1;
```

From here on, we typically use the ++ operator, as do most C++ programmers.

When designing loops, it is the programmer's responsibility to see that the condition to be tested is set correctly (initialized) before the While statement begins. The programmer also must make sure that the condition changes within the loop so that it eventually becomes `false`; otherwise, the loop is never exited.

```
loopCount = 1;                      ←——— Variable loopCount must be initialized
while (loopCount <= 10)
{
   .
   .
   .
   loopCount++;                     ←——— Variable loopCount must be incremented
}
```

A loop that never exits is called an *infinite loop* because, in theory, the loop executes forever. In the preceding code, omitting the incrementation of `loopCount` at the bottom of the loop leads to an infinite loop; the While expression is always `true` because the value of `loopCount` is forever 1. If your program goes on running for much longer than you expected, chances are that you've created an infinite loop. You may have to issue an operating system command to stop the program.

How many times does the loop in our Hello program execute—9 or 10? To answer this question, we have to look at the initial value of the loop control variable and then at the test to see what its final value is. Here we've initialized `loopCount` to 1, and the test indicates that the loop body is executed for each value of `loopCount` up through 10. If `loopCount` starts out at 1 and runs up to 10, the loop body is executed 10 times. If we want the loop to execute 11 times, we have to either initialize `loopCount` to 0 or change the test to

```
loopCount <= 11
```

Remember the program we developed in Chapter 2 that prints a chessboard? Here is the algorithm:

> Repeat four times
>   Output five whiteRows
>   Output five blackRows

Because we didn't know how to write loops then, we had to repeat the code four times. Here is the revised program with the code written using a loop:

```
//****************************************************************
// This program prints a chessboard pattern that is built up from
// basic strings of white and black characters.
//****************************************************************
#include <iostream>
#include <string>
using namespace std;
```

```cpp
const string BLACK = "********";   // Define a line of a black square
const string WHITE = "        ";   // Define a line of a white square

int main ()
{
  string whiteRow;            // A row beginning with a white square
  string blackRow;            // A row beginning with a black square
  int loopCount = 0;          // A loop counter initialized to zero

  // Create a white-black row by concatenating the basic strings
  whiteRow = WHITE + BLACK + WHITE + BLACK +
             WHITE + BLACK + WHITE + BLACK;
  // Create a black-white row by concatenating the basic strings
  blackRow = BLACK + WHITE + BLACK + WHITE +
             BLACK + WHITE + BLACK + WHITE;

  while (loopCount < 4)
  // Print four copies of white-black/black-white
  {
    // Print five white-black rows
    cout << whiteRow << endl;
    cout << whiteRow << endl;
    cout << whiteRow << endl;
    cout << whiteRow << endl;
    cout << whiteRow << endl;

    // Print five black-white rows
    cout << blackRow << endl;
    cout << blackRow << endl;
    cout << blackRow << endl;
    cout << blackRow << endl;
    cout << blackRow << endl;

    loopCount++;
  }

  return 0;
}
```

Event-Controlled Loops

Several kinds of event-controlled loops exist: sentinel controlled, end-of-file controlled, and flag controlled. In all of these loops, the termination condition depends on some event occurring while the loop body is executing.

Sentinel-Controlled Loops

Loops are often used to read in and process long lists of data. Each time the loop body is executed, a new piece of data is read and processed. Often a special data value, called a *sentinel* or *trailer value*, is used to signal the program that no more data remains to be processed. Looping continues as long as the data value read is *not* the sentinel; the loop stops when the program recognizes the sentinel. In other words, reading the sentinel value is the event that controls the looping process.

A sentinel value must be something that never shows up in the normal input to a program. For example, if a program reads calendar dates, we could use February 31 as a sentinel value:

```
// This code is incorrect:

while ( !(month == 2 && day == 31) )
{
  cin >> month >> day;   // Get a date
    ⋮                    // Process it
}
```

There is a problem in the loop in this example. The values of **month** and **day** are not defined before the first pass through the loop. Somehow we have to initialize these variables. We could assign them arbitrary values, but then we would run the risk that the first values input are the sentinel values, which would then be processed as data. Also, it's inefficient to initialize variables with values that are never used.

We can solve this problem by reading the first set of data values *before* entering the loop. This practice is called a *priming read*. (The idea is similar to priming a pump by pouring a bucket of water into the mechanism before starting it.) Let's add the priming read to the loop:

```
// This is still incorrect:

cin >> month >> day;                    // Get a date--priming read
while ( !(month == 2 && day == 31) )
{
  cin >> month >> day;                  // Get a date
    ⋮                                   // Process it
}
```

With the priming read, if the first values input are the sentinel values, then the loop correctly does not process them. We've solved one problem, but now there is a problem when the first values input are valid data. The first thing the program does inside the loop is to get a date, thereby destroying the values obtained by the priming read. Thus the first date in the data list is never processed. Given the priming read, the *first* thing that the loop body should do is process the data that's already been read. But at what point do we then read the next data set? We do this *last* in the loop. In this way, the While condition is applied to the next data set before it gets processed. Here's how it looks:

```
// This version is correct:

cin >> month >> day;                    // Get a date--priming read
while ( !(month == 2 && day == 31) )
{
    ⋮                                   // Process it
  cin >> month >> day;                  // Get the next date
}
```

This segment works correctly. The first data set is read in; if it is not the sentinel, it gets processed. At the end of the loop, the next data set is read in, and we go back to the beginning of the loop. If the new data set is not the sentinel, it gets processed just like the first. When the sentinel value is read, the While expression becomes `false` and the loop exits (*without* processing the sentinel).

Often the problem dictates the value of the sentinel. For example, if the problem does not allow data values of 0, then the sentinel value should be 0. Sometimes a combination of values is invalid. The combination of February and 31 as a date is such a case. Sometimes a range of values (negative numbers, for example) is the sentinel.

When you process `char` data one line of input at a time, the newline character (`'\n'`) often serves as the sentinel. Here's a program that reads and prints all of the characters from one line of an input file:

```cpp
//************************************************************
// EchoLine program
// This program reads and echoes the characters from one line
// of an input file
//************************************************************
#include <iostream>
#include <fstream>            // For file I/O

using namespace std;

int main()
{
  char    inChar;              // An input character
  ifstream inFile;             // Data file

  inFile.open("text.dat");     // Attempt to open input file
  if (!inFile)                 // Was it opened?
  {
    cout << "Can't open the input file.";  // No--print message
    return 1;                  // Terminate program
  }
  inFile.get(inChar);          // Get first character
  while (inChar != '\n')
  {
    cout << inChar;            // Echo it
    inFile.get(inChar);        // Get next character
  }
  cout << endl;
  return 0;
}
```

Notice that for this particular task we use the `get` function, not the `>>` operator, to input a character. Recall that the `>>` operator skips whitespace characters—including blanks and newlines—to find the next data value in the input stream. In this program, we want to input *every* character, even a blank and especially the newline character.

What if there aren't any invalid data values that you can use as a sentinel? Then you may have to input an extra value in each iteration, a value whose only purpose is to signal the end of the data. For example, the second value on each line of the following data set is used to indicate whether more data is present. When the sentinel value is 0, there is no more data; when it is 1, there is more data.

Data Values	Sentinel Values
10	1
0	1
−5	1
8	1
−1	1
47	0

It's extremely rare to encounter a problem that needs to be solved with this technique. Most programs input multiple data values in each iteration. As a program's input becomes more complex, the more likely it is that some combination of values will be invalid. (That also implies we need to be more careful to check that the input is correct!)

What happens if you forget to enter the sentinel value? In an interactive program, the loop executes again, prompting for input. At that point, you can enter the sentinel value. If the input to the program comes from a file, once all the data has been read, the loop body is executed again. However, there isn't any data left—because the computer has reached the end of the file—so the file stream enters the fail state. In the next section, we describe a way to use the end-of-file situation as an alternative to using a sentinel.

Before we move on, we should mention an issue that is related not to the design of loops but rather to C++ language usage. In Chapter 5, we talked about the common mistake of using the assignment operator (=) instead of the relational operator (==) in an If condition. This same mistake can happen when you write While statements. See what happens when we use the wrong operator in the previous example:

```
cin >> dataValue >> sentinel;
while (sentinel = 1)             // Whoops
{
   ⋮
   cin >> dataValue >> sentinel;
}
```

This mistake creates an infinite loop. The While expression is now an assignment expression, not a relational expression. The expression's value is 1 (interpreted in the loop test as **true** because it's nonzero), and its side effect is to store the value 1 into sentinel, replacing the value that was just input into the variable. Because the While expression is always **true**, the loop never stops.

End-of-File-Controlled Loops

You have already learned that an input stream (such as `cin` or an input file stream) goes into the fail state (1) if it encounters unacceptable input data, (2) if the program tries to open a nonexistent input file, or (3) if the program tries to read past the end of an input file. Let's look at the third of these three possibilities.

After a program has read the last piece of data from an input file, the computer is at the end of the file (EOF, for short). At this moment, the stream state is in a successful state. But if we try to input even one more data value, the stream goes into the fail state. We can use this fact to our advantage: To write a loop that inputs an unknown number of data items, we can use the failure of the input stream as a form of sentinel.

In Chapter 5, we described how to test the state of an I/O stream. In a logical expression, we use the name of the stream as though it were a Boolean variable:

```
if (inFile)
    ⋮
```

In such a test, the result is `true` if the most recent I/O operation succeeded, or `false` if it failed. In a While statement, testing the state of a stream works in the same way. Suppose we have a data file containing integer values. If `inData` is the name of the file stream in our program, here's a loop that reads and echoes all of the data values in the file:

```
inData >> intVal;              // Get first value
while (inData)                 // While the input succeeded . . .
{
  cout << intVal << endl;      // Echo it
  inData >> intVal;            // Get next value
}
```

Let's trace this code, assuming the file contains three values: 10, 20, and 30. The priming read inputs the value 10. The While condition is `true` because the input succeeded, and the computer executes the loop body. First the body prints out the value 10, and then it inputs the second data value, 20. Looping back to the loop test, the expression `inData` is `true` because the input succeeded. The body executes again, printing the value 20 and reading the value 30 from the file. Looping back to the test, the expression is `true`. Even though we are at the end of the file, the stream state is still okay—the previous input operation succeeded. The body executes a third time, printing the value 30 and executing the input statement. This time, the input statement fails, because we're trying to read beyond the end of the file. The stream `inData` enters the fail state. Looping back to the loop test, the value of the expression is `false` and we exit the loop.

When we write EOF-controlled loops like the previous example, we expect that the end of the file will be the reason for stream failure. But keep in mind that *any* input error causes stream failure. The preceding loop terminates, for example, if input fails because of invalid characters in the input data. This fact emphasizes again the importance of echo printing. It helps us verify that all the data was read correctly before the EOF was encountered.

EOF-controlled loops are similar to sentinel-controlled loops in that the program doesn't know in advance how many data items will be input. In the case of sentinel-controlled loops, the program reads data until it encounters the sentinel value. With EOF-controlled loops, it reads data until it reaches the end of the file.

The following program uses an EOF-controlled loop to read and print the `int` values from a file.

```
//****************************************************************
// Program ReadFile reads and prints all integer numbers on file
// myData.dat using an EOF-controlled loop.
//****************************************************************
#include <iostream>
#include <fstream>
using namespace std;
```

```
int main ()
{
  ifstream inData;
  inData.open("myData.dat");

  int intValue;

  cout << "Numbers on file myData.dat: " << endl;
  inData >> intValue;
  while (inData)
  {
    cout << intValue << " ";
    inData >> intValue;
  }
  cout << endl;
  inData.close();
  return 0;
}
```

Here is its output from a sample run:

```
Numbers on file myData.dat:
1066 1492 766 1918 1935 1941 2008 2010
```

Flag-Controlled Loops

A *flag* is a Boolean variable that is used to control the logical flow of a program. We can set a Boolean variable to `true` before a While loop; then, when we want to stop executing the loop, we can reset it to `false`. That is, we can use the Boolean variable to record whether the event that controls the process has occurred. For example, the following code segment reads and sums values until the input value is negative. (`nonNegative` is the Boolean flag; all of the other variables are of type `int`.)

```
sum = 0;
nonNegative = true;         // Initialize flag
while (nonNegative)
{
  cin >> number;
  if (number < 0)           // Test input value
    nonNegative = false;    // Set flag if event occurred
  else
    sum = sum + number;
}
```

Notice that we can code sentinel-controlled loops with flags. In fact, this code uses a negative value as a sentinel.

You do not have to initialize flags to `true`; you can initialize them to `false`. If you do, you must use the NOT operator (`!`) in the While expression and reset the flag to `true` when the event occurs. The following program, which calculates the square root of an input value, uses this approach. An initial value for the square root (**guess**) is calculated, **goodEnough** is set to **false**, and the loop continues recalculating **guess** until the absolute value of **guess*guess** is within 0.001 of the original value. Function **fabs** in **<cmath>** calculates the absolute value.

```cpp
//************************************************************
// This program calculates a square root using approximations.
//************************************************************
#include <iostream>
#include <cmath>
using namespace std;

int main ()
{
  float square;
  float guess;
  cout << "Enter a floating-point value" << endl;
  cin >> square;
  guess = square / 4.0;
  bool goodEnough = false;
  while (!goodEnough)
  {
    guess = ((square/ guess) + guess) / 2.0;
    cout << guess << endl;
    goodEnough = fabs(square - guess*guess) < 0.001;
  }
  cout << "The square root of " << square << " is " << guess
       << endl;
  return 0;
}
```

Here is the output from a sample run:

```
Enter a floating-point value
66.3
10.2875
8.36611
8.14547
8.14248
The square root of 66.3 is 8.14248
```

Looping Subtasks

We have been looking at ways to use loops to affect the flow of control in programs. In fact, looping by itself does nothing. The loop body must perform a task for the loop to accomplish something. In this section, we look at three tasks—counting, summing, and keeping track of a previous value—that often are performed in loops.

Counting

A common task in a loop is to keep track of the number of times the loop has been executed. For example, the following program fragment reads and counts input characters until it comes to a period. (`inChar` is of type `char`; `count` is of type `int`.) The loop in this example has a counter variable, but the loop is not a count-controlled loop because the variable is not being used as a loop control variable.

```
count = 0;                  // Initialize counter
cin.get(inChar);            // Read the first character
while (inChar != '.')
{
  count++;                  // Increment counter
  cin.get(inChar);          // Get the next character
}
```

The loop continues until a period is read. After the loop is finished, `count` contains one less than the number of characters read. That is, it counts the number of characters up to, but not including, the sentinel value (the period). Notice that if a period is the first character, the loop body is not entered and `count` contains 0, as it should. We use a priming read here because the loop is sentinel controlled.

The counter variable in this example is called an *iteration counter* because its value equals the number of iterations through the loop.

According to our definition, the loop control variable of a count-controlled loop is an iteration counter. However, as you've just seen, not all iteration counters are loop control variables.

> **Iteration counter** A counter variable that is incremented with each iteration of a loop.

Summing

Another common looping task is to sum a set of data values. Notice in the following example that the summing operation is written the same way, regardless of how the loop is controlled.

```
sum = 0;                    // Initialize the sum
count = 1;
while (count <= 10)
{
  cin >> number;            // Input a value
  sum = sum + number;       // Add the value to sum
  count++;
}
```

We initialize `sum` to 0 before the loop starts so that the first time the loop body executes, the statement

```
sum = sum + number;
```

adds the current value of `sum` (0) to `number` to produce the new value of `sum`. After the entire code fragment has executed, `sum` contains the total of the ten values read, `count` contains 11, and `number` contains the last value read.

In the preceding example, `count` is being incremented in each iteration. For each new value of `count`, there is a new value for `number`. Does this mean we could decrement `count` by 1 and inspect the previous value of `number`? No. Once a new value has been read into `number`, the previous value is gone forever—that is, unless we've saved it in another variable. We'll see how to do so in the next section.

Let's look at another example. We want to count and sum the first ten odd numbers in a data set. We need to test each number to see if it is even or odd. (We can use the modulus operator to find out: If **number % 2** equals 1, **number** is odd; otherwise, it's even.) If the input value is even, we do nothing. If it is odd, we increment the counter and add the value to our sum. We use a flag to control the loop because this is not a normal count-controlled loop. Here is a listing of the application and the output.

```cpp
//*************************************************************
// This program reads and sums odd numbers until 10 numbers
// have been read.
//*************************************************************
#include <iostream>
using namespace std;

int main ()
{
  int count = 0;                       // Initialize event counter
  int sum = 0;                         // Initialize sum
  bool lessThanTen = true;             // Initialize loop control flag
  int number;                          // Used for reading
  cout << "Enter a data set that contains at least 10 odd numbers"
    << endl;
  while (lessThanTen)
  {
    cin >> number;                     // Get the next value
    if (number % 2 == 1)               // Is the value odd?
    {
      count++;                         // Yes--increment counter
      sum = sum + number;              // Add value to sum
      lessThanTen = (count < 10);      // Update loop control flag
    }
  }
  cout << "The sum of the first 10 odd numbers is " << sum
       << "." << endl;
  return 0;
}
```

Sample output:

```
Enter a data set that contains at least 10 odd numbers
21 23 25 35 39 22 44 97 99 99 21 35 46 99
The sum of the first 10 odd numbers is 494.
```

In this example, there is no relationship between the value of the counter variable and the number of times the loop is executed. We could have written the While expression this way:

```cpp
while (count < 10)
```

but this might mislead a reader into thinking that the loop is count controlled in the normal way. Instead, we control the loop with the flag lessThanTen to emphasize that count is incremented only when an odd number is read. The counter in this example is an *event counter*; it is initialized to 0 and incremented only when a certain event occurs. The counter in the previous example was an iteration counter; it was initialized to 1 and incremented during each iteration of the loop.

> **Event counter** A variable that is incremented each time a particular event occurs.

Before we leave this example, we need to point out a shortcut we used in the code. Look at the following two statements:

```
int count = 0;   // Initialize event counter
int sum = 0;     // Initialize sum
```

We declared these two variables and initialized them in the same statement. This practice is quite legal. In fact, we used this shortcut once before in an earlier program. Did you notice it? In Chapter 9, we look at this construct a little more closely.

Keeping Track of a Previous Value

Sometimes we want to remember the previous value of a variable. Suppose we want to write a program that counts the number of not-equal operators (!=) in a file that contains a C++ program. We can do so by simply counting the number of times an exclamation mark (!) followed by an equal sign (=) appears in the input. One way in which to accomplish this task is to read the input file one character at a time, keeping track of the two most recent characters—that is, the current value and the previous value. In each iteration of the loop, a new current value is read and the old current value becomes the previous value. When EOF is reached, the loop is finished. Here's a program that counts not-equal operators in this way:

```cpp
//************************************************************
// This program counts the occurrences of "!=" in a data file
//************************************************************
#include <iostream>
#include <fstream>              // For file I/O
using namespace std;

int main()
{
    int count;                  // Number of != operators
    char prevChar;              // Last character read
    char currChar;              // Character read in this iteration
    ifstream inFile;            // Data file

    inFile.open("myfile.dat");  // Attempt to open file
    if ( !inFile )
    { // If file wouldn't open, print message, terminate program
        cout << "Can't open input file" << endl;
        return 1;
    }
    count = 0;                  // Initialize counter
    inFile.get(prevChar);       // Initialize previous value
    inFile.get(currChar);       // Initialize current value
```

```
    while (inFile)                  // While input succeeds . . .
    {
      if (currChar == '=' &&        // Test for !=
          prevChar == '!')
        count++;                    // Increment counter
      prevChar = currChar;          // Update previous value to current
      inFile.get(currChar);         // Get next value
    }
    cout << count << " != operators were found." << endl;
    return 0;
}
```

File `myfile.dat`:

`<= !!! === != ! = !=`

Output:

```
2 != operators were found.
```

Study this loop carefully, because it's going to come in handy. There are many problems in which you must keep track of the last value read in addition to the current value.

SOFTWARE MAINTENANCE CASE STUDY: Make a Program General

MAINTENANCE TASK: In Chapter 5, we updated program `Mortgage` to read from the keyboard and take interest rates as either decimals or percentages. Several friends are currently using the program and one has asked if it could be modified to give the total amount of interest paid over the term of the loan. Now that you know about loops, you can enclose the program in loop. A negative loan amount doesn't make any sense, so let's use a negative value to end the program.

You realize that what started out as a program to help your parents has turned into a general-purpose program to handle loans of many kinds. Rather than modify program `Mortgage`, you decide to create a new program called `LoanPayments` based on program `Mortgage`. The original functionality will remain, the total amount of interest over the period of the loan will be shown, and the user can continue entering values.

CHANGES: Because you worked on the program so recently, you do not need to study a listing. The following changes will be required:

- Change the name of the program and update its documentation.
- Update the prompt to say that a negative loan amount ends the program.
- Calculate the total amount of interest.
- Print the total amount of interest.
- Enclose the whole program within a loop.

SOFTWARE MAINTENANCE CASE STUDY: Make a Program General

You look back over the program to see if any of the output needs changing and find that all the labels are neutral; that is, they do not refer to mortgage payments. You finish the changes, run the program, and it goes into an infinite loop. You isolate the loop and examine it.

```
cin >> loanAmount >> yearlyInterest >> numberOfPayments;
numberOfPayments = numberOfYears * 12;

while (loanAmount > 0)
{
  // Calculate values
  if (yearlyInterest >= 0.25)                    // Assume percent entered
    yearlyInterest = yearlyInterest / 100.0;
  monthlyInterest = yearlyInterest / 12;
  payment = (loanAmount * pow(1 + monthlyInterest, numberOfPayments)
    * monthlyInterest)/
    (pow(1 + monthlyInterest, numberOfPayments) - 1 );

  // Output results
  . . .
}
```

The solution jumps out at you: New values for the variables weren't read in. The input statement must be repeated at the end of the loop. Is there anything else? Of course! The prompt must be repeated. You make these changes and try again. Now the program doesn't quit when you enter a negative loan amount; it just sits there waiting for something. This new behavior draws your attention to the input statements.

```
cin >> loanAmount >> yearlyInterest >> numberOfPayments;
numberOfPayments = numberOfYears * 12;
while (loanAmount > 0)
{
  ...
  cin >> loanAmount >> yearlyInterest >> numberOfPayments;
}
```

The program is waiting for something—it is waiting for the rest of the data. Because we didn't need it, we just entered a negative loan amount and stopped. We could tell the user to always enter three values, but a better solution exists: We can read the loan amount outside the loop, and finish reading the data in the loop. Then the last statement can read just the loan amount. The calculation of **numberOfPayments** must also be moved inside the loop.

Here is a listing of the new program with the new or changed lines highlighted:

```
//****************************************************************
// LoanPayment program
// This program determines the monthly payments on a loan given
// the loan amount, the yearly interest rate, and the number of
// months (payments).
// The process repeats until a negative loan amount is entered.
//****************************************************************
```

SOFTWARE MAINTENANCE CASE STUDY: Make a Program General

```cpp
#include <cmath>
#include <iomanip>
#include <iostream>
using namespace std;

int main()
{
  // Input variables
  float loanAmount;
  float yearlyInterest;
  int numberOfYears;

  // Local variables
  float monthlyInterest;
  int numberOfPayments;
  float payment;

  // Prompts
  cout << "Input loan amount, interest rate, and number of years."
      << endl;
  cout << "An interest rate of less than 0.25 is assumed to be "
      << endl;
  cout << "a decimal rather than a percent." << endl;
  cout << "A negative loan amount ends the program." << endl;
  // Read values
  cin >> loanAmount;
  while (loanAmount > 0)
  {
    cin >> yearlyInterest >> numberOfPayments;
    numberOfPayments = numberOfYears * 12;
    // Calculate values
    if (yearlyInterest >= 0.25)                        // Assume percent entered
      yearlyInterest = yearlyInterest / 100.0;
    monthlyInterest = yearlyInterest / 12;
    payment = (loanAmount * pow(1 + monthlyInterest, numberOfPayments)
        * monthlyInterest)/
      (pow(1 + monthlyInterest, numberOfPayments) - 1 );

    // Output results
    cout << fixed << "Loan amount:          " << setprecision(2)
        << loanAmount << endl << "Interest rate:       "
        << setprecision(4) << yearlyInterest*100.0 << "%"  << endl
        << "Number of payments:  " << numberOfPayments << endl;
    cout << fixed
        << "Monthly payments:    " << setprecision(2) << payment << endl;
    cout << fixed << "Total Interest:      " << setprecision(2)
        << (payment * numberOfPayments - loanAmount) << endl;
    // Prompts
    cout << "Input loan amount, interest rate, and number of months."
        << endl;
    cout << "An interest rate of less than 0.25 is assumed to be "
        << endl;
```

SOFTWARE MAINTENANCE CASE STUDY: Make a Program General

```
       cout << "a decimal rather than a percent." << endl;
       cout << "A negative loan amount ends the program." << endl;
       cin >> loanAmount;
   }
   return 0;
}
```

This program looks long and complicated, more so than it actually is. In Chapter 8, we cover a way to make the code look much cleaner and simpler. Here is sample output from the program:

```
Input loan amount, interest rate, and number of years.
An interest rate of less than 0.25 is assumed to be
a decimal rather than a percent.
A negative loan amount ends the program.
3000 6.8 24
Loan amount:        3000.00
Interest rate:      6.8000%
Number of payments: 288
Monthly payments:   21.16
Total Interest:     3092.92
Input loan amount, interest rate, and number of months.
An interest rate of less than 0.25 is assumed to be
a decimal rather than a percent.
A negative loan amount ends the program.
25000 5.4 60
Loan amount:        25000.00
Interest rate:      5.4000%
Number of payments: 720
Monthly payments:   117.12
Total Interest:     59326.53
Input loan amount, interest rate, and number of months.
An interest rate of less than 0.25 is assumed to be
a decimal rather than a percent.
A negative loan amount ends the program.
-2
```

The amount of interest looked so high that you calculated it by hand to be sure. However, it is correct.

QUICK CHECK

6.3.1 What are the two major types of loops encountered when solving problems? (p. 246)
6.3.2 Give a real-life example of the two major types of loops when solving problems. (p. 246)
6.3.3 How is a flag-controlled loop like a sentinel-controlled loop, and how do the two types of loops differ? (pp. 249–255)
6.3.4 Does averaging a set of values that are input by a loop involve summing, counting, or both? (pp. 255–259)
6.3.5 Write a While statement that exits when the `int` variable `count` is greater than 10 or the Boolean flag `found` is `true`. (pp. 247–255)
6.3.6 Add a test for the condition end-of-file on `cin` to the loop in Question 6.3.5, and add statements to the loop that perform a priming read and an updating read of `inData` from `cin`. (pp. 252–254)
6.3.7 Add initialization and update operations to the loop in Question 6.3.6 that cause it to count the occurrences of the value 1 that are input to variable `inData`, and to sum all of the values read into `inData`. (p. 256)

6.4 How to Design Loops

It's one thing to understand how a loop works when you look at it, and something else again to design a loop that solves a given problem. In this section, we consider the process of designing loops. We can divide this process into two tasks: designing the control flow and designing the processing that takes place in the loop. We can, in turn, break each task into three phases: the task itself, initialization, and update. It's also important to specify the state of the program when it exits the loop, because a loop that leaves variables and files in a mess is not well designed.

There are seven points to consider in designing a loop:

1. What is the condition that ends the loop?
2. How should the condition be initialized?
3. How should the condition be updated?
4. What is the process being repeated?
5. How should the process be initialized?
6. How should the process be updated?
7. What is the state of the program on exiting the loop?

We will use these questions as a checklist. The first three help us design the parts of the loop that control its execution. The next three help us design the processing within the loop. The last question reminds us to make sure that the loop exits in an appropriate manner.

Designing the Flow of Control

The most important step in loop design is deciding what should make the loop stop. If the termination condition isn't well thought out, our program might potentially contain infinite loops and other mistakes. So here is our first question:

- What is the condition that ends the loop?

This question usually can be answered through a close examination of the problem statement. The following table lists some examples:

Key Phrase in Problem Statement	Termination Condition
"Sum 365 temperatures"	The loop ends when a counter reaches 365 (count-controlled loop).
"Process all the data in the file"	The loop ends when EOF occurs (EOF-controlled loop).
"Process until ten odd integers have been read"	The loop ends when ten odd numbers have been input (event counter).
"The end of the data is indicated by a negative test score"	The loop ends when a negative input value is encountered (sentinel-controlled loop).

Now we need statements that make sure the loop gets started correctly and statements that allow the loop to reach the termination condition. At this point, we ask the next two questions:

- How should the condition be initialized?
- How should the condition be updated?

The answers to these questions depend on the type of termination condition.

Count-Controlled Loops
If the loop is count controlled, we initialize the condition by giving the loop control variable an initial value. For count-controlled loops in which the loop control variable is also an iteration counter, the initial value is usually 1. If the process requires the counter to run through a specific range of values, the initial value should be the lowest value in that range.

The condition is updated by increasing the value of the counter by 1 for each iteration. (Occasionally, you may come across a problem that requires a counter to count from some value *down* to a lower value. In this case, the initial value is the greater value, and the counter is *decremented* by 1 for each iteration.) So, for count-controlled loops that use an iteration counter, these are the answers to the key questions:

- Initialize the iteration counter to 1.
- Increment the iteration counter at the end of each iteration.

If the loop is controlled by a variable that is counting an event within the loop, the control variable is usually initialized to 0 and is incremented each time the event occurs. For count-controlled loops that use an event counter, these are the answers to the key questions:

- Initialize the event counter to 0.
- Increment the event counter each time the event occurs.

Sentinel-Controlled Loops
In sentinel-controlled loops, a priming read may be the only initialization necessary. If the source of input is a file rather than the keyboard, it may also be necessary to open the file

in preparation for reading. To update the condition, a new value is read at the end of each iteration. So, for sentinel-controlled loops, we answer our key questions this way:

- Open the file, if necessary, and input a value before entering the loop (priming read).
- Input a new value for processing at the end of each iteration.

EOF-Controlled Loops
EOF-controlled loops require the same initialization as sentinel-controlled loops. You must open the file, if necessary, and perform a priming read. Updating the loop condition happens implicitly; the stream state is updated to reflect success or failure every time a value is input. However, if the loop doesn't read any data, it can never reach EOF; thus updating the loop condition means the loop must keep reading data.

Flag-Controlled Loops
In flag-controlled loops, the Boolean flag variable must be initialized to `true` or `false` and then updated when the condition changes.

- Initialize the flag variable to `true` or `false`, as appropriate.
- Update the flag variable as soon as the condition changes.

In a flag-controlled loop, the flag variable essentially remains unchanged until it is time for the loop to end. Then the code detects some condition within the process being repeated that changes the value of the flag (through an assignment statement). Because the update depends on what the process does, sometimes we may have to design the process before we can decide how to update the condition.

Designing the Process Within the Loop

Once we've selected the type of looping structure, we can fill in the details of the process. In designing the process, we first must decide what we want a single iteration to do. Assume for a moment that the process will execute only once. Which tasks must the process perform?

- What is the process being repeated?

To answer this question, we have to take another look at the problem statement. The definition of the problem may require the process to sum up data values or to keep a count of data values that satisfy some test. For example:

> Count the number of integers in the file `howMany`.

This statement tells us that the process to be repeated is a counting operation.
Here's another example:

> Read a stock price for each business day in a week and compute the average price.

In this case, part of the process involves reading a data value. We conclude from our knowledge of how an average is computed that this process must also involve summing the data values.

In addition to counting and summing, another common loop process is reading data, performing a calculation, and writing out the result. Many other operations can appear in looping processes. We've mentioned only the simplest here; we look at some other processes later on.

After we've determined the operations to be performed if the process is executed only once, we design the parts of the process that are necessary for it to be repeated correctly. We often have to add some steps to account for the fact that the loop executes more than once. This part of the design typically involves initializing certain variables before the loop and then reinitializing or updating them before each subsequent iteration, and it leads to our next two questions:

- How should the process be initialized?
- How should the process be updated?

For example, if the process within a loop requires that several different counts and sums be performed, each must have its own statements to initialize variables, increment counting variables, or add values to sums. Just deal with each counting or summing operation by itself—that is, first write the initialization statement, and then write the incrementing or summing statement. After you've done this for one operation, go on to the next.

The Loop Exit

When the termination condition occurs and the flow of control passes to the statement following the loop, the variables used in the loop still contain values. If the `cin` stream has been used, the reading marker has also been left at some position in the stream. Or maybe an output file has new contents. If these variables or files are used later in the program, the loop must leave them in an appropriate state. Thus the final step in designing a loop is answering this question:

- What is the state of the program on exiting the loop?

To answer this question, we have to consider the consequences of our design and double-check its validity. For example, suppose we've used an event counter and that later processing depends on the number of events. It's important to make sure (with an algorithm walk-through) that the value left in the counter is the exact number of events—that it is not off by 1. Off-by-one bugs are sometimes referred to as OBOBs.

Look at this code segment:

```
commaCount = 1;        // This code is incorrect
cin.get(inChar);
while (inChar != '\n')
{
  if (inChar == ',')
     commaCount++;
  cin.get(inChar);
}
cout << commaCount << endl;
```

This loop reads characters from an input line and counts the number of commas on the line. However, when the loop terminates, `commaCount` equals the actual number of commas plus 1 because the loop initializes the event counter to 1 before any events take place. By determining the state of `commaCount` at loop exit, we've detected a flaw in the initialization. `commaCount` should be initialized to 0.

Designing correct loops depends as much on experience as it does on the application of design methodology. At this point, you may want to read through the Problem-Solving Case Study at the end of the chapter to see how the loop design process is applied to a real problem.

> **QUICK CHECK** ✓
>
> **6.4.1** Which type of loop would you use to read a file of drivers' license numbers until a specific number is input? (pp. 263–264)
>
> **6.4.2** Write the initialization and update portions for the termination condition of the loop in Question 6.3.5. The variable `found` becomes `true` when the `int` variable `inData` contains 0. The count starts at 1 and is incremented in each iteration. (pp. 263–264)
>
> **6.4.3** What are the seven points to consider in designing a loop? (p. 263)
>
> **6.4.4** Write a loop that will count the number of lines of an input file named `inFile`. Assume that you have the variable `inChar` of type `char` used to store the current character in the file and `lineCount` of type `int` to keep track of the number of lines. (pp. 263–266)

6.5 Nested Logic

In Chapter 5, we described nested If statements. It's also possible to nest While statements. Both While and If statements contain statements and are themselves statements. As a consequence, the body of a While statement or the branch of an If statement can contain other While and If statements. By nesting, we can create complex control structures.

Suppose we want to extend our code for counting commas on one line, repeating it for all the lines in a file. We put an EOF-controlled loop around it:

```
cin.get(inChar);           // Initialize outer loop
while (cin)                // Outer loop test
{
  commaCount = 0;          // Initialize inner loop
                           // (Priming read is taken care of
                           //  by outer loop's priming read)
  while (inChar != '\n')   // Inner loop test
  {
    if (inChar == ',')
      commaCount++;
    cin.get(inChar);       // Update inner termination condition
  }
  cout << commaCount << endl;
  cin.get(inChar);         // Update outer termination condition
}
```

In this code, we omitted the priming read for the inner loop. The priming read for the outer loop has already "primed the pump." It would be a mistake to include another priming read just before the inner loop, because the character read by the outer priming read would be destroyed before we could test it.

Let's examine the general pattern of a simple nested loop. The dots represent places where the processing and update may take place in the outer loop.

```
Initialize outer loop
while ( Outer loop condition )
{
    ⋮
    Initialize inner loop
    while ( Inner loop condition )
    {
        Inner loop processing and update
    }
    ⋮
}
```

Notice that each loop has its own initialization, test, and update operation. It's possible for an outer loop to do no processing other than to execute the inner loop repeatedly. Conversely, the inner loop might be just a small part of the processing done by the outer loop; there could be many statements preceding or following the inner loop.

Let's look at another example. For nested count-controlled loops, the pattern looks like this (where `outCount` is the counter for the outer loop, `inCount` is the counter for the inner loop, and `limit1` and `limit2` are the number of times each loop should be executed):

```
outCount = 1;                    // Initialize outer loop counter
while (outCount <= limit1)
{
  ⋮
  inCount = 1;                   // Initialize inner loop counter
  while (inCount <= limit2)
  {
    ⋮
    inCount++;                   // Increment inner loop counter
  }
  ⋮
  outCount++;                    // Increment outer loop counter
}
```

Here, both the inner and outer loops are count-controlled loops, but the pattern can be used with any combination of loops.

The following program shows a count-controlled loop nested within an event-controlled loop. The outer loop inputs an integer value telling how many asterisks to print out across a row of the screen.

```cpp
//***********************************************
// Program Stars reads in a number and prints that
// many asterisks.
//***********************************************
#include <iostream>
using namespace std;

int main ()
{
  int starCount;
  int loopCount;
  cout << "Enter the number of stars;" << endl
       << "'Q' ends the program." << endl;
  cin >> starCount;                               // 1
  while (cin)                                     // 2
  {
    loopCount = 1;                                // 3
    while (loopCount <= starCount)                // 4
    {
      cout << '*';                                // 5
      loopCount++;                                // 6
    }
    cout << endl;                                 // 7
    cout << "Enter the number of stars; "         // 8
         << "'Q' ends the program." << endl;
    cin >> starCount;                             // 9
  }
  cout << "Goodbye" << endl;                      // 10
  return 0;
}
```

Output:

```
Enter the number of stars; 'Q' ends the program.
3
***
Enter the number of stars; 'Q' ends the program.
5
*****
Enter the number of stars; 'Q' ends the program.
1
*
Enter the number of stars; 'Q' ends the program.
Q
Goodbye
```

To see how this code works, let's trace its execution with the data values shown in the sample session. Notice that the event that controls the loop is the keying of a letter when `cin` expects a number. This puts the input stream into the fail state, returning `false` when tested.

We'll keep track of the variables `starCount` and `loopCount`, as well as the logical expressions. To do so, we've numbered each line within the loops (except those containing only a left or right brace). As we trace the program, we indicate the first execution of line 3 by 3.1, the second by 3.2, and so on. Each loop iteration is enclosed by a large brace, and `true` and `false` are abbreviated as T and F (see **TABLE 6.1**).

TABLE 6.1 Code Trace

Statement	Variables		Logical Expressions		Output
	starCount	loopCount	cin	loopCount <= starCount	
1.1	3	—	—	—	—
2.1	3	—	T	—	—
3.1	3	1	—	—	—
4.1	3	1	—	T	—
5.1	3	1	—	—	*
6.1	3	2	—	—	—
4.2	3	2	—	T	—
5.2	3	2	—	—	*
6.2	3	3	—	—	—
4.3	3	3	—	T	—
5.3	3	3	—	—	*
6.3	3	4	—	—	—
4.4	3	4	—	F	—
7.1	3	4	—	—	\n (newline)
8.1	3	4	—	—	(Prompt)
9.1	1	4	—	—	—
2.2	1	4	T	—	—
3.2	1	1	—	—	—
4.5	1	1	—	T	—
5.4	1	1	—	—	*
6.4	1	2	—	—	—
4.6	1	2	—	F	—
7.2	1	2	—	—	\n (newline)
8.2	1	2	—	—	(Prompt)
9.2	1	2	—	—	— (null operation)
2.3	1	2	F	—	—
10.1	1	2	—	—	Goodbye

Because `starCount` and `loopCount` are variables, their values remain the same until they are explicitly changed, as indicated by the repeating values in Table 6.1. The values of the logical expressions `cin` and `loopCount <= starCount` exist only when the test is made. We indicate this fact with dashes in those columns at all other times.

Designing Nested Loops

To design a nested loop, we begin with the outer loop. The process being repeated includes the nested loop as one of its steps. Because that step is more complex than a single statement, our functional decomposition methodology tells us to make it a separate module. We can come back to it later and design the nested loop just as we would any other loop.

For example, here's the design process for the preceding code segment:

1. *What is the condition that ends the loop?* `'Q'` entered.
2. *How should the condition be initialized?* A priming read should be performed before the loop starts.
3. *How should the condition be updated?* An input statement should occur at the end of each iteration.
4. *What is the process being repeated?* Using the value of the current input integer, the code should print that many asterisks across one output line.
5. *How should the process be initialized?* No initialization is necessary.
6. *How should the process be updated?* A sequence of asterisks is output and then a newline character is output. There are no counter variables or sums to update.
7. *What is the state of the program on exiting the loop?* The `cin` stream is in the fail state (because the program encountered a letter when an integer was expected), `starCount` contains the last integer read from the input stream, and the rows of asterisks have been printed along with a concluding message.

From the answers to these questions, we can write this much of the algorithm:

```
Read starCount
WHILE Stream okay
    Print starCount asterisks
    Output newline
    Prompt
    Read starCount
Print "Goodbye"
```

After designing the outer loop, it's obvious that the process in its body (printing a sequence of asterisks) is a complex step that requires us to design an inner loop. So we repeat the methodology for the corresponding lower-level module:

1. *What is the condition that ends the loop?* An iteration counter exceeds the value of `starCount`.
2. *How should the condition be initialized?* The iteration counter should be initialized to 1.
3. *How should the condition be updated?* The iteration counter is incremented at the end of each iteration.

4. *What is the process being repeated?* The code should print a single asterisk on the standard output device.
5. *How should the process be initialized?* No initialization is needed.
6. *How should the process be updated?* No update is needed.
7. *What is the state of the program on exiting the loop?* A single row of asterisks has been printed, the writing marker is at the end of the current output line, and `loopCount` contains a value one greater than the current value of `starCount`.

Now we can write the algorithm:

```
Read starCount
WHILE Stream okay
    Set loopCount = 1
    WHILE loopCount <= starCount
        Print "*"
        Increment loopCount
    Output newline
    Read starCount
Print "Goodbye"
```

Of course, nested loops themselves can contain nested loops (called *doubly nested loops*), which can also contain nested loops (*triply nested loops*), and so on. You can use this design process for any number of levels of nesting. The trick is to defer details by using the functional decomposition methodology—that is, focus on the outermost loop first and treat each new level of nested loop as a module within the loop that contains it.

It's also possible for the process within a loop to include more than one loop. For example, we rewrote the chessboard program earlier in this chapter using a loop. Now let's rewrite it again, this time using two loops nested within the outer loop. Here is the algorithm followed by the code.

Chessboard program

```
Set up whiteRow
Set up blackRow
Set loopCount to 0
WHILE loopCount < 4
    Print whiteRows
    Print blackRows
    Increment loopCount
```

Print whiteRows

```
Set loopCount2 to 0
WHILE loopCount2 < 5
    Print whiteRow
    Increment loopCount2
```

Print blackRows

Set loopCount2 to 0
WHILE loopCount 2 < 5
    Print blackRow
    Increment loopCount2

```cpp
//****************************************************************
// Chessboard program
// This program prints a chessboard pattern that is built up from
// basic strings of white and black characters.
//****************************************************************
#include <iostream>
#include <string>
using namespace std;

const string BLACK = "********";  // Define a line of a black square
const string WHITE = "        ";  // Define a line of a white square

int main ()
{
  string whiteRow;       // A row beginning with a white square
  string blackRow;       // A row beginning with a black square
  int loopCount;         // A loop counter
  int loopCount2;        // Second loop counter

  // Create a white-black row by concatenating the basic strings
  whiteRow = WHITE + BLACK + WHITE + BLACK +
             WHITE + BLACK + WHITE + BLACK;
  // Create a black-white row by concatenating the basic strings
  blackRow = BLACK + WHITE + BLACK + WHITE +
             BLACK + WHITE + BLACK + WHITE;
  loopCount = 0;
  while (loopCount < 4)
  // Print four copies of white-black/black-white
  {
    // Print five white-black rows
    loopCount2 = 0;
    while (loopCount2 < 5)
    {
      cout << whiteRow << endl;
      loopCount2++;
    }
    loopCount2 = 0;
    // Print five black-white rows
    while (loopCount2 < 5)
    {
      cout << blackRow << endl;
      loopCount2++;
    }
    loopCount++;
  }
  return 0;
}
```

THEORETICAL FOUNDATIONS
Analysis of Algorithms

If you were given the choice of cleaning a room with a toothbrush or a broom, you probably would choose the broom. Using a broom sounds like less work than using a toothbrush. True, if the room were in a dollhouse, it might be easier to use the toothbrush, but in general a broom is the faster way to clean. If you were given the choice of adding numbers together with a pencil and paper or a calculator, you would probably choose the calculator because it is usually less work. If you were given the choice of walking or driving to a meeting, you would probably choose to drive; it sounds like less work.

What do these examples have in common? What do they have to do with computer science? In each of the situations mentioned, one of the choices seems to involve significantly less work. Precisely measuring the amount of work is difficult in each case because there are unknowns. How large is the room? How many numbers are there? How far away is the meeting? In each case, the unknown information is related to the size of the problem. If the problem is especially small (for example, adding 2 plus 2), our original estimate of which approach to take (using the calculator) might be wrong. However, our intuition is usually correct, because most problems are reasonably large.

In computer science, we need a way of measuring the amount of work done by an algorithm relative to the size of a problem, because there is usually more than one algorithm that solves any given problem. We often must choose the most efficient algorithm—the algorithm that does the least work for a problem of a given size.

The amount of work involved in executing an algorithm relative to the size of the problem is called the **complexity** of the algorithm. We would like to be able to look at an algorithm and determine its complexity. Then we could take two algorithms that perform the same task and determine which completes the task faster (requires less work).

Complexity A measure of the effort expended by the computer in performing a computation, relative to the size of the computation.

How do we measure the amount of work required to execute an algorithm? We use the total number of *steps* executed as a measure of work. One statement, such as an assignment, may require only one step; another, such as a loop, may require many steps. We define a step as any operation roughly equivalent in complexity to a comparison, an I/O operation, or an assignment.

Given an algorithm with just a sequence of simple statements (no branches or loops), the number of steps performed is directly related to the number of statements. When we introduce branches, however, we make it possible to skip some statements in the algorithm. Branches allow us to subtract steps without physically removing them from the algorithm because only one branch is executed at a time. But because we usually want to express work in terms of the worst-case scenario, we use the number of steps in the longest branch.

Now consider the effect of a loop. If a loop repeats a sequence of 15 simple statements 10 times, it performs 150 steps. Loops allow us to multiply the work done in an algorithm without physically adding statements.

Now that we have a measure for the work done in an algorithm, we can compare algorithms. For example, if algorithm A always executes 3124 steps and algorithm B always does the same task in 1321 steps, then we can say that algorithm B is more efficient—that is, it takes fewer steps to accomplish the same task.

If an algorithm, from run to run, always takes the same number of steps or fewer, we say that it executes in an amount of time bounded by a constant. Such algorithms are referred to as having

THEORETICAL FOUNDATIONS Analysis of Algorithms, continued

constant-time complexity. Be careful: Constant time doesn't mean small; it means that the amount of work done does not exceed some amount from one run to another.

If a loop executes a fixed number of times, the work done is greater than the physical number of statements but is still constant. What happens if the number of loop iterations can change from one run to the next? Suppose a data file contains N data values to be processed in a loop. If the loop reads and processes one value during each iteration, then the loop executes N iterations. The amount of work done then depends on a variable, the number of data values. The variable N determines the size of the problem in this example.

If we have a loop that executes N times, the number of steps to be executed is some factor times N. The factor is the number of steps performed within a single iteration of the loop.

Specifically, the work done by an algorithm with a data-dependent loop is given by the following expression:

$$\underbrace{S_1 \times N}_{\text{Steps performed by the loop}} + \underbrace{S_0}_{\text{Steps performed outside the loop}}$$

where S_1 is the number of steps in the loop body (a constant for a given simple loop), N is the number of iterations (a variable representing the size of the problem), and S_0 is the number of steps outside the loop. Mathematicians call expressions of this form *linear*; hence, algorithms such as this are said to have *linear-time* complexity. Notice that if N grows very large, the term $S_1 \times N$ dominates the execution time. That is, S_0 becomes an insignificant part of the total execution time. For example, if S_0 and S_1 are each 20 steps, and N is 1,000,000, then the total number of steps is 20,000,020. The 20 steps contributed by S_0 are merely a tiny fraction of the total.

What about a data-dependent loop that contains a nested loop? The number of steps in the inner loop, S_2, and the number of iterations performed by the inner loop, L, must be multiplied by the number of iterations in the outer loop:

$$\underbrace{(S_2 \times L \times N)}_{\text{Steps performed by the nested loop}} + \underbrace{(S_1 \times N)}_{\text{Steps performed by the outer loop}} + \underbrace{S_0}_{\text{Steps performed outside the outer loop}}$$

By itself, the inner loop performs $S_2 \times L$ steps, but because it is repeated N times by the outer loop, it accounts for a total of $S_2 \times L \times N$ steps. If L is a constant, then the algorithm still executes in linear time.

Now suppose that for each of the N outer loop iterations, the inner loop performs N steps (L = N). Here the formula for the total steps is

$$(S_2 \times N \times N) + (S_1 \times N) + S_0$$

THEORETICAL FOUNDATIONS Analysis of Algorithms, continued

or

$$(S_2 \times N^2) + (S_1 \times N) + S_0$$

Because N^2 grows much faster than N (for large values of N), the inner loop term ($S_2 \times N^2$) accounts for the majority of steps executed and of the work done. The corresponding execution time is thus essentially proportional to N^2. Mathematicians call this type of formula quadratic. If we have a doubly nested loop in which each loop depends on N, then the expression is

$$(S_3 \times N^3) + (S_2 \times N^2) + (S_1 \times N) + S_0$$

and the work and time are proportional to N^3 whenever N is reasonably large. Such a formula is called *cubic*.

The following table shows the number of steps required for each increase in the exponent of N, where N is a size factor for the problem, such as the number of input values.

N	N^0 (Constant)	N^1 (Linear)	N^2 (Quadratic)	N^3 (Cubic)
1	1	1	1	1
10	1	10	100	1,000
100	1	100	10,000	1,000,000
1,000	1	1,000	1,000,000	1,000,000,000
10,000	1	10,000	100,000,000	1,000,000,000,000
100,000	1	100,000	10,000,000,000	1,000,000,000,000,000

As you can see, each time the exponent increases by 1, the number of steps is multiplied by an additional order of magnitude (factor of 10). That is, if N is made 10 times greater, the work involved in an N^2 algorithm increases by a factor of 100, and the work involved in an N^3 algorithm increases by a factor of 1000. To put this in more concrete terms, an algorithm with a doubly nested loop in which each loop depends on the number of data values takes 1000 steps for 10 input values and 1 quadrillion steps for 100,000 values. On a computer that executes 1 billion instructions per second, the latter case would take about 12 days to run.

The table also shows that the steps outside of the innermost loop account for an insignificant portion of the total number of steps as N gets bigger. Because the innermost loop dominates the total time, we classify the complexity of an algorithm according to the highest order of N that appears in its complexity expression, called the *order of magnitude*, or simply the *order*, of that expression. So we talk about algorithms having "order N squared complexity" (or cubed or so on) or we describe them with what is called *Big-O notation*. We express the complexity by putting the highest-order term in parentheses with a capital O in front. For example, $O(1)$ is constant time, $O(N)$ is linear time, $O(N^2)$ is quadratic time, and $O(N^3)$ is cubic time.

Determining the complexities of different algorithms allows us to compare the work they require without having to program and execute them. For example, if you had an $O(N^2)$ algorithm and a linear algorithm that performed the same task, you probably would choose the linear algorithm. We say *probably* because an $O(N^2)$ algorithm actually may execute fewer steps than an $O(N)$ algorithm

THEORETICAL FOUNDATIONS Analysis of Algorithms, continued

for small values of N. Remember that if the size factor N is small, the constants and lower-order terms in the complexity expression may be significant.

Let's look at an example. Suppose that algorithm A is $O(N^2)$ and that algorithm B is $O(N)$. For large values of N, we would normally choose algorithm B because it requires less work than A. But suppose that in algorithm B, $S_0 = 1000$ and $S_1 = 1000$. If $N = 1$, then algorithm B takes 2000 steps to execute. Now suppose that for algorithm A, $S_0 = 10$, $S_1 = 10$, and $S_2 = 10$. If $N = 1$, then algorithm A takes only 30 steps. Here is a table that compares the number of steps taken by these two algorithms for different values of N.

N	Algorithm A	Algorithm B
1	30	2,000
2	70	3,000
3	130	4,000
10	1,110	11,000
20	4,210	21,000
30	9,310	31,000
50	25,510	51,000
100	101,010	101,000
1,000	10,010,010	1,001,000
10,000	1,000,100,010	10,001,000

From this table we can see that the $O(N^2)$ algorithm A is actually faster than the $O(N)$ algorithm B, up to the point that N equals 100. Beyond that point, algorithm B becomes more efficient. Thus, if we know that N is always less than 100 in a particular problem, we would choose algorithm A. For example, if the size factor N is the number of test scores on an exam and the class size is limited to 30 students, algorithm A would be more efficient. Conversely, if N is the number of scores at a university with 25,000 students, we would choose algorithm B.

Constant, linear, quadratic, and cubic expressions are all examples of *polynomial* expressions. Algorithms whose complexity is characterized by such expressions are, therefore, said to execute in *polynomial time* and form a broad class of algorithms that encompasses everything we've discussed so far.

In addition to polynomial-time algorithms, we encounter a logarithmic-time algorithm in Chapter 13. There are also factorial ($O(N!)$), exponential ($O(N^N)$), and hyperexponential ($O(N^{N^N})$) classes of algorithms, which can require vast amounts of time to execute and are beyond the scope of this book. For now, the important point to remember is that different algorithms that solve the same problem can vary significantly in the amount of work they do.

QUICK CHECK

6.5.1 Write a loop that will output the total number of characters per line (excluding the `'\n'` character) from an input file named `inFile`. Assume that you have the variable `inChar` of type `char` used to store the current character, `lineCount` of type `int` to keep track of the number of lines, and `count` of type `int` to keep track of the number of characters. (pp. 267–268)

6.5.2 What is the term given to an algorithm that measures the effort expended by the computer in performing a computation? (p. 274)

6.5.3 What measurement is used to determine the amount of work performed by an algorithm? (p. 274)

6.5.4 How would you extend the loop from Question 6.3.7 so that it would be repeated in its entirety five times? (pp. 271–272)

Problem-Solving Case Study

Recording Studio Design

PROBLEM: You've gone to work for a consulting firm that specializes in converting existing rooms into recording studios. Your employers have asked you to write a program that inputs a set of loudness measurements for a room and prints out basic statistics. The measurements are made by playing a series of 12 different tones, and recording the readings from a sound-level meter onto a file. The meter readings range from 50 to 126 decibels (a measure of loudness). Your program, however, is to output the measurements relative to the first tone—that is, to show how much each individual reading differs from the first. After all the data has been read, the program is to print out the highest and lowest readings.

INPUT: Twelve real numbers, representing the meter readings, on file `acoustic.dat`.

OUTPUT

- The 12 input values (echo print) and their values relative to the first reading
- At the end of the program, the actual value, relative value, and sequence number of both the highest reading and the lowest

DISCUSSION: This problem is easy to calculate by hand. We simply scan the list, subtracting the first value from each value in the list. As we scan the list, we also keep track of which value from the list is the highest and which is the lowest.

How do we translate this process into an algorithm? Let's take a closer look at what we are doing. To find the largest number in a list, we compare the first and second numbers and remember the larger one. Then we compare that number with the third one, remembering the larger number. We repeat the process for all of the numbers, and the one we remember at the end is the largest. We use the same process to find the smallest number, except that we remember the smaller number instead of the larger one.

Problem-Solving Case Study

Consider a sample data set:

Reading Number	Actual Reading	Relative Reading
1	86.0	0.0
2	86.5	0.5
3	88.0	2.0
4	83.5	−2.5
5	88.3	2.3
6	89.6	3.6
7	80.1	−5.9
8	84.0	−2.0
9	86.7	0.7
10	79.3	−6.7
11	74.0	−12.0
12	73.5	−12.5

The maximum reading for this data set was number 6 at 89.6 decibels. The lowest was reading 12 at 73.5 decibels.

"Scan the list" in our by-hand algorithm translates into a loop. Now that we understand the process, let's design the looping algorithm using our checklist.

1. *What is the condition that ends the loop?* Because there are exactly 12 values in a set of readings, we use a counter to control the loop. When it exceeds 12, the loop exits.

2. *How should the condition be initialized?* The first value will be input before the loop because it is a special case—it is the value that is subtracted from all the other values to get their relative values. Also, its relative value is automatically 0.0. Thus the first iteration of the loop gets the second value, so the counter will start at 2.

3. *How should the condition be updated?* The counter should be incremented at the end of each iteration.

4. *What is the process being repeated?* The process reads a value, echo prints it, subtracts the first value from the new value, prints the result, and checks whether the new value should replace the current high or low value.

5. *How should the process be initialized?* The first number must be read in. Its relative value is automatically printed as 0.0. It is the initial high and low, and it is also saved as the base reading. The sequence number for both the high and low values will be set to 1 and their relative values will be 0.0.

6. *How should the process be updated?* In each iteration, a new current reading is input. If the current reading is greater than **high**, it replaces the current **high**. If the current reading is lower than the current **low**, then it becomes the new **low**. We must also save the reading number of the highest and lowest values, and their relative values.

7. *What is the state of the program on exiting the loop?* Twelve readings have been input and echo printed together with 12 relative values. The loop control variable equals 13. **high** contains the greatest value read, **highNumber** the number of that value, and **highRelative** the relative value

Problem-Solving Case Study

for that reading. `low` contains the lowest value, `lowNumber` holds the number of that reading, and `lowRelative` has the corresponding relative value.

ASSUMPTIONS: At least 12 real numbers will be input, and all will be within the proper range.

Main Module — Level 0

```
Initialize process
Initialize loop ending condition
WHILE readingNumber <= 12 DO
    Update process
    Update ending condition
Print high and low readings
Close file
```

Initialize Process — Level 1

```
Open input file
IF not opened okay
   Write error message
   Return 1
Print heading for output
Get baseValue
Print readingNumber 1, baseValue, relativeValue 0.0
Set high to baseValue
Set highNumber to 1
Set highRelative to 0.0
Set low to baseValue
Set lowNumber to 1
Set lowRelative to 0.0
```

Initialize Loop Ending Condition

```
Set readingNumber to 2
```

Update Process

```
Get current
Set relative to current - baseValue
Print readingNumber, current, relative
Check for new high
Check for new low
```

Problem-Solving Case Study

Update Loop Ending Condition

Increment readingNumber

Print High and Low Readings

Print 'Highest reading number is ', highNumber
Print 'Highest reading is ', high
Print 'Highest relative value is ', highRelative
Print 'Lowest reading number is ', lowNumber
Print 'Lowest reading is ', low
Print 'Lowest relative value is ', lowRelative

Check for New High   Level 2

IF current > high
    Set high to current
    Set highNumber to readingNumber
    Set highRelative to relative

Check for New Low

IF current < low
    Set low to current
    Set lowNumber to readingNumber
    Set lowRelative to relative

MODULE STRUCTURE CHART

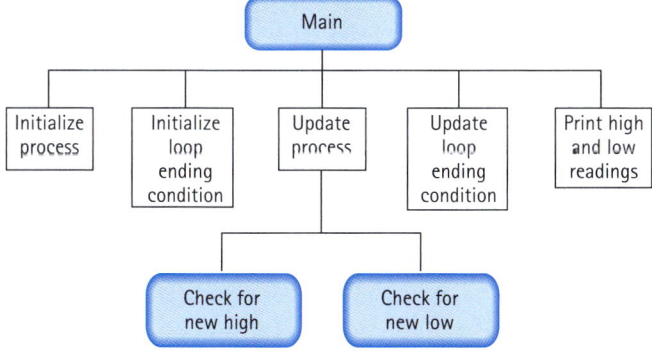

Problem-Solving Case Study

Here is the program:

```cpp
//*****************************************************************
// Acoustic program
// This program inputs 12 sound-level readings, taken in a room
// at different frequencies.  The first reading is used as a
// base value.  For each reading, a value relative to the base is
// calculated and printed.  The program ends by printing the
// highest reading and the lowest reading.
//*****************************************************************

#include <iostream>
#include <fstream>
#include <iomanip>

using namespace std;

int main()
{
  // Declare variables
  float baseValue;                // First reading
  float current;                  // Input during each iteration
  float relative;                 // Current minus base value
  float high;                     // Highest value input
  float highRelative;             // High minus base value
  float low;                      // Lowest value input
  float lowRelative;              // Low minus base value
  int highNumber;                 // Sequence number of high
  int lowNumber;                  // Sequence number of low
  int readingNumber;              // Sequence number of current reading
  // Declare and open input file
  ifstream inData;                // Input file of readings
  inData.open("acoustic.dat");
  if ( !inData )                  // Did input file open correctly?
  {   // no
    cout << "Can't open input file." << endl;
    return 1;                     // Terminate program
  }

  // Initialize variables and output
  readingNumber = 1;
  relative = 0.0;
  cout << setw(14) << "Reading Number" << setw(15)
       << "Actual Reading" << setw(18) << "Relative Reading"
       << endl;

  inData >> baseValue;            // Input base value
```

Problem-Solving Case Study

```
// Write first line of output
  cout << fixed << showpoint << setprecision(2) << setw(7)
       << readingNumber << setw(19) << baseValue << setw(15)
       << relative << endl;

  // Initialize process
  high = baseValue;
  highNumber = 1;
  highRelative = 0.0;
  low = baseValue;
  lowNumber = 1;
  lowRelative = 0.0;
  readingNumber = 2;                     // Initialize loop ending

  while (readingNumber <= 12)
  {
    inData >> current;                   // Input new reading
    relative = current - baseValue;      // Calculate new relative
    cout << setw(7) << readingNumber << setw(19) << current
         << setw(15) << relative << endl;

    if (current > high)                  // Check for new high
    {
      high = current;
      highNumber = readingNumber;
      highRelative = relative;
    }

    if (current < low)                   // Check for new low
    {
      low = current;
      lowNumber = readingNumber;
      lowRelative = relative;
    }
    readingNumber++;                     // Increment reading number

  }

  // Print high and low readings
  cout << endl;
  cout << "Highest reading number is " << highNumber << endl;
  cout << "Highest reading is "  << high << endl;
  cout << "Highest relative value is " << highRelative << endl;
  cout << endl;
  cout << "Lowest reading number is " << lowNumber << endl;
  cout << "Lowest reading is " << low << endl;
  cout << "Lowest relative value is " << lowRelative << endl;

  inData.close();
  return 0;
}
```

Problem-Solving Case Study

Here is the output:

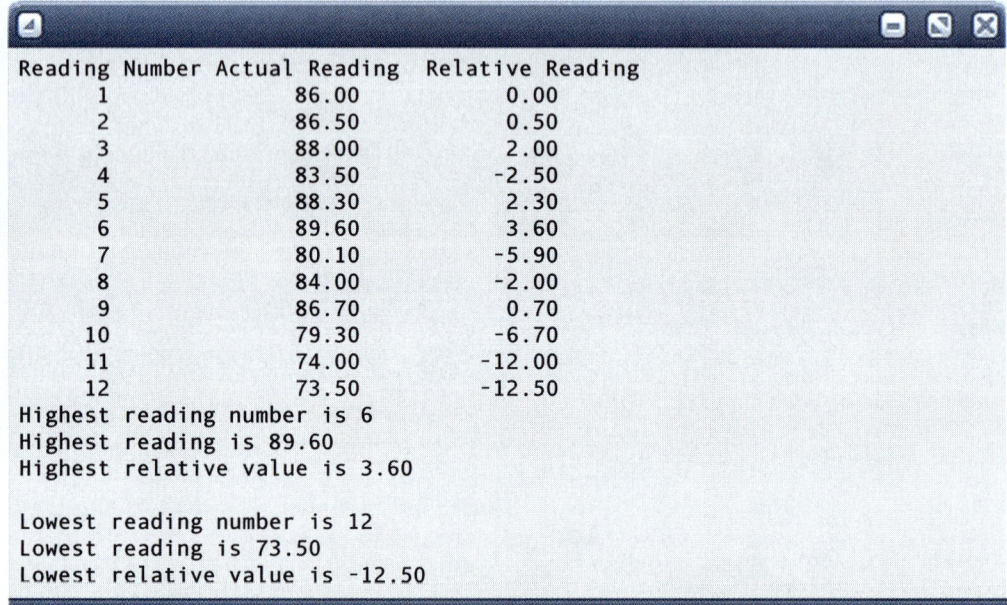

```
Reading Number  Actual Reading   Relative Reading
       1             86.00            0.00
       2             86.50            0.50
       3             88.00            2.00
       4             83.50           -2.50
       5             88.30            2.30
       6             89.60            3.60
       7             80.10           -5.90
       8             84.00           -2.00
       9             86.70            0.70
      10             79.30           -6.70
      11             74.00          -12.00
      12             73.50          -12.50
Highest reading number is 6
Highest reading is 89.60
Highest relative value is 3.60

Lowest reading number is 12
Lowest reading is 73.50
Lowest relative value is -12.50
```

Now that you have written the program, you call the president of the consulting firm and fax her the results. After studying the results, she is silent for a moment. "Oh. Right. I'm sorry," she says, "but I told you to keep track of the wrong value. We're not interested in the lowest value, but in the lowest dip in the readings. You see, the last value is almost always the lowest because it's the lowest tone, and we know that most rooms respond poorly to bass notes. There's nothing we can do about that. But the lowest dip in the readings often occurs with a higher tone, and that's usually a sign of a problem that we can fix. Can you change the program to output the lowest dip?" You confirm that a dip is a reading followed by a higher reading.

Now you have to figure out how to recognize a dip in the readings. You draw some graphs with random squiggles on them and pick out the lowest dips by hand. Then you make up some data sets that would generate the graphs. You find that a dip is usually a series of decreasing values followed by increasing values. But it can also just be a series of equal values followed by greater values. The bottom of a dip is merely the lowest value before values start increasing. You know how to keep track of a lowest value, but how do you tell if it is followed by a greater value?

Problem-Solving Case Study

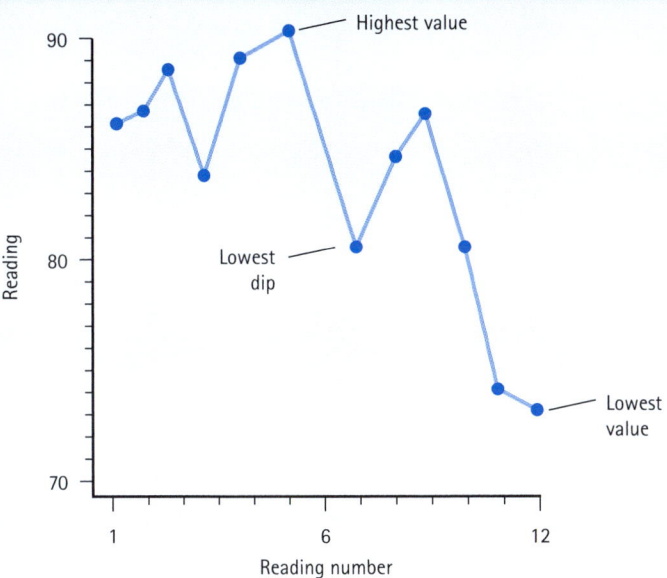

The answer is that you check for this condition after the next value is input. That is, when you read in a new value, you check whether the preceding value was lower. If it was, then you check whether it was the lowest value input so far. You've seen the algorithm for keeping track of a previous value—now you just have to add it to the program.

Now we can return to the checklist and see what must change. The control of the loop stays the same; only the process changes. Thus we can skip the first three questions.

4. *What is the process being repeated?* It is the same as before, except where we check for the lowest value. Instead, we first check whether the preceding value is less than the current value. If it is, then we check whether `preceding` should replace the lowest value so far. In replacing the lowest value, we must assign `readingNumber` minus one to `lowNumber`, because the dip occurred with the previous reading. We could also keep track of the previous value of `readingNumber`, but it is easier to calculate it.

5. *How should the process be initialized?* The change here is that we must initialize `preceding`. We can set it equal to the first value. We also have to initialize the `precedingRelative` value to 0.0.

6. *How should the process be updated?* We add steps to set `preceding` equal to `current` at the end of the loop, and to save `Relative` in `precedingRelative` for use in the next iteration.

7. *What is the state of the program on exiting the loop?* At this point, `preceding` holds the last value input and `precedingRelative` holds the last relative value computed. `low` holds the value of the lowest dip, `lowNumber` contains the reading number of the lowest dip, and `lowRelative` is the difference between the lowest dip and the first value.

Problem-Solving Case Study

Now let's look at the modules that have changed. We'll use highlighting to indicate the steps that are different:

Initialize Process   Level 1

Open input file
If not opened OK
  Write error message
  Return 1
Print heading for output
Get baseValue
Print readingNumber 1, baseValue, relativeValue 0.0
Set preceding to baseValue
Set precedingRelative to 0.0
Set high to baseValue
Set highNumber to 1
Set highRelative to 0.0
Set low to baseValue
Set lowNumber to 1
Set lowRelative to 0.0

Update Process

Prompt for current
Get current
Set relative to current − baseValue
Print readingNumber, current, relative
Check for new high
Check for new low
Set preceding to current
Set precedingRelative to relative

Print High and Low Readings

Print 'Highest reading number is ', highNumber
Print 'Highest reading is ', high
Print 'Highest relative value is ', highRelative
Print 'Lowest dip is number ', lowNumber
Print 'Lowest dip reading is ', low
Print 'Lowest relative dip is ', lowRelative

Problem-Solving Case Study

Check for New Low

```
IF current > preceding
   IF preceding < low
      Set low to preceding
      Set lowNumber to readingNumber – 1
      Set lowRelative to precedingRelative
```

Here's the new version of the program:

```cpp
//****************************************************************
// Acoustic program
// This program inputs 12 sound-level readings, taken in a room
// at different frequencies.  The first reading is used as a base
// value.  For each reading, a value relative to the base is
// calculated and printed.  The program ends by printing the
// lowest dip in the readings, where a dip is defined as a reading
// followed by a higher reading
//****************************************************************

#include <iostream>
#include <fstream>
#include <iomanip>

using namespace std;

int main()
{
  // Declare variables
  float baseValue;           // First reading
  float preceding;           // Reading preceding current
  float precedingRelative;   // Relative preceding current
  float current;             // Input during each iteration
  float relative;            // Current minus base value
  float high;                // Highest value input
  float highRelative;        // High minus base value
  float low;                 // Lowest dip in the readings
  float lowRelative;         // Relative value of low
  int highNumber;            // Sequence number of high
  int lowNumber;             // Sequence number of lowest dip
  int readingNumber;         // Sequence number of current reading

  // Declare and open input file
  ifstream inData;                    // Input file of readings
  inData.open("acoustic.dat");
      if ( !inData )                  // Did input file open correctly?
      {   // no
        cout << "Can't open input file." << endl;
        return 1;                     // Terminate program
      }
```

Problem-Solving Case Study

```cpp
    // Initialize variables and output
    cout << setw(14) << "Reading Number" << setw(15)
         << "Actual Reading" << setw(18) << "Relative Reading"
         << endl;
    inData >> baseValue;
    preceding = baseValue;
    precedingRelative = 0.0;
    highNumber = 1;
    lowNumber = 1;
    high = baseValue;
    low = baseValue;
    highRelative = 0.0;
    lowRelative = 0.0;
    readingNumber = 1;
    relative = 0.0;

    // Write first line of output
    cout << fixed << showpoint << setprecision(2) << setw(7)
         << readingNumber << setw(19)
         << baseValue << setw(15) << relative << endl;

    readingNumber = 2;                       // Initialize loop end
    while (readingNumber <= 12)
    {
      inData >> current;                     // Input new reading
      relative = current - baseValue;        // Calculate new relative
      cout << setw(7) << readingNumber << setw(19) << current
           << setw(15) << relative << endl;

      if (current > high)                    // Check for new high
      {
        high = current;
        highNumber = readingNumber;
        highRelative = relative;
      }

      if (current > preceding)               // Check for new low
      {
        if (preceding < low)
        {
          low = preceding;
          lowNumber = readingNumber - 1;
          lowRelative = precedingRelative;
        }
      }
      preceding = current;
      precedingRelative = relative;
      readingNumber++;
    }

    // Print high and low readings
    cout << endl;
    cout << "Highest reading number is " << highNumber << endl;
```

Problem-Solving Case Study

```
    cout << "Highest reading is "  << high << endl;
    cout << "Highest relative value is " << highRelative
         << endl;
    cout << endl;
    cout << "Lowest dip is number " << lowNumber << endl;
    cout << "Lowest dip reading is " << low << endl;
    cout << "Lowest relative dip is " << lowRelative << endl;

    inData.close();
    return 0;
}
```

Here is the output:

```
Reading Number Actual Reading  Relative Reading
       1                86.00             0.00
       2                86.50             0.50
       3                88.00             2.00
       4                83.50            -2.50
       5                88.30             2.30
       6                89.60             3.60
       7                80.10            -5.90
       8                84.00            -2.00
       9                86.70             0.70
      10                79.30            -6.70
      11                74.00           -12.00
      12                73.50           -12.50

Highest reading number is 6
Highest reading is 89.60
Highest relative value is 3.60

Lowest dip is number 7
Lowest dip reading is 80.10
Lowest relative dip is -5.90
```

Testing and Debugging

Loop-Testing Strategy

Even if a loop has been properly designed and verified, it is still important to test it rigorously: The chance of an error creeping in during the implementation phase is always present. Because loops allow us to input many data sets in one run, and because each iteration may be affected by preceding ones, the test data for a looping program is usually more extensive than that for a program with just sequential or branching statements. To test a loop thoroughly, we must check for the proper execution of both a single iteration and multiple iterations.

Remember that a loop has seven parts (corresponding to the seven questions in our checklist). A test strategy must test each part. Although all seven parts aren't implemented separately in every loop, the checklist reminds us that some loop operations serve multiple purposes, each of which should be tested. For example, the incrementing statement in a count-controlled loop may be updating both the process and the ending condition, so it's important to verify that it performs both actions properly with respect to the rest of the loop.

To test a loop, we try to devise data sets that could cause the variables to go out of range or leave the files in improper states that violate either the loop postcondition (an assertion that must be true immediately after loop exit) or the postcondition of the module containing the loop.

It's also good practice to test a loop for four special cases: (1) when the loop is skipped entirely, (2) when the loop body is executed just once, (3) when the loop executes some normal number of times, and (4) when the loop fails to exit.

Statements following a loop often depend on its processing. If a loop can be skipped, those statements may not execute correctly. If it's possible to execute a single iteration of a loop, the results can show whether the body performs correctly in the absence of the effects of previous iterations; this strategy can be very helpful when you're trying to isolate the source of an error. Obviously, it's important to test a loop under normal conditions, with a wide variety of inputs. If possible, you should test the loop with real data in addition to mock data sets. Count-controlled loops should be tested to confirm they execute exactly the right number of times. Finally, if there is any chance that a loop might never exit, your test data should try to make that happen.

Testing a program can be as challenging as writing it. To test a program, you need to step back, take a fresh look at what you've written, and then attack it in every way possible to make it fail. This isn't always easy to do, but it's necessary if your programs are going to be reliable. (A *reliable program* is one that works consistently and without errors regardless of whether the input data is valid or invalid.)

Test Plans Involving Loops

In Chapter 5, we introduced formal test plans and discussed the testing of branches. Those guidelines still apply to programs with loops, but here we provide some additional guidelines that are specific to loops.

Unfortunately, when a loop is embedded in a larger program, it may be difficult to control and observe the conditions under which the loop executes using test data and output alone. In some cases we must use indirect tests. For example, if a loop reads floating-point values from a file and prints their average without echo printing those values, you cannot tell directly that the loop processes all the data—if the data values in the file are all the same, then the average appears correct as long as even one of them is processed. You must construct the input file so that the average is a unique value that can be arrived at only by processing all the data.

To simplify our testing of such loops, we would like to observe the values of the variables associated with the loop at the start of each iteration. How can we observe the values of variables while a program is running? Two common techniques are to use the system's *debugger* program and to include extra output statements designed solely for debugging purposes. We discuss these techniques in the "Testing and Debugging Hints" section.

Now let's look at some test cases that are specific to the different types of loops that we've seen in this chapter.

Count-Controlled Loops

When a loop is count controlled, you should include a test case that specifies the output for all the iterations. It may help to add an extra column to the test plan that lists the iteration number. If the loop reads data and outputs a result, then each input value should produce a different output to make it easier to spot errors. For example, in a loop that is supposed to read and print 100 data values, it is easier to tell that the loop executes the correct number of iterations when the values are 1, 2, 3, . . . , 100 than when they are all the same.

If the program inputs the iteration count for the loop, you need to test the cases in which an invalid count, such as a negative number, is input (an error message should be output and the loop should be skipped), a count of 0 is input (the loop should be skipped), a count of 1 is input (the loop should execute once), and some typical number of iterations is input (the loop should execute the specified number of times).

Event-Controlled Loops

In an event-controlled loop, you should test the situation in which the event occurs before the loop, in the first iteration, and in a typical number of iterations. For example, if the event is that EOF occurs, then try test data consisting of an empty file, a file with one data set, and another file with several data sets. If your testing involves reading from test files, you should attach printed copies of the files to the test plan and identify each in some way so that the plan can refer to them. It also helps to identify where each iteration begins in the Input and Expected Output columns of the test plan.

When the event is the input of a sentinel value, you need the following test cases: The sentinel is the only data set, the sentinel follows one data set, and the sentinel follows a typical number of data sets. Given that sentinel-controlled loops involve a priming read, it is especially important to verify that the first and last data sets are processed properly.

Testing and Debugging Hints

1. Plan your test data carefully to test all sections of a program.
2. Beware of infinite loops, in which the expression in the While statement never becomes `false`. The symptom: The program doesn't stop. If you are on a system that monitors the execution time of a program, you may see a message such as `"TIME LIMIT EX-CEEDED."`

    If you have created an infinite loop, check your logic and the syntax of your loops. Be sure no semicolon appears immediately after the right parenthesis of the While condition:

```
while (Expression);    // Wrong
    Statement
```

This semicolon causes an infinite loop in most cases; the compiler thinks the loop body is the null statement (the do-nothing statement composed solely of a semicolon). In a count-controlled loop, make sure the loop control variable is incremented within the loop. In a flag-controlled loop, make sure the flag eventually changes.

As always, watch for the = versus == problem in While conditions as well as in If conditions. The line

```
while (someVar = 5)    // Wrong (should be ==)
```

produces an infinite loop. The value of the assignment (not relational) expression is always 5, which is interpreted as `true`.

3. Check the loop termination condition carefully and be sure that something in the loop causes it to be met. Watch closely for values that cause one iteration too many or too few (the "off-by-one-bug" syndrome).
4. Remember to use the `get` function rather than the >> operator in loops that are controlled by detection of a newline character.
5. Perform an algorithm walk-through to verify that all of the appropriate preconditions and postconditions occur in the right places.
6. Trace the execution of the loop by hand with a code walk-through. Simulate the first few passes and the last few passes very carefully to see how the loop really behaves.
7. Use a *debugger* if your system provides one. A debugger is a program that runs your program in "slow motion," allowing you to execute one instruction at a time and to examine the contents of variables as they change. If you haven't already done so, check whether a debugger is available on your system.
8. If all else fails, use *debug output statements*—output statements inserted into a program to help debug it. They output messages that indicate the flow of execution in the program or report the values of variables at certain points in the program.

    For example, if you want to know the value of variable `beta` at a certain point in a program, you could insert this statement:

```
cout << "beta = " << beta << endl;
```

If this output statement appears in a loop, you will get as many values of `beta` output as there are iterations of the body of the loop.

After you have debugged your program, you can remove the debug output statements or just precede them with // so that they'll be treated as comments. (This practice is referred to as commenting out a piece of code.) You can remove the double slashes if you need to use the statements again.

9. An ounce of prevention is worth a pound of debugging. Use the checklist questions to design your loop correctly at the outset. It may seem like extra work, but it pays off in the long run.

Summary

The While statement is a looping construct that allows a program to repeat a statement as long as the value of an expression is `true`. When the value of the While expression becomes `false`, the body of the loop is skipped and execution continues with the first statement following the loop.

With the While statement, you can construct several types of loops that you will use again and again. These types of loops are classified into one of two categories: count-controlled loops and event-controlled loops.

In a count-controlled loop, the loop body is repeated a specified number of times. You initialize a counter variable right before the While statement. This loop control variable is then tested against the limit in the While expression. The last statement in the loop body increments the control variable.

Event-controlled loops continue executing until something inside the body signals that the looping process should stop. Event-controlled loops include those that test for a sentinel value in the data, for end of file, or for a change in a flag variable.

Sentinel-controlled loops are input loops that use a special data value as a signal to stop reading. EOF-controlled loops are loops that continue to input (and process) data values until no more data remains. To implement them with a While statement, you must test the state of the input stream by using the name of the stream object as if it were a Boolean variable. The test yields `false` when there are no more data values. A flag is a variable that is set in one part of the program and tested in another part of the same program. In a flag-controlled loop, you must set the flag before the loop begins, test it in the While expression, and change it somewhere in the body of the loop.

Counting is a looping operation that keeps track of how many times a loop is repeated or how many times some event occurs. This count can be used in computations or to control the loop. A counter is a variable that is used for counting. It may take the form of a loop control variable in a count-controlled loop, an iteration counter in a counting loop, or an event counter that counts the number of times a particular condition occurs in a loop.

Summing is a looping operation that keeps a running total of certain values. It is like counting in that the variable that holds the sum is initialized outside the loop. The summing operation, however, adds up unknown values; the counting operation adds a constant (1) to the counter each time.

When you design a loop, you should consider seven points: how the termination condition is initialized, tested, and updated; how the process in the loop is initialized, performed, and updated; and the state of the program upon exiting the loop. By answering the checklist questions, you can bring each of these points into focus.

To design a nested loop structure, begin with the outermost loop. When you get to where the inner loop must appear, make it a separate module and come back to its design later.

The process of testing a loop is based on the answers to the checklist questions and the patterns the loop might encounter (for example, executing a single iteration, multiple iterations, an infinite number of iterations, or no iterations at all).

Quick Check Answers

6.1.1 While statement **6.1.2** bool **6.1.3** It is coerced to `false` for a zero value and `true` for any nonzero value. **6.1.4** repeat. **6.2.1** Entry, iteration, test, exit. **6.3.1** count-controlled loops and event-controlled loops. **6.3.2** count-controlled loop: Hop on one foot 10 times; event-controlled loop: Hop on one foot until you are tired. **6.3.3** Both types of loops exit when an event occurs. The sentinel-controlled loop tests for the event at the start of each iteration, while the flag-controlled loop checks for the event in the middle of the iteration, setting a flag to be tested at the start of the next iteration. **6.3.4** Both. **6.3.5** `while (count <= 10 && !found)`

6.3.6
```
count = 1;
found = false;
cin >> inData;
while (count <= 10 && !found && cin)
{
  count++;
  found = inData == 0;
  cin >> inData;
}
```
6.3.7
```
onesCount = 0;
sum = 0;
count = 1;
found = false;
cin >> inData;
while (count <= 10 && !found && cin)
{
  if (inData == 1)
    onesCount++;
  sum = sum + inData;
  count++;
  found = inData == 0;
  cin >> inData;
}
```
6.4.1 An event-controlled loop. (The events would be the input of the number, or reaching end-of-file).
6.4.2
```
count = 1;
found = false;
while (count <= 10 && !found)
{
  count++;
  found = inData == 0;
}
```
6.4.3 1. What is the condition that ends the loop?, 2. How should the condition be initialized?, 3. How should the condition be updated?, 4. What is the process being repeated?, 5. How should the process be initialized?, 6. How should the process be updated?, 7. What is the state of the program on exiting the loop?
6.4.4
```
lineCount = 0;
while (inFile.get(inChar))
{
    if (inChar == '\n')
        lineCount++;
}
```
6.5.1
```
while (inFile.get(inChar))
{
    count = 0;
    while (inFile && inChar != '\n')
    {
        count++;
        inFile.get(inChar);
    }
    cout << "Line " << lineCount << ": " << count << endl;
    lineCount++;
}
```
6.5.2 complexity. 6.5.3 The total number of steps required to execute an algorithm. 6.5.4 Nest it within a counting loop that counts from 1 to 5.

Exam Preparation Exercises

1. The While statement exits when the termination condition becomes true. True or false?

2. The body of the While statement is always executed at least once. True or false?
3. Using a block as the body of the While statement enables us to place any number of statements within a loop. True or false?
4. Match the following list of terms with the definitions given below.
   a. Loop entry.
   b. Iteration.
   c. Loop test.
   d. Loop exit.
   e. Termination condition.
   f. Count-controlled loop.
   g. Event-controlled loop.
   h. Iteration counter.
   i. Event counter.
      i. A loop that executes a specified number of times.
      ii. When the flow of control reaches the first statement inside a loop.
      iii. A variable that is incremented each time a particular condition is encountered.
      iv. When the decision is made whether to begin a new iteration or to exit.
      v. A loop that exits when a specific condition is encountered.
      vi. The condition that causes the loop to exit.
      vii. A variable that is incremented with each iteration of a loop.
      viii. When control passes to the statement following the loop.
      ix. An individual pass through a loop.
5. How many times does the following loop execute, and what is its output?

```
count = 1;
while (count <= 12)
{
  cout << count << endl;
  count++;
}
```

6. How many times does the following loop execute, and what is its output?

```
count = 0;
while (count <= 11)
{
  cout << count << ", ";
  count++;
}
```

7. How many times does the following loop execute, and what is its output?

```
count = 1;
while (count < 13)
{
  cout << "$" << count << ".00" << endl;
  count++;
}
```

8. What does the following nested loop structure output?

```
count = 1;
while (count <= 11)
{
  innerCount = 1
  while (innerCount <= (12 - count) / 2)
  {
    cout << " ";
    innerCount++;
  }
  innerCount = 1;
  while (innerCount <= count)
  {
    cout << "@";
    innerCount++;
  }
  cout << endl;
  count++;
}
```

9. What does the following nested loop structure output?

```
count = 1;
while (count <= 10)
{
  innerCount = 1;
  while (innerCount <= 10)
  {
    cout << setw(5) << count * innercount;
    innerCount++;
  }
  cout << endl;
  count++;
}
```

10. The following loop is supposed to sum all of the input values on file `indata`. What's wrong with it? Change the code so that it works correctly.

```
sum = 0;
indata >> number;
while (indata)
{
  indata >> number;
  sum = sum + number;
}
```

11. Which sentinel value would you choose for a program that reads names as strings?

12. The following code segment is supposed to write out the odd numbers from 1 to 19. What does it actually output? Change the code so that it works correctly.

```
number = 1;
while (number < 10)
{
  number++;
  cout << number * 2 - 1 << " ";
}
```

13. Priming reads aren't necessary when a loop is controlled by a sentinel value. True or false?
14. What are the seven questions that must be answered to design a loop?
15. The following code segment is supposed to output the average of the five numbers on each input line, for all of the lines in the file. Instead, it simply outputs the sum of all of the numbers in the file. What's wrong with the code segment? Change the code so that it works correctly.

```
sum = 0;
while (indata)
{
  count = 1;
  while (count <= 5 && indata)
  {
    cin >> number;
    sum = sum + number;
  }
  cout << sum / count << endl;
}
```

Programming Warm-Up Exercises

1. Write a code segment using a While loop that outputs the numbers from −10 to 10.
2. Write a code segment using a While loop that sums the integers, counting up from 1, and stops when the sum is greater than 10,000, printing out the integer that was most recently added to the sum.
3. Write a looping code segment that takes as input up to 20 integer scores from file `indata`, and outputs their average. If the file contains fewer than 20 scores, the segment should still output the correct average. If the file contains more than 20 scores, the additional numbers should be ignored. Be sure to consider what happens if the file is empty.
4. Write a code segment that reads lines of text from file `chapter6`, and outputs the number of lines in the file that contain the string `"code segment"`.
5. Write a code segment that reads a string from `cin`. The string should be one of the following: `"Yes"`, `"No"`, `"yes"`, or `"no"`. If it is not, the user should be prompted to input an appropriate response, and the process should repeat. Once a valid response is received, the `bool` variable `yes` should be assigned `true` if the response is `"Yes"` or `"yes"` and `false` if the response is `"No"` or `"no"`.
6. Write a code segment that prints the days of a month in calendar format. The day of the week on which the month begins is represented by an `int` variable `startDay`. When `startDay` is zero, the month begins on a Sunday. The `int` variable `days` contains the number of days in the month. Print a heading with the days of the week as the first line of output. The day numbers should be neatly aligned under these column headings.
7. We could extend the code from Exercise 6 to print a calendar for a year by nesting it within a loop that repeats the code 12 times.
   a. Which formula would you use to compute the new start day for the next month?
   b. Which additional information would you need to print the calendar for each month?
8. Write a code segment that reads all of the characters on file `textData`, and then outputs the percentage of the characters that are the letter `'z'`.

9. Change the code segment in Exercise 8 so that it stops reading either at the end of the file or after 10,000 characters have been input.
10. Write a code segment that outputs the Fibonacci numbers that are less than 30,000. Each Fibonacci number is the sum of its two predecessors. The first two Fibonacci numbers are 1 and 1. Thus, the sequence begins with

$$1, 1, 2, 3, 5, 8, 13, 21, 34, \ldots$$

Output each number on a separate line.
11. Modify the code segment in Exercise 10 so that it also outputs the position of the Fibonacci number in the sequence. For example:

```
1    1
2    1
3    2
4    3
5    5
6    8
7    13
```

12. Write a code segment that inputs an integer from `cin`, and then outputs a row of that many stars on `cout`.
13. How did you answer the loop checklist questions for the code segment you wrote in Exercise 12?
14. Change the code segment for Exercise 12 to read a series of numbers from file `indata`, and print a row of stars on `cout` for each number read. (You can think of this problem as printing a bar graph of a data file.)
15. What sort of test data would you use to test the code segment in Exercise 14?

Programming Problems

1. Write a C++ program that computes student grades for an assignment as a percentage given each student's score and the total points. The final score should be rounded up to the nearest whole value using the `ceil` function in the `<cmath>` header file. You should also display the floating-point result up to 5 decimal places. The input to the program must come from a file containing multiple lines with the student's last name, score, and total separated by a space. In addition, you should print to the console "Excellent" if the grade is greater than 90, "Well Done" if the grade is greater than 80, "Good" if the grade is greater than 70, "Need Improvement" if the grade is greater than or equal to 60, and "Fail" if the grade is less than 50. Here is an example of what the input file might look like:

```
Weems 50 60
Dale 51 60
Richards 57 60
Smith 36 60
Tomlin 44 60
Bird 45 60
...
```

The output of your program should look like this:

```
Weems 83% .83333 Well Done
Dale 85% .85000 Well Done
Richards 95% .95000 Excellent
Smith 60% .60000 Need Improvement
Tomlin 73% .73333 Good
Bird 75% .75000 Good
...
```

2. ROT13 (rotate by 13 places) is a simple letter substitution cipher that is an instance of a Caesar cipher developed in ancient Rome and used by Julius Caesar who used it in his private correspondence. ROT13 replaces a letter with the letter 13 letters after it in the alphabet. The following table demonstrates the translation in ROT13:

    A ↔ N
    B ↔ O
    C ↔ P
    D ↔ Q
    E ↔ R
    F ↔ S
    G ↔ T
    H ↔ U
    I ↔ V
    J ↔ W
    K ↔ X
    L ↔ Y
    M ↔ Z

    Thus, the translation of the word JULIUS using ROT13 would be WHYVHF. Write a C++ program that asks the user for the name of an input file and translates the contents of that input file using ROT13. Your program should output the translation into a secondary file with a ".rot13" file extension.

3. Design and write a C++ program that inputs a series of 24 hourly temperatures from a file, and outputs a bar chart (using stars) of the temperatures for the day. The temperature should be printed to the left of the corresponding bar, and there should be a heading that gives the scale of the chart. The range of temperatures should be from −30 to 120. Because it is hard to display 150 characters on the screen, you should have each star represent a range of 3 degrees. That way, the bars will be at most 50 characters wide. Here is a partial example, showing the heading, the output for a negative temperature, and the output for various positive temperatures. Note how the temperatures are rounded to the appropriate number of stars.

```
Temperatures for 24 hours:
      -30         0        30          60          90         120
-20         *******|
  0                |
  1                |
  2                |*
  3                |*
  4                |*
  5                |**
 10                |***
 50                |******************
100                |**********************************
```

Use meaningful variable names, proper indentation, and appropriate comments. Thoroughly test the program using your own data sets.

4. The standard deviation of a set of data values gives us a sense of the dispersion of values within their range. For example, a set of test scores with a small standard deviation indicates that most people's scores were very close to the average score. Some instructors use the standard deviation as a way of determining the range of values to assign a particular grade.

   Design and write a C++ program that reads a set of scores from the file **scores.dat**, and outputs their mean and standard deviation on **cout**. The formula for the standard deviation is

   $$s = \frac{\sum_{i=1}^{n} x_i^2 - \left(\sum_{i=1}^{n} x_i\right)^2}{n(n-1)}$$

   where n is the number of values and x_i represents the individual values. Thus, to compute the standard deviation, you must sum the squares of the individual values, and also square the sum of the values. All of this reading and summing can be done with a single loop, after which the mean and standard deviation of the scores are computed. Be sure to properly label the output. Use meaningful variable names, proper indentation, and appropriate comments. Thoroughly test the program using your own data sets.

5. You are burning some music CDs for a party. You've arranged a list of songs in the order in which you want to play them. However, you would like to maximize your use of space on the CD, which holds 80 minutes of music. To do so, you want to figure out the total time for a group of songs and see how well they fit. Write a design and a C++ program to help you accomplish this task. The data are on file **songs.dat**. The time is entered as seconds. For example, if a song takes 7 minutes and 42 seconds to play, the data entered for that song would be

   462

   After all the data has been read, the application should print a message indicating the time remaining on the CD.

The output should be in the form of a table with columns and headings written on a file. For example:

```
Song            Song Time           Total Time
Number      Minutes  Seconds     Minutes  Seconds
------      -------  -------     -------  -------
1              5       10           5       10
2              7       42          12       52
5              4       19          17       11
3              4       33          21       44
4             10       27          32       11
6              8       55          41        6
7              5        0          46        6
There are 33 minutes and 54 seconds of space left on the 80-minute CD.
```

Note that the output converts the input from seconds to minutes and seconds. Use meaningful variable names, proper indentation, and appropriate comments. Thoroughly test the program using your own data sets.

6. A palindrome is a phrase that reads the same both forward and backward. Write a C++ program that reads a line from `cin`, prints its characters in reverse order on `cout`, and then pronounces judgment on whether the input line is a palindrome. For example, here are two sample runs of the program:

```
Enter string: able was I ere I saw elba
able was I ere I saw elba
is a palindrome.
Enter string: madam I'm adam
madam I'm adam
is not a palindrome
```

Hint: Use the `substr` function within a loop to extract and print the characters one by one from the string, starting at the end of the string; at the same time, extract the corresponding character starting at the beginning of the string to compare with it.

Use a prompting message, meaningful variable names, proper indentation, and appropriate comments. Thoroughly test the program using your own data sets.

7. You're working for a company that's building an email list from files of mail messages. Your boss would like you to write a program that reads a file called `mail.dat`, and that outputs every string containing the @ sign to file `addresses.dat`. For the purpose of this project, a string is defined as it is by the C++ stream reader—a contiguous sequence of non-whitespace characters. Given the data

```
From:  sharon@marzipan.edu
Date:  Wed, 13 Aug 2003 17:12:33 EDT
Subject: Re: hi
To:    john@meringue.com
John,
Dave's email is dave_smith@icing.org.
ttyl,
sharon
```

the program would output the following information on file `addresses.dat`:

```
sharon@marzipan.edu
john@meringue.com
dave_smith@icing.org.
```

Use meaningful variable names, proper indentation, and appropriate comments. Thoroughly test the program using your own data sets.

Case Study Follow-Up

1. The first version of program `Acoustic` remembers the reading number of the highest reading. If there are multiple readings with the same value, it remembers only the first one. Change the program so that it remembers the last of these values instead. *Hint:* You need to add only one character to the program.
2. The second version of program `Acoustic` keeps track of the lowest dip in the readings. If there are two dips that are equal, it remembers the first one. Change the program so that it remembers the last one.
3. Does the loop in program `Acoustic` use a priming read?
4. Which type of loop, event-controlled or count-controlled, is used in program `Acoustic`?
5. The problem for the Case Study states that the readings are on a file. They could equally well have been entered from the keyboard. Change the revised program so that the values are entered in real time.
6. How might you determine whether it is better to enter data from a file or from the keyboard?
7. Discuss how you might go about devising a test plan for program `Acoustic`.

Additional Control Structures

KNOWLEDGE GOALS

- To know how to choose the most appropriate looping statement for a given problem.
- To understand the purpose of the Break and Continue statements.
- To be familiar with specialized C++ operators and expressions.

SKILL GOALS

To be able to:
- Write a Switch statement for a multiway branching problem.
- Write a Do-While statement and contrast it with a While statement.
- Write a For statement to implement a count-controlled loop.
- Cast a value from one type to another.

CHAPTER 7 Additional Control Structures

In the preceding chapters, we introduced C++ statements for sequence, selection, and loop structures. In some cases, we introduced more than one way of implementing these structures. For example, selection may be implemented by an If-Then structure or an If-Then-Else structure. The If-Then statement is sufficient to implement any selection structure, but C++ provides the If-Then-Else statement for convenience because the two-way branch is frequently used in programming.

This chapter introduces five new statements that are also nonessential to, but nonetheless convenient for, programming. One, the Switch statement, makes it easier to write selection structures that have many branches. Two new looping statements, For and Do-While, make it easier to program certain types of loops. The other two statements, Break and Continue, are control statements that are used as part of larger looping and selection structures.

7.1 The Switch Statement

> **Switch expression** The expression whose value determines which switch label is selected. It cannot be a floating-point or string expression.

The Switch statement is a selection control structure that allows us to list any number of branches. In other words, it is a control structure for multiway branches. A Switch is similar to nested If statements. The value of the switch expression—an expression whose value is matched with a label attached to a branch—determines which one of the branches is executed. For example, look at the following statement:

```
switch (letter)
{
  case 'X' : Statement1;
             break;
  case 'L' :
  case 'M' : Statement2;
             break;
  case 'S' : Statement3;
             break;
  default  : Statement4;
}
Statement5;
```

In this example, `letter` is the switch expression. The statement means "If `letter` is `'X'`, execute Statement1 and break out of the Switch statement, and proceed with Statement5. If `letter` is `'L'` or `'M'`, execute Statement2 and break out to Statement5. If `letter` is `'S'`, execute Statement3 and go to Statement5. If `letter` is none of the characters mentioned, execute Statement4 and exit to Statement5." The Break statement causes an immediate exit from the Switch statement. We'll see shortly what happens if we omit the Break statements.

The syntax template for the Switch statement is

SwitchStatement

```
switch ( IntegralOrEnumExpression )
{
    SwitchLabel ... Statement
         :
         :
}
```

IntegralOrEnumExpression is an expression of integral type—`char`, `short`, `int`, `long`, `bool`—or of **enum** type (we discuss **enum** in Chapter 10). The optional SwitchLabel in front of a statement is either a case label or a default label:

SwitchLabel

```
{ case ConstantExpression :
  default :
```

In a case label, ConstantExpression is an integral or **enum** expression whose operands must be literal or named constants. The following are examples of constant integral expressions (where `CLASS_SIZE` is a named constant of type `int`):

```
3
CLASS_SIZE
'A'
2 * CLASS_SIZE + 1
```

The data type of ConstantExpression is coerced, if necessary, to match the type of the switch expression.

In our opening example that tests the value of `letter`, the case labels have the following form:

```
case 'X' :
case 'L' :
case 'M' :
case 'S' :
```

As that example shows, a single statement may be preceded by more than one case label. Each case value may appear only once in a given Switch statement. If a value appears more than once, a syntax error results. Also, there can be only one default label in a Switch statement.

The flow of control through a Switch statement goes like this. First, the switch expression is evaluated. If this value matches one of the values in the case labels, control branches to the statement following that case label. From there, control proceeds sequentially until either a Break statement or the end of the Switch statement is encountered. If the value of the switch expression doesn't match any case value, then one of two things happens. If there is a default label, control branches to the statement following that label. If there is no default label, all statements within the Switch are skipped and control simply proceeds to the statement following the entire Switch statement.

The following Switch statement prints an appropriate comment based on a student's grade (`grade` is of type `char`):

```
switch (grade)
{
  case 'A' :
  case 'B' : cout << "Good Work";
             break;
  case 'C' : cout << "Average Work";
             break;
  case 'D' :
```

```
        case 'F' : cout << "Poor Work";
                   numberInTrouble++;
                   break;              // Unnecessary, but a good habit
}
```

Notice that the final Break statement is unnecessary. Programmers often include it anyway, because it's easier to insert another case label at the end if a Break statement is already present.

If `grade` does not contain one of the specified characters, none of the statements within the Switch is executed. Unless a precondition of the Switch statement is that `grade` is definitely one of 'A', 'B', 'C', 'D', or 'F', it would be wise to include a default label to account for an invalid grade:

```
switch (grade)
{
  case 'A' :
  case 'B' : cout << "Good Work";
             break;
  case 'C' : cout << "Average Work";
             break;
  case 'D' :
  case 'F' : cout << "Poor Work";
             numberInTrouble++;
             break;
  default  : cout << grade << " is not a valid letter grade.";
             break;
}
```

A Switch statement with a Break statement after each case alternative behaves exactly like an If-Then-Else-If control structure. For example, our Switch statement is equivalent to the following code:

```
if (grade == 'A' || grade == 'B')
  cout << "Good Work";
else if (grade == 'C')
  cout << "Average Work";
else if (grade == 'D' || grade == 'F')
{
  cout << "Poor Work";
  numberInTrouble++;
}
else
  cout << grade << " is not a valid letter grade.";
```

Is either of these two versions better than the other? There is no absolute answer to this question. For this particular example, the Switch statement seems easier to understand because of its two-dimensional, table-like form—but some people may find the If-Then-Else-If version easier to read. When implementing a multiway branching structure, our advice is to write both a Switch and an If-Then-Else-If, and then compare the two for readability. Keep in mind that C++ provides the Switch statement as a matter of convenience. Don't feel obligated to use a Switch statement for every multiway branch.

Finally, we said we would look at what happens if you omit the Break statements inside a Switch statement. Let's rewrite our letter grade example without the Break statements:

```
switch (grade)                                      // Wrong version
{
  case 'A' :
  case 'B' : cout << "Good Work";
  case 'C' : cout << "Average Work";
  case 'D' :
  case 'F' : cout << "Poor Work";
             numberInTrouble++;
  default  : cout << grade << " is not a valid letter grade.";
}
```

If `grade` happens to be 'H', control branches to the statement at the default label and the output is

`H is not a valid letter grade.`

Unfortunately, this case alternative is the only one that works correctly. If `grade` is 'A', the resulting output is this:

`Good WorkAverage WorkPoor WorkA is not a valid letter grade.`

Remember—after a branch is taken to a specific case label, control proceeds sequentially until either a Break statement or the end of the Switch statement is encountered. Forgetting a Break statement in a case alternative is a very common source of errors in C++ programs.

On page 210 in Chapter 5, we showed a listing of a program that printed a message depending on the temperature and whether it was raining. Here is the same program using a Switch statement rather than Boolean assignment statements and If Statements.

```
//****************************************************************
// Activity program
// This program outputs an appropriate activity
// for a given temperature
//****************************************************************
#include <iostream>
#include <string>
using namespace std;

int main()
{
  int temperature;     // The outside temperature
  int raining;

  // Read and echo temperature
  cout << "Enter the outside temperature:" << endl;
  cin >> temperature;
  cout << "Enter 1 if it is raining and 0 if it is not." << endl;
  cin >> raining;
  cout << "The current temperature is " << temperature;
  switch (raining)
  {
    case 0 : cout << " and it is not raining." << endl;
             if (temperature > 60)
```

```
                    cout << "Go for a walk." << endl;
               else
                    cout << "Read a good book." << endl;
               break;
       case 1 : cout << " and it is raining." << endl;
                if (temperature > 60)
                    cout << "Go to a movie." << endl;
                else
                    cout << "Read a good book." << endl;
                break;
    }
    return 0;
}
```

When this program was run four times, it produced the following output. It should be easy to convince yourself that this program is functionally equivalent to the other one.

```
Enter the outside temperature:
65
Enter 1 if it is raining and 0 if it is not.
1
The current temperature is 65 and it is raining.
Go to a movie.

Enter the outside temperature:
65
Enter 1 if it is raining and 0 if it is not.
0
The current temperature is 65 and it is not raining.
Go for a walk.

Enter the outside temperature:
55
Enter 1 if it is raining and 0 if it is not.
0
The current temperature is 55 and it is not raining.
Read a good book.

Enter the outside temperature:
55
Enter 1 if it is raining and 0 if it is not.
1
The current temperature is 55 and it is raining.
Read a good book.
```

MAY WE INTRODUCE Admiral Grace Murray Hopper

From 1943 until her death on New Year's Day in 1992, Admiral Grace Murray Hopper was intimately involved with computing. In 1991, she was awarded the National Medal of Technology "for her pioneering accomplishments in the development of computer programming languages that simplified computer technology and opened the door to a significantly larger universe of users."

Admiral Hopper was born Grace Brewster Murray in New York City on December 9, 1906. She attended Vassar College and received a Ph.D. in mathematics from Yale University. For the next ten years, she taught mathematics at Vassar.

In 1943, Admiral Hopper joined the U.S. Navy and was assigned to the Bureau of Ordnance Computation Project at Harvard University as a programmer on the Mark I. After the war, she remained at Harvard as a faculty member and continued work on the Navy's Mark II and Mark III computers. From her time there, she loved to tell the story of the discovery of the first computer "bug"—a moth caught in the hardware. In 1949, she joined Eckert-Mauchly Computer Corporation and worked on the UNIVAC I.

Admiral Hopper had a working compiler in 1952, at a time when the conventional wisdom was that computers could do only arithmetic. Although not on the committee that designed the computer language COBOL, she was active in its design, implementation, and use. COBOL (which stands for Common Business-Oriented Language) was developed in the early 1960s and is still widely used in business data processing.

Admiral Hopper retired from the Navy in 1966, only to be recalled within a year to full-time active duty. Her mission was to oversee the Navy's efforts to maintain uniformity in programming languages. It has been said that just as Admiral Hyman Rickover was the father of the nuclear navy, Rear Admiral Hopper was the mother of computerized data automation in the Navy. She served with the Naval Data Automation Command until she retired again in 1986 with the rank of rear admiral. At the time of her death, she was a senior consultant at Digital Equipment Corporation.

During her lifetime, Admiral Hopper received honorary degrees from more than 40 colleges and universities. She was honored by her peers on several occasions, including the first Computer Sciences Man of the Year award given by the Data Processing Management Association, and the Contributions to Computer Science Education Award given by the Special Interest Group for Computer Science Education of the ACM (Association for Computing Machinery).

Admiral Hopper loved young people and enjoyed giving talks on college and university campuses. She often handed out colored wires, which she called nanoseconds because they were cut to a length of about one foot—the distance that light travels in a nanosecond (one billionth of a second). Her advice to the young was, "You manage things; you lead people. We went overboard on management and forgot about leadership."

When asked which of her many accomplishments she was most proud of, she answered, "All the young people I have trained over the years."

310 CHAPTER 7 Additional Control Structures

QUICK CHECK

7.1.1 A Switch statement is specifically designed for what type of branches? (p. 304)
7.1.2 What does a `break` statement do? (p. 304)
7.1.3 The expression in a Switch statement must be of what type? (pp. 304–305)
7.1.4 Describe the flow of control followed in a Switch statement. (p. 305)
7.1.5 In converting an If-Then-Else-If multiway branching structure to a Switch statement, which part of the Switch corresponds to the final Else branch? (pp. 304–307)

7.2 The Do-While Statement

The Do-While statement is a looping control structure in which the loop condition is tested at the end (bottom) of the loop. This format guarantees that the loop body executes at least once. Here is the syntax template for the Do-While:

DoWhileStatement

```
do
   Statement
while ( Expression ) ;
```

As usual in C++, Statement is either a single statement or a block. Also, note that the Do-While ends with a semicolon.

The statement

```
do
{
   Statement1;
   Statement2;
      :
   StatementN;
} while (Expression);
```

means "Execute the statements between `do` and `while` as long as Expression still has the value `true` at the end of the loop."

Let's compare a While loop and a Do-While loop that do the same task: They find the first period in a file of data. Assume that there is at least one period in the file.

While Solution

```
dataFile >> inputChar;
while (inputChar != '.')
  dataFile >> inputChar;
```

Do-While Solution

```
do
  dataFile >> inputChar;
while (inputChar != '.');
```

The While solution requires a priming read so that `inputChar` has a value before the loop is entered. This isn't required for the Do-While solution because the input statement within the loop executes before the loop condition is evaluated.

Let's look at another example. Suppose a program needs to read a person's age interactively. The program requires that the age be positive. The following loops ensure that the input value is positive before the program proceeds any further.

While Solution
```
cout << "Enter your age: ";
cin >> age;
while (age <= 0)
{
  cout << "Your age must be positive." << endl;
  cout << "Enter your age: ";
  cin >> age;
}
```

Do-While Solution
```
do
{
  cout << "Enter your age: ";
  cin >> age;
  if (age <= 0)
    cout << "Your age must be positive." << endl;
} while (age <= 0);
```

Notice that the Do-While solution does not require the prompt and input steps to appear twice—once before the loop and once within it—but it does test the input value twice.

We can also use the Do-While to implement a count-controlled loop if we know in advance that the loop body should always execute at least once. Following are two versions of a loop to sum the integers from 1 through **n**.

While Solution
```
sum = 0;
counter = 1;
while (counter <= n)
{
  sum = sum + counter;
  counter++;
}
```

Do-While Solution
```
sum = 0;
counter = 1;
do
{
  sum = sum + counter;
  counter++;
} while (counter <= n);
```

If **n** is a positive number, both of these versions are equivalent. But if **n** is **0** or negative, the two loops give different results. In the While version, the final value of **sum** is **0** because the loop body is never entered. In the Do-While version, the final value of **sum** is **1** because the body executes once, after which the loop test is made.

Because the While statement tests the condition before executing the body of the loop, it is called a pretest loop. The Do-While statement does the opposite and thus is known as a posttest loop. **FIGURE 7.1** compares the flow of control in the While and Do-While loops.

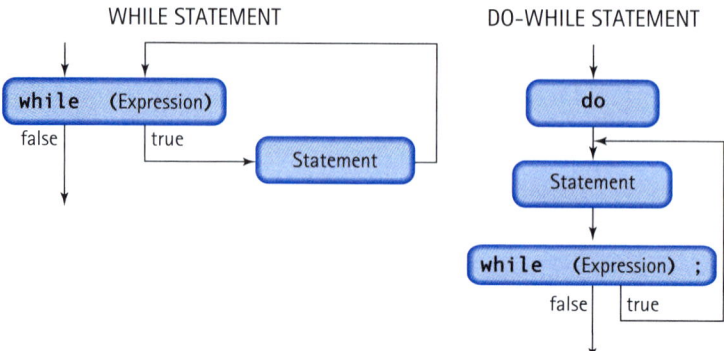

FIGURE 7.1 While and Do-While Loops

After we look at some additional looping constructs, we offer some guidelines for determining when to use each type of loop.

Here is a program that encloses the activity message code in a Do-While statement:

```cpp
//*****************************************************************
// Activity program
// This program outputs an appropriate activity
// for a given temperature
//*****************************************************************
#include <iostream>
#include <string>
using namespace std;

int main()
{
  int temperature;     // The outside temperature
  int raining;
  char signal;
  do                   // Repeat while signal is 'c'
  {
    // Read and echo temperature
    cout << "Enter the outside temperature:" << endl;
    cin >> temperature;
    cout << "Enter 1 if it is raining and 0 if it is not." << endl;
    cin >> raining;
    cout << "The current temperature is " << temperature;

    switch (raining)
    {
      case 0 : cout << " and it is not raining." << endl;
               if (temperature > 60)
                 cout << "Go for a walk." << endl;
               else
                 cout << "Read a good book." << endl;
               break;
```

```
            case 1 : cout << " and it is raining." << endl;
                     if (temperature > 60)
                        cout << "Go to a movie." << endl;
                     else
                        cout << "Read a good book." << endl;
                     break;
         }
         cout << "Enter a 'c' to continue or a 'q' to quit." << endl;
         cin >> signal;
    } while (signal == 'c');
    return 0;
}
```

Here is a sample run of this program:

```
Enter the outside temperature:
65
Enter 1 if it is raining and 0 if it is not.
1
The current temperature is 65 and it is raining.
Go to a movie.
Enter a 'c' to continue or a 'q' to quit.
c
Enter the outside temperature:
65
Enter 1 if it is raining and 0 if it is not.
0
The current temperature is 65 and it is not raining.
Go for a walk.
Enter a 'c' to continue or a 'q' to quit.
c
Enter the outside temperature:
55
Enter 1 if it is raining and 0 if it is not.
1
The current temperature is 55 and it is raining.
Read a good book.
Enter a 'c' to continue or a 'q' to quit.
c
Enter the outside temperature:
55
Enter 1 if it is raining and 0 if it is not.
0
The current temperature is 55 and it is not raining.
Read a good book.
Enter a 'c' to continue or a 'q' to quit.
q
```

You might wonder why we would want to repeat this particular process. After all, the weather doesn't change that often, in spite of how it may seem on some days! The preceding loop is an example of what is called a test harness (or driver)—a very simple program that surrounds a module so that we can directly enter a series of test data values. In many situations, a module's implementation can be destined for placement deep inside a complex program, where it would be difficult to thoroughly test. By separately enclosing it in a test driver, we gain complete control of its environment and can directly supply the module's inputs and check its outputs to ensure that it is correct. Once it has been tested, the code can be transplanted to its final place in the real program, where we can have confidence that it will work correctly.

> **QUICK CHECK**
>
> **7.2.1** Which looping statement always executes its body at least once? (pp. 310–312)
>
> **7.2.2** Translate the following While loop into a Do-While loop: (p. 311)
>
> ```
> int x = 1;
> int y = 0;
> while (x <= 10)
> {
>     y = x + y;
> }
> ```
>
> **7.2.3** What is another name for a Do-While loop? (p. 311)

7.3 The For Statement

The For statement is designed to simplify the writing of count-controlled loops. The following statement prints out the integers from 1 through n:

```
for (count = 1; count <= n; count++)
  cout << count << endl;
```

This For statement means "Initialize the loop control variable **count** to 1. While **count** is less than or equal to **n**, execute the output statement and increment **count** by 1. Stop the loop after **count** has been incremented to n + 1."

In C++, a For statement is merely a compact notation for a While loop. In fact, the compiler essentially translates a For statement into an equivalent While loop as follows:

```
for ( count = 1 ; count <= n ; count++ )
  cout << count << endl;

count = 1;
while (count <= n)
{
    cout << count << endl;
    count++;
}
```

The syntax template for a For statement is shown here:

ForStatement

```
for (InitStatement Expression1 ; Expression2 )
    Statement
```

Expression1 is the While condition. InitStatement can be one of the following: the null statement (just a semicolon), a declaration statement (which always ends in a semicolon), or an expression statement (an expression ending in a semicolon). Therefore, a semicolon always appears before Expression1. (This semicolon isn't shown in the syntax template because InitStatement always ends with its own semicolon.)

Most often, a For statement is written such that InitStatement initializes a loop control variable and Expression2 increments or decrements the loop control variable. Here are two loops that execute the same number of times (50):

```
for (loopCount = 1; loopCount <= 50; loopCount++)
    ⋮

for (loopCount = 50; loopCount >= 1; loopCount--)
    ⋮
```

Just like While loops, Do-While and For loops may be nested. For example, this nested For structure

```
for (lastNum = 1; lastNum <= 7; lastNum++)
{
    for (numToPrint = 1; numToPrint <= lastNum; numToPrint++)
        cout << numToPrint;
    cout << endl;
}
```

prints the following triangle of numbers:

```
1
12
123
1234
12345
123456
1234567
```

Although For statements are used primarily to implement count-controlled loops, C++ allows you to write any While loop by using a For statement. To use For loops intelligently, you should know the following facts.

1. In the syntax template, InitStatement can be the null statement, and Expression2 is optional. If Expression2 is omitted, there is no statement for the compiler to insert at the bottom of the loop. As a result, you could write the While loop

    ```
    while (inputVal != 999)
        cin >> inputVal;
    ```

    as the equivalent For loop

    ```
    for ( ; inputVal != 999; )
        cin >> inputVal;
    ```

2. According to the syntax template, Expression1—the While condition—is optional. If you omit it, the expression is assumed to be true. The loop

    ```
    for ( ; ; )
        cout "Hi" << endl;
    ```

is equivalent to the While loop

```
while (true)
   cout << "Hi" << endl;
```

Both of these structures are infinite loops that print "Hi" endlessly.

3. As highlighted here, the initializing statement, InitStatement, can be a declaration with initialization:

```
for (int i = 1; i <= 20; i++)
   cout << "Hi" << endl;
```

Here, the variable i has local scope, even though the statement does not have any braces that explicitly create a block. The scope of i extends only to the end of the For statement. Like any local variable, i is inaccessible outside its scope (that is, outside the For statement). Because i is local to the For statement, it's possible to write code like this:

```
for (int i = 1; i <= 20; i++)
   cout << "Hi" << endl;
for (int i = 1; i <= 100; i++)
   cout << "Ed" << endl;
```

This code does not generate a compile-time error (such as **MULTIPLY DEFINED IDENTIFIER**). We have declared two distinct variables named i, each of which is local to its own For statement.

As you have seen by now, the For statement in C++ is a very flexible structure. Its use can range from a simple count-controlled loop to a general-purpose, "anything goes" While loop. Some programmers squeeze a lot of work into the heading (the first line) of a For statement. For example, the program fragment

```
cin >> ch;
while (ch != '.')
   cin >> ch;
```

can be compressed into the following For loop (the density of the highlighting shows the corresponding parts of the two loops):

```
for (cin >> ch; ch != '.'; cin >> ch)
   ;
```

Because all the work is done in the For heading, there is nothing for the loop body to do. The body is simply the null statement.

With For statements, our advice is to keep things simple. The trickier the code is, the harder it will be for another person (or you!) to understand your code and track down errors. In this book, we use For loops for count-controlled loops only.

The following program contains both a For statement and a Switch statement. It analyzes the first 100 characters read from the standard input device and reports how many of the characters were letters, periods, question marks, and exclamation marks. For the first category (letters), we use the library function `isalpha`, which returns **true** if its argument is a letter and **false** otherwise.

```cpp
//****************************************************************
// CharCounts program
// This program counts the number of letters, periods, question
// marks, and exclamation marks found in the first 100 input
// characters
// Assumption: Input consists of at least 100 characters
//****************************************************************
#include <iostream>
#include <cctype>            // For isalpha()

using namespace std;

int main()
{
  char inChar;             // Current input character
  int  loopCount;          // Loop control variable
  int  letterCount = 0;    // Number of letters
  int  periodCount = 0;    // Number of periods
  int  questCount = 0;     // Number of question marks
  int  exclamCount = 0;    // Number of exclamation marks

  cout << "Enter your text:" << endl;
  for (loopCount = 1; loopCount <= 100; loopCount++)
  {
    cin.get(inChar);
    if (isalpha(inChar))
      letterCount++;
    else
      switch (inChar)
      {
        case '.' : periodCount++;
                   break;
        case '?' : questCount++;
                   break;
        case '!' : exclamCount++;
                   break;
        default  : ;                            // Unnecessary, but OK
      }
  }
  cout << endl;
  cout << "Input contained" << endl
       << letterCount << " letters" << endl
       << periodCount << " periods" << endl
       << questCount << " question marks" << endl
       << exclamCount << " exclamation marks" << endl;
  return 0;
}
```

Here is the output of a sample run:

The totals here look strange: They add up to only 85 characters. Where are the other 15? Well, the numbers are not counted in the totals, so that gives 94. But that still leaves 6 unaccounted for. Careful examination of the data shows that reading must end partway through the seventh line. Aha! The end-of-line characters on the first 6 lines of input account for the other missing characters!

Now we see that the code is actually correct—it was just our expectation of the results that was off. As you can see, sometimes the expected output in a test plan fails to take everything into consideration. Testing isn't always a one-way street where we have all the answers ahead of time and simply verify the code. In some cases, we find errors in the test plan, and need to fix it instead.

SOFTWARE MAINTENANCE CASE STUDY: Changing a Loop Implementation

MAINTENANCE TASK: You are given a program you have never seen before and asked to change the loop from a While loop to a For loop. The first step in converting one loop to another is to identify the parts of the loop that relate to its control.

1. Identify the loop control variable (LCV).
2. Determine where the LCV is declared.
3. Determine where the LCV is initialized.
4. Determine where and how the LCV is updated.
5. Identify the loop termination condition.

How can we do this in an unfamiliar program? We begin by reading the documentation to see what the program is supposed to accomplish.

SOFTWARE MAINTENANCE CASE STUDY: Changing a Loop Implementation

```
//****************************************************************
// BMI Program
// This program calculates the body mass index (BMI) given a weight
// in pounds and a height in inches and prints a health message
// based on the BMI. Input in English measures.
// The user is prompted to enter the number of cases to be read.
//****************************************************************
```

This calculation sounds vaguely familiar, but the key is the last statement—the program prompts the user to input the number of data cases to be input. The next step is to examine the declarations.

```
const int BMI_CONSTANT = 703;   // Constant in non-metric formula
float weight;                   // Weight in pounds
float height;                   // Height in inches
float bodyMassIndex;            // Appropriate BMI
int count;                      // Number of data sets
```

The first four lines are not of interest, but the fifth is. The variable **count** will be used in the loop. Next we examine the parts of the code that use **count**:

```
cout << "Enter the number of cases to run." << endl;
cin >> count;
while (count != 0)
{
  ...
  count--;
}
```

Now we have all the information we need:

- **count** is the LCV.
- **count** is initialized by prompting for and reading its value.
- **count** is updated by decrementing its value by 1.
- The loop termination condition is when **count** is equal to 0.

Here is the complete code, with the For statement highlighted:

```
//****************************************************************
// BMI Program
// This program calculates the body mass index (BMI) given a weight
// in pounds and a height in inches and prints a health message
// based on the BMI. Input in English measures.
// The user is prompted to enter the number of cases to be read.
//****************************************************************
#include <iostream>
using namespace std;

int main()
{
  const int BMI_CONSTANT = 703;    // Constant in non-metric formula
```

SOFTWARE MAINTENANCE CASE STUDY: Changing a Loop Implementation

```cpp
  float weight;                  // Weight in pounds
  float height;                  // Height in inches
  float bodyMassIndex;           // Appropriate BMI
  int count;                     // Number of data sets

  cout << "Enter the number of cases to run." << endl;
  cin >> count;
  for (; count != 0; count--)
  {
    // Prompt for and input weight and height
    cout << "Enter your weight in pounds. " << endl;
    cin >> weight;
    cout << "Enter your height in inches. " << endl;
    cin >> height;
    // Calculate body mass index
    bodyMassIndex = weight * BMI_CONSTANT / (height * height);
    // Print message indicating status
    cout << "Your body mass index is " << bodyMassIndex
         << ". " << endl;
    cout << "Interpretation and instructions. " << endl;
    if (bodyMassIndex < 20)
      cout << "Underweight: Have a milk shake." << endl;
    else if (bodyMassIndex <= 25)
      cout << "Normal: Have a glass of milk."  << endl;
    else if (bodyMassIndex <=  30)
      cout << "Overweight: Have a glass of iced tea."  << endl;
    else
      cout << "Obese: See your doctor." << endl;
  }
  return 0;
}
```

QUICK CHECK

7.3.1 Write a For statement that counts from −10 to 10. (pp. 314–316)

7.3.2 What does a For loop try to simplify? (p. 314)

7.3.3 Translate the following While loop into a For loop: (p. 315)

```
int x = 1;
int y = 0;
while (x <= 10)
{
    y = x + y;
}
```

7.3.4 Write a For loop that reads characters from `cin` until a `'\n'` character is encountered. (p. 316)

7.4 The Break and Continue Statements

The Break statement, which we introduced with the Switch statement, is also used with loops. A Break statement causes an immediate exit from the innermost Switch, While, Do-While, or For statement in which it appears. Notice the word *innermost*. If **break** is found in a loop that is nested inside another loop, control exits the inner loop but not the outer loop.

One of the more common ways of using **break** with loops is to set up an infinite loop and use If tests to exit the loop. Suppose we want to input ten pairs of integers, performing data validation and computing the square root of the sum of each pair. For data validation, assume that the first number of each pair must be less than 100 and the second must be greater than 50. Also, after each input, we want to test the state of the stream for EOF. Here's a loop using Break statements to accomplish the task:

```
loopCount = 1;
while (true)
{
  cin >> num1;
  if ( !cin || num1 >= 100)
    break;
  cin >> num2;
  if (!cin || num2 <= 50)
    break;
  cout << sqrt(float(num1 + num2)) << endl;
  loopCount++;
  if (loopCount > 10)
    break;
}
```

Note that we could have used a For loop to count from 1 to 10, breaking out of it as necessary. However, this loop is both count controlled and event controlled, so we prefer to use a While loop. When someone is reading code and sees a For loop, that person expects it to be purely count controlled.

The preceding loop contains three distinct exit points. Many programmers adhere to the *single-entry, single-exit* approach to writing a loop. With this philosophy, control enters a loop at one point only (the first executable statement) and exits at one point only (the end of the body). These programmers argue that multiple exits from a loop make the program logic hard to follow and difficult to debug. Other programmers take the position that it is acceptable to use **break** within a loop when the logic is clear. If we did not use **break** in this loop, it would contain multiple nested If statements with compound Boolean expressions that would obscure the actual computation.

Our advice is to use **break** sparingly; overuse can lead to confusing code. A good rule of thumb is this: Use **break** within loops only as a last resort. Specifically, use it only to avoid baffling combinations of compound Boolean expressions and nested Ifs.

Another statement that alters the flow of control in a C++ program is the Continue statement. This statement, which is valid only in loops, terminates the current loop iteration (but not the entire loop). It causes an immediate branch to the bottom of the loop—skipping the rest of the statements in the loop body—in preparation for the next iteration. Here is an example of a reading loop in which we want to process only the positive numbers in an input file:

```
for (dataCount = 1; dataCount <= 500; dataCount++)
{
  dataFile >> inputVal;
  if (inputVal <= 0)
    continue;
  cout << inputVal;
  .
  .
  .
}
```

If `inputVal` is less than or equal to `0`, control branches to the bottom of the loop. Then, as with any For loop, the computer increments `dataCount` and performs the loop test before going on to the next iteration.

The Continue statement is not used often, but we present it for completeness (and because you may run across it in other people's programs). Its primary purpose is to avoid obscuring the main process of the loop that would result from indenting the process within an If statement. For example, the previously given code would be written without a Continue statement as follows:

```
for (dataCount = 1; dataCount <= 500; dataCount++)
{
  dataFile >> inputVal;
  if (inputVal > 0)
  {
    cout << inputVal;
    .
    .
    .
  }
}
```

Be sure to note the difference between `continue` and `break`. The Continue statement means "Abandon the current iteration of the loop, and go on to the next iteration." The Break statement means "Exit the entire loop immediately."

QUICK CHECK

7.4.1 Write a For loop that reads numbers from `cin` until a `'\n'` character is encountered, *continues* if it encounters a number less than 10, *breaks* if it encounters a number greater than 20, and outputs the number otherwise. (p. 321)

7.4.2 When it is executed within a loop, to where does a Break statement transfer control? Where does control proceed from a Continue statement? (pp. 321–322)

7.5 Guidelines for Choosing a Looping Statement

Here are some guidelines to help you decide when to use each of the three looping statements (While, Do-While, and For):

1. If the loop is a simple count-controlled loop, the For statement is a natural. Collecting the three loop control actions—initialize, test, and increment/decrement—into one location (the heading of the For statement) reduces the chances of forgetting to include one of them.

2. If the loop is an event-controlled loop whose body should execute at least once, a Do-While statement is appropriate.
3. If the loop is an event-controlled loop and nothing is known about the first execution, use a While statement.
4. When in doubt, use a While statement.
5. An infinite loop with Break statements sometimes clarifies the code but more often reflects an undisciplined loop design. Use it only after careful consideration of While, Do-While, and For.

Bear in mind that most programmers, when encountering a For statement in the code, expect the loop to be purely count controlled. Using a For statement to implement an event-controlled loop leads to tricky code and is to be avoided.

QUICK CHECK

7.5.1 If a problem calls for a pure count-controlled loop, would you use a While, a Do-While, or a For statement to implement the loop? (pp. 322–323)

7.6 Additional C++ Operators

C++ has a rich, sometimes bewildering, variety of operators that allow you to manipulate values of the simple data types. Operators you have learned about so far include the assignment operator (=), the arithmetic operators (+, -, *, /, %), the increment and decrement operators (++, --), the relational operators (==, !=, <, <=, >, >=), and the logical operators (!, &&, ||). In certain cases, a pair of parentheses is also considered to be an operator—namely, the function call operator,

```
ComputeSum(x, y);
```

and the type cast operator,

```
y = float(someInt);
```

C++ also has many specialized operators that are seldom found in other programming languages. Here is a table of these additional operators. As you inspect the table, don't panic—a quick scan will do.

Operator		Remarks
Combined Assignment Operators		
+=	Add and assign	
-=	Subtract and assign	
*=	Multiply and assign	
/=	Divide and assign	

Operator		Remarks
Increment and Decrement Operators		
++	Pre-increment	Example: `++someVar`
++	Post-increment	Example: `someVar++`
--	Pre-decrement	Example: `--someVar`
--	Post-decrement	Example: `someVar--`
Bitwise Operators		Integer operands only
<<	Left shift	
>>	Right shift	
&	Bitwise AND	Logical AND of the bits in its operands
|	Bitwise OR	Logical OR of the bits in its operands
^	Bitwise exclusive OR	Logical XOR of the bits in its operands
~	Complement (invert all bits)	Single operand
More Combined Assignment Operators		*Integer operands only*
%=	Modulus and assign	
<<=	Shift left and assign	
>>=	Shift right and assign	
&=	Bitwise AND and assign	
|=	Bitwise OR and assign	
^=	Bitwise exclusive OR and assign	
Other Operators		
()	Cast	
`sizeof`	Size of operand in bytes	Form: `sizeof` Expr or `sizeof`(Type)
?:	Conditional operator	Form: Expr1 **?** Expr2 **:** Expr3

The operators in this table, along with those you already know, account for most—but not all—of the C++ operators. We introduce a few more operators in later chapters as the need arises.

Assignment Operators and Assignment Expressions

Assignment expression A C++ expression with (1) a value and (2) the side effect of storing the expression value into a memory location.

Expression statement A statement formed by appending a semicolon to an expression.

C++ has several assignment operators. The equal sign (=) is the basic assignment operator. When combined with its two operands, it forms an assignment expression (not an assignment statement). Every assignment expression has a value and a side effect—namely, that the value is stored into the object denoted by the left-hand side. For example, the expression

```
delta = 2 * 12
```

has the value 24 and the side effect of storing this value into `delta`.

In C++, any expression becomes an expression statement when it is terminated by a semicolon. All three of the following are valid C++ statements, although the first two have no effect at run time:

```
23;
2 * (alpha + beta);
delta = 2 * 12;
```

The third expression statement is useful because of its side effect of storing 24 into `delta`.

Because an assignment is an expression, not a statement, you can use it anywhere an expression is allowed. Here is a statement that stores the value 20 into `firstInt`, the value 30 into `secondInt`, and the value 35 into `thirdInt`:

```
thirdInt = (secondInt = (firstInt = 20) + 10) + 5;
```

Some C++ programmers use this style of coding because they think it is clever, but most find it hard to read and error prone.

In Chapter 5, we cautioned against the mistake of using the = operator in place of the == operator:

```
if (alpha = 12)     // Wrong
  ⋮
else
  ⋮
```

The condition in the If statement is an assignment expression, not a relational expression. The value of the expression is 12 (interpreted in the If condition as `true`), so the else-clause is never executed. Worse yet, the side effect of the assignment expression is to store 12 into `alpha`, destroying its previous contents.

In addition to the = operator, C++ has several combined assignment operators (+=, *=, and the others listed in our table of operators). The combined assignment operators are another example of "ice cream and cake." They are sometimes convenient for writing a line of code more compactly, but you can do just fine without them.

Increment and Decrement Operators

The increment and decrement operators (++ and --) operate only on variables, not on constants or arbitrary expressions. Suppose a variable `someInt` contains the value 3. The expression ++`someInt` denotes pre-incrementation. The side effect of incrementing `someInt` occurs first, so the resulting value of the expression is 4. In contrast, the expression `someInt`++ denotes post-incrementation. The value of the expression is 3, and then the side effect of incrementing `someInt` takes place. The following code illustrates the difference between pre- and post-incrementation:

```
int1 = 14;
int2 = ++int1;    // int1 == 15  &&  int2 == 15

int1 = 14;
int2 = int1++;    // int1 == 15  &&  int2 == 14
```

Using side effects in the middle of larger expressions is always a bit dangerous. It's easy to make semantic errors, and the code may be confusing to read. Look at this example:

```
a = (b = c++) * --d / (e += f++);
```

Some people make a game of seeing how much they can do in the fewest keystrokes possible. But they should remember that serious software development requires writing code that other programmers can read and understand. Overuse of side effects hinders this goal. By far the most common use of ++ and -- is to do the incrementation or decrementation as a separate expression statement:

```
count++;
```

Here, the value of the expression is unused, but we get the desired side effect of incrementing `count`. In this example, it doesn't matter whether you use pre-incrementation or post-incrementation. The choice is up to you.

Bitwise Operators

The bitwise operators listed in the operator table (`<<`, `>>`, `&`, `|`, and so forth) are used for manipulating individual bits within a memory cell. This book does not explore the use of these operators; the topic of bit-level operations is most often covered in a course on computer organization and assembly language programming. However, we point out two things about the bitwise operators.

First, the built-in operators `<<` and `>>` are the left shift and right shift operators, respectively. Their purpose is to take the bits within a memory cell and shift them to the left or right. Of course, we have been using these operators all along, but in an entirely different context—stream input and output. The header file `iostream` uses an advanced C++ technique called operator overloading to give additional meanings to these two operators. An overloaded operator is one that has multiple meanings, depending on the data types of its operands. When looking at the `<<` operator, the compiler determines by context whether a left shift operation or an output operation is desired. Specifically, if the first (left-hand) operand denotes an output stream, then it is an output operation. If the first operand is an integer variable, it is a left shift operation.

Second, we repeat our caution from Chapter 5: Do not confuse the `&&` and `||` operators with the `&` and `|` operators. The statement

```
if (i == 3 & j == 4)     // Wrong
    k = 20;
```

is syntactically correct because `&` is a valid operator (the bitwise AND operator). The program containing this statement compiles correctly but executes incorrectly. Although we do not examine what the bitwise AND and OR operators do, just be careful to use the relational operators `&&` and `||` in your logical expressions.

The Cast Operation

You have seen that C++ is very liberal about letting the programmer mix data types in expressions, assignment operations, argument passing, and returning a function value. However, implicit type coercion takes place when values of different data types are mixed together. Instead of relying on implicit type coercion in a statement such as

```
intVar = floatVar;
```

we have recommended using an explicit type cast to show that the type conversion is intentional:

```
intVar = int(floatVar);
```

In C++, the cast operation comes in three forms:

```
intVar = int(floatVar);                  // Functional notation
intVar = (int)floatVar;                  // Prefix notation
intVar = static_cast<int>(floatVar);     // Keyword notation
```

The first form is called functional notation because it looks like a function call. It isn't really a function call (there is no user-defined or predefined subprogram named `int`), but it has the syntax and visual appearance of a function call. The second form, prefix notation, doesn't look like any familiar language feature in C++. In this notation, the parentheses surround the name of the data type, not the expression being converted. The third form uses a keyword and angle brackets to explicitly document that a cast operation is to be performed. Prefix notation is the only form available in the C language; the original version of C++ added functional notation and, with the definition of the C++ standard, keyword notation was included.

Functional notation has one restriction on its use: The data type name must be a single identifier. If the type name consists of more than one identifier, you must use prefix notation or keyword notation. For example,

```
myVar = unsigned int(someFloat);            // Not allowed
myVar = (unsigned int) someFloat;           // Yes
myVar = static_cast<unsigned int> someFloat;  // Yes
```

Most software engineers now recommend the use of the keyword cast. From the viewpoint of documentation, it is much easier to find these keywords within a large program. And although `static_cast` is very similar to the other two casts for values of the simple data types, there are more advanced aspects of C++, involving object-oriented programming, where it causes the compiler to perform additional checks that help to spot errors.

C++ defines three additional forms of the keyword cast that have special purposes. We do not explain them further in this book, but we list them here so that you will be aware of their existence: `const_cast`, `dynamic_cast`, and `reinterpret_cast`.

The `sizeof` Operator

The `sizeof` operator is a unary operator that yields the size, in bytes, of its operand. The operand can be a variable name, as in

```
sizeof someInt
```

Alternatively, the operand can be the name of a data type, enclosed in parentheses:

```
sizeof(float)
```

You could find out the sizes of various data types on your machine by using code like this:

```
cout << "Size of a short is " << sizeof(short) << endl;
cout << "Size of an int is " << sizeof(int) << endl;
cout << "Size of a long is " << sizeof(long) << endl;
```

The ?: Operator

The last operator in our operator table is the ?: operator, sometimes called the conditional operator. It is a ternary (three-operand) operator with the following syntax:

ConditionalExpression

> Expression1 ? Expression2 : Expression3

Here's how it works. First, the computer evaluates Expression1. If the value is **true**, then the value of the entire expression is Expression2; otherwise, the value of the entire expression is Expression3. (Only one of Expression2 and Expression3 is evaluated, but both of them must evaluate to the same data type.) A classic example of the ?: operator's use is to set a variable **max** equal to the larger of two variables **a** and **b**. Using an If statement, we would do it this way:

```
if (a > b)
    max = a;
else
    max = b;
```

With the ?: operator, we can use the following assignment statement:

```
max = (a > b) ? a : b;
```

Here is another example. The absolute value of a number x is defined as

$$|x| = \begin{cases} x, & \text{if } x \geq 0 \\ -x, & \text{if } x < 0 \end{cases}$$

To compute the absolute value of a variable **x** and store it into **y**, you could use the ?: operator as follows:

```
y = (x >= 0) ? x : -x;
```

In both the **max** and the absolute value examples, we placed parentheses around the expression being tested. These parentheses are unnecessary because, as we'll see shortly, the conditional operator has very low precedence. Even so, it is customary to include the parentheses for clarity.

Operator Precedence

The following table summarizes operator precedence for the C++ operators we have encountered so far, excluding the bitwise operators. (Appendix B contains the complete list.) In the table, the operators are grouped by precedence level, and a horizontal line separates each precedence level from the next-lower level.

Operator	Associativity	Remarks
()	Left to right	Function call and function-style cast
++ --	Right to left	++ and -- as postfix operators
++ -- ! Unary + Unary -	Right to left	++ and -- as prefix operators
(cast) sizeof	Right to left	
* / %	Left to right	
+ -	Left to right	
< <= > >=	Left to right	
== !=	Left to right	
&&	Left to right	
||	Left to right	
?:	Right to left	
= += -= *= /=	Right to left	

The column labeled *Associativity* describes grouping order. Within a precedence level, most operators group from left to right. For example,

```
a - b + c
```

means

```
(a - b) + c
```

and not

```
a - (b + c)
```

Certain operators, though, group from right to left—specifically, the unary operators, the assignment operators, and the ?: operator. Look at the assignment operators, for example. The expression

```
sum = count = 0
```

means

```
sum = (count = 0)
```

This associativity makes sense because the assignment operation is naturally a right-to-left operation.

A word of caution: Although operator precedence and associativity dictate the grouping of operators with their operands, C++ does not define the order in which subexpressions are evaluated. Therefore, using side effects in expressions requires extra care. For example, if i currently contains 5, the statement

```
j = ++i + i;
```

stores either 11 or 12 into j, depending on the particular compiler being used. Let's see why. There are three operators in this expression statement: =, ++, and +. The ++ operator has the highest precedence, so it operates just on i, not the expression i + i. The addition operator has higher precedence than the assignment operator, giving implicit parentheses as follows:

```
j = (++i + i);
```

So far, so good. But now we ask this question: In the addition operation, is the left operand or the right operand evaluated first? The C++ language doesn't dictate the order. If a compiler generates code to evaluate the left operand first, the result is 6 + 6, or 12. Another compiler might generate code to evaluate the right operand first, yielding 6 + 5, or 11. To be assured of left-to-right evaluation in this example, you should force the ordering with two separate statements:

```
++i;
j = i + i;
```

The moral here is that if you use multiple side effects in expressions, you increase the risk of unexpected or inconsistent results. For the newcomer to C++, it's better to avoid unnecessary side effects altogether.

Type Coercion in Arithmetic and Relational Expressions

Promotion (widening) The conversion of a value from a "lower" type to a "higher" type according to a programming language's precedence of data types.

Suppose that an arithmetic expression consists of one operator and two operands—for example, 3.4*sum or var1/var2. If the two operands are of different data types, then one of them is temporarily promoted (or widened) to match the data type of the other. To understand exactly what promotion means, let's look at the rule for type coercion in an arithmetic expression.[1]

Step 1: Each char, short, bool, or enumeration value is promoted (widened) to int. If both operands are now int, the result is an int expression.

Step 2: If Step 1 still leaves a mixed type expression, the following precedence of types is used:

```
Lowest ─────────────────────────────────────────► Highest
int, unsigned int, long, unsigned long, float, double, long double
```

The value of the operand of the "lower" type is promoted to that of the "higher" type, and the result is an expression of that type.

A simple example is the expression someFloat+2. This expression has no char, short, bool, or enumeration values in it, so Step 1 leaves a mixed type expression. In Step 2, int is a "lower" type than float, so the value 2 is coerced temporarily to the float value—say, 2.0. Then the addition takes place, and the type of the entire expression is float.

This description of type coercion also holds for relational expressions such as

```
someInt <= someFloat
```

The value of someInt is temporarily coerced to floating-point representation before the comparison takes place. The only difference between arithmetic expressions and relational

---

[1]. The rule we give for type coercion is a simplified version of the rule found in the C++ language definition. The complete rule has more to say about unsigned types, which we rarely use in this book.

expressions is that the resulting type of a relational expression is always **bool**—the value **true** or **false**.

Here is a table that describes the result of promoting a value from one simple type to another in C++:

From	To	Result of Promotion
`double`	`long double`	Same value, occupying more memory space
`float`	`double`	Same value, occupying more memory space
Integral type	Floating-point type	Floating-point equivalent of the integer value; fractional part is zero
Integral type	Its **unsigned** counterpart	Same value, if original number is non-negative; a radically different positive number, if original number is negative
Signed integral type	Longer signed integral type	Same value, occupying more memory space
Unsigned integral type	Longer integral type (either signed or unsigned)	Same nonnegative value, occupying more memory space

Note: The result of promoting a `char` to an `int` is compiler dependent. Some compilers treat `char` as `unsigned char`, so promotion always yields a nonnegative integer. With other compilers, `char` means signed `char`, so promotion of a negative value yields a negative integer.

The note at the bottom of the table suggests a potential problem if you are trying to write a portable C++ program. If you use the `char` type only to store character data, there is no problem. C++ guarantees that each character in a machine's character set (such as ASCII) is represented as a nonnegative value. Using character data, promotion from `char` to `int` gives the same result on any machine with any compiler.

If you try to save memory by using the `char` type for manipulating small signed integers, however, then promotion of these values to the `int` type can produce different results on different machines! That is, one machine may promote negative `char` values to negative `int` values, whereas the same program on another machine might promote negative `char` values to positive `int` values. The moral is this: Unless you are squeezed to the limit for memory space, do not use `char` to manipulate small signed numbers; use `char` only to store character data.

QUICK CHECK

7.6.1 What is the value of **y** and **z** after executing the following statements? (p. 325)

```
int x = 5;
int y = ++x;
int z = x++;
```

7.6.2 Give an example of a common problem associated with assignment expressions. (p. 325)

7.6.4 What is the difference between the **&&** operator and the **&** operator? (pp. 325–326)

Problem-Solving Case Study

The Rich Uncle

PROBLEM: Your rich uncle has just died, and in his desk you find two wills. One of them, dated several months ago, leaves you and your relatives a substantial part of his fortune; the other, dated last week, gives everything to his next-door neighbor. Being suspicious that the second will is a forgery, you decide to write a program to analyze writing style and compare the wills. The program reads and categorizes each character. When the entire file has been read, it prints a summary table showing the percentage of uppercase letters, lowercase letters, decimal digits, blanks, and end-of-sentence punctuation marks in the data file. The names of the input and output files are read from the keyboard. The name of the input file should be printed on the output.

INPUT: Text on a file whose name is read from the keyboard.

OUTPUT: A table giving the name of each category and the percentage of the total that the category represents on the file whose name is read from the keyboard.

DISCUSSION: Doing this task by hand would be tedious but quite straightforward. You would set up five places to make hash marks, one for each of the categories of symbols to be counted. You would then read the text character by character, determine in which category to put each character, and make a hash mark in the appropriate place.

You can look at a character and tell immediately which category to mark. You can simulate "looking" with an If statement with branches for the uppercase letters, the lowercase letters, the digits, a blank, and end-of-sentence punctuation marks. An uppercase letter is defined as one between `'A'` and `'Z'` inclusive; a lowercase letter is defined as one between `'a'` and `'z'` inclusive. *But wait:* Before you start writing algorithms to recognize these categories, shouldn't you look in the library to see if they already exist? Sure enough, header file `<cctype>` contains functions to recognize uppercase letters, lowercase letters, and digits.

Another function recognizes whitespace. Will that do for counting blanks? Function `isspace` returns `true` if the character is a blank, newline, tab, carriage return, or form feed. The problem specifies a count of the number of blanks. A newline might function as the end of a word like a blank, but the problem doesn't ask for the number of words; it asks for the number of blanks.

There is a function to recognize punctuation, but not end-of-sentence punctuation. The problem doesn't state what end-of-sentence marks are. What kinds of sentences are there? Regular sentences, ending in a period; questions, ending in a question mark; and exclamations, ending in an exclamation mark.

Here is a summary of the function in `<cctype>` that we will use:

`isupper()`	Returns 1 if its argument is an uppercase letter
`islower()`	Returns 1 if its argument is a lowercase letter
`isdigit()`	Returns 1 if its argument is a numeric digit

These functions don't return Boolean values. How can they be used in a Boolean expression? They return an `int` value that is nonzero (coerced to `true` in an If or While condition) or 0 (coerced to `false` in an If or While condition). We have more to say about these functions in Chapter 9.

ASSUMPTIONS: File is not empty.

Main — Level 0

```
Open files for processing
IF files not opened okay
    Write error message
    return 1
Get a character
```

Problem-Solving Case Study

```
DO
    Increment appropriate character count
    Get a character
WHILE (more data)
Print table
```

Several of the counters are incremented based on the results of a function; others are based on the character itself. We must use If statements for the group characters, but we can use a Switch statement for the individual characters.

Increment Counters — Level 1

```
IF (isupper(character))
    Increment uppercaseCounter
ELSE IF (islower(character))
    Increment lowercaseCounter
ELSE IF (isdigit(character))
    Increment digitCounter
SWITCH (character)
    Case ' ' : Increment blankCounter
    Case '.' :
    Case '!' :
    Case '?' : Increment punctuationCounter
```

At this point you realize that the instructions do not indicate whether the percentages are to be taken of the total number of characters read, including those that do not fit any of the categories, or of the total number of characters that fall into the five categories. You decide to assume that all characters should be counted. Thus you add an Else branch to this module that increments a counter (called `allElseCounter`) for all characters that do not fall into one of the five categories. This assumption needs to be added to the program. This count can be placed in the default option of the Switch statement.

Calculate and Print Percentages

```
Set Total to sum of 6 counters
Print "Percentage of uppercase letters:", uppercaseCounter / Total * 100
Print "Percentage of lowercase letters:", lowercaseCounter / Total * 100
Print "Percentage of decimal digits:", digitCounter / Total * 100
Print "Percentage of blanks:", blankCounter / Total * 100
Print "Percentage of end-of-sentence punctuation:", punctuationCounter / Total * 100
```

Problem-Solving Case Study

MODULE STRUCTURE CHART

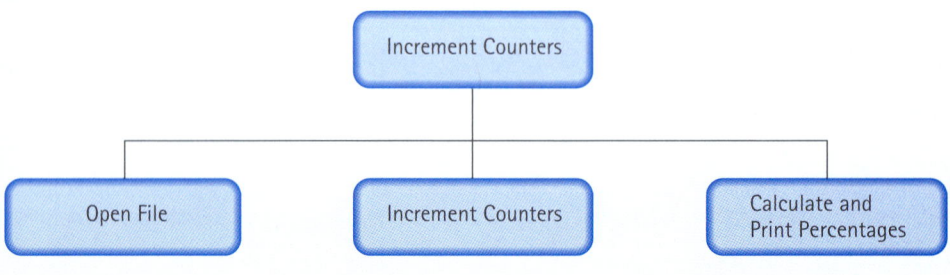

```
//*****************************************************************
// Rich Uncle Program
// Percentage of characters in the file that belong to five categories:
// uppercase characters, lowercase characters, decimal digits, blanks,
// and end-of-sentence punctuation marks
// Assumptions: Input file is not empty and percentages are based
// on total number of characters in the file
//*****************************************************************

#include <fstream>
#include <iostream>
#include <iomanip>
#include <cctype>

using namespace std;
int main()
{
  // Prepare files for reading and writing
  ifstream text;
  char character;

  // Declare and initialize counters
  int uppercaseCounter = 0;      // Number of uppercase letters
  int lowercaseCounter = 0;      // Number of lowercase letters
  int blankCounter = 0;          // Number of blanks
  int digitCounter = 0;          // Number of digits
  int punctuationCounter = 0;    // Number of end '.', '?', '!'
  int allElseCounter = 0;        // Remaining characters

  string inFileName;             // User-specified input file name
  cout << "Enter the name of the file to be processed" << endl;
  cin >> inFileName;
  text.open(inFileName.c_str());
  if (!text)
  {
    cout << "File did not open successfully." << endl;
    return 1;
  }
```

Problem-Solving Case Study

```
  text.get(character);              // Input one character
do
{
  // Process each character
  if (isupper(character))
    uppercaseCounter++;
  else if (islower(character))
    lowercaseCounter++;
  else if (isdigit(character))
    digitCounter++;
  else
    switch (character)
    {
      case ' ' : blankCounter++;
                 break;
      case '.' :
      case '?' :
      case '!' : punctuationCounter++;
                 break;
      defualt  : allElseCounter++;
                 break;

    }
  text.get(character);
} while (text);

// Calculate total number of characters
float total = uppercaseCounter + lowercaseCounter
    + blankCounter + digitCounter + punctuationCounter
    + allElseCounter;
cout << "Analysis of characters on input file " << inFileName << endl;

// Write output on standard output device
cout << fixed << setprecision(3)
     << "Percentage of uppercase characters: "
     << uppercaseCounter / total * 100 << endl;
cout << fixed << setprecision(3)
     << "Percentage of lowercase characters: "
     << lowercaseCounter / total * 100 << endl;
cout << fixed << setprecision(3) << "Percentage of blanks: "
     << blankCounter / total * 100 << endl;
cout << fixed << setprecision(3) << "Percentage of digits: "
     << digitCounter / total * 100 << endl;
cout << fixed << setprecision(3) << "Percentage of end-of-sentence "
     << "punctuation " << punctuationCounter / total * 100 << endl;
return 0;
}
```

Problem-Solving Case Study

TESTING: To be tested thoroughly, the `RichUncle` program must be run with all possible combinations of the categories of characters being counted. Following is the minimum set of cases that must be tested:

1. All the categories of characters are present.
2. Four of the categories are present; one is not. (This alone will require five test runs.)
3. Only characters that fall into one of the five categories are present.
4. Other characters are present.

The output listed below was run on a file containing more than 4000 characters. (It isn't a will, but it is sufficient for testing.)

```
Enter the name of the file to be processed
UncleData
Analysis of characters on input file UncleData
Percentage of uppercase characters: 2.978
Percentage of lowercase characters: 75.609
Percentage of blanks: 16.805
Percentage of digits: 0.331
Percentage of end-of-sentence punctuation 1.040
```

Testing and Debugging

The same testing techniques we used with While loops apply to Do-While and For loops. There are, however, a few additional considerations with these loops.

The body of a Do-While loop always executes at least once. Thus you should try data sets that show the result of executing a Do-While loop for the minimal number of times.

With a data-dependent For loop, it is important to test for proper results when the loop executes zero times. This occurs when the starting value is greater than the ending value (or less than the ending value if the loop control variable is being decremented).

When a program contains a Switch statement, you should test it with enough different data sets to ensure that each branch is selected and executed correctly. You should also test the program with a switch expression whose value is not found in any of the case labels.

Testing and Debugging Hints

1. In a Switch statement, make sure there is a Break statement at the end of each case alternative. Otherwise, control "falls through" to the code in the next case alternative.
2. Case labels in a Switch statement are made up of values, not variables. They may, however, include named constants and expressions involving only constants.

3. A switch expression cannot be a floating-point or string expression, and a case constant cannot be a floating-point or string constant.
4. If there is a possibility that the value of the switch expression might not match one of the case constants, you should provide a default alternative. In fact, it is a good practice to always include a default alternative.
5. Double-check long Switch statements to make sure that you haven't omitted any branches.
6. The Do-While loop is a posttest loop. If there is a possibility that the loop body should be skipped entirely, use a While statement or a For statement.
7. The For statement heading (the first line) always has three pieces within the parentheses. Most often, the first piece initializes a loop control variable, the second piece tests the variable, and the third piece increments or decrements the variable. The three pieces must be separated by semicolons. Any of these pieces can be omitted, but the semicolons must still be present.
8. With nested control structures, the Break statement can exit from only one level of nesting—the innermost Switch or loop in which the `break` keyword is located.

Summary

The Switch statement is a multiway selection statement. It allows the program to choose among a set of branches. A Switch containing Break statements can always be simulated by an If-Then-Else-If structure. If a Switch can be used, however, it often makes the code easier to read and understand. A Switch statement cannot be used with floating-point or string values in the case labels.

The Do-While is a general-purpose looping statement. It is like the While loop except that its test occurs at the end of the loop, guaranteeing at least one execution of the loop body. As with a While loop, a Do-While continues as long as the loop condition is true. A Do-While is convenient for loops that test input values and repeat if the input is not correct.

The For statement is also a general-purpose looping statement, but its most common use is to implement count-controlled loops. The initialization, testing, and incrementation (or decrementation) of the loop control variable are centralized in one location, the first line of the For statement.

C++ provides a wealth of additional operators. Many of these—such as the extra assignment operations, increment and decrement—involve a combination of a side effect the return of a value. Although use of side effects can save a few keystrokes, it usually results in code that is harder to understand.

The For, Do-While, and Switch statements are the "ice cream and cake" of C++. We can live without them if we absolutely must, but they are very nice to have.

Quick Check Answers

7.1.1 multiway branches **7.1.2** It causes an immediate exit from the Switch statement. **7.1.3** An integral type **7.1.4** First, the Switch expression is evaluated. If this value matches one of the values in the case labels, control branches to the statement following the case label. From there, control proceeds sequentially until a Break statement is encountered or the end of the Switch statement. **7.1.5** The default branch. **7.2.1** Do-While.
7.2.2
```
int x = 1;
int y = 0;
do
{
  y = x + y;
} while (x <= 10);
```

7.2.3 A posttest loop. 7.3.1 `for (int count = -10; count <= 10; count++)` 7.3.2 The writing of count-controlled loops.

7.3.3
```
int  x;
    int y = 0;
    for (x = 1; x <= 10; x++)
        y = x + y;
```
7.3.4 `for (cin >> ch; ch != '\n'; cin >> ch);`
7.4.1
```
for (cin >> ch; ch != '\n'; cin >> ch) {
    if (ch < 10)
       continue;
    if (ch > 20)
       break;
    cout << ch;
}
```
7.4.2 The Break statement immediately exits the loop; the Continue statement sends control to the end of the loop. 7.5.1 A For statement. 7.6.1 `y = 6, z = 5;` 7.6.2 `if (x == 10)` ... 7.6.3 `&&` is a logical AND of a pair of `bool` values; `&` is a bitwise AND of a pair of integral values.

Exam Preparation Exercises

1. A switch expression may be of type `bool`, `char`, `int`, or `long`, but not of type `float`. True or false?
2. A variable declared in the initialization statement of a For loop has global scope. True of false?
3. Any While loop can be directly rewritten as a Do-While merely by changing the statement syntax and moving the exit condition to the end of the loop. True or false?
4. A Break statement is not allowed in a For loop, but a Continue statement is. True or false?
5. Which of the looping statements in C++ are pretest loops and which are posttest loops?
6. What happens when you forget to include the Break statements in a Switch statement?
7. If you omit all of the clauses within a For loop (`for ( ; ; )`), what would be the condition in an equivalent While loop?
8. How many times is the inner loop body executed in the following nested loop?

    ```
    for (int x = 1; x <= 10; x++)
       for (int y = 1; y <= 10; y++)
          for (int z = 1; z <= 10; z++)
             cout << x + y + z;
    ```

9. Which looping statement would you choose for a problem in which the decision to repeat a process depends on an event, and the event cannot occur until the process is executed at least once?
10. Which looping statement would you choose for a problem in which the decision to repeat the process depends on an iteration counter and on the state of an input file, and the process may be skipped if the file is empty?
11. What is output by the following code segment if `wood` contains `'O'`?

    ```
    switch (wood)
    {
      case 'P' : cout << "Pine";
      case 'F' : cout << "Fir";
      case 'C' : cout << "Cedar";
    ```

```
      case 'O' : cout << "Oak";
      case 'M' : cout << "Maple";
      default  : cout << "Error";
   }
```

12. What is output by the following code segment if `month` contains 8?

    ```
    switch (month)
    {
      case 1  : cout << "January"; break;
      case 2  : cout << "February"; break;
      case 3  : cout << "March"; break;
      case 4  : cout << "April"; break;
      case 5  : cout << "May"; break;
      case 6  : cout << "June"; break;
      case 7  : cout << "July"; break;
      case 8  : cout << "August"; break;
      case 9  : cout << "September"; break;
      case 10 : cout << "October"; break;
      case 11 : cout << "November"; break;
      case 12 : cout << "December"; break;
      default : cout << "Error";
    }
    ```

13. What is output by the following code segment?

    ```
    outCount = -1;
    do
    {
      inCount = 3;
      do
      {
        cout << outCount + inCount << endl;
        inCount--;
      } while (inCount > 0);
      outCount++;
    } while (outCount < 2);
    ```

14. What is output by the following code segment?

    ```
    for (int outCount = -1; outCount < 2; outCount++)
      for (int inCount = 3; inCount > 0; inCount--)
        cout << outCount + inCount << endl;
    ```

15. Rewrite the code segment in Exercise 14 using While loops.
16. What is printed by the following code segment?

    ```
    for (int count = 1; count <= 4; count++)
      switch (count)
      {
        case 4 : cout << " cow?"; break;
        case 2 : cout << " now"; break;
        case 1 : cout << "How"; break;
        case 3 : cout << " brown"; break;
      }
    ```

17. Write a single simple statement that has the same effect on `cout` as the code segment in Exercise 16.

18. What does the following code segment (which is written in poor style) output?

    ```
    count = 1;
    for ( ; ; count++)
      if (count < 3)
        cout << count;
      else
        break;
    ```

19. The difference between an assignment expression and an assignment statement is a semicolon. True or false?
20. The `sizeof` operator can be used to determine whether a machine's `int` type is 32 or 64 bits long. True or false?
21. Which group of C++ operators has the lowest precedence of all?
22. What is the difference in effect of writing `count++` versus `++count`?
23. In what situation is it necessary to use prefix notation for the cast operation instead of functional notation?

■ Programming Warm-Up Exercises

1. Write a Switch statement that outputs the day of the week to `cout` according to the `int` value in `day` that ranges from 0 to 6, with 0 being Sunday.
2. Extend the Switch statement in Exercise 1 so that it outputs `"Error"` if the value in `day` is not in the range of 0 through 6.
3. Write a For loop that outputs the days of the week, each on a separate line, starting from Saturday and working backward to Sunday.
4. Change the For loop in Exercise 3 so that it outputs the days of the week in forward order, starting on Wednesday and going through Tuesday.
5. Write a Do-While loop that prompts for and inputs a user entry of "Y" or "N". If the user fails to enter a correct value, the loop outputs an error message and then repeats the request for the user to enter the value.
6. Write a code segment that adds up the positive integers, starting at 1, until the sum equals or exceeds a value read from the keyboard, and then prints the last integer added to the sum. Use a Do-While loop to do the summing.
7. Write a nested For loop that prints out a multiplication table for the integers 1 through 10.
8. Write a nested For loop that prints a filled right triangle of stars, one star on the first line, two on the next, and so on, up to the tenth line having ten stars.
9. Rewrite the nested loop in Exercise 8 with Do-While loops.
10. Rewrite the nested loop in Exercise 8 with While loops.
11. Write a code segment, using For loops, that prints a hollow rectangle of stars whose width and height are specified by two values read from the keyboard. The top and bottom of the rectangle is a solid row of stars, each row between the top and bottom consists of a star, then width − 2 spaces, and another star.
12. Write a nested For loop that outputs the hours and minutes in the period from 3:15 to 7:30.
13. Extend the loop in Exercise 12 to also output seconds.
14. How many lines do the loops in Exercises 12 and 13 output?

15. Write assignment expression statements that do the following:
    a. Add 7 to the variable **days**
    b. Multiply the value in variable **radius** by 6.2831853
    c. Subtract 40 from variable **workHours**
    d. Divide variable **average** by variable **count**
16. Write an expression whose result is the number of bits in a value of type **long**.
17. Use the C++ precedence rules to remove any unnecessary parentheses from the following expressions:
    a. `((a * b)) + (c * d)`
    b. `((a * b) / (c * d))`
    c. `((a + b) + ((c / (d + e)) * f))`
    d. `(((a + b) / (c + d)) * (e + f))`
    e. `((-a + b) <= (c * d)) && ((a + b) >= (c - d))`

Programming Problems

1. Programming Problem 3 in Chapter 5 asked you to write a program that takes a letter as input and outputs the corresponding word in the International Civil Aviation Organization Alphabet. Extend the program so that it inputs a string and outputs the series of ICAO words that would be used to spell it out. For example:

   ```
   Enter string: program
   Phonetic version is: Papa Romeo Oscar Golf Romeo Alpha Mike
   ```

   Write the program so that it determines the word corresponding to a specified letter using a Switch statement instead of an If structure. For ease of reference, the ICAO alphabet is repeated here:

A	Alpha
B	Bravo
C	Charlie
D	Delta
E	Echo
F	Foxtrot
G	Golf
H	Hotel
I	India
J	Juliet
K	Kilo
L	Lima
M	Mike
N	November
O	Oscar
P	Papa
Q	Quebec
R	Romeo
S	Sierra

T	Tango
U	Uniform
V	Victor
W	Whiskey
X	X-ray
Y	Yankee
Z	Zulu

Be sure to use proper formatting and appropriate comments in your code. Provide appropriate prompts to the user. The output should be clearly labeled and neatly formatted.

2. Programming Problem 4 in Chapter 5 asked you write a C++ program that asks the user to enter his or her weight and the name of a planet. The program was then to output how much the user would weigh on that planet. Rewrite that program so that the selection of the factor to use in computing the weight is made with a Switch statement instead of an If structure.

    For ease of reference, the information for the original problem is repeated here. The following table gives the factor by which the weight must be multiplied for each planet. The program should output an error message if the user doesn't type a correct planet name. The prompt and the error message should make it clear to the user how a planet name must be entered. Be sure to use proper formatting and appropriate comments in your code. The output should be clearly labeled and neatly formatted.

Mercury	0.4155
Venus	0.8975
Earth	1.0
Moon	0.166
Mars	0.3507
Jupiter	2.5374
Saturn	1.0677
Uranus	0.8947
Neptune	1.1794
Pluto	0.0899

3. You are working for a company that has traveling salespeople. The salespeople call in their sales to a fulfillment desk, where the sales are all entered into a file. Each sale is recorded as one line on the file `sales.dat` as a salesperson ID number, an item number, and a quantity, with all three items separated by blanks. There are 10 salespeople, with IDs of 1 through 10. The company sells eight different products, with IDs of 7 through 14 (some older products have been discontinued). The unit prices of the products are given here:

Product Number	Unit Price
7	345.00
8	853.00
9	471.00

10	933.00
11	721.00
12	663.00
13	507.00
14	259.00

You have been asked to write a program that reads in the sales file, and generates a separate file for each salesperson containing just that individual's sales. Each line from the sales file is copied to the appropriate salesperson file (`salespers1.dat` through `salespers10.dat`), with the salesperson ID omitted. The total for the sale (quantity times unit price) is appended to the record. At the end of processing, the total sales for each salesperson should be output with informative labels to `cout`. Use functional decomposition to design the program. Be sure that the program handles invalid ID numbers. If a salesperson ID is invalid, write an error message to `cout`. If a product number is invalid, write the error message to the salesperson's file and don't compute a total for that sale. There should be ample opportunity to use Switch statements and value-returning functions in this application.

4. Write a number-guessing game in which the computer selects a random number in the range of 0 to 100, and users get a maximum of 20 attempts to guess it. At the end of each game, users should be told whether they won or lost, and then be asked whether they want to play again. When the user quits, the program should output the total number of wins and losses. To make the game more interesting, the program should vary the wording of the messages that it outputs for winning, for losing, and for asking for another game. Create as many as 10 different messages for each of these cases, and use random numbers to choose among them. See Appendix C.7 for information on the C++ random-number generator functions. This application should provide a good opportunity for you to use a Do-While statement and Switch statements. Use functional decomposition to solve the problem, write your C++ code using good style and documenting comments, and have fun thinking up some messages that will surprise the user.

5. Write a functional decomposition and a C++ program that reads a time in numeric form and prints it in English. The time is input as hours and minutes, separated by a space. Hours are specified in 24-hour time (15 is 3 P.M.), but the output should be in 12-hour A.M./P.M. form. Note that noon and midnight are special cases. Here are some examples:

```
Enter time: 12 00
Noon

Enter time: 0 00
Midnight

Enter time: 6 44
Six forty four AM

Enter time: 18 11
Six eleven PM
```

Write your C++ code using good style and documenting comments. This application should provide you with ample opportunity to use Switch statements.

6. Extend the program in Problem 5 so that it asks the user if he or she wants to enter another time, and then repeats the process until the response to the question is "no." You should be able to code this easily using a Do-While statement.

Case Study Follow-Up

1. Which changes would be necessary in the `RichUncle` program if uppercase letters and lowercase letters were to be counted as members of the same category?
2. You decide that you are interested in counting the number of words in the text. How might you estimate this number?
3. Given that you can calculate the number of words in the text, how can you calculate the average word length?
4. Can you think of any other characteristics of a person's writing style that you might be able to measure?

Functions

KNOWLEDGE GOALS
- To know how functions can be used to reflect the structure of a functional decomposition.
- To understand the difference between value and reference parameters.
- To know how to use arguments and parameters.

SKILL GOALS

To be able to:
- Write a module of your own design as a void function.
- Design the parameter list for each module of a functional decomposition.
- Code a program using functions.
- Define and use local variables correctly.
- Write a program that uses multiple calls to a single function.

You have been using C++ functions since we introduced standard library routines such as `sqrt` and `abs` in Chapter 3. By now, you should be quite comfortable with the idea of calling these subprograms to perform a task. So far, however, we have not considered how the programmer can create his or her own functions other than `main`. That is the topic of this chapter and the next.

You might wonder why we waited until now to look at user-defined subprograms. The reason—and the major purpose for using subprograms—is that we write our own functions to help organize and simplify larger programs. Until now, our programs have been relatively small and simple, so we didn't need to write subprograms. Now that we've covered the basic control structures, we are ready to introduce subprograms so that we can begin writing larger and more complex programs.

8.1 Functional Decomposition with Void Functions

As a brief refresher, let's review the two kinds of subprograms with which the C++ language works: value-returning functions and void functions. A value-returning function receives some data through its argument list, computes a single function value, and returns this function value to the calling code. The caller invokes (calls) a value-returning function by using its name and argument list in an expression:

```
y = 3.8 * sqrt(x);
```

In contrast, a void function does not return a value, nor is it called from within an expression. Instead, the call appears as a complete, standalone statement. An example is the `get` function associated with the `istream` and `ifstream` classes:

```
cin.get(inputChar);
```

In this chapter, we concentrate exclusively on creating our own void functions. In Chapter 9, we examine how to write value-returning functions.

From the early chapters on, you have been designing your programs as collections of modules. Many of these modules are naturally implemented as *user-defined void functions*. We now look at how to do this explicitly in C++

When to Use Functions

In general, you can code any module as a function, although some are so simple that this step really is unnecessary. In designing a program, then, we frequently need to decide which modules should be implemented as functions. The decision should be based on whether the overall program is easier to understand as a result. Other factors can affect this decision, but for now this is the simplest heuristic (strategy) to use.

If a module is a single line only, it is usually best to write it directly in the program. Turning it into a function merely complicates the code, which defeats the purpose of using functions. Conversely, if a module is many lines long, it is natural to turn it into a function.

One case where we might implement a short module as a function is when the module is used in several places within the program. Coding the module in one place and calling it from many places yields a better design for two reasons. First, if we code the module directly in multiple places, there are more opportunities for us to make a mistake. We are less likely to introduce an error if we code the module once and just call it where it's needed. Second, if we later must change the module algorithm, we would need to search the code for every place that it was directly inserted. But given a function implementation, we need make the change only once within the function, and it affects every place that the function is called.

Keep in mind that implementing a module as a function should affect only the readability of the program and may make it more or less convenient to change the program later. It should not alter the functioning of the program. We say *should* because whether this is true depends on what we call the module's interface. We have not yet examined this aspect of module design, which we now consider.

Why Do Modules Need an Interface Design?

Before we look at how to convert a module to a function, we need to revisit how we design a module. Until now, our modules have simply been groups of statements that have access to all of the values in a program. That's fine for small problems, but it doesn't work when we have big problems with lots of modules.

To see why allowing every module to access every value is a bad idea, consider an analogy. At home, people tend to keep their doors open, and they share most of their belongings. Now suppose that you check into a hotel that's based on the same principle—none of the rooms have doors. There would be no privacy or security. Everyone would have free access to everyone else's things. (And the snoring would be terrible!) To make the hotel safe, we need to have a lockable door on each room.

Modules in larger problems need to be designed with the equivalent of doors. They should not have direct access to each other's values, and information should enter and leave them via just one carefully controlled route. We call this aspect of a module's design its interface. There are two views that we can take of the interface: external and internal. In our hotel room analogy, from outside you can see just the door to the room. From inside, you can see the door and the contents of the room. We start the interface design process with the external view.

Designing Interfaces

From now on, we consider a module as a separate block within a design whose implementation details are "hidden" (walled-off) from view.

How can we work with such a module? From the external perspective, as long as you know what a module does and how to call it, you can use the module without knowing how it accomplishes its task. For example, you don't know how the code for a library function like `sqrt` is written (its implementation is hidden from view), yet you still can use it effectively.

FIGURE 8.1 Module Interface (Visible) and Implementation (Hidden)

The specification of what a module does and how it is invoked defines its interface (see **FIGURE 8.1**). Hiding a module implementation is called encapsulation. When a module is encapsulated, we don't have to worry that it will accidentally access the values in other modules, or that other modules will be able to change its values.

Another advantage of encapsulation is that we can make internal changes to a module, as long as the interface remains the same. For example, you can rewrite the body of an encapsulated module using a more efficient algorithm.

One way to specify the interface to a module is to write down its purpose, its precondition and postcondition, and the information it takes and returns. If the specification is sufficiently complete, we could hand it to someone else, and that person could then implement the module for us. Interfaces and encapsulation are the basis for *team programming*, in which a group of programmers work together to solve a large problem.

Thus designing a module can (and should) be divided into two tasks: designing the external interface and designing the internal implementation. For the external interface, we focus on the *what*, not the *how*. We define the behavior of the module (what it does) and the mechanism for communicating with it.

To define the mechanism for communicating with the module, we make a list of the following items:

> **Interface** The formal description of what a subprogram does and how we communicate with it.
> **Encapsulation** Hiding a module implementation in a separate block with a formally specified interface.
> **Module parameter list** A set of variables within a module that hold values that are either incoming to the module or outgoing to the caller, or both.
> **Data flow** The direction of flow of information between the caller and a module through each parameter.

1. *Incoming values* that the module receives from the caller.
2. *Outgoing values* that the module produces and returns to the caller.
3. *Incoming/outgoing values*—values the caller has that the module changes (receives and returns).

Next, we turn to the internal view of the interface as the starting point for our implementation. We choose names for identifiers that will exist as variables inside the module, each of which matches a value in our list. These identifiers become what we call the parameter list for the module.

Henceforth, we write the parameters in the module heading. Any other variables that the module needs are said to be *local* and we declare them within its body. We do this for any module that we anticipate implementing as a function. As part of the module interface, we also document the direction of data flow for each parameter.

Now that we've seen how to design a module for implementation as a function, we are ready to start coding modules in C++.

Writing Modules as Void Functions

It is quite a simple matter to turn a module into a void function in C++. Basically, a void function looks like the `main` function except that the function heading uses `void` rather than `int` as the data type of the function. Additionally, the body of a void function does *not* contain a statement like

```
return 0;
```

as does `main`. That's because a void function doesn't return a value to its caller.

Let's look at a program using void functions. We'll start with a very simple example that doesn't have any parameters. A friend of yours is returning from a long trip, and you want to write a program that prints the following message:

```
**************
**************
 Welcome Home!
**************
**************
**************
**************
```

Here is a design for the program:

Main Level 0

Print two lines of asterisks
Print "Welcome Home!"
Print four lines of asterisks

Print 2 Lines Level 1

Print "**************"
Print "**************"

Print 4 Lines Level 1

Print "**************"
Print "**************"
Print "**************"
Print "**************"

If we write the two first-level modules as void functions, the `main` function is simply this:

```
int main()
{
  Print2Lines();
  cout << "Welcome Home!" << endl;
  Print4Lines();
  return 0;
}
```

Notice how similar this code is to the `main` module of our functional decomposition. It contains two function calls—one to a function named `Print2Lines` and another to a function named `Print4Lines`. Both of these functions have empty argument lists.

The following code should look familiar to you, but look carefully at the function heading.

```
void Print2Lines()                              // Function heading
{
  cout << "***************" << endl;
  cout << "***************" << endl;
}
```

This segment is a *function definition*. A function definition is the code that extends from the function heading to the end of the block that is the body of the function. The function heading begins with the word `void`, signaling the compiler that this is not a value-returning function. The body of the function executes some ordinary statements and does *not* contain a `return` statement.

Now look again at the function heading. Just like any other identifier in C++, the name of a function cannot include blanks, even though our paper-and-pencil module names do. Following the function name is an empty parameter list—that is, there is nothing between the parentheses. Later we will see what goes inside the parentheses if a function uses arguments.

Now let's put `main` and the other two functions together to form a complete program.

```
//*****************************************************************
// Welcome program
// This program prints a "Welcome Home" message
//*****************************************************************
#include <iostream>
using namespace std;

void Print2Lines();                             // Function prototypes
// This function prints two lines of asterisks

void Print4Lines();
// This function prints four lines of asterisks

int main()
{
  Print2Lines();                                // Function call
  cout << " Welcome Home!" << endl;
  Print4Lines();                                // Function call
  return 0;
}

//*****************************************************************

void Print2Lines()                              // Function heading
{
  cout << "***************" << endl;
  cout << "***************" << endl;
}
```

```
//*********************************************************************
void Print4Lines()                              // Function heading
{
    cout << "***************" << endl;
    cout << "***************" << endl;
    cout << "***************" << endl;
    cout << "***************" << endl;
}
```

C++ function definitions can appear in any order. We could have chosen to place the `main` function last instead of first, but C++ programmers typically put `main` first and any supporting functions after it.

In the `Welcome` program, the two statements just before the `main` function are called *function prototypes*. These declarations are necessary because C++ requires you to declare an identifier before you can use it. Our `main` function calls functions `Print2Lines` and `Print4Lines`, but their definitions don't appear until later. We supply the function prototypes to inform the compiler in advance that `Print2Lines` and `Print4Lines` are void functions that have no arguments. In addition, we include comments describing these two functions for the reader so that the `main` function makes sense. We say more about function prototypes later in the chapter.

Because the `Welcome` program is so simple initially, it may seem more complicated with its modules written as functions. Upon closer inspection, however, it is clear that it much more closely resembles our functional decomposition. If you handed this code to someone, the person could look at the `main` function and tell you immediately what the program does—it prints two lines of something, prints "Welcome Home!", and prints four lines of something. If you asked the person to be more specific, he or she could then look up the details in the other function definitions. The person is able to begin with a top-level view of the program and then study the lower-level modules as necessary, without having to read the entire program or look at a module structure chart. As our programs grow to include many modules nested several levels deep, the ability to read a program in the same manner as a functional decomposition aids greatly in the development and debugging process.

MAY WE INTRODUCE   Charles Babbage

The British mathematician Charles Babbage (1791–1871) is generally credited with designing the world's first computer. Unlike today's electronic computers, however, Babbage's machine was mechanical. It was made of gears and levers, the predominant technology of the 1820s and 1830s.

MAY WE INTRODUCE Charles Babbage, continued

Babbage actually designed two different machines. The first, called the Difference Engine, was to be used in computing mathematical tables. For example, the Difference Engine could produce a table of squares:

x	x^2
1	1
2	4
3	9
4	16
⋮	⋮

Babbage's Difference Engine was essentially a complex calculator that could not be programmed. It was designed to improve the accuracy of the computation of similar mathematical tables, not the speed. At that time, all tables were produced by hand, a tedious and error-prone job. Because much of science and engineering in Babbage's day depended on accurate tables of information, an error could have serious consequences. Even though the Difference Engine could perform the calculations only a little faster than a human could, it did so without error. In fact, one of its most important features was that the device would stamp its output directly onto copper plates, which could then be placed into a printing press, thereby avoiding even typographical errors.

By 1833, the project to build the Difference Engine had run into financial trouble. The engineer whom Babbage had hired to do the construction was dishonest and had drawn the project out as long as possible to extract more money from Babbage's sponsors in the British government. Eventually the sponsors became tired of waiting for the machine and withdrew their support. At about the same time, Babbage lost interest in the project because he had developed the idea for a much more powerful machine, which he called the Analytical Engine—a truly programmable computer.

The idea for the Analytical Engine came to Babbage as he toured Europe to survey the best technology of the time in preparation for constructing the Difference Engine. One of the technologies that he saw was the Jacquard automatic loom, in which a series of paper cards with punched holes was fed through the machine to produce a woven cloth pattern. The pattern of holes constituted a program for the loom and made it possible to weave patterns of arbitrary complexity automatically. In fact, its inventor even had a detailed portrait of himself woven by one of his machines.

Babbage realized that this sort of device could be used to control the operation of a computing machine. Instead of calculating just one type of formula, such a machine could be programmed to perform arbitrarily complex computations, including the manipulation of algebraic symbols. As his associate, Ada Lovelace (the world's first computer programmer), elegantly put it, "We may say most aptly that the Analytical Engine weaves algebraical patterns." It is clear that Babbage and Lovelace fully understood the power of a programmable computer and even contemplated the notion that someday such machines could achieve artificial thought.

Unfortunately, Babbage never completed construction of either of his machines. Some historians believe that he never finished them because the technology of the period could not support such complex machinery. But most feel that Babbage's failure was his own doing. He was both brilliant and somewhat eccentric (it is known that he was afraid of Italian organ grinders, for example). As a consequence, he had a tendency to abandon projects midstream so that he could concentrate on newer and better ideas. He always believed that his new approaches would enable him to complete a machine in less time than his old ideas would.

MAY WE INTRODUCE Charles Babbage, continued

When he died, Babbage had many pieces of computing machines and partial drawings of designs, but none of the plans were complete enough to produce a single working computer. After his death, his ideas were dismissed and his inventions ignored. Only after modern computers were developed did historians realize the true importance of his contributions. Babbage recognized the potential of the computer an entire century before one was fully developed. Today, we can only imagine how different the world would be if he had succeeded in constructing his Analytical Engine.

QUICK CHECK

8.1.1 Which elements of a functional decomposition correspond to functions in C++? (pp. 346–347)
8.1.2 If the same module appears in multiple places in a functional decomposition, how do you convert it into code in a program? (pp. 349–351)
8.1.3 What items define the mechanism for communicating with a module? (p. 348)
8.1.4 What is the name of the specification of what a module does and how it is invoked? (p. 348)
8.1.5 Write a void function called `PrintName` that prints your name. (pp. 349–351)

8.2 An Overview of User-Defined Functions

Now that we've seen an example of how a program is written with functions, let's look briefly and informally at some of the more important points of function construction and use.

Flow of Control in Function Calls

We said that C++ function definitions may be arranged in any order. During compilation, the functions are translated in the order in which they physically appear. When the program is executed, however, control begins at the first statement in `main`, and the program proceeds in logical order (recall that the flow of control is normally sequential, unless it is altered by a control structure statement).[1]

When a function call is encountered, control passes to the first statement in that function's body, with its remaining statements being executed in logical order. After the last statement is executed, control returns to the point immediately following the function call. Because function calls alter the order of execution, functions are considered control structures. **FIGURE 8.2** illustrates this physical versus logical ordering of functions. In the figure, functions A, B, and C are written in the physical order A, B, C but are executed in the order C, B, A.

In the `Welcome` program, execution begins with the first executable statement in the `main` function (the call to `Print2Lines`). When `Print2Lines` is called, control passes to its first statement and subsequent statements in its body. After the last statement in `Print2Lines` has executed, control returns to `main` at the point following the call (the output statement that prints "Welcome Home!").

---

[1]. Actually, some parts of a C++ program execute prior to `main`, such as the initialization of `cin` and `cout`. For the programs we are writing, however, it is simplest to think of execution as starting with `main`.

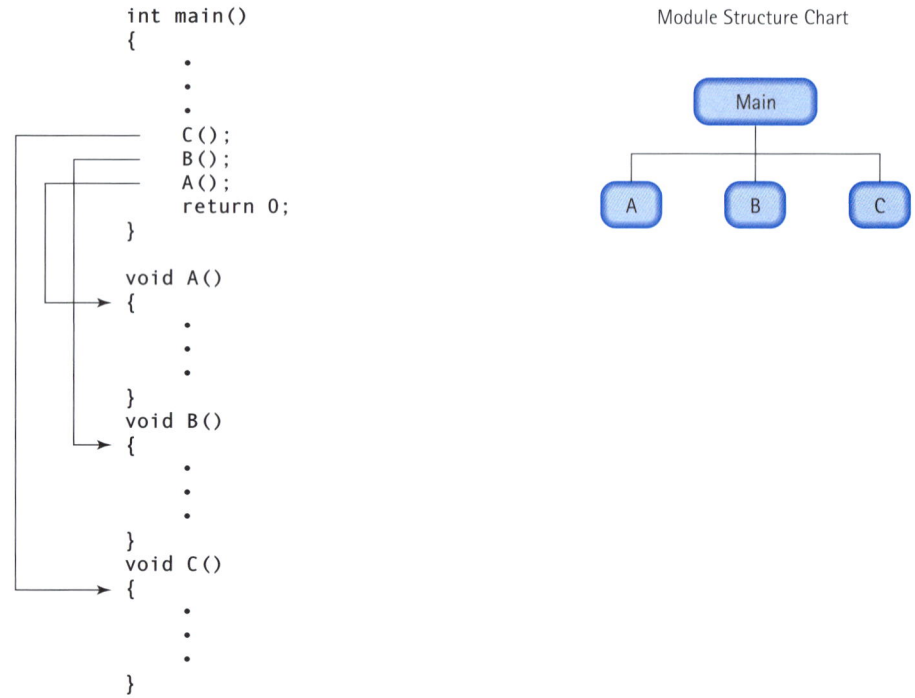

FIGURE 8.2 Physical Versus Logical Order of Functions

Function Parameters

Looking at the `Welcome` program, you can see that `Print2Lines` and `Print4Lines` are very similar functions. They differ only in the number of lines that they print. Do we really need two different functions in this program? Maybe we should write just one function that prints any number of lines, where the "any number of lines" is passed as an argument by the caller (`main`). Deciding to use only one function changes the design.

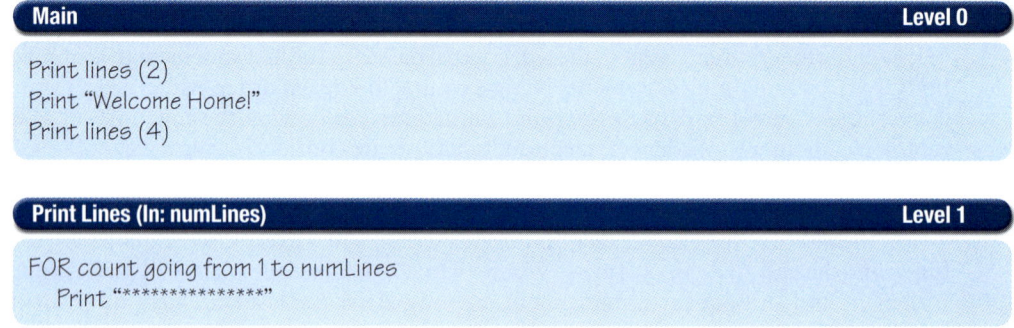

Here is a second version of the program, which uses just one function to do the printing. We call it `NewWelcome`.

```cpp
//***************************************************************
// NewWelcome program
// This program prints a "Welcome Home" message
//***************************************************************
#include <iostream>
using namespace std;

void PrintLines(int numLines);          // Function prototype
// This function prints lines of asterisks, where
// numLines specifies how many lines to print

int main()
{
  PrintLines(2);
  cout << " Welcome Home!" << endl;
  PrintLines(4);
  return 0;
}

//***************************************************************

void PrintLines(int numLines)
{
  for (int count = 1; count <= numLines; count++)
    cout << "***************" << endl;
}
```

In the function heading of `PrintLines`, you see some code between the parentheses that looks like a variable declaration. This code is a *parameter declaration*.

As you learned in earlier chapters, the items listed in the call to a function are the arguments. We have been using arguments, which constitute the external view of a function interface, for some time now.

The variables declared in the function heading are parameters. They provide identifiers within the function by which we can refer to the values supplied through the arguments. Parameters are the internal view of the function interface.

Argument A variable or expression listed in a call to a function.

Parameter A variable declared in a function heading.

In the `NewWelcome` program, the arguments in the two function calls are the constants 2 and 4, and the parameter in the `PrintLines` function is named `numLines`. The `main` function first calls `PrintLines` with an argument of 2. When control is turned over to `PrintLines`, the parameter `numLines` is initialized to 2. Within `PrintLines`, the count-controlled loop executes twice and the function returns. The second time `PrintLines` is called, the parameter `numLines` is initialized to the value of the argument, 4. The loop executes four times, after which the function returns.

Here is another version of the `main` function, just to show that the arguments can be variables instead of constants:

```cpp
int main()
{
  int lineCount;
  lineCount = 2;
  PrintLines(lineCount);
  cout << " Welcome Home!" << endl;
```

```
        lineCount = 4;
        PrintLines(lineCount);
        return 0;
}
```

In this version, each time `main` calls `PrintLines`, a copy of the value in `lineCount` is passed to the function to initialize the parameter `numLines`. As you can see, the argument and the parameter can have different names.

`NewWelcome` illustrates that a function can be called from many places in `main` (or from other functions). If a task must be done in more than one place in a program, we can avoid repetitive coding by writing it as a function and then calling it wherever we need it.

If more than one argument is passed to a function, the arguments and parameters are matched by their relative positions in the two lists. For example, if you want `PrintLines` to print lines consisting of any selected character, not only asterisks, you could rewrite the function so that its heading is

```
void PrintLines(int numLines, char whichChar)
```

A call to this function might look like this:

```
PrintLines(3, '#');
```

The first argument, 3, is matched with `numLines` because `numLines` is the first parameter. Likewise, the second argument, `'#'`, is matched with the second parameter, `whichChar`.

QUICK CHECK ✓

8.2.1 When a function call is encountered where does control pass to? (p. 353)
8.2.2 When a function returns where is control passed to? (p. 353)
8.2.3 What is the difference between a function **argument** and a function **parameter**? (p. 355)
8.2.4 If more than one argument is passed to a function, in what order are they matched with the parameters? (p. 356)

8.3 Syntax and Semantics of Void Functions

Function Call (Invocation)

As we've seen, to call (or invoke) a void function, we use its name as a statement, with the arguments in parentheses following the name. Here is the syntax template of a function call to a void function:

FunctionCall (to a void function)

> FunctionName (ArgumentList) ;

Note that the argument list is optional, but the parentheses are required even if the list is empty.

If the list includes two or more arguments, you must separate them with commas. Here is the syntax template for ArgumentList:

ArgumentList

> Expression , Expression . . .

When a function call is executed, the arguments are passed to the parameters according to their positions, left to right, and control is then transferred to the first executable statement in the function body. When the last statement in the function has executed, control returns to the point from which the function was called.

Function Declarations and Definitions

In C++, a function's declaration must physically precede any function call. The declaration gives the compiler the name of the function, the form of the function's return value (either `void` or a data type like `int` or `float`), and the data types of the parameters.

The `NewWelcome` program contains three function declarations. The first one (the statement labeled "Function prototype") does not include the body of the function. The remaining two—for `main` and `PrintLines`—include bodies for the functions.

In C++ terminology, a function declaration that omits the body is called a *function prototype*, and a declaration that does include the body is called a *function definition*. We can use a Venn diagram to illustrate that all definitions are declarations, but not all declarations are definitions:

> **Function prototype** A function declaration without the body of the function.
>
> **Function definition** A function declaration that includes the body of the function.

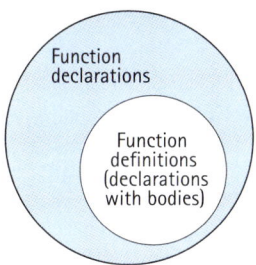

In general, C++ distinguishes declarations from definitions by whether memory space is allocated for the item. For example, a function prototype is merely a declaration—that is, it specifies only the unique properties of a function. By comparison, a function definition does more: it causes the compiler to allocate memory for the instructions in the body of the function.[2]

The rule throughout C++ is that you can declare an item as many times as you wish, but you can define it only once. In the `NewWelcome` program, we could include many function prototypes for `PrintLines` (though we have no reason to do so), but only one function definition is allowed.

Function Prototypes

Function prototypes allow us to declare functions before they are defined, so that we can arrange their definitions in any order. As we've noted, C++ programmers typically define `main` first, followed by all other functions.

Aside from style, there is a situation in C++ where function prototypes are essential. Suppose that two functions, A and B, call each other. If we write the definition of A followed by the definition of B, then within A the call to B generates a message that identifier B is undeclared. Of course, reversing the order of the definitions won't solve the problem. The solution is to write a prototype for B preceding the definition of A, so that B is declared

---

[2]. Technically, all of the variable declarations we've used so far have been variable *definitions* as well as declarations—they allocate memory for the variable. In Chapter 9, we see examples of variable declarations that aren't variable definitions.

before it is used in A. Because the prototype for B omits the function body, it doesn't contain a call to A. As a result, it avoids referring to A before it is declared. Notice that this special case is automatically covered when we adopt the style of writing prototypes for all of our functions preceding `main`.

A prototype for a void function has the following syntax:

FunctionPrototype (for a void function)

> **void** FunctionName (ParameterList) ;

As you can see in the template, no body is included for the function, and a semicolon terminates the declaration. The parameter list is optional, to allow for parameterless functions. If the parameter list is present, it has the following form:

ParameterList (in a function prototype)

> Datatype **&** VariableName , DataType **&** VariableName ...

The ampersand (**&**) attached to the name of a data type is optional and has a special significance that we cover later in the chapter.

In a function prototype, the parameter list must specify the data types of the parameters, but their names are optional. You could write either

```
void DoSomething(int, float);
```

or

```
void DoSomething(int velocity, float angle);
```

Sometimes it's useful for documentation purposes to supply names for the parameters, but be aware that the compiler ignores them.

Function Definitions

You learned in Chapter 2 that a function definition consists of two parts: the function heading and the function body, which is syntactically a block (compound statement). Here's the syntax template for a function definition—specifically, for a void function:

FunctionDefinition (for a void function)

> **void** FunctionName (ParameterList)
> {
>   Statement
>   ⋮
> }

Notice that the function heading does *not* end in a semicolon the way a function prototype does. Putting a semicolon at the end of the line will generate a syntax error.

The syntax of the parameter list differs slightly from that of a function prototype in that you must specify the names of all the parameters. Also, it's our style preference (but not a C++ language requirement) to declare each parameter on a separate line:

ParameterList (in a function definition)

```
Datatype & VariableName ,
Datatype & VariableName
    ⋮
```

Local Variables

Because a function body is a block, any function—not just `main`—can include variable declarations. These variables are called local variables because they are accessible only within the block in which they are declared. As far as the calling code is concerned, they don't exist. If you tried to print the contents of a local variable from another function, a compile-time error such as `UNDECLARED IDENTIFIER` would occur. You saw an example of a local variable in the `NewWelcome` program—the `count` variable declared within the `PrintLines` function.

Local variable A variable declared within a block and not accessible outside of that block.

In contrast to local variables, variables declared outside of all the functions in a program are called global variables. We return to the topic of global variables in Chapter 9.

Local variables occupy memory space only while the function is executing. At the moment the function is called, memory space is created for its local variables. When the function returns, its local variables are destroyed.[3] Therefore, every time the function is called, its local variables start out with their values undefined. Because every call to a function is independent of every other call to that same function, you must initialize the local variables within the function itself. Also, because local variables are destroyed when the function returns, you cannot use them to store values between calls to the function.

The following code segment illustrates each of the parts of the function declaration and calling mechanism that we have discussed.

```
#include <iostream>
using namespace std;

void TryThis(int, int, float);     // Function prototype for TryThis

int main()                         // Function definition for main
{
  int    int1;                     // Variables local to main
  int    int2;
  float  someFloat;
    ⋮
  TryThis(int1, int2, someFloat);  // Function call with
                                   //    three arguments
    ⋮
}

void TryThis(int    param1,        // Function definition for TryThis
             int    param2,        //    with three parameters
             float  param3)
```

---
3. We'll see an exception to this rule in Chapter 9.

```
{
  int i;                              // Variables local to TryThis
  float x;
   ⋮
}
```

The Return Statement

The `main` function uses the statement

```
return 0;
```

to return the value 0 to its caller, the operating system.

As we've seen, a void function does not return a function value. Control returns from the function when it "falls off" the end of the body—that is, after the final statement has executed. As you saw in the `NewWelcome` program, the `PrintLines` function simply prints some lines of asterisks and then returns.

Alternatively, you can use a second form of the Return statement. It looks like this:

```
return;
```

This statement is valid *only* for void functions. It can appear anywhere in the body of the function; it causes control to exit the function immediately and return to the caller. Here's an example:

```
void SomeFunc(int n)
{
  if (n > 50)
  {
    cout << "The value is out of range.";
    return;
  }
  n = 412 * n;
  cout << n;
}
```

In this (nonsense) example, there are two ways for control to exit the function. At function entry, the value of n is tested. If it is greater than 50, the function prints a message and returns immediately without executing any more statements. If n is less than or equal to 50, the If statement's then-clause is skipped and control proceeds to the assignment statement. After the last statement, control returns to the caller.

Another way of writing this function is to use an If-Then-Else structure:

```
void SomeFunc(int n)
{
  if (n > 50)
    cout << "The value is out of range.";
  else
  {
    n = 412 * n;
    cout << n;
  }
}
```

If you asked different programmers about these two versions of the function, you would get differing opinions. Some prefer the first version, saying that it is most straightforward to use Return statements whenever it logically makes sense to do so. Others insist on a *single-entry*, *single-exit* approach. With this philosophy, control enters a function at one point only (the first executable statement) and exits at one point only (the end of the body). These programmers argue that multiple exits from a function make the program logic hard to follow and difficult to debug. Other programmers take a position somewhere between the two extremes, allowing occasional use of the Return statement when the logic is clear. Our advice is to use the Return statement sparingly; overuse can lead to confusing code.

MATTERS OF STYLE Naming Void Functions

When you choose a name for a void function, keep in mind how calls to it will look. A call is written as a statement; therefore, it should sound like a command or an instruction to the computer. For this reason, it is a good idea to choose a name that is an imperative verb or has an imperative verb as part of it. (In English, an imperative verb is one representing a command: *Listen! Look! Do something!)* For example, the statement

```
Lines(3);
```

has no verb to suggest that it's a command. Adding the verb *Print* makes the name sound like an action:

```
PrintLines(3);
```

When you are picking a name for a void function, write down sample calls with different names until you come up with one that sounds like a command to the computer.

QUICK CHECK

8.3.1 Where do declarations of functions that are called by `main` appear in the program with respect to `main`? (pp. 356–359)

8.3.2 Which parts of a program can access a local variable declared within a function's block? (pp. 359–360)

8.3.3 What is a function prototype? (p. 357)

8.3.4 Why are function prototypes useful? (p. 357)

8.3.5 Write a void function prototype for a function called `UpdateRace` that takes an integer and floating-point parameter in that order. (pp. 357–359)

8.3.6 What is a variable called when it is declared within a block and not accessible outside of that block? (p. 359)

8.4 Parameters

When a function is executed, it uses the arguments given to it in the function call. How is this done? The answer to this question depends on the nature of the parameters. C++ supports two kinds of parameters: value parameters and reference parameters. With a value parameter, which is declared without an ampersand (**&**) at the end of the data type name, the function receives a copy of the argument's value. With a reference parameter, which is declared by

Value parameter A parameter that receives a copy of the value of the corresponding argument.

Reference parameter A parameter that receives the location (memory address) of the caller's argument.

adding an ampersand (**&**) to the data type name, the function receives the location (memory address) of the caller's argument. Before we examine in detail the difference between these two kinds of parameters, let's look at an example of a function heading with a mixture of reference and value parameter declarations:

```
void Example(int&  param1,      // A reference parameter
             int    param2,      // A value parameter
             float  param3)      // Another value parameter
```

With simple data types—**int**, **char**, **float**, and so on—a value parameter is the default (assumed) kind of parameter. In other words, if you don't do anything special (add an ampersand), a parameter is assumed to be a value parameter. To specify a reference parameter, you have to do something extra (attach an ampersand).

Now let's look at both kinds of parameters, starting with value parameters.

Value Parameters

In the **NewWelcome** program, the **PrintLines** function heading is

```
void PrintLines(int numLines)
```

The parameter **numLines** is a value parameter because its data type name doesn't end in **&**. If the function is called using an argument **lineCount**,

```
PrintLines(lineCount);
```

then the parameter **numLines** receives a copy of the value of **lineCount**. At this moment, there are two copies of the data—one in the argument **lineCount** and one in the parameter **numLines**. If a statement inside the **PrintLines** function were to change the value of **numLines**, this change would not affect the argument **lineCount** (remember, there are two copies of the data). As you can see, using value parameters helps us avoid unintentional changes to arguments.

Because value parameters are passed copies of their arguments, anything that has a value may be passed to a value parameter. This includes constants, variables, and even arbitrarily complicated expressions. (The expression is simply evaluated and a copy of the result is sent to the corresponding value parameter.) For the **PrintLines** function, the following function calls are all valid:

```
PrintLines(3);
PrintLines(lineCount);
PrintLines(2 * abs(10 - someInt));
```

There must be the same number of arguments in a function call as there are parameters in the function heading.[4] Also, each argument should have the same data type as the parameter in the same position. Notice how each parameter in the following example is matched to the argument in the same position (the data type of each argument is what you would assume from its name):

Function heading: void ShowMatch(float num1, int num2, char letter)

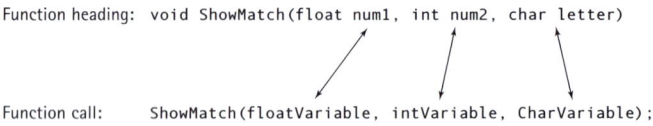

Function call: ShowMatch(floatVariable, intVariable, CharVariable);

---

4. This statement is not the whole truth. C++ has a special language feature—called *default parameters*—that lets you call a function with fewer arguments than parameters. We do not cover default parameters in this book.

If the matched items are not of the same data type, implicit type coercion takes place. For example, if a parameter is of type `int`, an argument that is a `float` expression is coerced to an `int` value before it is passed to the function. As usual in C++, you can avoid unintended type coercion by using an explicit type cast or, better yet, by not mixing data types at all.

As we have stressed, a value parameter receives a copy of the argument and, therefore, the caller's argument cannot be accessed directly or changed. When a function returns, the contents of its value parameters are destroyed, along with the contents of its local variables. The difference between value parameters and local variables is that the values of local variables are undefined when a function starts to execute, whereas value parameters are automatically initialized to the values of the corresponding arguments.

Because the contents of value parameters are destroyed when the function returns, they cannot be used to return information to the calling code. What if we *do* want to return information by modifying the caller's arguments? We must use the second kind of parameter available in C++: reference parameters. Let's look at these in more detail now.

Reference Parameters

A reference parameter is one that you declare by attaching an ampersand to the name of its data type. It is called a reference parameter because the called function can refer to the corresponding argument directly. Specifically, the function is allowed to inspect *and modify* the caller's argument.

When a function is invoked using a reference parameter, it is the *location* (memory address) of the argument—not its value—that is passed to the function. Only one copy of the information exists, and it is used by both the caller and the called function. When a function is called, the argument and the parameter become synonyms for the same location in memory. When a function returns control to its caller, the link between the argument and the parameter is broken. They are synonymous only during a particular call to the function. The only evidence that a matchup between the two ever occurred is that the contents of the argument may have changed (see **FIGURE 8.3**).

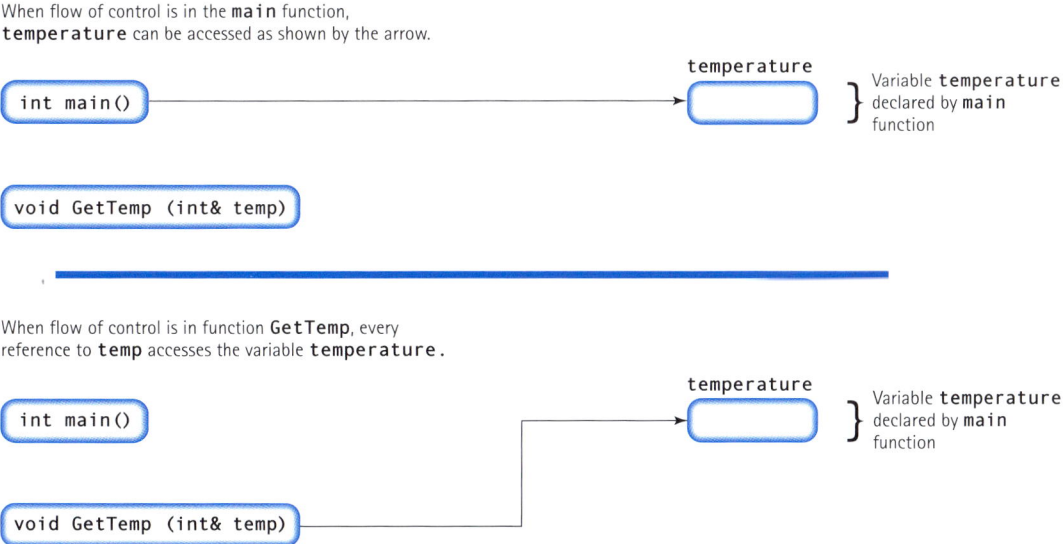

FIGURE 8.3 Using a Reference Parameter to Access an Argument

Whatever value is left by the called function in this location is the value that the caller will find there. You must be careful when using a reference parameter, because any change made to it affects the argument in the calling code. Here is an example of a heading and a call:

Function heading: `void ShowMatch(float& num1, int num2, char& letter)`

Function call: `ShowMatch(floatVar, intVar, CharVar);`

For the highlighted arguments, the *addresses* of `floatVar` and `charVar` are passed to `num1` and `letter`, respectively. Because `num2` is a value parameter, it receives the value stored in `intVar`.

Another important difference between value and reference parameters relates to matching arguments with parameters. With value parameters, we said that implicit type coercion occurs (the value of the argument is coerced, if possible, to the data type of the parameter). In contrast, reference parameters require that the matched items must have *exactly the same* data type.

Earlier in this chapter, we discussed documenting data flow direction in modules. Function parameters corresponding to Out and In/out module parameters must have an ampersand attached to their type when converting them to C++ code. We do not attach an ampersand to In parameters.

The following table summarizes the usage of arguments and parameters.

Item	Usage
Argument	Appears in a function *call*. The corresponding parameter may be either a reference parameter or a value parameter.
Value parameter	Appears in a function *heading*. Receives a *copy* of the value of the corresponding argument, which will be coerced if necessary.
Reference parameter	Appears in a function *heading*. Receives the *address* of the corresponding argument. Its corresponding type must have an ampersand (**&**) appended to it. The type of an argument must exactly match the type of the parameter.

SOFTWARE MAINTENANCE CASE STUDY: Refactoring a Program

MAINTENANCE TASK: For the Problem-Solving Case Study in Chapter 3, we wrote a mortgage payment calculator. In the Software Maintenance Case Study in Chapter 4, we changed it to use file I/O. In Chapter 5, we revised the input to allow interest to be entered either as a decimal or as a percentage. In Chapter 6, we expanded the program's capabilities, including calculation of the total interest paid over the period of the loan, and allowing entry of data for multiple loans in one run. Needless to say, by now this program has gotten quite long and complicated. It's time to *refactor it*.

When the goal of a maintenance project is to improve the maintainability of a program without changing its functionality, the process is called refactoring. Because this program has been changed so often, let's start over with a problem statement and a functional decomposition. In a refactoring situation, however, our functional decomposition is done in light of the known solution to the problem. In many cases, the process involves arranging existing statements into encapsulated functions so that the code is easier to understand and to modify.

> **Refactoring** Modifying code to improve its quality without changing its functionality.

PROBLEM STATEMENT: Write a program that calculates the monthly payment for a loan, given the loan amount, the length of the loan in years, and the interest rate either in decimal or percentage form. The input values, the monthly payment, and the total interest paid should be printed on the standard input device.

The loop that we added was based on a loan payment: A negative loan payment ended the processing. We do the same here. The main module can be written from this problem statement with no further discussion.

Main   Level 0

```
Get loan amount
WHILE loan amount is greater than zero
    Get rest of input (interest and number of years)
    Set numberOfPayments to numberOfYears * 12
    Determine payment
    Set totalInterest to payment * numberOfPayments - loanAmount
    Print results
    Get loan amount
```

GetLoanAmt(Out: loanAmount)   Level 1

In the original design, we printed all the prompts together, and printed them all again at the end of the loop. A better design is to separate the prompt for the loan amount from the prompts for the other values, and to issue each kind of prompt just before the respective value is to be read.

```
Print "Input loan amount. A negative loan amount ends the processing."
Read loanAmount
```

SOFTWARE MAINTENANCE CASE STUDY: Refactoring a Program

GetRest(Out: monthlyInterest, numberOfYears) — Level 1

  Get monthlyInterest
  Get Years

GetInterest(Out: monthlyInterest) — Level 2

Remember that the yearly interest can be entered either as a percentage or as a decimal value. The GetInterest module can decide which form was used for input and send the appropriate value back to the calling module.

  Print "Input interest rate. An interest rate of less than 0.25 is assumed to be "
      " a decimal rather than a percentage."
  Read yearlyInterest
  IF (yearlyInterest greater than or equal to 0.25)
    Set yearlyInterest to yearlyInterest / 100
  Set monthlyInterest to yearlyInterest / 12

GetYears(Out: numberOfYears) — Level 2

  Print "Enter number of years of the loan."
  Read numberOfYears

DeterminePayment(Out: payment;
             In: loanAmount, monthlyInterest, numberOfPayments) — Level 1

  Set payment to (loanAmount * pow(1 + monthlyInterest, numberOfPayments)
      * monthlyInterest)/(pow(1 + monthlyInterest, numberOfPayments) - 1);

PrintResults(In: loanAmount, yearlyInterest, numberOfPayments,
           payment, totalInterest) — Level 1

In the original versions, we computed the total amount of interest in the output statement because the calculation was an add-on feature. Here we have put it where it belongs in the main module. However, we leave the conversion of the interest rate to a percentage as part of the output.

  Print "Loan amount: " loanAmount
  Print "Interest rate: " interestRate * 100, "%"
  Print "Number of payments: " numberOfPayments
  Print "Monthly payments: " payment
  Print "Total interest: " totalInterest

SOFTWARE MAINTENANCE CASE STUDY: Refactoring a Program

There are several things to note about this decomposition. First, issuing the prompts when they are needed keeps us from repeating an extra request for the interest rate and length of the loan. Second, one module—GetLoanAmt—is called from two different places in the design. Third, module PrintResults has no formatting information. At the design stage, we can specify what the output should look like, but not how the formatting is done, which is specific to the C++ implementation. If there are specific formatting requirements, they would appear in the problem statement.

MODULE STRUCTURE CHART

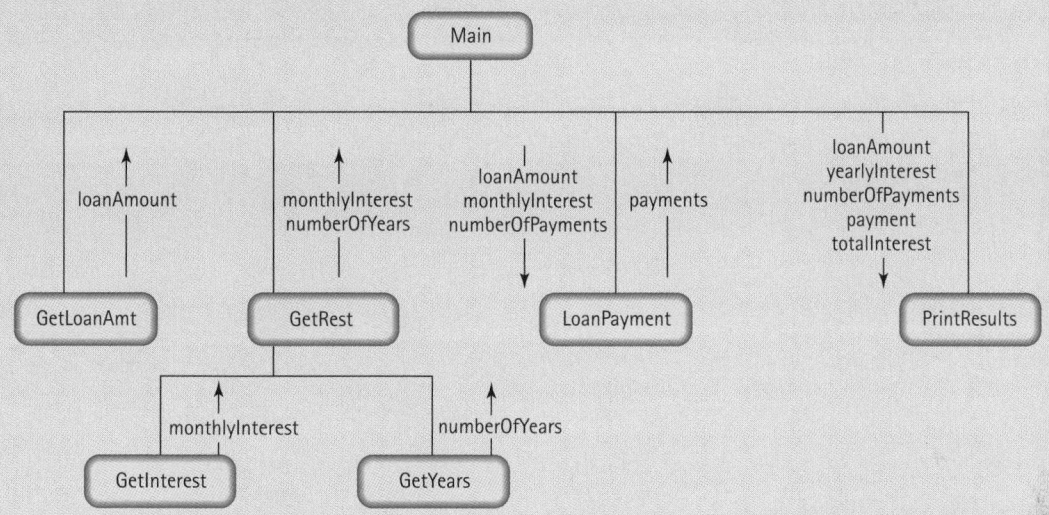

This looks like a very complicated design for such a simple problem. Do we really need to represent each module as a C++ function? The answer depends on your programming style. Some modules definitely should be functions—for example, PrintResults. Other modules probably should not be functions—for example, GetYears. Whether to implement the remaining modules as functions is up to the programmer. As we stated earlier, the key question is whether using a function makes the program easier to understand. "Easier to understand" is open to individual interpretation.

Here, we choose to turn all of the modules except GetYears into functions. Although GetLoanAmt is only two lines long, it is called from two places and, therefore, should be a function. Module DeterminePayment is only one statement long, but it is a complicated statement. It is appropriate to push the formula to a lower level. The reader does not need to know how the payment amount is calculated.

The first step is to create the function prototypes, being sure that all Out and In/out parameters have ampersands attached to the respective data types. Notice that we include the parameter names in the prototypes because our use of meaningful identifiers helps to automatically document what each parameter does.

```
void GetLoanAmt(float& loanAmount)
void GetRest(float& monthlyInterest, int& numberOfYears)
void GetInterest(float& monthlyInterest)
void DeterminePayment(float loanAmount, int yearlyInterest,
                     int numberOfPayments, float& payment)
```

SOFTWARE MAINTENANCE CASE STUDY: Refactoring a Program

We have suggested documenting modules with a descriptive comment beside each parameter, and marking the direction of flow. We do show the direction of flow on each module parameter, but it is necessary to document (comment) a parameter only when the name isn't self-explanatory.

In C++, the absence of an ampersand on the type indicates that its direction of flow is In. If the parameter has an ampersand, it is either an Out or an In/out parameter. Out is more common, so we do not explicitly document this case. When the value is both used and changed, then adding a comment identifying it as In/out would be useful. There is no such example in this problem.

```cpp
//*****************************************************************
// Loan Calculator program
// This program determines the monthly payments on a loan given
// the loan amount, the yearly interest rate, number of years,
// and total interest paid over the period of the loan.
// The process repeats until a negative loan amount is entered.
//*****************************************************************
#include <cmath>
#include <iomanip>
#include <iostream>
using namespace std;

// Function prototypes
void GetLoanAmt(float& loanAmount);
void GetRest(float& monthlyInterest, int& numberOfYears);
void GetInterest(float& monthlyInterest);
void DeterminePayment(float loanAmount, float monthlyInterest,
                     int numberOfPayments, float& payment);
void PrintResults(float loanAmount, float yearlyInterest,
                  int numberOfPayments, float payment,
                  float totalInterest);

int main()
{
  // Variable declarations
  float loanAmount;
  int numberOfYears;
  float monthlyInterest;
  int numberOfPayments;
  float payment;
  float totalInterest;

  // Calculate payments
  GetLoanAmt(loanAmount);
  while (loanAmount > 0)
  {
    GetRest(monthlyInterest, numberOfYears);
    numberOfPayments = numberOfYears * 12;
```

SOFTWARE MAINTENANCE CASE STUDY: Refactoring a Program

```
    DeterminePayment(loanAmount, monthlyInterest,
                     numberOfPayments, payment);
    totalInterest = payment * numberOfPayments - loanAmount;
    PrintResults(loanAmount, monthlyInterest, numberOfPayments,
                 payment, totalInterest);
    GetLoanAmt(loanAmount);
  }

  return 0;
}
//******************************************************************

void GetLoanAmt(float& loanAmount)
{
  cout << "Input loan amount.  "
       << "A negative loan amount ends the processing."
       << endl;
  cin >> loanAmount;
}
//******************************************************************

void GetRest(float& monthlyInterest, int& numberOfYears)
{
  GetInterest(monthlyInterest);
  cout << "Enter the number of years of the loan." << endl;
  cin >> numberOfYears;
}
//******************************************************************

void GetInterest(float& monthlyInterest)
{
  float yearlyInterest;                      // Local variable
  cout << "Input interest rate.  "
       << "An interest rate of less than 0.25 is assumed "
       << " to be a decimal rather than a percent." << endl;
  cin >> yearlyInterest;
  if (yearlyInterest >= 0.25)                // Assume percent entered
    yearlyInterest = yearlyInterest / 100.0;
  monthlyInterest = yearlyInterest / 12;
}
//******************************************************************

void DeterminePayment(float   loanAmount, float   monthlyInterest,
                      int     numberOfPayments, float& payment)
```

SOFTWARE MAINTENANCE CASE STUDY: Refactoring a Program

```cpp
{
  using namespace std;
  payment = (loanAmount * pow(1 + monthlyInterest, numberOfPayments)
          * monthlyInterest)/
          (pow(1 + monthlyInterest, numberOfPayments) - 1);
}

//****************************************************************

void PrintResults(float loanAmount, float yearlyInterest,
                  int numberOfPayments, float payment,
                  float totalInterest)
{
  cout << fixed << "Loan amount:        " << setprecision(2)
       << loanAmount << endl << "Interest rate:      "
       << setprecision(4) << yearlyInterest*100.0 << "%"  << endl
       << "Number of payments: " << numberOfPayments  << endl;
  cout << fixed << "Monthly payments:   " << setprecision(2)
       << payment << endl;
  cout << fixed << "Total Interest:     " << setprecision(2)
       << (payment * numberOfPayments - loanAmount) << endl;
}
```

Sample output:

```
Input loan amount.  A negative loan amount ends the processing.
3000
Input interest rate.  An interest rate of less than 0.25 is assumed to be
a decimal rather than a percent.
6.8
Enter the number of years of the loan.
2
Loan amount:        3000.00
Interest rate:      0.5667%
Number of payments: 24
Monthly payments:   134.05
Total Interest:     217.13
Input loan amount.  A negative loan amount ends the processing.
-1
```

> ### THEORETICAL FOUNDATIONS
> **Argument-Passing Mechanisms**
>
> There are two major ways of passing arguments to and from subprograms. C++ supports both mechanisms. Some languages, such as Java, support just one.
>
> C++ reference parameters employ a mechanism called *pass by address* or *pass by location*, in which a memory address is passed to the function. Another name for this technique is *pass by reference*, so called because the function can refer directly to the caller's variable that is specified in the argument list.
>
> C++ value parameters are an example of the *pass by value* mechanism. The function receives a copy of the value of the caller's argument. Passing by value can be less efficient than passing by address because the value of an argument may occupy many memory locations (as we see in Chapter 11), whereas an address usually occupies only a single location. For the simple data types `int`, `char`, `bool`, and `float`, the efficiency of either mechanism is about the same. Java supports only pass by value, although many of its data types are represented by an address that references the actual information, so in practice it passes arguments with efficiency comparable to C++.
>
> A third method of passing arguments is called *pass by name*. With this mechanism, the argument is passed to the function as a character string that must be interpreted by special run-time support software called a *thunk*. Passing by name is less efficient than the other two argument-passing mechanisms. It is supported by the older ALGOL and LISP programming languages, but not by C++. More recently, a research language called Haskell has implemented a variation of pass by name, called *pass by need*, which remembers the interpretation of the string between calls so that subsequent calls can be more efficient.
>
> There are two different ways of matching arguments with parameters, although C++ supports only one of them. Most programming languages (C++ among them) match arguments and parameters based on their relative positions in the argument and parameter lists. This technique is called *positional matching*, *relative matching*, or *implicit matching*. A few languages, such as Ada, also support *explicit* or *named matching*. In explicit matching, the argument list specifies the name of the parameter to be associated with each argument. Explicit matching allows arguments to be written in any order in the function call. The real advantage is that each call documents precisely which values are being passed to which parameters.

Using Expressions with Parameters

Only a variable should be passed as an argument to a reference parameter because a function can assign a new value to the argument.[5] (In contrast, an arbitrarily complicated expression can be passed to a value parameter.) Suppose that we have a function with the following heading:

```
void DoThis(float val,      // Value parameter
            int&  count)    // Reference parameter
```

---

5. C++ does allow some special cases of expressions that can be arguments to reference parameters, but their definition is beyond the scope of this text.

Then the following function calls are all valid:

```
DoThis(someFloat, someInt);
DoThis(9.83, intCounter);
DoThis(4.9 * sqrt(y), myInt);
```

In the `DoThis` function, the first parameter is a value parameter, so any expression is allowed as the argument. The second parameter is a reference parameter, so the argument *must* be a variable name. The statement

```
DoThis(y, 3);
```

generates a compile-time error because the second argument isn't a variable name. Earlier we said the syntax template for an argument list is

ArgumentList

> Expression , Expression ...

Keep in mind, however, that Expression is restricted to a variable name if the corresponding parameter is a reference parameter.

The following table summarizes the appropriate forms of arguments.

Parameter	Argument
Value parameter	A variable, constant, or arbitrary expression (type coercion may take place)
Reference parameter (**&**)	A variable *only*, of exactly the same data type as the parameter

A Last Word of Caution About Argument and Parameter Lists

It is the programmer's responsibility to make sure that the argument list and parameter list match up semantically as well as syntactically. For example, suppose we had written the modification to the `LoanCalculator` program as follows. Can you spot the error?

```
int main()
{
    .
    .
    .
    GetRest(monthlyInterest, numberOfYears);
    numberOfPayments = numberOfYears * 12;
    DeterminePayment(monthlyInterest, loanAmount,
                     numberOfPayments, payment);
    .
    .
    .
}
```

The argument list in the last function call matches the corresponding parameter list in its number and type of arguments, so no syntax error message would be generated. However, the output would be wrong because the first two arguments are switched. If a function has two parameters of the same data type, you must be careful that the arguments appear in the correct order.

SOFTWARE ENGINEERING TIP   Conceptual Versus Physical Hiding of a Function Implementation

In many programming languages, the encapsulation of an implementation is purely conceptual. If you want to know how a function is implemented, you simply look at the function body. C++, however, permits function implementations to be written and stored separately from `main`.

Larger C++ programs are usually split into separate files. One file might contain just the source for `main`; another file, the source for two functions invoked by `main`; and so on. This organization is called a *multifile program*. To translate the source code into object code, the compiler is invoked for each file. A program called the *linker* then collects all the resulting object code into a single executable program.

When you write a program that invokes a function located in another file, it isn't necessary for that function's source code to be available. You just need to include a function prototype so that the compiler can check the syntax of the call. After the compiler finishes its work, the linker finds the object code for that function and links it with your `main` function's object code. We do this kind of thing all the time when we invoke library functions. C++ systems supply only the object code—not the source code—for library functions like `sqrt`. The source code for their implementations is physically hidden from view.

One advantage of physical hiding is that it helps the programmer avoid the temptation to take advantage of any unusual features of a function's implementation. For example, suppose we want a program to read temperatures and output activities repeatedly. Knowing that the `GetTemp` function that reads the data doesn't perform range checking on the input value, we might be tempted to use −1000 as a sentinel for the loop reading temperatures:

```
int main()
{
  int temperature;

  GetTemp(temperature);
  while (temperature != -1000)
  {
    PrintActivity(temperature);
    GetTemp(temperature);
  }
  return 0;
}
```

> **SOFTWARE ENGINEERING TIP**   Conceptual Versus Physical Hiding of a Function Implementation, continued
>
> This code works fine for now, but later another programmer decides to improve `GetTemp` so that it checks for a valid temperature range (as it should):
>
> ```
> void GetTemp(int& temp)
>
> // This function prompts for and reads a temperature
> // and checks to be sure it is between -50 and 130
>
> {
>   cout << "Enter the outside temperature (-50 through 130): ";
>   cin >> temp;
>   while (temp < 50 || temp > 130))     //   temp is invalid . . .
>   {
>     cout << "Temperature must be"
>          << " -50 through 130." << endl;
>     cout << "Enter the outside temperature: ";
>     cin >> temp;
>   }
> }
> ```
>
> Unfortunately, this improvement causes **main** to become stuck in an infinite loop because `GetTemp` won't let us enter the value –1000. If the original implementation of `GetTemp` had been physically hidden, we would not have relied on the knowledge that it does not perform error checking.

Later in the book, you will learn how to write multifile programs and hide implementations physically. In the meantime, conscientiously avoid writing code that depends on the internal workings of a function.

Writing Assertions as Function Documentation

We have been talking informally about preconditions and postconditions. From now on, we include preconditions and postconditions as comments to document function interfaces. Here's an example:

```
void PrintAverage(float sum
                  int   count)
// Pre:  sum has been assigned and count is greater than 0
// Post: The average has been output on one line
{
  cout <<  "Average is " <<  sum / float(count) << endl;
}
```

The precondition is an assertion describing everything that the function requires to be true at the moment when the caller invokes the function. The postcondition describes the state of the program at the moment when the function finishes executing.

You can think of the precondition and the postcondition as forming a contract. The contract states that if the precondition is true at function entry, then the postcondition must be true at function exit. The *caller* is responsible for ensuring the precondition, and the *function body* must ensure the postcondition. If the caller fails to satisfy its part of the contract (the precondition), the contract is off; the function cannot guarantee that the postcondition will be true.

In the preceding example, the precondition warns the caller to make sure that `sum` has been assigned a meaningful value and that `count` is positive. If this precondition is true, the function guarantees it will satisfy the postcondition. If `count` isn't positive when `PrintAverage` is invoked, the effect of the module is undefined. (For example, if `count` equals 0, the postcondition surely isn't satisfied—any code that implements this module crashes!)

Sometimes the caller doesn't need to satisfy any precondition before calling a function. In this case, the precondition can be written as the value `true` or simply omitted. In the following example, no precondition is necessary:

```
void Get2Ints(int& int1,
              int& int2)
// Post: User has been prompted to enter two integers
//       int1 is the first input value
//       int2 is the second input value
{
  cout << "Please enter two integers: " << endl;
  cin >> int1 >> int2;
}
```

MATTERS OF STYLE   Function Documentation

Preconditions and postconditions, when well written, provide a concise but accurate description of the behavior of a function. A person reading your function should be able to see at a glance how to use the function simply by looking at its interface (the heading and the precondition and postcondition). The reader should never have to look into the function body to understand its purpose or use.

A function interface describes what the function does, not the details of *how* it works its magic. For this reason, the postcondition should mention (by name) each outgoing parameter and its value but should not mention any local variables. Local variables are implementation details; they are irrelevant to the module's interface.

In this book, we write pre/postconditions informally. However, some programmers use a very formal notation to express them. For example, function `Get2Ints` might be documented as follows:

```
// Postcondition:
//    User has been prompted to enter two integers
//    && int1 == first input value
//    && int2 == second input value
```

MATTERS OF STYLE Function Documentation, continued

Some programmers place comments next to the parameters to explain how each parameter is used and use embedded comments to indicate which of the data flow categories each parameter belongs to.

```
Print(/*In*/     float val,    // Value to be printed
      /*In/out*/ int   count)  // Number of lines printed so far
```

To write a postcondition that refers to parameter values that existed at the moment the function was invoked, you can attach the symbol **@entry** to the end of the variable name. An example of the use of this notation follows. The **Swap** function exchanges, or swaps, the contents of its two parameters.

```
void Swap(/*In/out*/ int& firstInt,
          /*In/out*/ int& secondInt)
//Precondition:
//    firstInt and secondInt are assigned
//Postcondition:
//    firstInt == secondInt@entry
// && secondInt == firstInt@entry
{
  int temporaryInt;

  temporaryInt = firstInt;
  firstInt = secondInt;
  secondInt = temporaryInt;
}
```

QUICK CHECK

8.4.1 Why does C++ mostly allow only variables to be passed as an argument to a reference parameter? (p. 371)

8.4.2 Why is it important for a programmer to not only make sure that the argument list and parameter list match up syntactically but also *semantically*? (p. 372)

8.4.3 Which character do we use to indicate a reference parameter, and where does it appear in the parameter's declaration? (pp. 361–365)

8.4.4 Where do arguments appear, and where do parameters appear? (pp. 361–366)

8.4.5 You are writing a function to return the first name from a string containing a full name. How many parameters does the function have, and which of them are reference parameters and which are value parameters? (pp. 361–366)

8.4.6 Which kind of parameter would you use for an incoming value from an argument? For an outgoing value? For a value that comes in, is changed, and returns to the argument? (pp. 361–366)

Problem-Solving Case Study

Lawn Care Company Billing

PROBLEM: A lawn care company has hired you to write a program to help with monthly billing. The company works for each client several times a month. Customers are billed by the number of hours spent on each job. The monthly record for a client consists of a sheet with the client's name, address, and a series of times in hours and minutes. Your program will read this information from a file, print a bill for each client, and output the monthly total and average of the time and charges for the company.

INPUT: A file contains a series of client records. Each client record begins with the customer's name and address. On the following line is a number indicating how many jobs were done for the client that month. Following that number are a series of times, one on each line, made up of a pair of integer values (hours and minutes). The name is written in last, first, middle format, with blanks separating the three parts. An address consists of a street address, a city, a state, and a ZIP code. The street address is on one line, and the city, state, and ZIP code are on the next line, separated by blanks. Here's an example of a client record:

```
Llewelynn Francis Gene
518034 West Elm Street
Cypressville SD 58234
3
1 30
2 15
1 50
```

The input file name may change, so the user should be prompted to enter the input file name.

OUTPUT

- File: A file made up of each client's bill, which contains a labeled echo-print of the input record, the total hours worked, and the payment amount. The output file name may change, so the user must be prompted to enter the output file's name. The file on which the output is based (the input file's name) must be written on the output file.
- Screen: A summary statement showing the monthly total of all charges and the average time and charges for the company.

DISCUSSION: The processing takes place in two parts: producing the client's bill and calculating the summary statistics. The input file doesn't contain the number of records, so the processing must be based on reaching the end-of-file condition. What about the hourly rate? We should ask the user to input the hourly rate at the beginning of each run.

Main   Level 0

Open files
IF files don't open properly
    Print "Error opening files"
    Quit
Get hourly rate
Process Clients
Close files

OpenFiles(In/out: inFile, outFile)   Level 1

Problem-Solving Case Study

We have marked the files as In/out. Although we only read from the input file, it must be marked In/out because the reading pointer in the file changes during the reading process. Likewise, we only write to the output file, but the file itself is input to the module, which then changes the file's contents.

```
Print "Enter the name of the input file."
Read inFileName
Open inFile with inFileName
Print "Enter the name of the output file."
Read outFileName
Open outFile with outFileName
Write on outFile "Billing for clients on file " inFileName
```

GetHourlyRate(Out: hourlyRate) — Level 1

```
Print "Enter hourly rate."
Read hourlyRate
```

ProcessClients(In/out: inFile, outFile; In: hourlyRate) — Level 1

Module ProcessClients reads and processes all the bills. The loop is an end-of-file loop, so we need a priming read before the loop. We read the name before the loop and again at the end of each iteration of the loop. We then print the name as the first step in the loop body. We do not need to keep a running total of the charges, because we can calculate it given the total time and the hourly rate. We do, however, have to keep a count of the number of clients so that we can calculate the averages.

```
Set totalTime to 0
Set numberOfBills to 0
Get name
WHILE inFile
    Write name
    ProcessAClient
    Increment numberOfBills
    Get name
Print results
```

Before we continue with the decomposition, we need to think more about printing the bills. The client's name is written in last, first, middle format on the file. Is it okay to print the bills with the name still in this format? If so, the name can simply be kept as a string; it doesn't have to be broken up into first, last, and middle parts. There is nothing in the instructions that gives us any information about what the format of the name should be on the bill, so we call the customer. She says that any format is fine for the output. Thus modules GetName and WriteName do not need further decomposition.

ProcessAClient(In/out: inFile, outFile, totalTme; In: hourlyWages) — Level 2

Problem-Solving Case Study

The number of jobs follows the client address. This value can be used to control a loop that reads and sums hours and minutes. For calculating purposes, we would prefer to have the time in a form that can be multiplied by the hourly rate. We can convert the time either to a **float**, representing hours and the fraction of an hour, or to an **int**, representing minutes. For calculating the individual charges, it makes no difference which way we represent the time. In summing up the total time, however, it will be more accurate to add up a series of **int** values than **float** values. As we noted in Chapter 5, **float** values can have small errors in their least significant digits. The more of them we add up, the greater this total error will be. Thus we change the time to minutes, divide it by 3600 (the number of minutes in an hour), and multiply that value by the hourly rate. We'll also keep totalTime in minutes. We can convert the minutes back to hours and minutes before printing the final summary.

```
Set time to 0
Read numberOfJobs
Write "Number of jobs: " numberOfJobs
Get Address
Print Address
FOR count going from 1 through numberOfJobs
    Read hours
    Read minutes
    Set time to hours * 60 + minutes + time
Write "Job ", count, ": ", hours, " and ", minutes, " minutes "
Set cost to totalTime / 60 * hourlyRate
Write "Amount of bill: $" cost
Set totalTime to totalTime + time
```

The address is formatted in the file as it should be on the bill, so the address can just be written to the output file as it is read. Thus GetAddress and WriteAddress should be combined into one module.

GetAndPrintAddress(In/out: inFile, outFile) — Level 3

```
Read street line
Write street line
Read city line
Write city line
```

PrintResults(In: numberOfBills, totalMinutes) — Level 2

```
Print "Total amount billed this month is " totalMinutes/60 * hourlyRate
Print "Average time worked per job is " totalMinutes / numberOfBills / 60
Print "Average customer bill is " totalMinutes/60 * hourlyRate / numberOfBills
```

Problem-Solving Case Study

```
                          Main
         ┌──────────┬──────────┬──────────┐
     OpenFiles  Get Hourly  Process    CloseFiles
                   Rate      Clients
                    ┌──────────┬──────────┬──────────┐
                Write Name  Process A  Get Name   Print Results
                             Client
                                │
                           Get And Print
                              Address
```

The only module that is simple enough to code directly is GetHourlyRate. All of the other modules should be coded as functions. However, before we start to code these functions, we need to consider whether any problems might come up in the translation from pseudocode to C++. Two popular places where errors often lurk are complex input and mixed-mode arithmetic; both occur here.

Let's first look at the input, which occurs across several modules. The following table shows the variables in the order in which they are read, the function in which the reads occur, the types of input statement to use, and the positions in which the reads leave the file. Recall that the stream input operator (>>) cannot be used with strings that might contain blanks.

Variable	Module	Operator Used	Position of the Reading Pointer
`hourlyRate`	Main	`>>`	Only item read from keyboard
`name`	ProcessClients	`getline`	Pointer left at next line
`address` (two lines)	GetAndPrintAddress	`getline`	Pointer left at line following address
`numberOfJobs`	ProcessAClient	`>>`	Pointer left on same line
`hours`, `minutes`	ProcessAClient	`>>`	Pointer left on same line
`name`	ProcessClients	`getline`	Pointer left at next line

We input `hourlyRate` from the keyboard, and the remaining input comes from the file. The name and address (two lines) are read, leaving the file pointer positioned at the beginning of the line following the address, ready to read the integer `numberOfJobs`. The three integer values (`numberOfJobs`, `hours`, and `minutes`) are read, skipping any extra blanks or lines that might be there. There is, however, a problem. Look at where the input operator leaves the file pointer after the last numeric read: at the blank or end of line (eoln) that ended the numeric read. Thus the input statement that should read the name reads the eoln and stores it into **name**. How can we get around this problem? We issue a `getline` command immediately after the minutes are read. This moves the file pointer to the beginning of the next line.

What about mixed-mode arithmetic? Let's examine the variables, their types, and the expressions in which they occur. Here is a table listing the variables, the places where they are declared, and their data types.

Variable	Location Declared	Type
hourlyRate	main	float
totalTime	ProcessClients	int
time	ProcessAClient	int
hours	ProcessAClient	int
minutes	ProcessAClient	int
cost	ProcessAClient	float
numberOfJobs	ProcessAClient	int

Now let's look at the types of the variables in the context of the expressions in which they are used. We show each expression rewritten as a comment where we've replaced the variable names with their types. Here's **ProcessAClient**:

```
ProcessAClient(...totalTime, hourlyRate)
  time = hours * 60 + minutes + time;     // int=int*int+int+int
  cost = time / 60 * hourlyRate;          // float=int/int*float
  totalTime = totalTime + time;           // int=int+int
```

The calculations of **time** and **totalTime** are okay, but the calculation of **cost** will give the wrong answer. The first **int** value (**time**) must be cast to a **float** for the calculations to be accurate. We should also change the **int** constant 60 to the **float** constant 60.0.

Next we look at **PrintResults**:

```
PrintResults(numberOfBills, totalMinutes, hourlyRate)
  cout << "Total amount billed this month is "
       << totalMinutes / 60 *  hourlyRate << endl;
      // int/int*float
  cout << "Average time worked per job is "
       << totalMinutes / numberOfBills / 60 << endl;
      // int/int/int
  cout << "Average customer bill is "
       << totalMinutes / 60 * hourlyRate / numberOfBills
      // int/int*float/int
       << endl;
```

There are problems in all three of these expressions. For starters, **totalMinutes** is an **int** parameter. The first statement in the function should declare a local **float** variable and set it to the argument cast as a **float**. The expressions should all be written using this local variable. We should also use 60.0 instead of 60, and explicitly cast **numberOfBills** to **float**.

Problem-Solving Case Study

Now the modules can be converted to C++ and the program tested. If we had not looked at these two possible problem areas in advance, we would have spent much time trying to decipher why the output was wrong. Here is the code:

```cpp
//****************************************************************
// Program LawnCare calculates and writes the bills for a lawn care
// service company.  The names of the input and output files are
// prompted for and read from the keyboard.
//****************************************************************
#include <iostream>
#include <fstream>
#include <string>
#include <iomanip>

using namespace std;

// Function prototypes
void OpenFiles(ifstream& inFile, ofstream& outFile);
// OpenFiles reads in the names of the input file and the
// output file and opens them for processing
void ProcessClients(ifstream& inFile, ofstream& outFile,
                    float hourlyRate);
// ProcessClients writes bills for all of the clients
// whose records are on inFile
void ProcessAClient(ifstream& inFile, ofstream& outFile,
                    int& totalTime,  float hourlyRate);
// ProcessAClient writes the bill for one client
void GetAndPrintAddress(ifstream& inFile, ofstream& outFile);
// GetAndPrintAddress reads the address from inFile and
// prints it on outFile
void PrintResults(int numberOfBills, int totalMinutes,
                  float hourlyRate);
// PrintRest prints total billed, average time per job,
// and average bill

int main ()
{
  float hourlyRate;
  ifstream inFile;
  ofstream outFile;
  OpenFiles(inFile, outFile);
  if (!inFile || !outFile)
  {
    cout << "Error opening files " << endl;
    return 1;
  }
  cout << "Enter hourly rate." << endl;
  cin >> hourlyRate;
  ProcessClients(inFile, outFile, hourlyRate);
  inFile.close();
  outFile.close();
  return 0;
}
```

Problem-Solving Case Study

```
//******************************************************************

void OpenFiles(ifstream& inFile, ofstream& outFile)
// Post: Files have been opened and filesOK reflects the result
//       of the opening process
{
  string inFileName;      // User-specified input file name
  string outFileName;     // User-specified output file name
  cout << "Enter the name of the input file." << endl;
  cin >> inFileName;
  inFile.open(inFileName.c_str());

  cout << "Enter the name of the output file." << endl;
  cin >> outFileName;
  outFile.open(outFileName.c_str());
  outFile << "Billing for clients on file " << inFileName << endl;
  outFile << fixed;
}

//******************************************************************

void ProcessClients(ifstream& inFile, ofstream& outFile,
                    float hourlyRate)
// Pre:  Files have been opened and the hourly rate has been set
// Post: Each bill has been written and the summary values have
//       been written to the screen
{
  int totalTime = 0;
  int numberOfBills = 0;
  string name;
  getline(inFile, name);
  while (inFile)
  {
    outFile << name << endl;
    ProcessAClient(inFile, outFile, totalTime, hourlyRate);
    numberOfBills++;
    getline(inFile, name);
  }
  // Print summary information
  PrintResults(numberOfBills, totalTime, hourlyRate);
}

//******************************************************************

void PrintResults(int numberOfBills, int totalMinutes,
                  float hourlyRate)
// Pre:  number of bills and total minutes have been calculated
// Post: total billing and average time and bill have been printed
{
  float minutes = static_cast<float>(totalMinutes);
  cout << "Total amount billed this month is "
       << minutes / 60.0 * hourlyRate << endl;
```

Problem-Solving Case Study

```
    cout << "Average time worked per job is "
         << minutes / float(numberOfBills) / 60.0 << endl;
    cout << "Average customer bill is "
         << minutes / 60.0 * hourlyRate / float(numberOfBills) << endl;
}

//*****************************************************************

void GetAndPrintAddress(ifstream& inFile, ofstream& outFile)
// Pre:  files have been opened and name has been read
// Post: address has been read from inFile and
//       written on outFile
{
    string line;
    getline(inFile, line);      // Process street line
    outFile << line << endl;
    getline(inFile, line);      // Process city line
    outFile << line << endl << endl;
}

//*****************************************************************

void ProcessAClient(ifstream& inFile, ofstream& outFile,
                    int& totalTime,  float hourlyRate)
// Pre:  Files have been opened, totalTime is total minutes
//       billed so far, and hourlyRate has been set
// Post: Bill has been written on outFile
{
    int time = 0;
    int hours;
    int minutes;
    float cost;
    int numberOfJobs;
    // Process
    GetAndPrintAddress(inFile, outFile);
    inFile >> numberOfJobs;
    outFile << "Number of jobs: " << numberOfJobs << endl;
    for (int count = 1; count <= numberOfJobs; count++)
    {
        inFile >> hours >> minutes;
        time = hours * 60 + minutes + time;
        outFile << "Job " << count << ": " << hours << " hours and "
                << minutes << " minutes " << endl;
    }
    cost = static_cast<float>(time) / 60.0 * hourlyRate;
    totalTime = totalTime + time;

    outFile << "Amount of bill: $" << setprecision(2) << cost
            << endl << endl;
    string skip;
    getline(inFile, skip);
}
```

Problem-Solving Case Study

TESTING: Devising a test plan for this program brings up an interesting question: Whose responsibility is it to check for errors in the input file? That is, should the application program include tests to confirm that the input file is correctly formatted or should a correctly formatted file be a precondition for the program? In this case, we included no tests for formatting because the billing program is given a task to process a file with a certain format. If we had decided to include some checks, how would the program recognize errors? For example, how would the application recognize that an address contains only one line? It might check that the second line of the address contains both numbers and letters—but what if the name line is missing? And if the program did check for correct formatting, what should it do in the case of errors? When checking the formatting of the input becomes more complicated than the required calculations, make the correct format a precondition.

Given that the program assumes correct input, which cases do we need to check for during testing? In testing the `LawnCare` application we need to have customers who have no jobs, one job, and more than one job. We also need runs with no customers, one customer, and more than one customer.

The following input file contains multiple customers with varying numbers of jobs. You are asked to test the program with no customers and one customer in the Case Study Follow-Up exercises.

Input File `LawnCare.txt`

```
Davis Allan James
223 Red Wing Terrace
Altamont WY 67606
5
1 45
2 0
0 30
1 30
2 50
Soucy Steven Carl
12 Wildblossom Court
Englebrook WY 67628
1
8 45
Castor Julia Maude
18472 East Main Street
Egremont WY 67624
4
1 30
1 30
1 30
1 30
Marengoni Christina Louise
25 Pomegranate Loop
Egremont WY 67624
0
```

Problem-Solving Case Study

Output File `Lawn.out`

```
Billing for clients on file LawnCare.txt
Davis Allan James
223 Red Wing Terrace
Altamont WY 67606

Number of jobs: 5
Job 1: 1 hours and 45 minutes
Job 2: 2 hours and 0 minutes
Job 3: 0 hours and 30 minutes
Job 4: 1 hours and 30 minutes
Job 5: 2 hours and 50 minutes
Amount of bill: $300.42

Soucy Steven Carl
12 Wildblossom Court
Englebrook WY 67628

Number of jobs: 1
Job 1: 8 hours and 45 minutes
Amount of bill: $306.25

Castor Julia Maude
18472 East Main Street
Egremont WY 67624

Number of jobs: 4
Job 1: 1 hours and 30 minutes
Job 2: 1 hours and 30 minutes
Job 3: 1 hours and 30 minutes
Job 4: 1 hours and 30 minutes
Amount of bill: $210.00

Marengoni Christina Louise
25 Pomegranate Loop
Egremont WY 67624

Number of jobs: 0
Amount of bill: $0.00
```

Testing and Debugging

The parameters declared by a function and the arguments that are passed to the function by the caller must satisfy the interface to the function. Errors that occur with the use of functions often are due to incorrect use of the interface between the calling code and the called function.

One source of errors is mismatched argument and parameter lists. The C++ compiler ensures that the lists have the same number of items and that they are compatible in type. It is the programmer's responsibility, however, to verify that each argument list contains the correct items. This task is a matter of comparing the parameter declarations to the argument list in every call to the function. This job becomes much easier if the function heading gives each parameter a distinct name and further describes its purpose in a comment, if necessary. You can avoid mistakes in writing an argument list by using descriptive variable names in the calling code to suggest exactly which information is being passed to the function.

Another source of errors is failure to ensure that the precondition for a function is met before it is called. For example, if a function assumes that the input file is not at EOF when it is called, then the calling code must ensure that this assumption holds before making the call to the function. If a function behaves incorrectly, review its precondition, then trace the program execution up to the point of the call to verify the precondition. You can waste a lot of time trying to locate an error in a correct function when the error is really in the part of the program prior to the call.

If the arguments match the parameters and the precondition is correctly established, then the source of the error is most likely in the function itself. Trace the function to verify that it transforms the precondition into the proper postcondition. Determine whether all local variables are initialized properly. Parameters that are supposed to return data to the caller must be declared as reference parameters (with an **&** symbol attached to the data type name).

An important technique for debugging a function is to use your system's debugger, if one is available, to step through the execution of the function. If a debugger is not available, you can insert debug output statements to print the values of the arguments immediately before and after calls to the function. It also may help to print the values of all local variables at the end of the function. This information provides a snapshot of the function (a picture of its status at a particular moment in time) at its two most critical points, which is useful in verifying hand traces.

To test a function thoroughly, you must arrange the incoming values so that the precondition is pushed to its limits; then the postcondition must be verified. For example, if a function requires a parameter to be within a certain range, try calling the function with values in the middle of that range and at its extremes.

The `assert` Library Function

We have discussed how function preconditions and postconditions are useful for debugging (by checking that the precondition of each function is true prior to a function call, and by verifying that each function correctly transforms the precondition into the postcondition) and for testing (by pushing the precondition to its limits and even violating it). To state the preconditions and postconditions for our functions, we've been writing the assertions as program comments:

```
// Pre: studentCount > 0
```

Of course, the compiler ignores all comments. They are not executable statements; they are for humans to examine.

The C++ standard library also gives us a way to write *executable assertions*. Through the header file `cassert`, the library provides a void function named `assert`. This function takes a logical (Boolean) expression as an argument and halts the program if the expression is `false`. Here's an example:

```
#include <cassert>
    ⋮
assert(studentCount > 0);
average = sumOfScores / studentCount;
```

The argument to the `assert` function must be a valid C++ logical expression. If its value is `true`, nothing happens; execution continues on to the next statement. If its value is `false`, execution of the program terminates immediately with a message stating (1) the assertion as it appears in the argument list, (2) the name of the file containing the program source code, and (3) the line number in the program. In the preceding example, if the value of `studentCount` is less than or equal to 0, the program halts after printing a message like this:

```
Assertion failed: studentCount > 0, file myprog.cpp, line 48
```

(This message is potentially confusing. It doesn't mean that `studentCount` *is* greater than 0. In fact, it's just the opposite. The message tells you that the assertion `studentCount > 0` is *false*.)

Executable assertions have a profound advantage over assertions expressed as comments: The effect of a false assertion is highly visible (the program terminates with an error message). The `assert` function is, therefore, valuable in software testing. A program under development might be filled with calls to the `assert` function to help identify where errors are occurring. If an assertion is false, the error message gives the precise line number of the failed assertion.

There is also a way to "remove" the assertions without really removing them. Suppose you use the preprocessor directive `#define NDEBUG` before including the header file `cassert`, like this:

```
#define NDEBUG
#include <cassert>
    ⋮
```

Then all calls to the `assert` function are ignored when you run the program. (`NDEBUG` stands for "No debug," and a `#define` directive is a preprocessor feature that we won't discuss right now.) After program testing and debugging, programmers often like to "turn off" debugging statements yet leave them physically present in the source code in case they might need the statements later. Inserting the line `#define NDEBUG` turns off assertion checking without having to remove the assertions.

As useful as the `assert` function is, it has two limitations. First, the argument to the function must be expressed as a C++ logical expression. We can turn a comment such as

```
//    yearlyInterest is greater than 0.0 AND
//    numberOfYears is less than or equal to 30
```

into an executable assertion with the following statement:

```
assert(0.0 <= yearlyInterest && numberOfYears <= 30);
```

Conversely, there is no easy way to turn the comment

```
//   The file contains a loan amount,
//   interest rate, and number of years
```

into a C++ logical expression.

The second limitation is that the `assert` function is appropriate only for testing a program that is under development. A production program (one that has been completed and released to the public) must be robust and must furnish helpful error messages to the user of the program. You can imagine how baffled a user would be if the program suddenly quit and displayed an error message such as this:

`Assertion failed: sysRes <= resCount, file newproj.cpp, line 298`

Despite these limitations, you should consider using the `assert` function as a regular tool for testing and debugging your programs.

Testing and Debugging Hints

1. Follow documentation guidelines carefully when writing functions (see Appendix F). As your programs become more complex and, therefore, prone to errors, it becomes increasingly important to adhere to documentation and formatting standards. Include comments that state the function precondition (if any) and postcondition and that explain the purposes of all parameters and local variables whose roles are not obvious.
2. Provide a function prototype near the top of your program for each function you've written. Make sure that the prototype and its corresponding function heading are an exact match (except for the absence of parameter names in the prototype).
3. Be sure to put a semicolon at the end of a function prototype, but do not put a semicolon at the end of the function heading in a function definition. Because function prototypes look so much like function headings, it's a common mistake to get one of them wrong.
4. Make sure the parameter list gives the data type of each parameter.
5. Use value parameters unless a result is to be returned through a parameter. Reference parameters can change the contents of the caller's argument; value parameters cannot. However, file names must be reference parameters.
6. In a parameter list, make sure the data type of each reference parameter ends with an ampersand (`&`). Without the ampersand, the parameter is a value parameter.
7. Make sure that the argument list of every function call matches the parameter list in terms of number and order of items, and be very careful with their data types. The compiler will trap any mismatch in the number of arguments. If a mismatch in data types occurs, however, there may be no compile-time error message generated. Specifically, with the pass by value mechanism, a type mismatch can lead to implicit type coercion rather than a compile-time error.
8. Remember that an argument matching a reference parameter must be a variable, whereas an argument matching a value parameter can be any expression that supplies a value of the same data type (except as noted above in Hint 7).
9. Become familiar with all the tools available to you when you're trying to locate the sources of errors—the algorithm walk-through, hand tracing, the system's debugger program, the `assert` function, and debug output statements.

Summary

C++ allows us to write programs in modules expressed as functions. The structure of a program, therefore, can parallel its functional decomposition even when the program is complicated. To make your `main` function look exactly like Level 0 of your functional decomposition, simply write each lower-level module as a function. The `main` function then executes these other functions in logical sequence.

Functions communicate by means of two lists: the parameter list (which specifies the data type of each identifier) in the function heading, and the argument list in the calling code. The items in these lists must agree in number and position, and they should agree in data type.

Part of the functional decomposition process involves determining which data must be received by a lower-level module and which information must be returned from it. The names of these data items, together with the precondition and postcondition of a module, define its interface. The names of the data items become the parameter list, and the module name becomes the name of the function. With void functions, a call to the function is accomplished by writing the function's name as a statement, enclosing the appropriate arguments in parentheses.

C++ supports two kinds of parameters: reference and value. Reference parameters have data types ending in `&` in the parameter list, whereas value parameters do not. Parameters that return values from a function must be reference parameters. All others should be value parameters. This practice minimizes the risk of errors, because only a copy of the value of an argument is passed to a value parameter, which protects the argument from change.

In addition to the variables declared in its parameter list, a function may have local variables declared within it. These variables are accessible only within the block in which they are declared. Local variables must be initialized each time the function containing them is called because their values are destroyed when the function returns.

You may call functions from more than one place in a program. The positional matching mechanism allows the use of different variables as arguments to the same function. Multiple calls to a function, from different places and with different arguments, can simplify greatly the coding of many complex programs.

Quick Check Answers

8.1.1 Modules. **8.1.2** You code the module once, placing it, or its prototype, before any reference to it in the rest of the program. You then call the module from each place in the program that corresponds to its appearance in the functional decomposition. **8.1.3** 1. Incoming values, 2. Outgoing values, 3. Incoming/outgoing values. **8.1.4** interface
8.1.5 `void PrintName()`
```
{
    cout << "Tim" << endl;
}
```
8.2.1 To the first statement in that function's body, with its remaining statements executed in logical order. **8.2.2** To the statement immediately following the function call. **8.2.3** An argument is a variable or expression listed in a call to a function, whereas a parameter is a variable declared in a function heading. **8.2.4** Arguments and parameters are matched by their relative ordering in the two lists. **8.3.1** They must be declared before they are used, so they appear before `main`. However, the declaration may simply be a function prototype and the actual definition can then appear anywhere. **8.3.2** Only the statements within the block, following the declaration. **8.3.3** A function declaration without the body of the function. **8.3.4** They allow you to declare a function before they are defined so that we can arrange function definitions in any order. **8.3.5** `void UpdateRace(int, float);` **8.3.6** local variable **8.4.1** Because a function can assign a new value to the argument. **8.4.2** Because a function could possibly have two or more parameters of the same data type. **8.4.3** The `&` character appears at the end of the type name of the parameter. **8.4.4** Arguments appear in function calls; parameters appear in function headings. **8.4.5** It should have two parameters, one for each string. The full name parameter should be a value parameter,

and the first name parameter should be a reference parameter. **8.4.6** Incoming values use value parameters. Values that return to the argument (Out or In/out) must be passed through reference parameters.

Exam Preparation Exercises

1. What three things distinguish a void function from `main`?
2. A function prototype must specify the name of a function and the name and type of each of its parameters. True or false?
3. When and to where does control return from a void function?
4. Match the following terms with the definitions given below.
    a. Argument
    b. Parameter
    c. Function call
    d. Function prototype
    e. Function definition
    f. Local variable
    g. Value parameter
    h. Reference parameter
        i. A function declaration without a body.
        ii. A parameter that receives a copy of the argument's value.
        iii. A variable declared in a function heading.
        iv. A function declaration with a body.
        v. A variable or expression listed in a call to a function.
        vi. A statement that transfers control to a function.
        vii. A parameter that receives the location of the argument.
        viii. A variable declared within a block.
5. In the following function heading, which parameters are value parameters and which are reference parameters?

    ```
    void ExamPrep (string& name, int age, float& salary, char level)
    ```

6. If a function has six parameters, how many arguments must appear in a call to the function?
7. What happens if a function assigns a new value to a value parameter? What happens if it assigns a new value to a reference parameter?
8. What's wrong with this function prototype?

    ```
    void ExamPrep (phone& int, name string, age& int)
    ```

9. Arguments can appear in any order as long as they have the correct types and C++ will figure out the correspondence. True or false?
10. Define encapsulation.
11. For which direction(s) of data flow do you use reference parameters?
12. What is wrong with the following function?

    ```
    void Square (int& x)
    {
      x = x * x;
      return 0;
    }
    ```

13. What is wrong with the following function?

    ```
    void Power (int x, int y)
    {
      int result;
      result = 1;
      while (y > 0)
      {
        result = result * x;
        y--;
      }
    }
    ```

14. What is wrong with the following function?

    ```
    void Power (int x, int y, int result)
    {
      result = 1;
      while (y > 0)
      {
        result = result * x;
        y--;
      }
    }
    ```

15. What is wrong with the following function?

    ```
    void Power (int& x, int& y, int& result)
    {
      result = 1;
      while (y > 0)
      {
        result = result * x;
        y--;
      }
    }
    ```

16. A local variable can be referenced anywhere within the block in which it is declared. True or false?
17. Functions can be called from other functions in addition to `main`. True or false?
18. What would be the precondition for a function that reads a file of integers and returns their mean?

Programming Warm-Up Exercises

1. Write the heading for a void function called `Max` that has three `int` parameters: `num1`, `num2`, and `greatest`. The first two parameters receive data from the caller, and `greatest` returns a value. Document the data flow of the parameters with appropriate comments.
2. Write the function prototype for the function in Exercise 1.
3. Write the function definition of the function in Exercise 1 so that it returns the greatest of the two input parameters.
4. Write the heading for a void function called `GetLeast` that takes an `ifstream` parameter called `infile` as an input parameter that is changed, and that has an `int` parameter

called `lowest` that returns a value. Document the data flow of the parameters with appropriate comments.

5. Write the function prototype for the function in Exercise 4.
6. Write the function definition for the function in Exercise 4 so that it reads all of `infile` as a series of `int` values and returns the lowest integer input from `infile`.
7. Add comments to the function definition you wrote in Exercise 6 that state its precondition and postcondition.
8. Write the heading for a function called `Reverse` that takes two string parameters. In the second parameter, the function returns a string that is the character-by-character reverse of the string in the first parameter. The parameters are called `original` and `lanigiro`. Document the data flow of the parameters with appropriate comments.
9. Write the function prototype for the function in Exercise 8.
10. Write the function definition for the function in Exercise 8.
11. Add comments to the function definition you wrote in Exercise 10 that state its precondition and postcondition.
12. Write a void function called `LowerCount` that reads a line from `cin`, and that returns an `int` (`count`) containing the number of lowercase letters in the line. In Appendix C, you will find the description of function `islower`, which returns `true` if its `char` parameter is a lowercase character. Document the data flow of the parameters with appropriate comments.
13. Add comments to the function definition you wrote in Exercise 12 that state its precondition and postcondition.
14. Write a void function called `GetNonemptyLine` that takes an `ifstream` (`infile`) as an In/out parameter, and that reads lines from the file until it finds a line that contains characters. It should then return the line via a `string` parameter called `line`. Document the data flow of the parameters with appropriate comments.
15. Write a void function called `SkipToEmptyLine` that takes an `ifstream` (`infile`) as an In/out parameter, and that reads lines from the file until it finds a line that contains no characters. It should then return the number of lines skipped via an `int` parameter called `skipped`. Document the data flow of the parameters with appropriate comments.
16. Write a void function called `TimeAdd` that takes parameters representing two times in days, hours, and minutes, and then adds those parameters to get a new time. Each part of the time is an `int`. Hours range from 0 to 23, while minutes range from 0 to 59. There is no limit on the range of days. We assume that the time to be added is positive. The values in the parameters representing the first time are replaced by the result of adding the two times.

    Here is an example call in which 3 days, 17 hours, and 49 minutes is added to 12 days, 22 hours, and 14 minutes:

    ```
    days = 12;
    hours = 22;
    minutes = 14;
    TimeAdd(days, hours, minutes, 3, 17, 49)
    ```

    After the call, the values in the variables are as follows:

    ```
    days = 16
    hours = 16
    minutes = 3
    ```

17. Extend function `TimeAdd` in Exercise 16 to include seconds.
18. Write a void function called `SeasonPrint` that takes `int` parameters representing a month and a day and that outputs to `cout` the name of the season. For the purposes of this exercise, spring begins on March 21, summer begins June 21, fall begins September 21, and winter begins December 21. Note that the year begins and ends during winter. The function can assume that the values in the `month` and `day` parameters have been validated before it is called.

Programming Problems

1. Write a C++ program that computes student grades for an assignment as a percentage given each student's score and the total points. The final score should be rounded up to the nearest whole value using the `ceil` function in the `<cmath>` header file. You should also display the floating-point result up to 5 decimal places. You should have a function to print the last name of the student and another function to compute and print the percentage as well as "Excellent" if the grade is greater than 90, "Well Done" if the grade is greater than 80, "Good" if the grade is greater than 70, "Need Improvement" if the grade is greater than or equal to 60, and "Fail" if the grade is less than 50. The main function is responsible for reading the input file and passing the appropriate arguments to your functions. Here is an example of what the input file might look like:

```
Weems 50 60
Dale 51 60
Richards 57 60
Smith 36 60
Tomlin 44 60
Bird 45 60
...
```

The output of your program should look like this:

```
Weems 83% .83333 Well Done
Dale 85% .85000 Well Done
Richards 95% .95000 Excellent
Smith 60% .60000 Need Improvement
Tomlin 73% .73333 Good
Bird 75% .75000 Good
...
```

2. ROT13 (rotate by 13 places) is a simple letter substitution cipher that is an instance of a Caesar cipher developed in ancient Rome and used by Julius Caesar who used it in his private correspondence. ROT13 replaces a letter with the letter 13 letters after it in the alphabet. The following table demonstrates the translation in ROT13:

A	↔	N
B	↔	O
C	↔	P
D	↔	Q
E	↔	R
F	↔	S
G	↔	T
H	↔	U

I ↔ V
J ↔ W
K ↔ X
L ↔ Y
M ↔ Z

Thus, the translation of the word JULIUS using ROT13 would be WHYVHF. Write a C++ program that asks the user for the name of an input file and translates the contents of that input file using ROT13. Your `main` function should be responsible for reading the input file and coordinating calls to a function named `Rot13` that will do the translation for each character and `WriteTranslatedChar` that will write the translated character to a secondary file. The `Rot13` function should be defined with a reference parameter that will be the initial character as input and the translated character as output. The second function named `WriteTranslatedChar` will have two parameters, the translated character and a reference to an `ifstream` data type for a secondary file named "`output.rot13`", and write that translated character to this file.

3. In mathematics, the Fibonacci numbers are the series of numbers that exhibit the following pattern:

   0, 1, 1, 2, 3, 5, 8, 13, 21, 34, 55, 89, 144, ...

   In mathematical notation the sequence F_n of Fibonacci numbers is defined by the following recurrence relation:

   $F_n = F_{n-1} + F_{n-2}$

   With the initial values of $F_0 = 0$ and $F_1 = 1$. Thus, the next number in the series is the sum of the previous two numbers. Write a program that asks the user for a positive integer N and generates the Nth Fibonacci number. Your main function should handle user input and pass that data to a function called Fib that takes an integer value N as input and a reference parameter that is assigned the Nth Fibonacci number.

4. Consider the following maze:

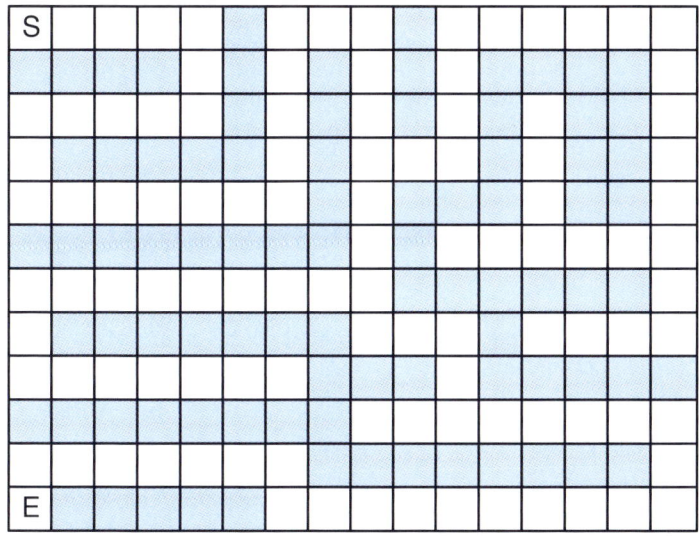

The maze begins at S and ends at E. We represent the current position in the maze using two integer variables named posX and posY. The starting location (S) is thus represented as posX = 0 and posY = 0. Movement through the maze is defined by the following rules:

1. MoveRight(spaces): posY = posY + spaces
2. MoveLeft(spaces): posY = posY − spaces
3. MoveDown(spaces): posX = posX + spaces
4. MoveUp(spaces): posX = posX − spaces

Define functions for each of the above rules such that each function has an integer reference parameter. Use these function declarations to write a C++ program that defines posX and posY, initialized to 0, and the corresponding calls to your functions that will correctly move your position in the maze from S to E ending at posX = 0, posY = 11. Print out the value of posX and posY after each function call.

5. Rewrite the program from Programming Problem 3 of Chapter 6 using functions. The program is to print a bar chart of the hourly temperatures for one day, given the data on a file. You should have a function to print the chart's heading, and another function that prints the bar of stars for a given temperature value. Note that the second function does not print the value to the left of the bar graph. The main program coordinates the process of inputting values and calling these functions as necessary. Now that your programs are becoming more complex, it is even more important for you to use proper indentation and style, meaningful identifiers, and appropriate comments.

6. You're working for a company that lays ceramic floor tile, and its employees need a program that estimates the number of boxes of tile for a job. A job is estimated by taking the dimensions of each room in feet and inches, and converting these dimensions into a multiple of the tile size (rounding up any partial multiple) before multiplying to get the number of tiles for the room. A box contains 20 tiles, so the total number needed should be divided by 20 and rounded up to get the number of boxes. The tiles are assumed to be square.

The program should initially prompt the user for the size of the tile in inches and the number of rooms to be covered with tile. It should then input the dimensions for each room and output the number of tiles needed for that room. After data for the last room is input, the program should output the total number of tiles needed, the number of boxes of tile needed, and how many extra tiles will be left over.

Here is an example of how a run might appear:

```
Enter number of rooms: 2
Enter size of tile in inches: 12
Enter room width (feet and inches, separated by a space): 17 4
Enter room length (feet and inches, separated by a space): 9 3
Room requires 180 tiles.
Enter room width (feet and inches, separated by a space): 11 6
Enter room length (feet and inches, separated by a space): 11 9
Room requires 144 tiles.
Total tiles required is 324.
Number of boxes needed is 17.
There will be 16 extra tiles.
```

Use functional decomposition to solve this problem, and code the solution using functions wherever it makes sense to do so. Your program should check for invalid data such as nonpositive dimensions, number of rooms less than 1, number of inches greater than 11, and so on. It should prompt the user for corrected input whenever it detects invalid input. Now that your programs are becoming more complex, it is even more important for you to use proper indentation and style, meaningful identifiers, and appropriate comments.

7. Programming Problem 8 in Chapter 5 asked you to write a program to compute the score for one frame in a game of tenpin bowling. In this exercise, you will extend this algorithm to compute the score for an entire game for one player. A game consists of 10 frames, but the tenth frame has some special cases that were not described in Chapter 5.

    A frame is played by first setting up the 10 pins. The player then rolls the ball to knock them down. If all 10 are knocked down on the first throw, it is called a strike, and the frame is over. If fewer than 10 are knocked down on the first throw, the number knocked down is recorded and the player gets a second throw. If the remaining pins are all knocked down on the second throw, it is called a spare. The frame ends after the second throw, even if there are pins left standing. If the second throw fails to knock all of the pins down, then the number that it knocked down is recorded, and the score for the frame is just the number of pins knocked down by the two throws. However, in the case of a strike or a spare, the score for the frame depends on throws in the next frame and possibly the frame after that.

    If the frame is a strike, then the score is equal to 10 points plus the number of pins knocked down in the next two throws. Thus the maximum score for a frame is 30, which occurs when the frame is a strike and the two following frames are also strikes. If the frame is a spare, then the score is those 10 points plus the number of pins knocked down on the next throw.

    The last frame is played somewhat differently. If the player gets a strike, then he or she gets two more throws so that the score for the strike can be computed. Similarly, if it is a spare, then one extra throw is given. If the first two throws fail to knock down all of the pins, then the score for the last frame is just the number knocked down, and there is no extra throw. Here is an example of how the I/O might appear for the start of a run:

```
Enter throw for frame 1: 10
Strike!
Enter throw for frame 2: 7
Enter throw for frame 2: 3
Spare!
Score for frame 1 is 20. Total is 20.
Enter throw for frame 3: 5
Score for frame 2 is 15. Total is 35.
Enter throw for frame 3: 2
Score for frame 3 is 7. Total is 42.
Enter score for frame 4: 12
Input error. Please enter number of pins in range of 0 to 10.
Enter score for frame 4:
```

Your program should take as input the number of pins knocked down by each throw, and output the score for each frame as it is computed. The program must recognize when a frame has ended (due to either a strike or a second throw). The program also should check for erroneous input. For example, a throw may be in the range of 0 through 10 pins, and the total of the two throws in any of the first nine frames must be less than or equal to 10.

Use functional decomposition to solve this problem and code the solution using functions as appropriate. Be sure to use proper formatting and appropriate comments in your code. The output should be labeled clearly and formatted neatly, and the error messages should be informative.

8. Write a simple telephone directory program in C++ that looks up phone numbers in a file containing a list of names and phone numbers. The user should be prompted to enter a first and last name, and the program should then either output the corresponding number or indicate that the name isn't present in the directory. After each lookup, the program should ask the user whether he or she wants to look up another number, and then either repeat the process or exit the program. The data on the file should be organized so that each line contains a first name, a last name, and a phone number, separated by blanks. You can return to the beginning of the file by closing it and opening it again.

    Use functional decomposition to solve this problem and code the solution using functions as appropriate. Be sure to use proper formatting and appropriate comments in your code. The output should be labeled clearly and formatted neatly, and the error messages should be informative.

9. Extend the program in Problem 8 to look up addresses as well as phone numbers. Change the file format so that the name and phone number appear on one line, and the address appears on the following line for each entry. The program should ask the user whether he or she wants to look up a phone number, an address, or both, and then perform the lookup and output the requested information. The program should recognize an invalid request and prompt the user to enter the request again. As in Problem 8, the program should allow the user to keep entering queries until the user indicates that he or she is finished.

10. Programming Problem 3 in Chapter 5 asked you to write a program that inputs a letter and outputs the corresponding word in the International Civil Aviation Organization (ICAO) phonetic alphabet. This problem asks you to turn that program into a function, and use it to convert a string input by the user into the series of words that would be used to spell it out phonetically. For example:

```
Enter string: program
Phonetic version is: Papa Romeo Oscar Golf Romeo Alpha Mike
```

For ease of reference, the ICAO alphabet is repeated here:

A	Alpha
B	Bravo
C	Charlie
D	Delta
E	Echo
F	Foxtrot
G	Golf
H	Hotel
I	India
J	Juliet
K	Kilo

L	Lima
M	Mike
N	November
O	Oscar
P	Papa
Q	Quebec
R	Romeo
S	Sierra
T	Tango
U	Uniform
V	Victor
W	Whiskey
X	X-ray
Y	Yankee
Z	Zulu

Be sure to use proper formatting and appropriate comments in your code. Provide appropriate prompts to the user. The output should be labeled clearly and formatted neatly.

11. You've been asked to write a program to grade a multiple-choice exam. The exam has 20 questions, each answered with a letter in the range of `'a'` through `'f'`. The data are stored on a file (`exams.dat`) where the first line is the key, consisting of a string of 20 characters. The remaining lines on the file are exam answers; each consists of a student ID number, a space, and a string of 20 characters. The program should read the key, read each exam, and output the ID number and score to file `scores.dat`. Erroneous input should result in an error message. For example, given the data

```
abcdefabcdefabcdefab
1234567 abcdefabcdefabcdefab
9876543 abddefbbbdefcbcdefac
5554446 abcdefabcdefabcdef
4445556 abcdefabcdefabcdefabcd
3332221 abcdefghijklmnopqrst
```

the program would output the following data on `scores.dat`:

```
1234567  20
9876543  15
5554446  Too few answers
4445556  Too many answers
3332221  Invalid answers
```

Use functional decomposition to solve the problem and code the solution using functions as appropriate. Be sure to use proper formatting and appropriate comments in your code. The output should be formatted neatly, and the error messages should be informative.

Case Study Follow-Up

1. Test the `LawnCare` application using a file with no data. What happens? If this input causes an error, rewrite the program to handle this situation.
2. Test the `LawnCare` application using a file with only one customer. What happens? If this input causes an error, rewrite the program to handle this situation.
3. The current version writes a bill with a zero amount due if there are no jobs. Rewrite the application so that no bill is written if there are no jobs.

Scope, Lifetime, and More on Functions

KNOWLEDGE GOALS

- To know what a global reference is.
- To understand and be able to avoid unwanted side effects.
- To know when to use a value-returning function.

SKILL GOALS

To be able to:
- Determine which variables in a program are local.
- Determine which variables are accessible in a given block.
- Determine the lifetime of each variable in a program.
- Design and code a value-returning function for a specified task.
- Invoke a value-returning function properly.

As programs get larger and more complicated, the number of identifiers in a program increases. We invent function names, variable names, constant identifiers, and so on. Some of these identifiers we declare inside blocks. Other identifiers—function names, for example—we declare outside of any block. This chapter examines the C++ rules by which a function may access identifiers that are declared outside its own block. Using these rules, we return to the discussion of interface design that we began in Chapter 8.

Finally, we look at the second kind of subprogram provided by C++: the *value-returning function*. Unlike void functions, which return results (if any) through the parameter list, a value-returning function returns a single result—the function value—to the expression from which it was called. In this chapter, you learn how to write user-defined value-returning functions.

9.1 Scope of Identifiers

As we saw in Chapter 8, local variables are those declared inside a block, such as the body of a function. Recall that local variables cannot be accessed outside the block that contains them. The same access rule applies to declarations of named constants: Local constants may be accessed only in the block in which they are declared.

Any block—not just a function body—can contain variable and constant declarations. For example, this If statement contains a block that declares a local variable **n**:

```
if (alpha > 3)
{
  int n;                   // n is defined here
  cin >> n;
  beta = beta + n;
}                          // n becomes undefined here
```

Like any other local variable, **n** cannot be accessed by any statement outside the block containing its declaration. It is defined for all statements that follow it within its block, and it is undefined outside of the block.

If we listed all the places from which an identifier could be accessed legally, we would describe that identifier's *scope of visibility* or *scope of access*, often just called its scope.

> **Scope** The region of program code where it is legal to reference (use) an identifier.

C++ defines several categories of scope for any identifier. We begin by describing three of these categories.

1. *Class scope.* This term refers to the data type called a *class*, which we mentioned briefly in Chapter 4. We will postpone our detailed discussion of class scope until Chapter 12.

2. *Local scope.* The scope of an identifier declared inside a block extends from the point of declaration to the end of that block. Also, the scope of a function parameter extends from where it is declared in the heading to the end of the function body. You can think of a function parameter's scope as being the same as if it was a local variable declared before anything else in the function body.
3. *Global scope.* The scope of an identifier declared outside all functions and classes extends from the point of declaration to the end of the entire file containing the program code.

C++ function names have global scope. (We discuss an exception to this rule in Chapter 12.) Once a function name has been declared, it can be invoked by any other function in the rest of the program. In C++, there is no such thing as a local function—that is, you cannot nest a function definition inside another function definition.

Global variables and constants are those declared outside all functions. In the following code fragment, `gamma` is a global variable and can be accessed directly by statements in `main` and `SomeFunc`:

```
int gamma;            // Global variable

int main()
{
  gamma = 3;
  .
  .
  .
}

void SomeFunc()
{
  gamma = 5;
  .
  .
  .
}
```

When a function declares a local identifier with the same name as a global identifier, the local identifier takes precedence within the function. This principle is called name precedence or name hiding.

> **Name precedence** The precedence that a local identifier in a function has over a global identifier with the same name in any references that the function makes to that identifier; also called *name hiding*.

Here's an example that uses both local and global declarations:

```
//***********************************************************
// This program demonstrates global and local variables.
//***********************************************************
#include <iostream>
using namespace std;

void SomeFunc(float);

const int A = 17;          // A global constant
int b;                     // A global variable
int c;                     // Another global
```

```
int main()
{
  b = 4;                        // Assignment to global b
  c = 6;                        // Assignment to global c
  SomeFunc(42.8);
  return 0;
}

//***********************************************************

void SomeFunc(float c)          // Prevents access to global c
{
  float b;                      // Prevents access to global b

  b = 2.3;                      // Assignment to local b
  cout << " A = " << A;         // Output global A (17)
  cout << " b = " << b;         // Output local b (2.3)
  cout << " c = " << c;         // Output local c (42.8)
}
```

In this example, function **SomeFunc** accesses global constant **A** but declares its own local variable **b** and parameter **c**. Thus the output is

A = 17 b = 2.3 c = 42.8

Local variable **b** takes precedence over global variable **b**, effectively hiding global **b** from the statements in function **SomeFunc**. Parameter **c** also blocks access to global variable **c** from within the function. Function parameters act just like local variables in this respect; that is, parameters have local scope.

Scope Rules

When you write C++ programs, you rarely declare global variables. There are negative aspects to using global variables, which we discuss later. But when a situation crops up in which you have a compelling need for global variables, it pays to know how C++ handles these declarations. The rules for accessing identifiers that aren't declared locally are called scope rules.

Scope rules The rules that determine where in the program an identifier may be accessed, given the point where that identifier is declared.

Nonlocal identifier With respect to a given block, any identifier declared outside that block.

In addition to local and global access, the C++ scope rules define what happens when blocks are nested within other blocks. Anything declared in a block that contains a nested block is nonlocal to the inner block. (Global identifiers are nonlocal with respect to all blocks in the program.) If a block accesses any identifier declared outside its own block, it is termed a *nonlocal access*.

Here are the detailed scope rules, excluding class scope and certain language features we have not yet discussed:

1. A function name has global scope. Function definitions cannot be nested within function definitions.
2. The scope of a function parameter is identical to the scope of a local variable declared in the outermost block of the function body.
3. The scope of a global variable or constant extends from its declaration to the end of the file, except as noted in Rule 5.

4. The scope of a local variable or constant extends from its declaration to the end of the block in which it is declared. This scope includes any nested blocks, except as noted in Rule 5.
5. The scope of an identifier does not include any nested block that contains a locally declared identifier with the same name (local identifiers have name precedence).

Here is a sample program that demonstrates C++ scope rules. To simplify the example, only the declarations and headings are spelled out. Note how the While loop body labeled **Block3**, located within function **Block2**, contains its own local variable declarations.

```cpp
//*************************************************************
// This program shell demonstrates scope.
//*************************************************************
#include <iostream>
using namespace std;

void Block1(int, char&};
void Block2();

int  a1;         // One global variable
char a2;         // Another global variable

int main()
{
   ⋮
}

//*************************************************************

void Block1(int   a1,       // Prevents access to global a1
            char& b2)       // Has same scope as c1 and d2
{
  int c1;        // A variable local to Block1
  int d2;        // Another variable local to Block1
   ⋮
}

//*************************************************************

void Block2()
{
  int a1;        // Local to Block2; prevents access to global a1
  int b2;        // Local to Block2; no conflict with b2 in Block1

  while (. . .)
  {              // Block3
    int c1;      // Local to Block3; no conflict with c1 in Block1
    int b2;      // Local to Block3; Prevents nonlocal access to b2 in
                 //    Block2; no conflict with b2 in Block1
     ⋮
  }
}
```

Let's look at the **ScopeRules** program in terms of the blocks it defines and see just what these rules mean. **FIGURE 9.1** shows the headings and declarations in the **ScopeRules** program, with the scopes of visibility being indicated by boxes.

```
int a1;
char a2;

int main()
{

}
void Block1( int    a1,
             char&  b2 )
{
    int c1;
    int d2;

}
void Block2()
{
    int a1;
    int b2;

    while (...)
    {              // Block3
        int c1;
        int b2;
    }

}
```

FIGURE 9.1 Scope Diagram for Scope Rules Program

Anything inside a box can refer to anything in a larger surrounding box, but outside-in references aren't allowed. Thus a statement in **Block3** could access any identifier declared in **Block2** or any global variable. A statement in **Block3** could not access identifiers declared in **Block1** because it would have to enter the Block1 box from outside.

Notice that the parameters for a function are inside the function's box, but the function name itself is outside the box. If the name of the function were inside the box, no function could call another function. This point demonstrates merely that function names are globally accessible.

Imagine the boxes in Figure 9.1 as rooms with walls made of two-way mirrors, with the reflective side facing out and the see-through side facing in. If you stood in the room for **Block3**, you would be able to see out through all the surrounding rooms to the declarations of the global variables (and anything between). You would not be able to see into any other rooms (such as **Block1**), however, because their mirrored outer surfaces would block your view. Because of this analogy, the term *visible* is often used in describing a scope of access. For example, variable **a2** is visible throughout the program, meaning that it can be accessed from anywhere in the program.

Figure 9.1 does not tell the whole story; however, it represents only scope Rules 1 through 4, but not Rule 5. Variable **a1** is declared in three different places. Because of the name precedence rules, **Block2** and **Block3** access the **a1** declared in **Block2** rather than the global **a1**. Similarly, the scope of the variable **b2** declared in **Block2** does *not* include the "hole" created by the declaration of variable **b2** in **Block3**.

Name precedence rules are implemented by the compiler as follows. When an expression refers to an identifier, the compiler first checks the local declarations. If the identifier isn't local, the compiler works its way outward through each level of nesting until it finds an identifier with the same name. There it stops. If there is an identifier with the same name declared at a level even farther out, it is never reached.

If the compiler reaches the global declarations (including identifiers inserted by `#include` directives) and still can't find the identifier, an error message such as `UNDECLARED IDENTIFIER` is issued. Such a message most likely indicates a misspelling or an incorrect capitalization, or it could mean that the identifier was not declared before the reference to it or was not declared at all. It may also indicate that the blocks are nested so that the identifier's scope doesn't include the reference.[1]

Variable Declarations and Definitions

In Chapter 8, you learned that C++ distinguishes between function declarations and definitions. Definitions cause memory space to be reserved, whereas declarations do not.

C++ applies the same terminology to variable declarations. A variable declaration becomes a variable definition if it also reserves memory for the variable. All of the variable declarations we have seen so far have been variable definitions. What would a variable declaration look like if it was *not* also a definition?

In Chapter 8, we talked about multifile programs. C++ has a reserved word `extern` that lets you reference a global variable located in another file. A definition such as

```
int someInt;
```

causes the compiler to reserve a memory location for `someInt`. By contrast, the statement

```
extern int someInt;
```

is known as an *external declaration*. It states that `someInt` is a global variable located in another file and that no storage should be reserved for it here. In C++ terminology, the preceding statement is a declaration but not a definition of `someInt`. It associates a variable name with a data type so that the compiler can perform type checking. In C++, you can declare a variable or a function many times, but there can be only one definition.

Except where it's important to distinguish between declarations and definitions of variables, we'll continue to use the more general phrase *variable declaration* instead of the more specific *variable definition*.

Namespaces

For some time, we have been including the following `using` directive in our programs:

```
using namespace std;
```

In Chapter 2, we noted that without this directive, we would have to refer to `cout` using the qualified name

```
std::cout
```

---

1. C++ provides syntax to work around name precedence and access a global identifier even when an identifier with the same name is declared locally. We can use the `::` operator without specifying a namespace. For example, if we have declared a local constant called `A1`, we can write `::A1` to refer to a global constant called `A1`.

Now that we have explored the basic concept of scope, we are ready to answer the question: What exactly is a namespace? It is a mechanism by which the programmer can create a named scope.[2] For example, the standard header file `cstdlib` contains function prototypes for several library functions, one of which is the absolute value function, `abs`. The declarations are contained within a *namespace definition* as follows:

```
// In header file cstdlib:
namespace std
{
    ⋮
  int abs(int);
    ⋮
}
```

A namespace definition consists of the word **namespace,** then an identifier of the programmer's choice, and then the *namespace body* between braces. Identifiers declared within the namespace body are said to have *namespace scope*. Such identifiers cannot be accessed outside the body except by using one of three methods.

The first method is to use a qualified name: the name of the namespace, followed by the scope resolution operator (::), followed by the desired identifier. Here is an example:

```
#include <cstdlib>
int main()
{
  int alpha;
  int beta;
    ⋮
  alpha = std::abs(beta);    // A qualified name referring to abs
  std::cout << alpha;        // A qualified name referring to cout
    ⋮
}
```

The general idea is to inform the compiler that we are referring to the `abs` declared in the `std` namespace, and not to some other `abs` (such as a global function named `abs` that we might have written ourselves).

The second method is to use a statement called a **using** *declaration* as follows:

```
#include <cstdlib>
int main()
{
  int alpha;
  int beta;
  using std::abs;     // A using declaration for abs
  using std::cout;    // A using declaration for cout
    ⋮
  alpha = abs(beta);
  cout << alpha;
    ⋮
}
```

These **using** declarations allow the identifiers `abs` and `cout` to be used throughout the body of `main` as synonyms for the longer `std::abs` and `std::cout`, respectively.

---

2. As a general concept, *namespace* is another word for *scope*. Here we consider it as a specific C++ language feature.

The third method—one with which we are familiar—is to use a `using` directive (not to be confused with a `using` declaration):

```cpp
#include <cstdlib>
int main()
{
  int alpha;
  int beta;
  using namespace std;    // A using directive
    ⋮
  alpha = abs(beta);
  cout << alpha;
    ⋮
}
```

With a `using` directive, *all* identifiers from the specified namespace are accessible, but only in the scope in which the `using` directive appears. In the preceding fragment, the `using` directive is in local scope (it's within a block), so identifiers from the `std` namespace are accessible only within `main`. Conversely, suppose we put the `using` directive outside all functions (as we have been doing), like this:

```cpp
#include <cstdlib>
using namespace std;
int main()
{
  ⋮
}
```

Then the `using` directive is in global scope; consequently, identifiers from the `std` namespace are accessible globally.

Placing a `using` directive in global scope is a convenience. For example, all of the functions we write can refer to identifiers such as `abs`, `cin`, and `cout` without our having to insert a `using` directive locally in each function.

Creating global `using` directives is considered a bad idea when we are creating large, multifile programs, where programmers often use multiple libraries. Two or more libraries may, just by coincidence, use the same identifier for different purposes. Global `using` directives then lead to *name clashes* (multiple definitions of the same identifier), because all the library identifiers are in the same global scope. (C++ programmers refer to this problem as "polluting the global namespace.")

We continue to use global `using` directives for the `std` namespace because our programs are relatively small and, therefore, name clashes aren't likely. Also, the identifiers in the `std` namespace are so commonly used that most C++ programmers avoid duplicating them.

Given the concept of namespace scope, we refine our description of C++ scope categories as follows:

1. *Class scope.* This term refers to the *class* data type, which we discuss in Chapter 12.
2. *Local scope.* The scope of an identifier declared inside a block extends from the point of declaration to the end of that block. Also, the scope of a function parameter (formal parameter) extends from the point of declaration to the end of the block that is the body of the function.
3. *Namespace scope.* The scope of an identifier declared in a namespace definition extends from the point of declaration to the end of the namespace body, *and* its scope includes the scope of any `using` directive specifying that namespace.

4. *Global* (or *global namespace*) *scope*. The scope of an identifier declared outside all namespaces, functions, and classes extends from the point of declaration to the end of the entire file containing the program code.

Note that these are general descriptions of scope categories and not scope rules. The descriptions do not account for name hiding.

QUICK CHECK

9.1.1 If a function references a variable that is not declared in its block or its parameter list, is the reference global or local? (pp. 402–403)

9.1.2 What is the exception to the scope rule that dictates that a local variable or constant extends from its declaration to the end of the block in which it is declared? (p. 405)

9.1.3 What are the four scope categories mentioned in this section? (pp. 409–410)

9.2 Lifetime of a Variable

A concept related to, but separate from, the scope of a variable is its lifetime—the period of time during program execution when an identifier actually has memory allocated to it. We have said that storage for local variables is created (allocated) at the moment control enters a function. The variables remain "alive" while the function is executing, and the storage is destroyed (deallocated) when the function exits. In contrast, the lifetime of a global variable is the same as the lifetime of the entire program. Memory is allocated only once, when the program begins executing, and is deallocated only when the entire program terminates. Observe that scope is a *compile-time* issue, whereas lifetime is a *run-time* issue.

In C++, an automatic variable is one whose storage is allocated at block entry and deallocated at block exit. A static variable is one whose storage remains allocated for the duration of the entire program. All global variables are static variables. By default, variables declared within a block are automatic variables. However, you can use the reserved word `static` when you declare a local variable. If you do so, the variable is a static variable and its lifetime persists from function call to function call.

Lifetime The period of time during program execution when an identifier has memory allocated to it.

Automatic variable A variable for which memory is allocated and deallocated when control enters and exits the block in which it is declared.

Static variable A variable for which memory remains allocated throughout the execution of the entire program.

The next program contains a function that keeps track of the number of times it is called. The output is shown following the program.

```
//***********************************************************
// This program demonstrates the use of a static variable.
//***********************************************************
#include <iostream>
using namespace std;

void Counting();
// Function Counting prints the value of a counter
// each time it is called.
```

```
int main()
{
  for (int count = 1; count <=10; count++)
    counting();
  return 0;
}

//*********************************************************

void counting()
{
  static int counter = 0;    // counter is defined once, and its
                             // value is not reinitialized to 0 on
                             // subsequent calls to counting()
  counter++;
  cout << "count: " << counter << endl;
}                            // counter is not deallocated here
```

Here is the program's output:

```
count: 1
count: 2
count: 3
count: 4
count: 5
count: 6
count: 7
count: 8
count: 9
count: 10
```

It is usually a better idea to declare a local variable as `static` than to use a global variable. As for a global variable, the memory for a static variable remains allocated throughout the lifetime of the entire program. But unlike for a global variable, its local scope prevents other functions in the program from tinkering with it.

Initializations in Declarations

One of the most common things we do in programs is first declare a variable and then, in a separate statement, assign an initial value to the variable. Here's a typical example:

```
int sum;
sum = 0;
```

As we said in Chapter 8, C++ allows you to combine these two statements. The result is known as an *initialization in a declaration*. Here we initialize `sum` as part of its declaration:

```
int sum = 0;
```

In a declaration, the expression that specifies the initial value is called an *initializer*. In the preceding statement, the initializer is the constant 0. Implicit type coercion takes place if the data type of the initializer differs from the data type of the variable.

An automatic variable is initialized to the specified value each time control enters the block:

```
void SomeFunc(int someParam)
{
  int i = 0;                    // Initialized each time
  int n = 2 * someParam + 3;    // Initialized each time
     ⋮
}
```

In contrast, initialization of a static variable (either a global variable or a local variable explicitly declared static) occurs once only, the first time control reaches its declaration. Here's an example in which two local static variables are initialized only once (the first time the function is called):

```
void AnotherFunc(int param)
{
  static char ch = 'A';         // Initialized once only
  static int  m  = param + 1;   // Initialized once only
     ⋮
}
```

Although an initialization gives a variable an initial value, it is perfectly acceptable to reassign it another value during program execution.

SOFTWARE MAINTENANCE CASE STUDY: Debug a Simple Program

MAINTENANCE TASK: Most of our maintenance problems have involved enhancing a program and then testing the changes. This time a friend came to you with a short program that just reads a file and for each line in the file prints a line number and the number of characters on the line—or at least that is what it is supposed to do. How can such a simple program not work? You agree to look at it.

The first step is to look at the input and the results, which your friend supplies. He has counted the number of characters on each line of test data: 61, 62, 60, 61, 59, 63, 54, 62, 29.

```
Ada Augusta, Countess of Lovelace, was a most romantic figure
in the history of computing.  Ada, the daughter of Lord Byron
(the English poet), was herself quite a mathematician.  She
became interested in Babbage's work on the analytical engine
and extended his ideas (and corrected some of his errors).
Ada is credited with being the first programmer.  The concept
of the loop--a series of instructions that repeat--is
attributed to her.  Ada, the language used by the Department
of Defense, is named for her.
```

SOFTWARE MAINTENANCE CASE STUDY: Debug a Simple Program

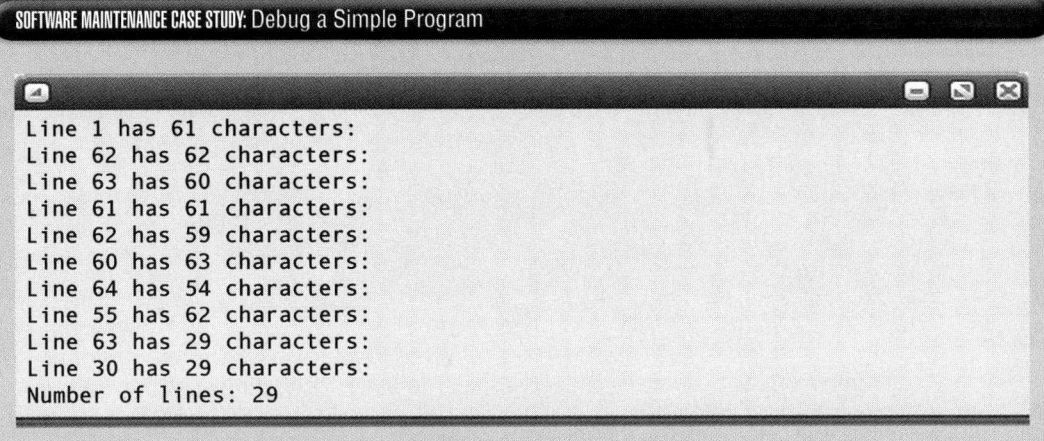

```
Line 1 has 61 characters:
Line 62 has 62 characters:
Line 63 has 60 characters:
Line 61 has 61 characters:
Line 62 has 59 characters:
Line 60 has 63 characters:
Line 64 has 54 characters:
Line 55 has 62 characters:
Line 63 has 29 characters:
Line 30 has 29 characters:
Number of lines: 29
```

The next step is to determine what is correct and what is not. The first line number is correct, and the number of characters on each line seems okay. The rest of the line numbers are way off, and the number of lines at the bottom is off. But you notice what seems to be a pattern: Each incorrect line number is one more than the number of characters on the previous line, except for the last line, which is the same as the number of characters on the previous line. It looks as if the *line* counter and the *letter* counter are getting confused. Now we know where to begin our debugging. Let's examine the code line by line and isolate the interaction between the two counters.

```cpp
#include <iostream>
#include <fstream>
#include <string>

using namespace std;

void LetterCount(string line, int& count);
// Number of letters in line is returned in count

void LineCount(istream& file, int& count);
// Number of lines in file is returned in count

int main()
{
  ifstream inFile;
  inFile.open("test.dat");
  int count = 0;
  LineCount(inFile, count);
  cout << "Number of lines: " << count << endl;
  return 0;
}

void LetterCount(string line, int& count)
{
  count = line.length();
  cout << " has "<< count << " characters: " << endl;
}
```

SOFTWARE MAINTENANCE CASE STUDY: Debug a Simple Program

```
void LineCount(istream& file, int& count)
{
  string line;
  while (file)
  {
    getline(file, line);
    count++;
    cout << "Line " << count;
    LetterCount(line, count);
  }
}
```

The first problem you see is that there is no documenting header for the program. You make a note to chide your friend for leaving out this information. Continuing, you see that the first few lines access the necessary files and determine the namespace. The next two statements are prototypes of the two functions used: **LetterCount** and **LineCount**. The documentation states that **LineCount** returns the number of lines, and **LetterCount** returns the number of characters. Does each function do what it is supposed to do? **LineCount** inputs a line, increments and prints the line counter, and invokes **LetterCount**. The documentation may not be complete, but the function is not incorrect. **LetterCount** takes a line and prints the number of characters in the line. It doesn't return anything; this function's documentation is incorrect. No, the function *does return a value:* The reference parameter **count** is used as a local variable to store a value temporarily. However, this value is being sent back to the calling program, corrupting the line count.

Both functions have **count** as a reference parameter; thus both functions are accessing the same place in memory. The same parameter is being used for two distinct purposes: counting the lines and counting the characters. **LetterCount** doesn't need a counter as a parameter; the **count** in this function should be a local variable. Let's make that correction and rerun the program. Be careful: Changing a parameter means changing the code in three places: the prototype, the function heading, and the invoking statement.

```
Line 1 has 61 characters:
Line 2 has 62 characters:
Line 3 has 60 characters:
Line 4 has 61 characters:
Line 5 has 59 characters:
Line 6 has 63 characters:
Line 7 has 54 characters:
Line 8 has 62 characters:
Line 9 has 29 characters:
Line 10 has 29 characters:
Number of lines: 10
```

Well, you are making progress. The only problem seems to be that the program says there are 10 lines when there are only 9. Also, note that line 10 has the same number of characters as line 9. It looks like the last line is being read twice. Let's examine the code that does the reading:

SOFTWARE MAINTENANCE CASE STUDY: Debug a Simple Program

```
while (file)
{
  getline(file, line);
  count++;
  cout << "Line " << count;
  LetterCount(line, count);
}
```

Of course! Because the loop is an EOF loop, we need a priming read. When the last read causes the file to go into the fail state but the program continues, the variable `line` is unchanged, so the last line is actually processed twice. Once this change is made, the results are correct.

Here is the corrected program. Note that documentation has been added and updated.

```cpp
//*******************************************************
// Program reads a file and prints the line number
// and the number of characters in the line.
//*******************************************************
#include <iostream>
#include <fstream>
#include <string>

using namespace std;

void LetterCount(string line);
// The number of characters in line is printed

void LineCount(istream& file, int& count);
// Number of lines in file is returned in count

int main()
{
  ifstream inFile;
  inFile.open("test.dat");
  int count = 0;
  LineCount(inFile, count);
  cout << "Number of lines: " << count << endl;
  return 0;
}

//*******************************************************

void LetterCount(string line)
{
  int count = line.length();
  cout << " has "<< count << " characters: " << endl;
}
```

SOFTWARE MAINTENANCE CASE STUDY: Debug a Simple Program

```
//***********************************************************
void LineCount(istream& file, int& count)
{
  string line;
  getline(file, line);

  while (file)
  {
    count++;
    cout << "Line " << count;
    LetterCount(line);
    getline(file, line);
  }
}
```

QUICK CHECK

- **9.2.1** A program has two functions, `Quick1` and `Quick2`. The program itself declares variables `check` and `qc`. Function `Quick1` declares variables called `quest` and `qc`. Function `Quick2` declares one variable called `quest` and a static variable called `forever`. Which of these variables are local? (pp. 410–412)
- **9.2.2** In Question 9.2.1, which variables are accessible within function `Quick1`? (pp. 410–412)
- **9.2.3** In Question 9.2.1, what is the lifetime of each of the six variables? (pp. 410–412)
- **9.2.4** At what point in time is the concept of a variable's lifetime considered? (p. 410)
- **9.2.5** How is a variable's lifetime related to memory? (p. 410)
- **9.2.6** What is an automatic variable? (p. 410)
- **9.2.7** What is the lifetime of a static variable? (p. 410)
- **9.2.8** In a declaration what do we call the expression that specifies the initial value? (p. 412)
- **9.2.9** How many times is a static variable initialized? (p. 412)
- **9.2.10** How many times is an automatic variable initialized? (p. 412)

9.3 Interface Design

We return now to the issue of interface design, which we first discussed in Chapter 8. Recall that the data flow through a module interface can take three forms: incoming only (In), outgoing only (Out), and incoming/outgoing (In/out). Any item that can be classified as purely incoming should be coded as a value parameter. Items in the remaining two categories (outgoing and incoming/outgoing) must be reference parameters; the only way the function can deposit results into the caller's arguments is to use the addresses of those arguments. Remember that stream objects passed as parameters must be reference types.

Sometimes it is tempting to skip the interface design step when writing a module, letting it communicate with other modules by referencing global variables. Don't! Without the interface design step, you would actually be creating a poorly structured and undocumented interface. Except in well-justified circumstances, the use of global variables is a poor programming practice that can lead to program errors. These errors are extremely hard to locate and usually take the form of unwanted side effects.

Side Effects

Suppose you made a call to the `sqrt` library function in your program:

`y = sqrt(x);`

You expect the call to `sqrt` to do one thing only: compute the square root of the variable `x`. You would be surprised if `sqrt` also changed the value of your variable `x` because `sqrt`, by definition, does not make such changes. This outcome would be an example of an unexpected and unwanted side effect.

> **Side effect** Any effect of one function on another function that is not a part of the explicitly defined interface between them.

Side effects are sometimes caused by a combination of reference parameters and careless coding in a function. Perhaps an assignment statement in the function stores a temporary result into one of the reference parameters, accidentally changing the value of an argument back in the calling code. As we mentioned earlier, use of value parameters avoids this type of side effect by preventing the change from reaching the argument. We saw these errors demonstrated in the last Software Maintenance Case Study.

Side effects also can occur when a function accesses a global variable. For example, forgetting to declare a local variable that has name precedence over a global variable with the same name is another source of side-effect errors. While you may think the function is accessing a local variable, it is actually changing a global variable. The error doesn't appear until after the function returns and `main` or some other function makes use of the value left in the global variable. Because of how nonlocal scope works in C++, every function interface has the potential to produce this kind of unintended side effect.

The symptoms of side-effect errors are especially misleading about their source because the trouble shows up in one part of the program when it really is caused by something in another part that may be completely unrelated. Every programmer has had the experience of spending several days attempting to isolate a bug that makes no sense at all, and even seems to violate the rules of the programming language. When you begin to think that an error must be the compiler's fault, it's a good bet that you're really looking at a side-effect bug!

Given their challenging nature, avoiding such errors is extremely important. The only external effect that a module should have is to transfer information through the well-structured interface of the parameter list (see **FIGURE 9.2**). To be more explicit: *The only variables used in a module should be either parameters or local.* In addition, incoming-only parameters should be value parameters. If these steps are taken, then each module is essentially isolated from other parts of the program and side effects cannot occur. When a module is free of side effects, we can treat it as an independent module and reuse it in other programs. It is hazardous or impossible to reuse modules with side effects.

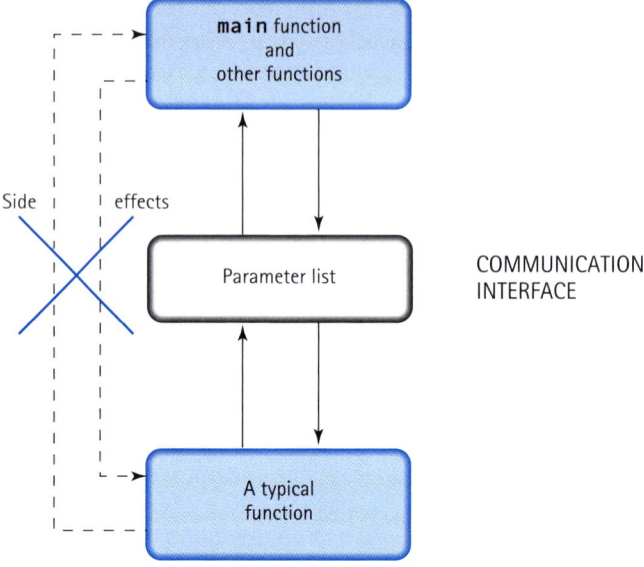

FIGURE 9.2 Side Effects

The following program, called **Trouble**, runs but produces incorrect results because of global variables and side effects:

```
//*************************************************************
// This is an example of poor program design, which
// causes an error when the program is executed
//*************************************************************
#include <iostream>
using namespace std;

void CountInts();

int count;         // Supposed to count input lines, but does it?
int intVal;        // Holds one input integer

int main()
{
  count = 0;
  cin >> intVal;
  while (cin)
  {
    count++;
    CountInts();
    cin >> intVal;
  }
  cout << count << " lines of input processed." << endl;
  return 0;
}
```

```
//*****************************************************************
void CountInts()
// Counts the number of integers on one input line (where 99999
// is a sentinel on each line) and prints the count
// Note: main() has already read the first integer on a line
{
  count = 0;                              // Side effect
  while (intVal != 99999)
  {
    count++;                              // Side effect
    cin >> intVal;
  }
  cout << count << " integers on this line." << endl;
}
```

Program `Trouble` is supposed to count and print the number of integers on each line of input. As a final output, it should print the number of lines. But each time the program is run, it reports that the number of lines of input is the same as the number of integers in the last line. Your first thought would be to look closely at `main` for a logic error in keeping track of the number of lines. But the algorithm in `main` is fine. Where could the bug be? The problem is that the `CountInts` function uses the global variable `count` to store the number of integers on each input line. The programmer probably intended to declare a local variable called `count` and forgot.

Furthermore, there is no reason for `count` to be a global variable. If a local variable `count` had been declared in `main`, then the compiler would have reported that `CountInts` was using an undeclared identifier. With local variables called `count` declared in both `main` and `CountInts`, the program works correctly. There is no conflict between the two variables, because each is visible only inside its own block.

This side-effect error was easy to locate because we had just one other function to examine. Of course, in a program with hundreds of functions, it would be much more challenging to determine which one was causing `main` to behave strangely.

The `Trouble` program also demonstrates one common exception to the rule of not accessing global variables. Technically, `cin` and `cout` are global objects declared in the header file `iostream`. The `CountInts` function reads and writes directly to these streams. To be absolutely correct, `cin` and `cout` should be passed as arguments to the function. However, `cin` and `cout` are fundamental I/O facilities supplied by the standard library, and by convention C++ functions access them directly.

Global Constants

Contrary to what you might think, it is acceptable to reference named constants globally. Because the values of global constants cannot be changed while the program is running, no side effects can occur.

There are two advantages to referencing constants globally: ease of change and consistency. If you need to change the value of a constant, it's easier to change only one global declaration than to change a local declaration in every function. By declaring a constant in only one place, we also ensure that all parts of the program use exactly the same value.

This is not to say that you should declare *all* constants globally. If a constant is needed in only one function, then it makes sense to declare it locally within that function.

At this point, you may want to turn to the Problem-Solving Case Study at the end of this chapter, which further illustrates interface design and the use of value and reference parameters.

MAY WE INTRODUCE Ada Lovelace

On December 10, 1815 (the same year in which George Boole was born), a daughter—Augusta Ada Byron—was born to Anna Isabella (Annabella) Byron and George Gordon, Lord Byron. In England at that time, Byron's fame derived not only from his poetry, but also from his wild, scandalous behavior. The marriage was strained from the beginning, and Annabella left Byron shortly after Ada's birth. By April 1816, the two had signed separation papers. Byron left England, never to return. Throughout the rest of his life, he regretted being unable to see his daughter. At one point, he wrote of her:

> I see thee not. I hear thee not.
> But none can be so wrapt in thee.

Before he died in Greece at age 36, he exclaimed, "Oh my poor dear child! My dear Ada! My God, could I but have seen her!"

Meanwhile, Annabella, who would eventually become a baroness in her own right, and who was educated as both a mathematician and a poet, carried on with Ada's upbringing and education. Annabella gave Ada her first instruction in mathematics, but it soon became clear that Ada was gifted in the subject and should receive more extensive tutoring. Ada received further training from Augustus DeMorgan, famous today for one of the basic theorems of Boolean algebra (DeMorgan's law), the logical foundation for modern computers. By age 8, Ada had also demonstrated an interest in mechanical devices and was building detailed model boats.

When she was 18, Ada visited the Mechanics Institute to hear Dr. Dionysius Lardner's lectures on the Difference Engine, a mechanical calculating machine being built by Charles Babbage. She became so interested in the device that she arranged to be introduced to Babbage. It was said that, upon seeing Babbage's machine, Ada was the only person in the room to understand immediately how it worked and to recognize its significance. Ada and Charles Babbage became lifelong friends. She worked with him, helping to document his designs, translating writings about his work, and developing programs for his machines. In fact, today Ada is recognized as the first computer programmer in history, and the modern Ada programming language is named in her honor.

When Babbage designed his Analytical Engine, Ada foresaw that it could go beyond arithmetic computations and become a general manipulator of symbols and, therefore, would have far-reaching capabilities. She even suggested that such a device could eventually be programmed with rules of harmony and composition so that it could produce "scientific" music. In effect, Ada foresaw the field of artificial intelligence more than 150 years ago.

MAY WE INTRODUCE Ada Lovelace, continued

In 1842, Babbage gave a series of lectures in Turin, Italy, on his Analytical Engine. One of the attendees was Luigi Menabrea, who was so impressed that he wrote an account of Babbage's lectures. At age 27, Ada decided to translate the account into English with the intent of adding a few of her own notes about the machine. In the end, her notes were twice as long as the original material, and the document, "The Sketch of the Analytical Engine," became the definitive work on the subject.

It is obvious from Ada's letters that her "notes" were entirely her own and that Babbage was sometimes making unsolicited editorial changes. At one point, Ada wrote to him,

> I am much annoyed at your having altered my Note. You know I am always willing to make any required alterations myself, but that I cannot endure another person to meddle with my sentences.

Ada gained the title Countess of Lovelace when she married Lord William Lovelace. The couple had three children, whose upbringing was left to Ada's mother while Ada pursued her work in mathematics. Her husband was supportive of her work, but for a woman of that day, such behavior was considered almost as scandalous as some of her father's exploits.

Ada Lovelace died of cancer in 1852, just one year before a working Difference Engine was built in Sweden from one of Babbage's designs. Like her father, Ada lived only to age 36. Even though they led very different lives, she had undoubtedly admired him and taken inspiration from his unconventional, rebellious nature. In the end, Ada asked to be buried beside him at the family's estate.

QUICK CHECK

9.3.1 How do references to global variables contribute to the potential for unwanted side effects? (pp. 416–419)

9.3.2 What is a side effect? (p. 416)

9.3.3 What important property of interface design is maintained if a module is free of side effects? (p. 417)

9.3.4 Which global variables used by convention are exceptions to the rule of not using global variables? (p. 419)

9.3.5 What type of variable is acceptable to use globally? (p. 419)

9.4 Value-Returning Functions

In Chapter 8 and the first part of this chapter, we have been writing our own void functions. We now look at the second kind of subprogram in C++, the value-returning function. You are already familiar with several value-returning functions supplied by the C++ standard library: `sqrt`, `abs`, `fabs`, and others. From the caller's perspective, the main difference between void functions and value-returning functions is the way in which they are called. A call to a void function is a complete statement; a call to a value-returning function is part of an expression.

From a design perspective, value-returning functions are used when a function will return only one result and that result is to be used directly in an expression. For example, the C++ standard library provides a power function, `pow`, that raises a floating-point number to a floating-point power. This library does not supply a power function for `int` values, however, so let's build one of our own. The function receives two integers, `number` and `n` (where `n` is greater than or equal to 0), and computes $number^n$. We use a simple approach to this calculation, multiplying repeatedly by `number`. Because the number of iterations is known in advance, a count-controlled loop is appropriate for implementing our new function. The loop counts down to 0 from the initial value of `n`. For each iteration of the loop, `number` is multiplied by the previous product.

```cpp
int Power(int number,   // Base number
          int n)        // Power to raise base to
// This function calculates and returns number to the
// nth power
// Pre:  n must be greater than or equal to 0
{
  int result = 1;       // Holds intermediate powers of x
  while (n > 0)
  {
    result = result * number;
    n--;
  }
  return result;
}
```

The first thing to note is that the function definition looks like a void function, except for the fact that the heading begins with the data type `int` instead of the word `void`. The second thing to observe is the Return statement at the end, which includes an integer expression between the word `return` and the semicolon.

A value-returning function returns one value—not through a parameter, but rather by means of a Return statement. The data type at the beginning of the heading declares the type of value that the function returns. This data type is called the *function type*, although a more precise term is function value type (or *function return type* or *function result type*).

Function value type The data type of the result value returned by a function.

```
#include <iostream>
using namespace std;

int Power(int, int);

int main ()
{ cout
    << "5 raised to the 4th power is"
    << Power(5, 4) << endl;
  return 0;
}
```

```
int Power(int number,
          int n)
{
  int result = 1;
  while (n > 0)
  {
    result = result*number;
    n--;
  }
  return result;
}
```

FIGURE 9.3 Returning a Function Value to the Expression That Called the Function

The program shown in **FIGURE 9.3** invokes function `Power`. The last statement in the `Power` function returns the result as the function value.

You now have seen two forms of the Return statement. The form

`return;`

is valid *only* in void functions. It causes control to exit the function immediately and return to the caller. In contrast, the form

`return` *Expression*;

is valid *only* in value-returning functions. It returns control to the caller, sending back the value of Expression as the function value. (If the data type of Expression is different from the declared function type, its value is coerced to the correct type.)

In Chapter 8, we presented a syntax template for the function definition of a void function. We now update the syntax template to cover both void functions and value-returning functions:

FunctionDefinition

> DataType FunctionName (ParameterList)
> {
>   Statement
>   ⋮
> }

If DataType is the word **void**, the function is a void function; otherwise, it is a value-returning function. Notice from the shading in the syntax template that DataType is optional. If you omit the data type of a function, a data type of `int` is assumed. We mention this point only because you sometimes encounter programs where DataType is missing from the function heading. Many programmers consider this practice to be poor programming style.

The parameter list for a value-returning function has exactly the same form as for a void function: a list of parameter declarations, separated by commas. Also, a function prototype for a value-returning function looks just like the prototype for a void function except that it begins with a data type instead of **void**.

Remember your friend's program that was so buggy? The function `LineCount` had a reference parameter that was used to return the number of lines in the file. This function should be written as a value-returning function, where the return value is the number of lines. The change requires the following steps:

1. Replace the word `void` with the word `int` in the prototype for function `LineCount`.
2. Remove `count` from the parameter list.
3. Make the same changes in the function definition.
4. Declare a local variable to keep a count of the number of lines.
5. Return the value of the line count variable.
6. Remove the declaration of `count` from the main program.
7. Insert the call to `LineCount` into the output statement.
8. Correct the documentation.

Here is this program with `LineCount` with these steps taken. The changed lines are shaded.

```
//*******************************************************
// This program reads a file and prints the line number
// and the number of characters for each line
//*******************************************************
#include <iostream>
#include <fstream>
#include <string>

using namespace std;

void LetterCount(string line);
// The number of characters in line is printed

int LineCount(istream& file);
// Number of lines in file is returned

int main()
{
  ifstream inFile;
  inFile.open("test.dat");
  cout << "Number of lines: " << LineCount(inFile) << endl;
  return 0;
}

//*******************************************************

void LetterCount(string line)
{
  int count = line.length();
  cout << " has "<< count << " characters: " << endl;
}

//*******************************************************
```

```
int LineCount(istream& file)
{
  int count = 0;
  string line;
  getline(file, line);

  while (file)
  {
     count++;
     cout << "Line " << count;
     LetterCount(line);
     getline(file, line);
  }
  return count;
}
```

Complete Example

Let's look at another problem. Suppose we are writing a program that calculates a prorated refund of tuition for students who withdraw in the middle of a semester. The amount to be refunded is the total tuition times the remaining fraction of the semester (the number of days remaining divided by the total number of days in the semester). The people who use the program want to be able to enter the dates on which the semester begins and ends and the date of withdrawal, and they want the program to calculate the fraction of the semester that remains.

Because each semester at this particular school begins and ends within one calendar year, we can calculate the number of days in a period by determining the day number of each date and subtracting the starting day number from the ending day number. The day number is the number associated with each day of the year if you count sequentially from January 1. December 31 has the day number 365, except in leap years, when it is 366. For example, if a semester begins on 1/3/09 and ends on 5/17/09, the calculation is as follows:

The day number of 1/3/09 is 3
The day number of 5/17/09 is 137
The length of the semester is $137 - 3 + 1 = 135$

We add 1 to the difference of the days because we count the first day as part of the period.

The algorithm for calculating the day number for a date is complicated by leap years and by months of different lengths. We could code this algorithm as a void function named ComputeDay. The refund could then be computed by the following code segment:

```
ComputeDay(startMonth, startDay, startYear, start);
ComputeDay(lastMonth, lastDay, lastYear, last);
ComputeDay(withdrawMonth, withdrawDay, withdrawYear, withdraw);
fraction = static_cast<float>(last - withdraw + 1) /
           static_cast<float>(last - start + 1);
refund = tuition * fraction;
```

The first three arguments to ComputeDay are received by the function, and the last one is returned to the caller. Because ComputeDay returns only one value, we can write it as a value-returning function instead of a void function.

Let's look at how the calling code would be written if we had a value-returning function named `Day` that returned the day number of a date in a given year:

```
start = Day(startMonth, startDay, startYear);
last = Day(lastMonth, lastDay, lastYear);
withdraw = Day(withdrawMonth, withdrawDay, withdrawYear);
fraction = static_cast<float>(last - withdraw + 1) /
           static_cast<float>(last - start + 1);
refund = tuition * fraction;
```

This second version of the code segment is much more intuitive. Because `Day` is a value-returning function, you know immediately that all its parameters receive values and that it returns just one value (the day number for a date).

Let's look at the function definition for `Day`. Don't worry about how `Day` works; for now, you should concentrate on its syntax and structure.

```
int Day(int month, int dayOfMonth, int year)
// This function computes and returns the day number within a year,
// given the date. It accounts correctly for leap years.
// Pre:  The month, day, and year are within the proper range
{
  int correction = 0;     // Correction factor to account for leap year

  if (IsLeapYear(year))
    correction = 1;       //   Then add one for leap year
  // Correct for different-length months
  switch (month)
  {
    case 3 : correction = correction - 1;
             break;
    case 8 : correction = correction + 2;
             break;
    case 2 :
    case 6 :
    case 7 : correction = correction + 1;
             break;
    case 9 :
    case 10: correction = correction + 3;
             break
    case 11:
    case 12: correction = correction + 4;
             break;
  }
  return (month - 1) * 30 + correction + dayOfMonth;
}
```

See how useful it is to have a collection of functions that we can use later? We created the `IsLeapYear` function in Chapter 1. We can now use it here without bothering to see how the function works. We can embed function `Day` in a driver (test) program that prompts for and reads three dates and prints the tuition refund. Here we just set the tuition as a constant, although in the real program it would be input.

```
//*****************************************************************
// This program calculates and prints the tuition refund
// owed a student given the beginning and ending dates of the
// semester and the withdrawal date.
//*****************************************************************

#include <iostream>
#include <iomanip>
using namespace std;

const float TUITION = 35000.0f;

bool IsLeapYear(int year);        // Prototype for subalgorithm
// Returns true if the year is a leap year

int Day(int month, int dayOfMonth, int year);
// This function computes and returns the day number within a year,
// given the date. It accounts correctly for leap years.
// Pre:  The month, day, and year are within the proper range

int main ()
{
  int month, day, year;
  int start, last, withdraw;
  float fraction;
  float refund;

  cout << "Enter the month, day, and year of beginning of semester."
       << endl;
  cin >> month >> day >> year;
  start = Day(month, day, year);

  cout << "Enter the month, day, and year of end of semester."
       << endl;
  cin >> month >> day >> year;
  last = Day(month, day, year);

  cout << "Enter the month, day, and year of withdrawal."
       << endl;
  cin >> month >> day >> year;
  withdraw = Day(month, day, year);

  fraction = static_cast<float>(last - withdraw + 1) /
             static_cast<float>(last - start + 1);
  refund = TUITION * fraction;
  cout << "The student gets a refund of $" << fixed
       << setprecision(2) << refund << endl;

  return 0;
}

//*****************************************************************

int Day(int month, int dayOfMonth, int year)
// This function computes and returns the day number within a year,
```

```cpp
// given the date. It accounts correctly for leap years.
// Pre:  The month, day, and year are within the proper range
{
  int correction = 0;   // Correction factor to account for leap year

  if (IsLeapYear(year))
    correction = 1;     //   Then add one for leap year
  // Correct for different-length months
  switch (month)
  {
    case 3 : correction = correction - 1;
             break;
    case 8 : correction = correction + 2;
             break;
    case 2 :
    case 6 :
    case 7 : correction = correction + 1;
             break;
    case 9 :
    case 10: correction = correction + 3;
             break;
    case 11:
    case 12: correction = correction + 4;
             break;
  }
  return (month - 1) * 30 + correction + dayOfMonth;
}

//*******************************************************

bool IsLeapYear( int year )
// IsLeapYear returns true if year is a leap year and
// false otherwise

{
  if (year % 4 != 0)              // Is year not divisible by 4?
    return false;                 // If so, can't be a leap year
  else if (year % 100 != 0)       // Is year not a multiple of 100?
    return true;                  // If so, is a leap year
  else if (year % 400 != 0)       // Is year not a multiple of 400?
    return false;                 // If so, then is not a leap year
  else
    return true;                  // Is a leap year
}
```

Here is the output:

```
Enter the month, day, and year of beginning of semester.
1 15 2008
Enter the month, day, and year of end of semester.
5 15 2008
Enter the month, day, and year of withdrawal.
3 3 2008
The student gets a refund of $21404.96
```

Boolean Functions

Value-returning functions are not restricted to returning numerical results, as the previous example shows. Boolean functions can be useful when a branch or loop depends on some complex condition. Rather than code the condition directly into the If or While statement, we can call a Boolean function to form the controlling expression.

Suppose we are writing a program that works with triangles. The program reads three angles as floating-point numbers. Before performing any calculations on those angles, however, we want to check that they really form a triangle by adding the angles to confirm that their sum equals 180 degrees. We can write a value-returning function that takes the three angles as parameters and returns a Boolean result. Such a function would look like this (recall from Chapter 5 that you should test floating-point numbers only for near equality):

```
#include <cmath>     // For fabs()
  ⋮
bool IsTriangle(float angle1, float angle2, float angle3)
// This function returns true if its three incoming values
// add up to 180 degrees, forming a valid triangle, and
// false otherwise
{
  return (fabs(angle1 + angle2 + angle3 - 180.0) < 0.00000001);
}
```

The following program shows how the `IsTriangle` function is called. (The function definition is shown without its documentation to save space.)

```
//************************************************************
// Triangle program
// This program uses the IsTriangle function
//************************************************************
#include <iostream>
#include <cmath>        // For fabs()

using namespace std;

bool IsTriangle(float, float, float);

int main()
{
  float angleA;         // Three angles of a potential triangle
  float angleB;
  float angleC;
  cout << "Triangle testing program; "
       << "a negative first angle ends the processing." << endl;
  cout << "Enter 3 angles: ";
  cin >> angleA;
  while (angleA >= 0)
```

```
    {
      cin >> angleB >> angleC;
      if (IsTriangle(angleA, angleB, angleC))
        cout << "The 3 angles form a valid triangle." << endl;
      else
        cout << "The 3 angles do not form a triangle." << endl;
      cout << "Enter 3 angles: ";
      cin >> angleA;
    }
    return 0;
}

//*************************************************************

bool IsTriangle(float angle1, float angle2, float angle3)
{
    return (fabs(angle1 + angle2 + angle3 - 180.0) < 0.00000001);
}
```

Here is the output:

```
Triangle testing program; a negative first angle ends the processing.
Enter 3 angles:
45 10 35
The 3 angles do not form a triangle.
Enter 3 angles:
45 45 90
The 3 angles form a valid triangle.
Enter 3 angles:
90 80 35
The 3 angles do not form a triangle.
Enter 3 angles:
-10
```

In the `main` function of the `Triangle` program, the If statement is much easier to understand with the function call than it would be if the entire condition were coded directly. When a conditional test is at all complicated, a Boolean function is in order.

MATTERS OF STYLE Naming Value-Returning Functions

In Chapter 8, we said that it's good style to use imperative verbs when naming void functions. The reason for this preference is that a call to a void function is a complete statement and should look like a command to the computer:

```
PrintResults(a, b, c);
DoThis(x);
DoThat();
```

This naming scheme, however, doesn't work well with value-returning functions. A statement such as

```
z = 6.7 * ComputeMaximum(d, e, f);
```

sounds awkward when you read it aloud: "Set *z* equal to 6.7 times the *compute maximum* of *d*, *e*, and *f*."

With a value-returning function, the function call represents a value within an expression. Things that represent values, such as variables and value-returning functions, are best given names that are nouns or, occasionally, adjectives. See how much better this statement sounds when you pronounce it out loud:

```
z = 6.7 * Maximum(d, e, f);
```

You would read this as "Set *z* equal to 6.7 times the *maximum* of *d*, *e*, and *f*." Other names that suggest values rather than actions include `SquareRoot`, `Cube`, `Factorial`, `StudentCount`, `SumOfSquares`, and `SocialSecurityNum`. As you see, they are all nouns or noun phrases.

Boolean value-returning functions (and variables) are often named using adjectives or phrases beginning with *Is*. Here are a few examples:

```
while (Valid(m, n))
if (Odd(n))
if (IsTriangle(s1, s2, s3))
```

When you are choosing a name for a value-returning function, try to stick with nouns or adjectives so that the name suggests a value, not a command to the computer.

Interface Design and Side Effects

The interface to a value-returning module is designed in much the same way as the interface to a void module. We simply write down a list of what the module needs and what it must return. Because value-returning modules return only one value, there is only one item labeled "Out" in the list: the module return value. Everything else in the list is labeled "In," and there aren't any items labeled "In/out."

Returning more than one value from a value-returning module (by modifying the caller's arguments) is a side effect and, as such, should be avoided. If your interface design calls for multiple values to be returned, then you should use a void function instead of a value-returning function.

A rule of thumb is to avoid reference parameters in the parameter list of a value-returning module, and to use value parameters exclusively. Let's look at a function that demonstrates the importance of this rule. Suppose we define the following function:

```
int SideEffect(int& n}
{
  int result = n * n;

  n++;                    // Side effect
  return result;
}
```

This function returns the square of its incoming value, but it also increments the caller's argument before returning. Now suppose we call this function with the following statement:

```
y = x + SideEffect(x);
```

If `x` is originally 2, what value is stored into `y`? The answer depends on the order in which your compiler generates code to evaluate the expression. If the compiled code calls the function first, then the answer is 7. If it accesses `x` first in preparation for adding it to the function result, then the answer is 6. This uncertainty is precisely why you should not use reference parameters with value-returning functions. A function that causes an unpredictable result has no place in a well-written program.

An exception to this rule is when a module is being designed for C++ implementation using an I/O stream object as a parameter. Recall that C++ requires stream objects to be passed as reference parameters. Keep in mind that reading from or writing to a file within a function is really a side effect. If you choose to go this route, be sure that your decision is clearly documented in the postcondition.

There is another advantage to using only value parameters in a value-returning function definition: You can use constants and expressions as arguments. For example, we can call the `IsTriangle` function using literals and other expressions:

```
if (IsTriangle(30.0, 60.0, 30.0 + 60.0))
  cout << "The three angles form a valid triangle.";
else
  cout << "The 3 angles do not form a triangle.";
```

When to Use Value-Returning Functions

There aren't any formal rules that specify when to use a void function and when to use a value-returning function, but here are some guidelines:

1. If the module must return more than one value or modify any of the caller's arguments, do not use a value-returning function.
2. Avoid using value-returning functions to perform I/O. If you must, clearly document the side effect in the postcondition.
3. If only one value is returned from the module and it is a Boolean value, a value-returning function is appropriate.
4. If only one value is returned and it is to be used immediately in an expression, a value-returning function is appropriate.
5. When in doubt, use a void function. You can recode any value-returning function as a void function by adding an extra outgoing parameter to carry back the computed result.

6. If both a void function and a value-returning function are acceptable, use the form you feel more comfortable implementing.

Value-returning functions were included in C++ to provide a way of simulating the mathematical concept of a function. The C++ standard library supplies a set of commonly used mathematical functions through the header file **cmath**. A list of these appears in Appendix C.

> **QUICK CHECK**
>
> 9.4.1 If a module has three In parameters and one Out parameter, should it be implemented as a void function or a value-returning function? (p. 432)
>
> 9.4.2 What distinguishes a value-returning function from a void function? (pp. 422–424)
>
> 9.4.3 Given the following function heading, how would you write a call to it that will pass it the value 98.6 and assign the result to the variable **fever**? (pp. 422–424)
>
> ```
> bool TempCheck(float temp)
> ```
>
> 9.4.4 How many values are returned from a value-returning function? (p. 422)
>
> 9.4.5 What is a function value type? (p. 422)
>
> 9.4.6 What are the two forms of the Return statement? (p. 423)

9.5 Type Coercion in Assignments, Argument Passing, and Return of a Function Value

In general, promotion of a value from one type to another does not cause loss of information. Think of promotion as the process of moving your baseball cards from a small shoe box to a larger shoe box. All of the cards still fit into the new box and there is room to spare. By comparison, demotion (or narrowing) of data values can potentially cause loss of information. Demotion is like moving a shoe box full of baseball cards into a smaller box—something has to be thrown out.

> **Demotion (narrowing)** The conversion of a value from a "higher" type to a "lower" type according to a programming language's precedence of data types. Demotion may cause loss of information.

Consider the assignment operation

```
v = e
```

where **v** is a variable and **e** is an expression. Regarding the data types of **v** and **e**, there are three possibilities:

1. If the types of **v** and **e** are the same, no type coercion is necessary.
2. If the type of **v** is "higher" than that of **e**, then the value of **e** is promoted to **v**'s type before being stored into **v**.
3. If the type of **v** is "lower" than that of **e**, the value of **e** is demoted to **v**'s type before being stored into **v**.

Demotion, which you can think of as shrinking a value, may cause loss of information:

- Demotion from a longer integral type to a shorter integral type (such as from **long** to **int**) results in discarding the leftmost (most significant) bits in the binary number representation. The result may be a drastically different number.
- Demotion from a floating-point type to an integral type causes truncation of the fractional part (and an undefined result if the whole-number part will not fit into the destination variable). The result of truncating a negative number varies from one machine to another.

- Demotion from a longer floating-point type to a shorter floating-point type (such as from `double` to `float`) may result in a loss of digits of precision.

Our description of type coercion in an assignment operation also holds for argument passing (the mapping of arguments onto parameters) and for returning a function value with a Return statement. For example, assume that `INT_MAX` on your machine is 32767 and that you have the following function:

```
void DoSomething( int n )
{
     ⋮
}
```

If the function is called with the statement

```
DoSomething(50000);
```

then the value 50000 (which is implicitly of type `long` because it is larger than `INT_MAX`) is demoted to a completely different, smaller value that fits into an `int` location. In a similar fashion, execution of the function

```
int SomeFunc( float x )
{
     ⋮
   return 70000;
}
```

causes demotion of the value 70000 to a smaller `int` value because `int` is the declared type of the function return value.

One interesting consequence of implicit type coercion is the futility of declaring a variable to be unsigned, in hopes that the compiler will prevent you from making a mistake like this:

```
unsignedVar = -5;
```

The compiler does not complain at all. It generates code to coerce the `int` value to an unsigned `int` value. But if you now print out the value of `unsignedVar`, you'll see a strange-looking positive integer. As we have pointed out before, unsigned types are most appropriate for advanced techniques that manipulate individual bits within memory cells. It's best to avoid using `unsigned` for ordinary numeric computations.

To be safe, avoid implicit coercion whenever you can!

BACKGROUND INFORMATION
Ignoring a Function Value

A peculiarity of the C++ language is that it lets you ignore the value returned by a value-returning function. For example, you could write the following statement in your program without any complaint from the compiler:

```
sqrt(x);
```

BACKGROUND INFORMATION Ignoring a Function Value, continued

When this statement is executed, the value returned by `sqrt` is promptly discarded. This function call has absolutely no effect except to waste the computer's time by calculating a value that is never used.

Clearly, this call to `sqrt` is a mistake. No programmer would write that statement intentionally. But C++ programmers occasionally write value-returning functions in a way that allows the caller to ignore the function value.

Consider this example from the C++ standard library. The library provides a function named `remove`, the purpose of which is to delete a file from the system. It takes a single argument—a C string specifying the name of the file—and returns a function value. This function value is an integer notifying you of the status: 0 if the operation succeeded, and nonzero if it failed. Here is how you might call the `remove` function:

```
status = remove("junkfile.dat");
if (status != 0)
    PrintErrorMsg();
```

If you assume that the system always succeeds at deleting a file, you can ignore the returned status by calling `remove` as though it were a void function:

```
remove("junkfile.dat");
```

The `remove` function is sort of a hybrid between a void function and a value-returning function. Conceptually, it is a void function; its principal purpose is to delete a file, not to compute a value to be returned. Literally, though, it's a value-returning function. It does return a function value—the status of the operation (which you can choose to ignore).

In this book, we don't write hybrid functions. We prefer to keep the concept of a void function distinct from a value-returning function. Nevertheless, there are two reasons why every C++ programmer should know about the possibility of ignoring a function value. First, if you accidentally call a value-returning function as if it were a void function, the compiler won't prevent you from making the mistake. Second, you sometimes encounter this style of coding in other people's programs and in the C++ standard library. Several of the library functions are technically value-returning functions, but the function value is used simply to return something of secondary importance, such as a status value.

QUICK CHECK

9.5.1 What can occur with the demotion of a data value? (p. 433)
9.5.2 What happens when we assign a long value to an int value? (p. 433)
9.5.3 Give an example of automatic coercion that may be dangerous and lead to unexpected results. (p. 434)
9.5.4 What parts of a function are affected by type coercion? (p. 433)

Problem-Solving Case Study

Health Profile

PROBLEM: Your grandmother has just come back from the doctor's office and is confused about all the numbers that were used to evaluate her health. The nurse weighed her, took her blood pressure, noted her cholesterol levels from her lab work, and told her to sit down, because the doctor would be in to see her shortly. After half an hour the doctor came in, looked at your grandmother's chart, smiled, and said she was fine. In looking over the report she gave your grandmother, you realize that there could be a market for a program that explains this information to patients. You have a project due in your software engineering class, so you decide to write the program to do exactly that.

Before you can state the input and output from this program, you need to go to the Web and do some research. You find that there are two important types of cholesterol: high-density lipoprotein (HDL; good) and low-density lipoprotein (LDL; bad). The ratio of the two is also important. You find several references that give you interpretations for a range of HDL and LDL values.

The interpretation of your weight depends on a ratio of your weight to your size as represented in the body mass index (BMI). Good! You already have a program to calculate the BMI.

Blood pressure is made up of two values: systolic and diastolic. When talking about blood pressure, the readings are usually given as "something" over "something," such as 120/80. The first value is the systolic pressure, and the second value is the diastolic pressure.

Now, you have enough information to determine the input.

INPUT: Patient's name, HDL, LDL, weight in pounds, height in inches, systolic pressure, and diastolic pressure.

OUTPUT: Patient's name, each of the input values, and interpretations of the cholesterol, weight, and blood pressure readings are written on file "Profile."

DISCUSSION: The decomposition of this problem into tasks is very straightforward. The data values are prompted for, entered, and evaluated. The only question is whether to enter the data all at once and evaluate it or whether to have each evaluation module enter its own data. The principle of information hiding suggests that we embed the data-gathering process within the modules that evaluate the data.

Here are the interpretations you found on the Web concerning cholesterol:

HDL	Interpretation
< 40	Too low
≥ 40 and < 60	Is okay
≥ 60	Excellent

LDL	Interpretation
< 100	Optimal
≥ 100 and < 130	Near optimal
≥ 130 and < 160	Borderline high
≥ 160 and < 190	High
≥ 190	Very high

Problem-Solving Case Study

Ratio HDL/LDL	Interpretation
> 0.3	Ratio is good
≤ 0.3	Ratio is not good

Fortunately, you already have the BMI calculator that can simply be turned into a function with the food suggestions removed. What about blood pressure readings? Again, here is what you found on the Web concerning blood pressure readings:

Systolic	Interpretation
< 120	Optimal
< 130	Normal
< 140	Normal high
< 160	Stage 1 hypertension
< 180	Stage 2 hypertension
≥ 180	Stage 3 hypertension

Diastolic	Interpretation
< 80	Optimal
< 85	Normal
< 90	High normal
< 100	Stage 1 hypertension
< 110	Stage 2 hypertension
≥ 110	Stage 3 hypertension

Main   Level 0

Open output file
IF output file not opened okay
  Write error message
  Return 1
Get name
Evaluate cholesterol
Evaluate BMI
Evaluate blood pressure
Close output file

Get Name (Out: String function value)   Level 1

Prompt for first name
Get first name
Prompt for last name
Get last name
Prompt for middle initial
Get middle initial
return first + ' ' + middle + ". " + last

Problem-Solving Case Study

Evaluate Cholesterol (In/out: healthProfile; In: name)

    Prompt for name's input
    Get data
    Print data
    Evaluate input according to charts
    Print message

Name has been added to the parameter list so that the user can prompt for the specific patient's data. The first two lines can be directly translated into C++. We can print as we evaluate, so these two tasks are implemented together.

Evaluate Input and Print (In: HDL, LDL)

    IF (HDL < 40)
        Print on healthProfile " HDL is too low"
    ELSE if (HDL < 60)
        Print on healthProfile " HDL is okay"
    ELSE
        Print on healthProfile " HDL is excellent"

    IF (LDL < 100)
        Print on healthProfile " LDL is optimal"
    ELSE IF (LDL < 130)
        Print on healthProfile " LDL is near optimal"
    ELSE IF (LDL < 160)
        Print on healthProfile " LDL is borderline high"
    ELSE IF (LDL < 190)
        Print on healthProfile " LDL is high"
    ELSE
        Print on healthProfile " LDL is very high"

    IF (ratio > 0.3)
        Print on healthProfile " Ratio of HDL to LDL is good";
    ELSE
        Print on healthProfile " Ratio of HDL to LDL is not good"

The algorithm for Evaluate BMI is discussed in Chapter 5. We can use it here by changing only the output. Evaluate Blood Pressure is identical in form, so we leave its development to you as Case Study Follow-Up Exercise 3.

Which modules should be functions and which should be coded inline? GetName should be a value-returning function; Evaluate Cholesterol, Evaluate BMI, and Evaluate Blood Pressure should be void functions. The question is whether the Evaluate Input and Print modules should be coded as separate functions. If we were coding this problem in a language that allowed us to embed a function within a function, good style would suggest that we make the Evaluate Input and Print modules separate functions. However, C++ does not. These modules would have to be coded at the same level as the functions that would call them. Thus

Problem-Solving Case Study

they will be coded inline. Another reason for doing so is that Evaluate Cholesterol, Evaluate BMI, and Evaluate Blood Pressure are tightly knit functions with a clearly stated purpose and interface.

```
//*****************************************************************
// Profile Program
// This program inputs a name, weight, height, blood pressure
// readings, and cholesterol values.  Appropriate health messages
// are written for each of the input values on file healthProfile.
//*****************************************************************

#include <fstream>
#include <iostream>
#include <string>
#include <iomanip>

using namespace std;

// Function prototypes

string Name();
// This function inputs a name and returns it in first,
// middle initial, and last order

void EvaluateCholesterol(ofstream& healthProfile, string name);
// This function inputs HDL (good cholesterol) and LDL (bad
// cholesterol) and prints out a health message based on their
// values on file healthProfile.
// Pre: Input file has been successfully opened

void EvaluateBMI(ofstream& healthProfile, string name);
// This function inputs weight in pounds and height in inches and
// calculates the body mass index (BMI), then prints a health message
// based on the BMI. Input is in English weights.
// Pre: Input file has been successfully opened
```

Problem-Solving Case Study

```
void EvaluateBloodPressure(ofstream& healthProfile, string name);
// This function gets blood pressure readings (systolic/diastolic)
// and prints out a health message based on their values
// on file healthProfile.
// Pre: Input file has been successfully opened

int main()
{
  // Declare and open the output file
  ofstream healthProfile;
  healthProfile.open("Profile");
  string name;
  name = Name();

  // Write patient's name on output file
  healthProfile << "Patient's name " << name << endl;

  // Evaluate the patient's statistics
  EvaluateCholesterol(healthProfile, name);
  EvaluateBMI(healthProfile, name);
  EvaluateBloodPressure(healthProfile, name);
  healthProfile << endl;

  healthProfile.close();
  return 0;
}

//*****************************************************************

string Name()
// This function inputs a name and returns it in first,
// middle initial, and last order
{
  // Declare the patient's name
  string firstName;
  string lastName;
  char middleInitial;

  // Prompt for and enter the patient's name
  cout << "Enter the patient's first name: ";
  cin >> firstName;
  cout << "Enter the patient's last name: ";
  cin >> lastName;
  cout << "Enter the patient's middle initial: ";
  cin >> middleInitial;
  return firstName + ' ' + middleInitial + ". " + lastName;
}

//*****************************************************************
```

Problem-Solving Case Study

```cpp
void EvaluateCholesterol(ofstream& healthProfile, string name)
// This function inputs HDL (good cholesterol) and LDL (bad
// cholesterol) and prints out a  health message based on their
// values on file healthProfile.
{
  int HDL;
  int LDL;

  // Prompt for and enter HDL and LDL
  cout << "Enter HDL for " << name << ": ";
  cin >> HDL;
  cout << "Enter LDL for " << name << ": ";
  cin >> LDL;
  float ratio = static_cast<float>(HDL)/
                static_cast<float>(LDL);   // Calculate HDL to LDL ratio

  healthProfile << "Cholesterol Profile " << endl
                << "   HDL: " << HDL << "  LDL: " << LDL << endl
                << "   Ratio: " << fixed << setprecision(4)
                << ratio << endl;

  // Print message based on HDL value
  if (HDL < 40)
    healthProfile << "    HDL is too low" << endl;
  else if (HDL < 60)
    healthProfile << "    HDL is okay" << endl;
  else
    healthProfile << "    HDL is excellent" << endl;
  // Print message based on LDL value
  if (LDL < 100)
    healthProfile << "    LDL is optimal" << endl;
  else if (LDL < 130)
    healthProfile << "    LDL is near optimal" << endl;
  else if (LDL < 160)
    healthProfile << "    LDL is borderline high" << endl;
  else if (LDL < 190)
    healthProfile << "    LDL is high" << endl;
  else
    healthProfile << "    LDL is very high" << endl;

  if (ratio > 0.3)
    healthProfile << "    Ratio of HDL to LDL is good"
                  << endl;
  else
    healthProfile << "    Ratio of HDL to LDL is not good"
                  << endl;
}

//*****************************************************************

void EvaluateBMI(ofstream& healthProfile, string name )
// This function inputs weight in pounds and height in inches and
// calculates the body mass index. Input in English weights.
```

Problem-Solving Case Study

```cpp
{
  const int BMI_CONSTANT = 703;  // Constant in English formula
  int pounds;
  int inches;

  // Enter the patient's weight and height
  cout << "Enter the weight in pounds for " << name << ": ";
  cin >> pounds;
  cout << "Enter the height in inches for " << name << ": ";
  cin >> inches;
  int bodyMassIndex = pounds * BMI_CONSTANT / (inches * inches);

  healthProfile << "Body Mass Index Profile" << endl
                << "   Weight: " << pounds << "  Height: "
                << inches << endl;
  // Print bodyMassIndex
  healthProfile << "   Body mass index is " << bodyMassIndex
                << endl;
  healthProfile << "   Interpretation of BMI " << endl;

  // Print interpretation of BMI
  if (bodyMassIndex <20)
    healthProfile << "   Underweight"
                  << endl;
  else if (bodyMassIndex <=25)
    healthProfile << "   Normal"  << endl;
  else if (bodyMassIndex <= 30)
    healthProfile << "   Overweight"
                  << endl;
  else
    healthProfile << "   Obese"
                  << endl;
}

//******************************************************************

void EvaluateBloodPressure(ofstream& healthProfile, string name)
// This function gets blood pressure readings (systolic/diastolic)
// and prints out a health message based on their values
// on file healthProfile.
{
  // Declare the blood pressure readings
  int systolic;
  int diastolic;

  // Enter the patient's blood pressure readings
  cout << "Enter the systolic blood pressure reading for "
       << name << ": ";
  cin >> systolic;
  cout << "Enter the diastolic blood pressure reading for "
       << name << ": ";
  cin >> diastolic;
```

Problem-Solving Case Study

```cpp
// Print interpretation of systolic reading
healthProfile << "Blood Pressure Profile " << endl
              << "    Systolic: " << systolic
              << "    Diastolic: " << diastolic << endl;
if (systolic < 120)
  healthProfile << "   Systolic reading is optimal" << endl;
else if (systolic < 130)
  healthProfile << "   Systolic reading is normal" << endl;
else if (systolic < 140)
  healthProfile << "   Systolic reading is high normal"
                << endl;
else if (systolic < 160)
  healthProfile <<
    "   Systolic indicates hypertension Stage 1" << endl;
else if (systolic < 180)
  healthProfile <<
    "   Systolic indicates hypertension Stage 2" << endl;
else
  healthProfile <<
    "   Systolic indicates hypertension Stage 3" << endl;

// Print interpretation of diastolic reading
if (diastolic < 80)
  healthProfile << "   Diastolic reading is optimal" << endl;
else if (diastolic < 85)
  healthProfile << "   Diastolic reading is normal" << endl;
else if (diastolic < 90)
  healthProfile << "   Diastolic reading is high normal"
                << endl;
else if (diastolic < 100)
  healthProfile <<
    "   Diastolic indicates hypertension Stage 1" << endl;
else if (diastolic < 110)
  healthProfile <<
    "   Diastolic indicates hypertension Stage 2" << endl;
else
  healthProfile <<
    "   Diastolic indicates hypertension Stage 3" << endl;
}
```

Problem-Solving Case Study

Here is sample input and output.

Console

```
Enter the patient's first name: Stephen
Enter the patient's last name: Stark
Enter the patient's middle initial: S
Enter HDL for Stephen S. Stark: 60
Enter LDL for Stephen S. Stark: 120
Enter the weight in pounds for Stephen S. Stark: 180
Enter the height in inches for Stephen S. Stark: 72
Enter the systolic blood pressure reading for Stephen S. Stark: 130
Enter the diastolic blood pressure reading for Stephen S. Stark: 80
```

File Profile

```
Patient's name Steven S. Stark
Cholesterol Profile
   HDL: 60   LDL: 120
   Ratio: 0.5000
   HDL is excellent
   LDL is near optimal
   Ratio of HDL to LDL is good
Body Mass Index Profile
   Weight: 180   Height: 72
   Body mass index is 24
   Interpretation of BMI
   Normal
Blood Pressure Profile
   Systolic: 130   Diastolic: 80
   Systolic reading is high normal
   Diastolic reading is normal
```

TESTING: There are nine inputs to this program: two strings and a character in **Name**, two integer values in **EvaluateCholesterol**, two floating-point values in **EvaluateBMI**, and two integer values in **EvaluateBloodPressure**. The input to **Name** is just printed, so a simple test to see that it does read in and concatenate its input is sufficient. Each of the other functions needs to be checked separately, choosing values that occur at the break points in the If statements of each function. We demonstrate this testing process in the Testing and Debugging section.

SOFTWARE ENGINEERING TIP   Conceptual Versus Physical Hiding of a Function Implementation

Although program `Profile` is quite complex, the `main` function looks simple; it doesn't even contain a control structure. All of the control structures are contained within the individual functions. This is an example of how the complexity of a program is hidden by reducing each of the major control structures to an abstract action performed by a function call. In the `Profile` program, for example, evaluating a patient's BMI is an abstract action that appears as a call to `EvaluateBMI`. The logical properties of the action are separated from its implementation. This aspect of a design is called control abstraction.

Control abstraction can serve as a guideline for deciding which modules to code as functions and which to code directly. If a module contains a control structure, it is a good candidate for being implemented as a function. Even if a module does not contain a control structure, however, you still want to consider other factors. Is the module lengthy, or is it called from more than one place? If so, you should use a function.

Somewhat related to control abstraction is the concept of functional cohesion, which states that a module should perform exactly one abstract action. If you can state the action that a module performs in one sentence with no conjunctions (*and*s), then it is highly cohesive. A module that has more than one primary purpose lacks cohesion. Apart from `main`, all of the functions in program `Profile` have good cohesion.

A module that only partially fulfills a purpose also lacks cohesion. Such a module should be combined with whatever other modules are directly related to it. For example, it would make no sense to have a separate function that prints the first digit of a date, because printing a date is one abstract action.

A third and related aspect of a module's design is its communication complexity, which reflects the amount of data that passes through a module's interface—for example, the number of arguments. A module's communication complexity is often an indicator of its cohesiveness. Usually, if a module requires a large number of arguments, either it is trying to accomplish too much or it is only partially fulfilling a purpose. In such a case, you should step back and see if there is an alternative way of dividing up the problem so that a minimal amount of data is communicated between modules. The modules in `Profile` have low communication complexity.

> **Control abstraction**   The separation of the logical properties of an action from its implementation.
>
> **Functional cohesion**   The principle that a module should perform exactly one abstract action.
>
> **Communication complexity**   A measure of the quantity of data passing through a module's interface.

Testing and Debugging

One of the advantages of a modular design is that you can test the program long before the code has been written for all of the modules. If we test each module individually, then we can assemble the modules into a complete program with much greater confidence that the program is correct. In this section, we introduce a technique for testing a module separately.

Stubs and Drivers

Suppose you were given the code for a module and your job was to test it. How would you test a single module by itself? First, it must be called by something (unless it is `main`). Second, it may have calls to other modules that aren't available to you. To test the module, you must fill in these missing links.

When a module contains calls to other modules, we can write dummy functions called stubs to satisfy those calls.

A stub usually consists of an output statement that prints a message such as "Function such-and-such just got called." Even though the stub is a dummy, it allows us to determine whether the function is called at the right time by `main` or another function.

A stub also can be used to print the set of values that are passed to it; this output tells us whether the module being tested is supplying the correct information. Sometimes a stub assigns new values to its reference parameters to simulate data being read or results being computed to give the calling module something on which to keep working. Because we can choose the values that are returned by the stub, we have better control over the conditions of the test run.

Here is a stub that simulates the `Name` function in the `Profile` program by returning an arbitrarily chosen string:

> **Stub** A dummy function that assists in testing part of a program. A stub has the same name and interface as a function that actually would be called by the part of the program being tested, but is usually much simpler than the real function.
>
> **Driver** A simple main function that is used to call a function being tested. The use of a driver permits direct control of the testing process.

```
string Name()
// Stub for Name function in the Profile program
{
  cout << "Name was called here. Returning \"John J. Smith\"."
       << endl;
  return "John J. Smith";
}
```

This stub is simpler than the function it simulates, which is typical because the object of using a stub is to provide a simple, predictable environment for testing a module.

In addition to supplying a stub for each call within the module, you must provide a dummy program—a driver—to call the module itself. A driver program contains the bare minimum of code required to call the module being tested.

By surrounding a module with a driver and stubs, you gain complete control of the conditions under which it executes. This allows you to test different situations and combinations that may reveal errors. You write a test plan for a module, and then a driver implements that test plan.

Here is a test plan and a driver for the `EvaluateCholesterol` function in the `Profile` program. This test plan is based on the interpretation guidelines used to write the function. Each category is taken once. Case Study Follow-Up Exercise 1 asks you to determine if this test plan is sufficient.

Test Plan for EvaluateCholesterol Function

Reason for Test	Input	Expected Output	Observed
HDL too low	39, 99	HDL is too low LDL is optimal Ratio of HDL to LDL is good	
HDL is okay	59, 99	HDL is okay LDL is optimal Ratio of HDL to LDL is good	
HDL is excellent	69, 99	HDL is excellent LDL is optimal Ratio of HDL to LDL is good	
LDL is optimal	39, 99	HDL is too low LDL is optimal Ratio of HDL to LDL is good	
LDL is near optimal	39, 129	HDL is too low LDL is near optimal Ratio of HDL to LDL is good	
LDL is borderline	39, 159	HDL is too low LDL is borderline high Ratio of HDL to LDL is not good	
LDL is high	39, 189	HDL is too low LDL is high Ratio of HDL to LDL is not good	
LDL is very high	39, 195	HDL is too low LDL is very high Ratio of HDL to LDL is not good	

```
//*****************************************************************
// This program provides an environment for testing the
// EvaluateCholesterol function in isolation from program Profile.
//*****************************************************************
#include <iostream>
#include <fstream>
#include <iomanip>
using namespace std;
void EvaluateCholesterol(ofstream&, string);
```

```cpp
int main()
{
  ofstream healthProfile;
  healthProfile.open("Profile");
  string name = "John J. Smith";
  for (int test = 1; test <= 8; test++)
    EvaluateCholesterol(healthProfile, name);
  healthProfile.close();
  return 0;
}

//*********************************************************************

void EvaluateCholesterol(ofstream& healthProfile, string name)
// This function inputs HDL (good cholesterol) and LDL (bad
// cholesterol) and prints out a health message based on their
// values on file healthProfile.
// Pre: Input file has been successfully opened
{
  int HDL;
  int LDL;

  // Prompt for and enter HDL and LDL
  cout << "Enter HDL for " << name << ": ";
  cin >> HDL;
  cout << "Enter LDL for " << name << ": ";
  cin >> LDL;
  float ratio = static_cast<float>(HDL)/
                static_cast<float>(LDL);    // Calculate HDL to LDL ratio

  healthProfile << "Cholesterol Profile " << endl
                << "   HDL: " << HDL << "  LDL: " << LDL << endl
                << "   Ratio: " << fixed << setprecision(4)
                << ratio << endl;

  // Print message based on HDL value
  if (HDL < 40)
    healthProfile << "   HDL is too low" << endl;
  else if (HDL < 60)
    healthProfile << "   HDL is okay" << endl;
  else
    healthProfile << "   HDL is excellent" << endl;
  // Print message based on LDL value
  if (LDL < 100)
    healthProfile << "   LDL is optimal" << endl;
  else if (LDL < 130)
    healthProfile << "   LDL is near optimal" << endl;
  else if (LDL < 160)
    healthProfile << "   LDL is borderline high" << endl;
  else if (LDL < 190)
    healthProfile << "   LDL is high" << endl;
  else
    healthProfile << "   LDL is very high" << endl;
```

```
    if (ratio > 0.3)
      healthProfile << "   Ratio of HDL to LDL is good"
                    << endl;
    else
      healthProfile << "   Ratio of HDL to LDL is not good"
                    << endl;
}
```

The driver calls the function eight times, which allows the points in the If statements to be executed. Here are the input and the output for this code:

Input

```
Enter HDL for John J. Smith: 39
Enter LDL for John J. Smith: 99
Enter HDL for John J. Smith: 59
Enter LDL for John J. Smith: 99
Enter HDL for John J. Smith: 69
Enter LDL for John J. Smith: 99
Enter HDL for John J. Smith: 39
Enter LDL for John J. Smith: 99
Enter HDL for John J. Smith: 39
Enter LDL for John J. Smith: 129
Enter HDL for John J. Smith: 39
Enter LDL for John J. Smith: 159
Enter HDL for John J. Smith: 39
Enter LDL for John J. Smith: 189
Enter HDL for John J. Smith: 39
Enter LDL for John J. Smith: 195
```

Output

```
Cholesterol Profile
   HDL: 39   LDL: 99
   Ratio: 0.3939
   HDL is too low
   LDL is optimal
   Ratio of HDL to LDL is good
Cholesterol Profile
   HDL: 59   LDL: 99
   Ratio: 0.5960
   HDL is okay
   LDL is optimal
   Ratio of HDL to LDL is good
Cholesterol Profile
   HDL: 69   LDL: 99
   Ratio: 0.6970
   HDL is excellent
   LDL is optimal
   Ratio of HDL to LDL is good
```

```
Cholesterol Profile
    HDL: 39   LDL: 99
    Ratio: 0.3939
    HDL is too low
    LDL is optimal
    Ratio of HDL to LDL is good
Cholesterol Profile
    HDL: 39   LDL: 129
    Ratio: 0.3023
    HDL is too low
    LDL is near optimal
    Ratio of HDL to LDL is good
Cholesterol Profile
    HDL: 39   LDL: 159
    Ratio: 0.2453
    HDL is too low
    LDL is borderline high
    Ratio of HDL to LDL is not good
Cholesterol Profile
    HDL: 39   LDL: 189
    Ratio: 0.2063
    HDL is too low
    LDL is high
    Ratio of HDL to LDL is not good
Cholesterol Profile
    HDL: 39   LDL: 195
    Ratio: 0.2000
    HDL is too low
    LDL is very high
    Ratio of HDL to LDL is not good
```

Stubs and drivers are important tools in a team programming environment. With this approach, the programmers develop the overall design and the interfaces between the modules. Each programmer then designs and codes one or more of the modules and uses drivers and stubs to test the code. When all of the modules have been coded and tested, they are assembled into what should be a working program.

For team programming to succeed, it is essential that all of the module interfaces be defined explicitly and that the coded modules adhere strictly to the specifications for those interfaces. Obviously, global variable references must be carefully avoided in a team-programming situation because it is impossible for each person to know how the rest of the team is using every variable.

Testing and Debugging Hints

1. Make sure that variables used as arguments to a function are declared in the block where the function call is made.
2. Carefully define the precondition, postcondition, and parameter list to eliminate side effects. Variables used only in a function should be declared as local variables. *Do not* use global variables in your programs. (Exception: It is acceptable to reference `cin` and `cout` globally.)

3. If the compiler displays a message such as **UNDECLARED IDENTIFIER**, check that the identifier isn't misspelled (and that it is, in fact, declared), that the identifier is declared before it is referenced, and that the scope of the identifier includes the reference to it.
4. If you intend to use a local name that is the same as a nonlocal name, be aware that a misspelling in the local declaration will wreak havoc. The C++ compiler won't complain, but will cause every reference to the local name to go to the nonlocal name instead.
5. Remember that the same identifier cannot be used in both the parameter list and the outermost local declarations of a function.
6. With a value-returning function, be sure the function heading and prototype begin with the correct data type for the function return value.
7. With a value-returning function, don't forget to use a statement

    return *Expression*;

    to return the function value. Make sure the expression is of the correct type, or implicit type coercion will occur.
8. Remember that a call to a value-returning function is part of an expression, whereas a call to a void function is a separate statement. (C++ softens this distinction, however, by letting you call a value-returning function as if it were a void function, ignoring the return value. Be careful here.)
9. In general, don't use reference parameters in the parameter list of a value-returning function. A reference parameter must be used, however, when an I/O stream object is passed as a parameter.
10. If necessary, use your system's debugger (or use debug output statements) to determine when a function is called and if it is executing correctly. The values of the arguments can be displayed immediately before the call to the function (to show the incoming values) and immediately after the call completes (to show the outgoing values). You also may want to display the values of local variables in the function itself to indicate what happens each time it is called.

Summary

The scope of an identifier refers to the parts of the program in which it is visible. C++ function names have global scope, as do the names of variables and constants that are declared outside all functions and namespaces. Variables and constants declared within a block have local scope; they are not visible outside the block. The parameters of a function have the same scope as local variables declared in the outermost block of the function.

With rare exceptions, it is not considered good practice to declare global variables and reference them directly from within a function. All communication between the modules of a program should be through the argument and parameter lists (and via the function value sent back by a value-returning function). The use of global constants, by contrast, is considered to be an acceptable programming practice because it adds consistency and makes a program easier to change while avoiding the pitfalls of side effects. Well-designed and well-documented functions that are free of side effects can often be reused in other programs. Many programmers, in fact, keep a library of functions that they use repeatedly.

The lifetime of a variable is the period of time during program execution when memory is allocated to it. Global variables have a static lifetime: Memory remains allocated for the duration of the program's execution. By default, local variables have an automatic lifetime:

Memory is allocated and deallocated at block entry and block exit. A local variable may be given static lifetime by using the word `static` in its declaration. This variable has the lifetime of a global variable but the scope of a local variable.

C++ allows a variable to be initialized in its declaration. For a static variable, the initialization occurs once only—when control first reaches its declaration. An automatic variable is initialized each time control reaches the declaration.

C++ provides two kinds of subprograms, void functions and value-returning functions. A value-returning function is called from within an expression and returns a single result that is used in the evaluation of the expression. For the function value to be returned, the last statement executed by the function must be a Return statement containing an expression of the appropriate data type.

All the scope rules, as well as the rules about reference and value parameters, apply to both void functions and value-returning functions. It is considered poor programming practice, however, to use reference parameters in a value-returning function definition. Doing so increases the potential for unintended side effects. (An exception is when I/O stream objects are passed as parameters. Other exceptions are noted in later chapters.)

We can use stubs and drivers to test functions in isolation from the rest of a program. They are particularly useful in the context of team-programming projects.

■ **Quick Check Answers**

9.1.1 Global. **9.1.2** When a nested block contains a locally declared identifier with the same name. **9.1.3** Class scope, Local scope, Namespace scope, and Global scope. **9.2.1** Variables declared within the functions are local. In `Quick1`, `quest`, and `qc`. In `Quick2`, `quest` and `forever`. **9.2.2** `check`, `quest`, and the locally declared `qc`. **9.2.3** `check` and `qc` in the program, together with `forever`, are static. The variables in `Quick1` and the variable `quest` in `Quick2` are automatic. **9.2.4** During the execution time of a program. **9.2.5** The lifetime of a variable is the period of time in which memory has actually been allocated to it. **9.2.6** A variable whose storage is allocated at block entry and deallocated at block exit. **9.2.7** The duration of the entire program. **9.2.8** An initializer. **9.2.9** Only once. **9.2.10** An automatic variable is initialized each time control enters the block in which it is declared. **9.3.1** They enable a function to affect the state of the program through a means other than the well-defined interface of the parameter list. **9.3.2** Any effect of one function on another function that is not part of the explicitly defined interface between them. **9.3.3** Reusability **9.3.4** The `cin` and `cout` I/O facilities provided by the standard libraries. **9.3.5** Global constants. **9.4.1** A value-returning function. **9.4.2** Using a type name in place of `void`, and using a Return statement to pass a value back to the caller. **9.4.3** `fever = TempCheck(98.6);` **9.4.4** one. **9.4.5** The data type of the result value returned by a function. **9.4.6** `return;` and `return Expression;` **9.5.1** Loss of information. **9.5.2** The long value is demoted and the leftmost bits in the binary number will be discarded. **9.5.3** unsigned x = -1; **9.5.4** A function's parameters and return values.

■ **Exam Preparation Exercises**

1. A function parameter is local to the entire block that is the body of the function. True or false?
2. A reference parameter has the same scope as a global variable. True or false?
3. A global variable can be referenced anywhere within the program. True or false?
4. Function names have global scope. True or false?
5. Match the following terms with the definitions given below.
    a. Scope
    b. Name precedence
    c. Scope rules
    d. Nonlocal identifier

e. Lifetime
f. Automatic variable
g. Static variable
h. Side effect
   i. The semantics that specify where we can reference nonlocal identifiers.
   ii. A variable for which memory is allocated for the duration of the program.
   iii. When one function affects another function in a manner that isn't defined by their interface.
   iv. The precedence that a local identifier has over a global identifier with the same name.
   v. The region of program code where it is legal to reference an identifier.
   vi. A variable that has memory allocated at block entry and deallocated at block exit.
   vii. An identifier declared outside of the current block.
   viii. The period in which an identifier has memory allocated to it.

6. Identify the side effect in the following function.

```
int ExamPrep (int param1, int& param2)
{
  if (param2 = param1)
    return param2;
  else if (param2 > param1)
    return param1;
  else
    return param1 * param2;
}
```

7. Identify the side effect in the following program (which uses poor style for naming variables).

```
#include <iostream>
using namespace std;

string a;
int w;

bool GetYesOrNo();

int main ()
{
  cout << "Enter name:";
  cin >> a;
  w = 0;
  cout << "Is there a weight value?";
  if (GetYesOrNo());
  {
    cout << "Enter weight:";
    cin >> w;
  }
  cout << "Name is " << a << " weight is " << w << endl;
}
```

```
bool GetYesOrNo()
{
  cout << "Enter yes or no: ";
  cin >> a;
  return a == "yes";
}
```

8. What is the scope of a namespace that is specified in a `using` directive outside of all functions?

9. What is the scope of the `std` namespace in the following code?

   ```
   // Include directives and function prototypes here
   int main()
   {
     using namespace std;
     // Rest of main body is here
   }
   // Function definitions are here
   ```

10. What is the lifetime of each of the following?
    a. A global variable.
    b. A local variable in a function.
    c. A local, static variable in a function.

11. Rewrite the following declaration and initialization as a single statement.

    ```
    float pi;
    pi = 3.14159265;
    ```

12. If a local, static variable is initialized in its declaration within a function, when does the variable get initialized and how often?

13. If a local, nonstatic variable is initialized in its declaration within a function, when does the variable get initialized and how often?

14. A value-returning function can have just one Return statement. True or false?

15. What's wrong with the following function?

    ```
    bool Greater (int a, int b)
    {
      if (a > b)
        return true;
    }
    ```

16. What's wrong with the following function?

    ```
    int Average (int a, int b, int c)
    {
      return (a + b + c)/3.0;
    }
    ```

17. What's wrong with the following function?

    ```
    void Maximum (int a, int b, int& max)
    {
      if (a > b)
        max = a;
    ```

```
      else
        max = b;
      return max;
    }
```

18. Using a reference parameter in a value-returning function makes which kind of programming error more likely?

Programming Warm-Up Exercises

1. The following program is written in a very poor style that uses global variables instead of parameters and arguments, resulting in unwanted side effects. Rewrite it using good style.

    ```
    #include <iostream>
    using namespace std;
    int Power ();
    int pow;
    int x;
    int result;
    int main ()
    {
      cout << "Enter power: ";
      cin >> pow;
      cout << "Enter value to be raised to power: ";
      cin >> x;
      cout << Power(x, pow);
    }
    int Power ()
    {
      result = 1;
      while (pow > 0)
      {
        result = result * x;
        pow--;
      }
      return result;
    }
    ```

2. Write the heading for a `bool` function `Equals` that has two value `float` parameters, x and y.
3. Write the function prototype for the function in Exercise 2.
4. Write a body for the function in Exercise 2 that compares x and y, returning `true` if their difference is less than 0.00000001, and `false` otherwise.
5. Write the heading and function prototype for a `float` function called `ConeVolume` that takes two value `float` parameters, radius and height.
6. Write the body for the function heading in Exercise 5. The body computes the volume of a cone using the following formula:

$$\frac{1}{3} \pi \times \text{radius}^2 \times \text{height}$$

7. Rewrite the void function described in Programming Warm-Up Exercises 4 and 6 in Chapter 8 as a value-returning function. The function, which is called `GetLeast`, takes an `ifstream` parameter called `infile` as an input parameter that is changed. It returns an `int` value that is the lowest value read from the file.

8. Rewrite the void function called `Reverse` that is described in Programming Warm-Up Exercises 8 and 10 in Chapter 8 as a value-returning function. It should take a `string` parameter as input. The function returns a string that is the character-by-character reverse of the string in the parameter. The parameter is called `original`.

9. Rewrite the void function called `LowerCount` that is described in Programming Warm-Up Exercise 12 of Chapter 8 as a value-returning function. The function reads a line from `cin`, and returns an `int` containing the number of lowercase letters in the line. In Appendix C, you will find the description of function `islower`, which returns `true` if its `char` parameter is a lowercase character.

10. Write a value-returning `float` function called `SquareKm` that takes two `float` parameters, length and width, and outputs a return value that is in square kilometers. The parameters are the length and width of an area in miles. The conversion factor for kilometers from miles is 1.6.

11. Write a value-returning `bool` function called `Exhausted` that takes an `int` parameter called `filmRolls`. The function keeps track of how many prints have been processed by the chemistry in a photo-processing machine. When the total number of prints exceeds 1000, it returns `true`. Each time the function is called, the value in the parameter is added to the total. When the total exceeds 1000, the variable containing the total is reset to zero before the function returns, under the assumption that the exhausted chemistry will be replaced before more prints are processed.

12. Write a value-returning `string` function called `MonthAbbrev` that takes an `int` value as a parameter. The parameter, `month`, represents the number of the month. The function returns a string containing the three-letter abbreviation for the corresponding month number. Assume that the month number is in the range of 1 to 12.

13. Modify the function in Exercise 12 to handle month numbers that are not in the valid range by returning the string `"Inv"`.

14. Write a value-returning `float` function called `RunningAvg` that takes a `float` variable, `value`, as its input and returns the running average of all the values that have been passed to the function since the program first called it.

■ Programming Problems

1. Write a C++ program that defines value-returning functions for the arithmetic integer binary operations *plus*, *minus*, *multiply*, and *divide*. You should also write a value-returning function for the unary operation negate. Use your function declarations to compute the following as a single expression:

    $-(((5-4)*(8/2))+7)$

    Your `main` function should not declare a single variable, but it should print as output the result of computing this expression. Your implementation is correct if your output yields the value −11.

2. Use your function declarations in Problem 1 to define two additional integer functions for *power* and *factorial*. Use your new function declarations to compute as a single expression the following:

$(5! + 4!)^3$

Your `main` function should not declare a single variable but it should print as output the result of computing this expression. Your implementation is correct if your output yields the value 2985984.

3. ROT13 (rotate by 13 places) is a simple letter substitution cipher that is an instance of a Caesar cipher developed in ancient Rome and used by Julius Caesar who used it in his private correspondence. ROT13 replaces a letter with the letter 13 letters after it in the alphabet. The following table demonstrates the translation in ROT13:

A ↔ N
B ↔ O
C ↔ P
D ↔ Q
E ↔ R
F ↔ S
G ↔ T
H ↔ U
I ↔ V
J ↔ W
K ↔ X
L ↔ Y
M ↔ Z

Thus, the translation of the word JULIUS using ROT13 would be WHYVHF. Write a C++ program that asks the user for the name of an input file and translates the contents of that input file using ROT13. Your `main` function should be responsible for reading the input file and coordinating calls to a value-returning function named `Rot13` that will do the translation for each character and `WriteTranslatedChar` that will write the translated character to a secondary file. The `Rot13` function takes as input the character to be translated and returns the translated character. The second function named `WriteTranslatedChar` will have two parameters, the translated character and a reference to an `ifstream` data type for a secondary file named "`output.rot13`", and write that translated character to this file.

4. In mathematics, the Fibonacci numbers are the series of numbers that exhibit the following pattern:

0, 1, 1, 2, 3, 5, 8, 13, 21, 34, 55, 89, 144, ...

In mathematical notation the sequence F_n of Fibonacci numbers is defined by the following recurrence relation:

$F_n = F_{n-1} + F_{n-2}$

With the initial values of $F_0 = 0$ and $F_1 = 1$. Thus, the next number in the series is the sum of the previous two numbers. Write a program that asks the user for a positive integer N and generates the Nth Fibonacci number. Your `main` function should handle user input and pass that data to a function called Fib that takes an integer value N as input and returns the Nth Fibonacci number.

5. You are working on a project that requires climate data for a location. The maximum daily change in barometric pressure is one aspect of climate that your company needs. You have a file (`barometric.dat`) containing hourly barometer readings taken over the course of a year. Each line of the file contains the readings for a single day, separated by blanks. Each reading is expressed in inches of mercury, so it is a decimal number ranging from approximately 28.00 to 32.00. For each line of data, you need to determine the maximum and minimum readings, and output the difference between those readings to file `differences.dat`. Each output value should appear on a separate line of the file. Once the file has been read, the program should output the greatest and least differences for the year on `cout`. Develop the program using functional decomposition, and use proper style and documentation in your code. Your program should make appropriate use of value-returning functions in solving this problem.

6. Extend the program in Problem 5 so that it also outputs the maximum and minimum barometric readings for each day on file `differences.dat`, and then outputs the maximum and minimum readings for the year on `cout` at the end of the run.

7. You're working for a lumber company, and your employer would like a program that calculates the cost of lumber for an order. The company sells pine, fir, cedar, maple, and oak lumber. Lumber is priced by board feet. One board foot equals one square foot, one inch thick. The price per board foot is given in the following table:

Pine	0.89
Fir	1.09
Cedar	2.26
Maple	4.50
Oak	3.10

The lumber is sold in different dimensions (specified in inches of width and height, and feet of length) that need to be converted to board feet. For example, a 2 × 4 × 8 piece is 2 inches wide, 4 inches high, and 8 feet long, and is equivalent to 5.333 board feet. An entry from the user will be in the form of a letter and four integer numbers. The integers are the number of pieces, width, height, and length. The letter will be one of P, F, C, M, O (corresponding to the five kinds of wood) or T, meaning total. When the letter is T, there are no integers following it on the line. The program should print out the price for each entry, and print the total after T is entered. Here is an example run:

Develop the program using functional decomposition, and use proper style and documentation in your code. Your program should make appropriate use of value-returning functions in solving this problem. Be sure that the user prompts are clear, and that the output is labeled appropriately.

8. Write a program that determines the day of the week for a given date. You can invent your own complex algorithm that takes into account the special leap year rules, and changes in calendars, but this is a case where it makes sense to look for things that are familiar. Who else might need to compute values from dates over a wide span of time? Historians work with dates, but generally don't compute from them. Astronomers, however, need to know the difference in time between orbital events in the solar system that span hundreds of years. Consulting an astronomy text, you will find that there is a standard way of representing a date, called the Julian Day Number (JDN). This value is the number of days that have elapsed since January 1, 4713 B.C. Given the JDN for a date, there is a simple formula that tells the day of the week:

```
DayOfWeek = (JDN + 1) % 7
```

The result is in the range of 0 to 6, with 0 representing Sunday.

The only remaining problem is how to compute the JDN, which is not so simple. The algorithm computes several intermediate results that are added together to give the JDN. We look at the computation of each of these three intermediate values in turn.

If the date comes from the Gregorian calendar (later than October 15, 1582), then compute `intRes1` with the following formula; otherwise, let `intRes1` be zero.

```
intRes1 = 2 - year / 100 + year / 400     (integer division)
```

The second intermediate result is computed as follows:

```
intRes2 = static_cast<int>(365.25 * Year)
```

We compute the third intermediate value with this formula:

```
intRes3 = static_cast<int>(30.6001 * (month + 1))
```

Finally, the JDN is computed this way:

```
JDN = intRes1 + intRes2 + intRes3 + day + 1720994.5
```

Your program should make appropriate use of value-returning functions in solving this problem. These formulas require nine significant digits; you may have to use the integer type `long` and the floating-point type `double`. Your program should prompt the user appropriately for input of the date; it should also properly label the output. Use proper coding style with comments to document the algorithm as needed.

9. Reusing functions from Problem 8 as appropriate, write a C++ program that computes the number of days between two dates. If your design for Problem 8 used good functional decomposition, this should be a trivial program to write. You merely need to input two dates, convert them to their JDNs, and take the difference of the JDNs.

Your program should make appropriate use of value-returning functions in solving this problem. These formulas require nine significant digits; you may have to use the integer type `long` and the floating-point type `double`. Your program should prompt the user appropriately for input of the date; it should also properly label the output. Use proper coding style with comments to document the algorithm as needed.

■ Case Study Follow-Up

1. Was the test plan outlined for function `EvaluateCholesterol` complete? If not, why not?
2. The BMI measure is calculated as an integer. Is this sufficient? Would it be a better idea to make this a real value? What would have to be changed to do so?
3. Write the algorithm for the Evaluate Blood Pressure module.
4. Write a test plan and a driver to test function `EvaluateBloodPressure`.
5. Add a Boolean function to the three Evaluate modules, which is `true` if the data are okay and `false` otherwise. Test the input within each module for negative or zero input values, which should be considered errors. If an error occurs, state in which module it occurs and set the error flag.
6. Rewrite the `main` program to test the flag set in Exercise 5 after each call and exit the program if an error occurs.

User-Defined Data Types

KNOWLEDGE GOALS

- To know all of the simple data types provided by the C++ language.
- To understand the concept of an enumerated type.
- To understand the difference between external and internal representations of character data.
- To understand the concept of a record type.
- To understand the concept of a pointer variable.
- To understand the general concept of a C++ union type.

SKILL GOALS

To be able to:

- Use a Typedef statement.
- Declare and use an enumeration type.
- Use the For and Switch statements with user-defined enumeration types.
- Distinguish a named user-defined type from an anonymous user-defined type.
- Declare a **struct** (record) data type, a data structure whose components may be heterogeneous.
- Access a member of a **struct** variable.
- Define a hierarchical record structure.
- Access values stored in a hierarchical record.
- Declare variables of pointer types.
- Take the addresses of variables and access the variables through pointers.
- Write an expression that selects a member of a class, struct, or union that is pointed to by a pointer.

This chapter represents a transition point in your study of computer science and C++ programming. So far, we have emphasized simple variables, control structures, and named processes (functions). After this chapter, the focus shifts to ways to structure (organize) data and to the algorithms necessary to process data in these structured forms. To make this transition, we must examine the concept of data types in greater detail.

Until now, we have worked primarily with the data types `int`, `char`, `bool`, and `float`. These four data types are adequate for solving a wide variety of problems. Certain programs, however, need other kinds of data. Sometimes the built-in data types cannot adequately represent all the data in a program. C++ has several mechanisms for creating user-defined data types; that is, we can define new data types ourselves. This chapter introduces one of these mechanisms, the enumeration type.

In this chapter, we also expand the definition of a data type to include structured types, which represent collections of components that are referred to by a single name. We begin with a discussion of structured types in general and then examine two structured types provided by the C++ language: `struct` and `union`.

10.1 Built-In Simple Types

In Chapter 2, we defined a data type as a specific set of data values (which we call the domain) along with a set of operations on those values. For the `int` type, the domain is the set of whole numbers from `INT_MIN` through `INT_MAX`, and the allowable operations we have seen so far are +, -, *, /, %, ++, --, and the relational and logical operations. The domain of the `float` type is the set of all real numbers that a particular computer is capable of representing, and the operations are the same as those for the `int` type except that modulus (%) is excluded. For the `bool` type, the domain is the set consisting of the two values `true` and `false`, and the allowable operations are the logical (!, &&, ||) and relational operations. The `char` type, although used primarily to manipulate character data, is classified as an integral type because it uses integers in memory to stand for characters. Later in the chapter we will see how this process works.

> **Simple (atomic) data type** A data type in which each value is atomic (indivisible).

The `int`, `char`, `bool`, and `float` types have a property in common: The domain of each type is made up of indivisible, or atomic, data values. Data types with this property are called simple (or atomic) data types. When we say that a value is atomic, we mean that it is not defined to have component parts that are accessed separately. For example, a single character of type `char` is atomic, but the string "Good Morning" is not (it is composed of 12 individual characters that we can also access).

Another way of describing a simple type is to say that only one value can be associated with a variable of that type. In contrast, a structured type is one in which an entire collection of values is associated with a single variable of that type. For example, a string object represents a collection of characters that are given a single name.

FIGURE 10.1 shows the simple types that are built into the C++ language. This figure is a portion of the complete diagram of C++ data types presented in Figure 3.1.

In this figure, one of the types—`enum`—is not actually a single data type in the sense that `int` and `float` are data types. Instead, it is a mechanism with which we can define our own simple data types. We will look at `enum` later in this chapter.

10.1 Built-In Simple Types

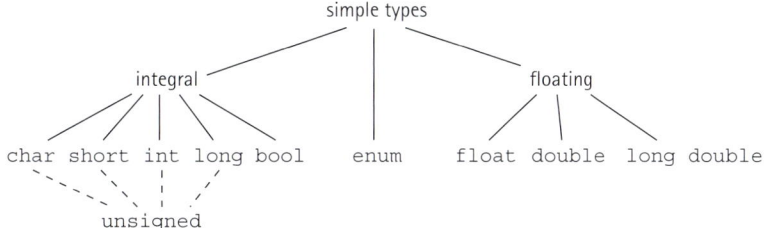

FIGURE 10.1 C++ Simple Types

Numeric Types

The integral types `char`, `short`, `int`, and `long` represent nothing more than integers of different sizes. Similarly, the floating-point types `float`, `double`, and `long double` simply refer to floating-point numbers of different sizes. What do we mean by sizes?

In C++, sizes are measured in multiples of the size of a `char`. By definition, the size of a `char` is 1. On most—but not all—computers, the 1 means one byte. (Recall from Chapter 1 that a byte is a group of eight consecutive bits [1s or 0s].)

Let's use the notation *sizeof* (SomeType) to denote the size of a value of type SomeType. Then, by definition, *sizeof* (`char`) = 1. Other than `char`, the sizes of data objects in C++ are machine dependent. On one machine, it might be the case that

sizeof (`char`) = 1
sizeof (`short`) = 2
sizeof (`int`) = 4
sizeof (`long`) = 8

On another machine, the sizes might be as follows:

sizeof (`char`) = 1
sizeof (`short`) = 2
sizeof (`int`) = 2
sizeof (`long`) = 4

Despite these variations, the C++ language guarantees that the following statements are true:

- 1 = *sizeof* (`char`) <= *sizeof* (`short`) <= *sizeof* (`int`) <= *sizeof* (`long`).
- 1 <= *sizeof* (`bool`) <= *sizeof* (`long`).
- *sizeof* (`float`) <= *sizeof* (`double`) <= *sizeof* (`long double`).
- A `char` is at least 8 bits.
- A `short` is at least 16 bits.
- A `long` is at least 32 bits.

> **Range of values** The interval within which values of a numeric type must fall, specified in terms of the largest and smallest allowable values.

For numeric data, the size of a data object determines its range of values. We showed a table of the range of values for numeric data types in Chapter 3 on page 93. Be careful: The actual range of values of a numeric data type is machine dependent. The only constraints on the C++ compiler are the relative sizes of the ranges given earlier. Making an implicit assumption about the actual range in a particular program may cause portability problems when the program is run on another machine.

Recall that the reserved word `unsigned` may precede the name of certain integral types—`unsigned char`, `unsigned short`, `unsigned int`, `unsigned long`. Values of these types are nonnegative integers with values from 0 through some machine-dependent maximum value. Although we rarely use unsigned types in this book, we include them in this discussion for thoroughness.

C++ systems provide the header file `climits`, from which you can determine the maximum and minimum values for your machine. This header file defines the constants `CHAR_MAX` and `CHAR_MIN`, `SHRT_MAX` and `SHRT_MIN`, `INT_MAX` and `INT_MIN`, and `LONG_MAX` and `LONG_MIN`. The unsigned types have a minimum value of 0 and maximum values defined by `UCHAR_MAX`, `USHRT_MAX`, `UINT_MAX`, and `ULONG_MAX`. To find out the values specific to your computer, you could print them out like this:

```
#include <climits>
using namespace std;
    ⋮
cout << "Max. long= " << LONG_MAX << endl;
cout << "Min. long= " << LONG_MIN << endl;
    ⋮
```

Code designed for portability should check these adjectives where needed within the program.

Likewise, the standard header file `cfloat` defines the constants `FLT_MAX` and `FLT_MIN`, `DBL_MAX` and `DBL_MIN`, and `LDBL_MAX` and `LDBL_MIN`. To determine the ranges of values for your machine, you could write a short program that prints out these constants.

We should note that the C++ standard adds header files called `limits.h` and `float.h` that also contain these definitions.

Characters

Each computer uses a particular character set, the set of all possible characters with which it is capable of working. ASCII, which consists of 128 different characters, has historically been used by the vast majority of computers. The extended version of the ASCII character set provides 256 characters, which is enough for English but not enough for international use. This limitation gave rise to the Unicode character set, which has a much wider international following.

Unicode allows many more distinct characters than either ASCII or extended ASCII. It was invented primarily to accommodate the larger alphabets and symbols of various international human languages. In C++, the data type `wchar_t` rather than `char` is used for Unicode characters. In fact, `wchar_t` can be used for other, possibly infrequently used, "wide character" sets in addition to Unicode. In this book, we do not examine Unicode or the `wchar_t` type. Instead, we focus our attention on the `char` type and the ASCII character set.

External representation The printable (character) form of a data value.

Internal representation The form in which a data value is stored inside the memory unit.

Whichever character set is being used, each character has an external representation—the way it looks on an I/O device like a printer—and an internal representation—the way it is stored inside the computer's memory unit. If you use the `char` constant `'A'` in a C++ program, its external representation is the letter A. That is, if you print it out, you will see an A, as you would expect. Its internal representation, though, is an integer value. The 128 ASCII characters have internal representations 0 through 127. For example, the ASCII table in Appendix E shows that the character `'A'` has internal representation 65, and the character `'b'` has internal representation 98.

Let's look again at the following statement:

```
someChar = 'A';
```

Assuming our machine uses the ASCII character set, the compiler translates the constant `'A'` into the integer 65. We could also have written the statement as follows:

```
someChar = 65;
```

Both statements have exactly the same effect—that of storing 65 into `someChar`. However, the first is certainly more understandable.

Earlier we mentioned that the computer cannot tell the difference between character and integer data in memory because both are stored internally as integers. However, when we perform I/O operations, the computer does the right thing—it uses the external representation that corresponds to the data type of the expression being printed. Look at this code segment, for example:

```
// This example assumes use of the ASCII character set
int  someInt = 97;
char someChar= 97;
cout << someInt << endl;
cout << someChar << endl;
```

When these statements are executed, the output is

```
97
a
```

When the << operator outputs `someInt`, it prints the sequence of characters 9 and 7. To output `someChar`, it prints the single character a. Even though both variables contain the value 97 internally, the data type of each variable determines how it is printed.

What do you think is output by the following sequence of statements?

```
char ch = 'D';
ch++;
cout << ch;
```

If you answered E, you are right. The first statement declares `ch` and initializes it to the integer value 68 (assuming ASCII). The next statement increments `ch` to 69, and then its external representation (the letter E) is printed. Extending this idea of incrementing a `char` variable, we could print the letters A through G as follows:

```
ch arch;
for (ch = 'A'; ch <= 'G'; ch++)
   cout << ch;
```

This code initializes `ch` to `'A'` (65 in ASCII). Each time through the loop, the external representation of `ch` is printed. On the final loop iteration, the `'G'` is printed and `ch` is incremented to `'H'` (72 in ASCII). The loop test is then false, so the loop terminates.

QUICK CHECK

10.1.1 Is `bool` considered an integral type or an `enum` type? (p. 463)
10.1.2 What property do the built-in types `int`, `char`, `bool`, and `float` have in common? (p. 462)
10.1.3 Other than `char`, what are the sizes of data objects in C++ dependent on? (p. 463)
10.1.4 What is the name of the character set that provides enough characters for the English language? How many characters can it represent? (p. 464)
10.1.5 What is the name of the character set that can accommodate larger alphabets? (p. 464)
10.1.6 What is the difference between the external and internal representation of a character? (pp. 464–465)

10.2 User-Defined Simple Types

The concept of a data type is fundamental to all of the widely used programming languages. One strength of the C++ language is that it allows programmers to create new data types, tailored to meet the needs of a particular program. Much of the remainder of this book deals with user-defined data types. In this section, we consider how to create our own simple types.

The Typedef Statement

The Typedef statement allows you to introduce a new name for an existing type. Its syntax template is

TypedefStatement

```
typedef ExistingTypeName  NewTypeName ;
```

Before the `bool` data type was part of the C++ language, many programmers used code like the following to simulate a Boolean type:

```
typedef int Boolean;
const int TRUE = 1;
const int FALSE = 0;
    ⋮
Boolean dataOK;
    ⋮
dataOK = TRUE;
```

In this code, the Typedef statement causes the compiler to substitute the word `int` for every occurrence of the word `Boolean` in the rest of the program.

The Typedef statement provides us with a very limited way of defining our own data types. In fact, Typedef does not create a new data type at all: It merely creates an additional name for an existing data type. As far as the compiler is concerned, the domain and operations of the `Boolean` type in the previous example are identical to the domain and operations of the `int` type.

Despite the fact that Typedef cannot truly create a new data type, it is a valuable tool for writing self-documenting programs. Before `bool` was a built-in type, program code that used the identifiers `Boolean`, `TRUE`, and `FALSE` was more descriptive than code that used `int`, `1`, and `0` for Boolean operations.

Names of user-defined types obey the same scope rules that apply to identifiers in general. Most types, like the `Boolean` example, are defined globally, although it is reasonable to define a new type within a subprogram if that is the only place it is used. The guidelines that determine where a named constant should be defined also apply to data types.

In Chapter 3, we said that the various string operations took as parameters or returned as results unsigned integers, but that we could use `int` instead. Actually these values should be of type `size_type`, a type defined in `string` as

```
typedef std::size_t size_type;
```

But what is `size_t`? It is a type provided in the C `std` header file that is implementation dependent. This unsigned integer type defines the maximum length of a string in a program compiled by a particular compiler. Given this fact, it is better style to use `string::size_type` rather than `int` when working with string operations, because the former type limits precisely the range of values that can be stored in these variables.

`string::npos` is the largest possible value of type `string::size_type`, a number like `4294967295` on many machines. This value is suitable for "not a valid position" because the `string` operations do not let any string become this long.

Enumeration Types

C++ allows the user to define a new simple type by listing (enumerating) the literal values that make up the domain of the type. These literal values must be identifiers, not numbers. The identifiers are separated by commas, and the list is enclosed in braces. Data types defined in this way are called enumeration types. Here's an example:

> **Enumeration type** A user-defined data type whose domain is an ordered set of literal values expressed as identifiers.
>
> **Enumerator** One of the values in the domain of an enumeration type.

```
enum Days {SUN, MON, TUE, WED, THU, FRI, SAT};
```

This declaration creates a new data type named `Days`. Whereas Typedef merely creates a synonym for an existing type, an enumeration type like `Days` is truly a new type and is distinct from any existing type.

The values in the `Days` type—`SUN`, `MON`, `TUE`, and so forth—are called enumerators. The enumerators are ordered, in the sense that `SUN < MON < TUE ... < FRI < SAT`. Applying relational operators to enumerators is like applying them to characters: The relation that is tested is whether an enumerator "comes before" or "comes after" in the ordering of the data type.

Earlier we saw that the internal representation of a `char` constant is a nonnegative integer. As we mentioned previously, the 128 ASCII characters are represented in memory as the integers 0 through 127. Values in an enumeration type are also represented internally as integers. By default, the first enumerator has the integer value 0, the second has the value 1, and so forth. Our declaration of the `Days` enumeration type is similar to the following set of declarations:

```
typedef int Days;
const int SUN = 0;
const int MON = 1;
const int TUE = 2;
    ⋮
const int SAT = 6;
```

If there is some reason that you want different internal representations for the enumerators, you can specify them explicitly like this:

```
enum Days {SUN = 4, MON = 18, TUE = 9, ... };
```

Nevertheless, there is rarely any reason to assign specific values to enumerators. With the **Days** type, we are interested in the days of the week, not in the way the machine stores this data internally. We do not discuss this feature any further, although you may occasionally see it in C++ programs.

Notice the style we use to capitalize enumerators. Because enumerators are, in essence, named constants, we capitalize the entire identifier. This is purely a style choice. Many C++ programmers use both uppercase and lowercase letters when they invent names for the enumerators.

Here is the syntax template for the declaration of an enumeration type. It is a simplified version; later in the chapter we expand it.

EnumDeclaration

```
enum Name { Enumerator , Enumerator ... } ;
```

Each enumerator has the following form:

Enumerator

```
Identifier = ConstIntExpression
```

where the optional ConstIntExpression is an integer expression composed only of literal or named constants.

The identifiers used as enumerators must follow the rules for any C++ identifier. For example,

```
enum Vowel {'A', 'E', 'I', 'O', 'U'};      // Error
```

is not legal because the items are not identifiers. The declaration

```
enum Places {1st, 2nd, 3rd};               // Error
```

is not legal because identifiers cannot begin with digits. In the declarations

```
enum Starch {CORN, RICE, POTATO, BEAN};
enum Grain {WHEAT, CORN, RYE, BARLEY, SORGHUM};   // Error
```

type **Starch** and type **Grain** are legal individually, but together they are not. Identifiers in the same scope must be unique, so **CORN** cannot be defined twice.

Suppose you are writing a program for a veterinary clinic. The program must keep track of many different kinds of animals. The following enumeration type might be used for this purpose:

```
                Type identifier              Literal values in the domain

                enum Animals {RODENT, CAT, DOG, BIRD, REPTILE, HORSE, BOVINE, SHEEP};

                Animals inPatient;
                                        }   Creation of two variables of type Animals
                Animals outPatient;
```

Here **RODENT** is a literal, one of the values in the data type **Animals**. Be sure you understand that **RODENT** is not a variable name. Instead, **RODENT** is one of the values that can be stored into the variables **inPatient** and **outPatient**.

Next, let's look at the kinds of operations we might want to perform on variables of enumeration types.

Assignment

The assignment statement

```
inPatient = DOG;
```

does not assign the character string **"DOG"** to **inPatient**, nor the contents of a variable named **DOG**. Instead, it assigns the value **DOG**, which is one of the values in the domain of the data type **Animals**.

Assignment is a valid operation, as long as the value being stored is of type **Animals**. Both of the statements

```
inPatient = DOG;
outPatient = inPatient;
```

are acceptable. Each expression on the right-hand side is of type **Animals**—**DOG** is a literal of type **Animals**, and **inPatient** is a variable of type **Animals**. Although we know that the underlying representation of **DOG** is the integer 2, the compiler prevents us from making this assignment:

```
inPatient = 2;    // Not allowed
```

Here is the precise rule:

> Implicit type coercion is defined from an enumeration type to an
> integral type but not from an integral type to an enumeration type.

Applying this rule to the statements

```
someInt = DOG;      // Valid
inPatient = 2;      // Error
```

we see that the first statement stores 2 into **someInt** (because of implicit type coercion), but the second produces a compile-time error. The restriction against storing an integer value into a variable of type **Animals** is intended to keep you from accidentally storing an out-of-range value:

```
inPatient = 65;     // Error
```

Incrementation

Suppose that you want to "increment" the value in `inPatient` so that it becomes the next value in the domain:

```
inPatient = inPatient + 1;    // Error
```

This statement is illegal for the following reason. The right-hand side is acceptable because implicit type coercion lets you add `inPatient` to 1; the result is an `int` value. But the assignment operation is not valid because you can't store an `int` value into `inPatient`. The statement

```
inPatient++;    // Error
```

is also invalid because the compiler considers it to have the same semantics as the earlier assignment statement. However, you can escape the type coercion rule by using an explicit type conversion—a type cast—as follows:

```
inPatient = static_cast<Animals>(inPatient + 1);    // Correct
```

When you use the type cast, the compiler assumes that you know what you are doing and allows it.

The ability to increment a variable of an enumeration type is very useful in loops. Sometimes we need a loop that processes all the values in the domain of the type. We might try the following For loop:

```
Animals patient;
for (patient=RODENT; patient <= SHEEP; patient++)    // Error
    ⋮
```

However, as we explained earlier, the compiler will complain about the expression `patient++`. To increment `patient`, we must use an assignment expression and a type cast:

```
for (patient=RODENT; patient <= SHEEP;
     patient=static_cast<Animals>(patient + 1))
    ⋮
```

The only caution here is that when control exits the loop, the value of `patient` is 1 greater than the largest value in the domain (`SHEEP`). If you want to use `patient` outside the loop, you must reassign it a value that is within the appropriate range for the `Animals` type.

Comparison

The operation most commonly performed on values of enumeration types is comparison. When you compare two values, their ordering is determined by the order in which you listed the enumerators in the type declaration. For instance, the expression

```
inPatient <= BIRD
```

has the value `true` if `inPatient` contains the value `RODENT`, `CAT`, `DOG`, or `BIRD`.

You can also use values of an enumeration type in a Switch statement. Because `RODENT`, `CAT`, and so on are literals, they can appear in case labels:

```
switch (inPatient)
{
  case RODENT  :
  case CAT     :
  case DOG     :
  case BIRD    : cout << "Cage ward";
                 break;
  case REPTILE : cout << "Terrarium ward";
                 break;
  case HORSE   :
  case BOVINE  :
  case SHEEP   : cout << "Barn";
}
```

Input and Output

Stream I/O is defined only for the basic built-in types (`int`, `float`, and so on), but not for user-defined enumeration types. Values of enumeration types must be input or output indirectly.

To input values, one strategy is to read a string that spells one of the constants in the enumeration type. The idea is to input the string and translate it to one of the literals in the enumeration type by looking at only as many letters as are necessary to determine what the string is.

For example, the veterinary clinic program could read the kind of animal as a string, then assign one of the values of type `Animals` to that patient. *Cat*, *dog*, *horse*, and *sheep* can be determined by their first letter. *Bovine*, *bird*, *rodent*, and *reptile* cannot be determined until the second letter is examined. The following program fragment reads in a string representing an animal name and converts it to one of the values in type `Animals`:

```
cin >> animalName;
switch (toupper(animalName.at(0)))
{
  case 'R' : if (toupper(animalName.at(1)) == 'O')
                inPatient = RODENT;
             else
                inPatient = REPTILE;
             break;
  case 'C' : inPatient = CAT;
             break;
  case 'D' : inPatient = DOG;
             break;
  case 'B' : if (toupper(animalName.at(1)) == 'I')
                inPatient = BIRD;
             else
                inPatient = BOVINE;
             break;
  case 'H' : inPatient = HORSE;
             break;
  default :  inPatient = SHEEP;
}
```

Enumeration type values cannot be printed directly, either. Printing is accomplished by using a Switch statement that prints a character string corresponding to the value.

```cpp
switch (inPatient)
{
  case RODENT  : cout << "Rodent";
                 break;
  case CAT     : cout << "Cat";
                 break;
  case DOG     : cout << "Dog";
                 break;
  case BIRD    : cout << "Bird";
                 break;
  case REPTILE : cout << "Reptile";
                 break;
  case HORSE   : cout << "Horse";
                 break;
  case BOVINE  : cout << "Bovine";
                 break;
  case SHEEP   : cout << "Sheep";
}
```

The following program reads in a value of an enumerated type and prints what it is:

```cpp
//***********************************************************
// This program demonstrates input/output of enumerated
// types.
//***********************************************************
#include <cctype>    // For toupper()
#include <string>    // For string type
#include <iostream>
using namespace std;

enum Animals {RODENT, CAT, DOG, BIRD, REPTILE, HORSE, BOVINE, SHEEP};
int main()
{
  string animalName;
  Animals inPatient;
  cout << "Enter the name of an animal." << endl;
  cout << "Enter Quit to stop." << endl;

  cin >> animalName;
  while ((toupper(animalName.at(0))) != 'Q')
  {
    switch (toupper(animalName.at(0)))
    {
      case 'R' : if (toupper(animalName.at(1)) == 'O')
                    inPatient = RODENT;
                 else
                    inPatient = REPTILE;
                 break;
      case 'C' : inPatient = CAT;
                 break;
      case 'D' : inPatient = DOG;
                 break;
```

```
        case 'B' : if (toupper(animalName.at(1)) == 'I')
                       inPatient = BIRD;
                   else
                       inPatient = BOVINE;
                   break;
        case 'H' : inPatient = HORSE;
                   break;
        default :  inPatient = SHEEP;
    }
    cout << "You entered ";
    switch (inPatient)
    {
       case RODENT  : cout << "Rodent";
                      break;
       case CAT     : cout << "Cat";
                      break;
       case DOG     : cout << "Dog";
                      break;
       case BIRD    : cout << "Bird";
                      break;
       case REPTILE : cout << "Reptile";
                      break;
       case HORSE   : cout << "Horse";
                      break;
       case BOVINE  : cout << "Bovine";
                      break;
       case SHEEP   : cout << "Sheep";
    }
    cout << endl;
    cout << "Enter the name of an animal." << endl;
    cout << "Enter Quit to stop." << endl;
    cin >> animalName;
  }
  return 0;
}
```

Here is sample output of this program:

```
Enter the name of an animal.
Enter Quit to stop.
Rodent
You entered Rodent
Enter the name of an animal.
Enter Quit to stop.
Cat
You entered Cat
Enter the name of an animal.
Enter Quit to stop.
Dog
You entered Dog
```

```
Enter the name of an animal.
Enter Quit to stop.
Bird
You entered Bird
Enter the name of an animal.
Enter Quit to stop.
Reptile
You entered Reptile
Enter the name of an animal.
Enter Quit to stop.
Horse
You entered Horse
Enter the name of an animal.
Enter Quit to stop.
Bovine
You entered Bovine
Enter the name of an animal.
Enter Quit to stop.
Sheep
You entered Sheep
Enter the name of an animal.
Enter Quit to stop.
Quit
```

You might ask, Why not use just a pair of letters or an integer number as a code to represent each animal in a program? The answer is that we use enumeration types to make our programs more readable; they are another way to make the code more self-documenting.

Returning a Function Value

So far, we have been using value-returning functions to compute and return values of built-in types such as `int`, `float`, and `char`:

```
int Factorial( int );
float CargoMoment( int );
```

C++ allows a function return value to be of any data type—built in or user defined—except an array (a data type we examine in later chapters, and for which there are special rules regarding return from a function).

In the last section, we wrote a Switch statement to convert an input string into a value of type `Animals`. Now let's write a value-returning function that performs this task. Notice how the function heading declares the data type of the return value to be `Animals`:

```
Animals StrToAnimal(string str)
{
  switch (toupper(str.at(0)))
  {
    case 'R' : if (toupper(str.at(1)) == 'O')
                  return RODENT;
               else
                  return REPTILE;
    case 'C' : return CAT;
```

```
      case 'D' : return DOG;
      case 'B' : if (toupper(str.at(1)) == 'I')
                   return BIRD;
                else
                   return BOVINE;
      case 'H' : return HORSE;
      default :  return SHEEP;
  }
}
```

In this function, why didn't we include a Break statement after each case alternative? Because when one of the alternatives executes a Return statement, control immediately exits the function. It's not possible for control to "fall through" to the next alternative.

Here is the `main` function of the previous program, which calls the `StrToAnimal` function to convert a string into a value of type `Animals`:

```
int main()
{
  string animalName;
  Animals inPatient;
  cout << "Enter the name of an animal." << endl;
  cout << "Enter Quit to stop." << endl;

  cin >> animalName;
  while ((toupper(animalName.at(0))) != 'Q')
  {
    cout << "You entered ";
    switch (StrToAnimal(animalName))    // Converts string to Animals
    {
      case RODENT  : cout << "Rodent";
                     break;
      case CAT     : cout << "Cat";
                     break;
      case DOG     : cout << "Dog";
                     break;
      case BIRD    : cout << "Bird";
                     break;
      case REPTILE : cout << "Reptile";
                     break;
      case HORSE   : cout << "Horse";
                     break;
      case BOVINE  : cout << "Bovine";
                     break;
      case SHEEP   : cout << "Sheep";
    }
    cout << endl;
    cout << "Enter the name of an animal." << endl;
    cout << "Enter Quit to stop." << endl;
    cin >> animalName;
  }
}
```

Named and Anonymous Data Types

The enumeration types we have looked at, `Animals` and `Days`, are called named types because their declarations included names for the types. Variables of these new data types are declared separately using the type identifiers `Animals` and `Days`.

C++ also lets us introduce a new type directly in a variable declaration. Instead of the declarations

```
enum CoinType {NICKEL, DIME, QUARTER, HALF_DOLLAR};
enum StatusType {OK, OUT_OF_STOCK, BACK_ORDERED};

CoinType change;
StatusType status;
```

we could write

```
enum {NICKEL, DIME, QUARTER, HALF_DOLLAR} change;
enum {OK, OUT_OF_STOCK, BACK_ORDERED} status;
```

Anonymous type A type that does not have an associated type identifier.

A new type declared in a variable declaration is called an anonymous type because it does not have a name—that is, it does not have a type identifier associated with it.

If we can create a data type in a variable declaration, why bother with a separate type declaration that creates a named type? Named types, like named constants, make a program more readable, more understandable, and easier to modify. Also, declaring a type and declaring a variable of that type are two distinct concepts; it is best to keep them separate.

We now give a more complete syntax template for an enumeration type declaration. This template shows that the type name is optional (yielding an anonymous type) and that a list of variables may optionally be included in the declaration.

EnumDeclaration

```
enum Name { Enumerator , Enumerator ... } VariableName , VariableName ... ;
```

QUICK CHECK

10.2.1 Write an enumeration type definition for the four seasons. (p. 468)
10.2.2 Write a For loop heading that iterates through the `Seasons` type defined in Question 10.2.1. (p. 470)
10.2.3 What is the Typedef statement used for? (p. 466)
10.2.4 What is the difference between a Named and Anonymous data type? (p. 476)

10.3 Simple Versus Structured Data Types

A value in a simple type is a single data item; it cannot be broken down into component parts. For example, each `int` value is a single integer number and cannot be further decomposed.

10.3 Simple Versus Structured Data Types

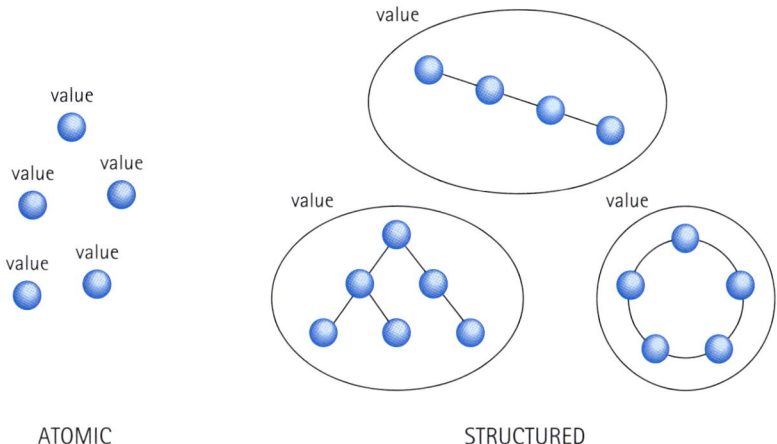

FIGURE 10.2 Atomic (Simple) and Structured Data Types

In contrast, a *structured data type* is a type in which each value is a *collection* of component items. The entire collection is given a single name, yet each component can still be accessed individually.

An example of a structured data type in C++ is the **string** class, which is used for creating and manipulating strings. When you declare a variable **myString** to be of type **string**, **myString** does not represent just one atomic data value; rather, it represents an entire collection of characters. Even so, each of the components in the string can be accessed individually by using an expression such as **myString.at(3)**, which accesses the **char** value at position 3.

> **Structured data type** A data type in which each value is a collection of components and whose organization is characterized by the method used to access individual components. The allowable operations on a structured data type include the storage and retrieval of individual components.

Simple data types, both built in and user defined, are the building blocks for structured types. A structured type gathers together a set of component values and usually imposes a specific arrangement on them (see **FIGURE 10.2**). The method used to access the individual components of a structured type depends on how the components are arranged. As we discuss various ways of structuring data, we will look at the corresponding access mechanisms.

FIGURE 10.3 shows the structured types available in C++. This figure is a portion of the complete diagram presented in Figure 3.1.

The **struct** and **union** data types are discussed in this chapter. The array is presented in Chapter 11; the class is the topic of Chapter 12.

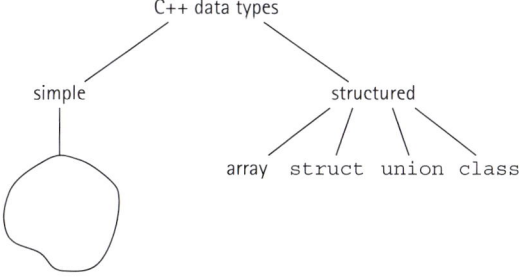

FIGURE 10.3 C++ Structured Types

> **QUICK CHECK**
>
> 10.3.1 Simple data types are the building blocks of what? (p. 477)
> 10.3.2 What are the four structured types in C++? (p. 477)

10.4 Records (Structs)

Record (struct, in C++) A structured data type with a fixed number of components that are accessed by name. The components may be heterogeneous (of different types).

Field (member, in C++) A component of a record.

In computer science, a record is a heterogeneous structured data type. By *heterogeneous*, we mean that the individual components of a record can be of different data types. Each component of a record is called a field of the record, and each field is given a name called the *field name*. C++ uses its own terminology with records. A record is a structure called a struct, the fields of a record are called members of the struct, and each member has a *member name*.[1]

In C++, record data types are most commonly declared according to the following syntax:

StructDeclaration

```
struct TypeName
{
    MemberList
};
```

where TypeName is an identifier giving a name to the data type, and MemberList is defined as

MemberList

```
DataType MemberName ;
DataType MemberName ;
        ⋮
```

The reserved word **struct** is an abbreviation for *structure*. Because the word *structure* has many other meanings in computer science, we'll use *struct* or *record* to avoid any possible confusion about what we are referring to.

You probably recognize the syntax of a member list as being nearly identical to a series of variable declarations. Be careful: A **struct** declaration is a type declaration, and we still must declare variables of this type for any memory locations to be associated with the member names. Let's look at an example that groups together the parts of a mailing address:

```
// Type declaration
struct MailingAddress
{
  string street;
  string city;
  string state;
  int    zipcode;
};
```

---

[1]. Technically, a C++ **struct** type is almost identical to the **class** type that we introduce in Chapter 12. However, in C a struct has the properties of a record, and most C++ programmers continue to use the struct in its traditional role of directly representing a record. In this book we retain this standard practice.

```
// Variable definitions
MailingAddress homeAddress;
MailingAddress businessAddress;
```

The `MailingAddress` struct contains four members representing the street address, city name, state, and ZIP code. Note that each member name is given a type. Also, member names must be unique within a `struct` type, just as variable names must be unique within a block.

The declaration of the `MailingAddress` data type just specifies the form that variables of this type will have; it doesn't allocate any space in which to store member values. When we define variables of type `MailingAddress`, the C++ compiler allocates space within each of the variables that will hold the four members.

Notice, both in this example and in the syntax template, that a `struct` declaration ends with a semicolon. By now, you have learned not to put a semicolon after the right brace of a compound statement (block). However, the member list in a `struct` declaration is not considered to be a compound statement; the braces are simply required syntax in the declaration. A `struct` declaration, like all C++ declaration statements, must end with a semicolon.

Let's look at another example. We can use a `struct` to describe a student in a class. We want to store the student's first and last names, the overall grade-point average prior to this class, the grade on programming assignments, the grade on quizzes, the final exam grade, and the final course grade.

```
// Type declarations
enum GradeType {A, B, C, D, F};

struct StudentRec
{
  string    firstName;
  string    lastName;
  float     gpa;              // Grade-point average
  int       programGrade;     // Assume 0..400
  int       quizGrade;        // Assume 0..300
  int       finalExam;        // Assume 0..300
  GradeType courseGrade;
};
// Variable definitions
StudentRec firstStudent;
StudentRec student;
int grade;
```

In this example, `firstName`, `lastName`, `gpa`, `programGrade`, `quizGrade`, `finalExam`, and `courseGrade` are member names within the `struct` type `StudentRec`. These member names make up the member list. `firstName` and `lastName` are of type `string`. `gpa` is a `float` member. `programGrade`, `quizGrade`, and `finalExam` are `int` members. `courseGrade` is of an enumeration data type made up of the grades A through D and F.

Just as we saw with our `MailingAddress` example, none of the `struct` members are associated with memory locations until we declare a variable of the `StudentRec` type. `StudentRec` is merely a *pattern* for a `struct` (see **FIGURE 10.4**).

The variables `firstStudent` and `student` are variables of type `StudentRec`. Each variable contains space for storing seven member values, according to the pattern specified in the type declaration.

FIGURE 10.4 Pattern for a Struct

Accessing Individual Components

Member selector The expression used to access components of a struct variable. It is formed by using the struct variable name and the member name, separated by a dot (period).

To access an individual member of a **struct** variable, you give the name of the variable, followed by a dot (period), and then the member name. This expression is called a member selector. The syntax template is

MemberSelector

StructVariable . MemberName

This syntax for selecting individual components of a **struct** is often called *dot notation*. To access the grade-point average of **firstStudent**, we would write

`firstStudent.gpa`

To access the final exam score for a student, we would write

`student.finalExam`

The component of a **struct** accessed by the member selector is treated just like any other variable of the same type. It may be used in an assignment statement, passed as an argument, and so on. **FIGURE 10.5** shows the **struct** variable **student**, along with the member selector for each member. In this example, we assume that some processing has already taken place, so values are stored in some of the components.

Let's demonstrate the use of these member selectors. Using our **student** variable, the following function takes in a **student** record as a parameter; adds up the program grade, the quiz grade, and the final exam grade; and returns a letter grade as the result:

```
GradeType CalculateGrade(StudentRecord aStudent)
{
   int grade = student.finalExam + student.programGrade +
               student.quizGrade;
```

FIGURE 10.5 Struct Variable `student` with Member Selectors

```
  if (grade >= 900)
     return A;
  else if (grade >= 800)
     return B;
  else if (grade >= 700)
     return C;
  else if (grade >= 600)
     return D;
  else
     return F;
}
```

Aggregate Operations on Structs

In addition to accessing individual components of a `struct` variable, we can in some cases use aggregate operations. An aggregate operation is one that manipulates the `struct` as an entire unit.

The following table summarizes the aggregate operations that C++ supports for `struct` variables:

Aggregate operation An operation on a data structure as a whole, as opposed to an operation on an individual component of the data structure.

Aggregate Operation	Supported for Structs?
I/O	No
Assignment	Yes
Arithmetic	No
Comparison	No
Argument passage	Yes, by value or by reference
Return as a function's return value	Yes

According to the table, one `struct` variable can be assigned to another. To do so, however, both variables must be declared to be of the same type. For example, given the declarations

```
StudentRec student;
StudentRec anotherStudent;
```

the statement

```
anotherStudent = student;
```

copies the entire contents of the `struct` variable `student` to the variable `anotherStudent`, member by member.

In contrast, aggregate arithmetic operations and comparisons are not supported (primarily because they wouldn't make sense):

```
student = student * anotherStudent;    // Not allowed
if (student < anotherStudent)          // Not allowed
```

Furthermore, aggregate I/O is not supported:

```
cin >> student;                        // Not allowed
```

We must input or output a `struct` variable one member at a time:

```
cin >> student.firstName;
cin >> student.lastName;
⋮
```

According to the table, an entire `struct` can be passed as an argument, as we did in the previous example. The `struct` variable `student` was passed as a value parameter because we did not change any field. Had we needed to do so, we would have passed it as a reference parameter. A `struct` can also be returned as the value of a value-returning function.

Let's define another function that takes a `StudentRec` variable as a parameter. The task of this function is to determine if a student's grade in a course is consistent with his or her overall grade-point average (GPA). We define *consistent* to mean that the course grade corresponds correctly to the rounded GPA. The GPA is calculated on a four-point scale, where A is 4, B is 3, C is 2, D is 1, and F is 0. If the rounded GPA is 4 and the course grade is A, then the function returns `true`. If the rounded GPA is 4 and the course grade is not A, then the function returns `false`. Each of the other grades is tested in the same way.

The `Consistent` function is coded below. The parameter `aStudent`, a `struct` variable of type `StudentRec`, is passed by value.

```
bool Consistent(StudentRec aStudent)
// Returns true if the course grade is consistent
// with the overall GPA; false, otherwise
{
    int roundedGPA = int(aStudent.gpa + 0.5);

    switch (roundedGPA)
    {
        case 0: return (aStudent.courseGrade == F);
```

```
      case 1: return (aStudent.courseGrade == D);
      case 2: return (aStudent.courseGrade == C);
      case 3: return (aStudent.courseGrade == B);
      case 4: return (aStudent.courseGrade == A);
   }
}
```

More About Struct Declarations

To complete our initial look at C++ structs, we give a more complete syntax template for a **struct** type declaration:

StructDeclaration

```
struct TypeName
{
      MemberList
} VariableList ;
```

As you can see in the syntax template, two items are optional: TypeName (the name of the **struct** type being declared) and VariableList (a list of variable names between the right brace and the semicolon). Our examples thus far have declared a type name but have not included a variable list. The variable list allows you not only to declare a **struct** type, but also to declare variables of that type, all in one statement. For example, you could write the declarations

```
struct StudentRec
{
  string firstName;
  string lastName;
     ⋮
};

StudentRec firstStudent;
StudentRec student;
```

more compactly in the form

```
struct StudentRec
{
  string firstName;
  string lastName;
     ⋮
} firstStudent, student;
```

In this book, we avoid combining variable declarations with type declarations, preferring to keep the two notions separate.

If you omit the type name but include the variable list, you create an anonymous type:

```
struct
{
  int    firstMember;
  float  secondMember;
} someVar;
```

Here, `someVar` is a variable of an anonymous type. No other variables of that type can be declared because the type has no name. Therefore, `someVar` cannot participate in aggregate operations such as assignment or argument passage. The cautions given previously against anonymous typing of enumeration types apply to `struct` types as well.

Binding Like Items

When data are obviously related, they should be collected into a record. For example, a name is made up of a first name, a middle name (or initial), and a last name. Rather than keeping these three values as separate variables, they should be bound into a record.

```
struct Name
{
  string: firstName;
  string: middleName;
  string: lastName;
};
```

In the billing program for a lawn care service in Chapter 8, input and output files were passed to each module. It would be easier to bind these files into a record and pass them as one variable rather than two.

```
struct Files
{
  istream: inFile;
  ostream: outFile;
};
```

SOFTWARE MAINTENANCE CASE STUDY: Changing a Loop Implementation

MAINTENANCE TASK: Remember the Rich Uncle case study in Chapter 7? This problem counted the number of times certain characters were used in a text file. Now that we know how to implement modules as functions, let's rewrite the program. Rather than looking at the code, we go back to the top-down design.

Main — Level 0

```
Open files for processing
IF file not opened okay
   Write error message
   Return 1
Get a character
DO
   Process character
   Get a character
WHILE (more data)
Print table
Close files
```

SOFTWARE MAINTENANCE CASE STUDY: Changing a Loop Implementation

Let's incorporate the file processing within a separate module, which takes the name of the file as a parameter.

PrepareFile (In/out: text)

Prompt for file name
Read file name
Open file
IF file not opened okay
   Write error message
   Return 1
Return

The next module is where the counters get incremented. The counters should be bound together in a record (**Counters**) and the record should be passed as a parameter to the module, along with the character.

IncrementCounters(In/out: counters, In: character)   **Level 1**

IF (isupper(character))
   Increment uppercaseCounter
ELSE IF (islower(character))
   Increment lowercaseCounter
ELSE IF (isdigit(character))
   Increment digitCounter
SWITCH (character)
   Case ' ' : Increment blankCounter
   Case '.' :
   Case '!' :
   Case '?' : Increment punctuationCounter

The last module calculates and prints the percentages. Because the output goes to the standard input device, only the record containing the counters is passed as a parameter.

Calculate and Print Percentages(In: counters)

Set Total to sum of 6 counters
Print 'Percentage of uppercase letters:', uppercaseCounter / Total * 100
Print 'Percentage of lowercase letters:', lowercaseCounter / Total * 100
Print 'Percentage of decimal digits:', digitCounter / Total * 100
Print 'Percentage of blanks:', blankCounter / Total * 100
Print 'Percentage of end-of-sentence punctuation:', punctuationCounter / Total * 100

SOFTWARE MAINTENANCE CASE STUDY: Changing a Loop Implementation

Coding these modules is very straightforward. We show the declaration of the record and the function prototypes here and leave the rest of the coding as an exercise. Note that because the counters are encapsulated into a record named `Counters`, we remove the word "Counter" from the variable names. Also, we need to add one more module: Initialize Counters. This initialization could be done within `main`, but creating a separate function to handle this task would be better style.

```
struct Counters
{
  int uppercase;      // Number of uppercase letters
  int lowercase;      // Number of lowercase letters
  int blank;          // Number of blanks
  int digit;          // Number of digits
  int punctuation;    // Number of end '.', '?', '!'
  int allElse;        // Remaining characters
};

void PrepareFile(ifstream& text);
// This function reads in a file name and opens the file.
// If the file is not found, an error code is returned

void IncrementCounters(Counters& counters, char character);
// This function increments the appropriate character counter

void InitializeCounters(Counters& counters);
// This function initializes the counter fields to zero

void CalculateAndPrint(Counters counters);
// This function prints the percentage of the total of each
// character category
```

QUICK CHECK

10.4.1 Can an anonymous user-defined type be a parameter in a function? (p. 484)
10.4.2 What is contained between the braces of a `struct` definition? (p. 478)
10.4.3 Which operator is used as the member selector of a `struct`? (p. 480)
10.4.4 When is memory allocated to a C++ `struct`? (p. 478)

10.5 Hierarchical Records

Hierarchical record A record in which at least one of the components is itself a record.

We have seen examples in which the components of a record are simple variables and strings. A component of a record can also be another record. Records whose components are themselves records are called hierarchical records.

Let's look at an example in which a hierarchical structure is appropriate. Suppose a small machine shop keeps information about each of its machines. These data include descriptive information, such as the identification number, a description of the machine, the purchase date, and the cost. They also include statistical information, such as

10.5 Hierarchical Records

the number of down days, the failure rate, and the date of last service. What is a reasonable way of representing all this information? First, let's look at a flat (nonhierarchical) record structure that holds this information.

```
struct MachineRec
{
  int     idNumber;
  string  description;
  float   failRate;
  int     lastServicedMonth;    // Assume 1..12
  int     lastServicedDay;      // Assume 1..31
  int     lastServicedYear;     // Assume 1900..2050
  int     downDays;
  int     purchaseDateMonth;    // Assume 1..12
  int     purchaseDateDay;      // Assume 1..31
  int     purchaseDateYear;     // Assume 1900..2050
  float   cost;
};
```

The `MachineRec` type has 11 members. There is so much detailed information here that it is difficult to quickly get a feeling for what the record represents. Let's see if we can reorganize it into a hierarchical structure that makes more sense. We can divide the information into two groups: information that changes and information that does not. There are also two dates to be kept: date of purchase and date of last service. These observations suggest use of a record describing a date, a record describing the statistical data, and an overall record containing the other two as components. The following type declarations reflect this structure.

```
struct Date
{
  int month;   // Assume 1..12
  int day;     // Assume 1..31
  int year;    // Assume 1900..2050
};
struct Statistics
{
  float failRate;
  Date  lastServiced;
  int   downDays;
};
struct MachineRec
{
  int         idNumber;
  string      description;
  Statistics  history;
  Date        purchaseDate;
  float       cost;
};

MachineRec machine;
```

The contents of a `machine` record are now much more obvious. Two of the components of the `struct` type `MachineRec` are themselves `struct`s: `purchaseDate` is of `struct` type `Date`, and `history` is of `struct` type `Statistics`. One of the components of `struct` type `Statistics` is, in turn, a `struct` of type `Date`.

FIGURE 10.6 Hierarchical Records in `machine` Variable

How do we access the components of a hierarchical structure such as this one? We build the accessing expressions (member selectors) for the members of the embedded `struct`s from left to right, beginning with the `struct` variable name. Here are some expressions and the components they access:

Expression	Component Accessed
`machine.purchaseDate`	`Date struct` variable
`machine.purchaseDate.month`	`month` member of a `Date struct` variable
`machine.purchaseDate.year`	`year` member of a `Date struct` variable
`machine.history.lastServiced.year`	`year` member of a `Date struct` variable contained in a `struct` of type `Statistics`

FIGURE 10.6 is a pictorial representation of `machine` with values. Look carefully at how each component is accessed.

> **QUICK CHECK**
>
> **10.5.1** What do we call a data structure that is implemented by a `struct` that contains other `struct` types? (p. 486)
>
> **10.5.2** How would you write an expression to access the `hour` member of a `struct` that is itself a member, called `time`, of a `struct` variable called `date`? (pp. 486–488)
>
> **10.5.3** Why are hierarchical records useful? (pp. 486–488)

10.6 Unions

In Figure 10.3, we presented a diagram showing the four structured types available in C++. We have discussed `struct` types and now look briefly at `union` types.

In C++, a union is defined to be a struct that holds only one of its members at a time during program execution. Here is a declaration of a `union` type and a `union` variable:

```
union WeightType
{
  long wtInOunces;
  int wtInPounds;
  float wtInTons;
};

WeightType weight;
```

The syntax for declaring a `union` type is identical to the syntax that we showed earlier for the `struct` type, except that the word `union` is substituted for `struct`.

At run time, the memory space allocated to the variable `weight` does *not* include room for three distinct components. Instead, `weight` can contain only one of the following: *either* a `long` value *or* an `int` value *or* a `float` value. The assumption is that the program will never need a weight in ounces, a weight in pounds, and a weight in tons simultaneously while executing. The purpose of a union is to conserve memory by forcing several values to use the same memory space, one at a time. The following code shows how the `weight` variable might be used:

```
weight.wtInTons = 4.83;
    ⋮
// Weight in tons is no longer needed. Reuse the memory space.

weight.wtInPounds = 35;
    ⋮
```

After the last assignment statement, the previous `float` value 4.83 is gone, replaced by the `int` value 35.

It's quite reasonable to argue that a union is not a data structure at all. It does not represent a collection of values; it represents only a single value from among several *potential* values. Nevertheless, unions are grouped together with the structured types because of their similarity to structs.

There is much more to be said about unions, including subtle issues related to their declaration and usage. However, these issues are more appropriate in an advanced study of data structures and systems programming. We have introduced unions here solely so that we could present a complete picture of the structured types provided by C++ and to acquaint you with the general idea in case you encounter unions in other C++ programs.

In the previous sections, we looked at the simple types and structured types available in C++. Now we have only two built-in data types left to cover: *pointer types* and *reference types* (see **FIGURE 10.7**). These types are simple data types, yet in Figure 10.7 we list them separately from the other simple types because their purpose is so special. We refer to pointer types and reference types as *address types*.

A variable of one of these types does not contain a data value; it contains the *memory address* of another variable or structure. Address types have two main purposes: They can make a program more efficient—either in terms of speed or in terms of memory usage—and they can be used to build complex data structures. It is this latter use that we emphasize here.

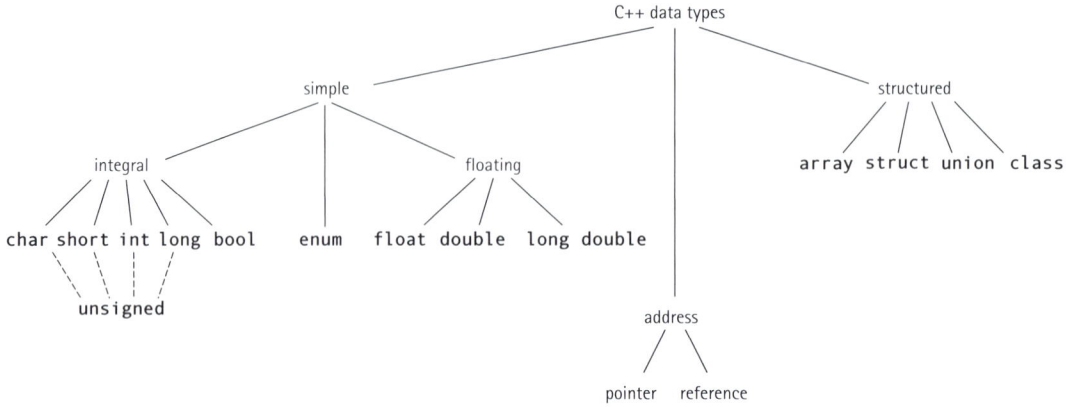

FIGURE 10.7 C++ Data Types

> **QUICK CHECK**
>
> **10.6.1** What is a C++ union? (p. 489)
> **10.6.2** How much space is allocated to a union? (p. 489)
> **10.6.3** How does a C++ union conserve memory space? (pp. 488–489)

10.7 Pointers

Pointer type A simple data type consisting of an unbounded set of values, each of which addresses or otherwise indicates the location of a variable of a given type. Among the operations defined on pointer variables are assignment and testing for equality.

In many ways, we've saved the best for last. Pointer types are the most interesting data types of all. Pointers are what their name implies: variables that tell where to find something else. That is, pointers contain the addresses or locations of other variables. Technically, a pointer type is a simple data type that consists of a set of unbounded values, each of which addresses the location of a variable of a given type.

Let's begin this discussion by looking at how pointer variables are declared in C++.

Pointer Variables

Surprisingly, the word "pointer" isn't used in declaring pointer variables; the symbol * (asterisk) is used instead. The declaration

```
int* intPtr;
```

states that `intPtr` is a variable that can point to (that is, contain the address of) an `int` variable. Here is the syntax template for declaring pointer variables:

PointerVariableDeclaration

{ DataType *Variable ;
  DataType *Variable , *Variable ... ; }

This syntax template shows two forms, one for declaring a single variable and the other for declaring several variables. In the first form, the compiler does not care where the asterisk is placed; it can be placed either to the right of the data type or to the left of the variable. Both of the following declarations are equivalent:

```
int* intPtr;
int *intPtr;
```

Although C++ programmers use both styles, we prefer the first. Attaching the asterisk to the data type name instead of the variable name readily suggests that `intPtr` is of type "pointer to `int`."

According to the syntax template, if you declare several variables in one statement, you must precede each variable name with an asterisk. Otherwise, only the first variable is taken to be a pointer variable; subsequent variables are not. To avoid unintended errors when declaring pointer variables, it is safest to declare each variable in a separate statement.

Given the declarations

```
int   beta;
int*  intPtr;
```

we can make `intPtr` point to `beta` by using the unary `&` operator, which is called the *address-of* operator. At run time, the assignment statement

```
intPtr = &beta;
```

takes the memory address of `beta` and stores it into `intPtr`. Alternatively, we could initialize `intPtr` in its declaration as follows:

```
int   beta;
int*  intPtr = &beta;
```

Suppose that `intPtr` and `beta` happen to be located at memory addresses 5000 and 5008, respectively. Then storing the address of `beta` into `intPtr` results in the relationship pictured in **FIGURE 10.8**.

Because the actual numeric addresses are generally unknown to the C++ programmer, it is more common to display the relationship between a pointer and a pointed-to variable by using rectangles and arrows, as illustrated in **FIGURE 10.9**.

To access a variable that a pointer points to, we use the unary `*` operator—the *dereference* or *indirection* operator. The expression `*intPtr` denotes the variable pointed to by `intPtr`. In our example, `intPtr` currently points to `beta`, so the statement

```
*intPtr = 28;
```

dereferences `intPtr` and stores the value 28 into `beta`. This statement represents indirect addressing of `beta`: The machine first accesses `intPtr`, then uses its contents to locate `beta`. In contrast, the statement

```
beta = 28;
```

represents direct addressing of `beta`. Direct addressing is like opening a post office box (P.O. Box 15, for instance) and finding a package, whereas indirect addressing is like opening P.O. Box 23 and finding a note that says your package is sitting in P.O. Box 15.

Indirect addressing Accessing a variable in two steps by first using a pointer that gives the location of the variable.

Direct addressing Accessing a variable in one step by using the variable name.

Continuing with our example, if we execute the statements

```
*intPtr = 28;
cout << intPtr<< endl;
cout << *intPtr<< endl;
```

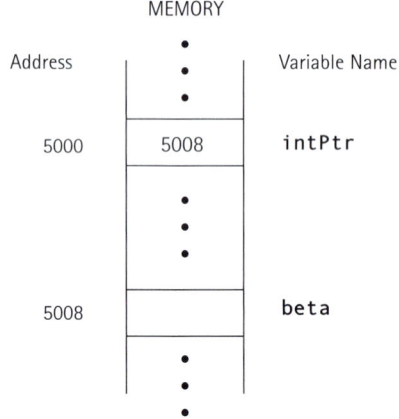

FIGURE 10.8 Machine-Level View of a Pointer Variable

FIGURE 10.9 Graphical Representation of a Pointer

then the output is

5008
28

The first output statement prints the contents of `intPtr` (5008); the second prints the contents of the variable pointed to by `intPtr` (28).

Pointers can point to any type of variable. For example, we can define a pointer to a struct as highlighted here:

```
struct PatientRec
{
  int idNum;
  int height;
  int weight;
};
PatientRec patient;
PatientRec* patientPtr = &patient;
```

The expression `*patientPtr` denotes a `struct` variable of type `PatientRec`. Furthermore, the expressions `(*patientPtr).idNum`, `(*patientPtr).height`, and `(*patientPtr).weight` denote the `idNum`, `height`, and `weight` members of `*patientPtr`. Notice how the accessing expression is built.

`patientPtr`	A pointer variable of type "pointer to `PatientRec`."
`*patientPtr`	A `struct` variable of type `PatientRec`.
`(*patientPtr).weight`	The `weight` member of a `struct` variable of type `PatientRec`.

The expression `(*patientPtr).weight` is a mixture of pointer dereferencing and `struct` member selection. The parentheses are necessary because the dot operator has higher precedence than the dereference operator (see Appendix B for C++ operator precedence). Without the parentheses, the expression `*patientPtr.weight` would be interpreted incorrectly as `*(patientPtr.weight)`.

When a pointer points to a struct (or a class or a union) variable, enclosing the pointer dereference within parentheses can become tedious. In addition to the dot operator, C++ provides another member selection operator: `->`. This arrow operator consists of two consecutive symbols: a hyphen and a greater-than symbol. By definition,

`PointerExpression -> MemberName`

is equivalent to

`(*PointerExpression).MemberName`

As a consequence, we can write

`(*patientPtr).weight` as `patientPtr->weight`.

The general guideline for choosing between the two member selection operators (dot and arrow) is the following: Use the dot operator if the first operand denotes a struct, class, or union variable; use the arrow operator if the first operand denotes a pointer to a struct, class, or union variable.

Pointer Expressions

You learned in the early chapters of this book that an arithmetic expression is made up of variables, constants, operator symbols, and parentheses. Similarly, pointer expressions are composed of pointer variables, pointer constants, certain allowable operators, and parentheses. We have already discussed pointer variables—variables that hold addresses of other variables. Let's look now at pointer constants.

In C++, there is only one literal pointer constant: the value 0. The pointer constant 0, called the `NULL` *pointer*, points to absolutely nothing. The statement

`intPtr = 0;`

stores the `NULL` pointer into `intPtr`. This statement does not cause `intPtr` to point to memory location zero, however; the `NULL` pointer is guaranteed to be distinct from any actual memory address. Because the `NULL` pointer does not point to anything, we diagram the `NULL` pointer as follows, instead of using an arrow to point somewhere:

Instead of using the constant 0, many programmers prefer to use the named constant NULL that is supplied by the standard header file cstddef:[2]

```
#include <cstddef>
   .
   .
   .
intPtr = NULL;
```

As with any named constant, the identifier NULL makes a program more self-documenting. Its use also reduces the chance of confusing the NULL pointer with the integer constant 0.

It is an error to dereference the NULL pointer, as it does not point to anything. The NULL pointer is used only as a special value that a program can test for:

```
if (intPtr == NULL)
  DoSomething();
```

We have now seen three C++ operators that are valid for pointers: =, *, and ->. In addition, the relational operators may be applied to pointers. For example, we can ask if a pointer points to anything with the following test:

```
if (ptr != NULL)
  DoSomething();
```

It is important to keep in mind that the operations are applied to pointers, *not* to the pointed-to variables. For example, if intPtr1 and intPtr2 are variables of type int*, the test

```
if (intPtr1 == intPtr2)
```

compares the pointers, not the variables to which they point. In other words, we are comparing memory addresses, not int values. To compare the integers that intPtr1 and intPtr2 point to, we would need to write

```
if (*intPtr1 == *intPtr2)
```

10.7.1 In declaring a pointer variable called compass that points to an int, there are two ways that you can write the declaration in C++. What are they? (p. 491)

---

2. The C++ standard was recently amended with a new keyword, called nullptr, which will eventually replace NULL. Because nullptr is a keyword, it is not necessary to include a header file to use it.

10.8 Reference Types

According to Figure 10.7, there is only one built-in type remaining: the reference type. Like pointer variables, reference variables contain the addresses of other variables. The statement

```
int& intRef;
```

declares that `intRef` is a variable that can contain the address of an `int` variable. Here is the syntax template for declaring reference variables:

> **Reference type** A simple data type consisting of an unbounded set of values, each of which is the address of a variable of a given type. The only operation defined on a reference variable is initialization, after which every appearance of the variable is implicitly dereferenced. Unlike a pointer, a reference cannot be set to 0.

ReferenceVariableDeclaration

```
{ DataType& Variable ;
  DataType &Variable , &Variable ... ;
```

Although both reference variables and pointer variables contain addresses of data objects, there are two fundamental differences between them. First, the dereferencing and address-of operators (`*` and `&`) are not used to dereference reference variables. After a reference variable has been declared, the compiler invisibly dereferences every single appearance of that reference variable. If you were to use `*` or `&` with a reference variable, it would be applied instead to the object that the variable references.

Using a Reference Variable	*Using a Pointer Variable*

`int  gamma = 26;`
`int& intRef = gamma;`
`// intRef is a reference`
`// variable that points`
`// to gamma`
	`int  gamma = 26;`
	`int* intPtr = &gamma;`
	`// intPtr is a pointer`
	`// variable that points`
	`// to gamma`

`intRef = 35;` `// gamma == 35`	`*intPtr= 35;` `// gamma == 35`
`intRef = intRef + 3;` `// gamma == 38`	`*intPtr= *intPtr+ 3;` `// gamma == 38`

Some programmers like to think of a reference variable as an alias for another variable. In the preceding code, we can think of `intRef` as an alias for `gamma`. After `intRef` is initialized in its declaration, everything we do to `intRef` is actually happening to `gamma`.

The second difference between reference and pointer variables is that the compiler treats a reference variable as if it were a constant pointer. Thus the value of this variable cannot be reassigned after being initialized. That is, we cannot assign `intRef` to point to another variable. Any attempt to do so just assigns the new value to the variable to which `intRef` points. It should also be noted that a reference variable cannot be initialized to 0 or `NULL`; a reference has to point to something that actually exists. In contrast, a pointer can be set to `NULL` to indicate that it points to nothing.

By now, you have probably noticed that the ampersand (`&`) has several meanings in the C++ language. To avoid errors, it is critical to recognize these distinct meanings. The following table summarizes the different uses of the ampersand. Note that a prefix operator precedes its operand(s), an infix operator lies between its operands, and a postfix operator comes after its operand(s).

Position	Usage	Meaning
Prefix	&Variable	Address-of operation
Infix	Expression & Expression	Bitwise AND operation (See Appendix B)
Infix	Expression && Expression	Logical AND operation
Postfix	DataType&	Data type (specifically, a reference type) *Exception: To declare two variables of a reference type, the & must be attached to each variable name:* `int &var1, &var2;`

Problem-Solving Case Study

Stylistical Analysis of Text

PROBLEM: Earlier in this chapter, we rewrote the Rich Uncle case study program, implementing the modules as functions. The Case Study Follow-Up Exercises to the original program intrigued you, so you decide to change and enhance the program. Rather than calculating percentages of groups of characters, you will just show counts. You also will determine the average word length and the average sentence length. Because you have just learned about enumerated types, you decide to redo the design using these constructs.

DISCUSSION: The Case Study Follow-Up exercise answers in Chapter 7 suggest that the number of new lines, punctuation marks, and blanks give a good approximation to the number of words. However, if any of these characters appear consecutively, only the first should be counted as an end-of-word symbol. You can use a Boolean variable `endOfWord` that is set to `true` when an end-of-word symbol is found. The word counter should be incremented only when `endOfWord` is `false`, after which `endOfWord` is set to `true`. When an alphanumeric character is read, `endOfWord` is set to `false`.

INPUT: Text on the file whose name is read from the keyboard.

OUTPUT: A table giving the file whose name is read from the keyboard, showing the following values:

```
Total number of alphanumeric characters
Number of uppercase letters
Number of lowercase letters
Number of digits
Number of characters ignored
Number of words
Number of sentences
Average word length
Average sentence length
```

The `main` and `OpenFiles` modules are almost the same as those for the revision in the Software Maintenance Case Study. It is the `IncrementCounters` module that will change.

Problem-Solving Case Study

INCREMENT COUNTERS: In the Rich Uncle program, you used a combination of If and Switch statements to determine to which category a character belonged. In the revised program, you will use a Switch statement with case labels of an enumerated type. The categories are uppercase, lowercase, digits, end-of-word, end-of-sentence, and ignore.

```
enum Features {UPPER, LOWER, DIGIT, EOW, EOS, IGNORE};
```

This module is where the **endOfWord** switch must be set. It should be set to **false** when it is declared, set to **true** when an end-of-word symbol is found, and reset to **false** when an alphanumeric character is found. For this process to work properly, **endOfWord** must be marked as a static variable. Recall that a static variable is a local variable that maintains its value from invocation to invocation.

IncrementCounters (In/out: counters, character) — Level 1

```
Set (static) endOfWord to false
SWITCH (Decode(character))
   UPPER :  Increment counters.uppercase
            Set endOfWord to false
   LOWER :  Increment lowercase
            Set endOfWord to false
   DIGIT :  Increment digit
            Set endOfWord to false
   EOW :    IF NOT endOfWord
               Increment word
               Set endOfWord to true;
   EOS:     Increment sentence
   IGNORE:  Increment ignore
```

DECODE: This module takes a character and returns the enumerated type for the category into which it falls. We can use part of the algorithm from the original version, adding the code for the end of a word and the end of a sentence.

Decode(In: character)
Out: function value—Features

```
IF isupper(character)
   Return UPPER
ELSE IF islower(character)
   Return LOWER
ELSE IF isdigit(character)
   Return DIGIT
ELSE
   SWITCH (character)
      '.' :
      '?' :
```

Problem-Solving Case Study

```
    '!' : return EOS
    '.' :
    ';' :
    '?' :
    ':' :
    '\n' : return EOW;
Return IGNORE;
```

Notice that a Switch statement can be used in the last else-clause because characters can be used as case labels. If neither of the first two are matched, control flows into the third case, which has a return beside it that causes execution to jump to the end of the Switch statement. The same is true of the fourth through seventh case labels, which flow through into the last case label, which has a return beside it.

As you look at this algorithm, you realize that the end-of-sentence markers are also end-of-word markers! Yet, you also want to keep the counts separate. You decide to take care of this problem in module CalculateAndPrint by adding the number of sentences to the number of words.

CalculateAndPrint (In/out: table, In: counters)   Level 1

Set totalAlphaNum to counters.uppercase + counters.lowercase + counters.digit

Print on table "Total number of alphanumeric characters: "   totalAlphaNum
Print on table "Number of uppercase letters: " counters.uppercase
Print on table "Number of lowercase letters: " counters.lowercase
Print on table "Number of digits: " counters.digit
Print on table "Number of characters ignored: " counters.ignore

Set counters.word to counters.word + counters.sentence

Print on table "Number of words: " counters.word
Print on table "Number of sentences: " counters.sentence
Print on table "Average word length: " float(totalAlphaNum)/counters.word
Print on table "Average sentence length: " float(counters.word)/counters.sentence

"CalculateAndPrint" is a little long. Let's call the function `PrintTable` instead.

Problem-Solving Case Study

MODULE STRUCTURE CHART

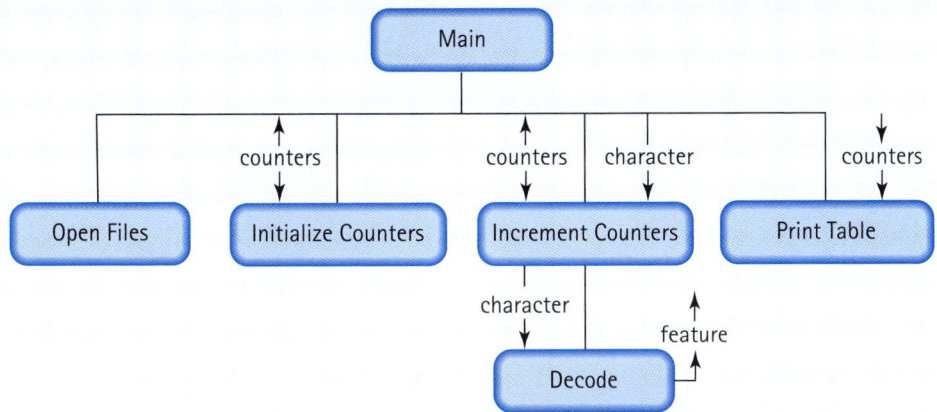

```
//*****************************************************************
// Style Program
// The program calculates number of words, average word length,
// number of sentences, average sentence length, number of
// uppercase letters, number of lowercase letters, and number of
// digits in a file of text.
//*****************************************************************

#include <fstream>
#include <iostream>
#include <iomanip>
#include <cctype>

using namespace std;

enum Features {UPPER, LOWER, DIGIT, IGNORE, EOW, EOS};

struct Counters
{
  int uppercase;
  int lowercase;
  int digit;
  int word;
  int sentence;
  int ignore;
};

// Function prototypes
void OpenFile(ifstream&);
// This function reads in a file name and opens the file.
// If the file is not found, an error code is returned
```

Problem-Solving Case Study

```
Features Decode(char character);
// This function reads in the names of the input file and the
// output file and opens them for processing
void IncrementCounters(Counters& counters, char character);
// This function increments the appropriate character counter.
void PrintTable(Counters counters);
// Table is printed
void InitializeCounters(Counters& counters);
// This function prints the resulting count

int main()
{
  // Prepare files for reading and writing
  ifstream text;
  Counters counters;
  OpenFile(text);
  if (!text)
  {
    cout << "Files did not open successfully." << endl;
    return 1;
  }

  InitializeCounters(counters);
  char character;                        // Input character

  text.get(character);                   // Input one character
  do
  { // Process each character
    IncrementCounters(counters, character);
    text.get(character);                 // Input one character
  } while (text);

  PrintTable(counters);
  text.close();
  return 0;
}

//****************************************************************

Features Decode(char character)
// This function examines the character and returns its type
{
  if (isupper(character))
    return UPPER;
  else if (islower(character))
    return LOWER;
  else if (isdigit(character))
    return DIGIT;
  else
  switch (character)
  {
    case '.' :
    case '?' :
```

Problem-Solving Case Study

```cpp
    case ' ' :
    case ',' :
    case ';' :
    case ':' :
    case '\n' :   return EOW;
  }
  return IGNORE;
}

//*********************************************************************

void OpenFile(ifstream& text)
{
  string inFileName;         // User-specified input file name
  cout << "Enter the name of the file to be processed" << endl;
  cin >> inFileName;
  text.open(inFileName.c_str());
  cout << "Analysis of characters on input file " << inFileName
       << endl << endl;
}


//*********************************************************************

void PrintTable(Counters counters)
// Function PrintTable prints the percentages represented by each
// of the five categories
{
  int totalAlphaNum;
  totalAlphaNum = counters.uppercase + counters.lowercase
     + counters.digit;

  // Print results on file cout
  cout << "Total number of alphanumeric characters: "
       << totalAlphaNum << endl;
  cout << "Number of uppercase letters: " << counters.uppercase
       << endl;
  cout << "Number of lowercase letters: " << counters.lowercase
       << endl;
  cout << "Number of digits: " << counters.digit << endl;
  cout << "Number of characters ignored: " << counters.ignore
       << endl;

  // Add number of end-of-sentence markers to the word count
  counters.word = counters.word + counters.sentence;

  // Write rest of results on file cout
  cout << "Number of words: " <<  counters.word << endl;
  cout << "Number of sentences: " << counters.sentence << endl;
  cout << "Average word length: " << fixed << setprecision(2)
       << static_cast<float>(totalAlphaNum)/ counters.word  << endl;
```

Problem-Solving Case Study

```
    cout << "Average sentence length: " << fixed << setprecision(2)
         << static_cast<float>(counters.word) / counters.sentence << endl;
}

//******************************************************************

void IncrementCounters(Counters& counters, char character)
// This function examines character and increments the
// appropriate counter.
{
    static bool endOfWord = false;

    switch (Decode(character))
    {
        case UPPER :    counters.uppercase++;
                        endOfWord = false;
                        break;
        case LOWER :    counters.lowercase++;
                        endOfWord = false;
                        break;
        case DIGIT :    counters.digit++;
                        endOfWord = false;
                        break;
        case EOW   :    if (!endOfWord)
                        {
                            counters.word++;
                            endOfWord = true;
                        }
                        break;
        case EOS   :    counters.sentence++;
                        break;
        case IGNORE:    counters.ignore++;
                        break;
    }
}

//******************************************************************

void InitializeCounters(Counters& counters)
{
    counters.uppercase = 0;
    counters.lowercase = 0;
    counters.digit = 0;
    counters.word = 0;
    counters.sentence = 0;
    counters.ignore = 0;
}
```

Problem-Solving Case Study

TESTING: Let's take a sample of text, calculate the statistics by hand, and compare the results with the output from the program.

Input

```
The Abacus (which appeared in the sixteenth century) was the first calcu-
lator. In the middle of the seventeenth century Blaise Pascal, a French
mathematician, built and sold gear-driven mechanical machines which per-
formed whole number addition and subtraction.  (Yes, the language Pascal
is named for him.)
Later in the seventeenth century a German mathematician Gottfried Wil-
helm von Leibniz built the first mechanical device designed to do all four
whole number operations: addition, subtraction, multiplication and divi-
sion.  The state of mechanical gears and levers at that time was such that
the Leibniz machine was not very reliable.
```

Expected Results

Total number of alphanumeric characters:	527
Number of uppercase letters:	15
Number of lowercase letters:	512
Number of digits:	0
Number of characters ignored:	5 (two pairs of parentheses and a hyphen)
Number of words:	96
Number of sentences:	5
Average word length:	5.489
Average sentence length:	19.2

Output from the Program

```
Total number of alphanumeric characters: 527
Number of uppercase letters: 15
Number of lowercase letters: 512
Number of digits: 0
Number of characters ignored: 5
Number of words: 100
Number of sentences: 5
Average word length: 5.27
Average sentence length: 20.00
```

The number of words, average word length, and average sentence length are wrong. You recount the number of words and again come up with 96. You took care of the case where end-of-sentence markers end words by adding the number of sentences to the number of words. But **endOfWord** wasn't reset when end-of-sentence markers were found. You correct the problem in function **ProcessCharacter** like this:

```
case EOS    :   counters.sentence++;
                endOfWord = true;
                break;
```

When you rerun the program, you get this output:

```
Number of uppercase letters: 15
Number of lowercase letters: 512
Number of digits: 0
Number of characters ignored: 5
Number of words: 95
Number of sentences: 5
Average word length: 5.55
Average sentence length: 19.00
```

The number of words is still off by one. Now you see it. You counted "gear-driven" as two words; the program counts it as one. You are asked to examine a solution to this problem in the Case Study Follow-Up Exercises.

Testing and Debugging

Coping with Input Errors

Several times in this book, we've had our programs test for invalid data and write error messages if they encountered incorrect input. Writing an error message is certainly necessary, but it is only the first step in handling errors. We must also decide what the program should do next. The problem itself and the severity of the error should determine which action is taken in any error condition. The approach taken also depends on whether the program is being run interactively.

In a program that reads its data only from an input file, there is no interaction with the person who entered the data. The program, therefore, should try to account for the bad data items, if at all possible.

If the invalid data item is not essential, the program can skip it and continue; for example, if a program averaging test grades encounters a negative test score, it could simply skip the negative score. If an educated guess can be made about the probable value of the bad data, it can be set to that value before being processed. In either event, a message should be written stating that an invalid data item was encountered and outlining the steps that were taken. Such messages form an exception report.

If the data item is essential and no guess is possible, processing should be terminated. A message should be written to the user containing as much information as possible about the invalid data item.

In an interactive environment, the program can prompt the user to supply another value. The program should indicate to the user what is wrong with the original data. Another possibility is to write out a list of actions and ask the user to choose among them.

These suggestions on how to handle bad data assume that the program recognizes bad data values. There are two approaches to error detection: passive and active. *Passive error detection* leaves it to the system to detect errors. This may seem easier, but the programmer relinquishes control of processing when an error occurs. An example of passive error detection is the system's division-by-zero error.

Active error detection means that the program checks for possible errors and determines an appropriate action if an error occurs. An example of active error detection would be to read a value and use an If statement to see if the value is 0 before dividing it into another number.

Debugging with Pointers

Programs that use pointers are more difficult to write and debug than programs without pointers. Indirect addressing never seems quite as "normal" as direct addressing when you want to get at the contents of a variable.

Two errors commonly associated with the use of pointer variables are as follows:

1. Confusing the pointer variable with the variable it points to.
2. Trying to dereference the NULL pointer or an uninitialized pointer.

Let's look at each of these potential problems in turn.

If `ptr` is a pointer variable, care must be taken not to confuse the expressions `ptr` and `*ptr`. The expression

`ptr`

accesses the variable `ptr` (which contains a memory address). The expression

`*ptr`

accesses the variable that `ptr` points to.

`ptr1 = ptr2`	Copies the contents of `ptr2` into `ptr1`.
`*ptr1 = *ptr2`	Copies the contents of the variable pointed to by `ptr2` into the variable pointed to by `ptr1`.
`*ptr1 = ptr2`	Illegal—one is a pointer and one is a variable being pointed to.
`ptr1 = *ptr2`	Illegal—one is a pointer and one is a variable being pointed to.

The second common error is to dereference the NULL pointer or an uninitialized pointer. On some systems, an attempt to dereference the NULL pointer produces a run-time error message such as NULL POINTER DEREFERENCE, followed immediately by termination of the program. When this event occurs, you have at least some notion of what went wrong with the program. The situation is worse, though, if your program dereferences an uninitialized pointer. In the code fragment

```
int  num;
int* intPtr;

num = *intPtr;
```

the variable `intPtr` has not been assigned any value before we dereference it. Initially, it contains some meaningless value such as 315988, but the computer does not know that it is meaningless. The machine simply accesses memory location 315988 and copies whatever it finds there into `num`. There is no way to test whether a pointer variable contains an undefined value. The only advice we can give for avoiding this problem is to check the code carefully to make sure that every pointer variable is assigned a value before being dereferenced.

Testing and Debugging Hints

1. Avoid using unnecessary side effects in expressions. The test

   ```
   if ((x = y) < z)
       ⋮
   ```

   is less clear and more prone to error than the equivalent sequence of statements

   ```
   x = y;
   if (y < z)
       ⋮
   ```

   Also, if you accidentally omit the parentheses around the assignment operation, like this:

   ```
   if (x = y < z)
   ```

   then, according to C++ operator precedence, `x` is not assigned the value of `y`. Instead, it is assigned the value 1 or 0 (the coerced value of the Boolean result of the relational expression `y < z`).

2. Programs that rely on a particular machine's character set may not run correctly on another machine. Check which character-handling functions are supplied by the standard library used by the machine on which the program is run. Functions such as `tolower`, `toupper`, `isalpha`, and `iscntrl` automatically account for the character set being used.

3. If your program increases the value of a positive integer and the result suddenly becomes a negative number, you should suspect integer overflow. On most computers, adding 1 to `INT_MAX` yields `INT_MIN`, a negative number.

4. Consider using enumeration types to make your programs more readable, understandable, and modifiable.

5. Avoid anonymous data typing. Give each user-defined type a name.

6. Enumeration type values cannot be input or output directly.

7. The declarations of a `struct` type must end with semicolons.

8. Be sure to specify the full member selector when referencing a component of a `struct` variable or class object.

9. To declare two pointer variables in the same statement, you must use

    ```
    int *p, *q;
    ```

    You cannot use

    ```
    int* p, q;
    ```

    Similarly, you must use

    ```
    int &m, &n;
    ```

    to declare two reference variables in the same statement.
10. Do not confuse a pointer with the variable to which it points.
11. Before dereferencing a pointer variable, be sure it has been assigned a meaningful value other than `NULL`.
12. Pointer variables must be of the same data type to be compared or assigned to one another.

■ Summary

A data type is a set of values (the domain) along with the operations that can be applied to those values. Simple data types are data types whose values are atomic (indivisible).

The integral types in C++ are `char`, `short`, `int`, `long`, and `bool`. The most commonly used integral types are `int` and `char`. The `char` type can be used for storing small (usually one-byte) numeric integers or, more often, for storing character data. Character data includes both printable and nonprintable characters.

C++ allows the programmer to define additional data types. The Typedef statement is a simple mechanism for renaming an existing type, although the result is not truly a new data type. In contrast, an enumeration type, which is created by listing the identifiers that make up the domain, is a new data type that is distinct from any existing type. Values of an enumeration type may be assigned, compared in relational expressions, used as case labels in a Switch statement, passed as arguments, and returned as function values. Enumeration types are extremely useful in the writing of clear, self-documenting programs. In succeeding chapters, we look at language features that let us create even more powerful user-defined types.

In addition to being able to create user-defined atomic data types, we can create structured data types. In a structured data type, a name is given to an entire group of components. With many structured types, the group can be accessed as a whole, or each individual component can be accessed separately.

A record is a data structure for grouping together heterogeneous data—that is, data items that are of different types. Individual components of a record are accessed by name. In C++, records are referred to as *structures* or simply *structs*. We can use a `struct` variable to refer to the struct as a whole, or we can use a member selector to access any individual member (component) of the struct. Entire structs of the same type may be assigned directly to each other, passed as arguments, or returned as function return values. Comparison of structs, however, must be done member by member. Reading and writing of structs must also be done member by member.

Pointer types and reference types are simple data types for storing memory addresses. Variables of these types do not contain data; rather, they contain the addresses of other variables or data structures. Pointer variables require explicit dereferencing using the * operator. Reference variables are dereferenced implicitly and are commonly used to pass nonarray arguments by reference.

■ Quick Check Answers

10.1.1 It is an integral type. **10.1.2** The domain of each type is made up of indivisible, or atomic, data values. **10.1.3** The machine the C++ program is executing on. **10.1.4** ASCII; 256 **10.1.5** Unicode **10.1.6** The external representation is what you see when it is printed. The internal representation is the numeric code used by the computer to represent the character. **10.2.1** `enum Seasons {SPRING, SUMMER, WINTER, AUTUMN};`
10.2.2 `for (quarter = SPRING; quarter <= AUTUMN; quarter = static_cast<Seasons>(quarter + 1))`
10.2.3 It is used to introduce a new name for an existing type. **10.2.4** A named data type is associated with a name as part of its declaration and can be used by any number of subsequent declarations. An anonymous data type is used only once and is included directly in a variable declaration. **10.3.1** Structured data types. **10.3.2** array, struct, union, and class **10.4.1** No. **10.4.2** A list of the members of the struct. **10.4.3** The dot (period). **10.4.4** When you declare a variable of the type of the struct. **10.5.1** A hierarchical record. **10.5.2** `date.time.hour` **10.5.3** They help organize the information they represent making it easier to understand. **10.7.1** `int* compass; int *compass;` **10.6.1** A C++ union is defined to be a struct that holds only one of its members at a time during program execution. **10.6.2** The maximum of the union's members. **10.6.3** By allowing a type to have values of different types at different times, avoiding the need to allocate storage for all of the different types at once.

■ Exam Preparation Exercises

1. All of the integral types in C++ can be signed or unsigned. True or false?
2. The `sizeof` operator can be used to determine whether a machine's `int` type is 32 or 64 bits long. True or false?
3. Floating-point numbers are seldom exactly equal. True or false?
4. The values of enumerator types must be written in uppercase letters. True or false?
5. What are the five integral types in C++?
6. What is wrong with the following pair of enumeration type declarations?

   ```
   enum Colors {RED, ORANGE, YELLOW, GREEN, BLUE, INDIGO, VIOLET};
   enum Flowers{ROSE, DAFFODIL, LILY, VIOLET, COSMOS, ORCHID};
   ```

7. Given the declaration of `Colors` in Exercise 6, what is the value of the expression (YELLOW + 1)?
8. Given the code segment:

   ```
   enum Flowers{ROSE, DAFFODIL, LILY, VIOLET, COSMOS, ORCHID};
   Flowers choice;
   choice = LILY;
   choice++;
   ```

   Why does the compiler give an invalid type error message for the last line?
9. Why is it impossible to use an anonymous type with a function parameter?
10. A struct cannot have another struct as a member. True or false?
11. A union is a struct that can hold just one of its members at a time. True or false?
12. Given the following declarations:

    ```
    struct Name
    {
      string first;
      string middle;
      string last;
    };
    ```

```
Name yourName;
Name myName;
```

What are the contents of the two **Name** variables after each of the following statements, assuming they are executed in the order listed?

a. `yourName.first = "George";`
b. `yourName.last = "Smith";`
c. `myName = yourName;`
d. `myName.middle = "Nathaniel";`
e. `yourName.middle = myName.middle.at(0) + ".";`

13. What are the three aggregate operations allowed on structs?
14. How does a union differ from an enumeration type?
15. Given the declaration of the **Name** type in Exercise 12, and the following declarations:

    ```
    struct studentRecord
    {
      Name studentName;
      Name teacherName;
      int gradeNumber;
      string grades;
    }

    studentRecord sally;
    ```

    a. How would you assign the name Sally Ellen Strong to the **studentName** field of variable **sally**?
    b. How would you assign the grade number 7 to that field of **sally**?
    c. How would you assign the fourth letter from the **grades** field to **char** variable **spring**?

16. What happens when a **struct** is passed as an argument to a value parameter of a function? How does this differ from passing it to a reference parameter?
17. Given the following union declaration:

    ```
    union GradeUnion
    {
      char gradeLetter;
      int gradeNumber;
    }

    GradeUnion grade;
    ```

    What does each of the following statements do, assuming they are executed in the order shown?

    a. `cin >> grade.gradeLetter;`
    b. `if (grade.gradeLetter >= 'A' && grade.gradeLetter <= 'D')`
    c. `grade.gradeNumber = 4 - int(grade.gradeLetter - 'A');`

18. Assigning the value **NULL** to a pointer causes it to point to nothing. True or false?
19. A reference variable can be reassigned a new address value at any time. True or false?

Programming Warm-Up Exercises

1. Declare an enumeration type consisting of the nine planets in their order by distance from the Sun (Mercury first, Pluto last).
2. Write a value-returning function that converts the name of a planet given as a `string` parameter to a value of the enumeration type declared in Exercise 1. If the string isn't a proper planet name, return `"EARTH"`.
4. Write a value-returning function that converts a planet of the enumeration type declared in Exercise 1 into the corresponding string. The planet is an input parameter and the string is returned by the function. If the input is not a valid planet, return `"Error"`.
4. Write a For statement that prints out the names of the planets in order, using the enumeration type declared in Exercise 1 and the function declared in Exercise 3.
5. Declare a `struct` type, `Time`, that represents an amount of time consisting of minutes and seconds.
6. Write statements that assign the time 6 minutes and 54 seconds to a variable, `someTime`, of type `Time`, as declared in Exercise 5.
7. Declare a `struct` type, `Song`, that represents a song entry in an MP-3 library. It should have fields for title, album, artist, playing time in minutes and seconds (use the type declared in Exercise 5), and music category. The music category is represented by an enumeration type called `Category`.
8. Write statements to declare a variable called `mySong` of type `Song`, and assign it a set of values. For the playing time, use the variable `someTime` declared in Exercise 6. Make up values for the other fields. Assume that the enumeration type `Category` includes any song category that you wish to use.
9. Write a statement to output the playing time from `mySong`, as declared in Exercise 8, in the format `mm:ss`.
10. Write a declaration of a `union` type called `Temporal` that can hold a time represented as a string, as an integer, or as a value of type `Time`, as declared in Exercise 5.
11. Write the declaration of a variable called `shift` of type `Temporal`, as declared in Exercise 10, and a statement that assigns the value of `someTime`, as declared in Exercise 6, to `shift`.
12. Declare a pointer variable `intPointer` and initialize it to point to an `int` variable named `someInt`. Write two assignment statements, the first of which stores the value 451 directly into `someInt`, and the second of which indirectly stores 451 into the variable pointed to by `intPointer`.

Programming Problems

1. Programming Problem 4 in Chapter 5 asked you to write a C++ program that asks the user to enter his or her weight and the name of a planet. In Chapter 7, Programming Problem 2 asked you to rewrite the program using a Switch statement. Now, rewrite the program so it uses an enumerated type to represent the planet.

    For ease of reference, the information for the original problem is repeated here. The following table gives the factor by which the weight must be multiplied for each planet. The program should output an error message if the user doesn't input a correct planet name. The prompt and the error message should make it clear to the user how a planet name must be entered. Be sure to use proper formatting and appropriate comments in your code. The output should be labeled clearly and formatted neatly.

Mercury	0.4155
Venus	0.8975
Earth	1.0
Moon	0.166
Mars	0.3507
Jupiter	2.5374
Saturn	1.0677
Uranus	0.8947
Neptune	1.1794
Pluto	0.0899

2. Programming Problem 3 in Chapter 7 asked you to write a program that generates sales-report files for a set of traveling salespeople. In the original problem, we used an integer in the range of 1 through 10 to represent ID numbers for the salespeople. Rewrite the program so that it uses an enumeration type whose values are the names of the salespeople (you can make up the names). The sales file format should replace the salesperson ID number with a string that is the person's last name, so that a line of the file contains a name, an item number, and a quantity. For convenience, the other information concerning the problem is repeated here.

The company sells eight different products, with IDs numbered 7 through 14 (some older products have been discontinued). The unit prices of the products are given here:

Product Number	Unit Price
7	345.00
8	853.00
9	471.00
10	933.00
11	721.00
12	663.00
13	507.00
14	259.00

The program reads in the sales file, and generates a separate file for each salesperson containing just his or her sales. Each line from the sales file is copied to the appropriate salesperson's file, with the salesperson's name omitted. The file names should be the name of the salesperson with .dat appended (you may have to adjust names that don't work as file names on your computer, such as hyphenated names or names with apostrophes). The total for the sale (quantity times unit price) is then appended to the record. At the end of processing, the total sales for each salesperson should be output with informative labels to **cout**. Use functional decomposition to design the program. Make sure that the program handles invalid salesperson's names. If a salesperson's name is invalid, write out an error message to **cout**. If a product number is invalid, write the error message to the salesperson's file and don't compute a total for the sale.

3. You are taking a geology class, and the professor wants you to write a program to help students learn the periods of geologic time. The program should let the user enter a range of prehistoric dates (in millions of years), and then output the periods that are included in that range. Each time this output is done, the user is asked if he or she wants to continue. The goal of the exercise is for the student to try to figure out when each period began, so that he or she can make a chart of geologic time.

    Within the program, represent the periods with an enumeration type made up of their names. You will probably want to create a function that determines the period corresponding to a date, and another function that returns the string corresponding to each identifier in the enumeration. Then you can use a For loop to output the series of periods in the range. The periods of geologic time are given here:

Period Name	Starting Date (millions of years)
Neogene	23
Paleogene	65
Cretaceous	136
Jurassic	192
Triassic	225
Permian	280
Carboniferous	345
Devonian	395
Silurian	435
Ordovician	500
Cambrian	570
Precambrian	4500 or earlier

    Use functional decomposition to solve this problem. Be sure to use good coding style and documenting comments. The prompts and error messages that are output should be clear and informative.

4. The educational program that you wrote for Problem 3 was a big success. Now the geology professor wants you to write another program to help teach geologic time. In this program, the computer picks a date in geologic time and presents it to the student. The student then guesses which period corresponds to the date. The student is allowed to continue guessing until he or she gets the right answer. Then the program asks the student whether he or she wants to try again, and repeats the process if the answer is "yes." To solve this problem, you should again use an enumeration type consisting of the names of the periods. In this case, you'll probably want to make a function that returns the period corresponding to a string containing the name of a period (the program should work with any style of capitalization of the names). You also may want a function that returns the period for a given date.

    Use functional design to solve this problem. Be sure to use good coding style and include helpful documenting comments. The prompts and error messages that are output should be clear and informative. You may want to add some interest to the program by keeping track of the number of guesses taken by the user, and offering differing levels of praise and encouragement depending on how well the user is doing.

5. Write a C++ program that determines the largest number for which your computer can represent its factorial exactly using the `longdouble` type. A factorial is the product of all numbers from 1 to the given number. For example, 10 factorial (written 10!) is

   $1 \times 2 \times 3 \times 4 \times 5 \times 6 \times 7 \times 8 \times 9 \times 10 = 3{,}628{,}800$

   As you can see, the factorial grows to be a large number very quickly. Your program should keep multiplying the prior factorial by the next integer, then subtract 1 and check whether the difference between the factorial and the factorial minus 1 is less than 1—an error tolerance. When the maximum precision of the type is reached, and least significant digits are truncated to allow the most significant digits of the product to be stored, then subtracting 1 should have no effect on the value. Because floating-point representations may not be exact, however, the expression

   ```
   abs((number - 1) - number)
   ```

   may not exactly equal 1. That's why you need to include a small error tolerance in the comparison.
      Use functional decomposition to solve this problem. Code the program using good style and include helpful documenting comments. To keep the user informed of progress, you may wish to output all of the intermediate factorial values. The greatest number and its factorial should be clearly labeled.

Case Study Follow-Up

1. How could you determine whether a hyphen should be counted as an end-of-word symbol or a break in the word due to spacing issues?
2. Implement the change outlined in your answer to Exercise 1.
3. The `endOfWord` variable is reset to `false` every time an alphanumeric character is read. Thus it is set to itself over and over again. Can you think of a scheme that would allow you to set it only once?
4. Should error detection be added to program `Style`? Explain.

Arrays

KNOWLEDGE GOALS

- To understand the structure of a one-dimensional array.
- To know how to use a one-dimensional array in solving a problem.
- To understand the structure of arrays of records.
- To know how index values can be chosen to have semantic content.
- To understand the structure of a two-dimensional array.
- To understand the structure of a multidimensional array.

SKILL GOALS

To be able to:
- Declare a one-dimensional array, with and without initialization.
- Perform fundamental operations on one-dimensional arrays.
- Apply subarray processing to a one-dimensional array.
- Declare a two-dimensional array.
- Perform fundamental operations on a two-dimensional array.
- Use arrays as parameters and arguments.
- Declare and process a multidimensional array.

Data structures play an important role in the design process. The choice of data structure directly affects the design because it determines the algorithms used to process the data. In Chapter 10, we saw how the record (struct) gave us the ability to refer to an entire group of components by one name. This simplifies the design of many programs.

In many problems, however, a data structure has so many components that it is difficult to process them if each component must have a unique member name. For example, suppose we needed to represent a collection of 100 integer values, such as the male and female population figures for each state. If we used a struct to hold these values, we would have to invent 100 different member names. Then we would have to write 100 input statements to read the values and 100 output statements to display them—an incredibly tedious task! An *array*—the third of the structured data types supported by C++—allows us to program operations of this kind with ease.

11.1 One-Dimensional Arrays

If we want to input 1000 integer values and print them in reverse order, we could write a program of this form:

```
//****************************
// ReverseNumbers program
//****************************
#include <iostream>

using namespace std;

int main()
{
  int value0;
  int value1;
  int value2;
     .
     .
     .
  int value999;

  cin >> value0;
  cin >> value1;
  cin >> value2;
     .
     .
     .
  cin >> value999;
  cout << value999 << endl;
  cout << value998 << endl;
  cout << value997 << endl;
     .
     .
     .
  cout << value0 << endl;
  return 0;
}
```

This program is more than 3000 lines long, and we have to use 1000 separate variables. Note that all the variables have the same name except for an appended number that distinguishes them. Wouldn't it be convenient if we could put the number into a counter variable and use For loops to go from 0 through 999, and then from 999 back down to 0? For example, if the counter variable is **number,** we can replace the 2000 original input/output statements with the following four lines of code (where highlighted below, we enclose **number** in brackets to set it apart from **value**):

```
for (number = 0; number < 1000; number++)
  cin >> value[number];
for (number = 999; number >= 0; number--)
  cout << value[number] << endl;
```

This code fragment is correct in C++ *if* we declare **value** to be a *one-dimensional array*. A one-dimensional array is a collection of variables—all of the same type—in which the first part of each variable name is the same, and the last part is an *index value* enclosed in square brackets. In our example, the value stored in **number** is called the *index*.

The declaration of a one-dimensional array is similar to the declaration of a simple variable (a variable of a simple data type), with one exception: You also declare the size of the array—that is, the number of values it can hold. To do so, you indicate within brackets the number of components in the array:

```
int value[1000];
```

This declaration creates an array with 1000 components, all of type **int**. The first component has index value 0, the second component has index value 1, and the last component has index value 999.

Here is the complete ReverseNumbers program, using array notation. It is certainly much shorter than our first version of the program.

```
//************************************************
// This program reverses the numbers in an array
//************************************************
#include <iostream>

using namespace std;
int main()
{
  int value[1000];
  int number;

  for (number = 0; number < 1000; number++)
    cin >> value[number];
  for (number = 999; number >= 0; number--)
    cout << value[number] << endl;
  return 0;
}
```

Here is the input and the output for our program. We changed the array to be just 10 numbers long to keep from having to enter 1000 data values! Note that we show the input and output in two columns to save space.

Input	Output
1	10
2	9
3	8
4	7
5	6
6	5
7	4
8	3
9	2
10	1

As a data structure, an array differs from a struct in two fundamental ways:

1. An array is a *homogeneous* data structure (all of its components are of the same data type), whereas structs are heterogeneous types (their components may be of different types).
2. A component of an array is accessed by its *position* in the structure, whereas a component of a struct is accessed by an identifier (the member name).

Let's now define arrays formally and look at the rules for accessing individual components.

Declaring Arrays

One-dimensional array A structured collection of components, all of the same type, that is given a single name. Each component (array element) is accessed by an index that indicates the component's position within the collection.

A **one-dimensional array** is a structured collection of components (often called *array elements*) that can be accessed individually by specifying the position of a component with a single index value. (Later in this chapter, we introduce multidimensional arrays, which are arrays that have more than one index value.)

Here is a syntax template describing the simplest form of a one-dimensional array declaration:

ArrayDeclaration

```
DataType  ArrayName [ ConstIntExpression ] ;
```

In the syntax template, DataType describes what is stored in each component of the array. Array components may be of almost any type, but for now we limit our discussion to atomic components.

In the syntax template, ConstIntExpression is an integer expression composed only of literal or named constants. This expression, which specifies the number of components in

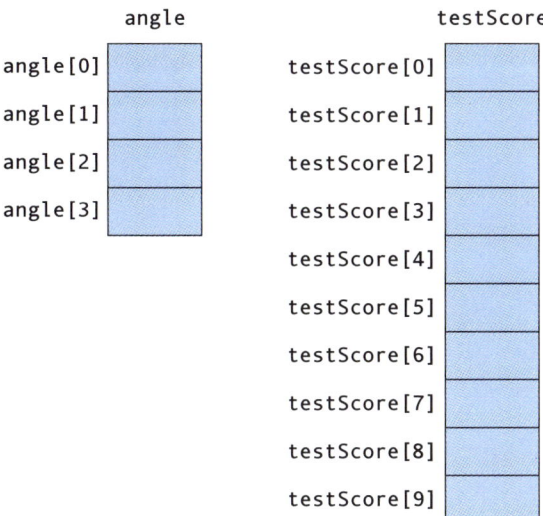

FIGURE 11.1 `angle` and `testScore` Arrays

the array, must have a value greater than 0. If the value is *n*, the range of index values is 0 through *n* − 1, not 1 through *n*. For example, the declarations

```
float  angle[4];
int    testScore[10];
```

create the arrays shown in **FIGURE 11.1**. The `angle` array has four components, each capable of holding one `float` value. The `testScore` array has a total of ten components, all of type `int`.

Accessing Individual Components of an Array

Recall that to access an individual component of a struct or class, we use dot notation—the name of the struct variable or class object, followed by a period, followed by the member name. In contrast, to access an individual array component, we write the array name, followed by an expression enclosed in square brackets. The expression specifies which component to access.

ArrayComponentAccess

> ArrayName [IndexExpression]

The index expression may be as simple as a constant or a variable name or as complex as a combination of variables, operators, and function calls. Whatever the form of the expression, it must result in an integer value. Index expressions can be of type `char`, `short`, `int`, `long`, or `bool`, because these are all integral types. Additionally, values of enumeration types can be used as index expressions, with an enumeration value implicitly being coerced to an integer.

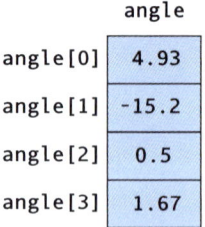

FIGURE 11.2 angle Array with Values

The simplest form of index expression is a constant. Using our **angle** array, the sequence of assignment statements

```
angle[0] = 4.93;
angle[1] = -15.2;
angle[2] = 0.5;
angle[3] = 1.67;
```

fills the array components one at a time (see **FIGURE 11.2**).

Each array component—**angle[2]**, for instance—can be treated exactly the same way as any simple variable of type **float**. For example, we can do the following to the individual component **angle[2]**:

`angle[2] = 9.6;`	Assign it a value.
`cin >> angle[2];`	Read a value into it.
`cout << angle[2];`	Write its contents.
`y = sqrt(angle[2]);`	Pass it as an argument.
`x = 6.8 * angle[2] + 7.5;`	Use it in an arithmetic expression.

Now let's look at index expressions that are more complicated than constants. Suppose we declare a 1000-element array of **int** values with the following statement:

```
int value[1000];
```

We then execute these two statements:

```
value[counter] = 5;
if (value[number+1] % 10 != 0)
    .
    .
    .
```

In the first statement, 5 is stored into an array component. If **counter** is 0, 5 is stored into the first component of the array. If **counter** is 1, 5 is stored into the second place in the array, and so forth.

In the second statement, the expression **number+1** selects an array component. The specific array component accessed is divided by 10 and checked to see if the remainder is nonzero. If **number+1** is 0, we are testing the value in the first component; if **number+1** is 1, we are testing the second-place value; and so on. **FIGURE 11.3** shows the index expression as a constant, a variable, and a more complex expression.

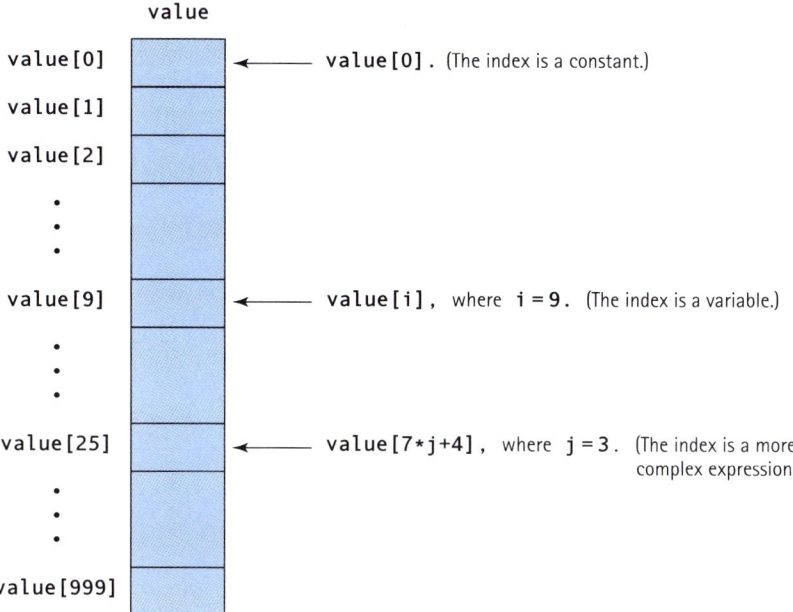

FIGURE 11.3 An Index as a Constant, a Variable, and an Arbitrary Expression

In earlier chapters, we saw how the **string** class allows us to access an individual character within a string:

```
string aString;

aString = "Hello";
cout << aString.at(1);    // Prints 'e'
```

Although **string** is a class (not an array), the **string** class was written using the advanced C++ technique of *operator overloading* to give the **[ ]** operator another meaning (string component selection) in addition to its standard meaning (array element selection). As a consequence, a **string** object is similar to an array of characters but has special properties. Thus we can write the last statement in the preceding example in an alternative manner:

```
cout << aString[1];       // Also prints 'e'
```

Even though C++ supports this alternative syntax, we recommend using the **at** operation because it checks whether the requested position is within the valid range of positions for the given string. Accessing the string with array index notation doesn't perform this check.

Out-of-Bounds Array Indexes

Given the declaration

```
float alpha[100];
```

the valid range of index values is 0 through 99. What happens if we execute the statement

```
alpha[i] = 62.4;
```

> **Out-of-bounds array index** An index value that, in C++, is either less than 0 or greater than the array size minus 1.

when i is less than 0 or when i is greater than 99? The result is that a memory location outside the array is accessed. C++ does not check for invalid (out-of-bounds) array indexes either at compile time or at run time. If i happens to be 100 in the preceding statement, the computer stores 62.4 into the next memory location past the end of the array, destroying whatever value was previously found there.

It is entirely the programmer's responsibility to make sure that an array index does not step off either end of the array.

Array-processing algorithms often use For loops to step through the array elements one at a time. Here is a loop to zero out our 100-element `alpha` array (`i` is an `int` variable):

```
for (i = 0; i < 100; i++)
    alpha[i] = 0.0;
```

We could also write the first line as

```
for (i = 0; i <= 99; i++)
```

However, C++ programmers typically prefer to use the first version so that the number in the loop test (100) is the same as the array size. With this pattern, it is important to remember to test for *less-than*, not less-than-or-equal.

The following program shows what happens when you access places beyond the array bounds.

```
//***************************************************
// This program creates an array of four
// items, stores values into the four
// places, and overruns the array by two places
// ***************************************************

#include <iostream>
using namespace std;
int main ()
{
  int data[4];
  for (int i = 1; i <= 4; i++)   // Fill all 4 places of array
    data[i] = i;
  for (int i = 1; i <= 6; i++)   // Print 6 places--error
    cout << data[i] << endl;
  return 0;
}
```

Output:

```
1
2
3
4
0
-1881139893
```

The first four values are the ones stored by the program. The next two are whatever happened to be in the two places in memory beyond the array.

Initializing Arrays in Declarations

You learned in Chapter 8 that C++ allows you to initialize a variable in its declaration:

```
int delta = 25;
```

The value 25 is called an initializer. You also can initialize an array in its declaration, using a special syntax for the initializer. To do so, you specify a list of initial values for the array elements, separate them with commas, and enclose the list within braces:

```
int age[5] = {23, 10, 16, 37, 12};
```

In this declaration, `age[0]` is initialized to 23, `age[1]` is initialized to 10, and so on. If you specify too many initial values, C++ generates a syntax error message. If you specify too few, the remaining array elements are initialized to zero.

Arrays follow the same rule as simple variables about the time(s) at which initialization occurs. A static array (one that is either global or declared as `static` within a block) is initialized once only, when control reaches its declaration. An automatic array (one that is local and not declared as `static`) is reinitialized each time control reaches its declaration.

An interesting feature of C++ is that you are allowed to omit the size of an array when you initialize it in a declaration:

```
float temperature[] = {0.0, 112.37, 98.6};
```

The compiler figures out the size of the array (here, 3) based on how many initial values are listed. In general, this feature is not particularly useful.

(Lack of) Aggregate Array Operations

In Chapter 10, we defined an aggregate operation as an operation on a data structure as a whole. Some programming languages allow aggregate operations on arrays, but C++ does not. In other words, if **one** and **two** are declared as

```
int one[50];
int two[50];
```

there is no aggregate assignment of **two** to **one**:

```
one = two;          // Not valid
```

To copy array **two** into array **one**, you must do it yourself, element by element:

```
for (index = 0; index < 50; index++)
  one[index] = two[index];
```

Similarly, there is no aggregate I/O of arrays:[1]

```
cout << one;        // Not valid
```

---

1. C++ allows one exception: Aggregate I/O is permitted for C strings, which are implemented as special `char` arrays. We cover C strings at the end of this section.

Nor is there aggregate arithmetic on arrays:

```
one = one + two;    // Not valid
```

Comparison of arrays is possible, but it doesn't do what you expect:

```
if (one == two)     // Not what you expect
```

Rather than comparing the values stored in the two arrays, this statement checks whether the arrays are stored at the same address in memory. Similarly, attempting to return an array as the value of a value-returning function passes back the memory address of the first element of the array:

```
return one;         // Returns address of the first element of one
```

The only thing you can do to an array as a whole is to pass it as an argument to a function:

```
DoSomething(one);
```

Passing an array as an argument gives the function access to the entire array. The following table compares arrays and structs with respect to aggregate operations.

Aggregate Operation	Arrays	Structs
I/O	No (except C strings)	No
Assignment	No	Yes
Arithmetic	No	No
Comparison	No	No
Argument passage	By reference	By value or by reference
Return as a function's return value	No	Yes

Later in this chapter, we look in detail at the process of passing arrays as arguments.

Examples of Declaring and Accessing Arrays

Let's look at some specific examples of declaring and accessing arrays. Here are some declarations that a program might use to analyze occupancy rates in an apartment building:

```
const int BUILDING_SIZE = 350;   // Number of apartments

int occupants[BUILDING_SIZE];    // occupants[i] is the number of
                                 //   occupants in apartment i
int totalOccupants;              // Total number of occupants
int counter;                     // Loop control and index variable
```

Here `occupants` is a 350-element array of integers (see **FIGURE 11.4**). `occupants[0]` = 3 if the first apartment has three occupants; `occupants[1]` = 5 if the second apartment has five occupants; and so on. If values have been stored into the array, then the following code totals the number of occupants in the building:

```
totalOccupants = 0;
for (counter = 0; counter < BUILDING_SIZE; counter++)
  totalOccupants = totalOccupants + occupants[counter];
```

FIGURE 11.4 occupants Array

The first time through the loop, `counter` is 0. We add the contents of `totalOccupants` (that is, 0) to the contents of `occupants[0]`, storing the result into `totalOccupants`. Next, the value of `counter` becomes 1 and the loop test occurs. The second loop iteration adds the contents of `totalOccupants` to the contents of `occupants[1]`, storing the result into `totalOccupants`. Now the value of `counter` becomes 2 and the loop test is made. Eventually, the loop adds the contents of `occupants[349]` to the sum and increments `counter` to have the value 350. At this point, the loop condition is false, and control exits the loop.

Note how we used the named constant `BUILDING_SIZE` in both the array declaration and the For loop. When constants are used in this manner, changes are easy to make. If the number of apartments changes from 350 to 400, we need to change only one line: the `const` declaration of `BUILDING_SIZE`. If we had used the literal value 350 in place of `BUILDING_SIZE`, we would need to update several of the statements in our previous code, and probably many more throughout the rest of the program.

The following is a complete program that uses the `occupants` array. The program fills the array with occupant data read from an input file and then lets the user interactively look up the number of occupants in a specific apartment.

```cpp
//****************************************************************
// This program allows a building owner to look up how many
// occupants are in a given apartment
//****************************************************************
#include <iostream>
#include <fstream>                 // For file I/O
using namespace std;

const int BUILDING_SIZE = 10;      // Number of apartments

int main()
{
  int occupants[BUILDING_SIZE];    // occupants[i] is the number of
                                   //    occupants in apartment i
  int totalOccupants;              // Total number of occupants
  int counter;                     // Loop control and index variable
```

```cpp
   int apt;                          // An apartment number
   ifstream inFile;                  // File of occupant data (one
                                     //   integer per apartment)
   inFile.open("apt.dat");
   totalOccupants = 0;
   for (counter = 0; counter < BUILDING_SIZE; counter++)
   {
     inFile >> occupants[counter];
     totalOccupants = totalOccupants + occupants[counter];
   }
   cout << "No. of apts. is " << BUILDING_SIZE << endl
        << "Total no. of occupants is " << totalOccupants << endl;

   cout << "Begin apt. lookup..." << endl;
   do
   {
     cout << "Apt. number (1 through " << BUILDING_SIZE
          << ", or 0 to quit): ";
     cin >> apt;
     if (apt > 0)
       cout << "Apt. " << apt << " has " << occupants[apt-1]
            << " occupants" << endl;
   } while (apt > 0);
   return 0;
}
```

Look closely at the last output statement in this program. The user enters an apartment number (apt) in the range 1 through BUILDING_SIZE, but the array has indexes 0 through BUILDING_SIZE − 1. Therefore, we must subtract 1 from apt to ensure that the index refers to the proper place in the array.

The constant BUILDING_SIZE was changed to 10 for the following test run.

Input on apt.dat: 3 4 0 3 4 1 1 2 3 2

Output:

```
No. of apts. is 10
Total no. of occupants is 23
Begin apt. lookup...
Apt. number (1 through 10, or 0 to quit): 1
Apt. 1 has 3 occupants
Apt. number (1 through 10, or 0 to quit): 3
Apt. 3 has 0 occupants
Apt. number (1 through 10, or 0 to quit): 5
Apt. 5 has 4 occupants
Apt. number (1 through 10, or 0 to quit): 6
Apt. 6 has 1 occupants
Apt. number (1 through 10, or 0 to quit): 7
Apt. 7 has 1 occupants
Apt. number (1 through 10, or 0 to quit): 9
Apt. 9 has 3 occupants
Apt. number (1 through 10, or 0 to quit): 10
Apt. 10 has 2 occupants
Apt. number (1 through 10, or 0 to quit): 0
```

Because an array index is an integer value, we access the components based on their position in the array—that is, the first, the second, the third, and so on. Using an `int` index is the most common way of thinking about an array. C++, however, provides more flexibility by allowing an index to be of any integral type or enumeration type. (The index expression still must evaluate to an integer in the range from 0 through one less than the array size.)

The next example shows an array in which the indexes are values of an enumeration type:

```
enum Drink {ORANGE, COLA, ROOT_BEER, GINGER_ALE, CHERRY, LEMON};

float salesAmt[6]; // Array of 6 floats, to be indexed by Drink type
Drink flavor;      // Variable of the index type
```

Here `Drink` is an enumeration type in which the enumerators ORANGE, COLA, . . . , LEMON have internal representations 0 through 5, respectively. `salesAmt` is a group of six `float` components representing sales figures (in dollars) for each kind of drink (see **FIGURE 11.5**). The following code prints the values in the array:

```
for (flavor = ORANGE; flavor <= LEMON; flavor = Drink(flavor + 1))
  cout << salesAmt[flavor] << endl;
```

Here is another example:

```
const int NUM_STUDENTS = 10;

char grade[NUM_STUDENTS];   // Array of 10 student letter grades
int  idNumber;              // Student ID number (0 through 9)
```

The `grade` array is pictured in **FIGURE 11.6**. Values are shown in the components, which implies that some processing of the array has already occurred. Following are some simple examples showing how the array might be used:

`cin >> grade[2];`	Reads the next nonwhitespace character from the input stream and stores it into the component in `grade` indexed by 2.
`grade[3] = 'A';`	Assigns the character 'A' to the component in `grade` indexed by 3.
`idNumber = 5;`	Assigns 5 to the index variable `idNumber`.

salesAmt

salesAmt[ORANGE]   (i.e., salesAmt[0])
salesAmt[COLA]   (i.e., salesAmt[1])
salesAmt[ROOT_BEER] (i.e., salesAmt[2])
salesAmt[GINGER_ALE] (i.e., salesAmt[3])
salesAmt[CHERRY]   (i.e., salesAmt[4])
salesAmt[LEMON]   (i.e., salesAmt[5])

FIGURE 11.5 salesAmt Array

```
                    grade
    grade[0]    'F'
    grade[1]    'B'
    grade[2]    'C'
    grade[3]    'A'
    grade[4]    'F'
    grade[5]    'C'
    grade[6]    'A'
    grade[7]    'A'
    grade[8]    'C'
    grade[9]    'B'
```

FIGURE 11.6 grade Array Filled with Values

Code	Description
`grade[idNumber] = 'C';`	Assigns the character 'C' to the component of **grade** indexed by **idNumber** (that is, by 5).

`for (idNumber = 0; idNumber`
`    < NUM_STUDENTS; idNumber++)`
`  cout << grade[idNumber];`
	Loops through the **grade** array, printing each component. For this loop, the output would be FBCAFCAACB.

`for (idNumber = 0; idNumber`
`    < NUM_STUDENTS; idNumber++)`
`  cout << "Student " << idNumber`
`      << " Grade "`
`      << grade[idNumber] << endl;`
	Loops through **grade**, printing each component in a more readable form.

In the last example, `idNumber` is used as the index, but it also has semantic content—it is the student's identification number. Here is the output of executing the code:

```
Student 0 Grade F
Student 1 Grade B
    ⋮
Student 9 Grade B
```

Here is one last example. Suppose we want to count the occurrences of characters within a text. We can set up an array of 26 positions in which each position serves as a counter for one letter in the alphabet (uppercase or lowercase). Because array indexes must be integral values, we can't use a letter as an index, so how will we recognize a letter? Use an If statement with 25 tests? No, fortunately, there is a better way.

Recall that in ASCII (or Unicode) the uppercase letters are in order and the lowercase letters are in order. If we subtract 'A' from any uppercase letter, we get the letter's position

FIGURE 11.7 counters Array

in the collating sequence. Likewise, if we subtract 'a' from any lowercase letter, we get its position in the collating sequence. That is,

```
'A' - 'A' = 0
'B' - 'B' = 1
. . .
'a' - 'a' = 0
'b' - 'b' = 1
. . .
```

We can read a character and, if it is a letter, convert it to uppercase and use the result of subtracting `'A'` from it as an index into the array of counters. See **FIGURE 11.7**.

Here is the program that uses the array to count the letters in text. The output is based on the same data that were used to test the Rich Uncle program in Chapter 7.

```cpp
//*****************************************************
// This program counts and prints the frequency of
// occurrence of alphabetic characters in a file
//*****************************************************
#include <iostream>
#include <fstream>
#include <string>
#include <cctype>
using namespace std;
int main ()
{
    // Declarations
    int counters[26];
    ifstream inFile;
    inFile.open("text.dat");
```

```
      string line;
      int limit;                    // Number of characters in a line
      int index;

      // Zero out the array of counters
      for (int counter = 0; counter < 26; counter++)
        counters[counter] = 0;
      getline(inFile, line);        // Read a line
      while (inFile)
      {
        limit = line.length();
        for (int counter = 0; counter < limit; counter++)
          // Access each character in the line
          if (isalpha(line.at(counter)))
          {
            // Increment the character's counter
            index = toupper(line.at(counter)) - 'A';
            counters[index]++;
          }
        }
        getline(inFile,line);       // Read a line
      }
      for (int counter = 0; counter < 26; counter++)
        cout << static_cast<char> (counter + 'A') << ": "
             << counters[counter] << endl;
      return 0;
    }
```

Output (in four columns to save space):

A: 305	H: 192	O: 204	V: 32
B: 54	I: 254	P: 60	W: 48
C: 142	J: 6	Q: 6	X: 5
D: 150	K: 9	R: 195	Y: 41
E: 421	L: 114	S: 184	Z: 5
F: 59	M: 109	T: 327	
G: 49	N: 258	U: 96	

Notice that the index has to be converted back to a character before it is output. This conversion is the reverse of the original operation: The letter 'A' is added to the index and the result cast back to a character.

Passing Arrays as Arguments

In Chapter 8, we said that if a variable is passed to a function and it should not be changed by the function, then the variable should be passed by value instead of by reference. We specifically excluded stream variables (such as those representing data files) from this rule and noted that one more exception would be discussed later in the book. Now we can clarify this point: Arrays are the exception.

By default, C++ simple variables are always passed by value. To pass a simple variable by reference, you must append an ampersand (**&**) to the data type name in the function's parameter list:

```
int SomeFunc(float param1,      // Pass-by-value
             char& param2)      // Pass-by-reference
{
   ⋮
}
```

C++ doesn't allow arrays to be passed by value; arrays are *always* passed by reference.[2] Therefore, you should never use **&** when declaring an array as a parameter. When an array is passed as an argument, its base address—the memory address of the first element of the array—is sent to the function. The function then knows where the caller's actual array is located and can access any element of the array.

Base address The memory address of the first element of an array.

Here is a C++ function that will zero out a one-dimensional **int** array of any size:

```
void ZeroOut(int intArray[], int numElements)
{
  int i;
  for (i = 0; i < numElements; i++)
    intArray[i] = 0;
}
```

In the parameter list, the declaration of **intArray** does not include a size within the brackets. If you include a size, the compiler ignores it. The compiler wants to know only that it is an **int** array, not an **int** array of any particular size. Therefore, in the **ZeroOut** function you must include a second parameter—the number of array elements—if the For loop is to work correctly.

The calling code can invoke the **ZeroOut** function for an **int** array of any size. The following code fragment makes function calls to zero out two arrays of different sizes. Notice how an array parameter is declared in a function prototype.

```
void ZeroOut(int intArray[], int numElements)   // Function prototype
// This function sets the first numElements in intArray to zero.

int main()
{
  int counters[26];
  int someOtherArray[9000];
  ZeroOut(counters, 26);
  ZeroOut(someOtherArray, 9000);
     ⋮
}
```

---

2. Here we are referring to passing arrays directly via parameters. There is an indirect way in which an array can be passed by value. Because a struct is passed by value, when an array is a field within a struct, its values are copied along with all of the other members. The same is true when an array is passed as a member of a class.

Keep in mind that within a function, an array parameter is simply a variable that is passed the address of the first element of the argument array. As mentioned earlier, C++ doesn't support aggregate assignment of one array to another. However, you can assign a new address to an array parameter, causing it to refer to a different array. The assignment is not copying the array's element values in this scenario, so it isn't aggregate assignment. It's a common mistake to forget this distinction.

With simple variables, passing by value prevents a function from modifying the caller's argument. Although arrays are not passed by value in C++, you can still prevent the function from modifying the caller's array. To do so, you use the reserved word **const** in the declaration of the parameter. Following is a function that copies one **int** array into another. The first parameter—the destination array—is expected to be modified; the second array is not.

```
void Copy(int destination[], const int source[], int size)
{
  int i;
  for (i = 0; i < size; i++)
    destination[i] = source[i];
}
```

The word **const** guarantees that any attempt to modify the **source** array within the **Copy** function results in a compile-time error.

The following table summarizes argument passage for simple variables and one-dimensional arrays:

Argument	Parameter Declaration for a Pass by Value	Parameter Declaration for a Pass by Reference
Simple variable	int cost	int& price
Array	Not allowed*	int table[]

*Prefixing the array declaration with the word **const** prevents the function from modifying the parameter.

One final remark about argument passage: It is a common mistake to pass an array *element* to a function when you actually intended to pass the entire array. For example, our **ZeroOut** function expects the base address of an **int** array to be sent as the first argument. In the following code fragment, the function call is incorrect:

```
int counters[26];
    ⋮
ZeroOut(counters[26], 25);    // Error
```

The error arises because **counters[26]** denotes a single array element—one **int** number—and not an entire array. Furthermore, there is no array element with an index of 26. The indexes for the **counters** array run from 0 through 25.

BACKGROUND INFORMATION
C, C++, and Arrays as Arguments

Some programming languages allow arrays to be passed either by value or by reference. Remember that when passing by value, a copy of the argument is sent to the function. When an array is passed by value, the entire array is copied. Not only is extra space required in the function to hold the copy, but the copying itself also takes time. Passing by reference requires only that the address of the argument be passed to the function; thus, when an array is passed by reference, just the address of the first array component is passed. Obviously, passing large arrays by reference saves both memory and time.

The C programming language—the direct predecessor of C++—was designed to be a system programming language. System programs, such as compilers, assemblers, linkers, and operating systems, must be both fast and economical with memory space. In the design of the C language, passing arrays by value was judged to be an unnecessary language feature. System programmers never use pass by value when working with arrays. Therefore, both C and C++ pass arrays by reference.

Of course, using a reference parameter can lead to inadvertent errors if the values are changed within the function. In early versions of the C language, there was no way to protect the caller's array from being modified by the function.

C++ (and recent versions of C) added the ability to declare an array parameter as **const**. When the array is declared as **const**, a compile-time error will occur if the function attempts to modify the array. As a result, C++ supports the efficiency of passing arrays by reference yet also provides the protection (through **const**) of passing by value.

Whenever your design of a function's interface identifies an array parameter as incoming only (to be inspected but not modified by the function), declare the array as **const** to obtain the same protection as passing by value.

Commenting Arrays

In comments, we often need to refer to a range of array elements:

`// alpha[i] through alpha[j] have been printed`

To specify such ranges, it is more convenient to use an abbreviated notation consisting of two dots:

`// alpha[i]..alpha[j] have been printed`

or more briefly:

`// alpha[i..j] have been printed`

Note that this dot-dot notation is *not* valid syntax in C++ language statements. We can use it only in comments within a program.

As an example of the use of this notation, here is how we would write the precondition and postcondition for our `ZeroOut` function:

```
void ZeroOut(int intArray[], int numElements)
// Pre:  numElements is assigned
// Post: intArray[0..numElements-1] are zero
```

SOFTWARE MAINTENANCE CASE STUDY: Modularizing a Program

MAINTENANCE TASK: The character counting program mentioned earlier in this chapter consisted of straight-line code. The task here is to modularize it using functions. Let's examine the action part of the code.

```
// Zero out the array of counters
for (int counter = 0; counter < 26; counter++)
  counters[counter] = 0;
```

The comment says it all: We need a function to zero out the counters. In fact, we just discussed such a function as an example in the last section.

```
getline(inFile, line);   // Read a line
while (inFile)
{
  limit = line.length();
  for (int counter = 0; counter < limit; counter++)
    // Access each character in the line
    if (isalpha(line[counter]))
    {
      // Increment the character's counter
      . . .
    }
  getline(inFile, line);   // Read a line
}
```

Again, the comments tell us what the loop body does: It accesses each character and increments its counter if it is a letter. Processing the text should be carried out through a function that takes the array of counters and the file name as parameters. The following section of code prints the output:

```
for (int counter = 0; counter < 26; counter++)
  cout << (char) (counter + 'A') << ": " << counters[counter]
       << endl;
```

We can turn this code into a function that takes the array of counters as a parameter. Here is the character counting program reorganized using functions and proper documentation:

```
//**********************************************************
// This program counts and prints the frequency of
// occurrence of alphabetic characters in a file.
// Three functions are used, which take array parameters.
//**********************************************************
```

SOFTWARE MAINTENANCE CASE STUDY: Modularizing a Program

```cpp
#include <iostream>
#include <fstream>
#include <string>
#include <cctype>
using namespace std;

void ZeroOut(int intArray[], int numElements);
// Pre: numElements is assigned
// Post: intArray[0..numElements-1] are zero
void ProcessText(int counters[], istream& inFile);
// Post: counters[0..25] contain the frequency of each
//       character in inFile
void Print(int counters[]);
// Post: counters[0..25] have been printed

int main ()
{
  // Declarations
  int counters[26];
  ifstream inFile;
  inFile.open("text.dat");
  ProcessText(counters, inFile);
  Print(counters);
  return 0;
}

//**********************************************************

void ZeroOut(int intArray[], int numElements)
{
  for (int i = 1; i <= numElements; i++)
    intArray[i] = 0;
}

//**********************************************************

void ProcessText(int counters[], istream& inFile)
{
  string line;
  int limit;               // Number of characters in a line
  int index;

  getline(inFile, line);   // Read a line
  while (inFile)
  {
    limit = line.length();
    for (int counter = 0; counter < limit; counter++)
    {// Access each character in the line
      if (isalpha(line[counter]))
```

SOFTWARE MAINTENANCE CASE STUDY: Modularizing a Program

```
      {
        index = toupper(line[counter]) - 'A';
        counters[index]++;
      }
    }
    getline(inFile,line);
  }
}

//************************************************************

void Print(int counters[])
{
  for (int counter = 0; counter < 26; counter++)
    cout << static_cast<char> (counter + 'A') << ": "
         << counters[counter] << endl;
}
```

TESTING: The program was run with the same data, giving these results.

```
A: -1073743727        J: -1880951530       S: 184
B: -1073743898        K: 13                T: 327
C: 142                L: 114               U: -1881139797
D: 150                M: 109               V: 4128
E: 421                N: -1881143618       W: 48
F: 59                 O: 204               X: 5
G: 49                 P: 60                Y: -1073744011
H: 201                Q: 6                 Z: -1881141188
I: -1881143874        R: 195
```

This makes no sense whatsoever! Some of the totals are correct, some are off slightly, some are way off, and some are negative. This looks like an initialization problem, but why are some right and others wrong? The `ZeroOut` function is correct: It sets each counter to 0—BUT it is never called. Whatever collection of bits that happened to be in a cell was just incremented.

You add the call to `ZeroOut` and again run the program.

```
A: -1073743727        J: 6                 S: 184
B: 54                 K: 9                 T: 327
C: 142                L: 114               U: 96
D: 150                M: 109               V: 32
E: 421                N: 258               W: 48
F: 59                 O: 204               X: 5
G: 49                 P: 60                Y: 41
H: 192                Q: 6                 Z: 5
I: 254                R: 195
```

> **SOFTWARE MAINTENANCE CASE STUDY:** Modularizing a Program
>
> This is better, but the count for `'A'` is still incorrect. Let's look at the code for `ZeroOut`:
>
> ```
> void ZeroOut(int intArray[], int numElements)
> {
>   for (int i = 1; i <= numElements; i++)
>     intArray[i] = 0;
> }
> ```
>
> Of course! The loop should begin at 0 and stop when the counter is `numElements`. When this bug is corrected, the program gives the correct results.
>
> Note that the location one beyond the array was set to 0. This did not affect the program because this location was not assigned to a variable.

Using Typedef with Arrays

In Chapter 10, we discussed the Typedef statement as a way of giving an additional name to an existing data type. We noted then that before **bool** became a built-in type in C++, programmers often used a Typedef statement such as the following:

```
typedef int Boolean;
```

We can also use Typedef to give a name to an array type. Here's an example:

```
typedef float FloatArray[100];
```

This statement says that the type **FloatArray** is the same as the type "100-element array of **float**." (Notice that the array size in brackets comes at the very end of the statement.) We can now declare variables to be of type **FloatArray**:

```
FloatArray angle;
FloatArray velocity;
```

The compiler essentially translates these declarations into

```
float angle[100];
float velocity[100];
```

In this book, we rarely use Typedefs to give names to one-dimensional array types. However, when we discuss multidimensional arrays later in the chapter, we'll see that this technique can come in quite handy.

Pointer Expressions and Arrays

Although 0 is the only literal constant of the pointer type, another pointer expression is also considered to be a constant pointer expression: an array name without any index brackets. The value of this expression is the base address (the address of the first element) of the array. Given the declarations

```
int  anArray[100];
int* ptr;
```

the assignment statement

```
ptr = anArray;
```

has exactly the same effect as

```
ptr = &anArray[0];
```

Both of these statements store the base address of `anArray` into `ptr`. Because C++ allows us to assign an array to a pointer, it is a common misperception to think that the pointer variable and the array identifier are then effectively identical, but they are not. If you apply the `sizeof` operator to the *pointer*, it returns the number of bytes in the *pointer*. Applying it to the *array* identifier returns the number of bytes in the *array*.

Although we did not explain it at the time, you have already used the fact that an array name without brackets is a pointer expression. Consider the following code, which calls a `ZeroOut` function to zero out an array whose size is given as the second argument:

```
int main()
{
  float velocity[30];
    .
    .
    .
  ZeroOut(velocity, 30);
    .
    .
    .
}
```

In the function call, the first argument—an array name without index brackets—is a pointer expression. The value of this expression is the base address of the `velocity` array; this base address is passed to the function. We can write the `ZeroOut` function heading in one of two ways. The first approach—one that you have seen many times—declares the first parameter to be an array of unspecified size:

```
void ZeroOut(float velocity[], int size)
```

Alternatively, we can declare the parameter to be of type `float*`, because the parameter simply holds the address of a `float` variable (the address of the first array element):

```
void ZeroOut(float* velocity, int size)
```

Whether we declare the parameter as `float velocity[]` or as `float* velocity`, the result is exactly the same from the perspective of the C++ compiler: Within the `ZeroOut` function, `velocity` is a simple variable that points to the beginning of the caller's actual array. However, the first form is more self-documenting, because it tells the reader of the function definition that the parameter is meant to represent an array. Even though `velocity` is a pointer variable within the `ZeroOut` function, we are still allowed to attach an index expression to the name `velocity`:

```
velocity[i] = 0.0;
```

Indexing is valid for any pointer expression, not just an array name. (However, indexing a pointer makes sense only if the pointer points to an array.)

C-Style Strings

In Chapter 3, we introduced the C++ **string** data type and several of its associated functions, including `length()` and `size()`. In this section, we introduce an alternate string representation based on arrays and additional operations that are specific to this implementation.

Strings as Arrays

As we noted in Chapter 1, the C++ programming language is a superset of an older programming language named C, which was specifically designed for implementing the UNIX operating system. It focused on accessing low-level features of computer hardware and thus provided very little support for rich data types such as the C++ **string**. Even so, strings are very important for program input and output: they allow the user to interact with a program in a meaningful way. For this reason, C provides a primitive mechanism for representing strings, namely as an array of characters. Because C++ is a superset of the C programming language, it inherits all of C's support for array-style string representation.

In previous sections, we discussed the declaration and use of arrays. A *string* can naturally be viewed as an array of characters. For example, the string "dogs" can be viewed as the sequence of characters 'd', 'o', 'g', 's'. This can easily be transcribed into the following C++ code segment:

```
char mystring[4];
mystring[0] = 'd';
mystring[1] = 'o';
mystring[2] = 'g';
mystring[3] = 's';
```

In this case we are declaring an array of 4 `char`s and assigning to each entry in the array the characters that represent the string `"dogs"`. We can then view the `mystring` variable as corresponding to the string `"dogs"`. Although this works, it is cumbersome to declare strings this way, especially when they are longer. To ease the burden on the programmer, it is also possible to declare a C-style string using literal notation:

```
char mystring[] = "dogs";
```

This simplifies the effort for the programmer and lets the C++ *compiler* assign each character to individual locations in the array. In doing so, however, there is an important difference that results from this translation as compared with the previous manual approach. Instead of an array of length 4, it results in an array of length 5. The additional character is the *null character*, which is placed in the last element of the array to indicate the end of the string. The null character is represented by the special character `'\0'`. Thus, to *truly* declare a C-style string without the help of the string literal notation, we would write

```
char mystring[] = {'d', 'o', 'g', 's', '\0' };
```

using array initializer syntax. In this case, this `char` array declaration corresponds identically to the compiler-generated array using string literal notation.

C provides no built-in facilities for string manipulation (except using string literals to initialize a `char` array). In contrast, the C++ **string** data type provides a rich set of operations such as `size()`. The lack of built-in support will be important when we reference an array using pointers. For example, the same `"dogs"` string mentioned here can also be initialized using a pointer to `char`:

```
char* mystring = "dogs";
```

This is identical to using array notation and produces the same underlying array structure with the terminating null character. From understanding this representation, we can write functions for manipulating C-style strings such as the following **length** function that returns the length of the string given as an argument:

```
int length(char* str) {
  int len = 0;
  char* ch = str;
  while (*ch != '\0') {
    len++;
  }
  return len;
}
```

We could then use our `length` function to compute the length of the following C-style string:

```
char* mystring = "dogs and cats";
int someint = length(mystring);                        // Returns 13
```

C String Operations

Although the C-style *string* is not as rich as its C++ counterpart, there are a number of useful operations available in the `string.h` header file that can be used to achieve much the same effect. The following table shows samples of some of the functions provided:

Function	Description
`size_t strlen(const char *s);`	Computes the length of the string **s**.
`int strcmp(const char *s1,` `            const char *s2);`	Lexicographically compares strings **s1** and **s2** and returns an integer greater than, equal to, or less than 0.

`char* strncat(char *s1,`
`               const char *s2,`
`               size_t n);`
	Appends a copy of **n** characters from the string **s2** to the end of the string **s1**. The string **s1** must be sufficiently long to hold the result. Returns a pointer to the new string.

`char* strncpy(char *s1,`
`               const char *s2,`
`               size_t n);`
	Copies **n** characters from the string **s2** to the string **s1**. Returns a pointer to the new string.

`char* strchr(const char *s,` `              int c);`	Locates the first occurrence of the character **c** in the string **s**. Returns a pointer to the location of the character in the string.
`char* strstr(const char *s1,` `              const char *s2);`	Locates the first occurrence of the string **s2** in the string **s1** and returns a pointer to the start of that string.

It is important to note that C-style strings are *mutable*. For example, assigning a character to any location in the string will *overwrite* that character with the one that you specify. Likewise, many of the string operations in the table overwrite their arguments. For instance, the `strncpy` function overwrites the string referenced by its first argument **s1**. In addition, because C-style strings are just pointers, you must be very careful in using functions such as `strncat`. The strncat function requires that its first argument *must be sufficiently long* to hold the result of appending the second argument. If it is not, it could lead to problems when the program is executing, possibly causing the program to crash. To this end you must program defensively and use these string functions properly. Thus, always make sure you know the length of a string.

Converting C Strings to C++ Strings

Programming in C++ will eventually lead to using a library that requires C-style strings. We may need to call a function that requires a C-style string argument or a function that returns a C-style string. You will then be required to convert between the C and C++ string abstractions. Converting from C-style strings to C++ strings is easy. The C++ string provides a constructor for creating C++ strings from C strings:

```
char *cdog = "dog";
string cppdog(cdog);
```

Likewise, we can convert the C++ string into a C-style string by using the `c_str()` function:

```
char *ccat = cppcat.c_str();
```

In this case the c_str() operation provided by the C++ string returns a C-style string, which can then be assigned to a variable of type char*.

Which String Representation to Use

Given that we have access to two different string representations, which string abstraction is best to use? In most cases, the programmer should choose the C++ string over the C-style string because it provides a safer abstraction. Although the C-style string enables representation of character data, it is still just an array of characters that can be accessed and changed in arbitrary ways. C++ provides a real-string data type with associated operations that work only for that data type. It captures the length of the string as part of its abstraction and alleviates the burden on the programmer to worry about how the string is implemented. When you must use functions that expect C-style strings, it is important to handle C-style strings appropriately or convert them into the C++ string data type.

QUICK CHECK

11.1.1 Why do we say that an array is a homogeneous data structure? (p. 518)

11.1.2 You are solving a problem that requires you to store 24 temperature readings. Which structure would be most appropriate for this problem: a record, a union, a class, or an array? (p. 518)

11.1.3 Write a declaration of an array variable called **temps** that holds 24 values of type **float**. (pp. 518–519)

11.1.4 Write a For loop that fills every element of the **temps** array declared in Exercise 11.1.3 with the value 32.0. (pp. 524–526)

11.1.5 How is a component of an array accessed? (p. 519)

11.1.6 A string in C++ can be treated like an array using the **[ ]** operator. Why is it preferred to use the **at** operation to access a character in a string? (p. 521)

11.2 Arrays of Records

Although arrays with atomic components are very common, many applications require a collection of records. For example, a business needs a list of parts records, and a teacher needs a list of students in a class. Arrays are ideal for these applications. We simply define an array whose components are records.

Arrays of Records

In Chapter 10, we defined a student record using a struct. We now need a collection of these student records. How do we implement a "collection"? By a file or an array. Because this chapter focuses on arrays, let's declare an array of student records and look at how each field would be accessed. To make things a little more interesting, let's add a user-defined type GradeType and an array of exam scores. As this is the beginning of a program, we show the structure as code.

```
//**********************************************
// This program manipulates an array of grade records.
//**********************************************
#include <iostream>
#include <string>
#include <fstream>
using namespace std;
```

```
const int MAX_STUDENTS = 150;
enum GradeType {A, B, C, D, F};
struct StudentRec
{
  string stuName;
  float  gpa;
  int examScore[4];
  GradeType courseGrade;
};
StudentRec gradeBook[MAX_STUDENTS];
int main()
{}
```

This data structure can be visualized as shown in **FIGURE 11.8**.

An element of `gradeBook` is selected by an index. For example, `gradeBook[2]` is the third component in the array `gradeBook`. Each component of `gradeBook` is a record of type `StudentRec`. To access the course grade of the third student, for example, we use the following expression:

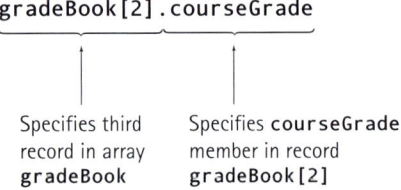

The record component `gradeBook[2].examScore` is an array. We can access the individual elements in this component just as we would access the elements of any other array: We give the name of the array followed by the index, which is enclosed in brackets.

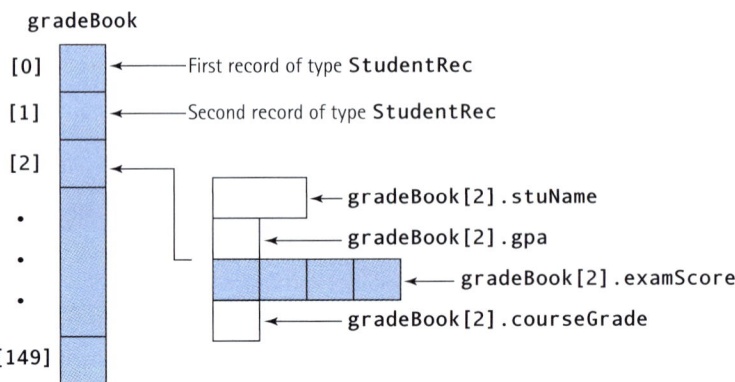

FIGURE 11.8 `gradeBook` Array with Records as Elements

The next step is to write a function that reads values from a file into the fields of the records. The file name and the record are parameters of the function. Both must be reference parameters: Files are always passed by reference, and we are sending back values to the calling code through the record.

```cpp
void ReadValues(ifstream& inFile, StudentRec& record)
{
  char letter;
  char throwAway;
  getline(inFile, record.stuName);
  inFile >> record.gpa >> record.examScore[0]
         >> record.examScore[1] >> record.examScore[2]
         >> record.examScore[3] >> letter;
  inFile.get(throwAway);
  switch (letter)        // Convert from char to GradeType
  {
    case 'A' : record.courseGrade = A;
               break;
    case 'B' : record.courseGrade = B;
               break;
    case 'C' : record.courseGrade = C;
               break;
    case 'D' : record.courseGrade = D;
               break;
    case 'F' : record.courseGrade = F;
               break;
  }
}
```

The only tricky part is getting past the eoln at the end of each student's entry. This eoln follows the letter grade entered as a character. We can't use a regular character read operation because it returns the first letter of the next student's name. Instead, we must use `inFile.get`.

The function to write each student's record is a mirror image of the input function.

```cpp
void PrintValues(ofstream& outFile, StudentRec& record)
{
  outFile << record.stuName << endl;
  outFile << record.gpa << ' ' << record.examScore[0] << ' '
          << record.examScore[1] << ' '
          << record.examScore[2] << ' '
          << record.examScore[3] << ' ';
  switch (record.courseGrade)
  {
    case A : outFile << 'A';
             break;
    case B : outFile << 'B';
             break;
    case C : outFile << 'C';
             break;
    case D : outFile << 'D';
             break;
```

```
        case F : outFile << 'F';
                break;
    }
    outFile << endl;
}
```

Now we must create a `main` program that uses these two functions to input the file of records, store them into an array, and print them on an output file.

```
int main()
{
  StudentRec record[MAX_STUDENTS];
  ofstream outFile;
  outFile.open("rec.out");
  ifstream inFile;
  inFile.open("rec.in");
  for (int count = 0; count < MAX_STUDENTS; count++)
    ReadValues(inFile, record[count]);
  for (int count = 0; count <= MAX_STUDENTS; count++)
    PrintValues(outFile, record[count]);
  inFile.close();
  outFile.close();
  return 0;
}
```

Here is an input file and the resulting output file. The constant for `MAX_STUDENTS` was changed to 5 for this run (for obvious reasons).

rec.in

```
Mary Abbott
3.4 80 90 60 99 B
Bob Baker
4.0 90 90 90 95 A
Sally Carter
2.0 70 70 70 65 C
Bill Dansk
3.0 65 50 60 70 D
JoEllen Zureck
1.9 90 95 80 99 A
```

rec.out

```
Mary Abbott
3.4 80 90 60 99 B
Bob Baker
4 90 90 90 95 A
Sally Carter
2 70 70 70 65 C
Bill Dansk
3 65 50 60 70 D
JoEllen Zureck
1.9 90 95 80 99 A
```

QUICK CHECK

11.2.1 How would you access the third letter in a string data member (called **street**) of a struct variable that is the twelfth element of an array called **mailList**? (pp. 541–542)

11.2.2 Imagine we are extending a web browser with functionality that requires an array of records to maintain the coordinates for HTML elements in the browser window. How might you declare the struct representing coordinates and an array of 1000 elements for holding these records? (pp. 541–542)

11.3 Special Kinds of Array Processing

Two types of array processing occur especially often: using only part of the declared array (a subarray) and using index values that have specific meaning within the problem (indexes with semantic content). We describe both of these methods briefly here and give further examples in the remainder of the chapter.

Subarray Processing

The *size* of an array—the declared number of array components—is established at compile time. We have to declare an array to be as big as it will ever need to be. Because the exact number of values to be put into the array often depends on the data itself, however, we may not fill all of the array components with values. The problem is that to avoid processing empty positions in the array, we must keep track of how many components are actually filled.

As values are put into the array, we keep a count of how many components are filled. We then use this count to process only those components that have values stored in them; any remaining places are not processed. For example, if there were 250 students in a class, a program to analyze test grades would set aside 250 locations for the grades. However, some students might be absent on the day of the test. So the number of test grades must be counted, and that number—rather than 250—is used to control the processing of the array.

If the number of data items actually stored in an array is less than its declared size, functions that receive array parameters must also receive the number of data items as a parameter. We handled this task in the **ZeroOut** function by passing the array and the number of elements as two parameters. However, there is a better way: The array and the number of actual items in the array can be bound together in a record.

Consider, for example, the collection of student records. We could change the problem a little and say that the actual number of student records is not known. The reading loop would be an eof loop rather than a For loop. Let's expand `ReadValues` and `PrintValues` to take the record containing the array and the number of items rather than just the array. Thus the loops would be found within the functions, not in `main`.

Here is the complete program with these changes. The definition of the data structure and the function prototypes are highlighted.

```cpp
//*****************************************************
// This program manipulates an array of grade records.
//*****************************************************
#include <iostream>
#include <string>
#include <fstream>
using namespace std;

const int MAX_STUDENTS = 150;
enum GradeType {A, B, C, D, F};
struct StudentRec
{
  string stuName;
  float  gpa;
  int    examScore[4];
  GradeType courseGrade;
};

struct GradeBook
{
  StudentRec grades[MAX_STUDENTS];
  int numElements;
};

void ReadValues(ifstream& inFile, GradeBook& book);
// Pre:  inFile has been opened
// Post: Values have been read from inFile and stored into the
//          proper fields of record
void PrintValues(ofstream& outFile, GradeBook& book);
// Pre:  outFile has been opened and record contains valid data
// Post: Values in record have been printed on outFile

int main ()
{
  ofstream outFile;
  outFile.open("rec.out");
  ifstream inFile;
  inFile.open("rec.in");
  GradeBook book;
  ReadValues(inFile, book);
  cout << book.numElements;
  PrintValues(outFile, book);
  return 0;
}

//*****************************************************
```

```cpp
void ReadValues(ifstream& inFile, GradeBook& book)
{
  char letter;
  char throwAway;
  int count = 0;
  getline(inFile, book.grades[count].stuName);
  while (inFile)
  {
    inFile >> book.grades[count].gpa
           >> book.grades[count].examScore[0]
           >> book.grades[count].examScore[1]
           >> book.grades[count].examScore[2]
           >> book.grades[count].examScore[3] >> letter;
    inFile.get(throwAway);
    switch (letter)
    {
      case 'A' : book.grades[count].courseGrade = A;
                 break;
      case 'B' : book.grades[count].courseGrade = B;
                 break;
      case 'C' : book.grades[count].courseGrade = C;
                 break;
      case 'D' : book.grades[count].courseGrade = D;
                 break;
      case 'F' : book.grades[count].courseGrade = F;
                 break;
    }
    count++;
    getline(inFile, book.grades[count].stuName);
  }
  book.numElements = count;
}

//***********************************************************

void PrintValues(ofstream& outFile, GradeBook& book)
{
  for (int count = 0; count < book.numElements; count++)
  {
    outFile << book.grades[count].stuName << endl;
    outFile << book.grades[count].gpa << ' '
            << book.grades[count].examScore[0] << ' '
            << book.grades[count].examScore[1] << ' '
            << book.grades[count].examScore[2] << ' '
            << book.grades[count].examScore[3] << ' ';
    switch (book.grades[count].courseGrade)
    {
      case A : outFile << 'A';
               break;
      case B : outFile << 'B';
               break;
      case C : outFile << 'C';
               break;
      case D : outFile << 'D';
               break;
```

```
            case F : outFile << 'F';
                     break;
        }
        outFile << endl;
    }
}
```

This program was run with the same data set used previously. It is always comforting to get the same results.

Indexes with Semantic Content

In some problems, an array index has meaning beyond simple position; that is, the index has *semantic content*. An example is the `salesAmt` array we showed earlier. This array is indexed by a value of enumeration type `Drink`. The index of a specific sales amount is the kind of soft drink sold; for example, `salesAmt[ROOT_BEER]` is the sales figure (in dollars) for root beer.

In the next section we will see some additional examples of indexes with semantic content.

QUICK CHECK

11.3.1 Explain how the index of an array of 24 hourly temperature readings has semantic content, if the index is an integer ranging from 0 through 23. (p. 548)

11.3.2 Write a loop that reads values from file `indata` into the `temps` array of Exercise 11.1.3, until either the end-of-file is reached or 24 values are input. The loop should keep track of the number of values in the array in an `int` variable called `count`. (pp. 545–546)

11.3.3 At what time is the *size* of an array established? (p. 545)

11.3.4 How might we avoid processing empty positions in an array? (p. 545)

11.4 Two-Dimensional Arrays

A one-dimensional array is used to represent items in a list or sequence of values. In many problems, however, the relationships between data items are more complex than can be depicted by a simple list. A two-dimensional array is used to represent items in a table with rows and columns, provided each item in the table is of the same data type. Two-dimensional arrays are useful for representing board games, such as chess, tic-tac-toe, or Scrabble, and in computer graphics, where the screen is thought of as a two-dimensional array.

Two-dimensional array A collection of components, all of the same type, structured in two dimensions. Each component is accessed by a pair of indexes that represent the component's position in each dimension.

A component in a two-dimensional array is accessed by specifying the row and column indexes of the item in the array. This is a familiar task. For example, if you want to find a street on a map, you look up the street name on the back of the map to find the coordinates of the street, usually a letter and a number. The letter specifies a column to look at, and the number specifies a row. You find the street where the row and column meet.

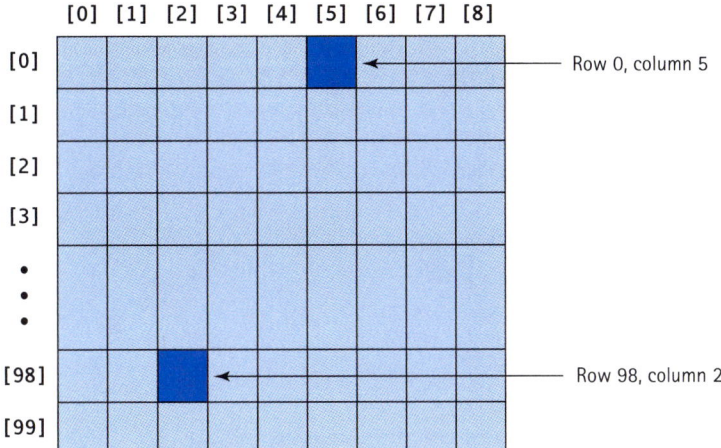

FIGURE 11.9 A Two-Dimensional Array

FIGURE 11.9 shows a two-dimensional array with 100 rows and 9 columns. The rows are accessed by an integer ranging from 0 through 99; the columns are accessed by an integer ranging from 0 through 8. Each component is accessed by a row–column pair—for example, 0, 5.

A two-dimensional array is declared in exactly the same way as a one-dimensional array, except that sizes must be specified for both of the two dimensions. Here is the syntax template for declaring an array with more than one dimension:

ArrayDeclaration

DataType ArrayName [ConstIntExpression] [ConstIntExpression] ... ;

The following example declares **alpha** to be a two-dimensional array, all of whose components are **float** values. The declaration creates the array that is pictured in Figure 11.9.

```
const int NUM_ROWS = 100;
const int NUM_COLS = 9;
  ⋮
float alpha[NUM_ROWS][NUM_COLS];
            ↑           ↑
          First       Second
        dimension   dimension
```

To access an individual component of the `alpha` array, two expressions (one for each dimension) are used to specify its position. Each expression appears in its own pair of brackets next to the name of the array:

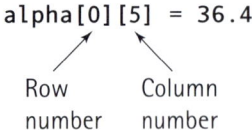

alpha[0][5] = 36.4;

Row number   Column number

The syntax template for accessing an array component is

ArrayComponentAccess

ArrayName [IndexExpression] [IndexExpression] ...

As with one-dimensional arrays, each index expression must result in an integer value.

Now let's look at some examples. Here is the declaration of a two-dimensional array with 364 integer components ($52 \times 7 = 364$):

`int hiTemp[52][7];`

`hiTemp` is an array with 52 rows and 7 columns. Each place in the array (each component) can contain any `int` value. Our intention is that the array will hold high temperatures for each day in a year. Each row represents one of the 52 weeks in a year, and each column represents one of the 7 days in a week. (To keep the example simple, we ignore the fact that there are 365—and sometimes 366—days in a year.) The expression `hiTemp[2][6]` refers to the `int` value in the third row (row 2) and the seventh column (column 6). Semantically, `hiTemp[2][6]` is the temperature for the seventh day of the third week. The code fragment shown in **FIGURE 11.10** would print the temperature values for the third week.

FIGURE 11.10 `hiTemp` Array

Another representation of the same data might be as follows:

```
enum DayType
{
  MONDAY, TUESDAY, WEDNESDAY, THURSDAY, FRIDAY, SATURDAY, SUNDAY
};

int hiTemp[52][7];
```

Here `hiTemp` is declared the same as before, but now we can use an expression of type `DayType` for the column index. `hiTemp[2][SUNDAY]` corresponds to the same component as `hiTemp[2][6]` in the first example. (Recall that enumerators such as `MONDAY`, `TUESDAY`, ... are represented internally as the integers 0, 1, 2, ...) If day is of type `DayType` and week is of type `int`, the code fragment shown in **FIGURE 11.11** sets the entire array to 0. (Notice that by using `DayType`, the temperature values in the array begin with the first Monday of the year, which is not necessarily January 1.)

Another way of looking at a two-dimensional array is to see it as a structure in which each component has two features. Consider the following code:

```
enum Colors {RED, ORANGE, YELLOW, GREEN, BLUE, INDIGO, VIOLET};
enum Makes
{
  FORD, TOYOTA, HYUNDAI, JAGUAR, CITROEN, BMW, FIAT, SAAB
};
const int NUM_COLORS = 7;
const int NUM_MAKES = 8;

float sales[NUM_COLORS][NUM_MAKES];   // Percent of sales by color
                                      //   for each manufacturer
    ⋮
sales[BLUE][JAGUAR] = 0.23;           // Blue cars make up 23% of
                                      //   Jaguar sales
sales[RED][FORD] = 0.19;              // Red cars make up 19% of
                                      //   Ford sales
```

FIGURE 11.11 `hiTemp` Array (Alternate Form)

This data structure uses one dimension to represent the color and the other dimension to represent the make of automobile. In other words, both indexes have semantic content—a concept we discussed in the previous section.

QUICK CHECK

11.4.1 How does a two-dimensional array differ syntactically from a one-dimensional array? (pp. 548–549)

11.4.2 Write the declaration for a two-dimensional array, called `allTemps`, that holds the 24 hourly readings for each day of a year (up to 366 days). (pp. 548–549)

11.4.3 What generic structure is a two-dimensional array typically used to represent? (p. 548)

11.4.4 Imagine we are using a two-dimensional array as the basis for creating the game *battleship*. In the game of battleship a '~' character entry in the array represents ocean (i.e., not a ship), a '#' character represents a place in the ocean where part of a ship is present, and an 'H' character represents a place in the ocean where part of a ship is present and has been *hit* by a torpedo. Thus, a ship with all 'H' characters means the ship has been sunk. Declare a two-dimensional array that is 25 × 25 that represents the entire ocean and an If statement that prints "HIT" if a torpedo hits a ship given the coordinates X and Y. (pp. 548–551)

11.5 Passing Two-Dimensional Arrays as Arguments

Earlier in the chapter, we said that when one-dimensional arrays are declared as parameters in a function, the size of the array usually is omitted from the square brackets:

```
void SomeFunc(float alpha[], int size)
{
    ⋮
}
```

If you include a size in the brackets, the compiler ignores it. As you learned, the base address of the caller's argument (the memory address of the first array element) is passed to the function. The function works for an argument of any size. Because the function cannot know the size of the caller's array, we either set the size as a constant, pass the size as an argument (as in `SomeFunc`), or, better still, bind the array and the number of elements together into a record and pass the record to the function.

When a two-dimensional array is passed as an argument, the base address of the caller's array is sent to the function. You cannot leave off the sizes of both of the array dimensions, however. You can omit the size of the first dimension (the number of rows) but not the second (the number of columns). Here is the reason.

In the computer's memory, C++ stores two-dimensional arrays in row order. If we think of memory as consisting of one long line of memory cells, the first row of the array is followed by the second row, which is followed by the third row, and so on (see **FIGURE 11.12**).

To locate `beta[1][0]` in Figure 11.12, a function that receives `beta`'s base address must be able to determine that there are four elements in each row—that is, that the array consists of four columns. Therefore, the declaration of a parameter must always state the number of columns:

```
void AnotherFunc(int beta[][4])
{
    ⋮
}
```

FIGURE 11.12 Memory Layout for a Two-Row by Four-Column Array

Furthermore, the number of columns declared for the parameter must be *exactly* the same as the number of columns in the caller's array. As you can tell from Figure 11.12, if there is any discrepancy in the number of columns, the function will access the wrong array element in memory.

Our **AnotherFunc** function works for a two-dimensional array of any number of rows, as long as the array has exactly four columns. In practice, we seldom write programs that use arrays with a varying number of rows but the same number of columns. To avoid problems with mismatches in argument and parameter sizes, it's practical to use a Typedef statement to define a two-dimensional array type and then declare both the argument and the parameter to be of that type. For example, we might make the declarations

```
const int NUM_ROWS = 10;
const int NUM_COLS = 20;
typedef int ArrayType[NUM_ROWS][NUM_COLS];
```

and then write the following general-purpose function that initializes all elements of an array to a specified value:

```
void Initialize(ArrayType table, int initialVal)
// Pre:  initialVal has an appropriate value
// Post: table[0..NUM_ROWS-1][0..NUM_COLS-1] has been set to initialVal
{
  int row;
  int col;
```

```
      for (row = 0; row < NUM_ROWS; row++)
        for (col = 0; col < NUM_COLS; col++)
          table[row][col] = initialVal;
    }
```

The calling code could then declare and initialize one or more arrays of type `ArrayType` by making calls to the `Initialize` function. For example:

```
ArrayType delta;
ArrayType gamma;

Initialize(delta, 0);
Initialize(gamma, -1);
      ⋮
```

QUICK CHECK

11.5.1 Write the heading for a function that accepts the `temps` array of Exercise 11.1.3 and its length as parameters. Call the function `Quick`, and have it be a `void` function. (pp. 552–554)

11.5.2 What does the C++ compiler do if you provide the size of an array of one dimension in a parameter declaration? (p. 552)

11.5.3 Why can you omit the size of the first dimension but not the second dimension in a two-dimensional array? (p. 552)

11.5.4 What part of an array is passed as an argument to a function? (p. 552)

11.6 Processing Two-Dimensional Arrays

Processing data in a two-dimensional array generally means accessing the array in one of four patterns: randomly, along rows, along columns, or throughout the entire array. Each of these methods may also involve subarray processing.

The simplest way to access a component is to look directly in a given location. For example, a user might enter map coordinates that we use as indexes into an array of street names to access the desired name at those coordinates. This process is referred to as *random access* because the user may enter any set of coordinates at random.

In many cases, we might wish to perform an operation on all the elements of a particular row or column in an array. Consider the `hiTemp` array defined previously, in which the rows represent weeks of the year and the columns represent days of the week. If we wanted to find the average high temperature for a given week, we would sum the values in that row and divide by 7. If we wanted to find the average high temperature for a given day of the week, we would sum the values in that column and divide by 52. The former case is access by row; the latter case is access by column.

Now suppose that we wish to determine the average high temperature for the year. We must access every element in the array, sum their values, and divide by 364. In this case, the order of access—by row or by column—is not important. (The same is true when we initialize every element of an array to zero.) This is access throughout the array.

Sometimes we must access every array element in a particular order, either by rows or by columns. For example, if we wanted the average high temperature for every week, we would run through the entire array, taking each row in turn. However, if we wanted the average high temperature for each day of the week, we would run through the array one column at a time.

Let's take a closer look at these patterns of access by considering four common examples of array processing.

1. Sum the rows.
2. Sum the columns.
3. Initialize the array to all zeros (or some special value).
4. Print the array.

First, let's define some constants and variables using general identifiers, such as `row` and `col`, rather than problem-dependent identifiers. Then, let's look at each algorithm in terms of generalized two-dimensional array processing.

```
const int NUM_ROWS = 50;
const int NUM_COLS = 50;

int table[NUM_ROWS][NUM_COLS];    // A two-dimensional array
int row;                          // A row index
int col;                          // A column index
int total;                        // A variable for summing
```

Sum the Rows

Suppose we want to sum row number 3 (the fourth row) in the array and print the result. We can do this easily with a For loop:

```
total = 0;
for (col = 0; col < NUM_COLS; col++)
  total = total + table[3][col];
cout << "Row sum: " << total << endl;
```

This For loop runs through each column of `table`, while keeping the row index fixed at 3. Every value in row 3 is added to total.

Now suppose we want to sum and print two rows—row 2 and row 3. We can use a nested loop and make the row index a variable:

```
for (row = 2; row < 4; row++)
{
  total = 0;
  for (col = 0; col < NUM_COLS; col++)
    total = total + table[row][col];
  cout << "Row sum: " << total << endl;
}
```

The outer loop controls the rows, and the inner loop controls the columns. For each value of `row`, every column is processed; then the outer loop moves to the next row. In the first iteration of the outer loop, `row` is held at 2 and `col` goes from 0 through `NUM_COLS-1`. Therefore, the array is accessed in the following order:

`table[2][0]    [2][1]    [2][2]    [2][3] . . .    [2][NUM_COLS-1]`

In the second iteration of the outer loop, `row` is incremented to 3, and the array is accessed as follows:

`table[3][0]    [3][1]    [3][2]    [3][3] . . .    [3][NUM_COLS-1]`

FIGURE 11.13 Partial Array Processing by Row

We can generalize this row processing to run through every row of the array by having the outer loop run from 0 through **NUM_ROWS-1**. However, if we want to access only part of the array (subarray processing), given variables declared as

```
int rowsFilled;     // Data is in 0..rowsFilled-1
int colsFilled;     // Data is in 0..colsFilled-1
```

then we write the code fragment as follows:

```
for (row = 0; row < rowsFilled; row++)
{
  total = 0;
  for (col = 0; col < colsFilled; col++)
    total = total + table[row][col];
  cout << "Row sum: " << total << endl;
}
```

FIGURE 11.13 illustrates subarray processing by row.

Sum the Columns Revised

Before we look at different processing algorithms, let's do what we did with our one-dimensional array: Let's redesign our structure to be a record that contains the array and two variables, `rowsFilled` and `colsFilled`. Rather than look at the algorithms as code fragments, we look at them as functions.

```
struct TwoDArray
{
  int rowsFilled;         // Rows with actual data
  int colsFilled;         // Columns with actual data
  ArrayType table;        // Two-dimensional array
};

TwoDArray structure;
```

The algorithm for summing a specific row in a two-dimensional array is encapsulated into the following function:

```
int SumRows(TwoDArray structure, int rowNum)
// This function returns the sum of
// structure.table[rowNum][0..colsFilled]
{
  int total = 0;
  for (int col = 0; col < structure.colsFilled; col++)
    total = total + structure.table[rowNum][col];
  return total;
}
```

The following function uses function `PrintRowSums` to print the sums of each of the rows, calling `SumRows` to do the summing:

```
void PrintRowSums(TwoDArray structure)
{
  for (int row = 0; row < structure.rowsFilled; row++)
  {
    cout << "Row " << row << ":  " << SumRows(structure, row)
         << endl;
  }
}
```

Why did we break the process of printing the sums of the rows of a two-dimensional array into two functions? Good style dictates that a function should accomplish only one task: The second function calls the first to return the row sum and then prints it.

Sum the Columns

Suppose we want to sum and print each column. The code to perform this task follows. Again, we have generalized the code to sum only the portion of the array that contains valid data.

```
int SumCols(TwoDArray structure, int colNum)
// This function returns the sum of
// structure.table[0..rowsFilled][colNum]
{
  int total = 0;
  for (int row = 0; row < structure.rowsFilled; row++)
    total = total + structure.table[row][colNum];
  return total;
}
```

In this case, the outer loop controls the column, and the inner loop controls the row. All of the components in the first column are accessed and summed before the outer loop index changes and the components in the second column are accessed. **FIGURE 11.14** illustrates subarray processing by column.

FIGURE 11.14 Partial Array Processing by Column

Initialize the Array

As with one-dimensional arrays, we can initialize a two-dimensional array either by initializing it in its declaration or by using assignment statements. If the array is small, it is simplest to initialize it in its declaration. To initialize a two-row by three-column array to look like this:

```
14   3  -5
 0  46   7
```

we can use the following declaration:

```
int table[2][3] =
{
  {14, 3, -5},
  {0, 46, 7}
};
```

In this declaration, the initializer list consists of two items, each of which is itself an initializer list. The first inner initializer list stores 14, 3, and −5 into row 0 of the array; the second stores 0, 46, and 7 into row 1. The use of two initializer lists makes sense if you think of each row of the two-dimensional array as being a one-dimensional array of three `int` values. The first initializer list initializes the first array (the first row), and the second list initializes the second array (the second row). Later in this chapter, we will revisit this notion of viewing a two-dimensional array as an array of arrays.

Initializing an array in its declaration is impractical if the array is large. For a 100-row by 100-column array, you don't want to list 10,000 values. If the values are all different, you should store them into a file and input them into the array at run time. If the values are all the same, the usual approach is to use nested For loops and an assignment statement. Here is a function that zeros out an array of type `TwoDArray`:

```
void ZeroArray(TwoDArray structure)
// This function assigns zero to every element of the
// array member of structure
{
  for (int row = 0; row < structure.rowsFilled; row++)
    for (int col = 0; col < structure.colsFilled; col++)
      structure.table[row][col] = 0;
}
```

In this case, we initialized the array one row at a time, but we could just as easily have run through each column instead. The order doesn't matter so long as we access every element.

Print the Array

If we wish to print out an array with one row per line, then we have another case of row processing:

```
#include <iomanip>    // For setw()
. . .
void PrintArray(TwoDArray structure)
// This function prints the values stored in the table by row
{
  for (int row = 0; row < structure.rowsFilled; row++)
  {
    for (int col = 0; col < structure.colsFilled; col++)
      cout << setw(5) << structure.table[row][col];
    cout << endl;
  }
}
```

This code fragment prints the values of the array in columns that are 15 characters wide. As a matter of proper style, this fragment should be preceded by code that prints headings over the columns to identify their contents.

There's no rule saying that we have to print each row on a line. If we liked, we could turn the array sideways and print each column on one line simply by exchanging the two For loops. When you are printing a two-dimensional array, you must consider which order of presentation makes the most sense and how the array fits on the page. For example, an array with 6 columns and 100 rows would be best printed as 6 columns, 100 lines long.

Almost all processing of data stored in a two-dimensional array involves either processing by row or processing by column. In most of our examples, the index type has been `int`; however, the pattern of operation of the loops is the same no matter what types the indexes are.

The looping patterns for row processing and column processing are so useful that we summarize them below. To make them more general, we use `minRow` for the first row number and `minCol` for the first column number. Remember that row processing places the row index in the outer loop, and column processing places the column index in the outer loop.

Row Processing

```
for (row = minRow; row < rowsFilled; row++)
  for (col = minCol; col < colsFilled; col++)
      ⋮           // Whatever processing is required
```

Column Processing

```
for (col = minCol; col < colsFilled; col++)
  for (row = minRow; row < rowsFilled; row++)
      ⋮           // Whatever processing is required
```

The following prototypes and **main** function use each of these functions to read the values into an array, print them, print the sum of the rows, and print the sum of the columns.

```cpp
//*****************************************************************
// This program reads in and manipulates data in a two-dimensional
// array bound into a record along with the number of actual values
// stored in the array.
//*****************************************************************
#include <iostream>
#include <iomanip>   // For setw()
using namespace std;

const int NUM_ROWS = 6;
const int NUM_COLS = 5;

typedef int ArrayType[NUM_ROWS][NUM_COLS];
struct TwoDArray
{
  int rowsFilled;        // Number of rows with actual data
  int colsFilled;        // Number of columns with actual data
  ArrayType table;       // Two-dimensional array
};

void PrintRowSums(TwoDArray structure);
// This function prints the sum of the rows in the structure
int SumRows(TwoDArray structure, int rowNum);
// This function returns the sum of
// structure.table[rowNum][0..colsFilled]
void PrintArray(TwoDArray structure);
// This functions prints the values stored in the table by row
void PrintColumnSums(TwoDArray structure);
// This function prints the sum of the columns in the structure
int SumCols(TwoDArray structure, int colNum);
// This function returns the sum of
// structure.table[0..rowsFilled][colNum]

int main ()
{
  TwoDArray structure;
  // Number of rows and columns is prompted for and read
  cout << "Enter the number of rows and the number of columns"
       << endl;
  cin >> structure.rowsFilled >> structure.colsFilled;
```

```
    // Values are read in by row
    cout << "Enter the data one row per line" << endl;
    for (int rows = 0; rows < structure.rowsFilled; rows++)
      for (int cols = 0; cols < structure.colsFilled; cols++)
        cin >> structure.table[rows][cols];
  PrintArray(structure);
  PrintRowSums(structure);
  PrintColumnSums(structure);
  return 0;
}
```

Output:

```
Enter the number of rows and the number of columns
4 5
Enter the data one row per line
1 2 3 4 5
5 4 3 2 1
6 7 8 9 0
0 9 8 7 6
     1     2     3     4     5
     5     4     3     2     1
     6     7     8     9     0
     0     9     8     7     6
Row Sums
Row 0:    15
Row 1:    15
Row 2:    30
Row 3:    30
Column Sums
Column 0:    12
Column 1:    22
Column 2:    22
Column 3:    22
Column 4:    12
```

QUICK CHECK

11.6.1 Write a nested For loop that outputs the contents of the **allTemps** array declared in Exercise 11.4.2, with the 24 temperatures for a day on a line and 366 lines of days. (pp. 559–560)

11.6.2 What is the process called when a two-dimensional array is accessed by index? (p. 554)

11.6.3 What are the four patterns of accessing a two-dimensional array? (p. 554)

11.6.4 Write a nested For loop that outputs the average hourly temperature across 366 days of the **allTemps** array declared in Exercise 11.4.2, with the average hourly temperature on a line and 24 lines of hours. (pp. 559–560)

11.6.5 Write a declaration for a two-dimensional array for a tic-tac-toe board where we represent an empty square as O, a square with an X as 1, and a square with a O as 2, that is initialized without assignment statements with the following board state: (pp. 560–561)

X	O	O
EMPTY	X	EMPTY
X	EMPTY	O

11.7 Another Way of Defining Two-Dimensional Arrays

We hinted earlier that a two-dimensional array can be viewed as an array of arrays. This view is supported by C++ in the sense that the components of a one-dimensional array do not have to be atomic. The components can themselves be structured—structs, class objects (which we introduce in Chapter 12), or even arrays. For example, our hiTemp array could be declared as follows:

```
typedef int WeekType[7];    // Array type for 7 temperature readings

WeekType hiTemp[52];        // Array of 52 WeekType arrays
```

With this declaration, the 52 components of the hiTemp array are one-dimensional arrays of type WeekType. In other words, hiTemp has two dimensions. We can refer to each row as an entity: For example, hiTemp[2] refers to the array of temperatures for week 2. We can also access each individual component of hiTemp by specifying both indexes: For example, hiTemp[2][0] accesses the temperature on the first day of week 2.

Does it matter which way we declare a two-dimensional array? Not to C++. The choice should be based on readability and understandability. Sometimes the features of the data are shown more clearly if both indexes are specified in a single declaration. At other times, the code is clearer if one dimension is defined first as a one-dimensional array type.

The following example shows a case when it is advantageous to define a two-dimensional array as an array of arrays. If the rows have been defined first as a one-dimensional array type, each row can be passed to a function whose parameter is a one-dimensional array of the same type. For example, the following function calculates and returns the maximum value in an array of type WeekType.

```
int Maximum(const WeekType data )
// Post: Function return value is the maximum value in data[0..6]

{
  int max;        // Temporary max value
  int index;      // Loop control and index variable

  max = data[0];
  for (index = 1; index < 7; index++)
    if (data[index] > max)
      max = data[index];
  return max;
}
```

Our two-part declaration of hiTemp permits us to call Maximum using a component of hiTemp as follows:

```
highest = Maximum(hiTemp[20]);
```

Row 20 of hiTemp is passed to Maximum, which treats it like any other one-dimensional array of type WeekType (see **FIGURE 11.15**). It makes sense to pass the row as an argument because both it and the function parameter are of the same named type, WeekType.

With hiTemp declared as an array of arrays, we can output the maximum temperature of each week of the year with the following code:

```
cout << " Week      Maximum" << endl
     << "Number Temperature" << endl;
```

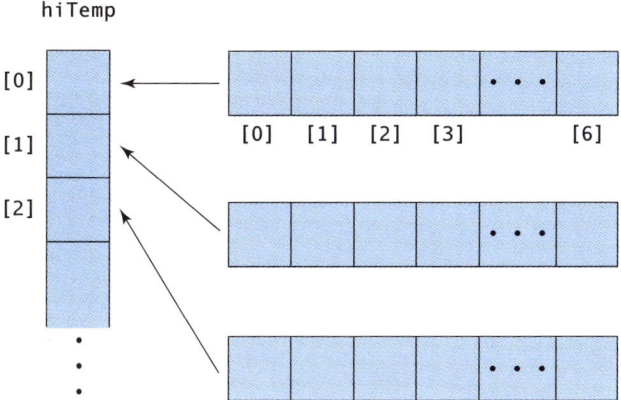

The components of hiTemp are one-dimensional arrays of type WeekType.

FIGURE 11.15 A One-Dimensional Array of One-Dimensional Arrays

```
for (week = 0; week < 52; week++)
  cout << setw(6) << week
       << setw(9) << Maximum(hiTemp[week]) << endl;
```

11.8 Multidimensional Arrays

C++ does not place a limit on the number of dimensions that an array can have. We can generalize our definition of an array to cover all cases.

You might have guessed from the syntax templates that you can have as many dimensions as you want. How many should you have in a particular case? Use as many as there are features that describe the components in the array.

> **Array** A collection of components, all of the same type, ordered on N dimensions (N ≥ 1). Each component is accessed by N indexes, each of which represents the component's position within that dimension.

Consider, for example, a chain of department stores. Monthly sales figures must be kept for each item by store. Three important pieces of information about each item are identified: the month in which it was sold, the store from which it was purchased, and the item number. We can define an array type to summarize this data as follows:

```
const int NUM_ITEMS = 100;
const int NUM_STORES = 10;
typedef int SalesType[NUM_STORES][12][NUM_ITEMS];

SalesType sales;     // Array of sales figures
int item;
int store;
int month;
int numberSold;
int currentMonth;
```

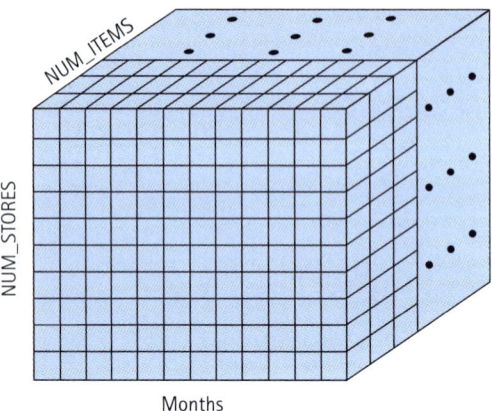

FIGURE 11.16 Graphic Representation of sales Array

FIGURE 11.16 provides a graphic representation of the sales array.

The number of components in sales is 12,000 (10 × 12 × 100). If sales figures are available only for January through June, then half of the array is empty. If we want to process the data in the array, we must use subarray processing. The following program fragment sums and prints the total number of each item sold this year to date by all stores:

```
for (item = 0; item < NUM_ITEMS; item++)
{
  numberSold = 0;
  for (store = 0; store < NUM_STORES; store++)
    for (month = 0; month <= currentMonth; month++)
      numberSold = numberSold + sales[store][month][item];
  cout << "Item #" << item << " Sales to date = " << numberSold
      << endl;
}
```

Because item controls the outer For loop, we are summing each item's sales by month and store. If we want to find the total sales for each store, we use store to control the outer For loop, summing its sales by month and item with the inner loops.

```
for (store = 0; store < NUM_STORES; store++)
{
  numberSold = 0;
  for (item = 0; item < NUM_ITEMS; item++)
    for (month = 0; month <= currentMonth; month++)
      numberSold = numberSold + sales[store][month][item];
  cout << "Store #" << store << " Sales to date = " << numberSold
      << endl;
}
```

It takes two loops to access each component in a two-dimensional array; it takes three loops to access each component in a three-dimensional array. The task to be accomplished determines which index controls the outer loop, the middle loop, and the inner loop. If we want to calculate monthly sales by store, month controls the outer loop and store controls the middle loop. If we want to calculate monthly sales by item, month controls the outer loop and item controls the middle loop.

If we want to keep track of the departments that sell each item, we can add a fourth dimension to the array:

```
enum Departments {A, B, C, D, E, F, G};
const int NUM_DEPTS = 7;
typedef int SalesType[NUM_STORES][12][NUM_ITEMS][NUM_DEPTS];
```

How would we visualize this new structure? Not very easily! Fortunately, we do not have to visualize a structure to use it. If we want the number of sales in store 1 during June for item number 4 in department C, we simply access the following array element:

```
sales[1][5][4][C]
```

When a multidimensional array is declared as a parameter in a function, C++ requires you to state the sizes of all dimensions except the first. For our four-dimensional version of `SalesType`, a function heading would look like this:

```
void DoSomething(int table[][12][NUM_ITEMS][NUM_DEPTS])
```

or, better yet, like this:

```
void DoSomething(SalesType arr)
```

The second version is the safest (and the most uncluttered for readers). It ensures that the sizes of all dimensions of the parameter match those of the argument exactly. With the first version, the reason that you must declare the sizes of all but the first dimension is the same as we discussed earlier for two-dimensional arrays: Because arrays are stored linearly in memory (one array element after another), the compiler must use this size information to locate correctly an element that lies within the array.

QUICK CHECK

11.8.1 Write a declaration for a multidimensional array for representing network access points in a building that has 15 floors, 10 rooms per floor, and up to 12 network access points per room. Each network access point is labeled with its state as being on or off and if it is on has the month it was turned on. (pp. 564–565)

11.8.2 Which aspect of a problem would lead you to consider using a multidimensional array as the representation of its data structure? (pp. 564–565)

11.8.3 Write a declaration for a multidimensional array that stores 24 hourly temperatures for each day of a year for a decade. Call the array `decadeTemps`. (pp. 564–565)

Problem-Solving Case Study

Calculating Exam Statistics

PROBLEM: You are the grader in your Government class. The teacher has asked you to prepare the following statistics for the last exam: average grade, maximum grade, minimum grade, number of grades above the average, and number of grades below the average. Because this is the first exam for the course, you decide to write a program to calculate these statistics so you can use the program for the remaining exams as well.

DISCUSSION: Let's abstract this problem from the given context and look at the tasks in isolation. Three separate things must be done in this problem: compute an average of values on a file, find the minimum value and maximum value in a file, and compare each value to the average. There are several approaches to the solution to this problem. In the next chapter, we will look at an entirely different solution technique; however, here we base our solution on the fact that the values in the list are between 0 and 100. We use an array where the indexes have semantic content: Each index represents a grade.

The by-hand analogy is to mark off 101 lines on a sheet of paper and number (or label) the lines from 0 to 100. Each line number represents a possible grade. As you read a grade, make a hash mark on the line whose number is the same as the grade. When you have finished recording each grade in this fashion, you compute the sum of the grades by summing the products of each grade (line number) times the number of hash marks on that line. You can either count the number of grades as you read them or later, as you go through the list to sum them up.

To calculate the lowest grade, start at line 0 and look down the list; the number of the first line with a hash mark is the lowest grade. To calculate the highest grade, start looking backward from line 100; the line number where you find the first hash mark is the highest grade. To determine how many grades are above average, start at the line whose number is the average grade plus 1 and count the hash marks on the lines from there through line 100. To determine how many grades are below the average, sum the hash marks from the line whose number is the truncated average through line 0.

The data structure equivalent of your sheet of paper is an integer array declared to be of size 101. The index is the line number; the component corresponds to where you make hash marks (increment the component) each time the grade corresponding to the index occurs.

FIGURE 11.17

Problem-Solving Case Study

INPUT: A file, whose name is input from the keyboard, containing test grades.

OUTPUT: A file, whose name is input from the keyboard, showing the following statistics properly labeled:

    Number of grades
    Average grade
    Lowest grade
    Highest grade
    Number of grades above the average
    Number of grades below the average

DATA STRUCTURE: The array of grades and the values to be calculated should be bound together into a record.

```
struct GradeStatistics
{
  int numGrades;         // Number of grades
  float average;         // Average grade
  int highest;           // Highest grade
  int lowest;            // Lowest grade
  int aboveAverage;      // Number of grades above the average
  int belowAverage;      // Number of grades below the average
  int grades[101];       // Array of grades
};
```

Main   Level 0

    Open files
    Calculate statistics
    Print results
    Close files

We can use the same "open files" function we have used in several other programs. However, the heading that is printed on the output needs to be changed.

Calculate Statistics

This function must input the grades and calculate the statistics. It needs the input file name and the record of type **GradeStatistics**. Let's call this parameter **statistics**. We pass it to all of the modules, letting each module decide which of the values to access.

CalculateStatistics(In/out: inData, statistics)

    Input grades
    Calculate average
    Calculate highest
    Calculate lowest
    Calculate number above average
    Calculate number below average

Problem-Solving Case Study

Input Grades   Level 1

This function must have the file name and the array as parameters. The program needs to know the number of grades. As we said, this value can be calculated either as the grades are read or as the grades are summed to get the average. Let's calculate it here and pass it as an argument to the function that computes the average.

InputGrades(In/out: statistics, inData)

```
Set numGrades to 0
Read grade
WHILE NOT eof
    Increment statistics.grades[grade]
    Increment statistics.numGrades
    Read grade
```

CalculateAverage(In/out: statistics)

```
Set sum to 0
FOR index going from 0 through 100
    Set sum to sum + statistics.grades[index] * index;
Set statisics.average to float(sum) / float(statistics.numGrades)
```

CalculateHighest(In/out: statistics)

```
Set highGrade to 100;
WHILE statistics.grades[highGrade] equal to 0
    Decrement highGrade
Set statistics.highest to highGrade
```

CalculateLowest(In/out: statistics)

```
Set lowGrade to 0
WHILE statistics.grades[lowGrade] equal to 0
    Increment lowGrade
Set statistics.lowest to lowGrade
```

CalculateAboveAverage(In/out: statistics)

```
Set averagePlus to int(statistics.average) + 1
Set number to zero
FOR index going from averagePlus to 100
    Set number to number + statistics.grades[index]
Set statistics.aboveAverage to number
```

Problem-Solving Case Study

CalculateBelowAverage(In/out: statistics)

Set truncatedAverage to (int) statistics.average
Set number to zero
FOR index going from 0 to truncatedAverage
    Set number to number + statistics.grades[index]
Set statistics.belowAverage to number

PrintResults(Inout: outData; In: statistics)

Print on outData "The average grade is " statistics.average
Print on outData "The highest grade is " statistics.highest
Print on outData "The lowest grade is " statistics.lowest
Print on outData "The number of grades above the average is " statistics.aboveAverage
Print on outData "The number of grades below the average is " statistics.belowAverage

MODULE STRUCTURE CHART

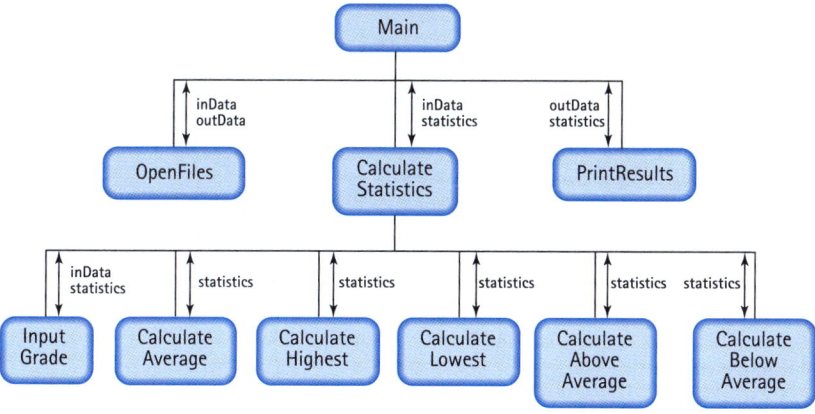

```
//***************************************************************
// This program calculates the average, high score, low score,
// number above the average, and number below the average for
// a file of test scores.
// Assumption: File contains at least one nonzero value
//***************************************************************

#include <iostream>
#include <fstream>
#include <iomanip>
```

Problem-Solving Case Study

```cpp
using namespace std;

struct GradeStatistics
{
  int numGrades;             // Number of grades
  float average;             // Average grade
  int highest;               // Highest grade
  int lowest;                // Lowest grade
  int aboveAverage;          // Number of grades above the average
  int belowAverage;          // Number of grades below the average
  int grades[101];           // Array of grades
};

// Declare function prototypes
void CalculateStatistics(GradeStatistics& statistics,
    ifstream& inData);
// Post: Data has been read and statistics calculated
void OpenFiles(ifstream& inData, ofstream& outData);
// Post: File names have been prompted for and files are opened;
//       Input file name has been written on output file
void InputGrades(GradeStatistics& statistics, ifstream& inData);
// Pre:  inData is assigned and not empty
// Post: Grades have been read from inData,
//       numGrades is the number of grades in inData
void CalculateAverage(GradeStatistics& statistics);
// Post: Average grade has been calculated
void CalculateHighest(GradeStatistics& statistics);
// Post: Highest grade has been calculated
void CalculateLowest(GradeStatistics& statistics);
// Post: Return value is the lowest grade
void CalculateAboveAverage(GradeStatistics& statistics);
// Post: Number of grades above the average has been calculated
void CalculateBelowAverage(GradeStatistics& statistics);
// Post: Number of grades below the average has been calculated
void PrintResults(GradeStatistics statistics, ofstream& outData);
// Pre:  outData has been opened
// Post: Output has been written on outData

int main()
{
  GradeStatistics statistics;
  // Declare and open files
  ifstream inData;
  ofstream outData;
  OpenFiles(inData, outData);
  if (!inData || !outData )
  {
    cout << "Files not opened successfully." << endl;
    return 1;
  }
```

Problem-Solving Case Study

```
    CalculateStatistics(statistics, inData);
    PrintResults(statistics, outData);
    inData.close();
    outData.close();
    return 0;
}

//**********************************************************************

void OpenFiles(ifstream& text, ofstream& outFile )
{
    string inFileName;
    string outFileName;
    cout << "Enter the name of the file to be processed"
         << endl;
    cin >> inFileName;
    text.open(inFileName.c_str());
    cout << "Enter the name of the output file" << endl;
    cin >> outFileName;
    outFile.open(outFileName.c_str());
    outFile << "Analysis of exams on file " << inFileName
            << endl << endl;
}

//**********************************************************************

void CalculateAverage(GradeStatistics& statistics )
{
    int sum = 0;
    // Sum number of grades for each index times the index
    for (int index = 0; index <= 100; index++)
        sum = sum + statistics.grades[index] * index;
    statistics.average =   static_cast<float>(sum) /
                           static_cast<float>(statistics.numGrades);
}

//**********************************************************************

void InputGrades(GradeStatistics& statistics, ifstream& inData)
{
    int grade;
    // Zero out the array of counters
    for (int index = 0; index <= 100; index++)
        statistics.grades[index] = 0;
    statistics.numGrades = 0;
    inData >> grade;           // Priming read
    while (inData)
    { // Process data
        statistics.grades[grade]++;
        statistics.numGrades++;
        inData >> grade;         // Subsequent reads
    }
}
```

Problem-Solving Case Study

```
//*******************************************************************

void CalculateLowest(GradeStatistics& statistics)
{
  // Index of first nonzero grade from the bottom is the low grade
  int lowGrade = 0;
  while (statistics.grades[lowGrade] == 0)
    lowGrade++;
    statistics.lowest =  lowGrade;
}

//*******************************************************************

void CalculateHighest(GradeStatistics& statistics)
{
  // Index of first nonzero grade from the top is the high grade
  int highGrade = 100;
  while (statistics.grades[highGrade] == 0)
    highGrade--;
  statistics.highest = highGrade;
}

//*******************************************************************

void CalculateAboveAverage(GradeStatistics& statistics)
{
  int averagePlus = (int)(statistics.average) + 1;
  int index;
  int number = 0;
  // Sum number of grades above average
  for (index = averagePlus; index <= 100; index++)
    number = number + statistics.grades[index];
  statistics.aboveAverage = number;
}

//*******************************************************************

void CalculateBelowAverage(GradeStatistics& statistics)
{
  int truncatedAverage = (int) (statistics.average);
  int index;
  int number = 0;
  // Sum number of grades at or below average
  for (index = 0; index <= truncatedAverage; index++)
    number = number + statistics.grades[index];
  statistics.belowAverage = number;
}

//*******************************************************************

void CalculateStatistics(GradeStatistics& statistics,
     ifstream& inData)
```

Problem-Solving Case Study

```
{
  // Read and process grades
  InputGrades(statistics, inData);
  CalculateAverage(statistics);
  CalculateHighest(statistics);
  CalculateLowest(statistics);
  CalculateAboveAverage(statistics);
  CalculateBelowAverage(statistics);
}

//****************************************************************

void PrintResults(GradeStatistics statistics, ofstream& outData)
{
  outData << "The number of grades is " << statistics.numGrades
          << endl;
  outData << fixed << setprecision(2)
          << "The average grade is " << statistics.average << endl;
  outData << "The highest grade is " << statistics.highest << endl;
  outData << "The lowest grade is " << statistics.lowest << endl;
  outData << "The number of grades above the average is "
          << statistics.aboveAverage  << endl;
  outData << "The number of grades below the average is "
          << statistics.belowAverage << endl;
}
```

TESTING: When testing this program, it is the values of **grades**—not the size of the file—that determines the test cases. We must include values of **MinGrade**, **MaxGrade**, and values in between. The following data set meets this criterion. It is shown below in columns to save space.

88	75	99
87	75	87
88	78	44
66	80	34
55	80	0
56	90	100

Here is the output:

```
Analysis of exams on file stat.data

The number of grades is 18
The average grade is 71.22
The highest grade is 100
The lowest grade is 0
The number of grades above the average is 12
The number of grades below the average is 6
```

Problem-Solving Case Study

Favorite Rock Group

PROBLEM: At a small college, four campus rock groups have organized a fund-raising project, in which there will be a playoff among the groups. Each student gets to vote for his or her favorite group. Two prizes will be awarded: The best group gets a prize and the class with the best participation gets a prize.

INPUT: An arbitrary number of votes in a file `voteFile`, with each vote represented as a pair of numbers: a class number (1 through 4) and a rock group number (1 through 4); and group names, entered from the keyboard (to be used for printing the output).

OUTPUT: The following three items, written to a file `reportFile`: a tabular report showing how many votes each rock group received in each class, the total number of votes for each rock group, and the total number of votes cast by each class.

DISCUSSION: The data consists of a pair of numbers for each vote. The first number is the class number; the second number is the rock group number.

If we were doing the analysis by hand, our first task would be to go through the data, counting how many people in each class voted for each group. We would probably create a table with classes down the side and rock groups across the top. Each vote would be recorded as a hash mark in the appropriate row and column (see **FIGURE 11.18**).

When all of the votes have been recorded, a sum of each column tells us how many votes each group received. A sum of each row tells us how many people voted in each class.

As is so often the case, we can use this by-hand algorithm directly in our program. We can create a two-dimensional array in which each component is a counter for the number of votes for a particular group in each class; for example, the value indexed by `[2][1]` would be the counter for the votes in class 2 (sophomore) for group 1. Well, not quite. C++ arrays are indexed beginning at 0, so the correct array component would be indexed by `[1][0]`. When we input a class number and a group number, we must remember to subtract 1 from each value before using the values as an index into the array. Likewise, we must add 1 to an array index that represents a class number or group number before printing it out.

DATA STRUCTURES: (1) A two-dimensional array named `votes`, where the rows represent classes and the columns represent groups. (2) A one-dimensional array of strings containing the names of the groups, to be used for printing (see **FIGURE 11.19**).

In our discussion we have used the word "class" to represent freshman, sophomore, junior, or senior. However, we need to be careful. We cannot use the word "class" in our program because it is a reserved word (as we will see in the next chapter). Let's make the switch here and use the word "level" instead. In the design that follows, we use the named constants `NUM_LEVELS` and `NUM_ROCK_GROUPS` in place of the literal constants 4 and 4.

	Group 1	Group 2	Group 3	Group 4
Class 1	‖‖‖ ‖	‖	‖‖‖ ‖‖‖ ‖	‖‖‖
Class 2	‖‖‖ ‖‖‖	‖	‖‖‖	‖‖
Class 3	‖	‖‖‖ ‖	‖‖‖ ‖‖‖ ‖‖‖	‖
Class 4	‖‖‖	‖‖‖ ‖	‖‖‖ ‖‖‖	‖

FIGURE 11.18 Vote-Counting Table

Problem-Solving Case Study

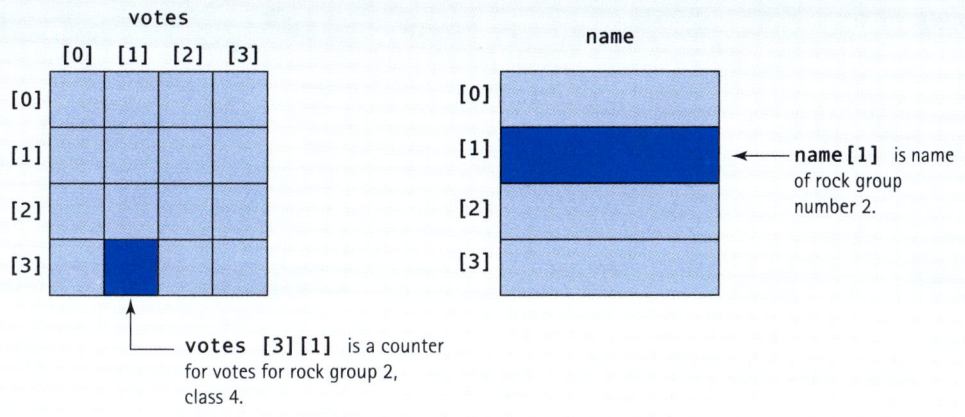

FIGURE 11.19 Data Structures for Favorite Rock Group Program

Main — Level 0

Get group names
Set votes array to 0
Read level, group from voteFile
WHILE NOT EOF on voteFile
    Increment votes[level–1][group–1] by 1
    Read level, rockGroup from voteFile
Write report to reportFile
Write totals per group to reportFile
Write totals per level to reportFile

Get RockGroup Names (Out: name) — Level 1

Print "Enter the names of the rock groups, one per line,
    in the order they appear on the ballot."
FOR rockGroup going from 0 through NUM_ROCK_GROUPS – 1
    Read name[rockGroup]

Note that each rock group's name is stored in the slot in the name array corresponding to its group's number (minus 1). These names are useful when the totals are printed.

Set Votes to Zero (Out: votes)

FOR each level
    FOR each group
        Set votes[level][group] to 0

Problem-Solving Case Study

Write Report (In: votes, name; In/out: reportFile)

FOR each rockGroup   // Set up headings
   Write name[rockGroup] to reportFile
FOR each level   // Print array by row
   FOR each rockGroup
      Write votes[level][rockGroup] to reportFile

Write Totals per RockGroup (In: votes, name; Inout: reportFile)

FOR each rockGroup
   Set total = 0
FOR each level   // Compute column sum
   Add votes[level][rockGroup] to total
   Write "Total votes for", name[rockGroup], total to reportFile

Write Totals per Level (In: votes; In/out: reportFile)

FOR each level
   Set total = 0
   FOR each rockGroup   // Compute row sum
      Add votes[level][rockGroup] to total
   Write "Total votes for level", level, ':', total to reportFile

MODULE STRUCTURE CHART

```
//*************************************************************
// Favorite Rock Group program
// This program reads votes represented by level number and
// rock group number from a data file, calculates the sums per
// level and per rock group, and writes all totals to an
// output file
//*************************************************************
```

Problem-Solving Case Study

```cpp
#include <iostream>
#include <iomanip>    // For setw()
#include <fstream>    // For file I/O
#include <string>     // For string type

using namespace std;

const int NUM_LEVELS = 4;
const int NUM_ROCK_GROUPS = 4;
typedef int VoteArray[NUM_LEVELS][NUM_ROCK_GROUPS];

void GetNames(string names[]);
// Rock group names have been prompted for and read
void OpenFiles(ifstream& voteFile, ofstream& reportFile);
// File names have been prompted for and read
void WritePerRockGroup(const VoteArray votes,
                       const string name[], ofstream& reportFile);
// The name of each rock group followed by the number of
// votes the group received have been written on reportFile
void WritePerLevel(const VoteArray votes, ofstream& reportFile);
// The level and the number of votes cast by the level
// have been written on reportFile
void WriteReport(const VoteArray votes, const string name[],
                 ofstream& reportFile);
// The array of votes has been written in tabular form on
// reportFile
void ZeroVotes(VoteArray votes);
// The array of votes has been set to all zeros

int main()
{
  string name[NUM_ROCK_GROUPS];   // Array of rockGroup names
  VoteArray votes;                // Totals for level vs. rockGroups
  int rockGroup;                  // Group number from voteFile
  int level;                      // Level number input from voteFile
  ifstream voteFile;              // Input file of level, rockGroups
  ofstream reportFile;            // Output file receiving summaries

  OpenFiles(voteFile, reportFile);
  if (!voteFile || !reportFile)
  {
    cout << "Files did not open successfully." << endl;
    return 1;
  }

  GetNames(name);
  ZeroVotes(votes);

  // Read and tally votes
  voteFile >> level >> rockGroup;
  while (voteFile)
```

Problem-Solving Case Study

```
  {
    votes[level-1][rockGroup-1]++;
    voteFile >> level >> rockGroup;
  }
  WriteReport(votes, name, reportFile);
  WritePerRockGroup(votes, name, reportFile);
  WritePerLevel(votes, reportFile);
  return 0;
}

//*********************************************************************

void OpenFiles(ifstream& text, ofstream& outFile)
{
  string inFileName;
  string outFileName;
  cout << "Enter the name of the file to be processed"
       << endl;
  cin >> inFileName;
  text.open(inFileName.c_str());
  cout << "Enter the name of the output file" << endl;
  cin >> outFileName;
  outFile.open(outFileName.c_str());
  outFile << "Analysis of exams on file " << inFileName
          << endl << endl;
}

//*********************************************************************

void GetNames(string name[])
{
  string inputStr;
  int rockGroup;

  cout << "Enter the names of the rock groups, one per line,"
       << endl << "in the order they appear on the ballot." << endl;
  getline(cin, inputStr);          // Bypass eoln
  for (rockGroup = 0; rockGroup < NUM_ROCK_GROUPS; rockGroup++)
  {
    getline(cin, inputStr);
    name[rockGroup] = inputStr.substr(0,16);
  }
}

//*********************************************************************

void ZeroVotes(VoteArray votes)
{
  int level;
  int rockGroup;
```

```
  for (level = 0; level < NUM_LEVELS; level++)
    for (rockGroup = 0; rockGroup < NUM_ROCK_GROUPS; rockGroup++)
      votes[level][rockGroup] = 0;
}

//*******************************************************************

void WriteReport(const VoteArray votes, const string name[],
                 ofstream& reportFile )
{
  int level;
  int rockGroup;

  reportFile << "              ";
  for (rockGroup = 0; rockGroup < NUM_ROCK_GROUPS; rockGroup++)
    reportFile << setw(17) << name[rockGroup];
  reportFile << endl;

  // Print array by row
  for (level = 0; level < NUM_LEVELS; level++)
  {
    reportFile << "level" << setw(4) << level + 1;
    for (rockGroup = 0; rockGroup < NUM_ROCK_GROUPS; rockGroup++)
      reportFile << setw(17) << votes[level][rockGroup];

    reportFile << endl << endl;
  }
}

//*******************************************************************

void WritePerRockGroup(const VoteArray votes, const string name[],
                       ofstream& reportFile)
{
  int level;
  int rockGroup;
  int total;          // Total votes for a rockGroup

  for (rockGroup = 0; rockGroup < NUM_ROCK_GROUPS; rockGroup++)
  {
    total = 0;

    // Compute column sum
    for (level = 0; level < NUM_LEVELS; level++)
      total = total + votes[level][rockGroup];
    reportFile << "Total votes for "
               << setw(17) << name[rockGroup] << ":"
               << setw(3) << total << endl;
  }
  reportFile << endl;
}

//*******************************************************************
```

Problem-Solving Case Study

```
void WritePerLevel(const VoteArray votes, ofstream& reportFile)
{
  int level;
  int rockGroup;
  int total;

  for (level = 0; level < NUM_LEVELS; level++)
  {
    total = 0;

    // Compute row sum
    for (rockGroup = 0; rockGroup < NUM_ROCK_GROUPS; rockGroup++)
      total = total + votes[level][rockGroup];

    reportFile << "Total votes for level"
               << setw(3) << level + 1 << ':'
               << setw(5) << total << endl;
  }
}
```

TESTING: This program was executed with the file data listed below. (We list the data in three columns to save space.) The keyboard I/O is shown below the file contents. In this data set, there is at least one vote for each group in each level. Case Study Follow-Up Exercise 7 asks you to outline a complete testing strategy for this program.

Input data on file `Votes.dat`:

```
1 1      3 1      3 3
1 1      4 3      4 4
1 2      3 4      4 4
1 2      3 2      4 3
1 3      3 3      4 4
1 4      2 1      4 4
2 2      2 3      4 1
2 2      4 3      4 2
2 3      4 4      2 4
2 1      3 2      4 4
```

Keyboard I/O:

```
Enter the name of the file to be processed
Votes.dat
Enter the name of the output file
Votes.out
Enter the names of the rock groups, one per line,
in the order they appear on the ballot.
Chas B Abbage
Boole's Brothers
Ada Love
Augie DeM
```

Problem-Solving Case Study

Output on file `Votes.out`:

```
             Chas B Abbage  Boole's Brothers    Ada Love      Augie DeM
level   1           1               2               1              1

level   2           2               2               2              1

level   3           1               2               2              1

level   4           1               1               3              6

Total votes for    Chas B Abbage:  5
Total votes for    Boole's Brothers:  7
Total votes for    Ada Love:  8
Total votes for    Augie DeM:  9

Total votes for level   1:    5
Total votes for level   2:    7
Total votes for level   3:    6
Total votes for level   4:    11
```

Testing and Debugging

One-Dimensional Arrays

The most common error in processing arrays is use of an out-of-bounds array index. That is, the program attempts to access a component using an index that is either less than 0 or greater than the array size minus 1. For example, given the declarations

```
char line[100];
int  counter;
```

the following For statement would print the 100 elements of the line array and then print a 101st value—the value that resides in memory immediately beyond the end of the array:

```
for (counter = 0; counter <= 100; counter++)
  cout << line[counter];
```

This error is easy to detect because 101 characters are printed instead of 100. The loop test should be `counter < 100`.

You won't always use a simple For statement when accessing arrays, however. Suppose we read data into the line array in another part of the program. Let's use a While statement that reads to the newline character:

```
counter = 0;
cin.get(ch);
while (ch != '\n')
{
  line[counter] = ch;
  counter++;
  cin.get(ch);
}
```

This code seems reasonable enough, but what if the input line has more than 100 characters? After the hundredth character is read and stored into the array, the loop continues to execute with the array index out of bounds. Characters are stored into memory locations past the end of the array, wiping out other data values (or even machine language instructions in the program!).

The moral of the story is this: When processing arrays, pay special attention to the design of loop termination conditions. Always ask yourself if the loop could possibly keep running after the last array component has been processed.

Whenever an array index goes out of bounds, your first suspicion should be that a loop has failed to terminate properly. The second thing to check is any array access involving an index that is based on input data or a calculation. When an array index is input as data, a data validation check is an absolute necessity.

Complex Structures

As we have demonstrated in many examples in this chapter and the last, data structures may be combined in various ways: structs whose components are structs, structs whose components are arrays, arrays whose components are structs, arrays whose components are arrays (multidimensional arrays), and so forth. When arrays and structs are combined, confusion can arise about precisely where to place the operators for array element selection ([]) and struct member selection (.).

To summarize the correct placement of these operators, let's use the **StudentRec** type we introduced earlier in this chapter:

```
struct StudentRec
{
  string    stuName;
  float     gpa;
  int       examScore[4];
  GradeType courseGrade;
};
```

If we declare a variable of type **StudentRec**,

```
StudentRec student;
```

then what is the syntax for selecting the first exam score of the student (that is, for selecting element 0 of the `examScore` member of `student`)? The dot operator is a binary (two-operand) operator; its left operand denotes a struct variable, and its right operand is a member name:

`StructVariable.MemberName`

The `[]` operator is a unary (one-operand) operator; it comes immediately after an expression denoting an array:

`Array[IndexExpression]`

Therefore, the expression

`student`

denotes a struct variable; the expression

`student.examScore`

denotes an array; and the expression

`student.examScore[0]`

denotes an integer—the integer located in element 0 of the `student.examScore` array.

With arrays of structs or class objects, you must once again make sure that the `[]` and `.` operators are in the proper positions. Given the declaration

`StudentRec gradeBook[150];`

we can access the `gpa` member of the first element of the `gradeBook` array with the following expression:

`gradeBook[0].gpa`

The index `[0]` is correctly attached to the identifier `gradeBook` because `gradeBook` is the name of an array. Furthermore, the expression

`gradeBook[0]`

denotes a struct, so the dot operator selects the `gpa` member of this struct.

Multidimensional Arrays

Errors made while working with multidimensional arrays usually fall into two major categories: index expressions that are out of order and index range errors.

Suppose we were to expand the rock group program to accommodate ten rock groups and four levels. Let's declare the `votes` array as

`int votes[4][10];`

The first dimension represents the levels, and the second represents the rock groups. An example of the first kind of error—incorrect order of the index expressions—would be to print out the `votes` array as follows:

```
for (level = 0; level < 4; level++)
{
  for (rockGroup = 0; rockGroup < 10; rockGroup++)
    cout << setw(4) << votes[rockGroup][level];
  cout << endl;
}
```

If you look closely at the highlighted part of the code, you will see that the output statement specifies the array indexes in the wrong order. The loops march through the array with the first index ranging from 0 through 9 (instead of 0 through 3) and the second index ranging from 0 through 3 (instead of 0 through 9). The effect of executing this code may vary from system to system. The program may output the wrong array components and continue executing, or it may crash with a memory access error.

An example of the second kind of error—an incorrect index range in an otherwise correct loop—can be seen in this code:

```
for (level = 0; level < 10; level++)
{
  for (rockGroup = 0; rockGroup < 4; rockGroup++)
    cout << setw(4) << votes[level][rockGroup];
  cout << endl;
}
```

Here the output statement correctly uses `level` for the first index and `rockGroup` for the second index. However, as the highlighting points out, the For statements use the opposite upper limits for the index variables—there are supposed to be four levels and ten groups. As with the preceding example, the effect of executing this code is undefined but is certainly wrong. A valuable way to prevent this kind of error is to use named constants instead of the literals 10 and 4. In the case study, we used `NUM_LEVELS` and `NUM_ROCK_GROUPS`. You are much more likely to spot an error (or to avoid making an error in the first place) if you write something like:

```
for (level = 0; level < NUM_LEVELS; level++)
```

than if you use a literal constant as the upper limit for the index variable.

Testing and Debugging Hints

1. When an individual component of a one-dimensional array is accessed, the index must be within the range 0 through the array size minus 1. Attempting to use an index value outside this range will cause the program to access memory locations outside the array.
2. The individual components of an array are themselves variables of the component type. When values are stored into an array, they should either be of the component type or be explicitly converted to the component type; otherwise, implicit type coercion occurs.
3. C++ does not allow aggregate operations on arrays; that is, it does not support aggregate assignment, aggregate comparison, aggregate I/O, or aggregate arithmetic. You must write code to do all of these operations, one array element at a time.
4. Omitting the size of a one-dimensional array in its declaration is permitted only in two cases: (1) when an array is declared as a parameter in a function heading and (2) when an array is initialized in its declaration. In all other declarations, you *must* specify the size of the array with a constant integer expression.
5. If an array parameter is incoming only, declare the parameter as `const` to prevent the function from accidentally modifying the caller's argument.

6. Don't pass an individual array component as an argument when the function expects to receive the base address of an entire array.
7. The size of an array is fixed at compile time, but the number of values actually stored there is determined at run time. Therefore, an array must be declared to be as large as it could ever be for the particular problem. Subarray processing is used to process only those components that contain data.
8. When functions perform subarray processing on a one-dimensional array, you must pass both the array and the number of items actually used or combine the array name and the number of items in a record.
9. With multidimensional arrays, you must use the proper number of indexes when referencing an array component. You should also make sure the indexes are in the correct order.
10. In loops that process multidimensional arrays, double-check the upper and lower bounds on each index variable to be sure they are correct for that dimension of the array.
11. When declaring a multidimensional array as a parameter, you must state the sizes of all but the first dimension. Also, these sizes must agree exactly with the sizes of the caller's argument.
12. To eliminate the chance of a size mismatch (see item 11), use a Typedef statement to define a multidimensional array type.
13. If subarray processing is being used, combine the multidimensional array type and the number of actual values stored in each dimension into a record. Pass the record as a parameter.
14. In an expression, an array name without any index brackets is a pointer expression; its value is the base address of the array. The array name is considered a constant expression, so no assignment to it is possible. The following code shows correct and incorrect assignments.

```
int   arrA[5] = {10, 20, 30, 40, 50};
int   arrB[5] = {60, 70, 80, 90, 100};
int*  ptr;

ptr = arrB;       // OK--you can assign to a variable
arrA = arrB;      // Wrong--you cannot assign to a constant
```

Summary

The one-dimensional array is a homogeneous data structure that gives a name to a sequential group of like components. Each component is accessed by its relative position within the group (rather than by name, as in a struct), and each component is a variable of the component type. To access a particular component, we give the name of the array and an index that specifies which component of the group we want. The index can be an expression of any integral type, as long as it evaluates to an integer from 0 through the array size minus 1. Array components can be accessed in random order directly, or they can be accessed sequentially by stepping through the index values one at a time.

Two-dimensional arrays are useful for processing information that is represented naturally in tabular form. Processing data in two-dimensional arrays usually takes one of two forms: processing by row or processing by column. An array of arrays, which is useful if rows of the array must be passed as arguments, is an alternative way of defining a two-dimensional array.

A multidimensional array is a collection of like components that are ordered on more than one dimension. Each component is accessed by a set of indexes, one for each dimension, that represents the component's position on the various dimensions. Each index may be thought of as describing a feature of a given array component.

If subarray processing is used, the array and the actual values stored in each dimension should be bound together into a record. This record should be passed as a parameter to functions.

Quick Check Answers

11.1.1 Because its elements are all of the same type. **11.1.2** An array.
11.1.3 `float temps[24];`
11.1.4 `for (int count = 0; count <=23; count++)`
`    temps[count] = 32.0;`
11.1.5 By its position. **11.1.6** The `at` operation checks the bounds of the array where as the `[ ]` operator does not.
11.2.1 `mailList[12].street.at(2)`
11.2.2 `struct Coord { int x; int y; };`
`    Coord elements[1000];`
11.3.1 The index represents the hour during which the reading was taken, based on a 24-hour clock.
11.3.2 `count = 0;`
`    cin >> inTemp;`
`    while (indata && count < 24)`
`    {`
`      temps[count] = inTemp;`
`      cin >> inTemp;`
`      count++;`
`    }`
11.3.3 At compile time. **11.3.4** We need to keep track of how many entries are actually filled. **11.4.1** It is declared and accessed with two index values instead of one. **11.4.2** `float allTemps[24][366];` **11.4.3** A table.
11.4.4 `char board[25][25]; if (board[X][Y] == '#') cout << "HIT" << endl;`
11.5.1 `void Quick (float table[], int numElements)`
11.5.2 Nothing, it ignores it. **11.5.3** Because C++ stores a two-dimensional array in row order. Thus, you can leave off the number of rows, but not the number of columns. **11.5.4** The base address.
11.6.1 `for (day = 0; day <= 365; day++)`
`    {`
`      for (hour = 0; hour <= 23; hour++)`
`        cout << allTemps[hour][day];`
`      cout << endl;`
`    }`
11.6.2 This process is referred to as *random access*. **11.6.3** randomly, along rows, along columns, and throughout the entire array.
11.6.4 `for (day = 0; day <= 365; day++) {`
`      average = 0;`
`      total   = 0;`
`      for (hour = 0; hour < 24; hour++) {`
`        total += allTemps[hour][day];`
`      }`
`      average = total / 24.0;`
`      cout << "Day " << day << " average = " << average << endl;`
`    }`
11.6.5 `int game[3][4] = { { 1, 2, 2 }, { 0, 1, 0 }, { 1, 0, 2 } };`
11.8.1 `struct AccessPoint { int state; string month; };`
`    AccessPoint building[15][10][12];`
11.8.2 If the problem has a homogeneous collection of data that is ordered by more than two indexes.
11.8.3 `float decadeTemps[24][366][10]`

Exam Preparation Exercises

1. The components of an array can be of different types. True or false?
2. Arrays can have any type for their components. True or false?
3. Multidimensional arrays are limited to no more than four dimensions. True or false?
4. When you are declaring a one-dimensional array, its size must be specified with an integer. True or false?

5. The type of an index expression can be any of the integral types or an enumeration type. True or false?
6. What happens if a program tries to access an array using an index of −1?
7. Which aggregate operations are allowed on arrays?
8. To what does the term "base address of an array" refer, and how is it used in a function call?
9. Which special type of array can be returned by a value-returning function?
10. If you want to use a nested loop to process a two-dimensional array row-by-row, which dimension's index (row or column) would you increment in the inner loop, and which would you increment in the outer loop?
11. How many elements are there in each of the following arrays?
    a. `int x[27];`
    b. `const int base = 10;`
       `int y[base + 5];`
    c. `int z[100][100][100][100];`
12. What's wrong with the following code segment?

    ```
    int prep[100];
    for (int index = 1; index <= 100; index++)
      prep[index] = 0;
    ```

13. What's wrong with the following code segment?

    ```
    const int limit = 100;
    int eprep[limit];
    int examp[limit];
    for (int index = 0; index <= limit - 1; index++)
    {
      eprep[index] = 0;
      examp[index] = 0;
    }
    if (eprep == examp)
      cout << "Equal";
    ```

14. What's wrong with the following code segment?

    ```
    typedef int Exrep[50];

    Exrep Init(Exrep); // Prototype
    ```

15. What's wrong with the following code segment?

    ```
    int prepex[3][4] =
    {
      {1, 2, 3},
      {4, 5, 6},
      {7, 8, 9},
      {0, -1, -2}
    };
    ```

16. What's the potential danger in the following code segment?

    ```
    int index;
    int value;
    int xeperp[100];
    cin >> index >> value;
    xeperp[index] = value;
    ```

17. What is the side effect of the following function?

    ```
    int Max (int trio[3])
    {
      int temp;
      if (trio[0] > trio[1])
      {
        temp = trio[1];
        trio[1] = trio[0];
        trio[0] = temp;
      }
      if (trio[1] > trio[2])
      {
        temp = trio[2];
        trio[2] = trio[1];
        trio[1] = temp;
      }
      return trio[2];
    }
    ```

18. What does the following code segment output?

    ```
    char pattern[5][5] =
    {
      {'*', ' ', '*', ' ', '*'},
      {' ', '*', ' ', '*', ' '},
      {'*', ' ', '*', ' ', '*'},
      {' ', '*', ' ', '*', ' '},
      {'*', ' ', '*', ' ', '*'}
    }
    for (int outer = 0; outer < 5; outer++)
    {
      for (int inner = 1; inner <= 5; inner++)
        cout << pattern[outer][inner % 5];
      cout << endl;
    }
    ```

19. Given the declaration of **pattern** in Exercise 18, what does the following loop output?

    ```
    for (int index = 0; index < 5; index++)
      cout << pattern[index][(index+2) % 5];
    ```

20. Given the declaration of **pattern** in Exercise 18, what does the following loop output?

    ```
    for (int outer = 0; outer < 5; outer++)
    {
      for (int inner = 0; inner < 5; inner++)
        cout << pattern[inner][outer];
      cout << endl;
    }
    ```

21. Given the following declaration:

    ```
    int examPrep [12][15];
    ```

a. Write a loop to print the first row of the array on one line on `cout`.
b. Write a loop to print the first column of the array on one line on `cout`.
c. Write a loop to print the first seven rows of the array, each on a single line.
d. Write a loop to print the entire array backward and upside down, so that the last line appears first, with the last column on the left.

22. An index expression (like those used with arrays) can be attached to any pointer variable, even if it doesn't point to an array. True or false?

Programming Warm-Up Exercises

1. Write the following declarations.
   a. An array called `topTenList`, containing ten values of type `string`.
   b. An enumeration type of the seven major colors of the spectrum, and a matching array declaration that can be indexed by the spectrum type. The array should be called `colorMix`, and should contain values of type `float`.
   c. A two-dimensional array representing the days on a calendar page with up to 6 weeks. Call the array `month`, and declare an enumeration type consisting of the names of the days, which can be used to index the array columns. The weeks should be indexed by an `int`. For the component type of the array, declare a `struct` consisting of an `int` field called `day`, and a `string` field called `activity`.
2. Write a declaration of a named array type, and then declare three arrays of that type. The array type should be called `DataSet`, and the three arrays should be called `input`, `output`, and `working`. Each array should hold five `float` values.
3. Using the `DataSet` type declared in Exercise 2, declare an array of three data sets, called `set`.
4. Using the `set` array declared in Exercise 3, write a nested For loop that initializes all of the values of the three data sets to 0.0.
5. Write a function heading for a function called `Equals` that takes two arrays of the `DataSet` type declared in Exercise 2 and returns a `bool` result. The array parameters should be `const`, as they are input-only parameters to the function.
6. Write the body of the `Equals` function described in Exercise 5. It should return `true` if each element of the first array is equal to its corresponding element in the second array.
7. A gallery needs to keep track of its paintings and photographs. It keeps at most 120 art works on its walls. Each one is described by the following information:

   Artist (`string`)
   Title (`string`)
   Medium (oil, watercolor, pastel, acrylic, print, color photo, black-and-white photo)
   Size (`struct`)
       Height (`int`)
       Width (`int`)
   Room where it is hung (main, green, blue, north, south, entry, balcony)
   Price (`float`)

   Write a declaration for a `struct` that represents a piece of art. Declare `struct` and enumeration types as needed to make up the fields of the `Artwork` type. Write an additional declaration of a named array type that holds the list of all the artworks in the gallery. Lastly, declare an array of this type called `currentList` and an `int` variable `numPieces`. The `numPieces` variable contains the number of pieces represented in the array.

8. Write expressions that retrieve the following values from the array declared in Exercise 7.
   a. The 37th work of art.
   b. The title of the 12th work of art.
   c. The width of the 85th work of art.
   d. The room for the 120th work of art.
   e. The first letter of the artist's name for the 78th work of art.
9. Write a For loop that prints a list of the artist, title, and price for every artwork in the `currentList` array defined in Exercise 7.
10. Write a code segment that sums the prices of the artworks in the gallery described in Exercise 7.
11. Write a code segment that outputs the titles of the artworks in the blue room of the gallery described in Exercise 7.
12. Write a code segment that sums the prices of the oil paintings in the gallery described in Exercise 7 that are larger than 400 square inches in size.
13. A piano is tuned in a scale that is slightly unequal (called a "well-tempered scale"), rather than a perfectly scientific scale in which each note sounds at twice the frequency of the same note an octave below (called a "just scale"). For this reason, we can't simply calculate the frequency of a note, but must keep it in a table. Declare a two-dimensional array (`scale`) to hold the frequencies of the well-tempered scale. A frequency is represented by a `float` value. The row dimension is indexed by an `int` value representing the octave (there are eight octaves, numbered 0 through 7), and the other should be indexed by an enumeration type (`Notes`) consisting of the names of the notes. When you write the declaration of the enumeration type, use only sharps (no flats). Thus the note names of an octave are `C, CSHARP, D, DSHARP, E, F, FSHARP, G, GSHARP, A, ASHARP,` and `B`, in that order.
14. Write a code segment that reads a table of frequencies into the `scale` array declared in Exercise 13 from a file called `frequencies.dat`. The frequency values are arranged one per line on the file.
15. Write a code segment that outputs the frequencies of the notes in the fourth octave of the `scale` array declared in Exercise 13.
16. Write a code segment that outputs the frequencies of all C notes in the `scale` array declared in Exercise 13.
17. Write a declaration for a four-dimensional array called `humidity` that is indexed by 10 years (0–9), 52 weeks (0–51), the 50 states (0–49), and an enumeration type consisting of `MAX, MIN,` and `AVERAGE`, called `Type`. The array holds humidity measurements (each component is a `float`).
18. Write a C++ function called `Reset`, which sets all of the components to zero in the humidity array declared in Exercise 17.
19. Write a declaration of a `struct` type called `TimePlace` that has three fields, one for each for the first three index values (year, week, state) in the `humidity` array declared in Exercise 17. `TimePlace` should have a fourth field called `difference`, which is a `float`. Then write a C++ function called `MaxSpread` that takes the `humidity` array as a parameter; scans through it to find the year, week, and state with the greatest difference in humidity over the course of a week; and returns these values as a `TimePlace struct`. If there is more than one week with the greatest difference, then the first one should be returned.

20. Write a code segment that outputs the AVERAGE component of the humidity array of Exercise 17, for all the weeks in the last 5 years for the 23rd state.

21. Declare a pointer variable charArrPointer and initialize it to point to the first element of a four-element char array named initials. Write assignment statements to indirectly store 'A', 'E', and 'W' into the first three elements of the array pointed to by charArrPointer.

Programming Problems

1. Imagine we are using a two-dimensional array as the basis for creating the game *battleship*. In the game of battleship a '~' character entry in the array represents ocean (i.e., not a ship), a '#' character represents a place in the ocean where part of a ship is present, and an 'H' character represents a place in the ocean where part of a ship is present and has been *hit* by a torpedo. Thus, a ship with all 'H' characters means the ship has been sunk. Declare a two-dimensional array that is 25 × 25 that represents the entire ocean and an If statement that prints "HIT" if a torpedo hits a ship given the coordinates X and Y. Write a C++ program that will read in a file representing a game board with 25 lines where each line has 25 characters corresponding to the description above. An example file might look like:

```
~~~~~~~~~~~~~~~~~~~~~~~~~
~~~~~~~~~~~~~~~~~~~~~~~~~
~~~~~~~~~~~~~~~~~~~~~~~~~
~~~~~#####~~~~~~~~~~~~~~~
~~~~~~~~~~~~~~~~~~~~~~~~~
~~~~~~~~~~~~~~#~~~~~~~~~~
~~~~~~~~~~~~~~#~~~~~~~~~~
~~~~~~~~~~~~~~#~~~~~~~~~~
~~~~~~~~~~~~~~#~~~~~~~~~~
~~~~~~~~~~~~~~#~~~~~~~~~~
~~~~~~~~~~~~~~~~~~~~~~~~~
~~~~~~~~~~~#####~~~~~~~~~
~~~~~~~~~~~~~~~~~~~~~~~~~
~#######~~~~~~~~~~~~~~~~~
~~~~~~~~~~~~~~~~~~~~~~~~~
~~~~~~~~~#####~~~~~~~~~~~
~~~~~~~~~~~~~~~~~~~#~~~~~
~~~~~~~~~~~~~~~~~~~#~~~~~
~~~~~~~~~~~~~~~~~~~#~~~~~
~~~~~~~~~~~~~~~~~~~#~~~~~
~~~######~~~~~~~~~~#~~~~~
~~~~~~~~~~~~~~~~~~~~~~~~~
~~~~~~~~~~~~~~~~~~~~~~~~~
~~~~~~~~~~~~~~~~~~~~~~~~~
~~~~~~~~~~~~~~~~~~~~~~~~~
```

You should write a function called Fire that will take an X and Y coordinate and print "HIT" if a ship is hit and "MISS" if a ship is missed. If a ship is HIT you should update the array with an 'H' character to indicate the ship was hit. If a ship is hit that has already been hit at that location you should print "HIT AGAIN". You should write a second function called FleetSunk that will determine if all the ships have been sunk. Your C++ program must then call these functions until all the ships have been sunk, at which point the program should display "The fleet was destroyed!".

2. Write a program to play a game in which you try to sink a fleet of five navy vessels by guessing their locations on a grid. The program uses random numbers to position its ships on a 15 × 15 grid. The ships are of different lengths as follows:

   Frigate: 2 locations
   Tender: 2 locations
   Destroyer: 3 locations
   Cruiser: 3 locations
   Carrier: 4 locations

   The program must pick one square as the starting location, then pick the direction of the ship on the board, and mark off the number of squares in that direction to represent the size of the ship. It must not allow a ship to overlap with another ship or to run off the board.

   The user enters coordinates in the range of 1 through 15 for the rows and A through O for the columns. The program checks this location, and reports whether it is a hit or a miss. If it is a hit, the program also checks whether the ship has been hit in every location that it occupies. If so, the ship is reported as sunk, and the program identifies which ship it is.

   The user gets 60 shots to attempt to sink the fleet. If the user sinks all of the ships before using all 60 shots, then he or she wins the game. At the end of the game, the program should output the grid, so that the user can see where the ships are located.

3. Programming Warm-Up Exercises 7 to 12 deal with an array representing the inventory for an art gallery. Using the same representation, write a C++ program that reads the gallery's inventory from a file called `art.dat` into the array. Then allow the user to look up the art by specifying any field in the record. As a reminder, here are the fields:

   Artist (`string`)
   Title (`string`)
   Medium (oil, watercolor, pastel, acrylic, print, color photo, black-and-white photo)
   Size (`struct`)
      Height (`int`)
      Width (`int`)
   Room where it is hung (main, green, blue, north, south, entry, balcony)
   Price (`float`)

   The user should be able to specify a field, and a value for that field, and the program then returns all artworks that match those criteria. For example, the user may specify Artist and Smithely, and the program will output all of the information concerning every work in the gallery by that artist.

4. Programming Problem 1 in Chapter 7 asked you to write a program that takes a string as input and then outputs the corresponding words in the International Civil Aviation Organization (ICAO) alphabet that would be used to spell it out phonetically. For that program, you should have used a large Switch statement. Rewrite that program using an array of strings to hold the words of the alphabet, and index the array by the positions of the letters of the alphabet. By using an index with semantic content, you can avoid the need for the Switch statement. Be sure that you don't try to index into the array using non-alphabetic characters, as that will result in an out-of-bounds access. For ease of reference, the ICAO alphabet is repeated here from Chapter 7:

A	Alpha
B	Bravo
C	Charlie
D	Delta
E	Echo
F	Foxtrot
G	Golf
H	Hotel
I	India
J	Juliet
K	Kilo
L	Lima
M	Mike
N	November
O	Oscar
P	Papa
Q	Quebec
R	Romeo
S	Sierra
T	Tango
U	Uniform
V	Victor
W	Whiskey
X	X-ray
Y	Yankee
Z	Zulu

Be sure to use proper formatting and appropriate comments in your code. Provide appropriate prompts to the user. The output should be clearly labeled and neatly formatted.

5. Programming Problem 6 in Chapter 6 asked you to write a program to check whether an input line is a palindrome (a word or phrase that is the same when read backward and forward). At that time, we needed to use the substring function to extract individual characters from a string. Because this is a cumbersome way to work with a string, we limited our definition of palindromes to just perfect palindromes—every letter and blank exactly the same in both forward and backward versions. Now that we know how to use arrays, we can expand the definition to ignore blanks, punctuation, and letter case. Thus

```
madam I'm adam
```

becomes

```
madamimadam
```

which is now a palindrome. Write a C++ program that reads a line of input and checks whether it is a palindrome on the basis of this less restrictive definition. Output the reversed line, with all blanks and punctuation removed, and all letters converted to lowercase along with the program's decision.

6. Create a record representing a song on a CD or in an MP3 library. Write a C++ program that allows the user to specify the name of a data file containing songs (assume there are fewer than 200 songs on the file) and then reads the song data from the file into an array of songs. The user should then be allowed to enter the name of an artist, and the program will output all of the songs by that artist, along with any other information about the song that is in the array.

■ Case Study Follow-Up

1. There is no error checking in the Calculating Exam Statistics program. List at least two errors that could easily be checked.
2. All of the functions in the Calculating Exam Statistics program except `OpenFiles`, `InputGrades`, and `PrintResults` are value-returning functions. Rather than calculating and storing the values these functions calculate, could the values be calculated as they are being printed in `PrintResults`? If so, would it be a good idea to do it?
3. The solution to the exam statistics problem makes use of a technique called indexes with semantic content. Explain what this means in relation to this problem.
4. The heading for the output of the Calculating Exam Statistics program is coded directly in the `OpenFiles` function. Remove this statement, prompt the user to enter a heading, and write this heading on the output file.
5. Exercise 4 had the heading in the exam statistics program written in the `OpenFiles` function. Would it be better to have the `PrintResults` function prompt for the heading?
6. Rewrite the Favorite Rock Group program using an enumerated type for class (or level). Which code is more readable and self-documenting?
7. Design a complete testing strategy for the Favorite Rock Group program.

Classes and Abstraction

KNOWLEDGE GOALS

- To understand the difference between specification and implementation of an abstract data type.
- To understand the concepts of encapsulation and abstraction.
- To understand how control and data abstraction facilitate modifiability and reuse.
- To understand the basic class design principles.
- To understand how encapsulation and information hiding are enforced by the C++ compiler.

SKILL GOALS

To be able to:
- Declare a C++ **class** type.
- Declare class objects, given the declaration of a **class** type.
- Write client code that invokes class member functions.
- Implement class member functions.
- Organize the code for a C++ class into two files: the specification (`.h`) file and the implementation file.
- Write a C++ class constructor.

Chapter 9 introduced the concept of control abstraction, in which the outward operation of a function is separated from its internal implementation. In the last two chapters, we learned how to define and use new data types. In this chapter, we add the analogous concept of *data abstraction*, the separation of a data type's logical properties from its implementation. Data abstraction, when combined with control abstraction, is embodied by the concept of the *abstract data type*. We first revisit the idea of abstract data types, and then introduce the C++ language feature through which we can implement them: the *class*. Using classes, we bind data and actions together into self-contained entities called objects—which is the foundation of object-oriented programming.

12.1 Abstract Data Types

We live in a complex world. Throughout the course of each day, we are constantly bombarded with information, facts, and details. To cope with complexity, the human mind engages in *abstraction*—the act of separating the essential qualities of an idea or object from the details of how it works or is composed.

With abstraction, we focus on the *what*, not the *how*. For example, our understanding of automobiles is largely based on abstraction. Most of us know *what* the engine does (it propels the car), but fewer of us know—or want to know—precisely *how* the engine works internally. Abstraction allows us to discuss, think about, and use automobiles without having to know everything about how they work.

In the world of software design, it is now recognized that abstraction is an absolute necessity for managing immense, complex software projects. In introductory computer science courses, programs are usually small (perhaps 50 to 200 lines of code) and understandable in their entirety by one person. By comparison, large commercial software products composed of hundreds of thousands—even millions—of lines of code cannot be designed, understood, or tested thoroughly without using abstraction in various forms. To manage complexity, software developers regularly use two important abstraction techniques: control abstraction and data abstraction.

In Chapter 9, we defined *control abstraction* as the separation of the logical properties of an action from its implementation. We engage in control abstraction whenever we write a function that reduces a complicated algorithm to an abstract action performed by a function call. By invoking a library function, as in the expression

`4.6 + sqrt(x)`

we depend only on the function's *specification*, a written description of what it does. We can use the function without having to know its *implementation* (the algorithms that accomplish the result). By invoking the `sqrt` function, our program is less complex because all the details involved in computing square roots remain hidden.

Abstract data type A data type whose properties (domain and operations) are specified independently of any particular implementation.

Abstraction techniques also apply to data. Every data type consists of a set of values (the domain) along with a collection of allowable operations on those values. As we mentioned in the introduction to this chapter, data abstraction is the separation of a data type's logical properties from its implementation details. Data abstraction comes into play when we need a data type that is not built into the programming language. We then define the new type as an abstract data type (ADT), concentrating only on its logical properties and deferring the details of its implementation.

As with control abstraction, an abstract data type has both a specification (the *what*) and an implementation (the *how*). The specification of an ADT describes the characteristics of the data values as well as the behavior of each of the operations on those values. The user of the ADT needs to understand only the specification, not the implementation, to use it.

Here's a very informal specification of a list ADT that contains integer numbers:

TYPE
  IntList
DOMAIN
  Each IntList value is a collection of up to 100 separate integer numbers.
OPERATIONS
  Create a list.
  Insert an item into the list.
  Delete an item from the list.
  Search the list for an item.
  Return the current length of the list.
  Sort the list into ascending order.
  Print the list.

Notice the complete absence of implementation details. We have not mentioned how the data might actually be stored in a program (it could be in an array, or on a file, or in a struct) or how the operations might be implemented (for example, the length operation could keep the number of elements in a variable, or it could count the elements each time it is called). Concealing the implementation details reduces complexity for the user and also shields the user from changes in the implementation.

Following is the specification of another ADT, one that might be useful for representing TimeOfDay in a program.

TYPE
  TimeOfDay
DOMAIN
  Each TimeOfDay value is a time of day in the form of hours, minutes, and seconds.
OPERATIONS
  Create a time object.
  Print (or write) the time.
  Return an object containing the time, incremented by one second.
  Compare two times for equality.
  Determine if one time is "less than" (comes before) another.

Although we refer to "time" in our informal list of operations, we are careful to call this ADT "TimeOfDay" to differentiate it from elapsed time, which also might be a useful ADT.

The specification of an ADT defines data values and operations in an abstract form that can be given as documentation to both the user and the programmer. Ultimately, of course, the ADT must be implemented in program code. To implement an ADT, the programmer must do two things:

1. Choose a concrete data representation of the abstract data, using data types that already exist.
2. Implement each of the allowable operations in terms of program instructions.

Data representation The concrete form of data used to represent the abstract values of an abstract data type.

To implement the IntList ADT, we could choose a concrete data representation consisting of a record with two items: a 100-element array in which to store the items and an `int` variable that keeps track of the number of items in the list. To implement the IntList operations, we must create algorithms based on the chosen data representation.

To implement the TimeOfDay ADT, we might use three `int` variables for the data representation—one for the hours, one for the minutes, and one for the seconds. Alternatively, we might use three strings as the data representation. Or we might keep the TimeOfDay as seconds and convert the TimeOfDay to hours, minutes, and seconds as needed. The specification of the ADT does not confine us to any particular data representation. As long as we satisfy the specification, we are free to choose among the various alternative data representations and their associated algorithms. Our choice may be based on time efficiency (the speed at which the algorithms execute), space efficiency (the economical use of memory space), or simplicity and readability of the algorithms. Over time, you will acquire knowledge and experience that will help you decide which implementation is best for a particular context.

> **THEORETICAL FOUNDATIONS**
> **Categories of Abstract Data Type Operations**
>
> In general, the basic operations associated with an abstract data type fall into one of three categories: **constructors**, **transformers**, and **observers**.
>
> An operation that initializes a new instance of an ADT (such as a list) is a constructor. Operations that change the value of an ADT, such as inserting an item into a list, are transformers (in the programming languages research community, they are also called mutators because they yield a mutation of the ADT's value). An operation that takes one list and appends it to the end of a second list is also a transformer.
>
> A Boolean function that returns `true` if a list is empty and `false` if it contains any components is an example of an observer (also known as an accessor). A Boolean function that tests whether a certain value is in the list is another kind of observer.
>
> Some operations are combinations of observers and constructors. An operation that takes two lists and merges them into a (new) third list is both an observer (of the two existing lists) and a constructor (of the third list).
>
> In addition to the three basic categories of ADT operations, two other categories are sometimes defined: **destructors** and **iterators**. A destructor is the opposite of a constructor; it cleans up an instance of an ADT just before its storage is released for reuse. An example of an iterator is an operation that returns the first item in a list when it is called initially and returns the next item with each successive call.
>
> **Constructor** An operation that initializes a new instance (variable) of an ADT.
>
> **Transformer** An operation that changes the value of the ADT; also known as a mutator.
>
> **Observer** An operation that allows us to observe the state of an instance of an ADT without changing it; also known as an accessor.
>
> **Destructor** An operation that cleans up the state of an ADT instance just prior to releasing its storage for reuse.
>
> **Iterator** An operation that allows us to process—one at a time—all the components in an instance of an ADT.

QUICK CHECK

12.1.1 What does the specification of an ADT describe? (pp. 596–597)

12.1.2 What two things must a programmer do to implement an ADT? (p. 597)

12.2 C++ Classes

In previous chapters, we have treated data values as passive quantities to be acted upon by functions. That is, we have passed values to and from functions as arguments, and our functions performed some operation. We took the same approach even when we defined new data types. For example, in Chapter 10, we viewed a student record as passive data, and we implemented operations on the data type as functions to which we passed a record. Similarly, in Chapter 11, we treated an array as a passive quantity, passing it to functions to be processed. (See **FIGURE 12.1**.)

This separation of operations and data does not correspond very well with the notion of an abstract data type. After all, an ADT consists of *both* data values and operations on those values. It is preferable to view an ADT as defining an *active* data structure—one that contains both data and operations within a single, cohesive unit (see **FIGURE 12.2**). C++ supports this view through the structured type known as a class.

> **Class** A data type in a programming language that is used to represent an abstract data type.

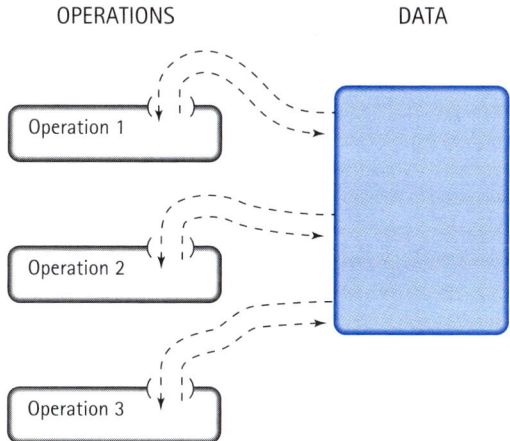

FIGURE 12.1 Data and Operations as Separate Entities

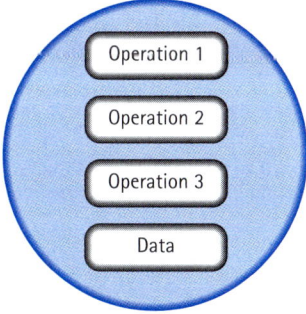

FIGURE 12.2 Data and Operations Bound into a Single Unit

> **Class member** A component of a class. Class members may be either data or functions.

In Figure 10.2, we listed the four structured types available in the C++ language: the array, the struct, the union, and the class. A class can be used to represent a record but is almost always designed so that its components (class members) include not only data but also functions that manipulate that data.[1]

Here is the syntax template for the C++ `class`:

Class Declaration

```
class TypeName
{
AccessModifier: MemberList
      .
      .
      .
} VariableList ;
```

AccessModifier is defined as either of the two keywords, `public` or `private`:

AccessModifier

$$\begin{cases} \text{public} \\ \text{private} \end{cases}$$

MemberList is one or more declarations of fields or functions:

MemberList

$$\begin{cases} \text{DataType MemberName ;} \\ \text{FunctionPrototype ;} \end{cases}$$
$$\begin{cases} \text{DataType MemberName ;} \\ \text{FunctionPrototype ;} \end{cases}$$
$$\quad \vdots$$

---

[1]. In C++, a struct is almost identical to a class. But because of its heritage from the C struct construct, most programmers use `class` to implement an ADT, and limit their use of `struct` to applications where a record is needed that has no associated operations.

Here is a C++ class declaration corresponding to the TimeOfDay ADT that we defined in the previous section:

```
class TimeOfDay
{
public:
  TimeOfDay();
  // Creates a zero TimeOfDay object
  TimeOfDay(int hours, int minutes, int seconds);
  // Creates a TimeOfDay object with the given time
  TimeOfDay Increment() const;
  // Returns a TimeOfDay object that is incremented by one second
  void Write() const;
  // Writes the TimeOfDay object to cout
  bool Equal(TimeOfDay otherTime) const;
  // Returns true if this TimeOfDay object equals otherTime
  bool LessThan(TimeOfDay otherTime) const;
  // Returns true if this TimeOfDay object is earlier than otherTime
private:
  int hours;
  int minutes;
  int seconds;
};
```

(For now, ignore the word **const** appearing in some of the function prototypes. We explain this use of **const** later in the chapter.)

The `TimeOfDay` class has nine members—four member functions (`Increment`, `Write`, `Equal`, `LessThan`), three member variables (`hours`, `minutes`, `seconds`), and two strange-looking constructs that look something like functions, but have no return value. The latter are examples of a special function called a *class constructor*. A constructor is a member function that is implicitly invoked whenever a class object is declared (created). A constructor function has an unusual name: the name of the class itself. It is not preceded by either a return type or the keyword **void**.

Our class declaration includes two constructors, differentiated by their parameter lists. The first constructor is parameterless and initializes a `TimeOfDay` object to some default value, such as 00:00:00, when it is declared. A parameterless constructor is known in C++ as a *default constructor*. The second has three **int** parameters, which are used to initialize the private data members when a class object is declared.

```
TimeOfDay startTime;              // Create a 0 TimeOfDay object
TimeOfDay endTime(10, 24, 3);     // Create a TimeOfDay object with 10
                                  //   hours, 24 minutes, and 3 seconds
```

As you might guess, the three data member variables (`hours`, `minutes`, and `seconds`) form the concrete data representation for the TimeOfDay ADT. The familiar-looking member functions correspond to the operations we listed for the TimeOfDay ADT: return a `TimeOfDay` object incremented by one second, print the time, compare two times for equality, and determine if one `TimeOfDay` object is less than another. Although the `Equal` function compares two `TimeOfDay` variables for equality, its parameter list has only one parameter—a `TimeOfDay` variable. Similarly, the `LessThan` function has only one parameter, even though it compares two times. We'll see why when we look at the implementation of the class.

Like a `struct` declaration, the declaration of the `TimeOfDay` class defines a data type but does not create variables of the type. Class variables (more often referred to as class objects or class instances) are created by using ordinary variable declarations, as shown earlier. Any software that declares and manipulates `TimeOfDay` objects is called a client of the class.

> **Class object (class instance)** A variable of a class type.
>
> **Client** Software that declares and manipulates objects of a particular class.

When you look at the preceding declaration of the `TimeOfDay` class, you will see the reserved words `public` and `private`, each followed by a colon. Data and/or functions declared following the word `public` and before the word `private` constitute the *public interface*; clients can access these class members directly. Class members declared after the word `private` are considered private information and are inaccessible to clients. If client code attempts to access a private item, the compiler will produce an error message.

Private class members can be accessed only by the class's member functions. In the `TimeOfDay` class, the private variables `hours`, `minutes`, and `seconds` can be accessed only within the member functions `Increment`, `Write`, `Equal`, and `LessThan`, not by client code. This separation of class members into private and public parts is a hallmark of ADT design. To preserve the properties of an ADT correctly, an instance of the ADT should be manipulated *only* through the operations that form the public interface. We will have more to say about this issue later in the chapter.

C++ does not require you to declare public and private class members in a fixed order. By default, class members are private; the word `public` is used to "open up" any members for public access. Once you have done so, if you wish to declare subsequent members as private, you must insert the `private` reserved word, as we did in the preceding example. A class can contain any number of public and private sections.

Regarding public versus private accessibility, we can now describe more fully the difference between C++ structs and classes. C++ defines a struct to be a class whose members are all, by default, public. In contrast, members of a class are, by default, private. Furthermore, it is common practice to use only data—not functions—as members of a struct. Note that you *can* declare struct members to be private and you *can* include member functions in a struct—but then you might as well use a class! Hence, most programmers use the struct in the manner that is traditional from C, as a way to represent a record structure, and implement ADTs only with classes.

MATTERS OF STYLE   Declaring Public and Private Class Members

Because the members of a class are private by default, we could write the **TimeOfDay** class declaration as follows:

```
class TimeOfDay
{                       // Declarations automatically start as private
  int hours;
  int minutes;
  int seconds;
public:                 // Here they switch to public
  TimeOfDay();
  TimeOfDay(int hours, int minutes, int seconds);
  TimeOfDay Increment() const;
  void Write() const;
  bool Equal(TimeOfDay otherTime) const;
  bool LessThan(TimeOfDay otherTime) const;
};
```

The variables **hours**, **minutes**, and **seconds** are automatically private. The public part in this example extends from the word **public** to the end of the class declaration.

Our preference is to locate the public part first so as to focus attention on the public interface and deemphasize the private data representation. This style of organizing the members of a class means that we must explicitly indicate those members that are private, which we also believe is more self-documenting.

```
class TimeOfDay
{
public:
  TimeOfDay();
  TimeOfDay(int initHours, int initMinutes, int initSeconds);
  TimeOfDay Increment() const;
  void Write() const;
  bool Equal(TimeOfDay otherTime) const;
  bool LessThan(TimeOfDay otherTime) const;
private:
  int hours;
  int minutes;
  int seconds;
};
```

In this version, the reader immediately sees the public interface for the class, and there is no question that the data members are private. We use this style throughout the remainder of the book.

Implementing the Member Functions

Let's take a look at how we implement the `TimeOfDay` class. There are many subtle details that we have yet to cover formally, and we'll point some of them out along the way. But don't worry: We'll come back to the C++ rules that govern all of these issues later. For now, we want to drill down into some concrete code, so that you can begin to get a sense of how a real class is implemented.

Constructors

The constructors for `TimeOfDay` are very straightforward. In the default constructor, 0 is stored in each data field.

```
TimeOfDay::TimeOfDay()
{
  hours = 0;
  minutes = 0;
  seconds = 0;
}
```

In the parameterized constructor, the first parameter is stored in `hours`, the second is stored in `minutes`, and the third is stored in `seconds`.

```
TimeOfDay::TimeOfDay(int initHours, int initMinutes,
                    int initSeconds)
{
  hours = initHours;
  minutes = initMinutes;
  seconds = initSeconds;
}
```

Note that the name of the class must precede the name of each function, with the `::` scope resolution operator appearing in between. This format indicates to which class the function definition belongs.

Increment

In this function we are returning a new object that is the same as the current object, except that it has been incremented by one second. In C++, we also refer to the current object as the *instance*, meaning the object to which a member function is *applied*. Keep in mind that member functions are defined within a class; thus, when you invoke one of them, it is running within the context of the other declarations within its class. This is a different notion of executing a function than we're used to—the member function is not running separately at the level of `main`.

We'll soon take a closer look at the semantics of member function execution. For now, just note that we use different terminology (instance to which it is applied) as a way to remind ourselves that a function is executing in a different environment.

The first step in **Increment** is to declare a duplicate of the `TimeOfDay` object to which the function is applied. To do so, we need to call the parameterized constructor, passing it the data members of the current object.

```
TimeOfDay TimeOfDay::Increment() const
{
  // Create a duplicate of instance
  TimeOfDay result(hours, minutes, seconds); // Constructor call
```

Notice that we do not pass anything into the `Increment` function. Because it resides inside the current object (instance), it has access to all of the values it needs to create the new object.

Next the `seconds` data member (of the duplicate) is incremented. If this action makes the value greater than 59, `seconds` must be set to 0, and the `minutes` data member must be incremented. If it makes the value of `minutes` greater than 59, then it must be set to 0, and the `hours` data member must be incremented. If the `hours` data member becomes greater than 23, it must be set to 0.

```
  result.seconds++;                    // Increment seconds
  if (result.seconds > 59)             // Adjust if seconds carry
  {
    result.seconds = 0;
    result.minutes++;
    if (result.minutes > 59)           // Adjust if minutes carry
    {
      result.minutes = 0;
      result.hours++;
      if (result.hours > 23)           // Adjust if hours carry
        result.hours = 0;
    }
  }
  return result;
}
```

Look closely at the difference between how we accessed the member fields of the instance in the constructor call and how we access the fields of the `result` object. We can refer directly to members of the instance (`hours, minutes, seconds`). When we want to access members of another object, however, we must use dot notation, just as we did for a struct (`result.hours, result.minutes, result.seconds`).

Wait—how can we access the data members of the `result` object? Aren't they private? Yes, but in C++, the `private` keyword only restricts access by client code. Within the implementation of a class, we are allowed to access the private members of any objects of the same class.

Write
To make the time uniform, we want to print two digits for each field, so we must check whether the value in each field is a single digit. If it is, we must print a 0 before we print the value. Again, notice that nothing is passed into `Write`—it automatically has access to the member fields of the instance.

```
void TimeOfDay::Write() const
{
  if (hours < 10)
    cout << '0';
  cout << hours << ':';
  if (minutes < 10)
    cout << '0';
  cout << minutes << ':';
  if (seconds < 10)
    cout << '0';
  cout << seconds;
}
```

LessThan

This Boolean operation compares two objects of class `TimeOfDay`: The first is the instance, and the second is passed in through a parameter of the function. As we saw with **Increment**, the data members of the instance can be accessed directly, but the data members of the other object must be accessed with dot notation.

How do we compare times? First we check the hours. If they are the same, we then check the minutes. If they are the same, we check the seconds. Let's look at this process in algorithm form.

```
LessThan(In: otherTime)
   Return value: Boolean

IF (hours < otherTime.hours)
   Return True
ELSE IF (hours > otherTime.hours)
   Return False
ELSE IF (minutes < otherTime.minutes)
   Return True
ELSE IF (minutes > otherTime.minutes)
   Return False
ELSE IF (seconds < otherTime.seconds)
   Return True
ELSE
   Return False
```

This algorithm can also be expressed using logical operators, as shown here:

```
hours < otherTime.hours || hours == otherTime.hours
    && minutes < otherTime.minutes || hours == otherTime.hours
    && minutes == otherTime.minutes
    && seconds < otherTime.seconds)
```

Which depiction is better? This is purely a matter of style. The first version is easier to read and, therefore, to debug. The second version is more elegant. In this case we opt for elegance.

```
bool TimeOfDay::LessThan(TimeOfDay otherTime) const
{
  return (hours < otherTime.hours || hours == otherTime.hours
          && minutes < otherTime.minutes || hours == otherTime.hours
          && minutes == otherTime.minutes
          && seconds < otherTime.seconds);
}
```

Equal

As in the `LessThan` function, the two objects being compared by `Equal` are the instance to which the function is applied and the parameter. The function returns `true` if all three data fields are identical and `false` otherwise.

```
bool TimeOfDay::Equal(TimeOfDay otherTime) const
{
  return (hours == otherTime.hours
         && minutes == otherTime.minutes
         && seconds == otherTime.seconds);
}
```

Classes, Objects, and Members

It is important to restate that a class is a type, not an object. Like any type, a class is a pattern from which you can create many concrete values of that type. With a class, these values are called objects. We say that we *instantiate* the class to make an object. An object is an instance (concrete example) of its class. Think of a class as a cookie cutter and objects of that class as the cookies.

The declarations

```
TimeOfDay time1;
TimeOfDay time2(17, 58, 2);
```

create two objects that are instances of the `TimeOfDay` class: `time1` and `time2`.

The pattern specified by the private data member declarations in the class is that each object of class `TimeOfDay` should have member variables called `hours`, `minutes`, and `seconds`. Thus `time1` has its own variables called `hours`, `minutes`, and `seconds`, and `time2` has a separate set of variables called `hours`, `minutes`, and `seconds`. `time1`'s `hours`, `minutes`, and `seconds` contain the values 0, 0, and 0, whereas `time2`'s variables contain the values 17, 58, and 2. **FIGURE 12.3** provides a visual image of the objects `time1` and `time2`.

(In truth, the C++ compiler does not waste memory by placing duplicate copies of a member function—say, `Increment`—into both `time1` and `time2`. Instead, the compiler

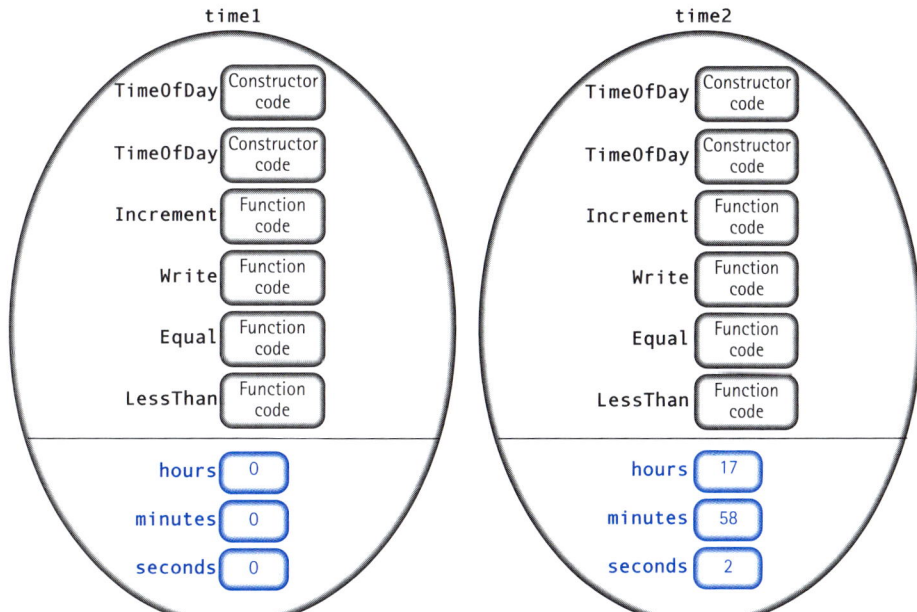

FIGURE 12.3 Conceptual View of Two Objects

generates just one physical copy of `Increment`, and it executes this one copy of the function whenever it is called from any class instance. Nevertheless, the diagram in Figure 12.3 is a good mental picture of two different class objects.)

Be sure you are clear about the difference between the terms *object* and *member*. Figure 12.3 depicts two objects of the `TimeOfDay` class, and each object has nine members.

Built-in Operations on Objects

In many ways, programmer-defined classes are like built-in types. For example, you can declare as many objects of a class as you like. You can pass objects as arguments to functions and return them as function values. Like any variable, an object can be automatic (that is, it is created each time control reaches its declaration and destroyed when control exits its surrounding block) or static (that is, it is created once when control reaches its declaration and destroyed when the program terminates).

In other ways, C++ treats structs and classes differently from built-in types. Most of the built-in operations do not apply to structs or classes. For example, you cannot use the + operator to add two `TimeOfDay` objects, nor can you use the == operator to compare two `TimeOfDay` objects for equality.

Two built-in operations that are valid for struct and class objects are member selection (.) and assignment (=). As with structs, you select an individual member of a class by using dot notation. That is, you write the name of the class object, then a dot, then the member name. The statement

```cpp
TimeOfDay time3 = time1.Increment();
```

invokes the `Increment` function for the `time1` object, presumably to create an object that is one second later than `time1`. The other built-in operation, assignment, performs aggregate assignment of one class object to another with the following semantics: If x and y are objects of the same class, then the assignment x = y copies the data members of y into x. Following is a fragment of client code that demonstrates member selection and assignment:

```cpp
int    inputHours;
int    inputMinutes;
int    inputSeconds;

TimeOfDay time1(5, 20, 0);

cout << "Enter hours, minutes, seconds: ";
cin >> inputHours >> inputMinutes >> inputSeconds;
TimeOfDay time2(inputHours, inputMinutes, inputSeconds);

if (time1.LessThan(time2))
   DoSomething();
time2 = time1;                   // Member-by-member assignment
time2.Write();                   // 05:20:00 has been output
```

From the very beginning, you have been working with C++ classes in a particular context: input and output. The standard header file `iostream` contains the declarations of two classes—`istream` and `ostream`—that manage a program's I/O. The C++ standard library declares `cin` and `cout` to be objects of these classes:

```cpp
istream cin;
ostream cout;
```

The `istream` class has many member functions, two of which—the `get` function and the `ignore` function—you have already seen in statements like these:

```
cin.get(someChar);
cin.ignore(200, '\n');
```

As with any C++ class object, we use dot notation to select a particular member function to invoke.

You have also used C++ classes when performing file I/O. The header file `fstream` contains declarations for the `ifstream` and `ofstream` classes. The client code

```
ifstream dataFile;
dataFile.open("input.dat");
```

declares an `ifstream` class object named `dataFile`, then invokes the class member function `open` to try to open the file `input.dat` for input.

We will not examine in detail the `istream`, `ostream`, `ifstream`, and `ofstream` classes and all of their member functions. To study these classes would be beyond the goals of this book. What is important to recognize is that classes and objects are fundamental to all I/O activity in a C++ program.

Class Scope

We said earlier that member names must be unique within a struct. Additionally, in Chapter 9 we mentioned four kinds of scope in C++: local scope, global scope, namespace scope, and *class scope*. Class scope applies to the member names within structs, unions, and classes. To say that a member name has class scope means that the name is bound to that class (or struct or union). If the same identifier happens to be declared outside the class, the two identifiers are unrelated.

Let's look at an example. The `TimeOfDay` class has a member function named `Write`. In the same program, another class (say, `SomeClass`) could also have a member function named `Write`. Furthermore, the program might have a global `Write` function that is completely unrelated to any classes. If the program has statements like

```
TimeOfDay checkInTime;
SomeClass someObject;
int n;
    .
    .
    .
checkInTime.Write();
someObject.Write();
Write(n);
```

then the C++ compiler has no trouble distinguishing among the three `Write` functions. The first two are function applications, where the dot notation denotes member selection in the context of the specific class instance (object). The first statement invokes the `Write` function of the `TimeOfDay` class for the `checkInTime` object, and the second statement invokes the `Write` function of the `SomeClass` class for the `someObject` instance of that class. The final statement does not use dot notation, so the compiler knows that the global `Write` function is being called.

QUICK CHECK

12.2.1 Which C++ construct is designed to implement ADTs? (p. 599)

12.2.2 What distinguishes a class constructor from other member functions? (p. 601)

12.2.3 What is an *active* data structure? (p. 599)

12.2.4 Any software that declares and manipulates objects of a particular class X is called what? (p. 602)

12.2.5 Write the declaration of a class object, called `today`, of class `Date`. (pp. 607–608)

12.2.6 How would you call member function `GetDay` (which takes no parameters) of an object called `today` of class `Date`? (pp. 608–609)

12.3 Information Hiding

Abstraction barrier The invisible wall around an object that encapsulates implementation details. The wall can be breached only through the public interface.

Black box A device whose inner workings remain hidden from view.

Information hiding The encapsulation and hiding of implementation details to keep the user of an abstraction from depending on or incorrectly manipulating these details.

Conceptually, an object has an invisible wall around it. This wall, called the abstraction barrier, protects private data and functions from being accessed by client code. The same barrier also prohibits the object from directly accessing data and functions outside the object. This barrier is a critical characteristic of classes and abstract data types.

For an object to share information with the outside world (that is, with clients), there must be a gap in the abstraction barrier. This gap is the public interface—the members declared to be `public`. If the only public members are functions and constants, and if we keep all of the member variables private, then the only way that a client can manipulate the internal values of the object is indirectly—through the operations in the public interface.

Electrical engineers work with a similar concept called a black box. A black box is a module or device whose inner workings remain hidden from view. The user of the black box depends only on the written specification of *what* it does, not on *how* it does it. The user connects wires to the interface and assumes that the module works correctly if it satisfies the specification (see **FIGURE 12.4**).

In software design, the black box concept is referred to as information hiding. Information hiding protects the user of a class from having to know all of the details of its implementation. Information hiding also assures the class's implementor that the user cannot directly access any private code or data to compromise the correctness of the implementation.

You have already been introduced to encapsulation and information hiding in this book. In Chapter 8, we discussed the possibility of hiding a function's implementation in a separate file. In this chapter, we will see how to hide the implementations of class member functions by placing them in files that are kept separate from the client code.

The creator of a C++ class is free to choose which members will be private and which will be public. However, making data members public (as in a struct) allows the client to

FIGURE 12.4 A Black Box

inspect and modify the data directly. Because information hiding is so fundamental to data abstraction, most classes exhibit a typical pattern: The private part contains data, and the public part contains the functions that manipulate the data.

The `TimeOfDay` class exemplifies this organization. The data members `hours`, `minutes`, and `seconds` are private, so the compiler prohibits a client from accessing them directly. As a consequence, the following client statement results in a compile-time error:

```
TimeOfDay checkInTime;

checkInTime.hours = 9;     // Prohibited in client code
```

Because only the class's member functions can access the private data, the creator of the class can offer a reliable product, knowing that external access to the private data is impossible. If it is acceptable to let the client *inspect* (but not modify) private data members, then a class might provide observer functions. The `TimeOfDay` class has four such functions: `Write`, `Increment`, `Equal`, and `LessThan`. Because these observer functions are not intended to modify the private data, they are declared with the word `const` following the parameter list:

```
void Write() const;
TimeOfDay Increment() const;
bool Equal(TimeOfDay) const;
bool LessThan(TimeOfDay) const;
```

C++ refers to these functions as `const` *member functions*. Within the body of a `const` member function, a compile-time error occurs if any statement tries to modify any of the private instance variables. Although not required by the language, it is good practice to declare as `const` those member functions that should not modify private data within the object.

User-Written Header Files

As you create your own user-defined data types, you will often find that a data type can be useful in more than one program. For example, suppose you are working on several programs that need an enumeration type consisting of the names of the 12 months of the year. Instead of typing the statement

```
enum Months
{
   JANUARY, FEBRUARY, MARCH, APRIL, MAY, JUNE,
   JULY, AUGUST, SEPTEMBER, OCTOBER, NOVEMBER, DECEMBER
};
```

at the beginning of every program that uses the `Months` type, you can put this statement into a separate file named, say, `months.h`. You can then use `months.h` just as you use system-supplied header files such as `iostream` and `cmath`. By using an `#include` directive, you ask the C++ preprocessor to physically insert the contents of the file into your program. (Although many C++ systems use the filename extension `.h` [or no extension at all] to denote header files, other systems use extensions such as `.hpp` or `.hxx`.)

When you enclose the name of a header file in angle brackets, as in

```
#include <iostream>
```

```
                                          Standard include directory
                                                iostream
                                          ┌─────────────────┐
                                          │ ─────────────── │
                                   Insert │ ─────────────── │
                                ◄──────   │ ─────────────── │
  ┌─────────────────────────┐             └─────────────────┘
  │ #include <iostream>     │
  │                         │                Local directory
  │ #include "months.h"     │                   months.h
  │                         │             ┌─────────────────────────┐
  │ int main( )      Insert │             │ enum Months             │
  │                ◄──────  │             │ {                       │
  │ {                       │             │   JANUARY, FEBRUARY, MARCH, │
  │   ─────                 │             │   APRIL, MAY, JUNE, JULY,   │
  │   ─────                 │             │   AUGUST, SEPTEMBER, OCTOBER,│
  │   ─────                 │             │   NOVEMBER, DECEMBER    │
  │                         │             │ };                      │
  └─────────────────────────┘             └─────────────────────────┘
```

FIGURE 12.5 Including Header Files

the preprocessor looks for the file in the standard **include** directory, which contains all the header files supplied by the C++ system. If you enclose the name of a header file in double quotes,

`#include "months.h"`

then the preprocessor will look for the file in the programmer's current directory. This mechanism allows us to write our own header files that contain type declarations and constant declarations. We can use a simple **#include** directive instead of retyping the declarations in every program that needs them (see **FIGURE 12.5**).

Header files also play an important role in preserving information hiding when we implement a class, as we see next.

Specification and Implementation Files

An abstract data type consists of two parts: a specification and an implementation. The specification describes the behavior of the data type without reference to its implementation. The implementation creates an abstraction barrier by hiding both the concrete data representation and the code for the operations.

The **TimeOfDay** class declaration serves as the specification of **TimeOfDay**. This declaration presents the public interface to the user in the form of function prototypes. To implement the **TimeOfDay** class, we provided function definitions for all the member functions.

In C++, it is customary (but not required) to package the class declaration and the class implementation into separate files. One file—the *specification file*—is a header (.h) file containing only the class declaration. The second file—the *implementation file*—contains the function definitions for the class member functions. Let's look first at the specification file.

The Specification File
Following is the specification file for the **TimeOfDay** class. This class declaration is the same as the one we presented earlier with one exception: We include function preconditions and postconditions to specify the semantics of the member functions as unambiguously as possible for the user of the class.

```
//*****************************************************************
// SPECIFICATION FILE (TimeOfDay.h)
// This file gives the specification
// of a TimeOfDay abstract data type
//*****************************************************************

class TimeOfDay
{
public:
  // Constructors
  TimeOfDay();
  // Post: hours, minutes, and seconds have been set to 0
  TimeOfDay(int initHours, int initMinutes, int initSeconds);
  // Pre:  0 <= hours <= 23, 0 <= minutes <= 59, 0 <= seconds <= 59
  // Post: TimeOfDay is set according to the incoming parameters
  TimeOfDay Increment() const;
  // Post: Returns a TimeOfDay that is the instance plus one,
  //       23:59:59 wrapping around to 0:0:0
  void Write() const;
  // Post: Instance has been output in the form HH:MM:SS
  bool Equal(TimeOfDay otherTimeOfDay) const;
  // Post: Returns true if this instance equals otherTime,
  //       false otherwise
  bool LessThan(TimeOfDay otherTimeOfDay) const;
  // Post: Returns true if this instance comes earlier than
  //       otherTime, false otherwise
private:
  int hours;
  int minutes;
  int seconds;
};
```

In principle, a specification file should not reveal any implementation details to the user of the class. The file should specify *what* each member function does without disclosing *how* it does it. However, as you can see in the preceding class declaration, one implementation detail is visible to the user: The concrete data representation of our ADT is listed in the private part. Nonetheless, the data representation is still considered hidden information in the sense that the compiler prohibits client code from accessing the data directly.

Here is a client program that manipulates two objects of class `TimeOfDay`. This program is written without knowing how the class is implemented.

```
//******************************************
// A program to create two time objects
// and manipulate them.
//******************************************
#include <iostream>
#include "TimeOfDay.h"            // For TimeOfDay class
using namespace std;
```

```cpp
int main()
{
  TimeOfDay time1(5, 30, 0);      // Instantiate two TimeOfDay objects
  TimeOfDay time2;
  int   loopCount;

  cout << "time1: ";              // Print them and compare them
  time1.Write();
  cout << "  time2: ";
  time2.Write();
  cout << endl;
  if (time1.Equal(time2))
    cout << "Times are equal" << endl;
  else
    cout << "Times are NOT equal" << endl;

  time2 = time1;                  // Set them equal

  cout << "time1: ";              // Print them and compare them
  time1.Write();
  cout << "  time2: ";
  time2.Write();
  cout << endl;

  if (time1.Equal(time2))
    cout << "Times are equal" << endl;
  else
    cout << "Times are NOT equal" << endl;

  time2.Increment();              // Increment one, print and compare
  cout << "New time2: ";
  time2.Write();
  cout << endl;
  if (time1.LessThan(time2))
    cout << "time1 is less than time2" << endl;
  else
    cout << "time1 is NOT less than time2" << endl;

  if (time2.LessThan(time1))
    cout << "time2 is less than time1" << endl;
  else
    cout << "time2 is NOT less than time1" << endl;

  TimeOfDay time4(23, 59, 55);    // Instantiate one near the maximum
  cout << "Incrementing time1 from 23:59:55:" << endl;
  for (loopCount = 1; loopCount <= 10; loopCount++)
  {
    time4.Write();
    cout << ' ';
    time4 = time4.Increment();    // Check that it overflows properly
  }
  cout << endl;
  return 0;
}
```

Output:

```
time1: 05:30:00   time2: 00:00:00
Times are NOT equal
time1: 05:30:00   time2: 05:30:00
Times are equal
New time2: 05:30:00
time1 is NOT less than time2
time2 is NOT less than time1
Incrementing time1 from 23:59:55:
23:59:55 23:59:56 23:59:57 23:59:58 23:59:59 00:00:00 00:00:01 00:00:02
00:00:03 00:00:04
```

The Implementation File

The specification (.h) file for the `TimeOfDay` class contains only the class declaration. The implementation file must provide the function definitions for all the class member functions. In the opening comments of the implementation file below, we document the file name as `TimeOfDay.cpp`. Your system may use a different file name suffix for source code files—perhaps .c, .C, or .cxx.

Here is the code shown previously. We do not repeat the documentation from the function prototypes in the specification file. We do add documentation for the programmers who must maintain the code in case clarification is necessary. Immediately following the program code, we explain the new features.

```cpp
//*****************************************************************
// IMPLEMENTATION FILE (TimeOfDay.cpp)
// This file implements the TimeOfDay member functions
//*****************************************************************
#include "TimeOfDay.h"
#include <iostream>

using namespace std;

TimeOfDay::TimeOfDay()
{
   hours = 0;
   minutes = 0;
   seconds = 0;
}

//*****************************************************************

TimeOfDay::TimeOfDay(int initHours, int initMinutes, int initSeconds)
{
   hours = initHours;
   minutes = initMinutes;
   seconds = initSeconds;
}
```

```cpp
//*******************************************************************
TimeOfDay TimeOfDay::Increment() const
{
  // Create a duplicate of instance and increment duplicate
  TimeOfDay result(hours, minutes, seconds);
  result.seconds = result.seconds++;   // Increment seconds
  if (result.seconds > 59)             // Adjust if seconds carry
  {
    result.seconds = 0;
    result.minutes = result.minutes++;
    if (result.minutes > 59)           // Adjust if minutes carry
    {
      result.minutes = 0;
      result.hours = result.hours++;
      if (result.hours > 23)           // Adjust if hours carry
        result.hours = 0;
    }
  }
  return result;
}

//*******************************************************************
void TimeOfDay::Write() const
{
  // Insert extra 0 if there is only one digit in a place
  if (hours < 10)
    cout << '0';
  cout << hours << ':';
  if (minutes < 10)
    cout << '0';
  cout << minutes << ':';
  if (seconds < 10)
    cout << '0';
  cout << seconds;
}

//*******************************************************************
bool TimeOfDay::Equal(TimeOfDay otherTime) const
{
  return (hours == otherTime.hours
          && minutes == otherTime.minutes
          && seconds == otherTime.seconds);
}

//*******************************************************************
bool TimeOfDay::LessThan(TimeOfDay otherTime) const
{
  return (hours < otherTime.hours || hours == otherTime.hours
          && minutes < otherTime.minutes || hours == otherTime.hours
          && minutes == otherTime.minutes
          && seconds < otherTime.seconds);
}
```

This implementation file demonstrates several important points.

1. The file begins with the preprocessor directive

   `#include "TimeOfDay.h"`

   Both the implementation file and the client code must **#include** the specification file. **FIGURE 12.6** illustrates this shared access to the specification file, which guarantees that all declarations related to an abstraction are consistent. That is, both `client.cpp` and `TimeOfDay.cpp` must reference the same declaration of the `TimeOfDay` class located in `TimeOfDay.h`.

2. In the heading of each function definition, the name of the member function is prefixed by the class name (`TimeOfDay`) and the C++ scope resolution operator (`::`). As discussed earlier, several different classes might potentially have member functions with the same name—say, `Write`. In addition, there may be a global `Write` function that is not a member of any class. The scope resolution operator eliminates any uncertainty about which particular function is being defined.

3. Although clients of a class must use the dot operator to refer to class members (for example, `startTime.Write()`), members of a class refer to one another directly without using dot notation. Looking at the body of the `Increment` function, you can see that the statements refer directly to the member variables `hours`, `minutes`, and `seconds` without using the dot operator.

   An exception to this rule occurs when a member function manipulates two or more class objects. Consider the `Equal` function. Suppose that the client code has two class objects, `startTime` and `endTime`, and uses the statement

   ```
   if (startTime.Equal(endTime))
       .
       .
       .
   ```

   At execution time, the `startTime` object is the object to which the `Equal` function is applied. In the body of the `Equal` function, the relational expression

   `hours == otherTime.hours`

   refers to members of two different objects. The unadorned identifier `hours` refers to the `hours` member of the object (instance) for which the function is invoked (that is,

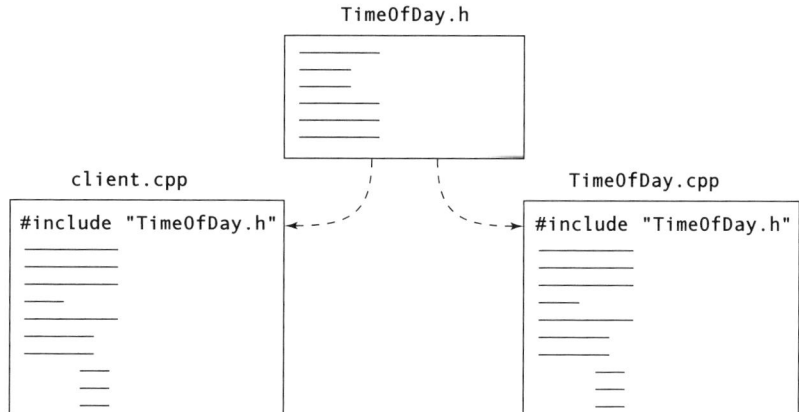

FIGURE 12.6 Shared Access to a Specification File

startTime). The expression `otherTime.hours` refers to the `hours` member of the object that is passed to the parameter, `otherTime`, as a function argument: `endTime`.

4. `Increment`, `Write`, `Equal`, and `LessThan` are observer functions; they do not modify the private data. Because we have declared them to be `const` member functions, the compiler prevents these functions from assigning new values to the private data. The use of `const` is both an aid to the user of the class (a visual signal that this function does not modify any private data) and an aid to the class implementor (a way of preventing accidental modification of the data). Note that the word `const` must appear in both the function prototype (in the class declaration) and the heading of the function definition.

Compiling and Linking a Multifile Program

Now that we have created a specification file and an implementation file for our `TimeOfDay` class, how do we (or any other programmer) make use of these files in our programs? Let's begin our exploration of this issue by looking at the notion of *separate compilation* of source code files.

In earlier chapters, we have referred to the concept of a multifile program—a program divided up into several files containing source code. In C++, each of these files may be compiled separately and at different times. In this process, the compiler translates each source code file into an object code file. **FIGURE 12.7** shows a multifile program consisting of the source code files `myprog.cpp`, `file2.cpp`, and `file3.cpp`. We can compile each of these files independently, yielding the object code files `myprog.obj`, `file2.obj`, and `file3.obj`. Although each `.obj` file contains machine language code, it is not yet in executable form. The system's linker program brings the object code together to form an executable program file. (In Figure 12.7, we use the file name suffixes `.cpp`, `.obj`, and `.exe`. Your C++ system may use different file name conventions.)

Files such as `file2.cpp` and `file3.cpp` typically contain function definitions for functions that are called by the code in `myprog.cpp`. An important benefit of separate compilation is that modifying the code in just one file requires recompiling only that file. The new `.obj` file is then relinked with the other existing `.obj` files. Of course, if a modification to one file affects the code in another file—for example, if it changes a function's interface by altering the data types of the function parameters—then the affected files must also be modified and recompiled.

FIGURE 12.7 Separate Compilation and Linking

Returning to our `TimeOfDay` class, let's assume we have created the `TimeOfDay.h` and `TimeOfDay.cpp` files. Now we can compile `TimeOfDay.cpp` into object code. You are probably using a C++ system that provides an *integrated environment*—a program that bundles the editor, the compiler, and the linker into one package. Integrated environments put you back into the editor when a compile-time or link-time error occurs, pinpointing the location of the error. Some integrated environments also manage *project files*. Project files contain information about all the constituent files of a multifile program. With project files, the system automatically recompiles or relinks any files that have become out of date because of changes to other files of the program.

If you are using a command line system, you will write one-line commands to the operating system telling it to compile or link certain files. Whichever environment you use—integrated environment or the command line—the overall effect is the same: The source code files are compiled into object code files, which are linked into an executable program, which is then executed.

Before leaving the topic of multifile programs, we must stress an important point. In the example in Figure 12.7, the files `TimeOfDay.h` and `TimeOfDay.obj` must be available to users of the `TimeOfDay` class. The user needs to examine `TimeOfDay.h` to see what `TimeOfDay` objects do and how to use them. The user must also be able to link his or her program with `TimeOfDay.obj` to produce an executable program. However, the user does *not* need to see `TimeOfDay.cpp`. To use the terminology introduced earlier, the implementation of `TimeOfDay` should be treated as a black box.

The main purpose of abstraction is to simplify the programmer's job by reducing complexity. Users of an abstraction should not have to look at its implementation to learn how to use it, nor should they have to write programs that depend on implementation details. In the latter case, any changes in the implementation could "break" the user's programs. In Chapter 8, the Software Engineering Tip box entitled "Conceptual Versus Physical Hiding of a Function Implementation" discussed the hazards of writing code that relies on implementation details.

QUICK CHECK

12.3.1 How does the use of a specification file help to provide encapsulation and information hiding for a class? (pp. 612–613)

12.3.2 Where does the `::` scope resolution operator appear in a member function definition within an implementation file? (p. 617)

12.3.3 What is information hiding? (p. 610)

12.3.4 What type of file is created as part of the compilation of a multifile program before an executable is produced? (p. 618)

12.3.5 Which file, specification or implementation, omits member function bodies? (pp. 612–615)

12.4 What Is an Object?

We started this chapter by talking about abstraction and abstract data types. We then examined the class construct, which is the C++ mechanism for implementing an ADT. We have discussed how information hiding can be accomplished through the design of the public interface and by having specification and implementation files. Now let's step back and take a broader view of objects and their use.

In object-oriented programming (OOP), the term *object* has a very specific meaning: It is a self-contained entity encapsulating data and operations on the data. In other words, an object represents an instance of an ADT. More specifically, an object has an *internal state* (the current values of its data, called attributes), and it has a *set of methods* (operations, which are implemented by functions in C++). If a class has been properly designed, the methods should be the only means by which an object's state can be modified by another object. To inspect the state of the object, methods are also employed; in addition, some objects provide public constants that can be inspected. For example, the `string` class makes the `npos` constant public, so that we can determine the maximum size of a string.

> **Attributes** The data represented by an object; its internal state.

An object-oriented program consists of a collection of objects, which communicate with one another by *message passing*. If object A wants object B to perform some task, object A sends a message containing the name of the object (B, in this case) and the name of the particular method to execute. Object B responds by executing this method in its own way, possibly changing its state and sending messages to other objects as well.

As you can tell, an object is conceptually quite different from a traditional data structure. A C struct is a passive data structure that contains only data and is acted upon by a program. In contrast, an object is an active data structure; the data and the code that manipulates the data are bound together within the object. In OOP jargon, an object knows how to manipulate its own state.

The vocabulary of the Smalltalk programming language, which pioneered many ideas related to object-oriented programming, has influenced the vocabulary of OOP. The literature of OOP is full of phrases such as "methods," "attributes," and "sending a message to." Here are some OOP terms and their C++ equivalents:

OOP	C++
Object	Object or class instance
Attribute	Data member
Method	Member function
Message passing	Function application (of a public member function)

> **Responsibilities** The public operations provided by a class for outside use.

Let's review the `TimeOfDay` class, albeit changed slightly to reflect object-oriented terminology and principles. There are six public methods (called responsibilities in object-oriented terminology): `Increment`, `Write`, `Equal`, `LessThan`, and the two constructors. One constructor takes the hours, minutes, and seconds as parameters, and the other sets the `TimeOfDay` to zero.

In object-oriented terminology, two types of responsibilities (operations) exist: *action responsibilities* and *knowledge responsibilities*. All of `TimeOfDay`'s public methods are either constructors or knowledge responsibilities. None of them takes action (changes the state of the object). As you can see, it is important for an object to be able to report on its own status; that is, each object should have methods that report the internal state of its private data in a manner that is appropriate to the information hiding goals of its public interface. Given such methods, we do not need a `Write` method. If the client code can *inspect* the internal state (not *change* it), then the code can print a `TimeOfDay` object in a form that is relevant to the problem using the ADT.

Here is the revised specification for the `TimeOfDay` class, in which the `Write` function has been removed. We omit the documentation that hasn't changed.

```
class TimeOfDay
{
public:
  // Constructors
  TimeOfDay();
  TimeOfDay(int initHours, int initMinutes, int initSeconds);
  // Knowledge responsibilities
  TimeOfDay Increment() const;
  int GetHours() const;
  // Post: Returns hours
  int GetMinutes() const;
  // Post: Returns minutes
  int GetSeconds() const;
  // Post: Returns seconds
  bool Equal(TimeOfDay otherTimeOfDay) const;
  bool LessThan(TimeOfDay otherTimeOfDay) const;
private:
  int hours;
  int minutes;
  int seconds;
};
```

Here is the part of the implementation file for class `TimeOfDay` that implements the new functions:

```
#include TimeOfDay.h
using namespace std;
. . .
int TimeOfDay::GetHours() const
{
  return hours;
}
int TimeOfDay::GetMinutes() const
{
  return minutes;
}
int TimeOfDay::GetSeconds() const
{
  return seconds;
}
```

MAY WE INTRODUCE John von Neumann

John von Neumann was a brilliant mathematician, physicist, logician, and computer scientist. His astonishing memory and the phenomenal speed at which he solved problems are legendary. Von Neumann used his talents not only for furthering his mathematical theories, but also for memorizing entire books and reciting them years after he had read them.

John von Neumann was born in Hungary in 1903, the oldest son of a wealthy Jewish banker. He was able to divide eight-digit numbers in his head by the age of 6. He entered high school by the time he was 11, and it wasn't long before his math teachers recommended that he be tutored by university professors. In spite of his interest in mathematics, von Neumann enrolled at the University of Berlin in 1921 to study chemistry. This decision was a compromise with his father, who wanted him to have a career that would allow him to make money. Five years later, he received his diploma in chemical engineering from the Technische Hochschule in Zürich. In the same year, however, von Neumann also received his doctorate in mathematics from the University of Budapest, with a thesis on set theory! During the period from 1926 to 1929, von Neumann lectured in Berlin and Hamburg while holding a Rockefeller fellowship for postdoctoral studies at the University of Göttingen.

Von Neumann came to the United States in the early 1930s to teach at Princeton, while still keeping his academic posts in Germany. He resigned the German posts when the Nazis came to power. While at Princeton, he worked with the talented British student Alan Turing, who would later become an important figure in computing theory. During World War II, von Neumann was hired as a consultant for the U.S. Armed Forces. Because of his knowledge of hydrodynamics, he was also called upon to participate in the construction of the atomic bomb in 1943.

Even though bombs and their performance fascinated von Neumann for many years, a fortuitous meeting in 1944 with Herbert Goldstine, a developer of one of the first electronic digital computers, introduced the mathematician to this new field. Von Neumann's chance conversation with Goldstine in a train station sparked a new fascination for him. He started working on the stored program concept and concluded that internally storing a program eliminated the hours of tedious labor required to reprogram computers (in those days). He also developed a new computer architecture to perform this storage task. In fact, today's computers are often referred to as von Neumann machines because the principles he described have proven so successful. Changes in computers over the past 40 years have been primarily in terms of the speed and composition of the circuits; the basic concepts developed by von Neumann have remained largely intact.

During the 1950s, von Neumann was a consultant for IBM, where he reviewed advanced technology projects. One such project was John Backus's FORTRAN, one of the first high-level programming languages. Von Neumann reportedly questioned why its development was necessary, asking why anyone would want more than one machine language. Von Neumann died in Washington, D.C., at the age of 54. We can only imagine the contributions that his brilliant mind might have made to computer science, had he lived longer.

QUICK CHECK

12.4.1 What is an object? (p. 620)
12.4.2 What is *message passing*? (p. 620)

12.5 Class Design Principles

Because classes are a fundamental building block of object-oriented programming, we now consider the principles that result in a well-designed class that can be used in the context of larger problems.

Encapsulation

A primary principle for class design is *encapsulation*. The dictionary tells us that a capsule is a sealed container that protects its contents from outside contaminants or harsh conditions to keep them intact. To encapsulate something is to place it into a capsule. In object-oriented programming, the capsule is a class, and its attributes are the contents we want to protect. By itself, the class construct doesn't protect its attributes. Instead, we must consciously provide that protection by defining a *formal interface* that limits access from other classes.

> **Encapsulation** Designing a class so that its attributes are isolated from the actions of external code except through the formal interface.
>
> **Formal interface** The components of a class that are externally accessible, which consist of the class's nonprivate attributes and responsibilities.
>
> **Reliable** The property of a unit of software that it can be counted on to always operate consistently, according to the specification of its interface.

What is a formal interface? In terms of class design, it is a written description of all the ways that the class may interact with other classes. The collection of responsibilities and nonprivate attributes defines the formal interface. In C++, we implement responsibilities with functions, and attributes are data fields within a class.

If the contents of an object can be changed only through a well-designed interface, then we don't have to worry about bugs in the rest of the application affecting it in unintended ways. As long as we design the class so that its objects can handle any data that are consistent with the interface, we know that it is a *reliable* unit of software.

Here's an analogy that illustrates the difference between a class that is encapsulated and one that is not. Suppose you are a builder, building a house in a new development. Other builders are working in the same development. If each builder keeps all of his or her equipment and materials within the property lines of the house that he or she is building, and enters and leaves the site only via its driveway, then construction proceeds smoothly. The property lines encapsulate the individual construction sites, and the driveway is the only interface by which people, equipment, and materials can enter or leave a site.

Now imagine the chaos that would occur if builders started putting their materials and equipment in other sites without telling one another. And what would happen if they began driving through other sites with heavy equipment to get to their own? The materials would get used in the wrong houses, tools would be lost or run over by stray vehicles, and the whole process would break down. **FIGURE 12.8** illustrates this situation.

Let's make this analogy concrete in C++ by looking at two interface designs for the same Date class—one encapsulated, and the other not encapsulated.

FIGURE 12.8 Encapsulation Draws Clear Boundaries Around Classes; Failing to Encapsulate Classes Can Lead to Chaos

```
// Encapsulated interface --
// avoids errors due to misuse
private:
  int month;
  int day;
  int year;

public:
  void setDate
    (int newMonth, int newDay,
     int newYear);
// Checks that the new date is
// valid; otherwise, leaves the
// value unchanged
```

```
// Unencapsulated interface --
// potential source of bugs
public:
  int month;
  int day;
  int year;
```

The interface on the right allows client code to directly change the fields of a `Date` object. Thus, if the client code assigns the values 14, 206, and 83629 to these fields, you end up with a nonsense date of the 206th day of the 14th month of the year 83629. The encapsulated implementation on the left makes these fields `private`. It then provides a `public` method that takes date values as arguments, and checks that the date is valid before changing the fields within the object.

This example shows that there is no special C++ syntax for encapsulation. Rather, we achieve encapsulation by carefully designing the class interface to ensure that its objects have complete control over what information enters and leaves them.

Encapsulation greatly simplifies the work of a programming team, because each class can be developed by a different team member, without worrying about how other classes are being implemented. In a large project, encapsulation permits each programmer to work independently on a different part. As long as each class meets its design specification, then the separate classes can interact safely.

> **Design specification** The written description of the behavior of a class with respect to its interface.

What do we mean by design specification? Given a formal interface to a class, the design specification is additional written documentation that describes how a class will behave for each possible interaction through the interface. We should be very clear here that we are referring to the problem-solving phase. The design specification is part of stating the problem. It is distinct from the specification file in the implementation phase, which defines the interface to a class. Depending on the context, we may refer to the design specification simply as the specification.

The formal interface is where we define how we will call a method, and the design specification is where we describe what the method will do. You can think of the formal interface as the syntax of a class, and the specification as its semantics. By definition, the specification includes the formal interface. We have seen how this information can be written as preconditions and postconditions.

Abstraction

Encapsulation is the basis for abstraction in programming. We've seen that there are two types of abstraction: data abstraction and control abstraction. As an example of data abstraction, consider that the external representation of a date might be integer values for the day and year, and a string that specifies the name of the month. But we might implement the date within the class using a standard value that calendar makers call the Julian day, which is the number of days since January 1, 4713 B.C.

> **Abstraction** The separation of the logical properties (interface and specification) of an object from its implementation (internal data representation and algorithms)

The advantage of using the Julian day is that it simplifies arithmetic on dates, such as computing the number of days between dates. All of the complexity of dealing with leap years and the different number of days in the months is captured in formulas that convert between the conventional representation of a date and the Julian day. From the user's perspective, however, the methods of a `Date` object receive and return a date as two integers and a string. **FIGURE 12.9** shows the two implementations, having the same external abstraction.

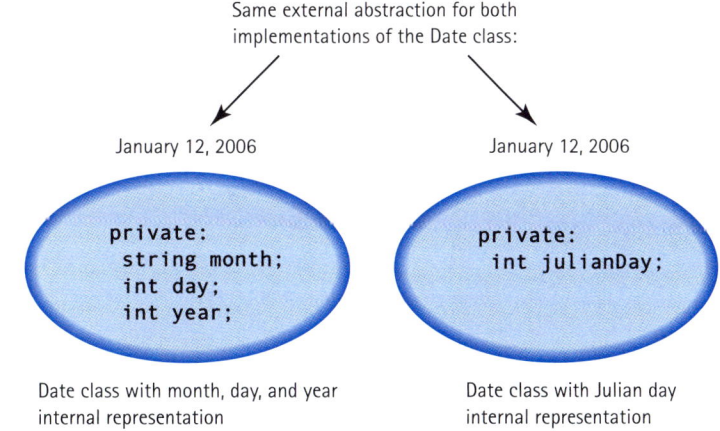

FIGURE 12.9 Data Abstraction Permits Different Internal Representations for the Same External Abstraction

In many cases, the external and internal representations are identical. We don't tell the user that, however, because we may want to change the implementation in the future. For example, we might initially develop a `Date` class using variables for the month, day, and year. Later, if we decide that a Julian day representation is more efficient, we can rewrite the implementation of the class. Because encapsulation has provided data abstraction, the change doesn't affect the client code.

This example also illustrates control abstraction. Suppose that the specification for the `Date` class says that it takes into account all of the special leap-year rules. In the Julian day implementation, only the Julian day conversion formulas handle those rules; the other responsibilities merely perform integer arithmetic on the Julian day number.

A user may assume that every `Date` responsibility separately deals with leap years. Control abstraction lets us program a more efficient implementation and then hide those details from the user.

Designing for Modifiability and Reuse

Applying the principle of abstraction has two additional benefits: modifiability and reuse.

Modifiability The property of an encapsulated class definition that allows the implementation to be changed without having an effect on code that uses it (except in terms of speed or memory space).

Reuse The ability to include a class in client code, without additional modification to either the class or the client code.

Encapsulation enables us to modify the implementation of a class after its initial development. Perhaps we are rushing to meet a deadline, so we create a simple but inefficient implementation. In the maintenance phase, we then replace the implementation with a more efficient version. The modification is undetectable with the exception that applications run faster and require less memory.

An encapsulated class is self-contained, which means we can import and use it in other applications. Whether we want to do so depends on whether the class provides a useful abstraction. For example, a `Date` class that assumes all years are in the range of 1900 to 1999 is not very useful today, even though that was a common approach used by twentieth-century programmers.

Reuse also means that a class can be extended to form new related classes. For example, a utility company has software to manage its fleet of vehicles. As shown in **FIGURE 12.10**, a class that describes a `Vehicle` can be used in multiple applications. Each application can add extensions to the `Vehicle` class to suit its particular requirements. Reuse is a way to save programming effort. It also ensures that objects have the same behavior every place that they are used—and consistent behavior helps us to avoid programming errors.

Of course, preparing a class that is suitable for wider reuse requires us to think beyond the immediate situation. Such a class should provide certain basic services that enable it to

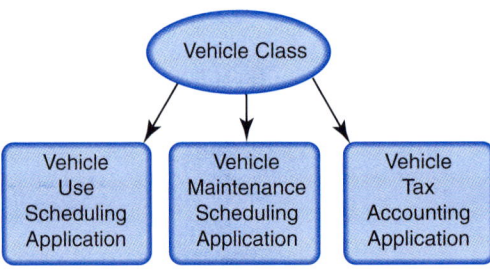

FIGURE 12.10 Reuse

be used more generally. For example, it should have observers that enable client code to retrieve any information from an object that we envision as potentially useful.

Not every class needs to be designed for general reuse. In some cases, we merely need a class that has specific properties for the problem at hand, and that won't be used elsewhere. If you are designing a class that may be used in other situations, however, then it is a good idea to make it more general.

Keep in mind that even though C++'s class construct provides a mechanism to *support* encapsulation, it is up to the programmer to use this capability in a way that results in actual encapsulation. There is no keyword or construct that distinguishes a class as encapsulated. Instead, the programmer must draw the boundaries around the class in a manner that keeps other code out.

There are two types of boundaries that we can draw: physical and visual. We can physically keep a user from accessing members in a class by declaring them to be private, and we can make the class implementation invisible to a user by the appropriate use of the header and implementation files.

Mutability

An *immutable* object cannot be changed after it is instantiated; a *mutable* object has at least one function (method) that allows the client to change the value of a data member in the object. Although many objects can be immutable, others require the client's ability to change the internal contents of an object after instantiation. Mutability is a key distinguishing characteristic of the interface of an object. While immutable objects are naturally encapsulated, because they are immune to change, we must take special care to ensure that mutable objects remain encapsulated.

> **Mutability** The ability of a client to change the value(s) of an object's state (data members) after it is created.

Our `TimeOfDay` class is immutable because we did not define a function that allowed the client to change any of its values. Had the `Increment` function actually changed the instance to which it was applied, the class would have been mutable instead.

Let's look at an example of a mutable object. Suppose we are creating a database of birth records for a hospital. A birth record is an object that contains the following information:

Birth Record

Date of birth
Time of day of birth
Mother's name
Father's name
Baby's name
Baby's weight
Baby's length
Baby's gender

A nurse enters all of this information into the database shortly after the baby is born. In some cases, the parents may not have chosen a name for the baby yet. Rather than keep the nurse waiting for the parents to make up their minds, the database allows all of the other information to be entered and creates a Birth Record object with an empty string for the name of the baby. Later, when the name is chosen, the nurse changes the name in the database.

There are two ways to change this database record. One would be to call a method that directly changes the value in the baby's name field. For example, we could write the function as follows:

```
void SetBabyName (Name newName)
{
  babysName = newName;
}
```

Given an instance of the `BirthRecord` class called `newBaby`, we can call this method with the following statement:

```
newBaby.SetBabyName(someName);   // Changes the baby name field
```

Such a method is called a transformer or a mutator. A transformer is an example of an action responsibility. Having a transformer makes `BirthRecord` a mutable class. Note that there is no special C++ syntax to denote that `SetBabyName` is a transformer. Instead, a method is a transformer simply by virtue of what it does: It changes the information stored in an existing object. We can ensure that a method is *not* a transformer only by using `const` in its heading.

Wouldn't it be easier to just make the `babysName` field `public` and to assign a new value to it without calling a method? Yes, but that would destroy the encapsulation of the `BirthRecord` class. Making the change through a transformer preserves encapsulation because it permits us to employ data and control abstraction. For example, we could later enhance this transformer to check that the new name contains only alphabetic characters.

The second way to change the name assumes that `BirthRecord` is an immutable class. We create a new record, copy into it all of the information except the name from the old record, and insert the new name at that point. For example, the following is a constructor that takes another `BirthRecord` object as an argument, and automatically does the copying:

```
BirthRecord (BirthRecord oldRecord,    // Constructor
             Name newName)
{
  dateOfBirth = oldRecord.dateOfBirth;
  timeOfBirth = oldRecord.timeOfBirth;
  mothersName = oldRecord.mothersName;
  fathersName = oldRecord.fathersName;
  babysName = newName;                 // Change name to new name
  babysWeight = oldRecord.babysWeight;
  babysLength = oldRecord.babysLength;
  babysGender = oldRecord.babysGender;
}
```

We would then update the birth record as follows:

```
BirthRecord updatedBaby(newBaby, someName);
```

Note that this statement doesn't change the old object, but rather it creates a new object containing the required information from the old object, together with the new name.

As you can see, using the transformer is simpler. It is also much faster for the computer to call a method that assigns a new value to a field than to create a whole new object.

12.5 Class Design Principles

SOFTWARE MAINTENANCE CASE STUDY: Comparing Two TimeOfDay Objects

MAINTENANCE TASK: The **TimeOfDay** class has two Boolean functions: **LessThan** and **Equal**. You are asked to enhance this class with a Boolean function that compares two **TimeOfDay** objects and returns the value of an enumerated type that describes the relationship between the instance and the parameter. The return type of this function must be a member of **RelationType**, an enumeration type with three values:

```
enum RelationType {BEFORE, SAME, AFTER};
```

If the object to which the function is applied comes before the parameter object, the function returns **BEFORE**. If the instance object comes after the parameter object, the function returns **AFTER**. Otherwise, the function returns **SAME**.

You may wonder why the enumeration type doesn't have **EARLIER**, **SAME**, and **LATER** values, which would make more sense with time. But we are designing **RelationType** to make sense in comparing almost anything from money to names to dates—another example of abstraction at work again, and especially in the service of reuse.

This looks easy. The following algorithm should work:

ComparedTo(In: otherTime)
Return value: RelationType

```
IF (time.LessThan(otherTime))
    Return BEFORE
ELSE IF (otherTime.LessThan(time))
    Return AFTER
ELSE
    Return SAME
```

This certainly works, but the **TimeOfDay** class seems to be a work in progress, so why not remove the **LessThan** and **Equal** functions and keep just the **ComparedTo** function? You check with the person asking for the enhancement and she says that this was her plan all along.

Now the algorithm has to be rewritten so that it does not depend on **LessThan**. First we compare to see if **hours** is greater or less than the hours in the other time. If it is neither, then it is equal and we go on to repeat the comparison for **minutes**. If the minutes are equal, we test the seconds. At each stage we either return **BEFORE** or **AFTER** or we go on to the next stage, until we get to **seconds**. Then, if the seconds are also equal, we return **SAME**.

ComparedTo(In: otherTime)
Return value: RelationType

```
IF (hours < otherTime.hours)
    Return BEFORE
ELSE IF (hours > otherTime.hours)
    Return AFTER
ELSE IF (minutes < otherTime.minutes)
    Return BEFORE
```

SOFTWARE MAINTENANCE CASE STUDY: Comparing Two `TimeOfDay` Objects

```
    ELSE IF (minutes > otherTime.minutes)
        Return AFTER
    ELSE IF (seconds < otherTime.seconds)
        Return BEFORE
    ELSE IF (seconds > otherTime.seconds)
        Return AFTER
    ELSE
        Return SAME
```

If `RelationType` is going to be used with other classes, then its declaration should be put into a header file and included in the `TimeOfDay` class. Here is the revised class and a client class that creates and manipulates the new version.

File `RelationType.h`:
`enum RelationType {BEFORE, SAME, AFTER};`

Here is the revised `TimeOfDay.h` specification file:

```cpp
//*****************************************************************
// SPECIFICATION FILE (TimeOfDay.h)
// This file gives the specification of a TimeOfDay abstract data
// type as revised to show object-oriented features and a
// comparison function.
//*****************************************************************
#include "RelationType.h"
class TimeOfDay
{
public:
  // Constructors
  TimeOfDay();
  // Post: hours, minutes, and seconds have been set to 0
  TimeOfDay(int initHours, int initMinutes, int initSeconds);
  // Pre: 0 <= hours <= 23, 0 <= minutes <= 59, 0 <= seconds <= 59
  // Post: Time is set according to the incoming parameters

  // Knowledge responsibilities
  TimeOfDay Increment() const;
  // Post: Returns a time that is the instance plus one,
  //       23:59:59 wrapping around to 0:0:0
  int GetHours() const;
  // Returns hours
  int GetMinutes() const;
  // Returns minutes
  int GetSeconds() const;
  // Returns seconds
  RelationType ComparedTo(TimeOfDay otherDay);
  // Post: Returns BEFORE if instance comes before otherDay;
  //       Returns SAME if instance and otherDay are the same;
  //       Returns AFTER if instance comes after otherDay
```

SOFTWARE MAINTENANCE CASE STUDY: Comparing Two `TimeOfDay` Objects

```cpp
private:
  int hours;
  int minutes;
  int seconds;
};
```

Here is the revised **TimeOfDay.cpp** implementation file:

```cpp
//*********************************************************************
// IMPLEMENTATION FILE (TimeOfDay.cpp)
// This file implements the TimeOfDay member functions as revised.
//*********************************************************************
#include "TimeOfDay.h"
#include <iostream>

using namespace std;

TimeOfDay::TimeOfDay()
{
  hours = 0;
  minutes = 0;
  seconds = 0;
}

//*********************************************************************

TimeOfDay::TimeOfDay(int initHours, int initMinutes,
                    int initSeconds)
{
  hours = initHours;
  minutes = initMinutes;
  seconds = initSeconds;
}

//*********************************************************************

TimeOfDay TimeOfDay::Increment() const
{
  // Create a duplicate of instance and increment duplicate
  TimeOfDay result(hours, minutes, seconds);
  result.seconds = result.seconds++;   // Increment seconds
  if (result.seconds > 59)             // Adjust if seconds carry
  {
    result.seconds = 0;
    result.minutes = result.minutes++;
    if (result.minutes > 59)           // Adjust if minutes carry
    {
      result.minutes = 0;
      result.hours = result.hours++;
```

SOFTWARE MAINTENANCE CASE STUDY: Comparing Two `TimeOfDay` Objects

```cpp
      if (result.hours > 23)           // Adjust if hours carry
        result.hours = 0;
    }
  }
  return result;
}

//*********************************************************************

int TimeOfDay::GetHours() const
{ return hours; }

//*********************************************************************

int TimeOfDay::GetMinutes() const
{ return minutes; }

//*********************************************************************

int TimeOfDay::GetSeconds() const
{ return seconds; }

//*********************************************************************

RelationType TimeOfDay::ComparedTo(TimeOfDay otherTime)
{
  if (hours < otherTime.hours)
    return BEFORE;
  else if (hours > otherTime.hours)
    return AFTER;
  else if (minutes < otherTime.minutes)
    return BEFORE;
  else if (minutes > otherTime.minutes)
    return AFTER;
  else if (seconds < otherTime.seconds)
    return BEFORE;
  else if (seconds > otherTime.seconds)
    return AFTER;
  else
    return SAME;
}
```

Here is a driver program to demonstrate use of the new **TimeOfDay** class:

```cpp
//*********************************************************************
// This program creates two time objects and manipulates them using
// get functions and a comparison function.
//*********************************************************************
#include <iostream>
#include "TimeOfDay.h"    // For TimeOfDay class
```

SOFTWARE MAINTENANCE CASE STUDY: Comparing Two `TimeOfDay` Objects

```cpp
using namespace std;

int main()
{
  TimeOfDay time1(5, 30, 0);
  TimeOfDay time2;

  cout << "time1: " << time1.GetHours() << ':'
       << time1.GetMinutes() << '/'
       << time1.GetSeconds() << endl;
  cout << "time2: " << time1.GetHours() << ':'
       << time2.GetMinutes() << ':'
       << time2.GetSeconds()  << endl;

  switch (time1.ComparedTo(time2))
  {
    case BEFORE : cout << "first time comes before second time"
                       << endl;
                  break;
    case SAME   : cout << "times are the same" << endl;
                  break;
    case AFTER  : cout << "second time comes before first time"
                       << endl;
                  break;
  }

  switch (time2.ComparedTo(time1))
  {
    case BEFORE : cout << "first time comes before second time"
                       << endl;
                  break;
    case SAME   : cout << "times are the same" << endl;
                  break;
    case AFTER  : cout << "second time comes before first time"
                       << endl;
                  break;
  }

  switch (time1.ComparedTo(time1))
  {
    case BEFORE : cout << "first time comes before second time"
                       << endl;
                  break;
    case SAME   : cout << "times are the same" << endl;
                  break;
    case AFTER  : cout << "second time comes before first time"
                       << endl;
                  break;
  }
  return 0;
}
```

SOFTWARE MAINTENANCE CASE STUDY: Comparing Two `TimeOfDay` Objects

Finally, here is the output:

```
time1: 5:30:0
time2: 5:0:0
second time comes before first time
first time comes before second time
times are the same
```

QUICK CHECK

12.5.1 What is design specification? (p. 625)
12.5.2 What do we call a method that changes the state of an object? (p. 628)
12.5.3 How can you determine if a class is immutable? (pp. 627–628)

12.6 The Name ADT

We have presented the ADT TimeOfDay and implemented it as a C++ class. It sits in a file ready to be used in any program that needs a `TimeOfDay` object. Now let's look at another ADT that will be useful in the future: the Name ADT.

In Chapter 4, we displayed a name in different formats. In Chapter 9, the Health Profile program used a name. Adding a name to the BMI and the Mortgage programs would make sense. Names are often necessary pieces of information. Let's stop this duplication of effort and do the job once and for all—let's write the code to support a name as an abstract data type.

We need to make the domain and operations general enough that they can be used in any program that keeps track of a name. The informal specification of the ADT is given here:

TYPE
  Name
DOMAIN
  Each Name is a name in the form of first name, middle name, and last name.
OPERATIONS
  Construct a Name instance
  Inspect the first name
  Inspect the middle name
  Inspect the last name
  Inspect the middle initial
  Compare two names for "before," "same," and "after"

Note that there is no operation to output the name in any particular format. Because we are allowing the user to inspect the parts of the name, the user can combine the parts to suit his or her purpose.

We create the Name ADT in two stages: specification, followed by implementation. The result of the first stage is a C++ specification (`.h`) file containing the declaration of a `Name` class. This file must also describe for the user the precise semantics of each ADT operation.

The second stage—implementation—requires us to (1) choose a concrete data representation for a name, and (2) implement each of the operations as a C++ function definition. The result is a C++ implementation file.

Specification of the ADT

The domain of our ADT is the set of all names made up of a first, middle, and last name. To represent the Name ADT as program code, we use a C++ class named `Name`. The ADT operations become public member functions of the class. Let's now specify the operations more carefully.

Construct a Name Instance

We use a C++ default constructor to create an instance of a Name ADT. The default constructor for `TimeOfDay` sets the hours, seconds, and minutes to zero. Blanks would be the logical equivalent for class `Name`.

The parameterized constructor must supply three arguments for this operation: the first name, the middle name, and the last name. Although we haven't yet determined a concrete data representation for a name, we must decide which data types the client should use for these arguments. The logical choice is for each value to be represented by a string. But what if we want to change a name after it has already been constructed? Let's not allow the user to do this; that is, let's make `Name` an immutable class.

Inspect the Name's First, Middle, and Last Names

All three of these operations are observer operations. They give the client access—albeit indirectly—to the private data. In the `Name` class, we represent these operations as value-returning member functions with the following prototypes:

```
string GetFirstName();
string GetMiddleName();
string GetLastName();
```

Inspect the Middle Initial

This operation requires that the first letter of the middle name be extracted and returned. In Chapter 4, we accessed the middle initial as a one-character string. Should we return it as a string here or as a `char` variable? It really doesn't matter as long as we are consistent in our code and in our documentation. Let's make this function a `char` function, just for the sake of variety.

Compare Two Names

This operation compares two names and determines whether the first name comes before the second, the names are the same, or the first name comes after the second. To indicate the result of the comparison, we use the enumeration type we used for the `TimeOfDay` class:

```
enum RelationType {BEFORE, SAME, AFTER};
```

Then we can code the comparison operation as a class member function that returns a value of type `RelationType`. Here is the function prototype:

```
RelationType ComparedTo(Name otherName) const;
```

Because this is a class member function, the name being compared to `otherName` is the object (instance) for which the member function is invoked. For example, the following client code tests whether `name1` comes before `name2`:

```
Name name1(string, string, string);
Name name2(string, string, string);
 .
 .
 .
switch (name1.ComparedTo(name2))
{
  case BEFORE : . . .
  case SAME   : . . .
  case AFTER  : . . .
}
```

We are now almost ready to write the C++ specification file for our `Name` class. However, the class declaration requires us to include the private part—the private variables that are the concrete data representation of the ADT. Choosing a concrete data representation properly belongs in the ADT implementation phase, not the specification phase. To satisfy the C++ class declaration requirement, however, we now choose a data representation. The simplest representation for a name is three string values—one each for the first, middle, and last. Here, then, is the specification file containing the `Name` class declaration.

```
//*****************************************************************
// SPECIFICATION FILE (Name.h)
// This file gives the specification of the Name abstract
// data type. There are two constructors: one takes the first,
// middle, and last name as parameters and the second sets first,
// middle, and last to blanks
//*****************************************************************

#include <iostream>
#include <string>
#include "RelationType.h"
using namespace std;

class Name
{
public:
  Name();
  // Default constructor
  // Post: first, middle, and last have been set to blanks
  Name(string firstName, string middleName, string lastName );
  // Parameterized constructor
  // Post: Data fields have been set to parameters

  // Knowledge Responsibilities
  string GetFirstName() const;
  // Post: Return value is this person's first name
  string GetLastName() const;
  // Post: Return value is this person's last name
```

```
    string GetMiddleName() const;
    // Post:  Return value is this person's middle name
    char GetMiddleInitial() const;
    // Post: Return value is this person's middle initial

    RelationType ComparedTo(Name otherName ) const;
    // Post: Return value is
    //       BEFORE, if this name comes before otherName
    //       SAME, if this name and otherName are the same
    //       AFTER, if this name is after otherName
private:
    string first;      // Person's first name
    string last;       // Person's last name
    string middle;     // Person's middle name
};
```

Notice that we use the word "Get" in the name of our observer functions. We did the same in the `TimeOfDay` class. Using "Get" as a prefix to the field name is an object-oriented convention used by many programmers. The corresponding name for transformers that change the value of a field would be "Set" preceding the field. In fact, many programmers refer to these kinds of operations generically as *getters* and *setters*.

Implementation File

We have already chosen a concrete data representation for a name, shown in the specification file as the string variables `first`, `middle`, and `last`. Now we must implement each class member function, placing the function definitions into a C++ implementation file named `Name.cpp`. The implementations of all but the `ComparedTo` function are so straightforward that no discussion is needed.

If we were to compare two names in our heads, we would look first at the last name. If the last names were different, we would immediately know which name came first. If the last names were the same, we would look at the first names. If the first names were the same, we would have to look at the middle name. As so often happens, we can use this algorithm directly in our function.

```
//****************************************************************
// IMPLEMENTATION FILE (Name.cpp)
// The file implements the Name member functions.
//****************************************************************
#include "Name.h"
#include <iostream>
Name::Name()
{
    first = " ";
    middle = " ";
    last = " ";
}

//****************************************************************
```

```cpp
Name::Name(string firstName, string middleName, string lastName )
{
  first = firstName;         // Assign parameters
  last = lastName;
  middle = middleName;
}

//*****************************************************************

string Name::GetFirstName() const
{ return first; }

//*****************************************************************

string Name::GetLastName() const
{ return last; }
//*****************************************************************

string Name::GetMiddleName() const
{ return middle; }

//*****************************************************************

char Name::GetMiddleInitial() const
{ return middle.at(0); }

//*****************************************************************

RelationType Name::ComparedTo(Name otherName ) const
{
  if (last < otherName.last)
    return BEFORE;
  else if (otherName.last < last)
    return AFTER;
  else if (first < otherName.first)
    return BEFORE;
  else if (otherName.first < first)
    return AFTER;
  else if (middle < otherName.middle)
    return BEFORE;
  else if (otherName.middle < middle)
    return AFTER;
  else
    return SAME;
}
```

Here is a driver program that creates two **Name** objects and manipulates them:

```cpp
//*****************************************************************
// This program creates two name objects and manipulates them.
//*****************************************************************
#include <iostream>
#include <string>
#include "Name.h"
```

```
using namespace std;

int main ()
{
  Name herName("Susy", "Sunshine", "Smith");
  Name hisName("Marvin", "Moonlight", "Morgan");
  cout << "Her name is " << herName.GetFirstName() << " "
       << herName.GetMiddleName()
       << " " << herName.GetLastName() << endl;
  cout << "Her middle initial is " << herName.GetMiddleInitial()
       << endl;
  cout << "His name is "<< hisName.GetFirstName() << " "
       << hisName.GetMiddleName()
       << " " << hisName.GetLastName() << endl;
  switch (hisName.ComparedTo(herName))
  {
    case BEFORE: cout << "His name comes before her name" << endl;
                 break;
    case SAME:   cout << "His name and her name are the same"
                      << endl;
                 break;
    case AFTER:  cout << "His name comes after her name" << endl;
  }
  return 0;
}
```

Finally, here, is the output:

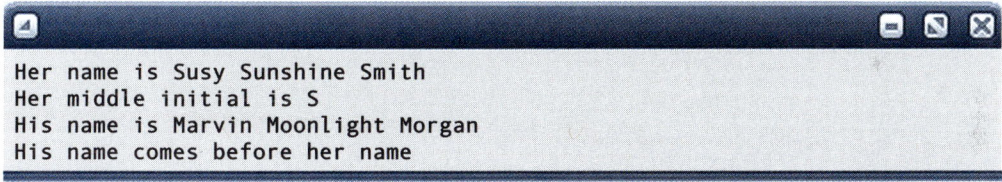

```
Her name is Susy Sunshine Smith
Her middle initial is S
His name is Marvin Moonlight Morgan
His name comes before her name
```

QUICK CHECK

12.6.1 Does the Name ADT create instances of mutable or immutable objects? (pp. 635–638)

12.6.2 What are the observer methods of the Name ADT? (p. 635)

12.7 Composition

Two classes typically exhibit one of three relationships: They are independent of each other, they are related by inheritance, or they are related by composition. Here we cover *composition*: the relationship in which the internal data of one class includes an object of another class as a data member. Stated another way, an object is contained within another object.

> **Composition** The relationship between classes in which one class contains an instance of another class as one of its attributes.

C++ does not have (or need) any special language notation for composition. You simply declare an object of one class to be one of the data members of another class. Let's look at an example.

Design of an Entry Class

You are developing a program to represent an appointment book. Each `Day` object will be a sorted list of `Appointment` objects. In preparation, you decide to build an Entry ADT with two fields, an object of a Name ADT and an object of a TimeOfDay ADT. You may need to add more information for an `Appointment` object later, but this gives you a start. Constructing this object should be easy because you already have a `TimeOfDay` class and a `Name` class. For the purpose of an appointment calendar, you decide to ignore the person's middle name or initial and the seconds in the time. You can always add the middle name later if you decide that you need it. Of course, you do need operations that return the name and `TimeOfDay` to the client program.

Let's call the operations `GetNameStr`, which returns a name composed of the first and last names, and `GetTimeStr`, which returns the hours and minutes with a colon between the two values. Of course, we need constructors. How many? Well, you know that the `Name` class has two constructors: one that takes the parts of the name as parameters and one that sets the fields to blanks. The same is true of the `TimeOfDay` class. Thus we should have a default constructor for the `Entry` class, which calls the default constructors for `Name` and `TimeOfDay`, and a parameterized constructor, which passes its parameters to `Name`'s and `Time`'s parameterized constructors.

We now know enough to write the specification file.

```cpp
//****************************************************************
// SPECIFICATION FILE (Entry.h)
// This file contains the specification of the Entry ADT, which has
// two contained classes, Name and Time
//****************************************************************

#include "TimeOfDay.h"
#include "Name.h"
#include <string>

class Entry
{
public:
  Entry();
  // Default constructor
  // Post: Entry object has been constructed
  //       Name and TimeOfDay objects have been constructed using
  //       their default constructors
  Entry(string firstName, string middleName, string lastName,
        int initHours, int initMinutes, int initSeconds);
  // Parameterized constructor
  // Post: Entry object has been constructed
  //       Name and TimeOfDay objects have been constructed using
  //       their parameterized constructors
  string GetNameStr() const;
  // Post: Returns the first and last name of Name object
  //       with a blank in between
  string GetTimeStr() const;
  // Post: Returns the hours and minutes from TimeOfDay object
  //       with a colon in between
```

```
private:
  Name name;
  TimeOfDay time;
}
```

Implementing the default class constructors involves invoking the default constructors for the `Name` object and the `TimeOfDay` object. The default `Entry` constructor has nothing else to do. In C++, default constructors are called automatically (although we've shown them explicitly in prior examples, as a matter of good documentation). Therefore, we can also leave the body of the default constructor for `Entry` empty, which we do here so that you can see an example of this coding style.

The parameterized constructor must pass its parameters to the `Name` and `Time` constructors. To do so, we use a *constructor initializer*. This C++ construct allows you to pass the information needed to construct an object that is declared in another class. The syntax is the heading of the containing class's constructor followed by a colon (:) and the name of a member object followed by a parameter list corresponding to the parameterized constructor for the class of the member object. If multiple constructor initializers are present, they are separated by commas.

```
Entry::Entry (string firstName, string middleName, string lastName,
              int initHours, int initMinutes, int initSeconds)
      : name (firstName, middleName, lastName),
        time (initHours, initMinutes, initSeconds)         ⟵ Constructor initializers
```

The body for this function will be empty. The system takes care of constructing the `Name` and `TimeOfDay` objects. Here is the implementation file for class `Entry`:

```
//****************************************************************
// IMPLEMENTATION FILE (Entry.cpp)
// This file contains the specification of the Entry ADT,
// which has two contained classes, Name and Time
//****************************************************************
#include "Entry.h"
#include <string>
#include <iostream>
using namespace std;

Entry::Entry()
{ }
Entry::Entry(string firstName, string middleName, string lastName,
             int  initHours, int  initMinutes, int  initSeconds )
           : name(firstName, middleName, lastName),
             time(initHours, initMinutes, initSeconds)
{ }
string Entry::GetNameStr() const
{ return (name.GetFirstName() + ' ' + name.GetLastName()); }
string Entry::GetTimeStr() const
{ return (name.FirstName() + ' ' + name.LastName()); }
```

Here is a simple driver that creates and prints a couple of `Entry` objects:

```
//*****************************************************************
// DRIVER for class Entry
// This program tests the constructors and return functions
//*****************************************************************
#include <iostream>
#include "Entry.h"
#include <string>

using namespace std;

int main ()
{
  Entry entry1("Sally", "Jane", "Smith", 12, 20, 0);
  Entry entry2("Mary", "Beth", "Jones", 10, 30, 0);

  cout << "Entry 1: " << entry1.GetNameStr() << " "
       << entry1.GetTimeStr() << endl;
  cout << "Entry 2: " << entry2.GetNameStr() << " "
       << entry2.GetTimeStr() << endl;
  return 0;
}
```

When we try to run this simple program, we get the following error:

```
error: multiple definition of 'enum RelationType'
```

How can that be? There is only one copy of file `RelationType.h`, *but it is included in both* `TimeOfDay` *and* `Name`. As a consequence, the preprocessor thinks `RelationType` is defined more than once. This happens often, so we have to tell the preprocessor to include file `RelationType.h` *only if* it hasn't been included before. The widely used solution to this problem is to write `RelationType.h` this way:

```
#ifndef RELATION
#define RELATION
enum RelationType {BEFORE, SAME, AFTER};
#endif
```

The lines beginning with # are directives to the preprocessor. `RELATION` (or any identifier you wish to use) is a preprocessor identifier, not a C++ program identifier. In effect, these directives say:

If the preprocessor identifier `RELATION` has not already been defined, then

1. Define `RELATION` as an identifier known to the preprocessor, and
2. Let the declaration of the `enum RelationType` pass through to the compiler.

If a subsequent `#include "RelationType.h"` is encountered, the test `#ifndef RELATION` will fail. The declaration will not pass through to the compiler a second time.

The multiple definition error has now been resolved, but there is *another* error:

```
Error   : illegal operand
EntryEr.cpp line 33
return "" + time.GetHours() + ":" + time.GetMinutes();
```

What could be wrong with this statement? We just created a string out of a string, an integer value, a colon, and another integer value. We have used concatenation to build strings since Chapter 2. Numbers are converted to strings for output. What's different about this statement? The C++ system automatically converts integers to strings *for output*, but there is no type cast from integers to strings anywhere except for output.

To create a string including integers, we could write it out to a file and then read it back in as a string. This approach would work, but it would be extremely time-consuming (disk access is more than a million times slower than memory access). Fortunately, the designers of the C++ language realized that there might be times when a conversion from integer to string would be useful. Thus they created a class called **stringstream**, which allows us to write values to a string as if we were writing them to a file. Because the data is not actually sent to a file but rather is kept in memory, the conversion is completed quickly.

We declare an object of class **ostringstream**, and use the insertion operator (<<) to send the integers to the object. To get them back as a string, we use the **str** member function of class **ostringstream**. Here is the corrected version of **GetTimeStr**, using an object of class **ostringstream**, followed by the output from the driver:

```
#include <sstream>                              // ostringstream
string Entry::TimeStr() const
// This function makes use of class sstream to create and return
// a string containing numeric values
{
  string outStr;
  ostringstream tempOut;                        // Declare an ostringstream

  if (time.GetHours() < 10)
    tempOut << '0';
  tempOut << time.GetHours() << ":";
  if (time.GetMinutes() < 10)
    tempOut << '0';
  tempOut << time.GetMinutes() << ":";
  if (time.GetSeconds() < 10)
    tempOut << '0';
  tempOut << time.GetSeconds();
  outStr = tempOut.str();
  return outStr;
}
```

Once this function is inserted, the driver produces this output:

```
Entry 1: Sally Smith 12:20:00
Entry 2: Mary Jones 10:30:00
```

QUICK CHECK

12.7.1 What is composition? (p. 639)

12.7.2 Does C++ require a special language notation for composition? (p. 639)

12.7.3 What must we use to construct an object that is declared within another class that is dependent on information provided by the constructor of that class? (p. 641)

12.7.4 Which preprocessor directives are used to avoid multiple inclusion? (p. 642)

12.8 UML Diagrams

It can be difficult to understand the operation of an application just by looking at the written documentation. When many classes are interacting, keeping track of their relationships involves building a mental picture. Before long, we start drawing diagrams just to keep everything straight. Perhaps we use boxes to represent classes, and lines between them to represent collaborations (classes calling methods in other classes). Inside the boxes, we make notes about the classes. Then we start using solid and dashed lines to indicate different kinds of collaboration. Eventually, we have a diagram that captures all of the important structural information about the application. The trouble is, no one else knows what our diagram means! If programmers used a common set of symbols, then they could read one another's diagrams.

The Unified Modeling Language (UML) is just such a collection of symbols. It was developed specifically for diagramming object-oriented applications. Even though it has the word *language* in its name, UML is not a programming language; it is just a collection of graphical symbols. It is *unified* in the sense that it is made up from a combination of three different sets of symbols that were in use prior to its development. Each of those earlier conventions had its own strengths and weaknesses, so UML was created to provide a single set of symbols incorporating all of their best features.

The UML symbols are divided into subsets that are used for different purposes. There are UML diagrams for documenting just about every aspect of programming, from analyzing the problem to deploying the code on customer's computers. You could take an entire course in drawing UML diagrams!

We begin by looking at the simplest form of diagrams: the Class diagram.

Diagramming a Class

A class is represented in UML by a box that's divided into three sections. The top section holds the name of the class, the middle section lists its attributes (the data members of the class), and the bottom section lists responsibilities (methods). Here's a UML diagram of the `TimeOfDay` class:

```
TimeOfDay
-------------------------------------------------
-hours: int
-minutes: int
-seconds: int
-------------------------------------------------
+TimeOfDay(hours: int, minutes: int, seconds: int)
+TimeOfDay()
+Increment()
+GetHours(): int
+GetMinutes(): int
+GetSeconds(): int
+Increment(): TimeOfDay
+ComparedTo(Time: otherTime): Boolean
```

As you can see, the diagram lists the attributes and their types in the middle section. The minus sign in front of each attribute is shorthand for `private`. UML uses + to mean `public`. You can see that all of `TimeOfDay`'s responsibilities are listed in the bottom section, showing parameters and return types for value-returning methods. As you can also see by the plus signs, TimeOfDay's functions are all `public`.

Diagramming Composition of Classes

When a class contains an instance of another class, such as the `Name` class field contained in the `Entry` class, we draw a solid diamond at the end of the line next to the containing class. (We just show the constructor as an example responsibility—in a proper UML diagram, all of the responsibilities would be listed.)

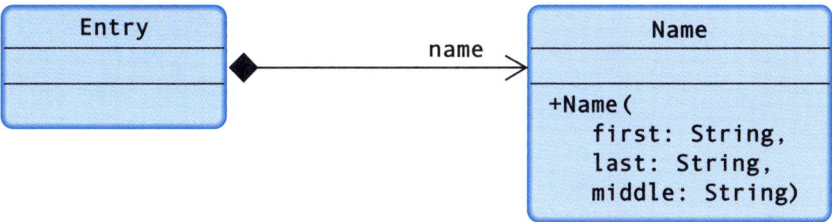

This is how UML documents composition. The class with the solid diamond is composed of (among other things) an instance of the class at the other end of the arrow. Notice that the name of the instance (`name`) is indicated beside the arrow.

QUICK CHECK

12.8.1 What is UML used for? (p. 644)

12.8.2 What symbols are used to represent public data and private data in a UML diagram? (p. 644)

Problem-Solving Case Study

Create an Array of Name Objects

PROBLEM: As a first pass of an appointment book, you decide to create a 24-hour listing of names organized by their associated hour. You have a file of entry data that needs to be converted to this form and then printed.

INPUT: The file of values that can be used to make `Entry` objects.

OUTPUT: The hour of the day and the associated name, ordered by hour.

DISCUSSION: We can read the data for an entry object, get the hour associated with the object, and use it as an index into the array. **FIGURE 12.11** describes this structure.

Problem-Solving Case Study

FIGURE 12.11 Names Array Indexed by Hours

What happens if there is more than one person with the same hour? Well, let's store the name the first time we see an hour. If a subsequent entry has the same hour, we can write an error message. Here is the `main` algorithm:

Main Level 0

```
Open files
IF files not ok
    Write error message
    Return 1
Get entry
WHILE more entries
    Process entry
    Get entry
Write time and name
Close files
```

We have been opening and checking files for many chapters now. We can consider this a concrete step.

Problem-Solving Case Study

GetEntry(In/out: inFile) — Level 1
Return value: Entry

Read Name
Read Time
Create newEntry
Return newEntry

ProcessEntry(In/out: array Names, In: entry)

Get Hours
Set Names[hours] to entry.GetNameStr

Get Hours . . . How are we going to do that? We can get a string with the hours embedded and try to access the hours. However, if we have a **TimeOfDay** object rather than an **Entry** object, we can access the hours directly. We don't need an **Entry** object: We need a **Name** object and a **TimeOfDay** object. We let the fact that the file contains data corresponding to **Entry** objects mislead us. This design needs to be redone, but first we need to see an example of the file format.

Sample File

```
Mary Jane Smith 12 30 0
Susy Olive Oliver 11 45 5
Jane Birdsong Wren 8 15 30
William Jennings Brian 0 35 35
. . .
```

This information makes the processing even easier. We read the first, middle, and last names and create a **Name** object. The next value on the line is the hours. We don't need the minutes and seconds, but we will have to read past them. In fact, we don't need a **TimeOfDay** object at all; we can just use the hours directly.

Main (Revised) — Level 0

Open files
IF files not ok
   Write error message
   Return 1
Get name
WHILE more data
   Get hours
   Set names[hours] to name
   Get name
Write time and name
Close files

Problem-Solving Case Study

GetName(In/out: inFile)
Return value: Name

Get first, middle, last from inFile
name = Name(first, middle, last)
Return name

WriteTimeName(In/out: outFile, In: names)

FOR hour going from 0 to 23
    Write "Hour: ", hour, "Name", names[hour].GetFirstName(),
       " ", names[hour].GetMiddleName(), " " on outFile

OpenFiles, GetName, and WriteTimeName should be coded as functions. Have we forgotten anything? Yes: We haven't taken care of duplicate hours. We must set every cell in the array to a default **Name** object. Before we store a **Name** object into the array, we must check whether an object there has a first name that is a blank. Again, we update the main module.

Main (Second revision)   **Level 0**

Open files
IF files not ok
    Write error message
    Return 1
Set array names to all default Name objects
Get name
WHILE more data
    Get hours
    IF names[hours].GetFirstName() is a blank
        Set names[hours] to name
    ELSE
        Write hours, " is already taken" on outFile
    Get name
Write time and name
Close files

WriteTimeName(In/out: outFile, In: names) (Revised)

FOR hour going from 0 to 23
IF names[hour].GetFirstName() != " "
    Write "Hour: ", hour, "Name", names[hour].GetFirstName(),
    " ", names[hour].GetMiddleName(), " ",
    names[hour].GetLastName(), endl on outFile
  ELSE
    Write "Hour: ", "None was scheduled.", endl on outFile

Problem-Solving Case Study

Here is a program listing, the input, and the output:

```cpp
//***************************************************
// This program reads a file of Entry objects and
// writes the hours from 0..23 and the associated
// name.  Duplicate hours are not recorded.
// **************************************************
#include <iostream>
#include <fstream>
#include "Name.h"

using namespace std;

void OpenFiles(ifstream& inFile, ofstream& outFile);
// Prompts for and reads file names.
// Opens files.
Name GetName(ifstream& inFile);
// Reads and returns Name object from inFile.
void WriteTimeName(ofstream& outFile, Name names[]);
// Writes each hour and the corresponding name.

int main ()
{
  // Declarations
  ifstream inFile;
  ofstream outFile;
  Name names[24];
  Name blankName;
  Name name;
  int hours, dummy;
  for (int index = 0; index < 24; index++)
    names[index] = blankName;
  OpenFiles(inFile, outFile);
  if (!(inFile && outFile))
  {
    cout << "Files did not open properly" << endl;
    return 1;
  }

  // Process file
  name = GetName(inFile);
  while (inFile)
  {
    inFile >> hours >> dummy >> dummy;
    if (names[hours].GetFirstName() == " ")
      names[hours] = name;
    else
      outFile << hours << " is already taken." << endl;
    name = GetName(inFile);
  }
```

Problem-Solving Case Study

```cpp
  WriteTimeName(outFile, names);
  outFile.close();
  inFile.close();
  return 0;
}

//**********************************************************************

void OpenFiles(ifstream& inFile, ofstream& outFile)
{
  string inFileName;       // User-specified input file name
  string outFileName;      // User-specified output file name
  cout << "Enter the name of the file to be processed" << endl;
  cin >> inFileName;
  inFile.open(inFileName.c_str());
  cout << "Enter the name of the output file" << endl;
  cin >> outFileName;
  outFile.open(outFileName.c_str());
}

//**********************************************************************

Name GetName(ifstream& inFile)
{
  string first, middle, last;
  inFile >> first >> middle >> last;
  Name name(first, middle, last);
  return name;
}

//**********************************************************************

void WriteTimeName(ofstream& outFile, Name names[])
{
  outFile << "A listing of the hour and the corresponding name"
          << endl;
  for (int hour = 0; hour < 24; hour++)
  {
    if (names[hour].GetFirstName() != " ")
      outFile << "Hour " << hour << ":  "
              << names[hour].GetFirstName()
              << " " << names[hour].GetMiddleName() << " "
              << names[hour].GetLastName() << endl;
    else
      outFile << "Hour " << hour<< ":   None was scheduled."
              << endl;
  }
}
```

Problem-Solving Case Study

Input File

```
Mary Jane Smith 12 30 0
Susy Olive Oliver 11 45 5
Jane Birdsong Wren 8 15 30
William Jennings Brian 0 35 35
Bill William Smith 2 4 5
Brad Smith Williams 4 5 6
Mary Margaret Jones 5 6 7
Andrew Bill Summer 6 7 9
Ann Betty Butler 6 7 8
```

Output File

```
6 is already taken.
A listing of the hour and the corresponding name
Hour 0:   William Jennings Brian
Hour 1:   None was scheduled.
Hour 2:   Bill William Smith
Hour 3:   None was scheduled.
Hour 4:   Brad Smith Williams
Hour 5:   Mary Margaret Jones
Hour 6:   Andrew Bill Summer
Hour 7:   None was scheduled.
Hour 8:   Jane Birdsong Wren
Hour 9:   None was scheduled.
Hour 10:  None was scheduled.
Hour 11:  Susy Olive Oliver
Hour 12:  Mary Jane Smith
Hour 13:  None was scheduled.
Hour 14:  None was scheduled.
Hour 15:  None was scheduled.
Hour 16:  None was scheduled.
Hour 17:  None was scheduled.
Hour 18:  None was scheduled.
Hour 19:  None was scheduled.
Hour 20:  None was scheduled.
Hour 21:  None was scheduled.
Hour 22:  None was scheduled.
Hour 23:  None was scheduled.
```

Testing and Debugging

Testing and debugging a C++ class amounts to testing and debugging each member function of the class. All of the techniques you have learned about so far—algorithm walk-throughs, code walk-throughs, hand traces, test drivers, verification of preconditions and postconditions, the system debugger, the `assert` function, and debug outputs—may be brought into play.

Consider how we might test this chapter's `TimeOfDay` class. Here is the class declaration, abbreviated by leaving out the function preconditions and postconditions:

```
class TimeOfDay
{
public:
  TimeOfDay(int initHours, int initMinutes, int initSeconds);
  TimeOfDay();
  // Action responsibilities
  TimeOfDay Increment() const;
  RelationType ComparedTo(TimeOfDay otherDay);
  // Knowledge responsibilities
  int GetHours() const;
  int GetMinutes() const;
  int GetSeconds() const;
private:
  int hours;
  int minutes;
  int seconds;
};
```

To test this class fully, we must test each of the member functions. Let's step through the process of testing just one of them: the `Increment` function.

Before we implemented the `Increment` function, we started with a pseudocode algorithm, performed an algorithm walk-through, and translated the pseudocode into the following C++ function:

```
TimeOfDay TimeOfDay::Increment() const
{
  // Create a duplicate of instance and increment duplicate
  TimeOfDay result(hours, minutes, seconds);
  result.seconds = result.seconds++;   // Increment seconds
  if (result.seconds > 59)             // Adjust if seconds carry
  {
    result.seconds = 0;
    result.minutes = result.minutes++;
    if (result.minutes > 59)           // Adjust if minutes carry
    {
      result.minutes = 0;
      result.hours = result.hours++;
      if (result.hours > 23)           // Adjust if hours carry
        result.hours = 0;
    }
  }
  return result;
}
```

Now we perform a code walk-through, verifying that the C++ code faithfully matches the pseudocode algorithm. At this point (or earlier, during the algorithm walk-through), we do a hand trace to confirm that the logic is correct.

For the hand trace, we should pick values of `hours`, `minutes`, and `seconds` that ensure code coverage. To execute every path through the control flow, we need cases in which the following conditions occur:

1. The first If condition is false.
2. The first If condition is true and the second is false.
3. The first If condition is true, the second is true, and the third is false.
4. The first If condition is true, the second is true, and the third is true.

Below is a table displaying values of `hours`, `minutes`, and `seconds` that correspond to these four cases. For each case we also write down what we hope will be the values of the variables after executing the algorithm.

Case	Initial Values			Expected Results		
	Hours	Minutes	Seconds	Hours	Minutes	Seconds
1	10	5	30	10	5	31
2	4	6	59	4	7	0
3	13	59	59	14	0	0
4	23	59	59	0	0	0

Using the initial values for each case, a hand trace of the code confirms that the algorithm produces the desired results.

Finally, we write a test driver for the `Increment` function, just to be sure that our understanding of the algorithm logic is the same as the computer's! Here is a possible test driver:

```cpp
//*************************************************************
// This program is a test driver for the Increment function
// in the TimeOfDay class.
//*************************************************************

#include <iostream>
#include "TimeOfDay.h"
using namespace std;

int main()
{
    int hours;
    int minutes;
    int seconds;
    cout << "Enter a TimeOfDay (use hours < 0 to quit): " << endl;
    cin >> hours >> minutes >> seconds;
    while (hours >= 0)
```

```
    {
      TimeOfDay time(hours, minutes, seconds);
      TimeOfDay timeInc = time.Increment();
      cout << "Incremented TimeOfDay is ";
      cout << timeInc.GetHours() << ':' << timeInc.GetMinutes() << ':'
           << timeInc.GetSeconds() << endl;
      cout << endl;
      cout << "Enter a TimeOfDay (use hours < 0 to quit): " << endl;
      cin >> hours >> minutes >> seconds;
    }
    return 0;
}
```

For input data, we supply at least the four test cases discussed earlier. The program's output should match the desired results—and it does. Notice that, because we are interested in checking the actual values from the observer methods, we do not have our driver apply output formatting to ensure that minutes and seconds have two digits when their values are less than ten.

```
Enter a TimeOfDay (use hours < 0 to quit):
10 5 30
Incremented TimeOfDay is 10:5:31

Enter a TimeOfDay (use hours < 0 to quit):
2 4 59
Incremented TimeOfDay is 2:5:0

Enter a TimeOfDay (use hours < 0 to quit):
13 59 59
Incremented TimeOfDay is 14:0:0

Enter a TimeOfDay (use hours < 0 to quit):
23 59 59
Incremented TimeOfDay is 0:0:0

Enter a TimeOfDay (use hours < 0 to quit):
-1 0 0
```

Now that we have tested the `Increment` function, we can apply the same steps to the remaining class member functions. We can create a separate test driver for each function, or we can write just one driver that tests all of the functions. The disadvantage of writing just one driver is that devising different combinations of input values to test several functions at once can quickly become complicated.

Before leaving the topic of testing a class, we must emphasize an important point: Even though a class has been tested thoroughly, it is still possible for errors to arise. Let's look at two examples using the `TimeOfDay` class. The first example is the client statement

```
TimeOfDay time1(24, 0, 0);
```

The precondition on the parameterized constructor requires the first argument to have a value from 0 through 23. We don't prevent an erroneous time from being constructed when the client ignores the precondition. The second example is the comparison

```
if (time1.ComparedTo(time2))
    .
    .
    .
```

where the programmer intends `time1` to be 11:00:00 on a Wednesday and `time2` to be 1:20:00 on a Thursday. (The result of the test is AFTER, not BEFORE as the programmer expects.) The implicit precondition of `ComparedTo` requires the two times to be on the same day, not on two different days. This implicit precondition should be made explicit.

Do you see the common problem? In each example, the client has violated the function precondition. If a class has been well tested but errors occur when the client code uses the class, always check the member function preconditions. You can waste many hours trying to debug a class member function when, in fact, the function is correct but the error lies in the client code.

Testing and Debugging Hints

1. The declaration of a `class` within the specification header file must end with a semicolon.
2. Be sure to specify the full member selector when referencing a component of a class object.
3. Regarding semicolons, the declarations and definitions of class member functions are treated the same as any C++ function. The member function prototype, which is located in the class declaration, ends with a semicolon. The function heading—the part of the function definition preceding the body—does not end with a semicolon.
4. When implementing a class member function, don't forget to prefix the function name with the name of the class and the scope resolution operator (::).

    ```
    TimeOfDay TimeOfDay::Increment() const
    {
        .
        .
        .
    }
    ```

5. For now, the only built-in operations that we apply to class objects are member selection (.) and assignment (=). To perform other operations, such as comparing two class objects, you must write class member functions.
6. If a class member function inspects but does not modify the private data, it is a good idea to make it a `const` member function.
7. A class member function does not use dot notation to access private members of the class object for which the function is invoked. In contrast, a member function *must* use dot notation to access the private members of a class object that is passed to it as an argument.
8. A class constructor is declared without a return value type and cannot return a function value.

9. If a client of a class has errors that seem to be related to the class, start by checking the preconditions of the class member functions. The errors may reside in the client, not the class.
10. If a class has a member that is an object of another class and this member object's constructor requires arguments, you must pass these arguments using a constructor initializer:

```
SomeClass::SomeClass( . . . ) : memberObject(arg1, arg2)
{
    .
    .
    .
}
```

If there is no constructor initializer, the member object's default constructor is invoked.

Summary

Abstraction is a powerful technique for reducing the complexity and increasing the reliability of programs. Separating the properties of a data type from the details of its implementation frees the user of the type from having to write code that depends on a particular implementation of the type. This separation also assures the implementor of the type that client code cannot accidentally compromise a correct implementation.

An abstract data type (ADT) is a type whose specification is separate from its implementation. The specification announces the abstract properties of the type. The implementation consists of (1) a concrete data representation and (2) the implementations of the ADT operations. In C++, an ADT can be realized by using the class mechanism. Class members can be designated as public or private. Most commonly, the private members are the concrete data representation of the ADT, and the public members are the functions corresponding to the ADT operations.

In object-oriented terminology, instances of ADTs are objects. That is, a class defines a pattern for instantiating an object. Among the public member functions of a class, the programmer often includes one or more class constructors—functions that are invoked automatically whenever a class object is created. When designing a class, the principles of abstraction, encapsulation, modifiability, and reuse must be considered. An immutable class provides no public function that changes a data value in the object; a mutable class does provide such a function.

Separate compilation of program units is central to the separation of specification from implementation. The declaration of a C++ class is typically placed in a specification (.h) file, and the implementations of the class member functions reside in the implementation file. The client code is compiled separately from the class implementation file, and the two resulting object code files are linked together to form an executable file. Through separate compilation, the user of an ADT can treat the ADT as an off-the-shelf component without ever seeing how it is implemented.

Quick Check Answers

12.1.1 The characteristics of the data values as well as the behavior of each of the operations on those values. **12.1.2** (1) Choose a concrete data representation using existing data types and (2) implement each of the allowable operations in terms of program instructions. **12.2.1** The `class` **12.2.2** Its name is identical to the name of the class; it is not void, nor does it have a return value type. **12.2.3** One that contains both data and operations within a single, cohesive unit. **12.2.4** A client of the class X. **12.2.5** `Date today;` **12.2.6** `today.GetDay();` **12.3.1** It enables client code to see the formal interface to the class, but none of the implementation details that the creator of the class wishes to hide. **12.3.2** In the heading, between the name of the class and the name of the function. **12.3.3** The encapsulation and hiding of implementation details to keep the user of an abstraction from depending on or incorrectly manipulating the details. **12.3.4** An object code file. **12.3.5** The specification file. **12.4.1** An object is a self-contained entity encapsulating data and operations on the data—an instance of an ADT. **12.4.2** When one object communicates to another object by invoking a method on that object. **12.5.1** The written description of the behavior of a class with respect to its interface. **12.5.2** A transformer or mutator method. **12.5.3** A class is immutable if there are no transformer (mutator) member functions. **12.6.1** immutable **12.6.2** `GetFirstName`, `GetMiddleName`, `GetLastName` **12.7.1** The relationship between classes in which one class contains an instance of another class as one of its attributes. **12.7.2** No, you simply declare an object of one class to be one of the data members of another class. **12.7.3** We must use a constructor initializer to pass the information needed to properly construct the contained object. **12.7.4** `#ifndef, #define, #endif` **12.8.1** To diagram object-oriented applications. **12.8.2** + and −

Exam Preparation Exercises

1. Dot notation is used only by class clients to refer to members. Other class members do not need to use dot notation. True or false?
2. Given the following declarations:

   ```
   class Name
   {
   public:
     string first;
     string middle;
     string last;
   };

   Name yourName;
   Name myName;
   ```

   What are the contents of the two **Name** variables after each of the following statements, assuming they are executed in the order listed?
   a. `yourName.first = "George";`
   b. `yourName.last = "Smith";`
   c. `myName = yourName;`
   d. `myName.middle = "Nathaniel";`
   e. `yourName.middle = myName.middle.at(0) + ".";`
3. What are the two major properties of an abstract data type that are defined in its specification?
4. How does the data representation differ from the domain of an abstract data type?
5. By default, are class members public or private?
6. Suppose you are given an object called **current**, of class **Time**: How would you write the call to its void member function, called **plus**, that adds an integer number of minutes to the current time? The number of minutes to add is found in variable **period**.

7. Which kind of operation—constructor, observer, transformer, or iterator—is implemented by a function that is declared as `const`?
8. A class may have multiple constructors, all with the same name. How does the compiler decide which one to call?
9. A class called `Calendar` has a default constructor and a constructor that accepts an integer value specifying the year. How would you invoke each of these constructors for an object called `primary`? Use the current year as the argument to the second constructor.
10. Which C++ language mechanism implements composition?
11. List three design principles for good class design.
12. What is a constructor initializer?
13. If a header file is used by more than one class, how do you keep the preprocessor from including the definition twice?
14. Distinguish between action responsibilities and knowledge responsibilities.

■ Programming Warm-Up Exercises

1. Write a specification of a Date ADT.
   a. What would be a good class representation?
   b. Name possible action responsibilities.
   c. Name possible knowledge responsibilities.
2. Write the specification file for class `Date` that implements the Date ADT as declared in Exercise 1.
3. Write the implementation for class `Date` from Exercise 2.
4. Write the specification for a Song ADT that represents a song entry in an MP3 library. It should have fields for title, album, artist, playing time in minutes and seconds, and music category. The music category is represented by an enumeration type called `Category`.
   a. What operations should Song ADT have?
   b. What observers should Song ADT have?
5. Write the specification file for class `Song` that implements the Song ADT from Exercise 4.
6. Write the implementation file for the class `Song` from Exercise 5.
7. Programming Problems 3 and 4 in Chapter 10 asked you to develop educational programs for teaching the periods of geologic time. Now that you know how to write classes, you can turn the Period ADT into a class. Write a specification file for class `Period`, which has a private field that's an enumeration type, representing the names of the periods. Class `Period` should have functions that return the period as a string, that return the period as an `int`, that return the starting date of the period, and that increment the period to the next most recent period (if the period is already `NEOGENE`, the increment operation should do nothing). It should have a default constructor that sets the period to `PRECAMBRIAN`, and a constructor with a parameter of the enumeration type to allow the user to create a `Period` object containing any period. For ease of reference, the table of the time periods is repeated here from Chapter 10. Be sure to use appropriate documenting comments.

Period Name	Starting Date (millions of years)
Neogene	23
Paleogene	65
Cretaceous	136
Jurassic	192
Triassic	225
Permian	280
Carboniferous	345
Devonian	395
Silurian	435
Ordovician	500
Cambrian	570
Precambrian	4500

8. Using the `Period` class as specified in Exercise 7, write a For statement that iterates through the periods of geologic times from earliest to most recent, writing out the name of the period and its starting date.

9. Write the function definitions of the two constructors for the `Period` class as specified in Exercise 7.

10. Write the function definition for the `ToInt` observer of the `Period` class specified in Exercise 7.

11. What would the file name be for the file containing the specification of the `Period` class in Exercise 7?

12. Write the `include` directive that would appear near the beginning of the `Period` class implementation file to include the specification file for the `Period` class as described in Exercise 7.

13. Because of floating-point representational errors, monetary amounts that need to be exact should not be stored in floating-point types. Code the specification for a class that represents an amount of money as dollars and cents. This class should have a default constructor that creates an object with zero dollars and zero cents, an observer for dollars, an observer for cents, and an observer that returns the amount as a `float`. It also should have transformers that add and subtract other values of class `Money`. Be sure to use appropriate documenting comments.

14. Write the function definitions of the two constructors for the `Money` class as specified in Exercise 13.

15. What would be the file name for the file containing the specification of the `Money` class in Exercise 13?

16. Write the `include` directive that would appear near the beginning of the `Money` class implementation file to include the specification file for the `Money` class as described in Exercise 13.

17. Write the function definitions for the observer in the `Money` class of Exercise 13 that returns the values as a float.

Programming Problems

1. Imagine you are working for an in-house software team for a company that wants to monitor network access points in a building. Each building has a specified number of

floors, a certain number of rooms per floor, and some number of network access points in a room. Each network access point is labeled with its state as being **on** or **off** and if it is **on** it has the month it was turned on. Design, implement, and test classes that represent buildings, floors, and network access points. Your classes should provide suitable observer methods that allow you to determine how many floors are in a building, how many rooms are on a floor, how many access points are in a room, and if an access point is on or off and which month it was turned on. You should also provide mutator methods that allow you to turn a network access point on or off and to set the month if it is turned on. You should use *composition* as a key strategy in designing these classes—thus, a building should contain floors, floors should contain rooms, and rooms should contain network access points.

2. A software company that develops games has just hired you! Before working on the next version of *Medieval Menace* they have given you the task of implementing the tic-tac-toe game in C++. Tic-tac-toe consists of a 3 × 3 game board of squares where each square is either empty, has an X marker, or has a O marker. Two players represented by an X or an O play the game. The objective is for one player to get three Xs or three Os in a row first. Design, implement, and test classes that represent a tic-tac-toe game board and X and O markers. Your classes should provide suitable observer and mutator methods for modifying the game board and displaying the state of the game. Use your classes to create a game that prompts for player X and player O to place markers at specified locations on the game board. After each move your program should display the current game board to the console. Your program should also check after each move if there is a winning configuration of the game board. If so, the game should complete indicating which player won.

3. Programming Problem 3 in Chapter 10 asked you to develop an educational program to teach users about geologic time. Rewrite that program using a class to implement an ADT representing a period of geologic time. If you did Programming Warm-Up Exercises 7 through 12, this will be a relatively easy task. The program should let the user enter a range of prehistoric dates (in millions of years), and then output the periods that are included in that range. Each time this is done, the user is asked if he or she wants to continue. The goal of the exercise is for the student to try to figure out when each period began, so that he or she can make a chart of geologic time. See Programming Warm-Up Exercise 7 for a list of the geologic time periods and their starting dates.

4. Programming Problem 4 in Chapter 10 asked you to write a second educational program for learning about geologic time. Rewrite that program using a class to implement an ADT representing a period of geologic time. If you did Programming Warm-Up Exercises 7 through 12, then you've already done some of this work. The ADT in those exercises needs to be enhanced with a constructor that takes a string as an argument and converts the string to the corresponding **Period** value (the constructor should work with any style of capitalization of the period names). In this program, the computer picks a date in geologic time and presents it to the student. The student guesses which period corresponds to the date. The student is allowed to continue guessing until he or she gets the right answer. The program then asks the user whether he or she wants to try again, and repeats the process if the answer is "yes." You also may want to write a function that returns the period for a given date; however, this function does not need to be part of the class.

5. Several chapters since Chapter 5 have included Programming Problems that ask you to develop or rewrite a program that outputs the user's weight on different planets. The

goal has been for you to see how the same program can be implemented in different ways. Here we would like you to rewrite the program using a class to represent the planet and its gravity. The class should include a constructor that allows a planet to be specified with a string, using any capitalization (if the string is not a planet name, then Earth should be assumed). The default constructor for the class will create an object representing Earth. The class has an observer operator that takes a weight on Earth as an argument and returns the weight on the planet. It should have a second observer that returns the name of the planet as a string with proper capitalization.

For ease of reference, the information for the original problem is repeated here. The following table gives the factor by which the weight must be multiplied for each planet. The program should output an error message if the user doesn't type a correct planet name. The prompt and the error message should make it clear to the user how a planet name must be entered. Be sure to use proper formatting and include appropriate comments in your code. The output should be labeled clearly and formatted neatly.

Planet	Factor
Mercury	0.4155
Venus	0.8975
Earth	1.0
Moon	0.166
Mars	0.3507
Jupiter	2.5374
Saturn	1.0677
Uranus	0.8947
Neptune	1.1794
Pluto	0.0899

6. Design, implement, and test a class that represents an amount of time in minutes and seconds. The class should provide a constructor that sets the time to a specified number of minutes and seconds. The default constructor should create an object for a time of zero minutes and zero seconds. The class should provide observers that return the minutes and the seconds separately, and an observer that returns the total time in seconds (minutes × 60 + seconds). Boolean comparison observers should be provided that test whether two times are equal, one time is greater than the other, or one time is less than the other. (You may use `RelationType` and function `ComparedTo` if you choose.) A function should be provided that adds one time to another, and another function that subtracts one time from another. The class should not allow negative times (subtraction of more time than is currently stored should result in a time of 0:00). This class should be immutable.

7. Design, implement, and test a class that represents a song on a CD or in an MP3 library. If you did Programming Warm-Up Exercises 4 through 6, you already have a good start. It should have members for title, album, artist, playing time in minutes and seconds, and music category. The music category is represented by an enumeration type called `Category`; make up an enumeration of your favorite categories. The class should have a constructor that allows all of the data members to be set, and a default constructor that sets all of the data members to appropriate empty values. It should have an observer operation for each data member, and an observer that returns all of the data for the song as a string. An observer that compares two songs for equality should be developed as well.

8. Design, implement, and test a class that represents a phone number. The number should be represented by a country code, an area code, a number, and a type. The first three values can be integers. The type member is an enumeration of `HOME`, `OFFICE`, `FAX`, `CELL`, and `PAGER`. The class should provide a default constructor that sets all of the integer values to zero and the type to `HOME`. A constructor that enables all of the values to be set should be provided as well. You also should provide a constructor that takes just the number and type as arguments, and sets the country and area codes to those of your location. The class will have observers that enable each data member to be retrieved, and transformers that allow each data member to be changed. An additional observer should be provided that compares two phone numbers for equality.

■ Case Study Follow-Up

1. Any duplicate time messages are written just before the listing of the events. Change the program so that duplicate time messages are written to `cout` instead, along with appropriate labels.
2. Add the name that goes with the duplicate time on the output.
3. Write a test plan for the case study program.
4. Implement the test plan written in Exercise 3.
5. The comparison function in class `Name` does not change the fields to all uppercase or all lowercase before comparing them. That would result, for example, in a comparison of the names MacTavish and Macauley indicating that MacTavish comes first alphabetically. Rewrite function `ComparedTo` in class `Name` so that all the strings are changed to all uppercase before the comparison is made.
6. Rerun the case study using the `Name` class as altered in Exercise 5.

Array-Based Lists

KNOWLEDGE GOALS

- To understand the structure of a list ADT.
- To know the basic operations associated with a list ADT.
- To recognize the difference between an array and a list.
- To know how a linear search algorithm works.
- To understand the properties of a sorted list ADT.
- To know how an insertion sort works.
- To understand the principle of "divide and conquer" as expressed in the binary search algorithm.

SKILL GOALS

To be able to:

- Represent a list ADT using a C++ class.
- Add an item into a list.
- Remove an item from a list.
- Search for an item in a list.
- Sort the items in a list into ascending or descending order.
- Build a list in sorted order.
- Search for an item in a sorted list using a linear search.
- Search for an item using a binary search.

> **Linear relationship** A relationship in which every element except the first has a unique predecessor, and every element except the last has a unique successor.
>
> **Length** The number of items in a list; it can vary over time.
>
> **Unsorted list** A list in which data items are placed in no particular order with respect to their content; the only relationships between data elements consist of the list predecessor and successor relationships.
>
> **Sorted list** A list whose predecessor and successor relationships are determined by the content of the keys of the items in the list; a semantic relationship exists among the keys of the items in the list.
>
> **Key** A member of a class whose value is used to determine the logical and/or physical order of the items in a list.

Chapter 11 introduced the array, a data structure that is a collection of components of the same type given a single name. In general, a one-dimensional array is a structure used to hold a list of items. In this chapter, we examine algorithms that build and manipulate data stored as a list in a one-dimensional array. We all know intuitively what a "list" is; in our everyday lives we use lists all the time—grocery lists, lists of things to do, lists of addresses, lists of party guests. In computer applications, lists are very useful and popular ways to organize the data. In this chapter, we examine algorithms that build and manipulate a list implemented using a one-dimensional array to hold the items.

These algorithms are implemented as general-purpose functions that can be modified easily to work with many kinds of lists. We conclude with a case study that uses an array as the main data structure.

13.1 What Is a List?

From a logical point of view, a list is a homogeneous collection of elements, with a linear relationship between elements. Here *linear* means that, at the logical level, every element in the list except the first one has a unique predecessor, and every element except the last one has a unique successor.[1] The number of items in the list, which we call the length of the list, is a property of a list. That is, every list has a length.

Lists can be unsorted—their elements may be placed into the list in no particular order—or they can be sorted in a variety of ways. For instance, a list of numbers can be sorted by value, a list of strings can be sorted alphabetically, and a list of addresses could be sorted by ZIP code. When the elements in a sorted list are of composite types, one of the members of the structure, called the key member, determines their logical (and often physical) order. For example, a list of students on a class roll can be sorted alphabetically by name or numerically by student identification number. In the first case, the name is the key; in the second case, the identification number is the key. (See **FIGURE 13.1**.)

If a list cannot contain items with duplicate keys, we say that it has unique keys. (See **FIGURE 13.2**.) This chapter deals with both unsorted lists and lists of elements with unique keys, sorted from smallest to largest key value. The items on the list can be of any type, atomic or composite. In the following discussion, "item," "element," and "component" are synonyms; they refer to what is stored in the list.

QUICK CHECK

13.1.1 What are the three main properties of a list? (p. 664)
13.1.2 What type can the elements of a list be? (p. 664)

13.2 The List as an Abstract Data Type

In this section, we will design a List ADT, which we implement as a general-purpose class in the next section. Let's think about this structure in terms of a to-do list. Before we begin to think about which operations we might need, however, we must ask an important question: For

---

1. At the implementation level, a relationship also exists between the elements, but the physical relationship may not be the same as the logical one.

FIGURE 13.1 List Sorted by Two Different Keys

FIGURE 13.2 List with Duplicate Keys and List with Unique Keys

whom are we designing the ADT? We may be designing it for ourselves to keep in our library of classes. We may be designing it for others to use in a team project. In our discussion, we use the terms "client" and "user" interchangeably, as we sometimes think of them as referring to the people writing the software that uses the class, rather than the software itself.

Let's think about which kinds of operations we might need in a to-do list. Ideally, we start with an empty list each morning and add things to it. Of course, there might also be items on the list left over from the previous day. As we accomplish a task on the list, we cross it off. We want to check whether an item is already on the list. We need to be able to check whether we can add one more item to the list. We also want to check whether the list is empty (we wish!). We ask how many things we have left to do. We go through the list one item at a time, looking for things to do.

Let's translate these observations into operations (responsibilities) for the list. Notice that constructors are obvious because they are prefaced by "create," knowledge observers have a "get" shown, and Boolean observers are prefaced with "is." Likewise, the choice of identifier for transformers gives their type away: "add" and "remove." Note that this is our first experience with using an iterator, an operation that allows us to access the items in a structure one at a time.

Type

    List

Domain

    Each instance of type List is a collection of up to MAX_LENGTH components, each of type ItemType.

Operations

    Create an initially empty list.
    Is the list empty?
    Is the list full?
    Get the current length of the list.
    Insert an item into the list.
    Delete an item from the list.
    Is an item in the list?
    Iterate through the list, returning each item in turn.

This list of operations differs somewhat from the one listed for the IntList ADT that we defined in Chapter 12. First, we have thought about the operations we might need within the context of a specific example. Second, we have used the object-oriented form of the operations, in which the name gives an indication of exactly what the operation does. From this representation of our ADT, we can begin to form the specification for the class that will eventually implement the List ADT.

Refining Responsibilities

Let's go back through the responsibilities, refining them and converting them into function headings. Because we are designing a general-purpose class, we will ask simplified questions that exemplify how we believe the class may be employed. Because the class is intended for widespread use, we should pay special attention to the documentation right from the design stage.

The observers, the tests for full and empty lists, and returning the number of items need no further discussion. Here are their function headings with the appropriate documentation:

```
bool IsEmpty() const;
// Post: Returns true if list is empty; false otherwise

bool IsFull() const;
// Post: Returns true if list if full; false otherwise

int GetLength() const;
// Post: Returns the length of the list
```

The observer that checks whether an item is in the list must take the item as a parameter. Calling this method isThere makes sense.

```
bool IsThere(ItemType item ) const;
// Post: Returns true if item is in the list and false otherwise
```

In designing the transformers, we must make some decisions. For example, do we allow duplicates in our list? This choice has implications for removing items as well as adding items. If we allow duplicates, what do we mean by "deleting an item"? Do we delete just one copy or all of them? Because this chapter focuses on algorithms, for now we just make a decision and design our algorithms to fit that decision. We will examine the effects of other choices in the exercises.

Let's allow only one copy of an item in the list. This decision means that deleting an item removes just one copy. But do we assume that the item to be deleted is in the list? Is it an error if it is not? Or does the deletion operation mean "delete, if there"? Let's use the last meaning.

We now incorporate these decisions into the documentation for the method headings.

```
void Insert(ItemType item);
// Pre:  List is not full and item is not in the list
// Post: item is in the list and length has been incremented

void Delete(ItemType item);
// Post: item is not in the list
```

The iterator allows the user to see each item in the list one at a time. Let's call the method that implements the "Get next item" responsibility `GetNextItem`. The list must keep track of the next item to return when the iterator is called. It does so with a data member that records the position of the next item to be returned. The constructor initializes this position to 0, and it is incremented in `GetNextItem`. The client could use the length of the list to control a loop. Another approach is to provide an observer `HasNext` that asks if the list contains another item that has not been seen. Let's use this second approach and explore the first approach in the exercises. Because invoking `GetNextItem` when `HasNext` is false causes an error, we must state the assumption in the documentation that there is an item to be accessed when `GetNextItem` is called.

What happens if a user adds or removes an item in the middle of an iteration? Nothing good, you can be sure! Depending on whether an insertion or deletion occurs before or after the iteration point, our iteration loop could end up skipping or repeating items.

We have several choices in how we handle this possibly dangerous situation. The list can handle this situation by resetting the current position when we are adding or deleting items, or it can disallow transformer operations while an iteration is taking place. We choose the latter option here by way of an assumption in the documentation. In case the user wants to restart an iteration, let's provide a `ResetList` method that reinitializes the current position.

```
void ResetList()
// The current position is reset to access the first item in the list
bool HasNext()
// Returns true if there is another item to be returned; false
// otherwise
ItemType GetNextItem()
// Assumptions:  No transformers are called during the iteration.
// There is an item to be returned; that is, hasNext is true when
// this method is invoked
// Pre:  ResetList has been called if this is not the first iteration
// Post: Returns item at the current position.
```

All we have left to write is the constructor.

```
List();
// Constructor
// Post: Empty list has been created
```

Data Representation

As defined in Chapter 11, a one-dimensional array is a built-in data structure that consists of a fixed number of homogeneous components. One use for an array is to store a list of values. A list then is made up of an array of values and an integer variable `length` that says how many list elements are stored in the array. Let's call our array `data`. The class construct is used to encapsulate the length and the array of values. From our previous discussion of `GetNextItem`, we know that the list must contain a variable that indicates where in the list the next item is to be found in an iteration. Because we are working with arrays, we assume that this variable will be an integer index. Let's call it `currentPos`.

In **FIGURE 13.3**, you can see that the array goes from `data[0]` through `data[MAX_LENGTH-1]`, but the list elements stored in the array go from `data[0]` through `data[length-1]`. The number of places in the array is fixed, but the number of values in the list that is stored there may vary.

We can use a C++ class named `List` to represent the List ADT in our programs. For the concrete data representation, we use three items: a one-dimensional array to hold the list items, an `int` variable that stores the current length of the list, and an `int` variable that is used for iteration. When we compile the `List` class, we need to supply definitions for `MAX_LENGTH` and `ItemType`, the type of the items in the list.

```
const int MAX_LENGTH = [     ]    // Maximum possible number of
                                  //    components needed
typedef [     ] ItemType;         // Type of each component
                                  //    (a simple type or the
                                  //    string class)
```

Here is the complete specification for the class `List` that implements the ADT List. For this implementation, we use a `MAX_LENGTH` of 100 and an `ItemType` of `string`.

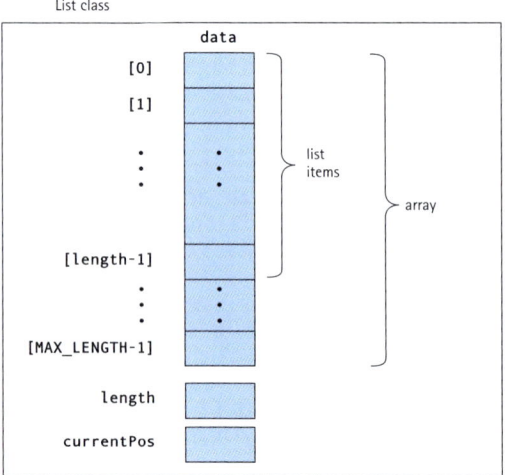

FIGURE 13.3 The Structure of the `List` Class

```cpp
//*****************************************************************
// SPECIFICATION FILE (list.h)
// This file gives the specification of a list abstract data type.
// The list components are not assumed to be in order by value.
//*****************************************************************
#include <string>
const int MAX_LENGTH =100;    // Maximum number of components
typedef int ItemType;         // Type of each component

class List
{
public:
  List();
  // Constructor
  // Post: Empty list has been created

  // Action responsibilities
  void Insert(ItemType item);
  // Pre:  List is not full and item is not in the list
  // Post: item is in the list and length has been incremented
  void Delete(ItemType item);
  // Post: item is not in the list
  void ResetList();
  // The current position is reset to access the first item in the list
  ItemType GetNextItem();
  // Assumptions:  No transformers are called during the iteration.
  // There is an item to be returned; that is, HasNext is true when
  // this method is invoked
  // Pre:  ResetList has been called if this is not the first iteration
  // Post: Returns item at the current position.

  // Knowledge responsibilities
  int GetLength() const;
  // Post: Returns the length of the list
  bool IsEmpty() const;
  // Post: Returns true if list is empty; false otherwise
  bool IsFull() const;
  // Post: Returns true if list is full; false otherwise
  bool IsThere  (ItemType item ) const;
  // Post: Returns true if item is in the list and false otherwise
  bool HasNext() const;
  // Returns true if there is another item to be returned; false
  // otherwise


  private:
    int length;
    int currentPos;
    ItemType data[MAX_LENGTH];
};
```

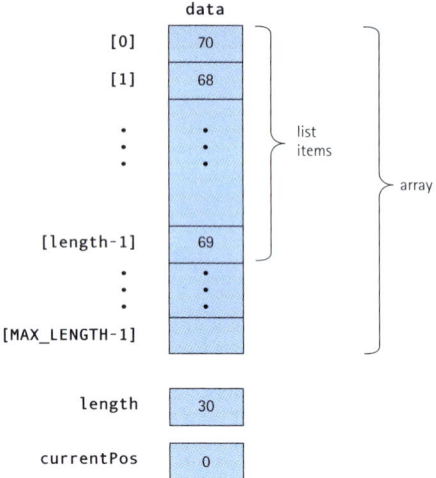

FIGURE 13.4 `myList`: An Instance of Class `List` with Values

In Chapter 12, we classified ADT operations as constructors, transformers, observers, and iterators. `IsEmpty`, `IsFull`, `GetLength`, and `IsThere` are observers. `Insert` and `Delete` are transformers. `GetNextItem` is an iterator. `ResetList` is a transformer that initializes the list before the iterator `GetNextItem` is called. `HasNext` is an observer associated with an iteration. `ResetList`, `HasNext`, and `GetNextItem` work together to allow an iteration to occur. The class constructor is an ADT constructor operation.

To get a `List` object, we have to declare one:

```
List myList;
```

`myList` contains three variables (two `int`, one array), the data representation for a list. (See **FIGURE 13.4**.)

Example Program

Let's look at an example of a client program. Suppose a data file contains a weather station's daily maximum temperature readings for one month, one integer value per day. Unfortunately, the temperature sensor is faulty and occasionally registers a temperature of 200 degrees. The following program uses the `List` class to store the temperature readings, delete any spurious readings of 200 degrees, and output the remaining readings in sorted order. Presumably, the data file contains no more than 31 integers for the month, so its length should be well within the `List` class's `MAX_LENGTH` of 100. However, just in case the file erroneously contains more than `MAX_LENGTH` values, the reading loop in the following program terminates not only if end-of-file is encountered but also if the list becomes full (`IsFull`). Another reason to use the `IsFull` operation in this loop can be found by looking at the function specifications in file `list.h`—namely, we must guarantee `Insert`'s precondition that the list is not full.

```cpp
//******************************************************************
// This program inputs one month's temperature readings from a file,
// stores unique readings in a list, prints the list, removes a value
// of 200, and prints the resulting list.
//******************************************************************
#include <fstream>      // For file I/O
#include "list.h"       // For List class
#include <iostream>
using namespace std;

int main()
{
  List temps;             // List of temperature readings
  int  oneTemp;           // One temperature reading
  ifstream inData;        // File of temperature readings
  ofstream outData;       // Output file

  inData.open("temps.dat");
  if (!inData)
  {
    outData << "Can't open file temps.dat" << endl;
    return 1;
  }

  outData.open("temps.ans");

  inData >> oneTemp;      // Get a temperature
  while (inData && !temps.IsFull())
  {
    if (!temps.IsThere(oneTemp))
      temps.Insert(oneTemp);
    inData >> oneTemp;
  }

  // Output original list
  // Set up for an iteration
  outData << "No. of unique readings: " << temps.GetLength() << endl;
  while (temps.HasNext())
  {
    oneTemp = temps.GetNextItem();
    outData << oneTemp << endl;
  }

  temps.Delete(200);      // Remove 200 if there, cannot be more than one
  temps.ResetList();
  outData << "Readings without value of 200. " << endl;

  while (temps.HasNext())
  {
    oneTemp = temps.GetNextItem();
    outData << oneTemp << endl;
  }

  inData.close();
  outData.close();
  return 0;
}
```

Here is the input file:

temps.dat

```
70 68 69 68 68 72 123 69 87 200
82 200 140 81 200 75 78 68 67 200
65 66 119 61 71 120 77 78 69
```

Given an implementation of the `List` class, this is the expected output file:

temps.ans

```
No. of unique readings: 20
70
68
69
72
123
87
200
82
140
81
75
78
67
65
66
119
61
71
120
77
Readings without value of 200.
70
68
69
72
123
87
77
82
140
81
75
78
67
65
66
119
61
71
120
```

We now consider how to implement each of the ADT operations, given that the list items are stored in an array.

QUICK CHECK

13.2.1 What are the observer methods of the List ADT discussed in this section? (p. 666)
13.2.2 What are the transformer methods of the List ADT discussed in this section? (p. 667)
13.2.3 Which two members of a list class are used to represent the data in a list? (p. 668)

13.3 Implementation of List ADT

Basic Operations

As we discussed in Chapter 12, an ADT should be implemented in C++ by using a pair of files: the specification file (such as the preceding `list.h` file) and the implementation file, which contains the implementations of the class member functions. Here is how the implementation file `list.cpp` starts out:

```
//*****************************************************************
// IMPLEMENTATION FILE (list.cpp)
// This file implements the List class member functions
//*****************************************************************
#include "list.h"
#include <iostream>

using namespace std;
```

Let's look now at the implementations of the basic list operations.

Creating an Empty List

As we saw in Figure 13.4, the list exists in the array elements `data[0]` through `data[length-1]`. To create an empty list, it is sufficient to set the `length` member to 0. We do not need to store any special values into the `data` array to make the list empty, because only those values in `data[0]` through `data[length-1]` are processed by the list algorithms. We also need to set `currentPos` to 0 to initialize the list for an iteration. We will have more to say about this initialization choice when we look at the implementation of the `GetNextItem` function.

```
List::List()
{
  length = 0;
  currentPos = 0;
}
```

The IsEmpty Operation

This operation returns `true` if the list is empty and `false` if the list is not empty. Using our convention that `length` equals 0 if the list is empty, the implementation of this operation is straightforward.

```
bool List::IsEmpty() const
{
  return (length == 0);
}
```

The IsFull Operation

The list is full if there is no more room in the array holding the list items—that is, if the list length equals `MAX_LENGTH`.

```
bool List::IsFull() const
{
  return (length == MAX_LENGTH);
}
```

The GetLength Operation

This operation simply returns to the client the current length of the list.

```
int List::GetLength() const
{
  return length;
}
```

Insertion and Deletion

To devise an algorithm for inserting a new item into the list, we first observe that we are working with an unsorted list. Nothing in the specification indicates that the values have to be maintained in any particular order. As a consequence, we can store a new value into the next available position in the array—`data[length]`—and then increment `length`. This algorithm brings up two questions: Do we need to check that the list has room for the new item? Do we need to be sure the item isn't in the list before we attempt to store it there? The answer to both questions is no. To see why, look back at the precondition on the `Insert` prototype in the specification:

```
void Insert(ItemType item);
// Pre:  List is not full and item is not in the list
// Post: item is in the list and length has been incremented
```

The user is responsible for checking these two conditions; this code is written assuming the precondition is true.

```
void List::Insert(ItemType item)
{
  data[length] = item;
  length++;
}
```

Deleting a component from a list consists of two steps: finding the component and removing it from the list. Before we can write the algorithm, we must know what to do if the component is not there. *Delete* can mean "Delete, if it's there" or "Delete, we know it *is* there" or "Delete one copy" or "Delete all copies." In our discussion of the delete operation earlier, we chose to make this operation mean "Delete, if it's there." This decision is reflected in the `Delete` prototype's documentation.

```
void Delete(ItemType item);
// Post: item is not in the list
```

We must start at the beginning of the list and search for the value to be deleted. If we find it, how do we remove it? We take the last value in the list (the one stored in `data[length-1]`), put it where the item to be deleted is located, and then decrement `length`. Moving the last item from its original position is appropriate only for an unsorted list because we don't need to preserve the order of the items in the list.

The definition "Delete, if it's there" requires a searching loop with a compound condition. We examine each component in turn and stop looking when we find the item to be deleted or when we have looked at all the items and know that it is not there.

```cpp
void List::Delete(ItemType item)
{
  int index = 0;
  while (index < length && item != data[index])
    index++;

  if (index < length)   // item found
  {
    data[index] = data[length-1];
    length--;
  }
}
```

To see how the While loop and the subsequent If statement work, let's look at the two possibilities: either `item` is in the list or it is not. If `item` is in the list, the loop terminates when the expression `index < length` is `true` and the expression `item != data[index]` is `false`. After the loop exit, the If statement finds the expression `index < length` to be `true` and removes the item. Conversely, if `item` is not in the list, the loop terminates when the expression `index < length` is `false`—that is, when `index` becomes equal to `length`. Subsequently, the If condition is `false`, and the function returns without changing anything.

Sequential Search

In the `Delete` function, the algorithm we used to search for the item to be deleted is known as a *sequential* or *linear search* in an unsorted list. We use the same algorithm to implement the `IsThere` function of the `List` class.

```cpp
bool List::IsThere(ItemType item) const
{
  int index = 0;            // Index variable
  while (index < length && item != data[index])
    index++;
  return (index < length);
}
```

This algorithm is called a sequential search because it starts at the beginning of the list and looks at each item in sequence. We stop the search as soon as we find the item we are looking for (or when we reach the end of the list, at which point we conclude that the desired item is not present in the list).

We can use this algorithm in any program requiring a list search. In the form shown here, it searches a list of `ItemType` components, provided that `ItemType` is an integral type or the `string` class; that is, values of `ItemType` can be compared using the relational operators. However, using the relational operators between floating-point values may give unexpected results. Perhaps a note should be added to the specification file giving this warning.

This sequential search algorithm begins at the beginning of the list and searches forward. We could just as easily have begun searching from the last item backward. How would we modify the algorithm to begin at the end? We would initialize `index` to `length-1` and decrement `index` each time through the loop, stopping when we found the item we wanted or when `index` became −1. These changes are highlighted in the following code:

```cpp
bool List::IsThere(ItemType item) const
{
  int index = length-1;      // Index variable
  while (index >= 0 && item != data[index])
    index--;
  return (index < length);
}
```

Before we leave this search algorithm, let's introduce a variation that makes the program more efficient, albeit a little more complex. The While loop contains a compound condition: It stops when it either finds `item` or reaches the end of the list. We can insert a copy of `item` into `data[length]`—that is, into the array component beyond the end of the list—to act as a sentinel. By doing so, we are guaranteed to find `item` in the list. Then we can eliminate the condition that checks for the end of the list (`index < length`).

```
bool List::IsThere(ItemType item) const   // Alternative version
// Copy of item is stored at end of the list to ensure it is found
{
  int index = 0;
  data[length] = item;             // Store item at position beyond end
  while (item != data[index])
    index++;
  return (index < length);
}
```

Is this algorithm really better? Eliminating a condition saves the computer the time that would be required to test it. In this case, we save time during every iteration of the loop, so the savings add up quickly. Note, however, that we are gaining efficiency at the expense of space. We must declare the array size to be one larger than the user's limit to hold the sentinel value if the list becomes full. That is, we must change the documentation to read

```
const int MAX_LENGTH = 100;       // Maximum number of components + 1
```

or change the declaration of the array to be

```
ItemType data[MAX_LENGTH + 1];
```

The comment describes the processing of this loop. Recall that prototype (specification) documentation is intended for the user and contains no implementation details. If the code uses an unusual algorithm, this fact should be noted in the function's definition documentation, which is for the maintainer of the code.

Iterators

Iterators are used with composite types to allow the user to process an entire structure component by component. To give the user access to each item in sequence, we provide three operations: one to initialize the iteration (a process analogous to `Open` with a file), one to determine if there are more items, and one to return a copy of the "next component" each time it is called. The user can then set up a loop that processes each component. We call these operations `ResetList`, `HasNext`, and `GetNextItem`. Note that `ResetList` and `HasNext` are not iterators themselves, but rather are auxiliary functions that support the iteration. Yet another type of iterator takes an operation and applies it to every element in the list.

The `ResetList` function is analogous to the open operation for a file in which the file pointer is positioned at the beginning of the file so that the first input operation accesses the first component of the file. Where is the first item? At position 0; thus `currentPos` must be initialized to 0. Because the constructor sets up the list for the first iteration, `ResetList` is called only on subsequent iterations. However, if it is called for the first iteration, no harm is done: `currentPos` is just set twice.

The `GetNextItem` operation is analogous to an input operation; it accesses the next item (the one at `currentPos`), increments `currentPos`, and returns the item it accessed. What happens if the last item has been accessed? `HasNext` will return false. How can `HasNext` recognize when the last item has been accessed? By testing whether `currentPos` is equal to `length`.

```cpp
void List::ResetList()
{
  currentPos = 0;
}

bool List::HasNext() const
{
  return (currentPos != length);
}

ItemType List::GetNextItem()
{
  ItemType item;
  item = data[currentPos];
  currentPos++;
  return item;
}
```

`Reset` and `GetNextItem` are designed to be used in a loop in the client program that iterates through all of the items in the list. The precondition in the specifications for `GetNextItem` protects against trying to access an array element that is not in the list. Look back at the `Temperature` program. `HasNext` and `GetNextItem` were used once to print the original list; `ResetList`, `HasNext`, and `GetNextItem` were used once to print the corrected list.

SOFTWARE MAINTENANCE CASE STUDY: Enhancing Class List with a Sort

Although we are implementing an unsorted list ADT, sometimes the user of the `List` class may want to rearrange the list components into a certain order just before printing the list. For example, the user might want to put a list of stock numbers into either ascending or descending order, or the user might want to put a list of words into alphabetical order. In software development, arranging list items into order is a very common operation and is known as sorting.

If you were given a sheet of paper with a column of 20 numbers on it and were asked to write the numbers in ascending order, you would probably do the following:

1. Make a pass through the list, looking for the smallest number.
2. Write it on the paper in a second column.
3. Cross the number off the original list.
4. Repeat the process, always looking for the smallest number remaining in the original list.
5. Stop when all the numbers have been crossed off.

Sorting Arranging the components of a list into order (for instance, words into alphabetical order or numbers into ascending or descending order).

We can implement this algorithm directly in C++, but we need two arrays—one for the original list and a second for the sorted list. If the list is large, we might not have enough memory for two copies of it. Also, how do we "cross off" an array component? We could simulate crossing off a value by replacing it with some dummy value like `INT_MAX`. That is, we would set the value of the crossed-off variable to something that would not interfere with the processing of the rest of the components. However, a slight variation of our hand-done algorithm allows us to sort

SOFTWARE MAINTENANCE CASE STUDY: Enhancing Class List with a Sort

the components *in place.* We do not have to use a second array; we can put a value into its proper place in the list by having it swap places with the component currently in that position.

We can state the algorithm as follows: We search for the smallest value in the list and exchange it with the component in the first position in the list. We search for the next-smallest value in the list and exchange it with the component in the second position in the list. This process continues until all the components are in their proper places. **FIGURE 13.5** illustrates how this algorithm works.

Observe that we perform `length-1` passes through the list because `count` runs from 0 through `length-2`. The loop does not need to be executed when `count` equals `length-1` because the last value, `data[length-1]`, is in its proper place after the preceding components have been sorted.

This sort, known as the *straight selection sort,* belongs to a class of sorts called selection sorts. There are many types of sorting algorithms. Selection sorts are characterized by finding the smallest (or largest) value left in the unsorted portion at each iteration and swapping it with the value indexed by the iteration counter. Swapping the contents of two variables requires a temporary variable so that no values are lost (see **FIGURE 13.6**).

Here is the code for the sorting operation of the `List` class. Note that the documentation for the function declaration says *what* the function does; the documentation for the function definition says *how* the function does it.

FIGURE 13.5 Straight Selection Sort

FIGURE 13.6 Swapping the Contents of Two Variables, x and y

SOFTWARE MAINTENANCE CASE STUDY: Enhancing Class `List` with a Sort

```cpp
void Sort();
// Post: List items have been put into ascending order either alphabetical
//       or numeric depending on ItemType.
void List::Sort ()
// Post:  Straight selection sort has been used to sort the list items
{
  ItemType temp;
  int passCount;         // Outer loop control variable
  int searchIndex;       // Inner loop control variable
  int minIndex;          // Index of minimum so far

  for (passCount = 0; passCount < length - 1; passCount++)
  {
    minIndex = passCount;
    // Find the index of the smallest component
    // in data[passCount..length-1]
    for (searchIndex = passCount + 1; searchIndex < length;
        searchIndex++)
      if (data[searchIndex] < data[minIndex])
        minIndex = searchIndex;
    // Swap data[minIndex] and data[passCount]
    temp = data[minIndex];
    data[minIndex] = data[passCount];
    data[passCount] = temp;
  }
}
```

We are looking for the minimum value in the rest of the list (`data[passCount]` through `data[length-1]`) on each pass through the loop. Therefore, `minIndex` is initialized to `passCount` and the inner loop runs from `searchIndex` equal to `passCount+1` through `length-1`. Upon exit from the inner loop, `minIndex` contains the position of the smallest value. (Note that the If statement is the only statement in the loop.)

We may also swap a component with itself—an event that occurs if no value in the remaining list is smaller than `data[passCount]`. We could avoid this unnecessary swap by checking whether `minIndex` is equal to `passCount`. Because this comparison would be made in each iteration of the outer loop, it is more efficient not to check for this possibility and just to swap something with itself occasionally. If the components we are sorting are much more complex than simple numbers, we might reconsider this decision.

Here is the line inserted in the temperature program and the correct output with the values sorted.

```
temps.Sort();
```

```
Valid readings in sorted order.
61
65
66
```

SOFTWARE MAINTENANCE CASE STUDY: Enhancing Class List with a Sort

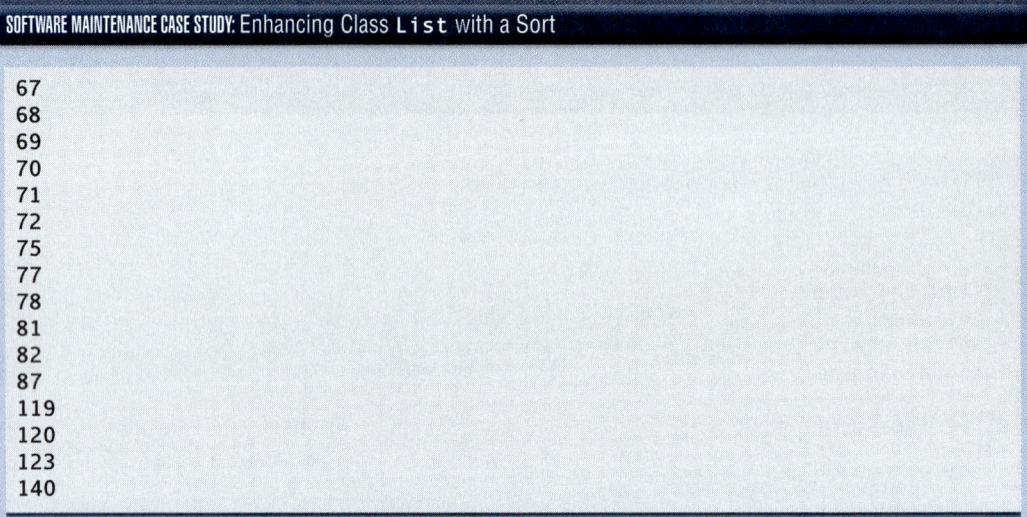

This algorithm sorts the components into ascending order. To sort them into descending order, we would scan for the maximum value instead of the minimum value. To do so, we would simply change the relational operator in the inner loop from < to >. Of course, `minIndex` would no longer be an appropriate identifier and should be changed to `maxIndex`.

By providing the user of the `List` class with a sorting operation, we have *not* turned our unsorted list ADT into a sorted list ADT. The `Insert` and `Delete` algorithms we wrote do not preserve ordering by value. `Insert` places a new item at the end of the list, regardless of its value, and `Delete` moves the last item to a different position in the list. After `Sort` has executed, the list items remain in sorted order only until the next insertion or deletion takes place. In the next section, we look at a sorted list ADT in which all the list operations cooperate to preserve the sorted order of the list components.

QUICK CHECK

13.3.1 Where do we insert a new value into a list that isn't sorted? (p. 674)

13.3.2 If an item isn't in the list, when does a linear search discover that it is missing? (p. 675)

13.3.3 What are the major steps in deleting a value from a list? (p. 674)

13.3.4 How many For loops are there in an implementation of a selection sort? (pp. 677–679)

13.3.5 To create an empty list, what must the length member of the List ADT be initialized to? (p. 673)

13.3.6 What must the `IsEmpty` operation check to determine if a list is empty? (p. 673)

13.3.7 In your own words, what does sequential search do to find an element in the list? (p. 675)

13.4 Sorted Lists

In the `List` class, both of the searching algorithms assume that the list to be searched is unsorted. A drawback to searching an unsorted list is that we must scan the entire list to discover that the search item is *not* there. Think what it would be like if your city telephone book contained people's names in random order rather than alphabetical order. To look up Mary Anthony's phone number, you would have to start with the first name in the phone book and scan sequentially, page after page, until you found it. In the worst case, you might have to examine tens of thousands of names, only to find out that Mary's name is not in the book.

Of course, telephone books *are* alphabetized, and the alphabetical ordering makes searching easier. If Mary Anthony's name is not in the book, you discover this fact quickly by starting with the A's and stopping the search as soon as you have passed the place where her name should be.

Let's define a sorted list ADT in which the components always remain in order by value, no matter which operations are applied. Following is the `SortedList.h` file that contains the declaration of a `SortedList` class.

```cpp
//****************************************************************
// SPECIFICATION FILE (SortedList.h)
// This file gives the specification of a SortedList abstract data
// type. The components are assumed to be in order by value.
//****************************************************************
const int MAX_LENGTH = 100;   // Maximum number of components
typedef int ItemType;          // Type of each component

class SortedList
{
public:
  // Action responsibilities
  void Insert(ItemType item);
  // Pre:  List is not full, item is not in the list, and
  //       the list items are sorted in ascending order
  // Post: item is in the list, length has been incremented, and
  //       the list items are sorted in ascending order
  void Delete(ItemType item);
  // Pre:  The list items are sorted in ascending order
  // Post: item is not in the list and the list items are sorted
  //       in ascending order
  void ResetList();
  // The current position is reset to access the first item in the list
  ItemType GetNextItem();
  // Assumptions:  No transformers are called during the iteration.
  // There is an item to be returned; that is, HasNext is true when
  // this method is invoked.
  // Pre:  ResetList has been called if this is not the first iteration.
  // Post: Returns item at the current position.
```

```cpp
  // Knowledge responsibilities
  bool IsEmpty() const;
  // Post: Returns true if list is empty; false otherwise
  bool IsFull() const;
  // Post: Returns true if list if full; false otherwise
  int GetLength() const;
  // Post: Returns the length of the list
  bool IsThere(ItemType item) const;
  // Post: Returns true if item is in the list and false otherwise
  bool HasNext() const;
  // Returns true if there is another item to be returned; false
  // otherwise

  SortedList();
   // Constructor
   // Post: Empty list has been created

  private:
    int length;
    int currentPos;
    ItemType data[MAX_LENGTH];
    void BinarySearch(ItemType item, bool& found, int& position);
};
```

How does the declaration of **SortedList** differ from the declaration of our original **List** class? Apart from a few changes in the documentation comments, there are only two differences:

1. The **SortedList** class does not supply a sorting operation to the client. Such an operation is not needed, because the list components are assumed to be kept in sorted order at all times.
2. The **SortedList** class has an additional class member in the private part: a **BinarySearch** function. This function is an auxiliary ("helper") function that is used only by other class member functions and is inaccessible to clients. We discuss its purpose when we examine the class implementation.

Let's look at which changes, if any, are required in the algorithms for the ADT operations, given that we are now working with a sorted list instead of an unsorted list.

Basic Operations

The algorithms for the class constructor, **IsEmpty**, **IsFull**, **GetLength**, **ResetList**, **HasNext**, and **GetNextItem** are identical to those used for the **List** class. The constructor sets the private data member **length** to 0, **IsEmpty** reports whether **length** equals 0, **IsFull** reports whether **length** equals **MAX_LENGTH**, **GetLength** returns the value of **length**, and the three iteration-related functions set up subsequent iterations, determine whether there is an unseen item, and get the next item.

Insertion

To add a new value to an already sorted list, we could store the new value at `data[length]`, increment `length`, and sort the array again. However, such a solution is *not* an efficient way of solving the problem. Inserting five new items results in five separate sorting operations.

If we were to insert a value by hand into a sorted list, we would write the new value out to the side and draw a line showing where it belongs. To find this position, we start at the top and scan the list until we find a value greater than the one we are inserting. The new value goes in the list just before that point.

We can use a similar process in our `Insert` function. We find the proper place in the list using the by-hand algorithm. Instead of writing the value to the side, we shift all the values larger than the new one down one place to make room for it. The main algorithm is expressed as follows, where `item` is the value being inserted.

```
WHILE place not found AND more places to look
    IF item > current component in list
        Increment current position
    ELSE
        Place found
Shift remainder of list down
Insert item
Increment length
```

Assuming that `index` is the place where `item` is to be inserted, the algorithm for Shift List Down is

```
Set data[length]     =   data[length–1]
Set data[length–1]   =   data[length–2]
       .                       .
       .                       .
       .                       .
Set data[index+1]    =   data[index]
```

This algorithm is illustrated in **FIGURE 13.7**. It is based on how we would accomplish the task by hand. Often, such an adaptation is the best way to solve a problem. However, in this case, further thought reveals a slightly better way. Notice that we search from the front of the list (people always do), and we shift down from the end of the list upward. We can combine the searching and shifting by beginning at the *end* of the list.

If `item` is the new item to be inserted, we can compare `item` to the value in `data[length-1]`. If `item` is *less* than this value, we put `data[length-1]` into `data[length]` and compare `item` to the value in `data[length-2]`. This process continues until we find the place where `item`

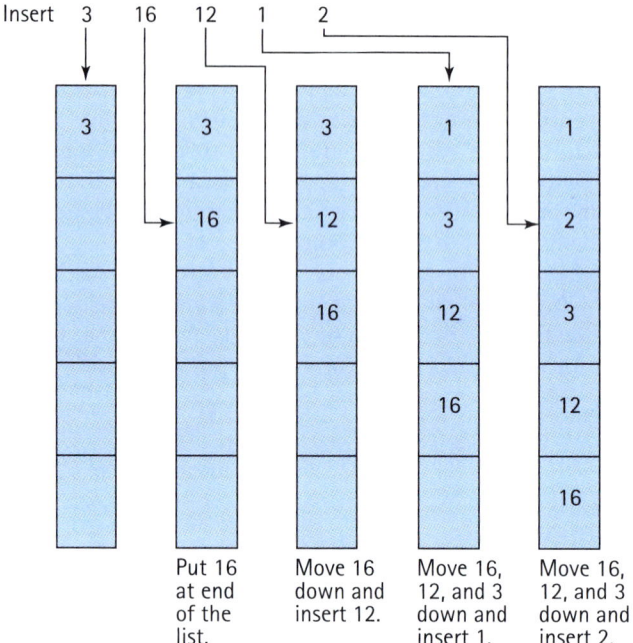

FIGURE 13.7 Inserting an Item into a Sorted List

is greater than or equal to the item in the list. We then store **item** directly below it. Here is the algorithm:

```
Set index = length – 1
WHILE index >= 0 AND item < data[index]
    Set data[index + 1] = data[index]
    Decrement index
Set data[index + 1] = item
Increment length
```

```
void SortedList::Insert(ItemType item)
// Search for insertion point begins at the end.  Items are compared
// and shifted until insertion place is found.
{
  int index;
  index = length - 1;
  while (index >= 0 && item < data[index])
  {
    data[index+1] = data[index];
    index--;
  }
  data[index+1] = item;          // Insert item
  length++;
}
```

Notice that this algorithm works even if the list is empty. When the list is empty, `length` is 0 and the body of the While loop is not entered. Thus `item` is stored into `data[0]`, and `length` is incremented to 1. Does the algorithm work if `item` is the smallest? The largest? Let's see: If `item` is the smallest, the loop body is executed `length` times, and `index` is -1. Thus `item` is stored into position 0, where it belongs. If `item` is the largest, the loop body is not entered. The value of `index` is still `length-1`, so `item` is stored into `data[length]`, where it belongs.

Are you surprised that the general case also takes care of the special cases? This situation does not happen all the time, but it occurs often enough that it is good programming practice to start with the general case. If we begin with the special cases, we usually generate a correct solution, but we may not realize that we don't need to handle the special cases separately. So begin with the general case, then treat as special cases only those situations that the general case does not handle correctly.

This algorithm is the basis for another general-purpose sorting algorithm—an *insertion sort*, in which values are inserted one at a time into a list that was originally empty. The insertion sort is often used when input data must be sorted; each value is put into its proper place as it is read. We use this technique in the Problem-Solving Case Study at the end of this chapter.

Sequential Search

When we search for an item in an unsorted list, we won't discover that the item is missing until we reach the end of the list. If the list is already sorted, we know that an item is missing when we pass the place where it should be in the list. For example, suppose a list contains these values:

7
11
13
76
98
102

If we are looking for 12, we need only compare 12 with 7, 11, and 13 to know that 12 is not in the list.

If the search item is greater than the current list component, we move on to the next component. If the item is equal to the current component, we have found what we are looking for. If the item is less than the current component, then we know that it is not in the list. In either of the last two cases, we stop looking. We can restate this process algorithmically with the following code, in which `found` is set to `true` if the search item was found.

```
// Sequential search in a sorted list

index = 0;
while (index < length && item > data[index])
  index++;
found = (index < length && item == data[index]);
```

On average, searching a sorted list in this way takes the same number of iterations to find an item as searching an unsorted list. The advantage of this new algorithm is that we find out sooner if an item is missing. Thus it is slightly more efficient. There is an even better approach to searching in a sorted list, however.

Binary Search

A second search algorithm on a sorted list is considerably faster than a sequential search both for finding an item and for discovering that an item is missing. This algorithm is called a *binary search*. A binary search is based on the principle of successive approximation. The algorithm divides the list in half (divides by 2—that's why it's called *binary* search) and decides which half to look in next. Division of the selected portion of the list is repeated until the item is found or it is determined that the item is not in the list.

This method is analogous to the way in which we look up a word in a dictionary. We open the dictionary in the middle and compare the word with one on the page that we turned to. If the word we're looking for comes before this word, we continue our search in the left-hand section of the dictionary. Otherwise, we continue in the right-hand section of the dictionary. We repeat this process until we find the word. If it is not there, we realize that either we have misspelled the word or our dictionary isn't complete.

The algorithm for a binary search is given below. In this algorithm, the list of values is in the array **data**, and the value being looked for is **item** (see **FIGURE 13.8**).

1. Compare **item** to **data[middle]**. If **item = data[middle]**, then we have found it. If **item < data[middle]**, then we look in the first half of **data**. If **item > data[middle]**, then we look in the second half of **data**.
2. Redefine **data** to be the half of **data** that we search next, and repeat Step 1.
3. Stop when we have found **item** or know it is missing. We know it's missing when there is nowhere else to look and we still have not found it.

This algorithm should make sense. With each comparison, at best, we find the item for which we are searching; at worst, we eliminate half of the remaining list from consideration.

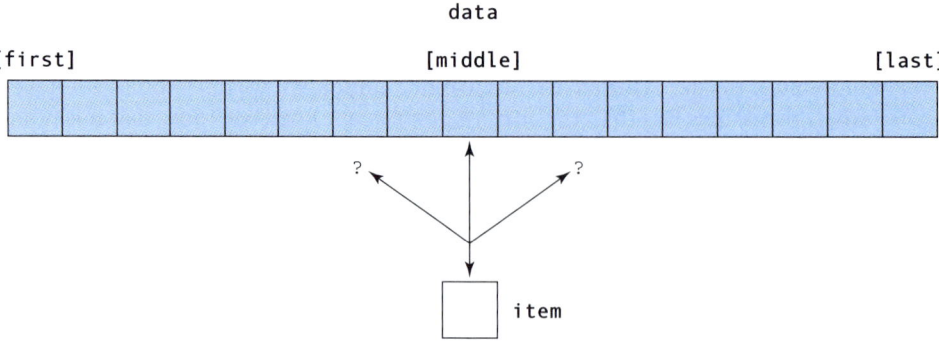

FIGURE 13.8 Binary Search

We need to keep track of the first possible place to look (`first`) and the last possible place to look (`last`). At any one time, we are looking only in `data[first]` through `data[last]`. When the function begins, `first` is set to 0 and `last` is set to `length-1` to encompass the entire list.

Our three previous search algorithms have been Boolean observer operations. They just answer a simple question: Is this item in the list? Let's code the binary search as a void function that not only asks whether the item is in the list, but also asks which one it is (if the item is there). To do so, we need to add two parameters to the parameter list: a Boolean flag `found` (to tell us whether the item is in the list) and an integer variable `position` (to tell us which item it is). If `found` is `false`, `position` is undefined.

```cpp
void SortedList::
    BinarySearch(ItemType item, bool& found, int& position)
// Uses binary search algorithm to search list for item.
// If item is found, found is true and position is its index;
// else found is false and position is undefined
{
  int first = 0;            // Lower bound on list
  int last = length - 1;    // Upper bound on list
  int middle;               // Middle index
  found = false;
  while (last >= first && !found)
  {
    middle = (first + last) / 2;
    if (item < data[middle])
      // item is not in data[middle..last]
      last = middle - 1;
    else if (item > data[middle])
      // item is not in data[first..middle]
      first = middle + 1;
    else
      // item == data[middle]
      found = true;
  }
  if (found)
    position = middle;
}
```

Should `BinarySearch` be a public member of the `SortedList` class? No. The function returns the index of the array element where the item was found. An array index is useless to a client of `SortedList`. The array containing the list items is encapsulated within the private part of the class and is inaccessible to clients. If you review the `SortedList` class declaration, you'll see that function `BinarySearch` is a *private* (not public), class member. We intend to use it as a helper function when we implement the public operations `IsThere` and `Delete`. The documentation reflects that it is a helper function: The function declaration has no documentation, and the function definition states what algorithm is used.

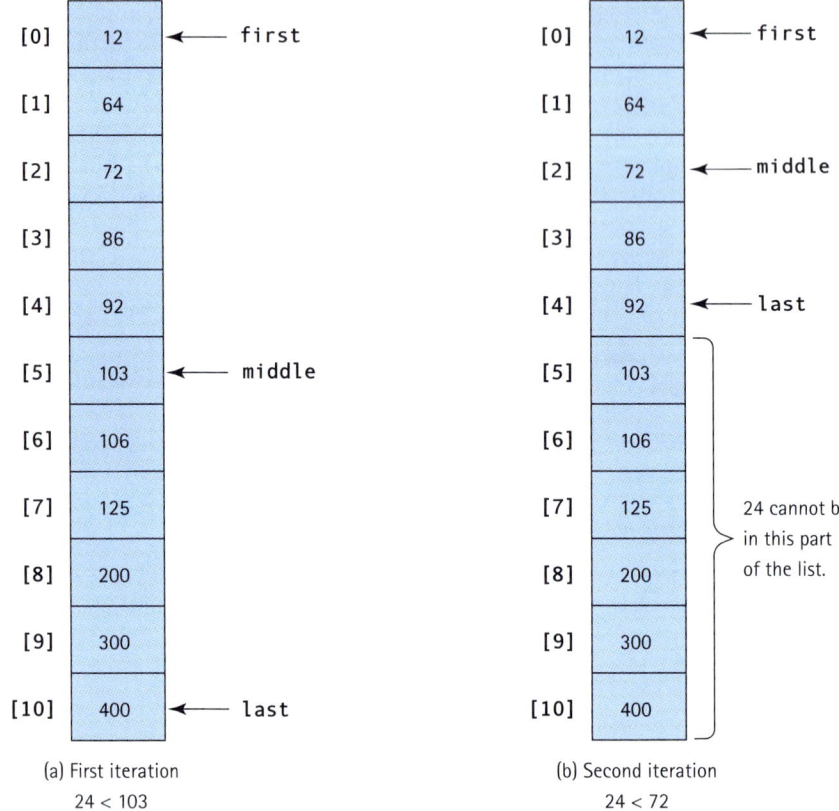

FIGURE 13.9A and B Code Walk-Through of `BinarySearch` Function (`item` is 13)

Let's do a code walk-through of the binary search algorithm. The value being searched for is 24. **FIGURE 13.9A** shows the values of `first`, `last`, and `middle` during the first iteration. In this iteration, 24 is compared with 103, the value in `data[middle]`. Because 24 is less than 103, `last` becomes `middle-1` and `first` stays the same. **FIGURE 13.9B** shows the situation during the second iteration. This time, 24 is compared with 72, the value in `data[middle]`. Because 24 is less than 72, `last` becomes `middle-1` and `first` again stays the same.

In the third iteration (**FIGURE 13.9C**), `middle` and `first` are both 0. The value 24 is compared with 12, the value in `data[middle]`. Because 24 is greater than 12, `first` becomes `middle+1`. In the fourth iteration (**FIGURE 13.9D**), `first`, `last`, and `middle` are all the same. Again, 24 is compared with the value in `data[middle]`. Because 24 is less than 64, `last` becomes `middle-1`. Now that `last` is less than `first`, the process stops; `found` is `false`.

The binary search is the most complex algorithm that we have examined so far. The following table shows `first`, `last`, `middle`, and `data[middle]` for searches of the values 106, 400, and 406, using the same data as in the previous example. Examine the results in this table carefully.

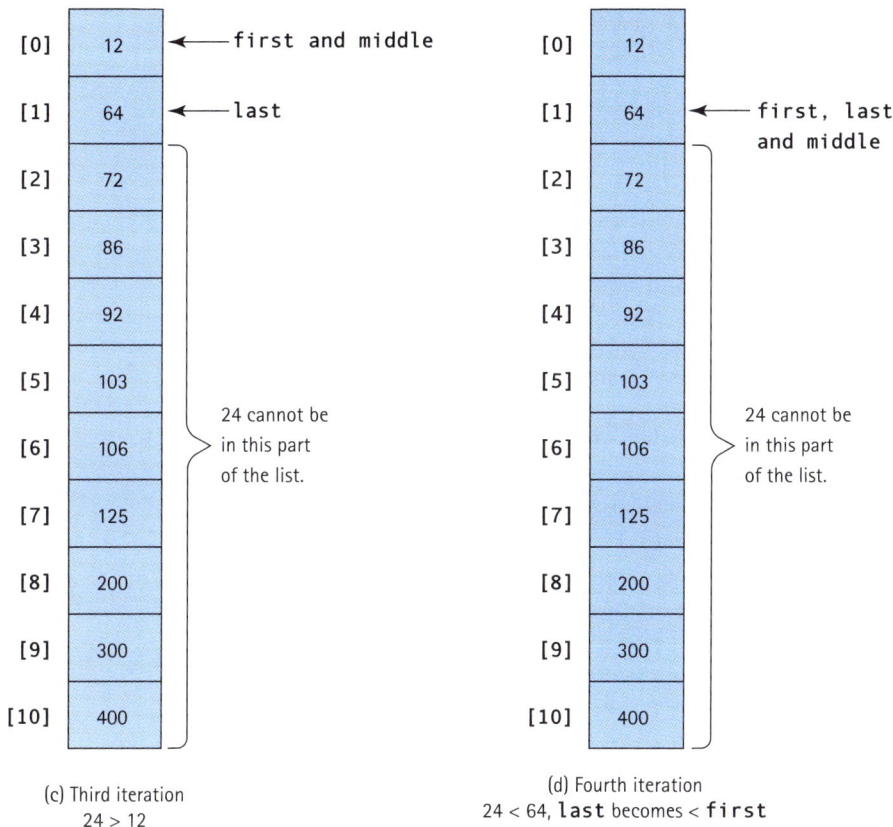

FIGURE 13.9C and D *(continued)*

item	first	last	middle	data[middle]	Termination of Loop
106	0	10	5	103	
	6	10	8	200	
	6	7	6	106	found = true
400	0	10	5	103	
	6	10	8	200	
	9	10	9	300	
	10	10	10	400	found = true
406	0	10	5	103	
	6	10	8	200	
	9	10	9	300	
	10	10	10	400	
	11	10			last < first
					found = false

Notice in this table that whether we searched for 106, 400, or 406, the loop never executed more than four times. In fact, it *never* executes more than four times in a list of 11 components because the list is being cut in half each time through the loop. The following table compares a sequential search and a binary search in terms of the average number of iterations needed to find an item.

| | Average Number of Iterations | |
Length of List	Sequential Search	Binary Search
10	5.5	2.9
100	50.5	5.8
1000	500.5	9.0
10,000	5000.5	12.4

If the binary search is so much faster, why not use it all the time? It certainly is faster in terms of the number of times through the loop, but more computations are performed within the binary search loop than in the other search algorithms. Thus, if the number of components in the list is small (say, fewer than 20 items), a sequential search algorithm is faster because it performs less work at each iteration. As the number of components in the list increases, the binary search algorithm becomes relatively more efficient. Remember, however, that the binary search requires the list to be sorted, and sorting takes time. Keep three factors in mind when you are deciding which search algorithm to use:

1. The length of the list to be searched
2. Whether the list is already sorted
3. The number of times the list is to be searched

Given the **BinarySearch** function (a private member of the **SortedList** class), it's easy to implement the **IsThere** function (a public member of the class).

```
bool SortedList::IsThere (ItemType item) const
// Calls helper function BinarySearch to look for item
{
  bool found;
  int position;        // Not used but required for BinarySearch
  BinarySearch(item, found, position);
  return found;
}
```

The body of **IsThere** calls **BinarySearch**, obtaining the result of the search in the variables **found** and **position**. Like the children's game of Pass It On, **IsThere** receives the value of **found** from **BinarySearch** and simply passes it on to the client (via the Return statement). The body of **IsThere** is not interested in where the item was found, so it ignores the value returned in the **position** argument. Why did we include this third argument when we designed **BinarySearch**? The answer is that the **Delete** operation, which we look at next, calls **BinarySearch** and *does* use the position argument.

Deletion

In the **List** class's **Delete** function, we deleted an item by moving up the last component in the list to fill the deleted item's position. Although this algorithm is fine for unsorted lists, it won't work for sorted lists. Moving the last component to an arbitrary position in the list is almost certain to disturb the sorted order of the components. Instead, we need a new algorithm for sorted lists.

Let's call **BinarySearch** to tell us the position of the item to be deleted. Then we can "squeeze out" the deleted item by shifting up all the remaining array elements by one position:

```
IF found
    Shift remainder of list up
    Decrement length
```

The algorithm for Shift List Up is

```
Set data[position]   = data[position+1]
Set data[position+1] = data[position+2]
       .                    .
       .                    .
       .                    .
```

Here is the coded version of this algorithm:

```
void SortedList::Delete( ItemType item)
// Calls helper function BinarySearch to find if the item is in the list
// and the index position if there
{
  bool found;      // True if item is found
  int position;    // Position of item, if found
  int index;       // Index and loop control variable

  BinarySearch(item, found, position);
  if (found)
  {
    // Shift data[position..length-1] up one position
    for (index = position; index < length - 1; index++)
      data[index] = data[index+1];
    length--;
  }
}
```

Here is a similar client program that reads words, rather than numbers:

```
//*******************************************************************
// This program inputs a file of words, stores the words, removing
// duplicates, and prints the list.
//*******************************************************************
#include <fstream>           // For file I/O
#include "SortedList.h"      // For List class

using namespace std;

int main()
{
  SortedList words;          // List of words
  string   oneWord;          // One word
  ifstream inData;           // File of temperature readings
  ofstream outData;          // Output file

  inData.open("words.dat");
  if (!inData)
  {
    outData << "Can't open file words.dat" << endl;
    return 1;
  }
```

```
  outData.open("words.ans");
  inData >> oneWord;          // Get a word
  while (inData && !words.IsFull())
  {
    if (!words.IsThere(oneWord))
      words.Insert(oneWord);
    inData >> oneWord;
  }

  // Output original list
  // Set up for an iteration
  outData << words.GetLength() << " unique words." << endl;
  while (words.HasNext())
  {
    oneWord = words.GetNextItem();
    outData << oneWord << endl;
  }

  inData.close();
  outData.close();
  return 0;
}
```

The only change necessary in the `SortedList` class was from

```
typedef int ItemType;          // Type of each component
```

to

```
using namespace std;
typedef string ItemType;       // Type of each component
```

Input (words.dat)

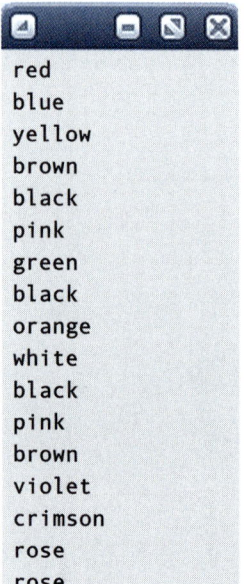

red
blue
yellow
brown
black
pink
green
black
orange
white
black
pink
brown
violet
crimson
rose
rose

Output (words.ans)

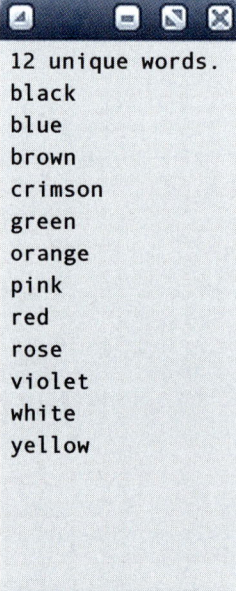

12 unique words.
black
blue
brown
crimson
green
orange
pink
red
rose
violet
white
yellow

THEORETICAL FOUNDATIONS
Complexity of Searching and Sorting

We introduced Big-O notation in Chapter 6 as a way of comparing the work done by different algorithms. Let's apply it to the algorithms that we've developed in this chapter and see how they compare with each other. In each algorithm, we start with a list containing some number of values, N.

In the worst case, our `List::IsThere` function scans all N values to locate an item. Thus, it requires N steps to execute. On average, `List::IsThere` takes roughly $N/2$ steps to find an item; however, recall that in Big-O notation, we ignore constant factors (as well as lower-order terms). Thus function `List::IsThere` is an order N—that is, an $O(N)$—algorithm.

The alternative version of `IsThere` is also an $O(N)$ algorithm because even though we saved a comparison on each loop iteration, the same number of iterations is performed. However, making the loop more efficient without changing the number of iterations decreases the constant (the number of steps) that N is multiplied by in the algorithm's work formula. Thus the alternative version of function `List::IsThere` is said to be a constant factor faster than `List::IsThere`.

What about the algorithm we presented for a sequential search in a sorted list? The number of iterations is decreased for the case in which the item is missing from the list. However, all we have done is take a case that would require N steps and reduce its time, on average, to $N/2$ steps. Therefore, this algorithm is also $O(N)$.

Now consider `BinarySearch`. In the worst case, it eliminates half of the remaining list components on each iteration. Thus the worst-case number of iterations is equal to the number of times N must be divided by 2 to eliminate all but one value. This number is computed by taking the logarithm, base 2, of N (written $\log_2 N$). Here are some examples of $\log_2 N$ for different values of N:

N	$\log_2 N$
2	1
4	2
8	3
16	4
32	5
1024	10
32,768	15
1,048,576	20
33,554,432	25
1,073,741,824	30

As you can see, for a list of more than 1 billion values, `BinarySearch` takes only 30 iterations. It is definitely the best choice for searching large lists. Algorithms such as `BinarySearch` are said to be of *logarithmic order*.

THEORETICAL FOUNDATIONS Complexity of Searching and Sorting, continued

Now let's turn to sorting. Function `Sort` contains nested For loops. The total number of iterations is the product of the iterations performed by the two loops. The outer loop executes $N - 1$ times. The inner loop also starts out executing $N - 1$ times, but steadily decreases until it performs just one iteration: The inner loop executes $N/2$ iterations. The total number of iterations is thus

$$\frac{(N-1) \times N}{2}$$

Ignoring the constant factor and lower-order term, this is N^2 iterations, and `Sort` is an $O(N^2)$ algorithm. Whereas `BinarySearch` takes only 30 iterations to search a sorted array of 1 billion values, putting the array into order takes `Sort` approximately 1 billion times 1 billion iterations!

We mentioned that the `SortedList::Insert` algorithm forms the basis for an insertion sort, in which values are inserted into a sorted list as they are input. On average, `SortedList::Insert` must shift down half of the values ($N/2$) in the list; thus it is an $O(N)$ algorithm. If `SortedList::Insert` is called for each input value, we are executing an $O(N)$ algorithm N times; therefore, an insertion sort is an $O(N^2)$ algorithm.

Is every sorting algorithm $O(N^2)$? Most of the simpler ones are, but $O(N \times \log_2 N)$ sorting algorithms exist. Algorithms that are $O(N \times \log_2 N)$ are much closer in performance to $O(N)$ algorithms than are $O(N^2)$ algorithms. For example, if N is 1 million, then an $O(N^2)$ algorithm takes 1 million times 1 million (1 trillion) iterations, but an $O(N \times \log_2 N)$ algorithm takes only 20 million iterations—that is, it is 20 times slower than the $O(N)$ algorithm but 50,000 times faster than the $O(N^2)$ algorithm.

QUICK CHECK

- **13.4.1** How does a sorted list ADT differ from a list ADT that includes a sort operation? (pp. 681–682)
- **13.4.2** When inserting into a sorted list, what happens to the components that precede the insertion point and the components that follow it? (pp. 683–685)
- **13.4.3** Where does the binary search algorithm get its name? (p. 686)
- **13.4.4** Which operations in a sorted list are different from the operations in an unsorted list, and how do they differ? (p. 682)
- **13.4.5** What condition ends a binary search? (p. 686)
- **13.4.6** What is binary search analogous to in the real world? (p. 686)

13.5 Sorted List of Classes

In Chapter 12, we created an `Entry` class in preparation for an appointment calendar. Now let's create a sorted list of `Entry` objects. Sorted—by what? Name or time? Because we are looking ahead toward creating an appointment calendar, let's keep the list sorted by time.

Can we use our `SortedList` class as is or must we make some changes? If the items on the list can be compared using the relational operators, then the only change necessary is the type of `ItemType`. If the items on the list are of a type that cannot be compared by the relational operators, the class must provide a comparison operator. Our `Entry` class does not have a comparison function, but our `TimeOfDay` class does: `ComparedTo`. We must enhance class `Entry` with a `ComparedTo` function, which merely calls the `TimeOfDay ComparedTo` function.

Which `SortedList` functions need to be changed because they compare objects? `IsThere`, `Insert`, and `Delete` compare two objects. First we add function `ComparedTo` to class `Entry`.

```
//*************************************************************
// SPECIFICATION FILE (Entry.h)
// This file contains the specification of the Entry ADT, which has
// two contained classes, Name and Time.
// A ComparedTo function has been added to this class.
//*************************************************************

#include "TimeOfDay.h"
#include "Name.h"
#include <sstream>
#include <string>
#include "RelationType"

class Entry
{
public:
  string GetNameStr() const;
  // Post: Returns the first and last name of Name object
  //       with a blank in between
  string GetTimeStr() const;
  // Post: Returns the hours and minutes from TimeOfDay object
  //       with a colon in between
  Entry();
  // Default constructor
  // Post: Entry object has been constructed
  //       Name and TimeOfDay objects have been constructed using
  //       their default constructors
  Entry(string firstName, string middleName, string lastName,
        int  initHours, int  initMinutes, int  initSeconds );
  // Parameterized constructor
```

```
      // Post: Entry object has been constructed
      //       Name and TimeOfDay objects have been constructed using
      //       their parameterized constructors
    RelationType ComparedTo(Entry otherEntry) const;
    // Post: Returns
    //       BEFORE if instance's time object is earlier than otherEntry's
    //       SAME if they are identical
    //       AFTER if instance's time object is later than otherEntry's
private:
  Name name;
  TimeOfDay time;
};

RelationType Entry::ComparedTo(Entry otherEntry) const
{
  return (time.ComparedTo(otherEntry.time))
}
```

Now we can examine the changes in the `SortedList` class.

IsThere

Because the list is sorted, we should first convert the BinarySearch algorithm. We need to replace the cascading If statements with a Switch statement using the result of `ComparedTo`. The initializations remain the same.

BinarySearch(In: item, Out: found, position)

WHILE last >= first and !found
    Set middle to (first + last) / 2
       SWITCH (item.ComparedTo(data[middle]))
          BEFORE: Set last to middle – 1
          SAME: Set found to true
                  Set position to middle
          AFTER: Set first to middle + 1

IsThere(In: item)
Return value: Boolean

BinarySearch(item, found, position)
return found

Here is the revised code for function `BinarySearch`. `IsThere` doesn't change; it only calls `BinarySearch`.

```
void SortedList::BinarySearch(ItemType item, bool& found, int& position)
     const
// Uses binary search algorithm to search list for item.
// If item is found, found is true and position is its index;
// else found is false and position is undefined
{
  int first = 0;            // Lower bound on list
  int last = length - 1;    // Upper bound on list
  int middle;               // Middle index
  found = false;
  while (last >= first && !found)
  {
    middle = (first + last) / 2;
    switch (item.ComparedTo(data[middle]))
    {
      case BEFORE:  last = middle - 1;
                    break;
      case SAME:    found = true;
                    position = middle;
                    break;
      case AFTER:   first = middle + 1;
                    break;
    }
  }
}
```

Insert and Delete

Function **Delete** calls **BinarySearch** to find the item to delete and makes no further comparison. Therefore, we don't need to make any changes in **Delete**. **Insert** repetitively compares **item** to a list value until one is found that is greater than **item** or there are no more values to check. Thus the code can be changed without having to rewrite the algorithm. The change is highlighted in the following code:

```
void SortedList::Insert(ItemType item)
// Search for insertion point begins at the end. Items are compared
// and shifted until insertion place is found
{
    int index;
    index = length - 1;
    while (index >= 0 && item.ComparedTo(data[index]) == BEFORE)
    {
      data[index+1] = data[index];
      index--;
    }
    data[index+1] = item;          // Insert item
    length++;
}
```

Here is a client program that inserts entries into a sorted list, demonstrates a test for a duplicate item, and then prints the list:

```cpp
//****************************************************************
// DRIVER for class SortedList of Entry objects
//****************************************************************
#include <iostream>
#include "Entry.h"
#include "RelationType.h"
#include "SortedList.h"
#include <string>

using namespace std;

int main ()
{
  SortedList list;
  Entry entry1("Sally", "Jane", "Smith", 12, 20, 0);
  Entry entry2("Mary", "Beth", "Jones", 10, 30, 0);
  Entry entry3("Bill", "John", "Baker", 8, 25, 30);
  list.Insert(entry1);
  list.Insert(entry2);
  list.Insert(entry3);
  if (list.IsThere(entry2))
    cout << "Duplicate: " << entry2.GetNameStr() << " not inserted"
         << endl;
  list.ResetList();
  while (list.HasNext())
  {
    entry1 = list.GetNextItem();
    cout << entry1.GetNameStr() << " " << entry1.GetTimeStr() << endl;
  }
}
```

Output:

```
Duplicate: Mary Jones not inserted
Bill Baker 08:25:30
Mary Jones 10:30:00
Sally Smith 12:20:00
```

A word of caution is in order here: When you have classes that contain other classes that contain other classes, you should use the preprocessor commands

```
#ifndef SOMECLASS
#define SOMECLASS
. . .
#endif
```

around the lower-level classes, to avoid duplicate definitions.

13.6 More on UML Diagrams

In Chapter 12, we introduced UML diagrams that show how classes relate to one another. It is clear that the sorted list of `Entry` objects is quite complex. Let's examine how the classes relate to one another.

Class `Entry` contains (through composition) objects of classes `Name` and `TimeOfDay`.

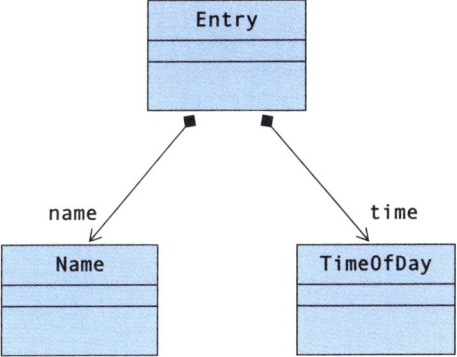

In turn, class `SortedList` contains an array of `Entry` objects.

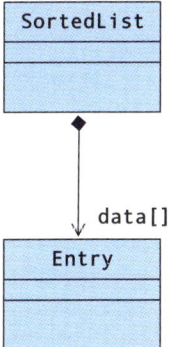

Now add the client program into the mix. What is its relationship to these classes? In our example, `main` declares three variables of type `Entry` and then inserts them into a variable of type `SortedList`. Through these our client program also contains objects of classes `Name` and `TimeOfDay`.

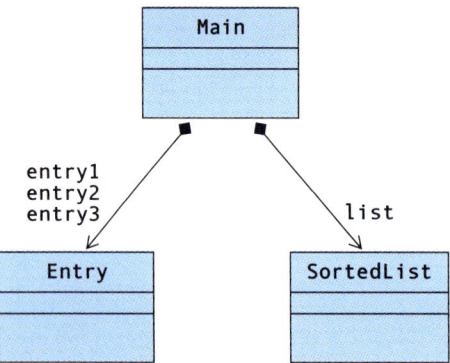

Technically, `main` is not a class, but rather a function. However, we give it a box in the UML diagram to show its relationship with the classes with which it interacts. In some other object-oriented programming languages, such as Java, `main` or its equivalent would be defined within a class because the class is the primary means of organizing code in those languages. Because C++ is more closely aligned with C, which is not object oriented, code in C++ can be organized into both classes and independent functions. Some programmers would argue that, to make a C++ application more purely object oriented, `main` should contain only a call to a method within a class; they would, therefore, omit `main` from the UML class diagram. Because we find it useful to have `main` do more than this, we diagram it as if it is in a separate class.

Problem-Solving Case Study

Calculating Exam Statistics Revisited

PROBLEM: You are the grader in your Government class. The teacher has asked you to prepare the following statistics. (*No, this isn't a misprint!* We are going to solve the same problem that we solved in Chapter 11, but in an entirely different way.) However, she has changed the input data and added some new output requirements. Each line in the input file contains a grade, which may be in either integer or real form, and a name. Three additional outputs must be provided: the name(s) of the students with the maximum grade, the names of the students above the average, and the names of the students below the average.

INPUT: A file, whose name is input from the keyboard, containing test grades.

Problem-Solving Case Study

OUTPUT: A file, whose name is input from the keyboard, showing the following statistics properly labeled:

Number of grades
Average grade
Lowest grade
Highest grade
Number of grades above the average
Number of grades below the average
Name of student(s) with the maximum grade
Names of students above the average
Names of students below the average

DISCUSSION: We have just designed and implemented several variations of a `List` class. Let's think about our current problem in terms of a list of grades. The first five tasks remain the same, but let's look at them in terms of list operations. We need to average the values in the list, find the maximum value in the list, find the minimum value in the list, count the number of values above the average, and count the number of values below the average. We know how to calculate an average: We sum the list of grades and divide by the number of grades. We found the minimum and maximum values in a file of numbers in the Studio Design program; the same algorithm can be used here. The third task involves looking at each grade, comparing it to the average, and incrementing one of two counters.

If all we had to do was find the average and the minimum and maximum grades, we could do the processing at the same time that we read the data values. However, the task of printing the number of grades above and below the average requires that each grade be examined twice: once to calculate the average, and again to compare each grade to the average. We can also find the minimum and maximum values as we initially read the grades.

The passive way of implementing this problem would be to pass the list of students/grades to functions that calculate the various statistics. The active (object-oriented) way of viewing the problem is to bind the list together with the operations into a class. But what would the structure look like? First we need a class that combines the student name and the grade. We have a `Name` class, but would a simple string do as well? You ask for a sample data file.

```
0 Bill Bly
100 Mary Jones
7 Anne Margaret
9 Susy Sunshine
78 Jim Jones
99 Alex Dale
67.5 Claire Clear
```

The grade comes first, followed by the first and last names. Thus the entire name could be read, stored, and printed as a single string. Should the grade be represented by an integer or a real number? Because both an integer and a real value can be read as a `float`, we can represent the grade as a real number. Which list class should we use to hold the grades? If we keep the list sorted by grade, we don't have to search for the minimum grade. Thus we need a `ComparedTo` function in the class that represents a student.

Problem-Solving Case Study

Here, then, is the specification for class `Student`:

```
class Student
// This class represents a student's name with a grade
{
public:
  Student(float initGrade, string initName);
  // Parameterized constructor
  // Post: Student object has been constructed with grade and name

  // Knowledge responsibilities
  string GetName() const;
  // Post: Returns the name from the Student object
  float GetGrade() const;
  // Post: Returns the grade from the Student object
  RelationType ComparedTo(Student otherStudent) const;
  // Post: Returns
  //       BEFORE if instance's grade is greater than otherStudent's
  //       SAME if they are identical
  //       AFTER if instance's grade is less than otherStudent's
private:
  string name; // First and last name in string form
  float grade;
}
```

Which other data members do we need in addition to our list? At first glance, it looks like we need variables to hold the average, maximum grade, minimum grade, number below the average, and number above the average. On second thought, however, we realize that we can access the minimum grade directly, and we can calculate the number above the average from the number of grades and the number below the average. Here we are assuming that if a student has the average grade that he or she will be counted in the above-average group. Checking with the teacher, she confirms that our assumption is correct.

Now we can write the specification of our `StatisticsList` class:

```
#include "SortedList.h"
class StatisticsList
{
public:
  StatisticsList(ifstream& inFile);
  // Parameterized constructor
  // Pre: inFile contains no more than 100 student records
  // Post: List of students has been created from file inFile
  //       Has calculated average, maxGrade, number below the average
```

Problem-Solving Case Study

```
  // Knowledge responsibilities
  float GetAverage();
  // Post: Returns average of the grades
  float GetMaxGrade();
  // Post: Returns maximum grade
  int GetAboveAverage();
  // Post: Returns the number of students whose grade was above the average
  int GetBelowAverage();
  // Post: Returns the number of students whose grade was below the average
  float GetMinGrade();
  // Post: Returns the minimum grade

  // Action responsibilities
  void StudentsMaxGrade(ofstream& outFile);
  // Post: Student(s) with the maximum grade output on file outFile
  void StudentsAbove(ofstream& outFile);
  // Post: Students whose grades were average or above output on outFile
  void StudentsBlow(ofstream& outFile);
  // Post: Students whose grades were below average output on outFile
private:
  float average;
  float maxGrade;
  int numBelow;
  SortedList list[100];   // List of grade/name pairs
}
```

Where do all the calculations take place? In the constructor! The operations are bound within the class.

StatisticsList(In/out: inFile) (only constructor)

Get student
WHILE more students
   Insert student into grade list
   Set sum to sum plus student.GetGrade()
   IF student.grade greater than maxSoFar
     Set maxSoFar to student.GetGrade()
   Get student
Set average to sum / list.GetLength()
WHILE (list.GetNextItem().GetGrade() < average)
   Increment numBelow

Get Student(In/out: inFile)
Return value: Student

inFile >> student.grade >> student.getline

GetStudent should be coded inline within the constructor.

Problem-Solving Case Study

The next five functions are just one line long and don't need further decomposition. The last three involve going through the list and writing the names of students who have the maximum grade, are above the average, or are below the average.

In getting the students with the maximum grade, there may be more than one such student. So first, we must look for the maximum grade and print the associated student. Then, we must cycle through the rest of the list printing associated names.

Students with Max Grade(In/out: outFile)

```
list.ResetList()
Set student to GetNextItem()
WHILE maxGrade > (student.GetGrade())
    Set student to GetNextItem()
Write on outFile student.GetName, " had the maximum score."
WHILE list.HasNext()
    Write on outFile list.GetNextItem().GetName, " had the maximum score."
```

Students Above Average(In/out: outFile)

We know that there are numBelow people whose scores are below the average. Thus we must simply access and skip these students; then we write the rest of the list.

```
list.ResetList()
FOR count going from 1 through numBelow
    Set item to list.GetNextItem()
Write on outFile "Students who scored above the average:"
FOR count going from numBelow+1 list.GetLength()
    Write on outFile list.GetNextItem.GetName()
```

Students Below(In/out: outFile)

We just need to access and print the first numBelow students, which are those students whose grades are below the average.

```
list.ResetList()
Write on outFile "Students who scored below the average:"
FOR count going from 1 through numBelow
    Write on outFile list.GetNextItem().GetName()
```

We show only `StatisticsList.cpp`, the driver, and the input and output files here. We've seen the other files in this application earlier. Note that the `SortedList` class must be changed so that `itemType` is defined as `Student`.

Problem-Solving Case Study

```cpp
//**********************************************************
// Implementation file for class StatisticsList
//**********************************************************

#include "StatisticsList.h"
StatisticsList::StatisticsList(ifstream& inFile)
{
  float grade;
  float sum = 0;
  maxGrade = 0;
  numBelow = 0;
  string name;
  inFile >> grade;
  // Build list and calculate maxGrade
  while (inFile)
  {
    getline(inFile, name);
    Student aStudent(grade, name);
    list.Insert(aStudent);
    sum = sum + grade;
    if (grade > maxGrade)
      maxGrade = grade;
    inFile >> grade;
  }

  average = sum / list.GetLength();
  // Calculate number of grades below average
  while (list.GetNextItem().GetGrade() < average)
    numBelow++;
}

//**********************************************************

float StatisticsList::GetAverage() const
{
  return average;
}

//**********************************************************

float StatisticsList::GetMaxGrade() const
{
  return maxGrade;
}

//**********************************************************

int StatisticsList::GetBelowAverage() const
{
  return numBelow;
}
```

Problem-Solving Case Study

```
//*********************************************************

int StatisticsList::GetAboveAverage() const
{
  return list.GetLength() - numBelow;
}

//*********************************************************

float StatisticsList::GetMinGrade()
{
  list.ResetList();
  return list.GetNextItem().GetGrade();
}

//*********************************************************

void StatisticsList::StudentsMaxGrade(ofstream& outFile)
{
  list.ResetList();
  Student aStudent = list.GetNextItem();
  outFile << endl << "The following student(s) had the maximum score: "
          << endl;
  while (maxGrade > aStudent.GetGrade())
    aStudent = list.GetNextItem();
  outFile << aStudent.GetName() << endl;
  while (list.HasNext())
    outFile << list.GetNextItem().GetName()
            << endl;
}

//*********************************************************

  void StatisticsList::StudentsAbove(ofstream& outFile)
  {
  list.ResetList();
  for (int count = 1; count <= numBelow; count++)
    list.GetNextItem();
  outFile << endl << "Students who scored above the average:" << endl;
  for (int count = numBelow + 1; count < list.GetLength(); count ++)
    outFile << list.GetNextItem().GetName() << endl;
}

//*********************************************************

void StatisticsList::StudentsBelow(ofstream& outFile)
{
  list.ResetList();
  outFile << endl << "Students who scored below the average: " << endl;
  for (int count = 1; count <= numBelow; count++)
    outFile << list.GetNextItem().GetName() << endl;
}
```

Problem-Solving Case Study

```cpp
//*****************************************************************
// DRIVER for class StatisticsList of Student objects
//*****************************************************************
#include <iostream>
#include "StatisticsList.h"
#include "RelationType.h"
#include <fstream>
#include <string>

using namespace std;
void OpenFiles(ifstream& inFile, ofstream& outFile);
// Post: Files have been opened

int main ()
{
  ofstream outFile;
  ifstream inFile;
  OpenFiles(inFile, outFile);
  if (!inFile || !outFile)
  {
    cout << "Error opening files " << endl;
    return 1;
  }
  StatisticsList grades(inFile);
  outFile << "Average: " << grades.GetAverage() << endl;
  outFile << "Minimum grade: " << grades.GetMinGrade() << endl;
  outFile << "Maximum grade: " << grades.GetMaxGrade() << endl;
  outFile << grades.GetBelowAverage()
          << " students had grades below the average. " << endl;
  outFile << grades.GetAboveAverage()
          << " students had grades above the average." << endl;
  grades.StudentsMaxGrade(outFile);
  grades.StudentsAbove(outFile) ;
  grades.StudentsBelow(outFile);
  inFile.close();
  outFile.close();
}

//*****************************************************************
void OpenFiles(ifstream& inFile, ofstream& outFile)
// Post: Files have been opened
{
  string inFileName;      // User specified input file name
  string outFileName;     // User specified output file name
  cout << "Enter the name of the input file." << endl;
  cin >> inFileName;
  inFile.open(inFileName.c_str());
```

Problem-Solving Case Study

```
    cout << "Enter the name of the output file." << endl;
    cin >> outFileName;
    outFile.open(outFileName.c_str());
    outFile << "Statistics for grades in file " << inFileName << endl;
    outFile << fixed;
}
```

Here is a sample input file and the output file generated by a run of the application:

Statistics.dat:

```
0 Bill Bly
100 Mary Jones
100 Martha Jones
65 Anne Margaret
82.0 Susy Sunshine
78 Jim Jones
99 Alex Dale
67.5 Claire Clear
99 Chris Dale
55 Mary Moonlight
```

Statistics.out:

```
Statistics for grades in file Statistics.dat
Average: 74.550003
Minimum grade: 0.000000
Maximum grade: 100.000000
4 students had grades below the average.
6 students had grades above the average.

The following student(s) had the maximum score:
 Mary Jones
 Martha Jones

Students who scored above the average:
 Jim Jones
 Susy Sunshine
 Alex Dale
 Chris Dale
 Mary Jones
 Martha Jones

Students who scored below the average:
 Bill Bly
 Mary Moonlight
 Anne Margaret
 Claire Clear
```

Problem-Solving Case Study

UML DIAGRAMS: Here are the UML class diagrams for the classes in this problem.

```
            Student
-name; string
-grade; float

+Student(initGrade: float, initName: string)
+GetName(): string
+GetGrade(): float
```

```
          StatisticsList
-average: float
-maxGrade: float
-numBelow: int

+StatisticsList(inFile: ifstream)
+GetAverage(): float
+GetMaxGrade(): float
+GetAboveAverage(): int
+GetBelowAverage(): int
+GetMinGrade(): float

+StudentsMaxGrade(outFile: ofstream)
+StudentsAbove(outFile: ofstream)
+StudentsBelow(outFile: ofstream)
```

```
           SortedList
-length: int
-currentPos: int
-data[MAX_LENGTH]: ItemType

+SortedList()
+GetLength(): int
+IsEmpty(): bool
+IsThere(item: ItemType): bool
+IsFull(): bool
+Insert(item: ItemType)
+Delete(item: ItemType)
+ResetList()
+HasNext(): bool
+GetNextItem(): ItemType
-BinarySearch(item: ItemType, found: bool,
              position: int)
```

Problem-Solving Case Study

Here is the UML diagram that shows how all of these classes are related.

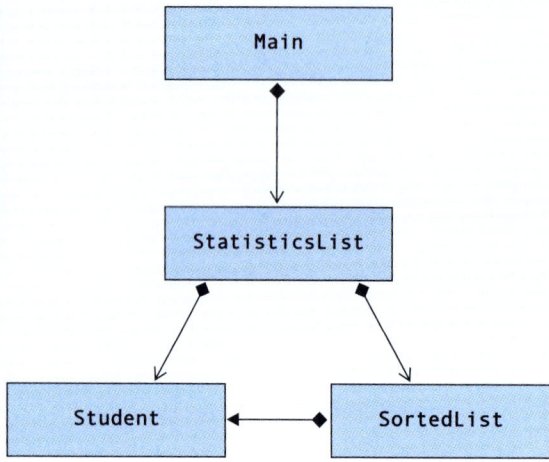

TESTING: This implementation is based on a list of values. We must test for cases in which there are no grades, one grade, a few grades, and exactly the maximum number of grades. We already took care of the case where there were just a few grades. You are asked in the Case Study Follow-Up questions to design a full test plan for this Problem-Solving Case Study.

Which algorithm is more efficient: the array algorithm from Chapter 11 or the list algorithm? We can't answer that question because it depends on the range of possible grades and the sizes of the data sets. The amount of work done in the first solution is based on the range of grades; the loops go from 0 to 100 (or somewhere in between). The amount of work done in the second solution is based on the number of grades; the loops go from 0 to the number of grades. Thus the choice of algorithm depends on the context in which it will be used.

Testing and Debugging

In this chapter, we have discussed, designed, and coded algorithms to construct and manipulate items in a list. In addition to the basic list operations `IsFull`, `IsEmpty`, `GetLength`, `ResetList`, `HasNext`, and `GetNextItem`, the algorithms included three sequential searches, a binary search, insertion into sorted and unsorted lists, deletion from sorted and unsorted lists, and a selection sort. We have partially tested the `List` and `SortedList` classes, in which the items are numeric values or strings, and the `SortedList` class, in which the items are objects. We have tested our algorithms with lists of intermediate sizes. We should also test them with lists containing no components, one component, two components, `MAX_LENGTH-1` components, and `MAX_LENGTH` components.

When we wrote the precondition stating that the list was not full for our list operations, we indicated that we could handle the problem another way—we could include an error flag in the function's parameter list. The function could call `IsFull` and set the error flag. With this approach, the insertion would not take place if the error flag were set to `true`. Both options are acceptable ways of handling the problem. The important point is that we clearly state whether the calling code or the called function is to check for the error condition. However, it is the calling code that must decide what to do when an error condition occurs. In other words, if errors are handled by means of preconditions, then the user must write the code to guarantee the preconditions. If errors are handled by flags, then the user must write the code to monitor the error flags.

Testing and Debugging Hints

1. Review the Testing and Debugging Hints for Chapter 12.
2. With string input, the >> operator stops at, *but does not consume*, the first trailing whitespace character. Likewise, if the `get` or `getline` function stops reading early because it encounters a newline character, the newline character is not consumed.
3. General-purpose functions (such as ADT operations) should be tested outside the context of a particular program, using a test driver.
4. Choose test data carefully so that you test all end conditions and some conditions in the middle. End conditions are those that reach the limits of the structure used to store them. For example, when testing a list, the test data should include cases in which the number of components is 0, 1, and `MAX_LENGTH`, as well as between 1 and `MAX_LENGTH`.
5. If a list ADT doesn't specify a precondition requiring the client to ensure that the number of items is less than a known maximum, be sure to include a test that verifies correct handling of an attempt to insert too many items.
6. Enclose lower-level classes in

```
#ifndef NAME
#define NAME
 . . .
#endif
```

■ **Summary**

This chapter provided practice in working with lists stored in one-dimensional arrays. We examined algorithms that insert, delete, search, and sort data stored in a list, and we wrote functions to implement these algorithms. We can use these functions again and again in different contexts because they are members of general-purpose C++ classes (`List` and `SortedList`) that represent list ADTs.

We also saw algorithms for sequential and binary search, and for selection and insertion sorts. In developing our list classes, we explored the semantic distinctions between an unsorted list, an unsorted list with a sort operation, and a sorted list. Through all of this design effort, we gained greater experience in object-oriented design and the use of UML class diagrams.

■ **Quick Check Answers**

13.1.1 There are variable length, linear, and homogenous. **13.1.2** any type. **13.2.1** `isEmpty`, `isFull`, `GetLength`, `IsThere`, `HasNext`, `GetNextItem` **13.2.2** `Insert`, `Delete`, `ResetList` **13.2.3** A data array containing the specified item type in each component, and a length represented by an `int`. **13.3.1** At the end of the list (assuming the list isn't already full). **13.3.2** When it has examined the last element in the list. **13.3.3** Search for the value, delete the value, shift any succeeding values up one place. **13.3.4** Two. **13.3.5** 0 **13.3.6** check if the length is equal to 0. **13.3.7** It starts at the beginning of the list and looks at each item in sequence until it finds the element it is looking for. **13.4.1** The components of a sorted list are always kept in order, but the components of a regular list are sorted only after the sort operation executes, and remain in order only until the next insertion or deletion. **13.4.2** The components that precede the insertion point remain where they are, and the ones following the insertion point shift over one place to make room. **13.4.3** The name comes from its pattern of dividing the area of the search by two on each iteration. **13.4.4** There is no sorting operation in the sorted list. The insert operation inserts a new value in its proper place rather than at the end of the list. The delete operation shifts the succeeding components up one place, rather than moving the last component into the vacated position. Searching in the sorted list can be done with a binary search rather than a linear search. **13.4.5** Either the value is found, or last is less than first and the value has not been found. **13.4.6** How we look up a word in the dictionary. **13.5.1** It depends on the class of the objects and how we want the list sorted. **13.5.2** Either name or time.

■ **Exam Preparation Exercises**

1. Why do we say that a list is a "linear data structure"?
2. What do we mean when we say that a list is "homogeneous"?
3. If the `Length` operation associated with an unsorted list returns 43, and we then call the `Delete` operation for the list, passing it a value that matches the 21st item in the list:
   a. What is the index of the component that is deleted?
   b. What is the index of the component that takes its place?
   c. What does the `Length` operation return after the deletion?
   d. How many components in the list change their positions as a result of the deletion?
4. If `ItemType` is `float`, how do we need to change the following While loop condition, as written in the sequential search, and why do we need to change it?

   ```
   while (index < length && item != data[index])
   ```

5. The following statements are supposed to swap two values in an array, but they are in the wrong order. Rearrange them into the proper order.

   ```
   data[value2] = temp;
   data[value1] = data[value2];
   temp = data[value1];
   ```

6. In a selection sort, what is accomplished by the inner loop each time it executes?
7. If the `GetLength` operation associated with a sorted list returns 43, and we then call the `Delete` operation for the list, passing it a value that matches the 21st item in the list:
   a. What is the index of the component that is deleted?
   b. What is the index of the component that takes its place?
   c. What does the `Length` operation return after the deletion?
   d. How many components in the list change their positions as a result of the deletion?
8. On average, a sequential search of a sorted list takes the same number of iterations as searching an unsorted list. True or false?
9. We should use a binary search for large sorted lists, but a sequential search is more efficient when a list has few components. True or false?
10. What is the log (base 2) of 32?
11. Why don't we need a separate sorting operation in a sorted list ADT?
12. A sorted list contains 16 elements, and the binary search operation is called with a value that matches the 12th value in the list. How many iterations does it take for the binary search to find this match?
13. Is the class `Entry`, as defined in this chapter, mutable?
14. Is our `SortedList` class mutable?

Programming Warm-Up Exercises

1. Write a C++ Boolean function named `Deleted` that has three parameters: `someItem` (of type `ItemType` as used in this chapter), `oldList`, and `newList` (both of type `List` as defined in this chapter). The function returns `true` if `someItem` is found in `oldList`, but is not present in `newlist`.
2. The `List` type in this chapter allows us to store only one copy of an item in the list. Sometimes it is useful to have a list in which an item can appear any number of times. Change the implementation of the `Insert` function so that it adds an item to the list any time it is inserted.
3. What is wrong with the following code segment, and what must be changed in type `List` to make it work correctly?

   ```
   List inVals;
   for (int count = 1; count <= 150; count++)
   {
     cin >> inVal;
     inVals.Insert(inVal);
   }
   ```

4. We would like to add a `DeleteAll` function to the `List` type from Exercise 2 that deletes all occurrences of an item from a list. Write the code that must be added to the specification file for the type to enable us to add this function.
5. Write the implementation of the `DeleteAll` function as described in Exercise 4.
6. We would like to add a `Replace` function to the `List` type in this chapter that takes two parameters, `oldItem` and `newItem` of `ItemType`. The function finds `oldItem` in the list, deletes it, and inserts `newItem` in its place. The list is unchanged if `oldItem` is not present in the list. Write the code that must be added to the specification file for the type to enable us to add this function.

7. Write the implementation of the `Replace` function as described in Exercise 6.
8. The `SortedList` type keeps items in ascending order. Which function(s) would need to be changed to make the list keep the items in descending order?
9. Change the implementation of the `BinarySearch` function so that it will work with a list that keeps items in descending order.
10. In Exercise 5, you wrote a `DeleteAll` function for the `List` type with duplicates. Implement a `DeleteAll` function for the `SortedList` type that allows duplicates, taking advantage of the fact that all occurrences of the item are stored in adjacent locations in the array. Note that the binary search does not necessarily return the position of the first occurrence of an item; it can return the position of any matching item. Thus, in this case, it may be more efficient to use a linear search to find the starting position for the matching items. Be sure that your function updates the length of the list as necessary.
11. In Exercise 6, you wrote a `Replace` function for the `List` type that deletes one value and replaces it with another. Reimplement the `Replace` function for the `SortedList` type. Note that in this case, the replacement value needs to be inserted in the proper position in the list to maintain the ordering of the items.
12. Write a code segment that fills a `SortedList` called `inData` with values that are input from a file called `unsorted`.

■ Programming Problems

1. Imagine you have been asked by a first grade teacher to create a hangman game for her students to help them with spelling and word recognition. In the game of hangman you are first presented with a list of blanks representing unknown letters of a hidden word. You must then guess a letter to see if that letter exists in the word. If it does the blank that corresponds to the guessed letter is then displayed along with blanks for the letters that have not been guessed yet. If you guess a previously guessed letter you get to try again. If you guess wrong you incrementally move toward being hung. You have 8 bad guesses until you lose the game. To represent the different states of "being hung" we will use the values PLATFORM, HEAD, BODY, LEFT_ARM, RIGHT_ARM, LEFT_LEG, RIGHT_LEG, and HUNG. To implement the game you should use the unsorted List ADT to represent the word being guessed. Each element in the list should be a struct that stores the letter of the word and a boolean that indicates if the letter is to be displayed or if a blank should be displayed. You should use a second list to represent the letters that have already been guessed and an enumeration to represent the states of the game. Your program should keep asking the user for another guess until either the entire word has been guessed or the state of the game is HUNG. After each guess the program should display the current state of the word to be guessed, the list of characters already guessed, and the state of the game.
2. Write a program using the `List` class from this chapter that implements a to-do list. The to-do items will be entered as strings. The user should be prompted to enter a command (add an item, mark an item as done or partially done, delete an item, and print the list) and data as necessary. Simply storing items in the list is easy, but the `List` class doesn't directly support the recording of the status of each task. You might want to go about this in several different ways. One approach would be to implement a struct or a class that represents an item and its status, and then modify the `List` class to work with this struct or class as its item type. Another way would be to keep three lists: `Done`,

Partial, and Undone. When an item is created, it enters the Undone list. When its status is changed, it moves to one of the other lists as appropriate. Choose the approach that you prefer, and implement the application using proper style, effective prompts, and sufficient documentation.

3. Many instructors like to see the distribution of scores on an exam before they assign grades. You're working for an art history professor who has asked you to develop a program that will read all of the scores from an exam and print out a bar chart that shows their distribution. The range of the scores varies from exam to exam, and there are at most 250 students in the class. Use or modify the SortedList class from this chapter as necessary to help you do this task. The integer scores are entered into a file called exams.dat in random order. Your program's job is to read in the data, sort it, and output a bar chart with one * (star) for each exam that has a particular score. The first bar in the chart should be the highest score, and the last bar in the chart should be the lowest score. Each line of output should start with the score value, followed by the appropriate number of stars. When there is a score value that didn't appear on any exams, just output the value and no stars, then go to the next line.

4. Enhance the program in Problem 3 as follows: The data file now contains a score and a name. Modify the SortedList class so that it uses a struct consisting of the score and the name as its fields. The program should input the file data into the modified list. In addition to displaying the bar chart, the program should output the sorted list to a file called byscore.dat.

5. You've gathered lists of email addresses from a variety of sources, and now you want to send out a mass mailing to all of the addresses. However, you don't want to send out duplicate messages. All of the email addresses (represented as strings) have been combined on a single file called rawlist.dat. You need to write a program that reads all of the addresses and discards any that have been previously input. Use one of the list classes from this chapter, modifying it as necessary to work with string data, and to deal with as many as 1000 items. After all of the data have been read, output the new mailing list to a file called cleanlist.dat.

6. You're working for the state vehicle registry, and it just has been discovered that the people who make the license plates have been mistakenly producing occasional duplicates. You have a file (platesmade.dat) containing a list of plate numbers, which are recorded as the license plates are made. You need to write a program that reads this file and identifies any duplicates in the list so that notices can be sent out to recall them. The plate numbers, which consist of letters and numbers, should be stored as strings. Output the duplicates into a file called recallplates.dat. Use the SortedList class from this chapter to help you in writing this application, modifying it if necessary.

Case Study Follow-Up

1. Which of the two implementations of the statistics program (Chapter 11 or Chapter 13) do you think is clearer? Why?
2. For which function did StatisticsList not ensure the preconditions? Correct this error and rerun the driver, being sure to test whether the precondition is checked.
3. Write a test plan for the statistics program.
4. Is the StatisticsList class mutable? Explain your answer.

Dynamic Data and Linked Lists

KNOWLEDGE GOALS

- To understand the concept of a linked data structure.
- To understand the difference between deep and shallow copy operations.
- To know and understand the four member functions that should be present in any class that manipulates dynamic data.

SKILL GOALS

To be able to:
- Create, access, and destroy dynamic data.
- Create linked data structures.
- Manipulate data in a linked structure.
- Distinguish between a reference variable and a pointer variable.

In Chapter 10 we looked at pointer types and reference types. A variable of one of these types does not contain a data value; it contains the *memory address* of another variable or structure. We focused on understanding how to create and manipulate pointers to static data defined in our C++ programs. The true power of pointers, however, becomes apparent with the introduction of dynamic data. Dynamic data allows programs to operate over data structures without a predetermined size and lifetime. Dynamic data structures can grow and shrink over the execution time of a program providing the ultimate in flexibility that can be both efficient in time and space. It is the creation and manipulation of dynamic data that we emphasize here by studying the *linked list* dynamic data structure.

14.1 Dynamic Data

In Chapter 9, we described two categories of program data in C++: static data and automatic data. Any global variable is static, as is any local variable explicitly declared as `static`. The lifetime of a static variable is the lifetime of the entire program. In contrast, an automatic variable—a local variable not declared as `static`—is allocated (created) when control reaches its declaration and is deallocated (destroyed) when control exits the block in which the variable is declared.

Dynamic data Variables created during execution of a program by means of special operations. In C++. These operations are `new` and `delete`.

With the aid of pointers, C++ provides a third category of program data: dynamic data. Dynamic variables are not declared with ordinary variable declarations; instead, they are explicitly allocated and deallocated at execution time by means of two special operators, `new` and `delete`. When a program requires an additional variable, it uses `new` to allocate the variable. When the program no longer needs the variable, it uses `delete` to deallocate it. The lifetime of a dynamic variable is, therefore, the time between the execution of `new` and the execution of `delete`. The advantage of being able to create new variables at execution time is clear: We don't have to create any more variables than we actually need.

Allocating Dynamic Data

The `new` operation has two forms, one for allocating a single variable and one for allocating an array. Here is the syntax template:

AllocationExpression

$$\begin{cases} \text{new } DataType \\ \text{new } DataType \text{ [} IntExpression \text{]} \end{cases}$$

The first form is used for creating a single variable of type `DataType`. The second form creates an array whose elements are of type `DataType`; the desired number of array elements is given by `IntExpression`.

Here is an example that demonstrates both forms of the **new** operation:

```
int* intPtr;
int* intArray;
```

`intPtr = new int;`	Creates a variable of type `int` and stores its address into `intPtr`.
`intArray = new int[6];`	Creates a six-element `int` array and stores the base address of the array into `intArray`.

Normally, the **new** operator does two things: It creates an uninitialized variable (or an array) of the designated type, and it returns the address of this variable (or the base address of an array). It is this address that is stored into the pointer variable. If the computer system has run out of space in which to store dynamic data, however, the program terminates with an error message. In Chapter 16, we show how to test for this condition and keep the program from terminating.

Variables created by **new** are said to reside on the free store (or heap), a region of memory set aside for dynamic variables. The **new** operator obtains a chunk of memory from the free store and, as we will see, the `delete` operator returns it to the free store.

Free store (heap) A pool of memory locations reserved for allocation and deallocation of dynamic data.

A dynamic variable is unnamed and cannot be addressed directly. Instead, it must be addressed indirectly through the pointer returned by the **new** operator. Following is an example of creating dynamic data and then accessing the data through pointers.

```
int* intPtr;         // Defines an int pointer variable
intPtr = new int;    // Creates a new int variable and stores its
                     // address in intPtr
PatientRec* patientPtr = new PatientRec; // Defines a PatientRec
                     // pointer variable, creates a new variable
                     // of type PatientRec, and stores its address in
                     // the PatientRec pointer variable
PatientRec* patientArray = new PatientRec[4];
                     // Defines an array of 4 variables of type
                     // PatientRec and stores the base address into
                     // patientArray
*intPtr = 250;                // Stores 250 into variable whose address
                              // is in intPtr
patientPtr -> idNum = 3245;   // Sets idNum field of the PatientRec struct
                              // whose address is in patientPtr to 3245
patientPtr -> height = 64;    // Sets height field to 64
patientPtr -> weight = 114;   // Sets weight field to 114
patientArray[3] = *patientPtr; // Stores what patientPtr points
                              // to in patientArray[3]
patientArray[3].weight = 120; // Changes weight field of
                              // patientArray[3] to 120
```

FIGURE 14.1 pictures memory after the effect of executing this code segment. Note that the contents of the struct to which `patientPtr` points have not been changed. What `patientPtr` points to was stored in the array, not a copy of the pointer.

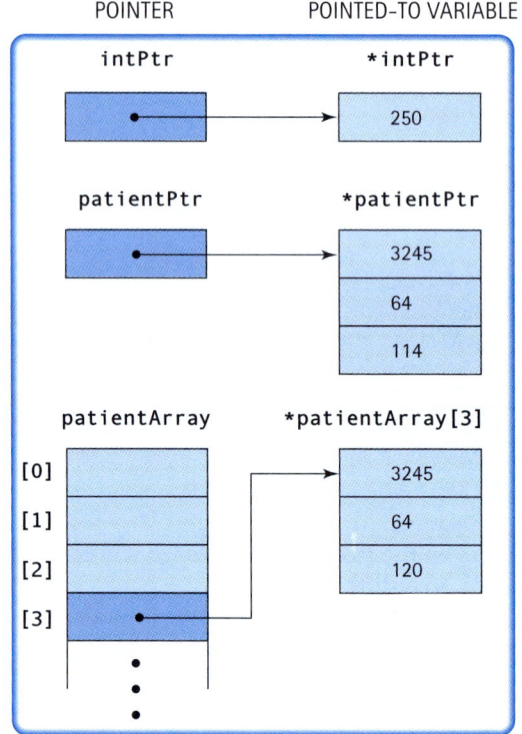

Figure 14.1 Picture of Memory After Execution of Code Segment

Deleting Dynamic Data

Dynamic data can (and should) be destroyed at any time during the execution of a program when it is no longer needed. The built-in operator **delete** is used to destroy a dynamic variable. The **delete** operation has two forms: one for deleting a single variable, the other for deleting an array.

DeallocationExpression

{ delete Pointer
  delete [] Pointer

Using the previous example, we can deallocate the dynamic data pointed to by **intPtr**, **patientPtr**, and **patientArray** with the following statements:

delete intPtr;   Returns the **int** variable pointed to by **intPtr** to the free store to be used again

`delete patientPtr;`	Returns the `struct` variable pointed to by `patientPtr` to the free store to be used again
`delete [] patientArray`	Returns the array pointed to by `patientArray` to the free store to be used again

After execution of these statements, the values pointed to by `intPtr`, `patientPtr`, and `patientArray` are undefined; that is, they may or may not still contain the deallocated data. Before using these pointers again, you must assign new values to them (that is, store new memory addresses into them).

Until you gain experience with the `new` and `delete` operators, it is important to pronounce the statement

```
delete intPtr;
```

accurately. Instead of saying, "Delete `intPtr`," it is better to say, "Delete the value to which `intPtr` points." The delete operation does not delete the pointer; it deletes the pointed-to value.

When using the `delete` operator, you should keep two rules in mind:

1. Applying `delete` to the `NULL` pointer does no harm; the operation simply has no effect.
2. Excepting Rule 1, the `delete` operator must only be applied to a pointer value that was obtained previously from the `new` operator.

The second rule is important to remember. If you apply `delete` to an arbitrary memory address that is not in the free store, the result is undefined and could prove to be very unpleasant.

The `new` operator lets you create variables only as they are needed. When you are finished using a dynamic variable, you should `delete` it. It is counterproductive to keep dynamic variables when they are no longer needed—a situation known as a memory leak. If a memory leak is permitted to occur too often, you may run out of memory.

> **Memory leak** The loss of available memory space that occurs when dynamic data is allocated but never deallocated.

Let's look at another example of using dynamic data.

```
int* ptr1 = new int;    // Create a dynamic variable
int* ptr2 = new int;    // Create a dynamic variable

*ptr2 = 44;             // Assign a value to a dynamic variable
*ptr1 = *ptr2;          // Copy one dynamic variable to another
ptr1 = ptr2;            // Copy one pointer to another
delete ptr2;            // Destroy a dynamic variable
```

Here is a more detailed description of the effect of each statement:

`int* ptr1 = new int;` `int* ptr2 = new int;`	Creates a pair of dynamic variables of type `int` and stores their locations into `ptr1` and `ptr2`. The values of the dynamic variables are undefined even though the pointer variables now have values (see **FIGURE 14.2A**).
`*ptr2 = 44;`	Stores the value 44 into the dynamic variable pointed to by `ptr2` (see **FIGURE 14.2B**).

INITIAL CONDITIONS

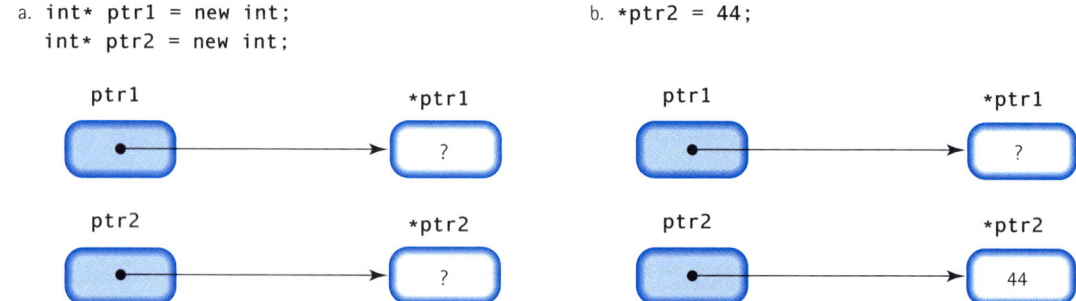

a. `int* ptr1 = new int;`
   `int* ptr2 = new int;`

b. `*ptr2 = 44;`

Figure 14.2A and B Results from Sample Code Segment

`*ptr1 = *ptr2;`   Copies the contents of the dynamic variable `*ptr2` to the dynamic variable `*ptr1` (see **FIGURE 14.2C**).

`ptr1 = ptr2;`   Copies the contents of the pointer variable `ptr2` to the pointer variable `ptr1` (see **FIGURE 14.2D**).

`delete ptr2;`   Returns the dynamic variable `*ptr2` back to the free store to be used again. The value of `ptr2` is undefined (see **FIGURE 14.2E**).

In Figure 14.2d, notice that the variable pointed to by `ptr1` before the assignment statement is still there. It cannot be accessed, however, because no pointer is pointing to it. This isolated variable is called an inaccessible object. Leaving inaccessible objects on the free store should be considered a logic error and is a cause of memory leaks.

Inaccessible object A dynamic variable on the free store without any pointer pointing to it.

Dangling pointer A pointer that points to a variable that has been deallocated.

Notice also that in Figure 14.2e `ptr1` is now pointing to a variable that, in principle, no longer exists. We call `ptr1` a dangling pointer. If the program later dereferences `ptr1`, the result will be unpredictable. The pointed-to value might still be the original one (44), or it might be a different value stored there if that space on the free store has been reused.

c. `*ptr1 = *ptr2;`   d. `ptr1 = ptr2;`

e. `delete ptr2;`

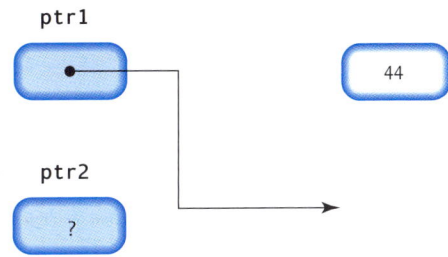

Figure 14.2C, D, and E Results from Sample Code Segment

Both situations shown in Figure 14.2e—an inaccessible object and a dangling pointer—can be avoided by deallocating `*ptr1` before assigning `ptr2` to `ptr1`, and by setting `ptr1` to `NULL` after deallocating `*ptr2`.

```
#include <cstddef>    // For NULL
   .
   .
   .
int* ptr1 = new int;
int* ptr2 = new int;

*ptr2 = 44;        // Give *ptr2 the value 44
*ptr1 = *ptr2;     // Copy 44 from *ptr2 into *ptr1
delete ptr1;       // Delete copy of 44, and avoid an inaccessible object
ptr1 = ptr2;       // ptr1 points to same value of 44 as ptr2
delete ptr2;       // The shared value 44 is deleted
ptr1 = NULL;       // Avoid a dangling pointer
```

FIGURE 14.3 shows the results of executing this revised code segment.

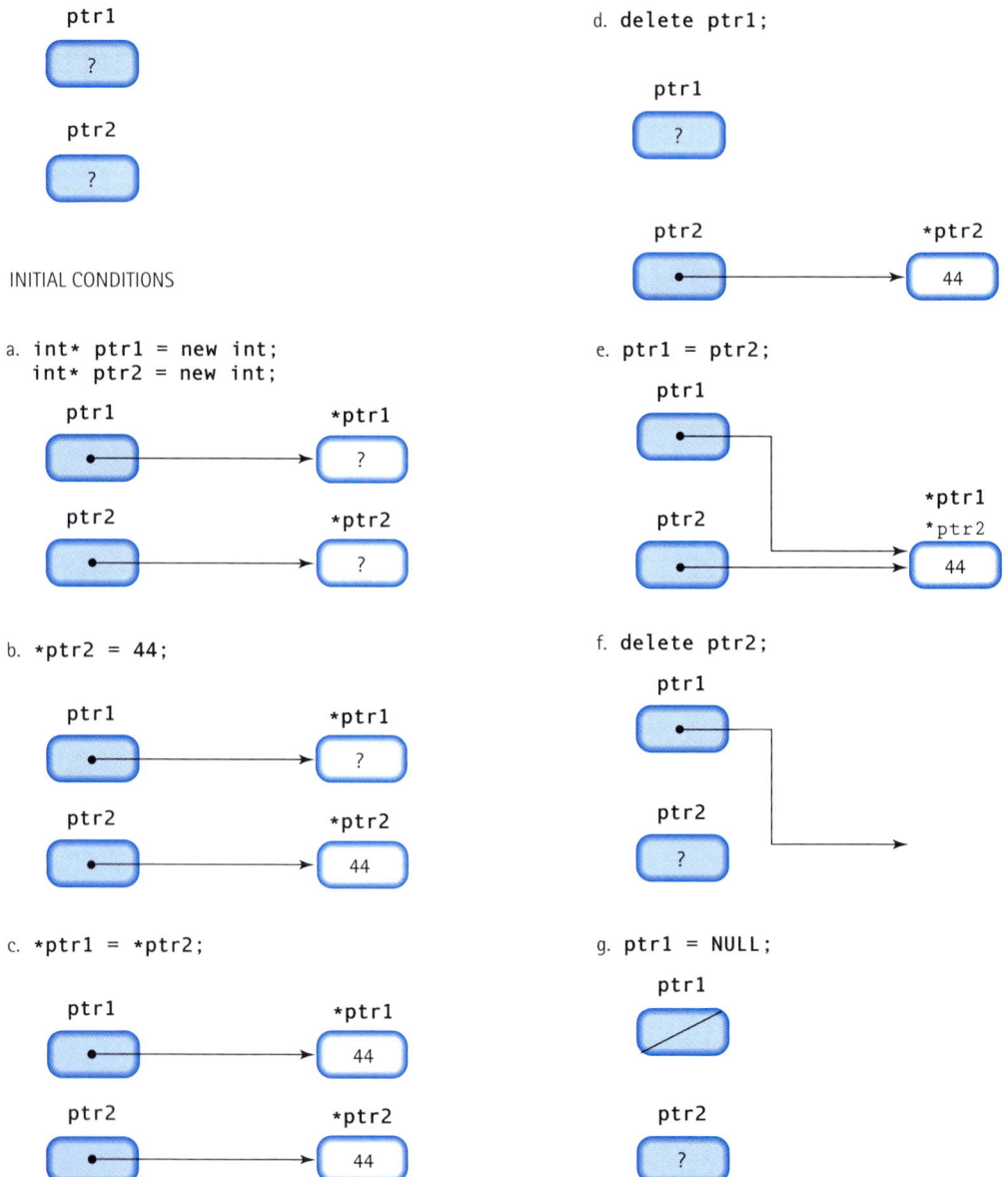

Figure 14.3 Results from Sample Code Segment After It Was Modified

Constants and Dynamic Data

There is another way to avoid the inaccessible object problem. Just as C++ allows us to define constants of other simple types, so a pointer can be made constant. In the following declaration, `patientPtr` is a constant pointer that is initialized to the address of a dynamic memory location representing a struct of type `PatientRec`:

```
PatientRec* const patientPtr = new PatientRec;    // patientPtr is constant
```

Once this code is executed, `patientPtr` will always point to the same location. We can change the values stored in that location by dereferencing `patientPtr`, but we cannot assign a new value to `patientPtr` itself. That is, we cannot make it point to another place in memory. As a result, the location it points to can never become inaccessible. When we apply `delete` to a constant pointer, we can be assured that we are deleting precisely what was originally allocated, thereby preventing a memory leak.

In the next section we look at the use of pointers in another form of list implementation.

> **QUICK CHECK** ✓
>
> **14.1.1** What is the keyword that we use in writing a C++ allocation expression? (pp. 718–719)
> **14.1.2** What is the keyword that we use in writing a C++ deallocation expression? (pp. 720–721)
> **14.1.3** What is dynamic data? (p. 718)
> **14.1.4** What are the two things the **new** operator does? (p. 719)
> **14.1.5** Where do variables created by **new** reside? (p. 719)
> **14.1.6** What does the **delete** operator do in terms of the free store? (p. 719)

14.2 Sequential Versus Linked Structures

As we pointed out in Chapter 13, many problems in computing involve lists of items. In that chapter, we implemented the List ADT using an array to store the items in the list. The size of an array is fixed, but the number of items in the list varies.

If the list we are implementing is a sorted list—one whose components must be kept in ascending or descending order—certain operations are efficiently carried out using an array representation. For example, searching a sorted list for a particular value is done quickly by using a binary search. However, inserting and deleting items from a sorted list are inefficient operations when we are using an array representation. To insert a new item into its proper place in the list, we must shift the array elements down to make room for the new item (see **FIGURE 14.4**). Similarly, deleting an item from the list requires that we shift up all the array elements following the one to be deleted.

When insertions and deletions will occur frequently, there is a better data representation for a list: the linked list. A linked list is a collection of items, called *nodes*, that can be scattered about in memory, not necessarily in consecutive memory locations. Each node, typically represented as a struct, consists of two members:

> **Linked list** A list in which the order of the components is determined by an explicit link member in each node, rather than by the sequential order of the components in memory.

- A component or item member, which contains one of the data values in the list
- A link member, which gives the location of the next node in the list

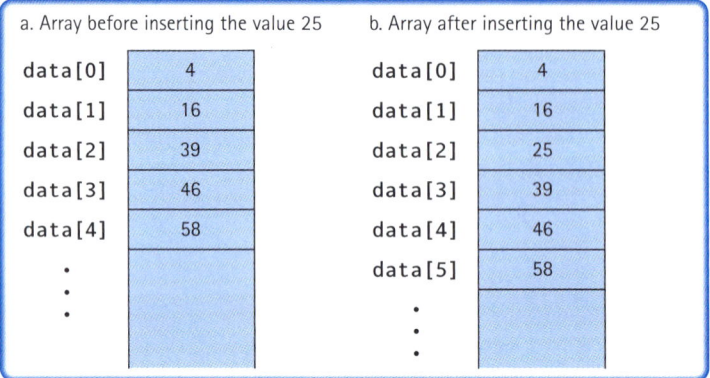

Figure 14.4 Inserting into a Sequential Representation of a Sorted List

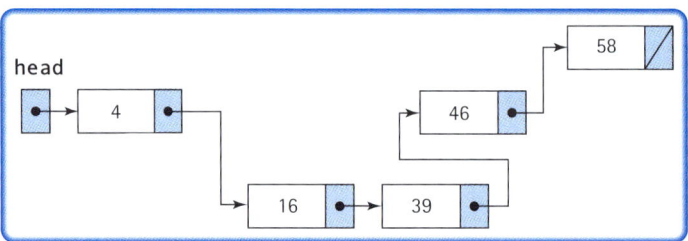

Figure 14.5 Linked List

FIGURE 14.5 shows an abstract diagram of a linked list. An arrow is used in the link member of each node to indicate the location of the next node. The slash (/) in the link member of the last node signifies the end of the list. A separate named variable points to the first node in the list; this pointer is called the external pointer to the list. This variable is not a pointer within the linked list; rather, its purpose is to give the location of the first node. The identifier "head" is sometimes used to refer to the external pointer to a list.

> **External pointer** A pointer that points to the first node in a linked list.

Accessing the items in a linked list is a little like playing the children's game of treasure hunt—each child is given a clue to the hiding place of the next clue, and the chain of clues eventually leads to the treasure.

As you look at Figure 14.5, you should observe two things. First, we have deliberately arranged the nodes in random positions. We have done so to emphasize the fact that the items in a linked list are not necessarily in adjacent memory locations (as they are in the array representation of Figure 14.4). Second, you may already be thinking of pointers when you see the arrows in the figure—and you would be right.

QUICK CHECK

14.2.1 Why is it often more space efficient to implement a list using pointers rather than with an array? (p. 708)

14.2.2 Which member do we need in addition to the data members of a struct to use the struct as a node in a linked list? (p. 709)

14.2.3 What is the primary difference between an array and a linked list? (pp. 708–709)

QUICK CHECK

14.2.4 What frequently occurring operations are more efficient for a linked list representation? (p. 725)

14.2.5 What is an external pointer? (p. 726)

14.3 Creating a Dynamic Linked List: A Walk-Through Example

In this section we walk through the creation of an example linked list so that we can see how the process works in one specific case. We represent the list as a linked structure whose nodes are dynamically allocated on the free store; the link member of each node contains the memory address of the next dynamic node. In this data representation, called a dynamic linked list, the arrows in the diagram of Figure 14.5 really do represent pointers (and the slash in the last node is the NULL pointer). We access the list with a pointer variable that holds the address of the first node in the list. This pointer variable, named head in Figure 14.5, is called the external pointer or head pointer. Every node after the first node is accessed by using the link member in the node before it.

Such a list can expand or contract as the program executes. To insert a new item into the list, we allocate more space from the free store. To delete an item, we deallocate the memory assigned to it. We don't have to know in advance how long the list will be (that is, how many items it will hold). The only limitation is the amount of available memory space. Data structures built using this technique are called dynamic data structures.

Dynamic linked list A linked list composed of dynamically allocated nodes that are linked together by pointers.

External (head) pointer A pointer variable that points to the first node in a dynamic linked list.

Dynamic data structure A data structure that can expand and contract during execution.

To create a dynamic linked list, we begin by allocating the first node and saving the pointer to it in the external pointer. We then allocate a second node and store the pointer to it into the link member of the first node. We continue this process—allocating a new node and storing the pointer to it into the link member of the previous node—until we have finished adding nodes to the list.

Let's look at how we can use C++ pointer variables to create a dynamic linked list of float values. We begin with the following declarations:

```
typedef float ItemType;
struct NodeType
{
  ItemType component;
  NodeType* link;
};
typedef NodeType* NodePtr;
NodePtr head;              // External pointer to list
NodePtr currPtr;           // Pointer to current node
NodePtr newNodePtr;        // Pointer to newest node
```

The order of these declarations is important. The Typedef for NodePtr refers to the identifier NodeType, so the declaration of NodeType must come first. (Remember that C++ requires every identifier to be declared before it is used.) Within the declaration of NodeType, we would like to declare link to be of type NodePtr, but we can't because the identifier NodePtr hasn't been declared yet. However, C++ allows *forward* (or *incomplete*) *declarations* of structs, classes, and unions:

```
typedef float ItemType;
struct   NodeType;                    // Forward (incomplete) declaration
typedef NodeType* NodePtr;

struct NodeType                       // Complete declaration
{
  ItemType component;
  NodePtr  link;
};
```

The advantage of using a forward declaration is that we can declare the type of `link` to be `NodePtr` just as we declare `head`, `currPtr`, and `newNodePtr` to be of type `NodePtr`.

Given the preceding declarations, the following code fragment creates a dynamic linked list with the values 12.8, 45.2, and 70.1 as the components in the list:

```
#include <cstddef>                    // For NULL
    .
    .
    .
head = new NodeType;
head->component = 12.8;
newNodePtr = new NodeType;
newNodePtr->component = 45.2;
head->link = newNodePtr;
currPtr = newNodePtr;
newNodePtr = new NodeType;
newNodePtr->component = 70.1;
currPtr->link = newNodePtr;
newNodePtr->link = NULL;
currPtr = newNodePtr;
```

Let's go through each of these statements, describing in words what is happening and showing the linked list as it appears after the execution of the statement.

| `head = new NodeType;` | A dynamic variable of type `NodeType` is created. The pointer to this new node is stored into `head`. Variable `head` is the external pointer to the list we are building. |

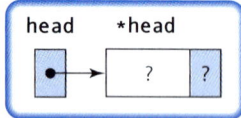

14.3 Creating a Dynamic Linked List: A Walk-Through Example

`head->component = 12.8;`   The value 12.8 is stored into the **component** member of the first node.

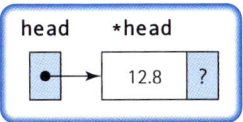

`newNodePtr = new NodeType;`   A dynamic variable of type **NodeType** is created. The pointer to this new node is stored into **newNodePtr**.

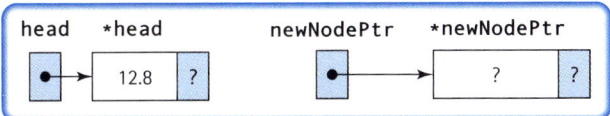

`newNodePtr->component = 45.2;`   The value 45.2 is stored into the **component** member of the new node.

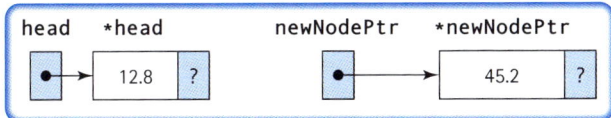

`head->link = newNodePtr;`   The pointer to the new node containing 45.2 in its **component** member is copied into the **link** member of ***head**. Variable **newNodePtr** still points to this new node. The node can be accessed either as ***newNodePtr** or as ***(head->link)**.

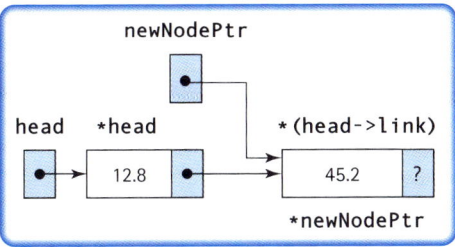

`currPtr = newNodePtr;`   The pointer to the new node is copied into `currPtr`. Now `currPtr`, `newNodePtr`, and `head->link` all point to the node containing 45.2 as its component.

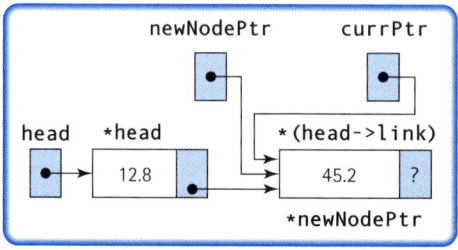

`newNodePtr = new NodeType;`   A dynamic variable of type `NodeType` is created. The pointer to this new node is stored into `newNodePtr`.

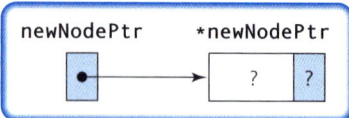

`newNodePtr->component = 70.1;`   The value 70.1 is stored into the `component` member of the new node.

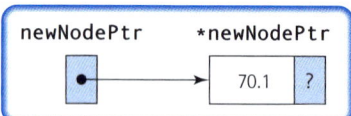

`currPtr->link = newNodePtr;`   The pointer to the new node containing 70.1 in the `component` member is copied into the `link` member of the node that contains 45.2.

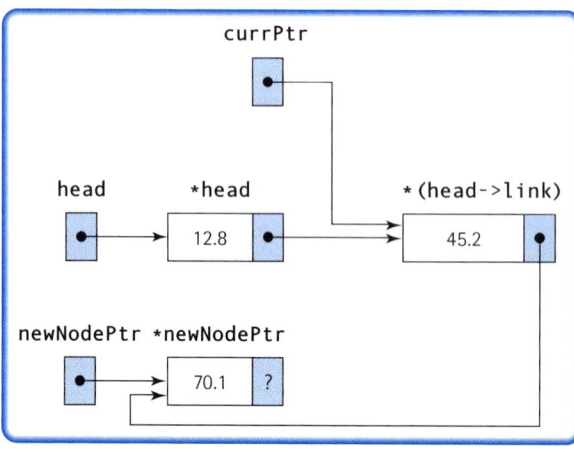

`newNodePtr->link = NULL;`	The special pointer constant **NULL** is stored into the `link` member of the last node in the list. When used in the `link` member of a node, **NULL** means the end of the list. **NULL** is shown in the diagram as a slash (/) in the `link` member.

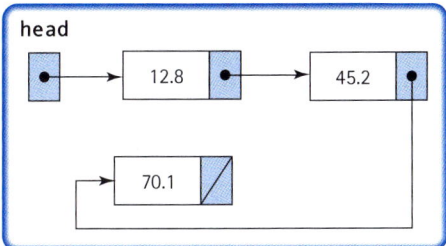

`currPtr = newNodePtr;`	`currPtr` is updated to point to the last node in the list (not shown).

We would like to generalize this algorithm so that we can use a loop to create a dynamic linked list of any length. In the algorithm, we used three pointers:

1. **head**, which was used in creating the first node in the list and became the external pointer to the list.
2. **newNodePtr**, which was used in creating a new node when it was needed.
3. **currPtr**, which was updated to always point to the last node in the linked list.

When building any dynamic linked list by adding each new node to the end of the list, we always need three pointers to perform these functions. The algorithm that we used is generalized here to build a linked list of ten integer values from the standard input device.

```
Set head to new node
Read a number
Set head->component to number
Set currPtr to head of list

FOR count going from 1 through 9
    Set newNodePtr to new node
    Set newNodePtr->component to next number
    Set currPtr->link to new node
    Set currPtr to newNodePtr
Set currPtr->link to NULL
```

Here is a program that implements this algorithm and prints the values in the order in which they were read. The part of the code that creates the linked list is highlighted. We cover how to print the list later in the chapter

```cpp
//***********************************************************
// This program creates a linked list of four values read
// from the keyboard.  The list is then printed.
//***********************************************************

#include <iostream>
using namespace std;
typedef int ItemType;

struct NodeType;                   // Forward declaration
typedef NodeType* NodePtr;

struct NodeType
{
  ItemType component;
  NodePtr  link;
};

int main ()
{
  NodePtr head;            // External pointer to list
  NodePtr newNodePtr;      // Pointer to newest node
  NodePtr currPtr;         // Pointer to last node

  cout << "Enter 4 integer values." << endl;
  head = new NodeType;
  cin >> head->component;
  currPtr = head;

  for (int count = 1; count <= 3; count++)
  {
    newNodePtr = new NodeType;          // Create new node
    cin >> newNodePtr->component;       // Set its component value
    currPtr->link = newNodePtr;         // Link node into list
    currPtr = newNodePtr;               // Set currPtr to last node
  }
  currPtr->link = NULL;                 // Mark end of list
  currPtr = head;
  for (int count = 0; count <= 3; count++)
  {
    cout << currPtr->component << endl;
    currPtr = currPtr->link;
  }
  return 0;
}
```

Here is a sample run:

Let's do a code walk-through and see just how this algorithm works.

`head = new NodeType;`	A variable of type `NodeType` is created. The pointer is stored into `head`. Variable `head` will remain unchanged as the pointer to the first node (that is, `head` is the external pointer to the list).
`cin >> head->component;`	The first number is read into the `component` member of the first node in the list.
`currPtr = head;`	`currPtr` now points to the last node (the only node) in the list.
`for (...)`	A count-controlled loop is used to read four integer values.
`{`	The loop begins.
`  newNodePtr = new NodeType;`	Another variable of type `NodeType` is created, with `newNodePtr` pointing to it.
`  cin >> newNodePtr->component;`	The current input value is stored into the `component` member of the newly created node.
`  currPtr->link = newNodePtr;`	The pointer to the new node is stored into the `link` member of the last node in the list.
`  currPtr = newNodePtr;`	`currPtr` is again pointing to the last node in the list.
`}`	The loop body repeats.
`currPtr->link = NULL;`	The `link` member of the last node is assigned the special end-of-list value `NULL`.

Here is the linked list that results when the program is run with the data 32, 78, 99, and 21 as input. The final values are shown for the auxiliary variables.

QUICK CHECK

14.3.1 What is a dynamic linked list? (p. 727)
14.3.2 What is a dynamic data structure? (p. 727)
14.3.3 What do we use to get access to the first node in a dynamic linked list? (p. 727)
14.3.4 Consider the task of adding a new node to a linked list of integers that already contains a single node. Describe the process of adding this new node to the existing linked list. (pp. 731–733)

14.4 Dynamic Implementation of ADT List

Now that we have looked at two examples of creating a dynamic linked list, let's examine the algorithms that process nodes in a linked list. We need to be able to insert a node into a list, delete a node from a list, search for a node, and traverse the list. For each of these operations, we make use of the fact that NULL is in the `link` member of the last node. NULL can be assigned to any pointer variable; it means that the pointer points to nothing. Its importance lies in the fact that we can compare the `link` member of each node to NULL, thereby determining when we have reached the end of the list.

As we develop these algorithms, we do so in the context of the ADT List. Here are the prototypes for the class `List`, which form the specification for the data type.

```
List();
// Constructor
// Post: Empty list has been created

// Action responsibilities
void Insert(ItemType item);
// Pre:  List is not full and item is not in the list
// Post: item is in the list and length has been incremented
void Delete(ItemType item);
// Post: item is not in the list
void ResetList();
// Post: The current position is reset to the first item in the list
ItemType GetNextItem();
// Assumptions:  No transformers are called during the iteration.
//   There is an item to be returned; that is, HasNext is true when
//   this method is invoked.
// Pre:  ResetList has been called if this is not the first iteration.
// Post: Returns item at the current position.

// Knowledge responsibilities
int GetLength() const;
// Post: Returns the length of the list
bool IsEmpty() const;
// Post: Returns true if list is empty; false otherwise
bool IsFull() const;
// Post: Returns true if list is full; false otherwise
bool IsThere(ItemType item ) const;
// Post: Returns true if item is in the list; false otherwise
bool HasNext() const;
// Post: Returns true if there is another item to be returned; false
// otherwise
```

In the class declaration, notice that the preconditions and postconditions of the member functions mention nothing about linked lists. The abstraction is a list, not a linked list. The user of the class is interested only in manipulating lists of items and does not care how we implement a list. If we decide to use a different implementation, the same public interface remains valid.

The private data in the array-based implementation of Chapter 13 consisted of a `data` array, a `length` field, and a `currentPos` field that held the current position for a traversal of the list. What would be the equivalent in a linked implementation? The array and the current position would be replaced with pointers.

```
class List
{
public:
...
private:
  NodeType* dataPtr;     // External pointer to the first node in the list
  int length;
  NodeType* currentPos;  // Pointer to current position in a traversal
}
```

Do we need to make other changes to the specification file for our new implementation? Yes, we must include a forward declaration for `NodeType` so that the private variable `dataPtr` can be specified. In the spirit of information hiding, we place the complete declaration of `NodeType` into the implementation file `List.cpp`. Now let's look at the linked implementation for the class, beginning with the constructor and the action responsibilities.

Creating an Empty Linked List

To create a linked list with no nodes, all that is necessary is to assign the external pointer the value `NULL`. For the `List` class, the appropriate place to do this is in the class constructor. `currentPos` and `length` must also be set. `length` should be set to 0—but what about `currentPos`? This data field should be initialized to point to the first item in the list: `dataPtr`.

```
List::List()
// Post: dataPtr == NULL
{
  dataPtr = NULL;
  currentPos = dataPtr;
  length = 0;
}
```

As we discussed in Chapter 13, the implementation documentation (the preconditions and postconditions appearing in the implementation file) is often stated differently from the abstract documentation (located in the specification file). Specification documentation is written in terms that are meaningful to the user of the ADT; implementation details should not be mentioned. In contrast, implementation documentation can be made more precise by referring directly to variables and algorithms in the implementation code. In the case of the `List` class constructor, the abstract postcondition simply states that an empty list (not a linked list) has been created. By comparison, the implementation postcondition

```
// Post: dataPtr == NULL
```

is stated in terms of how this is done.

Inserting into a Linked List

A function for inserting a component into a linked list must have an argument: the item to be inserted. The phrase *inserting into a linked list* could mean inserting the component as the first node, inserting the component as the last node, or inserting the component into its proper place according to some ordering (alphabetic or numeric). The list specification says nothing about order, however, so either of the first two meanings would be acceptable. In the case of the array-based list, we assumed the first meaning because inserting an item at the beginning of the list would have been grossly inefficient. In the case of a linked implementation, the logical place to insert an item is at the beginning of the list, because this place is directly accessible via the external pointer. If we want to insert an item at the end of the linked list, either we have to keep an additional pointer to the last node in the list or we must search for the end of the list with each insertion.

Because we are now providing an alternative implementation to an existing class, we want a traversal of the two implementations to be identical. Thus we implement the second meaning: The new item goes at the end of the list. What about the option of inserting the component in its proper place? That's the difference between an unordered list and a sorted list. We examine sorted lists later.

As we noted, there are two ways of managing insertion at the end of a linked list. We choose the approach of keeping a pointer to the last item in the list because it is faster than searching for the end of the list. Thus we add the data field `lastPtr` to our class private data. Our list now has the following general form:

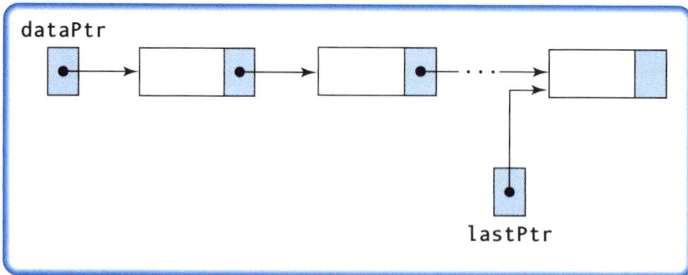

To what do we initialize `lastPtr`? We initialize `lastPtr` to `NULL`: The list is empty, so there is no last node. We insert the new node at the end and reset `lastPtr` to point to that node. This algorithm is very similar to the one we just used to build a list of four numbers.

Insert (In: item)

Set newNodePtr to new NodeType
Set newNodePtr->component to item
Set newNodePtr->link to NULL

Set lastPtr->link to newNodePtr
Set lastPtr to newNodePtr

Before we code this algorithm, we need to look at the end conditions. Does this algorithm work if the list is empty? No, it doesn't. Trying to access `lastPtr->link` when `lastPtr` is `NULL` will cause the program to crash. We need to make inserting into an empty list be a special case. If `lastPtr` is `NULL`, we need to set both `dataPtr` and `lastPtr` to the new node. Here is the revised algorithm:

Insert (In: item) Revised

Set newNodePtr to new NodeType
Set newNodePtr->component to item
Set newNodePtr->link to NULL

IF lastPtr is NULL
   Set dataPtr to newNodePtr
ELSE
   Set lastPtr->link to newNodePtr
   Set lastPtr to newNodePtr

Have we forgotten anything else? Yes—`length` must be incremented when an item is inserted. This algorithm is coded in the following function:

```
void List::Insert(ItemType item)
// Post: New node containing item is at the end of the linked list
//       and lastPtr points to the new node
{
  NodePtr newNodePtr = new NodeType;   // Get a new empty node
  newNodePtr->component = item;        // Give the node a component value
  newNodePtr->link = NULL;             // Set its link to NULL
  if (lastPtr == NULL)                 // If the list was empty
    dataPtr = newNodePtr;              //   Point external pointer to node
  else                                 // Otherwise
    lastPtr->link = newNodePtr;        //   Point last node to new node
  lastPtr = newNodePtr;                // New node becomes last node
  length++;                            // Increment length
}
```

Traversals of a Linked List

Many of the following list algorithms require a traversal—that is, going through the list node by node. Before considering the rest of the functions, let's examine the simple traversal of the four-element list that we used in the sample program in Section 14.3.

```
currPtr = head;
for (int count = 0; count <= 3; count++)
{
  cout << currPtr->component << endl;
  currPtr = currPtr->link;
}
```

In this code segment, the traveling pointer `currentPtr` is initialized to `head`, the first node in the list. This code segment goes through the nodes, printing the component part of each. When `count == 3`, `currPtr` is equal to `NULL`, and each element has been examined.

Do not confuse this internal traversal with the external traversal that a client would undertake using `ResetList`, `HasNext`, and `GetNextItem`. The preceding code segment illustrates the style of traversal that would be performed by a member function that needs to run through part or all of the list. However, because our linked list won't be fixed in size, we'll use a While loop instead of a For loop.

Deleting from a Linked List

To delete an existing node from a linked list, we must loop through the nodes until we find the node we want to delete. The postcondition says only that the item is not in the list; there is no precondition. Thus the item may be in the list or it may not be. However, we do know (by the precondition on `Insert`) that the list contains at most one copy of the item. Thus our search needs two ending conditions: The item is found or the end of the list is found. Here is the loop for the algorithms:

Delete(In: item)

Set currPtr to dataPtr
WHILE currPtr != NULL AND currPtr->component != item
    Set currPtr to currPtr->link
IF currPtr != NULL
  Delete currPtr

If `item` is in the list, at this point `currPtr->component` equals `item`. To delete the node, we must set the `link` portion of the node before it to its `link` field.

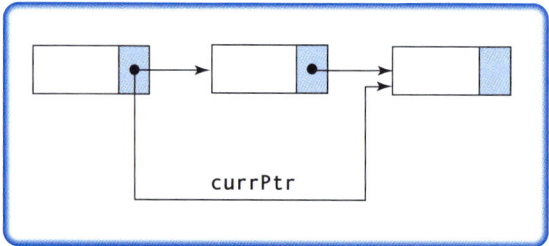

But we don't have access to the `link` field of the node before `currPtr`! Therefore, we must keep track of two nodes in this loop: `currPtr` and the node before it. Let's call it `prevPtr`. We must initialize `prevPtr` to `NULL`. Here is the revised algorithm:

Delete(In: item) Revised

```
Set currPtr to dataPtr
Set prevPtr to NULL
WHILE currPtr != NULL AND currPtr->component != item
    Set prevPtr to currPtr
    Set currPtr to currPtr->link
IF currPtr != NULL
    Set prevPtr->link to currPtr->link
    Delete currPtr
```

Are there any end conditions that we missed? If the node to be deleted is the first node, we must update **dataPtr**. If the node to be deleted is the last node, we must update **lastPtr**. If the node to be deleted is the only node in the list, both **dataPtr** and **lastPtr** must be updated. These tests must be done before the deletion is made.

```
...
IF currPtr != NULL                              // item is found
    IF currPtr == dataPtr                       // item is in first node
        Set dataPtr to currPtr->link            // delete first node
    ELSE
        Set prevPtr->link to currPtr->link      // delete item
    IF currPtr == lastPtr                       // item is in last node
        Set lastPtr to prevPtr                  // reset lastPtr
    Delete currPtr                              // deallocate currPtr
```

```cpp
void List::Delete(ItemType item)
{
  NodePtr prevPtr = NULL;       // Trailing pointer
  NodePtr currPtr = dataPtr;    // Loop control pointer
  while (currPtr != NULL && currPtr->component != item)
  {
    prevPtr = currPtr;
    currPtr = currPtr->link;
  }
  if (currPtr != NULL)
  {                             // item is found
    if (currPtr == dataPtr)
      dataPtr = currPtr->link;  // item is in first node
    else
      prevPtr->link = currPtr->link;
    if (currPtr == lastPtr)
       lastPtr = prevPtr;       // item is in last node
    delete currPtr;
    length--;
  }
}
```

As a walk-through example to check our algorithm, let's delete the node whose component is 20. The structure is shown below, with the nodes labeled as they are when the While statement is reached.

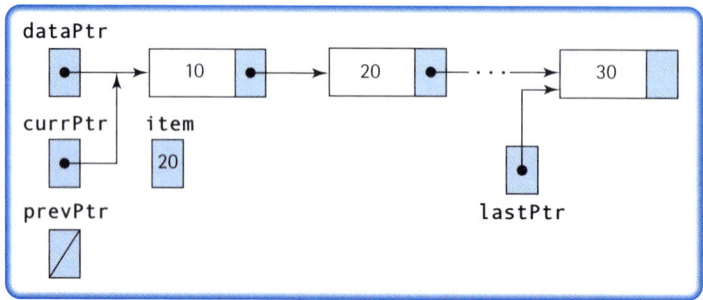

`while (currPtr != NULL` `   && currPtr->component != item)`	`currPtr` is not `NULL` and 10 is not equal to 20, so the loop body is entered.
`prevPtr = currPtr;` `currPtr = currPtr->link;`	The trailing pointer points to the first node. The current pointer points to the second node.
`while (currPtr != NULL` `   && currPtr->component != item)`	`currPtr` is not `NULL` but 20 equals 20, so the loop is exited.
`if (currPtr != NULL)`	`currPtr` is not `NULL` so the item is found.
`if (currPtr == dataPtr)`	`currPtr` is not equal to `dataPtr` so the item is not in the first node.
`prevPtr->link = currPtr->link;`	The node with the item is unlinked.
`if (currPtr == lastPtr)`	The item is not in the last node.
`delete currPtr;`	The node is deallocated.
`length--;`	The `length` of the list is decremented.

If the value to be deleted is in the first node, the node is unlinked by setting `dataPtr` to the `link` field of the first node. If the value to be deleted is in the last node, `lastPtr` is reset to the current last node (`prevPtr`).

Resetting the List

This function initializes `currentPos` for a traversal. The constructor sets it originally; this function must reset it to point to the head of the list: `dataPtr`.

```
void List::ResetList()
{
  currentPos = dataPtr;
}
```

Getting the Next Item

This algorithm is identical to the one in the array-based list implementation. We return the contents of the node pointed to by `currentPtr` and then set `currentPtr` to point to the next node. We don't have to worry about dereferencing the `NULL` pointer, because the precondition for the function states that there is another item to be returned.

```
ItemType List::GetNextItem()
{
  ItemType item;
  item = currentPos->component;
  currentPos = currentPos->link;
  return item;
}
```

Now we have finished looking at all the action responsibilities, leaving only the knowledge responsibilities to examine. Three of these are so straightforward that we show the code with no explanation: `GetLength`, `IsEmpty`, and `HasNext`.

```
int List::GetLength() const
{ return length; }

bool List::IsEmpty() const
{ return (dataPtr == NULL); }

bool List::HasNext() const
{ return (currentPos != NULL); }
```

Testing for the Full Linked List

Theoretically, a linked list cannot be full. However, there is a possibility that the list might be so long that the heap runs out of memory to supply to the `new` operator. We show how to handle this situation in Chapter 16 when we cover exceptions. Until then, we just let function `IsFull` return `false`.

```
bool List::IsFull() const
{ return false; }
```

Searching the List

We actually looked at this algorithm when we were searching the list for an item to delete. In fact, we can use the first part of the code directly. However, because we are not deleting a component, we do not need the pointer to the previous node.

```
bool List::IsThere() const
{
  NodePtr currPtr = dataPtr;        // Loop control pointer
  while (currPtr != NULL && currPtr->component != item)
    currPtr = currPtr->link;

  if (currPtr != NULL)
    return true;
  else
    return false;
}
```

Now we need to collect these functions in an implementation file and write a driver to test them. As this is an alternative implementation of a class, we can use the same driver that we used to test the array-based list implementation.

Here is the specification file:

```cpp
//****************************************************************
// SPECIFICATION FILE (list.h)
// This file gives the specification of a list abstract data type.
// The list components are not assumed to be in order by value.
//****************************************************************
typedef int ItemType;         // Type of each component
struct NodeType;              // Forward declaration
class List
{
public:
 List();
  // Constructor
  // Post: Empty list has been created

  // Action responsibilities
  void Insert(ItemType item);
  // Pre:  List is not full and item is not in the list
  // Post: item is in the list and length has been incremented
  void Delete(ItemType item);
  // Post: item is not in the list
  void ResetList();
  // Post: The current position is reset to the first item in the list
  ItemType GetNextItem();
  // Assumptions:  No transformers are called during the iteration.
  //   There is an item to be returned; that is, HasNext is true when
  //   this method is invoked.
  // Pre:  ResetList has been called if this is not the first iteration.
  // Post: Returns item at the current position.

  // Knowledge responsibility
  int GetLength() const;
  // Post: Returns the length of the list
  bool IsEmpty() const;
  // Post: Returns true if list is empty; false otherwise
  bool IsFull() const;
  // Post: Returns true if list if full; false otherwise
  bool IsThere  (ItemType item ) const;
  // Post: Returns true if item is in the list and false otherwise
  bool HasNext() const;
  // Post: Returns true if there is another item to be returned;
  // false otherwise
  private:
    NodeType* dataPtr;      // Pointer to the first node in the list
    int length;
    NodeType* currentPos;   // Pointer to the current position
                            // in a traversal
    NodeType* lastPtr;      // Pointer to the last node in the list
};
```

Here is the implementation file:

```cpp
//*****************************************************************
// IMPLEMENTATION FILE (list.cpp)
// This file implements the List class member functions
// List representation: A linked list with head and tail
// pointers, a length field, and a current position pointer.
//*****************************************************************
#include "list.h"
#include <iostream>
#include <cstddef>              // For NULL

using namespace std;

typedef NodeType* NodePtr;
struct NodeType
{
  ItemType component;
  NodePtr link;
};

List::List()
// Post: dataPtr == NULL
{
  dataPtr = NULL;
  currentPos = dataPtr;
  length = 0;
  lastPtr = NULL;
}

//*****************************************************************

void List::Insert(ItemType item)
// Post: New node containing item is at the end of the linked list
//       and lastPtr points to the new node
{
  NodePtr newNodePtr = new NodeType;
  newNodePtr->component = item;
  newNodePtr->link = NULL;
  if (lastPtr == NULL)
    dataPtr = newNodePtr;
  else
    lastPtr->link = newNodePtr;
  lastPtr = newNodePtr;
  length++;
}

//*****************************************************************
```

```cpp
void List::Delete(ItemType item)
{
  NodePtr prevPtr = NULL;          // Trailing pointer
  NodePtr currPtr = dataPtr;       // Loop control pointer
  while (currPtr != NULL && currPtr->component != item)
  {
    prevPtr = currPtr;
    currPtr = currPtr->link;
  }
  if (currPtr != NULL)
  { // item is found
    if (currPtr == dataPtr)
      dataPtr = currPtr->link;     // item is in first node
    else
      prevPtr->link = currPtr->link;
    if (currPtr == lastPtr)
      lastPtr = prevPtr;           // item is in last node
    delete currPtr;
    length--;
  }
}

//****************************************************************

void List::ResetList()
{
  currentPos = dataPtr;
}

//****************************************************************

ItemType List::GetNextItem()
{
  ItemType item;
  item = currentPos->component;
  currentPos = currentPos->link;
  return item;
}

//****************************************************************

int List::GetLength() const
{ return length; }

//****************************************************************

bool List::IsEmpty() const
{ return (dataPtr == NULL); }

//****************************************************************

bool List::HasNext() const
{ return (currentPos != NULL); }
```

```
//*****************************************************************
bool List::IsFull() const
{ return false; }

//*****************************************************************

bool List::IsThere(ItemType item) const
{
  NodePtr currPtr = dataPtr;        // Loop control pointer

  while (currPtr != NULL && currPtr->component != item)
    currPtr = currPtr->link;
  if (currPtr != NULL)
    return true;
  else
    return false;
}
```

The same driver was used with this implementation, and here is the output. If you look back to the last chapter, you will see the output is identical.

QUICK CHECK

14.4.1 What are the general steps necessary to insert a new node into a linked list following a specific node? (pp. 736–737)

14.4.2 What are the general steps necessary to delete a node from a linked list following a specific node? (pp. 738–739)

14.4.3 Write C++ code to traverse from beginning to end a linked list whose first element is pointed to by the variable **head** printing out the value of each node. Assume that each node consists of a variable called **value** for the value and **link** for the link to the next node. (pp. 737–738)

14.4.4 What does the **IsFull** method of a linked list return and why? (p. 741)

14.5 Destructors and Copy-Constructors

Classes whose objects manipulate dynamic data on the free store should provide three special operations: a *constructor*, a *destructor*, and a *copy-constructor*. You are familiar with constructors; now we look at the other two operations.

Destructor

The purpose of the destructor is to deallocate the nodes in a dynamic linked list when a `List` class object is destroyed. Without a destructor, the linked list would be left behind on the free store, still allocated but inaccessible. The code for the destructor is easy to write. We just traverse the list, deleting nodes as we go along. Note that the destructor is defined exactly like a constructor except that it has a tilde (~) before the class name.

```
List::~List()
// Destructor
// Post: All linked list nodes have been deallocated
{
  NodePtr tempPtr;
  NodePtr currPtr = dataPtr;
  while (currPtr != NULL)
  {
    tempPtr = currPtr;
    currPtr = currPtr->link;
    delete tempPtr;
  }
}
```

Shallow Versus Deep Copying

When we introduced arrays, we said that you could assign one array to another, but you wouldn't get what you expect. That's because you would just be copying the *address* of one array into another, not the *contents* of the array. The same is true of a linked list. After the following operations

```
List listOne;
List listTwo;
. . .
listOne = listTwo;
```

`listOne` just points to the first node of `listTwo`. With the built-in assignment operator (=), assignment of one class object to another copies only the class members; it does not copy any data pointed to by the class members. See **FIGURE 14.6**.

The result is called a shallow copy operation: The pointer is copied, but the pointed-to data is not. Shallow copying is perfectly fine if none of the class members are pointers. In the preceding example, `length`, `currentPos`, and `lastPtr` are copied as you would expect. But if one or more members are pointers to dynamic data, then shallow copying may not give the results you expect. Only the external pointer to the list (`dataPtr`) is copied into `listOne`, not the list to which it points. Thus there is only one copy of the linked list, not two as you would expect

> **Shallow copy** An operation that copies one class object to another without copying any pointed-to data.

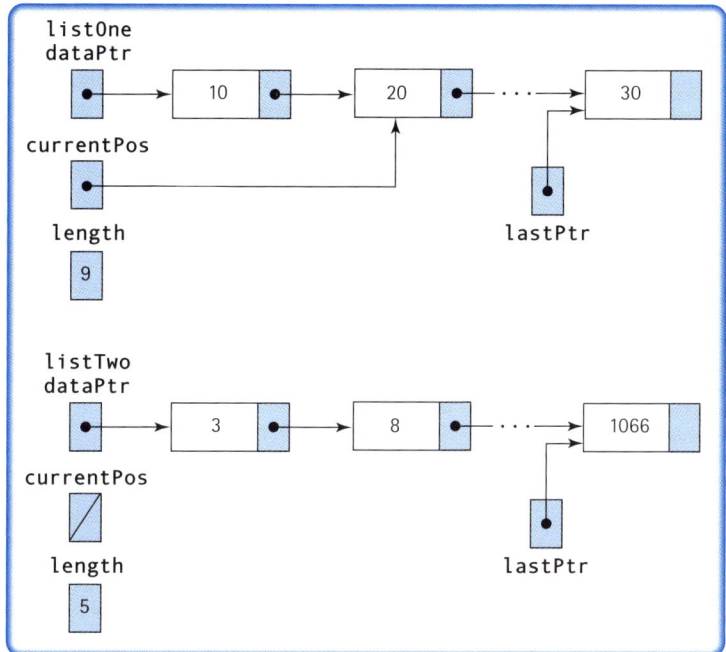

Figure 14.6 Shallow Copy (Initial State)

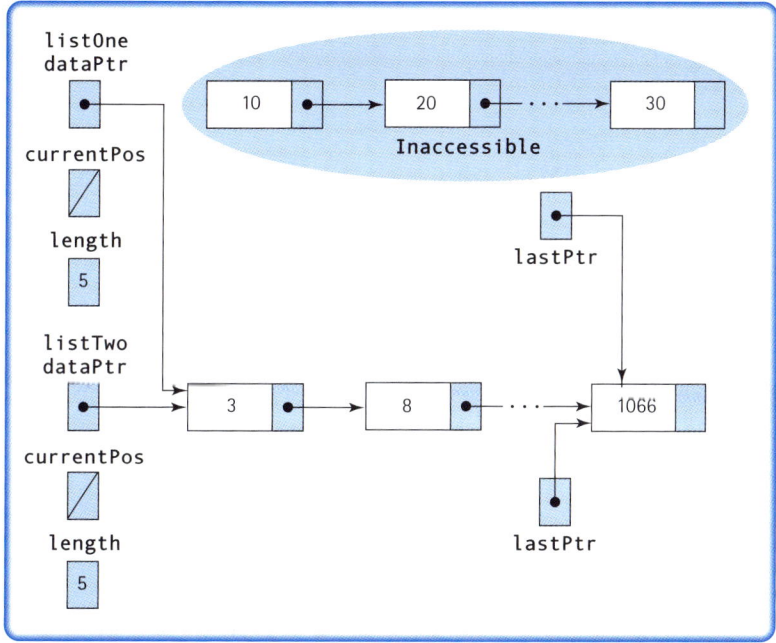

Figure 14.6 (continued) Shallow Copy After Executing `listOne = listTwo;`

> **Deep copy** An operation that not only copies one class object to another, but also makes copies of any pointed-to data.

when copying one instance to another. In addition, the dynamic data originally pointed to by the `listOne` object has been left inaccessible. See Figure 14.6.

What we really want is a *deep copy* operation—one that duplicates not only the class members, but also the pointed-to data.

Copy-Constructor

As we have just discussed, the built-in assignment operator (=) leads to a shallow copy when class data members point to dynamic data. The issue of deep versus shallow copying also can crop up in another context: initialization of one class object by another. C++ defines initialization to mean the following:

1. Initialization in a variable declaration:

   ```
   Name name1("Kenneth", "Charles", "Smith");
   Name name2 = name1;
   ```

2. Passing a copy of an argument to a parameter (that is, passing by value)
3. Returning an object as the value of a function:

   ```
   return someObject;
   ```

By default, C++ performs such initializations using shallow copy semantics. In other words, the newly created class object is initialized via a member-by-member copy of the old object without regard for any data to which the class members may point. Both `name1` and `name2` point to the same three strings; they do not each point to separate copies of the strings.

To handle this situation, C++ supports a special kind of constructor known as a copy-constructor. In a class declaration, its prototype has the following form:

```
class SomeClass
{
public:
    .
    .
    .
  SomeClass(const SomeClass& someObject);   // Copy-constructor
    .
    .
    .
};
```

Notice that the function prototype does not use any special words to suggest that this is a copy-constructor. You simply have to recognize the pattern of symbols: the class name followed by a parameter list, which contains a single `const` reference parameter of its own type:

```
const SomeClass&
```

The copy-constructor is more challenging to write than the destructor. Before we look at this task, we must stress the importance of providing a copy-constructor whenever we also provide a destructor. Pretend that `List` doesn't have a copy-constructor, and suppose that a client passes a class object to a function using pass by value. (Remember that passing an argument by value sends a *copy* of the value of the argument to the function.) Within the function, the parameter is initialized to be a copy of the caller's class object, including the caller's value of the private external pointer to the list. At this point, both the argument and the parameter are pointing to the same dynamic linked list. When the client function returns, the class destructor is invoked for the parameter, destroying the only copy of the linked list. Upon return from the function, the caller's linked list has disappeared!

By providing a copy-constructor, we ensure deep copying of an argument to a parameter whenever a pass by value occurs. The implementation of the copy-constructor, shown next, employs a commonly used algorithm for creating a new linked list as a copy of another: We set up the external pointer to the new list and copy the first node. We then use a While loop to traverse the original list, copying each node and linking the copy into the new list.

```
List::List(const List& otherList)
// Copy-constructor

// Post: A deep copy of otherList is created and the external pointer
//       now points to this list
{
  NodePtr fromPtr;    // Pointer into list being copied from
  NodePtr toPtr;      // Pointer into new list being built

  if (otherList.dataPtr == NULL)
  {
    dataPtr = NULL;
    return;
  }
  // Copy first node
  fromPtr = otherList.dataPtr;
  dataPtr = new NodeType;
  dataPtr->component = fromPtr->component;
  // Copy remaining nodes
  toPtr = dataPtr;
  fromPtr = fromPtr->link;
  while (fromPtr != NULL)
  // Copy nodes from original to duplicate
  {
    toPtr->link = new NodeType;              // Store new node in link of
                                             //    last node added to new list
    toPtr = toPtr->link;                     // toPtr points to new node
    toPtr->component = fromPtr->component;   // Copy component to new node
    fromPtr = fromPtr->link;                 // fromPtr points to next node
                                             //    of original list
  }
  toPtr->link = NULL;
  lastPtr = toPtr;                           // Set last pointer
}
```

If a copy-constructor is present, the default method of initialization (member-by-member copying) is circumvented. Instead, the copy-constructor is implicitly invoked whenever one object is initialized by another.

In summary, the default operations of assignment and initialization may be dangerous when objects point to dynamic data on the free store.[1] Member-by-member assignment and initialization cause only pointers to be copied, not the pointed-to data. If a class allocates and deallocates dynamic data, it almost certainly needs the following suite of member functions to ensure deep copying of dynamic data:

```
class SomeClass
{
public:
    .
    .
    .
  SomeClass( ... );
  // Constructor

  SomeClass(const SomeClass& anotherObject ;
   // Copy-constructor, for deep copying in initializations

  ~SomeClass();
   // Destructor, to clean up the free store
private:
    .
    .
    .
};
```

QUICK CHECK

14.5.1 If you want to copy all of the pointed-to data in a struct or class, should you use deep or shallow copying? (p. 746)

14.5.2 Two of the ways that C++ defines initialization are initialization in a variable declaration and passing an argument by value. What is the third way that C++ defines initialization? (pp. 748–749)

14.5.3 Every class that manipulates dynamic data should have a constructor, a destructor, and which other member function? (p. 746)

14.5.4 What is a copy constructor? (p. 748)

14.6 Sorted Linked List

As we saw in the array-based list implementation, the only operations that differ between an unsorted list and a sorted list are the insert operation and the delete operation. The same is true in the linked implementation.

To insert a component into its proper place in a sorted list, we must loop through the nodes until we find where the component belongs. Because the `SortedList` class keeps components in ascending order, we can recognize where a component belongs by finding the node that contains a value *greater than* the one being inserted. Our new node should be inserted directly before the node with that value; therefore, we must keep track of the

---

1. In Chapter 16, we will see how operators such as = can be given new meaning through a mechanism called overloading. Using overloading, it becomes possible to create an = operation for a class that implements deep copying. For example, that is how the `string` class avoids performing a shallow copy when one string is assigned to another.

node before the current one so that we can insert our new node. We use a pointer `prevPtr` to point to this previous node as we did in the delete operation.

What are the special cases? When the list is empty, when the value to be inserted is less than the first, and when the value to be inserted is greater than the last. Let's check for the empty list before we enter the loop. When the loop exits, there are two cases: If the current pointer is `NULL`, the node is inserted at the end; otherwise, the node is inserted between the trailing pointer and the current pointer. This method leads to the following algorithm:

Insert (In: item)

```
Set newNodePtr to new NodeType
Set newNodePtr->component to item

IF dataPtr is NULL                                    // Empty list
   Set newNodePtr->link to NULL
   Set dataPtr to newNodePtr
   Set lastPtr to newNodePtr
ELSE
   Set currPtr to dataPtr
   Set prevPtr to NULL
   WHILE currPtr != NULL AND currPtr->component < item
      Set prevPtr to currPtr
      Set currPtr to currPtr->link
   Set newNodePtr to currPtr
   IF prevPtr == NULL                                 // Insert as first node
      dataPtr = newNodePtr
   ELSE
      Set prevPtr to newNodePtr
   IF currPtr == NULL                                 // Insert as last node
      Set lastPtr to newNodePtr
```

The following function implements our algorithm with these changes incorporated:

```
void SortedList::Insert(ItemType item )
// Post: New node containing item is in its proper place and
//       component members of list nodes are in ascending order

{
  NodePtr currPtr;       // Moving pointer
  NodePtr prevPtr;       // Trailing pointer
  NodePtr newNodePtr;    // Pointer to new node

  newNodePtr = new NodeType;
  newNodePtr->component = item;

  if (dataPtr == NULL)    // Empty list
  {
    newNodePtr->component = NULL;
    dataPtr = newNodePtr;
    lastPtr = newNodePtr;
  }
```

```
else
{ // Find previous insertion point
  currPtr = dataPtr;
  prevPtr = NULL;
  while (currPtr != NULL && currPtr->component < item)
  {
    prevPtr = currPtr;
    currPtr = currPtr->link;
  }

  // Insert new node
  newNodePtr->link = currPtr;
  if (prevPtr == NULL)                   // Insert as first?
    dataPtr = newNodePtr;
  else
    prevPtr->link = newNodePtr;
  if (currPtr == NULL)                   // Insert as last?
    lastPtr = newNodePtr;
}
length++;
}
```

Let's go through this code for each of the three cases: inserting at the beginning (item is 20), inserting in the middle (item is 60), and inserting at the end (item is 100). Each insertion begins with the following list:

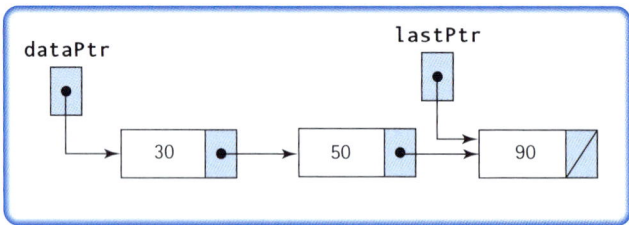

The next diagram shows the status after initialization. The only thing that changes is the value in the component field of newNodePtr.

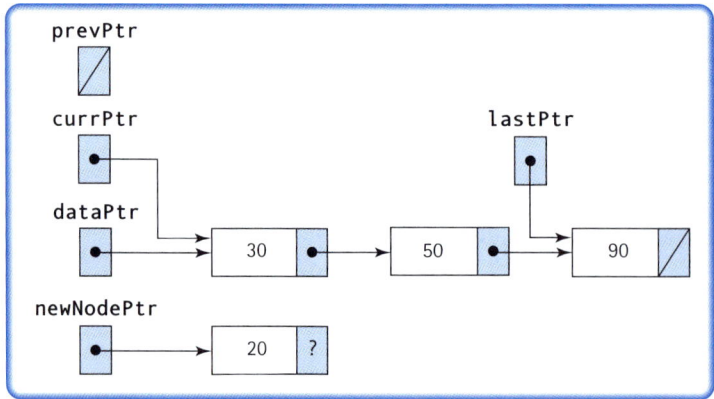

Insert(20)

`newNodePtr = new NodeType;` `newNodePtr->component = item;`	These two statements create and initialize the new node.
`if (dataPtr == NULL)` `else`	List is not empty.
`currPtr = data Ptr;` `prevPtr = NULL;`	Set up for traversal.
`while (currPtr != NULL &&` `currPtr->component < item)`	Because 20 is less than 30, the expression is `false` and the loop body is not entered.
`newNodePtr->link = currPtr;`	`link` member of `*newNodePtr` now points to `*currPtr`.
`if (prevPtr == NULL)` `dataPtr = newNodePtr;`	Because `prevPtr` is `NULL`, the then-clause is executed and 20 is inserted at the front of the list.

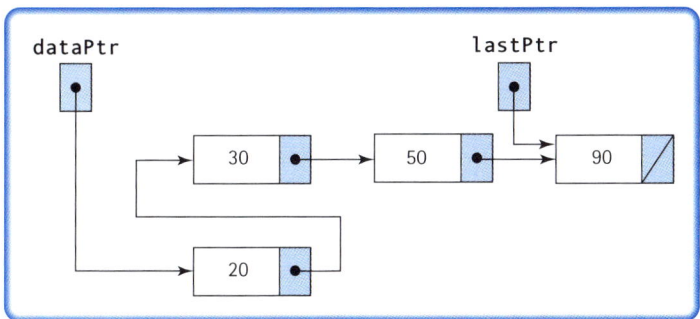

Insert(60) (pick up with loop)

`while (currPtr != NULL &&`
  `currPtr->component < item)`
  `prevPtr = currPtr;`
  `currPtr =  currPtr->link;`
	Because 30 is less than 60, this expression is `true` and the loop body is repeated. Pointer variables are advanced.

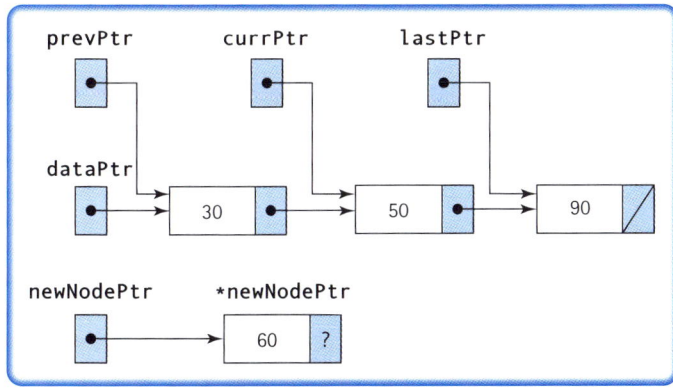

```
while (currPtr != NULL &&
    currPtr->component < item)
  prevPtr = currPtr;
  currPtr =  currPtr->link;
```
Because 50 is less than 60, the expression is
true and the loop body is repeated.
Pointer variables are advanced.

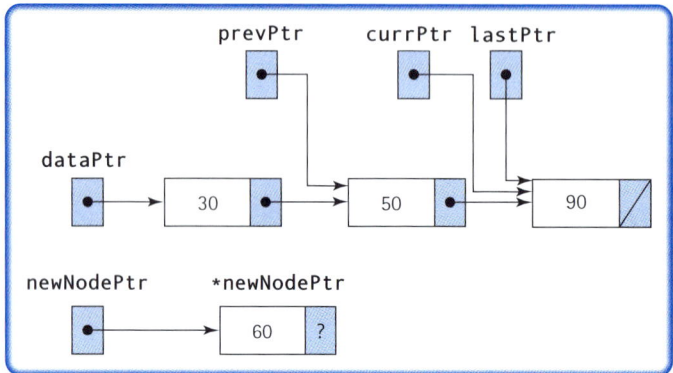

```
while (currPtr != NULL &&
    currPtr->component < item)
```
Because 90 is not less than 60, the expression
is false and the loop body is not repeated.

`newNodePtr->link = currPtr;`   link member of *newNodePtr now points to *currPtr.

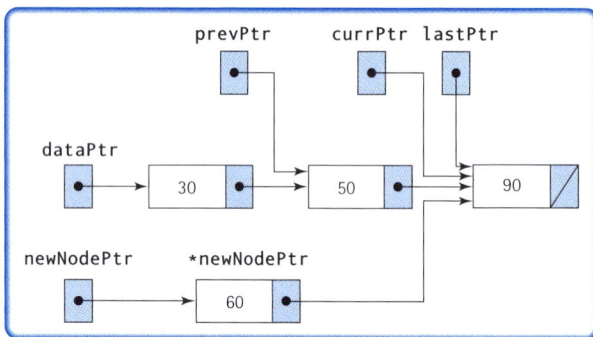

```
if (prevPtr == NULL)
  prevPtr->link = newNodePtr;
if (currPtr == NULL)
```
Because the node is not inserted as the first
component, the else-clause is executed.
Because the node is not inserted as the last component,
no further action is taken.

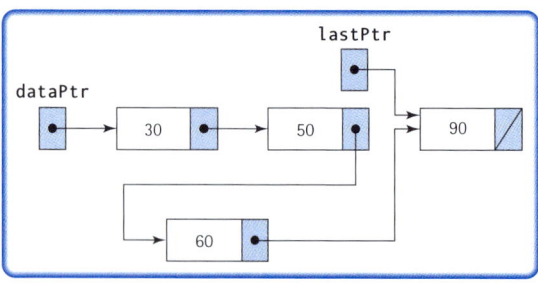

Insert(100)

We do not repeat the first part of the search, but pick up the walk-through where `prevPtr` is pointing to the node whose component is 50, and `currPtr` is pointing to the node whose component is 90.

```
while (currPtr != NULL &&
  currPtr->component < item)
  prevPtr = currPtr;
  currPtr = currPtr->link;
```

Because 90 is less than 100, this expression is **true** and the loop body is repeated. The pointer variables are advanced.

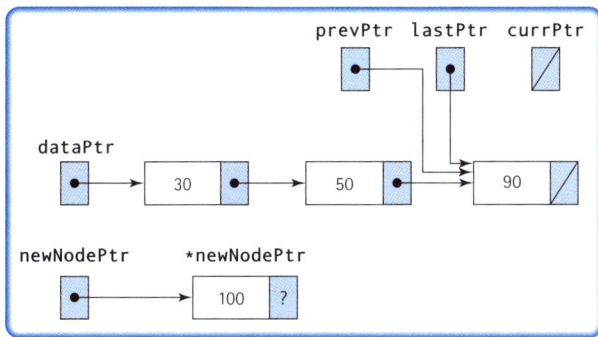

```
while (currPtr != NULL &&
  currPtr->component < item)
newNodePtr->link = currPtr;

if (prevPtr == NULL)
  prevPtr->link = newNodePtr;
if (currPtr == NULL)
  lastPtr = newNodePtr;
```

Because `currPtr` equals `NULL`, the expression is **false** and the loop body is not repeated. `NULL` is copied into the `link` member of `*newNodePtr`.
Because the node is not inserted as the first component, the else-clause is executed.
The node is inserted at the end, so `lastPtr` is updated.

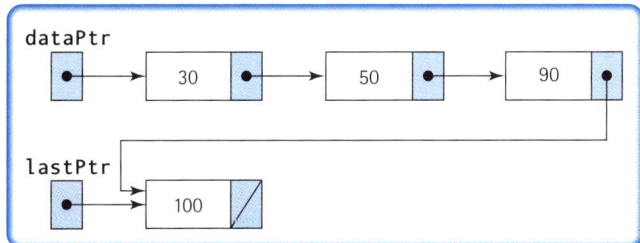

Deleting from a Linked List

To delete an existing node from a linked list, we have to loop through the nodes until we find the node we want to delete. In fact, the function written for the unordered list would work just fine here. However, we can determine that the item is not present when we pass a value that is greater than the one we are deleting. Thus the While expression needs an additional test (which we show as shaded).

```
while (currPtr != NULL && currPtr->component != item
       && currPtr->component < item)
```

Now there are two conditions that indicate that the item is not there: `currPtr` is `NULL` or `currPtr->component < item`. Here is the coded function with the changes shaded:

```
void SortedList::Delete(ItemType item)
{
  NodePtr prevPtr = NULL;         // Trailing pointer
  NodePtr currPtr = dataPtr;      // Loop control pointer
  while (currPtr != NULL && currPtr->component != item
         && currPtr->component < item)
  {
    prevPtr = currPtr;
    currPtr = currPtr->link;
  }
  if (currPtr != NULL && currPtr->component == item)
  { // item is found
    if (currPtr == dataPtr)
      dataPtr = currPtr->link;      // item is in first node
    else
      prevPtr->link = currPtr->link;
    if (currPtr == lastPtr)
      lastPtr = prevPtr;            // item is in last node
    delete currPtr;
    length--;
  }
}
```

Let's see what happens when we delete the node whose component is 30. The structure is shown below, with the nodes labeled with their state when the While statement is reached. Because the While and If expressions are so long, we show only the part of the expression responsible for the result.

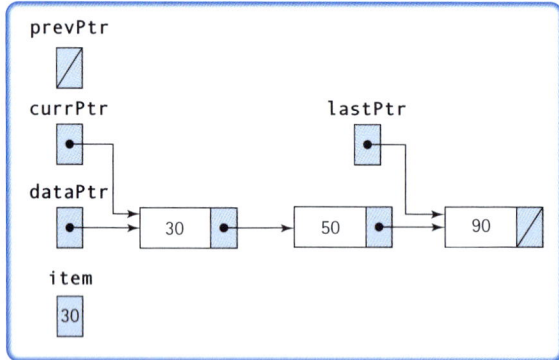

Delete(30)

`while (currPtr->component != item)`   The item is found so the loop is not entered.

`if (currPtr->component == item)`   The item is found.
  `if (currentPtr == dataPtr)`   The node is the first one.
    `dataPtr = currPtr;`   The external pointer points to the second node.

```
if (currPtr == lastPtr)                     The node is not the last.
delete currPtr;                             *currPtr is returned to the heap.
length--;                                   The length of the list is decremented.
```

Delete(50)

The picture is the same except that `item` contains 50.

```
while (...)                                 All of the expressions are true so the loop is
                                            entered.
  prevPtr = currPtr;                        Pointers are moved forward.
  currPtr = currPtr->link;
while (currPtr->component != item)          The node does contain the item to be deleted, so
                                            the loop is not entered again.

if (currPtr->component == item)             The item is found.
  if (currentPtr == dataPtr)                The node is not the first one.
  else
    prevPtr->link == currPtr->link;         The node with 30 is linked to the node with
                                            90.
if (currPtr == lastPtr)                     The node is not the last.
delete currPtr;                             *currPtr is returned to the heap.
length--;                                   The length of the list is decremented.
```

We leave the walk-through of the other cases as an exercise. We could use this same technique to improve the efficiency of `IsThere`. We leave its reimplementation as an exercise.

> **QUICK CHECK**
>
> **14.6.1** What are the special cases for inserting a node into a sorted linked list? (p. 751)

Problem-Solving Case Study

Creating a Sorted List of Entry Objects

PROBLEM: Create a sorted list of time/name pairs ordered by time.

DISCUSSION: We already have a `Name` class, a `TimeOfDay` class, and an `Entry` class made up of `Name` and `TimeOfDay` objects. (See Chapter 12.) We have two `List` classes, one unordered and one sorted. Because the list is to be returned in order by time, we must use the sorted list. It looks like the solution to this problem involves simply putting building blocks together, where the building blocks are classes. We can use each of these classes directly, except for the `List` class.

The `List` class is a list of `ItemType` objects in which `ItemType` is set by a Typedef statement. In the case study in Chapter 13, we used the `List` class to hold a list of integers. Here we have a list of `Entry`

Problem-Solving Case Study

objects, which should be ordered by time. That's okay; we have a `SortedList` class we can use. Uh oh, on second thought, it really isn't okay: The `SortedList` operations compare items using the relational operators, but our `TimeOfDay` class only supports a `ComparedTo` function that returns values of `RelationType`. If we are going to have a sorted list of objects of class `Entry`, we must add to the class a `ComparedTo` function that compares `TimeOfDay` objects. Then we need to change the `SortedList` implementation to use the `ComparedTo` operation instead of the relational operators.

As it stands now, there is only one parameterized constructor for class `Entry`, which takes parameters representing the separate parts of a name and time, so that it can build `Name` and `TimeOfDay` objects internally. Let's include a second parameterized constructor that takes already instantiated objects as parameters. Here are the prototypes for the new functions:

```
Entry(Name newName, TimeOfDay newTime);
// Creates an Entry object with newName as the name attribute and
// newTime as the time attribute
{
  name = newName;
  time = newTime;
}
RelationType ComparedTo(Entry otherEntry);
// Compares time with entry.time
// Post: Return value is
//       BEFORE if time comes before entry.time;
//       SAME if time is the same as entry.time;
//       AFTER if time comes after entry.time
{
  return (time.ComparedTo(otherEntry.time));
}
```

SORTED LIST: Is our current `SortedList` class useless? No; we must rewrite the functions that require comparisons: `Insert`, `Delete`, and `IsThere`. We replace the relational operators with the `ComparedTo` function from the `Entry` class, thereby specializing the list. But we can directly use the operations that do not require a comparison.

Is there some way that we could avoid this specialization and have a linked list that works for many different types? Yes—several advanced features of C++ will allow us to solve this problem by creating a general list. We look at one of them in Chapter 16.

Do we really need to change `Delete`? Our problem doesn't indicate that we need to delete an appointment, but we should anticipate such an operation in the future. Note that "item" is of class `Entry`, and our comparisons are based on time, so `ComparedTo` in class `Entry` just calls `ComparedTo` in class `TimeOfDay`. `IsThere` should also be changed because the client needs to be sure the item isn't in the list before inserting it.

Insert(In: item)

```
...
WHILE currPtr != NULL AND
   currPtr->component.ComparedTo (item) == BEFORE
...
```

Problem-Solving Case Study

Delete(In: item)

```
...
WHILE currPtr != NULL AND
    currPtr->component.ComparedTo(item) != SAME) AND
    currPtr->component.ComparedTo(item) == BEFORE
...

IF currPtr != NULL AND currPtr->component.ComparedTo(item) == SAME
    ...
```

We must remember to add to the specification file the Typedef statement that equates **itemtype** with **Entry**.

DRIVER: The calls to the **SortedList** functions to implement the tasks currently go into the driver. When we incorporate what we have done here into the bigger task, the driver will become part of the class that manipulates a day's events. We need to create **Entry** objects and insert them into the sorted list. We must precede each insertion with a test to be sure the item is not already present in the list. We should try to insert one copy to be sure **IsThere** works correctly. Here is the driver program:

```
//***************************************************************
// DRIVER for class sorted list of class Entry
// This program tests the constructors and return functions
//***************************************************************
#include <iostream>
#include "SortedList.h"
#include <string>

using namespace std;

int main ()
{
  SortedList list;
  Entry entry1("Sally", "Jane", "Smith", 12, 20, 0); // Create 1st entry
  if (!list.IsThere(entry1))
    list.Insert(entry1);                              // Insert 1st entry
  Entry entry2("Mary", "Beth", "Jones", 10, 30, 0);  // Create 2nd entry
  if (!list.IsThere(entry2))
    list.Insert(entry2);                              // Insert 2nd entry
if (!list.IsThere(entry2))
    list.Insert(entry2);                              // Try insert again
  Name name("Susy", "Nell", "Baxter");               // Create name
  TimeOfDay time(8, 30, 0);                          // Create time
  Entry entry3(name, time);                          // Test constructor
  if (!list.IsThere(entry3))
    list.Insert(entry3);                              // Insert 3rd entry
  list.ResetList();                                   // Reset position
```

Problem-Solving Case Study

```
    while (list.HasNext())                              // Output list items
    {
        entry1 = list.GetNextItem();
        cout << entry1.GetNameStr() << " " << entry1.GetTimeStr() << endl;
    };

    return 0;
}
```

Output:

```
Susy Baxter 08:30:00
Mary Jones 10:30:00
Sally Smith 12:20:00
```

Testing and Debugging

One common error—leaving inaccessible objects on the free store—usually results from either a shallow copy operation or incorrect use of the **new** operator. In Figure 14.6, we showed how the built-in assignment operator causes a shallow copy; the dynamic data object originally pointed to by one pointer variable remains allocated but is inaccessible. Misuse of the **new** operator also can leave dynamic data inaccessible. For example, execution of the code fragment

```
float* floatPtr;

floatPtr = new float;
*floatPtr = 38.5;
floatPtr = new float;
```

creates an inaccessible object: the dynamic variable containing 38.5. The problem is that we assigned a new value to `floatPtr` in the last statement without first deallocating the variable it pointed to. To guard against this kind of error, examine every use of the **new** operator in your code. If the associated variable currently points to data, delete the pointed-to data before executing the **new** operation.

Finally, dangling pointers are a source of errors and can be difficult to detect. One cause of dangling pointers is the deallocation of a dynamic data object that is pointed to by more than one pointer. Figures 14.2d and 14.2e picture this situation. A second cause of dangling pointers is returning a pointer to an automatic variable from a function. The following function, which returns a function value of type `int*`, is erroneous:

```
int* Func()
{
  int n;
    .
    .
    .
  return &n;
}
```

Remember that automatic variables are implicitly created at block entry and implicitly destroyed at block exit. The preceding function returns a pointer to the local variable n, but n disappears as soon as control exits the function. The caller of the function, therefore, receives a dangling pointer. Dangling pointers are hazardous for the same reason that uninitialized pointers are hazardous: When your program dereferences incorrect pointer values, it will access memory locations whose contents are unknown.

Testing and debugging a linked structure are complicated by the fact that each item in the structure contains not only a data portion but also a link to the next item. Algorithms must correctly account for both the data and the link.

Testing and Debugging Hints

1. A function must not return a pointer to automatic local data; otherwise, a dangling pointer will result.
2. If `ptrA` and `ptrB` point to the same dynamic data object, the statement

    `delete ptrA;`

    makes `ptrB` become a dangling pointer. You should now assign the value `NULL` to `ptrB` rather than leave it dangling.
3. Deallocate dynamic data when it is no longer needed. Memory leaks can cause you to run out of memory space.
4. Inaccessible objects—another cause of memory leaks—are caused by
    a. Shallow copying of pointers that point to dynamic data. When designing C++ classes whose data members point to dynamic data, be sure to provide a deep copy operation and a copy-constructor.
    b. Using the **new** operation when the associated variable already points to dynamic data. Before executing **new**, use `delete` to deallocate the data that is currently pointed to.
5. Make sure that the `link` member in the last node of a dynamic linked list has been set to `NULL`.
6. When visiting the components in a dynamic linked list, test for the end of the list in such a way that you don't try to dereference the `NULL` pointer. On many systems, dereferencing the `NULL` pointer will cause a run-time error.
7. Be sure to initialize the external pointer to each dynamic data structure.

8. Do not use

    ```
    currPtr++;
    ```

    to make `currPtr` point to the next node in a dynamic linked list. The list nodes are not necessarily in consecutive memory locations on the heap.
9. Keep close track of pointers. Changing pointer values prematurely may cause problems when you try to access the pointed-to variable.
10. If a C++ class that points to dynamic data has a class destructor but not a copy-constructor, do not pass a class object to a function using pass by value. A shallow copy will occur, and both the parameter and the argument will point to the same dynamic data. When the function returns, the parameter's destructor is executed, destroying the argument's dynamic data.
11. The `delete` operator must be applied to a pointer whose value was previously returned by `new`. Also, the `delete` operation leaves the value of the pointer variable undefined; do not use the variable again until you have assigned a new value to it.
12. A function must not return a pointer to automatic local data; otherwise, a dangling pointer will result.

■ Summary

A powerful use of pointers is to create dynamic variables. While a pointer variable can be declared at compile time, the data to which the pointer points is only created at run time. The built-in operator `new` creates a variable on the free store (heap) and returns the address of that variable, for storage in a pointer variable. A dynamic variable is not given a name, but rather is accessed through a pointer variable.

The use of dynamic data saves memory space because a variable is created only when it is needed at run time. When a dynamic variable is no longer needed, it can be deallocated (using `delete`) and the memory space can be reused. Use of dynamic data can also save machine (computing) time when large structures are being sorted. With this approach, we simply rearrange the pointers to the large structures, rather than the large structures themselves.

When C++ class objects point to data on the free store, it is important to distinguish between shallow copy and deep copy operations. A shallow copy of one class object to another copies only the pointers and results in two class objects pointing to the same dynamic variable. A deep copy results in two distinct copies of the pointed-to data. Classes that manipulate dynamic data usually require a complete collection of support routines: one or more constructors, a destructor (for cleaning up the free store), a deep copy operation, and a copy-constructor (for deep copying during initialization of one class object by another).

Dynamic data structures grow and contract during run time. They are made up of nodes that contain two kinds of members: (1) the component and (2) one or more pointers to nodes of the same type. The pointer to the first node is saved in a variable called the external pointer to the structure.

A linked list is a data structure in which the components are logically next to each other, rather than physically next to each other as they are in an array. A linked list can be represented as a collection of dynamic nodes, linked together by pointers. The end of a dynamic linked list is indicated by the special pointer constant `NULL`. Common operations on linked lists include inserting a node, deleting a node, and traversing the list (visiting each node from first to last).

In this chapter, we used linked lists to implement lists. Linked lists are also used to implement many data structures other than lists. The study of data structures forms a major topic in computer science. Indeed, entire books have been written and courses developed to cover the subject. A solid understanding of the fundamentals of linked lists is a prerequisite to creating more complex structures.

Quick Check Answers

14.1.1 `new` **14.1.2** `delete` **14.1.3** Variables created during execution of a program by means of special operators. In C++, these operators are `new` and `delete`. **14.1.4** It creates an uninitialized variable (or array) and returns the address of this variable. **14.1.5** free store or heap. **14.1.6** It returns allocated memory to the free store. **14.2.1** Because pointers allow us to dynamically create the list to be only as long as necessary. **14.2.2** A pointer to the next node in the list. **14.2.3** A linked list is a collection of items that can be scattered about in memory where as an array is a sequential collection of items that reside in consecutive memory locations. **14.2.4** insert and delete **14.2.5** A pointer that points to the first node in a linked list. **14.3.1** A linked list composed of dynamically allocated nodes that are linked together by pointers. **14.3.2** A data structure that can expand and contract during execution. **14.3.3** The external head pointer. **14.3.4** Set the pointer of the existing node in the linked list to point to the new node. **14.4.1** Allocate a new node. Assign the value from the node pointer of the current node to the node pointer of the new node. Assign the node pointer of the current node to equal the address of the new node. Assign any data members to the new node as appropriate. **14.4.2** Assign the value of the node pointer of the current node to a temporary pointer. Assign the value of the node pointer from the node pointed to by the node pointer field of the current node to the node pointer field of the current node. (Assign the address of the node following the one to be deleted to the node pointer of the current node.) Delete the data associated with the temporary pointer.
14.4.3
```
currPtr = head;
while (currPtr != NULL) {
    cout << currPtr->value << endl;
    currPtr = currPtr->link;
}
```
14.4.4 It always returns `false` because a linked list cannot be full. **14.5.1** Deep copying. **14.5.2** Returning an object as the value of a function. **14.5.3** A copy constructor. **14.5.4** A constructor that is specifically designed to construct a new object based on an old object using deep copy semantics. **14.6.1** When the list is empty, when the value to be inserted is less than the first, and when the value to be inserted is greater than the last.

Exam Preparation Exercises

1. Match the following terms with the definitions given below.
   a. Pointer type
   b. Indirect addressing
   c. Direct addressing
   d. Reference type
   e. Shallow copy
   f. Deep copy
      i. Accessing a variable using its name
      ii. Assigning the value of one object to another object, including the duplication of any pointed-to data
      iii. Accessing a variable using an address stored in a pointer
      iv. A simple type that can only be initialized with the address of a variable
      v. A simple type that can be assigned the address of a variable
      vi. Assigning the value of one object to another without duplicating any pointed-to data

2. Match the following terms with the definitions given below.
   a. Heap
   b. Memory leak
   c. Inaccessible object
   d. Dangling pointer
   e. Destructor

f. Dynamic data
   i. The loss of available space that occurs when dynamic data is not deallocated properly
   ii. The area of memory used for allocation and deallocation of dynamic data
   iii. An object that has been allocated but has no pointer pointing to it
   iv. Variables created with the **new** operation
   v. A pointer that points to a deallocated object
   vi. A member function invoked when an object goes out of scope

3. When an object goes out of scope, its pointer variables are automatically deleted, but their pointed-to values are *not* automatically deleted. True or false?
4. Does **delete** return the pointer variable to the heap or the pointed-to data?
5. What happens to the pointer(s) and pointed-to data in an object if the object goes out of scope without applying **delete** to the corresponding pointer(s)?
6. What is wrong with the following code segment?

   ```
   int* needle;
   needle = new int;
   *needle 100;
   cout << *needle;
   needle = new int;
   *needle = 32;
   cout << *needle;
   ```

7. What is wrong with the following code segment?

   ```
   int* birdDog;
   int* germanShortHair;
   birdDog = new int;
   germanShortHair = birdDog;
   *birdDog = 42;
   cout << *birdDog;
   delete birdDog;
   cout << *germanShortHair;
   ```

8. The copy-constructor for class **faxLog** should have one parameter. What should the type of this parameter be?
9. Why is it a problem if you perform a shallow copy of one object to another object and then delete the first object and all of its pointed-to dynamic data?
10. Which kind of member function does the following heading declare?

    ```
    ~phoneTree();
    ```

11. Applying **delete** to the **NULL** pointer produces an error message. True or false?
12. In the following expression, **index** is a pointer to an array and **book** is a member of a **struct** of type **libraryRecord**:

    ```
    index[12] -> book[5]
    ```

    What is the type of the components that are contained in the array that **index** points to?

13. Define the following terms:
    a. Node
    b. Component member
    c. Link member
    d. Current pointer
14. We only need an external pointer for a dynamic linked list. With an array-based list, we can find the head automatically. True or false?
15. Using a forward declaration of the node pointer type allows us to avoid using an anonymous type to declare the `link` field within the struct representing the node. True or false?
16. Which value does each of the following expressions access? The variable names have the same meanings as we have used them elsewhere in this chapter.
    a. `currPtr->link`
    b. `currPtr->component`
    c. `currPtr->link->component`
    d. `currPtr->link->link`
    e. `currPtr->link->link->component`
    f. `head->link->link->link->component`
17. a. Which special state of a list does the condition `listPtr == NULL` test for?
    b. Which special condition does the expression `currPtr == NULL` test for?
18. What are the algorithmic steps for inserting a new node into a sorted linked list?
19. What are the algorithmic steps for deleting the successor of the current node, assuming that the current node is not the last node in the list?
20. For each of the following operations, decide which is faster: a direct array representation of a list or a linked representation of a list.
    a. Inserting near the front of the list
    b. Deleting the last element of the list
    c. Accessing the nth element
    d. Searching for an item in a sorted list
21. Why does the following code segment produce a compiler error? What is missing from the declarations?

    ```
    typedef NodeType* NodePtr;
    struct NodeType
    {
      ComponentType component;
      NodePtr link;
    };
    ```

22. For each of the following, decide whether a direct array implementation or a dynamic linked list representation would be the best choice. Assume that memory capacity is limited and that good speed of execution is desirable.
    a. A list of CD titles in a personal library, with not more than 500 albums. CDs are rarely deleted and added occasionally, and the most frequent operation on the list is to search for a specific title.
    b. A list of shipping orders to be processed. The orders are inserted as they come in, and they are deleted as they are shipped out. The list can be quite large just before the December holidays, but may be nearly empty in January. The list is occasionally searched for a specific item, to check its status.

c. An itinerary of customer visits for a salesperson. Visits may be added anywhere within the itinerary, and they are deleted from the head after they have been completed. The itinerary can be of any length.

23. What does the following code do?

```
int number;
int& atlas = number;
number = 212;
atlas++;
```

a. Increments the contents of atlas.
b. Increments the contents of number.
c. Increments the contents of both atlas and number.
d. Adds 2 to number.
e. Produces a dangling pointer.

24. What does the following code do?

```
int number;
int* weathervane;
weathervane = &number;
number = 180;
(*weathervane)++;
```

a. Increments the contents of weathervane.
b. Increments the contents of number.
c. Increments the contents of both weathervane and number.
d. Adds 2 to number.
e. Produces a dangling pointer.

25. What does the following code do?

```
int number;
int* finger;
finger = &number;
number = 2;
*finger++;
```

a. Increments the contents of finger.
b. Increments the contents of number.
c. Increments the contents of both finger and number.
d. Adds 2 to number.
e. Produces a dangling pointer.

Programming Warm-Up Exercises

1. Extend the Sorted Linked List described in this chapter to include an additional method called Split. The Split method takes a single parameter that is the type of the element contained in the list and will search the list until it finds a matching element. If it finds a matching element it should return a new Linked List of the elements that start with the matching element until the end of the original linked list. The original Linked List should be modified such that the element before the matching element becomes the last element in the list. If the element is not found Split should return NULL. You should reuse all the NodeType nodes in the original linked list in the linked list that is returned.

2. Declare a pointer variable `structPointer` and initialize it to point to a `struct` variable called `newPhone`, of type `Phone`, that has three `int` fields called `country`, `area`, and `number`. Also write the declaration of the `Phone` type. Then write assignment statements to indirectly store the values 1, 888, and 5551212, respectively, into these fields.
3. Write a Boolean value-returning function called `ShallowCompare` that takes two variables of type `structPointer`, as defined in Exercise 2, and returns `true` if they point to the same struct and `false` otherwise.
4. Write a Boolean value-returning function called `DeepCompare` that takes two variables of type `structPointer`, as defined in Exercise 2, and returns `true` if the structs that they point to have identical values in their corresponding fields.
5. Write a For loop that scans through a dynamically allocated `int` array, pointed to by a variable called `dataPtr`, keeping track of the greatest value in a static `int` variable `max`. The array contains 100 values. At the end of the loop, the array should be deleted.
6. Wrap the For loop written in Exercise 5 in an `int`-returning function called `Greatest` that takes the array and its size as parameters and returns the value in `max` after the array is deleted. Be sure to change the loop to work with the given array size rather than the constant 100.
7. Write an `int`-returning function that prompts the user for the number of values to be entered, creates an `int` array of that size, and reads that many values into it. The function then passes this array to the `Greatest` function defined in Exercise 6, and returns the result from that function as its own result. Call the new function `GetGreatestInput`.
8. A class called `Circuit` has two private dynamic array data members called `source` and `sink`. Write a destructor for the class that ensures that the dynamic data is destroyed.
9. Write a code segment that checks whether the pointer `oldValue` actually points to a valid memory location. If it does, then its contents are assigned to `newValue`. If not, then `newValue` is assigned a new `int` variable from the heap.
10. Write a code segment that checks whether the pointers `oldValue` and `newValue` point to different locations. If they do, then delete the value pointed to by `oldValue`; otherwise, do nothing.
11. Given the dynamic linked implementation of a linked list shown below, write expressions that do the following, assuming that `currPtr` is somewhere in the middle of the list:
    a. Access the component member of the first list element.
    b. Advance `currPtr` to point to the next element.
    c. Access the component member of the next element (the one that follows the current element).
    d. Access the component member of the element that follows the next element.

    ```
    typedef int ComponentType;

    struct NodeType;
    typedef NodeType* NodePtr;

    struct NodeType
    {
      ComponentType component;
      NodePtr link;
    }
    ```

```
NodePtr lastPtr;
NodePtr listPtr;
NodePtr currPtr;
NodePtr newNodePtr;
```

12. Given the declarations in Exercise 11, write a code segment that creates a new node, assigns the value 100 to the component member, links `listPtr` to the new node, and sets `currPtr` to also point to the node.
13. Given the declarations in Exercise 11, and the fact that the first node has been inserted into the list as in Exercise 12, write a code segment that creates a new node with the component value equal to 212 and inserts this node at the end of the list, updating any pointers as necessary.
14. Given the declarations in Exercise 11, assume that the list has a large collection of members and that `currPtr` is somewhere in the middle of the list. Write a code segment to insert a new node with the component value of 32 following the node pointed to by `currPtr`, and update `currPtr` to point to the new node.
15. Given the declarations in Exercise 11, assume that the list has a large collection of members and that `currPtr` is somewhere in the middle of the list. Write a code segment to remove the node following the node pointed to by `currPtr` and reinsert it at the head of the list.
16. Given the declarations in Exercise 11, write a void function that sorts the elements of the list in ascending order. The sort algorithm will scan the list, keeping a pointer to the lowest value seen thus far. When the end of the list is reached, the lowest value will be removed from that point and inserted at the end of a new list. After all of the elements have been moved from the original list to the new sorted list, change `listPtr` and `currPtr` to point to the first element of the new list. That way, when the function returns, the client code will simply see the list as having been sorted.
17. Given the code for the sorted `delete` operation on page 739, walk through the following deletions.
    a. Delete from an empty list.
    b. Delete 20 from the list on page 740.
    c. Delete 30 from the list on page 740.
18. Write the code for the sorted version of `IsThere`.

Programming Problems

1. Imagine you have been asked by a first grade teacher to create a hangman game for her students to help them with spelling and word recognition. In the game of hangman you are first presented with a list of blanks representing unknown letters of a hidden word. You must then guess a letter to see if that letter exists in the word. If it does, the blank that corresponds to the guessed letter is then displayed along with blanks for the letters that have not been guessed yet. If you guess a previously guessed letter you get to try again. If you guess wrong you incrementally move toward being hung. You have eight bad guesses until you lose the game. To represent the different states of "being hung" we will use the values PLATFORM, HEAD, BODY, LEFT_ARM, RIGHT_ARM, LEFT_LEG, RIGHT_LEG, and HUNG. To implement the game you should use the Linked List ADT to represent the word being guessed. Each element in the list should be an object of type Slot that stores the letter of the word and a boolean that indicates if the letter is to be displayed or if a blank should be displayed. The Slot class should

provide the appropriate observer and mutator methods for accessing and manipulating a slot. You should use a second linked list to represent the letters that have already been guessed and an enumeration to represent the states of the game. Your program should keep asking the user for another guess until either the entire word has been guessed or the state of the game is HUNG. After each guess, the program should display the current state of the word to be guessed, the list of characters already guessed, and the state of the game.

2. You are working for your state's motor vehicle registry, and it has been discovered that some people in the driver's license database have multiple records. The license records are stored in alphabetical order on a set of files, one file per letter in the alphabet. The first file is `licensesa.dat`, and the last is `licensesz.dat`. For this problem, we'll just focus on getting the program to work for the `licensesa.dat` file. Each record consists of a license number (an eight-digit integer), a name, and an address, all on a single line. For the purposes of this problem, the name and address can be stored in a single string because they are not processed separately. The license number and the corresponding string should be kept together in a struct.

   Use the functions of the `SortedList` class to create a list of numbers that contains no duplicates. If a duplicate is found in the data file, write the contents of the original entry (first one encountered) and the contents of any duplicates in the file on file `duplicates.dat`.

3. You're working for a company that wants to take client contact information as it is entered by a salesperson from a stack of business cards that he or she has collected, and output the information to a file (`contacts.dat`) in alphabetical order. The program should prompt the salesperson for each of the following values for each card:

   Last name
   First name
   Middle name or initial
   Title
   Company name
   Street address
   City
   State
   ZIP code
   Phone number
   Fax number
   Email address

   After the data are entered for each card, the user should be asked if there is another card to enter. Each card should be inserted into a sorted list, whose key is the last name. After all the data are entered, iterate through the list, writing each card onto file `contacts.dat`. Use the `SortedList` modified in the Problem-Solving Case Study.

4. You are working for a company that has a collection of files, each of which contains information from business cards. The files are created by another program (see Problem 3 for a description of what this program outputs). The company would like to merge the files into a single file, sorted alphabetically by last name. The user should be prompted to enter the names of the files, until a file name of "done" is entered. Once

all of the data has been input, the sorted data should be written back out to a file called `mergedcontacts.dat`.

5. Create a new List ADT where duplicates are allowed. Define the `delete` operation to delete all copies of an item. Implement both an unordered version of the list and a sorted version.
6. Use the sorted list version defined and implemented in Problem 5 to solve Problem 2.
7. Use the sorted list version defined and implemented in Problem 5 to solve Problem 4.

■ **Case Study Follow-Up**

1. We did not discuss a copy-constructor or a destructor for the revised `SortedList` class. Would these functions have to be changed to use `ComparedTo`? Explain.
2. The classes in this case study have been built up over several chapters. Does this process demonstrate functional decomposition or object-oriented design? Explain.
3. Outline the next step in constructing an appointment calendar.

Inheritance, Polymorphism, and Object-Oriented Design

KNOWLEDGE GOALS

- To appreciate the distinction between structured (procedural) programming and object-oriented programming.
- To know the characteristics of an object-oriented language.
- To understand the difference between static and dynamic binding of operations to objects.

SKILL GOALS

To be able to:
- Create a new C++ class from an existing class by using inheritance.
- Create a new C++ class hierarchy with a virtual function.
- Apply the object-oriented design methodology to solve a problem.
- Take an object-oriented design and code it in C++.

In Chapter 12, we introduced the concept of data abstraction—the separation of the logical properties of a data type from the details of how it is implemented. We expanded on this concept by defining the notion of an abstract data type (ADT) and by using the C++ class mechanism to incorporate both data and operations into a single data type. In that chapter and Chapter 13, we saw how an object of a given class maintains its own private data and is manipulated by calling its public member functions.

In this chapter, we examine how classes and objects can be used to guide the entire software development process. Although the design phase precedes the implementation phase in the development of software, we reverse the order of presentation in this chapter. We begin with *object-oriented programming*, a topic that includes design but deals more with implementation issues. We describe the basic principles, terminology, and programming language features associated with the object-oriented approach. After presenting these concrete elements, we look more closely at the design phase—object-oriented design.

15.1 Object-Oriented Programming

> **Structured (procedural) programming** The construction of programs that are collections of interacting functions or procedures.

As you are now well aware, functional decomposition is a design methodology in which we decompose a problem into modules, each of which is a self-contained collection of steps that solves part of the overall problem. The process of implementing a functional decomposition is often called structured (or procedural) programming. Some modules are translated directly into C++ statements, whereas others are coded as functions. The resulting program is a collection of interacting functions (see **FIGURE 15.1**). With functional decomposition, data is considered a passive entity to be acted upon.

Functional decomposition is satisfactory for programming in the small (a concept we discussed in Chapter 4) but often does not "scale up" well for programming in the large. When we are building large software systems, this approach has two important limitations. First, the technique yields an inflexible structure. If the top-level algorithm requires modification, the changes may force many lower-level algorithms to be modified as well. Second,

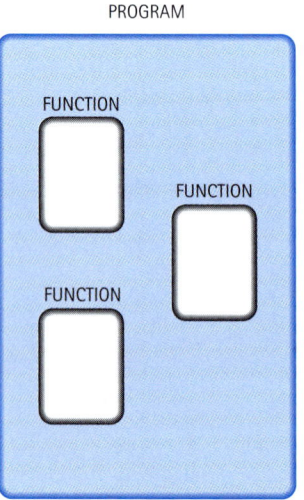

FIGURE 15.1 Program Resulting from Functional Decomposition

the technique does not lend itself easily to code reuse. By *code reuse*, we mean the ability to use pieces of code—either as they are or adapted slightly—in other sections of the program or in other programs. It is rare to be able to take a complicated C++ function and reuse it easily in a different context.

A methodology that often works better for creating large software systems is object-oriented design (OOD), which we introduced briefly in Chapter 4. OOD decomposes a problem into *objects*—self-contained entities composed of data and operations on the data. The process of implementing an object-oriented design is called object-oriented programming (OOP). The end result is a program that is a collection of interacting objects (see **FIGURE 15.2**). In OOD and OOP, data plays a leading role; the primary contribution of algorithms is to implement the operations on objects. In this chapter, we'll see why OOD tends to result in programs that are more flexible and conducive to code reuse than programs produced by functional decomposition.

> **Object-oriented programming (OOP)** The use of data abstraction, inheritance, and dynamic binding to construct programs that are collections of interacting objects.

Several programming languages have been created specifically to support OOD and OOP: C++, Java, Smalltalk, Simula, CLOS, Objective-C, Eiffel, Actor, Python, and others. These languages, which are called *object-oriented programming languages*, have facilities that support:

- Data abstraction
- Inheritance
- Dynamic binding

You have already seen that C++ supports data abstraction through the class mechanism. Some non-OOP languages also have facilities for data abstraction. But only OOP languages support the other two concepts—inheritance and dynamic binding.

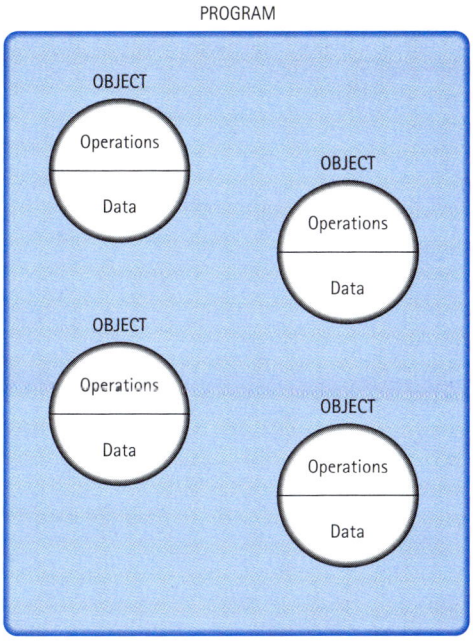

FIGURE 15.2 Program Resulting from Object-Oriented Programming

> **QUICK CHECK**
>
> **15.1.1** How do programs based on functional decomposition differ from object-oriented programs in terms of the components that interact with one another to solve a problem? (pp. 772–773)
>
> **15.1.2** What are the three main facilities that are provided by an object-oriented language that support object-oriented programming? (pp. 772–773)
>
> **15.1.3** What is procedural programming? (p. 772)
>
> **15.1.4** What plays a leading role in object-oriented programming? (p. 773)
>
> **15.1.5** What is the primary contribution of algorithms in object-oriented programming? (p. 773)

15.2 Inheritance

In the world at large, it is often possible to arrange concepts into an inheritance hierarchy—that is, a hierarchy in which each concept inherits the properties of the concept immediately above it in the hierarchy. For example, we might classify different kinds of vehicles according to the inheritance hierarchy shown in **FIGURE 15.3**. Moving down the hierarchy, each kind of vehicle is more specialized than its parent (and all of its ancestors) and is more general than its child (and all of its descendants). A wheeled vehicle inherits properties common to all vehicles (it holds one or more people and carries them from place to place) but has an additional property that makes it more specialized (it has wheels). A car inherits properties common to all wheeled vehicles but also has other, more specialized properties (four wheels, an engine, a body, and so forth).

The inheritance relationship can be viewed as an is-a relationship. Every two-door car *is a* car, every car *is a* wheeled vehicle, and every wheeled vehicle *is a* vehicle. This notion is distinct from the principle of composition, where one object is contained within another object. Composition is a has-a relationship: The enclosing object *has a* member that is another object.

To better understand the principles underlying inheritance, let's look at an analogy between the work of an architect and the work of a programmer. The way that an architect handles the complexity of a large building design sheds some light on how we can organize our own programming work. This analogy lets us consider the same concepts, but without the distraction of C++ syntax.

An Analogy

The architect begins by considering the overall requirements for a building: square footage, number of occupants, usage, and so on. The architect faces a basic aspect of any design: The

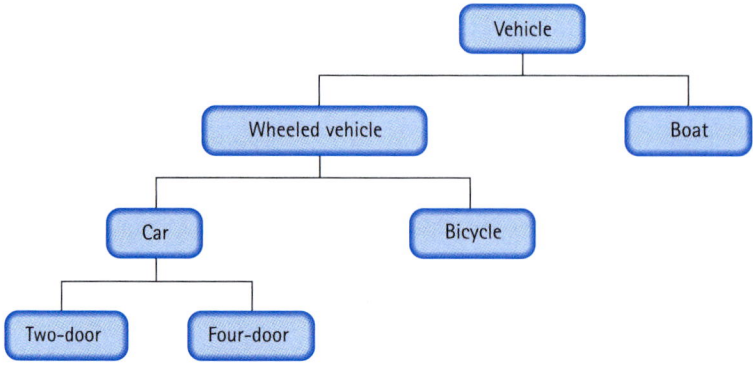

FIGURE 15.3 Inheritance Hierarchy

building is composed of floors. In many buildings, the floors all have common characteristics: the same size and shape; the same locations for elevator shafts, stairways, and utility trunks; and so on. The architect begins by designing a basic empty floor with these common elements. Once she installs this plan in the library of her computer-aided design (CAD) program, she can use it as the starting point for designing each floor of the building.

The architect may further decide that the building has two main types of floors: office floors and mechanical equipment floors. The office floors might be of two types: executive office space and standard office space. Starting from the basic empty floor design, the architect adds components such as lavatories and hallways to make an empty office floor. She can then add offices and conference rooms to the empty space. In this way, each of the four types of floor is derived from the basic empty floor and added to the library (see **FIGURE 15.4**). Drawing the entire building then becomes simply a matter of creating an instance of one of these four floor plans for each story.

The architect uses the same process to design the components that make up the floors. She might design a basic type of office, and then derive several types of offices from that one design. From a given type of office, such as secretarial, she might further refine the design into subtypes such as general secretarial, secretary/receptionist, and executive secretary.

Creating hierarchies of designs simplifies the architect's job. She begins each hierarchy with the most general form of a building component, such as the basic empty floor, and then derives new designs by adding details to the more general forms. The new designs inherit all of the characteristics of the general form, saving the architect from having to redraw the common pieces. In some cases she replaces existing parts of a design, such as when she substitutes a wider door for a reception area than appears in the basic secretarial office. The replacement part overrides what was originally specified in the more general form.

In addition to the components of individual floors, the architect can specify characteristics that are common to all floors, such as a color scheme. Each floor will then inherit these general properties. Sometimes she hides or deletes portions of the general properties, such as when she customizes the color scheme for a particular floor that has been rented in advance by a company with its own corporate colors.

Inheritance and the Object-Oriented Design Process

Now let's consider how a class hierarchy originates in the object-oriented design process. During the problem-solving phase, we discover that we need a class that is a variation of an existing one. For example, in the case study of Chapter 14, we discovered that the `Entry` class from Chapter 12 was appropriate, but noted that it lacked a `ComparedTo` member function. We also decided that the class should have a second parameterized constructor that took a `Name` object and a `TimeOfDay` object as parameters.

We solved this problem by copying the code for `Entry`, and then using that copy to create a new class with the extra responsibilities. The result was two classes named `Entry` that are unrelated. Later, if we find a bug in the original `Entry` class, we must remember to check the extended class for the same bug. But wouldn't it be nice if a fix or an improvement to the original could be automatically propagated to any derived classes?

We can achieve this goal by making `Entry` a base class or superclass, and defining the other class as a derived class or subclass of `Entry`. For example, if we add an email field and responsibilities to `Entry`, the property of inheritance causes it to be added to all of the derived classes automatically.

In general, you can take an existing class A, the base class, and create from it a new class B, the derived class. The derived class B inherits all of

> **Base class (superclass)** A class that is extended by one or more derived classes (its subclasses).
>
> **Derived class (subclass)** A class that is derived from another class (its base class).
>
> **Inheritance** A mechanism by which one class (a derived class) acquires the properties—the data and operations—of another class (its base class).

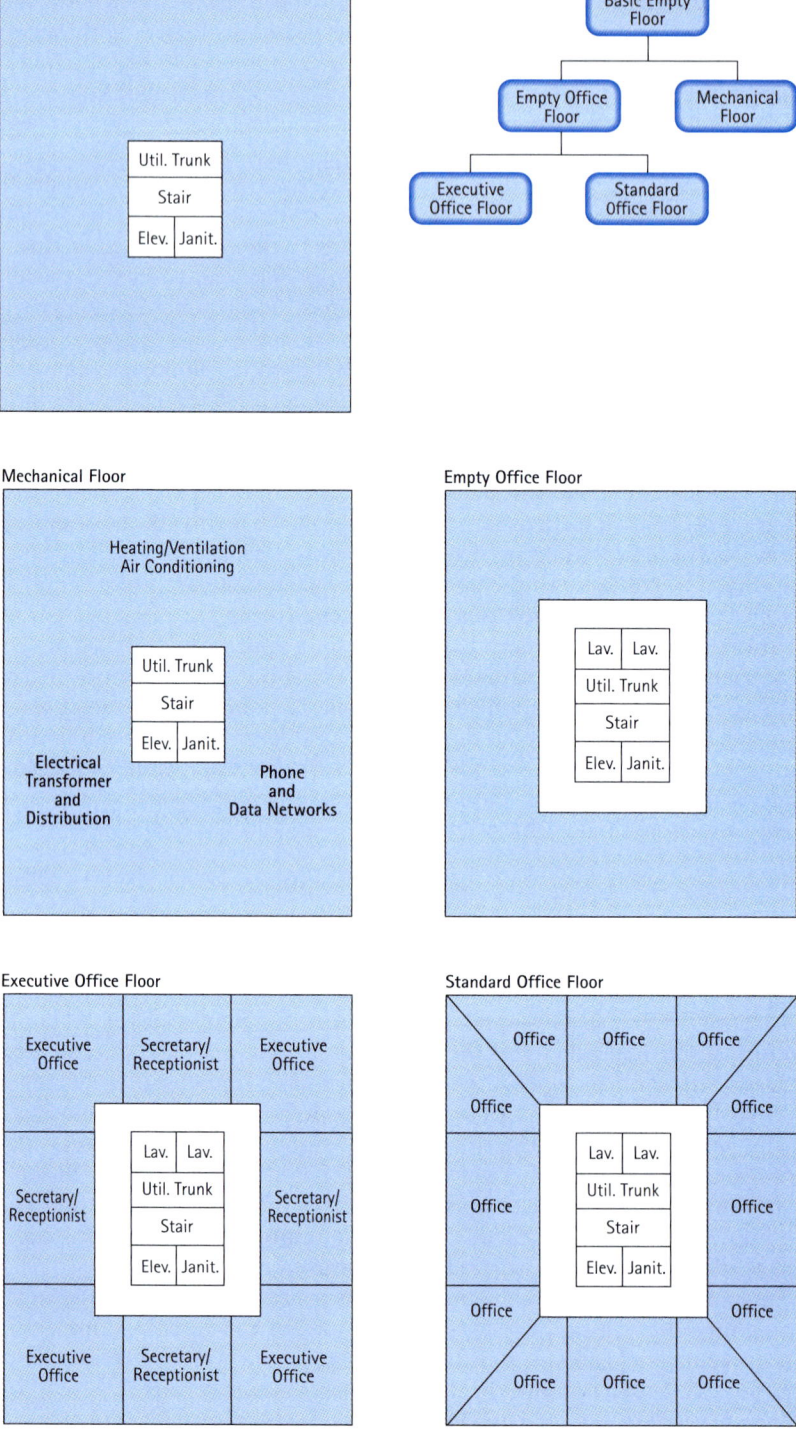

FIGURE 15.4 A Hierarchy of Floor Types

Deriving One Class from Another Class

Let's solve the `Entry` problem with inheritance. That is, let's create class `ExpandedEntry` that has the `ComparedTo` function and the additional parameterized constructor. Here is the specification file for the new class:

```
class ExpandedEntry : public Entry
{
public:
  ExpandedEntry(Name newName, TimeOfDay newTime);
  // Creates an ExpandedEntry object with newName as the name
  // attribute and newEntry as the Entry attribute
  RelationType ComparedTo(ExpandedEntry otherEntry);
  // Post: Returns
  //       BEFORE if instance's time object is earlier than entry's
  //       SAME if they are identical
  //       AFTER if instance's time object is later than entry's
}
```

The statement

```
class ExpandedEntry : public Entry
```

states that `ExpandedEntry` is derived from `Entry`. The reserved word `public` declares `Entry` to be a public base class of `ExpandedEntry`. As a consequence, all public members of `Entry` (except constructors) are also public members of `ExpandedEntry`. In other words, `Entry`'s member functions `GetNameStr` and `GetTimeStr` can also be invoked for `ExpandedEntry` objects.[1] However, the public part of `ExpandedEntry` specializes the base class by adding the `ComparedTo` function and providing an additional constructor. This relationship is pictured in **FIGURE 15.5**.

Figure 15.5 shows that each `ExpandedEntry` object is an `Entry` object, and more. C++ uses the terms "base class" and "derived class" instead of "superclass" and "subclass." The terms "superclass" and "subclass" can be confusing because the prefix *sub* usually implies something smaller than the original (for example, a subset of a mathematical set). In contrast, a subclass is often "bigger" than its superclass—that is, it has more data and/or functions.

Figure 15.5 includes arrows between the two ovals labeled `GetNameStr` and `GetTimeStr`. Because `Entry` is a public base class of `ExpandedEntry`, and because `GetNameStr` and

---

1. If a class declaration omits the word `public` and begins as

   ```
   class DerivedClass : BaseClass
   ```

   or if it explicitly uses the word `private`,

   ```
   class DerivedClass : private BaseClass
   ```

   then `BaseClass` is called a private base class of `DerivedClass`. Public members of `BaseClass` are not public members of `DerivedClass`. That is, clients of `DerivedClass` cannot invoke `BaseClass` operations on `DerivedClass` objects. We do not work with private base classes in this book.

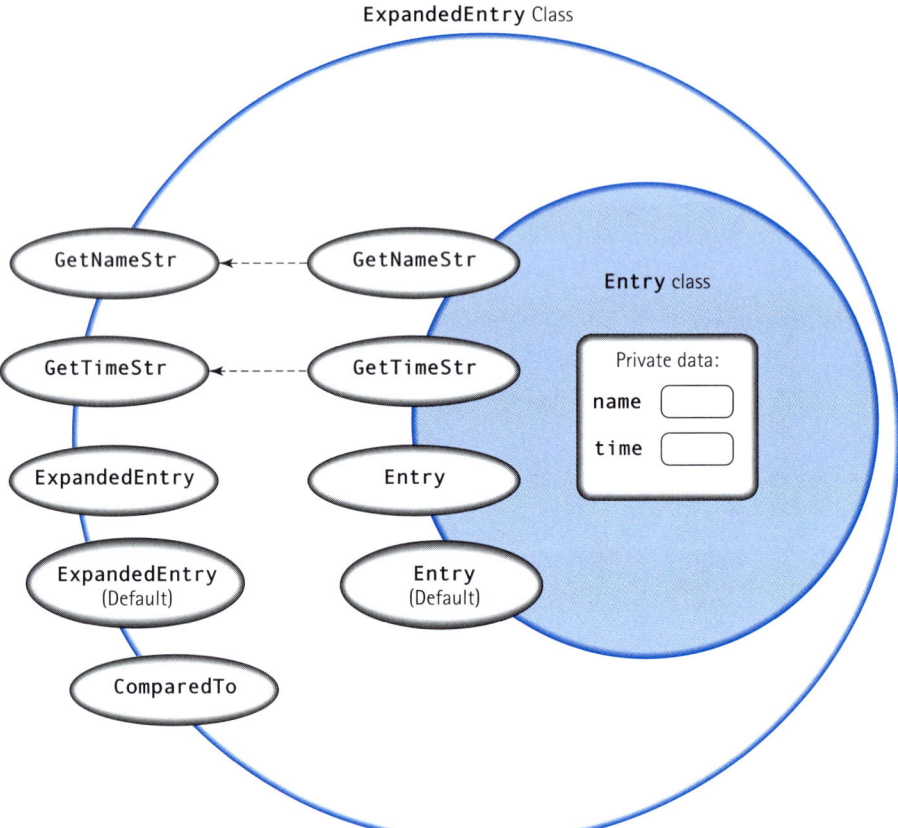

FIGURE 15.5 Class Interface Diagram for `ExpandedEntry` Class

`GetTimeStr` are not redefined by `ExpandedEntry`, the two functions available to clients of `ExpandedEntry` are the same as the ones inherited from `Entry`. We use the arrow between the corresponding ovals to indicate this fact. (Notice in Figure 15.5 that `Entry`'s constructors are operations on `Entry`, not on `ExpandedEntry`. The `ExpandedEntry` class must have its own constructors.)

Specification of the `ExpandedEntry` Class

Following is the fully documented specification of the `ExpandedEntry` class with the default constructor added. Notice that the preprocessor directive

```
#include "Entry.h"
```

is necessary for the compiler to verify the consistency of the derived class with its base class.

```
//********************************************************************
// SPECIFICATION FILE (ExpandedEntry.h)
// This file gives the specification of an ExpandedEntry abstract
// data type.  The Entry class is a public base class of
// ExpandedEntry, so public operations of Entry are also public
// operations of ExpandedEntry.
//********************************************************************
#include "Entry.h"

class ExpandedEntry : public Entry
{
public:
  // Constructors
  ExpandedEntry();
  // Default constructor
  ExpandedEntry(Name newName, TimeOfDay newTime);
  // Creates an entry object with newName as the name attribute and
  // newTime as the TimeOfDay attribute
  RelationType ComparedTo(ExpandedEntry otherEntry);
  // Post: Returns
  //       BEFORE if instance's time object is earlier than entry's
  //       SAME if they are identical
  //       AFTER if instance's time object is later than entry's
};
```

Implementation of the `ExpandedEntry` Class

When the default constructor of a derived class has no code, the default constructor for the base class is automatically called in its place. Because there are no new data fields in `ExpandedEntry` to be initialized, it makes sense to let the default constructor for `Entry` do the work for us. However, we will need a constructor initializer for the new parameterized constructor. We must take the `name` and `time` parameters and break them apart, because the constructor for the `Entry` class takes them as individual values.

```
ExpandedEntry::ExpandedEntry(Name newName, TimeOfDay newTime)  :
   Entry(newName.GetFirstName(), newName.GetMiddleName(),
         newName.GetLastName(), newTime.GetHours(),
         newTime.GetMinutes(), newTime.GetSeconds())
{ }
```

The `ComparedTo` function must compare the time in the instance with the time in the parameter. Now, we have a problem: We don't have access to the `time` field in the `Entry` class from the `ExpandedEntry` class.

With C++, *inheritance does not imply unrestricted access*. Although a derived class inherits the members of its base class, both private and public, it cannot directly access the private members of the base class. Figure 15.5 shows the variables `name` and `time` to be encapsulated within the `Entry` class. Neither external client code nor `ExpandedEntry` member functions can refer to these two variables directly. If a derived class could access the private members of its base class, any programmer could then write code to directly inspect or modify the private data, thereby defeating the benefits of encapsulation.

The solution to the problem is to add a getter function to the base class—in this case, `Entry`. The derived class can then see the value in the field, without having access to it. To make `Entry` as widely usable as possible, we should add two getter functions: `GetTime` and `GetName`.

We use `GetTime` to access the time in the instance and the time in the parameter.

```
RelationType ExpandedEntry::ComparedTo(ExpandedEntry otherEntry)
{
  return (GetTime().ComparedTo(otherEntry.GetTime()));
}
```

This little Return statement illustrates two important concepts. First, the function `GetTime` by itself applies to the class instance. Second, to get the time in the parameter, `GetTime` must be explicitly applied to it. Because we are adding getter functions to the class, we can remove the functions that return the name and time as strings. Users would then have the tools to format name and time themselves.

Following is the specification file for the revised `Entry` class.

```
//*****************************************************************
// SPECIFICATION FILE (Entry.h)
// This file contains the specification of the Entry ADT, which has
// two contained classes, Name and Time.
// A ComparedTo function has been added to this class.
//*****************************************************************

#include "TimeOfDay.h"
#include "Name.h"
#include "RelationType.h"

class Entry
{
public:
  Entry();
  // Default constructor
  // Post: Entry object has been constructed
  //       Name and TimeOfDay objects have been constructed using
  //       their default constructors
  Entry(string firstName, string middleName, string lastName,
        int  initHours, int  initMinutes, int  initSeconds );
  // Parameterized constructor
  // Post: Entry object has been constructed
  //       Name and TimeOfDay objects have been constructed using
  //       their parameterized constructors
```

```
  // Knowledge responsibilities
  TimeOfDay GetTime() const;
  // The function returns the time attribute
  Name GetName() const;
  // This function returns the name attribute
private:
  Name name;
  TimeOfDay time;
};
```

Here is the revised implementation file:

```
//**************************************************************
// IMPLEMENTATION FILE (Entry.cpp)
// This file contains the specification of the Entry ADT,
// which has two contained classes, Name and Time
//**************************************************************

#include "Entry.h"
#include <string>
#include <iostream>

using namespace std;

Entry::Entry()
{ }

//***********************************************************

Entry::Entry(string firstName, string middleName, string lastName,
        int  initHours, int  initMinutes, int  initSeconds )

  : name(firstName, middleName, lastName),
    time(initHours, initMinutes, initSeconds)
{ }

//***********************************************************


TimeOfDay Entry::GetTime() const
{ return time; }

//***********************************************************

Name Entry::GetName() const
{ return name; }
```

This experience illustrates why an important aspect of object-oriented design is planning ahead for reuse of classes. If we had thought about `Entry` in more general terms when we first designed it, we would have included these getter functions from the outset. Inheritance makes it so easy to reuse classes by extending them that we almost always want to generalize our designs to maximize their potential for future reuse.

Now we can write the implementation file for `ExtendedEntry`. As you look at this file, notice how little additional code is required to extend the base class with this new functionality. That's precisely the point behind the use of inheritance in object-oriented programming.

```cpp
//*****************************************************************
// IMPLEMENTATION FILE (ExpandedEntry.cpp)
// This file gives the implementation for the ExpandedEntry ADT.
//*****************************************************************
#include "ExpandedEntry.h"
#include <string>
#include <iostream>
using namespace std;

//*****************************************************************

ExpandedEntry::ExpandedEntry()
{ }

//*****************************************************************

ExpandedEntry::ExpandedEntry(Name newName, TimeOfDay newTime)  :
   Entry(newName.GetFirstName(), newName.GetMiddleName(),
         newName.GetLastName(), newTime.GetHours(),
         newTime.GetMinutes(), newTime.GetSeconds())
{ }

//*****************************************************************

RelationType ExpandedEntry::ComparedTo(ExpandedEntry otherEntry) const
{
   return (GetTime().ComparedTo(otherEntry.GetTime()));
}
```

We compile the file `ExpandedEntry.cpp` into an object code file—say, `ExpandedEntry.obj`. Next we write a test driver and compile it into `test.obj`. The development environment then creates an executable file by linking these two files with the existing `Entry.obj` file.

We're finally ready to test the resulting program. Here is the output from the same test driver that was used previously to test the revised `Entry` class in Chapter 13:

Here is a test driver and its output.

```cpp
//*****************************************************************
// DRIVER for class ExpandedEntry
// This program tests the constructors and return functions
//*****************************************************************

#include <iostream>
#include "ExpandedEntry.h"
#include "RelationType.h"
#include <string>

using namespace std;

int main ()
{
  Name name1("Sally", "Jane", "Smith");
  TimeOfDay time1( 12, 20, 0);
  Name name2("Mary", "Beth", "Jones");
  TimeOfDay time2(10, 30, 0);
  ExpandedEntry entry1(name1, time1);
  ExpandedEntry entry2(name2, time2);
  cout << "Entry 1: " << entry1.GetName().GetLastName() << endl
       << entry1.GetTime().GetHours()
       << ":" << entry1.GetTime().GetMinutes() << endl;
  cout << "Entry 2: " << entry2.GetName().GetLastName() << endl
       << entry2.GetTime().GetHours()
       << ":" << entry2.GetTime().GetMinutes() << endl;
  switch(entry1.ComparedTo(entry2))
  {
    case BEFORE: cout << "entry1 comes before entry2" << endl; break;
    case SAME:   cout << "two entries are the same" << endl; break;
    case AFTER:  cout << "entry1 comes after entry2" << endl; break;
  }
  switch(entry2.ComparedTo(entry1))
  {
    case BEFORE: cout << "entry2 comes before entry1" << endl; break;
    case SAME:   cout << "two entries are the same" << endl; break;
    case AFTER:  cout << "entry2 comes after entry1" << endl; break;
  }
  switch(entry1.ComparedTo(entry1))
  {
    case BEFORE: cout << "entry1 comes before entry2" << endl; break;
    case SAME:   cout << "two entries are the same" << endl; break;
    case AFTER:  cout << "entry1 comes after entry2" << endl; break;
  }

  return 0;
}
```

Output:

```
Entry 1: Smith
12:20
Entry 2: Jones
10:30
entry1 comes after entry2
entry2 comes before entry1
two entries are the same
```

The remarkable thing about extending a base class with inheritance is that modification of the base class is unnecessary, assuming it has the necessary getter operations. If these had already been present in the `Entry` class, we could have implemented `ExtendedEntry` even without having access to the source code for `Entry`. The C++ compiler is able to get all of the information it needs from the specification file for the base class, without having to recompile its implementation file. The linker then joins the object code for the derived class with the existing object code for the base class to produce the executable file.

Further variations of the `Entry` ADT can be created in ways the creator never considered. Through classes and inheritance, OOP languages facilitate code reuse. A class such as `Entry` can be used without modification in many different contexts, or it can be adapted to a particular context by using inheritance. Inheritance allows us to create extensible data abstractions—a derived class typically extends the base class by including additional private data or public operations or both.

Constructor Execution Order

Having discussed both inheritance and composition, we can give a complete description of the order in which constructors are executed:

> Given a class X, if X is derived from base class Y:
>
> 1. The base class (Y) constructor is executed first.
> 2. Constructors for X's member objects (if any) are then executed.
> 3. The body of X's constructor is executed last.

For example, when an `ExtendedEntry` object is created, the constructor for the `Entry` class is called first. This action triggers calls to the constructors for its `Name` and `TimeOfDay` members. After that, the body of `Entry`'s constructor is executed, which is empty. Then the body of `ExtendedEntry`'s constructor is executed, which also happens to be empty.

SOFTWARE MAINTENANCE CASE STUDY: Extending `TimeOfDay` with Support for a Time Zone

Maintenance Task: You've been given the task to modify the `TimeOfDay` class so that it includes the time zone within the continental United States. You are to represent the time zone as private data, using a variable of an enumeration type indicating the time zone—`EST` for Eastern Standard Time, `CST` for Central Standard Time, `MST` for Mountain Standard Time, and `PST` for Pacific Standard Time.

Existing Code: Before embarking on our solution to this task, we should review at least the public interface to the class we are preparing to extend. As you'll see, inheritance often enables us to add functionality to an existing class without looking any further than its interface.

`TimeOfDay` provides two constructors; separate getter functions for hours, minutes, and seconds; an observer that returns a new `TimeOfDay` that has been incremented by one second; and another observer that allows us to compare two `TimeOfDay` objects.

```
// Constructors
TimeOfDay();
// Post: hours, minutes, and seconds have been set to 0
TimeOfDay(int initHours, int initMinutes, int initSeconds);
// Pre:  0 <= hours <= 23, 0 <= minutes <= 59, 0 <= seconds <= 59
// Post: Time is set according to the incoming parameters

// Knowledge responsibilities
TimeOfDay Increment() const;
// Post: Returns a time that is the instance plus one,
//       with 23:59:59 wrapping around to 0:0:0
int GetHours() const;
// Returns hours
int GetMinutes() const;
// Returns minutes
int GetSeconds() const;
// Returns seconds
RelationType ComparedTo(TimeOfDay otherDay) const;
// Post: Returns BEFORE if instance comes before otherDay;
//       Returns SAME if instance and otherDay are the same;
//       Returns AFTER if instance comes after otherDay
```

Discussion: The approach in a language without inheritance would be to obtain the source code found in the `TimeOfDay.cpp` implementation file, analyze in detail how the class is implemented, and then modify and recompile the source code. This process has several drawbacks. If `TimeOfDay` is an off-the-shelf class on a system, the source code for the implementation is probably unavailable. Even if it is available, modifying this code may introduce bugs into a previously debugged solution. Access to the source code also violates a principal benefit of abstraction: Users of an abstraction should not need to know how it is implemented.

A better approach for adding this time zone feature to the `TimeOfDay` class is to use inheritance. Let's derive a new class from the `TimeOfDay` class and then specialize it. The new, extended time class—call it `ExtTime`—inherits the members of its base class, `TimeOfDay`. We'll need to modify the

SOFTWARE MAINTENANCE CASE STUDY: Extending `TimeOfDay` with Support for a Time Zone

class constructors to accommodate a time zone value. The **Increment** function, which returns a time incremented by one second, does not need to be changed, but the comparison function does need to change because of the time zones.

Here is the specification of **ExtTime**:

```
enum ZoneType {PST, MST, CST, EST};

class ExtTime : public TimeOfDay
{
public:
  // Constructors
  ExtTime(int newHours, int newMinutes, int newSeconds,
          ZoneType newZone);
  ExtTime();          //   setting time to 0:0:0 EST

  // Knowledge responsibilities
  ZoneType GetZone() const;
  // Returns the time zone
  RelationType ComparedTo(ExtTime otherTime) const;
  // Post: Returns
  //       BEFORE if instance is earlier than otherTime;
  //       SAME if they are identical;
  //       AFTER if instance is later than otherTime
private:
  ZoneType zone;
};
```

Notice how few functions and data members are included in this specification. Two new constructors must be provided because the name of the new class is different from the name of its base class. The private part of **ExtTime** declares a new private member: **zone**. The private members of **ExtTime** are, therefore, **hours**, **minutes**, **seconds** (all inherited from the base class, **TimeOfDay**), and **zone**.

All of the getters from **TimeOfDay** have been inherited, but we must add a new getter function for the **zone** member. **ExtTime** also inherits the **Increment** operation. Because a comparison that accounts for the time zone has a different semantic meaning than the original comparison, we provide a new **ComparedTo** function that overrides the version in the base class. **FIGURE 15.6** pictures the relationship between the **ExtTime** and **TimeOfDay** classes.

Implementing the constructors for **ExtTime** is easy because the constructors for **TimeOfDay** handle most of the work. All we have to do is initialize the **zone** member. The getter for **zone** is also quite simple: It merely returns the value of the variable.

The only tricky thing about the implementation is **ExtTime**'s **ComparedTo** function. If the two time zones are the same, then the times can be compared as before. If the time zones are different, however, then the time of one must be adjusted to be comparable with the other. Does it matter whether the instance or the parameter is adjusted? No, it doesn't. Let's adjust a copy of the instance to the same time zone as the parameter and use **TimeOfDay**'s **ComparedTo** function to compare the adjusted copy and the parameter.

We can take advantage of the numerical values of the time zones to simply compute the difference in hours between the two zones, and then add this value to the hours from the instance. The modulo operator provides an efficient way to ensure that when the new **hours** value is 24 or greater, it is readjusted to be within the proper range of 0 to 23.

SOFTWARE MAINTENANCE CASE STUDY: Extending `TimeOfDay` with Support for a Time Zone

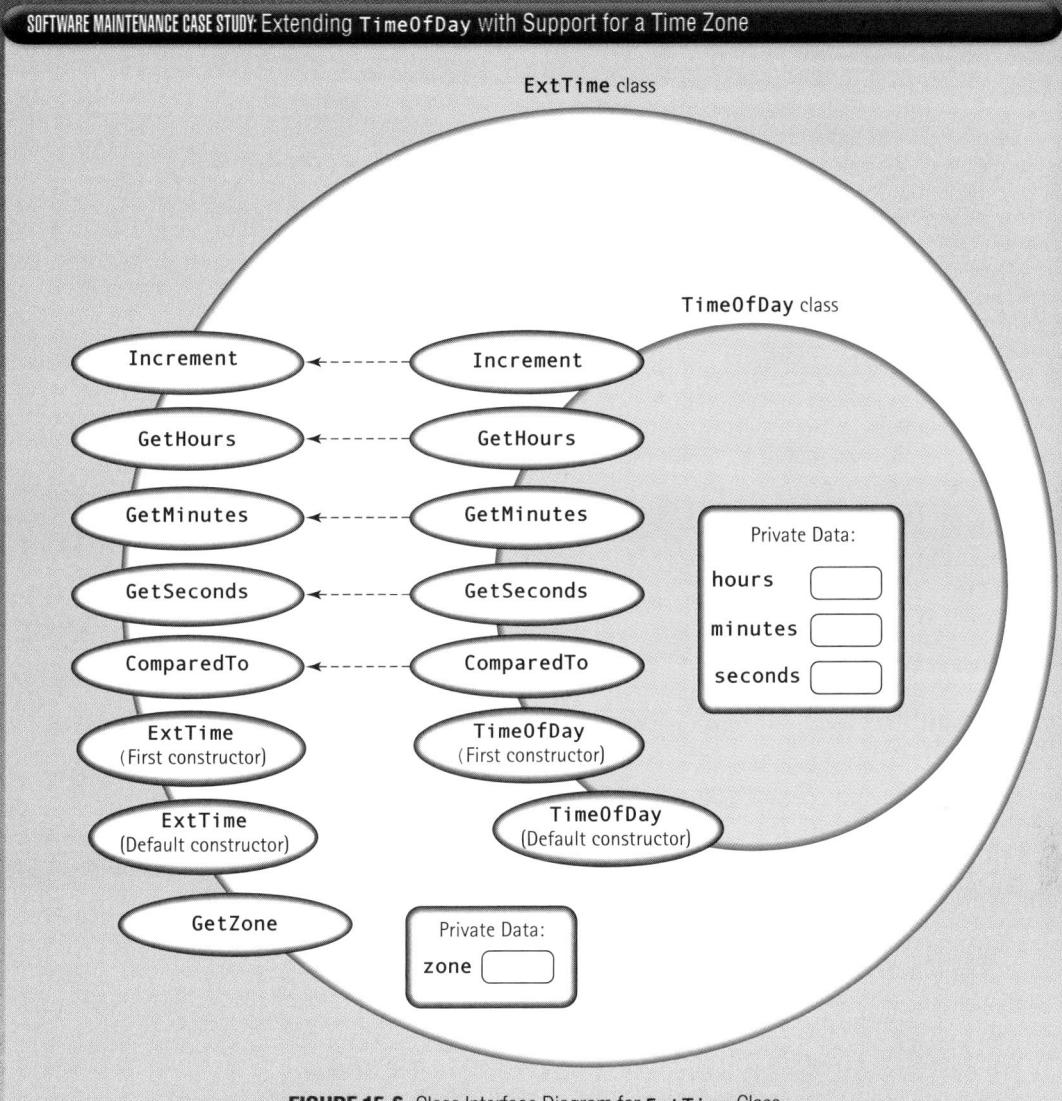

FIGURE 15.6 Class Interface Diagram for `ExtTime` Class

ComparedTo (In: otherTime)
Function Value: RelationType

Set difference to otherTime.zone minus zone
Set newHours to (GetHours() + difference) modulo 24
Create copy, a normalized TimeOfDay object initialized using newHours
RETURN copy.ComparedTo(otherTime)

SOFTWARE MAINTENANCE CASE STUDY: Extending `TimeOfDay` with Support for a Time Zone

Translating this algorithm into C++, we get the following implementation file:

```cpp
//****************************************************************
// IMPLEMENTATION FILE  for ExtTime, a derived
// class from TimeOfDay with a time zone.
//****************************************************************
#include "ExtTime.h"
#include "RelationType.h"
#include <iostream>
using namespace std;

ExtTime::ExtTime(int newHours, int newMinutes, int newSeconds,
  ZoneType newZone)
  : TimeOfDay(newHours, newMinutes, newSeconds)
{ zone = newZone; }


//****************************************************************

ExtTime::ExtTime()
{ zone = PST; }


//****************************************************************

ZoneType ExtTime::GetZone() const
{ return zone; }


//****************************************************************

RelationType ExtTime::ComparedTo(ExtTime otherTime) const
{
  // A copy of the instance is converted to the same
  // zone as otherTime; TimeOfDay's ComparedTo is
  // then used to compare the copy and the parameter

  int difference = int(otherTime.zone) - int(zone);
  int newHours = (GetHours() + difference) % 24;
  TimeOfDay copy(newHours, GetMinutes(), GetSeconds());
  return copy.ComparedTo(otherTime);
}
```

Testing: Here is a test driver and output:

```cpp
//****************************************************************
// Test driver for class ExtTime that inherits from TimeOfDay.
//****************************************************************
#include <iostream>
#include "ExtTime.h"                // For ExtTime class
#include "RelationType.h"
```

SOFTWARE MAINTENANCE CASE STUDY: Extending `TimeOfDay` with Support for a Time Zone

```cpp
using namespace std;
string TZString(ExtTime time);
// Returns a string representing the time zone
void Compare(ExtTime time1, ExtTime time2);
// Prints the result of comparison of time1 and time2

int main()
{
  ExtTime time1(5, 30, 0, EST);   // Parameterized constructor used
  ExtTime time2;                  // Create a time of 0:00:00 PST

  Compare(time1, time2);
  time2 = time1;
  Compare(time1, time2);
  ExtTime time3(5, 15, 0, CST);
  Compare(time1, time3);
  Compare(time3, time1);
  ExtTime time4(3, 5, 0,  MST);
  Compare(time1, time4);
  Compare(time4, time1);
  ExtTime time5(3, 30, 0, PST);
  Compare(time1, time5);
  Compare(time5, time1);
}

string TZString(ExtTime time)
{
  switch (time.GetZone())
  {
    case PST : return "PST";
    case MST : return "MST";
    case CST : return "CST";
    case EST : return "EST";
  }
}

void Compare(ExtTime time1, ExtTime time2)
{
  cout << "Time1: " << time1.GetHours() << ":"
       << time1.GetMinutes() << " " << TZString(time1) << endl;
  cout << "Time2: " << time2.GetHours() << ":"
       << time2.GetMinutes() << " " << TZString(time2) << endl;
  switch (time1.ExtTime::ComparedTo(time2))
  {
    case BEFORE : cout << "Time1 comes before time2"
                       << endl; break;
    case SAME   : cout << "Time1 is the same as time2"
                       << endl; break;
    case AFTER  : cout << "Time1 comes after time2"
                       << endl; break;
  }
}
```

SOFTWARE MAINTENANCE CASE STUDY: Extending `TimeOfDay` with Support for a Time Zone

Output:

```
Time1: 5:30 EST
Time2: 0:0 PST
Time1 comes after time2
Time1: 5:30 EST
Time2: 5:30 EST
Time1 is the same as time2
Time1: 5:30 EST
Time2: 5:15 CST
Time1 comes after time2
Time1: 5:15 CST
Time2: 5:30 EST
Time1 comes before time2
Time1: 5:30 EST
Time2: 3:5 MST
Time1 comes after time2
Time1: 3:5 MST
Time2: 5:30 EST
Time1 comes before time2
Time1: 5:30 EST
Time2: 3:30 PST
Time1 comes after time2
Time1: 3:30 PST
Time2: 5:30 EST
Time1 comes before time2
```

QUICK CHECK

15.2.1 Suppose you have a class called **Phone** and you want to extend it to support a country code, calling the new class **InternationalPhone**. How would you write the class heading for the new subclass? (p. 777)

15.2.2 Suppose that in Question 15.2.1, you wanted to create **InternationalPhone** as a separate class that contains an instance of **Phone**, rather than making it a subclass of **Phone**. Describe how you would accomplish this task. (p. 774)

15.2.3 What is the relationship as viewed by inheritance? (p. 774)

15.2.4 What is inheritance in terms of object-oriented programming? (p. 775)

15.2.5 What type of *access* of an instance variable is required by a derived class in order for the derived class to have direct access to the instance variable? (p. 779)

15.2.6 What part of a derived class constructor is required to invoke a constructor of a base class? (p. 779)

15.2.7 What is the execution order of constructors given a class X, if X is derived from a base class Y? (p. 784)

15.3 Dynamic Binding and Virtual Functions

Early in the chapter, we said that object-oriented programming languages provide language features that support three concepts: data abstraction, inheritance, and dynamic binding. Data abstraction is accomplished with the class construct; we have just covered inheritance. We now cover dynamic binding.

The term *dynamic binding* means, more specifically, "dynamic binding of an operation to an object." To explain this concept, let's look at an example. Given the `TimeOfDay` and `ExtTime` classes described in this chapter, the following code creates four class objects and compares them using the `ComparedTo` function:

```
TimeOfDay time1(8, 30, 30);
TimeOfDay time2;

ExtTime time3(10, 45, 0, CST);
ExtTime time4;

RelationType result1 = time1.ComparedTo(time2);
RelationType result2 = time3.ComparedTo(time4);
```

This code fragment invokes two different `ComparedTo` functions, even though the functions appear to have the same name. The first function call invokes the `ComparedTo` function of the `TimeOfDay` class; the second call invokes the `ComparedTo` function of the `ExtTime` class. In this code fragment, the compiler uses static (compile-time) binding of the operation (`ComparedTo`) to the appropriate object. The compiler can easily determine which `ComparedTo` function to call by checking the data type of the associated object.

> **Static binding** The compile-time determination of which function to call for a particular object.

In some situations, the compiler cannot determine the type of an object, however, so the binding of an operation to an object must occur at run time. One such situation involves passing class objects as arguments.

The basic C++ rule for passing class objects as arguments is that the argument and its corresponding parameter must be of identical types. With inheritance, C++ relaxes this rule to a certain extent. You may pass an object of a derived class as an argument to a function where the parameter is the type of the base class, but not the other way around—that is, you cannot pass an object of a base class as an argument where the parameter is of the derived type. More generally, you can pass an object of a descendant class as an argument to a function where the parameter is of any of its ancestor classes. This rule has a tremendous benefit: It allows us to write a single function that applies to any descendant class instead of having to write a different function for each subclass.

For example, let's assume that both `TimeOfDay` and `ExtTime` have a `Write` function. We could write a fancy Print function that takes as an argument an object of type `TimeOfDay` or any class descended from `TimeOfDay`:

```
void Print(TimeOfDay time)
{
  cout << "*************************" << endl;
  cout << "** The time is ";
  time.Write();
  cout << endl;
  cout << "*************************" << endl;
}
```

Given the code fragment

```
TimeOfDay startTime(8, 30, 0);
ExtTime endTime(10, 45, 0, CST);

Print(startTime);
Print(endTime);
```

the compiler lets us pass either a `TimeOfDay` object or an `ExtTime` object to the `Print` function. Unfortunately, the output is not what we would like. When `endTime` is printed, the zone `CST` is missing from the output. Let's see why.

The Slicing Problem

Our `Print` function uses passing by value for the parameter `time`. Passing by value sends a copy of the argument to the parameter. Whenever you pass an object of a derived class to an object of its base class using the pass by value technique, only the data members they have in common are copied. Recall that a derived class is often "larger" than its base class—that is, it contains additional data members. For example, a `TimeOfDay` object has three data members (`hours`, `minutes`, and `seconds`), but an `ExtTime` object has four data members (`hours`, `minutes`, `seconds`, and `zone`). When the larger class object is copied to the smaller parameter using pass by value, the extra data members are discarded or "sliced off." This situation is called the slicing problem (see **FIGURE 15.7**).

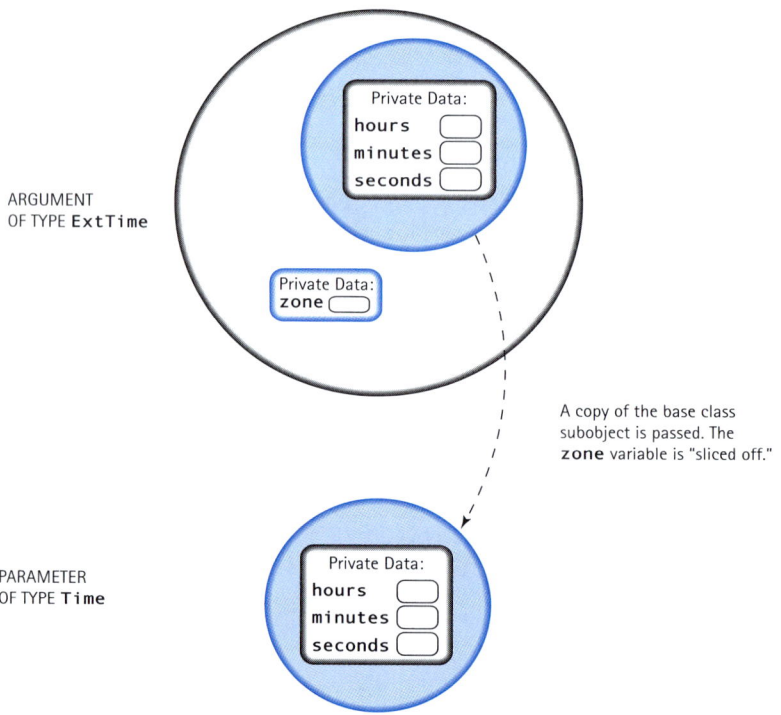

FIGURE 15.7 The Slicing Problem Resulting from Passing by Value

The slicing problem also occurs with assignment operations. In the statement

`baseClassObject = derivedClassObject;`

only the data members that the two objects have in common are copied. Additional data members contained in `derivedClassObject` are not copied.

With passing by reference, the slicing problem does not occur because the address of the caller's argument is sent to the function. To see how this approach works, let's change the heading of our `Print` function so that `someEntry` is a reference parameter:

`void Print(TimeOfDay& time)`

Now when we pass `endTime` as the argument, its address is sent to the function. Its `ExtTime` zone member is not sliced off because no copying takes place. But to our dismay, the `Print` function still prints only three of `endTime`'s data members—`hours`, `minutes`, and `seconds`.

Within the `Print` function, the difficulty is that static binding is used in the statement

`time.Write();`

The compiler must generate machine language code for the `Print` function at compile time, but the type of the actual argument (`TimeOfDay` or `ExtTime`) isn't known until run time. How can the compiler know which `Write` function to use—`TimeOfDay::Write` or `ExtTime::Write`? The compiler cannot know, so it uses `TimeOfDay::Write` because the parameter `time` is of type `TimeOfDay`. Therefore, the `Print` function always prints just three values—`hours`, `minutes`, and `seconds`—regardless of the type of the argument.

Fortunately, C++ provides a very simple solution to the slicing problem: *virtual functions*.

Virtual Functions

Suppose we make one small change to our `TimeOfDay` class declaration: We begin the declaration of the `Write` function with the reserved word `virtual`.

```
class TimeOfDay
{
public:
    ⋮
    virtual void Write() const;
    ⋮
private:
    ⋮
};
```

Declaring a member function to be `virtual` instructs the compiler to generate code that guarantees dynamic (run-time) binding of a function to an object. That is, the determination of which function to call is postponed until run time. (Note that to make `Write` a virtual function, the word `virtual` appears in one place only—the `TimeOfDay` class declaration. It does not appear in the `Write` function definition that is located in the `TimeOfDay.cpp` file, nor does it appear in any descendant class—such as `ExtTime`—that redefines the `Write` function.)

> **Dynamic binding** The run-time determination of which function to call for a particular object.

Virtual functions work in the following way. If a class object is passed by reference to some function, and if the body of that function contains a statement

```
param.MemberFunc( . . . );
```

then

1. If `MemberFunc` *is not* a virtual function, the type of the parameter determines which function to call. (Static binding is used.)
2. If `MemberFunc` *is* a virtual function, the type of the argument determines which function to call. (Dynamic binding is used.)

With the addition of just one word—`virtual`—the difficulties we encountered with our `Print` function disappear entirely. If we declare `Write` to be a virtual function in the `TimeOfDay` class, the function

```
void Print(TimeOfDay& time)
{
    ⋮
    time.Write();
    ⋮
}
```

works correctly for arguments of either type `TimeofDay` or type `ExtTime`. The correct `Write` function (`TimeOfDay::Write` or `ExtTime::Write`) is invoked because the argument includes the information needed at run time to choose the appropriate function. With this approach, deriving a new and unanticipated class from `TimeOfDay` presents no complications. If the new class redefines the `Write` function, then our `Print` function still works correctly. Dynamic binding ensures that each object knows how to print itself and that the appropriate version is invoked. In OOP terminology, `Write` is a polymorphic operation—an operation that has multiple meanings depending on the type of the object that responds to it at run time.

Polymorphic operation An operation that has multiple meanings depending on the type of the object to which it is bound at run time.

Here are some key points when using virtual functions in C++:

1. To achieve dynamic binding, you must use pass by reference when passing a class object to a function. If you use pass by value, the compiler does not use the `virtual` mechanism; instead, member slicing and static binding occur.
2. In the declaration of a virtual function, the word `virtual` appears only in the base class, not in any derived class.
3. If a base class declares a virtual function, it must implement that function, even if the body is empty.
4. A derived class is not required to provide its own reimplementation of a virtual function. In this case, the base class's version is used by default.
5. A derived class cannot redefine the function return type of a virtual function.

QUICK CHECK

15.3.1 Is a virtual function bound statically or dynamically? (pp. 793–794)
15.3.2 What is static binding of functions? (p. 791)
15.3.3 What is the slicing problem? (pp. 792–793)

15.4 Object-Oriented Design

Now that we've explored the language features that let us implement an object-oriented design, we turn to the phase that precedes implementation—object-oriented design itself.

A computer program usually models some real-life activity or concept. For example, a banking program models the real-life activities associated with a bank. A spreadsheet program models a real spreadsheet, which was a large paper form used in the past by accountants and financial planners. Programs for some kinds of robots model human perceptions and motions.

Nearly always, the aspect of the world that we are modeling (the application domain or problem domain) consists of objects—checking accounts, bank tellers, spreadsheet rows, spreadsheet columns, robot arms, robot legs. OOD is based on the philosophy that programs are easier to write and understand if the major objects in a program correspond closely to the objects in the problem domain. The programmer then focuses on how best to represent the real-world objects of the problem domain using the data types and operations provided by the programming language (the solution domain).

Object-oriented design can follow many different paths. Different software engineering researchers advocate different techniques. Our purpose here is not to teach you one particular technique in great detail or to present a summary of all the techniques. Rather, we will introduce you to a straightforward four-stage process that captures the essence of OOD. The four stages are brainstorming, filtering, scenario exploration, and responsibility algorithm design.

Brainstorming is the stage in which we make a first pass at identifying the objects in the problem. We freely list every possible object we can think of, in both the problem and solution domains.

Filtering is the stage in which we review the objects proposed in the brainstorming stage. We look for objects that are redundant or that can be combined, and perhaps notice some that are missing. Each object that survives the filtering stage becomes a class in the solution and is recorded on a *CRC card*. CRC stands for classes, responsibilities, and collaborations. A CRC card is a convenient way of recording important features of a class interface that emerge as we proceed through the design.

Scenario exploration is the stage in which the behavior of each class is determined. Because a class is responsible for its own behavior, we call these behaviors *responsibilities*. (You've already seen some use of this terminology. Recall that we have collectively referred to the getter functions of a class as its "knowledge responsibilities.") In this stage, we explore "what if" questions to be sure that we have examined all of the situations. When all of the responsibilities of each class have been determined, they are recorded on the class's CRC card. We also note the names of any other classes with which the class must collaborate (interact) to complete each responsibility.

In the last stage, *responsibility algorithm design*, we write the algorithms for each of the responsibilities outlined on the CRC cards. This stage is very similar to what happens in functional decomposition. However, in many cases the responsibility algorithms are so simple that further decomposition isn't necessary, and we can go directly to writing out the concrete steps. See **FIGURE 15.8** for an example of a CRC card.

Although these techniques were originally developed for use in programming teams, we can apply them to our own individual thought processes as well. Now that you have a general idea of how this OOD technique works, we can examine the specifics of each of the stages.

FIGURE 15.8 A Blank CRC Card

Brainstorming

Brainstorming The process of freely listing all the objects that may contribute to the solution of a problem.

Just exactly what is brainstorming? The dictionary defines it as a group problem-solving technique that involves the spontaneous contribution of ideas from all members of the group.[2] Brainstorming brings to mind a group of bright advertising people, tossing around ideas for a slogan for the latest revolutionary product. This picture seems at odds with the traditional concept of a computer programmer, slaving away for days in a cubicle, who finally jumps up, shouting, "It works!"

As computers have grown more powerful, the problems that can be solved with them have also grown increasingly more complex, and the picture of the solo coding genius has become obsolete. Solutions to complex problems need new and innovative solutions based on the creative collaborations of a diverse team.

In the context of object-oriented problem solving, brainstorming is a group activity designed to produce a list of candidate classes to be used to solve a particular problem. Just as the people brainstorming an advertising slogan know something about the product before the session begins, so brainstorming for classes requires that the participants know something about the problem. Each participant should be familiar with the requirements document and any additional information relating to the technical aspects of the project.

How does this process relate to individual problem solving? The equivalent step in the problem-solving process is "Understand the problem." Ask questions; try rewriting the problem statement in your own words. Take a sheet of paper and start writing down possible classes. Look for nouns in the problem statement that may indicate objects in the problem domain. Think about how the user will interact with the program. Review the

---

2. *Webster's New Collegiate Dictionary.*

classes that are available in libraries to see if any might be useful in the solution domain (including through inheritance in an extended class).

When you have a list of possible classes, you can then move to the next stage: *filtering*.

Filtering

The filtering step produces a smaller list of classes that we believe are sufficient to solve the problem. As part of the filtering stage we may recognize alternative approaches, and choose one set of objects over another set.

> **Filtering** The process of reviewing the initial list of objects to identify duplicate and unnecessary objects.

For example, when we are developing a highway traffic management system, we may list managers, drivers, lights, and cars as potential objects. In filtering the list, we might see that the problem can be solved either by representing managers and drivers or by representing lights and cars—but we don't need both. We may also find that the C++ Standard Template Library contains objects that we can use to implement items on our list.

Some classes may not really belong in the problem solution. For example, if we are simulating a calculator, we might list the user as an object in the problem domain. However, the user is not within the simulation; the user is an entity outside the problem that provides input to the simulation. Another problem domain object is the *on* button. A little thought shows that the *on* button is not actually part of the simulation; it is represented by the fact that the user has started the simulation program running.

Scenario Exploration

The goal of the scenario exploration phase is to assign responsibilities to each class. The responsibilities are the tasks that each class must perform. As we have seen, responsibilities are eventually implemented as functions. At this stage we are interested only in *what* the tasks are, not in *how* they might be carried out. To talk about what an object does, we need to determine its internal state, referred to as its attributes. We do *not* need to determine how these attributes are to be represented at this stage, only what they are.

> **Responsibilities** The operations associated with a class of objects.
> **Collaborations** The interactions between classes that are needed to solve a problem.

For example, our `TimeOfDay` class has three attributes: `hours`, `seconds`, and `minutes`. We have represented them as three integer values. In fact, we could keep the time as one integer value, `seconds`. `GetHours` and `GetMinutes` could then return these values by calculating them from `seconds`. Thus, at the logical (design) level, there are three values; at the implementation level, however, there may be only one value. The process we are describing is at the design (logical) level.

We distinguish two types of responsibilities: what a class must know about itself (knowledge) and what a class must be able to do (behavior). A class encapsulates its data (attributes); objects in one class cannot directly access data in another class. Encapsulation is a key to abstraction. However, each class has the responsibility of providing the information about itself that is needed by classes with which it collaborates.

For example, a `Student` class should "know" its name and address. The responsibilities for this knowledge might be called Get Name and Get Address. Whether the address is kept in the `Student` class or whether the `Student` class must ask some other class to access the address is irrelevant at this stage. The important fact is that the `Student` class is able to access and return (get) its own name and address.

The responsibilities for behavior look more like the tasks we described in functional decomposition. For example, a student object needs to calculate its GPA (grade-point average). In functional decomposition, we would say that a task is to calculate the GPA given the data. In OOD, we say that the student object is responsible for calculating its own GPA, perhaps by collaborating with an object that contains the student's grades.

This distinction is both subtle and profound. The final code for the calculation may be similar, but it is executed in different ways. In a procedural design, the main program calls the function that calculates the GPA, passing the student record as a parameter. In an object-oriented program, a message is sent to the student object to calculate its GPA. There are no parameters because the object to which the message is sent knows its own data.

How do we go about determining the responsibilities? The name for this phase gives a clue as to how we would assign responsibilities to classes. For our purposes, a scenario exploration is a sequence of steps that describes an interaction between a client (user or object) and any objects with which it must collaborate to satisfy a goal (which may include the `main` application).

> **Scenario exploration** A walk-through of the interactions between a client (the user or an object) and any objects (including the main application) with which the client must collaborate to achieve a particular goal.

Here is how the process works. The team uses play-acting to test different scenarios. During this exercise, each member of the team plays the role of one of the classes. Scenarios are "what if" scripts that allow participants to act out different situations. When a class has been sent a message, the actor holds up the CRC card and responds to the message, perhaps sending messages to others if necessary. As the scripts are being acted out, missing responsibilities are unearthed and unneeded responsibilities are detected. Sometimes the need for new classes surfaces. Although waving cards in the air when "you" are active might feel a little awkward at first, team members quickly get into the spirit of the action when they see how effective the technique is. See **FIGURE 15.9**.

FIGURE 15.9 A Scenario Walk-through in Progress

The output from this phase is a set of CRC cards representing the core classes in the problem solution. The responsibilities for each class are listed on the card, along with the classes with which each responsibility must collaborate.

Responsibility Algorithms

Eventually, the algorithms must be written for the responsibilities. Because we focus on data rather than actions in the object-oriented view of design, the algorithms for carrying out responsibilities tend to be fairly short. For example, knowledge responsibilities usually just return the contents of a variable in the object or send a message to another object to retrieve one of its attributes. Action responsibilities are a bit more complicated, often involving calculations. Thus the functional decomposition method of designing an algorithm is often appropriate for behavior responsibility algorithms.

A Final Word

To summarize, functional decomposition design methods focus on the *process* of transforming the input into the output, resulting in a hierarchy of tasks. By contrast, object-oriented design focuses on the *data objects* that are to be transformed, resulting in a hierarchy of objects. The nouns in the problem description become objects; the verbs become responsibilities. In a top-down design, the verbs are the primary focus; in an object-oriented design, the nouns are the primary focus.

The methodology that we have described makes use of the CRC card. This card is simply a notational device to help you organize your classes; its use is not a methodology.

BACKGROUND INFORMATION
What's the Best Solution?

As we discuss OOD, keep in mind that many different correct solutions exist for most problems. The techniques we use may seem imprecise, especially when contrasted with the precision required by the computer. In fact, the computer merely demands that we express (code) a solution precisely. The process of deciding which particular solution to use involves the skills of judgment and reasoning. It is our human ability to make choices without having complete information that enables us to solve problems.

For example, in developing a simulation of an air traffic control system, we might decide that airplanes and control towers are objects that communicate with one another. Alternatively, we might decide that pilots and controllers are the objects that communicate, as shown in **FIGURE 15.10**. This choice affects how we subsequently view the collaborations, and hence the responsibilities that we assign to the objects. Either choice can lead to a working application. We may simply prefer

BACKGROUND INFORMATION — What's the Best Solution, continued

the one with which we are most familiar (recall the "Look for things that are familiar" strategy from Chapter 1).

Some of our choices may lead to designs that are more or less efficient than others. For example, keeping a list of names in alphabetical order rather than in random order makes it possible for the computer to find a particular name much faster. Nevertheless, choosing to leave the list randomly ordered still produces a valid (albeit slower) solution.

The key point is this: Don't hesitate to begin solving a problem because you are waiting for some flash of genius that leads to the perfect solution. There is no such thing. It is better to jump in and try something, step back and see if you like the result, and then either proceed in the same direction or make changes. The CRC card technique is a way to easily explore different design choices and keep track of them.

FIGURE 15.10 Alternative Choices of Objects in an Air Traffic Control Application

QUICK CHECK

15.4.1 What are responsibilities in terms of object-oriented design? (p. 797)

15.4.2 What are the two types of responsibilities? (p. 797)

15.4.3 What are the four major steps in designing an object-oriented solution to a problem? (p. 795)

15.5 Implementing a Design

In OOD, when we first identify an object, it is an abstract entity. We do not immediately choose an exact data representation for that object's attributes. Similarly, the responsibilities of objects begin as abstract operations, because there is no initial attempt to provide algorithms. Of course, eventually we have to implement the attributes and operations. For each abstract object, we must complete two tasks:

- Choose a suitable data representation for its attributes
- Create algorithms for its responsibilities

To select a data representation for an object, the C++ programmer has three options:

1. Use a built-in data type.
2. Use or extend an existing class.
3. Create a new class.

For a given object, a good rule of thumb is to consider these three options in the order listed here. A built-in type is the most straightforward to use and understand, and operations on these types are already defined by the language. If a built-in type is not adequate to represent an object, you should survey the available ADTs in a class library (either the system's or your own) to see if any are a good match for the abstract object. Because we can use inheritance, it's not necessary to find an exact match, as long as an extension to the existing class will be sufficient. If no suitable ADT exists, you must design and implement a new ADT to represent the object.

In addition to choosing a data representation for the abstract object, we must implement the responsibility algorithms. With OOD, the algorithms for many responsibilities consist of a few concrete steps that can be directly translated into C++. Of course, this is not always the case. If an operation is complex, it may be best to treat the operation itself as a new problem and to use functional decomposition on the control flow. In this situation, it is appropriate to apply both functional decomposition and object-oriented methodologies together. Experienced programmers are familiar with both methodologies and often use them either independently or in combination with each other. However, the software development community is becoming increasingly convinced that although functional decomposition is important for designing low-level algorithms and operations on ADTs, the future in developing huge software systems lies in OOD and OOP.

QUICK CHECK

15.5.1 To select a data representation for an object, what three choices does a C++ programmer have? (p. 801)

15.5.2 In addition to the three data representations mentioned in the previous question, what else must be considered for an abstract object? (p. 801)

Problem-Solving Case Study

Creating an Appointment Calendar

Problem: Create an application that allows the user to edit entries on a list representing an appointment calendar. The input file contains a list of Entry objects similar to those defined in Chapter 12; however, each Entry object also contains a Date member. The user enters a name, and the application displays the entry for that name. After that, the user chooses which field to change and enters a new value. At the end of the processing, the list of updated entries is then written back to the file.

Identifying Initial Classes: Here is the list of potential objects, based on the problem statement and some brainstorming:

   Appointment Calendar
   List
   User
   Entry
   Name
   Time
   Date
   Input File
   Output File
   Format
   Field

Some of these items are clearly not a part of our solution, such as the User. The purpose of brainstorming, however, is to generate ideas without any inhibitions. Once we've run out of ideas, we move on to filtering them.

Filtering: After brainstorming, we filter the classes. The discussion that takes place during the filtering stage may reveal some classes that are really the same thing. For example, Appointment Calendar, List, Input File, and Output File all refer to the same information. Appointment Calendar is another name for the contents of the file on which the data is stored. That file is input when the program starts up, and it is output before the program exits. The List is the name of the data structure into which the information is stored within the program. Thus we have two representations for the Appointment Calendar: the external file and the internal representation. So do we need an Appointment Calendar class? Let's leave it in the filtered list; we may remove it later.

We may also find classes that were overlooked. For example, even though the User isn't an object in the problem, its presence in the brainstorming list reminds us that we need a User Interface that takes care of input and output. In the design, we call it a class; however, it can be implemented as the `main` program.

Here is our filtered list, indented to show objects that are contained within other objects:

   Appointment Calendar
   User Interface
   List
   Entry
       Name
       Time
       Date
   File
   Field

Problem-Solving Case Study

For each class that survives the filtering stage, we create a CRC card, which is just an index card with a line drawn down the middle. The name of the class is written at the top, and the two columns have the headings "Responsibilities" and "Collaborations." If a class is involved in a hierarchical relationship, that fact is noted at the top of the CRC card.

We already have an **Entry** class composed of a **Name** class and a **TimeOfDay** class. We do not need to make CRC cards for them: They are available to us from our library. We can use inheritance to create an **EntryWithDate** class from either our **Entry** class or our **ExpandedEntry** class. The **ComparedTo** operation provided in the **ExpandedEntry** class compares the **time** field. It is logical to keep an appointment ordered by date, so let's have **EntryWithDate** inherit its attributes directly from **Entry**.

Class Name: *EntryWithDate*	Superclass: *Entry*	Subclasses: *None*
Responsibilities	Collaborations	
Create EntryWithDate(Name, Time, Date)	*Name, TimeOfDay, Date*	
Get Date returns Date	*Date*	
RelationType ComparedTo(EntryWithDate)	*Date*	

Scenario Walk-through: To further expand the responsibilities of the classes and see how they collaborate, we process the scenarios by hand. We ask a question such as "What happens when the user wants to change the name?" We then answer the question by observing how each object is involved in accomplishing this task. In a team setting, the cards are distributed among team members. When an object of a class is doing something, its card is held in the air to visually signify that it is active. If you're walking through the scenario by yourself, you may set the card off to one side or put it on a bulletin board.

What are the responsibilities of the User Interface and Appointment Calendar for getting the Entry and displaying it? Let's have the User Interface input the name and date and retrieve the appropriate Entry. To do so, it must ask the Appointment Calendar to provide the Entry, based on the name and date. That responsibility is written down on the card. Once the name and date are input, the User Interface must collaborate with the **Name** and **Date** classes to instantiate Name and Date objects, and then ask the **AppointmentCalendar** class to retrieve the appropriate entry from the list.

After the User Interface gets the entry to be edited, it must get the field to be changed and input that changed field. If the name is to be changed, the User Interface must input the new name and collaborate with the **Name** class to instantiate a Name object. The same procedure would be carried out if the other fields were changed. The User Interface then must collaborate with the **Entry** class to instantiate a new Entry object, which is sent to the Appointment Calendar to be inserted.

What is the role of the Appointment Calendar? It must search the List for an entry with a certain name and date. In fact, the **AppointmentCalendar** class should be responsible for entering the original List of entries

Problem-Solving Case Study

and writing out the changed List of entries. Because our **Entry** hierarchy is a hierarchy of immutable objects, the object being changed must be removed from the List and the changed entry object then inserted.

Class Name: *AppointmentCalendar*	Superclass:		Subclasses:
Responsibilities		Collaborations	
Create AppointmentCalendar(File Name)		ifstream	
Get EntryBy(Name, Date) returns Entry		Name, Date	
Insert Entry(Entry)		List	
WriteListToFile(File Name)		ofstream	

Subsequent Scenarios: The preceding example illustrated using CRC cards in a single scenario. This particular scenario was selected from a list that was developed in a scenario brainstorming session. Here's a list of initial scenarios for our appointment calendar example:

What happens when the user

- Wants to change the date?
- Wants to change the name?
- Wants to change the address?
- Decides to not make any changes?
- Wants to change more than one field?
- Wants to change only one part of a field (such as the month)?

We walk through each scenario, adding responsibilities and collaborations to the CRC cards as necessary, and possibly extending the list of scenarios as we discover the need to do so (such as when we identify unanticipated error situations) or determining that we will not let the user perform that action. When every scenario we can envision seems to be feasible with the existing classes, responsibilities, and collaborations. The design is then finished.

Attributes and Their Internal Representations: Because we have used classes and subprograms already in our library—**Name**, **Time**, **Entry**, **ifstream**, and **ofstream**—only the **Date** class needs to have its internal representation determined. Before we do that, however, we should determine the responsibilities for ADT Date.

Our problem statement tells us nothing about the **Date** class except that we need one. What sorts of operations will our ADT Date need to perform? Of course, we need a default constructor and a parameterized constructor that takes month, day, and year as parameters. We should also have observer operations that let us observe the values for the month, day, and year. Finally, we should have an operation that lets us compare two dates.

Problem-Solving Case Study

Type

Date

Domain

Each **Date** value is a single date after the year 1582 A.D. in the form of month, day, and year.

Operations

Construct a new **Date** instance.
Construct a new **Date** instance with a given month, day, year.
Inspect the date's month.
Inspect the date's day.
Inspect the date's year.
Compare two dates for "before," "equal," or "after."

Here is the CRC card representing the Date ADT:

Class Name: Date	Superclass:	Subclasses:
Responsibilities	**Collaborations**	
Create Date(Month, Day, Year)		
Get Month returning Month		
Get Day returning Day		
Get Year returning Year		
ComparedTo(Date) returns RelationType		

The domain of our ADT is the set of all dates after the year 1582 A.D. in the form of a month, a day, and a year. We restrict the year to be after 1582 A.D. so as to simplify the ADT operations (10 days were skipped in 1582 in switching from the Julian to the Gregorian calendar).

Problem-Solving Case Study

Default Constructor

For this operation, we use a C++ default constructor that initializes the date to January 1 of the year 1583.

Parameterized Constructor

The client must supply three arguments for this operation: month, day, and year. Although we haven't yet determined a concrete data representation for a date, we must decide which data types the client should use for these arguments. We choose integers, where the month must be in the range 1 through 12, the day must be in the range 1 through the maximum number of days in the month, and the year must be greater than 1582. Notice that these range restrictions will become the precondition for invoking this operation.

Inspect the Date's Month, Inspect the Date's Day, and Inspect the Date's Year: All three of these operations are knowledge responsibilities. They give the client access—albeit indirectly—to the private data. As in the past, we represent knowledge responsibilities as value-returning member functions with the following prototypes:

```
int GetMonth();
int GetDay();
int GetYear();
```

Compare Two Dates: This operation compares two dates and determines whether the first one comes before the second one, they are the same, or the first one comes after the second one. To indicate the result of the comparison, we use enumeration type `RelationType` with three values:

```
enum RelationType {BEFORE, SAME, AFTER};
```

Then we can code the comparison operation as a class member function that returns a value of type `RelationType`. Here is the function prototype:

```
RelationType ComparedTo(Date otherDate) const;
```

Because this is a class member function, the date being compared to `otherDate` is the class object for which the member function is invoked. For example, the following client code tests whether `date1` comes before `date2`:

```
Date date1;
Date date2;
   .
   .
   .
if (date1.ComparedTo(date2) == BEFORE)
  DoSomething();
```

We are now almost ready to write the C++ specification file for our `Date` class. The simplest representation for a date is three `int` values—one each for the month, day, and year. Thus our internal structure is the same as the parameters. Here, then, is the specification file containing the `Date` class declaration:

Problem-Solving Case Study

```
//*****************************************
// SPECIFICATION File for a Date ADT
//*****************************************

#include "RelationType.h"
class Date
{
public:
  Date();
  Date(int initMonth, int initDay, int initYear);
  // Knowledge responsibilities
  int GetMonth() const;
  int GetDay() const;
  int GetYear() const;
  RelationType ComparedTo(Date otherDate) const;
  // Post: Returns BEFORE if instance comes before otherEntry;
  //       Returns SAME if instance and otherEntry are the same;
  //       Returns AFTER if instance comes after otherEntry

private:
  int month;
  int day;
  int year;
};
```

And here is the implementation file:

```
//********************************************************
// IMPLEMENTATION File for a Date ADT
// Month, day, and year are kept as integers
//********************************************************
#include <iostream>
#include "Date.h"
#include "RelationType.h"
using namespace std;

Date::Date()
{
  month = 1;
  day = 1;
  year = 1582;
}

//********************************************************
```

Problem-Solving Case Study

```
Date::Date(int initMonth, int initDay, int initYear)
{
  month = initMonth;
  day = initDay;
  year = initYear;
}

//*********************************************************

int Date::GetMonth() const
{ return month; }

//*********************************************************

int Date::GetDay() const
{ return day; }

//*********************************************************

int Date::GetYear() const
{ return year; }

//*********************************************************

RelationType Date::ComparedTo(Date otherDate) const
{
  if (year < otherDate.year)
    return BEFORE;
  else if (year > otherDate.year)
    return AFTER;
  else if (month < otherDate.month)
    return BEFORE;
  else if (month > otherDate.month)
    return AFTER;
  else if (day < otherDate.day)
    return BEFORE;
  else if (day > otherDate.day)
    return AFTER;
  else return SAME;
}
```

EntryWithDate Class

The CRC card can be translated directly into the specification file for this class.

Problem-Solving Case Study

```
//*******************************************
// SPECIFICATION FILE for class EntryWithDate
// This class inherits from Entry
//*******************************************

#include "Date.h"
class EntryWithDate : public Entry
{
public:
  // Constructors
  EntryWithDate();
  EntryWithDate(Date initDate, TimeOfDay initTime, Name initName);
  // Knowledge responsibility
  Date GetDate();
  RelationType ComparedTo(EntryWithDate otherEntry) const;
  // Post: Returns BEFORE if instance comes before otherEntry;
  //       Returns SAME if instance and otherEntry are the same;
  //       Returns AFTER if instance comes after otherEntry
private:
  Date date;
};
```

The algorithm for the **ComparedTo** function is a little complex. We are required to return an item of **RelationType**, but **AppointmentCalendar** is interested only in equality. If the name and the date are not equal, what do we send back: **BEFORE** or **AFTER**? In this case, let's use the comparison of the dates to determine the order.

```
//**********************************************************
// IMPLEMENTATION FILE for class EntryWithDate
//**********************************************************

#include "EntryWithDate.h"

EntryWithDate::EntryWithDate()
{ };

//**********************************************************

EntryWithDate::EntryWithDate(Date initDate,
  TimeOfDay initTime, Name initName) :
  Entry(initName.GetFirstName(), initName.GetMiddleName(),
    initName.GetLastName(), initTime.GetHours(),
    initTime.GetMinutes(), initTime.GetSeconds())
{
  date = initDate;
}

//**********************************************************
```

Problem-Solving Case Study

```
Date EntryWithDate::GetDate()
{ return date; }

//*******************************************************

RelationType EntryWithDate::ComparedTo(EntryWithDate otherDate)
  const
{
  if (GetDate().ComparedTo(otherDate.GetDate()) == SAME
    && GetName().ComparedTo(otherDate.GetName()) == SAME)
    return SAME;
  else if (GetDate().ComparedTo(otherDate.GetDate()) == BEFORE)
    return BEFORE;
  else return AFTER;
}
```

AppointmentCalendar Class

Which type of list should we use: sorted or unordered? It really doesn't matter in this case. All we plan to do is insert, search, and delete entries. Let's use an ordered array-based list. We must, however, change the comparison operations to use the `ComparedTo` function rather than the relational operators. This information, along with the CRC card, gives us enough information to write the specification file.

```
//*******************************************************
// SPECIFICATION FILE for class AppointmentCalendar
//*******************************************************

#include "List.h"
#include <fstream>
using namespace std;

class AppointmentCalendar
{
public:
  // Constructor
  AppointmentCalendar(ifstream& inFile);
  // Knowledge responsibility
  EntryWithDate GetEntry(Name name, Date date);
  // Returns entry with time field equal to time
  // Pre:  entry with time field equal to time exists

  // Action responsibilities
  void InsertEntry(EntryWithDate initEntry);
  // Inserts entry into list
  void WriteListToFile(ofstream& outFile);
  // Writes list to outFile

private:
  List list;
};
```

Problem-Solving Case Study

Constructor: The constructor should read in the entries and insert them in the list.

Because `AppointmentCalendar` will also write out the revised file, we must determine what the file looks like as well. There are three classes, each with three data values. `Date`'s and `TimeOfDay`'s data are integer values, while `Name`'s data consists of strings. Let's write the integer values first followed by the strings. Which kind of loop shall we use to input the data? Because we always update the file after each session, let's have `WriteListToFile` put the number of entries as the first value on the file. This value can be used in a count-controlled loop to read in the entries.

AppointmentCalendar (In: ifstream)

Read number of entries
FOR counter going from 0 to numberEntries − 1
    Read hours, minutes, seconds
    Read month, day, year
    Read first, middle, last
    TimeOfDay time(hours, minutes, seconds)
    Date date(month, day, year)
    Name name(first, middle, last)
    EntryWithDate entry(date, time, name)

Action Responsibilities: `GetEntry` takes a name and a date. The comparison operation used in the list compares only the name and date, but the object being compared must be an `EntryWithDate`. Thus, before we set up the iteration through the list, we must create a time object and then an `EntryWithDate` object using the time, name, and date.

GetEntry (In: name, date)
Function return value: EntryWithDate

TimeOfDay time;
EntryWithDate otherEntry(date, time, name)
Reset list
Set entry to list.GetNextItem()
WHILE entry.comparedTo(otherEntry) != SAME
    Set entry to list.GetNextItem()
Delete entry from list
Return entry

    What happens if there is no entry that matches the given date and time? In Chapter 16 we introduce a construct to handle such a case: exceptions and the `try-catch` statement. For the moment, we make it a precondition that such an entry exists. We then add an `IsThere` function to class `AppointmentCalendar`, thereby giving the client a tool to guarantee the precondition.

    `InsertEntry` just calls the `Insert` operation for the list. The `WriteListToFile` operation is the inverse of the constructor.

Problem-Solving Case Study

WriteListToFile (In: ofstream)

Reset the list
Write list.GetLength()
WHILE list.HasNext()
    Set entry to next item
    Set time to entry.GetTime()
    Set name to entry.GetName()
    Set date to entry.GetDate()
    Write time.GetHours(), time.GetMinutes(), time.GetSeconds()
    Write date.GetMonth(), date.GetDay(), date.GetYear()
    Write name.GetFirstName, name.GetMiddleName, name.GetLastName()

Here is the implementation file for class **AppointmentCalendar**:

```cpp
//*****************************************************
// IMPLEMENTATION FILE for AppointmentCalendar
//*****************************************************

#include "AppointmentCalendar.h"
#include <string>
#include <fstream>
#include <iostream>
using namespace std;

AppointmentCalendar::AppointmentCalendar(ifstream& inFile)
{
  int hours, minutes, seconds;   // For class TimeOfDay
  int month, day, year;          // For class Date
  string first, middle, last;    // For class Name
  int numberEntries;
  inFile >> numberEntries;
  for (int counter = 0; counter < numberEntries; counter++)
  {
    inFile >> hours >> minutes >> seconds;
    TimeOfDay time(hours, minutes, seconds);
    inFile >> month >> day >> year;
    Date date(month, day, year);
    inFile >> first >> middle >> last;
    Name name(first, middle, last);
    EntryWithDate entry(date, time, name);
    list.Insert(entry);
  }
}

//*****************************************************
```

Problem-Solving Case Study

```cpp
bool AppointmentCalendar::IsThere(Name name, Date date)
{
  TimeOfDay time;
  EntryWithDate entry(date, time, name);
  return list.IsThere(entry);
}

//********************************************************

EntryWithDate AppointmentCalendar::GetEntry(Name name, Date date)
{
  TimeOfDay time;
  EntryWithDate otherEntry(date, time, name);
  EntryWithDate entry;
  list.ResetList();
  entry = list.GetNextItem();
  while (entry.ComparedTo(otherEntry) != SAME)
    entry = list.GetNextItem();
  list.Delete(entry);
  return entry;
}

//********************************************************

void AppointmentCalendar::InsertEntry(EntryWithDate entry)
{ list.Insert(entry); }

//********************************************************

void AppointmentCalendar::WriteListToFile(ofstream& outFile)
{
  EntryWithDate entry;
  Name name;
  Date date;
  TimeOfDay time;
  list.ResetList();
  outFile << list.GetLength() << endl;
  while (list.HasNext())
  {
    entry = list.GetNextItem();
    time = entry.GetTime();
    outFile << time.GetHours() << ' ' << time.GetMinutes() << ' '
            << time.GetSeconds() << ' ';
    date = entry.GetDate();
    outFile << date.GetMonth() << ' ' << date.GetDay() << ' '
            << date.GetYear() << ' ';
    name = entry.GetName();
    outFile << name.GetFirstName() << ' ' << name.GetMiddleName()
            << ' ' << name.GetLastName() << endl;
  }
  outFile.close();
}
```

Problem-Solving Case Study

`UserInterface` Class (Implemented as `main`)

The `UserInterface` class is responsible for prompting for and inputting the name and date of the entry to be updated, then asking `AppointmentCalendar` to retrieve the entry. Once the entry is found and printed, `UserInterface` must ask the client which field is to be changed. Here we have a decision to make: Should we let the client change individual fields within the name, time, or date? For now, let's just have the client replace a complete name, time, or date.

We can create a menu of three characters: `'T'` for time, `'D'` for date, and `'N'` for name. Once the client has indicated which field is to be changed, `UserInterface` prompts for and inputs that field, creates an `EntryWithDate`, and inserts the revised entry back into the list. At that point, `UserInterface` asks the client if he or she wants to continue.

UserInterface (implemented as main)

```
Define input file
AppointmentCalendar calendar(inFile)
Get name and date of entry to change
DO
    IF calendar.IsThere(name, date)
        Set entry to calendar.GetEntry(name, date)
        Set time to calendar.GetTime()
        Print entry
        Set inputCode to GetInputCode()
        SWITCH (inputCode)
            'T' : GetTime()
            'D' : GetDate()
            'N' : GetName()
        EntryWithDate entry(date, time, name)
        calendar.InsertEntry(entry)
    ELSE
        Write "No entry exists with this name and date"
    Ask client to enter 'Y' to continue or 'N' to stop
    Read yesOrNo
    IF toupper(yesOrNo) == 'Y'
        Get name and date of entry to change
WHILE (toupper(yesOrNo) == 'Y')
Close inFile
Define outFile
calendar.WriteListToFile(outFile)
Close outFile
```

`GetInputCode`, `GetEntryToChange`, `GetTime`, `GetDate`, and `GetName` can be implemented as helper functions that prompt for and read the appropriate data. Here is the implementation file:

Problem-Solving Case Study

```cpp
//*********************************************************
// DRIVER for AppointmentCalendar problem
// Implements UserInterface class in design
//*********************************************************

#include <iostream>
#include <fstream>
#include <cctype>           // For toupper
#include <string>
#include "AppointmentCalendar.h"
using namespace std;

char GetInputCode();
// Prompts for and reads input code
TimeOfDay GetTime();
// Prompts for and reads a time object
Date GetDate();
// Prompts for and reads a date object
Name GetName();
// Prompts for and reads a name object
void GetEntryToChange(Name& name, Date& date);
// Prompts for and reads name and date of object to change

int main ()
{
  ifstream inFile;
  inFile.open("CalendarFile");
  if (!inFile)
  {
    cout << "File not found." << endl;
    return 1;
  }
  char inputCode;
  TimeOfDay time;
  Date date;
  Name name;
  EntryWithDate entry;
  char yesOrNo;
  AppointmentCalendar calendar(inFile);

  GetEntryToChange(name, date);
  do
  {
    if (calendar.IsThere(name, date))
    {
      entry = calendar.GetEntry(name, date);
      TimeOfDay time = entry.GetTime();
      cout << "Entry retrieved:" << endl;
      cout << "Time   " << entry.GetTime().GetHours() << ':'
           << entry.GetTime().GetMinutes() << endl;
```

Problem-Solving Case Study

```
      cout << "Date " << entry.GetDate().GetMonth() << '/'
           << entry.GetDate().GetDay() << '/'
           << entry.GetDate().GetYear() << endl;
      cout << "Name " << entry.GetName().GetFirstName() << ' '
           << entry.GetName().GetLastName() << endl << endl;
      inputCode = GetInputCode();
      switch (inputCode)
      {
        case 'T' : time = GetTime(); break;
        case 'D' : date = GetDate(); break;
        case 'N' : name = GetName(); break;
      }
      EntryWithDate entry(date, time, name);
      calendar.InsertEntry(entry);
    }
    else
      cout << "No entry exists with this name and date" << endl;
    cout << "Do you wish to continue changing entries? 'Y' or 'N'"
         << endl;
    cin >> yesOrNo;
    if (toupper(yesOrNo) == 'Y')
      GetEntryToChange(name, date);
  } while ((toupper(yesOrNo == 'Y')));
  inFile.close();
  ofstream outFile;
  outFile.open("CalendarFile");
  calendar.WriteListToFile(outFile);
  outFile.close();
  return 0;
}

//****************************************************************

char GetInputCode()
{
  char inputCode;
  cout << "Enter field to change: 'T' (time) 'D' (date) 'N' (name)"
       << endl;
  cin >> inputCode;
  return toupper(inputCode);
}

//****************************************************************

TimeOfDay GetTime()
{
  int hours, minutes, seconds;
  cout << "Enter time as hours, minutes, seconds " << endl;
  cin >> hours >> minutes >> seconds;
  TimeOfDay time(hours, minutes, seconds);
  return time;
}
```

Problem-Solving Case Study

```
//***********************************************************

Date GetDate()
{
  int month, day, year;
  cout << "Enter date as month, day, and year " << endl;
  cin >> month >> day >> year;
  Date date(month, day,year);
  return date;
}

//***********************************************************

Name GetName()
{
  string first, middle, last;
  cout << "Enter name as first, middle, last" << endl;
  cin >> first >> middle >> last;
  Name name(first, middle, last);
  return name;
}

//***********************************************************

void GetEntryToChange(Name& name, Date& date)
{
  cout << "Enter name of entry to change:"
       << endl;
  name = GetName();
  cout << "Enter date of entry to change"
       << endl;
  date = GetDate();
}
```

Here is the input file, followed by a scenario of three changes:

CalendarFile

```
5
8 20 0 10 12 2009 Boris Becker Brown
8 45 0 10 11 2009 Sara Jane Jones
12 30 0 10 11 2009 Susy Smiley Baker
8 30 0 10 12 2009 Bill Bradley Britton
9 30 0 11 5 2010 Mary Jane Smith
```

Problem-Solving Case Study

Script from interactive session (client input is shaded):

```
Enter name of entry to change:
Enter name as first, middle, last
Mary Jane Smith
Enter date of entry to change
Enter date as month, day, and year
11 5 2010
Entry retrieved:
Time  9:30
Date  11/5/2010
Name Mary Smith

Enter field to change: 'T' (time) 'D' (date) 'N' (name)
D
Enter date as month, day, and year
11 5 2009
Do you wish to continue changing entries? 'Y' or 'N'
y
Enter name of entry to change:
Enter name as first, middle, last
Bill Bradley Britton
Enter date of entry to change
Enter date as month, day, and year
10 12 2009
Entry retrieved:
Time  8:30
Date  10/12/2009
Name Bill Britton

Enter field to change: 'T' (time) 'D' (date) 'N' (name)
T
Enter time as hours, minutes, seconds
9 30 0
Do you wish to continue changing entries? 'Y' or 'N'
y
Enter name of entry to change:
Enter name as first, middle, last
Sara Jane Jones
Enter date of entry to change
Enter date as month, day, and year
10 11 2009
Entry retrieved:
Time  8:45
Date  10/11/2009
Name Sara Jones
```

Problem-Solving Case Study

```
Enter field to change: 'T' (time) 'D' (date) 'N' (name)
N
Enter name as first, middle, last
Sarah Jane Jones
Do you wish to continue changing entries? 'Y' or 'N'
y
Enter name of entry to change:
Enter name as first, middle, last
Sara Jane Jones
Enter date of entry to change
Enter date as month, day, and year
10 11 2009
No entry exists with this name and date
Do you wish to continue changing entries? 'Y' or 'N'
n
```

Testing and Debugging

Testing and debugging an object-oriented program is largely a process of testing and debugging the C++ classes on which the program is built. The top-level driver also needs testing, but this testing is usually uncomplicated—OOD tends to result in a simple driver.

To review how to test a C++ class, refer back to the "Testing and Debugging" section of Chapter 9. There we walked through the process of testing each member function of a class. We made the observation then that you could write a separate test driver for each member function or you could write just one test driver that tests all of the member functions. The latter approach is recommended only for classes that have a few simple member functions.

When an object-oriented program uses inheritance and composition, the order in which you test the classes is, in a sense, predetermined. If class X is derived from class Y, you cannot test X until you have designed and implemented Y. Thus it makes sense to test and debug class Y (the base class) before you test class X.

When class Y contains an object of class Z, then you should generally test Z before Y. If you're waiting for someone else to finish the implementation of Z, however, you can still perform some initial tests on Y by writing a stub class for Z. A stub class provides a minimal implementation of the interface that allows a client class to operate. For example, if we were adding a function to determine the difference between two dates, we could code a stub that always returns **BEFORE**. That's sufficient to enable the client code to make the call and receive a value.

Stub classes also allow you to control the testing of a class more precisely, because you can write the stubs for the functions to return specific values. Why would that approach be helpful? When your class uses an object of a very complex class, it can be challenging to force the other class to return the values you need for testing. With a stub class, you have total—and very direct—control over what is returned to the class you are testing.

Testing and Debugging Hints

1. Review the Testing and Debugging Hints in Chapter 12. They apply to the design and testing of C++ classes, which are at the heart of OOP.
2. When using inheritance, don't forget to include the word `public` when declaring the derived class:

   ```
   class DerivedClass : public BaseClass
   {
       .
       .
       .
   };
   ```

   The word `public` makes `BaseClass` be a public base class of `DerivedClass`. As a consequence, clients of `DerivedClass` can apply any public `BaseClass` operation (except constructors) to a `DerivedClass` object.
3. The header file containing the declaration of a derived class must `#include` the header file containing the declaration of the base class.
4. Although a derived class inherits the private and public members of its base class, it cannot directly access the inherited private members.
5. If a base class has a constructor, it is invoked before the body of the derived class's constructor is executed. If the base class constructor requires arguments, you must pass these arguments using a constructor initializer:

   ```
   DerivedClass::DerivedClass( ... )
       : BaseClass(arg1, arg2)
   {
       .
       .
       .
   }
   ```

   If you do not include a constructor initializer, the base class's default constructor is invoked.
6. If a class has a member that is an object of another class and this member object's constructor requires arguments, you must pass these arguments using a constructor initializer:

   ```
   SomeClass::SomeClass( ... )
       : memberObject(arg1, arg2)
   {
       .
       .
       .
   }
   ```

   If there is no constructor initializer, the member object's default constructor is invoked.

7. To achieve dynamic binding of an operation to an object when passing class objects as arguments, you must

   - Pass the object by reference, not by value.
   - Declare the operation to be `virtual` in the base class declaration.

8. If a base class declares a virtual function, it must implement that function even if the body is empty.
9. A derived class cannot redefine the function return type of a virtual function.

Summary

Object-oriented design (OOD) decomposes a problem into objects—self-contained entities in which data and operations are bound together. In OOD, data is treated as an active, rather than passive, quantity. Each object is responsible for one part of the solution, and the objects communicate by invoking one another's operations.

The OOD process begins by identifying potential objects and their operations. Brainstorming is used to produce a list of possible classes in the problem. Filtering reexamines the classes, looking for duplicate classes, unnecessary classes, and missing classes. CRC cards are then written for the classes that survive the filtering phase. Next, scenarios are examined to determine the responsibilities of the classes. Finally, algorithms are written to carry out the responsibilities and concrete data representations are chosen.

Object-oriented programming (OOP) is the process of implementing an object-oriented design by using language mechanisms for data abstraction, inheritance, and dynamic binding (polymorphism). Inheritance allows any programmer to take an existing class (the base class) and create a new class (the derived class) that inherits both the data and the operations of the base class. The derived class then specializes the base class by adding new private data, adding new operations, or reimplementing inherited operations—all without examining or modifying the implementation of the base class in any way.

Dynamic binding of operations to objects allows objects of many different derived types to respond to a single function name, each in its own way. C++ supports dynamic binding through the use of virtual functions. Together, inheritance and dynamic binding have been shown to dramatically reduce the time and effort required to customize existing ADTs. The result is truly reusable software components whose applications and lifetimes extend beyond those conceived of by the original creator.

Quick Check Answers

15.1.1 In a structured program, functions interact with one another and with the data in the program. In an object-oriented program, objects (which bind operations and data together) are the components that interact. **15.1.2** Abstraction, inheritance, dynamic binding. **15.1.3** The construction of programs that are collections of interacting functions or procedures. **15.1.4** data. **15.1.5** To implement the operations on objects.
15.2.1 `class InternationalPhone : public Phone`
15.2.2 By placing a member field within `InternationalPhone` that is of class **Phone**. **15.2.3** An is-a relationship. **15.2.4** A mechanism by which one class acquires the properties—the data and operations—of another class. **15.2.5** public. **15.2.6** A *constructor initializer*. **15.2.7** 1. The base class (Y) constructor is executed first; 2. Constructors for X's member objects (if any) are then executed; 3. The body of X's constructor is executed last. **15.3.1** Dynamically. **15.3.2** The compile-time determination of which function to call for a particular object. **15.3.3** When an object of a derived class X is assigned to an object of a base class Y, only the data members that X and Y have in common are copied to Y. **15.4.1** The operations associated with a class of objects. **15.4.2** knowledge: what a class must know about itself and behavior: what a class must be able to do. **15.4.3** Brainstorming, filtering, scenarios, responsibility algorithms. **15.5.1** Use a built-in type. Use or extend an existing class. Create a new class. **15.5.2** The implementation of the responsibility algorithms.

CHAPTER 15 Inheritance, Polymorphism, and Object-Oriented Design

■ Exam Preparation Exercises

1. Match the following terms with the definitions given below.
   a. Structured (procedural) program
   b. Object-oriented program
   c. Inheritance
   d. Superclass
   e. Subclass
   f. Composition
   g. Static binding
   h. Dynamic binding
   i. Polymorphic
      i. Determining, at run time, from which class to call a function.
      ii. A class from which properties are acquired.
      iii. A collection of classes designed using abstraction, inheritance, and polymorphism.
      iv. An operation that has different meanings depending on its binding to an object.
      v. Including an object of one class within another class.
      vi. A class that acquires properties from another class.
      vii. Determining, at compile time, from which class to call a function.
      viii. A collection of functions, designed using functional decomposition.
      ix. Acquiring the properties of another class.

2. Structured programming is better suited to developing small programs, whereas object-oriented programming is better for writing large programs. True or false?

3. Inheritance allows us to reuse functions from a base class and add new functions, but we cannot replace functions in the base class with new implementations. True or false?

4. To solve the slicing problem, we use a combination of pass by reference and virtual functions. True or false?

5. If we want a function to be virtual, where do we write the keyword: in the base class declaration file, in the base class definition file, in the derived class declaration file, or in the derived class definition file?

6. Which C++ language mechanism implements composition?

7. Suppose you have a subclass that contains several data members that are not defined in its superclass. What happens to those data members if you assign an object of the subclass to a variable of the superclass?

8. A client is supplied with the following declaration for a base class and a derived class:

```
class BaseClass
{
public:
  void PrintFields() const;
     .
     .
     .
};
```

```
class DerivedClass : BaseClass
{
public:
  void NewFunction();
  DerivedClass(int StartValue);
     .
     .
     .
};
```

The client writes the following code to call the constructor for an object of type `DerivedClass`, and then prints the fields in the newly created object.

```
DerivedClass anObject(10);
anObject.PrintFields();
```

The compiler reports an error for the second statement. What's wrong? How would you fix this problem?

9. Consider the following base and derived class declarations:

```
class BaseClass
{
public:
  void BaseAlpha();
private:
  void BaseBeta();
  float baseField;
};

class DerivedClass : public BaseClass
{
public:
  void DerivedAlpha();
  void DerivedBeta();
private:
  int derivedField;
};
```

For each class, do the following:
 a. List all private data members.
 b. List all private data members that the class's member functions can reference directly.
 c. List all functions that the class's member functions can invoke.
 d. List all member functions that a client of the class may invoke.

10. A class called `DerivedClass` is a subclass of a class called `BaseClass`. `DerivedClass` also has a member field that is an object of class `ComposedClass`.
 a. Which class's constructor is called first when an object of class `DerivedClass` is created?
 b. Which class's constructor is called last when an object of class `DerivedClass` is created?

11. Why does slicing occur with pass by value but not with pass by reference when a derived class object is passed to a parameter of its base class?

12. What's wrong with the following class declarations?

    ```
    class BaseClass
    {
    public:
      virtual void BaseAlpha();
    private:
      float baseField;
    };

    class DerivedClass : public BaseClass
    {
    public:
      virtual void BaseAlpha();
    private:
      int derivedField;
    };
    ```

13. Explain the difference between an *is-a* relationship and a *has-a* relationship.
14. When we code a derived class in separate files, which of the following steps do we take?
    a. Include the base class specification and implementation file in both the derived class specification file and its implementation files.
    b. Include the base class specification file in the derived class specification file, and include the base class implementation file in the derived class implementation file.
    c. Include the base class specification file in the derived class specification file.
    d. Include the base class implementation file in the derived class implementation file.
15. What is the task of the brainstorming phase?
16. What is the task of the filtering phase?
17. What is the task of the scenario exploration phase?
18. What is the task of the responsibility algorithm phase?
19. At which phase is a concrete data representation chosen?

Programming Warm-Up Exercises

1. Given the following declaration for a `TestScore` class, write a derived class declaration called `IDScore` that adds an integer student ID number as a private member, and that supplies (1) a constructor whose parameters correspond to the three member fields, and (2) an observer that returns the ID number.

    ```
    class TestScore
    {
    public:
      TestScore(string name, int score);
      string GetName() const;
      int GetScore() const;
    private:
      string studentName;
      int studentScore;
    };
    ```

2. Write the implementation file for the `TestScore` class in Exercise 1. The constructor just assigns its parameters to the private data members, and the observers simply return the corresponding member.
3. Write the implementation file for the `IDScore` class in Exercise 1. The constructor just assigns its parameters to the private data members, and the observer simply returns the corresponding member.
4. Write the specification file for a class called `Exam` that uses composition to create an array of 100 objects of class `IDScore` as defined in Exercise 1. The class can use the default constructor, and it will have a function that assigns an `IDScore` object to a location in the array, given the object and the location as parameters. The class should also have an observer that returns the `IDScore` object at the position specified by its parameter.
5. Write the implementation file for class `Exam` as defined in Exercise 4.
6. The following class represents a telephone number in the United States:

   ```
   // SPECIFICATION FILE (phone.h)

   enum PhoneType (HOME, OFFICE, CELL, FAX, PAGE);

   class Phone
   {
   public:
     Phone(newAreaCode, int newNumber, PhoneType newType);
     void Write() const;
   private:
     int areaCode;
     int number;
     PhoneType type;
   }
   ```

   Using inheritance, we want to derive an international phone number class, `InternPhone`, from the `Phone` class. For this exercise, we assume that the only change necessary is to add a country code (an integer) that identifies the country or region. The public operations of `InternPhone` are `Write`, which reimplements the `Write` function from the base class, and a class constructor, which takes four parameters corresponding to the four member fields in the class. Write the class declaration for the `InternPhone` class.
7. Implement the `InternPhone` class constructor as described in Exercise 6.
8. Implement the `Write` function of the `InternPhone` class as described in Exercise 6.
9. Write a global function `WritePhone` that takes a single parameter and uses dynamic binding to print either a U.S. phone number (`Phone` class) or an international phone number (`InternPhone` class). Make the necessary change(s) in the declaration of the `Phone` class from Exercise 6 so that `WritePhone` executes correctly.
10. Given the following declaration for a class that represents a computer in a company's inventory, write a derived class declaration (for a class called `InstallRecord`) that adds (1) a string field representing the location of the computer and (2) a field of class `SimpleDate` that holds the installation date. The new class should provide observers for each of the new fields. It should also reimplement the `Write` function.

    ```
    class Computer
    {
    public:
      Computer(string newName, string newBrand, string newModel,
               int newSpeed, string newSerial, int newNumber);
    ```

```
    string GetName() const;
    string GetBrand() const;
    string GetModel() const;
    int GetSpeed() const;
    string GetSerial() const;
    int GetNumber() const;
    void Write() const;
private:
    string name;
    string brand;
    string model;
    int speed;
    string serialNumber;
    int inventoryNumber;
};
```

11. Implement the constructor for the `Computer` class declared in Exercise 10.
12. Implement the constructor for the `InstallRecord` class declared in Exercise 10.
13. Implement the `Write` function for the `Computer` class declared in Exercise 10. It should output each member field on a separate line.
14. Implement the `Write` function for the `InstallRecord` class declared in Exercise 10. It should output each member field on a separate line. Assume that the `SimpleDate` class provides a `void` function called `Write()` that outputs the date in a standard format.

Programming Problems

1. Use object-oriented programming to develop an application for the game of memory. Memory consists of a 20 × 20 grid of face down cards where there is at most one pair of each card in the grid. The types of cards that are available in this version of the game are DOG, CAT, RAT, MOUSE, PENCIL, CRAYON, ROCK, BOOK, BAG, and KEY. Adding a new type of card to the game should only require the creation of a new class that inherits properties from an existing `Card` class. Each card has a unique description associated with it that will give the player something to remember that card by. Game play proceeds by flipping two cards over to determine if a matching pair has been found. After the pair has been chosen, the application should report the description of the card and if a match was found or not found. If a matching pair has been found, those cards are no longer able to be chosen and the application should report if a card is chosen that already corresponds to a match and will allow the player to choose a different card. The game continues until all matches have been found or the user types in the command 'quit'.

2. Use object-oriented programming to develop a game application that simulates a roulette table. The roulette table has 36 numbers (1 to 36) that are arranged in three columns of 12 rows. The first row has the numbers 1 through 3, the second row contains 4 through 6, and so on. There is also a number 0 that is outside the table of numbers. The numbers in the table are colored red and black (0 is green). The red numbers are 1, 3, 5, 7, 9, 12, 14, 16, 18, 19, 21, 23, 25, 27, 30, 32, 34, and 36. The other half of the numbers are black. In a simplified set of rules, players can bet on an individual number (including 0), the red numbers, the black numbers, the even numbers, the odd numbers, the numbers 1 to 18, the numbers 19 to 36, and any of the columns or rows in the table.

The user should be allowed to enter one of the bets, and the application uses the `rand` function from `<cstdlib>` as the basis for computing the number that would be rolled on the wheel. It then compares this number to the bet, and reports whether it won or lost. The process repeats until the user enters a quit command.

3. Use object-oriented programming to develop an extension to the application of Problem 2. The new application should allow the user to enter an initial amount of money into an account. In addition to placing a bet, the user specifies an amount to go with the bet. This amount is deducted from the account; any winnings are added to the account. The current winnings or losses (difference from the original amount) should be displayed in addition to the value of the account. Winnings are computed as follows:

   Single-number bets pay 36 times the amount placed
   Row bets pay 12 times the amount placed
   Column bets pay 3 times the amount placed
   Odd/even, red/black, and high/low half-bets pay 2 times the amount placed
   The user should not be allowed to bet more than the amount in the account.

4. Use object-oriented programming to develop a game application that plays the children's game of rock, paper, scissors. The user enters a letter, indicating his or her choice. When a choice is entered, the `rand` function from `<cstdlib>` is used to pick a value in the range of 1 through 3, with 1 corresponding to rock, 2 corresponding to paper, and 3 corresponding to scissors. The computer's choice is compared to the user's choice according to these rules: rock breaks scissors, scissors cut paper, paper covers rock. Choices that match are considered ties. Output a count of the wins by the user and the computer, and of the ties. The application ends when the user enters an invalid choice.

5. Use object-oriented programming to develop an extension to the application of Problem 4. The new application should accept either the original single letter or the full words (rock, paper, scissors). The capitalization of the words should not matter. The extended application should end only when the user enters "q" or "quit" as a choice and should prompt the user for one of the valid choices if an invalid value is entered.

6. Use the `Computer` and `InstallRecord` classes declared in Programming Warm-Up Exercises 10 to 14, together with the `SortedList` class developed in Chapter 13, as the basis for an object-oriented program that keeps track of a company's computer inventory. The company has at most 500 computers. The following operations should be supported:

   Add a new computer to the list.
   Delete a computer from the list.
   Change the location of a computer.
   Print a list of all computers in inventory-number order.
   Print a list of all computers in a given location.
   Print a list of all computers of a particular brand.
   Print a list of all computers installed before a given date.

   The application should keep the list sorted by inventory number. It should read an initial list from a file called `original.dat`. At the end of processing, it should write the current data in the list onto a file called `update.dat` in a format that could be read back in by the program as an initial list. You will also need to develop the `SimpleDate` class to the degree necessary to support the application.

■ **Case Study Follow-Up**

1. The name of the input file is given explicitly in the case study code. Write a function that prompts for and inputs the file name. The file should be a parameter of the function. The function should also have a Boolean parameter through which it returns `false` if the input file cannot be found after giving the user three tries to enter a correct file name. Have it return `true` if the file is opened properly. Change the code in `main` to use this function.
2. Write and implement a test plan to verify that the change made in Exercise 1 is correct.
3. We have implemented the `TimeOfDay` object, using three values for hours, minutes, and seconds. Seconds are not relevant in this problem; they are too fine a distinction. Explore the idea of keeping the time of day as a single variable that represents the time as a number of minutes. What changes would be required in the client code of the case study if this change were made? Explain your answer.
4. Implement the alternative version of `TimeOfDay` using the scheme outlined in Exercise 3.

Templates, Operator Overloading, and Exceptions

KNOWLEDGE GOALS
- To understand the concept of a template.
- To know what a generic operation is.
- To understand the concept of an exception.

SKILL GOALS

To be able to:
- Write a C++ class template.
- Code the instantiation of a class template.
- Write function definitions for members of a template class.
- Design and code a C++ function template.
- Write code that instantiates a function template.
- Overload the relational operators.
- Define an exception class and write code that throws an exception.
- Write an exception handler.

CHAPTER 16 Templates, Operator Overloading, and Exceptions

This chapter introduces C++ language features that can have a powerful impact on how we design and implement software: templates, operator overloading, and exceptions. A template, as the name suggests, is a pattern from which we can create multiple instances of something. You may be wondering, "What's new about that? Classes let us create multiple instances of objects." In reality, the C++ template mechanism carries the concept of "instance" to a higher level. It lets us create specialized instances of functions or entire classes without having to explicitly change or extend them.

Operator overloading allows us to redefine the standard C++ operators. In particular, we can redefine the relational operators so that they can be used to compare class objects.

Exceptions are unusual events that happen during execution. The C++ exception-handling mechanism allows one part of a program to detect that an exception has occurred and another part of the program to respond to it. The part that does the detection is said to throw an exception, and the part that responds (called an exception handler) is said to catch the exception.

16.1 Template Classes

In Chapter 13, we defined a List abstract data type (ADT) that represented a list of unsorted components, each of type `ItemType`. We coded this ADT as a C++ class named `List`, and the header file `List.h` was written as follows (abbreviated here by omitting the function preconditions and postconditions):

```cpp
const int MAX_LENGTH =100;    // Maximum number of components
typedef int ItemType;         // Type of each component

class List
{
public:
  List();
  // Action responsibilities
  void Insert(ItemType item);
  void Delete(ItemType item);
  void ResetList();
  ItemType GetNextItem();
  // Knowledge responsibilities
  int GetLength() const;
  bool IsEmpty() const;
  bool IsFull() const;
  bool IsThere(ItemType item ) const;
  bool HasNext() const;

private:
  int length;
  int currentPos;
  ItemType data[MAX_LENGTH];
};
```

The `typedef` statement lets us choose a particular type for `ItemType`, as long as it is a simple type or the `string` class. (This restriction exists because the `List` member functions use relational operators to compare list items. `ItemType` cannot be an array type, for example, because relational operations cannot be applied to an entire array as an aggregate.)

16.1 Template Classes

The `List` class is similar to a *generic data type* in the sense that the list items can be of (almost) any data type. If we change the `ItemType` by changing the `typedef` statement, we can recompile the class without changing any of the algorithms in the member functions.

However, the `List` class as written has two serious limitations. First, once the class is compiled using, say, `int` as the `ItemType`, a client program's `List` objects can only be lists of `int`s. There is no way for the client to maintain lists of `int`s, lists of `float`s, and lists of `char`s, all within the same program. Second, a client program cannot specify or change the `ItemType`; a human must go into the file `list.h` with an editor and change it manually.

To make a class such as `List` a truly generic type, we need a language construct that allows `ItemType` to be a parameter to the class declaration. Fortunately, C++ provides such a construct: the *class template*.

> **Generic data type** A type for which the operations are defined but the data types of the items being manipulated are not.
>
> **Class template** A C++ language construct that allows the compiler to generate multiple versions of a class through the use of parameterized data types.

Defining a Class Template

In C++, a class template allows you to write a class definition with "blanks" left in the definition to be filled in by the calling code. Most often, the "blanks" to be filled in are the names of data types.

Here is the syntax for a class template:

ClassTemplate

```
template < TemplateParamList >
ClassDefinition
```

where ClassDefinition is an ordinary class definition. The full syntax description of TemplateParamList in C++ is quite complicated, and we simplify it for our purposes as follows. TemplateParamList is a sequence of one or more parameter declarations separated by commas, where each is defined as follows:

TemplateParamDeclaration

```
{ class    } Identifier
{ typename }
```

Here is a class template for our `List` class, with the class name changed to `GList`:

```
template<class ItemType>
class GList
{
public:
  List();
  // Action responsibilities
  void Insert(ItemType item);
```

```
    void Delete(ItemType item);
    void ResetList();
    ItemType GetNextItem();
    // Knowledge responsibilities
    int GetLength() const;
    bool IsEmpty() const;
    bool IsFull() const;
    bool IsThere(ItemType item) const;
    bool HasNext() const;
private:
    int length;
    int currentPos;
    ItemType data[MAX_LENGTH];
};
```

As the highlighting indicates, this template is just like the declaration for the `List` type, except that it is preceded by `template<class ItemType>` and the class name is changed. Here, `ItemType` is the *template parameter*. Just as before, we use `ItemType` wherever we need to refer to the data type of an element of our list. The difference is that the type isn't hard-coded with a `typedef` statement in the class itself, but rather can be specified by the user when the class is instantiated. You can use any identifier for the template parameter; we just happen to use `ItemType` in this example because we have been using it in our `List` classes.

There are two things to note about template parameters. First, the use of the word `class` in `template<class ItemType>` is simply required syntax and does not mean that the list items must be objects of a C++ class. A list created from this template can hold any data type that we specify, including built-in or user-defined types. (For this reason, some C++ programmers are moving toward using the recently added reserved word `typename`, although `class` is more traditional.) In the example code in the next section, we use `int`, `char`, and `float` to instantiate three specific classes from this template.

Second, the template parameter takes the place of an explicit type name within the code. So what do we pass to this parameter? A data type name. This may seem strange at first, because when we pass arguments to functions, we always pass variable names or expressions, not data type names. Furthermore, passing an argument to a template has an effect at *compile* time—the compiler generates a new class definition from the template. In contrast, passing an argument to a function has an effect at *run* time.

Instantiating a Class Template

Given the `GList` class template, the client program can use code like the following to create several lists whose components are of different data types:

```
// Client code

GList<int> list1;
GList<float> list2;
GList<string> list3;

list1.Insert(356);
list2.Insert(84.375);
list3.Insert("Muffler bolt");
```

In the declarations of list1, list2, and list3, the data type name enclosed in angle brackets is the *template argument*. When the compiler encounters the declarations of list1, list2, and list3, it generates (instantiates) three distinct class types and gives its own internal name to each of the three types. You might imagine that the declarations are transformed internally into something like this:

```
GList_int list1;
GList_float list2;
GList_string list3;
```

In C++ terminology, the three new class types are called *template classes* or *generated classes* (as opposed to the class template from which they were created). Individually, each concrete class that is generated from a template is known as a *specialization* of the template.

When the compiler instantiates a template, it literally substitutes the template argument for the template parameter throughout the class template. For example, the first time the compiler encounters GList<int> in the client code, it generates a new class by substituting int for every occurrence of ItemType in the class template:

```
class GList_int
{
public:
    ⋮
    void Insert( ItemType item );
    void Delete( ItemType item );
    bool IsPresent( ItemType item ) const;
    ⋮
private:
    int       length;
    ItemType data[MAX_LENGTH];
};
```

A useful perspective on class templates is this: Whereas an ordinary class declaration is a pattern for stamping out individual objects, a class template is a pattern for stamping out individual data types.

Now that we've seen how to write the definition of a class template, what do we do about the definitions of the class member functions? We need to write them as function templates so that the compiler can associate each one with the proper template class. Here is the syntax diagram for a function template:

> **Function template** A C++ language construct that allows the compiler to generate multiple versions of a function by allowing parameterized data types.

FunctionTemplate

```
template < TemplateParamList >
FunctionDefinition
```

As you can see, the FunctionTemplate is very similar to the ClassTemplate, with two exceptions: the TemplateParamList can be omitted under some special circumstances[1] and the template parameter specification is followed by a FunctionDefinition rather than a ClassDefinition.

For example, we code the `Insert` function as the following function template:

```
template<class ItemType>
void GList<ItemType>::Insert(ItemType item)
{
  data[length] = item;
  length++;
}
```

Notice how we must write `GList` with `<ItemType>` appended to it so that the compiler knows to which specialization of `GList` we are referring. Multiple specializations within a class are also possible (though no examples are provided here), and the compiler needs to be told which one is which in every case.

If the client declares a type `GList<float>`, the compiler generates a function definition similar to the following:

```
void GList<float>::Insert(float item)
{
  data[length] = item;
  length++;
}
```

Another Way of Implementing Incoming Parameters: `const` References

Thus far we have used a very simple rule for implementing parameters in our functions: Incoming parameters are passed by value, and all other parameters are passed by reference. This rule is necessary because value parameters are copies of their arguments, meaning that those arguments are protected from being changed by the function. In this way, we avoid certain kinds of side-effect errors. Reference parameters allow the function to directly access the argument, which is necessary whenever a value must be passed back through a parameter.

For parameters of built-in types and simple, small objects, the copying that takes place for a value parameter is comparable in efficiency to the passing of an address that occurs with a reference parameter. When we use objects that are larger in size, however, copying them consumes much more time. Templates make it simple to generate large and complex data structures—for example, we can instantiate either a list of large objects or a list of `int`s from the same implementation. As a result, we can create a template that is efficient for simple types, yet horribly slow for complex types. Even when the operations performed by the template on the complex types are fast, the cost of copying to value parameters dominates the processing time.

---

1. Once a template function is defined, an additional definition, called an explicit specialization, can be written that redefines the function for a specific type. This redefinition is preceded by `template<>`, and the heading of the function includes the type to appear in angle brackets following the function name. There is controversy in the C++ community about the use of explicit specializations, and their definition may change in a future version of the language. Thus we do not discuss them further here. Even so, you should be aware of the implications of seeing `template` followed by empty brackets, in case you encounter such code elsewhere.

What we need is a parameter-passing mechanism that is as efficient as pass by reference, but as safe as pass by value. C++ provides such a mechanism by allowing us to specify a reference parameter as being constant. It is, therefore, important that we bring the constant reference parameter mechanism to bear on our template function definitions. For example, the following code shows how we should implement the `GList` insert operation, with the changes highlighted:

```
template<class ItemType>
void GList<ItemType>::Insert(const ItemType& item)
{
  data[length] = item;
  length++;
}
```

All that we have to do to convert a value parameter to a constant reference is precede the type name with `const` and follow it with the `&` character. Is that the only difference? Are the value parameter and the constant reference equivalent? Definitely not! Within the function, the constant reference parameter really is a constant—you cannot assign a new value to it. This stands in contrast to the value parameter, which is a variable within the function. Because a value parameter contains a copy of its argument, we can assign a new value to it or modify its contents without affecting the argument.

Constant reference parameters cannot be changed in any way. In addition to the restriction that we cannot assign a new value to a constant reference, when the type of the parameter is a class, we are not allowed to apply its transformer (mutator) methods. We can call only observer functions for an object passed as a constant reference. Recall from Chapter 12 that we append `const` to the headings of functions that do not change the values within an object. When an object is passed to a constant reference parameter, those are the only functions the compiler permits us to call on that object. It issues an error message if we try to call any of the object's nonconstant functions.

Organization of Program Code

When working with template classes, we must change the ground rules regarding the file(s) into which we put the source code. Previously, we placed the class declaration into a header file called `list.h` and the member function definitions into an implementation file called `list.cpp`. As a result, `list.cpp` could be compiled into object code independently of any client code. This strategy won't work with templates. The compiler cannot instantiate a template unless it knows the argument to the template, and this argument is located in the client code. Different compilers have different mechanisms to solve this problem.

The C++ standard itself defines a solution in the form of a new keyword, `export`, that is used at the beginning of a template declaration to indicate that the compiler should encode additional information to allow clients to specialize the template without having access to the definition's source code. Unfortunately, `export` has been implemented in only a few compilers to date. For now, to keep code portable, we must resort to other means.

A general solution that works with any compiler is to compile the client code and the class definition at the same time. With our `GList` template, one technique is to dispense with an implementation file `glist.cpp`, and instead place the template class declarations and member function definitions in the same file, `glist.h`. Another technique is to retain two distinct files, `glist.h` and `glist.cpp`, but place the directive `#include "glist.cpp"` at the end of the file `glist.h`. Either way, the compiler has all the source code—both for the client code and for the class—available to it at once.

In the following code for the `GList` template, we use the first technique—namely, appending the implementation to the specification in a single file.

```cpp
//****************************************************************
// SPECIFICATION (glist.h)
// This is the specification of a generic List ADT.
// The list components are not assumed to be in order by value,
// the maximum length of the list is 100 components, and the
// components must be comparable with the relational operators.
//****************************************************************

const int MAX_LENGTH =100;      // Maximum number of components

template<class ItemType>         // Type of each component
class GList
{
public:
  GList();
  // Action responsibilities
  void Insert(const ItemType& item);
  void Delete(const ItemType& item);
  void ResetList();
  ItemType GetNextItem();
  // Knowledge responsibilities
  int GetLength() const;
  bool IsEmpty() const;
  bool IsFull() const;
  bool IsThere(const ItemType& item) const;
  bool HasNext() const;
private:
  int length;
  int currentPos;
  ItemType data[MAX_LENGTH];
};

//****************************************************************
// IMPLEMENTATION Code
// Following is the implementation of the GList member functions
// List representation: a one-dimensional array and a length
//   variable
//****************************************************************

#include <iostream>

using namespace std;

template<class ItemType>
GList<ItemType>::GList()      // Constructor
{
  length = 0;
  currentPos = 0;
}
```

```
//*****************************************************************

template<class ItemType>
bool GList<ItemType>::IsEmpty() const
{
  return (length == 0);
}

//*****************************************************************

template<class ItemType>
bool GList<ItemType>::IsFull() const
{
  return (length == MAX_LENGTH);
}

//*****************************************************************

template<class ItemType>
int GList<ItemType>::GetLength() const
{
  return length;
}

//*****************************************************************

template<class ItemType>
void GList<ItemType>::Insert(const ItemType& item)
{
  data[length] = item;
  length++;
}

//*****************************************************************

template<class ItemType>
void GList<ItemType>::Delete(const ItemType& item)
{
  int index = 0;

  while (index < length && item != data[index])
    index++;
  if (index < length)
  {
    data[index] = data[length-1];
    length--;
  }
}

//*****************************************************************
```

```
template<class ItemType>
bool GList<ItemType>::IsThere(const ItemType& item) const
{
  int index = 0;

  while (index < length && item != data[index])
    index++;
  return (index < length);
}
//*****************************************************************

template<class ItemType>
void GList<ItemType>::ResetList()
{
  currentPos = 0;
}
//*****************************************************************

template<class ItemType>
bool GList<ItemType>::HasNext() const
{
  return (currentPos != length);
}
//*****************************************************************

template<class ItemType>
ItemType GList<ItemType>::GetNextItem()
{
  ItemType item;
  item = data[currentPos];
  currentPos++;
  return item;
}
```

Here is the same driver program that we used to test the **List** class in Chapter 13. The changes necessary to run **GList** instead of **List** are shaded. (Yes, only two lines need to be changed.) Because the output is the same as in Chapter 13, we do not repeat it here.

```
//*****************************************************************
// This program inputs one month's temperature readings from a file,
// stores unique readings in a list, prints the list, removes a value
// of 200, and prints the resulting list.
//*****************************************************************
#include <fstream>      // For file I/O
#include "GList.h"      // For List class
#include <iostream>
using namespace std;
```

```cpp
int main()
{
  GList<int> temps;       // List of temperature readings
  int   oneTemp;          // One temperature reading
  ifstream inData;        // File of temperature readings
  ofstream outData;       // Output file

  inData.open("temps.dat");
  if (!inData)
  {
    outData << "Can't open file temps.dat" << endl;
    return 1;
  }

  outData.open("temps.ans");

  inData >> oneTemp;      // Get a temperature
  while (inData && !temps.IsFull())
  {
    if (!temps.IsThere(oneTemp))
       temps.Insert(oneTemp);
    inData >> oneTemp;
  }

  // Output original list
  // Set up for an iteration
  outData << "No. of unique readings: " << temps.GetLength() << endl;
  while (temps.HasNext())
  {
    oneTemp = temps.GetNextItem();
    outData << oneTemp << endl;
  }

  temps.Delete(200);      // Remove 200 if there; cannot be more than one
  temps.ResetList();
  outData << "Readings without value of 200. " << endl;

  while (temps.HasNext())
  {
    oneTemp = temps.GetNextItem();
    outData << oneTemp << endl;
  }

  inData.close();
  outData.close();
  return 0;
}
```

The file name in the `include` statement and the declaration of the list are the only changes. The declaration is the type name with the definition of `ItemType` in brackets next to it. For example,

```cpp
GList<int> temps;
```

declares a `GList` named `temps`, for which the items on the list are specialized to be `int`s. If we wanted the items on the list to be `float`s or `string`s, the following statements would declare them:

```
GList<float> listOfFloats;
GList<string> listOfStrings;
```

Although using templates allows us to create generic data types, as noted in the comments, our implementation of the `GList` operations requires the items on the list to be comparable using the relational operators. Thus we cannot define

```
GList<Name> listOfNames;
```

because class `Name` uses function `ComparedTo` rather than the relational operators. It is important to document any restrictions on the types that can be used to instantiate a generic class. In a later section, we discuss ways to redefine the relational operators so that they can be applied to a class such as `Name`.

Another aspect of our `GList` type that's not fully generic is that its size is fixed to 100 components. It would be useful if the client code could specify a value for `MAX_LENGTH` when instantiating `GList`. C++ provides another mechanism to enable this behavior.

In addition to listing type names in the template parameter list, C++ permits us to include non-type parameters there as well. We can use these parameters to initialize the specialization. Non-type template parameters are restricted to just a few types: `int`s, `enum`s, pointers, and references. In this book, we look only at the use of `int` non-type template parameters. Another restriction is that the value of an argument to such a parameter must be fixed at compile time. Thus, for example, we can't instantiate a template using an argument value that is input by the user at run time.

Here is how we can enable instantiation of any size of `GList`. In the template declaration and in each of the function templates, we change the heading to include an `int` parameter called `MAX_LENGTH`, as highlighted here:

```
template<class ItemType, const int MAX_LENGTH>
```

Here we have made the parameter a constant, and written the identifier in the style of a constant. We're not required to use `const`, but in this case we want to ensure that `MAX_LENGTH` is not allowed to change. In the temperatures program, we then change the instantiation of the `GList` class to the following:

```
GList<int, 100> temps;          // List of temperature readings
```

The result is identical to that produced by the earlier code. But now, if we discover that we are running out of space in the list, we can just change the instantiation in the client code as follows, rather than having to edit the declaration of `GList`:

```
GList<int, 275> temps;          // List of temperature readings
```

You are asked in the exercises to make these changes to the code and test them.

A Word of Caution

If you develop your programs using an integrated development environment (IDE) in which the editor, compiler, and linker are bundled into one application, you must be careful when using templates. With an IDE, you typically are asked to define a "project"—a list of the individual files that constitute a program. With Chapter 13's `List` class comprising two files (`list.h` and `list.cpp`) and your client code located in a file `myprog.cpp`, you would specify `myprog.cpp` and `list.cpp` in your project. The key idea is that these two files are compiled separately and then their object code files are linked (by the linker) to form an executable file.

With templates, this situation may change. We do not want to separately compile `myprog.cpp` and `glist.h` (or `glist.cpp` if we're using the second approach to organizing the code). The solution in this case is to specify only `myprog.cpp` in the project. Because `myprog.cpp` says to include `glist.h`, and `glist.h` either contains the implementation code or says to include `glist.cpp`, the compiler receives all of the source code to compile at once.

QUICK CHECK

16.1.1 What kind of ADT does a template enable us to write? (pp. 830–831)

16.1.2 In mathematics, an ordered pair is a pair of numbers written in the form (*a*, *b*). Rewrite the following `OrdPair` declaration as a class template so that clients can manipulate ordered pairs of any simple type, not just ordered pairs of `int`s. (pp. 831–832)

```
class OrdPair
{
public:
   int  First() const;         // Returns first component of the pair
   int  Second() const;        // Returns second component of the pair
   void Print() const;         // Outputs the pair
   OrdPair(int m, int n);      // Constructor; creates ordered pair (m,n)
private:
   int first;
   int second;
};
```

16.1.3 Given the `OrdPair` class template from Question 16.1.2, write client code that declares three class objects named `pair1`, `pair2`, and `pair3` that represent the ordered pairs (5, 6), (2.95, 6.34), and ('+', '#'), respectively, and prints the ordered pairs represented by `pair1`, `pair2`, and `pair3`. (pp. 832–834)

16.1.4 Given the `OrdPair` class template from Question 16.1.2, write function definitions for the member functions. (pp. 832–834)

16.1.5 What is a **generic data type**? (p. 831)

16.1.6 What is a **class template**? (p. 831)

16.1.7 What are the two limitations of the List ADT defined in Chapter 13 as discussed in this section? (pp. 830–831)

16.1.8 What is the concrete class known as once it is generated from a template class? (p. 833)

16.1.9 What mechanism is used in C++ to pass a reference parameter to a function that is as safe as passing a parameter by value? (p. 834)

16.2 Generic Functions

Sometimes when we are designing or testing software, we discover a need for a single algorithm that might be applied to objects of different data types at different times. We want to be able to describe this algorithm without having to specify the data types of the items being manipulated. Such an algorithm is often referred to as a **generic algorithm**. C++ supports generic algorithms by providing two mechanisms: *function overloading* and *template functions*.

> **Generic algorithm** An algorithm in which the actions or steps are defined but the data types of the items being manipulated are not.
>
> **Function overloading** The use of the same name for different functions, distinguished from each other by their parameter lists.

Function Overloading

Function overloading is the use of the same name for different functions, as long as their parameter types are sufficiently different for the compiler to tell them apart. To see how it works, let's look at an example.

Suppose we are debugging a program and want to trace its execution by printing the values of certain variables as the program executes. The variables we want to trace are of the following six data types: `int`, `char`, `float`, `double`, `short`, and `long`. We could create six functions with different names, such as `PrintInt`, `PrintFloat`, and so on, to output values of different types. Instead of forcing us to invent different names for these similar functions, however, C++ lets us use function overloading to call them by the same name—`Print`:

```
void Print(int number)
{
  cout << "***Debug" << endl;
  cout << "Value is " << number << endl;
}
void Print(char character)
{
  cout << "***Debug" << endl;
  cout << "Value is " << character << endl;
}
void Print(float realValue)
{
  ⋮
}
void Print(double doubleValue)
{
  ⋮
}
  ⋮    // Etc.
```

The calls to these functions look like this:

```
Print(someInt);
Print(someFloat);
Print(someDouble);
```

We can think of `Print` as a generic algorithm in the sense that the algorithm itself—printing the string "`***Debug`" and then the value of a variable—is independent of the data type of the variable being printed. As we program, we have to use only one name for this algorithm (`Print`), even though there are really six distinct functions.

How does function overloading work? When the compiler encounters the function call

```
Print(someVar);
```

it compares the type of the actual argument with the types of the formal parameters of the six functions. If `someVar` is of type `int`, then the compiler generates code to call the `Print` function that has an `int` parameter. If `someVar` is of type `float`, then the compiler generates code to call the `Print` function that has a `float` parameter, and so forth.

As you can see, function overloading benefits the programmer by eliminating the need to come up with different names for functions that perform identical tasks on arguments of different data types. Despite the benefits of function overloading, in our `Print` function example we still had to supply six distinct function definitions. This entails a tedious amount of copy-and-paste work in an editor, and the resulting code is cluttered with nearly identical function definitions.

Defining a Function Template Outside a Class

A cleaner way to solve this problem is to use template functions. We have already seen that this approach offers a way to implement the member functions of a template class. However, C++ doesn't restrict template functions to classes. They can be defined anywhere that we can define a normal function. Here we'll use the alternate keyword, `typename`, just to emphasize that `Print` doesn't have to be part of a class.

```cpp
template<typename SomeType>
void Print(SomeType val)
{
    cout << "***Debug" << endl;
    cout << "Value is " << val << endl;
}
```

Instantiating a Function Template

Given this `Print` function template, we can make function calls as follows:

```cpp
Print<int>(sum);
Print<char>(initial);
Print<float>(angle);
```

In this code, the type name enclosed in angle brackets is the *template argument*. At compile time, the compiler generates (*instantiates*) three different functions, each of which is specialized for the particular template argument.

When the compiler instantiates a template, it literally substitutes the template argument for the template parameter throughout the function template, just as you would do with a search-and-replace operation in a word processor. For example, the first time the compiler encounters `Print<float>` in the calling code, it generates a new function by substituting `float` for every occurrence of `SomeType` in the function template:

```
                               float
                                 ↑
void Print(SomeType val)
{
  cout << "***Debug" << endl;
  cout << "Value is " << val << endl;
}
```

Here is the syntax template for a call to a template function:

TemplateFunctionCall

FunctionName **< TemplateArgList >** (FunctionArgList)

As you can see, the template argument list in angle brackets is optional. In fact, most programmers omit it. In that case, the compiler is said to deduce the template argument(s) by examining the function argument list.

For example, our earlier example of calling code using explicit template arguments would more likely be written as follows:

```
Print(sum);        // Implicit: Print<int>(sum)
Print(initial);    // Implicit: Print<char>(initial)
Print(angle);      // Implicit: Print<float>(angle)
```

In this code, when the compiler encounters `Print(sum)`, it looks at the data type of the function argument `sum` (which is `int`) and deduces that the template argument must be `int`. Therefore, the function call is to the `Print<int>` specialization of the template.

In some situations, however, the compiler cannot deduce the proper specialization of a function. For example, if the parameter is an object of a polymorphic class, the compiler doesn't know which subclass will be passed to the function at run time. Keep in mind that the compiler must be able to do all of the work to instantiate a generic function at compile time. If it can't deduce the specialization from the code, you must specify the type explicitly.

QUICK CHECK

16.2.1 Write a function template for a value-returning function **Thrice** that receives a parameter of any simple type and returns three times that value. (p. 843)

16.2.2 Write calling code that calls **Thrice** (from Question 16.2.1) two times, once with an integer argument and once with a floating-point argument. (pp. 843–844)

16.2.3 What is a **generic algorithm**? (p. 842)

16.2.4 What is **function overloading**? (p. 842)

16.2.5 How does function overloading benefit the programmer? (p. 843)

16.2.6 How can function overloading be improved when the function body performs the same operations over many types? (p. 843)

16.3 Operator Overloading

In Chapter 14, we created a sorted linked list that contained items of class `Entry`. To accomplish this task, we had to rewrite the list algorithms using function `ComparedTo` rather than the relational operators. We can avoid that step by using another advanced feature of C++: operator overloading.

Here is the `Date` class from the last chapter enhanced with functions that overload the relational operators <, >, and ==. The function prototypes are shaded.

```
//*****************************************
// SPECIFICATION File for a Date ADT
//*****************************************

class Date
{
public:
  Date();
  Date(int initMonth, int initDay, int initYear);
  // Knowledge responsibilities
  int GetMonth() const;
  int GetDay() const;
  int GetYear() const;
  bool operator<(const Date& otherDate) const;
  bool operator>(const Date& otherDate) const;
  bool operator==(const Date& otherDate) const;

private:
  int month;
  int day;
  int year;
};
```

The syntax for overloading a symbol is the word **operator** followed by the symbol to be overloaded. When we use these operators, they each have two operands, yet only one parameter is shown in the parameter list. Where is the other operand? The first operand is the object to which the operator is applied and the second operand is the parameter. Such functions are known in C++ as *operator functions*. Here are their implementations:

```
bool Date::operator<(const Date& otherDate) const
{
  if (year < otherDate.year)
    return true;
  else if (year > otherDate.year)
    return false;
  else if (month < otherDate.month)
    return true;
```

```cpp
    else if (month > otherDate.month)
      return false;
    else if (day < otherDate.day)
      return true;
    else return false;
}

//******************************************
bool Date::operator>(const Date& otherDate) const
{
  if (year > otherDate.year)
    return true;
  else if (year < otherDate.year)
    return false;
  else if (month > otherDate.month)
    return true;
  else if (month < otherDate.month)
    return false;
  else if (day > otherDate.day)
    return true;
  else return false;
}

//******************************************
bool Date::operator==(const Date& otherDate) const
{
  return (month==otherDate.month) && (day==otherDate.day)
         && (year==otherDate.year);
}
```

Here is a test driver to show how we use these functions. In the exercises, you are asked to build a test plan for class **Date** and to overload the remaining relational operators.

```cpp
//******************************************
// This is a test driver for class Date
//******************************************
#include <iostream>
#include "Date.h"
using namespace std;

int main ()
{
  Date date1(1, 1, 2008);
  Date date2(2, 2, 2007);
  if (date1 > date2)
    cout << "date1 is greater than date2" << endl;
  if (date2 < date1)
    cout << "date2 is less than date1" << endl;
  if (date1 == date1)
    cout << "date1 is equal to date1" << endl;
  return 0 ;
}
```

Output:

```
date1 is greater than date2
date2 is less than date1
date1 is equal to date1
```

As you can see, objects of class `Date` can now be compared using the relational operators <, >, and ==. In these examples, the operand to the left of the operator is passed as the argument to the first operand in the function; that is, it is the object to which the function is applied. The operand to the right of the operator is passed as the argument to the parameter in the function's parameter list.

Here are some guidelines for overloading operators:

1. All C++ operators may be overloaded except ::, ., `sizeof`, and ?:.
2. One operand of the overloaded operator must be a class instance.
3. You cannot change the standard order of operator precedence, define new operator symbols, change the number of operands of an operator, or change an operator's associativity.
4. Overloading unary operators: If `data` is of type `SomeClass`, and you want to overload, say, the unary minus operator, then you would write the operator function heading as `data.operator-()`. The empty parameter list tells the compiler that you mean the unary version of the minus operator. When you invoke the overloaded unary minus, the operand to the right of the operator is the object to which the function is applied.[2]
5. Overloading binary operators: If `data` is of type `SomeClass` and you have overloaded, say, the addition operator (+) in class `SomeClass`, then `data + otherData` is equivalent to `data.operator+(otherData)`.

As we noted in Guideline 1, all but a few of the C++ operators can be overloaded, including assignment, array indexing, function calls, pointer dereferencing, and the stream (shift) operators. You should consult a C++ reference before attempting to overload (), [], ->, <<, and >>, as some additional considerations arise with these operators that we do not cover here.

Using *this

In the preceding example, the > function is basically identical to the < function except that we used the > relational operator in all of the If statements. Once < has been defined for `Date`, it would be nice if we could avoid checking every member of a `Date`, and just write the body of the > function as follows:

`return otherDate < thisDate;   // Would be nice, but doesn't work`

The problem with this statement is that `thisDate` isn't defined anywhere. How can we refer to a whole object from within itself? C++ solves this problem by providing a reserved

---

[2]. For the increment and decrement operators, this syntax overloads their prefix (e.g., ++x) forms. Early C++ compilers did not allow overloading of the postfix (i.e., x++) forms of ++ and --. Newer compilers, however, support a heading of the form `data.operator++(int dummy)`. Nothing is actually passed to the parameter `dummy`, and it automatically has the value 0. The name of the parameter doesn't have to be `dummy`; any identifier will work. The presence of this unused `int` parameter is just a syntactic trick to signal to the compiler that the function should be applied to the object to the left of the operator.

word, `this`, that represents a pointer to the current object. To access the object, we have to dereference `this` with the `*` operator. The `>` function can then be rewritten as follows:

```
bool Date::operator>(const Date& otherDate) const
{
  return otherDate < *this;    // Compares parameter with current object
}
```

Operator overloading is a very powerful feature of C++ that can make a user-defined type look nearly identical to a built-in type in terms of how it can be used in expressions and I/O. Some debate has arisen within the programming languages community about the desirability of operator overloading (the designers of Java, for example, deliberately omitted the capability from that language). Within a particular context, such as creating a matrix algebra package for scientific computing, the effect can enable programmers to express algorithms in very natural and compact syntax. However, heavy use of operator overloading can also lead to confusing code where it appears that expressions are manipulating built-in types when they are actually operating on user-defined types. For this reason, careful documentation and use of explanatory comments is an important adjunct to operator overloading.

> **QUICK CHECK**
>
> **16.3.1** Write a function heading for an operator function that overloads the less than operator (<). (pp. 845–847)
> **16.3.2** What is a benefit of using operator overloading? (p. 848)
> **16.3.3** What is a drawback of using operator overloading? (p. 848)

16.4 Exceptions

Suppose we're writing a program in which we frequently need to divide two integers and obtain the quotient. In every case, we need to check for division by 0, so we write a function named `Quotient` that returns the quotient of any two integers unless the denominator is 0:

```
int Quotient(int numer, int denom)
{
  if (denom != 0)
    return numer / denom;
  else
    // What to do?
}
```

We are faced with a problem: What should this function *do* if the denominator is 0? This is not an easy question to answer. Here are some possibilities, none of which is entirely satisfactory:

1. Don't perform the division, and silently return to the calling code.
2. Print an error message and return an arbitrary integer value.
3. Return a special value such as −9999 to the caller as a signal that something went wrong.
4. Rewrite the function with a third parameter, a Boolean flag indicating success or failure.
5. Print an error message and halt the program.

Choice 1 is clearly irresponsible. Choice 2 might help the human running the program by displaying an error message, but will not notify the calling code that anything went wrong. Choice 3 might be acceptable in some circumstances, but in general is not a good solution. If the numerator and the denominator are allowed to be any integers, then −9999 is a perfectly valid quotient and cannot be distinguished from a special signal value. Choice 4 is a reasonable approach and is used quite often by programmers. Its disadvantage in our case is that we should change our value-returning function (which returns just one value) into a void function so that two values can be returned through the parameter list as reference parameters: the quotient and the Boolean flag. Choice 5 is almost never satisfactory. The calling code—not the called function—should be allowed to decide what to do in case of an error. Perhaps the caller would like to take steps to recover from the error and keep executing the program rather than terminating it.

One way out of our dilemma is to eliminate the dilemma! Use a function precondition as follows:

```
int Quotient(int numer, int denom)
// Pre: denom is not zero
// Post: Return value is numer / denom
{
   return numer / denom;
}
```

Here, the caller must ensure that the precondition is true before calling the function; as a consequence, the function does not have to do any error detection. Instead, with this approach, the caller is responsible for both error detection and error handling. Throughout this book, we have used this strategy of using preconditions to eliminate error detection from called functions. In some situations, however, errors can be detected only *after* an action has been attempted, not before.

For example, a function `ReadInt` that is supposed to read an integer value from the keyboard may find that the user has erroneously typed some letters of the alphabet (in which case the input variable is not changed, and the `cin` stream goes into the fail state). In this case, we cannot state a precondition for `ReadInt` that "The next input value is a valid integer" because there is no way for the caller of `ReadInt` to predict what the human at the keyboard will type. To deal with errors of this kind (and for programmers who prefer not to use the precondition approach), the C++ language provides an *exception-handling* mechanism.

In the world of software, an exception is an unusual event, often an error, that requires special processing. A section of program code that provides the necessary special processing is called an exception handler. When a section of code announces that an exception has occurred, it is said to throw (or raise) an exception, hoping that another section of code (the exception handler) will catch the exception and process it. If no exception handler exists for that particular exception, the entire program terminates with an error message.

> **Exception** An unusual, often unpredictable event, detectable by software or hardware, that requires special processing; also, in C++, a variable or class object that represents an exceptional event.
>
> **Exception handler** A section of program code that is executed when a particular exception occurs.
>
> **Throw (raise)** To signal the fact that an exception has occurred.
>
> **Catch** To process a thrown exception. (The catching is performed by an exception handler.)

Let's look now at the mechanisms C++ provides for throwing and catching exceptions.

The `throw` Statement

In C++, the term "exception" not only has the general meaning of an unusual event, but also has a more specific meaning: a variable or class object that represents such an event.

To throw (raise) an exception, the programmer uses a **throw** statement, whose syntax is as follows:

ThrowStatement

```
throw Expression ;
```

In the **throw** statement, Expression can be a value or a variable of any data type, either built in or user defined. Let's look at three examples of **throw** statements.

Here is Example 1:

```
throw 5;
```

In this example, we throw an exception of type **int** with the expectation that one or more exception handlers wants to catch an exception of type **int** (we see how this is done in the next section).

In Example 2, we throw an exception of type **string**, the standard library class:

```
string str = "Invalid customer age";
throw str;
```

Example 3 throws an exception of a class type that we define ourselves:

```
class SalaryError
{};              // Member list is empty
    ⋮
SalaryError sal;
throw sal;
```

In Example 3, observe how we first declare a class object named **sal** and then throw that object.

More commonly, C++ programmers do the following:

```
class SalaryError
{};              // Member list is empty
    ⋮
throw SalaryError();
```

In this code, the **throw** statement creates an anonymous (unnamed) object of type **SalaryError** by explicitly calling its default constructor (signified by the empty argument list) and then passes this anonymous object to an exception handler. It would be a syntax error to leave off the parentheses:

```
throw SalaryError;    // Invalid
```

The reason is that the syntax for the **throw** statement requires an expression, not the name of a data type.

Finally, notice in the syntax template that Expression is optional. We discuss later what happens if the **throw** expression is absent.

The try-catch Statement

If one part of a program throws an exception, how does another part of the program catch the exception and process it? The answer is by using a **try-catch** statement, which has the following form:

TryCatchStatement

```
try
   Block
catch ( FormalParameter )
   Block
catch ( FormalParameter )
   Block
      :
```

The syntax of FormalParameter is as follows:

FormalParameter

```
{ DataType VariableName
  ...
```

(In the latter syntax template, the three dots are literally three periods that are typed into the program.)

As the first syntax template shows, the **try-catch** statement consists of a try-clause followed by one or more catch-clauses. The try-clause consists of the reserved word **try** and a block (a pair of brackets { } enclosing any number of statements). Each catch-clause consists of the reserved word **catch**, a single parameter declaration enclosed in parentheses, and a block. Each catch-clause is, in fact, an exception handler.

When a statement or group of statements in a program might result in an exception, we enclose them in a try-clause. For each type of exception that can be produced by the statements, we write a catch-clause (exception handler). Here is an example of a **try-catch** statement involving the three types of exceptions (**int**, **string**, and **SalaryError**) discussed previously with the **throw** statement:

```
try
{
    :      // Statements that process personnel data and may throw
           // exceptions of type int, string, and SalaryError
}
catch(int)
{
    :      // Statements to handle an int exception
}
catch(string s)
{
  cout << s << endl;   // Prints "Invalid customer age"
    :      // More statements to handle a string exception
}
```

```
catch(SalaryError)
{
    ⋮      // Statements to handle a salary error
}
```

The `try-catch` statement is meant to sound like a coach telling a gymnast, "Go ahead and try this flip; I'll catch you if you fall." In our case, we tell the computer to try executing some operations that might fail, and then we provide code to catch the potential exceptions.

Execution of `try-catch`

Execution of the preceding `try-catch` statement works as follows. If none of the statements in the try-clause throws an exception, control transfers to the statement following the entire `try-catch` statement. That is, we try some statements, and if everything goes according to plan, we just continue with the succeeding statements. However, if an exception is thrown by a statement in the try-clause, control immediately transfers to the appropriate exception handler (catch-clause). Note that control jumps directly from whatever statement caused the exception to the exception handler. If there are statements in the try-clause following the one that caused the exception, they are skipped. When control reaches the exception handler, statements to deal with the exception are executed. If these statements do not cause any new exceptions and do not transfer control elsewhere (as with a return statement), then control passes to the next statement following the entire `try-catch` structure.

Formal Parameters in Exception Handlers

When an exception is thrown, how does the computer know which of several exception handlers is appropriate? It looks at the data type of the formal parameter declared in each handler and selects the first one whose data type matches that of the thrown exception. A formal parameter consisting solely of an ellipsis (three dots or periods), as shown earlier in the syntax template for FormalParameter, is a "wild card"—it matches any exception type. Because the computer searches the exception handlers for a matching parameter in sequential or "north to south" order, a final exception handler with an ellipsis parameter serves as a "catch-all" handler for any exception whose type hasn't been listed:

```
try
{
    ⋮      // Statements that may throw an exception
}
catch(Type1)
{
    ⋮      // Handle a Type1 exception
}
catch(Type2)
{
    ⋮      // Handle a Type2 exception
}
catch(...)                     // Catch-all handler
{
  cout << "Panic! Unexpected exception." << endl;
    ⋮      // Statements to deal with this situation
}
```

Note that the "north to south" search for a matching parameter type requires us to place the catch-all handler last. If we placed it first in the structure, it would trap *every* exception, and the remaining handlers would be ignored.

Another issue related to formal parameters in exception handlers is this: Should the parameter declaration include a name for the parameter? (If you look at the syntax template for FormalParameter, you'll see that the parameter's data type is required but its name is optional.) In fact, the parameter's name is needed only if statements in the body of the exception handler use that variable. In our earlier example of catching `int`, `string`, and `SalaryError` exceptions, the parameter lists for the first and third exception handlers contain data type names only. In contrast, the parameter list for the second handler specifies `string s` because the body of that handler uses the statement

```cpp
cout << s << endl;    // Prints "Invalid customer age"
```

to print the message contained in `s`.

Finally, we must address a very important issue in the programming of exceptions: the data types of the exceptions themselves. In our `int`, `string`, and `SalaryError` example, we used all three exception types simply to demonstrate the possibilities for the programmer and to show how exception handlers are written to catch exceptions of these types. In practice, exceptions of built-in types (`int`, `float`, and so on) and even of class `string` have limited usefulness. If a try-clause throws several exceptions of type `int` with different integer values, then an exception handler receiving an `int` value becomes complicated. It must include logic that tests the integer to determine exactly which kind of error occurred. Furthermore, statements such as

```cpp
throw 23;
```

are much less readable and self-documenting than statements such as

```cpp
throw SalaryError();
```

Consequently, it is a better idea to use only user-defined classes (or structs) as exception types, defining one type for each kind of exception and using descriptive identifiers:

```cpp
class SalaryError     // Exception class
{};
class BadRange        // Exception class
{};
    ⋮
if (condition)
  throw SalaryError();
    ⋮
if (condition)
  throw BadRange();
```

With all of our example exception handlers, the parameter has been passed by value. This approach is sufficient for any of the standard types, and for the simple user-defined exception types that we use in this text. However, it is possible to develop exception classes that are quite complex, passing a considerable amount of information to a handler. These

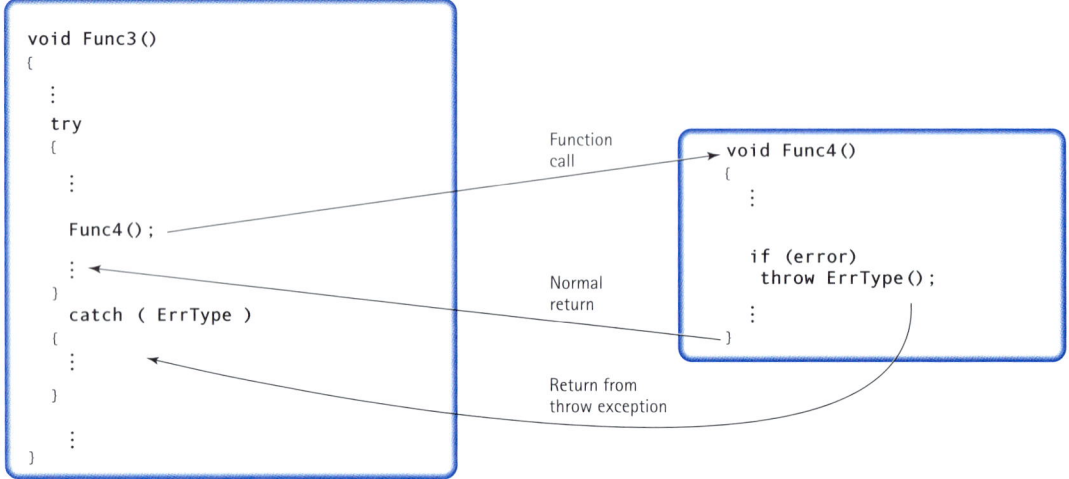

FIGURE 16.1 Throwing an Exception to Be Caught by the Calling Code

classes may also be part of an entire class hierarchy. In such cases, passing by reference will be more efficient, and will also avoid the slicing problems that can occur when a subclass of an exception is passed up to a level where only a parent class is defined.[3]

Nonlocal Exception Handlers

In our discussion so far, we have assumed that a `throw` statement is physically located within the `try-catch` statement that is intended to catch the exception. In that case, if the exception is thrown, control transfers to the catch-clause with the corresponding data type.

In C++ programs, it is actually more common for the `throw` to occur inside a function that is called from within a try-clause, as shown with functions `Func3` and `Func4` in **FIGURE 16.1**. At run time, the computer first looks for a `catch` within `Func4`. When it fails to find one, it causes `Func4` to return immediately and pass the exception back to its caller, `Func3`. The computer then looks around the point where `Func4` was called, finds an appropriate catch-clause, and executes the `catch`. As you can see in Figure 16.1, the exception was thrown in `Func4`, but the exception handler is nonlocal (it is found in the calling function, `Func3`).

Suppose that there was no matching catch-clause in `Func3` in Figure 16.1. Then `Func3` would return immediately and pass the exception back to its caller, perhaps `Func2`. This process is like the child's game of "Hot Potato." Each function that doesn't know how to deal with the problem passes the potato (the exception) back to the previous function. This sequence of returns continues working its way back through the chain of function calls until either a matching exception handler is found or control reaches `main`. If `main` fails to catch the exception (a situation known as an uncaught exception), the system terminates the program and displays a relatively unhelpful message like "Abnormal program termination." **FIGURE 16.2** illustrates this process.

---

3. Hierarchies of exception classes also affect how we order catch clauses. An exception superclass in a catch-clause matches any of its subclasses as well as itself. Thus, when a `try-catch` is used to catch exceptions at different levels of an exception class hierarchy, the catch-clauses should be ordered so that the lowest-level subclasses come first, and the top-level class comes last.

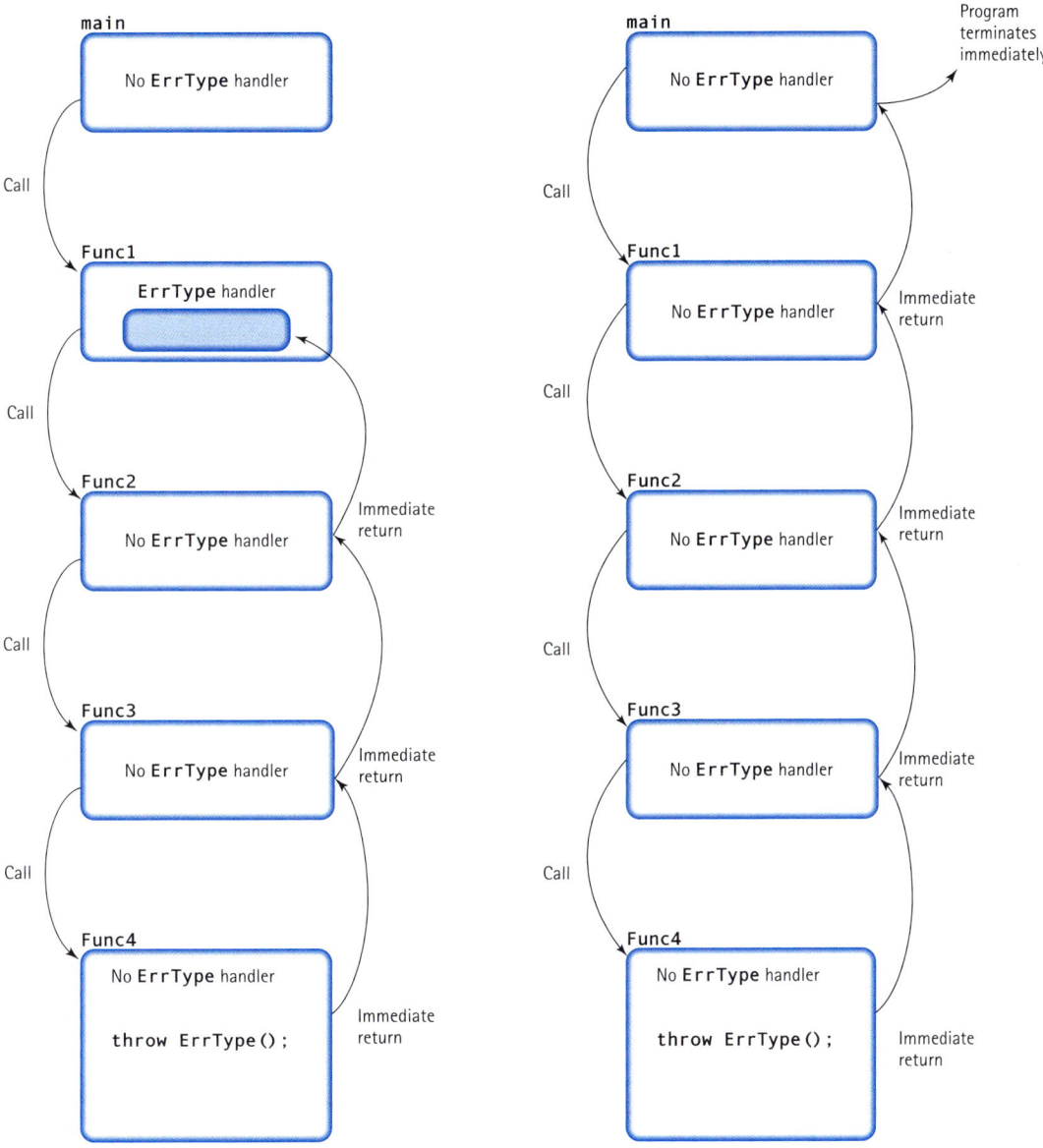

FIGURE 16.2 Exception Handling Over Multiple Levels of Function Calls

Even if a **throw** statement is physically present in the try-clause of a **try-catch**, if there is no matching exception handler in that **try-catch** statement, the result is the same as we have just described—namely, the enclosing function returns immediately and passes the exception back up the calling chain.

You may wonder why C++ programs typically use nonlocal exception handlers. The reason lies at the very heart of exception handling, no matter which programming language is used. The fundamental purpose of exceptions is to allow one part of a program to report an error to another part of the program if the error cannot be handled locally. When one function calls another function, the two generally exhibit a master–slave relationship. The master (the calling function) tells the slave (the called function) to do something for it. If the slave encounters an exceptional situation, it may not have enough information about the "outside world" to know how to recover from the error. As a consequence, the slave gives up and simply reports the error to the master by throwing an exception. If the master knows how to recover from the error, it catches the exception with an exception handler; otherwise, it passes the exception back to its own master, and so on. Often, the exception must be passed all the way back to `main` before a decision can be made as to whether to terminate the program or to recover from the error and continue executing.

Rethrowing an Exception

We have been using `throw` statements of the following form:

```
throw SalaryError();
```

The syntax template for the `throw` statement, presented earlier in this chapter, shows that we use the word `throw`, followed optionally by an expression. Therefore, the `throw` expression may be omitted, as in

```
throw;
```

This statement is used within an exception handler that has caught an exception and performed some actions, and then wishes to pass the exception along to its caller (rethrow the exception) for further processing. Here is an example:

```
void WriteToFile( parameters )
{
  ⋮    // Open a file for output
  try
  {
    while (condition)
    {
      DoSomething(arguments);   // May throw a BadData exception
        ⋮                       // Write to output file
    }
  }
  catch ( BadData )
  {
    ⋮        // Write message to output file and close it
    throw;   // Rethrow the exception
  }
  ⋮          // Continue processing and close the output file
}
```

Rethrowing an exception is C++'s way of allowing partial exception handling. In the preceding code, the catch-clause handles the `BadData` exception partially (by writing an error message to the file and closing it) and then returns, rethrowing the exception up the chain of function calls until it is caught.

What would happen in this code if we deleted the `throw` statement? What would happen if we changed `throw` to `return`? An Exam Preparation exercise at the end of this chapter asks you to consider these questions.

Standard Exceptions

Not all exceptions are defined by you as a C++ programmer. Several exception classes are predefined in the C++ standard library and are thrown either by C++ operations or by code that is supplied in standard library routines.

Exceptions Thrown by the Language

Certain C++ operations throw exceptions if errors occur during their execution. These operations are `new`, `dynamic_cast`, `typeid`, and something called an exception specification. The last three are not covered in this book; instead, we discuss only the `new` operator here. If you did not read the coverage of dynamic allocation of data in Chapter 14, you may want to skip this discussion.

In Chapter 14, we said that the `new` operator obtains a chunk of memory from the free store (heap) and returns a pointer to (the address of) the beginning of that chunk. For example, the code

```
int* intPtr;
intPtr = new int[1000];
```

creates a 1000-element `int` array on the free store and assigns the base address of the array to `intPtr`. We also said that if the system has run out of space on the free store, execution of `new` causes the program to terminate with an error message. Now that we know about exceptions, we can describe more completely what happens. If the `new` operator finds that the free store is exhausted, it throws an exception of type `bad_alloc`, a C++ class that is predefined in the standard library. If this exception is not caught by any exception handler, then—as with any uncaught exception—the program halts with a generic message such as "Abnormal program termination." Alternatively, our program could catch the exception and take some corrective action (or at least display a more specific error message). For example, we might write the following code in our `main` function:

```
float* arr;
try
{
  arr = new float[50000];
}
catch(bad_alloc)
{
  cout << "*** Out of memory. Can't allocate array." << endl;
  return 1;      // Terminate the program
}
  // Continue. Allocation succeeded
```

Notice the return statement in this exception handler. This statement will terminate the program only if it is in the `main` function. If we want the preceding code to be located in some other function, we must change the return statement to something else. For example, we could rethrow the `bad_alloc` exception to a higher-level function or throw a new exception (naming it, say, `OutOfMem`) for a higher-level function to catch.

Exceptions Thrown by Standard Library Routines

The C++ standard library is really two libraries: facilities inherited from the C language (called the C library) and facilities designed specifically for C++. In general, header files beginning with the letter "c"—`cmath` and `cctype`, for example—are found in the C library, and other header files are specific to C++. The C library doesn't throw exceptions. Instead, it uses a global integer `errno` that is a nonzero value after an error occurs in a library routine.

If you want to check for an error, set `errno` to 0, call the library routine, and then check if `errno` is nonzero. One option at that point is to throw your own exception.

The portion of the library that is specific to C++ defines exception classes and throws exceptions. For example, the exception classes include `out_of_range` and `length_error`, both of which can be thrown when working with strings. Let's see how we might work with these exceptions.

In Chapter 3, we examined the substring function: `str.substr(pos, len)`. We said then that if `pos` is too large, the program terminates with an error message. What really happens is that an `out_of_range` exception is thrown; if it isn't caught, the program terminates with an error message. The `length_error` exception is thrown if you try to construct a string whose length is greater than `string::npos`. Now we know enough to catch these exceptions and handle them:

```
void SomeFunc(parameters)
{
    ⋮
  string s1, s2;
  try
  {
    s2 = s1.substr(pos, len);   // May throw out_of_range()
    s1 = s1 + s1 + s2;          // May throw length_error()
  }
  catch(out_of_range)
  {
    cout << "Exception: out_of_range in SomeFunc" << endl;
    ⋮
  }
  catch (length_error)
  {
    cout << "Exception: length_error in SomeFunc" << endl;
    ⋮
  }
    ⋮   // Continue if no errors
}
```

Both of these exceptions are defined in the header file `<stdexcept>`, which must be included in a program that uses them.

We've looked at just two library exception classes to give you a sense of how they work. A full description of the C++ library could fill a book by itself, so we do not cover the others here. You will want to check for information about exceptions in the library documentation as you expand your use of its capabilities.

QUICK CHECK

16.4.1 What is an exception? (pp. 848–849)

16.4.2 **a.** Write the declaration of a user-defined exception type named **BadData**. (pp. 849–850)

   b. Write a void function **GetAge** that prompts for and inputs the user's age (type **int**) from the keyboard. The function returns the user's age through the parameter list unless the input value is a negative number, in which case a **BadData** exception is thrown. (pp. 849–850)

16.4.3 Write a **try-catch** statement that calls the **GetAge** function of Question 16.4.2b. If a **BadData** exception is thrown, print an error message and rethrow the exception to a caller; otherwise, execution should just continue. (pp. 851–852)

16.4 Exceptions

QUICK CHECK

16.4.4 When are preconditions not enough to deal with an erroneous argument to a function? (p. 849)
16.4.5 What is an exception handler? (p. 849)
16.4.6 What statement is used in a section of code to announce that an exceptional condition occurred? (p. 849)
16.4.7 What is the formal parameter and how is it used in an exception handler declaration? (p. 851)

SOFTWARE MAINTENANCE CASE STUDY: Adding Exceptions to the Date Class

When we were designing our **Date** class, we said that the year must start with the year 1582 or the date would be incorrect. Let's redesign the **Date** class to check its input parameters for the parameterized constructor and throw exceptions if the input values are not within proper ranges.

There are three possible errors: The month is not between 1 and 12, the day is not within the day-range of the month, and the year is before 1582. We will create an exception class for each possibility. Let's call them **MonthError**, **DayError**, and **YearError**:

```
class MonthError
{};
class DayError
{};
class YearError
{};
```

Within the code of the parameterized constructor, we must recognize and throw the appropriate error. It is easy to recognize a month error and a year error, but how do we recognize if a day is not within the month's bounds? We could write a complicated If statement built on the little rhyme "Thirty days hast September, April, June, and November . . ."—but there is a simpler way if we are willing to give up a little memory space. We can define an array of 12 values, each of which represents the days in the months for that index. How do we handle a leap year? We can use the function we wrote in Chapter 1 to test for a leap year.

Here is class **Date** that includes the exception handling. The code related to the exceptions is shaded.

```
//*****************************************
// SPECIFICATION File for a Date ADT
//*****************************************
// Exception classes
class MonthError
{};
class DayError
{};
class YearError
{};

class Date
{
public:
  Date();
```

SOFTWARE MAINTENANCE CASE STUDY: Adding Exceptions to the `Date` Class

```cpp
  Date(int initMonth, int initDay, int initYear);
  // Knowledge responsibilities
  int GetMonth() const;
  int GetDay() const;
  int GetYear() const;
  bool operator<(const Date& otherDate) const;
  bool operator>(const Date& otherDate) const;
  bool operator==(const Date& otherDate) const;
private:
  int month;
  int day;
  int year;
};


//******************************************
// IMPLEMENTATION File for a Date ADT
// Month, day, and year are kept as integers
//******************************************
#include <iostream>
#include "Date.h"

bool IsLeapYear(int year);
using namespace std;
Date::Date()
{
  month = 1;
  day = 1;
  year = 1582;
}

//******************************************

Date::Date(int initMonth, int initDay, int initYear)
{
  static int daysInMonth[12] =
    {31, 29, 31, 30, 31, 30, 31, 31, 30, 31, 30, 31};
  if (initMonth <= 0 || initMonth > 12)
    throw MonthError
  month = initMonth;
  if (month == 2 && initDay == 29 && !IsLeapYear(initYear))
    throw DayError();
  if (initDay <= 0 || initDay > daysInMonth[initMonth-1])
    throw DayError();
  day = initDay;
  if (initYear < 1582)
    throw YearError();
  year = initYear;
}
}

//******************************************
```

SOFTWARE MAINTENANCE CASE STUDY: Adding Exceptions to the `Date` Class

```cpp
int Date::GetMonth() const
{ return month; }

//******************************************

int Date::GetDay() const
{ return day; }

//******************************************

int Date::GetYear() const
{ return year; }

//******************************************

bool Date::operator<(const Date& otherDate) const
{
  if (year < otherDate.year)
    return true;
  else if (year > otherDate.year)
    return false;
  else if (month < otherDate.month)
    return true;
  else if (month > otherDate.month)
    return false;
  else if (day < otherDate.day)
    return true;
  else return false;
}

//******************************************

bool Date::operator>(const Date& otherDate) const
{
  return otherDate < *this;
}

//******************************************

bool Date::operator==(const Date& otherDate) const
{
  return (month==otherDate.month) && (day==otherDate.day)
         && (year==otherDate.year);
}

//******************************************

bool IsLeapYear(int year)
// IsLeapYear returns true if year is a leap year and
// false otherwise
```

SOFTWARE MAINTENANCE CASE STUDY: Adding Exceptions to the `Date` Class

```
{
  if (year % 4 != 0)      // Is year not divisible by 4?
    return false;         // If so, can't be a leap year
                          // Must be divisible by 4 at this point
  if (year % 100 != 0)    // Is year not a multiple of 100?
    return true;          // If so, is a leap year
                          // Must be divisible by 100 at this point
  if (year % 400 != 0)    // Is year not a multiple of 400?
    return false;         // If so, then is not a leap year
                          // Must be divisible by 400 at this point
  return true;            // Is a leap year
}
```

To test this enhanced class, we must try to instantiate an object of class **Date** with values that are within the range and values that are not correct. Here is a test plan that covers the possible errors:

Reason for Test Case	Input Values	Expected Output	Observed Output
Month error	13, 1, 2009	Attempt to create date with invalid month.	
Month error	0, 1, 2009	Attempt to create date with invalid month.	
Day error	1, 0, 2010	Attempt to create date with invalid day.	
Day error	2, 29, 2007	Attempt to create date with invalid day.	
Valid date	2, 29, 2008	Valid date.	
Day error	2, 30, 2010	Attempt to create date with invalid day.	
Day error	4, 31, 1945	Attempt to create date with invalid day.	
Day error	6, 31, 2000	Attempt to create date with invalid day.	
Day error	9, 31, 2000	Attempt to create date with invalid day.	
Day error	11, 31, 2012	Attempt to create date with invalid day.	
Year error	1, 30, 1066	Attempt to create date with invalid year.	
Valid date	12, 25, 2010	Valid date.	
Valid date	6, 3, 2009	Valid date.	

Let's set up a loop in the test driver to continue reading in dates until a negative month is read. The attempt to instantiate a **Date** object must be within a **try** statement. This is fairly complex; let's write the algorithm first.

TestDriver

```
Prompt for a month
Read month
WHILE month >= 0
    Prompt for day and year
    Read day and year
    TRY
        Instantiate Date with month, day, year
```

SOFTWARE MAINTENANCE CASE STUDY: Adding Exceptions to the `Date` Class

> CATCH MonthError
> CATCH DayError
> CATCH YearError
> Prompt for a month
> Read month

Here is the driver:

```cpp
//*******************************************
// Test driver for class Date, which
// is the Date class with exception handling
//*******************************************
#include <iostream>
#include "Date.h"
using namespace std;
int main()
{
  int month;
  int day;
  int year;

  cout << "Enter month. Negative month stops test." << endl;
  cin >> month;
  while (month >=  0)
  {
    cout << "Enter day and year" << endl;
    cin >> day >> year;
    try
    {
      Date date1(month, day, year);
      cout << "Valid date." << endl;
    }
    catch (MonthError error)
    {
      cout << "Attempt to create date with invalid month." << endl;
    }
    catch (DayError error)
    {
      cout << "Attempt to create date with invalid day." << endl;
    }
    catch (YearError error)
    {
      cout << "Attempt to create date with invalid year." << endl;
    }
    cout << "Enter month.  Negative month stops test." << endl;
    cin >> month;
  }
  return 0;
}
```

SOFTWARE MAINTENANCE CASE STUDY: Adding Exceptions to the `Date` Class

Here is the output:

```
Enter month.  Negative month stops test.
13
Enter day and year
1 2009
Attempt to create date with invalid month.
Enter month.  Negative month stops test.
0
Enter day and year
1 2009
Attempt to create date with invalid month.
Enter month.  Negative month stops test.
1
Enter day and year
0 2010
Attempt to create date with invalid day.
Enter month.  Negative month stops test.
2
Enter day and year
29 2007
Attempt to create date with invalid day.
Enter month.  Negative month stops test.
2
Enter day and year
29 2008
Valid date.
Enter month.  Negative month stops test.
2
Enter day and year
30 2010
Attempt to create date with invalid day.
Enter month.  Negative month stops test.
4
Enter day and year
31 1945
Attempt to create date with invalid day.
Enter month.  Negative month stops test.
6
Enter day and year
31 2000
Attempt to create date with invalid day.
Enter month.  Negative month stops test.
9
Enter day and year
31 2000
Attempt to create date with invalid day.
Enter month.  Negative month stops test.
11
```

SOFTWARE MAINTENANCE CASE STUDY: Adding Exceptions to the `Date` Class

```
Enter day and year
31 2000
Attempt to create date with invalid day.
Enter month.  Negative month stops test.
1
Enter day and year
30 1066
Attempt to create date with invalid year.
Enter month.  Negative month stops test.
12
Enter day and year
25 2010
Valid date.
Enter month.  Negative month stops test.
6
Enter day and year
3 2009
Valid date.
Enter month.  Negative month stops test.
-1
```

Problem-Solving Case Study

Starship Weight and Balance

Problem: The company you work for has just added a Beechcraft Starship-1 to its corporate aircraft fleet. As with any airplane, it is essential that the pilot know the total weight of the loaded plane at takeoff and its center of gravity. If the plane weighs too much, it won't be able to lift off. If the center of gravity is outside the limits established for the plane, it might be impossible to control. Either situation could potentially lead to a crash. You have been asked to write a program that determines the weight and center of gravity of this plane, based on the number and weight of crew members, the number and weight of passengers and their luggage, the weight of the closet contents, and the amount of fuel. The pilot will use the output of this program to determine if it is safe to take off.

Problem-Solving Case Study

Here are the formulas for total weight and center of gravity:

totalWeight = (empty weight + Σ(crew * weight) + Σ(passenger * weight)
            + Σ(baggage) + closet + fuel * 6.7)

centerOfGravity = Σ(weights * distance from front of the plane) / totalWeight

Brainstorming Initial Classes: The nouns in the problem provide a starting point for the objects in the problem. Here is a list of them:

   Company
   Fleet
   Aircraft
   Beechcraft Starship-1
   Center of gravity
   Pilot
   Weight of plane
   Loaded plane
   Number of crew members
   Number of passengers
   Crew member
   Weight of crew member
   Passenger
   Weight of passenger
   Weight of luggage
   Closet
   Fuel
   Distance from front of plane
   Names
   Service desk

This is quite a daunting list. In fact, it contains objects with which we are not familiar, such as "center of gravity" and "distance from front of plane." Let's filter this list and then go back for more information.

Filtering: The company and the fleet are not part of the solution. Aircraft and Beechcraft Starship-1 are the same object. The aircraft has a closet and fuel. These are not objects, but rather numeric attributes of the aircraft. The pilot, crew members, and passenger are all people with names, who have weight. Passengers have luggage, which has weight. The service desk is the person in charge of the processing. We will also need a user interface to represent the service desk.

Here is the filtered list:

   Aircraft
      Closet
      Fuel
      Luggage

Problem-Solving Case Study

List of people
    Name
    Weight
    Role {CREW, PASSENGER}
    Luggage
User interface

    We usually write the CRC cards at this point, one for each object. However, we need to look at center of gravity a little more closely before we are ready to do so, because we may need more information. The center of gravity is the sum of each weight multiplied by its distance from the front of the airplane divided by the total weight. A weight times its distance from the front of the plane is called a *moment arm* or simply a *moment*.

    Distance from the front of the plane? We need to know where each passenger is sitting, where the closet is, and where the baggage is stored. We go back to the Starship-1 manual and find the following table:

Loading Station	Distance from Nose (inches)
Crew seats	143
Row 1 seats (2)	219
Row 2 seats (2)	265
Row 3 seats (2)	295
Row 4 seats (2)	341
Closet	182
Baggage	386

← Passengers × 265 inches = Passenger Moment →

    The manual also tells us that the aircraft has several fuel tanks, which are found in different places in the plane. As fuel is added, it automatically flows into different tanks so that the center of gravity changes as the tanks are filled. There are four formulas for computing the distance from the nose to the "center" of the fuel tanks, depending on how much fuel is being loaded into the plane. The following table lists these distance formulas:

Gallons of Fuel (G)	Distance Formula (D)
0–59	$D = 314.6 \times G$
60–360	$D = 305.8 + [-0.01233 \times (G - 60)]$
361–520	$D = 303.0 + [0.12500 \times (G - 361)]$
521–565	$D = 323.0 + [-0.04444 \times (G - 521)]$

CHAPTER 16 Templates, Operator Overloading, and Exceptions

Problem-Solving Case Study

Before we finalize the design, let's do a scenario walk-through. We usually perform this check later, after the classes are determined, but our current problem is quite complex and we need to get a better feel for what is happening.

Let's look at the problem from the perspective of what the gate agent does now. She says she enters the closet weight and the amount of fuel. She then enters the crew members' names and weights. As the passengers arrive, she enters their names, weights, and baggage weights, and assigns row numbers. When the passengers are all on board, the gate agent calculates the weights and center of gravity. If the pilot approves these figures, she prints out the names of all on board, with each person marked as either crew or passenger. If the pilot does not approve the weights and center of gravity, the flight is halted.

At first glance, there appear to be two distinct ways to continue this design. The first option is to collect the data and store it into the classes we listed in our first brainstorming pass. After all of the data is collected, the total weight and center of gravity can be calculated. This strategy mirrors what the gate agent does.

On reflection, however, we see that the only data that needs to be kept consists of the names of those on board the aircraft. All of the other data can be processed as it is input. Thus the only attributes that we need are a running total of the weights and a running total of the moments. This streamlining makes a much simpler design. We do, however, need a user interface that will be responsible for inputting the data.

Aircraft
    Weight
    Moment
    List of people
        Name
        Role {'C', 'P'}
User interface

Now we are ready to create the CRC cards for the classes. The weight and moment are just running sums. We have a `Name` class, so we do not need to make a CRC card for `Name`. Role is a `char` attribute, not a class. Here is the CRC card for the `People` class, followed by the specification file for the class.

People Class

Class Name: *People*	Superclass:	
Responsibilities	Collaborations	
Create Person(Name, Role)	Name	
GetName returns Name		
GetRole returns Role		

Problem-Solving Case Study

```cpp
//*****************************************************
// SPECIFICATION FILE for People Class
//*****************************************************

#include "Name.h"

class People
{
public:
  People();
  People(Name initName, char initRole);
  Name GetName() const;
  char GetRole() const;
private:
  Name name;
  char role;
};
```

The implementation of these functions is so straightforward that we can go directly to the code.

```cpp
//****************************************
// IMPLEMENTATION FILE for People class
//****************************************
#include "People.h"

People::People()
{
  Name name(" ", " ", " ");
  role = 'C';
}

//****************************************

People::People(Name initName, char initRole)
{
  name = initName;
  role = initRole;
}

//****************************************

Name People::GetName() const
{ return name; }

//****************************************

char People::GetRole() const
{ return role; }
```

Problem-Solving Case Study

Aircraft Class

Class Name: People	Superclass:	
Responsibilities	Collaborations	
Create Aircraft()		
SetClosetAndFuel(ClosetWgt, FuelWgt)		
InsertPassenger(Name, Weight, RowNo)		
InsertCrew(Name, Weight)	Name	
GetTotalWeight returns float		
GetCenterOfGravity returns float		
WriteNamesOnBoard(outFile)	ofstream	

The class representing the plane is of prime importance. It keeps a list of crew and passengers, a running total of weights, and a running total of moments. It returns the total weight and center of gravity, and writes a list of people on board. We can use **GList** (defined earlier in this chapter) to keep the list of **People** objects.

Are there any exceptions that might occur? Yes, the gate agent might assign more than two people to a row. For the moment, we just throw an exception when this happens (class **RowOverflow**). In addition, we need to throw an exception if the weight is too high (class **TooHeavy**) and an exception if the center of gravity is not within bounds (class **CofGWrong**).

Here is the specification file:

```
//*******************************************
// SPECIFICATION FILE for class Aircraft
//*******************************************

#include "People.h"
#include "GList.h"
class RowOverflow      // More than 2 assigned to a row
{};
class TooHeavy         // Plane is too heavy to take off
{};
class CofGWrong        // Center of gravity not within bounds
{};

class Aircraft
{
public:
  Aircraft();
```

Problem-Solving Case Study

```
    // Knowledge responsibilities
    float GetTotalWeight();
    // Returns total weight
    float GetCenterOfGravity();
    // Calculates and returns center of gravity

    // Action responsibilities
    void SetClosetAndFuel(float closetWgt, float fuel);
    // Post: Closet weight and fuel weight have been added to the total
    //       weight;
    //       Closet moment and fuel moment have been added to total moment
    void InsertPassenger(Name initName, float pWeight, float bWeight,
                        int rowNo);
    // Post: Name and role inserted into list;
    //       Passenger and baggage weight have been added to total weight;
    //       Passenger and baggage moment have been added to total moment
    void InsertCrew(Name initName, float cWeight);
    // Post: Name and role inserted into list;
    //       Crew weight added to total weight;
    //       Crew moment added to total moment
    void WriteNamesOnBoard(ofstream& outFile);
    // Post: Names and role of all on board written to outFile

private:
    float weight;           // Running weight
    float moment;           // Running moments
    GList<People> list;     // List of people on board
                            //  (People specialization of GList template)
};
```

We need two auxiliary arrays to help with the calculations. First, we need a one-dimensional array to hold the number of people assigned to each row. Let's call it `row` and initialize the values to 0. Second, we need a parallel array that holds the distance each row is located from the front of the plane. Let's call this array `rowDistance`.

We also need to define certain constants, such as weight of the empty plane, moment of the empty plane, and weight of a gallon of fuel. We find these values in the plane's manual.

Here, then, are the declarations that go in the front of the implementation file:

```
const float EMPTY_WEIGHT = 9887.0;         // Weight of empty airplane
const float EMPTY_MOMENT = 3153953.0;      // Moment of empty airplane
const float FUEL_WEIGHT = 6.7;             // Fuel weight per gallon
static int rows[4] = {0, 0, 0, 0};         // Number in row
static int rowDistance[4] = {219, 265, 295, 341}; // Distance of row
```

The constructor needs to initialize `weight` to `EMPTY_WEIGHT` and `moment` to `EMPTY_MOMENT`. The algorithm GetTotalWeight returns the weight, and GetCenterOfGravity returns the moment divided by the weight. SetClosetAndFuel is more complex, so we decide to write the algorithm first, based on the fuel moments in the manual.

Problem-Solving Case Study

SetClosetAndFuel (In: closetWgt, fuel)

Set fuelWgt to fuel * FUEL_WEIGHT
Set weight to weight + closetWgt + fuelWgt
Set moment to moment + closetWgt * 182
IF fuel <60
   Set moment to moment + 314.6 * fuel * fuelWgt
ELSE IF fuel < 361
   Set moment to moment + (305.8 + (-0.01233 * (fuel − 60))) * fuelWgt
ELSE IF fuel < 521
   Set moment to moment + (303.0 + (-.12500 * (fuel -361))) * fuelWgt
ELSE
   Set moment to moment + (323.0 + (-0.0444 * (fuel − 521))) * fuelWgt

InsertPassenger (In: name, pWeight, bWeight, rowNo)

Increment row[rowNo]
   THROW RowOverflow if row[rowNo] > 2
Set weight to weight + pWeight + bWeight
Set moment to moment + pWeight * row[rowNo-1] + bWeight * 386
Create People person(name, 'P')
Insert person into list

InsertCrew is a simpler version of InsertPassenger. WriteNamesOnBoard is an algorithm that we have used many times before.

UserInterface Class

Class Name: *UserInterface*	Superclass:	
Responsibilities	Collaborations	
CreateUserInterface		
Input closet and fuel	iostream	
InputCrew	Aircraft	
InputPassenger	Aircraft	
Close Doors	Aircraft	

Problem-Solving Case Study

```
//***************************************************
// SPECIFICATION FILE for class UserInterface
// This class acts as the gate agent.
//***************************************************

#include <iostream>
#include "Aircraft.h"
class UserInterface
{
public:
  UserInterface();
  // Action responsibilities
  void InputClosetAndFuel();
  void InputCrew();
  void InputPassenger();
  void CloseDoors(ofstream& outFile);
private:
  Aircraft plane;
};
```

Scenarios: Before we write the implementation file for the `UserInterface` class, let's further examine these responsibilities by creating a scenario from the algorithms. The `UserInterface` (gate agent) prompts for and reads the closetWgt and fuelWgt and sends them as parameters to the `Aircraft` function `SetClosetAndFuel`. The gate agent enters each crew member's name and weight and passes them as parameters to the `Aircraft` function InsertCrew. The passengers come up to the gate and give their names. They are weighed, their luggage is weighed, and they are given a row number. Each passenger's information is sent to the plane, and each passenger is then allowed to board. When the gate agent closes the gate, the total weight and center of gravity are accessed, printed, and tested. If these values are within the appropriate range, the names of those on board are written to the file and the plane takes off. If the weight or the center of gravity is not within limits, an exception is thrown and the plane remains at the gate.

Which brings us to some questions: What is the maximum weight over which the plane can't fly? What is the range of the center of gravity within which it is safe to fly? We go back to the manuals and find that the plane is safe to fly if its weight is less than or equal to 14,440 pounds. The safe center-of-gravity range is between 307 and 321.

The task for each of these functions is quite straightforward. Here, then, is the implementation file for class `UserInterface`.

```
//*******************************************************
// IMPLEMENTATION FILE for class UserInterface
//*******************************************************

#include "UserInterface.h"
#include <iostream>
#include <fstream>
#include <string>
using namespace std;
```

Problem-Solving Case Study

```
UserInterface::UserInterface()
{}

//************************************************************

void UserInterface::InputClosetAndFuel()
{
  float closet;
  float fuel;
  cout << "Enter the closet weight and the gallons of fuel"
       << endl;
  cin >> closet >> fuel;
  plane.SetClosetAndFuel(closet, fuel);
}

//************************************************************

void UserInterface::InputCrew()
{
  string first;
  string last;
  float weight;
  cout << "Enter first name, last name, weight of crew member" << endl;
  cin >> first >> last >> weight;
  Name name(first, " ", last);
  plane.InsertCrew(name, weight);
}

//************************************************************

void UserInterface::InputPassenger()
{
  string first;
  string last;
  float weight;
  float baggage;
  int rowNo;
  cout << "Enter first name, last name of passenger, " << endl;
  cout << "passenger's weight, and weight of luggage." << endl;
  cin >> first >> last >> weight >> baggage;
  cout << "Enter row number" << endl;
  cin >> rowNo;
  Name name(first, " ", last);
  plane.InsertPassenger(name, weight, baggage, rowNo);
}

//************************************************************
```

Problem-Solving Case Study

```cpp
void UserInterface::CloseDoors(ofstream& outFile)
{
  float weight = plane.GetTotalWeight();
  cout << "Weight: " << weight << endl;;
  float CofG = plane.GetCenterOfGravity();
  cout << "Center of Gravity: " << CofG << endl;
  if (weight > 14440)
    throw TooHeavy();
  else if (CofG <= 307 && CofG <= 321)
    throw CofGWrong();
  else
    plane.WriteNamesOnBoard(outFile);
}
```

Testing: We must now write a test driver that sets all this activity in motion. The driver will need to prompt for and enter the number of crew members and the number of passengers. The gate agent must be told to enter the closet and fuel, the crew, and the passengers, and then to close the doors. All of these tasks must be done within a `try-catch` structure. Recall that there are three possible exceptions: `RowOverflow`, `TooHeavy`, and `CofGWrong`. Here we have the handlers in the `main` driver, which is shown next:

```cpp
#include <iostream>
#include "UserInterface.h"
#include <fstream>
using namespace std;
int main()
{
  UserInterface gateAgent;
  ofstream outFile;
  int crew;                      // Number of crew members
  int passengers;                // Number of passengers
  outFile.open("PassengerList");
  cout << "Enter number of crew members" << endl;
  cin >> crew;
  cout << "Enter number of passengers" << endl;
  cin >> passengers;
  try
  {
    gateAgent.InputClosetAndFuel();
    for (int number = 1; number <= crew; number++)
      gateAgent.InputCrew();
    for (int number = 1; number <= passengers; number++)
      gateAgent.InputPassenger();
    gateAgent.CloseDoors(outFile);
  }
  catch (TooHeavy)
  {
    cout << "Cancel flight: Weight is too heavy" << endl;
  }
```

Problem-Solving Case Study

```
    catch (CofGWrong)
    {
      cout << "Cancel flight: Center of Gravity is wrong " << endl;
    }
    catch (RowOverflow)
    {
      cout << "Too many passengers assigned to one row" << endl;
    }
    return 0;
}
```

Here is the output from a run where all of the parameters are acceptable and no exceptions are thrown:

```
Enter number of crew members
2
Enter number of passengers
3
Enter the closet weight and the gallons of fuel
50 200
Enter first name, last name, weight of crew member
Josh Smith 170
Enter first name, last name, weight of crew member
Jerry Jones 165
Enter first name, last name of passenger,
passenger's weight, and weight of luggage
Bill Brown 170 25
Enter row number
1
Enter first name, last name of passenger,
passenger's weight, and weight of luggage
Mary Magenta 150 40
Enter row number
4
Enter first name, last name of passenger,
passenger's weight, and weight of luggage
Sally Slew 130 25
Enter row number
3
Weight: 12152
Center of Gravity: 311.051
```

Testing and Debugging

When working with templates, it's important to remember that a generated template function or template class becomes an ordinary function or class and is subject to all the usual rules of syntax and semantics.

To test a template function or template class, one approach is to start with a nontemplate version, using a specific data type such as `int` or whatever type is most appropriate to your needs. Apply the usual testing strategies we have outlined in previous chapters for algorithms and classes. After all errors have been noted and corrected, convert the function or class into a templatized form, and continue testing by supplying different data types as template arguments.

Another approach is to begin with the templatized class, but specialize it initially to a type that you are confident is correct, such as `int` or `string`. It can be very frustrating to try to find a bug in a template when it is actually in a class that is specified in its type argument. Once you are confident that the template works for this type, you should test it for a range of classes that you anticipate using with it.

A program that handles exceptions must be tested to ensure that the exceptions are generated appropriately and then handled properly. Test cases must be included to cause exceptions to be thrown and to specify the expected results from handling them.

The Problem-Solving Case Study program has three exceptions:

1. More than two people are assigned to a row.
2. The loaded plan is too heavy to take off.
3. The center of gravity is outside the acceptable limits.

At least four runs would be required to test these three cases: (1) Three people would be assigned to a row; (2) the plane would be too heavy; (3) the center of gravity would be too low; and (4) the center of gravity would be too high. You are asked to create test data that would support these four cases in the Case Study Follow-Up exercises.

Testing and Debugging Hints

1. When declaring a template parameter, as in

   ```
   template<class ItemType>
   ```

   remember to use the word `class` (or `typename`). However, the template argument used when instantiating a template is not required to be the name of a C++ class. Any data type, built in or user defined, is allowed.

2. In the restricted form discussed in this book, template arguments are data type names, not variable names or expressions.

3. Template functions are usually called with implicit template arguments, but template classes must use explicit template arguments.

4. Just as with nontemplate functions, if template function definitions are physically placed after the code that calls the functions, then function prototypes (forward declarations) must precede the calling code.

5. With template classes, the member function definitions must be compiled together with the client code, not independently. One strategy is to group the class template and the member function definitions into a single file (the `.h` file). Another strategy is to place the class template into a `.h` file and the member function definitions into a `.cpp` file,

with the `.h` file including the `.cpp` file. In the latter approach, if you are using an IDE, do not list this `.cpp` file in your "project." Instead, include only the client code file in the project.

6. Avoid using built-in types as exception types. Throw objects of a user-defined class or struct whose name suggests the nature of the error or exceptional event.

7. If `BadData` is the name of an exception class, be sure to throw an object of that class by writing

    ```
    throw BadData();    // Throw a constructed object
    ```

    rather than

    ```
    throw BadData;      // Syntax error
    ```

8. Make sure that all exceptions are caught. An uncaught exception results in program termination with a vague error message. It is best practice to catch exceptions at the point nearest to their source where they can be properly handled.

■ Summary

C++ templates are a powerful and convenient mechanism for implementing generic data types and algorithms. With a class template, we can define an entire family of class types that differ only in terms of the data types of their internal data representations. With a function template, we can define an entire family of functions that are the same except for the data types of the items they manipulate.

A template is instantiated by placing the template argument in angle brackets next to the name of the class or function. In the examples shown in this chapter, a template argument is the name of a data type, not the name of a variable or expression. The compiler then generates a new function or class by substituting the template argument for the template parameter wherever the parameter appears in the template. With template classes, the template argument must be explicit for the compiler to instantiate the template. With template functions, the template argument is usually omitted, and the compiler deduces the template argument by examining the function's argument list.

Nearly all of the C++ operators can be overloaded. This goal is achieved by defining a function called "operator," followed by the symbol to be overloaded. When the symbol is used between two instances of the class for which the symbol has been overloaded, the operator function is called.

An exception is an unusual event that requires special processing. The primary purpose of exception handling is to allow one part of a program to report an error to another part of the program if the error cannot be handled locally. C++ supports exception handling by means of the `throw` and `try-catch` statements. A section of code that detects an error uses the `throw` statement to throw an exception, which is an object of some data type—usually a class. The thrown exception is then caught by an enclosing `try-catch` statement that has a catch-clause (exception handler) with a parameter whose type matches that of the exception. If no matching exception handler is found, the enclosing function immediately returns and passes the exception up to its calling function. This process continues up the call chain until either a matching exception handler is found or control reaches the `main` function. If `main` does not catch the exception, then the program terminates with an error message.

Quick Check Answers

16.1.1 Generic ADT.
16.1.2
```
template<class SomeType>
    class OrdPair
    {
    public:
      SomeType First() const;
      SomeType Second() const;
      void Print() const;
      OrdPair(SomeType m, SomeType n);
    private:
      SomeType first;
      SomeType second;
    };
```
16.1.3
```
OrdPair<int>   pair1(5, 6);
OrdPair<float> pair2(2.95, 6.34);
OrdPair<char>  pair3('+', '#');

pair1.Print();
pair2.Print();
pair3.Print();
```
16.1.4
```
template<class SomeType>
OrdPair<SomeType>::OrdPair( SomeType m, SomeType n )
// Constructor
{
  first = m;
  second = n;
}

template<class SomeType>
SomeType OrdPair<SomeType>::First() const
{
  return first;
}

template<class SomeType>
SomeType OrdPair<SomeType>::Second() const
{
  return second;
}

template<class SomeType>
void OrdPair<SomeType>::Print() const
{
  cout << '(' << first << ", " << second << ')' << endl;
}
```
16.1.5 A type for which the operations are defined but the data types of the items being manipulated are not.
16.1.6 A C++ language construct that allows the compiler to generate multiple versions of a class through the use of parameterized data types. **16.1.7** 1. Once the List ADT is compiled for a specific item type X (e.g., int) a client program can only use lists of that type X; 2. A client program cannot change the item type X. **16.1.8** A *specialization* of the template class. **16.1.9** The reference parameter is specified as being *constant*.
16.2.1
```
template<class SimpleType>
    SimpleType Thrice( SimpleType val )
    {
      return 3*val;
    }
```
16.2.2 `cout << Thrice(75) << ' ' << Thrice(64.35);`
or
`cout << Thrice<int>(75) << ' ' << Thrice<float>(64.35);`

16.2.3 An algorithm in which the actions or steps are defined but the data types of the items being manipulated are not. **16.2.4** The use of the same name for different functions, distinguished from each other by their parameter lists. **16.2.5** It allows functions that perform the same action on different parameter types to have the same name. **16.2.6** Function overloading can be improved by using a function template.

16.3.1 `bool operator<(some class)`
```
{...}
```
16.3.2 It can lead to algorithms that are specified in a natural and compact syntax for a particular context (e.g., matrix multiplication). **16.3.3** Overuse of operator overloading can lead to confusing code where it appears that expressions are manipulating built-in types when they are actually operating on user-defined types. **16.4.1** An unusual, often unpredictable event that requires special processing.

16.4.2 a. `class BadData`
```
      {};             // Don't forget the semicolon
```
  b. `void GetAge( int& age )`
```
      {
        cout << "Enter your age: ";
        cin >> age;
        if (age < 0)
          throw BadData();
      }
```
16.4.3 `try`
```
   {
     GetAge(age);
   }
   catch ( BadData )
   {
     cout << "Age must not be negative." << endl;
     throw;
   }
```
16.4.4 When an argument is unpredictable. **16.4.5** An exception handler is a section of program code that is executed when a particular exception occurs. **16.4.6** The `throw` statement. **16.4.7** The formal parameter is the exact type of an exception that was thrown and is used to determine which exception handler to execute.

■ Exam Preparation Exercises

1. In C++, two (nontemplate) functions can have the same name. True or false?
2. In C++, two (nontemplate) classes can have the same name. True or false?
3. Is the following a function template, a template function, or neither?

   ```
   template<class T>
   T OneLess(T var)
   {
      return var-1;
   }
   ```

4. In the statement

   `Group<char> oneGroup;`

   a. Is `Group<char>` a class template, a template class, or neither?
   b. Is `oneGroup` a class template, a template class, or neither?

5. Define the following terms:
   a. instantiate (a template)
   b. specialization (of a template)
   c. template parameter
   d. user-defined specialization (of a template)
   e. template argument

6. Consider this function call:

   ```
   DoThis<float>(3.85)
   ```

   a. Which item is the template argument?
   b. Which item is the function argument?
   c. Could the call be written as `DoThis(3.85)`?
7. Which C++ control structure should you use if you think an operation might throw an exception?
8. Which C++ statement raises an exception?
9. Which part of the `try-catch` statement must be written with a formal parameter?
10. Mark the following statements as true or false. If a statement is false, explain why.
    a. There can be only one catch-clause for each `try-catch` statement.
    b. A catch-clause is an exception handler.
    c. A `throw` statement must be located within a try-clause.
11. In the `WriteToFile` function of Section 16.4:
    a. What would happen if we deleted the `throw` statement in the exception handler?
    b. What would happen if we changed `throw` to `return`?
12. Consider the division-by-zero program at the end of Section 16.4. How would you change the `main` function so that the program terminates if a denominator is found to be 0?
13. What happens if you call a function that throws an exception, without placing the call in a try-clause?
14. What does the following statement do if it is written within an exception handler?

    ```
    throw;
    ```

15. Which type of exception would be written as the parameter of a catch-clause if the try-clause is calling `new` and we want to check whether the free store has run out of space?
16. What do you call the following function?

    ```
    bool operator==(Name otherName)
    {..}
    ```

Programming Warm-Up Exercises

1. Write a function template for a void function that squares and outputs the value passed to its parameter. The type of the parameter is the template type.
2. Write statements that call the function in Exercise 1 for values of type `int`, `long`, and `float`.
3. Write a user specialization of the function in Exercise 1 that accepts a string argument and "squares" it by printing it twice with no intervening spaces.
4. We would like to have a value-returning function that returns twice the value of its incoming parameter.
   a. Using function overloading, write two C++ function definitions for such a function: one with an `int` parameter and one with a `float` parameter.
   b. Write calling code that makes calls to both functions.

5. Write a function template for a function that returns the sum of all the elements in a one-dimensional array. The array elements can be of any simple numeric type, and the function has two parameters: the base address of the array and the number of elements in the array.

6. Write a function template for a void function, `GetData`, that receives a string through the parameter list, uses that string to prompt the user for input, reads a value from the keyboard, and returns that value (as a reference parameter) through the parameter list. The data type of the input value can be any type for which the `>>` operator is defined.

7. Assume you have the following enumeration type:

    ```
    enum AutoType {SEDAN, COUPE, OTHER};
    ```

    Write a user-defined specialization of the `GetData` template (see Exercise 6) that accommodates the `AutoType` type. For input, the user should type the character `s` for sedan, `c` for coupe, and `o` (or anything else) otherwise.

8. Consider the `GList` class template of Section 16.1.
   a. Write client code to instantiate the template twice, creating a list of `int`s and a list of `float`s.
   b. Assume that at some point in the client code the list of `int`s already contains values known to be in the range 10 through 80 and the list of `float`s is empty. Write client code that empties the list of `int`s as follows: As each item is removed from the list of `int`s, multiply it by 0.5 and insert the result into the list of `float`s.

9. Write a `MixedPair` class template that is similar to the `OrdPair` template of Quick Check Question 16.1.2 except that the pair of items can be of two different data types. *Hint:* Begin the template with

    ```
    template<class Type1, class Type2>
    ```

10. Given the `MixedPair` class template of Exercise 9, write client code that creates two class objects representing the pairs (5, 29.48) and ("Book", 36).

11. Given the `MixedPair` class template of Exercise 9, write function definitions for the class member functions.

12. a. Declare a user-defined exception class named `MathError`.
    b. Write a statement that throws an exception of type `MathError`.

13. Write a `try-catch` statement—assumed to be in the `main` function—that attempts to concatenate two `string` objects, but prints an error message and terminates the program if an exception is thrown. You may wish to review Section 16.4 to see which exceptions are thrown by the `string` class.

14. Write a `Sum` function that returns the sum of its two nonnegative `int` parameters unless the sum would exceed `INT_MAX`, in which case it throws an exception. (*Caution:* You cannot check for overflow after adding the numbers. On most machines, integer overflow results in a change of sign, but you should not write code that depends on this fact.)

15. Write a `try-catch` statement that calls the `Sum` function of Exercise 14 and, if an exception is thrown, prints an error message and rethrows the exception to a caller.

16. Make the changes described in this chapter to the `GList` class and `Temperatures` program so that `Temperatures` can instantiate a `GList` of any size. Test the change by experimenting with different sizes of `GList` for a given input file to see which size is necessary to accommodate all of the different temperature values.

17. The `Date` class in Section 16.3 overloads the <, > , and == operators. Add functions to this class that overload the <=, >=, and != operators as well. You can code these modifications very compactly by using `*this`.

Programming Problems

1. Imagine you are working for an in-house software team for a company that wants to monitor network access points in a building. Each building has a specified number of floors, a certain number of rooms per floor, and some number of network access points in a room. Each network access point is labeled with its state as being **on** or **off** and if it is **on** it has the month it was turned on. Design, implement, and test classes that represent buildings, floors, and network access points. Your classes should provide suitable observer methods that allow you to determine how many floors are in a building, how many rooms are on a floor, how many access points are in a room, and if an access point is on or off and which month it was turned on. You should also provide mutator methods that allow you to turn a network access point on or off and to set the month if it is turned on. You should use *composition* as a key strategy in designing these classes—thus, a building should contain floors, floors should contain rooms, and rooms should contain network access points. Your program should allow a user to add additional floors, rooms, and access points as well as turn access points on and off. Your program should also report errors using exceptions if a room, floor, or access point is chosen that does not exist.

2. A software company that develops games has just hired you! Before working on the next version of *Medieval Menace* they have given you the task of implementing the tic-tac-toe game in C++. Tic-tac-toe consists of a 3 × 3 game board of squares where each square is either empty, has an X marker, or has an O marker. Two players represented by an X or an O play the game. The objective is for one player to get three X's or three O's in a row first. Design, implement, and test classes that represent a tic-tac-toe game board and X and O markers. Your classes should provide suitable observer and mutator methods for modifying the game board and displaying the state of the game. Use your classes to create a game that prompts for player X and player O to place markers at specified locations on the game board. After each move, your program should display the current game board to the console. Your program should also check after each move if there is a winning configuration of the game board and use exceptions if an invalid board location is chosen. If there is a winning configuration, the game should complete indicating which player won.

3. Write a simple calculator program that allows a user to indicate simple arithmetic operations from the console. Your calculator should support at least addition, subtraction, multiplication, and division. The calculator should keep a running total after each operation and use exceptions to handle erroneous input such as division by 0. You can also introduce other constraints on the running total such as restricting the total by some maximum and minimum value. Here is an example of a typical interaction:

```
> 32
total = 32
> +
> 4
total = 36
> /
> 0
```

```
Error: Cannot  Divide by Zero!
Total = 36
> quit
```

4. Programming Problem 1 in Chapter 7 asked you to output the ICAO word corresponding to each letter in a word. Change the function that converts a letter to the matching word so that it throws an exception if the letter is not in the alphabet, and add an exception handler to the program that outputs "Invalid letter" and the offending letter whenever the exception is thrown.

5. Programming Problem 2 in Chapter 7 asked you to compute a person's weight on a specified planet. Rewrite that program so that an erroneous planet name results in an exception being thrown by the input routine and caught by the caller.

6. Programming Problem 3 in Chapter 11 asked you to write a simple database program for an art gallery. The problem required that a user be able to search the database using any of the values in a record for an artwork. Rewrite the program using a template for the equality test function so that a single search function can be used for the different types of values in the database.

7. You're working for an observatory that keeps a database of stars. The most prominent stars are indexed by name (a string); less prominent stars are indexed by the name of the constellation in which they are found and a sequentially assigned number (an `int`); and the least prominent stars are indexed by coordinates consisting of two floating-point numbers. Each star record also contains a measurement of the star's brightness, called its magnitude (a `float`), and a letter indicating its color (a `char`).

    Write a C++ program that reads the star data from three files (`named.dat`, `numbered.dat`, and `coord.dat`) and places all of the data into a single list. The program should then allow the user to retrieve the data for any star using the different kinds of indexes. Use templates to simplify the coding of this application.

8. Programming Problem 5 in Chapter 7 asked you to write a program to input a time in numeric form and print it in English. Rewrite the program to check for entry of erroneous times in the input function, and throw an exception that is handled by the caller.

■ Case Study Follow-Up

1. Complete the test plan for the Problem-Solving Case Study such that the three exceptions are called as specified in the "Testing" section.

2. Catch the `RowOverflow` exception in the `Aircraft` class. If a row is full, find a seat in another row and put the passenger there. Continue with the processing. Note that if one person is moved, another row may then be full. Thus passengers may be shifting out of their assigned row, but as long as there are only 8 passengers, all will find a seat. (*Hint:* You will have to put a `try` statement in `InsertPassenger`.)

3. Consider the exception `TooHeavy`. Is there any reasonable action that the program could take to solve the situation rather than causing the plane to not fly? Discuss your answer.

4. Consider the exception `CofGWrong`. Is there any reasonable action that the program could take to solve the situation rather than causing the plane to not fly? Discuss your answer.

17 Introduction to Data Structures Using the Standard Template Library

KNOWLEDGE GOALS

- To appreciate the distinction between the Standard Template Library (STL) and data structures in the abstract sense.
- To understand the operation of stacks, queues, and deques.
- To understand the set and map as abstract data types.
- To be aware of the structure and operations associated with tree and hash table abstract types.

SKILL GOALS

To be able to:
- Instantiate and use specializations of STL templates.
- Work with STL iterators.
- Apply STL algorithms to STL data structures.
- Use the basic STL sequence containers: `vector`, `list`, and `deque`.
- Use the STL sequence container adapters: `stack` and `queue`.
- Use the associative STL containers: `set` and `map`.

In Chapter 10, we began our exploration of user-defined data types. In Chapter 11, we introduced the array. Chapters 13 and 14 focused on the list data structure as a vehicle for appreciating the general principles of how data can be organized in the abstract sense, and for recognizing how an ADT can have many different implementations that offer advantages under different circumstances. We are now ready to survey a broader range of ways to organize data.

The study of data structures is a major area of computer science research and education. Most computer science curricula include one or more complete courses on data structures, their related algorithms, and efficient implementation techniques. In this chapter, we can merely whet your appetite for those more advanced studies by giving you a preview of what's to come.

That doesn't mean, however, that we cannot delve into some practical uses of these more advanced structuring techniques. The C++ library provides a wealth of existing implementations of generic structured types, which we can use directly. In fact, the Standard Template Library (STL) is so rich that entire books have been devoted to explaining the subtleties of its operation! In this chapter, we concentrate on the basic principles and practical aspects of those STL types that support the more commonly used structured ADTs.

17.1 Abstract Data Structures Versus Implementations

By this point you are quite familiar with the array and list data structures. We describe both of them as belonging to the family of linear data structures, because their components can be arranged in a straight sequence from one end to the other. The array is sequenced by its index values, and the list is sequenced by the logical relationship between each node and the nodes that immediately precede or follow it, as shown in **FIGURE 17.1**. As you know, lists may be implemented either with arrays or via pointers (linked lists).

With a little thought, you should also appreciate that nothing prevents us from implementing the abstract idea of the array using a linked list. Under normal circumstances, a linked implementation of an array would be inefficient. When an array with a large index range is sparsely filled with values, however, a linked implementation can save a lot of space. As an example, imagine that a wildlife biologist is plotting the location of geese on a lake using GPS coordinates received from the geese's tracking collars. The natural representation of this data is with a two-dimensional array indexed by the coordinates, with each element representing the number of geese in that area of the lake. Of course, when there are only a few geese on the lake, an array implementation wastes a huge amount of memory space, which can be saved by switching to a linked implementation, as shown in **FIGURE 17.2**.

This discussion is simply meant to convey the idea that every data structure has two aspects: its abstract (conceptual) form and its implementation. Through the control and data abstraction supported in object-oriented programming using classes, it is possible to entirely divorce one of these aspects from the other. The advantage is that client code can use a natural representation that is easier to understand, while obtaining the benefits of an efficient underlying implementation.

As we proceed through this chapter, you might have thoughts such as, "But a stack is just a restricted kind of list. Why do we need it as a separate type?" We all fall into this trap of mixing abstract representation with implementation. It's true that once we have an implementation of a general list, it can do everything a stack can do. But as you'll see when we demonstrate the use of the stack, sometimes that simpler abstract type is all we need to solve a problem, and coding the solution is made easier by its simplicity. Underneath the stack interface, however, we can have either a list-based or an array-based implementation.

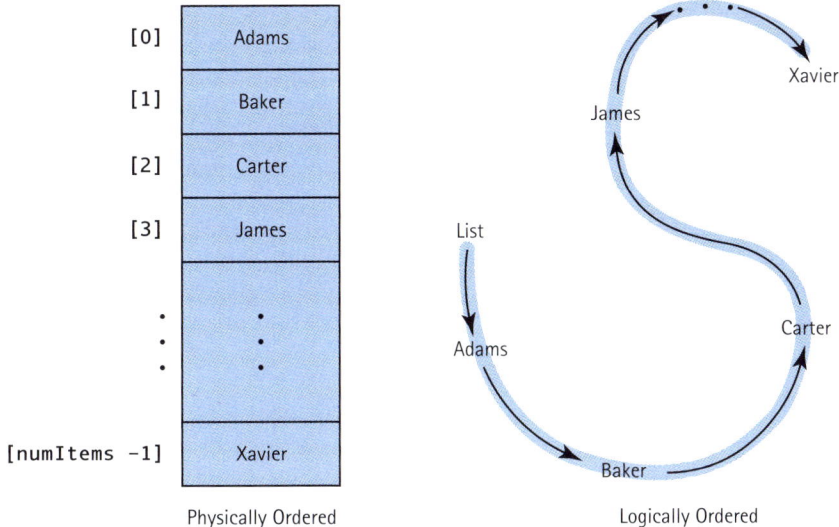

FIGURE 17.1 The Array and List as Linear Structures

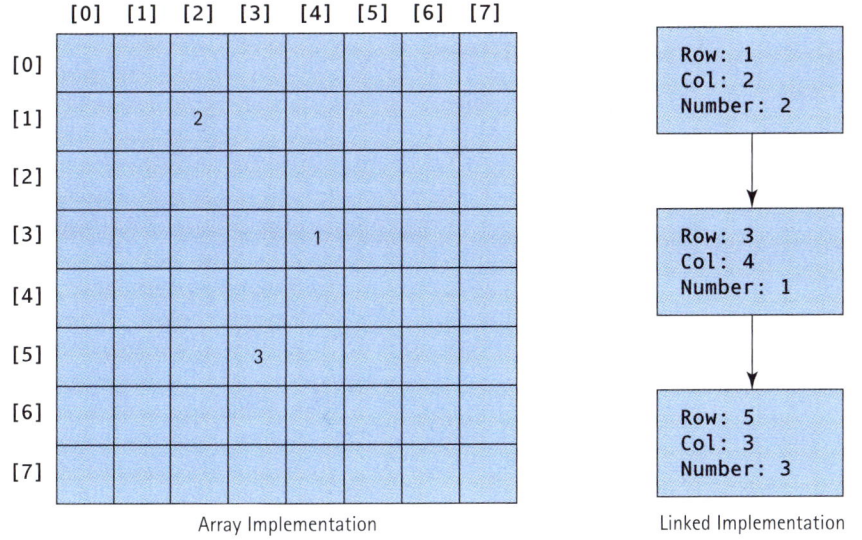

FIGURE 17.2 A Linked Implementation of a Sparsely Filled Array Conserves Space

Something else to keep in mind is that any implementation of a data structure is representing a corresponding ADT. For example, a `list` class has an interface that represents a list ADT. Because of this, when we look at a library of implementations such as the STL, it is tempting to automatically use the provided linked `list` type to implement the abstract list in a problem. But what if the problem requirements specify that the list is built from file data at the start of the run, with few subsequent deletions and additions? That argues for an array-based implementation.

The problem-solving strategy we use with data structures is as follows. In the problem-solving phase, we design the structure and interface that most naturally solves the problem. In the implementation phase, we consider how the structure will be used and which kind of structure actually provides the most efficient solution. Next we define a class that wraps the implementation structure with an interface for the abstract type. Lastly, we go to the library to see if it provides a suitable data structure implementation that can be used within the class.

Having just spelled out this strategy, we need to note that many of the goals of this chapter involve demonstrating the use of the STL. It's much easier to see how an STL type works without wrapping it in an interface for a different type. So be forewarned that our examples aren't necessarily meant to illustrate this approach: This is definitely a case of "Do as we say, not as we do!"

> **QUICK CHECK** ✓
>
> **17.1.1** Why would you choose one data structure in the problem-solving phase and then implement it with a different structure? (pp. 886–888)
>
> **17.1.2** Every data structure has two aspects. What are they? (p. 886)

17.2 Additional Linear Structures

Outside of the context of a specific problem, it's difficult to imagine how we could invent a linear data structure that's not conceptually an array or a list—so let's consider an example problem. Do shopping carts at the supermarket wear out evenly? You've seen them arranged in their neat columns, with people taking them from the back, and clerks wheeling them back into place. But do the ones at the front of the column ever get used? Are they rearranged enough so that all carts get the same amount of wear in the long run? Or is there a reason that you always seem to get one with a sticky wheel that won't roll straight?

Other than curiosity, understanding how carts are used can help a supermarket decide how many to buy. If it turns out that they don't wear evenly, a manager might decide to have a clerk manually rearrange the carts periodically.

Solving such a problem involves simulation. We can model the carts in their rows and the time that they spend roaming the aisles, and record how much total time of use each one acquires. The speed of the computer enables us to evaluate years of use in a matter of seconds.

Which data structures should we use to represent this situation? Given what we've seen so far, an array would be a good choice for modeling a column of carts. When a simulated customer arrives, we remove a cart from the back end of the column. Then what do we do with it? We can randomly assign it a return time and put it into a sorted list. As each minute passes, we check the list to see if the cart at the head of the list is ready to be returned. Then we remove it from the head of the list, and place it at the back of the column array. **FIGURE 17.3** shows this arrangement.

Let's consider these structures more closely. Do we really need all of their capabilities to solve our problem? Not really. For example, we won't index into the array in random locations; instead, we merely add and delete elements from one end of the array. In computer science, such a structure is called a stack. What about the list? Do we ever

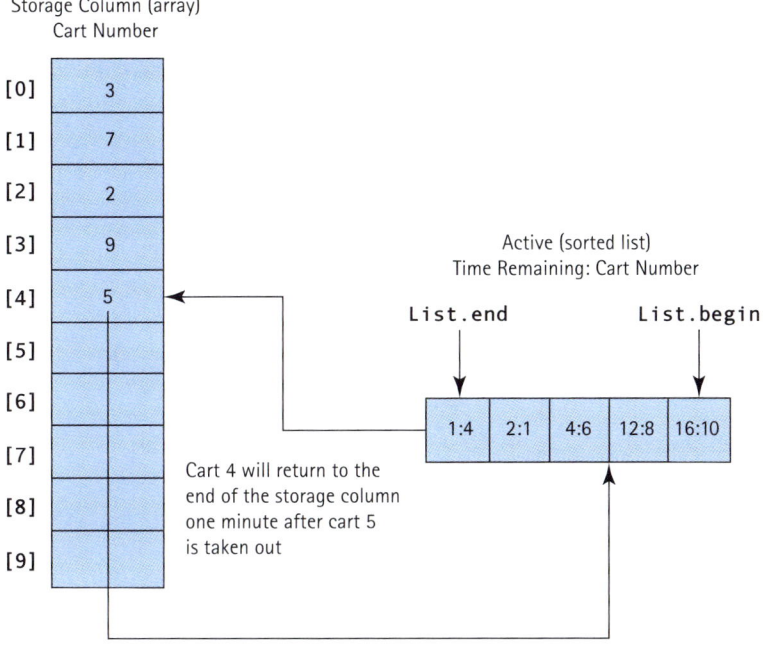

FIGURE 17.3 Using an Array and a Sorted List to Simulate Shopping Carts

traverse it from one end to the other, or delete elements from the middle? No, we just insert elements into place and remove them from one end. This structure, which is called a priority queue (pronounced like the letter "Q"), is one member of a broader family of queue data structures.

At this point, you should start to see that differences in linear data structures are based on how they are accessed. Arrays and lists support very general access. If access is restricted in some way, however, we can define a data structure with a simpler interface. Also, in some cases, the restrictions permit us to create a more efficient implementation.

Let's take a closer look at stacks and queues.

Stacks

A stack is a data structure that can be accessed from only one end. We can insert an element at the top (as the first element) and we can remove the top (first) element. This structure models a property commonly encountered in real life. Accountants call it LIFO, which stands for "last in, first out." The plate holder in a cafeteria has this property. You can take only the top plate. When you do, the one below it rises to the top so the next person can take a plate. Cars in a noncircular driveway exhibit this property: The last car in must be the first car out.

Stack A data structure in which insertions and deletions can be made from only one end.

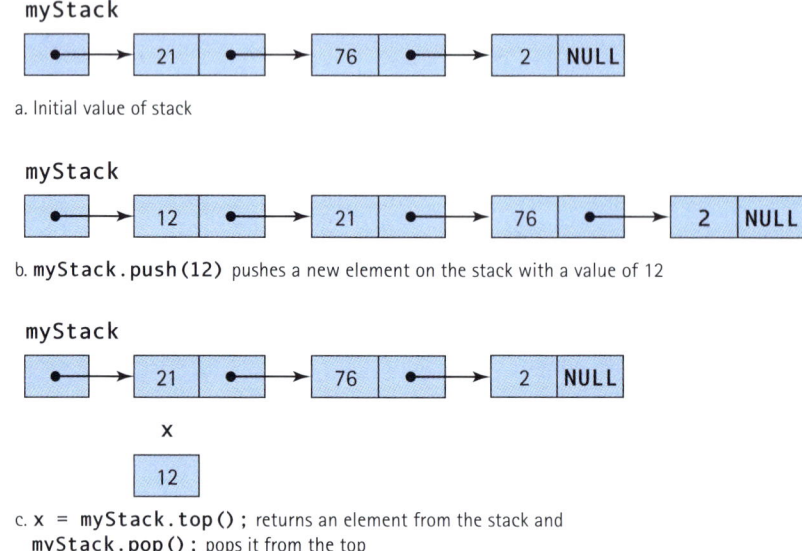

FIGURE 17.4 A Stack Showing Push, Top, and Pop Operations

The term **push** is used for the insertion operation, and the term **pop** is used for the deletion operation. In some implementations of a stack, **pop** also returns the top element. In other implementations, a separate operation, **top**, retrieves the top value and **pop** simply deletes it. **FIGURE 17.4** shows what happens when you **push** an element on a given stack and then **pop** the stack.

Stacks are used frequently in systems software. For example, C++ uses a stack at run time to keep track of nested method calls. The compiler uses a stack to translate arithmetic expressions. Stacks are used whenever we wish to remember a sequence of objects or actions in the reverse order from their original occurrence. An algorithm to read in a file containing a series of lines and print the lines out in reverse order using a stack of strings is shown here:

Reverse File

Create stack
Create file in
while in
   stack.push(in.getline)
while not stack.empty
   print stack.top
   stack.pop

As you can see from this algorithm, in addition to **push**, **pop**, and **top**, we need a way to test whether the stack is empty. We may also want a way to find the size of a stack. Even with those additions, the stack interface has only five responsibilities, making it a very simple abstract type.

Queues

A queue is a data structure in which elements are entered at one end and removed from the other end. Accountants call this property FIFO, which stands for "first in, first out." A waiting line in a bank or supermarket and a line of cars on a one-way street are types of queues.[1] Indeed, queues are often used in computer simulations of similar situations.

> **Queue** A data structure in which insertions are made at one end and deletions are made at the other.

Whereas the terminology for the insert and remove responsibilities on stacks is standard (**push, pop**), no such standardization exists with queues. The operation of inserting an element at the rear of the queue has many names in the literature: Insert, add, push, and enqueue are four common ones. Correspondingly, the operation for removing from the front of the queue is variously called delete, remove, pop, and dequeue.

C++ uses stack terminology for queues, where **push** applies to the back of the structure and **pop** applies to the front. In place of **top**, the operation **front** returns the element at the head of the queue. As with the stack, we need operations to check for an empty queue and to determine the size of a queue. The C++ implementation of a queue is atypical in that one more operation, **back**, returns the element at the rear of the queue. **FIGURE 17.5** shows an empty queue (a), insertion into a queue (b), and deletion from a queue (c).

Priority Queues

As we said in our shopping cart problem, a priority queue is a member of the queue family of structures. It behaves like a queue in that data is removed only from its front. Instead of inserting elements at the rear, however, elements are inserted so that they are in some given order, as shown in **FIGURE 17.6**. For example, passengers boarding an airplane are often called to line up in order of their seat assignments. Schoolchildren preparing to have their portraits taken may be told to line up in alphabetical order. In each case, the people enter the line at whatever point puts them in the proper order, but they leave the line only at the front.

> **Priority queue** A data structure in which insertions are made according to a specified ordering and deletions are made at one end.

As with queues, there is no standard terminology for priority queue responsibilities. C++ simply uses the stack terminology: **push, pop, top, empty,** and **size**. As a result, it is important to be careful in naming stack and priority queue objects so that it's easy to tell what kind of object each one is. Unlike with other structures, we can't rely on the operation names to help us identify the data type.

Here we should reiterate a key point made in Section 17.1: Data structures have a conceptual structure and an implementation structure, which may differ. We have just described the priority queue from the conceptual perspective. The STL typically uses a more complex and more efficient structure to implement the priority queue. As we describe other data

---

[1]. The word *queue* originates from French, but is in more widespread use around the globe. For example, where Americans would ask people to "line up," the British would ask them to "queue up."

a. An empty queue

b. Insertion into a queue

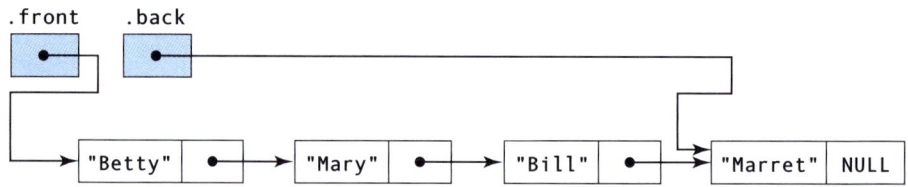

c. Deletion from a queue

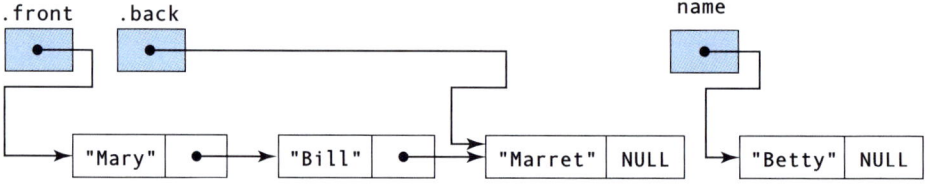

FIGURE 17.5 A Queue, Showing Insertion and Deletion Operations

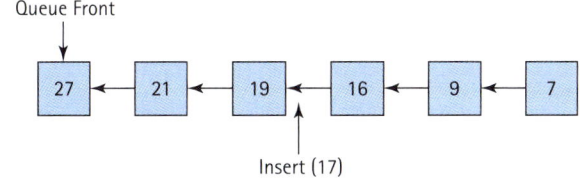

FIGURE 17.6 A Priority Queue, ADT Showing Insertion and Removal Points

structures in this chapter, keep in mind that we are looking at their conceptual arrangement. Except for a few cases, we do not describe how the STL implements them.

> **QUICK CHECK**
>
> **17.2.1** What are the two basic operations on a stack? (pp. 889–891)
> **17.2.2** Is a queue a LIFO structure or a FIFO structure? (p. 891)
> **17.2.3** What aspect of linear data structures dictates their differences? (p. 889)
> **17.2.4** What benefit arises when a data structure requires restricted access? (p. 889)
> **17.2.5** Describe how a priority queue could be used to implement software for a garage that performs an oil change on cars that are dropped off and given a specific pick-up time. (p. 891)

17.3 Bidirectional Linear Structures

Like the linked lists discussed in Chapter 14, queues are unidirectional structures. We traverse our lists from front to back. Elements in queues move from back to front. In a linked implementation, the components of the structures carry a link member that points to the next component. Even though elements in a stack may move down and up, they, too, can be implemented by links that point from the top down. It's more difficult to traverse the elements of these structures against the direction of their chain of links—analogous to petting a cat's fur in the wrong direction.

Bidirectional Lists

When we want a structure that can be traversed in either direction, an array is a natural choice. But when insertions and deletions in the middle of the data structure are common and random access is not as important, the array is appropriate neither as an ADT nor as an implementation. Instead, we want a list structure that provides for bidirectional traversal. Such a structure is known as a **bidirectional list**.

> **Bidirectional list** A list data structure in which traversals can be made in either direction.

In a linked implementation of the bidirectional list, we augment our list nodes with a second link that points in the opposite direction. We keep external references to the front and the back of the list, and we can step through the nodes by going either forward or backward, as shown in **FIGURE 17.7**.

With this structure, every insertion and every deletion require twice as many pointer operations, and the nodes have twice as much space allocated to pointer members, so there is an overall loss of efficiency. Thus, even though the bidirectional list is a more general structure with many attractive capabilities, it should be reserved for use only in those cases that need its extra features. Just as you wouldn't trim your houseplants with a chainsaw,

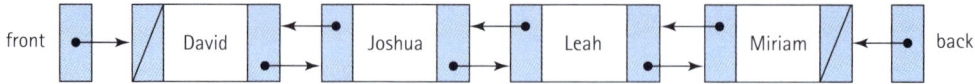

FIGURE 17.7 A Bidirectional Linked List

similarly there are many places where a bidirectional linked list is overkill. Having said that, be aware that the STL provides only a bidirectional implementation of the list ADT. Instead of a unidirectional list, it provides similar functionality with the **set** type, which has a much different implementation that we describe later in the chapter.

Deques

> **Deque** A data structure in which insertions and deletions are made at either end.

A *deque* (pronounced like "deck") is the bidirectional equivalent to the queue. With it, we can insert and delete elements at either end, as shown in **FIGURE 17.8**. In fact, the name is a word invented by computer scientists as a contraction of double-ended queue. If you want to simulate a waiting line in which people get frustrated and also leave from the back, a deque would be a good choice. It could also represent a train of railroad cars in a switchyard, where cars can be added and removed from either end of the train.

There is no consensus on the naming of deque operations. C++ uses **push_front** and **push_back** for insertion, **pop_front** and **pop_back** for deletions, and **front** and **back** for accessing the head and tail values. As we see when we look at the STL implementation, the C++ deque is really one huge class that combines a combination of the interfaces for the abstract bidirectional list, the deque, and the array.

Now it's time to take a look at the STL. We will focus on how it implements the interfaces for these linear ADTs—that is, how it implements the conceptual view of them. Data and control abstraction allow us to write whatever client code is needed to make use of these structures, without concerning ourselves about their internal implementations. We will return to our survey of abstract data structures later in the chapter, when we shift our focus to nonlinear organizations of data.

QUICK CHECK

17.3.1 What is the efficiency trade-off in using a bidirectional list? (pp. 893–894)
17.3.2 What is the difference between a *queue* and a *dequeue* data structure? (p. 894)

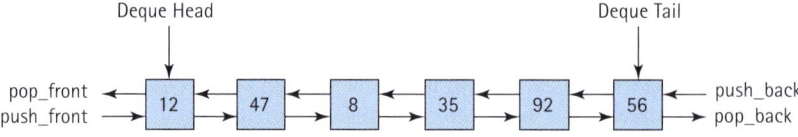

FIGURE 17.8 A Deque (Double-Ended Queue)

17.4 An Introduction to the STL

As the name Standard Template Library implies, the STL is made up primarily of templates. There are two main sections of the library: containers and algorithms. The containers portion has templates for 11 generic structured data types. Three of these data types are beyond the scope of this text: `bitset`, `multiset`, and `multimap`. The other 8 are summarized in the following table.

> **Container** The name used with respect to the C++ STL to refer to its generic data structures that hold an arbitrary number of elements.

Name	Description
`deque`	A double-ended queue. Also has bidirectional list and array (direct random access via an index) functionality.
`list`	A bidirectional list with similar capabilities to **deque**, but no direct index access.
`map`	Associates a lookup value (the key) with a value to be looked up. An example use would be a telephone directory.
`priority_queue`	A priority queue of elements ordered by a key value.
`queue`	A simple FIFO queue of elements.
`set`	An ordered collection of values that can be searched. Duplicates are not allowed. Similar in capability to the sorted list implemented in Chapter 13.
`stack`	A simple LIFO push-down stack of elements.
`vector`	Equivalent to an array, but able to change its size at runtime.

To declare and specialize any of these template classes, simply use its name, followed by the type in angle brackets. For example:

```
list<string> strList;     // Create an empty list of strings
vector<int> intVec;       // Create an empty vector of ints
```

We'll see different forms of constructors for each type as we look at them individually. The type of a container's elements can be either a built-in type or a class. The STL does impose some requirements on element objects. In particular, they must support at least a minimal subset of the overloaded relational operators. For most compilers, overloading < and == is sufficient, but a few require more of the operators to be overloaded.

The algorithms portion of the STL has a large number of function templates that can be used in many different contexts. In this text, we cover just a few of the algorithms in detail. The following table summarizes some of the more commonly used functions. Not all of these can be applied to every type of container.

Name	Description of Operation
copy	Copies a given range of elements in a container.
copy_backward	Copies a given range of elements in a container in reverse order.
equal	Compares a range of elements in two containers for equality.
find	Searches a range of elements in a container for a match with a specified value.
max	Given two elements comparable with the <, operator returns the greater one.
min	Given two elements comparable with the <, operator returns the lesser one.
random_shuffle	Randomly reorders the elements in a container within a specified range.
replace	Searches a container over a given range for elements that match a given value, replacing them with a second given value.
search	Searches a container within a given range for a series of elements that match a series from another container. Can be thought of as a generic equivalent of the string find operation for containers.
set_difference	Given two sets, returns their difference—that is, the values in the first set that are not present in the second set. Can be applied over specified ranges within each set.
set_intersection	Given two sets, returns their intersection—that is, the values in the first set that are also present in the second set. Can be applied over specified ranges within each set.
set_union	Given two sets, returns their union—that is, a set containing all of the values from both sets, but without duplicates. Can be applied over specified ranges within each set.
sort	Sorts the elements of a container within a given range.
transform	Applies a supplied function to all of the elements of a container within a given range.

We will look in more detail at each of the container classes, bringing in some of these algorithms as examples. Keep in mind that we are just skimming the surface of the capabilities of these templates so that you can get a sense of how they work. For a deeper treatment, you should consult one of the dedicated STL reference books.

Iterators

Before we begin, we must explore one key concept associated with container classes: the iterator. We've discussed iterators in the past, as one kind of responsibility a class can have. In the STL, an iterator is an object that points to some place in a container. One way to think of an iterator is as a pointer that has been wrapped in a class to provide additional functionality. It is called an iterator because the extra functionality includes operations that cause it to move in a step-by-step fashion through an STL container.

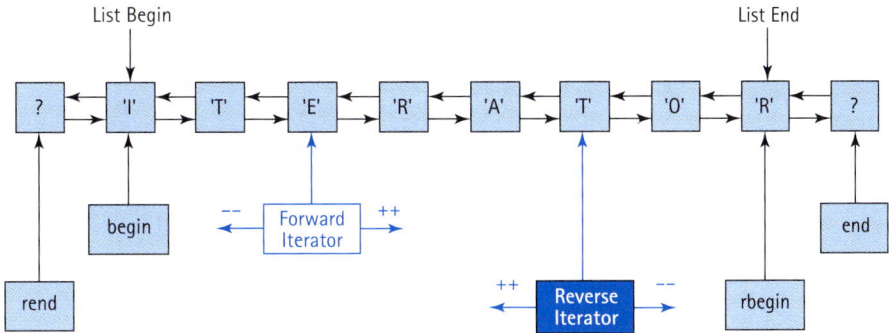

FIGURE 17.9 Forward and Reverse Iterators Associated with a List

Iterators in the STL come in two flavors: forward and reverse.[2] Typically, a container has methods called **begin** and **end** that return forward iterators pointing to its beginning and its end, respectively. You can use the ++ operator to advance a forward iterator through the container. Using -- shifts the iterator backward.

Methods called **rbegin** and **rend** return reverse iterators. The iterators returned by **rbegin** and **rend** point to the end and the beginning of a container, respectively. Using ++ with a reverse iterator moves it from the back toward the front, and applying -- causes a move toward the back. That is, the semantics of a reverse iterator are the opposite of those of a forward iterator. A reverse iterator begins at the end of a container and "advances" toward the front. **FIGURE 17.9** illustrates this relationship.

The design of these iterators is meant to make it especially easy to traverse a container with a For loop. What **end** returns is actually an iterator referring to a point just beyond the last element. Similarly, the iterator returned by **rend** refers to a position just before the start of the container. As we'll see, this odd-sounding convention simplifies the termination condition in For loops. Be aware, however, that you cannot use the values returned by **end** and **rend** to directly access the ends of the container.

With random-access containers (such as **deque** and **vector**), the arithmetic operators + and - can be applied to iterators, just as we would use them with array indexes to compute the location of another element. Many C++ programmers think of an iterator as just another kind of pointer. In reality, the STL classifies a pointer the other way around—as a kind of iterator. Keep in mind that an iterator is an object. Not only does it provide extra operations, but it may also have restrictions that constrain its capabilities as compared to the capabilities of a pointer. For example, a unidirectional data structure limits its iterators to forward motion alone.

One very important aspect of iterators is the fact that they remain valid only as long as the contents of the container do not change. When an element is inserted into or deleted from a container, its iterators become invalid because C++ doesn't guarantee how the contents of a container are arranged after a change has occurred. The idea is that STL implementors

---

[2]. The STL actually defines five types of iterators. To keep things simple, however, we focus on just these two kinds of iterator behavior.

are free to reorganize the data so as to improve efficiency. The container class cannot keep track of every iterator that's pointing to it, so there is no way to update these iterators when a change takes place.

Each iterator must be declared for the specific type of container with which it will be used. For example, if we need iterators for a list of strings, we would declare them as follows:

```
list<string>::iterator place;          // Create a forward iterator
list<string>::reverse_iterator rplace; // Create a reverse iterator
```

The `vector` Template

Our tour of the STL's containers begins with one that, in the abstract, is very easy to understand. The `vector` class template implements an array. Why would we want another way to define an array? Well, there is one more thing about `vector`—it doesn't have to be fixed in size. As a consequence, we don't have to worry about subarray processing or decide how big to make the array when we declare it. Otherwise, however, you can almost directly substitute this container for the built-in array.

We say "almost" because a `vector` is an object rather than a built-in structure. Thus it must be instantiated with a constructor at run time. For this reason, we cannot declare it using an initialization list, as we can an array. Here are some simple calls to `vector` constructors:

```
vector<int> intVec(20);     // A vector holding 20 integers,
                            //    all initialized to 0
vector<string> noSizeVec;   // A vector holding 0 strings
```

The first statement makes sense—it's similar to writing this code:

```
int intVec[20];
```

But why would we want to declare a `vector` with no space in it? The reason is that a `vector` automatically expands to hold as much data as we put into it. Thus, if we don't have any idea of how many strings we will put into `noSizeVec`, we simply declare it with no elements and let the structure grow as we insert values.

If a `vector` always adjusts its size to hold the data, why do we ever need to bother with specifying a size? The answer is that this flexibility comes at a price. Every time a `vector` grows, it can take quite a bit of work. The underlying implementation is an array, and the template simply allocates a new, larger array and moves the old contents into it. Thus, when we know a maximum size in advance, it makes sense to indicate that value in the constructor.

Let's see an example of a `vector` in action. In Chapter 11, we wrote a demonstration program that allows the user to look up the number of occupants in a given apartment. Here is that program rewritten to use a `vector` directly with the changes highlighted. Recall that we fixed the number of apartments at 10.

```cpp
//*****************************************************************
// This program allows a building owner to look up how many
// occupants are in a given apartment
//*****************************************************************
#include <iostream>
#include <fstream>              // For file I/O
#include <vector>               // For vector template
using namespace std;

const int BUILDING_SIZE = 10;   // Number of apartments

int main()
{
  vector<int> occupants(BUILDING_SIZE);  // occupants[i] is the number of
                                         //    occupants in apartment i
  int totalOccupants;           // Total number of occupants
  int counter;                  // Loop control and index variable
  int apt;                      // An apartment number
  ifstream inFile;              // File of occupant data (one
                                //    integer per apartment)
  inFile.open("apt.dat");
  totalOccupants = 0;
  for (counter = 0; counter < BUILDING_SIZE; counter++)
  {
    inFile >> occupants[counter];
    totalOccupants = totalOccupants + occupants[counter];
  }
  cout << "No. of apts. is " << BUILDING_SIZE << endl
       << "Total no. of occupants is " << totalOccupants << endl;

  cout << "Begin apt. lookup..." << endl;
  do
  {
    cout << "Apt. number (1 through " << BUILDING_SIZE
         << ", or 0 to quit): ";
    cin >> apt;
    if (apt > 0)
      cout << "Apt. " << apt << " has " << occupants[apt-1]
           << " occupants" << endl;
  } while (apt > 0);
  return 0;
}
```

As you can see, the **vector** almost directly replaces the array. Because the class overloads the **[]** operator, we can access the elements using index notation, both in storing values in the **vector** and in retrieving them. Our example, however, doesn't fully illustrate the potential power of the **vector** template. Let's rewrite the program so that it grows the **vector** to hold as much apartment data as is on the input file.

Of course, we have to change the loop from a For to a While, testing the state of the `inFile` stream and using a priming read. The constant `BUILDING_SIZE` is no longer useful, so we remove it. But how do we determine the size value to output? We use the `vector` `size` method. For example:

```
cout << "No. of apts. is " << occupants.size() << endl
```

Well, that's simple enough. But what about adding elements to the `vector`? For that we have to call the `push_back` method, which appends the element passed as its argument to the end of the `vector`, increasing its size if necessary.

In the original program, we didn't check whether the apartment number input by the user was in the valid range. We could use the `size` method again, with an If statement that guards the access to `occupants[apt-1]`, but that solution also ignores another useful feature of `vector`. If we use the `at` method instead of index access, the range is automatically checked, and we can easily catch an `out_of_range` exception (remember that we have to include `<stdexcept>` to access this exception class).

Here then, is the revised code with the changes highlighted, followed by a new data file containing 18 values, and the output from a sample run.

```cpp
//*****************************************************************
// This program allows a building owner to look up how many
// occupants are in a given apartment
//*****************************************************************
#include <iostream>
#include <fstream>              // For file I/O
#include <vector>               // For vector template
#include <stdexcept>            // For out_of_range exception
using namespace std;

int main()
{
    vector<int> occupants;      // occupants vector with 0 elements
    int totalOccupants;         // Total number of occupants
    int apt;                    // An apartment number
    int aptOccupants;           // Occupants in one apartment
    ifstream inFile;            // File of occupant data (one
                                //    integer per apartment)
    inFile.open("apt.dat");
    totalOccupants = 0;
    inFile >> aptOccupants;
    while (inFile)
    {
      occupants.push_back(aptOccupants);
      totalOccupants = totalOccupants + aptOccupants;
      inFile >> aptOccupants;
    }
    cout << "No. of apts. is " << occupants.size() << endl
         << "Total no. of occupants is " << totalOccupants << endl;

    cout << "Begin apt. lookup..." << endl;
```

```
  do
  {
    cout << "Apt. number (1 through " << occupants.size()
         << ", or 0 to quit): ";
    cin >> apt;
    if (apt > 0)
      try
      {
         cout << "Apt. " << apt << " has " << occupants.at(apt-1)
              << " occupants" << endl;
      }
      catch(out_of_range)
      {
        cout << "Invalid apartment number. Enter ";
      }

  } while (apt > 0);
  return 0;
}
```

Data file:

```
3 4 0 3 4 1 1 2 3 2 1 4 2 3 0 5 2 3
```

Test run:

```
No. of apts. is 18
Total no. of occupants is 43
Begin apt. lookup...
Apt. number (1 through 18, or 0 to quit): 4
Apt. 4 has 3 occupants
Apt. number (1 through 18, or 0 to quit): 14
Apt. 14 has 3 occupants
Apt. number (1 through 18, or 0 to quit): 18
Apt. 18 has 3 occupants
Apt. number (1 through 18, or 0 to quit): 19
Invalid apartment number. Enter Apt. number (1 through 18, or 0 to quit): 15
Apt. 15 has 0 occupants
Apt. number (1 through 18, or 0 to quit): 0
```

The preceding example demonstrates just a few of the operators available with `vector`. The following table summarizes these and lists additional operators that are commonly used:

Name	Parameters	Returns	Description
at	int	reference	Returns a reference to the value at the specified location, checking the range.
back		reference	Returns a reference to the last element.
begin		iterator	Returns an iterator to the first element.
capacity		int	Returns the number of elements that can be held.
clear			Removes all elements. Sets `size` to 0.
empty		bool	Returns `true` if there are no elements in the `vector`.
end		iterator	Returns an iterator beyond the end of the `vector`.
erase	iterator		Removes the element at the iterator position. The `size` decreases.
front		reference	Returns a reference to the first element.
insert	iterator, value		Inserts the value at the location specified by the iterator. The `size` increases.
push_back	value		Inserts the value at the end of the vector. The `size` increases.
rbegin		reverse_iterator	Returns a reverse iterator to the last element.
rend		reverse_iterator	Returns a reverse iterator before the start of the `vector`.
reserve	int		Indicates that the `capacity` of the `vector` should increase to the amount specified.
size		int	Returns the number of elements in the `vector`.

There are a few additional things to note about these methods. The `at` method returns a reference that can be used for either access or assignment. That is, we can also write

`occupants.at(3) = 5;`

to set the fourth element of the `vector` to 5, with range checking of the index.

The **capacity** of a **vector** is not the same as its **size**. The **capacity** is the number of spaces allocated for elements. In simple cases, the values of **capacity** and **size** may be the same. We can also use **reserve** to increase the **capacity** beyond the **size**, however. The advantage of doing so is that as the number of elements grows, the **vector** doesn't have to allocate larger and larger arrays, in addition to copying data between them. For example, if we insert

```
occupants.reserve(20);
```

after declaring **occupants**, then our program would not have to do any reallocations or make any copies of the data set we gave it. The test run would still show that **size** is 18, but if we were to insert

```
cout << occupants.capacity();
```

in the program, the value 20 would be output. **FIGURE 17.10** shows a **vector<char>** for which 10 spaces have been reserved and 6 elements have been inserted.

This is also different from calling the **vector** constructor with a number of elements specified, as we did in the previous version of our program:

```
vector<int> occupants(BUILDING_SIZE);
```

In this case, **occupants** is constructed with 10 elements, all initialized to the default value for the type (0 for **int**). Thus its initial **size** and **capacity** are both 10.

One other form of constructor is particularly useful. We may not be able to use an initializer list with a **vector**, but we can initialize it from an array of values. For example:

```
int occData[] = {3,4,0,3,4,1,1,2,3,2,1,4,2,3,0,5,2,3};
vector<int> occupants(occData, occData+sizeof(occData)/sizeof(int));
```

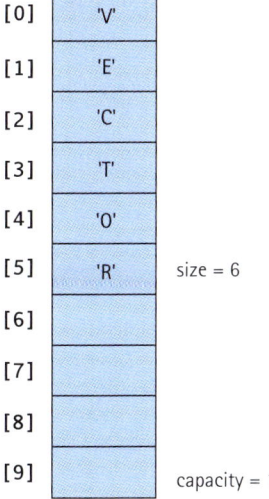

FIGURE 17.10 A **vector<char>** with **capacity** 10, After Insertion of 6 Elements

This constructor takes two iterators as its parameters. Recall that whenever we pass an array as an argument, what actually gets sent to the parameter is the memory address of the first element (the base address). Thus the first argument, `occData`, is the base address of the already initialized array. The second argument,

```
occData+sizeof(occData)/sizeof(int)
```

is the address that is one greater than the location of the last element of the array. The formula first determines the number of elements in `occData` by dividing its size (in bytes) by the size of its element (in bytes). The number of elements is added to the address for the beginning of the array to produce the address for the end of the array. C++ automatically casts these addresses into iterators of the appropriate type as they are passed to the constructor. The constructor is designed so that the address just beyond the end of the array is a sentinel value—it doesn't copy that location into the vector.

Lastly, the `vector` template provides a copy constructor that lets us simply pass another `vector` as an argument, and a new `vector` is created with the same size and content.

The `list` Template

Now that we've seen how `vector` works, we can quickly introduce the remaining containers. Many of their operations have similar functionality. For example, `list` also defines `back`, `begin`, `clear`, `empty`, `end`, `erase`, `front`, `insert`, `push_back`, `rbegin`, `rend`, and `size`, with essentially the same meanings as for `vector`. Because it is a linked implementation, `list` does not define a `capacity` or `reserve`. Also, because it doesn't support random access, the `[]` operator is not overloaded, nor is the `at` operation supported.

The same four forms of constructors are also defined for `list`. That is, we can create a `list` with zero elements, a `list` with a specific number of elements initialized to a default value, a `list` initialized from an array or another container, or a `list` created by using a copy constructor. The following table describes some additional operators that `list` supports.

Name	Parameters	Description
merge	list	Inserts the elements of the parameter `list` into the current `list`, in order. The elements are deleted from the parameter `list`. If the `lists` were already sorted, the result is a sorted `list` containing both sets of elements.
pop_back		Removes the last element.
pop_front		Removes the first element.
push_front	value	Inserts the value as the first element.
remove	value	Removes all elements with the specified value.
reverse		Reverses the order of the elements in the `list`.
sort		Sorts the elements from least to greatest.
unique		Removes all but the first element in any group of adjacent elements with the same value. If the `list` is sorted, the result is that it contains only unique values.

To see how `list` works, we present the following nonsense example program that creates a `list` from user input, displays its contents in different ways, applies various mutator operations, and merges it with another `list`. Here is the code:

```cpp
//*******************************************************
// This program demonstrates various list methods
//*******************************************************
#include <iostream>
#include <list>
using namespace std;

int main ()
{
  list<string> demo;              // Create an empty list
  string word;
  cout << "Enter a line with six words:" << endl;
  for (int i = 1; i <= 6; i++)
  {
    cin >> word;
    demo.push_back(word);         // Insert elements at back
  }
  // Access front, back, and size
  cout << "Front element: " << demo.front() << endl
       << "Back element: " << demo.back() << endl
       << "Size of list: " << demo.size() << endl;
  // Create a forward iterator
  list<string>::iterator place;
  cout << "List contents from beginning to end: " << endl;
  // Traverse list in forward direction
  for (place = demo.begin(); place != demo.end(); place++)
    cout << *place << " ";
  // Create a reverse iterator
  list<string>::reverse_iterator rplace;
  cout << endl << "List contents from end to beginning: " << endl;
  // Traverse list in backward direction
  for (rplace = demo.rbegin(); rplace != demo.rend(); ++rplace)
    cout << *rplace << " ";
  cout << endl << "Enter a word to insert after the first word: ";
  cin >> word;
  place = demo.begin();           // Point forward iterator to front
  ++place;                        // Advance one place
  demo.insert(place, word);       // Insert an element
  place = demo.end();             // Point forward iterator past end
  --place;                        // Move back to last element
  --place;                        // Move back one more place
  demo.erase(place);              // Delete element
  cout << "Next to last word has been erased." << endl;
  cout << "Enter a word to add at the front: ";
  cin >> word;
  demo.push_front(word);          // Insert at front
  cout << "List contents from beginning to end: " << endl;
```

```cpp
      for (place = demo.begin(); place != demo.end(); ++place)
        cout << *place << " ";
      demo.sort();                  // Sort the elements
      cout << endl
           << "After sorting, list contents from beginning to end: "
           << endl;
      for (place = demo.begin(); place != demo.end(); ++place)
        cout << *place << " ";
      // Create a three element list from an array of strings
      string init[] = {"large", "medium", "small"};
      list<string> demo2(init, init+sizeof(init)/sizeof(string));
      cout << endl << "After merging with: ";
      for (place = demo2.begin(); place != demo2.end(); ++place)
        cout << *place << " ";
      demo.merge(demo2);            // Merge the two lists
      cout << endl << "List contents are: " << endl;
      for (place = demo.begin(); place != demo.end(); ++place)
        cout << *place << " ";
      return 0;
}
```

Here is the output from a test run:

```
Enter a line with six words:
quick fox jumped over lazy dog
Front element: quick
Back element: dog
Size of list: 6
List contents from beginning to end:
quick fox jumped over lazy dog
List contents from end to beginning:
dog lazy over jumped fox quick
Enter a word to insert after the first word: brown
Next to last word has been erased.
Enter a word to add at the front: the
List contents from beginning to end:
the quick brown fox jumped over dog
After sorting, list contents from beginning to end:
brown dog fox jumped over quick the
After merging with: large medium small
List contents are:
brown dog fox jumped large medium over quick small the
```

The `stack` Template

Unlike `list`, which provides a very general set of container operations, the goal of the `stack` type is to model a LIFO push-down stack as simply as possible. It has only five methods associated with it, which are listed in the following table.

17.4 An Introduction to the STL

Name	Parameters	Returns	Description
empty		bool	Returns **true** if there are no elements in the **stack**.
top		reference	Returns a reference to the value of the top element.
push	value		Inserts the value as the top element.
pop			Removes the top element.
size		int	Returns the number of elements in the **stack**.

There are two ways to create a **stack**, either as an empty container or as a copy of a **vector**, **list**, or **deque**.

```
stack<float> fltStack;          // Create an empty stack of floats
stack<string> strStack(demo);   // Create string stack from list demo
```

Here is a short demonstration program that inputs some words, pushing them on the stack and printing them in reverse order as they are popped from the top.

```cpp
//*****************************************************
// This program demonstrates various stack methods
//*****************************************************
#include <iostream>
#include <stack>
using namespace std;

int main ()
{
  stack<string> strStack;              // Create an empty stack
  string word;
  cout << "Enter a line with six words:" << endl;
  for (int i = 1; i <= 6; i++)
  {
    cin >> word;
    strStack.push(word);               // Insert elements at top
  }
  // Access top and size
  cout << "Top element: " << strStack.top() << endl
       << "Size of stack: " << strStack.size() << endl;
  // Print the stack
  cout << "Stack contents:" << endl;
  while (!strStack.empty())
  {
    cout << strStack.top() << endl;
    strStack.pop();                    // Remove elements from top
  }
  return 0;
}
```

```
Enter a line with six words:
four score and seven years ago
Top element: ago
Size of stack: 6
Stack contents:
ago
years
seven
and
score
four
```

The queue Template

The design philosophy behind **queue** is the same as for **stack**: Keep it simple. The most significant difference is that **push** inserts elements at one end of the data structure and **pop** removes them from the other end. In addition to the observer, **front**, for the element that is about to be popped, **queue** provides **back** to allow us to look at the element most recently pushed. Here is a summary of its operations:

Name	Parameters	Returns	Description
empty		bool	Returns **true** if there are no elements in the **queue**.
front		reference	Returns a reference to the value of the front element.
back		reference	Returns a reference to the value of the back element.
push	value		Inserts the value as the back element.
pop			Removes the front element.
size		int	Returns the number of elements in the **queue**.

As with **stack**, there are two forms of constructor for **queue**. The default creates an empty **queue**, and the other form lets us initialize the **queue** with a copy of the contents of a **vector**, **list**, or **deque**.

Here is a sample program, very similar to the one we showed for **stack**, illustrating the basic differences between the two types.

```
//*****************************************************
// This program demonstrates various queue methods
//*****************************************************
#include <iostream>
#include <queue>
using namespace std;
```

```cpp
int main ()
{
  queue<string> strQueue;           // Create an empty queue
  string word;
  cout << "Enter a line with six words:" << endl;
  for (int i = 1; i <= 6; i++)
  {
    cin >> word;
    strQueue.push(word);            // Insert elements at back
  }
  // Access front, back, and size
  cout << "Front element: " << strQueue.front() << endl
       << "Back element: " << strQueue.back() << endl
       << "Size of queue: " << strQueue.size() << endl;
  // Print the queue
  cout << "Queue contents:" << endl;
  while (!strQueue.empty())
  {
    cout << strQueue.front() << endl;
    strQueue.pop();                 // Remove elements from front
  }
  return 0;
}
```

Here is a test run with the same data that we used for our **stack** example. As you can see, the words emerge in the order that they were entered, rather than in reverse order.

```
Enter a line with six words:
four score and seven years ago
Front element: four
Back element: ago
Size of queue: 6
Queue contents:
four
score
and
seven
years
ago
```

The `priority_queue` Template

The `priority_queue` is a variation on the idea of a queue that also bears some resemblance to a **stack**. The major difference is that the elements in the structure are kept in sorted order. Thus **push** inserts elements using an insertion sort so that they go directly to their proper places in the ordering. At one end, **top** observes the element with the greatest value and application of **pop** removes it. An example of a priority queue is what happens in an emergency room at the hospital: Cases are arranged with the most urgent at the head of the waiting line, and then the cases are taken in order. As subsequent cases arrive, they are inserted in the waiting line according to their urgency.

Here is a summary of the `priority_queue` operations:

Name	Parameters	Returns	Description
empty		bool	Returns `true` if the priority queue contains no elements.
top		reference	Returns a reference to the value of the top element.
push	value		Inserts the value according to the ordering of the type.
pop			Removes the top element.
size		int	Returns the number of elements in the priority queue.

One of the quirks of the STL's organization is that `priority_queue` is not kept in its own header file. Instead, it shares the same file with `queue`; thus we include `<queue>` instead of `<priority_queue>`. This type supports the empty constructor, and more like `list` and company, it provides a second constructor that allows us to initialize the values from another container. Unlike with `stack` and `queue`, there is no straight copy constructor.

Here is a revision of our example `stack` program, adapted to the `priority_queue` so that we can appreciate the difference in this structure's behavior. Note that the queue outputs its contents in reverse alphabetical order.

```cpp
//***********************************************************
// This program demonstrates various priority_queue methods
//***********************************************************
#include <iostream>
#include <queue>
using namespace std;

int main ()
{
  priority_queue<string> strQueue; // Create an empty priority_queue
  string word;
  cout << "Enter a line with six words:" << endl;
  for (int i = 1; i <= 6; i++)
  {
    cin >> word;
    strQueue.push(word);           // Insert elements in place
  }
  // Access top and size
  cout << "Top element: " << strQueue.top() << endl
       << "Size of priority_queue: " << strQueue.size() << endl;
  // Print the priority_queue
  cout << "Priority queue contents:" << endl;
  while (!strQueue.empty())
  {
    cout << strQueue.top() << endl;
    strQueue.pop();                // Remove elements from top
  }
  return 0;
}
```

Here is the output for the revised program:

```
Enter a line with six words:
four score and seven years ago
Top element: years
Size of priority_queue: 6
Priority queue contents:
years
seven
score
four
and
ago
```

The deque Template

Whereas **stack** and **queue** strive to keep things simple, the design for **deque** takes the opposite approach. With **deque**, we get a panoply of features taken from the containers we've already seen.

For example, **deque** replicates most of the operations of **list**: back, begin, clear, empty, end, erase, front, insert, pop_back, pop_front, push_back, push_front, rbegin, rend, and size, with essentially the same meanings. Like **vector**, it overloads [] and at to provide random access. Being linked, it does not need to support capacity or reserve operations. Nor does it directly support merge, remove, reverse, sort, or unique, because equivalent function templates with the same names are defined in the algorithms section of the STL, all of which can be applied to **deque**. This template provides constructors of the same four forms that **list** supplies: We can create a **deque** with zero elements, a **deque** with a specific number of elements initialized to a default value, a **deque** initialized from an array or another container, and a **deque** created with a copy constructor.

If **deque** encompasses **list** and **vector**, why shouldn't we always use it? As always, this increase in capability costs us in terms of efficiency. The underlying array implementation of a **vector** is usually much faster than that of a **deque**. We say "usually" because, if a large **vector** must change its capacity frequently, the linked implementation of a **deque** can outperform it. Random access in a **deque** is also not as efficient as for a **vector**. How does **deque** compare with **list**? Because a **list** doesn't have to support random access, deletions and insertions at points other than its ends can be much faster. However, when you really need the combination of **vector** and **list** features in one structure, **deque** is quite useful to have in the library.

The naming of **list** and **deque** in the STL is really somewhat misleading, because both can act as either a list or a deque in the abstract sense. The STL **list** is a general bidirectional list with support for deque operations. The STL **deque** is also a bidirectional list, with support for both deque operations and random-access indexing.

Because we've already seen the features of **deque** with other containers, an operation summary table is redundant. We will demonstrate the use of a **deque** in the Problem-Solving Case Study at the end of the chapter.

MAY WE INTRODUCE Sir Charles Antony Richard Hoare

Tony Hoare's interest in computing was awakened in the early fifties, when he studied philosophy (together with Latin and Greek) at Oxford University, under the tutelage of John Lucas. He was fascinated by the power of mathematical logic as an explanation of the apparent certainty of mathematical truth. During his National Service (1956–1958), he studied Russian in the Royal Navy. Then he took a qualification in statistics (and incidentally) a course in programming given by Leslie Fox. In 1959, as a graduate student at Moscow State University, he studied the machine translation of languages (together with probability theory) in the school of Kolmogorov. To assist in efficient look-up of words in a dictionary, he discovered the well-known sorting algorithm Quicksort.

On return to England in 1960, he worked as a programmer for Elliott Brothers, a small scientific computer manufacturer. He led a team (including his later wife Jill) in the design and delivery of the first commercial compiler for the programming language Algol 60. He attributes the success of the project to the use of Algol itself as the design language for the compiler, although the implementation used decimal machine code. Promoted to the rank of Chief Engineer, he then led a larger team on a disastrous project to implement an operating system. After managing a recovery from the failure, he moved as Chief Scientist to the computing research division, where he worked on the hardware and software architecture for future machines.

These machines were cancelled when the company merged with its rivals, and in 1968 Tony took a chance to apply for the Professorship of Computing Science at the Queen's University, Belfast. His research goal was to understand why operating systems were so much more difficult than compilers, and to see if advances in programming theory and languages could help with the problems of concurrency. In spite of civil disturbances, he built up a strong teaching and research department, and published a series of papers on the use of assertions to prove correctness of computer programs. He knew that this was long-term research, unlikely to achieve industrial application within the span of his academic career.

In 1977 he moved to Oxford University, and undertook to build up the Programming Research Group, founded by Christopher Strachey. With the aid of external funding from government initiatives, industrial collaborations, and charitable donations, Oxford now teaches a range of degree courses in Computer Science, including an external Master's degree for software engineers from industry. The research of his teams at Oxford pursued an ideal that takes provable correctness as the driving force for the accurate specification, design and development of computing systems, both critical and non-critical. Well-known results of the research include the Z specification language, and the CSP concurrent programming model. A recent personal research goal has been the unification of a diverse range of theories applying to different programming languages, paradigms, and implementation technologies.

Throughout more than thirty years as an academic, Tony has maintained strong contacts with industry, through consultancy, teaching, and collaborative research projects. He took a particular interest in the sustenance of legacy code, where assertions are now playing a vital role, not for his original purpose of program proof, but rather in instrumentation of code for testing purposes. On reaching retirement age at Oxford, he welcomed an opportunity to go back to industry as a senior researcher with Microsoft Research in Cambridge. He hopes to expand the opportunities for industrial application of good academic research, and to encourage academic researchers to continue

MAY WE INTRODUCE Sir Charles Antony Richard Hoare, continued

the pursuit of deep and interesting questions in areas of long-term interest to the software industry and its customers.

    The above biographical sketch was written by Sir Tony Hoare himself and reprinted with his permission. What he does not say is that he received the Turing Award in 1980, at the age of 46, for his fundamental contributions to the definition and design of programming languages and was awarded a Knighthood in 1999 for his services to education and computer science.

SOFTWARE MAINTENANCE CASE STUDY: Appointment Calendar Using STL List

MAINTENANCE TASK: In Chapter 15, we developed a set of classes to support an appointment calendar application, and a simple driver with which to test them. We used our linked implementation of a list to hold the calendar data. Now that we have learned how to use the STL **list** class, let's see how much work it will take to convert our prior work to make use of it. In theory, this should be fairly easy.

EXISTING CODE: Recall that our appointment calendar project had six underlying classes. Three of these provide the attributes of an entry: **Name**, **TimeOfDay**, and **Date**. We originally developed a base class called **Entry**, containing just **Name** and **TimeOfDay**. We then derived a subclass from **Entry**, called **EntryWithDate**, that added support for a **Date** attribute. The **AppointmentCalendar** class used our **List** class to create a list of **EntryWithDate** objects that we could search and update. To keep things simple, we did not actually make use of the **TimeOfDay** attribute, but distinguished appointments only by their date and name.

    Because our **List** class kept its data unsorted, we took the approach of performing a linear search on the list, removing the element to be updated, and then appending the new version to the end of the list.

    In Chapter 16, we changed the **Date** class so that it uses the overloaded relational operators rather than the **ComparedTo** function. Let's also make this update to our appointment calendar. That step will necessitate some changes to **EntryWithDate**, but we know that its use of **ComparedTo** likewise must be revised to overload at least the < and == operators so that we can use this class with the **list** container.

DISCUSSION: Looking over the classes in our original solution, even at the abstract level, we can see that **Name**, **TimeOfDay**, and **Entry** do not depend on any of the changes we are making. We should be able to use them unchanged. Our goal should be to hide the changes from the driver, within the encapsulating interface of **AppointmentCalendar**.

    We know that **EntryWithDate** must be updated to use the relational operators supplied by the revised **Date** class, and that it must itself supply overloaded relational operators for at least < and == to enable the STL **list** to work with it. For generality's sake, we can just include all of the relational operators. Once we have < and == implemented, we can write the others by cutting and pasting from them with minor changes (often called cookie-cutter coding).

    Recall that we defined equality for entries as having the same date and name. How should we define "less than"? For now, let's just use the date to order entries. The implication of this choice is that within

SOFTWARE MAINTENANCE CASE STUDY: Appointment Calendar Using STL List

a single date, the ordering of entries isn't significant. In the future, we would clearly amend this definition to take into account the time and perhaps to alphabetically order elements by name.

We now have enough information to code the new version of this class:

```cpp
//*******************************************
// SPECIFICATION File for class EntryWithDate
//*******************************************
#include "Date.h"
#include "Entry.h"
class EntryWithDate : public Entry
{
public:
  // Constructors
  EntryWithDate();
  EntryWithDate(Date initDate, TimeOfDay initTime, Name initName);
  // Knowledge responsibility
  Date GetDate() const;
  bool operator<(const EntryWithDate& otherEntry) const;
  // Post: Returns true if instance comes before otherEntry
  bool operator>(const EntryWithDate& otherEntry) const;
  // Post: Returns true if instance comes after otherEntry
  bool operator==(const EntryWithDate& otherEntry) const;
  // Post: Returns true if instance is the same date as otherEntry
  bool operator<=(const EntryWithDate& otherEntry) const;
  // Post: Returns true if instance is <= otherEntry
  bool operator>=(const EntryWithDate& otherEntry) const;
  // Post: Returns true if instance is >= otherEntry
  bool operator!=(const EntryWithDate& otherEntry) const;
  // Post: Returns true if instance is != otherEntry
private:
  Date date;
};
```

```cpp
//***********************************************************
// IMPLEMENTATION FILE for class EntryWithDate
//***********************************************************

#include "EntryWithDate.h"

EntryWithDate::EntryWithDate()
{ };

//***********************************************************
```

SOFTWARE MAINTENANCE CASE STUDY: Appointment Calendar Using STL List

```cpp
EntryWithDate::EntryWithDate
  (Date initDate, TimeOfDay initTime, Name initName) :
    Entry(initName.GetFirstName(), initName.GetMiddleName(),
          initName.GetLastName(), initTime.GetHours(),
          initTime.GetMinutes(), initTime.GetSeconds())

{
  date = initDate;
}

//*******************************************************

Date EntryWithDate::GetDate() const
{ return date; }

//*******************************************************

bool EntryWithDate::operator<(const EntryWithDate& otherEntry) const
{
  return date < otherEntry.GetDate();
}
//*******************************************************

bool EntryWithDate::operator>(const EntryWithDate& otherEntry) const
{
  return date > otherEntry.GetDate();
}

//*******************************************************

bool EntryWithDate::operator==(const EntryWithDate& otherEntry) const
{
  return (date == otherEntry.GetDate() &&
          (GetName().ComparedTo(otherEntry.GetName()) == SAME));
}

//*******************************************************

bool EntryWithDate::operator<=(const EntryWithDate& otherEntry) const
{
  return
    date < otherEntry.GetDate() || date == otherEntry.GetDate();
}
//*******************************************************

bool EntryWithDate::operator>=(const EntryWithDate& otherEntry) const
{
  return
    date > otherEntry.GetDate() || date == otherEntry.GetDate();
}
```

SOFTWARE MAINTENANCE CASE STUDY: Appointment Calendar Using STL List

```
//**********************************************************
bool EntryWithDate::operator!=(const EntryWithDate& otherEntry) const
{
  return !(otherEntry == *this);
}
```

Next we turn our attention to the **AppointmentCalendar** class, which makes use of the **list**. Let's look first at the original version of the specification file:

```
//**********************************************************
// SPECIFICATION FILE for class AppointmentCalendar
//**********************************************************

#include "List.h"
#include <fstream>
using namespace std;

class AppointmentCalendar
{
public:
  // Constructor
  AppointmentCalendar(ifstream& inFile);
  // Knowledge responsibility
  bool AppointmentCalendar::IsThere(Name name, Date date)
  // Returns true if an entry exists with the given name and date

  // Action responsibilities
  EntryWithDate GetEntry(Name name, Date date);
  // Returns entry with time field equal to time
  // Pre:  entry with time field equal to time exists
  void InsertEntry(EntryWithDate initEntry);
  // Inserts entry into list
  void WriteListToFile(ofstream& outFile);
  // Writes list to outFile

private:
  List list;
};
```

Obviously, we need to include `<list>` rather than `"List.h"` and we will use `list<EntryWithDate>` as the type for `list`. Oh no! We gave our entry list the same name as the STL type. We should change it to **entryList**. Is there anything else to change here? If we plan to hide the changes from the driver, then the only changes should be to the private part of the interface; that means we are done with updating the specification file.

SOFTWARE MAINTENANCE CASE STUDY: Appointment Calendar Using STL List

Here is the new version with the changes highlighted:

```
//*******************************************************
// SPECIFICATION FILE for class AppointmentCalendar
//*******************************************************

#include <list>
#include <fstream>
#include "EntryWithDate.h"
using namespace std;

class AppointmentCalendar
{
public:
  // Constructor
  AppointmentCalendar(ifstream& inFile);
  // Knowledge responsibility
  bool IsThere(Name name, Date date);
  // Returns true if an entry exists with the given name and date

  // Action responsibilities
  EntryWithDate GetEntry(Name name, Date date);
  // Returns entry with time field equal to time
  // Pre:  entry with time field equal to time exists
  void InsertEntry(EntryWithDate initEntry);
  // Inserts entry into list
  void WriteListToFile(ofstream& outFile);
  // Writes list to outFile

private:
  list<EntryWithDate> entryList;
};
```

Thus far the changes have been very straightforward. As we expected, all of the significant changes are confined to the implementation of **AppointmentCalendar**. Let's go through it method-by-method to see what we need to revise.

Here is the original version of the constructor, which reads a file and inserts it into the list. Everything in the code is concerned with building up the pieces of an entry, which hasn't changed (even though the implementation of **Date** is different, it still uses the same form of constructor).

```
AppointmentCalendar::AppointmentCalendar(ifstream& inFile)
{
  int hours, minutes, seconds;   // for class TimeOfDay
  int month, day, year;          // for class Date
  string first, middle, last;    // for class Name
  int numberEntries;
  inFile >> numberEntries;
```

SOFTWARE MAINTENANCE CASE STUDY: Appointment Calendar Using STL List

```
  for (int counter = 0; counter < numberEntries; counter++)
  {
    inFile >> hours >> minutes >> seconds;
    TimeOfDay time(hours, minutes, seconds);
    inFile >> month >> day >> year;
    Date date(month, day, year);
    inFile >> first >> middle >> last;
    Name name(first, middle, last);
    EntryWithDate entry(date, time, name);
    list.Insert(entry);
  }
}
```

Only the very last statement makes reference to **list**. Our class used **Insert** rather than **push_back** to add elements to the end of the list. We change this one line to the following and then move on to the next method:

```
entryList.push_back(entry);
```

The **IsThere** method checks whether an entry is in the calendar merely by constructing an entry from its parameters and calling **IsThere** for the list. Now we have a problem: The STL **list** template doesn't provide an operation equivalent to a search. But wait! There are more than 60 algorithms in the other portion of the STL. Maybe we can find something there that will help us. Searching through our STL reference, we discover an algorithm called **find** that sounds promising.

The documentation for **find** says that it searches a container, starting from a beginning **iterator** up to an ending **iterator**, looking for a specified element. If it finds the element, it returns an **iterator** pointing to it (when there are multiple copies, **find** stops with the first one). If the element isn't found, the iterator points to the same place that the **end** method returns. Because we want to search the entire list, we can use **begin** and **end** to get the range iterators. To convert the result of the search into a **bool** indicating whether the entry is there, we just compare it with **end**. All we have to do is insert

```
#include <algorithm>
```

at the top of the file and change the return statement to the following:

```
return find(entryList.begin(), entryList.end(), entry)
       != entryList.end();
```

Next comes the workhorse method of this class, **GetEntry**, which searches for an entry to update and deletes it from the list.

```
EntryWithDate AppointmentCalendar::GetEntry(Name name, Date date)
{
  TimeOfDay time;
  EntryWithDate otherEntry(date, time, name);
  EntryWithDate entry;
  list.ResetList();
  entry = list.GetNextItem();
  while (entry.ComparedTo(otherEntry) != SAME)
    entry = list.GetNextItem();
  list.Delete(entry);
  return entry;
}
```

SOFTWARE MAINTENANCE CASE STUDY: Appointment Calendar Using STL List

Our **List** class kept an iterator internally and allowed us to indirectly manage it by providing methods called **GetNextItem** and **ResetList**. The client code was responsible for looping through the list using these operations. The paradigm for the STL containers is to allow any number of iterators to be kept externally and to supply algorithms that traverse the data. We must now adapt this method to that alternate paradigm.

We already know that we can use **find** to replace the search operation. Obviously, that means we can delete the entire looping structure. But what do we do with the result from **find**? It returns a pointer to the entry, rather than the entry itself. We should declare an iterator of the appropriate type, assign the **find** result to it, and then dereference it before passing the entry back. At least the **Delete** operation has an equivalent form in **list**: We just call **erase**.

As we start coding, one other stylistic change comes to light. We named **otherEntry** because of how it would be used in the **ComparedTo** function. Given that it is the target of the **find** function, that name now seems inappropriate. Let's call it **searchEntry** instead.

Here is the revised code for **GetEntry**, with the changes highlighted.

```
EntryWithDate AppointmentCalendar::GetEntry(Name name, Date date)
{
  TimeOfDay time;
  EntryWithDate searchEntry(date, time, name);
  list<EntryWithDate>::iterator location =
    find(entryList.begin(), entryList.end(), searchEntry);
  EntryWithDate entry = *location;
  entryList.erase(location);
  return entry;
}
```

The change to the original **InsertEntry** method is trivial. We just replace the call to **Insert** with a call to **push_back**. Lastly, we review the **WriteListToFile** method.

```
void AppointmentCalendar::WriteListToFile(ofstream& outFile)
{
  EntryWithDate entry;
  Name name;
  Date date;
  TimeOfDay time;
  list.ResetList();
  outFile << list.GetLength() << endl;
  while (list.HasNext())
  {
    entry = list.GetNextItem();
    time = entry.GetTime();
    outFile << time.GetHours() << ' ' << time.GetMinutes() << ' '
            << time.GetSeconds() << ' ';
    date = entry.GetDate();
    outFile << date.GetMonth() << ' ' << date.GetDay() << ' '
            << date.GetYear() << ' ';
    name = entry.GetName();
```

```
    outFile << name.GetFirstName() << ' ' << name.GetMiddleName()
            << ' ' << name.GetLastName() << endl;
  }
  outFile.close();
}
```

As before, we have to account for the change in the paradigm of how we create and manage iterators in the STL versus our List ADT. However, we already know how to traverse a list from beginning to end: We simply use a For loop along with calls to **begin** and **end**. We also need to declare an iterator of the appropriate type, which we call **location**. Because **location** is a pointer to an entry, we must dereference it and assign the result to **entry**, instead of assigning the result of **GetNextItem**. Finally, our use of the **GetLength** method becomes a call to **size**.

Here, then, is the complete implementation for **AppointmentCalendar**, with all of the changes highlighted.

```
//****************************************************
// IMPLEMENTATION FILE for AppointmentCalendar
//****************************************************

#include <string>
#include <fstream>
#include <iostream>
#include <algorithm>
#include "AppointmentCalendar.h"
using namespace std;

AppointmentCalendar::AppointmentCalendar(ifstream& inFile)
{
  int hours, minutes, seconds;    // for class TimeOfDay
  int month, day, year;           // for class Date
  string first, middle, last;     // for class Name
  int numberEntries;
  inFile >> numberEntries;
  for (int counter = 0; counter < numberEntries; counter++)
  {
    inFile >> hours >> minutes >> seconds;
    TimeOfDay time(hours, minutes, seconds);
    inFile >> month >> day >> year;
    Date date(month, day, year);
    inFile >> first >> middle >> last;
    Name name(first, middle, last);
    EntryWithDate entry(date, time, name);
    entryList.push_back(entry);
  }
}

//****************************************************
```

SOFTWARE MAINTENANCE CASE STUDY: Appointment Calendar Using STL List

```cpp
bool AppointmentCalendar::IsThere(Name name, Date date)
{
  TimeOfDay time;
  EntryWithDate entry(date, time, name);
  return find(entryList.begin(), entryList.end(), entry)
         != entryList.end();
}

//*******************************************************

EntryWithDate AppointmentCalendar::GetEntry(Name name, Date date)
{
  TimeOfDay time;
  EntryWithDate searchEntry(date, time, name);
  list<EntryWithDate>::iterator location =
    find(entryList.begin(), entryList.end(), searchEntry);
  EntryWithDate entry = *location;
  entryList.erase(location);
  return entry;
}

//*******************************************************

void AppointmentCalendar::InsertEntry(EntryWithDate entry)
{ entryList.push_back(entry); }

//*******************************************************

void AppointmentCalendar::WriteListToFile(ofstream& outFile)
{
  EntryWithDate entry;
  Name name;
  Date date;
  TimeOfDay time;
  outFile << entryList.size() << endl;
  list<EntryWithDate>::iterator location;
  for (location = entryList.begin();
       location != entryList.end(), location++)
  {
    entry = *location;
    time = entry.GetTime();
    outFile << time.GetHours() << ' ' << time.GetMinutes() << ' '
            << time.GetSeconds() << ' ';
    date = entry.GetDate();
    outFile << date.GetMonth() << ' ' << date.GetDay() << ' '
            << date.GetYear() << ' ';
    name = entry.GetName();
    outFile << name.GetFirstName() << ' ' << name.GetMiddleName()
            << ' ' << name.GetLastName() << endl;
  }
  outFile.close();
}
```

SOFTWARE MAINTENANCE CASE STUDY: Appointment Calendar Using STL List

TESTING: Here is the driver's output, using the same test data as before. The results match what was output by the version in Chapter 15.

Here is the input file:

```
5
8 20 0 10 12 2009 Boris Becker Brown
8 45 0 10 11 2009 Sara Jane Jones
12 30 0 10 11 2009 Susy Smiley Baker
8 30 0 10 12 2009 Bill Bradley Britton
9 30 0 11 5 2010 Mary Jane Smith
```

Here is a test run:

```
Enter name of entry to change:
Enter name as first, middle, last
Mary Jane Smith
Enter date of entry to change
Enter date as month, day, and year
11 5 2010
Entry retrieved:
Time  9:30
Date  11/5/2010
Name Mary Smith

Enter field to change: 'T' (time) 'D' (date) 'N' (name)
D
Enter date as month, day, and year
11 5 2009
Do you wish to continue changing entries? 'Y' or 'N'
Y
Enter name of entry to change:
Enter name as first, middle, last
Bill Bradley Britton
Enter date of entry to change
Enter date as month, day, and year
10 12 2009
Entry retrieved:
Time  8:30
Date  10/12/2009
Name Bill Britton

Enter field to change: 'T' (time) 'D' (date) 'N' (name)
T
Enter time as hours, minutes, seconds
9 30 0
Do you wish to continue changing entries? 'Y' or 'N'
y
```

17.4 An Introduction to the STL

SOFTWARE MAINTENANCE CASE STUDY: Appointment Calendar Using STL List

```
Enter name of entry to change:
Enter name as first, middle, last
Sara Jane Jones
Enter date of entry to change
Enter date as month, day, and year
10 11 2009
Entry retrieved:
Time  8:45
Date  10/11/2009
Name Sara Jones

Enter field to change: 'T' (time) 'D' (date) 'N' (name)
N
Enter name as first, middle, last
Sarah Jane Jones
Do you wish to continue changing entries? 'Y' or 'N'
y
Enter name of entry to change:
Enter name as first, middle, last
Sara Jane Jones
Enter date of entry to change
Enter date as month, day, and year
10 11 2009
No entry exists with this name and date
Do you wish to continue changing entries? 'Y' or 'N'
N
```

Here is the output file:

```
5
8 20 0 10 12 2009 Boris Becker Brown
12 30 0 10 11 2009 Susy Smiley Baker
9 30 0 11 5 2009 Mary Jane Smith
9 30 0 10 12 2009 Bill Bradley Britton
8 45 0 10 11 2009 Sarah Jane Jones
```

QUICK CHECK

17.4.1 How would you declare an STL **queue** called **nums**, with a **float** specialization? (pp. 908–909)

17.4.2 Which **list** operation returns an iterator that points just beyond the last element? (pp. 904–906)

17.4.3 Which STL algorithm would you use to search a **deque** for a value? (pp. 918–919)

17.4.4 The STL **stack** and **queue** containers both have **pop** operations. How do they differ? (pp. 906–909)

17.4.5 What are the two main sections of the STL library? (p. 895)

17.4.6 What is a C++ STL **container**? (p. 895)

17.4.7 What is an important aspect of iterators with respect to the content in their associated container? (p. 897)

> **QUICK CHECK**
>
> **17.4.8** What does the **vector** template implement? (p. 898)
> **17.4.9** What is the primary reason why you might use a vector over the built-in C++ array? (p. 898)
> **17.4.10** What is the difference between a **vector**'s **size** and **capacity**? (p. 903)

17.5 Nonlinear Structures

Early in the chapter, we noted that all of the structured types we had seen were linear in nature. That's still true: Vectors, lists, stacks, queues, deques, and priority queues all arrange their elements one after another, either by indexing with an integral value or by following links. In this section, we open the door to some other arrangements. If you were surprised by how many different variations could be created within the limitations of a linear arrangement, it should be clear that when we remove this restriction, the number of possibilities grows tremendously. Here we can touch on only a few nonlinear arrangements.

We start with one of the simplest, in which elements have links that branch out in different directions. This branching behavior gives the structure its name: tree. In particular, we focus on the case where each node has just two branches and, therefore, is called a binary tree.

Binary Trees

> **Binary tree** A linked data structure, each of whose nodes contains links to a left and right child node.

We can expand the concept of a linked list to structures containing nodes with more than one forward link field. One of these structures is known as a binary tree (**FIGURE 17.11**). Such a tree is referenced by an external pointer to a specific node, called the *root* of the tree. The root has two pointers: one to its *left child* and one to its *right child*. Each child also has two pointers: one to its left child and one to its right child. The left and right children of a node are called *siblings*.

For any node in a tree, the left child of the node is the root of the *left subtree* of the node. Likewise, the right child is the root of the *right subtree*. Nodes whose left and right children are both **NULL** are called *leaf nodes*.

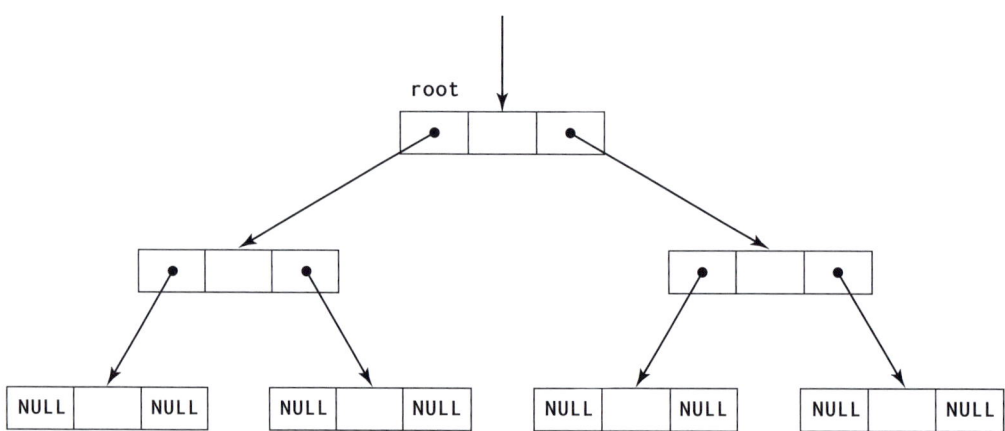

FIGURE 17.11 A Binary Tree

Although Figure 17.11 shows a binary tree with only seven nodes, there is no theoretical limit on the number of nodes in a tree. If you turn the figure upside down, you can see why it is called a tree.

A *binary search tree* is a special kind of binary tree with the additional property that the values are arranged in a particular order. In a binary search tree, the component in any node is greater than the component in its left child and any of its children (left subtree) and less than the component in its right child and any of its children (right subtree). This definition assumes no duplicates. The tree shown below is an example of a binary search tree.

> **Binary search tree** A binary tree in which the value in any node is greater than the value in its left child and any of its children and less than the value in its right child and any of its children.

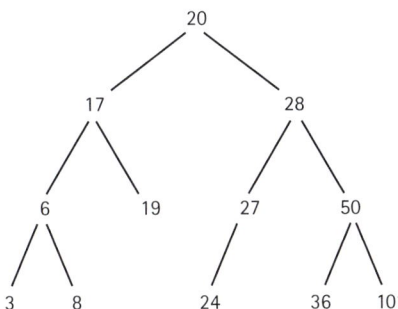

A binary search tree is useful because, if we are looking for a certain item, we can tell which half of the tree it is in by using just one comparison. We can then tell which half of that half the item is in with one more comparison. This process continues until either we find the item (a number in this case) or we determine that the item is not there. The process is analogous to a binary search of a sorted array.

Let's search for the number 50 in our binary search tree.

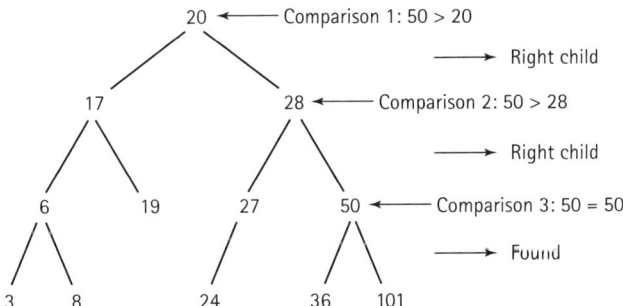

Now let's look for 18, a number that is not there.

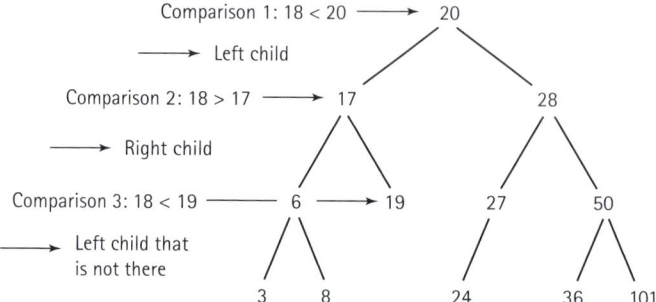

The left child of 19 is **NULL**, so we know that 18 isn't in the tree. Not only do we know that 18 is not there, but we are also at the right place to insert 18 if we want to do so.

To summarize, we compared the value we were looking for with the item in the tree and took the appropriate branch if the value and the item were not the same. When we started to take a branch that was **NULL**, we knew that the value was not in the tree. Just as the binary search has algorithmic complexity of $O(\log_2 N)$, so does searching in a binary search tree.

If we want to print all of the values in a binary search tree in order, we traverse it as follows:

Tree Traversal

If the left child isn't null, traverse the left subtree.
Print the current item.
If the right child isn't null, traverse the right subtree.

We start at the root of the tree. If it has a left child, we move to that node and repeat the process. We continue in the same way down the left side of the tree until we reach a leaf, which we print. Then we move back up to the parent of that leaf and print it before traversing the subtree to its right. As an example, suppose we are given the following binary search tree:

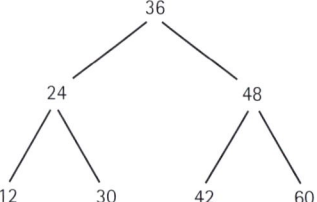

Traversal begins with the root (36), proceeds to its left child (24) and then to the left child of 24, which is 12. Because 12 is a leaf, it is printed, and we go back up to 24, which we also print. Then we traverse its right subtree, which is the leaf, 30. After printing 30, we go back to 24. Because we are done with this subtree, we back up to 36 and print it. Then the process is repeated with the right subtree, printing 42, 48, and 60.

As we see in Chapter 18, this kind of algorithm, which calls itself to process a smaller portion of the problem, is said to be *recursive*. In that chapter, we'll also see that a stack is the natural choice of structure for keeping track of where we are in the tree.

This particular form of traversal (visit left subtree, then root, then right subtree) is called an in-order traversal. There are two other commonly used traversal patterns for a tree.

> **In-order traversal** A traversal of a binary tree that proceeds in the pattern of "left subtree, visit the root, then visit right subtrees."

Pre-order Traversal

Visit the root.
Visit the left subtree.
Visit the right subtree.

Post-order Traversal

Visit the left subtree.
Visit the right subtree.
Visit the root.

The names come from the place within the order of traversal that we visit the root. If we visit it before we visit the subtrees, then it is pre-order traversal. If we visit the root after the subtrees, then it is post-order traversal. Depending on the data stored in a binary tree, each order of traversal may have a particular use.

Trees are not limited to a binary branching factor. If we define a node to have three link fields, we get a tree that has three branches per node. Nor are trees limited to having the same number of branches in each node. For example, we can construct a tree that represents a family genealogy, where the number of links from a node depends on the number of children who were born to a given set of parents. To store a variable number of child links, we might use a list as a field within a tree node.

Lists, stacks, queues, and trees all have the property that the links flow in one direction (from head to tail, from root to leaf, and so on). We can form even more sophisticated structures, called graphs, in which links can flow in any direction. We might use a graph to represent the roads connecting a set of cities, or the network connecting a set of computers. As you can see, linked structures can become quite complex.

> **Pre-order traversal** A traversal of a binary tree that proceeds in the pattern of "visit the root, then visit the left and right subtrees."
>
> **Post-order traversal** A traversal of a binary tree that proceeds in the pattern of "visit the left and right subtrees, then visit the root."
>
> **Graph** A data structure in which the links can be arranged in any pattern.

Just as we were able to implement a list as an array or a dynamic structure, so we can implement stacks, queues, trees, and graphs with dynamic structures or arrays. It is important to remember that a data structure has both a logical organization and an implementation structure. The two are distinct, and the choice of each depends on the requirements of any given problem.

The STL does not actually provide a container that implements a tree in the abstract sense. However, the `set` container that we examine in Section 17.6, "Associative Containers," is often implemented with a binary search tree.

Next we look at a different kind of logical structure that provides very fast searching under certain conditions. We'll again see that it can have multiple implementations.

Hash Tables

Your summer job at a drive-in theater includes changing the movie title on the sign each week. The letters are kept in a box in the projection booth. Your first day on the job, you discover that the letters are in random order, and you have to search through nearly all of them to find the ones you need. You sort the letters into alphabetical order, which allows you to use a binary search to locate each letter, but that's still tedious. Finally, you make a set of 26 cards to separate the letters, and then you are able to directly pull each letter from its place in the box.

Because you are searching for values within a known range, you've divided up the space so that you can directly locate them. In general, if the items you are searching have this property, you can merely index into an array based on their values and retrieve the items. Given a set of N values, the searching algorithms we've seen so far have a maximum of either N steps (linear search) or $\log_2 N$ steps (binary search). This new technique typically takes just a few steps, regardless of the amount of data. We refer to this approach as hashing.

> **Hashing** A technique used to perform insertion and access of elements in a data structure in approximately constant time, by using the value of each element to identify its location in the structure.
>
> **Hash function** A function used to manipulate the value of an element to produce an index that identifies its location in a data structure.
>
> **Collision** The condition resulting when a hash function maps multiple values to the same location.

Our letter-finding example is a perfect situation for using hashing because there are a small number of possible values, and we can use them as indexes. Unfortunately, most data are not equally well behaved. For example, if our data values are real numbers representing temperatures, then the number of potential values is immense. C++ does not let us create an array big enough to use a `float` value as an index.

Nevertheless, the temperatures might have a very limited range, such as 90.0 to 110.0 degrees Fahrenheit. If we are interested in precision only to one-tenth of a degree, then there are actually just 201 distinct values. We could develop a method that takes a temperature and returns an index in the range of 0 to 200; we could then store the temperatures using hashing. Such a method is called a hash function. Assuming that the hash function takes a small amount of time to compute, searching with hashing is still a very fast operation.

The preceding examples have ignored the problem of having duplicates in the data set. Also, some data sets can have an irregular distribution of values. For example, if you are sorting a group of names, you will find that many more begin with "A," "M," or "S" than with "Q," "X," or "Z" (although those frequencies change with where you are in the world). Thus we might end up trying to store multiple values into the same place in the array, a condition called a collision.

Several approaches can be taken to deal with collisions. For example, when we attempt to store a value into a location that's already full, we could simply increment the index until we find an empty location. Unfortunately, that strategy tends to produce clusters of filled locations. In the worst case, it can take as many accesses to find an empty slot as there are elements in the array. In another approach, known as rehashing, we feed the output of the hash function back into the function (or into another function) to select a new index.

Until now we've assumed the use of a simple linear array implementation, but hashing isn't limited to this kind of structure. We could, for example, use an array of linked lists. The hash function might then index into this array and add the item to the linked list at that location. With each collision on a given array slot, the associated list would simply grow one node longer. If the hash function is well designed, the lists would remain reasonably short (few collisions), so the search would still take just a few operations. **FIGURE 17.12** shows such a structure, called a chained hash table.

The efficiency of hashing depends on having an array or table that is large enough to hold the data set, with enough extra room to keep collisions to a minimum. Sometimes this is an impractical condition to satisfy; for many other problems, hashing is a very effective means of organizing data. For example, we could use a hash table to implement a list that

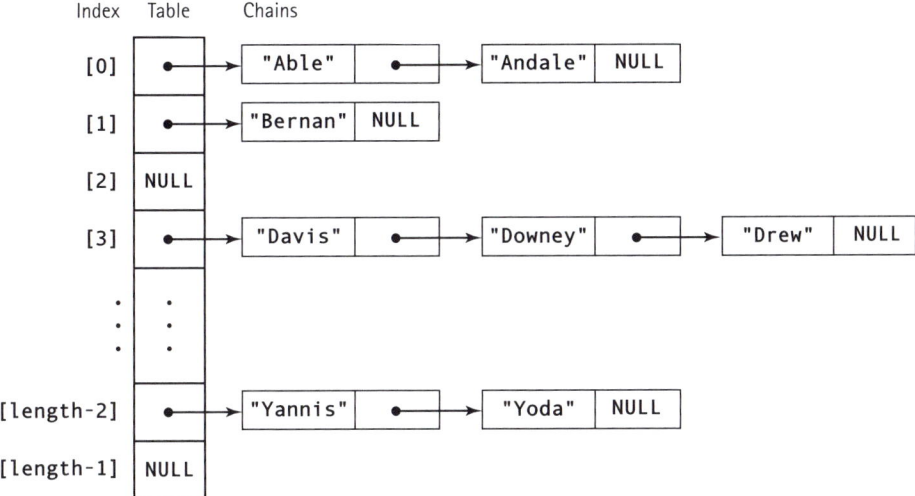

FIGURE 17.12 A Chained Hash Table

has fast insertion, deletion, and access capabilities, similar to the STL **deque**. A hash table is also a candidate implementation structure for another kind of container that we look at in the next section, the **map**.

Developing a good hash function can require a considerable amount of data analysis. Our goal here is not to show you how to develop such functions, but merely to give you an appreciation for both the benefits of hashing and its limitations.

> **QUICK CHECK**
>
> **17.5.1** In what order does post-order traversal visit the nodes of a binary tree? (pp. 926–927)
> **17.5.2** What is a collision in a hash table? (pp. 928–929)
> **17.5.3** What is a **binary tree**? (p. 924)
> **17.5.4** What is the difference between a **binary tree** and a **binary search tree**? (p. 925)
> **17.5.5** What do we call the node in a binary tree that is referenced from an external pointer? (p. 924)
> **17.5.6** What technique is used to access elements of a data structure in approximately constant time? (p. 928)
> **17.5.7** Describe a hash function that we could use to produce an index into a data structure where the input to the hash function is a value representing a student grade between 0 and 100 and the output would be a value between 0 and 4 where 0 represents the grade of F and 4 is an A (no +/− letter grades). (p. 928)

17.6 Associative Containers

The STL divides its containers into three groups. The vector, list, and deque are referred to as *sequence containers*. The simpler stack, queue, and priority queue types are called *container adapters* because they are actually built on top of the sequence containers to provide a simpler and more convenient interface. The third group includes the so-called *associative containers*.

We locate values within an associative container not by their positions, but by their values. Imagine, for example, that you have an array of structs, each of which contains a name and a phone number. You can access a number by name by conducting a search of the array and comparing a given name to the name stored in each location; you may eventually find a match with this approach. Now, suppose instead that you could just write

```cpp
cout << phonebook["Sylva Jones"];
```

to look up the number. That is, suppose you could find the phone number just by referring to its associated value.

> **Associative lookup (content-addressable access)** The process of retrieving a value based on an associated value called the key.

Computer scientists refer to this kind of lookup as access by association, **associative lookup**, or **content addressable access**. The value that is used for searching is called the key, and collectively these values must be ordered in a manner that allows two keys to be compared. In many cases, the keys must also be unique. Associative lookup is the basis for many kinds of database processing as well as having a wide variety of other uses.

The STL offers five different associative containers. Here we examine just two of them: **set** and **map**.

The `set` Template

The STL `set` template takes its name from the fact that, like the mathematical set, it stores only unique values. If you try to insert a value that is already in a set, the set will be unchanged. Not surprisingly, the STL takes the implementation of the set far beyond the mathematical concept.

Internally, the values in a `set` are sorted from least to greatest, so the STL provides the ability to use an `iterator` with `begin` and `end`, or a `reverse_iterator` with `rbegin` and `rend`, to traverse the set as if it was a sorted list (most implementations use a binary search tree as shown in **FIGURE 17.13**). However, this is less efficient than traversing a sequence container.

What the `set` excels at is finding elements by their values. Thus the `find` operation is built into the `set` interface, rather than being treated as a separate algorithm. After `find` provides

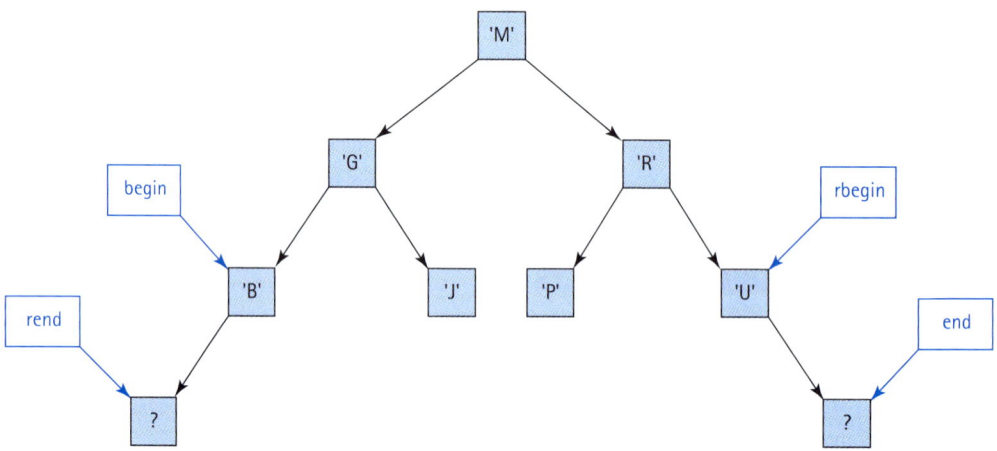

FIGURE 17.13 An Implementation of a `set` Using a Binary Search Tree

an `iterator` pointing to a value in a `set`, you can use it to `erase` the element or retrieve adjacent elements. Here is a table of some of the more commonly used `set` operations.

Name	Parameters	Returns	Description
`begin`		`iterator`	Returns an `iterator` to the first element.
`clear`			Removes all elements. Sets `size` to 0.
`count`	value	`int`	Returns the number of instances of this value in the `set`. Will be 1 if the value is in the set and 0 otherwise.
`empty`		`bool`	Returns `true` if there are no elements in the `set`.
`end`		`iterator`	Returns an `iterator` beyond the end of the `set`.
`erase`	`iterator`		Removes the element at the `iterator` position. The `size` decreases.
`find`	value	`iterator`	Returns an `iterator` to the element with the value.
`insert`	value		Inserts the value into the `set`. The `size` increases.
`lower_bound`	value	`iterator`	Returns an `iterator` to the first element that is greater than or equal to the value.
`rbegin`		`reverse_iterator`	Returns a reverse `iterator` to the last element.
`rend`		`reverse_iterator`	Returns a reverse `iterator` before the start of the `set`.
`size`		`int`	Returns the number of elements in the `set`.
`upper_bound`	value	`iterator`	Returns an `iterator` to the first element that is less than the value.

The `set` type provides a default constructor that creates an empty `set`. A second form of constructor follows the pattern of the sequence containers, in which another container or an array can be used to initialize the `set`. Of course, any duplicate elements in the container are not inserted into the `set`. A straight copy constructor that takes another `set` as a parameter is available for creating a duplicate `set`.

In addition to the class methods in the preceding table, three of the algorithms described in Section 17.4 apply to `set`: `set_difference`, `set_intersection`, and `set_union`. Keep in mind that you must include `<algorithm>` to use these algorithms, and they are called like traditional functions, rather than object methods. The example program later in this section demonstrates the use of `set_difference`. All of the `set` algorithms use the same arrangement of five parameters, all of which are iterators:

```
set_difference(start1, end1, start2, end2, output);
```

The first two iterators specify a range in the first **set**, the next two specify a range in the second **set**, and the last points to the beginning of the place where the result **set** should be placed.

Oddly enough, the **set** algorithms are not designed to output their results directly as a value of class **set**. Instead, they were written to be more generally applicable to other containers, so their output can't go directly into a **set**. (You can write the result directly to a **vector**, for example.)

Another function template in the **<iterator>** package of algorithms, **inserter**, must be used to force the **set** algorithms to generate their output in a way that enables a **set** to insert the output into itself. The **inserter** takes two arguments: the destination container, followed by an iterator that points to the place where the insertion should occur. Because **set** picks its own insertion point, it doesn't matter what the second value is, as long as it points to a place in the set. We can use **begin** or **end**, for example. Here is how a call to **set_difference** looks, once all of this has been factored in:

```
set_difference(set1.begin(), set1.end(),        // First set
               set2.begin(), set2.end(),        // Second set
               inserter(set3, set3.end()));     // Result set
```

In this example, **set3** contains all of the elements of **set1** that are not found in **set2**. We've shown this behavior as a void function call. In reality, each of the set algorithms returns an iterator pointing to the end of the result. Because we don't need this result in our example, we simply let the return value be discarded.

Here is a sample program using **set**:

```
//*******************************************************
// This program demonstrates various set methods
//*******************************************************
#include <iostream>
#include <set>
#include <algorithm>
#include <iterator>
using namespace std;

int main ()
{
  set<string> strSet;              // Create an empty set
  string word;
  cout << "Enter a line with six words:" << endl;
  for (int i = 1; i <= 6; i++)
  {
    cin >> word;
    strSet.insert(word);           // Insert elements
  }
  // Access size
  cout << "Size of set: " << strSet.size() << endl;
  // Print the set
  set<string>::iterator place;
  cout << "Set contents from beginning to end: " << endl;
  // Traverse set in forward order
```

```cpp
    for (place = strSet.begin(); place != strSet.end(); place++)
      cout << *place << " ";
  // Create a reverse iterator
  set<string>::reverse_iterator rplace;
  cout << endl << "Set contents from end to beginning: " << endl;
  // Traverse set in reverse order
  for (rplace = strSet.rbegin(); rplace != strSet.rend(); ++rplace)
      cout << *rplace << " ";
  // Prepare to illustrate set difference
  set<string> strSet2(strSet);            // Create a copy of strSet
  strSet2.erase(strSet2.begin());         // Delete first element
  strSet2.erase(--strSet2.end());         // Delete last element
  set<string> strSet3;                    // Create a set for the result
  // Need to use inserter because set doesn't allow copy iterator
  set_difference(strSet.begin(), strSet.end(),       // First set
                 strSet2.begin(), strSet2.end(),     // Second set
                 inserter(strSet3, strSet3.end()));  // Result set
  // Print result set
  cout << endl << "Set difference from beginning to end: " << endl;
  for (place = strSet3.begin(); place != strSet3.end(); place++)
      cout << *place << " ";
  return 0;
}
```

Here is a sample run of the program:

```
Enter a line with six words:
four score and seven years ago
Size of set: 6
Set contents from beginning to end:
ago and four score seven years
Set contents from end to beginning:
years seven score four and ago
Set difference from beginning to end:
ago years
```

The map Template

An STL **map** type is like a **set**, but with one major difference: Whereas the **set** stores only key values, a **map** associates a second value with each key. The **map** is, therefore, the standard example of an associative container. It lets us implement the kind of name-indexed array that we described at the beginning of this section, as shown in **FIGURE 17.14**. Although the **map** is conceptually an array, internally it may be implemented with a linked structure such as a binary search tree or a chained hash table.

The operations for a **map** are nearly identical to those for a **set**. Its elements are sorted and it supports **begin**, **clear**, **count**, **empty**, **end**, **erase**, **find**, **insert**, **lower_bound**, **rbegin**, **rend**, **size**, and **upper_bound**. As you might guess, however, the **insert** operation does not take a simple value as its argument. Instead, it expects a value of the template type **pair**.

Here is an example definition of a **map** that could be used for a phone book, and an **insert** operation that places an entry into it:

```cpp
map<string, int> phonebook;
phonebook.insert(pair<string, int>("Eben Johnson", 5550001));
```

["Helmand"]	5550101
["Jeng"]	5552345
["Kellaug"]	8881077
["Lepoutre"]	9994280
["Marini"]	7714444
["McCartney"]	5550003
["Meely"]	8884902
["Melchiore"]	5557391
["Smite"]	8883129
["Teernsma"]	7713618

FIGURE 17.14 A Conceptual Illustration of a `map`

The following statements

```
map<string, int>::iterator place;
place = phonebook.find("Eben Johnson");
cout << *place.first << ": " << *place.second << endl;
phonebook.erase(place);
```

cause `find` to return an `iterator` pointing to this `pair` element of `phonebook`. After dereferencing the iterator, we can use `first` and `second` to output the two parts of the `pair`. The last statement erases the element.

This is all well and good, but a bit tedious to code. Wouldn't it be nice if we could just use array syntax? That's the other big difference between the `set` and the `map`. With `map`, the `[]` operator is overloaded, enabling us to write the preceding code segment as follows:

```
map<string, int> phonebook;
string name = "Eben Johnson";
phonebook[name] = 5550001;
cout << name << ": " << phonebook[name] << endl;
phonebook.erase(name);
```

As we see in the following case study, a `map` can also be used to convert input strings to `enum` values.

> **QUICK CHECK**
>
> **17.6.1** What is an associative data structure? (p. 930)
> **17.6.2** What is the main difference between a **set** and a **map**? (p. 933)
> **17.6.3** Which operator is overloaded in a **map** container that makes it easy to store and retrieve values from it? (p. 934)
> **17.6.4** Why do we call a map an associative structure? (p. 933)
> **17.6.5** How would you insert the number 42 into a **map** called **matches**, at a location with the key value **"answer"**? (pp. 933–934)

Problem-Solving Case Study

Creating a Deck of Cards

PROBLEM: For a probability and statistics class, you are doing a project to empirically explore the odds of certain kinds of hands occurring in various card games. You want to begin by developing a set of classes that will allow you to simulate a deck of 52 cards consisting of the four suits (hearts, clubs, diamonds, spades) with 13 values (ace through king) in each suit. Once you have these working, you can easily construct the necessary drivers to try out your hypotheses.

IDENTIFYING INITIAL CLASSES: Here is the list of potential classes, based on the problem statement:

Deck
Card
Suits
Values
Hands
Games

FILTERING: With a little reflection, it's clear that the last two classes pertain to the larger problem rather than to the task immediately at hand. Clearly, we need a structure to represent the card deck as well as an individual card. Do we really need separate classes to represent suits and values, or can we just use a pair of **enum** values? You anticipate wanting to be able to enter names of cards for some of the experiments, and it would be nice to encapsulate the conversion of the **enum** values back into strings. So, yes, it makes sense to build classes representing these objects.

Here is our filtered list:

Deck
Card
Suits
Values

INITIAL CLASS DESIGNS: Let's begin by looking at the simplest classes, which represent the suits and values. They are likely to be nearly identical, with the exception of the particular enum. We can start with **Suits**, because it has a smaller range than **Values**. We would like to be able to construct a suit value from a string or from an integer. As a default, it should use the smallest value, **CLUBS**. We want observers to convert the value to an **int** or a **string**. We can call these responsibilities **toString** and **toInt**. For comparison purposes, we should also provide tests for less than and equal.

A quick walk-through of the responsibilities shows that most of them are straightforward. In **toString** we can use an array of strings, indexed by the **enum** to convert the value to a string. But how do we go in the other direction for the constructor that takes a string? As we've just seen, a **map** is a perfect choice for this task. But there's one more problem: We need to convert an input string into all uppercase to properly match it. We could use a loop to convert the string character-by-character to uppercase, but a quick brows-

Problem-Solving Case Study

ing of the STL reveals an algorithm called `transform` that can do the work for us. Here is a CRC card for this class design:

Class Name: *Suits*	Superclass: *None*		Subclasses: *None*
Responsibilities		Collaborations	
Create Suits()			
Create Suits(string)		*map, transform*	
Create Suits(int)			
toString() returns string			
toInt() returns int			
Operator < returns bool			
Operator == returns bool			

The `Values` class will be identical except for the name, so we don't show its CRC card. Here are the specification files for these two classes, based on the CRC card design. We wait until after we've finished the rest of the design before considering their implementations.

```cpp
//****************************************
// SPECIFICATION File for class Suits
//****************************************
#include <string>
using namespace std;

class Suits
{
public:
  // Constructors
  Suits();
  Suits(string initString);
  Suits(int initInt);
  // Observers
  string toString() const;
  int toInt() const;
  // Relational operators
  bool operator<(Suits otherSuit) const;
  bool operator==(Suits otherSuit) const;

  enum Suit {CLUBS, DIAMONDS, HEARTS, SPADES};
private:
  Suit mySuit;
};
```

Problem-Solving Case Study

```
//*****************************************
// SPECIFICATION File for class Values
//*****************************************
#include <string>
using namespace std;

class Values
{
public:
  // Constructors
  Values();
  Values(string initString);
  Values(int initInt);
  // Observers
  string toString() const;
  int toInt() const;
  // Relational operators
  bool operator<(Values otherValue) const;
  bool operator==(Values otherValue) const;

  enum Value {ACE, TWO, THREE, FOUR, FIVE, SIX, SEVEN,
              EIGHT, NINE, TEN, JACK, QUEEN, KING};
private:
  Value myValue;
};
```

Now let's move up to considering the responsibilities for a Card. We should provide a constructor that takes a value and a suit. We also want to be able to observe both of these members. Because it will be necessary to compare cards against one another, we should also support relational operators. Let's go ahead and include all of them, just for future convenience. Again a quick walk-through reveals that most of these responsibilities are trivial. However, comparisons require computing the rank of a card within the deck (its suit value $\times$ 13 plus its face value). It will simplify our work if we create a helper function to do this computation. Here is the CRC card for `Card`:

Problem-Solving Case Study

Class Name: *Card*	Superclass: *None*	Subclasses: *None*
Responsibilities		**Collaborations**
Create Card()		
Create Card(Values, Suits)		Values, Suits
Get Value returns Values		Values
GetSuit returns Suits		Suits
Operator < returns bool		
Operator > returns bool		
Operator == returns bool		
Operator <= returns bool		
Operator >= returns bool		
Operator != returns bool		

In fact, this class is so simple that we can implement it directly:

```cpp
//*****************************************
// SPECIFICATION File for class Card
//*****************************************
#include "Values.h"
#include "Suits.h"
class Card
{
public:
  // Constructors
  Card();
  Card(Values initValue, Suits initSuit);
  // Observers
  Values GetValue() const;
  Suits GetSuit() const;
  // Relational operators
  bool operator<(const Card& otherCard) const;
  bool operator>(const Card& otherCard) const;
  bool operator==(const Card& otherCard) const;
  bool operator<=(const Card& otherCard) const;
  bool operator>=(const Card& otherCard) const;
  bool operator!=(const Card& otherCard) const;
private:
  Values myValue;
  Suits mySuit;
  int rank() const;   // Helper function for relational ops
};
```

Problem-Solving Case Study

```
//*********************************************************
// IMPLEMENTATION FILE for class Card
//*********************************************************

#include "Card.h"

Card::Card()
{ }

//*********************************************************

Card::Card(Values initValue, Suits initSuit)
{
  myValue = initValue;
  mySuit = initSuit;
}

//*********************************************************

Values Card::GetValue() const
{ return myValue; }

//*********************************************************

Suits Card::GetSuit() const
{ return mySuit; }

//*********************************************************

bool Card::operator<(const Card& otherCard) const
{ return rank() < otherCard.rank(); }

//*********************************************************

bool Card::operator>(const Card& otherCard) const
{ return rank() > otherCard.rank(); }

//*********************************************************

bool Card::operator==(const Card& otherCard) const
{ return rank() == otherCard.rank(); }

//*********************************************************

bool Card::operator<=(const Card& otherCard) const
{ return rank() <= otherCard.rank(); }

//*********************************************************
```

Problem-Solving Case Study

```
bool Card::operator>=(const Card& otherCard) const
{ return rank() >= otherCard.rank(); }

//*********************************************************

bool Card::operator!=(const Card& otherCard) const
{ return rank() != otherCard.rank(); }

//*********************************************************

int Card::rank() const
{
   return mySuit.toInt() * 13 + myValue.toInt();
}
```

All that remains is determining the responsibilities for class **Deck**. Initially it will be sufficient to have the default constructor build a full deck of cards in order. We want the ability to shuffle the deck, to deal out an individual card, to ask whether the deck is empty, and to find out whether a given card is still in the deck. It's also helpful to know how many cards are left in the deck.

A walk-through reveals that we have a choice of STL containers with which we could collaborate to represent the deck. Let's use the **deque**, just to see it in action. We'll need to loop through the values and suits, creating the 52 cards to push into the **deque**. Once that's done, we can use the STL **find** algorithm to implement **isThere**. What about shuffling? Again, the STL algorithms come to the rescue with a **random_shuffle** operation. Dealing is just a matter of getting the front element of the **deque** and popping the card off of it. Here is a CRC card that outlines those responsibilities:

Class Name: *Deck*	Superclass: *None*	Subclasses: *None*
Responsibilities	**Collaborations**	
Create Deck()	*deque, Values, Suits, Card*	
Empty returns bool	*deque*	
IsThere returns bool	*find*	
Size returns int	*deque*	
void Shuffle	*Random_shuffle*	
Deal returns Card	*Card*	

Problem-Solving Case Study

Here is the specification file for class **Deck**:

```cpp
//*******************************************
// SPECIFICATION File for class Deck
//*******************************************
#include "Card.h"
#include <deque>

class Deck
{
public:
  // Constructor
  Deck();
  // Observers
  bool empty() const;
  bool isThere(Card aCard) const;
  int size () const;
  // Action responsibilities
  void Shuffle();      // Reorders the cards
  Card Deal();         // Takes one card from deck
private:
  deque<Card> theDeck;
};
```

The implementations of most of these methods are straightforward. We can use the **empty** and **size** functions from **deque** to implement the corresponding functions in this class. We already know that **find** and **random_shuffle** from the STL algorithms can implement the **isThere** and **Shuffle** functions, respectively. To deal a card, we just use the **front** and **pop_front** operations from **deque**. The only part that requires much thought is the constructor. It's clear that we'll use **push_back** to insert the cards into the **deque**—but how do we generate the cards in order? A nested For loop, counting through the enum values, with **Values** in the inner loop and **Suits** in the outer loop, can accomplish this task. A little refresher on how to iterate through an **enum**, from Chapter 10, and we're all set to write the implementation.

```cpp
//***********************************************************
// IMPLEMENTATION FILE for class Deck
//***********************************************************
#include "Deck.h"
#include <algorithm>

Deck::Deck()
{
  for(Suits::Suit suit = Suits::CLUBS;
      suit <= Suits::SPADES; suit=Suits::static_cast<Suit>(Suit+1))
    for(Values::Value value = Values::ACE;
        value <= Values::KING; value=Values::Value(value+1))
      theDeck.push_back(Card(Values(value), static_cast<Suit>(Suits)));
}
```

Problem-Solving Case Study

```
//*************************************************************

bool Deck::empty() const
{ return theDeck.empty(); }

//*************************************************************

bool Deck::isThere(Card aCard) const
{ return find(theDeck.begin(), theDeck.end(), aCard)
         != theDeck.end(); }

//*************************************************************

int Deck::size() const
{ return theDeck.size(); }

//*************************************************************

void Deck::Shuffle()
{
   random_shuffle(theDeck.begin(), theDeck.end());
}

//*************************************************************

Card Deck::Deal()
{
   Card next = theDeck.front();   // Get the next card
   theDeck.pop_front();           // Delete it from the deck
   return next;                   // Return it
}
```

Now we can return to the implementation of **Suits**. As we noted, the only method that needs further attention is the constructor that is initialized by a string. What we can do is assign the **string-enum** pairs to a **map** using statements like

```
map<string, Suit> lookup;
lookup["CLUBS"] = CLUBS;
```

To get the suit from the string, we just reverse the process:

```
mySuit = lookup[initString];
```

The one thing that stands in our way is converting the string to uppercase. The STL **transform** algorithm can handle this task for us. It takes four arguments: The first two are iterators to the start and end of the source container, the third is an iterator to the start of the destination container, and the last is a function that is applied to each element of the container as it is copied from the source to the destination. We can use the **toupper** function to perform the conversion. But can we actually apply **transform** to a string?

This is where we see that **string** really is a class in the C++ library. It is actually another container in the STL (albeit with some special properties). As a consequence, **string** also supports **begin** and **end** operations, and it can have many of the STL algorithms applied to its objects. The necessary call to `transform` looks like this:

```
transform(initString.begin(), initString.end(),
         initString.begin(), toupper);
```

At last, we can implement **Suits**:

```cpp
//**********************************************************
// IMPLEMENTATION FILE for class Suits
//**********************************************************

#include "Suits.h"
#include <map>
#include <cctype>           // For toupper
#include <algorithm>        // For transform
#include <string>

Suits::Suits()
{ mySuit = CLUBS; }


//**********************************************************

Suits::Suits(string initString)
{
  // Create a mapping between strings and enums
  map<string, Suit> lookup;
  lookup["CLUBS"] = CLUBS;
  lookup["DIAMONDS"] = DIAMONDS;
  lookup["HEARTS"] = HEARTS;
  lookup["SPADES"] = SPADES;
  // Convert the string to uppercase
  transform(initString.begin(), initString.end(),
            initString.begin(), toupper);
  // Get the corresponding enum
  mySuit = lookup[initString];
}

//**********************************************************

Suits::Suits(int initInt)
{ mySuit = Suit(initInt); }

//**********************************************************

string Suits::toString() const
{
  string suitString[4] = {"CLUBS", "DIAMONDS", "HEARTS", "SPADES"};
  return suitString[mySuit];
}
```

Problem-Solving Case Study

```
//************************************************************

int Suits::toInt() const
{ return int(mySuit); }

//************************************************************

bool Suits::operator<(Suits otherSuit) const
{
  return mySuit < otherSuit.toInt();
}

//************************************************************

bool Suits::operator==(Suits otherSuit) const
{
  return mySuit == otherSuit.toInt();
}
```

As we noted, the implementation of **Values** is virtually identical, except for the change in the variable names and the different **enum** values.

```
//************************************************************
// IMPLEMENTATION FILE for class Values
//************************************************************

#include "Values.h"
#include <map>
#include <cctype>              // For toupper
#include <algorithm>           // For transform
#include <string>

Values::Values()
{ myValue = ACE; }

//************************************************************

Values::Values(string initString)
{
  // Create a mapping between strings and enums
  map<string, Value> lookup;
  lookup["ACE"] = ACE;
  lookup["TWO"] = TWO;
  lookup["THREE"] = THREE;
  lookup["FOUR"] = FOUR;
  lookup["FIVE"] = FIVE;
  lookup["SIX"] = SIX;
  lookup["SEVEN"] = SEVEN;
  lookup["EIGHT"] = EIGHT;
  lookup["NINE"] = NINE;
```

Problem-Solving Case Study

```cpp
  lookup["TEN"] = TEN;
  lookup["JACK"] = JACK;
  lookup["QUEEN"] = QUEEN;
  lookup["KING"] = KING;
  // Convert the string to uppercase
  transform(initString.begin(), initString.end(),
            initString.begin(), toupper);
  // Get the corresponding enum
  myValue = lookup[initString];
}

//***********************************************************

Values::Values(int initInt)
{ myValue = Value(initInt); }

//***********************************************************

string Values::toString() const
{
  string valueString[13] = {"ACE", "TWO", "THREE", "FOUR",
    "FIVE", "SIX", "SEVEN", "EIGHT", "NINE", "TEN", "JACK",
    "QUEEN", "KING"};
  return valueString[myValue];
}

//***********************************************************

int Values::toInt() const
{ return int(myValue); }

//***********************************************************

bool Values::operator<(Values otherValue) const
{
  return myValue < otherValue.toInt();
}

//***********************************************************

bool Values::operator==(Values otherValue) const
{
  return myValue == otherValue.toInt();
}
```

TESTING: A proper driver for these classes should exercise them as much as possible. Here we are limited by space to some basic tests. We can create a deck and deal out some cards to see that they are initially in order. Then the deck can be shuffled before we test `isThere` with a random query that is input by the user. Using `empty`, we can control a second loop that deals out the rest of the cards. At each stage, we can test `size` by outputting the size of the deck. That covers all of the operations in `Deck`, which in turn runs through all of the values in `Card`, although it does not cover the relational operators (except as they are used by `find`). Again, with the exception of the relational operators, this strategy covers all of the operations in `Values` and `Suits`.

Problem-Solving Case Study

Here is the driver that implements these tests:

```cpp
//***********************************************************
// Driver for class Deck
//***********************************************************
#include <iostream>
#include "Deck.h"
using namespace std;

int main ()
{
  // Create a deck of 52 cards in order
  Deck myDeck;
  cout << "The deck has " << myDeck.size() << " cards."
       << endl << endl;
  // Deal out the first ten in order
  for (int i=1 ; i<=10; ++i)
  {
    Card aCard = myDeck.Deal();
    cout << aCard.GetValue().toString() << " of "
         << aCard.GetSuit().toString() << endl;
  }
  cout << endl << "The deck has " << myDeck.size()
       << " cards." << endl;
  // Shuffle the remaining cards
  cout << "Shuffling" << endl << endl;
  myDeck.Shuffle();
  // Input a card
  cout << "Enter the name of a suit: ";
  string suit;
  cin >> suit;
  cout << "Enter the name of a card (ace, two,..., king): ";
  string value;
  cin >> value;
  // Check if card is in the deck
  if (myDeck.isThere(static_cast<Card>(static_cast<Values>(value),
      static_cast<Suits>(suit))))
    cout << "The card is in the deck." << endl;
  else
    cout << "The card has already been dealt." << endl;
  // Deal out the remaining cards
  cout << "The remaining contents of the deck are:" << endl;
  while (!myDeck.empty())
  {
    Card aCard = myDeck.Deal();
    cout << aCard.GetValue().toString() << " of "
         << aCard.GetSuit().toString() << endl;
  }
  cout << endl << "The deck has " << myDeck.size()
       << " cards." << endl;
}
```

Problem-Solving Case Study

Following is a run of the driver with the user input shaded. As you can see, the cards are in order to start, and the last 42 are output in shuffled order. The user input mixes uppercase and lowercase and still matches the card. At each point the correct size is reported, and the final loop terminates when the deck is empty. After a little more testing, these classes can go into production use for your experiments.

```
The deck has 52 cards.

ACE of CLUBS
TWO of CLUBS
THREE of CLUBS
FOUR of CLUBS
FIVE of CLUBS
SIX of CLUBS
SEVEN of CLUBS
EIGHT of CLUBS
NINE of CLUBS
TEN of CLUBS

The deck has 42 cards.
Shuffling

Enter the name of a suit: Clubs
Enter the name of a card (ace, two,..., king): jack
The card is in the deck.
The remaining contents of the deck are:
QUEEN of SPADES
NINE of SPADES
TWO of SPADES
KING of DIAMONDS
EIGHT of DIAMONDS
FOUR of SPADES
SEVEN of HEARTS
NINE of HEARTS
SIX of DIAMONDS
TWO of DIAMONDS
FIVE of HEARTS
FIVE of DIAMONDS
TEN of HEARTS
KING of SPADES
QUEEN of CLUBS
JACK of HEARTS
TEN of SPADES
SIX of HEARTS
JACK of DIAMONDS
JACK of SPADES
TEN of DIAMONDS
EIGHT of HEARTS
FOUR of DIAMONDS
ACE of HEARTS
TWO of HEARTS
```

Problem-Solving Case Study

```
THREE of SPADES
SEVEN of SPADES
SIX of SPADES
THREE of DIAMONDS
SEVEN of DIAMONDS
QUEEN of DIAMONDS
EIGHT of SPADES
KING of CLUBS
FOUR of HEARTS
QUEEN of HEARTS
ACE of SPADES
KING of HEARTS
ACE of DIAMONDS
JACK of CLUBS
THREE of HEARTS
FIVE of SPADES
NINE of DIAMONDS

The deck has 0 cards.
```

Testing and Debugging

One of the advantages of working with the STL is that the classes and algorithms it provides have already been thoroughly tested. It's easy, however, to let this fact give you a false sense of security. In this chapter, we've been able to touch on only the highlights of the STL; there are many more features that we haven't seen. For example, many of the operations and constructors are overloaded by other versions or have default parameters. A mistake in writing a call may not trigger a compiler error, but instead call a version of an operation with which you're not familiar. If you will work extensively with the STL, it is important to have access to a complete reference for the STL, and to take the time to understand the sometimes cryptic notation of templatized functions and parameters.

When testing a program that uses a container, we must watch out for some special cases. Obviously, attempting to operate on an empty container and going beyond the bounds of the container are among those situations. Also watch for iterators that are moving the wrong direction or by the wrong distance on each step. Popping the first element off of a stack or queue at the start of a loop results in the equivalent of an off-by-one error, because the first element of the container is never processed. Be aware of the special properties and boundary conditions associated with each type of container you are using, and take the time to design tests that ensure your code is not inadvertently violating them.

Testing and Debugging Hints

1. When accessing a container, remember that the values returned by **end** and **rend** point outside of the structure.
2. An iterator must be dereferenced to obtain the value it points to.
3. When declaring an iterator, remember that it must be qualified by the type that it will point to—for example, `list<string>::iterator`.
4. Forward iterators are incremented to advance them and decremented to move them backward. Reverse iterators move backward when they are incremented.
5. Whenever the underlying structure of a container changes, its iterators become invalid. Accessing an invalid iterator after an insertion or deletion operation will cause errors.
6. Whenever you are deleting elements from a container, make sure that you check whether it is empty.
7. Keep in mind that not all algorithms work with all containers. Check the documentation carefully.
8. Remember to copy the top element of a stack or queue before you pop it.
9. Choose a container that has the functionality you need. Additional capability often comes at a cost in performance.
10. Many of the containers require that user-defined element types support some subset of the relational operators. Be sure that your classes provide this support.

Summary

In this chapter, we explored the realm of data structures beyond arrays and singly linked lists. Along the way we encountered vectors, bidirectional lists, stacks, queues, priority queues, deques, trees, graphs, hash tables, sets, and maps. The programming universe is full of other data structures, to the point that the options can sometimes feel overwhelming. Always keep in mind that there are two sides to every data structure. The abstract side is the interface that we use to clearly and conveniently solve a problem. The implementation side is chosen for efficiency of operation. It is usually possible to wrap an implementation within an interface in such a manner that we obtain the best of both worlds. In the end, almost any choice of data structure will be a compromise in one way or another, so the best strategy is to choose the abstract structure that best fits the problem, and then to determine whether the same or another structure provides the most effective implementation.

The stack is a structure in which we insert and delete elements at one end. It is useful when we need to recall information in the order that is the reverse of how it was inserted. We thus say that a stack is a "last in, first out" (LIFO) structure. The queue is another linear structure, but in this case elements are added at one end (the back) and removed from the other end (the front). Therefore, a queue is a "first in, first out" (FIFO) structure. Queues are often used in simulations of real-world waiting lines. A priority queue inserts information according to a given ordering, keeping the data sorted and returning it in order.

Linear structures that have links running in both directions are said to be bidirectional. We can traverse a bidirectional list from back to front as easily as we can go from front to back. A second form of bidirectional structure is the double-ended queue, or deque. With it, we can insert or remove elements at either end.

A binary tree is a branching data structure that has a root node with left and right subtrees. Each of the subtrees has a pair of links to its own subtrees, and so on. Nodes that have two **NULL** links are called leaves. A node with non-**NULL** links is said to be a parent, and the nodes directly below it are called its children. By arranging the values in a binary tree so that every left child's value is less than its parent's value, and every right child's value is greater than its parent's value, we create a binary search tree. Finding a value in a binary search tree containing N values takes $\log_2(N)$ steps. An in-order traversal of the tree will visit all of the elements in order; a binary tree may also be traversed in pre-order or post-order. Additional links enable us to build arbitrarily complex networks of nodes, called graphs.

Hashing is a technique that computes an index for storing and retrieving values in a structure in roughly constant time. The keys to effective hashing are developing a good hash function and having enough extra space in the structure to minimize collisions. A chained hash table uses an array of linked lists, where a collision results in a node being added to the list associated with the array element where the collision occurred.

Binary search trees and hash tables are often used to implement associative lookup, in which an arbitrarily complex key value may be used like an index to access associated data. The set is a structure that stores unique values associatively, enabling us to determine whether a given value is present in the set. A map extends the idea of a set by pairing another value with the key so that we can retrieve it once the key has been located.

The C++ Standard Template Library provides templatized classes and functions that represent many common data structures. Once you understand the principles behind the STL, working with data structures becomes much easier. However, it is important to be aware of the underlying properties of the STL classes so that you can choose the ones that are most appropriate for a given problem.

■ Quick Check Answers

17.1.1 In problem solving, we want a structure that naturally fits the problem. In implementation, efficiency is also a concern. **17.1.2** Its abstract form (interface) and its implementation. **17.2.1** `push` and `pop` **17.2.2** FIFO. **17.2.3** How they are accessed. **17.2.4** A simpler interface. **17.2.5** The cars could be ordered by priority where priority is the pick-up time. The car at the front of the priority queue will be the one that will be picked up the earliest. **17.3.1** A bidirectional list requires twice as many pointers per node and twice as many pointer manipulation operations for every insert and delete, however, it provides more flexibility than a unidirectional list. **17.3.2** The *dequeue* data structure allows us to insert and delete elements from either end of a queue. **17.4.1** `queue<float> nums;` **17.4.2** `end()` **17.4.3** `find` **17.4.4** The `stack pop` removes the element at the back; the `queue pop` removes the element at the front. **17.4.5** containers and algorithms. **17.4.6** A generic data structure that holds an arbitrary number of elements. **17.4.7** The iterator will remain valid only as long as the contents of the container do not change. **17.4.8** A C++ array. **17.4.9** The vector doesn't need to have a fixed size. **17.4.10** The size indicates the number of elements contained in the vector and the capacity is the maximum number of elements the vector may hold. **17.5.1** Left subtree, right subtree, root. **17.5.2** The condition in which the hash function maps two values to the same place in the structure. **17.5.3** A linked data structure whose nodes contain links to a left and right child node. **17.5.4** A binary search tree has an additional property where the elements are arranged in a particular order. **17.5.5** The *root* node. **17.5.6** Hashing. **17.5.7** The hash function would return the value 0 if the grade is less than 59, 1 if the grade is between 60 and 69, 2 if the grade is between 70 and 79, 3 if the grade is between 80 and 89, and 4 if the grade is between 90 and 100. **17.6.1** A data structure that associates values within it not by their indexes, but by their values. **17.6.2** A set stores only the key values where as a **map** associates a second value with each key. **17.6.3** The `[]` operator. **17.6.4** Because it associates key–value pairs and allows us to look up values using their associated keys. **17.6.5** `matches["answer"] = 42;`

■ Exam Preparation Exercises

1. Given the following operations on a stack:

   `push(5), push(4), push(3), pop(), push(2), push(1), pop(), pop()`

   a. How many elements are on the stack?
   b. What is the value at the top of the stack?

2. Given the following operations on a queue:

   `push(5), push(4), push(3), pop(), push(2), push(1), pop(), pop()`

a. How many elements are in the queue?
   b. What is the value at the front of the queue?
3. Given the following operations on a priority queue:

   `push(1), push(7), push(3), push(2), push(5), pop(), push(10), pop()`

   a. How many elements are in the priority queue?
   b. What is the value at the front of the priority queue?
   c. What was the last value popped from the priority queue?
   d. Where would the value 4 be inserted in the priority queue?
4. Given the following operations on a deque:

   `push_back(5), push_back(4), push_front(3), push_front(2), pop_back(),`
   `push_back(1), pop_front(), pop_front()`

   a. How many elements are in the deque?
   b. What is the value at the front of the deque?
   c. What is the value at the back of the deque?
   d. Write the current contents of the deque, indicating `front` and `back`.
5. a. Write an algorithm to perform in-order traversal of a binary tree.
   b. Write an algorithm to perform pre-order traversal of a binary tree.
   c. Write an algorithm to perform post-order traversal of a binary tree.
6. a. What is the relationship of the values in the parent node and its two children in a binary search tree?
   b. If a binary search tree contains 63 nodes, what is the maximum time required to search for a matching value among its nodes?
   c. How many leaves are there in a binary search tree with 7 nodes?
7. a. What problem can result from resolving a collision in a hash table by incrementing the index and using the next location in the table?
   b. What do we mean by the "chain" in a chained hash table?
8. a. Is an `iterator` the same as a pointer? Explain.
   b. What happens to an `iterator` after a deletion from a container?
   c. Which operator do you use to advance an `iterator`?
   d. Which operator causes an `iterator` to move backward?
   e. In which direction does a `reverse_iterator` move when it is incremented?
9. a. Which aspect of `vector` does `deque` implement?
   b. Which aspect of `list` does `deque` implement?
   c. What happens to a `deque` when the `clear` operation is called?
   d. What happens to a `deque` when the `erase` operation is called?
10. a. What are the five operations provided by `stack`?
    b. What are the six operations provided by `queue`?
11. a. What is the difference between the `size` and `capacity` of a `vector`?
    b. How does the `vector at` operator differ from the `[]` operator?
    c. When would you use the `reserve` operation with a `vector`?
12. a. For `map` and `set`, what is returned by the `upper_bound` operation?
    b. Which primary capability does a `map` add to those of the `set`?
    c. Name three set-theoretic operations from the STL algorithms library.
    d. You want a data structure that keeps track of whether shareholders are present at a corporate meeting. Would you choose a `map` or a `set`? Explain.

Programming Warm-Up Exercises

1. Given the following `vector` initialization:

   ```
   int fill[] = {1,2,3,4,5,6,7,8,9,10};
   vector<int> ex1(fill, fill+sizeof(fill)/sizeof(int));
   ```

   What is output by each of the following code segments?

   a. `cout << ex1.size() << " " << ex1.front() << " " << ex1.back();`
   b. `cout << ex1[3] << " " << ex1[5] << " " << ex1[9];`
   c. `ex1.erase(ex1.begin()+4);`
      `cout << ex1[3] << " " << ex1[4] << " " << ex1[5];`
   d. `vector<int>::iterator i;`

      ```
      ex1.erase(ex1.begin());
      for (i = ex1.begin()+2; i != ex1.end(); i++)
         cout << *i << endl;
      ```

2. Given the following `list` initialization:

   ```
   int fill[] = {12,15,7,42,43,9,11,52,30,10};
   list<int> ex2(fill, fill+sizeof(fill)/sizeof(int));
   ```

   What is output by each of the following code segments?

   a. `cout << ex2.size() << " " << ex2.front() << " " << ex2.back();`
   b. `cout << *ex2.begin() << " " << *(--ex2.end()) << " "`
      `   << *ex2.rbegin() << " " << *(--ex2.rend());`
   c. `ex2.insert(++ex2.begin(), 99);`
      `ex2.pop_back();`
      `cout << *ex2.begin();`
   d. `list<int>::iterator i = ex2.begin();`

      ```
      while (i != ex2.end())
         if (*i%2 == 0)
            i = ex2.erase(i);
         else
            i++;
      for (i = ex2.begin(); i != ex2.end(); i++)
         cout << *i << endl;
      ```

   e. `list<int>::iterator i;`

      ```
      ex2.sort();
      for (i = ++(++ex2.begin()); i != ex2.end(); i++)
         cout << *i << endl;
      ```

3. Given the following `deque` initialization:

   ```
   int fill[] = {27,16,81,42,22,75,3,49,12,3,7,2,4};
   deque<int> ex3(fill, fill+sizeof(fill)/sizeof(int));
   ```

   What is output by each of the following code segments?

   a. `cout << ex3.size() << " " << ex3.front() << " " << ex3.back();`
   b. `cout << *ex3.begin() << " " << *(--ex3.end()) << " "`
      `   << *ex3.rbegin() << " " << *(--ex3.rend());`
   c. `cout << ex3[2] << " " << ex3[6] << " " << ex3[8];`

d. `ex3.erase(ex3.begin()+4);`
      `cout << ex3[3] << " " << ex3[4] << " " << ex3[5];`
   e. `ex3.insert(++ex3.begin(), 99);`
      `ex3.pop_back();`
      `cout << *ex3.begin();`
   f. `deque<int>::iterator i = ex3.begin();`
      `while (i != ex3.end())`
         `if (*i%2 == 1)`
            `i = ex3.erase(i);`
         `else`
            `i++;`
      `for (i = ex3.begin(); i != ex3.end(); i++)`
         `cout << *i << endl;`

4. Given the following `list` initialization:

   ```
   int fill[] = {1,2,3,4,5};
   list<int> ex4(fill, fill+sizeof(fill)/sizeof(int));
   ```

   What is wrong with the following statement?

   ```
   cout << *ex4.rend() << endl;
   ```

5. Given the following `stack` operations:

   ```
   stack<char> ex5;
   ex5.push('r'); ex5.push('a'); ex5.push('h'); ex5.push('c');
   while(!ex5.empty())
      { cout << ex5.front(); ex5.pop(); }
   ```

   What is output?

6. Given the following `queue` operations:

   ```
   queue<string> ex6;
   ex6.push("Co"); ex6.push("nt"); ex6.push("ai"); ex6.push("ner");
   while(!ex6.empty())
      { cout << ex6.top(); ex6.pop(); }
   ```

   What is output?

7. Given the following `priority_queue` operations:

   ```
   priority_queue<float> ex7;
   ex7.push(1.8); ex7.push(5.2); ex7.push(3.4); ex7.push(6.7);
   while(!ex7.empty())
      { cout << ex7.top() << " "; ex7.pop(); }
   ```

   What is output?

8. a. Write the declaration for a **vector** of **int** values, initialized to the numbers 1 through 10. You will need to define an array as part of the initialization process.
   b. Write the declaration for an empty **deque** of **int** values.
   c. Write statements that twice copy the contents of the **vector** declared in part (a) into the **deque** declared in part (b). The first time, the elements should be pushed in order at the back of the **deque**; the second time, they should be pushed at the front so that they are in reverse order within the **deque**. Afterward, the values of **front**

and **back**, as applied to the **deque**, should both be 10, and the **size** of the **deque** should be 20.

    d. Assuming the operations in part (c) have been performed, write statements to output the **size** of the **deque**, its first and last elements, and the values in locations 9 and 10.

    e. Assuming the operations in part (c) have been performed, write a loop that pops an element from both ends of the **deque** on each iteration and outputs these values in two columns. The loop terminates when the **deque** is empty.

9. a. Write the declarations for three **set** containers that can hold **int** values. Initialize the first **set** to hold the odd numbers in the range 1 through 9. Initialize the second **set** to hold the even numbers from 2 to 10.

    b. Given the declarations in part (a), write statements to store their difference in the third **set**, and then output the contents of the third **set**. Does it matter whether you pass the first **set** or the second **set** as the first argument to the difference algorithm? That is, would the output differ if their places were reversed in the call?

    c. Given the declarations in part (a), write statements to store the intersection of the first two **set**s in the third **set** and then output its contents.

    d. Given the declarations in part (a), write statements to store the union of the first two **set**s in the third **set** and then output its contents.

10. a. Write the declaration for a **map** that associates values of type **long int** with values of type **string**. The **long int** will be the key (index), and the **string** will be its associated data. You can imagine this data structure as holding Social Security numbers (SSNs) and names.

    b. Write a simple driver that inputs ten SSNs, with corresponding names, and stores them in the **map** declared in part (a). It should then allow the user to input an SSN, after which the matching name is output. Be sure that you handle cases of SSNs that aren't in the **map**.

    c. Given the use of the **map** in part (b), explain why it is a better choice of data structure than an array indexed by the SSN.

11. a. Which STL algorithm would you use to search through a **list**?

    b. If you want to convert a **string** to uppercase, which STL algorithm makes that task easier?

    c. You want to rearrange the elements of **list** into random order. Which STL algorithm can take care of this task for you?

    d. You want to search through a **deque** of **int** values, replacing every occurrence of 21 with 18. Which STL algorithm would be a good choice?

Programming Problems

1. Write a program that will allow the user to evaluate postfix expressions. A postfix expression is an arithmetic expression where the operator occurs after the expression. For example, using infix notation we would add 4 and 5 using 4 + 5. In postfix notation we would arrange the operator to occur at the end: 4 5 +. A postfix expression can become arbitrarily complex such as 3 4 5 + − 2 *. This expression would be expressed using infix notation like this: ((4 + 5) − 3) * 2. As you can see, the postfix form does not require parentheses because the order of operations is made explicit. It turns out that evaluating postfix expressions is quite easy when combined with a stack data structure. We read

a postfix expression from left to right pushing values onto the stack when a number is encountered and popping numbers from the stack when an operator is encountered. For example, the expression **4 5 +** would require the following operations:

1. Push 4 onto the stack.
2. Push 5 onto the stack.
3. Pop the top two values of the stack, add them, and then push the
   result back onto the stack.

Your program should support the basic arithmetic operators such as +, –, *, and / for addition, subtraction, multiplication, and division. It should also provide the operator ^ that pops the top value off the stack and prints it to the console.

2. Extend Problem 1 above to allow multiline postfix expressions that may include variables. For example, we would like to evaluate the following postfix expression:

```
4 5 + X
$X 3 *
^ X
```

The result of evaluating these expressions would be the value **27** printed to the console. You should continue to use a **stack** to implement your postfix evaluator. To implement variables you should use the **map** data structure from the STL to map variable names (e.g., X) to integer values. You should extend your postfix evaluator to support variables such that when a variable is encountered from the input it should pop the current value off the top of the stack and associate it with that variable in the map. If the variable is preceded by a '$' the postfix evaluator should simply retrieve the variable's associated value from the map and push it onto the stack. You should use *exceptions* to handle erroneous input from the user.

3. You are registering people for a campus club that charges dues. New members receive a discount, and returning members pay the full fee. You have a file that contains the ID numbers (which are integers) of existing members, and a file containing the ID numbers for people who have signed up for this year. Write an application that determines which of the people who have signed up for this year are new members and which are returning members. The application should combine the two files so that there are no duplicates and write the result out as a new file of existing members. It should also write out three additional files: the first contains the ID numbers of past members who did not return, the second contains the ID numbers of returning members, and the third contains the ID numbers of new members.

4. A local movie theater has three ticket windows and two computerized ticket kiosks. Some transactions, such as group discounts, can only be done at the ticket windows. An arriving customer looks at the lines, and chooses to stand in the shortest one that can handle his or her transaction. Group sales take four minutes to process. Normal ticket sales take two minutes at a window and three minutes at a kiosk. Internet ticket sales pickups take one minute at a kiosk and two minutes at a window. Write a simulation of this process, using queues to represent the five lines. The data set should consist of randomly arranged customer arrivals, with 5% group sales, 20% Internet ticket sales pickups, and 75% regular ticket sales. A data set will contain 200 customers. All of the customers tend to arrive shortly before the start of a movie, so we are simplifying the simulation to say that they all arrive at the same time. From this simulation, the theater

wants you to determine the maximum length of each line, the average waiting time for each line, and the time required for each line to empty.

As a hint, think about using a `list` to create the data set by adding 10 group, 40 Internet, and 150 regular customers and then shuffling the list. The list is then traversed, transferring each customer to the shortest queue that can handle the customer's transaction.

5. Implement the shopping cart simulation described in Section 17.2 so that it runs for a specified number of minutes. A counter can be used to keep track of the current minute in the simulation. Each time the counter advances, the simulation code handles all of the actions to be performed during that minute. You can use a stack to represent the column of waiting carts, and a priority queue to represent the active carts.

    Each `Cart` object should keep track of the total time it has been active. Use the random-number generator to determine how many minutes (1 to 60) that a cart will be active when it is taken out, and how many customers take carts out in each minute. Keep in mind that the priority queue pops the element with the greatest value, so you will want the `Cart` object's < operator to indicate that carts with a later return time have lower values. One way to do so is to represent the time as a negative number. For example, a simulation of 1000 minutes would start at -1 and end at -1000. When a cart is taken out, its return time becomes the current minute minus the time it will be active. That way, the cart at the head of the priority queue will have the return time that is earliest in the simulation.

    At the start of every minute, check the front of the priority queue to see if the front cart's return time is the same as the current minute, and move it back to the stack. Be sure to check for more than one cart being returned in a given minute. Then determine the number of carts to be taken out during that minute and their activity times, and push them into the priority queue. Remember to watch out for empty container situations. At the end of the simulation, any carts that remain active should be transferred back to the stack. Then, for each cart, output its ID number and total activity time.

6. An application is needed to keep track of shareholders at an annual corporate meeting. The application takes as input a file containing the shareholder names. When a shareholder arrives, his or her name is checked against the list for permission to enter the meeting. That name is then moved to a list of those present, which management can request to see at any time. If the person leaves the meeting, his or her name should be moved from the present list back to the shareholder list. We've described these data structures as lists, but it should be apparent that a `set` is also a natural way of representing the data, given that the only operations are to search the `set` and move names in and out. You can also use the `Name` class that we developed for this book, but the `ComparedTo` function should be replaced with overloaded relational operators.

7. In Chapter 7, Programming Problem 2 involved an application to compute a person's weight on a different planet. Reimplement the application using a `map`, so that the planet's name (a `string`) can be used to retrieve the weight multiplication factor (a `float`).

8. Use the `Deck` class developed in this chapter as part of implementing a program that allows the user to play a game of solitaire. A `list` is a natural way to represent the columns of cards, because it provides an operator called `splice` that lets us move ranges of elements from one `list` to another. Here's an example call:

```
column5.splice(column5.end(), column3, column3.place, column3.end());
```

The result of the call is that the elements of the `column3 list`, starting from the one pointed to by the iterator `place` and going to its end, are removed from `column3` and inserted at the end of `column5`. The `Deck` class will provide a convenient way to deal out the initial arrangement, and the `Card` class can be used to create the `list` elements.

Case Study Follow-Up

1. Expand the test driver for the `Deck` class so that it exercises the relational operators supported by `Deck`, `Suits`, and `Values`.
2. Implement the remaining relational operators for the `Suits` and `Values` classes.
3. Some card games involve shuffling multiple decks. Add a parameterized constructor to the `Deck` class that lets the caller specify how many standard 52-card decks should be in the working deck.
4. Add support for `begin` and `end` operations that return iterators to the ends of the deck. Also implement overloading of the `[]` operator to enable access to deck elements. You can do so by simply calling the corresponding operators in the underlying `deque`.
5. After completing Exercise 4, implement a driver that lets you issue various commands to the deck: deal a given number of cards, reshuffle the deck, and view the current contents of the deck.
6. Write a simulation that empirically determines the odds of being dealt four of a kind in a 5-card hand. As input, it should take the number of hands to try. Note that if more than 10 hands are requested, the program will have to create a new deck after 50 cards have been dealt. You may have to simulate thousands of hands to get significant results. For each hand, check whether four cards with the same value are present, and increment a count. At the end, divide the total number of hands by this count to get the odds. For example, if the result is 35, you can report the odds as 1 in 35 hands.

Recursion

KNOWLEDGE GOALS

- To understand the concept of a recursive definition.
- To understand the difference between iteration and recursion.
- To understand the distinction between the base case(s) and the general case in a recursive definition.

SKILL GOALS

To be able to:
- Write a recursive algorithm for a problem involving only simple variables.
- Write a recursive algorithm for a problem involving structured variables.

> **Recursive call** A function call in which the function being called is the same as the one making the call.

In C++, any function can call another function. A function can even call itself! When a function calls itself, it is making a **recursive call**. The word *recursive* means "having the characteristic of coming up again, or repeating." In this case, a function call is being repeated by the function itself. Recursion is a powerful technique that can be used in place of iteration (looping).

Recursive solutions are generally less efficient than iterative solutions to the same problem. However, some problems lend themselves to simple, elegant, recursive solutions and are exceedingly cumbersome to solve iteratively. Some programming languages, such as early versions of Fortran, Basic, and COBOL, do not allow recursion. Other languages are especially oriented to recursive algorithms—LISP is one of these. C++ lets us take our choice: We can implement both iterative and recursive algorithms.

Our examples are broken into two groups: problems that use only simple variables and problems that use structured variables. If you are studying recursion before reading Chapters 11–16 on structured data types, then cover only the first set of examples and leave the rest until you have completed the chapters on structured data types.

18.1 What Is Recursion?

You may have seen a set of gaily painted Russian dolls that fit inside one another. Inside the first doll is a smaller doll, inside of which is an even smaller doll, inside of which is yet a smaller doll, and so on. A recursive algorithm is like such a set of Russian dolls. It reproduces itself with smaller and smaller examples of itself until a solution is found—that is, until there are no more dolls. The recursive algorithm is implemented by using a function that makes recursive calls to itself.

In Chapter 9, we wrote a function named `Power` that calculates the result of raising an integer to a positive power. If X is an integer and N is a positive integer, the formula for X^N is

$$X^N = \underbrace{X \times X \times X \times X \times \cdots \times X}_{N \text{ times}}$$

We could also write this formula as

$$X^N = X \times \underbrace{(X \times X \times \cdots \times X)}_{(N-1) \text{ times}}$$

or even as

$$X^N = X \times X \times \underbrace{(X \times X \times \cdots \times X)}_{(N-2) \text{ times}}$$

In fact, we can write the formula most concisely as

$$X^N = X \times X^{N-1}$$

This definition of X^N is a classic recursive definition—that is, a definition given in terms of a smaller version of itself.

X^N is defined in terms of multiplying X times X^{N-1}. How is X^{N-1} defined? Why, as $X \times X^{N-2}$, of course! And X^{N-2} is $X \times X^{N-3}$; X^{N-3} is $X \times X^{N-4}$; and so on. In this example, "in terms of smaller versions of itself" means that the exponent is decremented each time.

When does the process stop? When we have reached a case for which we know the answer without resorting to a recursive definition. In this example, it is the case where N equals 1: X^1 is X. The case (or cases) for which an answer is explicitly known is called the base case. The case for which the solution is expressed in terms of a smaller version of itself is called the recursive or general case. A recursive algorithm is an algorithm that expresses the solution in terms of a call to itself, a recursive call. A recursive algorithm must terminate; that is, it must have a base case.

The following program shows a recursive version of the **Power** function with the base case and the recursive call marked. The function is embedded in a program that reads in a number and an exponent and prints the result.

> **Recursive definition** A definition in which something is defined in terms of smaller versions of itself.
>
> **Base case** The case for which the solution can be stated nonrecursively.
>
> **General case** The case for which the solution is expressed in terms of a smaller version of itself; also known as the *recursive case*.
>
> **Recursive algorithm** A solution that is expressed in terms of (1) smaller instances of itself and (2) a base case.

```
//**************************************************************
// Exponentiation program
//**************************************************************
#include <iostream>
using namespace std;

int Power(int x, int n);

int main()
{
  int number;          // Number that is being raised to power
  int exponent;        // Power the number is being raised to

  cin >> number >> exponent;
  cout << Power(number, exponent);   // Nonrecursive call
  return 0;
}

//**************************************************************

int Power(int x, int n)
// Computes x to the n power by multiplying x times the result of
// computing x to the n - 1 power

// Pre: n > 0
{
  if (n == 1)
    return x;                        // Base case
  else
    return x * Power(x, n - 1);      // Recursive call
}
```

Each recursive call to `Power` can be thought of as creating a completely new copy of the function, each with its own copies of the parameters **x** and **n**. The value of **x** remains the same for each version of `Power`, but the value of **n** decreases by 1 for each call until it becomes 1.

Let's trace the execution of this recursive function, with **number** equal to 2 and **exponent** equal to 3. We use a new format to trace recursive routines: We number the calls and then discuss what is happening in paragraph form.

Call 1: `Power` is called by `main`, with **number** equal to 2 and **exponent** equal to 3. Within `Power`, the parameters **x** and **n** are initialized to 2 and 3, respectively. Because **n** is not equal to 1, `Power` is called recursively with **x** and **n** − 1 as arguments. Execution of Call 1 pauses until an answer is sent back from this recursive call.

Call 2: **x** is equal to 2 and **n** is equal to 2. Because **n** is not equal to 1, the function `Power` is called again, this time with **x** and **n** − 1 as arguments. Execution of Call 2 pauses until an answer is sent back from this recursive call.

Call 3: **x** is equal to 2 and **n** is equal to 1. Because **n** equals 1, the value of **x** is to be returned. This call to the function has finished executing, and the function return value (which is 2) is passed back to the place in the statement from which the call was made.

Call 2: This call to the function can now complete the statement that contained the recursive call because the recursive call has returned. Call 3's return value (which is 2) is multiplied by **x**. This call to the function has finished executing, and the function return value (which is 4) is passed back to the place in the statement from which the call was made.

Call 1: This call to the function can now complete the statement that contained the recursive call because the recursive call has returned. Call 2's return value (which is 4) is multiplied by **x**. This call to the function has finished executing, and the function return value (which is 8) is passed back to the place in the statement from which the call was made. Because the first call (the nonrecursive call in `main`) has now completed, this is the final value of the function `Power`.

This trace is summarized in **FIGURE 18.1**. Each box represents a call to the `Power` function. The values for the parameters for that call are shown in each box.

Infinite recursion The situation in which a function calls itself over and over endlessly.

What happens if there is no base case? We have infinite recursion, the recursive equivalent of an infinite loop. For example, if the condition

```
if (n == 1)
```

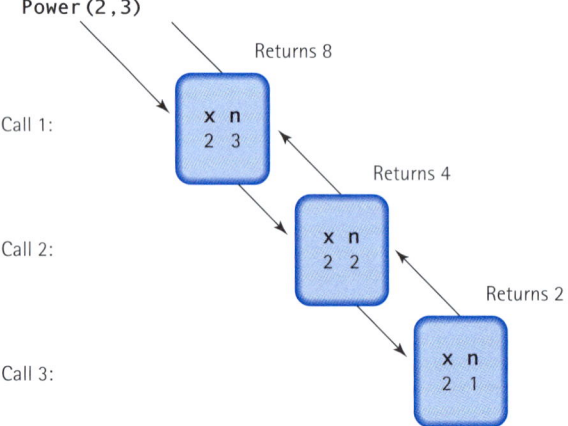

FIGURE 18.1 Execution of `Power(2,3)`

were omitted, `Power` would be called over and over again. Infinite recursion also occurs if `Power` is called with `n` less than or equal to 0.

In actuality, recursive calls cannot go on forever. Here's the reason. When a function is called, either recursively or nonrecursively, the computer system creates temporary storage for the parameters and the function's (automatic) local variables. This temporary storage is a region of memory called the *run-time stack*. When the function returns, its parameters and local variables are released from the run-time stack. With infinite recursion, the recursive function calls never return. Each time the function calls itself, a little more of the run-time stack is used to store the new copies of the variables. Eventually, all the memory space on the stack is used. At that point, the program crashes with an error message such as "Run-time stack overflow" (or the computer may simply hang).

> **QUICK CHECK** ✓
>
> **18.1.1** Which case causes a recursive algorithm to end its recursion: the base case or the general case? (p. 961)
> **18.1.2** What is a **recursive definition**? (p. 961)
> **18.1.3** What is a **recursive algorithm**? (p. 961)
> **18.1.4** What happens if a recursive function does not have a **base case**? (p. 962)

18.2 Recursive Algorithms with Simple Variables

Let's look at another example: calculating a factorial. The factorial of a number N (written $N!$) is N multiplied by $N - 1$, $N - 2$, $N - 3$, and so on. Another way of expressing factorial is

$N! = N \times (N - 1)!$

This expression looks like a recursive definition. $(N - 1)!$ is a smaller instance of $N!$—that is, it takes one less multiplication to calculate $(N - 1)!$ than it does to calculate $N!$ If we can find a base case, we can write a recursive algorithm. Fortunately, we don't have to look too far: $0!$ is defined in mathematics to be 1.

> **Factorial (In: n)**
>
> IF n is 0
>   Return 1
> ELSE
>   Return n * Factorial (n−1)

This algorithm can be coded directly as follows:

```
int Factorial(int n)
// Returns the factorial of n.
// Pre:    n >= 0
{
  if (n == 0)
    return 1;           ◄─────────────── // Base case
  else
    return n * Factorial(n - 1);  ◄───── // General case
}
```

Let's trace this function with an original `n` of 4.

Call 1: n is 4. Because n is not 0, the **else** branch is taken. The Return statement cannot be completed until the recursive call to **Factorial** with n - 1 as the argument has been completed.

Call 2: n is 3. Because n is not 0, the **else** branch is taken. The Return statement cannot be completed until the recursive call to **Factorial** with n - 1 as the argument has been completed.

Call 3: n is 2. Because n is not 0, the **else** branch is taken. The Return statement cannot be completed until the recursive call to **Factorial** with n - 1 as the argument has been completed.

Call 4: n is 1. Because n is not 0, the **else** branch is taken. The Return statement cannot be completed until the recursive call to **Factorial** with n - 1 as the argument has been completed.

Call 5: n is 0. Because n equals 0, this call to the function returns, sending back 1 as the result.

Call 4: The Return statement in this copy can now be completed. The value to be returned is n (which is 1) times 1. This call to the function returns, sending back 1 as the result.

Call 3: The Return statement in this copy can now be completed. The value to be returned is n (which is 2) times 1. This call to the function returns, sending back 2 as the result.

Call 2: The Return statement in this copy can now be completed. The value to be returned is n (which is 3) times 2. This call to the function returns, sending back 6 as the result.

Call 1: The Return statement in this copy can now be completed. The value to be returned is n (which is 4) times 6. This call to the function returns, sending back 24 as the result. Because this is the last of the calls to **Factorial**, the recursive process is over. The value 24 is returned as the final value of the call to **Factorial** with an argument of 4.

FIGURE 18.2 summarizes the execution of the **Factorial** function with an argument of 4.

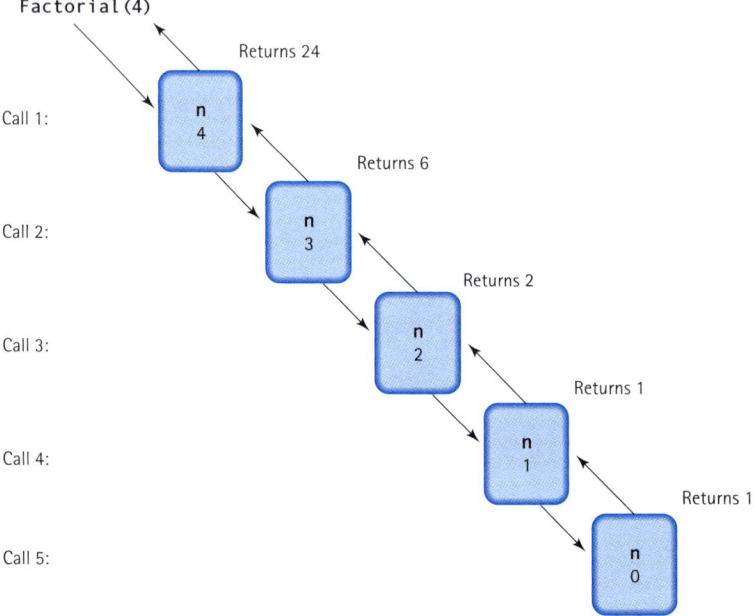

FIGURE 18.2 Execution of **Factorial(4)**

Let's organize what we have done in these two solutions into an outline for writing recursive algorithms:

1. Understand the problem. (We threw this one in for good measure; it is always the first step.)
2. Determine the base case(s).
3. Determine the recursive case(s).

We have used the factorial and the power algorithms to demonstrate recursion because they are easy to visualize. In practice, one would never want to calculate either of these functions using the recursive solution. In both cases, the iterative solutions are simpler and much more efficient because starting a new iteration of a loop is a faster operation than calling a function. Let's compare the code for the iterative and recursive versions of the factorial problem.

Iterative Solution

```
int Factorial (int n)
{
  int factor;
  int count;

  factor = 1;
  for (count = 2; count <= n;
       count++)
    factor = factor * count;
  return factor;
}
```

Recursive Solution

```
int Factorial(int n)
{
  if (n == 0)
    return 1;
  else
    return n * Factorial(n - 1);
}
```

The iterative version has two local variables, whereas the recursive version has none. There are usually fewer local variables in a recursive routine than in an iterative routine. Also, the iterative version always has a loop, whereas the recursive version always has a selection statement—either an If or a Switch. A branching structure is the main control structure in a recursive routine. A looping structure is the main control structure in an iterative routine.

In the next section, we examine a more complicated problem—one in which the recursive solution is not immediately apparent.

QUICK CHECK

18.2.1 In writing a recursive algorithm that computes the factorial of *N*, what would you use as the base case? What would be the general case? (p. 963)

18.2.2 What are the steps for outlining a recursive algorithm? (p. 965)

18.3 Towers of Hanoi

One of your first toys may have been three pegs with colored circles of different diameters. If so, you probably spent countless hours moving the circles from one peg to another. If we put some constraints on how the circles or discs can be moved, we have an adult game called the Towers of Hanoi. When the game begins, all the circles are on the first peg in order by size, with the smallest on the top. The object of the game is to move the circles, one at a time, to the third peg. The catch is that a circle cannot be placed on top of one that is smaller in diameter. The middle peg can be used as an auxiliary peg, but it must be empty at the beginning and at the end of the game.

To get a feel for how this might be done, let's look at some sketches of what the configuration must be at certain points if a solution is possible. We use four circles or discs. Here is the beginning configuration:

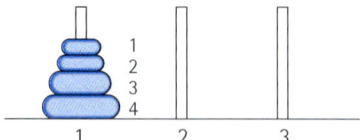

To move the largest circle (circle 4) to peg 3, we must move the three smaller circles to peg 2. Then circle 4 can be moved into its final place:

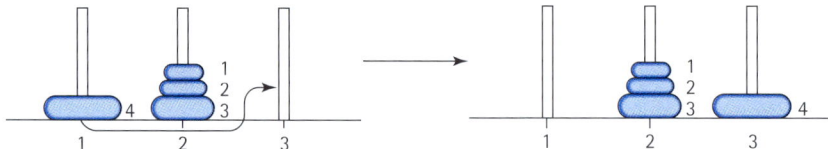

Let's assume we can do this. Now, to move the next largest circle (circle 3) into place, we must move the two circles on top of it onto an auxiliary peg (peg 1 in this case):

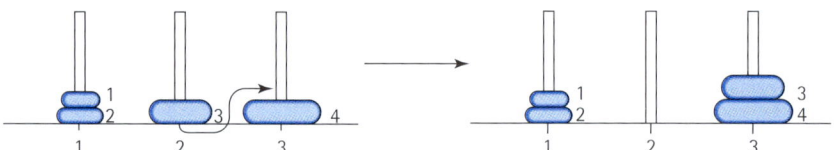

To get circle 2 into place, we must move circle 1 to another peg, freeing circle 2 to be moved to its place on peg 3:

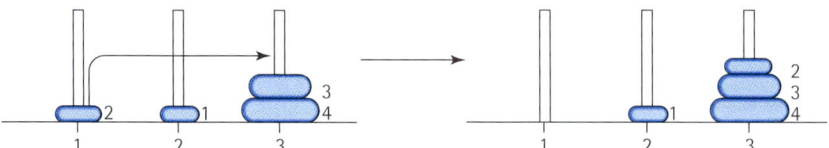

The last circle (circle 1) can now be moved into its final place, and we are finished:

Notice that to free circle 4, we had to move three circles to another peg. To free circle 3, we had to move two circles to another peg. To free circle 2, we had to move one circle to another peg. This sounds like a recursive algorithm: To free the *n*th circle, we have to move *n* − 1 circles. Each stage can be thought of as beginning again with three pegs, but with one less circle each time. Let's see if we can summarize this process, using *n* instead of an actual number.

> **Get *n* Circles Moved from Peg 1 to Peg 3**
>
> Get n–1 circles moved from peg1 to peg2
> Move nth circle from peg1 to peg3
> Get n–1 circles moved from peg2 to peg3

This algorithm certainly sounds simple; surely there must be more. But this really is all there is to it.

Let's write a recursive function that implements this algorithm. We can't actually move discs, of course, but we can print out a message to do so. Notice that the beginning peg, the ending peg, and the auxiliary peg keep changing during the algorithm. To make the algorithm easier to follow, we call the pegs `beginPeg`, `endPeg`, and `auxPeg`. These three pegs, along with the number of circles on the beginning peg, are the parameters of the function.

We have the recursive or general case, but what about a base case? How do we know when to stop the recursive process? The clue is in the statement "Get *n* circles moved." If we don't have any circles to move, we don't have anything to do. We are finished with that stage. Therefore, when the number of circles equals 0, we do nothing (that is, we simply return).

```
void DoTowers(
    int circleCount,    // Number of circles to move
    int beginPeg,       // Peg containing circles to move
    int auxPeg,         // Peg holding circles temporarily
    int endPeg)         // Peg receiving circles being moved
{
  if (circleCount > 0)
  {
    // Move n - 1 circles from beginning peg to auxiliary peg
    DoTowers(circleCount - 1, beginPeg, endPeg, auxPeg);
    cout << "Move circle from peg " << beginPeg
         << " to peg " << endPeg << endl;

    // Move n - 1 circles from auxiliary peg to ending peg
    DoTowers(circleCount - 1, auxPeg, beginPeg, endPeg);
  }
}
```

It's hard to believe that such a simple algorithm actually works, but we'll prove it to you. Following is a driver program that calls the `DoTowers` function. Output statements have been added so you can see the values of the arguments with each recursive call. Because there are two recursive calls within the function, we have indicated which recursive statement issued the call.

```cpp
//*********************************************************************
// TestTowers program
// This program, a test driver for the DoTowers function, reads in
// a value from standard input and passes this value to DoTowers
//*********************************************************************
#include <iostream>
#include <iomanip>       // For setw()

using namespace std;

void DoTowers(int circleCount, int beginPeg, int auxPeg, int endPeg);
// This function moves circleCount circles from beginPeg to
// endPeg, using auxPeg as a temporary holding peg

int main()
{
  int circleCount;       // Number of circles on starting peg

  cout << "Input number of circles: ";
  cin >> circleCount;
  cout << "OUTPUT WITH " << circleCount << " CIRCLES" << endl
       << endl;
  cout << "CALLED FROM  #CIRCLES" << setw(8) << "BEGIN"
       << setw(8) << "AUXIL." << setw(5) << "END"
       << "    INSTRUCTIONS" << endl
       << endl;
  cout << "Original     :";
  DoTowers(circleCount, 1, 2, 3);
  return 0;
}

//*********************************************************************
void DoTowers(int circleCount, int beginPeg, int auxPeg, int endPeg
// This recursive function moves circleCount circles from beginPeg
// to endPeg.  All but one of the circles are moved from beginPeg
// to auxPeg, then the last circle is moved from beginPeg to endPeg,
// and then the circles are moved from auxPeg to endPeg.
// The subgoals of moving circles to and from auxPeg are what
// involve recursion

// Pre:  circleCount >= 0
{
  cout << setw(6) << circleCount << setw(9) << beginPeg
       << setw(7) << auxPeg << setw(7) << endPeg << endl;
  if (circleCount > 0)
  {
    cout << "From  first:";
    DoTowers(circleCount - 1, beginPeg, endPeg, auxPeg);
    cout << setw(58) << "Move circle " << circleCount
         << " from " << beginPeg << " to " << endPeg << endl;
    cout << "From second:";
    DoTowers(circleCount - 1, auxPeg, beginPeg, endPeg);
  }
}
```

The output from a run with three circles follows. "Original" means that the parameters listed beside it are from the nonrecursive call, which is the first call to DoTowers. "From first" means that the parameters listed are for a call issued from the first recursive statement. "From second" means that the parameters listed are for a call issued from the second recursive statement. Notice that a call cannot be issued from the second recursive statement until the preceding call from the first recursive statement has completed execution.

OUTPUT WITH 3 CIRCLES

CALLED FROM	#CIRCLES	BEGIN	AUXIL.	END	INSTRUCTIONS
Original :	3	1	2	3	
From first:	2	1	3	2	
From first:	1	1	2	3	
From first:	0	1	3	2	
					Move circle 1 from 1 to 3
From second:	0	2	1	3	
					Move circle 2 from 1 to 2
From second:	1	3	1	2	
From first:	0	3	2	1	
					Move circle 1 from 3 to 2
From second:	0	1	3	2	
					Move circle 3 from 1 to 3
From second:	2	2	1	3	
From first:	1	2	3	1	
From first:	0	2	1	3	
					Move circle 1 from 2 to 1
From second:	0	3	2	1	
					Move circle 2 from 2 to 3
From second:	1	1	2	3	
From first:	0	1	3	2	
					Move circle 1 from 1 to 3
From second:	0	2	1	3	

QUICK CHECK

18.3.1 What is the **base case** in the recursive solution to the Tower of Hanoi problem? (p. 967)

18.3.2 How many recursive calls are in the recursive solution to the Tower of Hanoi problem and what do they do? (p. 967)

18.4 Recursive Algorithms with Structured Variables

In our definition of a recursive algorithm, we said there were two cases: the recursive or general case, and the base case for which an answer can be expressed nonrecursively. In the general case for all our algorithms so far, an argument was expressed in terms of a smaller value each time. When structured variables are used, the recursive case is often given in terms of a smaller structure rather than a smaller value; the base case occurs when there are no values left to process in the structure.

Let's examine a recursive algorithm for printing the contents of a one-dimensional array of n elements to show what this means.

Print Array

IF more elements
   Print the value of the first element
   Print the array of n–1 elements

The recursive case is to print the values in an array that is one element "smaller"; that is, the size of the array decreases by 1 with each recursive call. The base case is when the size of the array becomes 0—that is, when there are no more elements to print.

Our arguments must include the index of the first element (the one to be printed). How do we know when there are no more elements to print (that is, when the size of the array to be printed is 0)? We know we have printed the last element in the array when the index of the next element to be printed is beyond the index of the last element in the array. Therefore, the index of the last array element must be passed as an argument. We call these indexes `first` and `last`. When `first` is greater than `last`, we are finished. The name of the array is `data`.

```
void Print(const int data[], int first, int last)
// This function prints the values in data from data[first]
// through data[last]
{
  if (first <= last)
  {                                                // Recursive case
    cout << data[first] << endl;
    Print(data, first + 1, last);
  }
    // Empty else-clause is the base case
}
```

Here is a code walk-through of the function call

`Print(data, 0, 4);`

using the pictured array:

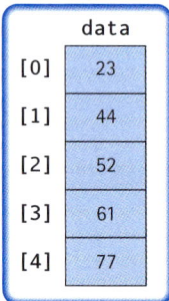

Call 1: `first` is 0 and `last` is 4. Because `first` is less than `last`, the value in `data[first]` (which is 23) is printed. Execution of this call pauses while the array from `first + 1` through `last` is printed.

Call 2: `first` is 1 and `last` is 4. Because `first` is less than `last`, the value in `data[first]` (which is 44) is printed. Execution of this call pauses while the array from `first + 1` through `last` is printed.

Call 3: `first` is 2 and `last` is 4. Because `first` is less than `last`, the value in `data[first]` (which is 52) is printed. Execution of this call pauses while the array from `first + 1` through `last` is printed.

Call 4: `first` is 3 and `last` is 4. Because `first` is less than `last`, the value in `data[first]` (which is 61) is printed. Execution of this call pauses while the array from `first + 1` through `last` is printed.

18.4 Recursive Algorithms with Structured Variables

Call 5: **first** is 4 and **last** is 4. Because **first** is equal to **last**, the value in **data[first]** (which is 77) is printed. Execution of this call pauses while the array from **first + 1** through **last** is printed.

Call 6: **first** is 5 and **last** is 4. Because **first** is greater than **last**, the execution of this call is complete. Control returns to the preceding call.

Call 5: Execution of this call is complete. Control returns to the preceding call.

Calls 4, 3, 2, and 1: Each execution is completed in turn, and control returns to the preceding call.

Notice that once the deepest call (the call with the highest number) was reached, each of the calls before it returned without doing anything. When no statements are executed after the return from the recursive call to the function, the recursion is known as tail recursion. Tail recursion often indicates that the problem could be solved more easily using iteration. We used the array example because it made the recursive process easy to visualize; in practice, an array should be printed iteratively.

> **Tail recursion** A recursive algorithm in which no statements are executed after the return from the recursive call.

FIGURE 18.3 shows the execution of the **Print** function with the values of the parameters for each call. Notice that the array gets smaller with each recursive call (**data[first]** through **data[last]**). If we want to print the array elements in reverse order recursively, all we have to do is interchange the two statements within the If statement.

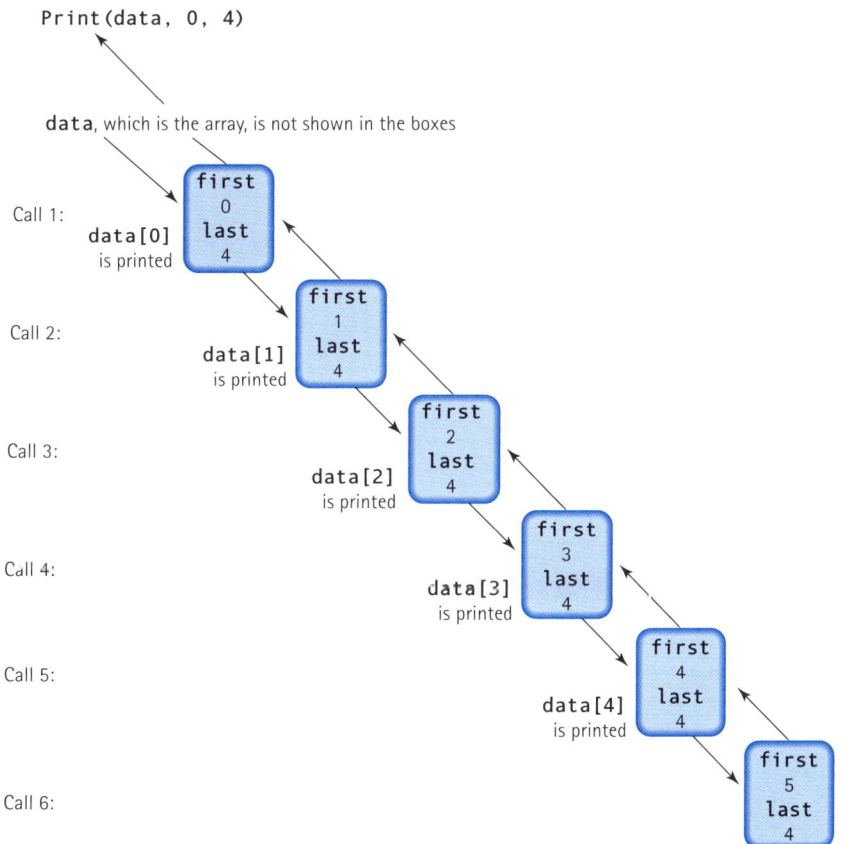

FIGURE 18.3 Execution of **Print(data, 0, 4)**

SOFTWARE MAINTENANCE CASE STUDY: Substituting Binary Search for Linear Search

MAINTENANCE TASK: In Chapter 13, we presented two algorithms that are often applied to values in an array: sorting and searching. If the values in an array are sorted, there is a better searching algorithm: *binary search*. Replace the sequential search used in the searching example in Chapter 13 with a binary search.

CHANGES: Here is a skeleton of that program to remind us of the processing. The function prototype and function call that are to be replaced are shaded. These clearly must be changed.

```
bool Search(string words[], int numWords, string aWord);
// Post: Returns true if aWord is in words; false otherwise

main ()
{
  // Declarations and definitions
  while (inFile)
  {
    numWords++;
    inFile >> words[numWords];
  }

  cout << "Enter a word; enter Quit to stop processing" << endl;
  cin >> aWord;
  while (aWord != "Quit")
  {
    if (Search(words, numWords, aWord))
      cout << aWord << " was found" << endl;
    else
      cout << aWord << " was not found" << endl;
    cout << "Enter a word; enter Quit to stop processing" << endl;
    cin >> aWord;
  }
}
```

Are there any other places that require changing? Yes: The words in the array must be sorted if the binary search algorithm is to be used. We can use the selection sort algorithm we coded in Chapter 13. The only change required is to change the data type of the values to be sorted from `int` to `string`.

BINARY SEARCH ALGORITHM: Now let's look at the binary search algorithm itself. Think of how you might go about finding a name in a phone book, and you can get an idea of a faster way to search. Let's look for the name "David." We open the phone book to the middle and see that the names there begin with M. M is larger than D, so we search the first half of the phone book, the section that contains A to M. We turn to the middle of the first half and see that the names there begin with G. G is larger than D, so we search the first half of this section, from A to G. We turn to the middle page of this section, and find that the names there begin with C. C is smaller than D, so we search the second half of this section—that is, from D to G—and so on, until we are down to the single page that contains the name "David." This algorithm is illustrated in **FIGURE 18.4**.

How can we translate this by-hand algorithm into operations on an array? We can define two integer values `first` and `last` that bracket where in the array the item for which we are looking might be. We then compute the index of the middle item (`middle`) in the bracketed portion of the array and compare the value at that place to the one for which we are looking. If the values are the same, we have found what we are looking for. If the value in that place is greater, we then look in the array from `first` to `middle-1`.

SOFTWARE MAINTENANCE CASE STUDY: Substituting Binary Search for Linear Search

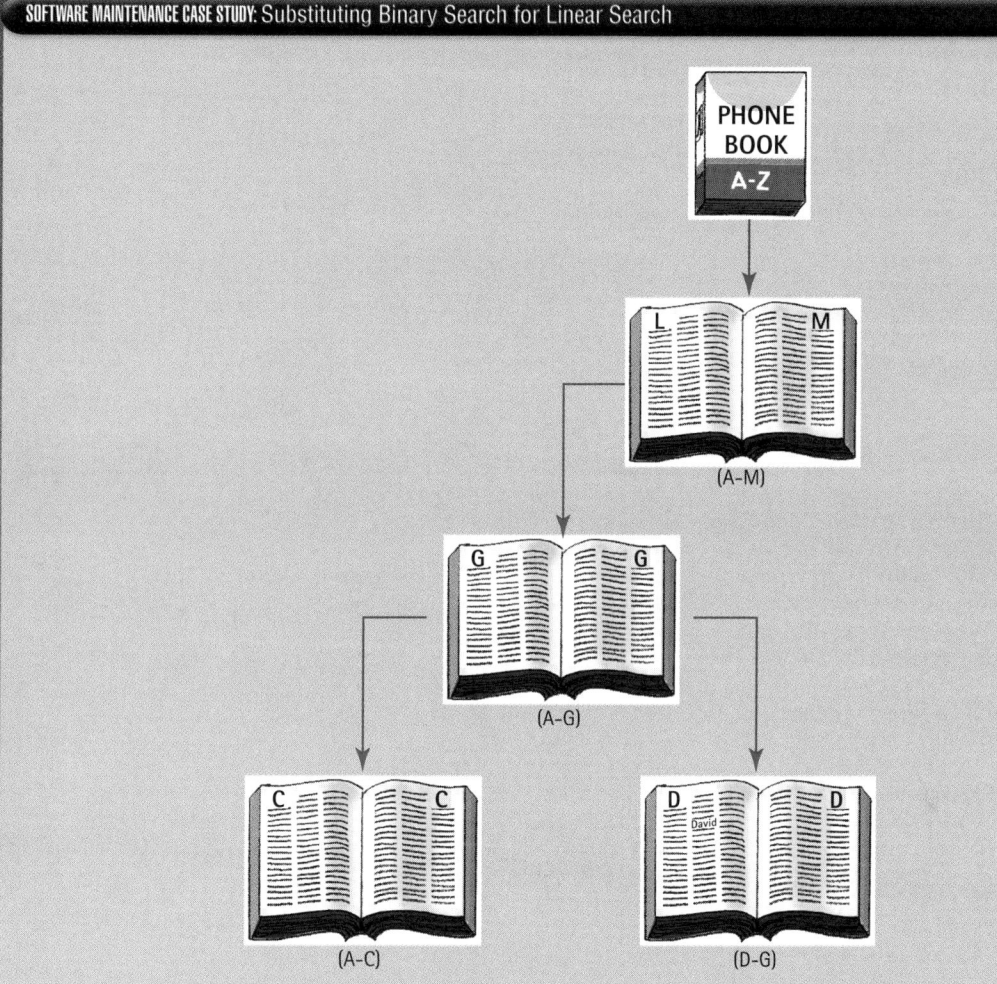

FIGURE 18.4 A Binary Search of the Phone Book

If the value in that place is less, we look in the array from **middle+1** to **last**. How do we know when the value isn't there? When **first** is greater than **last**, we know the item is not in the array.

Let's express the algorithm in terms of our problem: searching for a word in an array of words.

BinarySearch (In: string words[ ], aWord, first, last)
Return value: Boolean

```
IF first > last
    Return false
ELSE
    Set middle to (first + last) / 2
    IF words[middle] is equal to aWord
        Return true
```

SOFTWARE MAINTENANCE CASE STUDY: Substituting Binary Search for Linear Search

```
    ELSE
        IF words[middle] comes after aWord
            Search words[first]..words[middle−1]
    ELSE
        Search words[middle+1]..words[last]
```

This certainly looks like a recursive solution. There are two base cases: when we find the item and when we know it isn't there. What is the general case? There are two: when we look in the first half and when we look in the last half. So the two statements "Search . . ." become calls to the same binary search algorithm with changing parameters. Here is the revised program and the results.

```cpp
//****************************************************
// This program reads words from a file, storing
// them into an array.  The array is sorted.
// The user is prompted to enter a word.  The program
// reports whether or not the word was in the array
// of words.
//****************************************************

#include <iostream>
#include <fstream>         // For ifstream
#include <string>          // For string class
using namespace std;

void sort(string grades[], int numGrades);
// Post: Values in grades have been put into numeric order

bool BinarySearch(string words[], string aWord, int first, int last);
// Post: Returns true if aWord is in words; false otherwise

int main ()
{
  ifstream inFile;
  inFile.open("Words.in");
  string words[30];
  int numWords = 0;
  string aWord;
  inFile >> words[0];
  while (inFile)
  {
    numWords++;
    inFile >> words[numWords];
  }
```

SOFTWARE MAINTENANCE CASE STUDY: Substituting Binary Search for Linear Search

```cpp
  sort(words, numWords);
  cout << "Enter a word; enter Quit to stop processing" << endl;
  cin >> aWord;
  while (aWord != "Quit")
  {
    if (BinarySearch(words, aWord, 0, numWords))
      cout << aWord << " was found" << endl;
    else
      cout << aWord << " was not found" << endl;
    cout << "Enter a word; enter Quit to stop processing" << endl;
    cin >> aWord;
  }

  return 0;
}
//*****************************************************************
void sort(string grades[], int numGrades)
// Post:  Straight selection sort has been used to sort the values
{
  string temp;
  int passCount;        // Outer loop control variable
  int searchIndex;      // Inner loop control variable
  int minIndex;         // Index of minimum so far

  for (passCount = 0; passCount < numGrades - 1; passCount++)
  {
    minIndex = passCount;
    // Find the index of the smallest component
    // in grades[passCount..numGrades-1]
    for (searchIndex = passCount + 1; searchIndex < numGrades;
         searchIndex++)
      if (grades[searchIndex] < grades[minIndex])
        minIndex = searchIndex;
    // Swap data[minIndex] and data[passCount]

    temp = grades[minIndex];
    grades[minIndex] = grades[passCount];
    grades[passCount] = temp;
  }
}
//*****************************************************************
bool BinarySearch(string words[], string aWord, int first, int last)
// Binary search is used
{
  int middle;
  if (first > last)
    return false;
```

SOFTWARE MAINTENANCE CASE STUDY: Substituting Binary Search for Linear Search

```
    else
    {
      middle = (first + last) / 2;
      if (words[middle] == aWord)
        return true;
      else
        if (words[middle] > aWord)
          return BinarySearch(words, aWord, first, middle-1);
        else
          return BinarySearch(words, aWord, middle+1, last);
    }
}
```

Input file: `Words.in`

```
red
blue
gold
yellow
black
silver
purple
green
violet
orange
white
```

Interactive input:

```
Enter a word; enter Quit to stop processing
green
green was found
Enter a word; enter Quit to stop processing
gray
gray was not found
Enter a word; enter Quit to stop processing
red
red was found
Enter a word; enter Quit to stop processing
white
white was found
Enter a word; enter Quit to stop processing
Quit
```

> **QUICK CHECK**
>
> **18.4.1** In writing a recursive algorithm that outputs the values in an array, what would you use as the base case? What would be the general case? (pp. 969–970)
> **18.4.2** What is **tail recursion**? (p. 971)
> **18.4.3** What does **tail recursion** often indicate about a problem? (p. 971)

18.5 Recursion Using Pointer Variables

The recursive algorithm for printing a one-dimensional array could have been implemented much more easily using iteration. Now we look at two algorithms that cannot be handled more easily with iteration: printing a linked list in reverse order and creating a duplicate copy of a linked list. We call the external pointer to the list `listPtr`.

Printing a Dynamic Linked List in Reverse Order

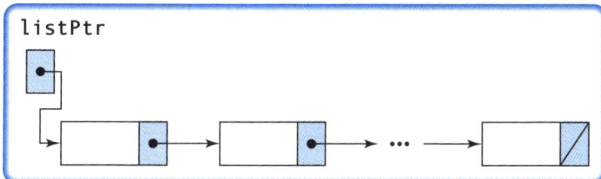

Printing a linked list in order from first to last is easy. We set a running pointer (`ptr`) equal to `listPtr` and cycle through the list until `ptr` becomes `NULL`.

Print List (In: listPtr)

Set ptr to listPtr
WHILE ptr is not NULL
    Print ptr->component
    Set ptr to ptr->link

To print the list in reverse order, we must print the value in the last node first, then the value in the next-to-last node, and so on. Another way of expressing this process is to say that we do not print a value until the values in all the nodes following it have been printed. We might visualize the process as the first node's turning to its neighbor and saying, "Tell me when you have printed your value. Then I'll print my value." The second node says to its neighbor, "Tell me when you have printed your value. Then I'll print mine." That node, in turn, says the same to its neighbor, and so on, until there is nothing to print.

Because the number of neighbors gets smaller and smaller, we seem to have the makings of a recursive solution. The end of the list is reached when the running pointer is `NULL`. When that happens, the last node can print its value and send the message back to the one before it. That node can then print its value and send the message back to the one before it, and so on.

RevPrint (In: listPtr)

IF listPtr is not NULL
    RevPrint rest of nodes in list
    Print current node in list

This algorithm can be coded directly as the following function:

```
void RevPrint(NodePtr listPtr)
// Pre:  listPtr points to a list node or is NULL
// Post: If listPtr is not NULL, all nodes after listPtr have
//       been printed followed by the contents of listPtr;
//       else no action has been taken.
{
  if (listPtr != NULL)
  {
    RevPrint(listPtr->link);                    // Recursive call
    cout << listPtr->component << endl;
  }
  // Empty else-clause is the base case
}
```

This algorithm seems complex enough to warrant a code walk-through. We use the following list:

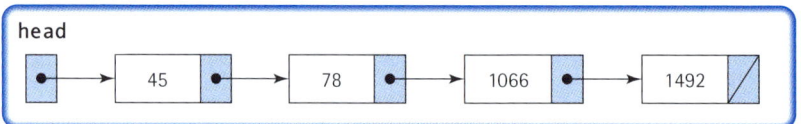

Call 1: `listPtr` points to the node containing 45 and is not **NULL**. Execution of this call pauses until the recursive call with the argument `listPtr->link` has been completed.

Call 2: `listPtr` points to the node containing 78 and is not **NULL**. Execution of this call pauses until the recursive call with the argument `listPtr->link` has been completed.

Call 3: `listPtr` points to the node containing 1066 and is not **NULL**. Execution of this call pauses until the recursive call with the argument `listPtr->link` has been completed.

Call 4: `listPtr` points to the node containing 1492 and is not **NULL**. Execution of this call pauses until the recursive call with the argument `listPtr->link` has been completed.

Call 5: `listPtr` is **NULL**. Execution of this call is complete. Control returns to the preceding call.

Call 4: `listPtr->component` (which is 1492) is printed. Execution of this call is complete. Control returns to the preceding call.

Call 3: `listPtr->component` (which is 1066) is printed. Execution of this call is complete. Control returns to the preceding call.

Call 2: `listPtr->component` (which is 78) is printed. Execution of this call is complete. Control returns to the preceding call.

Call 1: `listPtr->component` (which is 45) is printed. Execution of this call is complete. Because this is the nonrecursive call, execution continues with the statement immediately following `RevPrint(listPtr)`.

FIGURE 18.5 shows the execution of the `RevPrint` function. The parameters are pointers (memory addresses), so we use → 45 to mean the pointer to the node whose component is 45.

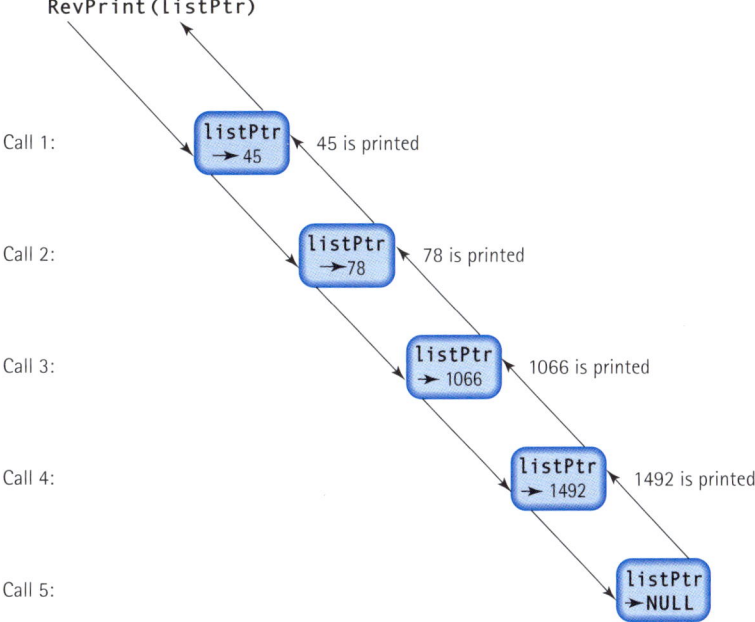

FIGURE 18.5 Execution of `RevPrint`

Copying a Dynamic Linked List

When working with linked lists, we sometimes need to create a duplicate copy (sometimes called a *clone*) of a linked list. For example, in Chapter 14, we wrote a copy-constructor for the `List` class. This copy-constructor creates a new class object that is a copy of another class object, including its dynamic linked list.

Suppose that we want to write a value-returning function that receives the external pointer to a linked list (`listPtr`), makes a clone of the linked list, and returns the external pointer to the new list as the function value. A typical call to the function would be the following:

```
NodePtr listPtr;
NodePtr newListPtr;
   .
   .
   .
newListPtr = PtrToCopy(listPtr);
```

Using iteration to copy a linked list is rather complicated. The following algorithm is essentially the same as the one used in the `List` copy-constructor.

```
PtrToCopy (In: listPtr)        // Iterative algorithm
Out: Function value
```

IF listPtr is NULL
  Return NULL

// Copy first node
Set fromPtr = listPtr
Set copyPtr = new NodeType
Set copyPtr->component = fromPtr->component

// Copy remaining nodes
Set toPtr = copyPtr
Set fromPtr = fromPtr->link
WHILE fromPtr is not NULL
   Set toPtr->link = new NodeType
   Set toPtr = toPtr->link
   Set toPtr->component = fromPtr->component
   Set fromPtr = fromPtr->link
Set toPtr->link = NULL
Return copyPtr

A recursive solution to this problem is far simpler, but it requires us to think recursively. To copy the first node of the original list, we can allocate a new dynamic node and copy the **component** value from the original node into the new node. However, we cannot yet fill in the **link** member of the new node: We must wait until we have copied the second node, so that we can store its address into the **link** member of the first node. Likewise, the copying of the second node cannot complete until we have finished copying the third node. Eventually, we copy the last node of the original list and set the **link** member of the copy node to **NULL**. At this point, the last node returns its own address to the next-to-last node, which stores the address into its **link** member. The next-to-last node returns its own address to the node before it, and so forth. The process is complete when the first node returns its address to the first (nonrecursive) call, yielding an external pointer to the new linked list.

```
PtrToCopy (In: fromPtr)        // Recursive algorithm
Out: Function value
```

IF fromPtr is NULL
  Return NULL
ELSE
  Set toPtr = new NodeType
  Set toPtr->component = fromPtr->component
  Set toPtr->link = PtrToCopy(fromPtr->link)
  Return toPtr

Like the solution to the Towers of Hanoi problem, this scheme looks too simple—yet it is the full algorithm. Because the argument that is passed to each recursive call is `fromPtr->link`, the number of nodes left in the original list becomes smaller with each call. The base case occurs when the pointer into the original list becomes `NULL`. Following is the C++ function that implements this algorithm.

```
NodePtr PtrToCopy(NodePtr fromPtr)
// Pre:  fromPtr points to a list node or NULL
// Post: If fromPtr is not NULL, a copy of the entire sublist
//          starting with *fromPtr is on the free store and
//          function value is the pointer to front of this sublist
//       else
//          Return value is NULL

{
  NodePtr toPtr;      // Pointer to newly created node

  if (fromPtr == NULL)
    return NULL;                        // Base case
  else
  {                                     // Recursive case
    toPtr = new NodeType;
    toPtr->component = fromPtr->component;
    toPtr->link = PtrToCopy(fromPtr->link);
    return toPtr;
  }
}
```

Let's perform a code walk-through of the function call

`newListPtr = PtrToCopy(listPtr);`

using the following list:

Call 1: `fromPtr` points to the node containing 49 and is not `NULL`. A new node is allocated and its `component` value is set to 49.

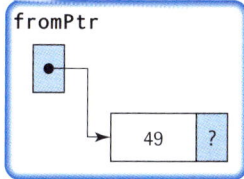

Execution of this call pauses until the recursive call with the argument `fromPtr->link` has been completed.

Call 2: `fromPtr` points to the node containing 50 and is not `NULL`. A new node is allocated and its `component` value is set to 50.

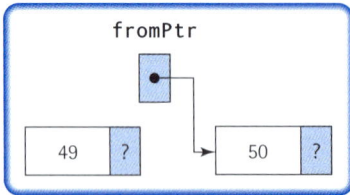

Execution of this call pauses until the recursive call with the argument `fromPtr->link` has been completed.

Call 3: `fromPtr` points to the node containing 58 and is not `NULL`. A new node is allocated and its component value is set to 58.

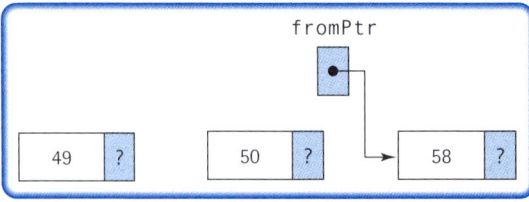

Execution of this call pauses until the recursive call with the argument `fromPtr->link` has been completed.

Call 4: `fromPtr` is `NULL`. The list is unchanged.

Execution of this call is complete. `NULL` is returned as the function value to the preceding call.

Call 3: Execution of this call resumes by assigning the returned function value (`NULL`) to `toPtr->link`.

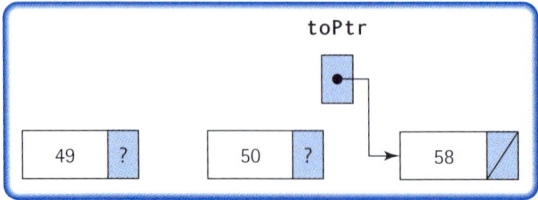

Execution of this call is complete. The value of `toPtr` is returned to the preceding call.

Call 2: Execution of this call resumes by assigning the returned function value (the address of the third node) to `toPtr->link`.

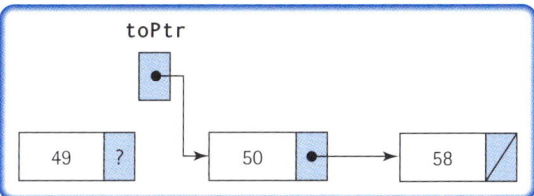

Execution of this call is complete. The value of `toPtr` is returned to the preceding call.

Call 1: Execution of this call resumes by assigning the returned function value (the address of the second node) to `toPtr->link`.

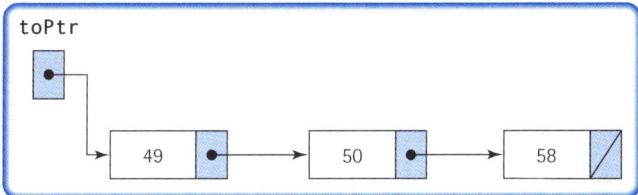

Execution of this call is complete. Because this is the nonrecursive call, the value of `toPtr` is returned to the assignment statement containing the original call. The variable `newListPtr` now points to a copy of the original list.

QUICK CHECK

18.5.1 In writing a recursive algorithm that outputs the values in a linked list in reverse order, what would you use as the base case? What would be the general case? (pp. 977–978)

18.6 Recursion or Iteration?

Recursion and iteration are alternative ways of expressing repetition in a program. When iterative control structures are used, processes are made to repeat by embedding code in a looping structure such as a While, For, or Do-While. In recursion, a process is made to repeat by having a function call itself; a selection statement is used to control the repeated calls.

Which is the better approach—recursion or iteration? There is no simple answer to this question. The choice usually depends on two issues: efficiency and the nature of the problem being solved.

Historically, the quest for efficiency, in terms of both execution speed and memory usage, has favored iteration over recursion. Each time a recursive call is made, the system must allocate stack space for all parameters and (automatic) local variables. The overhead involved in any function call is time-consuming. On early, slow computers with limited memory capacity, recursive algorithms were visibly—sometimes painfully—slower than the iterative versions. By contrast, on modern, fast computers, the overhead of recursion is often so small that the increase in computation time is almost unnoticeable to the user. Except in cases where efficiency is absolutely critical, then, the choice between recursion and iteration more often depends on the second issue—the nature of the problem being solved.

Consider the factorial and power algorithms discussed earlier in this chapter. In both cases, iterative solutions were obvious and easy to devise. We imposed recursive solutions on these problems simply to demonstrate how recursion works. As a rule of thumb, if an iterative solution is more obvious or easier to understand, use it; it will be more efficient. In some other problems, the recursive solution is more obvious or easier to devise, such as in the Towers of Hanoi problem. (It turns out that the Towers of Hanoi problem is surprisingly difficult to solve using iteration.) Computer science students should be aware of the power of recursion. If the definition of a problem is inherently recursive, then a recursive solution should certainly be considered.

QUICK CHECK

18.6.1 What factor dictates an iterative solution to an algorithm versus a recursive one? (p. 983)

Problem-Solving Case Study

Quicksort

PROBLEM: Throughout the last half of this book, we have worked with lists of items, both sorted and unsorted. At the logical level, sorting algorithms take an unsorted list and convert it into a sorted list. At the implementation level, sorting algorithms take an array and reorganize the data into some sort of order. We have used the straight selection algorithm to sort a list of numbers, and we have inserted entries into a list ordered by time. In this case study, we will create a function template that implements the Quicksort algorithm.

DISCUSSION: The Quicksort algorithm, which was developed by C. A. R. (Tony) Hoare, is based on the idea that it is faster and easier to sort two small lists than one larger one. The name comes from the fact that, in general, a Quicksort can sort a list of data elements quite rapidly. The basic strategy of this sort is to "divide and conquer."

If you were given a large stack of final exams to sort by name, you might use the following approach: Pick a splitting value—say, L—and divide the stack of tests into two piles, A–L and M–Z. (Note that the two piles do not necessarily contain the same number of tests.) Then take the first pile and subdivide it into two piles, A–F and G–L. The A–F pile can be further broken down into A–C and D–F. This division process goes on until the piles are small enough to be easily sorted by hand. The same process is applied to the M–Z pile. Eventually all of the small sorted piles can be stacked one on top of the other to produce a sorted set of tests. (See **FIGURE 18.6**.)

This strategy is based on recursion—on each attempt to sort the stack of tests, the stack is divided and then the same approach is used to sort each of the smaller stacks (a smaller case). This process goes on until the small stacks do not need to be further divided (the base case). The parameter list of the Quicksort algorithm specifies the part of the list that is currently being processed. Notice that we are sorting the list items stored in the array—not an abstract list about whose implementation we know nothing. To make this distinction clear, we call the array **data** rather than **list**.

Problem-Solving Case Study

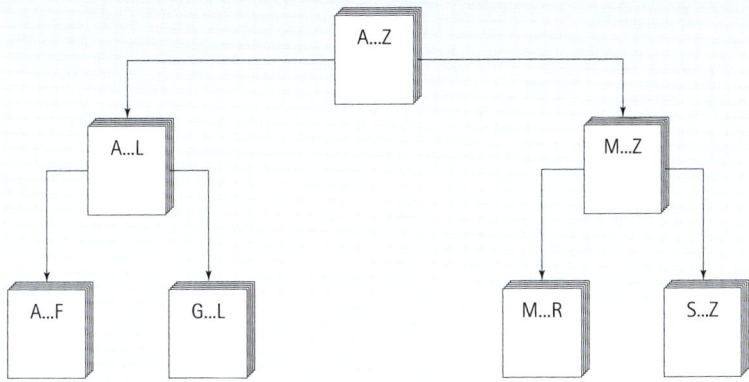

FIGURE 18.6 Ordering a List Using the Quicksort Algorithm

Quicksort (In: first, last)

IF there is more than one item in data[first]..data[last]
    Select splitVal
    Split the data so that
        data[first]..data[splitPoint-1] <= splitVal
        data[splitPoint] = splitVal
        data[splitPoint+1]..data[last] > splitVal
    Quicksort the left half
    Quicksort the right half

How do we select **splitVal**? One simple solution is to use whatever value is in **data[first]** as the splitting value. Let's look at an example using **data[first]** as **splitVal**.

After the call to **Split**, all of the items less than or equal to splitVal are on the left side of the data and all of those items greater than **splitVal** are on the right side of the data.

Problem-Solving Case Study

The two "halves" meet at `splitPoint`, the index of the last item that is less than or equal to `splitVal`. Note that we don't know the value of `splitPoint` until the splitting process is complete. We can then swap `splitVal` (`data[first]`) with the value at `data[split]`.

smaller data			larger data				
6	8	9	10	14	20	60	11
[first]		[splitPoint]					[last]

Our recursive calls to `Quicksort` use this index (`splitPoint`) to reduce the size of the problem in the general case.

`Quicksort(first, splitPoint-1)` sorts the left "half" of the data; `Quicksort(splitPoint+1, last)` sorts the right "half" of the data. (Note that the "halves" are not necessarily the same size.) `splitVal` is already in its correct position in `data[splitPoint]`.

What is the base case? When the segment being examined has only one item, we do not need to go on. So "there is more than one item in `data[first]..data[last]`" translates into "`if (first < last)`". We can now code the function `Quicksort`.

```
template<class ItemType>
void Quicksort(ItemType data[], int first, int last)

// Pre:  ComparedTo has been defined on ItemType
// Post: data are sorted

{
  if (first < last)
  {
    int splitPoint;
    Split(data, first, last, splitPoint);
    // data[first]..data[splitPoint-1] <= splitVal
    // data[splitPoint] = splitVal
    // data[splitPoint+1]..data[last] > splitVal

    QuickSort(data, first, splitPoint-1);
    QuickSort(data, splitPoint+1, last);
  }
}
```

Now we must find a way to get all of the elements that are equal to or less than `splitVal` on one side of `splitVal` and all of the elements that are greater than `splitVal` on the other side. We do so by moving a pair of the indexes toward the middle of the data, looking for items that are on the wrong side of the split point. When we find pairs that are on the wrong side, we swap them and continue working our way into the middle of the data.

FIGURE 18.7A shows the initial state of the array to be sorted. We start out by moving first to the right, toward the middle, comparing `data[first]` to `splitVal`. If `data[first]` is less or equal to `splitVal`, we keep incrementing `first`; otherwise, we leave `first` where it is and begin moving `last` toward the middle. (See **FIGURE 18.7B**.)

Problem-Solving Case Study

(a) Initialization

| 9 | 20 | 6 | 10 | 14 | 8 | 60 | 11 |

[saveFirst] [first]   [last]

(b) Increment `first` until `values[first]>splitVal`

| 9 | 20 | 6 | 10 | 14 | 8 | 60 | 11 |

[saveFirst] [first]   [last]

(c) Decrement `last` until `values[last]<= splitVal`

| 9 | 20 | 6 | 10 | 14 | 8 | 60 | 11 |

[saveFirst] [first]   [last]

(d) Swap `values[first]` and `values[last]`; move `first` and `last` toward each other

| 9 | 8 | 6 | 10 | 14 | 20 | 60 | 11 |

[saveFirst]   [first]   [last]

(e) Increment `first` until `values[first]>splitVal` or `first>last`
    Decrement `last` until `values[last]<= splitVal` or `first>last`

| 9 | 8 | 6 | 10 | 14 | 20 | 60 | 11 |

[saveFirst]   [last] [first]

(f) `first>last` so no swap occurs within the loop
    Swap `values[saveFirst]` and `values[last]`

| 6 | 8 | 9 | 10 | 14 | 8 | 60 | 11 |

[saveFirst]   [last]
                  [splitPoint]

FIGURE 18.7 Function Split

Problem-Solving Case Study

Now `data[last]` is compared to `splitVal`. If it is greater, we continue decrementing `last`; otherwise, we leave `last` in place (see **FIGURE 18.7C**). At this point it is clear that `data[last]` and `data[first]` are on the wrong sides of the array. Note that the elements to the left of `data[first]` and to the right of `data[last]` are not necessarily sorted; they are just on the correct side with respect to `splitVal`. To move `data[first]` and `data[last]` to the correct sides, we merely swap them, and then increment `first` and decrement `last` (see **FIGURE 18.7D**).

Now we repeat the whole cycle, incrementing `first` until we encounter a value that is greater than `splitVal`, and then decrementing `last` until we encounter a value that is less than or equal to `splitVal` (see **FIGURE 18.7E**).

When does the process stop? When `first` and `last` meet each other, no additional swaps are necessary. They meet at the `splitPoint`. This is the location where `splitVal` belongs, so we swap `data[saveFirst]`, which contains `splitVal`, with the element at `data[splitPoint]` (**FIGURE 18.7F**). The index `splitPoint` is returned from the function, to be used by `Quicksort` to set up the next recursive call.

To make the `Quicksort` function template truly generic, let's assume that the items to be sorted can be compared with the `ComparedTo` function.

```
template<class ItemType>
void Swap(ItemType& item1, ItemType& item2)
// Post: Contents of item1 and item2 have been swapped
{
  ItemType tempItem;
  tempItem = item1;
  item1 = item2;
  item2 = tempItem;
}

template<class ItemType>
void Split(ItemType data[], int first, int last, int& splitPoint)
// Pre:  ComparedTo has been defined on ItemType
// Post: All items greater than split value are to the left and all
//       items less than or equal to split value are to the right
{
  ItemType splitVal = data[first];
  int saveFirst = first;
  bool onCorrectSide;

  first++;
  do
  {
    onCorrectSide = true;
    while (onCorrectSide)              // Move first toward last
      switch (data[first].ComparedTo(splitVal))
      {
        case AFTER   : onCorrectSide = false;
                       break;
        case SAME    :
        case BEFORE  : first++;
                       onCorrectSide = (first <= last);
                       break;
      }
```

Problem-Solving Case Study

```
    onCorrectSide = (first <= last);
    while (onCorrectSide)              // Move last toward first
      switch (data[last].ComparedTo(splitVal))
      {
        case SAME      :
        case BEFORE    : onCorrectSide = false;
                         break;
        case AFTER     : last--;
                         onCorrectSide = (first <= last);
                         break;
      }

    if (first < last)
    {
      Swap(data[first], data[last]);
      first++;
      last--;
    }
  } while (first <= last);

  splitPoint = last;
  Swap(data[saveFirst], data[splitPoint]);
}
```

TESTING: These three functions are placed in a single file and included in a driver to be tested. Class **Name** defines **ComparedTo**, so let's read in names, sort them, and print them. Here is the driver and output from the run:

```
//***************************************************************
//  Driver for the Quicksort algorithm.
//***************************************************************
#include <iostream>
#include <string>
#include "Name.h"
#include "Quicksort.h"
using namespace std;
Name ReadName();
// Prompts for and reads a name from the standard input device

int main()
{
  Name data[15];
  Name name;
  // Read in 15 names
  for (int index = 0; index < 15; index++)
  {
    name = ReadName();
    data[index] = name;
  }
```

Problem-Solving Case Study

```cpp
  // Sort 15 names
  QuickSort(data, 0, 14);
  // Print first and last name in sorted order
  for (int index = 0; index < 15; index++)
    cout << data[index].GetFirstName() << " "
         << data[index].GetLastName() << endl;
  return 0;
}

//**************************************************************

Name ReadName()
{
  string first, middle, last;
  cout << "Enter first name: ";     // Prompt for first name
  cin >> first;                      // Get first name
  cout << "Enter middle name: ";    // Prompt for middle name
  cin >> middle;                     // Get middle name
  cout << "Enter last name: ";      // Prompt for last name
  cin >> last;                       // Get last name
  Name name(first, middle, last);
  return name;
}
```

Sample run:

```
Enter first name: Sam
Enter middle name: Sloan
Enter last name: Smith
Enter first name: Joe
Enter middle name: John
Enter last name: Jones
Enter first name: Bill
Enter middle name: Bradley
Enter last name: Black
Enter first name: Jane
Enter middle name: June
Enter last name: Jones
Enter first name: Gray
Enter middle name: G
Enter last name: Green
Enter first name: Pansy
Enter middle name: P
Enter last name: Potter
Enter first name: Rose
Enter middle name: Violet
```

Problem-Solving Case Study

```
Enter last name: Red
Enter first name: Yellow
Enter middle name: Y
Enter last name: Yarn
Enter first name: Calvin
Enter middle name: Charles
Enter last name: Carson
Enter first name: Alfred
Enter middle name: Albert
Enter last name: Alred
Enter first name: Nell
Enter middle name: Nancy
Enter last name: Night
Enter first name: Carol
Enter middle name: Carter
Enter last name: Carton
Enter first name: Zoe
Enter middle name: Z
Enter last name: Zebra
Enter first name: June
Enter middle name: May
Enter last name: July
Enter first name: Son
Enter middle name: Shine
Enter last name: Sunlight
Alfred Alred
Bill Black
Calvin Carson
Carol Carton
Gray Green
Jane Jones
Joe Jones
June July
Nell Night
Pansy Potter
Rose Red
Sam Smith
Son Sunlight
Yellow Yarn
Zoe Zebra
```

Testing and Debugging

Recursion is a powerful technique when it is used correctly. When improperly used, however, recursion can lead to difficult-to-diagnose errors. The best way to debug a recursive algorithm is to construct it correctly in the first place. To be realistic, we give a few hints about where to look if an error occurs.

Testing and Debugging Hints

1. Be sure there is a base case. If there is no base case, the algorithm continues to issue recursive calls until all memory has been used. Each time the function is called, either recursively or nonrecursively, stack space is allocated for the parameters and automatic local variables. If there is no base case to end the recursive calls, the run-time stack eventually overflows. An error message such as "Stack overflow" indicates that the base case is missing.

2. Make sure you have not used a While structure. The basic structure in a recursive algorithm is the If statement. There must be at least two cases: the recursive case and the base case. If the base case does nothing, the else-clause is omitted. The selection structure, however, must be present. If a While statement is used in a recursive algorithm, the While statement usually should not contain a recursive call.

3. As with nonrecursive functions, do not reference global variables directly within a recursive function unless you have justification for doing so.

4. Parameters that relate to the size of the problem must be value parameters, not reference parameters. The arguments that relate to the size of the problem are usually expressions. Arbitrary expressions can be passed only to value parameters.

5. Use your system's debugger program (or use debug output statements) to trace a series of recursive calls. Inspecting the values of parameters and local variables often helps to pinpoint the locations of errors in a recursive algorithm.

Summary

A recursive algorithm is expressed in terms of a smaller instance of itself. It must include a recursive case, for which the algorithm is expressed in terms of itself, and a base case, for which the algorithm is expressed in nonrecursive terms.

In many recursive problems, the smaller instance refers to a numeric argument that is being reduced with each call. In other problems, the smaller instance refers to the size of the data structure being manipulated. The base case is the one in which the size of the problem (in terms of either a value or a structure) reaches a point for which an explicit answer is known.

- In the example of printing an array using recursion, the size of the problem was the size of the array. When the array size became 0, the entire array had been printed.
- In the Towers of Hanoi game, the size of the problem was the number of discs to be moved. When only one was left on the beginning peg, it could be moved to its final destination.

Recursion incurs extra overhead that iteration doesn't. Thus, in most cases, iteration is more efficient. For some problems, however, a recursive algorithm is the natural solution. In those situations, the corresponding iterative solution is likely to be more complex—programming the iterative version often involves manually implementing the equivalent of the call stack. While you may not use recursion on a regular basis, it is a powerful tool to have in your programming toolkit.

Quick Check Answers

18.1.1 The base case. **18.1.2** A definition given in terms of a smaller version of itself. **18.1.3** An algorithm that expresses the solution in terms of a call to itself, a recursive call. **18.1.4** We have **infinite recursion**, the recursive equivalent of an infinite loop. **18.2.1** The base case would be that when N is 0, the result is 1. The general case would be that when N is greater than 0, we multiply it by the product of the numbers from 1 to $N - 1$, as returned from a recursive call. **18.2.2** 1. Understand the problem; 2. Determine the base case(s); 3. Determine the recursive case(s). **18.3.1** When the number of circles equals 0. **18.3.2** 2 recursive calls. The first is to move $n - 1$ circles from the beginning peg to auxiliary peg and the second is to move n–1 circles from the auxiliary peg to the ending peg. **18.4.1** The base case would be that if there are no elements remaining, we return. The general case would be that if there are elements remaining, we print the first one, then recurse to print the rest. **18.4.2** A recursive algorithm in which no statements are executed after the return from the recursive call. **18.4.3** That it could be solved more easily using iteration. **18.5.1** The base case would be that the link of the current node is **NULL**, so we print it. The general case would be that if the link of the current node is not **NULL**, we print the remainder of the list before printing the current node. **18.6.1** The nature of the problem in terms of its efficiency.

Exam Preparation Exercises

1. Recursion is an alternative to
    a. branching.
    b. looping.
    c. function invocation.
    d. event handling.
2. A recursive function can be void or value returning. True or false?
3. When a function calls itself recursively, its parameters and local variables are saved on the run-time stack until it returns. True or false?
4. Tail recursion occurs when all of the processing happens at the end of the function, after the return from the recursive call. True or false?
5. Given the recursive formula $F(N) = F(N - 2)$, with the base case $F(0) = 0$, what are the values of $F(4)$, $F(5)$, and $F(6)$? If any of the values are undefined, say so.
6. Given the recursive formula $F(N) = F(N - 1) * 2$, with the base case $F(0) = 1$, what are the values of $F(3)$, $F(4)$, and $F(5)$? If any of the values are undefined, say so.
7. What happens when a recursive function never encounters a base case?
8. Which practical limitation prevents a function from calling itself recursively forever?
9. A tail-recursive function would be more efficiently implemented with a loop in most cases. True or false?
10. When you develop a recursive algorithm to operate on a simple variable, what does the general case typically make smaller with each recursive call?
    a. The data type of the variable
    b. The number of times the variable is referenced
    c. The value in the variable

11. When you develop a recursive algorithm to operate on a data structure, what does the general case typically make smaller with each recursive call?
    a. The number of elements in the structure
    b. The number of times the variable is referenced
    c. The distance to the end of the structure
12. Given the following input data:

    ```
    10
    20
    30
    ```

    What is output by the following program?

    ```
    #include <iostream>
    using namespace std;

    void Rev();

    int main()
    {
      Rev();
      return 0;
    }

    //*******************

    void Rev()
    {
      int number;
      cin >> number;
      if (cin)
      {
        Rev();
        cout << number << endl;
      }
    }
    ```

13. Repeat Exercise 12, replacing the Rev function with the following version:

    ```
    void Rev()
    {
      int number;
      cin >> number;
      if (cin)
      {
        cout << number << endl;
        Rev();
        cout << number << endl;
      }
    }
    ```

14. What is output by the following program?

    ```cpp
    #include <iostream>

    using namespace std;

    void Rec(string word);

    int main()
    {
      Rec("abcde");
      return 0;
    }

    //*******************

    void Rec(string word)
    {
      if (word.length() > 0)
      {
        cout << word.substr(0, 1);
        Rec(word.substr(1, word.length()-2));
        cout << word.substr(word.length()-1, 1) << endl;
      }
    }
    ```

15. What does the program in Exercise 14 output if the initial call to `Rec` from `main` uses `"abcdef"` as the argument?

Programming Warm-Up Exercises

1. Write a value-returning recursive function called `DigitSum` that computes the sum of the digits in a given positive `int` argument. For example, if the argument is 12345, then the function returns 1 + 2 + 3 + 4 + 5 = 15.

2. Write a value-returning recursive function that uses the `DigitSum` function of Exercise 1 to compute the single digit to which the `int` argument's digits ultimately sum. For example, given the argument 999, the `DigitSum` result would be 9 + 9 + 9 = 27, but the recursive digit sum would then be 2 + 7 = 9.

3. Write a recursive version of a binary search of a sorted array of int values that are in ascending order. The function's arguments should be the array, the search value, and the maximum and minimum indexes for the array. The function should return the index where the match is found, or else −1.

4. Write a recursive function that asks the user to enter a positive integer number each time it is called, until zero or a negative number is input. The function then outputs the numbers entered in reverse order. For example, the I/O dialog might be the following:

    ```
    Enter positive number, 0 to end: 10
    Enter positive number, 0 to end: 20
    Enter positive number, 0 to end: 30
    Enter positive number, 0 to end: 0
    ```

The function then outputs

```
30
20
10
```

5. Extend the function of Exercise 4 so that it also outputs a running total of the numbers as they are entered. For example, the I/O dialog might be the following:

```
Enter positive number, 0 to end: 10
Total: 10
Enter positive number, 0 to end: 20
Total: 30
Enter positive number, 0 to end: 30
Total: 60
Enter positive number, 0 to end: 0
```

The function then outputs

```
30
20
10
```

6. Extend the function of Exercise 5 so that it also outputs a running total as the numbers are printed out in reverse order. For example, the I/O dialog might be the following:

```
Enter positive number, 0 to end: 10
Total: 10
Enter positive number, 0 to end: 20
Total: 30
Enter positive number, 0 to end: 30
Total: 60
Enter positive number, 0 to end: 0
```

The function then outputs

```
30 Total: 30
20 Total: 50
10 Total: 60
```

7. Extend the function of Exercise 4 so that it reports the greatest value entered, at the end of its output. For example, the I/O dialog might be the following:

```
Enter positive number, 0 to end: 10
Enter positive number, 0 to end: 20
Enter positive number, 0 to end: 30
Enter positive number, 0 to end: 0
```

The function then outputs

```
30
20
10
The greatest is 30
```

8. Change the function of Exercise 7 so that it outputs the greatest number entered thus far, as the user is entering the data. For example, the I/O dialog might be the following:

```
Enter positive number, 0 to end: 10
Greatest: 10
Enter positive number, 0 to end: 30
Greatest: 30
Enter positive number, 0 to end: 20
Greatest: 30
Enter positive number, 0 to end: 0
```

The function then outputs

```
20
30
10
The greatest is 30
```

9. Change the function of Exercise 8 so that it also outputs the greatest number thus far, as it outputs the numbers in reverse order. For example, the I/O dialog might be the following:

```
Enter positive number, 0 to end: 10
Greatest: 10
Enter positive number, 0 to end: 30
Greatest: 30
Enter positive number, 0 to end: 20
Greatest: 30
Enter positive number, 0 to end: 0
```

The function then outputs

```
20 Greatest: 20
30 Greatest: 30
10 Greatest: 30
The greatest is 30
```

10. Given the following declarations:

```
struct NodeType;
typedef NodeType* PtrType;
struct NodeType
{
    int info;
    PtrType link;
};

PtrType list1;
PtrType list2;
```

Assume that the list pointed to by `list1` contains an arbitrary number of nodes. Write a recursive function that makes a copy of this list in reverse order, which is pointed to by `list2`.

11. Given the declarations in Exercise 10, assume that the list pointed to by `list1` contains an arbitrary number of nodes. Write a recursive function that makes a copy of this list in the same order, which is pointed to by `list2`.

12. Given the declarations in Exercise 10, assume that the list pointed to by `list1` contains an arbitrary number of nodes. Write a recursive function that makes a single list containing two copies of the `list1` list. The first copy will be in the same order, and the second copy will be in reverse order. The new list is pointed to by `list2`.

Programming Problems

1. In mathematics, the Fibonacci numbers are the series of numbers that exhibit the following pattern:

    0, 1, 1, 2, 3, 5, 8, 13, 21, 34, 55, 89, 144, ...

    In mathematical notation the sequence F_n of Fibonacci numbers is defined by the following recursive definition:

    $F_n = F_{n-1} + F_{n-2}$

    With the initial values of $F_0 = 0$ and $F_1 = 1$. Thus, the next number in the series is the sum of the previous two numbers. Write a program that asks the user for a positive integer N and generates the Nth Fibonacci number. Your `main` function should handle user input and pass that data to a recursive function called `Fib` that takes an integer value N as input and returns the Nth Fibonacci number.

2. Write a recursive function that will display all permutations of characters in a user-provided string.

3. The greatest common divisor (GCD) of two positive integers is the largest integer that divides the numbers exactly. For example, the GCD of 14 and 21 is 7; for 13 and 22, it is 1; and for 45 and 27, it is 9. We can write a recursive formula for finding the GCD, given that the two numbers are called *a* and *b*, as:

    GCD(*a*, *b*) = *a*, if *b* = 0

    GCD(*a*, *b*) = GCD(*b*, *a*%*b*), if *b* > 0

    Implement this recursive formula as a recursive C++ function, and write a driver program that allows you to test it interactively.

4. Write a C++ program to output the binary (base-2) representation of a decimal integer. The algorithm for this conversion is to repeatedly divide the decimal number by 2, until it is 0. Each division produces a remainder of 0 or 1, which becomes a digit in the binary number. For example, if we want the binary representation of decimal 13, we would find it with the following series of divisions:

    ```
    13/2 = 6    remainder 1
    6/2  = 3    remainder 0
    3/2  = 1    remainder 1
    1/2  = 0    remainder 1
    ```

    Thus the binary representation of 13 (decimal) is 1101. The only problem with this algorithm is that the first division generates the low-order binary digit, the next division generates the second-order digit, and so on, until the last division produces the high-order digit. Thus, if we output the digits as they are generated, they will be in reverse order. You should use recursion to reverse the order of output.

5. Change the program for Problem 4 so that it works for any base up to 10. The user should enter the decimal number and the base, and the program should output the number in the given base.

6. Write a C++ program using recursion to convert a number in binary (from 1 to 10) to a decimal number. The algorithm states that each successive digit in the number is multiplied by the base (2) raised to the power corresponding to its position in the number. The low-order digit is in position 0. We sum together all of these products to get the decimal value. For example, if we have the binary number 111001, we convert it to decimal as follows:

$1 * 2^0 = 1$
$0 * 2^1 = 0$
$0 * 2^2 = 0$
$1 * 2^3 = 8$
$1 * 2^4 = 16$
$1 * 2^5 = 32$

Decimal value = 1 + 0 + 0 + 8 + 16 + 32 = 57

A recursive formulation of this algorithm can extract each digit and compute the corresponding power of the base by which to multiply. Once the base case (the last digit is extracted), the function can sum the products as it returns.

In C++ we can represent a binary number using integers. However, there is a danger—the user can enter an invalid number by typing a digit that's unrepresentable in the base. For example, the number 1011201 is an invalid binary number because 2 isn't allowed in the binary number system. Your program should check for invalid digits as they are extracted, handle the error in an appropriate way (that is, it shouldn't output a numerical result), and provide an informative error message to the user.

7. Modify the program from Problem 6 to work for any number base in the range of 1 through 10. The user should enter a number and a base, and the program should output the decimal equivalent. If the user enters a digit that is invalid for the base, the program should output an error message and not display a numerical result.

8. A maze is to be represented by a 12 × 12 array composed of three values: Open (O), Wall (W), or Exit (E). There is one exit from the maze. Write a program to determine whether it is possible to exit the maze from each possible starting point (any open square can be a starting point). You may move vertically or horizontally to any adjacent open square. You may not move to a square containing a wall. The input consists of a series of 12 lines of 12 characters each, representing the contents of each square in the maze; the characters are O, W, or E. Your program should check that the maze has only one exit. As the data are entered, the program should make a list of all of the starting-point coordinates. It can then run through this list, solving the maze for each starting point.

Case Study Follow-Up

1. In the Problem-Solving Case Study, both sorting versions have an implicit restriction on the data type of the elements in the array. What is the restriction?

2. If the array to be sorted and/or searched combined the array and the number of elements into a `struct`, could the number of parameters to `Sort`, `Search`, and `BinarySearch` be reduced? Explain.
3. In Chapter 16, we discussed operator functions. Rewrite the `Name` class, replacing `ComparedTo` with operator functions for the relational operators.
4. Rewrite `Quicksort` using the relational operators. Rerun the test driver with the new `Name` class and `Quicksort`.

Appendices

Appendix A Reserved Words

The following identifiers are *reserved words*—identifiers with predefined meanings in the C++ language. The programmer cannot declare them for other uses (for example, variable names) in a C++ program.

and	double	not	this
and_eq	dynamic_cast	not_eq	throw
asm	else	operator	true
auto	enum	or	try
bitand	explicit	or_eq	typedef
bitor	export	private	typeid
bool	extern	protected	typename
break	false	public	union
case	float	register	unsigned
catch	for	reinterpret_cast	using
char	friend	return	virtual
class	goto	short	void
compl	if	signed	volatile
const	inline	sizeof	wchar_t
const_cast	int	static	while
continue	long	static_cast	xor
default	mutable	struct	xor_eq
delete	namespace	switch	
do	new	template	

Appendix B Operator Precedence

The following table summarizes C++ operator precedence. Several operators are not discussed in this book (**typeid**, the comma operator, ->*, and .*, for instance). For information on these operators, see Stroustrup's *The C++ Programming Language,* Third Edition (Addison-Wesley, 1997).

In the table, the operators are grouped by precedence level (highest to lowest), and a horizontal line separates each precedence level from the next-lower level.

In general, the binary operators group from left to right; the unary operators, from right to left; and the **?:** operator, from right to left. Exception: The assignment operators group from right to left.

\multicolumn{3}{c}{Precedence (highest to lowest)}		
Operator	Associativity	Remarks
::	Left to right	Scope resolution (binary)
::	Right to left	Global access (unary)
()	Left to right	Function call and function-style cast
[] -> .	Left to right	
++ --	Right to left	++ and -- as postfix operators
typeid dynamic_cast	Right to left	
static_cast const_cast	Right to left	
reinterpret_cast	Right to left	
++ -- ! Unary + Unary -	Right to left	++ and -- as prefix operators
~ Unary * Unary &	Right to left	
(cast) sizeof new delete	Right to left	
->* .*	Left to right	
* / %	Left to right	
+ -	Left to right	
<< >>	Left to right	
< <= > >=	Left to right	
== !=	Left to right	
&	Left to right	
^	Left to right	
|	Left to right	
&&	Left to right	
||	Left to right	
?:	Right to left	
= += -= *= /= %=	Right to left	
<<= >>= &= |= ^=	Right to left	
throw	Right to left	
,	Left to right	The sequencing operator, not the separator

Appendix C   A Selection of Standard Library Routines

The C++ standard library provides a wealth of data types, functions, and named constants. This appendix details only some of the more widely used library facilities. It is a good idea to consult the manual for your particular system to see what other types, functions, and constants the standard library provides.

This appendix is organized alphabetically according to the header file your program must #include before accessing the listed items. For example, to use a mathematics routine such as sqrt, you would #include the header file cmath as follows:

```
#include <cmath>
using namespace std;
    ⋮
y = sqrt(x);
```

Note that every identifier in the standard library is defined to be in the namespace std. Without the using directive above, you would write

```
y = std::sqrt(x);
```

C.1   The Header File cassert

assert(booleanExpr)
Argument: A logical (Boolean) expression
Effect: If the value of booleanExpr is true, execution of the program simply continues. If the value of booleanExpr is false, execution terminates immediately with a message stating the Boolean expression, the name of the file containing the source code, and the line number in the source code.
Function return value: None (a void function)
Note: If the preprocessor directive #define NDEBUG is placed before the directive #include <cassert>, all assert statements are ignored.

C.2   The Header File cctype

isalnum(ch)
Argument: A char value ch
Function return value: An int value that is
- nonzero (true), if ch is a letter or a digit character ('A'–'Z', 'a'–'z', '0'–'9')
- 0 (false), otherwise

isalpha(ch)
Argument: A char value ch
Function return value: An int value that is
- nonzero (true), if ch is a letter ('A'–'Z', 'a'–'z')
- 0 (false), otherwise

`iscntrl(ch)`
Argument: A **char** value **ch**
Function return value: An **int** value that is
- nonzero (**true**), if **ch** is a control character (in ASCII, a character with the value 0–31 or 127)
- 0 (**false**), otherwise

`isdigit(ch)`
Argument: A **char** value **ch**
Function return value: An **int** value that is
- nonzero (**true**), if **ch** is a digit character ('0'–'9')
- 0 (**false**), otherwise

`isgraph(ch)`
Argument: A **char** value **ch**
Function return value: An **int** value that is
- nonzero (**true**), if **ch** is a nonblank printable character (in ASCII, '!' through '~')
- 0 (**false**), otherwise

`islower(ch)`
Argument: A **char** value **ch**
Function return value: An **int** value that is
- nonzero (**true**), if **ch** is a lowercase letter ('a'–'z')
- 0 (**false**), otherwise

`isprint(ch)`
Argument: A **char** value **ch**
Function return value: An **int** value that is
- nonzero (**true**), if **ch** is a printable character, including the blank (in ASCII, ' ' through '~')
- 0 (**false**), otherwise

`ispunct(ch)`
Argument: A **char** value **ch**
Function return value: An **int** value that is
- nonzero (**true**), if **ch** is a punctuation character (equivalent to `isgraph(ch) && !isalnum(ch)`)
- 0 (**false**), otherwise

`isspace(ch)`
Argument: A **char** value **ch**
Function return value: An **int** value that is
- nonzero (**true**), if **ch** is a whitespace character (blank, newline, tab, carriage return, form feed)
- 0 (**false**), otherwise

`isupper(ch)`
Argument: A **char** value **ch**
Function return value: An **int** value that is
- nonzero (**true**), if **ch** is an uppercase letter ('A'–'Z')
- 0 (**false**), otherwise

`isxdigit(ch)`
Argument: A `char` value `ch`
Function return value: An `int` value that is
- nonzero (`true`), if `ch` is a hexadecimal digit ('0'–'9', 'A'–'F', 'a'–'f')
- 0 (`false`), otherwise

`tolower(ch)`
Argument: A `char` value `ch`
Function return value: A character that is
- the lowercase equivalent of `ch`, if `ch` is an uppercase letter
- `ch`, otherwise

`toupper(ch)`
Argument: A `char` value `ch`
Function return value: A character that is
- the uppercase equivalent of `ch`, if `ch` is a lowercase letter
- `ch`, otherwise

C.3 The Header File `cfloat`

This header file supplies named constants that define the characteristics of floating-point numbers on your particular machine. Among these constants are the following:

`FLT_DIG`	Approximate number of significant digits in a `float` value on your machine
`FLT_MAX`	Maximum positive `float` value on your machine
`FLT_MIN`	Minimum positive `float` value on your machine
`DBL_DIG`	Approximate number of significant digits in a `double` value on your machine
`DBL_MAX`	Maximum positive `double` value on your machine
`DBL_MIN`	Minimum positive `double` value on your machine
`LDBL_DIG`	Approximate number of significant digits in a `long double` value on your machine
`LDBL_MAX`	Maximum positive `long double` value on your machine
`LDBL_MIN`	Minimum positive `long double` value on your machine

C.4 The Header File `climits`

This header file supplies named constants that define the limits of integer values on your particular machine. Among these constants are the following:

`CHAR_BITS`	Number of bits in a byte on your machine (8, for example)
`CHAR_MAX`	Maximum `char` value on your machine
`CHAR_MIN`	Minimum `char` value on your machine
`SHRT_MAX`	Maximum `short` value on your machine
`SHRT_MIN`	Minimum `short` value on your machine
`INT_MAX`	Maximum `int` value on your machine
`INT_MIN`	Minimum `int` value on your machine
`LONG_MAX`	Maximum `long` value on your machine
`LONG_MIN`	Minimum `long` value on your machine
`UCHAR_MAX`	Maximum `unsigned char` value on your machine
`USHRT_MAX`	Maximum `unsigned short` value on your machine
`UINT_MAX`	Maximum `unsigned int` value on your machine
`ULONG_MAX`	Maximum `unsigned long` value on your machine

C.5 The Header File `cmath`

In the `math` routines listed below, the following notes apply.
1. Error handling for incalculable or out-of-range results is system dependent.
2. All arguments and function return values are technically of type `double` (double-precision floating-point). However, single-precision (`float`) values may be passed to the functions.

`acos(x)`
Argument: A floating-point expression x, where $-1.0 \leq x \leq 1.0$
Function return value: Arc cosine of x, in the range 0.0 through π

`asin(x)`
Argument: A floating-point expression x, where $-1.0 \leq x \leq 1.0$
Function return value: Arc sine of x, in the range $-\pi/2$ through $\pi/2$

`atan(x)`
Argument: A floating-point expression x
Function return value: Arc tangent of x, in the range $-\pi/2$ through $\pi/2$

`ceil(x)`
Argument: A floating-point expression x
Function return value: "Ceiling" of x (the smallest whole number $\geq$ x)

`cos(angle)`
Argument: A floating-point expression angle, measured in radians
Function return value: Trigonometric cosine of `angle`

`cosh(x)`
Argument: A floating-point expression x
Function return value: Hyperbolic cosine of x

`exp(x)`
Argument: A floating-point expression x
Function return value: The value e (2.718...) raised to the power x

`fabs(x)`
Argument: A floating-point expression x
Function return value: Absolute value of x

`floor(x)`
Argument: A floating-point expression x
Function return value: "Floor" of x (the largest whole number $\leq$ x)

`log(x)`
Argument: A floating-point expression x, where x > 0.0
Function return value: Natural logarithm (base *e*) of x

`log10(x)`
Argument: A floating-point expression x, where x > 0.0
Function return value: Common logarithm (base 10) of x

pow(x, y)
Arguments: Floating-point expressions **x** and **y**. If **x** = 0.0, **y** must be positive; if **x** ≤ 0.0, **y** must be a whole number
Function return value: **x** raised to the power **y**

sin(angle)
Argument: A floating-point expression angle, measured in radians
Function return value: Trigonometric sine of **angle**

sinh(x)
Argument: A floating-point expression **x**
Function return value: Hyperbolic sine of **x**

sqrt(x)
Argument: A floating-point expression **x**, where **x** ≥ 0.0
Function return value: Square root of **x**

tan(angle)
Argument: A floating-point expression angle, measured in radians
Function return value: Trigonometric tangent of **angle**

tanh(x)
Argument: A floating-point expression **x**
Function return value: Hyperbolic tangent of **x**

C.6 The Header File `cstddef`

This header file defines a few system-dependent constants and data types. From this header file, the only item we use in this book is the following symbolic constant:

NULL   The null pointer constant 0

C.7 The Header File `cstdlib`

abs(i)
Argument: An **int** expression i
Function return value: An **int** value that is the absolute value of i

atof(str)
Argument: A C string (null-terminated **char** array) **str** representing a floating point number, possibly preceded by whitespace characters and a '+' or '−'
Function return value: A **double** value that is the floating-point equivalent of the characters in **str**
Note: Conversion stops at the first character in **str** that is inappropriate for a floating-point number. If no appropriate characters were found, the return value is system dependent.

atoi(str)
Argument: A C string (null-terminated **char** array) **str** representing an integer number, possibly preceded by whitespace characters and a '+' or '−'
Function return value: An **int** value that is the integer equivalent of the characters in **str**
Note: Conversion stops at the first character in **str** that is inappropriate for an integer number. If no appropriate characters were found, the return value is system dependent.

atol(str)
Argument: A C string (null-terminated **char** array) **str** representing a long integer, possibly preceded by whitespace characters and a '+' or '−'
Function return value: A **long** value that is the long integer equivalent of the characters in **str**
Note: Conversion stops at the first character in **str** that is inappropriate for a **long** integer number. If no appropriate characters were found, the return value is system dependent.

exit(exitStatus)
Argument: An **int** expression **exitStatus**
Effect: Program execution terminates immediately with all files properly closed
Function return value: None (a void function)
Note: By convention, **exitStatus** is 0 to indicate normal program completion and is nonzero to indicate an abnormal termination.

labs(i)
Argument: A **long** expression **i**
Function return value: A **long** value that is the absolute value of **i**

rand()
Argument: None
Function return value: A random **int** value in the range 0 through **RAND_MAX**, a constant defined in **cstdlib** (**RAND_MAX** is usually the same as **INT_MAX**)
Note: See **srand** below.

srand(seed)
Argument: An **int** expression **seed**, where **seed** ≥ 0
Effect: Using **seed**, the random number generator is initialized in preparation for subsequent calls to the **rand** function.
Function return value: None (a void function)
Note: If **srand** is not called before the first call to **rand**, a **seed** value of 1 is assumed.

`system(str)`

Argument: A C string (null-terminated `char` array) `str` representing an operating system command, exactly as it would be typed by a user on the operating system command line

Effect: The operating system command represented by `str` is executed.

Function return value: An `int` value that is system dependent

Note: Programmers often ignore the function return value, using the syntax of a void function call rather than a value-returning function call.

C.8 The Header File `cstring`

The header file `cstring` (not to be confused with the header file named `string`) supports manipulation of C strings (null-terminated `char` arrays).

`strcat(toStr, fromStr)`

Arguments: C strings (null-terminated `char` arrays) `toStr` and `fromStr`, where `toStr` must be large enough to hold the result

Effect: `fromStr`, including the null character `'\0'`, is concatenated (joined) to the end of `toStr`.

Function return value: The base address of `toStr`

Note: Programmers usually ignore the function return value, using the syntax of a void function call rather than a value-returning function call.

`strcmp(str1, str2)`

Arguments: C strings (null-terminated `char` arrays) `str1` and `str2`

Function return value: An `int` value < 0, if `str1` < `str2` lexicographically
The `int` value 0, if `str1` = `str2` lexicographically
An `int` value > 0, if `str1` > `str2` lexicographically

`strcpy(toStr, fromStr)`

Arguments: `toStr` is a `char` array and `fromStr` is a C string (null-terminated `char` array), and `toStr` must be large enough to hold the result

Effect: `fromStr`, including the null character `'\0'`, is copied to `toStr`, overwriting what was there.

Function return value: The base address of `toStr`

Note: Programmers usually ignore the function return value, using the syntax of a void function call rather than a value-returning function call.

`strlen(str)`

Argument: A C string (null-terminated `char` array) `str`

Function return value: An `int` value ≥ 0 that is the length of `str` (excluding the `'\0'`)

C.9 The Header File string

This header file supplies a programmer-defined data type (specifically, a *class*) named **string**. Associated with the **string** type are a data type **string::size_type** and a named constant **string::npos**, defined as follows:

string::size_type	An unsigned integer type related to the number of characters in a string
string::npos	The maximum value of type string::size_type

There are dozens of functions associated with the **string** type. Below are several of the most important ones. In the descriptions, **s** is assumed to be a variable (an *object*) of type **string**.

s.c_str()
Arguments: None
Function return value: The base address of a C string (null-terminated **char** array) corresponding to the characters stored in **s**

s.find(arg)
Argument: An expression of type **string** or **char**, or a C string (such as a literal string)
Function return value: A value of type **string::size_type** that gives the starting position in **s** where **arg** was found. If **arg** was not found, the return value is **string::npos**.
Note: Positions of characters within a string are numbered starting at 0.

getline(inStream, s)
Arguments: An input stream **inStream** (of type **istream** or **ifstream**) and a **string** object **s**
Effect: Characters are input from **inStream** and stored into **s** until the newline character is encountered. (The newline character is consumed but not stored into **s**.)
Function return value: Although the function technically returns a value (which we do not discuss here), programmers usually invoke the function as though it were a void function.

s.length()
Arguments: None
Function return value: A value of type **string::size_type** that gives the number of characters in the string

s.size()
Arguments: None
Function return value: The same as **s.length()**

`s.substr(pos, len)`
Arguments: Two unsigned integers, `pos` and `len`, representing a position and a length. The value of `pos` must be less than `s.length()`.
Function return value: A temporary `string` object that holds a substring of at most `len` characters, starting at position `pos` of `s`. If `len` is too large, it means "to the end" of the string in `s`.
Note: Positions of characters within a string are numbered starting at 0.

C.10 The Header File `sstream`

This header file supplies various classes derived from `iostream` that enable the user to apply stream-like operations to strings instead of files. In this text, we use only the `ostringstream` class, which enables us to convert numeric types to formatted string values. We can apply the insertion operator (`<<`) to an `ostringstream` object to append values to it, and then read back its contents in string form, using the `str` member function. In the following, `oss` is an `ostringstream` object.

`ostringstream()`
Argument: None
Return value: An empty `osstringstream` object

`ostringstream(arg)`
Argument: A string
Return value: An `ostringstream` object initialized to the argument string

Left argument: An `ostringstream` object
Right argument: An expression that can be converted to a string, including output manipulators.
Return value: An `ostringstream` object
Evaluated: Left to right

`oss.str()`
Argument: None
Return value: A string containing whatever has been appended to `oss`

`oss.str(arg)`
Argument: A string
Effect: Assigns the value of the argument to `oss`. Using the empty string as the argument effectively sets the content of the `ostringstream` object to be empty.

Appendix D Using This Book with a Prestandard Version of C++

D.1 Standard Header Files and Namespaces

Historically, the standard header files in both C and C++ had file names ending in `.h` (meaning "header file"). Certain header files—for example, `iostream.h`, `iomanip.h`, and `fstream.h`—related specifically to C++. Others, such as `math.h`, `stddef.h`, `stdlib.h`, and `string.h`, were carried over from the C standard library and were available to both C and C++ programs. When you used an `#include` directive such as

```
#include <math.h>
```

near the beginning of your program, all identifiers declared in `math.h` were introduced into your program in global scope (as discussed in Chapter 8). With the advent of the *namespace* mechanism in ISO/ANSI standard C++ (see Chapter 2 and, in more detail, Chapter 8), all of the standard header files were modified so that identifiers are declared within a namespace called `std`. In standard C++, when you `#include` a standard header file, the identifiers therein are not automatically placed into global scope.

To preserve compatibility with older versions of C++ that still need the original files `iostream.h`, `math.h`, and so forth, the new standard header files are renamed as follows: The C++-related header files have the `.h` removed, and the header files from the C library have the `.h` removed *and* the letter *c* inserted at the beginning. Here is a list of the old and new names for some of the most commonly used header files.

Old Name	New Name
iostream.h	iostream
iomanip.h	iomanip
fstream.h	fstream
assert.h	cassert
ctype.h	cctype
float.h	cfloat
limits.h	climits
math.h	cmath
stddef.h	cstddef
stdlib.h	cstdlib
string.h	cstring

Be careful: The last entry in the list above refers to the C language concept of a string and is unrelated to the `string` type defined in the C++ standard library.

If you are working with a prestandard compiler that does not recognize the new header file names or namespaces, simply substitute the old header file names for the new ones as you encounter them in the book. For example, where we have written

```
#include <iostream>
using namespace std;
```

you would write

```
#include <iostream.h>
```

For compatibility, C++ systems are likely to retain both versions of the header files for some time to come.

D.2 The `fixed` and `showpoint` Manipulators

Chapter 3 introduces five manipulators for formatting the output: `endl`, `setw`, `fixed`, `showpoint`, and `setprecision`. If you are using a prestandard compiler with the header file `iostream.h`, the `fixed` and `showpoint` manipulators may not be available.

Appendix D Using This Book with a Prestandard Version of C++

In place of the following code shown in Chapter 3,

```
#include <iostream>
using namespace std;
   ⋮
cout << fixed << showpoint;        // Set up floating-pt.
                                   //   output format
```

you can substitute the following code:

```
#include <iostream.h>
   ⋮
cout.setf(ios::fixed, ios::floatfield);
cout.setf(ios::showpoint);
```

These two statements employ some advanced C++ notation. Our advice is simply to use the statements just as you see them and not worry about the details. Here's the general idea. `setf` is a void function associated with the `cout` stream. (Note that the dot, or period, between `cout` and `setf` is required.) The first function call ensures that floating-point numbers are always printed in decimal form rather than scientific notation. The second function call specifies that the decimal point should always be printed, even for whole numbers. In other words, these two function calls accomplish the same effect as the `fixed` and `showpoint` manipulators.

Note: If your compiler complains about the syntax `ios::fixed`, `ios::floatfield`, or `ios::showpoint`, you may have to replace `ios` with `ios_base` as follows:

```
cout.setf(ios_base::fixed, ios_base::floatfield);
cout.setf(ios_base::showpoint);
```

D.3 The bool Type

Before the ISO/ANSI C++ language standard, C++ did not have a `bool` data type. Some prestandard compilers implemented the `bool` type before the standard was approved, but others did not. If your compiler does not recognize the `bool` type, the following discussion will assist you in writing programs that are compatible with those in this book.

In versions of C++ without the `bool` type, the value 0 represents *false*, and any nonzero value represents *true*. It is customary in pre–standard C++ to use the `int` type to represent Boolean data:

```
int dataOK;
   ⋮
dataOK = 1;    // Store "true" into dataOK
   ⋮
dataOK = 0;    // Store "false" into dataOK
```

To make the code more self-documenting, many pre-standard C++ programmers define their own Boolean data type by using a *Typedef statement*. This statement allows you to introduce a new name for an existing data type:

```
typedef int bool;
```

All this statement does is tell the compiler to substitute the word `int` for every occurrence of the word `bool` in the rest of the program. Thus, when the compiler encounters a statement such as

```
bool dataOK;
```

it translates the statement into

```
int dataOK;
```

With the Typedef statement and declarations of two named constants, `true` and `false`, the code at the beginning of this discussion becomes the following:

```
typedef int bool;
const int true = 1;
const int false = 0;
    ⋮
bool dataOK;
    ⋮
dataOK = true;
    ⋮
dataOK = false;
```

Throughout the book, our programs use the words `bool`, `true`, and `false` when manipulating Boolean data. If your compiler recognizes `bool` as a built-in type, there is nothing you need to do. Otherwise, here are three steps you can take.

1. Use your system's editor to create a file containing the following lines:

    ```
    #ifndef BOOL_H
    #define BOOL_H
    typedef int bool;
    const int true = 1;
    const int false = 0;
    #enif
    ```

    Don't worry about the meaning of the first, second, and last lines. They are explained in Chapter 14. Simply type the lines as you see them above.

2. Save the file you created in step 1, giving it the name `bool.h`. Save this file into the same directory in which you work on your C++ programs.

3. Near the top of every program in which you need `bool` variables, type the line

    ```
    #include "bool.h"
    ```

    Be sure to surround the file name with double quotes, not angle brackets (< >). The quotes tell the preprocessor to look for `bool.h` in your current directory rather than the C++ system directory.

With `bool`, `true`, and `false` defined in this fashion, the programs in this book run correctly, and you can use `bool` in your own programs, even if it is not a built-in type.

Appendix E   Character Sets

The following charts show the ordering of characters in two widely used character sets: ASCII (American Standard Code for Information Interchange) and EBCDIC (Extended Binary Coded Decimal Interchange Code). The internal representation for each character is shown in decimal. For example, the letter *A* is represented internally as the integer 65 in ASCII and as 193 in EBCDIC. The space (blank) character is denoted by a "□".

Left Digit(s)	Right Digit				ASCII					
	0	1	2	3	4	5	6	7	8	9
0	NUL	SOH	STX	ETX	EOT	ENQ	ACK	BEL	BS	HT
1	LF	VT	FF	CR	SO	SI	DLE	DC1	DC2	DC3
2	DC4	NAK	SYN	ETB	CAN	EM	SUB	ESC	FS	GS
3	RS	US	□	!	"	#	$	%	&	'
4	(	)	*	+	,	-	.	/	0	1
5	2	3	4	5	6	7	8	9	:	;
6	<	=	>	?	@	A	B	C	D	E
7	F	G	H	I	J	K	L	M	N	O
8	P	Q	R	S	T	U	V	W	X	Y
9	Z	[	\	]	^	_	`	a	b	c
10	d	e	f	g	h	i	j	k	l	m
11	n	o	p	q	r	s	t	u	v	w
12	x	y	z	{	|	}	~	DEL		

Codes 00–31 and 127 are the following nonprintable control characters:

NUL	Null character	VT	Vertical tab	SYN	Synchronous idle
SOH	Start of header	FF	Form feed	ETB	End of transmitted block
STX	Start of text	CR	Carriage return	CAN	Cancel
ETX	End of text	SO	Shift out	EM	End of medium
EOT	End of transmission	SI	Shift in	SUB	Substitute
ENQ	Enquiry	DLE	Data link escape	ESC	Escape
ACK	Acknowledge	DC1	Device control one	FS	File separator
BEL	Bell character (beep)	DC2	Device control two	GS	Group separator
BS	Back space	DC3	Device control three	RS	Record separator
HT	Horizontal tab	DC4	Device control four	US	Unit separator
LF	Line feed	NAK	Negative acknowledge	DEL	Delete

Left Digit(s)	Right Digit				EBCDIC					
	0	1	2	3	4	5	6	7	8	9
6					□					
7					¢	.	<	(	+	|
8	&									
9	!	$	*	)	;	¬	-	/		
10							^	,	%	_
11	>	?								
12		`	:	#	@	'	=	"		a
13	b	c	d	e	f	g	h	i		
14						j	k	l	m	n
15	o	p	q	r						
16		~	s	t	u	v	w	x	y	z
17								\	{	}
18	[	]								
19				A	B	C	D	E	F	G
20	H	I								J
21	K	L	M	N	O	P	Q	R		
22							S	T	U	V
23	W	X	Y	Z						
24	0	1	2	3	4	5	6	7	8	9

In the EBCDIC table, nonprintable control characters—codes 00–63, 250–255, and those for which empty spaces appear in the chart—are not shown.

Appendix F   Program Style, Formatting, and Documentation

Throughout this text, we encourage the use of good programming style and documentation. Although the programs you write for class assignments may not be looked at by anyone except the person grading your work, outside of class you will write programs that will be used by others.

Useful programs have very long lifetimes, during which they must be modified and updated. When maintenance work must be done, either you or another programmer will have to do it. Good style and documentation are essential if another programmer is to understand and work with your program. You will also discover that after not working with your own program for a few months, you'll be amazed at how many of the details you've forgotten.

F.1   General Guidelines

The style used in the programs and fragments throughout this text provides a good starting point for developing your own style. Our goals in creating this style were to make it simple, consistent, and easy to read.

Style is of benefit only for a human reader of your program—differences in style make no difference to the computer. Good style includes the use of meaningful variable names, comments, and indentation of control structures, all of which help others to understand and work with your program. Perhaps the most important aspect of program style is consistency. If the style within a program is not consistent, then it becomes misleading and confusing.

Sometimes, a particular style is specified for you by your instructor or by the company you work for. When you are modifying someone else's code, you should use his or her style in order to maintain consistency within the program. However, you will also develop your own, personal programming style based on what you've been taught, your own experience, and your personal taste.

F.2 Comments

Comments are extra information included to make a program easier to understand. You should include a comment anywhere the code is difficult to understand. However, don't overcomment. Too many comments in a program can obscure the code and be a source of distraction.

In our style, there are four basic types of comments: headers, declarations, in-line, and sidebar.

Header comments appear at the top of the program and should include your name, the date that the program was written, and its purpose. It is also useful to include sections describing input, output, and assumptions. Think of the header comments as the reader's introduction to your program. Here is an example:

```
// This program computes the sidereal time for a given date and
// solar time.
//
// Written By: Your Name
//
// Date Completed: 4/8/05
//
// Input: A date and time in the form MM DD YYYY HH MM SS
//
// Output: Sidereal time in the form HH MM SS
//
// Assumptions: Solar time is specified for a longitude of 0
//      degrees (GMT, UT, or Z time zone)
```

Header comments should also be included for all user-defined functions (see Chapters 8 and 9).

Declaration comments accompany the constant and variable declarations in the program. Anywhere that an identifier is declared, it is helpful to include a comment that explains its purpose. In programs in the text, declaration comments appear to the right of the identifier being declared. For example:

```
const float E = 2.71828;      // The base of the natural logarithms

float deltaX;                 // The difference in the x direction
float deltaY;                 // The difference in the y direction
```

Notice that aligning the comments gives the code a neater appearance and is less distracting.

In-line comments are used to break long sections of code into shorter, more comprehensible fragments. These are often the names of modules in your algorithm design, although you may occasionally choose to include other information. It is generally a good idea to surround in-line comments with blank lines to make them stand out. For example:

```
// Prepare file for reading

scoreFile.open("scores.dat");

// Get data

scoreFile >> test1 >> weight1;
scoreFile >> test2 >> weight2;
scoreFile >> test3 >> weight3;

// Print heading

cout << "Test Score   Weight" << endl;
```

Even if comments are not used, blank lines can be inserted wherever there is a logical break in the code that you would like to emphasize.

Sidebar comments appear to the right of executable statements and are used to shed light on the purpose of the statement. Sidebar comments are often just pseudocode statements from the lowest levels of your design. If a complicated C++ statement requires some explanation, the pseudocode statement should be written to the right of the C++ statement. For example:

```
while (file1 && file2)     // While neither file is empty...
{
    ⋮
```

In addition to the four main types of comments that we have discussed, there are some miscellaneous comments that we should mention. After the `main` function, we recommend using a row of asterisks (or dashes or equal signs or ...) in a comment before and after each function to help it to stand out. For example:

```
//****************************************************************

void PrintSecondHeading()
{
    ⋮
}

//****************************************************************
```

In this text, we use C++'s alternative comment form

```
/* Some comment */
```

to document the flow of information for each parameter of a function:

```
void GetData( /* out */ int age,        // Patient's age
              /* out */ int weight )    // Patient's weight
{
    ⋮
}
```

```
void Print( /* in    */    float val,      // Value to be printed
            /* inout */    int&  count )   // Number of lines printed
                                           //   so far
{
     ⋮
}
```

(Chapter 8 describes the purpose of labeling each parameter as /* in */, /* out */, or /* inout */.)

Programmers sometimes place a comment after the right brace of a block (compound statement) to indicate which control structure the block belongs to:

```
while (num >= 0)
{
     ⋮
    if (num == 25)
    {
         ⋮
    } // if
} // while
```

Attaching comments in this fashion can help to clarify the code and aid in debugging mismatched braces.

F.3 Identifiers

The most important consideration in choosing a name for a data item or function in a program is that the name convey as much information as possible about what the data item is or what the function does. The name should also be readable in the context in which it is used. For example, the following names convey the same information but one is more readable than the other:

`datOfInvc`   `invoiceDate`

Identifiers for types, constants, and variables should be nouns, whereas names of void functions (non-value-returning functions) should be imperative verbs or phrases containing imperative verbs. Because of the way that value-returning functions are invoked, their names should be nouns or occasionally adjectives. Here are some examples:

Variables	`address, price, radius, monthNumber`
Constants	`PI, TAX_RATE, STRING_LENGTH, ARRAY_SIZE`
Data types	`NameType, CarMakes, RoomLists, Hours`
Void functions	`GetData, ClearTable, PrintBarChart`
Value-returning functions	`CubeRoot, Greatest, Color, AreaOf, IsEmpty`

Although an identifier may be a series of words, very long identifiers can become quite tedious and can make the program difficult to read.

The best approach to designing an identifier is to try writing out different names until you reach an acceptable compromise—and then write an especially informative declaration comment next to the declaration.

Capitalization is another consideration when choosing an identifier. C++ is a case-sensitive language; that is, uppercase and lowercase letters are distinct. Different programmers use different conventions for capitalizing identifiers. In this text, we begin each variable name with a lowercase letter and capitalize the beginning of each successive English word. We begin each function name and data type name with a capital letter and, again, capitalize the beginning of each successive English word. For named constants, we capitalize the entire identifier, separating successive English words with underscore (_) characters. Keep in mind, however, that C++ reserved words such as `main`, `if`, and `while` are always lowercase letters, and the compiler will not recognize them if you capitalize them differently.

F.4 Formatting Lines and Expressions

C++ allows you to break a long statement in the middle and continue onto the next line. (However, you cannot split a line in the middle of an identifier, a literal constant, or a string.) When you must split a line, it's important to choose a breaking point that is logical and readable. Compare the readability of the following code fragments.

```
cout << "For a radius of " << radius << " the diameter of the cir"
    << "cle is " << diameter << endl;
cout << "For a radius of " << radius
    << " the diameter of the circle is " << diameter << endl;
```

When you must split an expression across multiple lines, try to end each line with an operator. Also, try to take advantage of any repeating patterns in the expression. For example,

```
meanOfMaxima = (Maximum(set1Value1, set1Value2, set1Value3) +
                Maximum(set2Value1, set2Value2, set2Value3) +
                Maximum(set3Value1, set3Value2, set3Value3)) / 3.0;
```

When writing expressions, also keep in mind that spaces improve readability. Usually you should include one space on either side of the = operator and most other operators. Occasionally, spaces are left out to emphasize the order in which operations are performed. Here are some examples:

```
if (x+y > y+z)
    maximum = x + y;
else
    maximum = y + z;
hypotenuse = sqrt(a*a + b*b);
```

F.5 Indentation

The purpose of indenting statements in a program is to provide visual cues to the reader and to make the program easier to debug. When a program is properly indented, the way the statements are grouped is immediately obvious. Compare the following two program fragments:

```
while (count <= 10)            while (count <= 10)
{                              {
cin >> num;                        cin >> num;
if (num == 0)                      if (num == 0)
{                                  {
count++;                               count++;
num = 1;                               num = 1;
}                                  }
cout << num << endl;               cout << num << endl;
cout << count << endl;             cout << count << endl;
}                              }
```

As a basic rule in this text, each nested or lower-level item is indented by four spaces. Exceptions to this rule are parameter declarations and statements that are split across two or more lines. Indenting by four spaces is a matter of personal preference. Some people prefer to indent by three, five, or even more than five spaces.

In this book, we indent the entire body of a function. Also, in general, any statement that is part of another statement is indented. For example, the If-Then-Else contains two parts, the then-clause and the else-clause. The statements within both clauses are indented four spaces beyond the beginning of the If-Then-Else statement. The If-Then statement is indented like the If-Then-Else, except that there is no else-clause. Here are examples of the If-Then-Else and the If-Then:

```
if (sex == MALE)
{
    maleSalary = maleSalary + salary;
    maleCount++;
}
else
    femaleSalary = femaleSalary + salary;

if (count > 0)
    average = total / count;
```

For nested If-Then-Else statements that form a generalized multiway branch (the If-Then-Else-If, described in Chapter 5), a special style of indentation is used in the text. Here is an example:

```
if (month == JANUARY)
    monthNumber = 1;
else if (month == FEBRUARY)
    monthNumber = 2;
else if (month == MARCH)
    monthNumber = 3;
else if (month == APRIL)
    ⋮
else
    monthNumber = 12;
```

The remaining C++ statements all follow the basic indentation guideline mentioned previously. For reference purposes, here are examples of each.

```
while (count <= 10)
{
    cin >> value;
    sum = sum + value;
    count++;
}

do
{
    GetAnswer(letter);
    PutAnswer(letter);
} while (letter != 'N');

for (count = 1; count <= numSales; count++)
    cout << '*';
```

```
for (count = 10; count >= 1; count--)
{
    inFile >> dataItem;
    outFile << dataItem << ' ' << count << endl;
}

switch (color)
{
    RED     : cout << "Red";
              break;
    ORANGE  : cout << "Orange";
              break;
    YELLOW  : cout << "Yellow";
              break;
    GREEN   :
    BLUE    :
    INDIGO  :
    VIOLET  : cout << "Short visible wavelengths";
              break;
    WHITE   :
    BLACK   : cout << "Not valid colors";
              color = NONE;
}
```

Appendix G More on Floating-Point Numbers

We have used floating-point numbers off and on since we introduced them in Chapter 2, but we have not examined them in depth. Floating-point numbers have special properties when used on the computer. In this appendix we consider them in detail.

G.1 Representation of Floating-Point Numbers

Let's assume we have a computer in which each memory location is the same size and is divided into a sign plus five decimal digits. When a variable or constant is defined, the location assigned to it consists of five digits and a sign. When an `int` variable or constant is defined, the interpretation of the number stored in that place is straightforward. When a `float` variable or constant is defined, the number stored there has both a whole number part and a fractional part, so it must be coded to represent both parts.

Let's see what such coded numbers might look like. The range of whole numbers we can represent with five digits is −99,999 through +99,999:

Appendix G More on Floating-Point Numbers

Our **precision** (the number of digits we can represent) is five digits, and each number within that range can be represented exactly.

What happens if we allow one of those digits (the leftmost one, for example) to represent an exponent?

> **Precision** The maximum number of significant digits.

Exponent

Then +82345 represents the number $+2345 \times 10^8$. The range of numbers we now can represent is much larger:

-9999×10^9 through 9999×10^9

or

$-9,999,000,000,000$ through $+9,999,000,000,000$

However, our precision is now only four digits; that is, only four-digit numbers can be represented exactly in our system. What happens to numbers with more digits? The four leftmost digits are represented correctly, and the rightmost digits, or least significant digits, are lost (assumed to be 0). **FIGURE G.1** shows what happens. Note that 1,000,000 can be represented exactly but $-4,932,416$ cannot, because our coding scheme limits us to four **significant digits**.

> **Significant digits** The digits from the first nonzero digit on the left to the last nonzero digit on the right (plus any 0 digits that are exact).

To extend our coding scheme to represent floating-point numbers, we must be able to represent negative exponents. Examples are

$7394 \times 10^{-2} = 73.94$

and

$22 \times 10^{-4} = .0022$

NUMBER	POWER OF TEN NOTATION	Sign	Exp				VALUE
+99,999	$+9999 \times 10^1$	+	1	9	9	9	+99,990
-999,999	-9999×10^2	−	2	9	9	9	-999,900
+1,000,000	-1000×10^3	+	3	1	0	0	+1,000,000
-4,932,416	-4932×10^3	−	3	4	9	3	-4,932,000

FIGURE G.1 Coding Using Positive Exponents

FIGURE G.2 Coding Using Positive and Negative Exponents

Because our scheme does not include a sign for the exponent, let's change it slightly. The existing sign becomes the sign of the exponent, and we add a sign to the far left to represent the sign of the number itself (see **FIGURE G.2**).

All the numbers between -9999×10^9 and 9999×10^9 can now be represented accurately to four digits. Adding negative exponents to our scheme allows us to represent fractional numbers as small as 1×10^{-9}.

FIGURE G.3 shows how we would encode some floating-point numbers. Note that our precision is still only four digits. The numbers 0.1032, -5.406, and 1,000,000 can be represented exactly. The number 476.0321, however, with seven significant digits, is represented as 476.0; the 321 cannot be represented. (We should point out that some computers perform *rounding* rather than simple truncation when discarding excess digits. Using our assumption of four significant digits, such a machine would store 476.0321 as 476.0 but would store 476.0823 as 476.1. We continue our discussion assuming simple truncation rather than rounding.)

NUMBER	POWER OF TEN NOTATION	Sign	Exp					VALUE
0.1032	$+1032 \times 10^{-4}$	+	−	4	1	0	3	2	0.1032
−5.4060	-5406×10^{-3}	−	−	3	5	4	0	6	−5.406
−0.003	-3000×10^{-6}	−	−	6	3	0	0	0	−0.0030
476.0321	$+4760 \times 10^{-1}$	+	−	1	4	7	6	0	476.0
1,000,000	$+1000 \times 10^{3}$	+	+	3	1	0	0	0	1,000,000

FIGURE G.3 Coding of Some Floating Point Numbers

G.2 Arithmetic with Floating-Point Numbers

When we use integer arithmetic, our results are exact. Floating-point arithmetic, however, is seldom exact. To understand why, let's add the three floating-point numbers x, y, and z using our coding scheme.

First, we add x to y and then we add z to the result. Next, we perform the operations in a different order, adding y to z, and then adding x to that result. The associative law of arithmetic says that the two answers should be the same—but are they? Let's use the following values for x, y, and z:

$$x = -1324 \times 10^3 \qquad y = 1325 \times 10^3 \qquad z = 5424 \times 10^0$$

Here is the result of adding z to the sum of x and y:

```
(x)    -1324 × 10³
(y)     1325 × 10³
           1 × 10³    = 1000 × 10⁰

(x + y) 1000 × 10⁰
(z)     5424 × 10⁰
        6424 × 10⁰    ← (x + y) + z
```

Now here is the result of adding x to the sum of y and z:

```
(y) 1325000 × 10⁰
(z)    5424 × 10⁰
    1330424 × 10⁰    = 1330 × 10³ (truncated to four digits)

(y + z) 1330 × 10³
(x)    -1324 × 10³
           6 × 10³    = 6000 × 10⁰ ← x + (y + z)
```

These two answers are the same in the thousands place but are different thereafter. The error behind this discrepancy is called representational error.

> **Representational Error** Arithmetic error that occurs when the precision of the true result of an arithmetic operation is greater than the precision of the machine.

Because of representational errors, it is unwise to use a floating-point variable as a loop control variable. Because precision may be lost in calculations involving floating-point numbers, it is difficult to predict when (or even *if*) a loop control variable of type **float** (or **double** or **long double**) will equal the termination value. A count-controlled loop with a floating-point control variable can behave unpredictably.

Also because of representational errors, you should never compare floating-point numbers for exact equality. Rarely are two floating-point numbers exactly equal, and thus you should compare them only for near equality. If the difference between the two numbers is less than some acceptable small value, you can consider them equal for the purposes of the given problem.

G.3 Implementation of Floating-Point Numbers in the Computer

All computers limit the precision of floating-point numbers, although modern machines use binary rather than decimal arithmetic. In our representation, we used only 5 digits to simplify the examples, and some computers really are limited to only 4 or 5 digits of precision. A more typical system might provide 6 significant digits for **float** values, 15 digits for **double** values, and 19 for the **long double** type. We have shown only a single-digit exponent, but most systems allow 2 digits for the **float** type and up to 4-digit exponents for type **long double**.

When you declare a floating-point variable, part of the memory location is assumed to contain the exponent, and the number itself (called the *mantissa*) is assumed to be in the balance of the location. The system is called floating-point representation because the number of significant digits is fixed, and the decimal point conceptually is allowed to float (move to different positions as necessary). In our coding scheme, every number is stored as four digits, with the leftmost digit being nonzero and the exponent adjusted accordingly. Numbers in this form are said to be *normalized*. The number 1,000,000 is stored as

+	+	3	1	0	0	0

and 0.1032 is stored as

+	−	4	1	0	3	2

Normalization provides the maximum precision possible.

Model Numbers Any real number that can be represented exactly as a floating-point number in the computer is called a *model number*. A real number whose value cannot be represented exactly is approximated by the model number closest to it. In our system with four digits of precision, 0.3021 is a model number. The values 0.3021409, 0.3021222, and 0.30209999999 are examples of real numbers that are represented in the computer by the same model number. The following table shows all of the model numbers for an even simpler floating-point system that has one digit in the mantissa and an exponent that can be −1, 0, or 1. Zero is a special case, because it has the same value regardless of the exponent.

0.1×10^{-1}	0.1×10^{0}	$0.1 \times 10^{+1}$
0.2×10^{-1}	0.2×10^{0}	$0.2 \times 10^{+1}$
0.3×10^{-1}	0.3×10^{0}	$0.3 \times 10^{+1}$
0.4×10^{-1}	0.4×10^{0}	$0.4 \times 10^{+1}$
0.5×10^{-1}	0.5×10^{0}	$0.5 \times 10^{+1}$
0.6×10^{-1}	0.6×10^{0}	$0.6 \times 10^{+1}$
0.7×10^{-1}	0.7×10^{0}	$0.7 \times 10^{+1}$
0.8×10^{-1}	0.8×10^{0}	$0.8 \times 10^{+1}$
0.9×10^{-1}	0.9×10^{0}	$0.9 \times 10^{+1}$

The difference between a real number and the model number that represents it is a form of representational error called *rounding error*. We can measure rounding error in

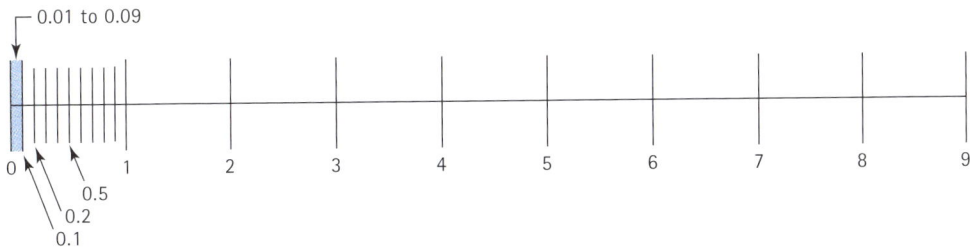

FIGURE G.4 A Graphical Representation of Model Numbers

two ways. The *absolute error* is the difference between the real number and the model number. For example, the absolute error in representing 0.3021409 by the model number 0.3021 is 0.0000409. The *relative error* is the absolute error divided by the real number and sometimes is stated as a percentage. For example, 0.0000409 divided by 0.3021409 is 0.000135, or 0.0135%.

The maximum absolute error depends on the *model interval*—the difference between two adjacent model numbers. In our example, the interval between 0.3021 and 0.3022 is 0.0001. The maximum absolute error in this system, for this interval, is less than 0.0001. Adding digits of precision makes the model interval (and thus the maximum absolute error) smaller.

The model interval is not a fixed number; it varies with the exponent. To see why the interval varies, consider that the interval between 3021.0 and 3022.0 is 1.0, which is 10^4 times larger than the interval between 0.3021 and 0.3022. This makes sense, because 3021.0 is simply 0.3021 times 10^4. Thus, a change in the exponent of the model numbers adjacent to the interval has an equivalent effect on the size of the interval. In practical terms, this means that we give up significant digits in the fractional part in order to represent numbers with large integer parts. **FIGURE G.4** illustrates this by graphing all of the model numbers listed in the preceding table.

We also can use relative and absolute error to measure the rounding error resulting from calculations. For example, suppose we multiply 1.0005 by 1000. The correct result is 1000.5, but because of rounding error, our four-digit computer produces 1000.0 as its result. The absolute error of the computed result is 0.5, and the relative error is 0.05%. Now suppose we multiply 100,050.0 by 1000. The correct result is 100,050,000, but the computer produces 100,000,000 as its result. If we look at the relative error, it is still a modest 0.05%, but the absolute error has grown to 50,000. Notice that this example is another case of changing the size of the model interval.

Whether it is more important to consider the absolute error or the relative error depends on the situation. It is unacceptable for an audit of a company to discover a $50,000 accounting error; the fact that the relative error is only 0.05% is not important. On the other hand, a 0.05% relative error is acceptable in representing prehistoric dates because the error in measurement techniques increases with age. That is, if we are talking about a date roughly 10,000 years ago, an absolute error of 5 years is acceptable; if the date is 100,000,000 years ago, then an absolute error of 50,000 years is equally acceptable.

Comparing Floating-Point Numbers   We have cautioned against comparing floating-point numbers for exact equality. Our exploration of representational errors in this chapter reveals why calculations may not produce the expected results even though it appears that they should. In Chapter 5, we wrote an expression that compares two floating-point variables r and s for near equality using the floating-point absolute value function fabs:

```
fabs(r - s) < 0.00001
```

From our discussion of model numbers, you now can recognize that the constant 0.00001 in this expression represents a maximum absolute error. We can generalize this expression as

```
fabs(r - s) < ERROR_TERM
```

where ERROR_TERM is a value that must be determined for each programming problem.

What if we want to compare floating-point numbers with a relative error measure? We must multiply the error term by the value in the problem to which the error is relative. For example, if we want to test whether r and s are "equal" within 0.05% of s, we write the following expression:

```
fabs(r - s) < 0.0005 * s
```

Keep in mind that the choice of the acceptable error and whether it should be absolute or relative depends on the problem being solved. The error terms we have shown in our example expressions are completely arbitrary and may not be appropriate for most problems. In solving a problem that involves the comparison of floating-point numbers, you typically want an error term that is as small as possible. Sometimes the choice is specified in the problem description or is reasonably obvious. Some cases require careful analysis of both the mathematics of the problem and the representational limits of the particular computer. Such analyses are the domain of a branch of mathematics called *numerical analysis* and are beyond the scope of this text.

Underflow and Overflow   In addition to representational errors, there are two other problems to watch out for in floating-point arithmetic: *underflow* and *overflow*.

Underflow is the condition that arises when the value of a calculation is too small to be represented. Going back to our decimal representation, let's look at a calculation involving small numbers:

$$\frac{4210 \times 10^{-8}}{\times\ 2000 \times 10^{-8}}$$
$$8420000 \times 10^{-16} = 8420 \times 10^{-13}$$

This value cannot be represented in our scheme because the exponent -13 is too small. Our minimum is -9. One way to resolve the problem is to set the result of the calculation to 0.0. Obviously, any answer depending on this calculation will not be exact.

Overflow is a more serious problem because there is no logical recourse when it occurs. For example, the result of the calculation

$$\frac{9999 \times 10^{9}}{\times\ 1000 \times 10^{9}}$$
$$9999000 \times 10^{18} = 9999 \times 10^{21}$$

cannot be stored, so what should we do? To be consistent with our response to underflow, we could set the result to 9999×10^{9} (the maximum representable value in this case). Yet this seems intuitively wrong. The alternative is to stop with an error message.

C++ does not define what should happen in the case of overflow or underflow. Different implementations of C++ solve the problem in different ways. You might try to cause an overflow with your system and see what happens. Some systems may print a run-time error message such as "FLOATING POINT OVERFLOW." On other systems, you may get the largest number that can be represented.

Although we are discussing problems with floating-point numbers, integer numbers also can overflow both negatively and positively. Most implementations of C++ ignore integer overflow. To see how your system handles the situation, you should try adding 1 to `INT_MAX` and -1 to `INT_MIN`. On most systems, adding 1 to `INT_MAX` sets the result to `INT_MIN`, a negative number.

Sometimes you can avoid overflow by arranging computations carefully. Suppose you want to know how many different five-card poker hands can be dealt from a deck of cards. What we are looking for is the number of *combinations* of 52 cards taken 5 at a time. The standard mathematical formula for the number of combinations of n things taken r at a time is

$$\frac{n!}{r!(n-r)!}$$

We could use the `Factorial` function we wrote in the Recursion chapter and write this formula in an assignment statement:

```
hands = Factorial(52) / (Factorial(5) * Factorial(47));
```

The only problem is that 52! is a very large number (approximately $8.065X \times 10^{67}$). And 47! is also large (approximately 2.5862×10^{59}). Both of these numbers are well beyond the capacity of most systems to represent exactly as integers (52! requires 68 digits of precision). Even though they can be represented on many machines as floating-point numbers, most of the precision is still lost. By rearranging the calculations, however, we can achieve an exact result on any system with 9 or more digits of precision. How? Consider that most of the multiplications in computing 52! are canceled when the product is divided by 47!

$$\frac{52!}{5! \times 47!} = \frac{52 \times 51 \times 50 \times 49 \times 48 \times 47 \times 46 \times 45 \times 44 \times \ldots}{(5 \times 4 \times 3 \times 2 \times 1) \times (47 \times 46 \times 45 \times 44 \times \ldots)}$$

So, we really only have to compute

```
hands = 52 * 51 * 50 * 49 * 48 / Factorial(5);
```

which means the numerator is 311,875,200 and the denominator is 120. On a system with 9 or more digits of precision, we get an exact answer: 2,598,960 poker hands.

Cancellation Error Another type of error that can happen with floating-point numbers is called cancellation error, a form of representational error that occurs when numbers of widely differing magnitudes are added or subtracted. Let's look at an example:

$$(1 + 0.00001234 - 1) = 0.00001234$$

The laws of arithmetic say this equation should be true. But is it true if the computer does the arithmetic?

$$\begin{array}{r} 100000000 \times 10^{-8} \\ +\quad 1234 \times 10^{-8} \\ \hline 100001234 \times 10^{-8} \end{array}$$

To four digits, the sum is 1000×10^{-3}. Now the computer subtracts 1:

$$\begin{array}{r} 1000 \times 10^{-3} \\ -1000 \times 10^{-3} \\ \hline 0 \end{array}$$

The result is 0, not .00001234.

Sometimes you can avoid adding two floating-point numbers that are drastically different in size by carefully arranging the calculations. Suppose a problem requires many small floating-point numbers to be added to a large floating-point number. The result is more accurate if the program first sums the smaller numbers to obtain a larger number and then adds the sum to the large number.

BACKGROUND INFORMATION
Practical Implications of Limited Precision

A discussion of representational, overflow, underflow, and cancellation errors may seem purely academic. In fact, these errors have serious practical implications in many problems. We close this section with three examples illustrating how limited precision can have costly or even disastrous effects.

During the Mercury space program, several of the spacecraft splashed down a considerable distance from their computed landing points. This delayed the recovery of the spacecraft and the astronaut, putting both in some danger. Eventually, the problem was traced to an imprecise representation of the Earth's rotation period in the program that calculated the landing point.

As part of the construction of a hydroelectric dam, a long set of high-tension cables had to be constructed to link the dam to the nearest power distribution point. The cables were to be several miles long, and each one was to be a continuous unit. (Because of the high power output from the dam, shorter cables couldn't be spliced together.) The cables were constructed at great expense and strung between the two points. It turned out that they were too short, however, so another set had to be manufactured. The problem was traced to errors of precision in calculating the length of the catenary curve (the curve that a cable forms when hanging between two points).

An audit of a bank turned up a mysterious account with a large amount of money in it. The account was traced to an unscrupulous programmer who had used limited precision to his advantage. The bank computed interest on its accounts to a precision of a tenth of a cent. The tenths of cents were not added to the customers' accounts, so the programmer had the extra tenths for all the

> **BACKGROUND INFORMATION** Practical Implications of Limited Precision, continued
>
> accounts summed and deposited into an account in his name. Because the bank had thousands of accounts, these tiny amounts added up to a large amount of money. And because the rest of the bank's programs did not use as much precision in their calculations, the scheme went undetected for many months.
>
> The moral of this discussion is twofold: (1) The results of floating-point calculations are often imprecise, and these errors can have serious consequences; and (2) if you are working with extremely large numbers or extremely small numbers, you need more information than this book provides and should consult a numerical analysis text.

Appendix H Using C Strings[1]

Starting with Chapter 2, we use the `string` class to store and manipulate character strings.

```
string name;
name = "James Smith"; len = name.length();
  ⋮
```

In some contexts, we think of a string as a single unit of data. In other contexts, we treat it as a group of individually accessible characters. In particular, we think of a string as a variable-length, linear collection of homogeneous components (of type `char`). The `string` class from the standard library is one approach to implementing a data type with these properties. However, before this class was developed, the C language, upon which C++ is built, had its own approach: the C string.

> **C string** In C and C++, a null-terminated sequence of characters stored in an array.

We are using a C string whenever we write a string constant. In C and C++, a string constant is a sequence of characters enclosed by double quotes:

`"Hi"`

A string constant is not a member of the `string` class, rather it is stored as a `char` array with enough components to hold each specified character plus one more—the *null character*. The null character, which is the first character in both the ASCII and EBCDIC character sets, is internally represented by the value 0. In C++, the escape sequence \0 stands for the null character. When the compiler encounters the string `"Hi"` in a program, it stores the

---

1. Note: This appendix assumes that you have already read about arrays in Chapter 11.

three characters 'H', 'i', and '\0' into a three-element, anonymous (unnamed) `char` array as follows:

The C string is the only kind of C++ array for which there exists an aggregate constant—the string constant. Notice that in a C++ program, the symbols `'A'` denote a single character, whereas the symbols `"A"` denote two: the character 'A' and the null character.[2]

In addition to C string constants, we can create C string *variables*. To do so, we explicitly declare a `char` array and store into it whatever characters we want to, finishing with the null character. Here's an example:

```
char myStr[8];  // Room for 7 significant characters plus '\0'

myStr[0] = 'H';
myStr[1] = 'i';
myStr[2] = '\0';
```

In C++, all C strings (constants or variables) are assumed to be null-terminated. This convention is agreed upon by all C++ programmers and standard library functions. The null character serves as a sentinel value; it allows algorithms to locate the end of the string. For example, here is a function that determines the length of any C string, not counting the terminating null character:

```
int StrLength(const char str[] )
// Precondition:
//    str holds a null-terminated string
// Postcondition:
//    Function value == number of characters in str (excluding '\0')
{
  int i = 0;  // Index variable
  while (str[i] != '\0')
    i++;
  return i;
}
```

---

[2]. C *string* is not an official term used in C++ language manuals. Such manuals typically use the term string. However, we use C *string* to distinguish between the general concept of a string, the built-in array representation defined by the C and C++ languages, and the `string` class in the standard library.

The value of i at loop exit is returned by the function. If the array being examined is

then i equals 2 at loop exit. The string length is therefore 2.

The argument to the `StrLength` function can be a C string variable, as in the function call

`cout << StrLength(myStr);`

or it can be a string constant:

`cout << StrLength("Hello");`

In the first case, the base address of the `myStr` array is sent to the function, as we discussed in Chapter 11. In the second case, a base address is also sent to the function—the base address of the unnamed array that the compiler has set aside for the string constant.

There is one more thing we should say about our `StrLength` function. A C++ programmer would not actually write this function. The standard library supplies several string-processing functions, one of which is named `strlen` and does exactly what our `StrLength` function does. Later in this appendix, we look at `strlen` and other library functions.

H.1 Initializing C Strings

In Chapter 11, we showed how to initialize an array in its declaration by specifying a list of initial values within braces, like this:

`int delta[5] = {25, -3, 7, 13, 4};`

To initialize a C string variable in its declaration, you could use the same technique:

`char message[8] = {'W', 'h', 'o', 'o', 'p', 's', '!', '\0'};`

However, C++ allows a more convenient way to initialize a C string. You can simply initialize the array by using a string constant:

`char message[8] = "Whoops!";`

This shorthand notation is unique to C strings because there is no other kind of array for which there are aggregate constants.

We said in Chapter 12 that you can omit the size of an array when you initialize it in its declaration (in which case, the compiler determines its size). This feature is often used with C strings because it keeps you from having to count the number of characters. For example,

```
char promptMsg[] = "Enter a positive number:";   // Size is 25
char errMsg[] = "Value must be positive.";       // Size is 24
```

Be very careful about one thing: C++ treats initialization (in a declaration) and assignment (in an assignment statement) as two distinct operations. Different rules apply. Remember that array initialization is legal, but aggregate array assignment is not.

```
char myStr[20] = "Hello";   // OK
    ⋮
myStr = "Howdy";            // Not allowed
```

H.2 C String Input and Output

In Chapter 11, we emphasized that C++ does not provide aggregate operations on arrays. There is no aggregate assignment, aggregate comparison, or aggregate arithmetic on arrays. We also said that aggregate input/output of arrays is not possible, with one exception. C strings are that exception. Let's look first at output.

To output the contents of an array that is *not* a C string, you aren't allowed to do this:

```
int alpha[100];
    ⋮
cout << alpha;   // Not allowed
```

Instead, you must write a loop and print the array elements one at a time. However, aggregate output of a null-terminated `char` array (that is, a C string) is valid. The C string can be a constant:

```
cout << "Results are:";
```

or it can be a variable:

```
char msg[8] = "Welcome";
    ⋮
cout << msg;
```

In both cases, the insertion operator (<<) outputs each character in the array until the null character is found. It is up to you to double-check that the terminating null character is present in the array. If not, the << operator will march through the array and into the rest of memory, printing out bytes until—just by chance—it encounters a byte whose integer value is 0.

To input C strings, we have several options. The first is to use the extraction operator (>>), which behaves exactly the same as with `string` class objects. When reading input characters into a C string variable, the >> operator skips leading whitespace characters and then reads successive characters into the array, stopping at the first trailing whitespace character (which is not consumed, but remains as the first character waiting in the input stream). The >> operator also takes care of adding the null character to the end of the string. For example, assume we have the following code:

```
char firstName[31];    // Room for 30 characters plus '\0'
char lastName[31];
cin >> firstName >> lastName;
```

If the input stream initially looks like this (where ◊ denotes a blank):

◊◊John◊Smith◊◊◊25

then our input statement stores 'J', 'o', 'h', 'n', and '\0' into `firstName[0]` through `firstName[4]`; stores 'S', 'm', 'i', 't', 'h', and '\0' into `lastName[0]` through `lastName[5]`; and leaves the input stream as

◊◊◊25

The >> operator, however, has two potential drawbacks.

1. If the array isn't large enough to hold the sequence of input characters (and the '\0'), the >> operator will continue to store characters into memory past the end of the array.
2. The >> operator cannot be used to input a string that has blanks within it. (It stops reading as soon as it encounters the first whitespace character.)

To cope with these limitations, we can use a variation of the **get** function, a member of the **istream** class. We have used the **get** function to input a single character, even if it is a whitespace character:

```
cin.get(inputChar);
```

The **get** function also can be used to input C strings, in which case the function call requires two arguments. The first is the array name and the second is an **int** expression.

```
cin.get(myStr, charCount + 1);
```

The **get** function does not skip leading whitespace characters and continues until it either has read `charCount` characters or it reaches the newline character '\n', whichever comes first. It then appends the null character to the end of the string. With the statements

```
char oneLine[81];      // Room for 80 characters plus '\0'
    ⋮
cin.get(oneLine, 81);
```

the **get** function reads and stores an entire input line (to a maximum of 80 characters), embedded blanks and all. If the line has fewer than 80 characters, reading stops at '\n' but does not consume it. The newline character is now the first one waiting in the input stream. To read two consecutive lines worth of strings, it is necessary to consume the newline character:

```
char dummy;
    ⋮
cin.get(string1, 81);
cin.get(dummy);        // Consume newline before next "get"
cin.get(string2, 81);
```

The first function call reads characters up to, but not including, the '\n'. If the input of **dummy** were omitted, then the input of **string2** would read *no* characters because '\n' would immediately be the first character waiting in the stream.

Finally, the **ignore** function can be useful in conjunction with the **get** function. The statement

```
cin.ignore(200, '\n');
```

says to skip at most 200 input characters but stop if a newline was read. (The newline character *is* consumed by this function.) If a program inputs a long string from the user but only wants to retain the first four characters of the response, here is a way to do it:

```
char response[5];        // Room for 4 characters plus '\0'

cin.get(response, 5);    // Input at most 4 characters
cin.ignore(100, '\n');   // Skip remaining chars up to and
                         //    including '\n'
```

The value 100 in the last statement is arbitrary. Any "large enough" number will do.

Here is a table that summarizes the differences between the >> operator and the **get** function when reading C strings:

Statement	Skips Leading Whitespace?	Stops Reading When?
`cin >> inputStr;`	Yes	At the first trailing whitespace character (which is not consumed)
`cin.get(inputStr, 21);`	No	When either 20 characters are read or '\n' is encountered (which is not consumed)

Certain library functions and member functions of system-supplied classes require C strings as arguments. An example is the **ifstream** class member function named **open**. To open a file, we pass the name of the file as a C string, either a constant or a variable:

```
ifstream file1;
ifstream file2;
char     fileName[51];     // Max. 50 characters plus '\0'

file1.open("students.dat");
cin.get(fileName, 51);     // Read at most 50 characters
cin.ignore(100, '\n');     // Skip rest of input line
file2.open(fileName);
```

If our file name is contained in a **string** class object, we still can use the **open** function, *provided* we use the **string** class member function named **c_str** to convert the string to a C string:

```
ifstream  inFile;
string    fileName;

cin >> fileName;
inFile.open(fileName.c_str());
```

Comparing these two code segments, you can observe a major advantage of the **string** class over C strings: A string in a **string** class object has unbounded length, whereas the length of a C string is bounded by the array size, which is fixed at compile time.

H.3 C String Library Routines

Through the header file `cstring`, the C++ standard library provides a large assortment of C string operations. In this section, we discuss three of these library functions: `strlen`, which returns the length of a string; `strcmp`, which compares two strings using the relations less-than, equal, and greater-than; and `strcpy`, which copies one string to another. Here is a summary of `strlen`, `strcmp`, and `strcpy`:

Header File	Function	Function Value	Effect
`<cstring>`	`strlen(str)`	Integer length of `str` (excluding '\0')	Computes length of `str`
`<cstring>`	`strcmp(str1, str2)`	An integer < 0, if `str1 < str2`	Compares `str1` and `str2`
		The integer 0, if `str1 = str2`	
		An integer > 0, if `str1 > str2`	
`<cstring>`	`strcpy(toStr, fromStr)`	Base address of `toStr` (usually ignored)	Copies `fromStr` (including '\0') to `toStr`, overwriting what was there; `toStr` must be large enough to hold the result

The `strlen` function is similar to the `StrLength` function we wrote earlier. It returns the number of characters in a C string prior to the terminating '\0'. Here's an example of a call to the function:

```
#include <cstring>
    ⋮
char subject[] = "Computer Science";

cout << strlen(subject);      // Prints 16
```

The `strcpy` routine is important because aggregate assignment with the = operator is not allowed on C strings. In the following code fragment, we show the wrong way and the right way to perform a string copy.

```
#include <cstring>
    ⋮
char myStr[100];
    ⋮
myStr = "Abracadabra";              // No
strcpy(myStr, "Abracadabra");       // Yes
```

In `strcpy`'s argument list, the destination string is the one on the left, just as an assignment operation transfers data from right to left. It is the caller's responsibility to make sure that the destination array is large enough to hold the result.

The `strcpy` function is technically a value-returning function; it not only copies one C string to another, but also returns as a function value the base address of the destination array. The reason why the caller would want to use this function value is not at all obvious, and we don't discuss it here. Programmers nearly always ignore the function value and simply invoke `strcpy` as if it were a void function (as we did above). You may wish to review the Background Information box in Chapter 9 entitled "Ignoring a Function Value."

The `strcmp` function is used for comparing two strings. The function receives two C strings as parameters and compares them in *lexicographic* order (the order in which they would appear in a dictionary)—the same ordering used in comparing `string` class objects. Given the function call `strcmp(str1, str2)`, the function returns one of the following `int` values: a negative integer, if `str1` < `str2` lexicographically; the value 0, if `str1` = `str2`; or a positive integer, if `str1` > `str2`. The precise values of the negative integer and the positive integer are unspecified. You simply test to see if the result is less than 0, 0, or greater than 0. Here is an example:

```
if (strcmp(str1, str2) < 0)    // If str1 is less than str2 . . .
    ⋮
```

We have described only three of the string-handling routines provided by the standard library. These three are the most commonly needed, but there are many more. If you are designing or maintaining programs that use C strings extensively, you should read the documentation on strings for your C++ system.

H.4 String Class or C Strings?

When working with string data, should you use a class like `string`, or should you use C strings? From the standpoints of clarity, versatility, and ease of use, there is no contest. Use a `string` class. The standard library `string` class provides strings of unbounded length, aggregate assignment, aggregate comparison, concatenation with the + operator, and so forth.

However, it is still useful to be familiar with C strings. Among the thousands of software products currently in use that are written in C and C++, most (but a declining percentage) use C strings to represent string data. In your next place of employment, if you are asked to modify or upgrade such software, understanding C strings is essential.

Appendix I C++ `char` Constants

In C++, `char` constants come in two different forms. The first form is a single printable character enclosed by apostrophes (single quotes):

```
'A'  '8'  ')'  '+'
```

Notice that we said *printable* character. Character sets include both printable characters and *control* characters (or *nonprintable* characters). Control characters are not meant to be printed. In the early days of computing, including the period when the C language was first developed, the primary interface to the computer was often a very simple printer or display screen. Control characters were used to direct the actions of the screen, printer, and other hardware devices. With modern graphical user interfaces, the control mechanisms are more complex, and their coverage is beyond the scope of this text. However, C++ (and C) still preserve the simpler interface in the form input and output to a console window, or terminal program, that simulates the old-style hardware.

If you look at the listing of the ASCII character set in Appendix E, you will see that the printable characters are those with integer values 32–126. The remaining characters (with values 0–31 and 127) are nonprinting control characters.

To accommodate control characters, C++ provides a second form of `char` constant: the *escape sequence*. An escape sequence is one or more characters preceded by a backslash (\), for example, the escape sequence `\n` represents the newline character. Here is the complete description of the two forms of `char` constant in C++:

1. A single printable character—except an apostrophe (') or backslash (\)—enclosed by apostrophes.
2. One of the following escape sequences, enclosed by apostrophes:

`\n`	Newline
`\t`	Horizontal tab
`\v`	Vertical tab
`\b`	Backspace
`\r`	Carriage return
`\f`	Form feed
`\a`	Alert (a bell or beep sound)
`\\`	Backslash
`\'`	Single quote (apostrophe)
`\"`	Double quote (quotation mark)
`\0`	Null character (all 0 bits)
`\ddd`	Octal equivalent (one, two, or three octal digits specifying the integer value of the desired character)
`\xddd`	Hexadecimal equivalent (one or more hexadecimal digits specifying the integer value of the desired character)

Even though an escape sequence is written as two or more characters, each escape sequence represents a single character in the character set. The alert character (`\a`) is the same as what is called the BEL character in ASCII. On old mechanical printers, it actually rang a bell. These days, it causes the terminal program to make a beeping sound. You can output the alert character like this:

```
cout << '\a';
```

In the list of escape sequences above, the entries labeled *Octal equivalent* and *Hexadecimal equivalent* let you refer to any character in your machine's character set by specifying its integer value in either octal (base-8) or hexadecimal (base-16). The reason for using these seemingly strange number bases is that, being powers of two, they translate more directly into binary.

Note that you can use an escape sequence within a string just as you can use any printable character within a string. The statement

```
cout << "\aWhoops!\n";
```

beeps the beeper, displays `Whoops!`, and terminates the output line. The statement

```
cout << "She said \"Hi\"";
```

outputs

```
She said "Hi"
```

and does not terminate the output line.

Index

Symbols

- - (double minus). *See* decrement operators (- -)
\# (pound sign), directive syntax, 642
% (modulus) operator, 95–96
& (ampersand)
   for declaring reference parameters, 361, 363
   for passing arrays by reference, 531
&& (AND operator), 207–209
/* */, comment syntax, 62, 63
*this, 847–848
:: (double colon), scope resolution operator, 408
@entry, function documentation, 376
_ (underscore), identifiers beginning with, 49
{ } (braces)
   block syntax, 65–66, 197
   C++ functions, 45
|| (OR operator), 207–209
} (right brace), C++ functions, 45
< > angle brackets, header syntax, 69
<< (left arrows)
   bitwise operator, 326
   insertion operator. *See* insertion operator (<<)
>> (right arrows)
   bitwise operator, 326
   extraction operator. *See* extraction operator (>>)
= (equals). *See* assignment operators (=)
== (double equals). *See* relational operators (==)
\ (backslash), printing strings, 61, 75
?: (conditional operator), 324, 328
/ (forward slash), division operator, 97–98
– (minus) sign, in integral types, 92
! (NOT operator), 207–209, 254–255
. (period), member selector, 608
; (semicolon)
   blocks and, 197
   Do-While statement ending in, 310–311
   expression statements and, 324
   function prototype ending with, 389
   infinite loops and, 291–292
   For statements and, 314
" (double quotes), printing strings, 61, 75
( ) (parentheses)
   overriding order or evaluation in expression, 213
   testing and debugging hints, 231–232

A

abstract data structures, 886–888
abstract data types (ADTs)
   array-based lists. *See* array-based lists
   dynamic lists. *See* dynamic ADT lists
   implementation of, 597–598
   operation categories, 598
   overview of, 596
   specification of, 597
abstract steps, 165
abstraction
   abstract data types. *See* abstract data types (ADTs)
   class design and, 625–626
   control abstraction, 445, 596
   data abstraction, 596
   modifiability and reuse and, 626–627

1041

abstraction barrier, 610. *See also* information hiding
access
   to components of one-dimensional arrays, 519–521
   in inheritance, 779–780
   to one-dimensional arrays, 524–530
action responsibilities
   public methods of objects, 620
   transformers as example of, 628
actions
   algorithms as logical sequence of, 4
   control unit controlling other component, 20
   means-end analysis of, 29
active error detection, 505
address-of operators, 495
ADTs. *See* abstract data types (ADTs)
aggregate operations
   Aggregate I/O, 523
   one-dimensional arrays, 523–524
   on structs, 481–483
air traffic control simulation, 800
Algol 60, 912
algorithms
   analysis of, 274–277
   coding, 5–6
   generic functions, 842
   overview of, 4–5
   problem-solving case study. *See* leap year program (case study)
   problem-solving using, 31–32
   responsibility, 795, 799, 801
   using control structures to express, 13–14
allocating dynamic data, 718–719
ALU (arithmetic/logic unit), 20
American National Standards Institute (ANSI), 32
American Standard Code for Information Interchange (ASCII)
   characters, 464–465
   defined, 8
analogy, problem-solving using, 28
analysis, in problem-solving phase, 163
Analytical Engine, Babbage, 352–353, 420
AND operator (**&&**), 207–209
angle arrays, 519–520

anonymous data types, 476, 506
ANSI (American National Standards Institute), 32
appointment calendar creation (case study), 802–819
   attributes in, internal representation of, 804–805
   constructors in, 806–808, 811
   CRC cards in, 803, 805, 809
   filtering in, 802
   responsibilities in, 811
   scenario explorations in, 803–804
appointment calendar using STL `list` (case study), 913–923
argument lists
   defined, 108
   parameter lists and, 372–373
   testing and debugging tips, 389
   testing functions, 387
   voiding function, 356–357
arguments
   C+, C++, and arrays and, 533
   defined, 355
   functions and, 146
   mechanisms for passing, 371
   one-dimensional arrays as, 533
   parameters and, 361–364
   type coercion in passing of, 433–435
   voiding function, 356–357
arithmetic expressions
   compound, 100–104
   mixed type expressions, 103–104
   relational operators for comparing values of, 190
   simple, 95–98
   type coercion in, 330–331
arithmetic operators
   overview of, 95–97
   precedence rules for, 213
arithmetic/logic unit (ALU), 20
array identifiers, 538
array-based lists, 663–715
   as abstract data types, 664–666
   of classes, generally, 695–696
   creating empty, 673
   data representation in, 668–670
   defined, 664

deletion, 674–675
example program for, 670–673
insertion, 674–675
iterators, 676–677
List, enhancing with sorts, 677–680
overview of, 663–664
responsibilities of, 666–668
sequential searches of, 675–676
sorted. *See* sorted lists
arrays, 515–594
    abstract form vs. implementation of, 886–888
    complex structures of, 581–585
    defined, 563
    elements of, 518
    indexes with semantic content, 548
    multidimensional, 563–565
    one-dimensional. *See* one-dimensional arrays
    overview of, 515–516
    processing, special kinds of, 545–548
    of records, 541–545
    as structured data type, 476–477
    subarray processing, 545–548
    testing and debugging, 581–585
    two-dimensional. *See* two-dimensional arrays
ASCII (American Standard Code for Information Interchange)
    characters, 464–465
    defined, 8
    assembler program, 10
assembly languages, 9–10
assert library function, 387–389
assertions
    asking questions as, 187
    as logical expressions, 188–192
    writing as function documentation, 374–375
assignment expressions
    common mistake when using, 199–200
    overview of, 324
assignment operators (=)
    built-in operations on objects, 608
    combined, 323, 324
    common mistakes, 199–200
    enumeration types and, 469

    overview of, 57–58, 324–325
    placing declarations and, 60
    simple arithmetic expressions, 98–99
    type casting, 102–103
    type coercion in, 102–103, 433–435
    writing If statements, 190
    writing While statements, 252
associative containers, 929–934
associative lookups, 930
atomic data types. *See* simple (atomic) data types
attributes
    internal representation of, 804–805
    of objects, 620
automatic variables, 410
auxiliary (storage) devices
    defined, 21
    input data coming from, 138

B

Babbage, Charles, 351–353, 420
Backus-Naur Form (BNF) metalanguage, 47
base addresses, 531
base cases, 961–967
base classes, 775
batch processing, as noninteractive I/O, 152
batch systems, 22
BCPL (Basic Combined Programming Language), 32
bidirectional linear structures, 893–894
bidirectional lists, 893–894
Big-O notation, 276
binary codes, data stored as, 9
binary operators, 97
binary representation of data
    approximating floating-point values, 95
    overview of, 7–9
binary search algorithms, 972–976
binary search trees, 925–927
binary searches
    linear searches vs., 972–976
    logarithmic order of, 693
    in sorted lists, 682, 686–690, 696
binary trees, 924–927
binding like items, structs, 483–484
bits, of data, 8–9

bitwise operators
    overview of, 326
    specialized, 323
black boxes, 610
black-box testing, 229
blank lines, creating, 74–75
blanks
    extraction operator (>>) skipping, 143–145
    output formatting using, 111
blocks (compound statements). *See also* scope, identifier
    body of loop as, 245
    braces and, 197
    declaring automatic variables within, 410
    overview of, 66–67
    using in If statements, 195–197
BMI calculator (case study), 217–232
    changing loop implementation (case study) and, 318–320
BNF (Backus-Naur Form) metalanguage, 47
body, of function, 45
body, of loop, 244–245
`bool` data type
    domain of, 462
    overview of, 188
    simulating, 466
Boole, George, 212–213
Boolean algebra, 212
Boolean expressions. *See* logical (Boolean) expressions
Boolean functions
    `LessThan` operation, 606
    naming, 431
    overview of, 429–430
Boolean operators. *See* logical (Boolean) operators
    brainstorming
    defined, 795
    in object-oriented design, 795–796
branching control structure. *See* selection (branching) control structure
Break statement
    flow of control using, 305–307
    overview of, 321–322
    testing and debugging, 337
building-block approach, to problem-solving, 29–30
built-in data types, 50

built-in operations, on objects, 608–609
built-in simple types, 462–465
    characters, 464–465
    numeric types, 463–464
    overview of, 462–463
Byron, Anna Isabella (Annabella), 420–421
Byron, Lord (George Gordon), 420–421
bytecode, Java, 12
bytes, 8

C

C language, 160–161
C strings, 664
C++ origins, 32
CAD (computer-aided) design, 775
calculators, Pascal, 105
case labels, Switch statement, 305–307
case studies. *See* problem-solving case studies
case-sensitivity
    in C++, 50
    enumerators, 468
    using capitalization of identifiers, 56
cast operator ()
    defined, 323
    overview of, 102–104, 326–327
catching exceptions
    defined, 849
    `try-catch` statement for, 851–854
central processing unit (CPU), 20
`cfloat` header file, 464
chained hash tables, 928–929
`char` data type
    concatenation working with, 59
    defined, 50
    domain of, 462
    as integral type, 92–94
    measuring sizes in multiples of, 463
    overview of, 51–52
    storing character data, 331
`char` literal, 76
character data
    input streams and extraction operator, 141–142
    overview of, 464–465
    reading marker and new line, 142–143
    reading with `get` function, 143–146
    skipping characters with `ignore` function, 146–147

using char to store, 331
character sets
   adding to string value, 59
   defined, 51–52
   testing and debugging hints, 506
chessboard program (case study), 78–82, 89
children (of tree node), 924–927
cin variable
   example of, 140–141
   input failure, 162
   inputting data from, 139
   mistaken use of, 176
   reading string data with, 147–148
class constructors, 601, 604
class design
   abstraction, 625–626
   encapsulation, 623–625
   modifiability and reuse, 626–627
   mutability, 627–628
class members, 600
class scope, 402, 410, 609–610
classes
   built-in operations on objects, 608–609
   class objects (class instances), 602
   composition, 639–643
   constructors, 601, 604
   design specification, 624
   information hiding. *See* information hiding
   instantiating, 832–834
   member functions, 604
   members, 600–601
   objects and members and, 607–608
   overview of, 599
   scope, 402, 410, 609–610
   as structured data type, 476–477
   syntax template for, 600
   in templates, 831–832
   testing and debugging, 652–656
   UML diagrams, 644–645
clients, class, 602
climits header file, 464
clock, 23
clones, 979
closing files, 155, 158–159
COBOL (Common Business-Oriented Language), 309
code coverage
   developing test plan with, 229
   testing using, 229
code editors
   defined, 17
   entering program using, 76–77
code walk-through, 225
coding
   algorithms, 5–6
   binary representations of data and, 8–9
collaborations, 797
collating sequence, 52
collisions, 928
column processing, 560
comments
   assertions as function documentation, 374–375
   on constant and variable declarations, 56
   creating from debug output statements, 292
   in one-dimensional arrays, 533
   program construction using, 65
   on programs, 62–63
   pseudocode from design process as, 171
communication complexity, 445
ComparedTo
   in binary searches, 695–696
   in dynamic binding, 791–792
comparison operations
   ADT operations, 635–636
   enumeration types and, 470
compilation/compilers
   computer speed and, 24
   defined, 11
   interpretation vs. compilation, 11–12
   multifile program compilation, 618–619
   program compilation, 77
   testing automatically during compilation, 230–231
compile time, 832
compile-time binding, 791
complexity, of algorithm, 274
composition, class
   diagramming, 645
   overview of, 639–643
compound arithmetic expressions
   precedence rules, 101
   type coercion and type casting, 101–104
compound statements. *See* blocks (compound statements)
computer programming, 2

computer programs, 9–19
    compilation vs. interpretation, 12
    defined, 2
    how it works, 9–12
    programming language instructions, 13
    software maintenance study, 13–19
    writing, 3–4
computer-aided (CAD) design, 775
computers
    components of, 19–23
    defined, 2
    designing world's first, 351–352
    factors affecting speed of, 23–24
    von Neumann's role in development of, 622
    resources and ethics, 25–26
concatenation, 58–59
conceptual hiding, of function implementation, 373–374, 445
concrete steps, hierarchical solution tree, 165
conditional (short-circuit) evaluation, 211–212
conditional operator (?:), 324, 328
conditions, 187–192
    `bool` data type, 188
    logical (Boolean) expressions, 188–192
    overview of, 187
    postconditions. See postconditions
    preconditions. See preconditions
`const` references, 834–835
constant pointers, 725, 731
constants
    adding comments to declarations, 63
    Boolean, 188
    declaring, 55–57
    dynamic data and, 724
    global, 403, 419–420
    identifiers, 53, 57
    as member functions, 611
    program construction using, 65–66
    relational operators for comparing, 188–190
constant-time complexity, of algorithm, 275
ConstIntExpression, enumerators, 468
constructor execution orders, 784
constructor initializers, 641
constructors
    in ADT operations, 598

class, 601
for dynamic linked lists, 746
implementing class member functions with, 604
for instances of objects, 635
constructs, 46
container adapters, 929
containers, 895
content addressable access, 930
Continue statement, 321–322
control abstraction, 445, 596. See also abstraction
control structures
    additional C++ operators, 323–324
    algorithms and, 13–14
    assignment operators and expressions, 324–325
    bitwise operators, 326
    Break statement, 321–322
    cast operation, 326–327
    conditional operator (?:), 328
    Continue statement, 321–322
    Do-While statement, 310–314
    increment and decrement operators, 325–326
    looping. See loops/looping
    nested, 203–207
    operator precedence, 328–330
    programming languages and, 13–14
    For statement, 314–318
    Switch statement, 304–308
    testing and debugging, 336
    type coercion and, 330–331
control unit, 20
copy-constructors, 746, 748–750
count-controlled loops
    defined, 246
    designing flow of control, 263–264
    implementing with For statement, 314–318, 322
    overview of, 247–249
    test plan for, 291
counters, variables as, 247
counting, looping and, 256
`cout` variable
    denoting output stream with, 60
    example of, 140
    mistaken use of, 176
    outputting values to, 139–140

CPU (central processing unit), 20
CRC (classes, responsibilities, and collaborations) cards
    as notational device, 799
    overview of, 795–796
    in scenario explorations, 795, 797–798
cubic expressions, 276–277

D

dangling pointers, 722
data
    binary representation of, 7–9
    defined, 7
    input failure from invalid, 162, 176
    privacy of, 25
    separating/combining with operations, 599
    storage, 51
data abstraction, 596, 625–626. *See also* abstraction
data coverage, 229
data flow, for parameters, 348
data objects, 53
data representation, of abstract data, 597–598
data representation of objects, 801
data structures, 885–957
    abstract date structures vs. implementations, 886–888
    associative containers, 929–934
    bidirectional linear structures, 893–894
    bidirectional lists, 893–894
    binary trees, 924–927
    deques, 894
    dynamic, 727
    hash tables, 928–929
    linear structures, additional, 888–889
    `map` template, 933–934
    nonlinear, 924–929
    overview of, 885–886
    priority queues, 891–893
    queues, 891
    `set` template, 930–933
    stacks, 889–891
    Standard Template Library for. *See* Standard Template Library (STL)
    testing and debugging, 948–949
data types
    abstract, 596–598
    arrays. *See* arrays
    built-in simple types, 462–465
    `char` data type, 51–52
    classes. *See* classes
    information hiding. *See* information hiding
    numeric. *See* numeric data types
    overview of, 50–51, 92
    string. *See* string data type
    type coercion and, 330
    user-defined. *See* user-defined data types
`data[length]`
    in sorted lists, 683–685
`Date` class, adding to (case study), 859–865
debug output statements, 292
debugging. *See also* testing
    array-based lists, 711
    C++ syntax and semantics and, 82–83
    classes, 652–656
    compiling and running program and, 77
    control structures, 336
    data structures, 948–949
    defined, 5
    functions, 387–389
    loops, 290–292
    modular design and, 445–451
    `Null` pointers, 761
    numeric types, expressions and output, 125
    object-oriented designs, 819–821
    pointers, 760–762
    process of elimination and, 105
    program input, 175–177
    recursion, 992
    templates, 877–878
    user-defined data types, 504–505
deck of cards creation (case study), 935–948
declarations
    assignment operations and, 60
    classes, 602, 603
    constants, 55–57
    defined, 53–57
    definitions vs., 357
    file streams, 153–154
    functions, 357
    initialization in, 411–412
    mixing with executable statements in blocks, 67
    numeric data types, 95–96

of one-dimensional arrays, 518–519, 524–530
overview of, 53
program construction using, 63–66
structs, 478–479, 483–484
variables, 53–55, 407
void functions, 357–359
decrement operators (- -)
overview of, 325
specialized, 323
unary operators, 100
deep copy operations, 748–749
default constructor, 601
default labels, Switch statement, 305–306
default parameters, 362
definitions
declarations vs., 357
function, 350–351, 353
namespace, 407–410
variable, 407
deleting
`delete` operators for, 718, 720–724
dynamic data, 720–724
from dynamic linked lists, 738–740
from sorted linked lists, 756–757
from sorted lists, 690–692
DeMorgan, Augustus, 420
demotion (narrowing), 433
`deque` template, 911
deques, 894
derived classes, 775
Descartes, René, 105
design
of classes. *See* class design
computer-aided, 775
documentation of, 171
of interfaces. *See* interface design
loops, 263–266
module interface, 347–348
in problem-solving phase, 163
of recording studios, 273–289
of software. *See* software design methodologies
structured. *See* functional decomposition
design specification, classes, 624
destructors
in ADT operations, 598

closing files, 155
for dynamic linked lists, 746–747
development models, software, 4
development process
compiling and running program, 77–78
constructing program, 63–73
data and data types, 50–52
declarations, 53–57
entering program, 76–77
executable statements, 57–63
identifiers, 49–50
output, 72–74
program structure, 44–46
syntax and semantics, 46–47
syntax templates, 47–49
testing and debugging, 82–83
diagrams, UML (Unified Modeling Language)
of classes, generally, 644–645
Difference Engine, Babbage, 352, 420
direct addressing, 491
directives, 642
disk drives, 21
divide and conquer problem-solving, 29
division (/) operator, 97–98
documentation
defined, 7
function, 374–376, 389
tips for, 171
dot notation
overview of, 119
using `get` function with, 144
`double` data type, 94
doubly nested loops, 272
Do-While statement
Break statement with, 321–322
guidelines for choosing, 322–323
overview of, 310–314
testing and debugging, 336–337
drivers, 446, 452
duplicate keys, 664–665
dynamic ADT lists. *See also* array-based lists
creating empty, 735
deleting from, 738–740
implementing generally, 740–746
inserting into, 736–738

overview of, 734–736
resetting, 740
retrieving items, 741
searching, 741–742
testing for full, 741
traversals of, 737
dynamic binding
overview of, 791–792
slicing issues in, 792–793
virtual functions in, 793–794
dynamic data
allocating, 718–719
constants and, 724–725
deleting, 720–724
in linked lists. *See* dynamic linked lists
overview of, 718
dynamic data structures, 727
dynamic linked lists
constructors for, 746
copy-constructors for, 746, 748–750
copying, 979–983
creating, 727–733
creating empty, 735
deleting from, 738–740
destructors for, 746–747
implementing generally, 734–736, 741–746
inserting into, 736–738
printing in reverse order, 977–979
resetting, 740
retrieving items, 741
searching, 741–742
shallow vs. deep copying of, 746–747
testing for full, 741
traversals of, 737–738

E
echo printing
interactive I/O using, 149–151
noninteractive I/O using, 152
testing and debugging, 177, 232
editors
defined, 23
entering existing code, 17
electric circuits
binary representations of data and, 7–9
clock generating, 23

elements, C++ programs
data and data types, 50–52
declarations, 53–57
executable statements, 57–63
identifiers, 49–50
program structure, 44–46
syntax and semantics, 46–47
syntax templates, 47–49
else clause
defined, 193
nested If statements and, 206–207
encapsulation
abstraction and, 625
class design and, 623–625
modifiability and reuse and, 626–627
mutability of objects and, 627
overview of, 348
`endl` manipulator
creating blank lines, 74–75
generating newline character in output statement, 142
inserting blanks within line, 75
`ofstream` data type, 154
output formatting using, 111, 116
terminating output line, 61–62
end-of-file (EOF)-controlled loops, 252–254, 264
end-of-file errors, 175
English statements, changing into logical expressions, 214
`Entry` class
deriving classes from other classes and, 777–778
expanded. *See* ExpandedEntry class
inheritance and object-oriented design for, 775–777
overview, 695–699
`Entry` objects (case study), 757–760
`EntryWithDate` class, 808–810, 913–916
enumeration data types
assignment, 469
comparison, 470–471
defining own simple types with, 462–463
incrementation, 470
input and output, 471–472
overview of, 467–469
returning function value, 474–475

testing and debugging, 504–505
EOF (end-of-file)-controlled loops, 252–254, 264
`Equal` operation, class member functions, 606–607
errors
   coping with input, 504–505
   function, 387–388
   messages, 17–18
   side effects in, 417–419
   software engineering tip for handling, 125
   syntactic or semantic tests, 230–231
ethical issues
   privacy of data, 25
   software piracy, 24
evaluate, 58
event counter, 258
event-controlled loops, 249–259
   defined, 246
   end-of-file-controlled loops, 252–254
   flag-controlled loops, 254–255
   guidelines for choosing looping statement, 322–323
   sentinel-controlled loops, 249–252
   test plan for, 291
exam statistics (case study), 566–573, 700–710
exception handlers
   defined, 849
   formal parameters in, 852–854
   nonlocal, 854–856
exceptions, 848–876
   defined, 849
   exception handlers, formal parameters in, 852–854
   exception handlers, nonlocal, 854–856
   overview of, 829–830, 848–849
   rethrowing, 856
   standard, 857
   in starship weight and balance (case study). *See* starship weight and balance (case study)
   `throw` statements for, 849–850
   thrown by language, 857
   thrown by standard library routines, 858
   `try-catch` statements for, 851–852
executable assertions, 388
executable statements
   mixing with declarations in blocks, 67
   overview of, 57–63

   program construction using, 66
execution
   overview of, 12
   programs, 5
   testing automatically during, 230–231
execution (hand) trace, 225–227
exit status, 66
exiting loops, 266–267
`ExpandedEntry` class. *See also* `Entry` class
   constructor execution order in, 784
   deriving classes from other classes with, 777–778
   implementation of, 779–784
   specifications for, 778–779
explicit matching, 371
explicit type casts, 103–104
exponentiation program, 961
exponents, floating-point values an, 94
expressions
   arithmetic. *See* arithmetic expressions
   assignment, 199–200, 324
   avoiding using side effects in, 506–507
   compound arithmetic, 100–104
   defined, 57, 324
   library functions in, 108–110
   logical, 188–192
   parameters in, 371–372
   performing calculations with, 97
   of pointers, 537–538
   relational, 330–331
   simple arithmetic, 97–100
   string, 58–59
   switch, 304
external declaration, 407
external pointers
   in copying dynamic linked lists, 979
   in empty linked lists, 735
   in linked lists, 726, 727, 730
   in recursion, 977
external representation, character, 464
extraction operator (>>)
   `ifstream` data type, 154
   and input streams, 139–142
   reading string data with getline function vs., 147–148
   review, 177
   skipping characters with `ignore` function, 146–147
   skipping newline characters, 142
   using `get` function with, 143–145

ExtTime class
   in dynamic binding generally, 791
   slicing issues in, 792–793
   virtual functions with, 793–794

F
factorials, 963–965
fail state, 162
failure, input
   causes of, 174–175
   overview of, 162–163
`false` value, `bool` type, 462
familiarity, problem-solving and, 27–28
fear of starting, as mental block to problem solving, 31
fetch-execute cycle
   computer speed and, 23
   overview of, 21
field, of record, 478
fieldwidth specification
   floating-point values, 113–116
   integer values, 112–113
FIFO (first in, first out), 891
file input/output (I/O), 152–161
   declaring file streams, 153
   including header file `fstream`, 153
   input failure from, 162
   opening files, 154–155
   reading data from files, 152
   runtime input of file names, 160–161
   specifying file streams in I/O statements, 156
   testing and debugging, 175–176
files
   closing, 155
   defined, 77
   opening, 154–155
filtering
   defined, 795
   in object-oriented design, 796
first in, first out (FIFO), 891
`fixed` manipulator, output formatting using, 111, 114–116
flag-controlled loops, 254–255, 264
flash memory, 21
flat (inline) implementation, 169
`float` data type
   in class templates, 831–834
   constructing complex arithmetic expressions, 97–100

   defined, 50
   domain of, 462
   as floating type, 94
   in function overloading, 842–844
floating data types
   division and, 98
   output formatting, 113–116
   overview of, 94
   relational operators with, 214–215
flow of control
   conditions and logical expressions and, 187–192
   defined, 186
   English statements changed into logical expressions, 214
   in function calls, 353–356
   If statements, 192–203
   logical operators. *See* logical (Boolean) operators
   loop design and, 263–267
   nested If statements, 203–207
   selection (branching) control structure, 186–187
   Switch statements, 305–307
   test plan for, 229–230
   testing state of I/O stream, 215–217
   tests performed automatically during compilation and execution, 230–231
   While and Do-While loops, 311
For loops
   in multidimensional arrays, 564
   summing rows with, 555–556
For statement
   Break statement used with, 321–322
   guidelines for choosing, 322–323
   overview of, 314–318
   testing and debugging, 336–337
formal interfaces, encapsulation and, 623–625
formatting output. *See* output formatting
Fortran language, 622
forward declarations, 728–733, 742
forward iterators, 897–898
free format language, 117–118, 129
free store, 719
`fstream` header file
   file I/O and, 153–154
function calls (invocation)
   abstraction and, 596
   defined, 107

in value-returning functions, 108
for void vs. value-returning functions, 110
function definitions
   defined, 83, 350
   flow of control in, 353
   function declarations vs., 357
   as heading followed by block, 66
   overview of, 358–359
   program construction using, 63–66
   scope rules for, 404–407
   testing and debugging tips, 389
   for void functions, 358–359
function overloading, 842–843
function prototypes
   defined, 351, 357
   testing and debugging tips, 389
   for void functions, 357–358
function templates
   outside classes, 843–844
   overview of, 833–834
function value (return or result) type, 422–423
functional cohesion, 166, 445
functional decomposition
   design perspective, 170
   developing test plan with, 229–230
   documentation in, 171
   implementing design, 166–170
   modules, 165–166
   object-oriented design vs., 163–164, 177
   overview of, 164–165
   review, 177
   software design using, 163
   tree structure in, 164–165
   with void functions, 346–351
functional equivalence, modules, 165
functional notation, cast operation, 326–327
functions
   arguments and, 146
   capitalization of, 56–57
   conceptual vs. physical hiding of, 373–374
   declarations, 357
   functional decomposition with void, 346–351
   interface design, 416–420
   library, 108–110
   modules implemented as, 168–170
   naming void, 361
   parameters. *See* parameters
   scope of identifiers, 402–410
   specification and implementation, 596
   `string` data type, 119–123
   as subprograms, 44–45
   syntax and semantics of void, 356–361
   testing and debugging, 387–389, 445–451
   type coercion and, 433–435
   user-defined, 353–356
   value-returning. *See* value-returning functions
   variable lifetime and, 410–412
   void, 110
   when to use, 346–347
   writing assertions as documentation of, 374–376

G

general cases, 961
generated classes, 833
generic algorithms, 842
generic data type, 831
generic functions
   algorithms, 842
   function overloading, 842–843
   function templates, defining outside classes, 843–844
`get` function
   accepting only variable as argument, 146
   `ifstream` data type, 154
   in loops controlled by newline character, 251, 292
   reading character data with, 143–146
`getline` function, 147–148
`GetNextItem`
   iterators and, 676–677
   overview of, 667–668, 670
GHz (gigahertz), 23–24
`GList` class template, 831–840. *See also* `List` class
   cautions regarding, 841
   `const` references and, 834–835
   defining, 831–832
   instantiating, 832–834
   in program code organization, 835–840
global constants
   defined, 403
   example using, 403–404
   interface design and, 419–420

global scope
  defined, 403
  namespaces, 410
  `using` directives and, 409
global variables
  defined, 403
  example using, 403–404
  local variables vs., 359
  scope rules for, 404–407
  side effects in, 417–419
  as static variables, 410
Goldstine, Herbert, 622
grade record arrays
  implementing, 541–545
  subarray processing of, 545–548
  using, 527–528
grammar. *See* syntax (grammar)
graphs, 927
grouping order (associativity), arithmetic expressions, 101

H
hardware, 21–22
hash function, 928
hash tables, 928–929
hashing, 928
head pointers, 725, 727–731
header files
  defined, 69
  file I/O with, 153–154
  user-written, 611–612
health profile program (case study)
  follow-up, 460
  overview of, 436–444
  testing and debugging, 446–450
heaps, 719
hiding, name precedence or, 403
hiding, of function implementation, 373–374, 445
hierarchical implementation, 169
hierarchical records, 486–488
hierarchical solution tree, 165
high-level languages, 10–12
Hoare, Sir Charles Anthony Richard, 912–913, 984
Hopper, Admiral Grace Murray, 309

I
identifiers
  capitalization of, 56–57
  declaring, 53–57
  meaningful, readable, 50
  naming memory locations with, 51
  overview of, 49–50
  scope of. *See* scope, identifier
  self-documenting code using meaningful, 171
IDEs (integrated development environments), 841–842
If statements
  blocks, 195–197
  Break statement used with, 321–322
  common mistake, 199–200
  If-Then, 198–199
  If-Then-Else, 193–195
  logical order vs. physical order and, 186, 244
  nested, 203–207
  overview of, 192–193
  testing and debugging, 232
  While statement vs., 245–246
`ifstream` data type
  closing files, 155
  defined, 153
  opening files, 154–155
  testing state of I/O stream, 215–216
If-Then statement, 198–199
If-Then-Else statement, 193–195
If-Then-Else-If control structure, 205, 306
`ignore` function
  `ifstream` data type, 153
  skipping characters with, 146–147
immutable objects, 627–628
implementation
  conceptual vs. physical hiding of functions and, 373–374
  defined, 5
  differences in, 5–6
  of dynamic linked lists, 732–734, 734–745
  functional decomposition and, 166–170
  functions, 596
  information hiding and, 612, 615–618
  overview, 3–4
  program life cycle and, 7
  testing during, 225–229
implicit matching, 371
inaccessible objects, 722–725
`#include` directive
  preprocessors and, 69

program construction using, 65
`include` statement, adding titles to names, 71
incoming parameters, 834–835
incomplete declarations, 728
incorrect output (case study), 200–203
`Increment` function, class member functions, 604–605
increment operators (++)
    enumeration types and, 470
    incrementing variables using, 247–248
    overview of, 325–326
    specialized, 323
    unary operators, 99–100
increment variable, loop control, 247
index values, 517
indexes
    as constants, variables, and complex expressions, 520–521
    defined, 517
    out-of-bounds array, 521–523
    with semantic content, 548
indirect addressing, 491, 505
indirection operators, 491
infinite loop
    Break statement with, 321–323
    defined, 5, 248
    testing and debugging, 291–292
infinite recursion, 963–965
information, 7
information hiding, 610–619
    compiling and linking multifile programs, 618–619
    implementation file and, 612, 615–618
    overview of, 610–611
    specification file and, 612–615
    user-written header files and, 611–612
inheritance
    constructor execution order in, 784
    deriving classes from other classes, 777–778
    in `ExpandedEntry` class, 779–784
    object-oriented design and, 775–777
    overview of, 771–774
    `TimeOfDay`, extending with time zone support, 785–790
initialization
    in declarations, 411–412

loop control variable, 247
of one-dimensional arrays, 523
of two-dimensional arrays, 558–560
initializer, defined, 412
InitStatement, For statement, 314–318
in-order traversals, 926–927
input
    compilation and execution of, 12
    error handling, 504
    failure, 162–163
    file I/O, 154–159
    If-Then-Else for checking validity of, 193–194
    input devices for, 13, 19–21, 138
    interactive I/O, 149–151
    manipulators for, 111
    noninteractive I/O, 152
    operating system carrying out, 22–23
    source program as, 11–12
    storing in auxiliary storage device, 21
    testing and debugging, 175–177
input, into programs
    input streams and extraction operator, 139–142
    reading character data with `get` function, 143–146
    reading marker and newline character, 142–143
    reading `string` data, 147–149
    skipping characters with `ignore` function, 146–147
input prompts, 149–151
input streams, 139–142
input values, of enumerated types, 471–473
input/output. *See* I/O (input/output)
inserting
    into dynamic linked lists, 734, 736–737
    into sorted lists, 683–685
insertion operator (<<)
    extraction operator compared with, 139–140
    `ofstream` data type, 154
    output statements and, 60
insertion sorts, 685
instances
    constructing, 635
    object, 604
instantiation, object, 607

int array, 531
int data type
    constructing complex arithmetic expressions, 97–98
    defined, 45–46, 50
    domain of, 462
    input failure from, 162
    as integral type, 92–93
    syntax template for main function, 48–49
integers
    converting to strings, 643
    output formatting, 111–113
    testing and debugging, 504
integral data types
    division and, 97
    overview of, 92–93
integrated development environments (IDEs), 841
integrated environment, C++, 619
interactive I/O
    defined, 177
    overview of, 149–151
interactive systems, 22
interface design, 416–421
    global constants, 419–420
    modules, 347–348
    overview of, 416–417
    side effects, 417–419
    value-returning functions and, 431–432
interfaces
    defined, 348
    encapsulation and, 623–625
    user/computer, 22
internal representation, characters, 464–465
International Standards Organization (ISO), 32
Internet, 23
interpretation, compilation vs., 12
invalid data
    coping with input errors, 504–505
    as source of input failure, 162, 176
An Investigation of the Laws of Thought . . . (Boole), 212
invocation. *See* function calls (invocation)
I/O (input/output)
    devices, 20–22
    file I/O. *See* file input/output (I/O)
    program I/O, 609

iostream header file, 153, 156
ISO (International Standards Organization), 32
IsThere
    in binary searches, 690
    in searching and sorting, 693
istream data type
    extraction operator. *See* extraction operator (>>)
    get function, 143–146
    ignore function, 146–147
    managing program I/O with, 609
    testing state of I/O stream, 215–216
iteration
    in ADT operations, 598
    defined, 246
    recursion vs., 983–984
iteration counter, 256
iterators
    in array-based lists, 676–677
    in Standard Template Library, 896–898

J

Java
    compiler and interpreter, 12
    Unicode and, 8
JVM (Java Virtual Machine), 12

K

keyboard
    as input device, 20, 138–142
    input failure, 162
    reading data from files vs., 152, 156
keys, 664–665
keyword cast, 327
knowledge responsibilities, public methods of objects, 620

L

LAN (local area network), 23
last in, first out (LIFO), 889
lawn care application (case study), 377–386
leaf nodes, 924–927
leap year program (case study)
    follow-up, 41–42
    overview of, 33–36
    reserved words in, 49–50
left children, 924–927

left subtrees, 924–927
length of lists, 664
library functions, 107–110
life cycle, program, 7
lifetime, variable, 410–412
LIFO (last in, first out), 889
linear relationships, 664
linear searches. *See* sequential searches
linear structures, 886–889
linear-time complexity, of algorithm, 275
linked lists
    bidirectional, 893–894
    defined, 725
    dynamic. *See* dynamic linked lists
    overview of, 718–725
    pointers and. *See* pointers
    sequential structures vs., 725–726
    sorted. *See* sorted linked lists
linking multifile programs, 618–619
`List` class
    class templates for, 830–832
    sorts, enhancing with, 677–680
`list` template, 904–906
lists
    abstract form vs. implementation of, 886–888
    argument. *See* argument lists
    array-based. *See* array-based lists
    bidirectional, 893–894
    dynamic. *See* dynamic linked lists
    length of, 664
    linked. *See* linked lists
    parameter. *See* parameter lists
    sorted. *See* sorted lists
    unsorted, 664
literal strings
    concatenation working with, 59
    output formatting, 111–113
    output statements printing, 61
literal values
    defined, 55
    enumeration types and, 467–468
literals, named constants instead of, 95–96
local area network (LAN), 23
local constants, access rules for, 402
local scope
    defined, 403, 410
    rules for, 404–407
local variables
    access rules for, 402
    scope rules for, 405–407
    `static` reserved word for declaring, 410
    void functions and, 359–360
    writing function documentation, 375
logarithmic order, 693
logic errors, handling, 77
logical (Boolean) expressions
    Boolean variables and constants, 188
    conditions in While statement as, 245
    English statements converted to, 214
    If statements. *See* If statements
    relational operators, 188–191
    string comparison, 191–192
    testing and debugging, 231
logical (Boolean) operators, 207–215
    overview of, 207–211
    precedence rules for, 213
    short-circuit evaluation, 211–212
logical order, 186
`long` data type, 92–93
`long double` data type, 92, 94
loop control pointers, 741, 756
loop control variables, 247
loop implementation (case study), 318–320, 484–486
loop termination condition
    defined, 246
    designing flow of control, 263–265
    loop exit and, 266–267
    nested logic, 267
    testing and debugging hints, 292
loop test, 246
loops/looping
    analysis of algorithms, 274–277
    Break statements, 321–322
    Continue statements, 321–322
    as control structure of programming language, 13–14
    count-controlled, 247–249
    count-controlled loops. *See* count-controlled loops
    counting and, 256
    Do-While statements, 310–314
    entry, 246

event-controlled. *See* event-controlled
    loops
exit, 246, 266–267
flow of control design, 263–265
For statements, 314–318
guidelines for choosing statement for,
    322–323
keeping track of previous value, 258–259
nested logic, 267–273
overview of, 244
phases of loop execution, 245
process design, 265–266
sentinel-controlled loops. *See* sentinel-
    controlled loops
summing and, 256–258
testing and debugging, 290–292
While statements, 244–245, 310–312
Lovelace, Ada, 420–421
Lovelace, Lord William, 421
Lucas, John, 912

M

machine language (code)
    defined, 9
    translating assembly language into, 10
    translating high-level languages into, 11
`main` function
    constructing programs, 65–66
    executing programs, 83
    overview of, 44–46
    syntax template for, 48–49
    writing modules as void functions,
        349–351
maintenance phase
    effort expended in, 6–7
    overview, 3–4
    program life cycle and, 7
    software, 13–15, 19
malware, 26
manipulators
    defined, 62
    specifying for floating-point values,
        114–116
    specifying for integer values, 111–113
`map` template, 933–934
markers, reading, 142–143
The Mathematical Analysis of Logic (Boole),
    212

meaning. *See* semantics (meaning)
means-end analysis, for problem-solving,
    29
member functions, `const`, 611
member selector, 480
members, class
    declaring public and private members,
        603
    implementing functions, 604
    objects and, 607–608
memory leaks, 721
memory unit (RAM)
    affecting computer speed, 24
    defined, 20
mental blocks, to problem solving, 31
merging solutions, for problem-solving,
    30–31
message passing, objects, 620
metalanguages
    defined, 46
    overview of, 47
    using identifiers to name things, 49
methods, object, 620
minimum complete coverage, 227
minus sign (-), in integral types, 92
mixed type (mode) expressions, 103–104
mnemonic, 9
modifiability, class design, 626–627
modular programming. *See* functional de-
    composition
modularizing programs, 534–537
modules
    coding as functions, 346–347, 367–370
    documentation of, 368
    functional decomposition and, 165–166
    hierarchical solution tree, 165
    implementing functional decomposition,
        168–170
    interface design for, 347–348
    summary, 177
    testing separately, 176
    writing as void functions, 349–351
modulus (`%`) operator, 97–98
mortgage program (case study)
    expanding capabilities in, 259–262
    functional decomposition implementation
        for, 166–170
    incorrect output in, 200–203

payment calculator in, 126–128, 135
  refactoring in, 365–370
mouse, as input device, 20
multidimensional arrays, 563–565, 583–584
multifile programs
  compiling and linking, 618–619
  defined, 373
multiway branches
  defined, 203–204
  nested If statements for coding, 203–204
  Switch statement as control structure for, 304–308
Murray (Hopper), Grace Brewster, 309
mutability, class design, 627–628
mutators. *See* transformers

N
\n (newline character)
  defined, 76
  `get` function in loops controlled by, 251, 292
  reading, 142–143
  review, 177
  sentinel-controlled loops, 251
named (symbolic) constants
  capitalization of identifiers representing, 57
  declarations for, 95–96
  defined, 55
named data types, 476
named matching, 371
names
  clashes, 409
  elements, 53
  memory locations, 51
  precedence (hiding), 403
  program elements, using identifiers, 49–50
  run time input of file, 160–161
  user-defined types, 466
  value-returning functions, 431
  void functions, 361
`namespace` keyword, 408–410
namespaces, 408–410
NDEBUG, 388
nested For statements, 315
nested If statements
  dangling `else` and, 206–207
  overview of, 203–206
  Switch statement similar to, 304
nested logic, 267–273
  analysis of algorithms, 274–277
  designing nested loops, 271–273
  overview of, 267–271
networks, 23
Neumann, John von, 622
`new` operators, 718–719
nodes
  copying, 749–750
  deallocating, 746–747
  deleting from linked lists, 738–740
  in dynamic implementation of ADT lists, 734–745
  in inserting into linked lists, 736–737
  leaf, 924–927
  in linked lists, 725–733
  in sorted link lists. *See* sorted linked lists
  in traversals of linked lists, 735
noninteractive I/O, 152, 177
nonlinear data structures, 924–929
nonlocal identifier, 404
NOT operator (!)
  flag-controlled loops using, 254–255
  overview of, 207–209
null (empty) string, 52
`Null` pointers
  in copying dynamic linked lists, 979–983
  in deleting from linked lists, 738–740
  in dynamic implementation of ADT lists, 734
  in dynamic linked lists, 727
  in empty linked lists, 735
  in inserting into linked lists, 736
  introducing, 495
  in recursion, 977–979
  reference types and, 505
  in sorted link lists, 751
  testing and debugging, 761–762
  in traversals of linked lists, 737–738
numeric data types. *See also* arithmetic expressions; output formatting
  as built-in simple types, 463–464
  declarations for, 95–96
  floating, 94
  integral, 92–93
  named constants vs. literals, 95–96

O

object program, 11
object-oriented design (OOD)
   in appointment calendar creation. *See* appointment calendar creation (case study)
   brainstorming in, 795–796
   dynamic binding and, 791–794
   filtering in, 795
   focus of, 792
   functional decomposition in, 170
   generally, 163–164, 170
   implementing, 801
   inheritance and. *See* inheritance
   object-oriented programming and, 772–774
   overview of, 771–772, 795–796
   responsibility algorithms in, 799
   scenario exploration in, 795–796
   software design using, 163–164
   solutions, assessing, 799
   testing and debugging, 819–821
object-oriented programming languages, 773–774
object-oriented programming (OOP)
   C++ equivalents of OOP terms, 620
   in object-oriented design, 772–774
   overview of, 620–622
objects
   attributes of, 620
   built-in operations on, 608–609
   as class values, 607–608
   instances of, 604
   mutability of, 627–628
   OOP and, 620–622
   overview of, 619–620
OBOBs (off-by-one bugs), 266
observer operations, ADTs, 598, 635
octal number system, 93
off-by-one bugs (OBOBs), 266
`ofstream` data type
   closing files, 155
   defined, 153
   opening files, 154
   testing state of I/O stream, 215–216
O(N) algorithms, 693
one-dimensional arrays
   accessing components of, 519–521
   accessing generally, 524–530
   aggregate operations in, 523–524
   as arguments, 533
   commenting, 533
   declaring, 518–519, 524–530
   defined, 518
   initializing, in declarations, 523
   introducing, 516–518
   modularizing programs with, 534–537
   out-of-bounds indexes and, 521–523
   passing as arguments, 530–532
   testing and debugging, 581–582
   `Typedef` with, 537
OOD (object-oriented design). *See* object-oriented design (OOD)
OOP (object-oriented programming). *See* object-oriented programming (OOP)
`open` function
   input failure from, 162–163
   opening files, 154–155
   testing and debugging, 176
opening files
   preparing for reading or writing, 154–155
operating systems
   calling `main` function, 46
   computer speed and, 24
   defined, 22–23
operations
   ADT categories, 598
   built-in operations on objects, 608–609
   separating/combining with data, 599
   of sorted lists, 681
operator functions, 845
operator overloading, 845–848
   `*this` for, 847–848
   overview of, 829–830, 845–847
   review, programming warm-up exercises, 881
   review, summary, 878
operators
   arithmetic, 97–99
   assignment expressions and, 324–325
   bitwise, 326
   cast operation, 326–327
   conditional, 328
   increment and decrement, 99–100, 325–326

logical. *See* logical (Boolean) operators
overview of, 323–324
precedence, 213, 328–330
relational. *See* relational operators (==)
`sizeof`, 327
specialized, 323
OR operator (||), 207–209
order of magnitude, 276
`ostream` data type
managing program I/O with, 608
testing state of I/O stream, 215–216
`ostringstream` class, 643
out-of-bounds indexes, 521–523
output
enumerated type output values, 471, 473–474
file. *See* file input/output (I/O)
interactive I/O, 149–151
noninteractive I/O, 152–153
output formatting, 110–118
creating blank lines, 74–75
floating-point numbers, 113–116
inserting blanks within line, 75
integers and strings, 111–113
matters of style, 116–118
output stream
denoting with `cout` variable, 60
terminating, 61–62
Oxford University, 912

P

parameter lists
modules, 348
testing and debugging, 389
testing functions, 387
parameters
argument-passing and, 371
arguments matched with, 371
cautions regarding argument and parameter lists, 372–373
declaring, 355
defined, 355
expressions and, 371–372
incoming, 834–835
overview of, 361–362
reference, 363–364
scope rules for, 404–407
user-defined functions and, 353–356
value, 362–363
writing function documentation, 376
Pascal, Blaise, 105–106
pass by reference, 371. *See also* reference parameters
pass by value, 371. *See also* value parameters
passing as arguments
one-dimensional arrays, 530–532
two-dimensional arrays, 552–554
passive error detection, 505
peripheral devices, computers, 21
physical hiding, of function implementation, 373–374, 445
physical order, of functions, 353–356
physical order of statements
flow of control vs., 244
If statements and, 186
piracy, software, 24–25
pointer variables, 977–979
pointers, 718–719
dynamic data and. *See* dynamic data
expressions of, 493–494
linked lists and. *See* linked lists
overview of, 718–719
reference types vs., 495–496
testing and debugging, 760–762
types of, 490
variables of, 490–493, 495
polymorphic operations, 794
polymorphism. *See* dynamic binding
polynomial expressions, 277
pop operations
in deques, 894
in priority queues, 891–893
in `priority_queue` templates, 909–911
in queues, 891
in stacks, 890–891
portable (machine-independent) code, 11
positional matching, 371
postconditions
assertions as function documentation, 374–375
developing test plan with, 229
problem-solving phase and, 223–224
testing functions, 387–388
writing function documentation, 374–376
postfix operators, 100

post-order traversals, 927
posttest loop, 311
precedence rules
    arithmetic expressions, 100–101
    operators, 213, 329–330
preconditions
    developing test plan with, 229
    testing functions, 387
    testing problem-solving phase by determining, 223–224
    writing assertions as function documentation, 374–375
    writing function documentation, 374–376
prefix notation, cast operation, 327
prefix operators, 100
pre-order traversals, 927
preprocessor, 68
preprocessor directive
    defined, 69
    file I/O and, 152–153
    stream I/O and, 139
pretest loops, 311
priming read, 250
printing
    echo. *See* echo printing
    two-dimensional arrays, 558–561
priority queues, 891–893
`priority_queue` template, 909–911
privacy of data, 25
`private`, declaring private class member, 602
problem-solving case studies
    adding to `Date` class, 859–865
    appointment calendar creation, 802–819
    appointment calendar using STL `list`. *See* appointment calendar using STL `list` (case study)
    BMI calculator, 217–223, 241
    chessboard program, 78–82, 89
    deck of cards creation, 935–948
    displaying name in multiple formats, 171–175
    `Entry` objects, 757–760
    exam statistics, 700–710
    health profile program, 436–444
    Hello Universe!, 16–19
    lawn care company billing, 377–386

    leap year program. *See* leap year program (case study)
    mortgage payment calculator, 126–128, 135
    Quicksort algorithm, 984–991
    recording studio design, 278–289, 302
    refactoring program, 365–370
    `RichUncle` program, 332–336, 344
    rock group, 574–581
    software maintenance. *See* software maintenance (case study)
    starship weight and balance. *See* starship weight and balance (case study)
    stylistic analysis of text, 496–504
    `TimeOfDay` objects, 629–634
problem-solving phase
    analysis and design in, 163
    computer programming, 3, 7
    testing in, 223–225
problem-solving techniques
    algorithms, 31–32
    analogies, 28
    building-block approach, 29–30
    divide and conquer, 29
    fear of starting, 31
    looking for familiar things, 27–28
    means-end analysis, 29
    merging solutions, 30–31
    questions, 27
procedural programming, 772
processing arrays, 545–548, 554–561
program code organization, 835–840
programming languages
    assembly languages, 9–10
    control structures and, 13–14
    high-level languages, 10–12
    metalanguages, 46, 47, 49
    OOP and, 620
    overview of, 5–6
    selection (branching) control structure and, 13–14
programs/programming. *See also* problem-solving techniques
    algorithms, 4–5
    binary representations of data and, 7–9
    computer components, 19–24
    computer programs. *See* computer programs

constructing programs, 64–70
definition of, 2–3
developing programs. *See* development process
entering programs, 76–77
ethics and responsibilities of, 24–27
executing programs, 5
linking multifile programs, 618–619
programming languages and, 5–9
running and compiling programs, 77
stages in writing, 3–4
structure of programs, 44–46
project files, in integrated environment, 619
promotion (widening), 330
prompts, input, 149–151
Provincial Letters (Pascal), 106
pseudocode, 166, 171
`ptr` (pointer)
   in copying dynamic linked lists, 979–983
   in printing dynamic linked lists in reverse order, 977–979
`public`, declaring public class member, 602
push operations
   in deques, 894
   in priority queues, 891–893
   in `priority_queue` templates, 909–911
   in queues, 891
   in stacks, 890–891

Q

quadratic expressions, 276–277
qualified names, namespaces, 407–408
questions
   asking as assertions in C++, 187
   programming and, 27
`queue` template, 908–909
queues, 891
Quicksort algorithm (case study), 984–991

R

raising exceptions, 849
RAM (memory unit)
   affecting computer speed, 24
   defined, 20
range of values, numeric data types, 463–464
reading
   character data with `get` function, 143–146
   marker and newline character, 142–143
   `string` data, 147–149
recording studio design (case study)
records (structs), 477–484
   accessing individual components, 480–481
   aggregate operations on, 481–483
   of arrays, 541–545
   binding like items, 484
   declarations, 483–484
   defined, 476–477
   hierarchical, 486–488
   overview of, 477–480
recursion, 959–1001
   defined, 960–963
   dynamic linked lists, copying, 979–983
   dynamic linked lists, printing in reverse order, 977–979
   iteration vs., 983–984
   overview of, 959–960
   pointer variables in, 977–979
   recursive algorithms with simple variables, 963–965
   recursive algorithms with structured variables, 969–971
   testing and debugging, 992
   in Towers of Hanoi game, 965–969
recursive algorithms
   defined, 961
   with simple variables, 963–965
   with structured variables, 969–971
recursive calls, 960
recursive definitions, 961
refactoring program (case study), 365–370
reference parameters
   avoiding side effects in value-returning module, 432
   coding outgoing and incoming/outgoing data as, 416–417
   `const`, 834–835
   defined, 361–362
   overview of, 363–364
   pass by address mechanism, 371
   testing and debugging tips, 389
   usage, 364
reference types, 495–496
relational expressions, 330–331
relational operators
   common mistake, 199–200

with floating point types, 214–215
If statements, 190
overview of, 188–191
precedence rules for, 213
While statements, 252
relative matching, 371
reliable, software unit, 623
reserved words
defined, 49
`public` and `private`, 602
resetting dynamic linked lists, 741
resources, ethics and, 25–26
responsibilities
algorithms for, 795, 799, 801
assigning to classes, 797–798
defined, 795
in public methods of objects, 620
responsibility algorithms, 795, 799, 801
rethrowing exceptions, 856
retrieving items, 741
Return statement
value-returning functions, 422–423
void functions, 360–361
reuse, class design and, 626–627
reverse iterators, 897–898
ReverseNumbers program, 516–518
right children, 924–927
right subtrees, 924–927
Ritchie, Dennis, 32
rock group (case study), 574–581
row processing, 560
`rowsFilled`, 556–557
run time, 832
running pointers, 972–976
run-time
binding. *See* dynamic binding
input of file names, 160–161
lifetime as issue of, 410–411

S

`sales` array, 564
scenario explorations
defined, 795
in object-oriented design, 797–798
scientific notation, 94
scope, class, 609–610
scope, identifier, 402–410
namespaces, 407–410
overview of, 402–404
scope rules, 404–408
variable declarations and definitions, 407
scope resolution operator (::), 408
scope rules
names of user-defined types obeying, 466
overview of, 404–407
searching
binary search trees in, 925–927
dynamic linked lists, 741
sorted lists, 693–694
selection (branching) control structure
overview of, 186–187
programming languages and, 13–14
Switch statement as, 321–322
testing, 225–229
self-documenting code, 171
semantics (meaning)
assignment operators and, 57
overview of, 46–47
semantic (logic) errors, 230–231
semihierarchical implementation, 169
sentinel (trailer) value, 249–252
sentinel-controlled loops
designing flow of control, 263–264
end-of-file-controlled loops vs., 253
overview of, 249–252
sequence, as control structure, 13–14
sequence containers, 929
sequential searches, 685–686
sequential structures, 725–726
`set` template, 930–933
`setprecision` manipulator
`ofstream` data type, 154
output formatting using, 111–112, 114–116
`setw` manipulator
`ofstream` data type, 154
output formatting using, 112, 115–116
shallow copy operations, 747–748
Shickard, Wilhelm, 105
`short` data type, 92–93
short-circuit (conditional) evaluation, 211–212
`showpoint` manipulator, 111, 114, 116
siblings, 924–927
side effects
avoiding using in expressions, 506–507
functions and, 417–419
interface design and, 431–432

testing and debugging, 450
simple (atomic) data types
   built-in, 462–465
   defined, 462
   enumerating. *See* enumeration data types
   vs. structured data types, 476–477
   user-defined, 466–476
simple arithmetic expressions, 97–100
size of arrays, 545
`sizeof` operator
   defined, 327
   measuring in multiples of `char`, 463–464
   overview of, 327–328
slicing issues, 792–793
Smalltalk programming language, 620
software
   affecting computer speed, 24
   defined, 21–22
   maintenance, 13–15, 19
   piracy, 24–25
   waterfall model of developing, 4
software design methodologies
   documentation, 171
   functional decomposition, 164–170
   object-oriented design, 163–164
   testing and debugging, 175–177
software engineering
   conceptual vs. physical hiding of functions, 373–374, 445
   documentation, 171
   English statements converted to logical expressions, 214
   named constants vs. literals, 95–96
   overview of, 26–27
   understanding errors before changing, 125
software maintenance (case study)
   adding file I/O to program, 156–159
   adding titles to names, 70–73
   changing loop implementation, 484–486
   in changing loop implementation (case study), 318–320
   in creating general program (case study), 259–262
   debugging simple program, 412–416
   essential steps of, 16–19, 70
   incorrect output in, 200–203
   modularizing programs with arrays in, 534–537
   precedence error in, 104–105
   refactoring program in, 365–370
solutions, problem-solving by merging, 30–31
sorted linked lists
   deleting from, 755–756
   of `Entry` objects (case study), 757–760
   overview of, 750–751
sorted lists, 681–694
   binary searches and, 686–690
   of classes, generally, 695–696
   defined, 664
   `Delete`, 697–698
   deletions generally, 690–692
   `Insert`, 697–698
   insertions generally, 682–684
   `IsThere` operation, 696
   linked. *See* sorted linked lists
   operations generally, 682
   overview of, 681–682
   searching, 693–694
   sequential searches, 685–686
   sorting, 693–694
sorting
   complexity of, 693–694
   defined, 677
   lists. *See* sorted lists
source program
   defined, 11
   using editor to create or modify, 23
special characters, 75–76
specialization of templates, 833–834
specification, of function, 596
specification files
   ADTs and, 635–637
   information hiding and, 612–615
speed, factors affecting computer, 23–24
spiral model, of software development, 4
splitting data, 985–989
`stack` template, 906–908
stacks, 889–891
stand-alone computers, 23
standard (built-in) data types, 50
standard exceptions, 857
Standard Template Library (STL)
   appointment calendar using. *See* appointment calendar using STL `list` (case study)
   data structures using. *See* data structures
   `deque` template in, 911

introduction to, 895–896
iterators in, 896–898
`list` template in, 904–906
`priority_queue` template in, 909–911
`queue` template in, 908–909
`stack` template in, 906–908
`vector` template in, 898–904
starship weight and balance (case study), 865–876
statement flow control, 186
static binding, 791
static variables, 410–411
`static_cast`, 326–327
`std` namespace, 69–70
stepwise refinement. *See* functional decomposition
STL (Standard Template Library). *See* Standard Template Library (STL)
storage
　data, 51
　storage (auxiliary) devices, 21, 138
Strachey, Christopher, 912
straight selection sorts, 678
stream input/output (I/O), 139
`string` class, 477
string constants, 59
`string` data type. *See* strings
string expressions, 58–59
string variables, 147–148, 160
strings
　character operations, 123–125
　comparison of, 191–192
　concatenation of, 58–59
　`find` function, 120–121
　`at` function, 123
　integers converted to, 643
　`length` and `size` functions, 119–120
　null (empty) string, 52
　output formatting, 111–113
　overview of, 52
　reading character string into, 176
　reading data into, 147–149
　`substr` function, 122–123
`stringstream` class, 643
Stroustrup, Bjarne, 32
`struct` data type. *See* records (structs)
structural programming, 772
structure
　C++ program, 44–46

programming language control, 13–14
structured data types
　arrays. *See* arrays
　classes. *See* classes
　vs. simple, 476–477
structured design. *See* functional decomposition
stubs, 446, 452
style
　braces and blocks, 197
　function documentation, 375–376
　naming value-returning functions, 431
　program formatting, 117–118
stylistical analysis of text (case study), 496–504, 513
subarray processing, 545–548
subclasses, 775
subprograms
　C++ program structure, 44
　as control structure, 13–14
subtrees, 924–927
summing
　columns, 556–557
　columns as functions, 556
　rows, 555–556
superclasses, 775
switch expression, 304
Switch statement
　overview of, 304–308
　testing and debugging, 336–337
　using Break statement with, 321–322
SwitchLabel, 305
syntax (grammar)
　assignment operators, 57
　blocks, 66
　C++ (generally), 47–49
　compound statements, 67
　Do-While statements, 310
　enumeration types, 468
　errors, 46, 77, 230
　function call to void function, 356
　If-Then, 198
　If-Then-Else, 193, 195
　input statements, 140
　overview of, 46–49
　programs, 63
　For statements, 314
　Switch statements, 304
　value-returning functions, 423

variable declarations, 54
void functions, 423
While statements, 244

T
tall recursions, 971
team programming, 348
template arguments, 833, 843
template class, 833
templates, 829–835, 884
  cautions regarding, 841
  class, defining, 831–832
  class, instantiating, 832–834
  `const` references and, 834–835
  exceptions and. *See* exceptions
  function, defining outside classes, 843
  generic functions and. *See* generic functions
  operator overloading and. *See* operator overloading
  overview of, 829–831
  parameters of, 832
  in program code organization, 835–840
  testing and debugging, 877–878
templates, C++, 47–49
test plans
  defined, 229
  implementation, 229–230
  for loops, 290–291
testing
  array-based lists, 711
  arrays, 581–585
  automatically during compilation and execution, 230–231
  classes, 652–656
  control structures, 336
  data structures, 948–949
  dynamic linked lists, 741
  functions, 387–389
  in implementation phase, 225–229
  loops, 290–292
  modular design, 445–451
  multidimensional arrays, 583–584
  `Null` pointers, 505–507
  numeric types, expressions and output, 125
  object-oriented designs, 819–821
  one-dimensional arrays, 581–582
  plan for, 229–230

  pointers, 504–507
  problem-solving phase and, 223–225
  program input, 175–177
  recursion, 992
  starship weight and balance, 875–876
  stream state, 215–217
  syntax and semantics, 82–83
  templates, 877–878
  user-defined data types, 504–505
then-clauses, 193
theoretical foundations, of algorithm, 274–277
`throw` statements, 849–850
throwing exceptions
  defined, 849
  by language, 857
  rethrowing, 856
  by standard library routines, 858
thunk, defined, 371
`TimeOfDay` class
  assigning responsibilities to, 798
  in dynamic binding generally, 791
  implementing `ExpandedEntry` class with, 779–780
  slicing issues in, 792–793
  virtual functions with, 793–794
`TimeOfDay` objects (case study), 629–634
top-down design. *See* functional decomposition
touch screens, as pointing device, 20
Towers of Hanoi game, 965–969
trackpads, as pointing device, 20
trailing pointers, 739, 740, 751
transformers
  in ADT operations, 598
  as example of action responsibility, 628
traversals, 735
  of dynamic linked lists, 737
  in-order, 926–927
  post-order, 927
  pre-order, 927
Treatise on Differential Equations (Boole), 212
Treatise on the Calculus of Finite Differences (Boole), 212
tree structure
  functional decomposition and, 164–165
  implementing, 166–170
triply nested loops, 272

true value, **bool** type, 462
try-catch statements, 851–852
Turing, Alan, 622
two-dimensional arrays
   defining, alternate method for, 562–563
   initializing, 558–559
   introducing, 548–549
   passing as arguments, 552–554
   printing, 558–561
   processing, 554–561
   summing columns as functions, 556–557
   summing columns, generally, 556–557
   summing rows, 555–556
type casting (conversion), 102–104
type coercion
   in arithmetic and relational expressions, 330–331
   in assignments, in argument passing, and in return of function values, 433–435
   overview of, 102–104
Typedef statement, 466–467, 537
TypeName, record data type, 478

U

UML (Unified Modeling Language), 644–645
unary operators
   defined, 97
   increment and decrement, 99–100
Unicode
   characters, 464
   defined, 8
union data types
   overview of, 488–489
   as structured data type, 477
unique keys, 664–665
unsigned reserved word
   defined, 93
   numeric data types, 464
unsorted lists, 664
user friendly, 201
user/computer interface, 22
user-defined data types
   built-in simple types, 462–465
   capitalization of, 56–57
   defined, 50
   hierarchical records, 486–488
   records (structs), 477–484
   simple types, 466–476

simple vs. structured data types, 476–477
testing and debugging, 504–505
unions, 488–490
user-defined functions
   flow of control, 353–356
   parameters, 354–356
user-written header files, 611–612
using declaration, namespaces, 408–409
using directive
   adding titles to names, 71
   namespaces, 409

V

value parameters
   arguments, 371
   coding incoming data as, 416–417
   defined, 361–362
   overview of, 362–363
   pass by value mechanism, 371
   testing and debugging tips, 389
   usage, 364
value-returning functions
   Boolean functions, 429–430
   complete example of, 425–428
   enumerated types as, 474
   ignoring value returned by, 434–435
   interface design and side effects, 431–432
   invoking void functions vs., 110
   naming, 431
   overview of, 107–108, 422–425
   testing and debugging, 450
   type coercion in, 433–435
   void functions vs., 346
   when to use, 432–433
values
   atomic, 462
   of enumerated types, 471
   literal. *See* literal values
   range of, 463–464
variable definition, 407
variables
   assignment statements and, 57
   Boolean, 188
   capitalization of identifiers, 56–57
   comments added to declarations, 56, 63
   as counters, 247
   declaring, 53–55, 407
   declaring numeric, 96
   defined, 53

in expressions, 98
in function headings, as parameters, 355
global, 403
identifiers, 53
input statements and, 141, 177
keeping track of previous value of, 258
lifetime of, 410–412
of pointers, 490–493, 494
program construction using, 66
relational operators for comparing, 188–190

`vector` template, 898–904
virtual functions, 793–794
viruses, 26
void functions
    declarations and definitions, 357–359
    function call to, 356–357
    functional decomposition with, 346–351
    local variables, 359–360
    naming, 361
    overview of, 110
    return statement and, 360–361
    when to use, 433–434

W
WAN (wide area network), 23
waterfall model, of software development, 4
`wchar_t` data type, Unicode, 464
While statement
    Break statement with, 321–322
    defined, 244
    Do-While statement vs., 310–312
    For statement for writing, 315
    guidelines for choosing, 321
white-box (clear-box) testing, 229
whitespace characters, 141–144
wide area network (WAN), 23
worms, 26

Y
Y2K problem, 13, 15

Z
`ZeroOut` function, 531, 534–538, 545
zombies, 26